FOURTH EDITION

Majority and Minority

The Dynamics of Race and Ethnicity in American Life

Edited by

Norman R. Yetman
The University of Kansas

ALLYN AND BACON, INC.

Boston   Sydney
London   Toronto

Production Coordinator: Louise A. Lindenberger
Production Services: Helyn Pultz
Cover Coordinator: Christy Rosso
Cover Designer: Robert Northup

Library of Congress Cataloging in Publication Data
Main entry under title:

Majority and minority.

    Bibliography: p.
    1. United States—Race relations—Addresses, essays,
lectures. 2. United States—Ethnic relations—
Addresses, essays, lecturers. 3. Minorities—United
States—Addresses, essays, lecturers. I. Yetman,
Norman R., 1938–
E184.A1M256 1985   305.8′00973   84–24537
ISBN 0–205–08458–3

Printed in the United States of America

10   9   8   7   6   5   4   3   2   1   90   89   88   87   86   85

For Jill and Doug

with hopes unaltered and no less urgently felt

Contents

Part IV   Race and Ethnicity in 1980s America   **385**

Preface

Majority and Minority began in 1968 as a collaborative effort with C. Hoy Steele, who was then a graduate student in American Studies at The University of Kansas. Hoy and I shared academic interests in race and ethnicity in American life. We also shared a commitment to the realization of a society free of inequality and injustice—the dream of which Martin Luther King, Jr., so eloquently spoke. The sense of urgency with which we approached the analysis of racial and ethnic relations was influenced not only by national protest movements to end racial oppression but equally, and more directly, by the racial tension and conflict that brought the community of Lawrence, Kansas, national notoriety. Thus we sought to emphasize the *practical* need, as well as the theoretical one, for a fundamental understanding of the dynamics of racial and ethnic relations. We were convinced of the irrelevance of analysis and understanding that are not complemented by action to alter existing systems.

At the time, the most common approaches to racial and ethnic relations were heavily psychological and social-psychological in orientation; they focused primarily on the phenomenon of prejudice. We devoted little attention to psychological and attitudinal factors, believing them to be far less significant as explanatory variables than other factors.

Instead, our basic assumption was that the study of racial and ethnic relations should focus primarily on patterns of differential power and intergroup conflict. We thought that the fundamental determinants were to be found in the institutional structures of society, and that sociological concepts, rather than psychological ones, were the most useful in explaining them.

I have retained the basic thrust of this orientation in this edition. However, I have sought, above all, to respond to changing perspectives in the field of racial and ethnic relations. Several developments have influenced my conceptualization, selection, and organization of the materials in this book. Foremost among these has been the increased attention devoted to ethnicity over the past decade. The growing recognition of its salience, not just in the United States but throughout the world, by historians and social scientists alike, suggests that it is not a superficial or fleeting factor in social life. Rather, it is a phenomenon that must be grasped in order to understand the dynamics of modern societies in general and the United States in particular.

Recognition of the universality and importance of ethnic and racial issues, of course, forced me to confront directly whether this edition's substantive focus should be on race and ethnicity in the United States alone, or more broadly comparative. Given the enormous amount of literature published in the field during the past five years, it would be impossible to do justice to both concerns in a single volume, and so I have included articles on the dynamics of these phenomena related specifically to American life.

However, my selection does not imply a lack of concern for comparative issues. Nor does it reinforce the parochial perspectives from which many American students view race and ethnicity. The major criterion for inclusion in this edition was that each article simultaneously illuminate some aspect of race and ethnicity in the United States *and* a broader conceptual issue or model. In other words, I have included articles whose conceptual approaches explain intergroup relations in general, but use materials on racial and ethnic relations from the United States as illustrative examples. Thus I believe the selections both treat the dynamics of race and ethnicity in America and are potentially applicable to other societies. I hope in this way to increase the volume's conceptual breadth while simultaneously making it attractive to students of race and ethnicity in American life.

One of the major objectives of this edition is to familiarize students with the *range* of conceptual perspectives or ways of interpreting American racial and ethnic relations. The primary audience for whom the book is intended is the upper division or graduate student; it is not intended as an introduction to the field. Nevertheless, in an effort to facilitate student interest and comprehension, I have edited several of the more difficult selections, with an eye toward emphasizing their central conceptual issues. Moreover, I have expanded the essays introducing each section to provide a context within which to consider each selection and to alert students to some of the salient issues raised therein.

The book's basic orientation remains historical and structural. I have tried to provide the historical depth necessary to understand the various ways different ethnic and racial groups have adapted to American society. Part II is explicitly devoted to historical perspectives, but in reality the historical dimension is stressed throughout the entire book, making the placement of some articles in some instances arbitrary. Subsequent sections build on the historical base established in Part II: patterns of assimilation in the American experience are examined in Part III, and the present and future significance of ethnicity are addressed in Part IV. The most apparent change from the third edition to the fourth occurs in this section. The topic of post–1968 immigration, its causes, characteristics, and consequences is becoming an increasingly important political, as well as social-scientific, issue, and is considered in greater depth than in any previous edition.

Finally, the statistical appendix in previous editions was based primarily on data from the 1970 census. For this edition, the appendix has been completely revised using data drawn from both the 1980 census and subsequent population surveys, thus providing students with the most current information available.

Finally, I would like to express my thanks to Allyn and Bacon's Sociology Editor, Al Levitt, and to Bob Antonio, Morteza Ardebili, Sharon Cox, Karyn Davis, Helyn Pultz, Bill Wilson, and Anne Yetman for the invaluable assistance they provided in completing this fourth edition.

Introduction: Definitions and Perspectives

The term *minority group* was originally derived from the European experience, particularly after the rise of nationalism and the emergence of the nation-state in the late eighteenth and early nineteenth centuries. In that context, it was used to characterize national or ethnic groups that had become subordinate to the peoples of another national group through the imposition of, or shifts in, political boundaries. Subsequently, the term was applied—by social scientist and laymen alike—to a diversity of groups and social categories.

In recent use, the term has generally been restricted to groups characterized by hereditary membership and endogamy—racial, caste, and ethnic groupings (Williams, 1964:304; Wagley and Harris, 1958:4–10). However, since differences in power comprise the distinctive feature of majority-minority relations, a more inclusive definition is appropriate. Joseph B. Gittler's comprehensive definition is consistent with this approach. According to Gittler, "Minority groups are those whose members experience a wide range of discriminatory treatment and frequently are relegated to positions relatively low in the status structure of a society" (Gittler, 1956:vii). This definition retains the crucial element of the term's original meaning: the reference to a distinct group or social category occupying a subordinate position of prestige, privilege, and power. In this book, I will devote particular attention to the power relation implied by the terms *minority* and *majority.*

Occasionally a so-called minority group will represent a numerical majority of the total population, as is the case today in South Africa, historically in some areas of the South in the United States, and in most colonial situations. Numerical superiority, therefore, does not necessarily ensure majority status. Many commentators have suggested that the terms *majority* and *minority* be replaced by *dominant* and *subordinate* to represent more accurately the differences in power that differentiate one from the other. However, since *majority* and *minority* have been so widely used, I will continue to employ them here with the understanding that the crucial feature of the minority's status is its inferior social position, in which its interests are not effectively represented in the political, economic, and social institutions of the society. I will use the term *dominant* as a synonym for *majority*

1

and *subordinate* as a synonym for *minority*. (It is possible that there are substantial differences in the nature of ethnic relations between circumstances in which the dominant group is a numerical minority and those in which it is in number, as well as in power, greater than the subordinate group. However, social scientists have not yet reached consensus on the pertinence of these factors.)

Many different dimensions, such as race, ethnicity, and religion, have been used to distinguish a minority from the majority. But, as Donald L. Noel argues in "The Origin of Ethnic Stratification" (see Part II, Article 6), ethnic, racial, or religious differences do not automatically generate conflict and social inequalities. Culturally, religiously, or racially distinct groups may coexist without a system of ethnic inequality developing. Majority-minority relations do not appear until one group is able to impose its will on another. By definition, minority groups are subordinate segments of the societies of which they are a part. Once people perceive ethnic differences and ethnic groups then compete against each other, the crucial variable in majority-minority relations is the differential power of one group relative to another.

Power refers to the ability of one group to realize its goals and interests, even in the face of resistance. This power may be derived from the superior size, weapons, technology, property, education, or economic resources of the dominant group. Hence, minority groups are categories of people that possess imperfect access to positions of equal power, prestige, and privilege in a society. Superior power is crucial not only to the establishment of a system of ethnic stratification but, as Noel points out, also to its maintenance and perpetuation. Having obtained control of a society's institutions, a majority group generally strives to solidify and consolidate its position.

Although conflict is not always overt, continuous, or apparent in a social system based on structured inequality, the potential for conflict is continually present. The extent to which conflict or stability manifests itself is related to a society's social structure. Pierre van den Berghe (1967) has contrasted the patterns of race relations characteristic of two structurally different types of societies. Under the *paternalistic* type, characteristic of a traditional, pre-industrial, predominantly agricultural society, race relations are highly stable and conflict is submerged—a function of both the mechanisms of social control used by the dominant group and the symbiotic nature of relations between dominant and subordinate groups. On the other hand, race relations in a *competitive* setting—an urbanized and highly industrialized society characterized by a complex division of labor—are less likely to remain stable. Overt conflict, initiated by both the dominant and subordinate groups, frequently erupts.

However, even in the most stable situations, dominant groups view minority groups as potentially threatening to their position. This is nowhere more apparent than in the American slave system, which exemplifies van den Berghe's paternalistic type of race relations. Proponents of the so-called peculiar institution frequently justified slaveholding on the grouds of the slave's docility, dependence, improvidence, and fear of freedom. Simultaneously, however, they saw slaves as "a troublesome presence" (Stampp, 1956), they initiated elaborate mechanisms (such as patrols, passes, and legal prohibitions against literacy and the possession of weapons) to reduce resistance to the slave regime, and they employed brutal sanctions to discourage noncompliance to the prescribed subservient roles.

The social inequalities inherent in majority-minority relations are, as Berreman points out in "Race, Caste, and Other Invidious Distinctions in Social Stratification," symbolically expressed in the institutionalized patterns of interpersonal relations between dominant and subordinate group members. Social interaction among majority and minority group members is never among status equals; it consistently involves what was known in the American context as *the etiquette of race relations.* Although the patterns of deference it demanded persisted long after slavery was legally abolished, the American slave regime vividly exemplified this point. One primary objective of slave socialization was to implant in slaves a sense of personal inferiority. Slaves were taught to "know their place," to recognize the difference between the status of master and slave. Whites interpreted any impudence on the part of slaves as an effort to reject their subordinate role. Frederick Douglass, the great nineteenth-century black leader, recalled that slaves could be labeled disobedient and punished for a variety of actions, including "the tone of an answer; in answering at all; in not answering; in the expression of countenance; in the motion of the head; in the gait, manner and bearing of the slave" (Stampp, 1956:145).

As events during the black protest movement of the 1960s in the United States demonstrated, attempts by a subordinate group to alter traditional relationships between dominant and subordinate groups and to achieve autonomy and equality of status are strenuously resisted by the majority group. Allen D. Grimshaw has summarized the history of changes in black-white relations by pointing out that:

> The most savage oppression, whether expressed in rural lynchings and pogroms or in urban race riots, has taken place when the Negro has refused to accept a subordinate status. The most intense conflict has resulted when the subordinate minority group has attempted to disrupt the accommodative pattern or when the superordinate group has defined the situation as one in which such an attempt is being made (Grimshaw, 1959:17).

Efforts to alter the relative power of the majority and the minority thus inevitably involve conflict between the two groups, the subordinate group attempting to decrease the inequalities in the system through a wide variety of means (including violence), the dominant group resorting to a multiciplity of techniques (also including violence—both legal and extralegal) to prevent such changes from occurring. Today, these efforts are most graphically and tragically depicted in conflict between blacks and whites in South Africa and between Protestants and Roman Catholics in Northern Ireland. The increasing white tyranny reflected in the repressive apartheid policy of the South African government developed in response to the political awakening of black Africa. Furthermore, the monopoly of power held by whites and their intransigent resistance to basic change offer little possibility that alteration of South Africa's power structure will be peaceful and nonviolent. Observers (for example, Moore, 1972) have been similarly pessimistic that the conflict in Northern Ireland can be peaceably resolved, arguing that changing the situation will require an entirely new society.

The discussion thus far has suggested that the concept of minority group must always be considered in relation to the existence of a majority, or dominant, group. Although this conclusion may appear self-evident, until the 1970s only a meager amount of the voluminous research on racial and ethnic relations had been devoted to the characteristics and attributes of the majority group and the mechanisms by which the relationships between majority and minority are created, maintained, and altered. A notable exception was the work of Robert Bierstedt. In "The Sociology of Majorities," written nearly four decades ago, Bierstedt said:

> It is the majority . . . which sets the culture pattern and sustains it, which is in fact responsible for whatever pattern or configuration there is in a culture. It is the majority which confers upon folkways, mores, customs, and laws the status of norms and gives them coercive power. It is the majority which guarantees the stability of a society. It is the majority which requires conformity to custom and which penalizes deviation—except in ways in which the majority sanctions and approves. It is the majority which is the custodian of the mores and which defends them against innovation. And it is the inertia of majorities, finally, which retards the processes of social change (Bierstedt, 1948:709).

Bierstedt's statement, which places the primary emphasis in the analysis of majority-minority relations on the dominant group, reflects one of the major themes of this book.

The principal focus of inquiry, therefore, should be not so much on the characteristics of the minority group as on the manner in which the dominant group controls the institutions of the society. As Preston Wilcox has argued, "Much of what has been written as sociology would suggest that . . . minorities suffer problems because of their unique characteristics rather than [because of] the systems which impinge upon them and the sanctioning of these systems by dominant groups" (Wilcox, 1970:44).

Lack of recognition of the importance of societal patterns of institutional control has meant that frequently, as John Horton (1966) has pointed out, sociologists and laypeople alike frequently define *social problems* as a minority group's deviation from dominant societal norms and standards; seldom do they critically examine the society's institutions, values, and social processes themselves. The importance of an institutional approach to the analysis of mass protest and violence in America was forcefully articulated in 1969 by the Violence Commission, which was appointed by President Lyndon Johnson to examine and explain the mass protest that swept the country during the turbulent 1960s. Mass protest, the Commission contended,

> . . . must be analyzed in relation to crises in American institutions. . . . [It] is an outgrowth of social, economic, and political conditions. . . . Recommendations concerning the prevention of violence which do not address the issue of fundamental social, economic, and political change are fated to be largely irrelevant and frequently self-defeating (Skolnick, 1969:3).

In other words, both the sources of, and the solutions to, problems of majority-minority conflict are institutional. Thus, the most realistic approach to their analysis must focus primarily on the majority group and the institutional structures of the society in question.

Examination of the ways majority group members typically approach intergroup conflict demonstrates the importance of an institutional perspective. As noted above, the majority determines whether a problem even exists—witness the classic statement advanced by proponents of the status quo in communities throughout America that "we have no problems here. Our _____ [insert appropriate minority group residing in the community] are happy." Whether or not one perceives social conditions as a problem depends on one's position within the social structure. And, as the Violence Commission noted, whether or not one classifies behavior as violent depends on whether one is challenging the existing institutional arrangements or seeking to uphold them (Skolnick, 1969:3–4).

In an important article examining the functions of racial conflict, Joseph Himes points out that conflict may have positive consequences: it can force the dominant group to be aware of, come to grips with, and respond to societal inequities. Himes argues that organized social conflict alters traditional power relations and the traditional etiquette of race relations. As the minority group develops the ability to mobilize power against the dominant group's interests, traditional race relations change to the point where minority grievances can be more realistically discussed (Himes, 1966). During the late 1950s and early 1960s, blacks, denied change through institutionalized political channels (voting, for example), used mass protest to mobilize power against the dominant group's entrenched interests. Nonviolent protest and conflict were integral strategies of power in the civil rights movement. Martin Luther King, Jr., one of history's most articulate advocates of the weapon of nonviolence, perceived that it represented a means of effecting a redistribution of power:

> Non-violent direct action seeks to create such a crisis and foster such a tension that a community which has constantly refused to negotiate is forced to confront the issue. It seeks so to dramatize the issue that it can no longer be ignored (King, 1964:81).

If the dominant group acknowledges the existence of social problems at all, they are invariably ascribed to the characteristics of the subordinate group rather than to defects in the social system controlled by the majority group. For many years, discussion of black-white relations in America was described as the *Negro problem*, a stance explicitly challenged by Gunnar Myrdal in his classic work, *An American Dilemma* (1944), excerpts of which are reprinted in Part II. Today, most white Americans deny that opportunity for black Americans is limited, and perceive that blacks themselves are primarily responsible for the conditions in which they find themselves (Schumann, 1969; Kluegel and Smith, 1982). This interpretation is also implicit in the idea of cultural deprivation (Baratz and Baratz, 1970). According to this ideology, the relatively higher dropout rates, academic failures, and lower achievement levels found among many minority groups are attributable to the internal deficiences and instabilities of the minority group itself—that is, to home and neighborhood factors—and not to the inadequacies of the schools. The result of this focus on the characteristics of the minority group is to deflect attention from the institutional factors that impinge upon it. In short, the emphasis is on the symptom rather than on the disease.

The resolution of intergroup conflict also reflects power differentials, for conflicts tend to be resolved within limits acceptable to the majority group. Efforts to alter the pattern of inequalities are therefore restricted to methods defined as legitimate or appropriate by the majority group, a requisite that seldom poses a threat to the continued functioning of the existing system. Nancy Oestreich Lurie's article, "The American Indian: Historical Background," (Part II), which sketches the background of American Indian encounters with white Americans, provides an excellent example of this pattern. Indian-white problems were always defined from the perspective of whites and generally involved the refusal of Native Americans to accede to white demands for cultural assimilation or to the ceding of their lands. Native American values, needs, and desires were seldom, if ever, a consideration in the solution of such confrontations. According to the humanitarian Thomas Jefferson, if Indians did not conform to white cultural patterns, the only viable solution was their forcible removal.

The role of the majority group in delimiting the context within which solutions to problems of intergroup conflict can be reached is exemplified by the analysis and recommendations of the 1968 Kerner Commission report and the nation's reactions to it. The Commission charged that white racism was the ultimate source of the civil disorders that rent the nation's cities for several summers during the 1960s. It concluded that "there can be no higher priority for national action and no higher claim on the nation's conscience" than the elimination of racism from American society (National Advisory Commission on Civil Disorders, 1968:2). However, it warned that implementation of its recommendations would necessitate "unprecedented levels of funding and performance." Since implementation on these terms would be unpopular with the dominant group, the response to the Kerner report—both officially and unofficially—was to discredit or (perhaps more significant) to ignore its findings.

Although the conclusion that white racism was primarily responsible for the period's pervasive racial conflict was unacceptable to most white Americans, the Commission's report demonstrated that majority solutions to social problems seldom entail basic alterations of the society's institutional patterns. On the one hand, the Kerner Commission indicted American institutions as the primary source of the racism that permeates the society. On the other, most of its recommendations involved changing blacks to conform to these institutions rather than substantially altering the institutions themselves. Such an approach, involving what Horton terms an *order model* of social problems, slights the basic institutional sources of racial inequality in American society, a subject that we will explore more fully in Parts III and IV.

Ethnic, Racial, and Caste Categories

The initial problem encountered in the analysis of racial and ethnic relations is that of definition: What is meant by the terms *racial* and *ethnic?*

The word *ethnic* is derived from the Greek word *ethnos,* meaning people. An *ethnic group* is socially defined on the basis of its *cultural* characteristics. *Ethnicity,* or the sense of belonging to a particular ethnic group, thus implies the existence of a distinct culture or subculture in which group members feel themselves bound together by a common history, values, attitudes, and behaviors—in its broadest sense, a sense of peoplehood—are are so regarded by other members of the society.

Ethnic groups differ in cultural characteristics as diverse as food habits, family patterns, sexual behaviors, modes of dress, standards of beauty, political orientations, economic activities, and recreational patterns. In American society, Chicanos, blacks, Jews, Poles, Filippinos, and white Anglo-Saxon Protestants can all be considered ethnic groups, however broad and diverse their internal composition. Killian (1970) has argued that white Southerners also comprise an important ethnic group in American society. Ethnicity was an important factor in the 1976 presidential campaign of Jimmy Carter, whose candidacy evoked a sense of ethnic identity among many Southerners. It was explicity articulated by Patrick Anderson, who served as Carter's aide:

> Perhaps you have to be a Southerner to understand what [Jimmy Carter's candidacy] means to some of us. There is a great sense of personal pride and personal vindication involved, a sense that after losing for a long, long time, our side is finally going to win one. I imagine that Jews and blacks will feel the same way when one of their own finally gets a shot at the White House.
>
> The emotions involved run deep, and are hard to communicate, but I think they must be considered by anyone who wants to understand why young Southerners . . . are driving themselves so relentlessly on Governor Carter's behalf. They are motivated, I think, not only by the personal ambition that afflicts us all, but by personal affection for the the candidate, by political commitment to certain goals, and by a regional pride that has its roots many generations in the past (Anderson, 1976:21).

Ethnic groups are inherently ethnocentric, regarding their own cultural traits as natural, correct, and superior to those of other ethnic groups, who are perceived as odd, amusing, inferior, or immoral. In his article "A Theory of the Origin of Ethnic Stratification" (Part II), Noel suggests that ethnocentrism is a necessary, but not sufficient, condition for the emergence of ethnic stratification. According to Noel, a majority-minority relationship between two ethnocentric groups will not come about unless the groups are competing for the same scarce resources and, most important, one group possesses superior power to impose its will on the other.

There is frequently an intimate relation between the concepts of race and ethnicity. Groups that the social scientist would classify as racial may be ethnically distinctive as well (American Indians, for example). Nationality, language, religion, and tribal identity have all been employed to distinguish among conflicting groups. Since the presence of cultural differences among social castes or classes is an important component of almost all theories of stratification, in its broadest sense the term *ethnic* can refer to a wide range of social phenomena in the study of structured social inequality. It is possible for a group to possess racial, religious, national, and linguistic characteristics similar to those of the dominant group (for example, the Buraku of Japan) and still identify itself and be identified as a distinct ethnic minority on the basis of different cultural or subcultural traits.

As a review of its use will reveal, the term *race* has been an extremely loose concept. Indeed, as Berreman points out, several scholars have chosen not to use it, preferring to subsume racially distinct groups under a broadly defined category of ethnic groups. Race has been used in a variety of ways: to refer to linguistic categories (Aryan, English-speaking), to religious categories (Hindu, Jewish), to national categories (French, Italian), and to mystical, quasiscientific categories

(Teutonic). The wide range of social categories that have been considered races is a reflection of the fact that racial designations are artificial; they serve the function of isolating and separating certain social categories based on an arbitrary selection of physical or biologically transmitted characteristics. As Berreman notes, "systems of 'racial' stratification are social phenomena based on social rather than biological facts."

A society therefore defines a social category as a race when it isolates certain physical characteristics, perceives them to be innate and inherited, and magnifies their importance as differentiating factors. Moreover, these physical characteristics are usually believed to be related to other immutable mental, emotional, or moral characteristics such as intelligence. Berreman contends that the definition of a group as a race is not a function of biological or genetic differences between groups, but is rather dependent on the society's perceptions that such differences exist and that they are important. Many groups possess physically identifiable characteristics, but these traits do not provide a basis for racial distinctions. The criteria selected to make racial distinctions in one society may be overlooked or considered insignificant or irrelevant by another. For instance, Pitt-Rivers (1967) has noted that in much of Latin America skin color and the shape of the lips—important differentiating criteria in the United States—are much less salient variables than are hair texture, eye color, and stature. A person defined as black in Georgia or Michigan might be considered white in Peru. In central Africa, the Tutsi (among whom men average six feet in height) and Hutu (who stand slightly over four feet) have similar skin pigmentation, but the physical characteristic of stature, not skin color, is the basis for group distinctions among these two groups (van den Berghe, 1967:12; Lemarchand, 1975).

The concept of race has been closely related to that of *caste,* which refers to a particular system of rigidly separated categories within a social structure. Indeed, Berreman contends that all systems of racial stratification and caste are qualitatively comparable. A caste system is a "hierarchy of endogamous divisions in which membership is hereditary and permanent" (Berreman, 1969:226). A caste society can be conceptualized as occupying one end of a continuum, its polar opposite being a class society. The distinction between these two types of stratification systems is that in a caste system one's status is birth-ascribed; that is, it is immutable, permanent, and fixed. In a class system, on the other hand, social mobility is possible because one's class status is determined by achievement. Tumin has observed, however, that pure caste and class systems do not exist. No stratification system is totally closed or totally open; virtually all societies display both ascription and achievement in some form (Tumin, 1969).

Race might be a basis for status distinctions in a caste system; however, a caste system can also be organized without reference to hereditary physical (that is, racial) characteristics so long as social categories are distinguished on a basis of traits believed to be birth-ascribed. The Japanese Buraku (Eta) present an excellent example of a caste system without racial distinctions. The Buraku occupy a pariah position in Japanese society and their undesirable characteristics are perceived by upper-caste individuals as attributable to biological inheritance, yet no physical differences can be detected between them. But caste and racially stratified systems function in a similar manner. Thus, De Vos and Wagatsuma, on the basis of their analysis of the Japanese Buraku, support Berreman's position that the two systems are analytically comparable: "From the viewpoint of comparative sociology or social anthropology, and from the viewpoint of human social psychology, racism and caste attitudes are one and the same phenomenon" (De Vos and Wagatsuma, 1966:xx).

Sources of Racial and Ethnic Affiliations

Why have people used racial and ethnic distinctions so frequently throughout history to rank a society's members? Why have racial and ethnic differences so often demarcated the lines of intergroup conflict? Two broad explanatory models have been advanced: the nonrational or primordialist perspective and the rational or situational perspective. The former position conceptualizes racial and ethnic identities as essentially biologically based, present at birth, instinctive, innate, and unchangeable, "attachments [that] seem to flow more from a sense of natural affinity than from social interaction" (Burgess, 1978:266). The rational position, on the other hand, locates the sources of ethnicity in the very structure and dynamics of human societies. From this perspective, race and ethnicity are functional, pragmatic, emergent, and constantly evolving and changing phenomena, "a rational group response to social pressures and a basis for group action, especially where none other exists. . . . Ethnicity [is] a strategy chosen to advance individual interest as the situation dictates" (Burgess, 1978:267).

During the past two decades Pierre van den Berghe has been one of the most prominent, prolific, and penetrating scholars of race and ethnicity. In numerous publications (van den Berghe, 1967, 1970, 1978), he has criticized American scholarship in the field of race and ethnicity for its narrow, myopic, and often-parochial focus on the United States, and he has urged sociologists to more broadly conceptualize the study of race and ethnicity through the adoption of a comparative, cross-cultural perspective. In his more recent work van den Berghe has urged that sociologists also extend the range within which these phenomena are conceptualized to the wider context of evolutionary biology.

Van den Berghe argues for what has been broadly termed a primordialist perspective—one that sees racial and ethnic distinctions as deeply rooted in the basic nature of human sociality. He contends that kin selection and its corollary, nepotism, are the basic principles on which societies have been based for most of human existence; and that ethnic and racial distinctions are merely extensions of kinship principles. The pervasiveness of ethnic distinctions and ethnocentrism in human societies suggest that these related phenomena provide means of establishing group boundaries. Most preliterate societies, for example, employ ethnic distinctions (such as language or body adornment), rather than racial ones, for the simple reason that they rarely encounter other peoples who are physically distinguishable from themselves. Racial distinctions, van den Berghe argues, are the consequence primarily of large-scale migrations, which have only occurred relatively recently in human existence:

> Humans, like other animals, are selected to favor kin, and whatever does a quick, easy, and accurate job of differentiating kin and non-kin will be used. In most cases, and until recently, cultural criteria have been predominantly used. Physical criteria became salient only after large, strikingly different-looking populations found themselves in sudden and sustained contact (van den Berghe, 1978:407–408).

Van den Berghe's article, "Race and Ethnicity: A Sociological Perspective," represents a brief statement of a position that he develops more fully in his recent book, *The Ethnic Phenomenon.*

Several articles in this book represent the rational or situational approach to race and ethnicity, each of which emphasizes that definitions of ethnic and racial categories are *socially* defined phenomena. Bonacich ("Class Approaches to Race and Ethnicity"), for example, argues that an ethnic identity is not natural or inherent in the nature of the group itself; rather it is socially constructed, a reflection of the more deeply rooted dynamics of class. As a consequence, new ethnic or racial categories can emerge over time. Yancey et al. ("Emergent Ethnicity") contend that among European-immigrant ethnic groups a sense of ethnicity was produced, not by the cultural commonalities, but by factors external to the group: a sense of ethnicity represented a response to the conditions in the cities in which they settled. Among these were "common occupational positions, residential stability and concentration, and dependence on common institutions and services, [which were] in turn directly affected by the process of industrialization." Historians of American ethnic groups have pointed out that a sense of national identity was not brought by many immigrants from their homelands; it often crystallized in the United States (e.g., Vecoli, 1964). For example, Italians who immigrated to the United States did not think of themselves as Italians; rather, they defined themselves by their village or regional identities. Consciousness of themselves as Italians emerged only as a consequence of their encounter with American society.

Similarly, several of the racial categories discussed in Part II—Indians, Asians, and Hispanics—are inclusive terms that ignore or obscure great internal diversity within each group. Bonacich notes that the Asian-American category is now comprised of diverse and often hostile national elements including Chinese, Japanese, Korean, Vietnamese, and Thai. Nagel points out how the terms *Indian* and *Native American* are consequences of their minority status in American society. Similarly, the terms *Hispanic* or *Latino,* which two decades ago were not even part of the common language, are increasingly employed to subsume into one category several extremely diverse ethnic categories. Although such distinctions are employed by social scientists, journalists, business people, and ultimately the people themselves, Enloe contends that the state has played a crucial role in defining these arbitrary social categories: "The state employs ethnic categories to suit its administrative-political needs. In so doing it requires individuals subject to certain laws to respond as 'Hispanics' or 'Indians' or 'Filipinos'."

Recently there has been a spate of newspaper and magazine accounts delineating the emergence of Asians or Hispanics as significant forces in American life. Indeed, in Part II, reflecting this tendency to lump diverse groups together, I argue (as have numerous other social scientists and journalists) that at some point in the not-so-distant future Hispanics will exceed blacks as the nation's largest minority group. Likewise, Lieberson (Part IV) contends that there may be a new ethnic category emerging in American society: what he terms *unhyphenated whites,* whose European national origins are so obscure or so mixed that their only ethnic identity is in reference to American society. In each case, the nature of these ethnic categories—Italian, Indian, Asian, Hispanic, and American—are socially and politically defined and created.

Finally, the principle that ethnic and racial categories are socially defined is vividly exemplified by the ways in which states, such as the United States, South Africa, and Nazi Germany, have sought to regulate relations between such categories, especially through laws concerning intermarriage. In the United States, and well into the twentieth century, many states stipulated that any person with one-fourth or more black ancestry (that is, with one "black" grandparent and three "white" grandparents) was legally defined as black. However, this definition did not prevent many individuals who were physically identified as black from marrying persons physically identified as white. Consequently, some states prohibited marriages between whites and anyone with Negro blood. Thus an individual who had fifteen great-great-grandparents who were white but one great-great-grandparent who was black—who was therefore one-sixteenth black and fifteen-sixteenths white biologically—could still be socially defined as black. The social, not the biological, definition of the individual was most significant.

Racism, Prejudice, and Discrimination

According to Allport, *prejudice* refers to "an avertive or hostile attitude toward a person who belongs to a group, simply because he [or she] belongs to that group, and is therefore presumed to have the objectionable qualities ascribed to the group" (Allport, 1958:8). Prejudice is an attitudinal phenomenon often involving an intense emotional component. Thus, many white Americans consciously and rationally reject the myths of black inferiority but react emotionally with fear, hostility, or condescension in the presence of blacks. The forms of prejudice may range from a relatively unconscious aversion to members of the out-group to a comprehensive, well-articulated, and coherent ideology, such as the ideology of racism. In any form, prejudice provides a justification for the status quo and a means of rationalizing the treatment to which the minority group is subject.

Note that prejudice cannot be equated with discrimination; the former refers to attitudes, the latter to behavior. *Discrimination* involves differential treatment of individuals because of their membership in a minority group. The relationship of prejudice to discriminatory behavior is problematic. In his classic article, "Discrimination and the American Creed," Robert Merton examines the distinctions between prejudice and discrimination and the interrelationship between them. "Prejudicial attitudes," he contends, "need not coincide with discriminatory behavior." To explore the interrelations of prejudice and discrimination, he developed a typology of ethnic prejudice and discrimination, which focuses on the attitudinal and behavioral dimensions of intergroup relations. The unprejudiced nondiscriminator is the all-weather liberal who adheres to the American creed of equality for all in both belief and practice. The unprejudiced discriminator has internalized the ideals of the American creed but may acquiesce to group pressures to discriminate. Similarly, the prejudiced non-discriminator conforms to social pressures not to discriminate despite prejudicial attitudes toward ethnic minorities. Finally, the prejudiced discriminator is, like the unprejudiced nondiscriminator, consistent in belief and practice; he or she rejects belief in the American creed and engages in personal discrimination.

Whether prejudice becomes translated into discriminatory behavior depends on many factors. It is therefore impossible to understand the dynamics of majority-minority relations by examinining prejudice alone; prejudice is most appropriately considered not as a causal factor but as a dependent variable. As Schermerhorn has cogently suggested, prejudice "is a product of situations, historical situations, economic situations, political situations; it is not a little demon that emerges in people because they are depraved" (Schermerhorn, 1970:6). To explain the dynamics of ethnic and racial relations fully, it is necessary to analyze the institutional conditions that have preceded and generated them.

During the past quarter century, the conceptualization of American race relations has undergone several significant changes. These changes have been profoundly influenced by the changing nature of the racial crisis in this country. Before the advent of the black protest movement that began during the 1950s, social scientists focused their attention primarily on racial attitudes, because prejudice was thought to be the key to understanding racial and ethnic conflict. This perception of the essential dynamics of race relations is perhaps best illustrated in Myrdal's classic, *An American Dilemma*, in which he defined race prejudice as "the whole complex of valuations and beliefs which are behind discriminatory behavior on the part of the majority group . . . and which are contrary to the equalitarian ideals in the American Creed" (Myrdal, 1944:52). Thus, as Paul Metzger points out, the liberal order model of race relations was predicated on the assumption that racial conflict in the United States was a problem of ignorance and morality that could best be solved by changing—through education and moral suasion—the majority's prejudicial attitudes toward racial minorities. "A great majority of white people in America," Myrdal wrote, "would be better prepared to give the Negro a substantially better deal if they knew the facts" (Myrdal, 1944:48).

The advent of the black protest era of the 1950s and '60s challenged the assumption that change in the patterns of racial inequality in American society could be brought about through a reduction in prejudicial attitudes alone. Sociologists and social activists focused increasingly on the dynamics of discrimination and sought means for eliminating discriminatory behavior. The numerous forms of direct protest, such as nonviolent sit-ins, boycotts, and voter registration drives, were tactics designed to alter patterns of discrimination. In keeping with this emphasis on discrimination were the prodigious efforts undertaken to secure enactment of the Civil Rights Act of 1964, which outlawed discrimination in public accommodations and employment, and the 1965 Voting Rights Act, which provided federal support to ensure that blacks had the right to vote throughout the South.

It was not until after these legislative victories had been achieved, however, that the greatest racial unrest of the black protest era occurred. Whereas the earlier civil rights phase of the black protest movement had been directed primarily against public discrimination and especially its manifestations in the South, the outbreak of urban riots in Northern cities focused attention on the nature of racial inequalities affecting blacks throughout the entire nation. For several summers during the late 1960s, the nation was torn with racial strife. Parts of cities were burned, property damage ran into the millions of dollars, and the toll of dead— primarily, although not exclusively, blacks—numbered almost a hundred (National Advisory Commission on Civil Disorders, 1968:116). In July, 1967, President Lyndon Johnson appointed a national commission (the Kerner Commission) to investigate the causes of these urban riots. In 1968 the commission issued its report, which concluded:

> What white Americans have never fully understood—but what the Negro can never forget—is that white society is deeply implicated in the ghetto. White society condones it. . . .
>
> Race prejudice has shaped our history decisively in the past; it now threatens to do so again. White racism is essentially responsible for the explosive mixture which has been accumulating in our cities since the end of World War II (National Advisory Commission on Civil Disorders, 1968:2, 203).

Although I concur with the Kerner Commission's conclusion that the ultimate responsibility for the racial disorders of the 1960s should be attributed to white racism, the term is extremely imprecise. This imprecision enabled President Johnson, who had created the Commission, to ignore its findings and his successor, Richard Nixon, to condemn and deny them. Consequently, the term *racism* is in urgent need of clarification if its significance in American society is to be fully understood. First, it is apparent that *racism* is a general term, subsuming several analytically distinct phenomena; namely, prejudice and several forms of discrimination. In attempting to clarify the nature of these components, Carmichael and Hamilton distinguished between *individual* racism and *institutional* racism (Carmichael and Hamilton, 1967:4):

> Racism is both overt and covert. It takes two closely related forms: individual whites acting against individual blacks and acts by the total white community against the black community. . . . The second type is less overt, far more subtle, less identifiable in terms of specific individuals committing the acts. But it is no less destructive of human life. . . . When white terrorists bomb a black church and kill five black children, that is an act of individual racism, widely deplored by most segments of the society. But when in that same city—Birmingham, Alabama— five hundred black babies die each year because of the lack of proper food, shelter, and medical facilities, and thousands more are destroyed and maimed physically, emotionally, and intellectually because of the conditions of poverty and discrimination in the black community, that is a function of institutional racism (Carmichael and Hamilton, 1967:4).

Yet, as I will note more fully below, prejudicial attitudes are causal factors in Carmichael and Hamilton's conceptualization of institutional racism. Moreover, their conceptualization does not analytically distinguish between psychological and sociological factors in its operation.

Another problem in the use of the word *racism* is that although it is inclusive, lumping together all forms of racial oppression, it is not a generic term. It does not encompass majority-minority situations based on criteria other than race— criteria such as religion, tribal identity, ethnicity, or sex. Therefore, in the following discussion, I define racism carefully and then avoid use of the word itself. This approach has practical as well as theoretical importance, since effective solutions to problems of intergroup relations depend on analytical clarity.

The term *racism* has traditionally referred to an *ideology*—a set of *ideas* and *beliefs*—used to explain, rationalize, or justify a racially organized social order.

There are two essential parts of racism: its content and its function. Racism is distinguished from ethnocentrism by its racial focus, which emphasizes the beliefs that differences among groups are biologically based. The in-group is believed to be innately superior to the out-group, and members of the out-group are defined as being "biogenetically incapable of ever achieving intellectual and moral equality with members of the in-group" (Noel, 1972:157). Howard Schuman has offered a commonly accepted definition of racism:

> The term racism is generally taken to refer to the belief that there are clearly distinguishable human races; that these races differ not only in superficial physical characteristics, but also innately in important psychological traits; and finally that the differences are such that one race (almost always one's own, naturally) can be said to be superior to another (Schuman, 1969:44).

Unlike ethnocentrism, racism is not a universal phenomenon. As van den Berghe has pointed out, "Only a few human groups have deemed themselves superior because of the content of their gonads" (van den Berghe, 1967a:12).

Racism's primary *function* has been to provide a rationale and ideological support for a racially based social order; to use beliefs in genetic superiority-inferiority as a means of justifying domination and exploitation of one racial group by another. Van den Berghe (1967:16–18) has suggested three major sources of Western racism. First, racism developed as a justification of capitalist forms of exploitation, most particularly slavery in the New World. As Noel has argued, "As slavery became ever more clearly the pivotal institution of Southern society, racism was continually strengthened and became an ever more dominant ideology" (Noel, 1972:162).

Second, racism was congruent with Darwinian notions of stages of evolution and survival of the fittest, and with the idea of Anglo-Saxon superiority. According to these doctrines, those people in inferior social positions were destined to their station because they were least evolved or least fit in the struggle for existence. In 1870, Francis A. Walker, United States Commissioner of Immigration, characterized the most recent immigrants in the following manner:

> They are beaten men from beaten races; representing the worst failures in the struggle for existence. Centuries are against them, as centuries were on the side of those who formerly came to us. They have none of the ideas and aptitudes which fit men to take up readily and easily the problem of self-care and self-government (quoted in Saveth, 1948:40).

The third explanation of racism, van den Berghe argues, is paradoxically related to the egalitarian ideas of the Enlightenment, which were expressed in the Declaration of Independence:

> Faced with the blatant contradiction between the treatment of slaves and colonial peoples and the official rhetoric of freedom and equality, Europeans and white North Americans began to dichotomize humanity between men and submen (or the "civilized" and the "savages"). The scope of applicability of the egalitarian ideals was restricted to "the people," that is, the whites, and there resulted . . . regimes such as those of the United States or South Africa that are democratic

for the master race but tyrannical for the subordinate groups. The desire to preserve both the profitable forms of discrimination and exploitation and the democratic ideology made it necessary to deny humanity to the oppressed groups (van den Berghe, 1967a:17–18).

There has been a substantial decline in racist ideology in the last four decades; especially since 1970, white Americans have increased their approval of racial integration (Taylor, Sheatsley, and Greeley, 1978). In 1942, only 42 percent of a national sample of whites reported that they believed blacks to be equal to whites in innate intelligence; since the late 1950s, however, around 80 percent of white Americans have rejected the idea of inherent black inferiority. The Kerner Commission was therefore misleading in lumping all white antipathy toward blacks into the category of racism. Rather than believing blacks are genetically inferior, the dominant white ideology is of free will: anyone can better himself or herself, if he or she is not too lazy to make the effort. This belief is not inherently racist, but rather a general judgment about human nature, and one that can be applied to all sorts of human conditions or groupings. However, when applied to black Americans, the belief system of free will is racist in that it refuses to recognize or acknowledge the existence of external impingements and disabilities (such as prejudice and discrimination) and instead imputes the primary responsibility for black disadvantages to blacks themselves. Blacks, by this definition, are still considered inferior people, otherwise they would be like whites.

But if the term *racism* referred merely to the realm of beliefs and not to behavior or action, its relevance for the study of race relations would be limited. To restrict the meaning of *racism* to ideology would be to ignore the external constraints and societally imposed disabilities—rooted in the power of the majority group—confronting a racial minority. As Noel points out in Part II, If one group does not possess the power to impose its belief system on another, ethnic stratification cannot occur. When critics charged that the ideology of Black Power was "racism in reverse," black spokesmen responded that their critics failed to consider the components of differential power that enabled the ideology of white supremacy to result in white domination:

> There is no analogy—by any stretch of definition or imagination—between the advocates of Black Power and white racists. Racism is not merely exclusion on the basis of race but exclusion for the purpose of subjugating or maintaining subjugation. The goal of the racists is to keep black people on the bottom, arbitrarily and dictatorially, as they have done in this country for over three hundred years (Carmichael and Hamilton, 1967:47).

Therefore, the most crucial component of a definition of *racism* is behavioral and implies the greater power held by the dominant racial group. Racism in its most inclusive sense refers to actions on the part of a racial majority that have discriminatory effects; that is, effectively prevent members of a group from securing access to prestige, power, and privilege. These actions may be intentional or unintentional. Racism therefore entails discrimination as well as an ideology that proclaims the superiority of one racial grouping over another.

As noted above, *discrimination* refers to the differential treatment of members of a minority group. Discrimination in its several forms comprises the means by which the unequal status of the minority group and the power of the majority group are preserved. In the ensuing discussion, I distinguish between *attitudinal* discrimination, which refers to discriminatory practices attributable to or influenced by prejudice, and *institutional* discrimination, which cannot be attributed to prejudice, but instead is a consequence of a society's normal functioning. Both of these types can be further elaborated according to the sources of the discriminatory behavior. In reality, these types are at times interrelated, and seldom is discrimination against a minority group member derived from one source alone.

Attitudinal Discrimination

According to the definition advanced above, discrimination involves differential treatment of individuals because of their membership in a minority group. It has traditionally referred to circumstances in which the privileges and rewards of society are arbitrarily denied to minority group members whose qualifications are equal to those of the majority group. It has implied the "unequal treatment of equals"; for example, the refusal to employ a qualified Puerto Rican or to sell a home to a black who is able to meet the stipulated price.

The most blatant form, and the one for which many white Americans would probably deny responsibility, is individual discrimination, which refers to actions motivated by personal prejudice or bigotry. In the hypothetical examples above, if the primary reason minority group members were not hired or were unable to purchase a home was because the personnel manager or the realtor was a racist (that is, he or she held feelings of personal prejudice toward individuals who were Puerto Rican or black) it would be a case of individual discrimination. The emphasis, at this point, is on the relationship between the individual's personal feelings and his or her actions. Although it has been the subject of a voluminous amount of research, we will not be concerned here with the essentially psychological and social-psychological issues concerning the etiology of prejudice—whether it arises from an actor's psychological needs, or conformity to relatively well-defined cultural definitions, or a combination of both.

As attitudinal surveys continue to confirm, consciously bigoted attitudes have declined substantially among Americans during recent years, or at least it has become less fashionable to express racial prejudice in public. However, it is problematic whether there has been a similar decline in discrimination. Feagin and Feagin contend that prejudiced attitudes of whites have declined to a much greater degree than discrimination; despite attitudinal support for increased integration, the economic, political, and social status of blacks has improved only slightly, if at all (Feagin and Feagin, 1978:7). Overt forms of individual discrimination are now condemned, most frequently through the force of public opinion and the law. Yet subtle, covert forms of individual discrimination are still prevalent.

But discrimination is not necessarily a function of individual prejudices. As Merton points out, it occurs without personal malice merely because the discriminating individual conforms to existing cultural patterns or acquiesces to the dictates of others who are prejudiced. *Adaptive* discrimination involves actions that can be attributed to the actor's conscious or unconscious perception of the negative effects that nondiscriminatory behavior will have. In our hypothetical examples, the personnel manager or realtor placed in a position of having to hire or sell may genuinely disclaim any personal prejudice for having refused the minority group member the desired job or home. The grounds for such discriminatory behavior could be other than prejudicial. Perhaps he or she felt constrained by the negative sanctions of peers, or by the fear of alienating customers. In this case, the discriminatory actor's judgment would be based on the existence of the prejudicial attitudes of a powerful reference group such as customers. Although the heart and mind of the actors in our hypothetical situations may be devoid of any personal prejudice, the effects or consequences of their actions—no job, no home—for the minority-group applicant are no different than they would be if the actors were old-fashioned, dyed-in-the-wool bigots.

Attitudinal discrimination remains an important component of intergroup relations. One of the most prominent examples is the world of sports, which is perceived by most Americans to be devoid of racism. Although there have been very substantial—even overwhelming—changes in the racial composition of sports teams during the past quarter of a century, the persistence of racial stacking, the omission of blacks from leadership and outcome-control positions, and the relative dearth of blacks in second-team positions indicate discrimination is still a factor in player selection. The effects of individual and adaptive discrimination are even more pronounced at management levels: while blacks are proportionately overrepresented in player roles, there is a dearth of black executives, managers, coaches, scouts, and officials (Yetman and Eitzen, 1982).

The mass media provide some of the most important means by which negative images of minority groups are (often unconsciously) perpetuated. Popular magazines and children's literature have been among the most conspicuous purveyors of racial stereotypes. Although social scientists have pointed out the racially biased nature of these publications for decades, a 1965 study found that of 5,206 children's trade books published from 1962 through 1964, only 349, or 6.7 percent, included one or more blacks (Larrick, 1965:63–65; Berelson and Steiner, 1946; Klineberg, 1963; Teague, 1968). Similarly, by omission, distortion, or misrepresentation, the role of racial and ethnic minorities has been slighted in the nation's history books (Henry, 1967; Stampp et al., 1968). Finally, Engelhardt (1971) has shown that the cultural stereotypes in American movies reinforce those found in other media forms. All positive, humanitarian virtues remain with whites: even if they represent the dregs of Western society, "any White is a step up from the rest of the world." Nonwhites, on the other hand, are depicted as alien intruders, helpless, dependent, or less than human. When they do assume center stage, they do so as villians—"the repository for Evil." Whether undertaken consciously or unconsciously, intentionally or unintentionally, perpetuation of these racially biased roles serves to reflect and reinforce cultural beliefs in the racial inferiority of nonwhites.

Institutional Discrimination

Both forms of attitudinal discrimination defined above are ultimately reducible to psychological variables: either the actor is prejudiced, defers to, or is influenced by the sanctions of a prejudiced reference group or the norms of a racially biased culture. The third type of discrimination—institutional discrimination—refers to the effects of inequalities rooted in the system-wide operation of a society. The effects have little relation to racially related attitudinal factors or to the majority group's racial or ethnic prejudices. This type of discrimnation involves "policies or practices which appear to be neutral in their effect on minority individuals or groups, but which have the effect of disproportionately impacting on them in harmful or negative ways" (Task Force on the Administration of Military Justice in the Armed Forces, 1972:19).

The existence of institutional inequalities that effectively exclude substantial portions of minority groups from participation in the dominant society has seldom been considered under the category of discrimination. According to Yinger, discrimination refers to "The persistent application of criteria that are arbitrary, irrelevant, or unfair *by dominant standards,* with the result that some persons receive an undue advantage and others, *although equally qualified,* suffer an unjustified penalty" (Yinger, 1968:449, emphasis added). The underlying assumption of this definition is that if all majority-group members would eliminate "arbitrary, irrelevant, and unfair criteria," discrimination would, by definition, cease to exist. However, if prejudice—and the attitudinal discrimination that emanates from it—were eliminated overnight, the inequalities rooted in the normal and impersonal operation of existing institutional structures would remain. Therefore, the crucial issue is not the equal treatment of those with equal qualifications, but the accessibility of minority-group members to the qualifications themselves.

Institutional discrimination is thus more subtle, more complex, and less visible than attitudinal discrimination. Because it does not result from the motivations or intentions of specific individuals, it is more impersonal than attitudinal discrimination. Nevertheless, it has the same discriminatory consequences for minority-group members. In examining institutional discrimination, therefore, it is more important to consider the *effect* of a particular policy or practice upon a minority group than it is to consider the *motivations* of the majority group.

Because it emphasizes the role of *impersonal* social forces, an institutional discrimination model focuses on the effects of broad structural changes in modern American society, especially in the economy. In his analysis of blacks in America during the 1980s (Part IV), William J. Wilson identifies several broad economic factors that have recently had a significant effect on the structure of the black community: "the shift from goods-producing to service-producing industries, the increasing segmentation of the labor market, the growing use of industrial technology, and the relocation of industries out of the central cities."

This emphasis on examining the impact of such broad structural changes raises the issue—a perennial concern among scholars in the field—of whether racial and ethnic relations are unique forms of structured social inequality or whether they are ultimately reducible to class factors. That the dynamics of race and ethnicity are influenced at a deeper level by class factors is Edna Bonacich's thesis in her article, "Class Approaches to Race and Ethnicity," in this section. Bonacich distinguishes between two broad types of social movements: *communalist,* which emphasize ethnic, racial, national, or tribal in-group solidarity and cut across class lines; and *class,* which emphasize common class interests and reject appeals to ethnic solidarity. From these two basic orientations she examines several class models (including the split labor market and middleman minority models that she has been instrumental in developing) that have been advanced to explain the salience of ethnic and racial divisions in modern societies.

Having elaborated several variants of class-oriented models of racial and ethnic relations, Bonacich then seeks to develop an integrated class model. She suggests that the dynamics of race and ethnicity in the modern world in general, and in contemporary United States in particular, must be conceptualized within the context of the world capitalist system. She contends that as the price of labor increases in developed nations, capital seeks alternative sources of labor. One consequence is the runaway shop, in which the labor is located in another country. The advantage of such an arrangement is that the capitalist is able to hire people who traditionally have worked basically for their own subsistence and, consequently, have low wage expectations. Moreover, such workers are unfamiliar with or disinclined to join trade unions and their standards of living are lower than those of workers in developed countries. All these factors enable capitalists to hire workers at much lower wages than would be possible in the developed country.

An alternative to taking the employment opportunity abroad is to induce foreign workers to immigrate to the developed country, where, lacking many of the advantages available to indigenous labor, such as wages, medical and retirement benefits, workmen's compensation, and the like, they work under conditions that undermine the bargaining power of indigenous labor.

Bonacich demonstrates how communalist factors (race, ethnicity, or nationality) affect the multiplicity of possible relationships that can develop between capitalist and worker classes in the two different countries. Her analysis shows how closely linked are the issues of the expanding American underclass and, simultaneously, the recent upsurge in immigration, especially of illegal immigrants, into the United States. On the one hand, the economic status of black workers, especially, has recently been severely injured by the flight of manufacturing jobs out of central cities in the industrial Northeast and Midwest to the suburbs, the Sunbelt, and overseas. On the other hand, illegal immigrants are encouraged to enter the United States, where they work under precarious economic and political conditions. "Immigrant labor, or the runaway shop to cheap countries or regions," writes Bonacich, "is used by capital in the form both of threat and reality to constrain its national working class." The nature and impact of these structural changes on the economy, and the increasing significance of contemporary immigration to these changes will be discussed more fully in Part IV.

In her effort to develop an integrated model of race and ethnicity Bonacich emphasizes the manner in which economic forces affect the dynamics of racial and ethnic relations and suggests that the *state* be considered as a "semi-autonomous" factor. However, Cynthia Enloe contends that the state is not merely a reflection of economic forces, but plays an independent role in generating ethnic distinctions. In other words, the dynamics of race and ethnicity cannot be understood solely in reference to economic factors but must consider the actions of the state as well.

Like Bonacich and Yancey et al., Enloe contends that ethnicity is an ever-changing and emergent phenomenon, being created, recreated, maintained, and perpetuated in response to humanly created situations. She differs from Bonacich in the relative importance that she attaches to state action: "The process of state-building, from its early days through its periods of elaboration and maturity, cannot help but involve the state with ethnic identifications and ethnic group dynamics." In her article, "The Growth of the State and Ethnic Mobilization," she sketches some of the mechanisms whereby the institutions of the state—the civil bureaucracy, the judiciary, and the military and police—have contributed to the intensification of racial and ethnic divisions in the American experience. Her specific concern is with the phenomenon of ethnic mobilization, "the process by which a group organizes along ethnic lines in pursuit of collective ends" (Nagel and Olzak, 1982:127), as a consequence of actions by the institutions of the state. Her analysis suggests that the state possesses a capacity—one frequently ignored by students of race and ethnicity—to shape ethnic relations and to generate ethnic awareness and identification, either intentionally or unintentionally. She suggests that, as the power of the American state continues to expand and penetrate more efficiently and pervasively into all sectors of modern life, the salience of ethnicity is unlikely to decline. In all probability, ethnicity will continue to have an important influence on American life, not because it reflects natural or primordial sentiments, but because the forces of the state elicit it.

1

Race, Caste, and Other Invidious Distinctions in Social Stratification

Gerald D. Berreman

A society is socially stratified when its members are divided into categories which are differentially powerful, esteemed, and rewarded. Such systems of collective social ranking vary widely in the ideologies which support them, in the distinctiveness, number, and size of the ranked categories, in the criteria by which inclusion in the categories is conferred and changed, in the symbols by which such inclusion is displayed and recognized, in the degree to which there is consensus upon or even awareness of the ranking system, its rationale, and the particular ranks assigned, in the rigidity of rank, in the disparity in rewards of rank, and in the mechanisms employed to maintain or change the system.

For purposes of study, such systems have been analysed variously depending upon the interests and motives of the analyst. One of the most frequently used bases for categorizing and comparing them has been whether people are accorded their statuses and privileges as a result of characteristics which are regarded as individually acquired, or as a result of characteristics which are regarded as innate and therefore shared by those of common birth. This dichotomy is often further simplified by application of the terms

Reprinted from RACE, (Volume XIII, no. 4, April 1972) by permission of the author and The Institute of Race Relations, London.

'achieved' versus 'ascribed' status. Actually, what is meant is *non*-birth-ascribed status versus birth-ascribed status. The former is usually described as class stratification, referring to shared statuses identified by such features as income, education, and occupation, while the latter is frequently termed caste or racial stratification or, more recently, ethnic stratification, referring to statuses defined by shared ancestry or attributes of birth.

Regardless of its characteristics in a particular society, stratification has been described as being based upon three primary dimensions: class, status, and power, which are expressed respectively as wealth, prestige, and the ability to control the lives of people (oneself and others).[1] These dimensions can be brought readily to mind by thinking of the relative advantages and disadvantages which accrue in Western class systems to persons who occupy such occupational statuses as judge, garbage man, stenographer, airline pilot, factory worker, priest, farmer, agricultural labourer, physician, nurse, big businessman, beggar, etc. The distinction between class and birth-ascribed stratification can be made clear if one imagines that he encounters two Americans, for example, in each of the above-mentioned occupations, one of whom is white and one of whom is black. This quite literally changes the complexion of the matter. A similar contrast could be drawn if, in India, one were Brahmin and one untouchable; if in Japan one were Burakumin and one were not; if in Europe one were Jew and one were Gentile; or if, in almost any society, one were a man and one a woman. Obviously something significant has been added to the picture of stratification in these examples which is entirely missing in the first instance—something over which the individual generally has no control, which is determined at birth, which cannot be changed, which is shared by all those of like birth, which is crucial to social identity, and which vitally affects one's opportunities, rewards, and social roles. The new element is race (colour), caste, ethnicity (religion, language, national origin), or sex. The differences in opportunities and behaviour accorded people as a result of these criteria are described by such pejorative terms as racism, casteism, communalism (including especially ethnic and religious discrimination), and sexism. To be sure, the distinctions are manifest in class, status, and power, but they are of a different order than those considered in the first examples: they are distinctions independent of occupation, income, or other individually acquired characteristics. While the list includes a variety of criteria for birth-ascription and rank with somewhat different implications for those to whom they are applied, they share the crucial facts that: 1. the identity is regarded as being a consequence of birth or ancestry and hence immutable; 2. the identity confers upon its possessor a degree of societally defined and affirmed worth which is regarded as intrinsic to the individual; 3. this inherent worth is evaluated relative to that of all others in the society—those of different birth are inherently unequal and are accordingly adjudged superior or inferior, while those regarded as being of similar birth are innately equal. The crucial fact about birth-ascription for the individual and for society lies not so much in the source of status (birth), as in the fact that it cannot be repudiated, relinquished, or altered. Everyone is sentenced for life to a social cell shared by others of like birth, separated from and ranked relative to all other social cells. Despite cultural differences, therefore, birth-ascribed stratification has common characteristics of structure, function, and meaning, and has common consequences in the lives of those who experience it and in the social histories of the societies which harbour it.

The specific question motivating the present discussion is this: is social ranking by race absolutely distinctive, not significantly distinctive at all, or is race one criterion among others upon which significantly similar systems of social ranking may be based? While identifying the last of these as 'correct' from my perspective, I shall insist that the answer depends entirely upon what one means by 'race,' and by 'distinctive,' and what one wishes to accomplish by the inquiry. No satisfactory answer can be expected without comparative, cross-cultural analysis encompassing a number of systems of social differentiation, social separation, and social ranking, based on a variety of criteria, embedded in a variety of cultural *milieux*, analysed by reference to various models of social organization, and tested against accounts of actual social experience. The attempt to do this leads to a number of issues central and tangential to the study of stratification and race, some of which have been overlooked or given short shrift in the scholarly literature, while others are well discussed in particular disciplinary, regional, or historical specialties without necessarily being familiar to students of other academic domains to whose work and thought they are nevertheless relevant.

There is not space here to present ethnographic and historical documentation for particular instances of birth-ascribed stratification. I have done so briefly in another paper, citing five societies on which there is fortunately excellent published material vividly exemplifying the kinds of social system I refer to in this paper, and their implications for those who comprise them: Ruanda, India, Swat, Japan, and the United States. I recommend those accounts to the reader.[2]

Models for Analysis

In the course of scholarly debate concerning the nature and comparability of systems of collective social ranking, a number of models and concepts have been suggested, implied, or utilized. A framework can be provided for the present discussion by identifying some of these and analysing whether and to what extent each is relevant and applicable to all or some systems of birth-ascribed social separation and inequality, with special attention to the five societies cited above.

Stratification

By definition, stratification is a common feature of systems of shared social inequality—of ranked social categories—whether birth-ascribed or not. Where membership in those categories is birth-ascribed, the ranking is based on traditional definitions of innate social equivalence and difference linked to a concept of differential intrinsic worth, rationalized by a myth of the origin, effect, and legitimacy of the system, perpetuated by differential power wielded by the high and the low, expressed in differential behaviour required and differential rewards accorded them, and experienced by them as differential access to goods, services, livelihood, respect, self-determination, peace of mind, pleasure, and other valued things including nourishment, shelter, health, independence, justice, security, and long life.

Louis Dumont, in *Homo Hierarchicus*, maintains that the entire sociological notion of stratification is misleading when applied to South Asia, for it is of European origin, alien and inapplicable to India. He holds that the term implies an equalitarian ideology wherein hierarchy is resented or denied, and that it therefore obscures the true nature of India's hierarchical society, based as it is on religious and ideological premises peculiar to Hinduism which justify it and result in its endorsement by all segments of Indian society. Stratification, he maintains, is thus a 'sociocentric' concept which cannot cope with the unique phenomenon of Indian caste.[3] My response to this is twofold; first, the caste hierarchy based on the purity-pollution opposition as Dumont insists, is well within any reasonable definition of stratification, for the latter refers to social structure and social relations rather than to their ideological bases; and second, Dumont's description of the functioning of, and ideological basis for, the caste hierarchy is idealized and similar to the one commonly purveyed by high caste beneficiaries of the system. Few low caste people would recognize it or endorse it. Yet their beliefs and understandings are as relevant as those of their social superiors to an understanding of the system. The low caste people with whom I have worked would find Dumont's characterization of 'stratification' closer to their experience than his characterization of 'hierarchy.'[4]

Use of the stratification model focuses attention upon the ranking of two or more categories of people within a society, and upon the criteria and consequences of that ranking. Often, but not inevitably, those who use this concept place primary emphasis upon shared values and consensus, rather than power and conflict, as the bases for social ranking and its persistence. This emphasis is misleading, at best, when applied to systems of birth-ascribed ranking, as I shall show. It is obvious, however, that while many systems of stratification are not birth-ascribed, all systems of birth-ascribed ranking are systems of social stratification, and any theory of social stratification must encompass them.

Ethnic Stratification

Probably the most recent, neutral, and nonspecific term for ascriptive ranking is 'ethnic stratification.' 'An ethnic group consists of people who conceive of themselves as being alike by virtue of common ancestry, real or fictitious, and are so regarded by others,'[5] or it comprises 'a distinct category of the population in a larger society whose culture is usually different from its own [and whose] members . . . are, or feel themselves, or are thought to be, bound together by common ties of race or nationality or culture.'[6] Undoubtedly the systems under discussion fit these criteria. Use of the adjective 'ethnic' to modify 'stratification' places emphasis upon the mode of recruitment, encompassing a wide variety of bases for ascription, all of which are determined at birth and derive from putative common genetic makeup, common ancestry, or common early socialization and are therefore regarded as immutable. This commonality is held responsible for such characteristics as shared appearance, intelligence, personality, morality, capability, purity, honour, custom, speech, religion, and so forth. Usually it is held responsible for several of these. The ranked evaluation of these charactertistics, together with the belief that they occur differentially from group to group and more or less uniformly within each group serves as the basis for ranking ethnic groups relative to one another.

Van den Berghe has held that 'ethnic' should be distinguished from 'race' or 'caste' in that the former implies real, important, and often valued social and cultural differences (language, values, social organization), while the latter are artificial and invidious distinctions reflecting irrelevant (and sometimes non-existent) differences in physiognomy, or artificial differences in social role.[7] This is a useful point. In the recent sociological literature, however, 'ethnic' has increasingly been used to refer to *all* social distinctions based on birth or ancestry, be they associated with race, language, or anything else. This is the usage adopted here. Moreover, as I shall elaborate in discussing pluralism below, race and caste entail the kinds of cultural distinctions cited by van den Berghe as diagnostic of ethnic diversity, for the social separation implied by those systems ensures social and cultural diversity. For example, van den Berghe's assertion that 'nonwithstanding all the African mystique, Afro-Americans are in fact culturally Anglo-American,'[8] has been countered by ample evidence that the African origin, social separation, and collective oppression of blacks in America *has* resulted in an identifiable Afro-American culture.[9]

All systems of ethnic stratification are thus based on ancestry, approximating a theory of birth-ascription, and if the definitions set forth by advocates of this term are accepted, most systems of birth-ascribed stratification can properly be designated ethnic stratification. Perhaps the only recurrent exception is sexual stratification, wherein inherent, birth-ascribed, and biologically determined characteristics which are *independent* of ancestry are the basis for institutionalized inequality. This instance, exceptional in several respects, will be discussed separately below, and hence will not be alluded to repeatedly in intervening discussions although most of what is said applies to it also.

Caste

A widely applied and frequently contested model for systems of birth-ascribed rank is that of 'caste,' deriving from the example of Hindu India where the *jati* (almost literally, 'common ancestry') is the type-case. *Jati* in India refers to interdependent, hierarchically ranked, birth-ascribed groups. The ranking is manifest in public esteem accorded the members of the various groups, in the rewards available to them, in the power they wield, and in the nature and mode of their interaction with others. *Jatis* are regionally specific and culturally distinct, each is usually associated with a tradi-

tional occupation and they are usually (but not always) endogamous. They are grouped into more inclusive, pan-Indian ranked categories called *varna* which are frequently confused with the constituent *jatis* by those using the term 'caste.' The rationale which justifies the system is both religious and philosophical, relying upon the idea of ritual purity and pollution to explain group rank, and upon the notions of right conduct (*dharma*), just deserts (*karma*), and rebirth to explain the individual's fate within the system. As an explanation of caste inequalities this rationale is advocated by those whom the system benefits, but is widely doubted, differently interpreted, or regarded as inappropriately applied by those whom the system oppresses.

Many students of stratification believe that the term 'caste' conveys an impression of consensus and tranquility that does not obtain in systems of rigid social stratification outside of India. That notion, however, is no more applicable to, or derivable from Indian caste than any other instance of birth-ascribed stratification.[10]

If one concedes that caste can be defined cross-culturally (i.e., beyond Hindu India), then the systems under discussion here are describable as caste systems. That is, if one agrees that a caste system is one in which a society is made up of birth-ascribed groups which are hierarchically ordered, interdependent, and culturally distinct, and wherein the hierarchy entails differential evaluation, rewards, and association, then whether one uses the term 'caste,' or prefers 'ethnic stratification,' or some other term is simply a matter of lexical preference. If one requires of a caste system that it be based on consensus as to its rationale, its legitimacy, and the legitmacy of the relative rank of its constituent groups, then none of the examples mentioned here is a caste system. If one requires social tranquillity as a characteristic, then too, none of these is a caste system. If one allows that a caste system is held together by power and the ability of people within it to predict fairly accurately one another's behaviour while disagreeing on almost anything or everything else, then all of these systems will qualify. If one requires a specifically Hindu rationale of purity and pollution and/or endogamy and/or strict and universal occupational specialization, then one restricts caste to India and to only certain regions and groups within India at that. If one requires for castes, as some do, a tightly organized corporate structure, then too one would exclude even in India some *jatis* and other groups commonly called 'castes'. (This, however, does seem to me to be the structural criterion which comes closest to differentiating Indian *jati* from other systems of birth-ascribed stratification such as that of the United States. Corporateness evidently emerges as a response to oppression and as a mechansim for emancipation even where it has been previously minimal, e.g., in Japan, Ruanda, and the United States. Thus, the corporateness of Indian *jatis* may represent a late stage of development in caste systems rather than a fundamental difference in the Indian system.)

Jati in Hindu India and the equivalent but non-Hindu *quom* organization in Swat and Muslim India, are each unique, yet both share the criteria by which I have defined caste, as do the tri-partite system of Ruanda and the essentially dual systems of Japan and the United States, and all share in addition (and in consequence, I believe) a wide variety of social and personal concomitants. Caste is a useful and widely used term because it is concise, well-known, and in fact (as contrasted to phantasy), the structural, functional, and existential analogy to Indian caste is valid for many other systems.

Race

Systems of 'racial' stratification are those in which birth-ascribed status is associated with alleged physical differences among social categories, which are culturally defined as present and important. Often these differences are more imagined than real, sometimes they are entirely fictional and always a few physical traits are singled out for attention while most, including some which might differently divide the society if they were attended to, are ignored. Yet systems so described share the principle that ranking is based on putatively inborn, ancestrally derived, and significant physical characteristics.

Those who use this model for analysis generally base it upon the negative importance attached by Europeans to the darker skin colour of those they have colonized, exterminated, or enslaved.

A good many have argued that racially stratified societies are *sui generis;* that they are unique and hence not comparable to societies stratified on any other basis.[11] There is often a mystical quality to these arguments, as though race were an exalted, uniquely 'real', valid, and important criterion for birth ascription, rendering it incomparable to other criteria. An element of inadvertent racism has in such instances infected the very study of race and stratification. In fact, as is by now widely recognized, there is no society in the world which ranks people on the basis of biological race, i.e., on the basis of anything a competent geneticist would call 'race,' which means on the basis of distinctive shared genetic makeup derived from a common gene pool. 'Race,' as a basis for social rank is always a *socially* defined phenomenon which at most only very imperfectly corresponds to genetically transmitted traits and then, of course, only to phenotypes rather than genotypes. Racists regard and treat people as alike or different because of their group membership defined in terms of socially significant ancestry, not because of their genetic makeup. It could not be otherwise, for people are rarely geneticists, yet they are frequently racists.

To state this point would seem to be superfluous if it were not for the fact that it is continually ignored or contested by some influential scholars and politicians as well as the lay racists who abound in many societies. To cite but one well known recent example, Arthur Jensen, in his article on intelligence and scholastic achievement, maintains that there is a genetic difference in learning ability between blacks and whites in the United States.[12] Nowhere, however, does he offer evidence of how or to what extent his 'Negro' and 'White' populations are genetically distinct. All of those, and only those, defined in the conventional wisdom of American folk culture to be 'Negro' are included by Jensen, regardless of their genetic makeup in the category whose members he claims are biologically handicapped in learning ability. Thus, large numbers of people are tabulated as 'Negroes,' a majority of whose ancestors were 'white,' and virtually all of Jensen's 'Negroes' have significant but highly variable percentages of 'white' ancestry. Although, also as a result of social definition, the 'whites' do not have known 'Negro' ancestry, the presumed genetic homogeneity of the 'whites' is as undemonstrated and unexplored as that of the 'Negroes.' In short, there was no attempt to identify the genetic makeup or homogeneity of either group, the genetic distinctiveness of the two groups, or whether or how genetic makeup is associated with learning ability, or how learning ability is transmitted. This kind of reasoning is familiar and expectable in American racism, but not in a supposedly scientific treatise—a treatise whose author berates those who deplore his pseudo-science as themselves unscientific for failing to seriously consider his 'evidence.' The fallacy in Jensen's case is that he has selected for investigation two socially defined groupings in American society which are commonly regarded as innately different in social worth and which as a result are accorded widely and crucially divergent opportunities and life experiences. Upon finding that they perform differentially in the context of school and test performance, he attributes that fact to assumed but undemonstrated and uninvestigated biological differences. Thus, socially defined populations perform differently on socially defined tasks with socially acquired skills, and this is attributed by Jensen to biology. There are other defects in Jensen's research, but none more fundamental than this.[13] One is reminded of E. A. Ross's succinct assessment of over fifty years ago, that ' "race" is the cheap explanation tyros offer for any collective trait that they are too stupid or too lazy to trace to its origin in the physical environment, the social environment, or historical conditions.'[14]

The point to be made here is that systems of 'racial' stratification are social phenomena based on social rather than biological facts. To be sure, certain conspicuous characteristics which are genetically determined or influenced (skin colour, hair form, facial conformation, stature, etc.) are widely used as convenient indicators by which ancestry and hence 'racial' identity is recognized. This is the 'colour bar' which exists in many societies. But such indicators are never sufficient in themselves to indicate group membership and in some instances are wholly unreliable, for it is percentage rather than appearance or genetics which is the basis for these distinctions. One who does not display the overt characteristics of his 'racial' group is still accorded its status if his relationship to the group is known or can be

discovered. The specific rules for ascertaining racial identity differ from society to society. In America, if a person is known to have had a sociologically black ancestor, he is black regardless of how many of his ancestors were sociologically white (and even though he looks and acts white). In South Africa, most American blacks would be regarded as 'coloured' rather than 'black.' Traditionally, in a mixed marriage, one is a Jew only if one's mother is a Jew. In contemporary India, an Anglo-Indian has a male European ancestor in the paternal line; female and maternal European ancestry are irrelevant. In racially stratified societies, phenotypical traits are thus never more than clues to a person's social identity.

As Shibutani and Kwan have noted, 'a color line is something existing in the presuppositions of men.'[15] '. . . what is decisive about "race relations" is not that people are genetically different but that they approach one another with dissimilar perspectives.'[16] Van den Berghe makes a similar point: 'Race, of course, has no intrinsic significance, except to a racist. To a social scientist, race acquires meaning only through its social definition in a given society.'[17]

This is illustrated by the title of DeVos and Wagatsuma's book, *Japan's Invisible Race*, dealing with the hereditarily stigmatized and oppressed Burakumin. The Japanese believe that these people are physically and morally distinct, and their segregation and oppression are explained on that basis when in fact they are not so at all. Instead they are recognizable only by family (ancestry), name, occupation, place of residence, life style, etc. The Burakumin thus comprise a 'race' in the sociological sense of Western racism, but an 'invisible' (i.e., not genetic or phenotypic) one. The authors subtitled the book, *Caste in Culture and Personality*, shifting the analogy from that of race (in the West) to that of caste (in India). The book could as well have been entitled: *Caste in Japan: Racial Stratification in Culture and Personality*.

The Japanese example brings up a point which needs to be made about the alleged uniqueness of 'racial' stratification. *All* systems of birth-ascribed stratification seem to include a belief that the social distinctions are reflected in biological (i.e., 'racial') differences. That is, caste and other ethnic differences are said to be revealed in physical makeup or appearance. Associated with these supposed natural and unalterable inherited physical characteristics are equally immutable traits of character, morality, intelligence, personality, and purity. This is the case in Japan, where no actual physical differences can be detected; it is true in India and Swat where physical stereotypes about castes abound but actual differences are minimal; it is true in Ruanda where the ranked groups all are black but are said to differ in stature and physiognomy as well as in culture; it is true in the United States where the physical differences are commonly and erroneously thought to be absolute. Cultural factors have to be relied upon in addition to whatever biological ones may be present, in order to make the important discriminations upon which ranked social interaction depends, and even then mistakes are frequently made. Throughout the world, people who look distinctive are likely to be regarded as socially different; people who are regarded as socially different are likely to be thought to look distinctive. They are also likely to be required to dress and act distinctively.

I suggest that, just as societies frequently dramatize the social differences among kin groups (e.g., sibs, clans, phratries) by giving to them totemic names and attributing to them characteristics of animals or plants, thereby identifying the social differences with biological species differences,[18] so also, societies with birth-ascribed status hierarchies dramatize and legitimize these crucial social differences by attributing to them innate biological, hence, 'racial' differences. As a result the concept of miscegenation arises, based on an ideology of innate difference contradicted by a persistent and recurrent perception of similarity by people of opposite sex across social boundaries.[19]

Thus, caste organization and ethnic stratification include racism; racial stratification is congruent with caste and ethnic stratification. Their ultimate coalescence is in the imputation of biological differences to explain and justify birth-ascribed social inequality. In this regard, sexual stratification can be seen to be a phenomenon of the same order.

This universality of racism in birth-ascribed stratification can be understood in the fact that physical traits not only dramatize social differentiation, but can also explain and justify it. The effect of such explanation is to make social inequality appear to be a natural necessity rather than a human choice and hence an artificial imposition. Social distinctions are man-made and learned; what man makes and learns he can unmake and unlearn. What God or biology has ordained is beyond man's control. The former may be defined as artificial, unjust, untenable, and remediable; the latter as inevitable or divinely sanctioned. This is important because birth-ascribed stratification is widely or universally resented by those whom it oppresses (at least as it affects them), and advocated by those it rewards. Both categories share the human capability of empathy, and it inspires envy and resentment in the one and fear or guilt in the other. Racism—the self-righteous rationalization in terms of biology—is a desperate and perhaps ultimately futile attempt to counteract those subversive emotions.

In sum, 'race,' as commonly used by social scientists, emphasizes common physical characteristics (as does 'sex'); 'caste' emphasizes common rank, occupational specialization, endogamy, and corporate organization; 'ethnic stratification' emphasizes cultural distinctiveness. These are real differences in meaning, but the degree of empirical overlap in systems so described, and the commonalities in the existential worlds of those who live within them are so great as to render the distinctions among them largely arbitrary, and irrelevant, for many purposes. Individual cases differ, but as types of social stratification, they are similar. With equal facility and comparable effect, they utilize as evidence of social identity anything which is passed on with the group: skin colour, hair form, stature, physiognomy, language, dress, occupation, place of residence, genealogy, behavior patterns, religion. None is wholly reliable, all are difficult to dissimulate. In any case, strong sanctions can be brought to bear to minimize the temptation to 'pass' among those who might be capable and tempted. As the case of India suggests and Japan confirms, social criteria can be as rigid as physical ones.

'Race' versus 'Caste'

Considerable controversy has surrounded the terms 'race' and 'caste' when applied outside of the contexts in which they originated and to which they have been most widely applied: Western colonialism and Hindu India, respectively. This is understandable because there are important peculiarities in each of these situations, and to extend the terms beyond them requires that those peculiarities be subordinated to significant similarities. Systems of birth-ascribed inequality are sufficiently similar, however, to invite comparative study, and some general term is needed to refer to them. 'Caste' has seemed to me more useful than 'race,' because it refers to social rather than allegedly biological distinctions, and it is the social distinctions which are universal in such systems. If it were a catchier term, 'ethnic stratification' might replace both in the social scientific literature. Unfortunately it is not, so we must probably await a better term or tolerate continuing terminological dispute and confusion. In any case, it is the nature of birth-ascribed stratification—the ideas, behaviours, and experiences which comprise it, the effects it has on persons and societies and, quite frankly, the means by which it may be eliminated—in which I am interested. The words applied to it are of little importance. When I try to explain American race relations to Indians, I describe and analyse America as a caste stratified society, with attention to the similarities and differences in comparison with India. If I am trying to explain Indian caste stratification to Americans, I describe and analyse India as a racist society, with attention to the similarities and differences in comparison to the United States. I do this as a matter of translation from the social idiom of one society to the other. It is the most economic, vivid, and accurate way I know to convey these phenomena to people whose experience is limited to one system or the other. I do not think Indian caste *is* American race, or vice versa, but neither do I think that race stratification in America *is* race stratification in South Africa or that caste in India *is* caste in Swat, or that caste in the Punjab *is* caste in Kerala. Neither do I think racial stratification and racism are the same for blacks, Chicanos, and whites in America, or that caste stratification and casteism are the same for sweepers, blacksmiths, and Rajputs in Hindu India. There are features in all of these which are the same in important ways, and by focusing on these I think we can understand and explain and predict the experience of people in these diverse situations

better than if we regard each of them as unique in every way.

Colonialism

The concept of colonialism has gained popularity in recent years for the analysis of racism and racial stratification in the West.[20] It therefore merits further discussion. This model focuses on the history of Western expansion and the exploitation of alien peoples, emphasizing notions of the superiority of the dominant, Western, white society whose members arrogated privilege to themselves through the exercise of power (usually technological, often military) to dominate, control, exploit, and oppress others. Racism has been an integral aspect of this process, for there usually have been differences in colour between the colonizer and the colonized which were used to account for the alleged inferiority in ability, character, and mentality which in turn were used to justify colonial domination. Colonialism has been most often described as the result of overseas conquest, in which case the colonizing group has usually comprised a numerical minority. Less often colonialism has included conquest or expansion across national boundaries overland, but the results are the same, if the romance is less. These phenomena have recently come to be termed 'external colonialism,' in contrast to 'internal colonialism' which refers to similar domination and exploitation, within a nation, of an indigenous, over-run, or imported minority. This distinction directs attention to the *locus* of colonial domination whereas the distinction between third-world and fourth-world colonies cited above, directs attention to the *sources* of that domination.

While it has not been much easier to gain acceptance of the colonial model for analysis of American race relations than it has been to gain acceptance of the caste model, it is clear that here again, the problem is semantic rather than substantive. Some of those who argue persuasively the cross-cultural and multi-situational applicability of the colonial model deny such applicability for the caste model and in so doing use precisely the logic and data they deplore and regard as faulty when their intellectual adversaries deny applicability of 'colonialsim' outside of the classical overseas context.[21]

Colonialism, external and internal, is a process which has occurred repeatedly, in many contexts with many specific manifestations and many common results. It long antedates the recent period of European and American expansion. Caste stratification, racial stratification, ethnic stratification, and 'pluralism' have been its recurrent products.[22] The point can be made with specific reference to caste in India. Rather than regarding colonialism as an antecedent condition which excludes traditional India from the category of racially or ethically stratified societies, it can well be used as a basis for assigning India historical priority among such societies, in the contemporary world. That is, traditional India may represent the most fully evolved and complex post-colonial society in the world. It is easy to obtain explanations of caste from informants or books in India which refer directly to the presumed early domination of primitive indigenes by advanced invaders. There is little doubt that the present caste system had its origins some 3,000 to 3,500 years ago in a socio-cultural confrontation that was essentially colonial. Low status was imposed on technologically disadvantaged indigenes by more sophisticated, militarily and administratively superior peoples who encroached or invaded from the north and west, arrogating to themselves high rank, privileges, and land. The large number of local and ethnically distinct groups on the sub-continent were fitted into a scheme of social hierarchy which was brought in or superimposed by the high status outsiders, culminating in the caste system we know today.[23] Social separation and social hierarchy based on ancestry became the essence of the system; colonial relations were its genesis. Even today, most tribal people—those who are geographically and economically marginal and culturally distinct—are incorporated into Hindu society, if at all, at the bottom of the hierarchy (except in those rare instances where they have maintained control over land or other important sources of income and power).

If one were to speculate on the course of evolution which ethnic stratification might take in the United States in the context of internal colonialism, of rigid separation, hierarchy, and discrimination which are part of it, and the demands for ethnic autonomy which arise in response to it, one possibility would be a caste system similar to, though less complex than that of India. The historical circumstances may be rather similar despite the separation of many hundreds of years, many thousands of miles and a chasm of cultural difference. Actually, development of the degree of social separation common in India seems at this point unlikely given the mass communications and mass education in the United States, its relative prosperity, and the rather widespread (but far from universal) commitment to at least the trappings of social equality. But surely if anything is to be learned from history and from comparison, the case of the Indian sub-continent should be of major interest to students of American race and ethnic relations, social stratification, and internal colonialism.

In sum, colonialism is as inextricable from caste and race as caste and race are from one another. There may be instances of colonialism where birth-ascription is or becomes irrelevant, but every instance of caste, race, and ethnic stratification includes, and relies for its perpetuation upon, the kind of ethnic domination and exploitation that defines colonialism.

Class
Closely associated with each of the models discussed here is that of social class. Class is a matter of acquired status rather than of birth-ascription, and is in this respect distinct from race, caste, and ethnic stratification, with different social consequences. In a class system, one is ranked in accord with his behaviour and attributes (income, occupation, education, life style, etc.). In a birth-ascribed system, by contrast, one behaves and exhibits attributes in accord with his rank. In a class system, individual mobility is legitimate, albeit often difficult, while in ascribed stratification it is explicitly forbidden. Systems of acquired rank—class systems—prescribe the means to social mobility; systems of ascribed rank proscribe them. As a consequence, a class system is a continuum; there are individuals who are intergrades, there are individuals in the process of movement, there are individuals who have experienced more than one rank. Miscegenation is not an issue because there are no ancestrally distinct groups to be inappropriately mixed. A birth-ascribed system is comprised of discrete ranks on the pattern of echelon organization,

without legitimate mobility, without intergrades; the strata are named, publicly recognized, clearly bounded. Miscegenation is therefore a social issue. In a system of acquired ranks, the strata may be indistinct, imperfectly known, or even unknown to those within the system. In fact, there is considerable debate among students of stratification as to whether or not awareness of class is essential to a definition of class. Some hold that social classes are properly defined by social analysts who use such criteria as income to designate categories which may be entirely unrecognized by those in the society.

In a class system individuals regard themselves as potentially able to change status legitimately within the system through fortune, misfortune, or individual and family efforts. In a birth-ascribed system, individuals know that legitimate status change is impossible—that only dissimulation, revolution, or an improbable change is publicly accorded social identity can alter one's rank and hence life-chances.

Despite these differences, class is in no way incompatible with birth-ascribed systems. In fact, in so far as it is a term for categories of people ranked by income, occupation, education, and life style, it co-occurs with them. Low castes, despised races, ethnic minorities, and colonized people comprise economically and occupationally depressed, exploited classes who are politically and socially oppressed; high castes, exalted races, privileged ethnic groups, and colonizers comprise economically and occupationally privileged, power-wielding, elite classes who live off the labour of others. In this respect, class differences pervade and reinforce systems of birth-ascribed stratification. Furthermore, it is not unusual to find significant class differentials within a caste, racial, or ethnic group or within a colonized or colonial group.[24] That is, class, in the conventional sense often occurs conspicuously within such groups, and may also bridge their boundaries without obscuring them. But it is not possible to analyse birth-ascribed stratification solely in terms of class, for no amount of class mobility will exempt a person from the crucial implications of his birth in such systems.

Those who have sought to identify the positions of European immigrants to America such as the Poles, Italians, and Irish, with the position of blacks, Native Americans, Chicanos, and Asians have failed to discern the essential fact that racism is the basis of American caste, and that it bestows upon those who experience it a unique social, political, and economic stigma which is not bestowed by class or national origin. Second generation white Europeans can meet all of the criteria for acceptance into the American white race-caste, for they are regarded as being only culturally different. A fifteenth generation American black, or a fifteen-hundredth generation American Indian cannot, for their differences are regarded as innate, immutable, and crucial. Equalitarianism has produced no 'American dilemma' among racists, as Myrdal believed, simply because it is an equality for whites only, and its extension to other groups has moved slowly, painfully, and with vehement opposition, even where it has moved at all.

Systems of collective social rank, whether ascribed or acquired, are systems for retaining privilege among the powerful and power among the privileged, reserving and maintaining vulnerability, oppression, and want for those upon whom it can be imposed with minimal risk while retaining their services and their deference. In this way they are similar. In the principles of recruitment and organization by which that similarity is effected and in the individuals' prospects for mobility they differ, and those differences have important consequences for individual life experience and social processes in the societies which harbour them.

Pluralism

Pluralism is a model which has been applied to socially and culturally diverse societies since the writings of Furnivall on South-East Asia.[25] Cultural pluralism obtains when 'two or more different cultural traditions characterize the population of a given society'; it is 'a special form of differentiation based on institutional divergences.'[26] Systems of birth-ascribed stratification are inevitably systems of social and cultural pluralism because they are accompanied by social separation. In a caste system, 'Because intensive and status-equal interaction is limited to the caste, a common and distinctive caste culture is assured. This is a function of the quality and density of communication within the group, for culture is learned, shared and transmitted.'[27] The same is true for any system of racial or ethnic stratification. M. G. Smith has noted, 'it is perfectly clear that in any social system based on intense cleavages and discontinuity between differentiated segments the community of values or social relations between these sections will be correspondingly low. This is precisely the structural condition of the plural society.'[28] And I have noted elsewhere that,

> . . . castes are discrete social and cultural entities. . . . They are maintained by defining and maintaining boundaries between castes; they are threatened when boundaries are compromised. Even when interaction between castes is maximal and cultural differences are minimal, the ideal of mutual isolation and distinctiveness is maintained and advertised among those who value the system. Similarly, even when mobility within, or subversion of the system is rampant, a myth of stability is stolidly maintained among those who benefit from the system.[29]

Mutual isolation of social groups inevitably leads to group-specific institutions (an important criterion for pluralism according to Furnivall), because members are excluded from participation in the institutions of other groups.

Caste, race, and ethnic stratification, like all plural systems therefore, are systems of social separation and cultural heterogeneity, maintained by common or over-riding economic and political institutions rather than by agreement or consensus regarding the stratification system and its rationale.[30] This does not deny consensus, it only defines its nature:

> In caste systems, as in all plural systems, highly differentiated groups get along together despite widely differing subjective definitions of the situation because they agree on the objective facts of what is happening and what is likely to happen— on who has the power, and how, under what circumstances, and for what purposes it is likely to be exercised. They cease to get along when this crucial agreement changes or is challenged.[31]

The constituent social elements of plural societies need not be birth-ascribed, and they need not be (and sometimes are not) ranked relative to one another, although by Furnivall's definition, one element must be dominant. In fact, unranked

pluralism is the goal many ethnic minorities choose over either stratification or assimilation. But a system of birth-ascribed stratification is always culturally, socially and hence institutionally heterogeneous, and thus pluralistic.

Hierarchy as Symbolic Interaction

I have elsewhere described the universality among social hierarchies of patterns of interaction which symbolize superiority and inferiority.[32] Social hierarchy, after all, exists only in the experiences, behaviours, and beliefs of those who comprise it. Interpersonal interaction becomes the vehicle for expression of hierarchy: for asserting, testing, validating or rejecting claims to status. Almost every interaction between members of ranked groups expresses rank claimed, perceived, or accorded. When the hierarchy is birth-ascribed, the membership of its component groups is ideally stable, well-known, and easily recognizable. In such systems people are perceived by those outside of their groups almost wholly in terms of their group identity rather than as individuals. They are regarded as sharing the characteristics which are conventionally attributed to the group and they share the obligations, responsibilities, privileges, and disabilities of their group. In intergroup relations, therefore, one individual is substitutable for another in his group, for all are alike and interchangeable. This is the setting for prejudice, discrimination, bigotry, chauvinism, and is an ideal situation for scapegoating. These attitudes and their behavioral consequences are designated and deplored by such terms as racism, casteism, communalism (referring to ethnic chauvinism of various sorts), and recently, sexism. They are characterized by domination, deprivation, oppression, exploitation, and denigration directed downward; obedience, acquiescence, service, deference, and honour demanded from above. They result in envy, resentment, dissimulation, and resistance arising from below, balanced from above by fear, guilt, and that combination of arrogant self-righteousness and rationalization which is found in all such systems. Maya Angelou has aptly characterized the result in American race relations as 'the humorless puzzle of inequality and hate'; 'the question of worth and values, of aggressive inferiority and aggressive arrogance'[33] which confronts and exacts its toll not only from black Americans, but from the denizens of all those jungles of inherited inequality I call caste systems. It is this quality of interpersonal relations rather than any particular event or structural feature which struck me most vividly, forcefully, and surprisingly as similar in Alabama and India when I first experienced them for over a year each within a period of five years.[34] For me, this is the hallmark of oppressive, birth-ascribed stratification.

A specifically interactional definition of caste systems applies equally to all systems of birth-ascribed stratification: *a system of birth-ascribed groups each of which comprises for its members the maximum limit of status-equal interaction, and between all of which interaction is consistently hierarchical.*[35] The cultural symbols of hierarchical interaction vary; the presence and importance of such symbols is universal and essential to racism, casteism, and their homologues.

Hierarchy as Ideology

Dumont has emphasized the point that Indian caste is unique in that it is based on an ideology of hierarchy defined in terms of ritual purity and pollution.[36] He regards other systems of hierarchical social separation as non-comparable because of the inevitable differences in the ideologies supporting them. In the comparative framework which I advocate, I maintain simply that the Hindu rationale is one of several ideologies (cf. those of Islamic Swat, of the South Indian Lingayats to whom purity is irrelevant, of Ruanda, of Japan, and the United States) which can and do underlie and justify systems of birth-ascribed social hierarchy. Each is unique to the culture in which it occurs; each is associated with remarkably similar social structures, social processes, and individual experiences. I believe that anyone who has experienced daily life in rural India and the rural American South, for example, will confirm the fact that there is something remarkably similar in the systems of social relations and attitudes. I believe that anyone who has experienced daily life in an urban slum, a public market, or a factory in India and the United States would come to the same conclusion. That similarity is generated by birth-ascribed stratification and it is not concealed by differential ideologies.[37]

Contrary to another of Dumont's assump-

tions (shared with Cox), there is nothing incompatible between an ideology which underwrites a hierarchy of groups and a notion of equality within each group. This combination, in fact, is found not only in the United States where it accounts for the above-mentioned absence of a real 'American dilemma' in race relations, but also in each of the other systems described here. Members of each ranked group are *inherently unequal* to those of each other group and are by birth *potentially equal* to those of their own group. More importantly, the existence of an ideology of hierarchy does not mean that this ideology is conceived and interpreted identically by all within the system it is presumed to justify or even that it is shared by them. Acquiescence must not be mistaken for concurrence. Dumont's assumption to the contrary is the most glaring weakness in his analysis of Indian caste.[38]

Sexual Stratification

Finally, in my discussion of models for analysis, I turn to the controversial and sociologically puzzling matter of sex as a basis for social separation and inequality. The special problems which the sexual criterion poses for the student of stratification are both academic and substantive. The academic problems derive from the history of the study of stratification. Although the role of women in various non-Western societies has been discussed by anthropologists (including prominently Margaret Mead), and the position of women in European societies has been discussed by some social historians, the sexual dichotomy rarely appears in sociological works on stratification. That this criterion has been largely ignored or dismissed by stratification theorists is attributable to several factors not the least of which is no doubt that members of the privileged sex have authored most of the work and to them such ranking has not been a problem and hence has not been apparent. Also, their culturally derived biases have been such that this kind of ranking was taken for granted as a manifestation of biological differences. 'Many people who are very hip to the implications of the racial caste system . . . don't seem to be able to see the sexual caste system and if the question is raised they respond with: "that's the way it's supposed to be. There are biological differences." Or with other statements which recall a white segregationist confronted with integration.'[39] The biological rationale—what Millett refers to as the 'view of sex as a caste structure ratified by nature'[40]— recalls also the justification offered for all birth-ascribed dominance-exploitation relationships be they caste in India, Burakumin status in Japan, sexual roles, or any other. In each instance the plea is that these are uniquely real, significant, unavoidable, and natural differences, and therefore they must be acted upon. Thus, in an interview about their book, *The Imperial Animal*, which is said to claim that males have dominated human history because 'the business of politics . . . is a business that requires skills and attitudes that are peculiarly male,' anthropologists Robin Fox and Lionel Tiger were reported to have vehemently denied that their theory about the reasons for women's roles might be a sexist theory. ' "These are the facts, don't accuse us of making up the species," Tiger said.' And again, ' "Because this is a racist country, people relate sexism to racism." But these two reactions are actually different because while there are no important biological differences between races, there are very important differences between the sexes.'[41] Whether the differences are real or not (and who would deny that males and females differ in important ways?), the sociological and humanistic question is whether the differences require or justify differential opportunities, privileges, responsibilities, and rewards or, put negatively, domination and exploitation.

Birth-ascribed stratification, be it sexual, racial, or otherwise, is always accompanied by explanations, occasionally ingenious but usually mundane and often ludicrous, as to why putative natural differences *do* require and justify social differences. Those explanations are widely doubted by those whose domination they are supposed to explain, and this includes increasing numbers of women.

The substantive issues which becloud the topic of sexual stratification have to do with the mode of recruitment, the socialization, membership, and structural arrangements of sexually ranked categories. First, there is the fact that while sex is determined at birth, it is not contingent upon ancestry, endogamy, or any other arrangement of marriage or family, and is not predictable. It is the only recurrent basis for birth-ascribed stratification that can be defensibly attributed solely to undeniably physical characteristics. Even here there are individual or categorical exceptions made for transvestites, hermaphrodites, homosexuals, etc., in some societies as in the case of *hijaras* in India.[42] The significance (as contrasted to the fact) of the diagnostic physical traits—of sexual differences—is, however, largely socially defined, so that their cultural expressions vary widely over time and space. Second, as a concomitant to the mode of recruitment, males and females have no distinct ethnic or regional histories. It must not be overlooked, however, that they do have distinct social histories in every society. Third, the universal co-residence of males and females within the household precludes the existence of lifelong, separate male and female societies as such, and usually assures a degree of mutual early socialization. But note that it does not preclude distinct male and female social institutions, distinct patterns of social interaction within and between these categories or distinguishable male and female subcultures (in fact the latter are universal) including, for example, distinct male and female dialects.

Partly as a consequence of these factors, the nature and quality of segregation of the sexes has not been defined by sociologists as comparable to that of the other ascriptive social categories discussed here. Nevertheless, most of the characteristics of birth-ascribed separation and stratification (racial, caste, ethnic, colonial, class, and pluralistic characteristics), and virtually all of the psychological and social consequences of inborn, lifelong superiority-inferiority relations are to be found in the relationship of males and females in most societies. These stem from similar factors in early socialization and from stereotypes and prejudices enacted and enforced in differential roles and opportunity structures, rationalized by ideologies of differential intrinsic capabilities and worth, sustained and defended through the combination of power and vested interest that is common to all birth-ascribed inequality. I have elsewhere contrasted some of the consequences of these assumptions and behaviours in the United States and India as reflected in the political participation of women in the two nations although this is dwarfed by Millett's more recent work on male domination, its sources, and manifestations in the West.[43]

If we agree with van den Berghe that 'race can be treated as a special case of invidious status differentiation or a special criterion of stratification,[44] I think we are bound to agree that sex is another.

Consequences of Inherited Inequality

Assuming that there are significant structural and interactional similarities among systems of birth-ascribed stratification, the question can still be legitimately asked, 'so what?' Is this merely a more or less interesting observation—even a truism—or does it have some theoretical or practical significance? My answer would be that it has both, for such systems have common and predictable consequences in the individual lives of those who live them and in the cumulative events which comprise the ongoing histories of the societies which harbour them.

> Caste systems are living environments to those who comprise them. Yet there is a tendency among those who study and analyse them to intellectualize caste, and in the process to squeeze the life out of it. Caste is people, and especially people interacting in characteristic ways and thinking in characteristic ways. Thus, in addition to being a structure, a caste system is a set of human relationships and it is a state of mind.[45]

Their 'human implications' are justification enough for studying and comparing systems of birth-ascribed stratification. There are neither the data nor the space to discuss these implications fully here, but I will suggest the nature of the evidence briefly, identifying psychological and social consequences. I am well aware that many features of such systems are found in all sharply stratified societies. Some are characteristic of all relationships of superordination and subordination, of poverty and affluence, of differential power. Others are found in all societies made up of distinct sub-groups whether stratified or not. It is the unique combination of characteristics in the context of the ideal of utter rigidity and unmitigable inequality which makes systems of stratification by race, caste, ethnicity, and sex distinctive in their impact on people, individually and collectively.

Psychological Consequences

Beliefs and attitudes associated with rigid stratification can be suggested by such terms as paternalism and dependence, *noblesse oblige*, arrogance, envy, resentment, hatred, prejudice, rationalization, emulation, self-doubt, and self-hatred. Those who are oppressed often respond to such stratification by attempting to escape either the circumstances or the consequences of the system. The realities of power and dependence make more usual an accommodation to oppression which, however, is likely to be less passive than is often supposed, and is likely to be unequivocally revealed when the slightest change in the perceived distribution of power occurs. Those who are privileged in the system seek to sustain and justify it, devoting much of their physical effort to the former and much of their psychic and verbal effort to the latter. When these systems are birth-ascribed, all of these features are exacerbated.

Kardiner and Ovesey conclude their classic, and by now outdated, study of American Negro personality, *Mark of Oppression*, with the statement: 'The psycho-social expressions of the Negro personality that we have described are the *integrated* end products of the process of oppression.'[46] Although it is appropriate to question their characterization of that personality in the light of subsequent events and research, there is no doubt that such oppression has recurrent psychological consequences for both the oppressor and the oppressed, as Robert Coles has demonstrated in *Children of Crisis* and subsequent works.[47]

Oppression does not befall everyone in a system of birth-ascribed inequality. Most notably, it does not befall those with power. What does befall all is the imposition by birth of unalterable membership in ranked, socially isolated, but interacting groups with rigidly defined and conspicuously different experiences, opportunities, public esteem and, inevitably, self-esteem. The black in America and in South Africa, the Burakumin of Japan, the Harijan of India, the barber or washerman of Swat, the Hutu or Twa of Ruanda, have all faced similar conditions as individuals and they have responded to them in similar ways. The same can be said for the privileged and dominant groups in each of these societies, for while painful consequences of subordination are readily apparent, the consequences of superordination are equally real and important. Thus, ethnic stratification leaves its characteristic and indelible imprint on all who experience it.

The consequences of birth-ascribed stratification are self-fulfilling and self-perpetuating, for although low status groups do not adopt views of themselves or their statuses which are consistent with the views held by their superiors, they are continually acting them out and cannot avoid internalizing some of them and the self-doubts they engender, just as high status groups internalize their superiority and self-righteousness. The oppression of others by the latter serves to justify and bolster their superiority complex and to rationalize for them the deprivation and exploitation of those they denigrate. 'Once you denigrate someone in that way,' say Kardiner and Ovesey, 'the sense of guilt makes it imperative to degrade the subject further to justify the whole procedure.'[48] Gallagher notes that in the southern United States,

> By the attitudes of mingled fear, hostility, deprecation, discrimination, amused patronage, friendly domination, and rigid authoritarianism, the white caste generates opposite and complementary attitudes in the Negro caste. It is a touch of consummate irony that the dominant group should then argue that the characteristics which exhibit themselves in the submerged group are 'natural' or 'racial.'[49]

The products of oppression are thus used to justify oppression.

Change and Emancipation

The self-reinforcing degradation described above combines with greed and fear of status-loss or revolt to comprise a dynamic of oppression which, in birth-ascribed stratification, probably accounts for the widespread occurrence of pariah status or untouchability. Elites characteristically justify oppression by compounding it; they enhance their own rewards by denying them ever more stringently to social inferiors, and they strive to protect themselves from challenges to status and privilege from below by rigidifying the status boundaries, reinforcing the sanctions which enforce them, and increasing the monopoly on power which makes the sanctions effective. This assures increasing social separation and hierarchical distance between groups until such time as it generates rebellion, reform, or disintegration.

The fact that social order prevails most of the time in any given instance of inherited inequality does not mean that all of those in the system accept it or their places within it willingly, nor does it mean that the system is either stable or static. It most often means that power is held and exercised effectively by those in superordinate statuses, for the time being. Such systems are based on conformity more than consensus, and are maintained by sanctions more than agreement. Nevertheless, change is inherent, resistance and mobility-striving are universal, and effective challenges to such systems are probably ultimately inevitable because the response they elicit from those they oppress is subversive. The possibility of acting out the subversion depends largely upon the balance of power among the stratified groups and the definitions of the situation their members hold. The processes of change and patterns of conflict which lead to them are major areas of commonality in such systems.[50]

The history of every caste system, of every racially stratified system, of every instance of birth-ascribed oppression is a history of striving, conflict and occasional revolt. That this is not generally acknowledged is largely a result of the fact that most of these actions occur in the context of overwhelming power and uncompromising enforcement by the hereditary elites and are therefore expressed in the form of day-to-day resentment and resistance handled so subtly and occurring so routinely that it goes unremarked.[51] Even conspicuous manifestations are likely to be quickly and brutally put down, confined to a particular locality or group, and knowledge of their occurrence suppressed by those against whom they have been directed. These phenomena often can only be discovered by consulting and winning the confidence of members of oppressed groups, and this is rarely done.

Only the most spectacular instances of resistance, and the few successful ones are likely to be well-known. Immediately to mind come such martyrs to the cause of emancipation of oppressed peoples as the Thracian slave Spartacus, who led a rebellion against Rome; the American slave rebellion leaders Gabriel and Nat Turner, the white abolitionist John Brown, and the contemporary leaders of black emancipation in America, Martin Luther King, Medgar Evers, and others (too many of them martyred) among their fellow leaders and supporters, black and white. No doubt there are many more, most of them unknown and unsung, in the history of all groups whose members society condemns by birth to oppression. In the folk history of every such group, and in the memory of every member, are instances of courageous or foolhardy people who have challenged or outwitted their oppressors, often at the cost of their own foreseeable and inevitable destruction.

Better-known and better-documented than the individuals who led and sometimes died for them, are the emancipation movements which have occurred in most such societies—movements such as those for black power and black separatism in the United States, anti-casteism and anti-touchability in India, Hutu emancipation in Rwanda and Burundi, Burakumin emancipation in Japan, and anti-apartheid in South Africa. All have depended primarily upon concerted efforts to apply political, economic, or military power to achieve their ends. They have comprised direct challenges to the systems. Most have followed after the failure of attempts less militant, less likely to succeed, and hence less threatening to social elites—attempts towards assimilation or mobility within the systems such as those of status emulation.

Henry Adams characterized the slave society of Virginia in 1800 as 'ill at ease.'[52] This seems to be the chronic state of societies so organized— the privileged cannot relax their vigilance against the rebellious resentment of the deprived. That such rigid, oppressive systems do function and persist is a credit not to the consensus they engender any more than to the justice or rationality of the systems. Rather, it is a tribute to the effectiveness of the monopoly on power which the privileged are able to maintain. When in such systems deprived people get the vote, get jobs, get money, get legal redress, get guns, get powerful allies, get public support for their aspirations, they perceive a change in the power situation and an enhancement of the likelihood of successful change in their situation, and they are likely to attempt to break out of their oppressed status. These conditions do not generate the desire for change, for that is intrinsic; they merely make it

seem worthwhile to attempt the change. Sometimes the triggering factor is not that the deprived believe conditions have changed so that success is more likely, but rather that conditions have led them to define the risk and consequences of failure (even its virtual certainty) as acceptable. Resultant changes are often drastic and traumatic of achievement, but they are sought by the oppressed and by enlightened people of all statuses precisely because of the heavy individual and societal costs of maintaining inherited inequality and because of its inherent inhumanity.

An important difference between the dynamics of inherited stratification and acquired stratification results from the fact that in the latter, power and privilege accompany achievable status, emulation is at least potentially effective, and mobility and assimilation are realistic goals. Therefore energies of status resentment may rationally be channelled toward mobility. Most immigrant groups in the United States, for example, have found this out as they have merged with the larger society after one or two generations of socialization. But in a system where inherited, unalterable group identity is the basis for rewards, emulation alone cannot achieve upward mobility, and assimilation is impossible so long as the system exists (in fact, prevention of assimilation is one of its main functions). Only efforts to destroy, alter, or circumvent the system make sense. In the United States, blacks, Chicanos, and Native Americans have found this out. Only in response to changes in the distribution of power is such inherited status likely to be re-evaluated and the distribution of rewards altered.

Conclusion

'Race' as the term is used in America, Europe, and South Africa, is not qualitatively different in its implications for human social life from caste, *varna*, or *jati* as applied in India, *quom* in Swat and Muslim India, the 'invisible race' of Japan, the ethnic stratification of Rwanda and Burundi. Racism and casteism are indistinguishable in the annals of man's inhumanity to man, and sexism is closely allied to them as man's inhumanity to woman. All are invidious distinctions imposed unalterably at birth upon whole categories of people to justify the unequal social distribution of power, livelihood, security, privilege, esteem, freedom—in short, life chances. Where distinctions of this type are employed, they affect people and the events which people generate in surprisingly similar ways despite the different historical and cultural conditions in which they occur.

If I were asked, 'What practical inference, if any, is to be drawn from the comparative study of inherited inequality—of ascriptive social ranking?' I would say it is this: There is no way to reform such institutions; the only solution is their dissolution. As Kardiner and Ovesey said long ago *'there is only one way that the products of oppression can be dissolved, and that is to stop the oppression.'*[53] To stop the oppression, one must eliminate the structure of inherited stratification upon which it rests. Generations of Burakumin, Hutu, blacks, untouchables, and their sympathizers have tried reform without notable success. Effective change has come only when the systems have been challenged directly.

The boiling discontent of birth-ascribed deprivation cannot be contained by pressing down the lid of oppression or by introducing token flexibility, or by preaching brotherly love. The only hope lies in restructuring society and redistributing its rewards so as to end the inequality. Such behavioral change must come first. From it may follow attitudinal changes as meaningful, status-equal interaction undermines racist, casteist, communalist, and sexist beliefs and attitudes, but oppressed people everywhere have made it clear that it is the end of oppression, not brotherly love, which they seek most urgently. To await the latter before achieving the former is futility; to achieve the former first does not guarantee achievement of the latter, but it increases the chances and makes life liveable. In any case, the unranked pluralism which many minorities seek requires only equality, not love.

To those who fear this course on the grounds that it will be traumatic and dangerous, I would say that it is less so than the futile attempt to prevent change. Philip Mason spoke for all systems of inborn inequality when he called the Spartan oppression of the Helots in ancient Greece a trap from which there was no escape.

It was the Helots who released the Spartans from such ignoble occupations as trade and agricul-

ture. . . . But it was the Helots who made it necessary to live in an armed camp, constantly on the alert against revolt. . . . They had a wolf by the ears; they dared not let go. And it was of their own making; they had decided—at some stage and by what process one can only guess—that the Helots would remain separate and without rights forever.[54]

That way, I believe, lies ultimate disaster for any society. A thread of hope lies in the possibility that people can learn from comparison of the realities of inherited inequality across space, time, and culture, and can act to preclude the disaster that has befallen others by eliminating the system which guarantees it. It is a very thin thread.

REFERENCES

1. Max Weber, *From Max Weber: Essays in Sociology*, H. H. Gerth and C. W. Mills trans. and ed. (New York, Oxford University Press, 1946); W. G. Runciman, 'Class, Status and Power?', in *Social Stratification*, J. A. Jackson, ed. (London, Cambridge University Press, 1968), pp. 25–61.

2. See for Ruanda: Jacques J. Maquet, *The Premise of Inequality in Ruanda* (London, Oxford University Press, 1961); for India: F. G. Bailey, 'Closed Social Stratification in India,' *European Journal of Sociology* (Vol. IV, 1963); Gerald D. Berreman, 'Caste: The Concept,' in *International Encyclopedia of the Social Sciences*, D. Sills, ed. (New York, Macmillan and The Free Press, 1968), Vol. II, pp. 333–9; André Béteille, *Castes Old and New* (Bombay, Asia Publishing House, 1969); Louis Dumont, *Homo Hierarchicus* (London, Weidenfeld and Nicolson, 1970); J. H. Hutton, *Caste in India, Its Nature, Functions and Origins* (London, Cambridge University Press, 1946); Adrian C. Mayer, 'Caste: The Indian Caste System,' in D. Sills, ed., op. cit., pp. 339–44; M. N. Srinivas, *Caste in Modern India and Other Essays* (Bombay, Asia Publishing House, 1962), and *Social Change in Modern India* (Berkeley, University of California Press, 1966); for Swat: Fredrik Barth, 'The System of Social Stratification in Swat, North Pakiston,' in *Aspects of Caste in South India, Ceylon and North-West Pakistan*, E. Leach, ed. (London, Cambridge University Press, 1960), pp. 113–48; for Japan: George DeVos and Hiroshi Wagatsuma, eds., *Japan's Invisible Race: Caste in Culture and Personality* (Berkeley, University of California Press, 1966); Shigeaki Ninomiya, 'An Inquiry Concerning the Origin, Development and Present Situation of the *Eta*

in Relation to the History of Social Classes in Japan,' *The Transactions of the Asiatic Society of Japan* (Second series, Vol. 10, 1933); cf. Herbert Passin, 'Untouchability in the Far East,' *Monumenta Nipponica* (Vol. 2, No. 3, 1955); for the United States: Allison Davis, B. Gardner, and M. R. Gardner, *Deep South: A Social Anthropological Study of Caste and Class* (Chicago, The University of Chicago Press, 1941); John Dollard, *Caste and Class in a Southern Town* (Garden City, New York, Doubleday, 1957); Gunnar Myrdal, *An American Dilemma: The Negro Problem in Modern Democracy* (New York, Harper, 1944); Alphonso Pinkney, *Black Americans* (Englewood Cliffs, New Jersey, Prentice-Hall, 1969); Peter I. Rose, ed., *Americans from Africa*, Vol. 1: *Slavery and its Aftermath* and Vol. II: *Old Memories, New Moods* (New York, Atherton Press, 1970). See also contrasts with South Africa: Pierre van den Berghe, *South Africa, a Study in Conflict* (Berkeley, University of California Press, 1967); Latin America: Marvin Harris, *Patterns of Race in the Americas* (New York, Walker, 1964); Julian Pitt-Rivers, 'Race, Color and Class in Central America and the Andes,' *Daedalus* (Spring, 1967); the Caribbean: M. G. Smith, *The Plural Society in the British West Indies* (Berkeley, University of California Press, 1965). G. D. Berreman, *Caste in the Modern World* (New York, General Learning Press, forthcoming).

3. Dumont, op. cit.

4. Gerald D. Berreman, 'A Brahmanical View of Caste: Louis Dumont's *Homo Hierarchicus,*' *Contributions to Indian Sociology* (New Series, No. V, 1972).

5. Tamotsu Shibutani and Kian M. Kwan, *Ethnic Stratification: A Comparative Approach* (New York, Macmillan, 1965), p. 572.

6. H. S. Morris, 'Ethnic Groups,' in D. Sills, ed., op. cit., Vol. 5, p. 167.

7. Pierre van den Berghe, 'The Benign Quota: Panacea or Pandora's Box,' *The American Sociologist* (Vol. 6, Supplementary Issue, June 1971).

8. Ibid., p. 43.

9. Cf. Robert Blauner, 'Black Culture: Myth or Reality?" in Rose, *Old Memories, New Moods*, pp. 417–43.

10. Gerald D. Berreman, 'Caste in India and the United States,' *The American Journal of Sociology* (Vol. LXVI, September, 1960); cf. Berreman, 'A Brahmanical View of Caste . . .'; op. cit.

11. Oliver C. Cox, 'Race and Caste: A Distinction,' *The American Journal of Sociology* (Vol. L, March, 1945); cf. Oliver C. Cox, *Caste, Class and Race* (Garden City, New York, Doubleday, 1948).

12. Arthur R. Jensen, 'How Much Can We Boost I.Q. and Scholastic Achievement?" *Harvard Educational Review* (Vol. 39, No. 1, Winter, 1969).

13. See the various articles comprising the 'Discussion,' of Jensen's article in *Harvard Educational Review* (Vol. 39, No. 2, Spring, 1969).

14. E. A. Ross, *Social Psychology* (New York, Macmillan, 1914), p. 3.

15. Shibutani and Kwan, op. cit., p. 37.

16. Ibid., p. 110.

17. Pierre van den Berghe, *Race and Racism* (New York, Wiley, 1967), p. 21.

18. Claude Lévi-Strauss, 'The Bear and the Barber,' *Journal of the Royal Anthropological Institute* (Vol. 93, Part 1, 1963).

19. Winthrop D. Jordan, *White Over Black* (Baltimore, Penguin Books, 1969), p. 137–8.

20. Robert Blauner, 'International Colonialism and Ghetto Revolt,' *Social Problems* (Vol. 16, No. 4, Spring 1969); Stokely Carmichael and Charles Hamilton, *Black Power* (New York, Random House, 1967); Frantz Fanon, *The Wretched of the Earth* (New York, Grove Press, 1966.); 0. Mannoni, *Prospero and Caliban: The Psychology of Colonization* (New York, Praeger, 1956); Albert Memmi, The Colonizer and the Colonized (Boston, Beacon Press, 1967).

21. Cf. Blauner, 'Internal Colonialism...' p. 395–6.

22. Gerald D. Berreman, 'Caste as Social Process,' *Southwestern Journal of Anthropology* (Vol. 23, No. 4, Winter, 1967); Blauner, *Racial Oppression in America*; S. F. Nadel, Caste and Government in Primitive Society,' *Journal of the Anthropological Society of Bombay* (Vol. 8, 1954); J. S. Furnivall, *Colonial Policy and Practice: A Comparative Study of Burma and Netherlands India* (London, Cambridge University Press, 1948); M. G. Smith, *The Plural Society in the British West Indies* (Berkeley, University of California Press, 1965); James B. Watson, 'Caste as a Form of Acculturation,' *Southwestern Journal of Anthropology* (Vol. 19, No. 4, Winter 1963).

23. Cf. Irawati Karve, *Hindu Society: An Interpretation* (Poona, Deccan College Postgraduate and Research Institute, 1961).

24. Davis, Gardner, and Gardner, op. cit.; St. Clair Drake and Horace R. Cayton, *Black Metropolis* (New York, Harcourt, Brace, 1945); Dollard, op. cit.; Marina Wikramanayake 'Caste and Class among Free Afro-Americans in Ante-bellum South Carolina,' paper delivered before the 70th Annual Meeting of the American Anthropological Association (New York, November 1971).

25. Furnivall, op. cit.; cf. Malcolm Cross, ed., *Special Issue on Race and Pluralism, Race* (Vol. XII, No. 4, April 1971).

26. M. G. Smith, op. cit., pp. 14, 83.

27. Gerald D. Berreman, "Stratification, Pluralism and Interaction: A Comparative Analysis of Caste,'

in *Caste and Race: Comparative Approaches*, A. deReuck and J. Knight, eds., p. 51.

28. M. G. Smith, op. cit, p. xi.

29. Berreman, 'Stratification, Pluralism and Interaction . . . ,' op. cit., p. 55.

30. Cf. Furnivall, op. cit.

31. Berreman, 'Stratification, Pluralism and Interaction . . . ,' op. cit., p. 55.

32. Ibid., cf. McKim Marriott, 'Interactional and Attributional Theories of Caste Ranking,' *Man in India* (Vol. 39, 1959).

33. Maya Angelou, *I Know Why the Caged Bird Sings* (New York, Bantam Books, 1971), p. 168.

34. Cf. Berreman, 'Caste in India and the United States,' op. cit.

35. Berreman, 'Stratification, Pluralism and Interaction . . . ,' op. cit., p. 51.

36. Dumont, op. cit.

37. Cf. Berreman, 'Caste in India and the United States,' op. cit.; Berreman, 'Caste in Cross-Cultural Perspective . . . ,' op. cit.; Gerald D. Berreman, 'Social Categories and Social Interaction in Urban India,' *American Anthropologist* (Vol. 74, No. 3).

38. Cf. Berreman, 'A Brahmanical View of Caste . . . ,' op. cit.

39. Kate Millett, *Sexual Politics* (New York, Avon Books, 1971), p. 19.

40. Casey Hayden and Mary King, 'Sex and Caste,' *Liberation* (April, 1966), p. 35; cf. Millett, op. cit.

41. Fran Hawthorne, 'Female Roles Examined by Rutgers Professors,' *Daily Californian* (Berkeley, 6 October, 1971), p. 5. See also Millett, op. cit., p. 57, for a summary of the common psychological traits and adaptational mechanisms attributed to blacks and women in American society as reported in three recent sociological accounts.

42. Cf., G. Morris Carstairs, *The Twice-Born* (Bloomington, Indiana University Press, 1958), pp. 59–62 *et passim;* Morris E. Opler, 'The Hijarā (Hermaphrodites) of India and Indian National Character: A Rejoinder,' *American Anthropologist* (Vol. 62, No. 3, June, 1960).

43. Gerald D. Berreman, "Women's Roles and Politics: India and the United States,' in *Readings in General Sociology*, R. W. O'Brien, C. C. Schrag, and W. T. Martin, eds., (4th Edition, Boston, Houghton Mifflin Co., 1969). First published, 1966. Cf. Millett, op cit.

44. van den Berghe, *Race and Racism*, op. cit., p. 22.

45. Berreman, 'Stratification, Pluralism and Interaction . . . ,' op. cit., p. 58.

46. Abram Kardiner and Lionel Ovesey, *Mark of Oppression* (Cleveland, The World Publishing Co., 1962), p. 387.

47. Robert Coles, *Children of Crisis* (Boston, Atlantic–Little, Brown, 1964); with Jon Erikson, *The Middle Americans* (Boston, Little, Brown, 1971).

48. Kardiner and Ovesey, op. cit., p. 379.

49. B. G. Gallagher, *American Caste and the Negro College* (New York, Columbia University Press, 1938), p. 109.

50. Berreman, 'Caste as Social Process,' op. cit.

51. Raymond Bauer and Alice Bauer, 'Day to Day Resistance to Slavery,' *Journal of Negro History* (Vol. 27, October 1942); Douglas Scott, 'The Negro and the Enlisted Man: An Analogy,' *Harpers* (October 1962), pp. 20–1; cf. Berreman, 'Caste in India and the United States,' op. cit.

52. Henry Adams, *The United States in 1800* (Ithaca, New York, Cornell University Press, 1961), p. 98.

53. Kardiner and Ovesey, op. cit., p. 387.

54. Philip Mason, *Patterns of Dominance* (London, Oxford University Press for the Institute of Race Relations, 1970), p. 75.

2

Discrimination and the American Creed

Robert K. Merton

The primary function of the sociologist is to search out the determinants and consequences of diverse forms of social behavior. To the extent that he succeeds in fulfilling this role, he clarifies the alternatives of organized social action in a given situation and of the probable outcome of each. To this extent, there is no sharp distinction between pure research and applied research. Rather, the difference is one between research with direct implications for particular problems of social action and research which is remote from these problems. Not infrequently, basic research which has succeeded only in clearing up previously confused concepts may have an immediate bearing upon the problems of men in society to a degree not approximated by applied research oriented exclusively to these problems. At least, this is the assumption underlying the present paper: clarification of apparently unclear and confused concepts in the sphere of race and ethnic relations is a step necessarily prior to the devising of effective programs for reducing intergroup conflict and for promoting equitable access to economic and social opportunities.

"Discrimination and the American Creed," by Robert K. Merton in *DISCRIMINATION AND THE NATIONAL WELFARE*, Edited by R. M. MacIver. Copyright, 1949 by Institute for Religious and Social Studies. By permission of Harper & Row, Publishers, Inc.

In an effort toward such clarification, I shall consider first the place of the creed of equitable access to opportunity in American culture; second, the relations of this creed to the beliefs and practices of Americans; third, the diverse types of orientation toward discrimination *and* prejudice; fourth, the implications for organized action of the recognition of these diverse types; and fifth, the expectable consequences of alternative lines of action in diverse social contexts.

The American Creed: As Cultural Ideal, Personal Belief and Practice

The American creed as set forth in the Declaration of Independence, the preamble of the Constitution and the Bill of Rights has often been misstated. This part of the cultural heritage does *not* include the patently false assertion that all men are created equal in capacity or endowment. It does *not* imply that an Einstein and a moron are equal in intellectual capacity or that Joe Louis and a small, frail Columbia professor (or a Mississippian Congressman) are equally endowed with brawny arms harboring muscles as strong as iron bands. It does *not* proclaim universal equality of innate intellectual or physical endowment.

Instead, the creed asserts the indefeasible principle of the human right to full equity—the right of equitable access to justice, freedom and opportunity, irrespective of race or religion or ethnic origin. It proclaims further the universalist doctrine of the dignity of the individual, irrespective of the groups of which he is a part. It is a creed announcing full moral equities for all, not an absurd myth affirming the equality of intellectual and physical capacity of all men everywhere. And it goes on to say that though men differ in innate endowment, they do so as individuals, not by virtue of their group memberships.

Viewed sociologically, the creed is a set of values and precepts embedded in American culture, to which Americans are expected to conform. It is a complex of affirmations, rooted in the historical past and ceremonially celebrated in the present, partly enacted in the laws of the land and partly not. Like all creeds, it is a profession of faith, a part of cultural tradition sanctified by the larger traditions of which it is a part.

It would be a mistaken sociological assertion, however, to suggest that the creed is a fixed and static cultural constant, unmodified in the course of time, just as it would be an error to imply that as an integral part of the culture, it evenly blankets all subcultures of the national society. It is indeed dynamic, subject to change and in turn promoting change in other spheres of culture and society. It is, moreover, unevenly distributed throughout the society, being institutionalized as an integral part of local culture in some regions of the society and rejected in others.

Nor does the creed exert the same measure of control over behavior in diverse times and places. In so far as it is a "sacred" part of American culture, hallowed by tradition, it is largely immune to direct attack. But it may be honored simply in the breach. It is often evaded, and the evasions themselves become institutionalized, giving rise to what I may call the "institutionalized evasion of institutional norms." Where the creed is at odds with local beliefs and practices, it may persist as an empty cultural form partly because it is so flexible. It need not prove overly obstructive to the social, psychological and economic gains of individuals, because there are still so many avenues for conscientiously ignoring the creed in practice. When necessary for peace of mind and psychological equilibrium, individuals indoctrinated with the creed who find themselves deviating from its precepts may readily explain

how their behavior accords with the spirit of the creed rather than with its sterile letter. Or the creed itself is re-interpreted. Only those of equal endowment should have equal access to opportunity, it is said, and a given race or ethnic group manifestly does not have the requisite capacity to be deserving of opportunity. To provide such opportunities for the inferior of mind would be only wasteful of national resources. The rationalizations are too numerous and too familiar to bear repetition. The essential point is that the creed, though invulnerable to direct attack in some regions of the society, is not binding on practice. Many individuals and groups in many areas of the society systematically deny through daily conduct what they affirm on periodic ceremonial or public occasions.

This gap between creed and conduct has received wide notice. Learned men and men in high public positions have repeatedly observed and deplored the disparity between ethos and behavior in the sphere of race and ethnic relations. In his magisterial volumes on the American Negro, for example, Gunnar Myrdal called this gulf between creed and conduct "an American dilemma," and centered his attention on the prospect of narrowing or closing the gap. The President's Committee on Civil Rights, in their report to the nation, and the President himself, in a recent message to Congress, have called public attention to this "serious gap between our ideals and some of our practices."

But valid as these observations may be, they tend so to simplify the relations between creed and conduct as to be seriously misleading both for social policy and for social science. All these high authorities notwithstanding, the problems of racial and ethnic inequities are not expressible as a discrepancy between high cultural principles and low social conduct. It is a relation not between two variables, official creed and private practice, but between three: first, the cultural creed honored in cultural tradition and partly enacted into law; second, the beliefs and attitudes of individuals regarding the principles of the creed; and third, the actual practices of individuals with reference to it.

Once we substitute these three variables of cultural ideal, belief and actual practice for the customary distinction between the two variables of cultural ideals and actual practices, the entire formulation of the problem becomes changed. We escape from the virtuous but ineffectual impasse of deploring the alleged hypocrisy of many Americans into the more difficult but potentially effectual realm of analyzing the problem in hand.

To describe the problem and to proceed to its analysis, it is necessary to consider the official creed, individuals' beliefs and attitudes concerning the creed, and their actual behavior. Once stated, the distinctions are readily applicable. Individuals may *recognize* the creed as part of a cultural tradition, *without having any private conviction of its moral validity or its binding quality.* Thus, so far as the beliefs of individuals are concerned, we can identify two types: those who genuinely believe in the creed and those who do not (although some of these may, on public or ceremonial occasions, profess adherence to its principles). Similarly, with respect to actual practices: conduct may or may not conform to the creed. But, and this is the salient consideration: *conduct may or may not conform with individuals' own beliefs concerning the moral claims of all men to equal opportunity.*

Stated in formal sociological terms, this asserts that attitudes and overt behavior vary independently. *Prejudicial attitudes need not coincide with discriminatory behavior.* The implications of this statement can be drawn out in terms of a logical syntax whereby the variables are diversely combined, as can be seen in the typology below.

By exploring the interrelations between prejudice and discrimination, we can identify four major types in terms of their attitudes toward the creed and their behavior with respect to it. Each type is found in every region and social class, though in varying numbers. By examining each type, we shall be better prepared to understand their interdependence and the appropriate types of action for curbing their ethnic discrimination. The folk-labels for each type are intended to aid in their prompt recognition.

Type 1: The Unprejudiced Non-Discriminator or All-Weather Liberal

These are the racial and ethnic liberals who adhere to the creed in both belief and practice. They are neither prejudiced nor given to discrimination. Their orientation toward the creed is fixed and stable. Whatever the environing situation, they are likely to abide by their beliefs: hence, the *all-weather* liberal.

This is, of course, the strategic group which *can* act as the spearhead for the progressive extension of the creed into effective practice. They represent the solid foundation both for the measure of ethnic equities which now exist and for the future enlargement of these equities. Integrated with the creed in both belief and practice, they would seem most motivated to influence others toward the same democratic outlook. They represent a reservoir of culturally legitimatized goodwill which can be channeled into an active program for extending belief in the creed and conformity with it in practice.

Most important, as we shall see presently, the all-weather liberals comprise the group which can so reward others for conforming with the creed, as to transform deviants into conformists. They alone can provide the positive social environment for the other types who will no longer

A Typology of Ethnic Prejudice and Discrimination

		Attitude Dimension:* Prejudice and Non-prejudice	Behavior Dimension:* Discrimination and Non-discrimination
Type I:	Unprejudiced non-discriminator	+	+
Type II:	Unprejudiced discriminator	+	−
Type III:	Prejudiced non-discriminator	−	+
Type IV:	Prejudiced discriminator	−	−

*Where (+) = conformity to the creed and (−) = deviation from the creed. For a brief note on the uses of paradigms such as this, see the appendix to this paper.

find it expedient or rewarding to retain their prejudices or discriminatory practices.

But though the ethnic liberal is a *potential* force for the successive extension of the American creed, he does not fully realize this potentiality in actual fact, for a variety of reasons. Among the limitations on effective action are several fallacies to which the ethnic liberal seems peculiarly subject. First among these is the *fallacy of group soliloquies.* Ethnic liberals are busily engaged in talking to themselves. Repeatedly, the same groups of like-minded liberals seek each other out, hold periodic meetings in which they engage in mutual exhortation and thus lend social and psychological support to one another. But however much these unwittingly self-selected audiences may reinforce the creed among themselves, they do not thus appreciably diffuse the creed in belief or practice to groups which depart from it in one respect or the other.

More, these group soliloquies in which there is typically whole-hearted agreement among fellow-liberals tend to promote another fallacy limiting effective action. This is the *fallacy of unanimity.* Continued association with like-minded individuals tends to produce the illusion that a large measure of consensus has been achieved in the community at large. The unanimity regarding essential cultural axioms which obtains in these small groups provokes an overestimation of the strength of the movement and of its effective inroads upon the larger population which does not necessarily share these creedal axioms. Many also mistake participation in the groups of like-minded individuals for effective action. Discussion accordingly takes the place of action. The reinforcement of the creed for oneself is mistaken for the extension of the creed among those outside the limited circle of ethnic liberals.

Arising from adherence to the creed is a third limitation upon effective action, the *fallacy of privatized solutions* to the problem. The ethnic liberal, precisely because he is at one with the American creed, may rest content with his own individual behavior and thus see no need to do anything about the problem at large. Since his own spiritual house is in order, he is not motivated by guilt or shame to work on a collective problem. The very freedom of the liberal from guilt thus prompts him to secede from any *collec-tive* effort to set the national house in order. He essays a *private* solution to a *social* problem. He assumes that numerous individual adjustments will serve in place of a collective adjustment. His outlook, compounded of good moral philosophy but poor sociology, holds that each individual must put his own house in order and fails to recognize that privatized solutions cannot be effected for problems which are essentially social in nature. For clearly, if each person *were* motivated to abide by the American creed, the problem would not be likely to exist in the first place. It is only when a social environment is established by conformists to the creed that deviants can in due course be brought to modify their behavior in the direction of conformity. But this "environment" can be constituted only through collective effort and not through private adherence to a public creed. Thus we have the paradox that the clear conscience of many ethnic liberals may promote the very social situation which permits deviations from the creed to continue unchecked. Privatized liberalism invites social inaction. Accordingly, there appears the phenomenon of the inactive or passive liberal, himself at spiritual ease, neither prejudiced nor discriminatory, but in a measure tending to contribute to the persistence of prejudice and discrimination through his very inaction.

The fallacies of group soliloquy, unanimity and privatized solutions thus operate to make the potential strength of the ethnic liberals unrealized in practice.

It is only by first recognizing these limitations that the liberal can hope to overcome them. With some hesitancy, one may suggest initial policies for curbing the scope of the three fallacies. The fallacy of group soliloquies can be removed only by having ethnic liberals enter into organized groups not comprised merely by fellow-liberals. This exacts a heavy price of the liberal. It means that he faces initial opposition and resistance rather than prompt consensus. It entails giving up the gratifications of consistent group support.

The fallacy of unanimity can in turn be reduced by coming to see that American society often provides large rewards for those who express their ethnic prejudice in discrimination. Only if the balance of rewards, material and psychological, is modified will behavior be modified. Sheer exhortation and propaganda are not enough. Exhortation verges on a belief in magic if it is not supported by appropriate changes in the social environment to make conformity with the exhortation rewarding.

Finally, the fallacy of privatized solutions requires the militant liberal to motivate the passive liberal to collective effort, possibly by inducing in him a sense of guilt for his unwitting contribution to the problems of ethnic inequities through his own systematic inaction.

One may suggest a unifying theme for the ethnic liberal: goodwill is not enough to modify social reality. It is only when this goodwill is harnessed to social-psychological realism that it can be used to reach cultural objectives.

Type II: The Unprejudiced Discriminator or Fair-Weather Liberal

The fair-weather liberal is the man of expediency who, despite his own freedom from prejudice, supports discriminatory practices when it is the easier or more profitable course. His expediency may take the form of holding his silence and thus implicitly acquiescing in expressions of ethnic prejudice by others or in the practice of discrimination by others. This is the expediency of the timid: the liberal who hesitates to speak up against discrimination for fear he might lose status or be otherwise penalized by his prejudiced associates. Or his expediency may take the form of grasping at advantages in social and economic competition deriving solely from the ethnic status of competitors. This is the expediency of the self-assertive: the employer, himself not an anti-Semite or Negrophobe, who refuses to hire Jewish or Negro workers because "it might hurt business"; the trade union leader who expediently advocates racial discrimination in order not to lose the support of powerful Negrophobes in his union.

In varying degrees, the fair-weather liberal suffers from guilt and shame for departing from his own effective beliefs in the American creed. Each deviation through which he derives a limited reward from passively acquiescing in or actively supporting discrimination contributes cumulatively to this fund of guilt. He is, therefore, peculiarly vulnerable to the efforts of the all-weather liberal who would help him bring his conduct into accord with his beliefs, thus removing this source of guilt. He is the most amenable to cure, because basically he wants to be cured. His is a split conscience which motivates him to cooperate actively with those who will help remove the source of internal conflict. He thus represents the strategic group promising the largest returns for the least effort. Persistent re-affirmation of the creed will only intensify his conflict; but a long regimen in a favorable social climate can be expected to transform the fair-weather liberal into an all-weather liberal.

Type III: The Prejudiced Non-Discriminator or Fair-Weather Illiberal

The fair-weather illiberal is the reluctant conformist to the creed, the man of prejudice who does not believe in the creed but conforms to it in practice through fear of sanctions which might otherwise be visited upon him. You know him well: the prejudiced employer who discriminates against racial or ethnic groups until a Fair Employment Practice Commission, able and willing to enforce the law, puts the fear of punishment into him; the trade union leader, himself deeply prejudiced, who does away with Jim Crow in his union because the rank-and-file demands that it be done away with; the businessman who foregoes his own prejudices when he finds a profitable market among the very people he hates, fears or despises; the timid bigot who will not express his prejudices when he is in the presence of powerful men who vigorously and effectively affirm their belief in the American creed.

It should be clear that the fair-weather illiberal is the precise counterpart of the fair-weather liberal. Both are men of expediency, to be sure, but expediency dictates different courses of behavior in the two cases. The timid bigot conforms to the creed only when there is danger or loss in deviations, just as the timid liberal deviates from the creed only when there is danger or loss in conforming. *Superficial similarity in behavior of the two in the same situation should not be permitted to cloak a basic difference in the meaning of this outwardly similar behavior*, a difference which is as important for social policy as it is for social science. Whereas the timid bigot is under strain when he conforms to the creed, the timid liberal is under strain when he deviates. For ethnic prejudice has deep roots in the character structure of the fair-weather bigot, and this will find overt expression unless there are powerful countervailing forces, institutional, legal and interpersonal. He does not accept the moral legitimacy of the creed; he conforms because he must, and will cease to conform when the pressure is removed. The fair-weather liberal, on the other hand, is effectively committed to the creed and does not require strong institutional pressure to conform; continuing interpersonal relations with all-weather liberals may be sufficient.

This is the one critical point at which the traditional formulation of the problem of ethnic discrimination as a departure from the creed can lead to serious errors of theory and practice. Overt behavioral deviation (or conformity) may signify importantly different situations, depending upon the underlying motivations. Knowing simply that ethnic discrimination is rife in a community does not, therefore, point to appropriate lines of social policy. It is necessary to know also the distribution of ethnic prejudices and basic motivations for these prejudices as well. Communities with the same amount of overt discrimination may represent vastly different types of problems, dependent on whether the population is comprised by a large nucleus of fair-weather liberals ready to abandon their discriminatory practices under slight interpersonal pressure or a large nucleus of fair-weather illiberals who will abandon discrimination only if major changes in the local institutional setting can be effected. Any statement of the problem as a gulf between creedal ideals and prevailing practice is thus seen to be over-simplified in the precise sense of masking this decisive difference between the type of discrimination exhibited by the fair-weather liberal and by the fair-weather illiberal. That the gulf-between-ideal-and-practice does not adequately describe the nature of the ethnic problem will become more apparent as we turn to the fourth type in our inventory of prejudice and discrimination.

Type IV: The Prejudiced Discriminator or the All-Weather Illiberal

This type, too, is not unknown to you. He is the confirmed illiberal, the bigot pure and unashamed, the man of prejudice consistent in his departures from the American creed. In some measure, he is found everywhere in the land, though in varying numbers. He derives large social and psychological gains from his conviction that "any white man (including the village idiot) is 'better' than any nigger (including George Washington Carver)." He considers differential treatment of Negro and white not as "discrimination," in the sense of unfair treatment, but as "discriminating," in the sense of showing acute discernment. For him, it is as clear that one "ought" to accord a Negro and a white different treatment in a wide diversity of situations, as it is clear to the population at large that one "ought" to accord a child and an adult different treatment in many situations.

This illustrates anew my reason for questioning the applicability of the usual formula of the American dilemma as a gap between lofty creed and low conduct. For the confirmed illiberal, ethnic discrimination does *not* represent a discrepancy between *his* ideals and *his* behavior. His ideals proclaim the right, even the duty, of discrimination. Accordingly, his behavior does not entail a sense of social deviation, with the resultant strains which this would involve. The ethnic illiberal is as much a conformist as the ethnic liberal. He is merely conforming to a different cultural and institutional pattern which is centered, not about the creed, but about a doctrine of essential inequality of status ascribed to those of diverse ethnic and racial origins. To overlook this is to overlook the well-known *fact* that our national culture is divided into a number of local subcultures which are not consistent among themselves in all respects. And again, to fail to take this fact of different subcultures into account is to open the door for all manner of errors of social policy in attempting to control the problems of racial and ethnic discrimination.

This view of the all-weather illiberal has one immediate implication with wide bearing upon social policies and sociological theory oriented toward the problem of discrimination. The extreme importance of the social surroundings of the confirmed illiberal at once becomes apparent. For as these surroundings vary, so, in some measure, does the problem of the consistent illiberal. The illiberal, living in those cultural regions where the American creed is widely repudiated and is no effective part of the subculture, has his private ethnic attitudes and practices supported by the local mores, the local institutions and the local power-structure. The illiberal in cultural areas dominated by a large measure of adherence to the American creed is in a social environment where he is isolated and receives small social support for his beliefs and practices. In both instances, the *individual* is an illiberal, to be sure, but he represents two significantly different *sociological types*. In the first instance, he is a *social conformist*, with strong moral and institutional reinforcement, whereas in the second, he is a *social deviant*, lacking strong social corroboration. In the one case, his discrimination involves him in further integration with his network of social relations; in the other, it threatens to cut him off from sustaining interpersonal ties. In the first cultural context, personal change in his ethnic behavior involves alienating himself from people significant to him; in the second context, this change of personal outlook may mean fuller incorporation in groups meaningful to him. In the first situation, modification of his ethnic view requires him to take the path of greatest resistance whereas in the second, it may mean the path of least resistance. From all this, we may surmise that any social policy aimed at changing the behavior and perhaps the attitudes of the all-weather illiberal will have to take into account the cultural and social structure of the area in which he lives.

Some Assumptions Underlying Social Policies for the Reduction of Racial and Ethnic Discrimination
To diagnose the problem, it appears essential to recognize these several types of men, and not to obscure their differences by general allusions to the "gulf between ideals and practice." Some of these men discriminate precisely because their local cultural ideals proclaim the duty of discrimination. Others discriminate only when they find it expedient to do so, just as still others fail to translate their prejudices into active discrimination when *this* proves expedient. It is the existence of these three types of men, in a society traditionally given over to the American creed, who constitute "the racial problem" or "the ethnic problem." Those who practice discrimination are *not* men of one kind. *And because they are not all of a*

piece, there must be diverse social therapies, each directed at a given type in a given social situation.

Were it not for widespread social policies to the contrary, it would be unnecessary to emphasize that there is no single social policy which will be adequate for all these types in all social situations. So far as I know, sociological science has not yet evolved knowledge for application to this problem sufficient to merit great confidence in the results. But it has reached the point where it can suggest, with some assurance, that different social types in different social contexts require different social therapies if their behavior is to be changed. To diagnose these several types, therefore, may not be an "academic" exercise, in the too-frequent and dolorous sense of the word "academic." However scanty our knowledge, if action is to be taken, such diagnoses represent the first step toward pragmatic social therapy. The unprejudiced discriminator will respond differently from the prejudiced non-discriminator and he, in turn, differently from the prejudiced discriminator or all-weather illiberal. And each of these will respond according to the social composition of the groups and community in which he is involved.

In setting forth my opinions on the strategy of dealing with ethnic and racial discrimination, I hope it is plain that I move far beyond the adequately accredited knowledge provided by sociology to this point. In 1948, neither the rigorous theory nor many needed data are at hand to "apply" sociological science to this massive problem of American society. But moving from the slight accumulation of sociological knowledge at my disposal, it may be possible to suggest some considerations which it presently seems wise to take into account. For at scattered points, our knowledge may be sufficient to detect probably erroneous assumptions, though it is not always adequate to set out probably sound assumptions.

It is sometimes assumed that discrimination and its frequent though not invariable adjunct, prejudice, are entirely the product of ignorance. To be sure, ignorance *may* support discrimination. The employer unfamiliar with the findings of current anthropology and psychology, for example, may discriminate against Negroes on the ground of the honest and ignorant conviction that they are inherently less intelligent than whites. But, in general, there is no indication that ignorance is the major source of discrimination. The evidence at hand does not show that ethnic and racial discrimination is consistently less common among those boasting a college education than among the less well educated.

To question the close connection between ignorance and discrimination is to raise large implications for social policy. For if one assumes that ignorance and error are alone involved, obviously all that need be done by way of curbing prevalent discriminatory practices is to introduce a program of education concerning racial and ethnic matters, on a scale yet unimagined. Mass education and mass propaganda would at once become the sole indicated tools for action. But there are few who will accept the implications of this assumption that simple ignorance is a major or exclusive source of discrimination and urge that formal education alone can turn the trick. If some seem to be saying this, it is, I suspect, because they are begging the question; they are using the phrase "education on racial and ethnic matters" in an equivocal sense to mean "eradication of racial and ethnic prejudices." But, of course, that is precisely the question at issue: what *are* the procedures most likely to eradicate prejudice and discrimination?

If the assumption of ignorance as the root-source of discrimination is put to one side, then we must be prepared to find that discrimination is in part sustained by a socialized reward-system. When a population is divided into sub-groups, some of which are set apart as inferior, even the lowliest member of the ostensibly superior group derives psychic gains from this institutionalized superiority of status. This system of discrimination also supplies preferential access to opportunity for the more favored groups. The taboos erect high tariff walls restricting the importation of talent from the ethnic outgroups. But we need not assume that such psychic, social and economic gains are *sufficient* to account for the persistence of ethnic discrimination in a society which has an ideal pattern proclaiming free and equal access to opportunity. To be sure, these rewards supply motivation for discrimination. But men favor practices which give them differential advantages only so long as there is a moral code which defines these advantages as "fair." In the absence of this code, special advantage is not typically exploited. Were this not the case, the doctrine of Hobbes would stand unimpaired: everyone would cheat—in personal, economic and other institutional relations. Yet even the most cynical observer would not suggest that chicanery and cheating are the typical order of the day in all spheres, even where fear of discovery is at a minimum. This suggests that discrimination is sustained not only by the direct gains to those who discriminate, but also by cultural norms which *legitimize* discrimination.

To the extent that the foregoing assumptions are valid, efforts to minimize discrimination must take into account at least three sets of factors sustaining discriminatory practices. And each of these points toward distinct, though interrelated, lines of attack on the forces promoting discrimination. First, mass education and propaganda would be directed toward the reduction of sheer ignorance concerning the objective attributes of ethnic groups and of the processes of intergroup relations and attitudes. Second, institutional and interpersonal programs would seek to reduce the social, psychic and economic gains presently accruing to those who discriminate. And third, long-range efforts would be required to reinforce the legitimacy of the American creed as a set of cultural norms applicable to all groups in the society.

One gains the impression that certain secular trends in the society are slowly affecting each of these three fronts. On the educational front, we find an increasing proportion of the American population receiving higher schooling. And in the course of schooling, many are exposed for the first time to salient *facts* regarding ethnic and racial groups. Preconceptions notwithstanding, higher educational institutions even in the Deep South do not teach discredited myths of race superiority; if race is treated at all, it is in substantially factual terms countering the cognitive errors now sustaining race discrimination. Without assuming that such education plays a basic role I suggest that in so far as it is at all effective, it undermines erroneous conceptions of racial and ethnic qualities.

On the economic front, secular change moves with geological speed but consistently in the same positive direction. This secular trend is represented in slow shifts in the occupational composition of Negroes and other ethnic groups toward a perceptibly higher level. Again, the importance of these slight shifts should not be exaggerated. As everyone knows, prejudice and its frequent corollary in action, discrimination, are resistant, if not entirely immune, to the coercion of sheer facts. Yet the white agricultural laborer does recognize, at some level of his self, the improbability of his "superiority" to the Negro physician or university president. The discrepancy between achieved occupational status and ascribed caste status introduces severe strains upon the persistence of rationalized patterns of social superiority. As occupational and educational opportunity expand for Negroes, the number of Negroes with class status higher than that of many whites will grow and with it the grounds for *genuinely believing*, no matter what one's protestations, that "any white man is better than any nigger" will be progressively eroded. This secular change is, of course, a two-edged sword: every economic advance of the Negro invites increased hostility and resentment. But no major change in social structure occurs without the danger of temporarily increased conflict (though it is a characteristic of the liberal to want the rose without the thorn, to seek major change without conflict). In any event, it seems plausible that the secular trend of occupational change presently militates against the unimpeded persistence of discrimination.

On the third front of the reinforcement of the American creed, the impressionistic picture is not so clear. But even here, there is one massive fact of contemporary history which points to a firmer foundation for this cultural doctrine. In a world riven with international fears, the pressure for national consensus grows stronger. Ethnic and racial fissures in the national polity cannot so lightly be endured. (Consider the concessions commonly given these groups in times of war.) This tendency is enhanced as men become sensitized to the balance of world population and recognize that firm alliances must be built with non-white peoples, ultimately, it is hoped, in a world alliance. From these pressures external to the nation, there develops an increasing movement toward translating the American creed from a less than fully effective ideology into a working code governing the behavior of men. Slight, yet

not unimpressive, signs of this change are evident. In the realm of institutional organizations, there is growing pressure upon government, universities, trade unions and churches to govern themselves by the words they profess. In the realm of interpersonal relations, one has a marked impression of increasing relations between members of diverse racial and ethnic groups. (This change in the pattern of private relations must remain conjectural, until social research searches out the needed *facts*. Periodic researches into the frequency of interracial and interethnic friendships would provide a barometer of interpersonal relations [necessarily invisible to the individual observer] which could be used to supplement current information on institutional changes and public decisions.)

These assumptions of the strategic significance of the three major fronts of social policy on race and ethnic relations and these impressions of secular trends now in progress on each front provide the basis for a consideration of social strategies for the reduction of discrimination.

Implications of the Typology for Social Policy
This necessary detour into the assumptions underlying social policy leads us back to the main path laid down in the account of the four main types appearing in our typology of prejudice and discrimination. And again, however disconcerting the admission may be, it is essential to note that we must be wholly tentative in drawing out the implications of this typology for social policy, for the needed sociological theory and data are plainly inadequate to the practical demands of the situation. Yet if we cannot confidently establish the procedures which should be followed, we can perhaps exclude the procedures which are likely to be unproductive. The successive elimination of alternative procedures is some small gain.

In approaching problems of policy, two things are plain. First, these should be considered from the standpoint of the militant ethnic liberal, for he alone is sufficiently motivated to engage in positive action for the reduction of ethnic discrimination. And second, the fair-weather liberal, the fair-weather illiberal and the all-weather illiberal represent types differing sufficiently to require diverse kinds of treatment.

Treatment of the Fair-Weather Liberal

The fair-weather liberal, it will be remembered, discriminates only when it appears expedient to do so, and experiences some measure of guilt for deviating from his own belief in the American creed. He suffers from this conflict between conscience and conduct. Accordingly, he is a relatively easy target for the all-weather liberal. He represents the strategic group promising the largest immediate returns for the least effort. Recognition of this type defines the first task for the militant liberal who would enter into a collective effort to make the creed a viable and effective set of social norms rather than a ceremonial myth. And though the tactics which this definition of the problem suggests are numerous, I can here only allude to one of these, while emphasizing anew that much of the research data required for fuller confidence in this suggestion are not yet at hand. But passing by the discomforts of our ignorance for the moment, the following would seem to be roughly the case.

Since the fair-weather liberal discriminates only when it seems rewarding to do so, the crucial need is so to change social situations that there are few occasions in which discrimination proves rewarding and many in which it does not. This would suggest that ethnic liberals self-consciously and deliberately seek to draw into the social groups where they constitute a comfortable majority a number of the "expedient discriminators." This would serve to counteract the dangers of self-selection through which liberals come to associate primarily with likeminded individuals. It would, further, provide an interpersonal and social environment for the fair-weather liberal in which he would find substantial social and psychological gains from abiding by his own beliefs, gains which would more than offset the rewards attendant upon occasional discrimination. It appears that men do not long persist in behavior which lacks social corroboration.

We have much to learn about the role of numbers and proportions in determining the behavior of members of a group. But it seems that individuals generally act differently when they are numbered among a minority rather than the majority. This is not to say that minorities abdicate their practices in the face of a contrary-acting majority, but only that the same people are subjected to different strains and pressures according to whether they are included in the majority or the minority. And the fair-weather liberal who finds himself associated with militant ethnic liberals may be expected to forego his occasional deviations into discrimination; he may move from category II into category I; this at least is suggested by our current Columbia-Lavanburg researches on ethnic relations in the planned community.

This suggestion calls attention to the possible significance for policy of the composition of a local population with respect to the four types found in our typology, a consideration to which I shall presently return in some detail. But first it is necessary to consider briefly the problems attending policies for dealing with the illiberal.

Treatment of the Fair-Weather Illiberal

Because his *beliefs* correspond to those of the full-fledged liberal, the fair-weather liberal can rather readily be drawn into an interpersonal environment constituted by those of a comparable turn of mind. This would be more difficult for the fair-weather illiberal, whose beliefs are so fully at odds with those of ethnic liberals that he may, at first, only be alienated by association with them. If the initial tactic for the fair-weather liberal, therefore, is a change in interpersonal environment, the seemingly most appropriate tactic for the fair-weather illiberal is a change in the institutional and legal environment. It is, indeed, probably this type which liberals implicitly have in mind when they expect significant changes in behavior to result from the introduction of controls on ethnic discrimination into the legal machinery of our society.

For this type—and it is a major limitation for planning policies of control that we do not know his numbers or his distribution in the country—it would seem that the most effective tactic is the institution of legal controls administered with strict efficiency. This would presumably reduce the amount of *discrimination* practiced by the fair-weather illiberal, though it might *initially* enhance rather than reduce his *prejudices*.

Despite large libraries on the subject, we have little by way of rigorous knowledge indicating how this group of prejudiced but coercible conformists can be brought to abandon their prejudices. But something is known on a research basis of two methods which are *not* effective, information important for social policy since groups of ethnic liberals do commonly utilize these two apparently ineffectual methods. I refer, first, to mass propaganda for "tolerance" and second, the information of interracial groups seeking to promote tolerance among their members.

Available evidence suggests rather uniformly that propaganda for ethnic equity disseminated through the channels of mass communication does not appreciably modify prejudice. Where prejudice is deep-seated, it serves too many psychological functions for the illiberal to be relinquished in response to propaganda, emanating from howsoever prestigeful a source. The propaganda is either evaded through misinterpretation or selectively assimilated into his prejudice-system in such a fashion as to produce a "boomerang" effect of intensified prejudice.[1] Seemingly, propaganda for ethnic tolerance has a more important effect upon the propagandist, who comes to feel that he "is doing something" about diffusing the American creed, than upon the prejudiced people who are the ostensible objects of the propaganda. It is at least plausible that *the great dependence of ethnic liberals upon propaganda for tolerance persists because of the morale function the propaganda serves for the liberals who feel that something positive is being accomplished.*

A second prevalent tactic for modifying the prejudice of the fair-weather illiberal is that of seeking to draw him into interethnic groups explicitly formed for the promotion of tolerance. This, too, seems largely ineffectual, since the deeply prejudiced individual will not enter into such groups of his own volition. As a consequence of this process of self-selection, these tolerance groups soon come to be comprised by the very ethnic liberals who initiated the enterprise.

This barrier of self-selection can be partially hurdled only if the ethnic illiberals are brought into continued association with militant liberals in groups devoted to significant common values, quite remote from objectives of ethnic equity as such. Thus, as our Columbia-Lavanburg researches have found, many fair-weather illiberals *will* live in interracial housing projects in order to enjoy the rewards of superior housing at a given rental. And some of the illiberals thus brought into personal contact with various ethnic groups under the auspices of prestigeful militant liberals come to modify their prejudices. It is, apparently, only through interethnic collaboration, initially enforced by pressures of the situation, for immediate and significant objectives (other than tolerance) that the self-insulation of the fair-weather illiberal from rewarding interethnic contacts can be removed.

But however difficult it may presently be to affect the *prejudicial sentiments* of the fair-weather liberal, his *discriminatory practices* can be lessened by the uniform, prompt and prestigeful use of legal and institutional sanctions. The critical problem is to ascertain the proportions of fair-weather and all-weather illiberals in a given local population in order to have some clue to the probable effectiveness or ineffectiveness of anti-discrimination legislation.

Treatment of the All-Weather Illiberal

It is, of course, the hitherto confirmed illiberal, persistently translating his prejudices into active discrimination, who represents the most difficult problem. But though he requires longer and more careful treatment, it is possible that he is not beyond change. In every instance, his social surroundings must be assiduously taken into account. It makes a peculiarly large difference whether he is in a cultural region of bigotry or in a predominantly "liberal" area, given over to verbal adherence to the American creed, at the very least. As this cultural climate varies, so must the prescription for his cure and the prognosis for a relatively quick or long delayed recovery.

In an unfavorable cultural climate—and this does not necessarily exclude the benign regions of the Far South—the immediate resort will probably have to be that of working through legal and administrative federal controls over extreme discrimination, with full recognition that, in all probability, these regulations will be systematically evaded for some time to come. In such cultural regions, we may expect nullification of the law as the common practice, perhaps as common as was the case in the nation at large with respect to the Eighteenth Amendment, often with the connivance of local officers of the law. The large gap between the new law and local mores will not *at once* produce significant change of prevailing practices; token punishments of violations will probably be more common than effective control. At best, one may assume that significant change will be fitful, and excruciatingly slow. But secular changes in the economy may in due course lend support to the new legal framework of control over discrimination. As the economic shoe pinches because the illiberals do not fully mobilize the resources of industrial manpower nor extend their local markets through equitable wage-payments, they may slowly abandon some discriminatory practices as they come to find that these do not always pay—even the discriminator. So far as discrimination is concerned, organized counteraction is possible and some small results may be expected. But it would seem that wishes father thoughts, when one expects basic changes in the immediate future in these regions of institutionalized discrimination.

The situation is somewhat different with regard to the scattered, rather than aggregated, ethnic illiberals found here and there throughout the country. Here the mores and a social organization oriented toward the American creed still have some measure of prestige and the resources of a majority of liberals can be mobilized to isolate the illiberal. In these surroundings, it is possible to move the all-weather liberal toward Type III—he can be brought to conform with institutional regulations, even though he does not surrender his prejudices. And once he has entered upon this role of the dissident but conforming individual, the remedial program designed for the fair-weather illiberal would be in order.

Ecological Bases of Social Policy

Where authenticated data are few and scattered and one must make *some* decision, whether it be the decision to act in a given fashion or not to take action at all, then one must resort to reasonable conjecture as the basis for policy. That is what I have done in assuming throughout that policies designed to curb ethnic discrimination must be oriented toward differences in the composition of a population with respect to the four types here under discussion. It is safe to assume that communities and larger areas vary in the proportion of these several types. Some communities may have an overwhelming majority of

militant liberals, in positions of authority and among the rank-and-file. Others may be short on ethnic liberals but long on fair-weather illiberals who respond promptly though reluctantly to the pressure of institutional controls. It would seem reasonable to suppose that different social policies of control over discrimination would be required as these ecological distributions of prejudice-discrimination types vary.

This assumption is concretized in the conjectural distributions of these types set forth in the following charts. Consider the same legislation aimed at curbing job discrimination against the Negro as this might operate in a community in the Far South and in New England. Since it runs counter to the strongly entrenched attitudes of the large majority in the one community and not in the other, we may suppose that the same law will produce different results in the two cases. This must be put in a reasonable time prespective. Conceivably, the short-term and the long-term effects may differ widely. But with respect to both the long and the short term, it matters greatly whether there is a sufficient local nucleus of ethnic liberals in positions of prestige and authority. The ecological and social distribution of the prejudice-discrimination types is of central importance in assessing the probable outcome. Whether a law providing for equitable access to jobs will in fact produce this result depends not only on the law itself as on the rest of the social structure. The law is a small, though important, part of the whole. Unless a strong economic and social base for its support exists in a community, the law will be nullified in practice.

Charts C and D set forth, again conjecturally, the distribution of the prejudice-discrimination types with respect to the Jew among middle-class "strainers" and industrial workers. Should research find that the industrial worker stratum indeed has a larger proportion of militant ethnic liberals than the middle classes, then initial support of an active anti-discrimination policy might most effectively be sought there. But whatever the actual facts might show, the policy-maker attuned to the realities as well as the objectives of the problem would do well to take these into account in the design of his program.

If makers of policy are to escape utopianism on the one hand and pessimistic inaction on the

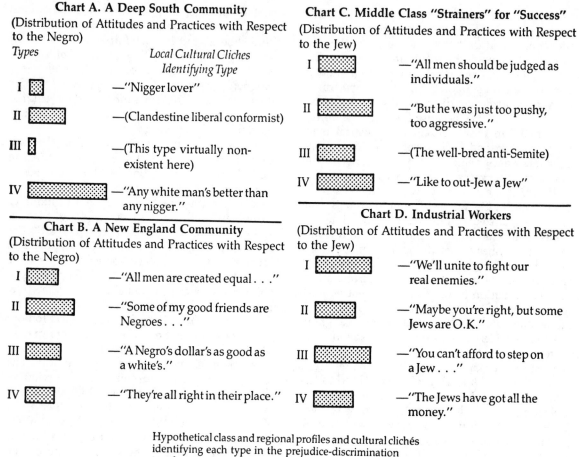

Chart A. A Deep South Community
(Distribution of Attitudes and Practices with Respect to the Negro)

Types   *Local Cultural Cliches Identifying Type*

I —"Nigger lover"

II —(Clandestine liberal conformist)

III —(This type virtually non-existent here)

IV —"Any white man's better than any nigger."

Chart B. A New England Community
(Distribution of Attitudes and Practices with Respect to the Negro)

I —"All men are created equal . . ."

II —"Some of my good friends are Negroes . . ."

III —"A Negro's dollar's as good as a white's."

IV —"They're all right in their place."

Chart C. Middle Class "Strainers" for "Success"
(Distribution of Attitudes and Practices with Respect to the Jew)

I —"All men should be judged as individuals."

II —"But he was just too pushy, too aggressive."

III —(The well-bred anti-Semite)

IV —"Like to out-Jew a Jew"

Chart D. Industrial Workers
(Distribution of Attitudes and Practices with Respect to the Jew)

I —"We'll unite to fight our real enemies."

II —"Maybe you're right, but some Jews are O.K."

III —"You can't afford to step on a Jew . . ."

IV —"The Jews have got all the money."

Hypothetical class and regional profiles and cultural clichés identifying each type in the prejudice-discrimination typology.

other, they must utilize diverse procedures for modifying attitudes and behavior according to the distribution of these prejudice-discrimination types.

Finally, though action cannot, perhaps, wait upon continued research, it is suggested that the following kinds of information are needed as a basis for effective anti-discrimination policy:

1. An inventory to determine the relative proportions in various areas of these four prejudice-discrimination types;
2. Within each area, an inventory of these proportions among the several social classes, major associations, and nationality groups;
3. Periodic audits of these proportions, thus providing a barometric map of ethnic attitudes and practices repeatedly brought up to date and marking the short-run and secular trends in diverse areas and groups;
4. Continuing studies of the consequences of various programs designed to promote ethnic equities, thus reducing the wastage presently entailed by well-intentioned, expensive and ineffectual programs.

This is a large research order. But the American creed, as set down in the basic moral documents of this nation, seems deserving of the systematic exercise of our social intelligence fully as much as it is deserving of our moral resolution.

ENDNOTE

1. There is a large literature bearing on this point. For recent discussions, see P. F. Lazarsfeld, "Some remarks on the role of mass media in so-called tolerance propaganda," *Journal of Social Issues*, Summer, 1947; P. F. Lazarsfeld and R. K. Merton, "Media of mass communication, popular taste, and organized social action," in Lyman Bryson (ed.), *Communication of Ideas* (New York, Institute for Religious and Social Studies, 1948); M. Jahoda and E. Cooper, "Evasion of propaganda: how prejudiced people respond to anti-prejudice propaganda," *Journal of Psychology*, 1947, 23, 15–25. For an appraisal of the inadequate research to date on this problem, see R. M. Williams, Jr., *The Reduction of Intergroup Tensions* (New York, Social Science Research Council, 1947), 32 ff. The absence of adequate evidence attesting the *pragmatic* (not statistical) significance of tolerance propaganda suggests that propaganda programs now present an act of faith on the part of propagandists.

3

Race and Ethnicity:
A Sociobiological Perspective

Pierre L. van den Berghe

Two contrasting positions on the nature of race and ethnicity have been taken or at least, have been implicit, in the literature. Some scholars have viewed ethnic and racial group affiliation as an ascribed 'primordial identity,' deeply rooted, given at birth, and largely unchangeable. Such was the dominant view until the 1920s when ethnically and racially defined collectivities were taken for granted and generally assumed to have an unquestionable objective reality of their own, beyond their constituent members. Both racist and nationalist ideologies were popular expressions of this early version of the 'primordialist' view. During the next half-century the dominant social science view became culturally determinist, and increasingly argued that ethnic and racial identities, far from being primordial, were, in fact, culturally defined, changeable, manipulable to political ends, situationally sensitive, and often ecologically determined (Barth, 1969). What we may term the 'subjectivist' view of ethnicity probably became the dominant position in the 1960s and early 1970s. Only recently is the primordialist view being once more cautiously advanced (Francis, 1976; Keyes, 1976; Stein and Hill, 1977).

From *Ethnic and Racial Studies* 1:4 (October 1978), pp. 401–411 by permission of the author and Routledge & Kegan Paul PLC.

Such crudely dichotomous ways of characterizing intellectual positions and periodizing intellectual history serve little purpose beyond clarifying basic issues, and they do violence to many scholars' thinking. In my own writings, I repeatedly stressed the need to consider both the objective and the subjective aspects of race and ethnicity (van den Berghe, 1970, 1974, 1978a), and I was far from alone in doing so (Hoetink, 1967; Kuper and Smith, 1969; Schermerhorn, 1970). I was also in good company in emphasizing the irreducibility of ethnic and/or racial membership to class affiliation, and vice versa. Class, ethnicity and race, I asserted, are fundamentally different principles of social affiliation, although each of them must be looked at in both subjective and objective terms. I now believe that what in my prior works I left at the level of analytical concepts and categorical assertions can be subsumed under a more comprehensive theoretical umbrella derived from sociobiology. This is what I propose to do here.

Unfortunately, there is room here only for the sketchiest presentation of sociobiological concepts. The reader will find early theoretical formulations in Hamilton (1964), and Maynard Smith (1964), more recent and extensive treatments in Wilson (1975), Barash (1977), and Dawkins (1976), and human applications in Alexander (1971), Parker (1976), van den Berghe and Barash (1977),

Hartung (1976), Greene (1978), Fox (1975), Chagnon and Irons (1978), Barkow (1978), and Dyson-Hudson and Smith (1978), among others. Although the label 'sociobiology' has only recently gained currency, thanks largely to Wilson's book (1975), the emerging new discipline is nothing but a systematic application of Darwinian evolutionary theory to animal behavior, especially to social behavior. Sociobiology is, in fact, little else than a more theoretically grounded, and less descriptive brand of ethology informed by behavior genetics.

The most basic question asked by sociobiology as well as sociology is: why are animals social, that is, why do they cooperate? Why are some species more social than others? The answer was long intuitively known: animals are social to the extent that cooperation is mutually beneficial. What sociobiology does is supply the main genetic mechanism for animal sociality, namely *kin selection* to maximize *inclusive fitness*. Natural selection operates through differential reproduction. Different alleles of the same gene compete with each other, and the ones that are carried by the more reproductively successful individuals have a greater probability of being replicated in the population's next generation. The successful alleles are the ones which, in a given environment, favor the reproductive success or 'fitness' of their carriers.

The great theoretical contribution of sociobiology has been to extend the concept of fitness to that of 'inclusive fitness' (Hamilton, 1964). Indeed, an animal can duplicate its genes directly through its own reproduction, or indirectly through the reproduction of relatives with which it shares specific proportions of genes. Animals, therefore, can be expected to behave cooperatively, and thereby enhance each other's fitness to the extent that they are genetically related. This is what is meant by kin selection (Maynard Smith, 1964). Animals, in short, are nepotistic, i.e. they prefer kin over non-kin, and close kin over distant kin. This may happen consciously, as in humans, or, more commonly, unconsciously. Kin selection does not presuppose consciousness in order to be operative.

The propensity to be 'altruistic,' i.e. to contribute to alter's fitness at the expense of ego's fitness, is directly proportional not only to the coefficient of relatedness between ego and alter, but also to the benefit/cost ratio of the altruistic act. To use a human example, a post-menopausal mother could be expected to sacrifice her life more readily for a young adult child about to reproduce than a young mother to forego her life for the benefit of her first foetus. The genetic relationship is the same in both cases (namely, one half), but the fitness cost is low in the first case, high in the second. Altruism, then, is directed mostly at kin, especially close kin, and is, in fact, a misnomer. It represents the ultimate form of genetic selfishness. It is but the blind expression of inclusive fitness maximization. In fact, a simple formula leads one to predict that 'altruism' can be expected if the cost/benefit ratio of the transaction is smaller than the coefficient of relatedness between alter and ego.

There is no reason to doubt that kin selection is a powerful cement of sociality in humans as it is in other animals. Yet, it is also clear that kin selection does not explain all of human sociality. There are, in my view, two additional bases of human sociality: reciprocity and coercion. Rudimentary forms of these are also present in many animals, but human forms of reciprocity and coercion greatly over-shadow in complexity and importance anything we know in other species. Not surprisingly, therefore, even the simplest and smallest human societies, though far less 'perfect' than those of the social insects (termites, ants, bees, wasps), are much more complex than those of any other known species. Reciprocity is cooperation for mutual benefit, and with expectation of return, and it can operate between kin or between non-kin. Coercion is the use of force for one-sided benefit, that is, for purposes of intraspecific parasitism or predation. All human societies continue to be organized on the basis of all three principles of sociality: kin selection, reciprocity, and coercion. However, the larger and the more complex a society becomes, the greater the importance of reciprocity, and, with the emergence of the state, coercion becomes in relation to kin selection.

This is the barest sketch of an argument which I develop elsewhere (van den Berghe, 1978b). In the last analysis, this view of human sociality seeks to reduce individual behavior, social structure and cultural superstructure to the competition for scarce resources between individual organisms, each one acting, consciously or unconsciously, to maximize its gains or minimize its losses. This view of human affairs is sufficiently at variance with much of contemporary social science to arouse passionate rejection as a return to simplistic instinct theory, biological reductionism, speculative evolutionism, social Darwinism, racism, hereditarianism, and so on. Lacking the space to present the full theory here, I can even less examine the objections and refute them. Suffice it to say that sociobiology is indeed reductionist (as all modern science), evolutionist (as all modern biology), and materialist (as much good social science), but that it is emphatically not a return to social Darwinism, instinct theories or racism, and that it does not belittle the importance of environmental factors, the unique characteristics of *Homo sapiens*, and the significance of human culture. It merely asserts in the most undogmatic fashion that human behavior is the product of a long process of adaptive evolution that involved the complex interplay of genotypical, ecological and cultural factors.

How do these prolegomena relate to race and ethnicity? My central thesis is that both ethnicity and 'race' (in the social sense) are, in fact, extensions of the idiom of kinship, and that, therefore, ethnic and race sentiments are to be understood as an extended and attenuated form of kin selection. Class relations, on the other hand, are in the realm of reciprocity, and are therefore of a fundamentally different nature. In more general form, I am suggesting that there are two broad types of human collectivities: the ones that I shall call Type I tend to be ascriptive, defined by common descent, generally hereditary, and often endogamous, and those of Type II that are joined in the defense of common interests. Type I includes racial, caste and ethnic groups, while Type II encompasses such varied associations as trade unions, political parties, professional bodies, sports clubs, neighborhood groups, parent-teacher associations, and so on. Empirically, of course, a group may have mixed characteristics, as an ethnically-based political party, or a hereditary occupational guild. Nevertheless, in their ideal-typical form, each kind of group has a clearly distinct basis of solidarity: kinship and interest respectively.

Type I groups are generally preferentially or prescriptively endogamous, but internally subdivided into exogamous kin groups: nuclear families, lineages, clans, kindreds. Indeed, until the last few thousand years of human history, Type I groups were synonymous with human societies. They were small in-bred populations of a few hundred individuals, prototypical 'tribes' that regarded themselves as 'the people,' sharing common descent, real or putative, and as children of the mythical founder couple or creator god. Members of the tribe, though subdivided into smaller kin groups, saw themselves as a single people, solidary against the outside world, and interlinked by a web of kinship and marriage making the tribe in fact a superfamily. A high rate of inbreeding insured that most spouses were also kinsmen. The cultural inventions of unilineal descent and lineage exogamy permitted the extension of that primordial model of social organization to much larger societies running into the tens of thousands of people, and yet where Type II organizations were almost totally absent (with the exception of age sets).

Ethnic groups, for nearly all of human history, were what geneticists call breeding populations, in-breeding superfamilies, in fact, which not only were much more closely related to each other than to even their closest neighbors, but which, almost without exception, explicitly recognized that fact, and maintained clear territorial and social boundaries with other such ethnic groups. This is, of course, not to deny that migration, conquest, and inter-breeding took place with some regularity, and thus that the common ancestry of 'the people' was always partially fictive. But this was also true of smaller kin groups: the *pater* is not necessarily the *progenitor*. That the extended kinship of the ethnic group was sometimes putative rather than real was not the important point. Just as in the smaller kin units, the kinship was real often enough to become the basis of these powerful sentiments we call nationalism, tribalism, racism, and ethnocentrism. The ease and speed with which these sentiments can be mobilized even in modern industrial societies where they have to compete with many Type II groups, the blind ferocity of the conflicts to which these sentiments can lead, the imperviousness of such sentiments to rational arguments are but a few indications of their continued vitality and their primordiality.

What I am suggesting is that ethnocentrism evolved during millions, or at least hundreds of thousands of years as an extension of kin selection. Reciprocity was also involved, especially in the exchange of women in marriage, but as spouses were typically also kinsmen there was no sharp distinction between kin selection and reciprocity. As hominids became increasingly formidable competitors and predators to their own and closely related species, there was a strong selective pressure for the formation of larger and more powerful groups. Group size in hunting and gathering societies was, of course, severely constrained by ecological factors, but, still, there was an obvious selective advantage for kin groups to form those solidary superfamilies we call tribes; this, in turn, as Bigelow (1969) so clearly argues, necessarily meant organizing *against* other competing groups, and therefore maintaining and defending ethnic boundaries.

Of Type II groups, little needs to be said here. With the exception of age sets, they tend to be characteristic of larger, more complex, state-organized societies, and therefore to have arisen much later in human evolution, and to be more exclusively cultural. They are, of course, also important, especially in industrial societies, but they are not primordial, they can be more readily formed and disbanded, they are more amenable to cool, rational calculations of interest, and they do not as readily unleash orgies of passion. Nor, of course, have they stamped out Type I groups. Another fundamental difference between Type I and Type II groups is that the former tend to be mutually exclusive in membership and thus to form the basis of most primary relationships, while the latter are segmental, and non-mutually exclusive. Millions of people in individual societies belong to a multiplicity of Type II groups, few of which involves them very deeply or permanently. Some people are ethnically alienated, marginal or mobile or they are the product of mixed marriages, but most people belong to a single ethnic group or sub-group, and remain there for life. Even allowing for all the complications of the real world, and the existence of mixed-type groups, the categorical distinction remains nevertheless quite striking.

Let us return to Type I groups, our special concern here. I have suggested that they evolved as an extension of kin selection, and thus probably have a partial biological basis, in the same sense as human kinship systems are rooted in biology. This contention is, of course, hotly contested by anthropologists such as Sahlins (1976), who counter that human kinship is cultural, not biological. Almost every aspect of human behavior takes a cultural form, from sneezing and defecating to writing poetry and riding a motorcycle. But this is not to say that some of these things do not *also* have a biological basis. I am definitely not arguing that we have a gene for ethnocentrism, or for recognizing kin; rather I am arguing that those societies that institutionalized norms of nepotism and ethnocentrism had a strong selective advantage over those that did not (assuming that any such ever existed), because kin selection has been the basic blueprint for animal sociality. To explain the universality of ethnocentrism and kinship organization in human societies by invoking culture is completely question begging. Culture is merely a *proximate* explanation of why people behave ethnocentrically and nepotistically. As every ethnographer knows, when natives are asked why they behave a certain way, they answer: because it is the custom. The anthropologist then translates: because of his culture; the sociologist says: because he has been socialized into the norms of his society; and the psychologist counters: because of his learning experiences. All of them are right as far as they go, but none of them has explained why all human societies practice kin selection and are ethnocentric.

So far, I have stressed ethnicity rather than race or caste in my treatment of Type I groups. Caste is a very special case, limited, even if one adopts a wide definition of the term, to highly differentiated, stratified societies, and may be considered an extreme case of the grafting of the principle of occupational specialization into what is basically a Type I group. Castes are not unique in being occupationally specialized Type I groups. Ethnic and racial groups also tend to become so (Hechter, 1976). Castes are merely extreme cases of occupational specialization linked with rigid endogamy and hierarchization.

Race is a different matter. First, I should make it clear that, even though I have presented a partially biological argument, I am most emphatically not using the word 'race' in the sense of a sub-species of *Homo sapiens*. Instead, I mean by 'race' the social definition which it is variously ascribed in different societies. Social race typically seizes on biologically trivial phenotypes, and, equally typically, corresponds only very imperfectly with genetically isolated populations. It thus has no intrinsic biological significance, as indicated by the fact that only a few of the world's societies use primarily morphological phenotypes to define themselves, and to differentiate outsiders.

At first blush, this would seem to invalidate my argument that ethnic and racial sentiments represent an extension of kin selection. If that is the case, why should most human societies seize primarily on such obviously culturally transmitted traits such as language and dialect, religious beliefs, dress, hair styles, manners, scarifications, and the like as badges of group recognition and membership? If the name of the game is to identify kinsmen in order to enhance one's inclusive fitness, then why are not inherited physical characteristics chosen as recognition signals, rather than acquired cultural traits? Sometimes, of course, morphological phenotypes such as skin color, facial features, stature, hair texture, eye color, and so on are used, not only to define group membership, but also, within the group, as tests of ever-questionable paternity. Generally, however, cultural criteria of membership are far more salient than physical ones, if the latter are used at all. Societies that stress physical phenotypes more than cultural traits are exceptional. Why?

The answer must again be sought in our evolutionary history. Until the last few millenia, that is, until the rise of conquest states, sudden, large-scale, human migration was rare, and human breeding populations were small. There was migration and interbreeding, but on an individual scale, and mostly between neighboring groups. The result was that neighboring populations were typically not sharply discontinuous in their genetic composition. The relative proportions of alleles of the same gene often constituted a gradient as one travelled through several breeding populations. Eye color in Europe would be a good example. The further north one goes, from, say, Sicily to Sweden, the higher the proportion of lightly pigmented eyes. Yet, at no point in the

journey is there a noticeable discontinuity. Eye color, therefore, is a poor criterion of national membership in Europe. Indeed, it varies much more *within* national groups, and indeed within families, than *between* groups.

Now, Europeans do use some morphological phenotypes to distinguish various ethnic groups. They speak loosely of 'Nordic', 'Mediterranean', 'Jewish,' and so on, types. In the absence of any other clue, probabilistic guesses are often made on the basis of physical appearance as to a stranger's ethnic origin. Most groups probably have what Hoetink (1967) termed a 'somatic norm image,' that is, a mental picture of what a model group member looks like. The point, however, is that morphological phenotypes tend to be used either in the absence of more reliable cultural clues (such as language), or when physical appearance is widely discrepant from the somatic norm image (as, for instance, in Europe with Asians or Africans).

A good test of group membership for the purpose of assessing kin relatedness must meet the basic requirement of discriminating more reliably *between* groups than *within* groups. That is, the criterion chosen must show more *inter*group than *intra*-group variance. Until recently, cultural criteria met that condition far more reliably than physical ones. The problem was for small groups to distinguish themselves from their immediate neighbors, not with unknown populations thousands of kilometers away. Even the most trivial differences of accent, dialect, vocabulary, body adornment, and so on, could be used far more reliably to assess *biological* relatedness or unrelatedness than any physical phenotype.[1] Therefore, whatever test was easiest to apply and correlated best with kin relatedness was used. That the correlation was spurious did not matter. What mattered was that it discriminated accurately.

This theory accounts not only for the general prevalence of cultural diacritica in assessing group membership. It also accounts for the appearance of racism when and where it does occur better than any competing theory. The kin selection argument predicts that physical criteria *will* be salient to the extent that they do a good and easy job of discriminating kin and non-kin. This obviously occurs in the aftermath of large-scale, long-distance migration, whether through conquest, incursions, slavery, indenture, or voluntary immigration. The colonial expansion of Europe beginning some five centuries ago, and all of the massive population transfers it brought in its wake are, of course, the overwhelmingly important genetic event of our species. Predictably, it brought about a great surge in racism, because all of a sudden, it became possible to make a fairly accurate kin selection judgment from a distance of several hundred meters. The Dutchman at the Cape, the Portuguese in Brazil, the Englishman in Kenya did not have to ask questions and pick up subtle clues of accent to detect kin relatedness. By using a simple test of skin pigmentation he could literally shoot and ask questions later at little risk of killing a kinsman.

Competing theories of racism based on arguments about the nature of capitalism, or normative differences betweeen Catholicism and Protestantism, explain little by comparison with the simple kin selection argument. Humans, like other animals are selected to favor kin, and whatever does a quick, easy and accurate job of differentiating kin and non-kin will be used. In most cases, and until recently, cultural criteria have been predominantly used. Physical criteria became salient only after large, strikingly different-looking populations found themselves in sudden and sustained contact.

The story of Western racism did not stop with the sudden contact of large numbers of different-looking people. As soon as strangers met, they started mating, as indeed any members of the same species can be expected to do. Interbreeding, in turn, began to blur physical differences between human groups, and obviously had the consequence of reducing the validity of physical traits as a predictor of kin relatedness. It has sometimes been argued that 'miscegenation' is evidence of the relative absence of racial prejudice. This is nonsense. Racism has never stopped dominant group men from mating with subordinate group women. But the reverse is probably true. Racism requires a special effort to sustain when most of your closest relatives belong to the despised race, that is, when phenotypes become poor preditors of genetic relatedness. Not only do the physical markers between races become blurred but they cut across kin ties. Fully institutionalized racism can only be maintained, in

short, in societies like South Africa and the United States that retain a high degree of racial endogamy, or that have reestablished racial endogamy after a phase of miscegenation under slavery.

Slavery was euphemistically referred to in the nineteenth-century United States as the 'peculiar institution.' There was, in fact, nothing very peculiar about slavery as such, for it had existed in the vast majority of stratified pre-industrial societies. What was indeed peculiar was the special brand of Western Hemisphere, *racial* slavery. All slavery systems involved extensive interbreeding between male masters and female slaves. Sexual exploitation is the inevitable concomitant of the situation of domination which characterizes slavery. The peculiarity of racially defined slavery, however, was the internal contradiction inherent in attempting to keep a racial boundary between kinsmen. In Brazil, much of the Caribbean and Spanish America, racial lines were so extensively blurred that, even though several of these societies remain race-conscious, no distinct, corporate racial groups can now be said to exist. In the United States, slavery was abolished in time to preserve a rigid racial dichotomy by establishing a segregated system of endogamous racial groups after the Civil War.

The American slave plantation was a big family of sorts, albeit an extraordinarily perverse one. Masters, overseers and slaves inhabited a little world which maximized inequality while at the same time fostering all kinds of intimacy. Slaves cooked their master's food, wetnursed their legitimate children, and bore their illegitimate ones. The legitimizing ideology of plantation slavery, not surprisingly was paternalistic. Paternalism was not new to slavery; indeed it is one of the commonest rationalizations for tyranny and exploitation. What better way of making the oppressed accept their lot than to disguise parasitism as kin selection? Exploitation is said to be in the best interest of the oppressed because the despot is a surrogate father who loves them. But whereas the paternalism of traditional despotic states was a fiction often maintained by an elaborate origin myth and an all-encompassing familistic ideology such as Confucianism, paternalism under chattel slavery often described actual kinship. Slave children of owners often did receive better treatment, and were more likely to be freed. Nevertheless, there was a fundamental incompatibility between the institution of slavery, the essence of which was parasitism, and kin selection.

Paternalism was simply not a workable ideology for slavery. Either the owner was not the father of his slaves, and it was little use pretending he was, as his exploitative behavior fooled no one, or else, he was his slaves' father, grandfather, or half-brother, in which case the master–slave relationship and the color line were difficult to maintain.

We suggested at the outset that there were three main mechanisms of human sociality: kin selection, reciprocity and coercion. Ethnic and racial groups command our unreasoned loyalty because they are in fact, or at least in theory, superfamilies. But ethnic and race relations are not only relations of cooperation and amity with the in-group; they are equally importantly relations of competition and conflict between groups. While intra-group relations are primarily dictated by kin selection, real or putative, intergroup relations are typically antagonistic. Occasionally, ethnic groups may enter a symbiotic, mutually beneficial relationship based, for instance, on the exploitation of two specialized and noncompetitive niches in the same habitat. Relations between some pastoralist and sedentary groups are of this type. More commonly, there is open competition for, and conflict over scarce resources, and not infrequently the establishment of multi-ethnic states dominated by one ethnic group at the expense of others. Coercion then becomes the basis of interethnic (or inter-racial) relations.

Unlike kin selection and reciprocity which require no justification because they contribute to the fitness of all actors in the system, coercion, which leads to asymmetrical parasitism, often does attempt to legitimate itself. Interestingly, there are but two basic ideologies in support of coercion. One seeks to disguise coercion as kin selection, and here we have the many brands of paternalism and familism that have been used to justify nearly all pre-industrial forms of despotism. The other attempts to present coercion as reciprocity and exchange, it is characteristic of the various 'democratic' ideologies of industrial societies in the last two centuries, from liberalism to socialism. Why this ideological shift from paternalism to *liberté, égalité, franternité* in justifying tyranny during the last two centuries?

Perhaps this ideological shift reflects in part the increasing incorporation of small nation-states into multi-national states. Paternalism is a peculiarly well suited ideology for the small, ethnically homogeneous nation-state. Not surprisingly, it was independently reinvented in societies as far distant as China, Japan, Inca Peru, Tzarist Russia, Ancient Egypt, Ottoman Turkey, Renaissance Europe and countless African kingdoms. Paternalism works in monoethnic states because the very concept of the nation is an extension of kin selection. For the same reason, it breaks down in multi-ethnic states. It was one thing for the Japanese peasant to look on his emperor as a divine super-father, the living incarnation of Nippon, quite another for the Hindu peasant to regard that polluted beef eater, Queen Victoria, as the living symbol of Mother India. An ideology based on reciprocity, on the other hand, can transcend ethnic boundaries. It is therefore a suitable one for the 90 percent of the world's states which are multi-ethnic conglomerates, and, furthermore, being ethnically neutral, it exports remarkably well as revolutionary ideology. It is no accident that France launched into the most imperialistic phase of its history immediately after the Revolution.

The ideas sketched here are still tentative. They do not so much supplant other theories of ethnicity and race as supplement them by putting them in the broader context of evolutionary thinking. They do not purport to explain everything about these phenomena; they do not predict detailed historical occurrences, nor account for subtle cultural differences. They do, however, suggest parsimonious hypotheses to account for features of race and ethnicity which had hitherto remained elusive and problematic. Their plausibility to the reader hinges on whether he accepts the most fundamental paradigm for the evolution of different life forms and societal organization on our planet, Darwinian evolutionary theory, and on whether he is willing to apply that enormously successful model to our own species, or prefers to invoke an act of special creation for mankind.

ENDNOTE

1. The classical historical anecdote is that the massacre of French occupation forces by Flemings in 1302, in Bruges. The insurgent Flemings massacred their enemies at night in their beds. To make sure that no Flemings would be accidentally killed, the person was made to repeat a sentence 'schilde ende vriend' containing Dutch phonemes which are virtually unpronounceable for a native speaker of French. I daresay this kin selection test was well over 99 percent effective, and no physical trait could have come closer to it for reliability.

4

Class Approaches to Ethnicity and Race*

Edna Bonacich

The field of ethnic and race relations has recently tended to be dominated by an assumption that race and ethnicity are "primordial" bases of affiliation, rooted in "human nature." This assumption is increasingly being challenged by authors who contend that, while race and ethnicity may appear to be primordial attachments, in fact they reflect a deeper reality, namely, class relations and dynamics. I believe that class approaches are the most fruitful way to study ethnicity and race. Not only are they more in accord with a "deeper" level of reality that enables us to understand phenomena at the surface of society, but they also provide us with the tools for changing that reality. The purpose of this paper is to briefly review and criticize primordial assumptions about ethnicity and race, to present several class approaches to the subject in an effort to demonstrate the richness of available ideas, and

Reprinted from *Insurgent Sociologist* 10:2 (Fall, 1980) by permission.

A version of this paper was presented at the Annual Meeting of the American Sociological Association in Boston, August, 1979. I would like to thank the following for their helpful suggestions: Phillip Bonacich, James Geschwender, Richard Platkin, Linda Pomerantz, the Binghamton Insurgent Sociologist Collective, and Red Wednesday, my women's group, namely, Johanna Brenner, Norma Chinchilla, Nora Hamilton, Barbara Laslett, and Julia Wrigley.

finally, to attempt a tentative synthesis of some of these ideas.

Before we start, let us define our terms. Ethnicity and race are "communalistic" forms of social affiliation, sharing an assumption of a special bond between people of like origins, and the obverse of a negative relation to, or rejection of, people of dissimilar origins. There are other bases of communalistic affiliation as well, notably, nationality and "tribe." For the sake of this discussion, I would like to treat all of these as a single phenomenon. Thus, ethnocentrism, racism, nationalism, and tribalism are similar kinds of sentiments, dividing people along lines of shared ancestry rather than other possible lines of affiliation and conflict, such as common economic or political interest.

Obviously there are other important bases of affiliation besides communalism. One important alternative form of solidarity is along class lines. Figure 1 presents schematically these two forms of affiliation and their interaction for capitalist societies. Needless to say, it is a very simplified sketch and could be elaborated along both dimensions, as well as by the addition of other dimensions. Still, the point to be made is that ethnic (or communalistic, or "vertical") forms of solidarity cross-cut class (or "horizontal") bases of affiliation. They represent competing principles, each calling on people to join together along one of two axes.

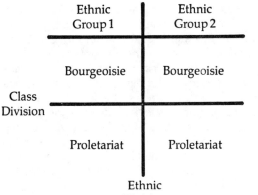

	Ethnic Group 1	Ethnic Group 2
	Bourgeoisie	Bourgeoisie
Class Division		
	Proletariat	Proletariat

Ethnic Division

Nationality, race, or tribe could be substituted for ethnicity.

FIGURE 1. *Ethnicity and Class in the Capitalist Mode of Production.*

Primordialism

The sociology of race and ethnic relations grew in reaction to a tradition that underplayed the importance of communalistic affiliations.[1] As many authors have pointed out, the early "classic" writers in sociology paid little heed to ethnicity.[2] They assumed that it would disappear with modernization and industrialization. Indeed, the early grand dichotomies, such as *gemeinschaft* and *gesellschaft*, assumed a movement from ethnic-type affiliations, based on irrational, kin-like bonds between people, to affiliation based on the rational principles of mutual interest and need. Organic solidarity would replace mechanical; horizontal bonds would destroy vertical ones. Ethnicity and race were "traditional" social forms. The exigencies of modern society would "liberate" people from these traditions.[3] It should be noted that this expectation was also held by early Marxists, who assumed that class solidarity would override national chauvinism (Nairn, 1975; Blauner, n.d.).

The obvious falseness of this premise, perhaps especially realized by American sociologists in the face of Nazi Germany, when one of the world's most "modern" societies proved capable of extreme racism, forced a reassessment. Similarly, the black uprising of the 1960s in the United States reawakened sociologists to the fact that the "race problem" was not simply disappearing.

Clearly these "traditional" sources of solidarity were far more resistant to change than had been realized.

Several authors began to call for revisions in our thinking. Criticizing earlier writers, they demanded that race and ethnicity be given prominence as phenomena that could not be ignored. Some, for example, writers in the "plural society" school (Smith, 1965; Kuper and Smith eds., 1969) suggested that we place this phenomenon at center stage. As they correctly pointed out, almost every society in the world has some degree of ethnic and racial diversity, and for most it is apparently a pivotal point of division and conflict.

The polemic against the obvious inadequacies of the belief that ethnicity would disappear has led to another extreme position: the view that it is such a "natural" bond between people as to be immutable or "primordial." Geertz (1963:109) defines this concept as follows:

> By a primordial attachment is meant one that stems from the "givens"—or, more precisely, as culture is inevitably involved in such matters, the assumed "givens"—of social existence: immediate contiguity and kin connection mainly, but beyond them the givenness that stems from being born into a particular religious community, speaking a particular language, or even a dialect of a language, and following particular social practices. These congruities of blood, speech, custom, and so on, are seen to have an ineffable, and at times overpowering, coerciveness in and of themselves. One is bound to one's kinsman, one's neighbor, one's fellow believer, *ipso facto*; as the result not merely of personal affection, practical necessity, common interest, or incurred moral obligation, but at least in great part by virtue of some unaccountable absolute import attributed to the very tie itself. The general strength of such primordial bonds, and the types of them that are important, differ from person to person, from society to society, and from time to time. But for virtually every person, in every society, at almost all times, such attachments seem to flow more from a sense of natural—some would say spiritual—affinity than from social interaction.

The primordial ethnic bond is assumed to have two faces. On the one hand, it leads to a special attachment to an "in-group" of similar people, on the other, to feelings of disdain or repulsion towards the "out-group" or people of dissimilar origins. "Ethnocentrism" is believed to be a "natural" human sentiment. For example, Gordon (1978:73) states:

> The sense of ethnicity (in the larger definition of racial, religious, or national origins identification), because it cannot be shed by social mobility, as for instance social class background can, since society insists on its inalienable ascription from cradle to grave, becomes incorporated into the self. This process would appear to account for the widespread, perhaps ubiquitous presence of ethnocentrism, and perhaps even more crucially means that injury to the ethnic group is seen as injury to the self.

This idea derives from a biologically rooted conception of "human nature."[4]

Gordon may be more explicit than most in stating the assumption that ethnicity is rooted in human nature, but it is widespread (Williams, 1964:17–27) in the discipline. The naturalness of the ethnic bond is extended to "racial" categories, even as authors recognize that these have questionable validity. Thus such categories as "blacks" and "whites" in the United States are treated as "groups." Whites naturally prefer the company of other whites, who are more similar to themselves, while disdaining the company of less similar blacks. The unquestioned assumption of the "group" nature of ethnic and racial "groups" extends even to authors who recognize that such groups may act as interest groups to attain political ends (Glazer and Moynihan eds., 1975).

Accepting the primordialness of ethnicity leads to a certain logic of inquiry. Since ethnic and racial affiliation requires no explanation in itself, one concentrates on its consequences.[5] These may be negative, in the form of prejudice and discrimination against "out-groups."[6] Or they may be positive, providing people with a meaningful and rich group life.[7] In the process of concentrating on intra-"group" solidarity and inter-"group" hostility, little attention is paid to intra-ethnic conflict let alone cross-ethnic alliances.

There are at least three reasons for questioning the primordial nature of communalistic ties. First, there are boundary problems in defining ethnic and racial groups (cf. Barth, ed., 1969;

Patterson, 1977). Because of the pervasive tendency for human beings to interbreed, a population of mixed ancestry is continually being generated. To consign these people to an ethnic identity requires a descent rule. There are a variety of such rules, including: tracing descent matrilineally (as found among the Jews), or by the presence of one particular ancestry (as in U.S. blacks), or by treating mixed ancestry as a separate ethnicity (as in the case of South African Coloureds), and so on. The variability in descent rules suggests their social rather than primordial nature. They reflect social "decisions," not natural, kin-like feeling.[8]

Apart from mixed ancestry problems, ethnic groups can redefine their boundaries in terms of whom they incorporate. As many authors (e.g. Yancey et al., 1976) have pointed out, several of the Eurpoean immigrant groups to the United States, such as Italians, had no sense of common nationality until they came here. And the construction of "whites" out of the enmity between old and "new" European immigrants took decades to achieve. Similarly today a new ethnic group, Asian-Americans, is being constructed out of previously quite distinctive, and often hostile, national elements. That such a creation is social and political, rather than primordial, seems clear.

A second reason for questioning the primordial nature of ethnicity is that shared ancestry has not prevented intra-ethnic conflict, including class conflict. If one considers the history of societies which were relatively homogeneous ethnically, such as France or England, one finds not only intense class conflict, but even class warfare. Even in ethnically diverse societies such as the United States, within ethnic groups, class conflict is not unknown. White workers have struck against white-owned plants and been shot down by co-ethnics without concern for "common blood." Chinese and Jewish businessmen have exploited their ethnic "brothers and sisters" in sweatshops and have bitterly resisted the efforts of their workers to gain independence. The prevalence of intra-ethnic conflict should lead us to question the idea that ethnicity necessarily provides a bond between people, let alone a primordial one.

Third, conflicts based on ethnicity, race, and nationality, are quite variable. In some cases they are fierce; in others, despite the presence of groups with different ancestry, conflict is limited or non-existent. A full range of ethnic relations is found in the world, extending from complete assimilation of diverse ethnic elements (as in the case of various European nationalities which came to make up the "WASP" group in the United States), to the total extermination of one ethnic group by another (as in the genocide of the Tasmanians). This variability should, again, lead us to question the primordial nature of ethnicity for if ethnicity were a natural and inevitable bond between people it should always be a prominent force in human affairs.

Of course, primordialists (e.g. Hoetnik, 1967) might reply that the level of conflict is based on the degree of difference between groups, in terms of color or culture. Thus variability in race and ethnic relations could be accounted for within a primordial framework. For instance, in the United States, degree of racial and ethnic difference would, on the surface, appear to account for patterns of assimilation or rejection (Warner and Srole, 1945). Yet the U.S. pattern finds limited replications on a world scale. Some of the worst ethnic-type conflicts have occurred among very similar groups, such as Protestants and Catholics in Northern Ireland, French and English speaking Canadians, Ibos and other "tribes" in Nigeria, Chinese and native populations in Southeast Asia, and Jews and Germans in Nazi Germany, to name a few. The "degree of difference" seems quite inadequate to explain the emergence of conflict or its intensity.

For all these reasons, and there are probably others, we cannot simply accept communalistic groups as natural or primordial units. Ethnic, national, and racial solidarity and antagonism are all socially created phenomena. True, they are social phenomena which call upon primordial sentiments and bonds based upon common ancestry. But these sentiments and bonds are not just naturally there. They must be constructed and activated. It is thus incumbent upon us not to take ethnic phenomena for granted, but to try to explain them.

Recently a new school of thought has emerged. While not moving back to the earlier errors of the "founding fathers" in ignoring the importance of ethnicity, racism, and nationalism it neverthe-less holds that these phenomena cannot be taken for granted as natural; they need to be explained. Without ignoring communalistic affiliations we can ask: Under what conditions will ethnic or racial affiliation be invoked? Under what conditions will this lead to extreme conflict? And under what conditions will ethnicity or race subside as major axes of social organization and conflict? Class theories constitute one broad category of attempted explanation of the ethnic phenomenon. They share in common the notion that ethnic movements are not only essentially political rather than primordial, but that they have *material* roots in the system and relations of production.

Class Theories of Ethnicity

There is no single class approach to the question of ethnicity. Indeed, in recent years, considerable creative work has proceeded on several fronts, not all of which are in communication with one another. Different disciplines and subdisciplines, such as economic anthropology, urban sociology, and immigrant history, are all developing class approaches to ethnicity. Scholars interested in different areas of the world tend to communicate poorly with one another. Thus there are class theories of ethnicity in African or Latin American studies, about South Africa, the U.S.-Mexican border, about guest workers in Europe, and so on. In addition, an abundance of theoretical models is available, some of which operate at different levels, but all of which address ethnicity to some extent. These include: theories of labor migration and immigration, dependency theory, dual labor markets, split labor markets, internal colonialism, theories of middleman minorities, labor aristocracy theories, world systems theory, and more. Bringing all these literatures together is a huge task, well beyond the scope of this paper. My goal here is to present a few of the available ideas.

Before examining particular theories, let us briefly return to Figure 1 to define what is being talked about. Positive (integrative) movements along the vertical axis may be termed "nationalist" movements. These are efforts to mobilize people of different classes within the same ethnic group to join together. Negative (conflictual) movements along the horizontal axis represent within-class inter-ethnic antagonisms. These two types of movements constitute the two faces of ethnicity: in-group solidarity and out-group rejection. In contrast, negative movements along the vertical axis represent intra-ethnic class struggle, while positive movements along the horizontal axis reflect cross-ethnic class solidarity. Diagonal movements are ambiguous, having both class and ethnic content. For instance, a negative diagonal could represent national and colonial oppression or movements for liberation from such oppression. Our main concern here is with the explanation of ethnic-type movements, i.e., positive vertical and negative horizontal.

Note that the figure should apply to inter-ethnic relations regardless of the territorial location of these groups. They can each occupy a discrete geographical territory, or a segment of one nation may have conquered and settled among another,[9] or a segment of one nation may have moved or been brought in as laborers to the territory of another, and so on. While there are important differences between these situations (Lieberson, 1961), they all juxtapose communalistic against class bases of affiliation.

Figure 2 presents very schematically several class approaches to the question of ethnic nationalism. They are intended not to represent a comprehensive coverage of all class theories of ethnicity but to illustrate the tremendous riches and diversity of ideas within a class orientation.

A. Nation-building

One of the simplest class theories of ethnicity or nationalism is that it is a movement reflecting an early stage of capitalistic development in which capitalists seek to integrate a "national" market. This movement achieved its peak in Europe in the late nineteenth century (Hobsbawm, 1977). When capitalism became imperialistic, the national bourgeoisies of the various Western nations came into conflict with one another, leading ultimately to the two world wars (Lenin, 1939). The participants in these wars espoused nationalist ideologies as a mechanism by which the capitalist class could mobilize workers to support their cause. Exponents of this view hold that workers are not nationalistic since they are all exploited. Rather, they are internationalist, sharing a common in-

terest in the overthrow of capitalism which transcends national boundaries. Nationalism is thus a movement representing the interests of the bourgeoisie. (This is illustrated in Figure 2A by showing that antagonism between national bourgeoisies leads to efforts at national mobilization by the bourgeoisies. The workers are objects, not generators, of this effort.)

B. Super-exploitation

The fact that workers of different nationalities have not easily joined with one another, and have apparently joined willingly with their "national bourgeoisie" in the oppression or exclusion of workers of other nationalities, revealed the limitation of this approach. Such cases as the U.S. South or South Africa, where white workers generally failed to join with blacks in a united working class movement, and instead identified with white capitalists and land-owners, led to some rethinking on the issue. An adequate explanation of communalism must take into account worker interests in it too.

"Super-exploitation," a crude designation for several schools of thought, provided an answer. Probably the most common class approach to ethnicity, it sees ethnicity or race as markers used by employers to divide the working class. One segment of workers, typically dark-skinned, are more oppressed than another, the latter typically of the same ethnicity as the exploiters. This enables the dominant bourgeoisie to make huge profits from the former segment, enough to pay off the more privileged sector of the working class, who then help to stabilize the system by supporting it and acting as the policemen of the specially oppressed.[10]

For several authors in this tradition (e.g. Cox, 1948), the super-exploitation of dark-skinned workers is rooted in the imperialistic expansion of Western European capitalism. Europe colonized the rest of the world in order to continue to accumulate capital more effectively. The ideology of racism grew as a justification for the exploitation of colonized peoples: they were "naturally" inferior and needed Europeans to "help" them move into the modern world. Racist ideology developed not only in relation to people living in the distant colonies, but also toward people living in "internal colonies," (Allen, 1970; Blauner, 1972) where either white settlers had become established or colonized workers had been brought under some degree of coercion. Even when separated in politically differentiated territories, the working class of the imperialist power could be used to keep the colonized in line. Thus, with imperialism, the major axis of exploitation shifted

A. Nation-Building

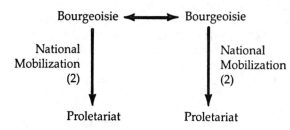

B. Super-Exploitation

C. Split Labor Market

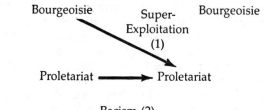

D. Middleman Minorities

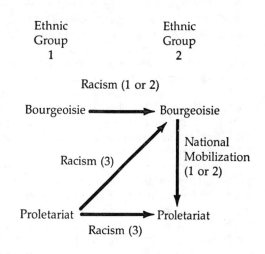

E. National Liberation

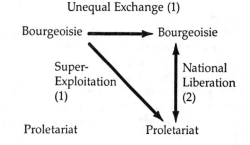

FIGURE 2. *Five Types of Class Theory of Ethnicity.*

from capitalist versus workers to oppressor "nations" and oppressed "nations."

Within a multi-ethnic society, having an especially exploited, ethnically delineated class serves several "functions" for the capitalist class: it can be used as a reserve army of labor, permitting flexibility in the system to deal with business cycles (Baran and Sweezy, 1966); it allows employers to fill diverse labor needs, such as the "dual" requirements of a stable, skilled labor force in the monopoly and state sectors of the economy, and a flexibly, unskilled, low wage labor force in the competitive sector (Gordon, 1972; O'Connor, 1973); it helps get done the "dirty work" that other workers are unwilling to do by creating a class that is desperate for work (Oppenheimer, 1974); it helps in the accumulation of capital because wealth is extracted from the "under-developed" sector of ethnic group and passed on to the bourgeoisie of the dominant group (Blauner, 1972; Frank, 1967, 1969); and it helps to stabilize the system by keeping the working class fragmented and disorganized (Reich, 1972; Szymanski, 1976).

Within this broad perspective are found some major differences. One important issue of debate is whether white workers gain or lose from the racial oppression of minorities. The "internal colonialism" school supports the idea that white workers benefit, by being paid extra from the surplus taken from minorities, by being cushioned against unemployment, and by getting other psychological and political rewards. In other words, in this view, the racism of white workers is a "rational" response, rooted in their vested interest in imperialism.

In contrast, authors such as Reich and Szymanski contend that white workers lose from racism. Since workers of different ethnicity are pitted against one another, the working class movement is weakened, and all lose. Thus white worker racism is seen more as a product of manipulation by capital than a rational pursuit of self-interest by white labor.

Despite these differences, both schools of thought see ethnicity as created, or at least nurtured, by the bourgeoisie of the dominant ethnic group or nationality. It is used to mark off the super-exploited as inferior, through ideologies like racism. And it is used to bind the more advantaged workers to the ruling class through the ideology of ethnic solidarity, thereby masking conflicting class interests within that group. White workers, for example, are taught that their whiteness makes them superior to other workers and gives them a common lot with their employers. A possibility is even held out to them that they too may become part of the ruling class because they are white. By the mobilization of ethnic solidarity, then, the capitalist class can induce these workers to support the system and align themselves against other workers. As Figure 2B suggests, the racism

of dominant group workers is a secondary phenomenon, while that of the bourgeoisie is primary.

C. Split Labor Market

This approach places labor competition at the center of racist-nationalist movements, challenging the idea that they are the creation of the dominant bourgeoisie.[11] Uneven development of capitalism on a world scale, exacerbated by imperialist domination, generates "backwardness" or "under-development" for certain "nationalities." Workers of these nations, unable to defend themselves against exploitation of the severest kind, became "cheap labor" (arrow 1 in Figure 2C). The availability of cheap labor leads dominant workers to be displaced or threatened with displacement, since employers would prefer to hire cheaper labor. The threat of displacement may be accompanied by other changes in production, such as deskilling. Dominant group workers react to the threat of displacement by trying to prevent or limit capital's access to cheap labor, through efforts to exclude members of "cheap labor" groups from full participation in the labor market (arrow 2). That these exclusionary efforts have a "nationalist" or "racist" character is a product of historical accident which produced a correlation between ethnicity and the price of labor.

In contrast to the "super-exploitation" school of thought, split labor market theory argues that dominant group workers do not share a "national" interest with capital in the exploitation of colonized people, nor are they even fooled into believing they share such an interest. Rather, dominant group capital and labor are engaged in struggle over this issue. Capital wants to exploit ethnic minorities while labor wants to prevent them from doing so. However, in attempting to exclude ethnic groups from certain jobs, labor's reactions may be just as devastating to minority workers as direct exploitation by capital. Where the dominant working class is successful, minority workers are kept out of the most advanced sectors of the economy, suffer high unemployment rates, and so on. In sum, this approach suggests that there are two distinct types of racial-national oppression, one stemming from capital, and the other from labor.

Split labor market theory sees the question of whether white workers gain or lose from racism as a false, or at least oversimplified, issue. It suggests that white workers are hurt by the existence of cordoned-off cheap labor sectors that can be utilized by capital to undercut them. White labor's efforts to protect itself may prevent undercutting, in the short run; however, in the long run, it is argued, a marked discrepancy in the price of labor is harmful to all workers, permitting capital to pit one group against another.

D. Middleman Minorities

Middleman minority theories deal with a particular class of ethnic phenomena, namely, groups which specialize in trade and concentrate in the petite bourgeoisie. Class explanations of this phenomenon vary. Some see these specialized minorities as creations of the dominant classes (not only bourgeoisies, since they arise in precapitalist societies as well) (Blalock, 1967; Hamilton, 1978; Rinder, 1958). By marking a group off as ethnically distinct, it can be forced to occupy a distinctive class position that is of special use to the ruling class, namely, to act as a go-between to the society's subordinate classes, while bearing the brunt of hostility towards the elite. The racist reactions of subordinate classes against the middleman group can thus be seen as secondary or tertiary phenomena, manipulated by ruling classes to protect themselves. (There are parallels in this tripartite system to the construction of ethnic divisions within the working class. In both cases, the creation of two ethnically distinct subordinate classes which are pitted against one another helps to keep the elite in power.)

Another interpretation of middleman minorities is to see them as internally generated by the minorities themselves. Bonds of ethnic loyalty are used by the dominant class within the minority to mobilize the group economically. The use of ethnic sentiments enables the group's leaders to mobilize resources cheaply and effectively. One of the most important of these cheap resources is ethnic labor. By emphasizing ethnic bonds, the ethnic elite is able to minimize class division within the ethnic group, thereby keeping labor effectively controlled (Benedict, 1968; Light, 1972). In this interpretation, the racist reactions of dominant group members in part derive from fears of competition. The dominant business class, as well as

the potential business class among subordinated segments of society, has access to a less pliable work force and fears being undercut. The dominant working class resents the competition of cheap-labor-based firms. Anti-middleman minority movements are seen (Bonacich, 1973) to be rooted in these class antagonisms.

Several authors have pointed to a strong correlation between class position in the petty trader category, and ethnic solidarity. Not only does ethnic solidarity support trading, but the reverse holds true, namely, petty trading helps to hold the ethnic group together. Leon even coined the term "people-class" to express this coincidence. The argument follows that, when members of the ethnic group no longer occupy a unique class position, they will gradually lose their ties to the ethnic group and assimilate. Jews, according to Leon, who have ceased to be members of the petite bourgeoisie, have tended to disappear from the ranks of Judaism. If true, here is a clear example of the dominance of class over primordial roots of ethnic affiliation.

The people-class idea has also been used to describe groups that are not middleman minorities (or in the petite bourgeoisie). For instance, Leggett (1968) and Oppenheimer (1974) develop a similar conception of blacks in the United States. Blackness represents not merely a racial category, but a class category as well: sub-proletarian, marginal working class, etc.[12] As blacks become less exclusively identified with a particular class position, the salience of "race" as a category tends to decrease (Wilson, 1978). In other words, racial terminology and antagonism reflect, to some extent, the common and distinctive class position of blacks and reactions to that position. A similar approach is developed for U.S. white ethnic groups by Hechter (1978) and Yancey, et al. (1976), who see ethnic solidarity as linked to a concentration in particular occupations or subcategories of the working class.[13]

E. National Liberation

Partly growing out of the notion that some national groups are particularly oppressed or occupy a unique class position in world capitalism, is a concern for movements of national liberation. While these movements are clearly reactions to external domination and underdevelopment, considerable debate has ensued over the conditions under which "nationalist" reactions are appropriate. On the one hand is the principle of the right of "nations" to self-determination (Lenin, 1968); on the other is the ambiguity of which groups actually constitute a viable nation and can therefore legitimately form separatist movements (Hobsbawm, 1977). For instance, a major debate ensued over whether or not U.S. blacks constituted a "nation" in the South which could reasonably aspire to statehood. More recently, the "internal colonialism" model of the black experience again suggests the legitimacy of a "nationalist" solution, this time for northern, urban, ghetto-dwellers, a position that has been challenged by those who feel that class solidarity should take precedence.[14]

An important aspect of this issue is the question of whether it is necessary to go through a capitalist (or at least not fully socialist) phase in order to develop economically. Most Third World "peoples," particularly those in separate states, but also some minorities within states, still live and work under systems with feudal or pre-capitalist remnants, such as peasant agriculture, or migrate between pre-capitalist and capitalist sectors. It has been suggested that, under colonial conditions, a two-stage revolution is necessary: first, workers and peasants must join their incipient national bourgeoisie in overthrowing the foreign oppressor. Once the national bourgeoisie is sufficiently liberated to begin to develop the "nation" economically, and a true proletariat is formed, then intra-national class struggle and true socialist revolution become possible. Note that, in a way, we have come full circle, back to Type A, though under very different historical circumstances. Nationalism in the Third World can represent the interests of the bourgeoisie or petite bourgeoisie (Saul, 1979) in establishing and consolidating modified forms of capitalism.

The necessity for a two-stage revolution has, of course, been challenged. On the one hand it is argued that the "national bourgeoisie" of oppressed nations is too linked to international capital to lead a liberation movement which will truly liberate. On the other, the ability of Third World peasants and other pre-capitalist classes as well as the incipient proletariat to engage in revolutionary movements has been proven. Indeed

Third World peasant and proletarian movements have been far more successful on this score than the "developed" proletariat of Western Europe and the United States, though the degree to which these revolutions have produced truly socialist societies remains in question. Similarly, black workers in the United States, despite their sub-proletarian status (or perhaps more accurately, because of it) are undoubtedly more class conscious and ready for socialist revolution than the white working class (Leggett, 1968, Geschwender, 1977). Thus exclusively "nationalist" alliances are seen to be both undesirable and unnecessary, though colonized workers' movements against "white" capital still have a "national" component.

The debate is not so much concerned with explaining nationalist movements as prescribing when they are appropriate. However, implicit is an explanatory theme: movements for ethnic self-determination are likely to arise under conditions of colonial or neo-colonial rule; they represent a temporary class alliance between the colonized bourgeoisie (or incipient bourgeoisie) and workers-peasants, in response to colonial domination.[15]

As stated earlier, the five types of class theory are not intended to be definitive, but rather, illustrative of the multiplicity and complexity of ideas on this topic. Although I have presented them as if they were competing approaches, in fact they are not necessarily all incompatible. For instance, different kinds of communalistic movements may be appropriate to different stages of capitalist development. Thus the five approaches presented here may, to some extent, reflect sequential stages in the development of capitalism and imperialism. True, there are some genuine theoretical debates which need to be resolved one way or another, for example, whether or not most white workers have a vested interest in imperialist domination. I shall not, at this point, attempt to critically evaluate each of the various approaches since the criticisms will be inherent in the synthesis attempted in the next section.

Before moving on to the synthesis, however, one lesson from this review needs to be stressed: "Nationalism" is not a unitary phenomenon. Not only must we distinguish between the nationalisms of the exploiters and the exploited (Mandel, 1972), but also between nationalisms with different class roots, such as petit-bourgeois nationalism versus working-class nationalism. Indeed all four classes in our schema generate communalistic movement at times, and for quite different reasons. Some of the debates among class theorists may, in part, result from confusing different kinds of ethnic movements. To use the same example again, the debate over whether or not white workers have a vested interest in "racism" may confuse different kinds of racism: exploitation by the bourgeoisie versus exclusion by the working class. Any comprehensive class theory of ethnicity must take these differences into account.

Towards an Integrated Class Approach

Since most of the important "ethnic relations" in the modern world have grown out of the rise of capitalism in Western Europe, and its resulting imperialist expansion, most of my analysis will concern this case. I assume that other capitalist imperialisms, notably that of Japan, produce a similar dynamic. Whether non-capitalist or state capitalist expansions, such as that of the Soviet Union, would fit the model, I do not know. The model will also not attempt to deal with precapitalist ethnic relations.

A promising new literature is developing which attempts to place ethnic phenomena within the context of the development of world capitalism.[16] The ideas which I am presenting here draw heavily upon their contributions.

A fully developed class analysis of ethnicity needs to consider all of the possible class relations between "ethnic groups" that result from imperialism. These are schematically presented in Figure 3, and again we must note that the figure is simplified along both dimensions. One ought to consider not only other classes, but also, perhaps, a semi-autonomous role for the state. And "ethnic" relations between imperialist powers (as in Figure 2A), let alone between colonized peoples, have been omitted. A total analysis would include all of these. Still, even this very simplified version enables us to begin to chart the relationships and demonstrates some of the complexities of the problem.

Before we start to examine each of the relationships, it is important to point out that I am using the term "colonized" loosely here to refer to any form of external domination by a capitalist power. It may range from a minimum of unequal trade relations, through foreign investment, to total political domination.[17] In addition, the geographical position of both nationalities may vary: they may each remain primarily in their homelands, or members of the imperialist nation may move into the territory of the colonized nation, or members of the colonized nation may move to the territory of the imperialist power (as in labor immigration or importation). While geographic location obviously affects the nature of the relations between national groups, there is, nevertheless, a fundamental similarity (or parallel) between these situations.

A final preliminary caution: The following attempt has numerous problems. For one thing, it is very general and abstract, glossing over differences in historical period let alone location. For another, it suffers from the ignorance, both theoretical and factual, of its author. My goal is mainly to *suggest* a way of tying these things together, and to stress that all the class relations generated by imperialism, in all its forms, need to be considered as a system if we are fully to understand the emergence of "nationalist" movements.

1. Class Relations within Imperialist Nations

Our analysis begins with class relations within imperialist nations. Needless to say, this encompasses the entire history of class struggle in the developed capitalist countries, a topic much too vast to cover here. I would like to examine one aspect of this topic, namely, the role of the "national" class struggle in the emergence of imperialism. While there is considerable debate over the roots of imperialism it seems to me that one important push towards overseas expansion by capital comes from problems with its "national" working class. Put another way, as capitalism develops, the price of labor-power tends to rise, leading capital to seek cheaper labor-power (or commodities based upon cheaper labor-power) abroad.

The price of labor-power rises with the advance of capitalism for at least four reasons. First, increasing numbers of people are drawn from pre-capitalist modes of production into the proletariat until the potential national labor force is completely absorbed. We can see this process

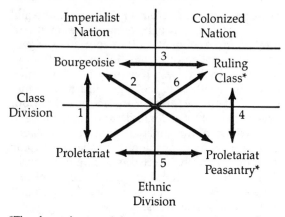

*The classes here are left somewhat ambiguous to indicate the possibility that full-blown capitalism has not yet emerged.

FIGURE 3.   *Class and Ethnic Relations Resulting from Imperialism.*

in the decline of independent farming and the rise of large cities, in the movement from self-employment to the predominance of wage and salary earners, and most recently, in the movement of women into the labor force. All of these shifts represent movements from pre-capitalist to capitalist relations of production. The complete absorption of the national labor force leads to a rise in the price of labor-power. Since the drive to accumulate capital continues unabated, the demand for labor exceeds supply, driving up the price.

Second, as workers become increasingly proletarianized, they are decreasingly able to provide any of the means of subsistence for themselves or their families. These need to be purchased from wages, which have to be increased in order to cover these new necessary expenses. In contrast, during transitional periods, when capitalism co-existed with pre-capitalist forms, part of the means of subsistence was provided by those forms. Women working in the home, processing food, making clothing, providing "free" child-care, and so on, meant that wages did not have to cover these items. But once the entire nation enters the proletariat, all goods and services become commodities, and they must be purchased with earnings.

A third factor in the rising cost of labor-

power is that the social conditions of production become increasingly conducive to political organization among workers. In particular, large factories enable workers to compare their grievances and form organizations to protect their mutual interests. And their increasing divorce from their own means of subsistence, or any independent ownership of productive property, strengthens the motivation to organize. Thus, as capitalism advances, labor unionism develops and contributes to the rise in the price of labor-power.

Fourth, as capitalism develops, the rising demands of workers are likely to receive some state support. For example, under pressure from organized labor many advanced capitalist countries set minimum wages, regulate work conditions, provide old age pensions, and protect the rights of labor unions to provide independent representation for workers. In other words, the state helps to set national labor standards. In so doing, it provides a prop to the price of labor-power, helping both to maintain and raise it.

One important aspect of state intervention is protection against the use of the "army of the unemployed" to lower the price of labor-power in core industries. If left to their own devices, individual capitalists would respond to the rising cost of labor-power by introducing labor-saving machinery, throwing some people out of work, thereby putting competitive pressure on wages. Through "welfare" and unemployment insurance, the state cushions workers from the last aspect of this process, so that high levels of unemployment can, in fact, coexist with rising wages.

It is very important to recognize that a rise in the price of labor-power does not necessarily mean that workers are better off. The price goes up in part because the cost of living rises as people are increasingly dependent upon commodities. Many of these commodities are necessities (e.g., a car in Los Angeles), and in some cases their quality may be lower than when they were produced by unpaid family labor (e.g., home-made bread versus Wonder Bread). The rising price of labor-power may actually be associated with a decline in the quality of life.

Regardless of its impact on workers, the rising price of labor-power puts a squeeze on profits.[18] While there are various responses to this problem, including investment in labor-saving technology, one important response is to turn to new sources of labor-power. Having exhausted the national reserve army of the unemployed inaccessible because of welfare, capital looks overseas, especially to countries where capitalism is less fully developed, for "fresh troops." Essentially the process is one of continuing to absorb pre-capitalist modes of production and transforming their personnel into wage workers, except that now the process spills across national borders.

2. Relations between Imperialist Capital and Colonized Workers

Imperialist domination and exploitation of colonized workers is the fundamental root of "racism." Out of this exploitation grow efforts by imperialist capital to mobilize its "national" proletariat in support of colonial domination, utilizing racist, or nationalist, ideology. Also growing out of it are important divisions in the world's working class which lead to "nationalist" reactions on both sides.

As we have seen, capital tends to move overseas in search of cheaper labor-power. Labor is cheaper there for two reasons: first, the lower level of development decreases the price of labor-power; and second, imperialism itself distorts development, contributing to the perpetuation of a low price for labor-power beyond what might be expected under conditions of non-domination. Let us deal briefly with each of these in turn.

Early stages of development are associated with a lower price of labor-power. Essentially the reason lies in the participation in pre-capitalist modes of production. In pre-capitalist modes, people mainly work for their own subsistence. When confronted with capitalist employers, they are likely, at first, to work for capital only on a supplementary basis. Most of their subsistence is provided by pre-capitalist forms. As a result, the capitalist employer need not pay the worker his or her complete subsistence, but only that part of it which is necessary to sustain the worker at that moment. In other words, the subsistence of his family, including health care, education, and housing, can be lift out of the wage calculation. This enables employers in transitional economies to "earn" extraordinary rates of surplus value and at the same time to undersell competitors who use fully proletarianized work-forces.

Other features of attachment to pre-capitalist modes of production also contribute to "cheap labor." For one thing, "new" workers are unfamiliar with trade unions. For another, because they are less dependent on the wage-earning job, they have less incentive to form or join organizations to further their long-term collective interests as workers. Stable labor organizing goes hand-in-hand with permanent proletarianization. In general, the more completely dependent upon wage labor, the more developed will be the labor organizations of a group of workers.

Another factor which lowers the price of labor-power in less developed societies is a lower standard of living. Such items as housing, furniture, even diet, and certainly gadgetry of all kinds, vary from society to society, but tend to be more "substantial" in advanced capitalist societies. This may partly reflect real differences in necessities (e.g., an urban worker must have a means of transportation to get to work, must have a radio to find out certain kinds of information, must have a can-opener because much of his food comes in cans, etc.), but also seems to reflect different experiences and expectations, or what Marx terms an historical and moral element (Emmanuel, 1972). Housing standards are a case in point. In one society, straw huts or shacks are perfectly acceptable. In another they are not even permitted.

Undoubtedly, these differences reflect the different levels of productivity of the two types of economy. Advanced capitalism spews forth an endless stream of commodities which come to be defined as necessities (in part through capitalist efforts). In poor, undeveloped societies, these necessities are luxuries which people have lived without for time immemorial. Imperialists can capitalize on these low expectations by lowering wages accordingly.

Imperialist capital introduces a special coercive element into the relations with colonized labor. Colonial and neo-colonial labor systems take on a variety of forms, e.g., the retention of peasant agriculture and crafts, but with increasing exaction of surplus from these workers; the retention of peasant agriculture associated with the migration of labor between the subsistence sector and capitalist enterprises; and the creation of plantation-type enterprises which employ semi-

or fully-coerced labor full time. They all share however, a coercive element which cannot be imposed upon the working class of the advanced capitalist nation.[19]

Imperialist-type exploitation can also arise with immigrant workers. If the immigrants are still attached to pre-capitalist modes of production in the homeland, some of the factors which cheapen labor-power there apply to them as well. More importantly, just as imperialist capital can utilize special coercion in its relations with labor in the colonies, so can it towards immigrant workers. Special legal constraints, justified by "national" differences, can be set up for immigrants, such as the denial of citizenship rights. The legal disabilities of immigrants permit capital to act in an unrestrained manner towards this special class of workers. As Castells states: "The utility of immigrant labour to capital derives primarily from the fact that it can act towards it as though the labour movement did not exist, thereby moving the class struggle back several decades."[20] The same could be said for all types of colonized labor.

In sum, imperialist capital is willing and eager to make use of all potential sources of labor-power. Capitalism is a system that seeks to proletarianize the world. Pre-capitalist remnants in colonized territories, combined with the ability of imperialist capital to introduce coercive elements into labor relations, serve to retard the ability of colonized workers to fully participate in, or develop, a labor movement. Thus capital can "exploit" these workers (in the sense of extracting surplus from them, even if not always directly via the wage relationship) more thoroughly than it can exploit its own workers.

3. Relations between Imperialist Capital and Colonized Ruling Classes

Imperialism has important consequences not only for the workers in colonized societies, but also for their ruling classes, including the incipient bourgeoisie. The relationship between these two classes can take two major forms: on the one hand, imperialist capital can retard and undermine the development of a colonized ruling class. On the other hand, it can utilize this class to help them dominate colonized workers more effectively.

Imperialist undermining of colonial ruling classes can take many forms. Perhaps the simplest is the exaction of tribute, or simple stripping of some of the wealth from the invaded area. This may be achieved by taxation, for instance. At another level, the imperialist power can impose unequal treaties, forcing colonies or neo-colonies to accept trade from the more advanced economy, thereby having their crafts and infant industries undermined by cheap imports. At still a "higher" level, when foreign capital is invested in colonial societies, their ruling classes lose control over the direction of development. Profits and interest are drained out of the territory, while technologies are monopolized by foreign capital. Since power is unevenly distributed, benefit and wealth tend to accrue to the imperialist bourgeoisie, often at the expense of the colonized bourgeoisie. This unequal relationship may also arise with ethnic minorities within the imperialist nation so that their petite bourgeoisie is kept in a "dependent" position.

The other face of this relationship concerns the utilization of colonial leaders as "middlemen" to help imperialist capital penetrate the territory more effectively. Again, this occurs at many levels, from using the local rulers to collect taxes, to having them conduct the trade in imperialist commodities and in the goods produced by colonized workers. Perhaps the most important level is their role in helping to control colonized labor, the topic of our next section.

In sum, relationship 3 can be either competitive or cooperative. When the latter predominates, members of the colonial ruling class can become very wealthy, and develop a vested interest in the continuation of imperialism. Under such circumstances, there is little incentive to be "nationalist." When the relationship is competitive, however, nationalism is a likely response in the form of calling for the removal of "foreign domination." Both of these aspects may, of course, be present in the same territory, producing conflict within this class.

4. Relationship between Colonial Ruling Classes and Workers

The colonial ruling class can be used to make the "cheap labor" of colonial territories even cheaper, by the suppression and coercion of the workers. This suppression can take place at a variety of levels, from the individual entrepreneur or landholder, to the state, where oppressive "national" regimes can keep labor subdued for the benefit of foreign capital. The number of right-wing dictatorships propped up by foreign capital (aided by their states), which actively crush any movement that would improve the position of labor need scarcely be mentioned. These intermediary classes often play a critical role in keeping the relations of production partially pre-capitalist.

"Nationalism" may be an important ideological tool in this effort. In particular, neo-colonial rulers may sometimes be able to persuade their workers to temper their demands, in the short run, in order to help the "nation" develop, and enable their exports to be competitive on the world market. While this effort may serve the interests of imperialist capital in its search for cheap labor, it also benefits colonial rulers and their bourgeoisies.

Ethnic minorities within capitalist societies may reveal both of these forms. The ethnic petite bourgeoisie can play a pivotal role in suppressing workers. Examples include labor contractors, padrones, and sweat shop owners. These people are able to take advantage of the vulnerable position of minority workers, while at the same time acting as intermediaries on behalf of big capital. They, too, can call upon "ethnic loyalty" as a technique of control. A garment sweatshop owner can appeal to his or her workers that it is in the "community interest" that the shop remain open, and provide jobs to community members. But this is conditional on their limiting their demands as workers, since the shop will only remain competitive if it can undersell others. Thus, ethnic solidarity can be used to retard the development of class consciousness as workers. Ultimately, this redounds to the benefit of big capital.

Since segments of the colonized ruling class are undermined by imperialist relations, another form of nationalism can emerge in this relationship, namely, an anti-imperialist alliance which calls for "national liberation." Although primordial symbolism may be invoked to bring the colonized ruling class together with workers and peasants, the coalition is still essentially the product of "class" forces: the exploitation of colonized labor,

and the unequal competition between imperialist and colonial bourgeoisies.

In sum, two quite different nationalisms can emerge in this relationship. In one case, nationalism is used as a tool of exploitation; in the other, as a tool of liberation. The difference between these two may not always be easy to disentangle.

5. Relations within the Working Class

National divisions in the working class arise, in part, out of the material differences in the situations of different national segments. The working class of the imperialist nation has been able to organize and wrest some concessions from capital. Colonized labor (including migrant labor), in contrast, is under a double layer of oppression, both from the imperialist bourgeoisie and from middlemen. They are frequently still tied to pre-capitalist economic forms, limiting their ability to participate fully in a working-class movement. And they can be placed under special legal statuses (such as "illegal aliens") which are much more coercive than the situation with which the rest of the proletariat has to deal.

Since colonized workers are especially exploitable by capital, they pose a threat to the proletariat of the imperialist nation, who fear that their hard-won labor standards will be undermined. Immigrant labor, or the runaway shop to cheap-labor countries or regions, is used by capital in the form both of threat and reality to constrain its national working class. The local working class can respond to this threat either by trying to limit capital's access to cheap labor (protectionism), or by fighting to raise the labor standards of cheap labor (inclusionism). The first of these is a "nationalist" response, the second, "internationalist."

Both nationalist and internationalist responses are found among the workers of advanced capitalist countries. The issue is usually a point of struggle within the working-class movement. Factors that affect which choice is made include: the extent to which capital controls colonized labor (making it difficult to coordinate transnational efforts), the immediacy of the competitive threat, the completeness of proletarianization of workers in the imperialist nation (or the degree to which there are petit-bourgeois remnants),[21] and so on. Undoubtedly a very important factor is the ability of capital to manipulate "nationalist" sentiment by weeding out internationalist-oriented leaders from the working class movement.

Four quite different kinds of nationalism serve to divide the working class. First is imperialist capital's efforts to whip up nationalist sentiment among the workers to get them to support the oppression of the colonized. Second is the proletariat's own protectionist reactions (reinforced by segments of capital), which invoke nationalism (e.g., Buy American). Third is the nationalism generated by the colonial ruling class in an effort to keep colonized labor cheap for the benefit of international capital. And fourth is the nationalism promoted by colonized workers to overthrow the double and triple layers of oppression they face.

Neither set of workers has to respond in a nationalist manner, and segments of both frequently do not. But once nationalism is the dominant response, it tends to be mutually reinforcing such that each segment of the working class continues to distrust the other.

6. Relations between the Proletariat of Imperialist Nations and the Colonized Ruling Class

These two classes are often in a struggle for the affiliation of colonized workers, hence their relationship is typically conflictual. Colonized workers are either asked to join the working class movement and become aware of their class antagonism with their ruling class (or middlemen), or they are asked to cooperate with the ruling class, which uses a nationalist pitch, to develop the "nation" (or ethnic community), and set aside class antagonisms.

To the extent that the colonized ruling class exercises control over "its" workers, they will be inaccessible to the proletariat of the advanced capitalist nation. Labor contractors, or sweat shop owners, for example, may be able to use a combination of coercion, paternalism, and desperation on the part of the workers, to keep them in the "nationalist" fold. If accomplished, another wedge is driven between the segments of the working class, and the dominant nation's proletariat continues to be threatened with displacement and undermining.

This kind of conflict can occur both within states and between them. For instance, at the international level, the existence of a right-wing, dictatorial, "nationalist" regime which severely suppresses its workers, may preclude any efforts on the part of advanced capitalist workers to attempt to help raise labor standards in that country. The discrepancy in labor standards can be used by the ruling class to attract international capital, and as a basis for cheap exports. Within a single state, the leadership of a minority community may exercise a similar labor-control function, though on a much reduced scale, with the same effect of keeping labor standards low within the minority community, in part for the benefit of big capital.

Since both the ruling class and workers of colonized nations appear to conspire in maintaining the low level of labor standards, the advanced capitalist nation's proletariat is likely to have nationalist reactions. It sees all segments of the colonized nations as threatening its position, and may make crude generalizations about the nature of "those people." On the other side, protectionist reactions by labor in the imperialist nation may interfere with the plans of the colonized ruling class to penetrate international markets and may jeopardize the jobs of Third World workers in the affected industries.

In sum, there can be a major struggle between the workers of imperialist nations and colonial ruling classes over the affiliation of colonized workers to determine whether these workers will choose a nationalist or internationalist strategy emphasizing class or nationalist solidarity. Of course, such a struggle is only likely when the proletariat of the imperialist nation is not staunchly protectionist.

We have now briefly considered all six relationships represented in Figure 3. All interact with one another, creating "higher" levels of relationship. For example, if relationship 5 between the imperialistic proletariat and the colonized proletariat, becomes conflictual or nationalistic, imperialist capital can utilize the division to mute the class struggle of its national proletariat (relationship 1). This may lead workers in the imperialist nation to temper their demands and seek narrow concessions instead of revolutionary change. Thus nationalist division may be an important factor in the preservation of capitalism.[22] There are other such reverberations through the system: nationalism at one level tends to provoke counter-nationalism at other levels, while cross-national class alliances probably support one another.

Another point of elaboration, as suggested earlier, would be the addition of other classes and other ethnic groups. For instance, the imperialist nation's class structure includes important intermediary classes, such as managers and small business owners, which may foster nationalist reactions and make it more difficult for workers to support internationalist positions. Or, in the colonized nation, a special ethnic group may play the role of middleman, diluting the class struggle by turning it into an anti-ethnic (nationalist) movement against the middlemen.

In some cases, key classes may be absent, also with ramifications for nationalism. Thus, the fact that countries like Brazil and Mexico draw a less harsh "race line" than the United States and South Africa (both of which developed clear descent rules to protect the category "white") may in part be due to the absence of a large white working class in the former. There was, in other words, no sizable class to develop protectionist reactions against the absorption of colonized workers. Or the absence of a large middleman element among immigrant workers may make cross-ethnic worker alliances easier to establish, thus blurring the lines of national difference.

Needless to say, there are numerous issues this model has not addressed, such as the effects of technological change, labor productivity, geography, natural resources, and population density.[23] To understand the rise of nationalism, or its absence, in each particular case, such factors would have to be taken into consideration.

Despite its incompleteness, the model enables us to make four important points. First, nationalist movements are generated by each class, for different reasons, and with different content. Second, non-nationalist options are available to each class, and are often acted upon. The call upon "primordial attachments" frequently fails, indicating beyond doubt its lack of universality or inevitability. Third, the emergence of nationalist versus non-nationalist reactions depends upon the structure of the entire system of relationships. It is not simply an orientation that one group chooses to adopt in isolation. The emergence of nationalism is contingent upon where a group fits within the entire world capitalist system, and how others react to it. And fourth, despite the fact that nationalism calls upon "primordial" bonds of affiliation, it both grows out of the class relations generated by the development of capitalism and imperialism, and represents efforts to create alliances across class lines, or, alternatively, to prevent alliances from developing within major classes across national lines. In other words, nationalist movements are, at root, the product of class forces.

ENDNOTES

1. Perhaps this position was itself a reaction to the belief that race and ethnicity were "real" and marked off some nationalities from others as biologically superior or inferior.

2. C.f. Banton, 1974; Glazer and Moynihan, 1975; Rex, 1970

3. For a more complete exposition of this position, see Blumer, 1965; pp. 220–253. For a criticism of this position see Wolpe, 1970, pp. 151–179.

4. For a similar position see Isaacs, 1975, pp. 29–52.

5. Perhaps I am overstating this case. Even authors who concentrate on the consequences of ethnic affiliations give some attention to origins. But these tend to be seen as rooted in the distant past, and firmly embedded in long-established cultural traditions, rather than requiring explanation in the present. Class theorists, in contrast, believe that ethnic affiliation must be created or reproduced in the present for its persistence to be understood.

6. See for example: Simpson and Yinger, 1972.

7. See for example, Gordon, M., 1964. In addition, see authors interested in the rise of "white ethnicity," such as Greeley (1974); Novak (1971).

8. A good example of an effort to uncover the social or class meaning of descent rules is M. Harris, 1964, in which he contrasts the United States' and Latin American descent rules for determining who is black.

9. This condition is itself quite variable depending on which classes move, i.e., a major distinction needs to be drawn between "white settler" colonies where members of the working class of the conquering nation settled in the colonized territory, and colonies where only foreign capitalists have been active. White settler colonies, such as the United States, Australia, and South Africa, have generally experienced much harsher ethnic problems, a fact that has raised considerable

debate regarding competing explanations (Foner and Genovese, eds, 1969).

10. There is some debate over whether ethnically or racially oppressed workers are more exploited, in a technical sense, than dominant workers. The term "exploitation" refers to the amount of surplus value extracted from labor. Since ethnic minority workers are often employed in the most backward, unproductive sectors, the rate of surplus extracted from them may, in fact, be lower than for more privileged workers who work in the high-productivity, monopoly sector of the economy. Especially when minority workers suffer high rates of unemployment, it is difficult to see how surpluses are generated here (Willhelm, 1971). Still, there are other mechanisms by which surplus is extracted from minority workers, such as "unequal exchange." It seems undeniable that some form of wealth moves from ethnically oppressed labor to the dominant bourgeoisie, even if not via direct employment as wage labor. In any case, this is a point of debate.

11. Bonacich, 1972; 1975; 1976; 1979. Some authors (Wilson, 1978) combine theories B and C, attributing them to different historical epochs.

12. Geschwender, 1978, uses the concept "nation-class" more broadly to allow for class differentiation within oppressed ethnic groups. Thus blacks are differentiated by class, although disproportionately in the proletariat, but within each class they also experience "national oppression." Each case of coincidence between class and national categories is considered a "nation-class." Using a figure similar to Figure 1, Geschwender (1978, pp. 264–267), concludes that alliances and enmities can arise along both class and national axes.

13. The concept "people-class" needs to be distinguished from Gordon's (1964) concept of "eth-class." For Gordon, class means status group rather than relations to the means of production. Gordon's eth-classes are social groupings which feel comfortable together because of similarity in style of life. They are not political-economic interest groups. Gordon's is not a class theory of ethnicity; it accepts ethnicity as a primordial tie.

14. Harris, 1972; Geschwender, 1978, Chapters 4 and 5 review this debate.

15. Focus on the national liberation movements of the colonized tends to lead to a disregard of class dynamics within the dominating nationalities. As stated earlier, national oppression is seen to have taken the place of class oppression as the major axis of world capitalist exploitation. This viewpoint again puts ethnicity at center stage, though it recognizes that national domination and colonialism are rooted in capitalism rather than in the "national" tendencies of nations to despise one another. Still, by focusing on national op-

pression, writers in this school of thought tend to ignore the internal class dynamics of both national groups.

16. A sample of this literature includes Amin, 1976; Bettelheim, 1970; Burawoy, 1976; Castells, 1975; Geschwender, 1978; Hechter, 1975; Petras, 1980; Portes, 1978; and many others. For an effort to develop a theoretical statement integrating some of this literature, see Bonacich and Hirata, 1979.

17. The use of the term "colonized" should not be taken as an endorsement of all the assumptions of the "internal colonialism" model.

18. An example of the "profit squeeze" argument is found in the work of Glyn and Sutcliffe (Glyn and Sutcliffe, 1971, 1972).

19. In some cases, the employees of foreign firms are among the most highly paid workers in a poor nation. They may be more fully proletarianized than other workers, and more likely to form unions. Foreign capital pays higher wages as a means of undercutting local manufacturers. Still, despite higher wages relative to other workers in the same country, they are paid considerably less than workers in the imperialist country.

20. Castells, 1972, p. 52. Some of the differences in experience between Eastern European and non-European immigrants in the United States may be accounted for by this. Eastern Europe was less thoroughly dominated by the advanced capitalist societies of Western Europe. Thus the immigrants came under a less coerced status and were more readily able to join the local labor movement.

21. This theme is developed, with respect to the United States, and its long tradition of an "independent household mode of production" associated with the availability of land and concomitant ability to withstand complete proletarianization, in Bonacich, 1980. There I argue that this class, which oriented itself towards a pre-capitalist "golden age," contributed importantly to the generation of a powerful racist ideology. Since it often formed coalitions with the proletariat against the "monopolists," the working-class movement sometimes developed a racist cast.

22. One may ask if nationalist movements are ever progressive. With important exceptions, I believe they are not. They always divide the working class movement. But sometimes they are necessary anyway, especially on the part of colonized workers who may have no other means to overthrow the double oppression that can stem from imperialist capital's super-exploitation, combined with protectionist reactions by workers of the imperialist nation. Under such conditions, self-determination may be the only route to liberation. When this is the case, nationalism is progressive.

23. An attempt is made to deal with some of these issues in Bonacich and Hirata, 1979, and Bonacich, 1980.

5

The Growth of the State and Ethnic Mobilization: The American Experience

Cynthia Enloe

This paper will explore a possibility neglected in most analyses of ethnic mobilization: that the state apparatus is not merely something that must 'cope with' the mobilization of ethnic groups, but is at times itself a critical factor in generating such ethnic mobilization. In other words, the discussion that follows is meant to challenge the conventional wisdom that politics is a dependent variable in ethnic phenomena, that politics typically only reflects the 'deeper realities' of either modes of production or psychological needs. Relegating politics to the status of a dependent variable in ethnic affairs is especially easy when one is considering American society: the state—the most potent dimension of modern political life—appears so ephemeral throughout most of American history. In fact, the concept of 'the state' is scarcely mentioned in most analyses of American politics and society. European societies, Asian or Arab societies may have states, but not American society.

It is true that state-building has been a slow process in American history. Institutions of the state have developed slowly and diffusely; they have trailed behind other, more quickly maturing American political institutions such as interest

From *Ethnic and Racial Studies* 4:2 (April 1981), pp. 123–136 by permission of the author and Routledge & Kegan Paul PLC.

groups, political parties, electoral institutions, legislatures, and the press. On the other hand, to say that state-building has been retarded in the United States is not to say that it has been non-existent or inconsequential. One of the clearest evidences of the state's steady, and recently rapid, growth on American soil is in the management of inter-ethnic relations. The political history of certain ethnic groups reveals both the existence of the state in American society and its important impact on American social relationships. In both its growth and its effects, the American state has frequently intensified ethnic identities and often mobilized ethnic groups, even as the forces of the state were intent instead upon assimilation or ethnic demobilization.

State-Building in America

The *state* is a vertical structure of public authority. It contrasts with the *nation*, which is essentially a horizontal network of trust and identity. The state's most visible expressions are those institutions which exert vertical authority: the civil bureaucracy, the judicial system and the military and police. A *nation-state*—a term used all too glibly in much contemporary social analysis—is a state whose vertical authority structures are rooted in, and dependent upon, horizontal bonds of trust and identification among all those persons who fall under its presumed jurisdiction. For the sake of ideological justification and political legitimation, most state elites today claim to preside over nation-states. Yet in reality there are few genuine nation-states, and even in those the relationships between the vertical and horizontal structures remain dynamic and usually tenuous.[1]

State-building in America was historically slow and ideologically suspect. Institutions of nation-building were more legitimate and vital from the outset. Legislatures, elections, an energetic (if not always 'free') press, competitive party organizations, and interest lobbies created and also reflected growing horizontal, national interrelationships, even while the formal organization of government was still being hammered out in the late eighteenth century. The state-building enterprise was proceeding, but under a cloud of suspicion. It smelled of centralization, autocracy and restriction of privacy, all of which had been discredited in the Revolution.

The bureaucracies of the individual states and the federal government were skeletal; the state civil service was treated with contempt rather than accorded the social prestige it enjoyed in more developed state systems such as those in Prussia or China. In addition, military institutions of the state were kept small, and a standing army was deemed anathema by a large segment of the public and their political representatives. Not until 1917 could military conscription be successfully implemented, although it was tried unsuccessfully during the Civil War. The police arm of the American state was rudimentary and fragmented into local units. The judicial system was perhaps the most assertive branch of the nascent state in its early years; much of the political debate that at least implicitly dealt with the character and scope of the state in American society focused on controversial court rulings and judges' presumptions of the courts' jurisdiction.

The American state today is still fragmented institutionally—due especially to the federal structure and partisan divisions in the legislature, press and bureaucratic lobbies—and is ambiguous enough ideologically to be left in the analytical shadows. But it is no longer nascent or attenuated. Its legal jurisdiction is expansive and its operational capabilities are impressive. The federal bureaucracy alone—excluding military personnel and state and local civil servants, who theoretically should be thought of in statist terms—employs over three million persons. The military establishment is awesome in the coercive capacity it provides the state. Police forces formally are still decentralized. But in numbers they are significant: the New York City police force alone is larger than the armed forces of Denmark. Perhaps more significant in terms of state-building processes, the police in the United States are increasingly centralized, both in their dependence on federally derived funds, and in their reliance upon the FBI for information and other services and standards. The state's judicial capacity has grown as legislation has brought public authority to bear on more and more spheres of society and as private citizens have become disenchanted with national institutions, such as elections and legislatures, and increasingly have sought to settle conflicts by resort to the state's judicial system.

Institutionalization, centralization, and penetration—these are the key processes at work in state-building. All had their beginnings in the United States in the eighteenth and nineteenth centuries, even if they have only blossomed in the mid-twentieth century. Particular ethnic groups felt the brunt of those state-building processes first. These groups—specifically new Asian and European immigrants, African slaves and American Indians—were more directly affected by the institutionalization, centralization and penetration of the American state in the early period because they touched upon some of the apparently essential conditions for state maintenance and survival.

States may be rather limited in scope and capacity and yet still require these conditions. First, to survive a state must be able to operationalize its alleged jurisdiction. This usually means that the persons acting with the state authority must be able to at least nominally defend territorial boundaries and control the movement of persons across those boundaries.[2] Second, a state must be capable of distinguishing between those who are subject to its authority and those who are exempt. This calls for some definition of the concepts of subject or citizenship, as well as some capacity to tabulate the numbers and types of persons within the state's jurisdiction: i.e., census-takers are as crucial to state-builders as soldiers. Third, perhaps less obviously, a state must have a pool and division of labor sufficient to generate revenues adequate for the administration of the state-paying bureaucrats, financing armies and usually building some public works such as fortifications and roads. Thus the state may exist even within a society wedded to a laissez-faire ideology. What may change over time, of course, is the extent to which the state not only provides the minimal conditions for that appropriate labor system but actually takes an active, direct part in generating necessary workers and distributing them within the economy.[3]

The operationalization of territorial jurisdiction, the counting and categorization of subjects and the insurance of at least that labor system that will generate adequate revenues for the state to govern, are the elemental conditions that even the most rudimentary state must guarantee. Significantly, each of these statist imperatives affects ethnic groups. As a result, the process of state-building, from its early days through its periods of elaboration and maturity, cannot help but involve the state with ethnic identifications and ethnic group dynamics.

State-Building and Ethnicity in the United States
The ethnic groups that were most immediately and profoundly affected by the earliest moves toward American state-building were those categorized by Europeans as 'Indians.' Before the arrival of Europeans the American continent already was ethnically plural. It was inhabited by numerous groups which recognized cultural-descent boundaries between themselves; they translated those boundaries into political demarcations, which in turn reinforced ethnic identities. The American state institution with which these Indian groups—collectively and individually—had the most contact was the fledgling United States military.

Prior to the United States military's formation, American Indian groups had had contact— as enemies and as formal allies—with the armies of more mature state systems: Spain, Britain and France. It is true that American Indian groups such as the Narragansett, Iroquois, and Cherokee were affected in their own sense of ethnic differen-

tiation and need for intra-communal cohesiveness or assimilation by non-state processes as well, particularly by contacts with European, and later white American, religious missionaries and land-seeking settlers and real estate speculators. These contacts and their consequences provide the stuff of most historical analyses of 'white-Indian relationships' (a phrase in itself which is far too undifferentiated). But such extra-statist contacts as these were not the sum of contacts which determined how Indian groups defined themselves. The American military became a critical factor even prior to the formal establishment of the American state. In a sense, there were state-ethnic relationships developing in America before there was an explicitly articulated state. The military, in the form of the admittedly fragmented, under-manned Continental Army, was the first of America's state institutions. Civil bureaucracy, courts and police all came later.

It is in the expansion of the American state's jurisdiction westward and southward that one can see the importance of state military–ethnic group relationships most dramatically. Far beyond the Mississippi the military was the state.[4] Indian groups had to be organized sufficiently to fight and negotiate with the United States military. The rest of the American state appratus was far too shallow and limited in its territorial reach in even the mid-1800s to have a direct and persistent effect on state-ethnic relations. To understand Indian ethnic boundary formations, communal institution building and efforts to sustain themselves materially one must examine United States military relationships with each Indian group in turn: the Cherokee, the Apache, the Miamis and numerous others.

It was not until 1849, when the Bureau of Indian Affairs was established in the Department of Interior, that the civilian state bureaucracy was elaborate enough to take over the handling ('handling' is rather a euphemistic term) of Indian affairs. Before 1849, it was the Department of the Army that had prime state responsibility—where it was not superseded by the increasingly elaborated federal state structures, as in New England and the South.

What I am suggesting here is that the American state was developing—becoming more centralized, penetrative, and instrumentally capable—

during the period from 1789 to 1860, and that state influence had significant effects on certain ethnic groups, particularly the Indians. To analyze white-Indian relationships and the *intra*-ethnic processes of each during that formative period as if they were shaped solely by social, cultural and economic forces is to leave ethnic analysis incomplete and, I would argue, unrealistic as well.

In most colonized societies, as well, ethnic-military relationships are important—both for the development of the state and of the particular ethnic group. In the Philippines, the Muslims in the South were dealt with chiefly by military means by the new interventionist United States colonizers from 1899 to 1905. There are numerous parallels between the experiences of the American Indians and the Philippine Muslims in their interaction with the United States military: they were, for example, both treated as a single category, despite historic internal differentiations, and both had to mobilize in order to protect themselves against the intruding military. In fact, United States military commanders drew explicit parallels between their task in the southern Philippines and their American battles against resistant Indians. Many officers sent to the Philippines during 1898 and 1905 had actually just come from assignments in the American west. They were selected for duty in the southern Philippines precisely because American officials saw the 'problem' of the Muslims as analogous to that of the American Indians.[5]

Other ethnic groups in the United States were affected by state institutions even when they had just arrived, though less with the military than with other arms of the new state and often more belatedly in the state-building process. New immigrants touched the American state's basic need to operationalize its formal territorial jurisdiction. But there was no central state apparatus authorized and capable of doing more than militarily protecting the most vulnerable borders until the late nineteenth century. The four basic needs of states interact with one another. Thus, for instance, in the first half of the nineteenth century the Indians were dismissed as pools of labor (as they were in the Caribbean, though not in Andean South America and Mexico) and thus were dealt with largely as a threat to the movement of the state's citizens out to new territories claimed by the state. But European and Asian immigrants posed a different problem. Initially, they were viewed chiefly as labor resources, additions to the economy which would, among other things, insure that the revenue-hungry new state would be underpinned by a healthy and expanding economy. Only in the latter half of the nineteenth century was the state's need to control movements across its boundaries, and to distinguish between its subjects and aliens, so important as to generate a new state institution. The Immigration and Naturalization Service was created by an act of Congress in 1891.

The expansion of the American state occurred rapidly in the post-civil war era, due in part to economic development as well as to the involvement of the United States in overseas affairs, including its colonization of Alaska, Hawaii and the Philippines, and its investments in Latin America. Testimony to this state building push was the growing elaboration of the civil bureaucracy, not simply in numbers of personnel but, more significantly, in organizational specialization and legal authorization. Establishment of the Immigration and Naturalization Service was part of that general development. It intruded the state ever more in the dynamics of ethnicity. For immigration in the United States, as it is virtually everywhere, is a policy matter that either explicitly or implicitly involves state authorities in making ethnic distinctions—between acceptable and/or useful foreign pools of potential immigrants as against unwanted and/or allegedly unuseful pools of such would-be entrants. The 1891 legislation—the first major legislation passed at the federal level to regulate immigration—made no specific mention of various ethnic groups. It referred instead to the need for new health standards administered at ports of entry as well as to the need to terminate the practice of contract labor recruited by American employers abroad.[6] In effect, however—it later would be made more ethnically explicit through quotas—this meant that the new federal service would be the arm of the state that No Nothings and other anti-immigrant political activists would look to to curtail the influx of German, Irish and Chinese immigrants.

The state's expansion and elaboration continued in the next decades prior to World War I in ways that deepened the impact of the state on ethnic formations. In 1902, the Bureau of the

Census was established. The first census had been carried out almost a century before this bureaucratic innovation, but now it was institutionalized. States may be of the most attenuated variety, but they invariably count, categorize and collect taxes. For control depends on information; information, to be functionally useful for a state apparatus, must allow for administrative differentiation. No state authorities, modern or pre-modern, govern the subjects in their proclaimed jurisdiction simply as an undifferentiated mass. Thus census-taking is something that touches the nerve center of a state.

What does differ among states is *what* is counted: age, occupation, sex, residence are most common. But most state elites hold some notion of ethnic differentiation as they relate to labor resources and national (i.e. state) security. State census-takers may not, and usually do not, employ categories derived from the subject population's own subjective perceptions of meaningful ethnic differentiations. They utilize ethnic/racial categories that best fit their—and their superiors'—notions of what is salient for economic and political order. The United States Bureau of the Census has itself become increasingly sophisticated in the last seventy-six years so that the state could meet the needs of a more politically and economically complex society. In that sense, this arm of the state is a dependent not independent variable.[7] But while the Census Bureau's bureaucratic history would reveal how state organizations reflect rather than shape ethnically plural societies, at various points in its history that same bureau has been an independent factor, shaping persons' perceptions of their own identities and the communal differentiations existing in American society as a whole through the questions they posed—and the questions they omitted. It is not surprising that state census operations have become the focal point of political dispute in such ethnically divided societies as Nigeria, Lebanon, Britain, Guyana, the USSR and of course the United States.[8]

In 1913 the United States Department of Labor was created. Labor and ethnicity had been intertwined in American history ever since the early importations of European indentured workers and African slaves. The creation of this new federal department, therefore, was not the beginning of the state's need to have a secure and productive pool of labor. But it was a step toward the American state taking a more direct role in insuring that labor would be distributed within the economy without labor-employee conflicts which can so dislocate a productive system and even undermine the state itself. Today the Department of Labor's manpower training and equal opportunity programs together with its migrant labor bureau operations impinge upon ethnic relations.

However, it would be a serious analytical mistake to presume that the state equips itself with the capacity to shape ethnic relations, and thus insure the maintenance of the state's own stability, merely by creating formal institutions such as the Bureau of Indian Affairs, Bureau of the Census, the Immigration and Naturalization Service and the Department of Labor. For there is ample evidence available today that—although the state has more capacity for affecting an ethnic group's situation than does any single ethnic group itself—American state capacities are incomplete.

Such state incompleteness is apparent in that critical area where control of territorial movement, management of the labor force and tabulating and categorizing citizens all intersect in the United States: the question of 'illegal aliens.'[9] This matter—it may or may not be a 'problem'—involves the Census Bureau, the Immigration and Naturalization Service, and the Department of Labor. All appear to be able to have impacts on the perception and operationalization of ethnic identities. Yet all three state institutions also seem to lack the capacity to fully control the movement and distribution of labor among citizens and non-citizens. The policy debate concerning this question provides a focus for a more far-reaching analysis of the American state-building process and its effects on ethnic identities and inter-ethnic relationships.

In a similar fashion, we could learn a great deal about the nature of the state, its historic development and the effect of its current level of capabilities on ethnicity in the United States by examining the present policy debate over the success or failure of the United States volunteer army. The American military perhaps has never had such wide-ranging state responsibilities and effect on certain inter-ethnic relationships as it did in the nineteenth century period of westward expansion. On the other hand, in terms of impact on the economy, social stratification and international structures, the United States military in the 1970s has more profound influence than ever.

State-building and military escalation have been intimately connected in the United States especially since World War I, insofar as military expansion has (1) increased the state's need for revenues, (2) increased the state's administrative capacities, (3) increased the state's need to structure the industrial sector, (4) increased the state's penetration of the labor market, (5) increased the state's impact on the use and distribution of technology and knowledge. But the volunteer army debate that has gone on since the end of the Vietnam War suggests that, nonetheless, the military has not been able to shape inter-ethnic relations *entirely* to its liking. Every time there is racial violence on an army base or aircraft carrier, or every time a military officer voices anxiety about the 'too high' (in his perception) proportion of Black enlistees in any unit—in each of these instances one is in fact hearing complaints about the inadequate level of state-building in the United States.[10]

Variations in State Impact on American Ethnic Groups

Ethnic groups in any country vary in the extent to which they are directly influenced by the state. 'Influenced by' does not simply mean oppressively manipulated by the state. For some ethnic groups are significantly shaped in their self perceptions, their levels of communal cohesion and their resources for communal action by the fact that they have such *access* to state power. This has been the case for Han Chinese in China, Great Russians in the Soviet Union, Afrikaners in South Africa, Hispanic whites in Peru and Bolivia, Malays in Malaysia, English in Britain and European Jews in Israel. It also has been true for Anglo-Saxons in the American state system. For this last group the effect has been to push explicit ethnic consciousness well below ground, to translate that communal ethnic awareness into a very diffuse political ideology which would legitimatize the state. In other words, state-building in the United States has had the effect on the members of the ethnic group that has had greatest entré into the corridors of state power of blurring ethnic awareness. So that today Anglo-Saxon ethnic consciousness is full of the sort of ambiguities and ideological contradictions that make public discussion of state-ethnic relationships extremely difficult to carry on with any precision or clarity.

The other groups that have been shaped by the patterns of state penetration, expansion and elaboration have ranged from those that have been constantly and directly affected by operations of the United States state to those that have been only intermittently, belatedly or indirectly affected by the course of state development. On the extreme end of statist impact scale are American Indians. Tracing the history of the American Indians—as tribes, individuals, and pan-Indians—is so valuable to any student of United States political history, or any student of the more general phenomenon of state creation for the very reason that the Indians have been the group that has experienced the expansion of state authority and institutional capacity most immediately and persistently. They have fought the state's military when it was a relatively small force; they have been made wards of the state when 'welfare state' still had not gained wide enough popular legitimacy to allow full state expansion; they have been among the first groups to experience the results of a tightening structural integration between private business and the United States state in the area of natural resources (e.g., coal, oil and gas) development.

On the low end of the state-impact scale, by contrast, are the American Gypsies. They have had relatively little—either indirect or spasmodic—state contact for two reasons. First Gypsies have been deemed inconsequential to American state elites over the centuries: Gypsies have not appeared to be crucial for any of the three state-building conditions. Secondly, Gypsies as an ethnic group have made a calculated effort to avoid contact with the state appratus.[11]

In between Indians and Gypsies are numerous other ethnic groups which vary in persistency and intensity of statist impact. Perhaps closest to the Indian end of the scale are Blacks and Chicanos (one might also add Puerto Ricans). Blacks entered this society defined as property; that property status was legitimized and enforced by the state, particularly by the state's young judicial system. After Emancipation, the state was crucial—through the Freedman's Bureau, the courts and the military (as recruiters of Blacks and as occupying forces in the Confederate states)—in defining the new status of Blacks, no longer property but still a legally distinguishable category of second-class citizens.

Today the state impact on Blacks is perhaps greater than it has ever been since the era of slavery, for the federal bureaucracy has expanded during the last twenty years to include an array of bureaucratic agencies to which Blacks must look for economic and legal protection. The Civil Rights Division of the Justice Department, FBI, HUD, HEW, EEOC, Department of Labor, Small Business Administration and, for employment, the United States Postal Service and Department of Defense—all are critical factors shaping Blacks' resources and political-social status. If the 1950s and 1960s was the era of extra-state politics for Blacks (through the press, cultural institutions, parties, legislatures—though of course also through the courts), then the 1970s represents a period of intense state-oriented politics for Blacks, thanks to notable state expansion.

Chicanos have been subject to state impact because from the outset of their American ethnic development they have been shaped by state policies and administrative operations regarding immigration control and labor market organization. Chicano development paralleled the rise of the federal immigration (including Border Patrol) and labor bureaucracies. When political forces based in the Western states pressed for the termination of Chinese and Japanese immigration, the economy—and thus too the state dependent on that economy—still needed a pool of cheap, pliable labor. Immigration and labor administrative policies were altered after 1910 to permit a greater influx of workers from Mexico. This move affected the ethnic awareness and ethnic resources of Japanese, Chinese and Chicanos.

European-derived ethnic groups have been more sporadic in their direct relationship as communities with the American state, but those contacts have not been inconsequential. The Swedes, Irish, Germans, East Europeans, Italians and other ethnic groups have been most potently affected by the state at the point of entry. This was particularly true for those ethnic groups whose greatest

numbers entered the country after the 1880s, that is, after the state-building process had gone so far as to equip the state with immigration and census bureaucratic capabilities. The second instance in which European-derived ethnic groups have been immediately affected by the state has been in wartime. For it is in wartime that a political system reveals most blatantly its statist character. The history of World War I is in part the history of the expansion of the American state and its impact on ethnic groups—categorizing ethnic groups in terms of loyalty and utility.[12]

State-Building and Ethnic Mobilization

Ethnic *identification* may be a mix of both internally-generated dynamics and pressures from the external environment. Ethnic group *mobilization*, on the other hand, virtually never occurs without some crucial external stimulus. The actions of state authorities frequently provide that necessary stimulus. Sometimes it is intentional; most often it is unintentional or even contrary to the state's intent.

The state is, among other things, a vehicle for mobilization. Pre-modern and modern states both have had the capacity for mobilization—of resources, allegiances, manpower, revenues—but they have differed in the persistence and effectiveness of their mobilizing efforts. Whereas pre-modern states typically have the will and capacity for only limited and sporadic mobilization (for road building and irrigation projects, periodic tax collections, occasional warfare), modern states incline toward perpetual mobilization due to the nature of industrialized economies and twentieth-century warfare.

This has meant that states and ethnic groups, which also have impressive mobilizing capacities, are often in direct competition. A state that is expanding and entrenching its authority usually attempts to reduce competing mobilizing institutions' influence (1) by cooptation (so that the ethnic group, for instance, still mobilizes resources but now channels them to serve state ends) or (2) by demobilization of the competitor.

Demobilizing efforts by the American state apparatus over the decades have taken several forms. First, as was the experience of the American Indians, the state dispersed them physically, driving them out of home territories and eventually confining them to state-prescribed reservations. Second, the state denied certain ethnic groups access to those processes—industrial labor, military service, elections—which often stimulate ethnic-based mobilization. This was most dramatically revealed in the experience of American Blacks. Third, the American state acted as a legitimizer of a public ideology which sanctioned individual rights but discredited the notion of communal rights.[13] For all ethnic groups in the United States, European, Indian, Black, Chicano, Chinese, the heavy hand of ideological individualism has thwarted ethnically-based mobilization or, even if it was launched, converted it quickly into merely a collaborative effort by group members to acquire individual benefits. Fourth, the state, especially in its contemporary phase of development, has demobilized certain groups by encouraging a dependent relationship between members of the group and state agencies. Dependency breeds a sense of vulnerability and inferiority that frustrates extra-state group mobilization. Such moves to create state dependency are often accompanied by state cooptation of the groups' potential leaders, recruiting them into state agencies or making them responsible for state programs.

Despite this general demobilizing inclination of the American state, state expansion has at times been a powerful factor in fostering ethnic group mobilization. There are several aspects in particular of state-building that have provided an ethnic mobilizing stimulus. First, the establishment of a specialized arm of the state to deal with certain ethnic groups (maybe not openly admitted in the authorizing legislation but still quite evident to the target ethnic group) provides an otherwise disparate, resource-poor group with a clear object for efficiently focusing its hostility, resistance or pressure. For example, there was a move in 1978 to disperse federal programs for Indians among a host of central agencies, thus in effect dismantling the Bureau of Indian Affairs. Indian activists have been closely monitoring this move (spearheaded by certain white Western Senators), but with considerable ambivalence. For, on the one hand, the BIA has always been viewed by Indian activists as a vehicle by which the American state made Indians poor and dependent. In this view, the dismantling of the BIA would cause no regrets.

On the other hand, the very existence of the BIA—despite its renowned weakness in federal bureaucratic infighting—has provided an important focus for Indian mobilization, especially mobilization that could cut across tribal lines. For this reason, most Indian leaders in 1978 were opposed to the proposed legislation. They saw it as the whites' way of not simply dispersing federal programs but of effectively demobilizing Indians as a political force.[14]

Second, as suggested above, the creation of state agencies often makes clear in administrative operations what may be left camouflaged in the extra-state politics of popular campaigning or party platform designing. As the state has expanded its reach in the last two centuries it literally has had to take more actions, articulate more decisions. These take the form of increasingly detailed administrative policies. What may be deliberately blurred in Congressional debate can become quite clear in its ethnic ramifications in administrative actions. Thus, for example, the ethnic consequences of immigration policy become most clear in the everyday decisions by the Immigration and Naturalization Service. The INS has become a stimulus for Chicano (and other Hispanic groups) mobilization. One result of that ethnic mobilization is that the INS today has its first Hispanic director, just as the BIA has its first Indian director. But one would be mistaken to start ethnic-state analysis by seeing these appointments as proof solely of the dependent status of politics, i.e., that the state is shaped by levels of ethnic pluralism and of ethnic mobilization. For, in fact, the reason that the INS has an Hispanic chief is that *first* the expansion of the state was a factor stimulating Hispanic mobilization and only *then* was pressure brought to bear on the INS.[15]

There is a third way in which the state-building process in the United States has had a mobilizing effect on ethnic groups. Just now reference was made to 'Hispanics' as if they constituted a discreet ethnic group that overarched earlier ethnic references such as Chicano, Puerto Rican, and Cuban. Whether in fact there is a distinguishable 'Hispanic' ethnic group developing now in the American society is still open to investigation. But if there is even a hint of such an ethnic group evolution it is in no small part the result of state categorization practices. In the past the American state has legitimized 'Blacks' as an ethnic category in law, despite the variety of ethnic groups from which Afro-Americans derived. The state has also established 'Filipino' as a legal category (in recent years Filipinos have represented the largest immigrant group coming into the United States, although in Philippines society there are numerous recognized ethnic distinctions). But the state employs ethnic categories to suit its administrative-political needs. In so doing it requires individuals subject to certain laws to respond as 'Hispanics' or 'Indians' or 'Filipinos.' Over time, this state practice may encourage individuals to see themselves as part of not just an artificial state category but as a group which shares important common experiences: oppression, deprivation, and also benefits.

Conclusion

The state dimension of American socio-political history has been sadly neglected. In other countries the state has been harder to ignore because of a tradition of monarchy *or* because of an historically powerful central bureaucracy *or* because of weak or retarded party and legislative organizations *or* because of a strong element of police and military coercion in political life. In the United States, however, the early development of extra-state political institutions such as elections and parties, together with a public ideology which denied the legitimacy of statist authority per se, put up a smoke screen that hid the development of the state. State-building involves the increased penetration and capacity of the institutions of vertical authority: the bureaucracy, judicial system, police and military. Such increasing penetration and capability usually are accompanied by greater centralization of authority. These classic processes of state-building may be more blatantly visible in countries such as France and Indonesia, but they were occurring in American society as early as the 1780s and they are still continuing to operate today.

The experiences of ethnic groups in any country are affected by the levels and patterns of state-building. State needs for territorial jurisdiction, mobility control and adequate supplies and distribution of labor all inevitably impinge upon ethnic definitions and inter-ethnic relationships.

Ethnic groups vary in how persistent the state's impact is (1) on the potential group members' self-perceptions of their identity, (2) on the ethnic group's resources for communal organization and mobilization, and (3) on the group's acceptance by other ethnic groups in the extra-state political processes such as elections and petitioning.

Perhaps one of the reasons that the effect of the state on ethnic groups in the United States has been so neglected is that those ethnic groups which have had the longest and greatest access to state power—English Americans and more belatedly, European-derived groups—have themselves been so at ease with state institutions that they were able to push out of their analytical consciousness the recognition of the state's important role in shaping the character of ethnic relationships. Today, as the reach and power of the state grows remarkably, such analytical blindness will be less and less possible. It may be that all students of American politics need to give serious thought to the historical experience of American Indians.

ENDNOTES

*An earlier version of this paper was first presented to the Indo–US symposium on ethnic mobilization, November 1978.

1. A recent exploration of the evolution of modern states is: Gianfranco Poggi, *The Development of the Modern State*, Stanford, Stanford University Press, 1978. Among the analyses prompting renewed interest in the state in contemporary politics are: Nicos Poulantzas, 'The Capitalist State: A Reply to Miliband and Laclau,' *New Left Review*, No. 95, Jan.–Feb. 1976, pp. 63–83; Hamza Alavi, 'The State in Post-Colonial Societies: Pakistan and Bangladesh,' *New Left Review*, No. 74, July–Aug. 1972, pp. 59–81; Michael von Freyhold, 'The Post-Colonial State and Its Tanzanian Version,' *Review of African Political Economy*, No. 8, Jan.–April, 1977, pp. 75–89. My own tentative efforts to comprehend the relationships between state-building and ethnicity include: Enloe, *Police, Military and Ethnicity: Foundations of State Power*, New Brunswick, NJ, Transaction Books, 1980; Enloe, 'Internal Colonialism, Federalism and Alternative State Development Formulas,' *Publius*, Vol. 7, No. 4, Fall, 1977, pp. 145–160.

2. A valuable case analysis of American Indians' experience in this early period of United States state-building is: Francis Paul Prucha, *American Indian Policy in the Formative Years*, Lincoln, Neb., University of Nebraska Press, 1970. A recent assessment of United

States Government policy's historical impact on Indians in the *Report of the American Indian Policy Review Commission, 1977* (chairman: Senator James Abourezk of South Dakota).

3. See, for example, Alexander Saxton, *The Indispensable Enemy: Labor and the Anti-Chinese Movement in California*, Berkeley, University of California Press, 1971. Also pertinent are works by historians of slavery such as Immanual Wallerstein, Eugene Genovese, Walter Rodney and Eric Williams. A collection of studies of the ways in which the ethnic distributions of labor are shaped in part by state needs is: Ronald Grant and S. Wellhoffer, eds., *Ethno-Nationalism, Multinational Corporations and the Modern State*, Denver, Colorado, University of Denver Monograph Series on World Affairs, 1978.

4. Prucha, *op. cit.*, Vine Deloria, *Custer Died for Your Sins*, New York, Macmillan, 1969; Alvin Josephy, *The Indian Heritage of America*, New York, Alfred A. Knopf, 1968; Angie Debo, *A History of the Indians of the United States*, Norman, University of Oklahoma Press, 1970; Enloe, *Ethnic Soldiers: State Security in Divided Societies*, London, Penguin Books, 1980 and Athens, University of Georgia Press, 1980.

5. Peter G. Gowing, *Mandate in Moroland: The American Government of Muslim Filipinos, 1899–1920*, Quezon City, Philippines, Philippine Center for Advanced Studies, 1977; Gowing, *Moros and Indians: Commonalities of Purpose, Policy and Practice in American Government of Two Hostile Subject Peoples*, Marawi City, Dansalan College, Dansalan Research Center, Occasional Paper No. 6, 1977.

6. Carl Wittke, 'Immigration Policy Prior to World War I,' in Benjamin Ziegler, ed., *Immigration: An American Dilemma*, Boston, DC Health & Co., 1953, p. 8.

7. See for instance a report of preparations for the 1980 census, *New York Times*, August 6, 1978.

8. Several of these debates are analyzed in Enloe, *Ethnic Conflict and Political Development*, Boston, Little, Brown and Co., 1973.

9. United States Department of State, Bureau of Public Affairs, 'The Undocumented Aliens Program,' Washington, DC, Government Printing Office, May, 1978; *New York Times*, April 16, 1978; *New York Times*, June 22, 1978.

10. As of mid-1978, 24 percent of the United States Army's uniformed personnel was Black. Warren Rogers, 'Volunteer Army: Is it Working?,' *Boston Globe*, August 27, 1978. A discussion of the racial and ethnic policies relevant to the formation of the United States volunteer army is found in Enloe, *Ethnic Soldiers, op. cit.*

11. Anne Sutherland, 'Gypsies, the Hidden Americans,' *Transaction/Society*, Vol. 12, No. 2, Jan.–Feb., 1975, pp. 27–33. For a comparative perspective see *"The Rom: The Gypsies of Europe,"* London, Minority Rights Group, Revised edition, 1975.

12. Edward George Hartmann, *The Movement to Americanize the Immigrant*, New York, Columbia University Press, 1948; John Hingham, *Strangers in the Land*, New York, Atheneum, 1973.

13. Frances Svensson, a University of Michigan political scientist who is both a political theorist and student of American Indian politics, discusses the intolerance of American ideology for communal rights in a forthcoming article in *American Political Science Review*.

14. Robert Levey, 'American Longest Battle for Juistice,' *Boston Globe*, August 20, 1978.

15. Discussions of the concept of 'representative bureaucracies' can be found in Enloe, 'Ethnicity, Bureaucracy and State-Building in Africa and Latin America', *Ethnic and Racial Studies*, Vol. 1, No. 3, Summer, 1978; Peta Sheriff, 'Sociology of Public Bureaucracies, 1965–1975,' *Current Sociology*, Vol. 24, No. 2, 1976, pp. 73–99; Frank Thompson, 'Minority Groups in Public Bureaucracies,' *Administration and Society*, Vol. 8, No. 2, August, 1976, pp. 201–226. Lee Sigelman and Robert Carter, 'American Indians in the Political Kingdom: A Note on the Bureau of Indian Affairs,' *Administration and Society*, Vol. 8, No. 3, Nov. 1976.

II

Historical Perspectives

The United States, which has been called a "nation of nations," is one of the most ethnically diverse societies in the modern world. Conflict for economic, social, and political preeminence among its numerous racial and ethnic groups has been one of the most salient features of the American experience. A separate section emphasizing the historical dimensions of racial and ethnic relations in the American experience is important for at least two reasons. First, analysis of the historical dimensions of racial and ethnic relations is essential to understanding the dynamics of race and ethnicity in American life today. Contemporary racial and ethnic relations have important historical roots, and present patterns of assimilation and inequality, of conflict and accommodation, are based on, and derived from, systems of intergroup relations initiated in the past. Adequate analysis of the dynamics of racial and ethnic relations is, therefore, inherently historical. In order to comprehend fully the nature of contemporary racial and ethnic patterns, considerable attention must be devoted to the manner in which they developed over time.

Second, a primary objective of this book is an understanding of the general phenomenon of racial and ethnic relations. Whether the specific cases in which the dynamics of race and ethnicity are examined occur in contemporary American society, in another society, or in a past society is irrelevant to this aim; historical as well as contemporary settings provide examples with which the validity of general theoretical and conceptual models can be assessed. Because of its extraordinary ethnic diversity, an analysis of American society can serve as an excellent laboratory for the study of racial and ethnic relations in general. Examination of the American experience, therefore, can illumine some of the most important features of majority-minority relations. For example, Noel's analysis of the genesis of American slavery not only illumines that subject but also provides a test of his theory of the origins of ethnic stratification. Thus understanding the history of race and ethnicity in America can suggest new ways of conceptualizing these phenomena.

However, one important qualification should be noted. Emphasizing the historical dimension of intergroup relations should not be permitted to obscure the significance of social-structural conditions in the present society. Too often, historical explanations of a society's patterns of inequality deflect attention from the extent to which these patterns are reinforced and perpetuated by contemporary institutions. For instance, the disabilities encountered by blacks, Chicanos, Puerto Ricans, and American Indians in the United States today are not merely a function of racism and oppression in the past, but of those same factors operating in the present. The implications of this fact are moral as well as analytical. Responsibility for the existence of unequal rewards, prestige, and power in a society cannot be relegated to the sins of one's ancestors; rather, it rests with all who participate in the society and benefit from existing institutional arrangements.

Given these broad objectives, it is impossible to provide more than a brief overview of the history of majority-minority relations in the United States. Thus Part II considers some of the salient features of the history of American ethnic relations. Our primary concern is not that the experience of each American ethnic group be examined in depth, but rather that the articles chosen provide conceptual and substantive continuity to the volume as a whole. Let us first look at a historical overview of several of the major ethnic and racial categories that collectively comprise the American people.

Native Americans

The first Americans migrated from Asia around 20,000 years ago, and dispersed throughout North, Central, and South America. Although the length of time that they inhabited the American continents is relatively brief when compared to human societies elsewhere in the world, Native American peoples developed a great diversity of cultures with widely different levels of technology and cultural complexity. As Enloe puts it in her article, "The Growth of the State and Ethnic Mobilization," "Before the arrival of Europeans the American continent was already ethnically plural." The large and highly sophisiticated Aztec, Inca, and Mayan civilizations contrast sharply with the relatively simple societies of the Yavapai, Onondaga, and Kansa. A good index of this diversity was the myriad number of languages found in the New World. Wax points out that Native American languages

> can be classed into about a dozen different stocks (each as distinct from the other as the Semitic from the Indo-European) and within each stock into languages as distinct as English from Russian. The Americas were linguistically as diverse as the Euroasian land mass (Wax, 1971:3).

To the present day, substantial differences can be found among Native Americans despite the popular perception of Indians as a single distinct ethnic group.

The arrival of Europeans, however, significantly affected Indian cultures. Examination of the effects of Indian-white contact shows the process by which a system of ethnic stratification develops. Ethnic stratification involves a system of social ranking in which one ethnic group acquires greater power, privilege, and prestige than another (or others). An unequal relationship between two or more ethnic groups is not inevitable, however. In other words, some groups are not inherently dominant and others inherently subordinate. In his article, "A Theory of the Origins of Ethnic Stratification," Noel suggests that three conditions are necessary for a system of ethnic stratification to be created: *ethnocentrism, competition,* and differences in *power.* Noel applied these conditions to the development of the caste system of black-white relations in the United States, but let us here examine how these variables influenced patterns of Indian-white relations.

Ethnocentrism refers to the idealization of the attributes of the group to which an individual belongs. It seems to be an inevitable outgrowth of the socialization process, during which cultural values and standards of right and wrong, beauty and ugliness, and so forth, are internalized. By the same process, individuals tend to reject or ridicule different groups to the extent that they differ from their own. European settlers regarded Indians as heathen savages, possessing cultures vastly inferior to their own. Indeed, among many Puritans of New England, Indians were regarded as agents of Satan, to be exterminated by gunfire or disease. The European invaders considered agriculture a superior economic activity and an index of their own cultural superiority. Therefore they perceived the lands they entered to be wilderness—in their eyes, unoccupied and unused territory. Europeans also sought to Christianize the Indians and to eliminate their traditional religious practices. The ethnocentrism that underlay the missionary impulse is exemplified by the following speech by a Boston missionary to a group of Seneca Indians:

> There is but one religion, and but one way to serve God, and if you do not embrace the right way, you cannot be happy hereafter. You have never worshipped the Great Spirit in a manner acceptable to him; but have all your lives, been in great errors and darkness. To endeavor to remove these errors, and open your eyes, so that you might see clearly, is my business with you (Washburn, 1964:210).

When two different ethnic groups come into initial contact, ethnocentrism is not restricted to one group. Rather, both sides respond with mutual ethnocentrism. Noel notes this reciprocal process when he cites the reply of representatives of the Six (Indian) Nations to an offer by the Virginia Commission in 1774 to educate Indian youth at the College of William and Mary:

> Several of our young people were formerly brought up at Colleges of the Northern Provinces; they were instructed in all your sciences; but when they came back to us, they were bad runners, ignorant of every means of living in the woods, unable to bear either cold or hunger, knew neither how to build a cabin, take a deer, or kill an enemy, spoke our language imperfectly, were therefore neither fit for hunters, warriors, or counsellors; they were totally good for nothing. We are, however, not the less obliged by your kind offer, though we decline accepting it; and to show our grateful Sense of it, if the Gentlemen of Virginia will sent us a Dozen of their Sons we will take great care of their education, instruct them in all we know and make Men of them.

It is clear that the Indian leaders felt their ways to be superior to those of the Virginians.

The second condition necessary for a system of ethnic stratification to develop is *competition;* that is, a situation in which two or more individuals or groups strive for a goal or objective that only one can achieve. From the beginning of Indian-

European contacts, competition between the two groups centered around land. Indian and white looked on land differently. The Indian concept of land ownership emphasized the notion of *usufruct,* or user's rights. The land could be occupied, hunted, cultivated, and otherwise used as long as an individual wished. Once it was abandoned, it became available for the use of others. To Native Americans, land therefore was not something that could be owned or bought or sold, as Europeans conceived of it. Many land transactions between Native Americans and Europeans were based on radically different conceptions of what rights were being conveyed.

Initially, the desire of Europeans for land they could cultivate did not strain Indian-white relationships. But, as the number of Europeans increased, so did the pressures for land acquisition. Moreover, cultivation soon reduced the supply of game and forced an Indian retreat. The process of European expansion westward also involved the expulsion of Indians from their tribal lands to settlements beyond the immediate frontier. Removal was frequently legitimated by treaties with British colonial and, later, with United States governments. The underlying white philosophy of the nineteenth century grew out of the Anglo-Saxon sense of cultural superiority, perhaps best exemplified by President Theodore Roosevelt's assertion that "this great continent could not have been kept as nothing but a game preserve for squalid savages" (quoted in Lurie's article, "The American Indian: Historical Background").

A system of ethnic stratification ultimately rests on differences in *power.* Initial contacts between Indian and white usually took place in a context of relative equality and were not necessarily destructive of Indian life. In fact, many items of white technology—especially guns, knives, cloth, fishhooks, pots, and other tools—were eagerly sought by Indians. For instance, it was only after the introduction of the horse by Europeans that the Plains Indian cultures flourished (Washburn 1964:66–70). The Indians' ability to maintain a posture of equality is reflected by the white recognition of them as independent powers and by numerous diplomatic treaties, gifts, and even politically arranged marriages between Indians and whites. (The marriage of Pocahontas and John Rolfe, for example, was primarily a political match to ensure the survival of early Virginia colonists.)

However, the advance of European settlement eventually overwhelmed even the most stalwart Indian resistance. Armed with superior military technology and bolstered by increasing numbers, whites moved inexorably westward. Indian tribes were forced to retreat as control of lands they had formerly occupied passed to whites. Diseases carried by the Europeans, such as smallpox, scarlet fever, measles, and cholera, were fatal to large numbers of Indian peoples. Epidemics ravaged Native American peoples throughout American history, frequently killing more than half of a tribe. Washburn concludes that "unwittingly, disease was the white man's strongest ally in the New World" (1975:107).

The reservation system that developed most fully during the nineteenth century symbolized the end of the era of Indian-white equality. Most Indians had to obtain passes to leave the reservation, were denied the vote, and were forcefully prohibited from engaging in native religious and ceremonial practices. Traditional patterns of authority were undermined because the administration and control of the reservation were placed in the hands of white agents. Reservation Indians lost control over their fate. The Native American population, which had numbered about ten million when Columbus reached America, had dwindled to less than 250,000 by 1900.

Although reservations reduced Indians to a subjugated status, they did preserve some of the dwindling Indian lands. Yet, despite efforts to extinguish them traditional Indian cultural values and practices persisted on the reservations, since they were usually isolated from the rest of society. In the last quarter of the nineteenth century, most white Americans agreed that forced assimilation—the socialization of Indians to white culture—represented the most humane means of dealing with the dilemma of the Native American's continued existence. To assimilate the Indians, whites employed a strategy of destroying tribal governments, breaking up the reservations, and granting land to Indians on an individual basis. The federal government subsidized Indian schools controlled by white religious groups. In many of these schools students were forcibly taken from their families, forced to adopt non-Indian styles of dress, and punished for speaking their own native languages.

The overall objective was to force Indians to rid themselves of their cultural heritage and to adopt white values of rugged individualism, competition, and private enterprise. To ethnocentric whites, these values represented more civilized forms of behavior. In 1887, Carl Schurz, the German-born Secretary of the Interior, justified these efforts: "The enjoyment and pride of individual ownership of property is one of the most effective civilizing agencies" (U.S. Commission on Civil Rights, 1961:122). Theodore Roosevelt, reflecting the late-nineteenth-century, Social Darwinist theory that emphasized the "survival of the fittest," agreed: "This will bring the whites and Indians into close contact, and while, of course, in the ensuing struggle and competition many of the Indians will go to the wall, the survivors will come out American citizens" (quoted in Washburn, 1975:242).

Throughout the history of Indian-white contacts, Europeans have consistently assumed that their cultures were superior to the cultures of Indian peoples. The basic U.S. government policy has been one of assimilation: of turning Indians into whites. Yet the striking feature of Indian life in twentieth-century America has been its ability to endure. Despite pressures to force them to assimilate into the mainstream of American society, Indians have tenaciously clung to their ancestral cultural values, standards, and beliefs. This resistance to assimilation is consistent with Lieberson's thesis (see Part III) that conflict, rather than assimilation, is the consequence of contact situations in which the indigenous group is subordinate. Although plagued by the nation's poorest health standards, the Native American population increased by 1980 to nearly one and a half million, a five-fold increase since 1900. Moreover, the rise of ethnic consciousness and militancy during the 1960s and 1970s found expression among American Indians, particularly among the younger and better educated.

European Americans

The migratory movement of European peoples from the seventeenth through the twentieth centuries has been the greatest in human history. Since the beginning of the seventeenth century, more than seventy million people have emigrated from Europe; about two-thirds of this number came to the United States. For nearly two centuries—from the beginning of the seventeenth to the beginning of the nineteenth centuries—the European population of America was overwhelmingly Protestant and British.

The first substantial migration to settle permanently in America occurred between 1607 and 1660. This almost exclusively English migration established the English character of American institutions, language, and culture. The economic, legal, and political traditions that English settlers brought to America served as the foundation of American society. Later ethnic groups were forced to adapt to the cultural and social systems that the English had created.

Although the English comprised the most substantial proportion of the colonial population, the middle colonies (New York, New Jersey, Pennsylvania, Delaware) contained substantial settlements of Germans, Dutch, Scotch-Irish, Scots, Swedes, and French Huguenots. These colonies contained the greatest variety of European cultures and therefore provided a context within which the first interethnic relations among European peoples can be examined. It was here that the ideal of America as a *melting pot,* in which diverse cultures come together to form a new people, was first formulated. As the eighteenth century Frenchman, Hector St. John de Crevecoeur, wrote:

> What then is the American, this new man? He is either an European, or the descendant of an European, hence that strange mixture of blood, which you will find in no other country.... Here [in America] individuals of all nations are melted into a new race of men, whose labours and posterity will one day cause great changes in the world (Crevecoeur, 1957:39).

As we will consider more fully in Part III, the idealistic notion of the melting pot has greatly influenced later conceptions of how the various cultures comprising the American people have adapted and interacted.

The reality of intergroup relations in the middle colonies appears to have been somewhat different. Spurred by William Penn's promotional efforts during the late-seventeenth and early-eighteenth centuries, substantial numbers of Germans settled in Pennsylvania, where they formed prosperous farming communities. Because the Germans insisted on maintaining their own language, churches, and culture, their presence generated some of the earliest recorded antagonism among European ethnic groups in America. In 1752, Benjamin Franklin openly expressed the widely held fears of the ''Germanization'' of Pennsylvania:

> Why should the *Palatine Boors* Germans be suffered to swarm into our Settlements, and by herding together, establish their Language and Mannaers, to the Exclusion of ours? Why should Pennsylvania, founded by the *English,* become a Colony of *Aliens,* who will shortly be so numerous as to Germanize us instead of our Anglifying them . . . ? (cited in Dinnerstein and Reimers, 1975:7).

Colonial attitudes toward immigrants were marked by considerable ambivalence. This same uncertainty still characterizes America's response to ethnic diversity. Throughout the American experience, immigrant groups have been regarded both positively and negatively. On the one hand, immigration has provided a steady source of labor necessary for the country's economic expansion. Until the twentieth century, inducements in the form of land, jobs, and exemption from taxation were offered to encourage settment and thus to assist American economic development. Americans have also celebrated the idea of America as a haven for the oppressed, as reflected in Emma Lazarus's classic poem, "Give me your tired, your poor/your huddled masses yearning to breathe free. . . ."

On the other hand, the concern expressed by Benjamin Franklin over the impact of ethnic diversity on the society's institutions has been a persistent one. Lazarus's poem, inscribed on the Statue of Liberty, further characterizes those "tired," "poor," "huddled masses" as "wretched refuse." Many immigrant groups have been perceived as wretched refuse. In practice, Americans have been less charitable than these idealized accounts indicate. Americans have frequently rejected ethnic differences as alien and undesirable. Some ethnic groups in particular have been rejected or excluded as un-American and incapable of assimilating. Thus, while the labor of immigrants was accepted, their cultural traditions usually were not.

In 1790, when the first United States census was taken, the population of the new American nation was nearly four million. It was overwhelmingly British in composition, with the English comprising 60 to 80 percent of the population, and with other peoples from the British Isles (Scots, Welsh, and Scotch-Irish) contributing substantially. Between 1830 and 1930, the United States population experienced its greatest growth and change. During this period, the nation changed from a small group of tenuously related state governments to the most politically and economically powerful nation on earth. The frontier of unsettled land moved progressively westward and diminished at the same time that the country became the world's leading industrial nation.

Peoples of many lands contributed to this dramatic growth. Between 1830 and 1930, nearly thirty-five million immigrants entered the country, swelling its total population to more than 123 million. In contrast to the relative ethnic homogeneity of colonial immigration, the immigrants who arrived in the nineteenth and early-twentieth centuries represented many different countries and peoples, including German, Russian, Mexican, British, Polish, Japanese, Scandinavian, Irish, Italian, Slavic, Greek, Chinese, and Portuguese. European immigration since 1790 has been divided into two broad categories: "old" immigrants from northern and western Europe and "new" immigrants from southern and eastern Europe.

The "Old" Immigration

Immigration to the United States increased dramatically throughout the nineteenth century. In the peak year of the 1830s slightly more than 70,000 immigrants entered. By the 1850s this annual figure had increased to 400,000; by the 1880s to 650,000; and by the first decade of the twentieth century, there were several years in which more than one million immigrants were admitted.

Until the 1890s, immigration drew principally from countries of northern and western Europe: Germany, Ireland, Great Britain (England, Scotland, and Wales), and Scandinavia (Norway, Sweden, and Denmark). With the exception of the Roman Catholic Irish, the old immigration was primarily Protestant. These groups, again with the exception of the Irish, were attracted by the opportunities of free or relatively cheap land, and therefore often settled in the rural areas of the country. There were several common factors in their countries of origin that led people to emigrate: drastic population increases, displacement of traditional handicraft industries by the industrial revolution, an upheaval in agriculture that transformed traditional agrarian land patterns, and migration of substantial numbers of people from rural to urban areas. Above all, the promise of economic opportunity in America lured people to the United States.

The "New" Immigration

Immigration into the United States reached its peak between 1890 and the outbreak of World War I in 1914. During this period, the United States received more than fourteen million immigrants. As dramatic as the numerical increase during this period was the shift in the sources of immigration. Prior to the 1880s, immigrants had come almost exclusively from northern and western Europe. By the first decade of the twentieth century, however, more than 70 percent of all immigrants came from southern and eastern Europe. This shift brought large numbers of immigrants from a great variety of countries—Greeks, Croatians, Italians, Russians (primarily Jews), Poles, Hungarians, Czechs, and Lithuanians. These groups were culturally different from those who had previously migrated to this country. Unlike the old immigration, which was heavily Protestant and followed agricultural pursuits, the new immigrants were overwhelmingly Roman Catholic or Jewish and were drawn primarily to the economic opportunities in the nation's rapidly expanding cities. The changes in the ethnic composition of this immigration caused "native" whites to fear the impact of non-English cultures on American institutions.

The shift in immigration patterns coincided with the flowering of the ideology of "scientific" racism, which reached its height about the turn of the twentieth century. As noted in the introduction to Part I, at this time scientific and lay opinion concurred in the idea of the inherent mental and moral inferiority of all those who were not of Anglo-Saxon or Teutonic ancestry. To already existing conceptions of black, Indian, and Asian inferiority was added the notion of the racial inferiority and unassimilability of immigrant groups from southern and eastern Europe. Never before or since have racist ideologies been so pervasive and so intellectually respectable in the United States as they were at this time.

These racist assumptions provided the foundations for American immigration policy from 1917 to 1965. The first general restrictive legislation, passed in 1917, was a literacy test, which was employed because people thought it would materially lessen the immigration from southern and eastern Europe while permitting immigration from northern and western Europe to continue. In the ensuing decade, even more stringent restrictive measures were enacted, each one based on the assumption of the desirability of restricting immigration to those from the countries of the old immigration. In 1921 and 1924 further legislation designed to curtail new immigration was enacted. And finally, in 1929, the National Origins Quota Act, based (as was preceding legislation) on the rationale of ensuring the maintenance of Anglo-Saxon "racial" purity, became law. The quota system limited total immigration to 150,000 annually and established quotas for each nation. Derived by a complicated means of calculation, each nation's quota was supposed to be "in proportion to its [the nation's] contribution to the American population." The measure assigned the highest quotas to those nations of northern and western Europe, whose racial stock was conceived to coincide most closely with that of the original settlers of the country. More than four-fifths of the total quota was allocated to countries of the old immigration. For instance, Great Britain had an admissions quota exceeding 65,000, but Italy was allocated fewer than 6,000 and Hungary fewer than 1,000. This policy was retained virtually intact until its repeal in 1965.

The process of uprooting that millions of immigrants experienced comprises one of the most dramatic sagas in American history. It has been widely described (e.g., Handlin, 1951; Taylor, 1971; Jones, 1960, 1976; Seller, 1977; Dinnerstein and Reimers, 1975). Moreover, the consequences of this massive migration—its effects on European immigrants and the manner in which they and their descendants adapted to American society—have been a source of considerable description, debate, and controversy among social historians and sociologists. In Part III we will examine in greater depth some of the competing explanations for differences in adaptation among ethnic groups in American society.

Black Americans

Racism, which provided a basis for restricting the immigration of southern and eastern European immigrants, has also been a pervasive characteristic of whites' interaction with blacks. From the earliest settlement to the present, the principal racial division in American society has been between white and black, between those of European ancestry and those whose ancestral origins can be traced to the African continent. From the arrival of the first African at Jamestown in 1619 to the present, the meaning attributed to the physical traits of black people has been more important than all other racial divisions in American society. America's blacks were enslaved for more than two centuries; and although more than a century has passed since slavery was legally abolished, the rationale for slavery that emphasized the racial and cultural differences between blacks and whites persists to this day. Numbering more than twenty-six million—more than 11 percent of the total American population—black Americans have been the largest racial minority in American society since the eighteenth century.

In his provocative article, "The Declining Significance of Race," William J. Wilson distinguishes among three major periods or stages of black-white relations in American history: preindustrial, industrial, and modern industrial. Let us review briefly here the black experience during the first two of these three periods. (We will examine the racial dynamics of the most recent period, the modern industrial stage, in Part IV).

During the preindustrial period, a plantation economy dominated and defined the lives of black people, the most important aspect of which was the institution of slavery. *Slavery* is a system of social relations in which some persons are involuntarily placed in perpetual servitude, are defined as property, and are denied rights generally given to other members of the society. Throughout human history, the creation of a great variety of social statuses has limited the freedom and rights of particular classes of individuals. Other systems of servile statuses, such as serfdom, debt bondage, and indentureship, involved some degree of unfreedom and rightlessness. The question of what distinguishes these statuses from slavery is therefore not an absolute one. "Slaves are [simply] the most deprived and oppressed class of serviles" (Noel, 1972:5). This definition of slavery is useful because it provides a standard against which social systems can be compared. In other words, if slavery is conceived as being located at the far end of a continuum ranging from absolute rightlessness, on the one hand, to absolute freedom on the other, one may examine each case of oppression in terms of its location between the extremes on this continuum.

Slavery, therefore, was not an American invention. It existed in ancient civilizations, persisted throughout the Middle Ages and into modern times, was practiced legally until 1962 on the Arabian peninsula, and persists, unofficially, to this day. Although it has existed in many different societies throughout virtually the whole of human history, the introduction of national monarchies and the growing industrial and commercial revolutions in the sixteenth through the nineteenth centuries acted as catalysts for the development of Western slave systems, in which slave labor was an indispensible component of economic systems.

Even though there has been a surge of historical interest in the institution of American slavery (e.g., Elkins, 1959; Davis, 1966, 1975; Genovese, 1974; Gutman, 1976; Yetman, 1970; Blassingame, 1972; Rawick, 1972; Fogel and Engerman, 1974; Levine, 1977), there has been a dearth of social-scientific attention directed to the analysis of slavery as a social institution, and to the more general question of the nature and effects of institutional regimentation. The implications of an analysis of slavery in America, therefore, could be used to examine the dynamics of other total institutions (Goffman, 1961) and other dominant-subordinate relationships (serfdom, caste systems, racial or ethnic ghettos, and various Indian reservation systems) that have not yet been considered in these terms.

Noel's article, "A Theory of the Origins of Ethnic Stratification," represents an effort to consider American slavery from a broader perspective. Noel identifies three major conditions—ethnocentrism, competition, and differences in power—as necessary for the emergence of a system of ethnic stratification, and he uses American slavery as a case study with which to test the utility of his general propositions. However, if one closely considers Noel's arguments, it is problematic whether the important feature of black-white relations in the United States was slavery per se. Crucial to an understanding of the dynamics of black-white relations in the United States are the features that undergirded the so-called peculiar institution: the conception of black inferiority and the capacity of the dominant group to restrict blacks to a permanent subordinate position.

Although slavery represented the most extreme form of institutionalized inequality between black and white in America, Leon Litwack (1961) has pointed out that during the slavery era the rights and privileges of free blacks were severely circumscribed throughout the entire society. Oppression of blacks was by no means restricted to the South or to slaveholders; throughout the North, too, the freedom, rights, and privileges of free blacks were severely curtailed. At no time did the words *free person* or *freedom* mean the same thing to blacks as to whites. In many states, barriers to voting were initiated for blacks at the same time that restrictions for whites were being liberalized or eliminated. Court testimony and the formation of legal contracts and lawsuits by blacks were also forbidden in many states. Several states prohibited immigration; others required that blacks carry identification passes (as is done in contemporary South Africa). Excluded from public schools, blacks were generally denied the benefits of formal education. In addition to these officially imposed disabilities, blacks in most areas were subjected to ridicule, harassment, and occasional mob violence (Litwack, 1961).

The most salient features of black-white relations in the United States, therefore, were that blacks, whether slave or free, occupied a lower *caste* status, and that severe sanctions were employed to restrict their freedoms. The American slave thus had to contend with the sanctions and effects of two inferior statuses—slave and lower caste—both of which were mutually reinforcing. Unlike many other slave societies, manumission was difficult, and people who had been freed could not anticipate assimilation into the society on an equal basis.

Immediately after the Civil War, a period of fluid race relations occurred. Bolstered by passage of the 13th Amendment, which abolished slavery; the 14th Amendment, which extended the equal protection of the law to blacks; and the 15th Amendment, which guaranteed the right to vote, black Americans actively sought to realize the opportunities and responsibilities of their new status. Nevertheless, the reality of caste persisted. Patterns of black-white relations formed under slavery did not automatically change after emancipation: race relations continued to be based on a rigid caste system. The roles of blacks after their emancipation became well defined and tightly circumscribed. The new legal status conferred by emancipation and the Reconstruction Amendments did little to alter the patterns of social relations in the plantation South, or to promote the acquisition of new values, habits, and attitudes by either black or white. Former slaves were formally given liberty but not the means (that is, economic, political, educational, and social equality) to realize it. Blacks remained largely unskilled and illiterate, most of them living lives of enforced dependence on the still-dominant whites. The result was a black peasantry dominated by an agricultural system that ensured dependence on the land and isolation from the main currents of society.

Northern troops, which had occupied the South during the period of Reconstruction, were removed in 1877, and Southern whites then resorted to a wide range of devices to ensure the maintenance of white dominance. Blacks, who during Reconstruction had voted and held public office, were systematically disenfranchised by a variety of mechanisms: white primary elections from which blacks were excluded; poll taxes; "grandfather clauses," which restricted voting to those (and their descendants) who had been eligible to vote before the Civil War; and literacy requirements, which, because they were selectively enforced, effectively restricted even the most educated and literate blacks from exercising the constitutionally mandated right to vote.

Moreover, to ensure that white dominance would be perpetuated, the Jim Crow system of racial segregation was created. Historian C. Vann Woodward (1955) has described the extraordinary variety of state and municipal ordinances requiring racial separation that Southern state legislatures enacted during the last decade of the nineteenth and first two decades of the twentieth centuries. The pervasiveness of the segregated system was signaled by a profusion of "Whites Only" and "Colored" signs that governed working conditions, public accommodations, state institutions, recreation, sports, cemeteries, and housing. In 1896, in the famous *Plessy* v. *Ferguson* decision, the United States Supreme Court provided judicial support for the doctrine of "separate but equal." Thereafter, virtually every aspect of contact between whites and blacks was legally regulated.

Finally, extralegal sanctions, including intimidation and violence in the form of lynching and terrorism, were employed to assure that the subservient status of blacks persisted long after slavery had been abolished. Writing in 1929, Charles S.

Johnson, a pioneer black sociologist, noted the continuity between the slave plantation and rural Macon County, Alabama, during the 1920s:

> There have been retained, only slightly modified, most of the features of the plantation under the institution of slavery. . . . The Negro population of this section of Macon County has its own social heritage which, in a relatively complete isolation, has had little chance for modification from without or within. Patterns of life, social codes, as well as social attitudes, were set in the economy of slavery. The political and economic revolution through which they have passed has affected only slightly the social relationships of the community or the mores upon which these relations have been based. The strength and apparent permanence of this early cultural set have made it virtually impossible for newer generations to escape the influence of the patterns of work and general social behavior transmitted by their elders (Johnson, 1934:16).

Similar reports noted the persistence of the slave plantation in many areas of the rural South well into the 1930s.

In response to these oppressive conditions, after the turn of the twentieth century blacks began to leave the South, a movement that has been called the Great Migration. Migrating primarily to Northern urban areas, blacks congregated in urban ghettos, geographically defined residential areas to which minority groups are restricted. The transformation of American blacks from an essentially rural to a predominantly urban people has been one of the most significant aspects in the black American experience and one of the most important demographic changes in American history. In 1900, almost 90 percent of the black population lived in the South; in 1980, the percentage in the South had declined to only 53 percent. In 1900, blacks were primarily rural residents, with only 22.7 percent living in urban areas. By 1980, this percentage had increased to 81.3 percent, indicating that blacks have become a more urbanized population than whites. Although a substantial portion of the increase in the number of urbanized blacks was in the North, many were living in Southern cities as well. Between 1900 and 1980, the percentage of the Southern black population residing in cities increased from 17.2 percent to 67.3 percent. Table 1 shows the percentage of the black population residing in major American cities for the years 1920, 1950, 1970, and 1980.

The massive movement of blacks out of the South provided the basis for a change in the nature of race relations. Wilson has characterized this as the *industrial* period of race relations. His description of the transition from preindustrial to industrial parallels van den Berghe's distinction between *paternalistic* race relations, which were characteristic of a plantation economy, and *competitive* race relations, which are found in an urban, industrial setting. In the industrial setting, racial competition for jobs generated considerable racial antagonism, tension, and conflict. (For a superb analysis of this conflict, see Tuttle, 1972, especially Chapter 4).

The Great Migration of blacks out of the South ultimately proved to be one of the most important factors underlying the black protest movement that swept the nation during the late 1950s and 1960s. Although discrimination against blacks in education, employment, housing, and the administration of justice also prevailed in the North, a greater range of opportunities for blacks were available in Northern urban areas than in the South. Especially after World War II, increasing numbers of blacks obtained college educations and found employment in skilled and white-

TABLE 1. Black population as percent of the total population of the twelve largest U.S. cities,* 1920, 1950, 1970, and 1980

	1920†	1950†	1970	1980
New York	2.7	9.8	21.1	25.2
Los Angeles	2.7	10.7	17.9	17.0
Chicago	4.1	14.1	32.7	39.8
Philadelphia	7.4	18.3	33.6	37.8
Houston	24.6	21.1	25.7	27.6
Detroit	4.1	16.4	43.7	63.1
Dallas	15.1	13.2	24.9	29.4
San Diego	1.2	4.5	7.6	8.9
Phoenix	3.7	6.0	4.8	4.8
Baltimore	14.8	23.8	46.4	54.8
San Antonio	8.9	6.7	7.6	7.3
Indianapolis	11.0	15.0	18.0	21.8

*These were the twelve largest cities in the United States in 1980.
†Figures pertain to "nonwhite" population.
Sources: U.S. Census of 1920; U.S. Census of 1950; U.S. Bureau of the Census, *Negroes in the United States, 1920–1932,* Washington, D.C: U.S. Government Printing Office, 1935; "Characteristics of the Population," *Statistical Abstract of the United States,* 1972, pp. 21–23; *Statistical Abstract of the United States, 1984,* pp. 28–30.

collar occupations. These changes expanded the black middle class, which provided the primary source of leadership for the black protest movement. The educated and articulate black middle class played an especially important role in providing legal challenges to the Southern Jim Crow system, which culminated in the Supreme Court's 1954 *Brown v. Board of Education* decision that segregated schools were unconstitutional. The *Brown* decision, which overturned the 1896 separate-but-equal doctrine, symbolized the beginning of an era in which the legal basis for the caste system would crumble. In Part IV, we will examine the changing status of black Americans during the past quarter century, the period that Wilson has identified as the *modern industrial* stage of American race relations.

Asian Americans
Stanford Lyman discusses the experience of Asian immigrants to this country in "Contrasts in the Community Organization of Chinese and Japanese in North America." Although the Chinese and Japanese differed dramatically in culture and social organization, the dominant group's response to their presence was basically identical: derogation; educational, political, social, and legal discrimination; and, ultimately, restriction of further immigration.

Asian immigration has been slight compared to the numbers of Europeans who have come to the United States. At no time did the numbers of Chinese or Japanese immigrants ever approximate those from Europe. Chinese immigration reached its peak during the decade from 1873 to 1882, when 161,000 Chinese entered the country. Peak Japanese immigration was reached during the ten years between 1900 and 1909, when 139,000 entered. In contrast, between 1840 and 1920 there were thirty-one different *years* when the number of immigrants from a *single* European country alone exceeded 150,000. As Tables 2 and 3 reveal, the total

TABLE 2. Racial and Hispanic population in the United States 1970–1980

	Number (in thousands)		Percent Distribution	
	1980	1970	1980	1970
TOTAL	226,546	203,212	100.0	100.0
White	188,341	177,749	83.2	87.5
Black	26,488	22,580	11.7	11.1
American Indian, Eskimo, and Aleut	1,418	827	0.6	0.4
Asian and Pacific Islander	3,501	1,539	1.5	0.8
Chinese	806	435	0.4	0.2
Filipino	775	343	0.3	0.2
Japanese	701	591	0.3	0.3
Asian Indian	362	NA	0.2	—
Korean	355	69	0.2	0.0
Vietnamese	262	NA	0.1	—
Hispanics#	14,609	9.073	6.4	4.5
Mexican-American	8,740	4,532	3.9	2.2
Puerto Rican	2,014	1,429	0.9	0.7
Cuban	803	544	0.4	0.3
Other	3,051	2,566	1.3	1.2
Other	6,757	517	3.0	0.3

NA–Not available
#–Hispanics included in white, black and "other" categories
Source: Bureau of the Census, *Census of Population,* Supplementary Reports.

number of immigrants from Asia, in general, and Japan and China, in particular, have been relatively insignificant when considered in the context of American immigration as a whole. What is significant is the response that the presence of Asian immigrants generated, and the adaptation of Asians to the discrimination they encountered.

TABLE 3. *United States Population of Indians, Chinese, Japanese, Filipinos, Koreans, and Puerto Ricans*

	Indian	Chinese	Filipino	Japanese	Korean	Puerto Rican[2]
1890	248,253	107,448		2,039		
1900	237,196	89,863		24,236		
1910	276,927	71,531	160	72,157		
1920	244,437	61,639	5,603	111,010		
1930	343,352	74,954	45,208	138,834		
1940	345,252	77,504	45,563	126,947		
1950	357,499	117,629	61,636	141,768		301,375
1960[1]	523,591	237,292	176,310	464,332		892,513
1970[1]	792,730	435,062	343,060	591,290	69,130	1,429,396
1980[1]	1,418,195	806,027	774,640	700,747	354,529	2,013,945

[1]The 1960, 1970 and 1980 census data include Hawaii and Alaska.
[2]Data on persons of Puerto Rican parentage were first collected in the 1950 census.
Source: Bureau of the Census, *Historical Statistics of the United States,* p. 9; Bureau of the Census, 1970 *Census of Population,* Subject Reports, American Indians, p. 5; Puerto Ricans, p. xi; Japanese, Chinese, and Filipinos in the United States, p. 148; Bureau of the Census, 1960 *Census of Population, Characteristics of the Population,* vol. 1, part 1, p. 145; Bureau of the Census, *1980 Census of Population,* Supplementary Reports, Race of Population by States:1980, pp. 6–14.

The initial migration of Chinese into North America began during the middle of the nineteenth century. The Chinese came as unskilled laborers. Since they filled a need for labor created by the California Gold Rush, they were welcomed initially. As their numbers grew, however, the Chinese became perceived as an economic threat to native labor, and racist opposition to them increased. Chinese were subjected to various forms of discriminatory legislation, including laws designed specifically to harass them; the Queue Ordinance, for example, which placed a tax on pigtails. Finally, in response to anti-Chinese agitation in California, Congress passed the Chinese Exclusion Act in 1882, which was the first law to restrict immigration of a specific nationality to the United States. In contrast, more than thirty years were to pass before substantial restrictions were placed on European immigration (Hsu, 1971; Lyman, 1974; Nee and Nee, 1974).

The fear of the "yellow peril," which pervaded the hysteria over Chinese immigration, was revived when the Japanese immigrated in the early twentieth century. Although the Japanese represented an extremely small proportion of the population of both California and the nation as a whole, their presence generated intense hostility. In 1906, the San Francisco Board of Education precipitated an international incident when it attempted to place all Japanese children, native and foreign born, in a segregated Oriental school in Chinatown. Immediate protests from the Japanese ambassador ultimately led the school board to rescind its order. But the Board of Education's segregation efforts in reality were stymied only because President Theodore Roosevelt was able to negotiate the so-called Gentleman's Agreement with Japan in which Japan pledged that it would halt further immigration of its citizens (other than family members of those who had previously immigrated) to the United States. In 1924, federal legislation restricted all Asian immigration into the United States. The anti-Japanese agitation drew support from the same "scientific" sources that led to the respectability of racist thought described earlier (Matthews, 1964). Ultimately, this fear of the yellow peril culminated in the forcible evacuation and relocation of more than 110,000 Japanese-Americans—more than half of them American citizens—by the federal government during World War II (Thomas and Nishimoto, 1969; Grodzins, 1966; Bosworth, 1967; Kitano, 1969; Daniels, 1972).

Despite early antipathy toward the Chinese and Japanese, and the particular hostility toward the Japanese during World War II, both groups have made substantial improvements in socioeconomic status. As Hirschman and Wong point out, both Chinese and Japanese now exceed all other racial groups, including whites, in educational attainments. By 1960, Japanese men and women had the highest median education of any racial group, and since then the educational achievements of Chinese- and Japanese-Americans have continued to increase to the point that "in recent years 90 percent of young Chinese and Japanese men have attended college and almost all continue to graduation" (Hirschman and Wong, 1981:503). Similarly, a disproportionate percentage of Japanese and Chinese are found in professional occupational categories. Finally, the mean incomes of Japanese and Chinese men exceed all other racial categories, including white males. Although they continue to encounter discrimination, the relative economic success of the Chinese and Japanese provides an interesting contrast to the status of other ethnic minorities in American society. Indeed, as we will consider more fully in Part III, their socioeconomic success, in spite of the considerable discrimination against them, has led to the characterization of Asians as "model" minorities and to the suggestion from some commentators (e.g., Sowell, 1981:176) that the discrimination may actually have improved their long-run mobility.

Hispanic Americans

Spanish-speaking Americans constitute one of the largest and the most rapidly growing ethnic categories in contemporary American society. The Hispanic or Latino population totaled more than fourteen-and-a-half million by 1980 and is growing four times more rapidly than any other ethnic segment of the nation. Demographers have estimated that, if Hispanic immigration (both legal and illegal) and fertility rates remain at their present levels, by the year 2020 Hispanics will number forty-six million and will exceed blacks as the country's largest minority (Davis, Haub, and Willette, 1983:39). This dramatic increase in the Hispanic population in the United States is the result of both higher Hispanic fertility rates and substantially increased rates of immigration from Latin America, especially from Mexico.

As we will examine more fully in Part IV, vast social inequalities, poverty, and political repression throughout the region all influence migration pressures in Latin America. A crucial dimension contributing to these problems is demographic: the recent rapid population growth in both Central and South America. During the 1950s the total Latin American population was approximately the same as that of the United States—about 150 million. However, by 2025 it is expected to be 845 million, or about three times the estimate of the U.S. population at that time (Fallows, 1983:45; Davis, Haub, and Willette, 1983:39).

However, to refer to Spanish-speaking people as a single ethnic category is misleading, since the terms *Hispanic* or *Latino,* which are of relatively recent origin, obscure the great diversity of historical, cultural, and geographic backgrounds that exist among them. The Hispanic category includes representatives from more than thirty Latin American nations, as well as Spain and Portugal. More than three-fourths of them are of Mexican, Puerto Rican, or Cuban descent, but there are also substantial communities of Dominicans, Colombians, Ecuadorans, Salvadoreans, and several other Latin nationalities in the United States. These groups also differ in their socioeconomic status as well as in their regional distribution in the United States.

Analysis of the historical backgrounds of Spanish-speaking Americans focuses, especially in this section, on Mexican-Americans, or Chicanos (from the Spanish *Mexicanos),* who comprise the largest Spanish-speaking group and the second largest minority group (after blacks) in American society. Today more than nine million Chicanos live in the United States, more than four-fifths (83 percent) in the five southwestern states of Texas, New Mexico, Arizona, Colorado, and California. Next to the American Indians, with whom they share a common ancestry, they represent the oldest ethnic group in American society. The Chicano people are the biological and cultural descendants of the Spanish military and religious conquest of the Indians of northern Central America. From the early 1600s to the mid-1800s, Spain, and, later, Mexico, colonized and exerted political, economic, and cultural dominance over the region. By the turn of the nineteenth century, Mexican culture, a mixture of Spanish and Indian influences, was well established throughout what is today the southwestern United States.

The process of contact between Mexicans and the Anglo immigrants who settled in Texas in increasing numbers during the early nineteenth century provides another opportunity to test Noel's model concerning the emergence of a system of ethnic stratification. Initially Anglo and Mexican peacefully coexisted, although each viewed the other with an antipathy and distrust that had grown out of two centuries of English and Spanish competition for world dominance. Mutual ethnocentrism between the two peoples occurred from the start, Anglos attributing notions of "racial" inferiority to the darker-skinned Mexicans, and Mexicans seeing in the growing encroachment of the Americans confirmation of their stereotypes of Yankee aggressiveness and greed. Anglo and Mexican also differed in religion and class structure. To ensure their loyalty, the Mexican government required that Anglo colonists, most of whom were Protestants, become Roman Catholics as well as Mexican citizens. More offensive to the sensibilities of Anglo settlers, many of whom were from the South and were slaveholders, was the Mexican prohibition of slavery. Although slavery was illegal, Mexican society was highly stratified, with a small, wealthy upper class and a large class of the very poor. Anglo-Americans, literate and middle class in outlook, developed a perception of the Mexican people as basically indolent and lazy (McLemore, 1973).

Yet despite these differences, Anglo and Mexican Texans coexisted, cooperated, and together fought a common enemy, the Mexican central government controlled by Santa Ana (both Anglos and Mexicans died fighting Santa Ana in the Alamo). After Santa Ana's defeat, however, competition for land became increasingly intense between Anglo and Mexican. The 1848 Treaty of Guadalupe-Hidalgo, in which Mexico ceded to the United States most of the land of the present-day Southwest, signaled the triumph of Anglo power. Despite the fact that the treaty guaranteed legal and property rights to Mexican citizens in the newly acquired territories, Mexican-Americans soon became the object of persistent discrimination. Anglos, especially in Texas, established a system of caste relations, which ensured Chicano political, social, and economic subservience. By the eve of the Civil War the American military conquest of Mexican lands in the Southwest had been completed. In the ensuing years those Mexicans who chose to remain in the annexed territories were largely dispossessed of both their land and the positions of prominence they had occupied in Mexican society. By the turn of the twentieth century, Mexicans had been "relegated to a lower-class status, [in which] they were overwhelmingly dispossessed landless laborers, politically and economically impotent," which was justified by notions of racial inferiority (Estrada et al., 1981:109). For this reason, Alvarez (1973) has argued that the subjugation experience of this "creation generation" after the Mexican War was formative, in much the same sense that Bryce-Laporte (1969) has characterized slavery as "the contextual baseline of Black American experience."

Although a substantial proportion of the contemporary Chicano population is derived from the migrant generation that followed the surge of European immigration into the United States during the early-twentieth century, the situation of Mexican immigrants differed substantially from that of European immigrant groups because Mexican immigrants entered a society that had already adopted a clearly defined lower-caste role for them, a result of the mid-nineteenth century conquest patterns of subordination.

Whereas the earliest Chicano population became an American minority through the annexation of Mexican lands by the United States, the primary source of the later Chicano population in the United States has been immigration, both legal and illegal. This immigration, most of which has occurred during the twentieth century, has been instrumental in the economic development of the American Southwest. As Estrada et al. indicate, Mexican immigrants have provided a readily available and exploitable source of cheap labor, especially for the expansion of the railroad industry, mining, and, above all, agriculture. Indeed, Mexican labor played an integral role in the dramatic expansion of agribusiness interests in the Southwest. During the first two decades of the twentieth century, many Mexicans fled to the United States from the upheavals of the Mexican Revolution. As European immigration to the United States was curtailed by the outbreak of World War I and the passage of the restrictive legislation of the 1920s, Mexican labor filled the growing demand for agricultural workers to replace those who had left for jobs in the nation's industrial sector. The defense employment boom generated by World War II produced a shift of the Chicano population away from rural areas and agricultural pursuits, while at the same time the *bracero* program, which ran from 1942 to 1965, ensured a continuing source of cheap agricultural labor from Mexico. Chicanos still comprise a substantial proportion of the nation's migratory farmworkers, but today more than 80 percent of Mexican Americans are urban residents, and are found especially in the major urban areas of the Southwest. Indeed, there are more people of Mexican descent living in Los Angeles than any city except Mexico City and Guadalajara. As their concentration in urban areas, their occupational status, and their educational levels have increased in recent decades, Mexican-Americans have also become an increasingly salient force in American politics, especially because of their substantial presence in the electorally significant states of Texas and California.

The other major groups of Spanish-speaking peoples are relatively recent immigrant groups who have settled primarily in urban areas on the East coast since the end of World War II. Although the number of immigrants from countries throughout the Caribbean and Central and South America has increased markedly during this period, the two Caribbean islands of Puerto Rico and Cuba have been the primary sources of this influx of Spanish-speaking peoples. These two groups provide an interesting contrast in backgrounds and adaptations to American society.

Among Hispanic groups, Puerto Ricans have a unique relationship with the United States. Although they are American citizens, their language and cultural tradition are both different from the dominant language and culture on the United States mainland. Today Puerto Ricans are the largest Hispanic group outside the Southwest. Residents of the island of Puerto Rico began immigrating to the United States early in the twentieth century, but it was not until the advent of relatively cheap commercial air travel after World War II that they began to arrive in substantial numbers. Today, one out of every three Puerto Ricans lives on the mainland, more than half of them in New York City, which historically has been the principal magnet for Puerto Rican immigrants. Puerto Rican migration to the mainland was prompted primarily by economic pressures among the impoverished lower strata of Puerto Rican society. Consequently, Puerto Ricans are concentrated in blue-collar, semiskilled, and unskilled occupations, which had previously been occupied by "new" immigrants. In 1974, for example, 33 percent of Puerto Ricans held white-collar jobs, compared with 58 percent of all New York residents and 43 percent of blacks (Gray, 1975:12). The Puerto Rican population is afflicted with higher levels of unemployment than any other Hispanic group. And Puerto Rican income levels are lower than those of any other ethnic group, including blacks. Puerto Ricans recently have begun to migrate away from New York City; although most Puerto Ricans remain on the East coast, midwestern and far western cities—such as Chicago, Cleveland, and Los Angeles—have lately had notable increases in the number of Puerto Rican residents.

The Cuban migration to the mainland has been comprised primarily of political refugees from Castro's proletarian revolution. Approximately three-quarters of a million Cubans have entered this country since Castro's rise to power in 1959. In contrast to most previous immigrations to the United States (with the notable exception of emigrés from Nazi Germany during the 1930s), these immigrants tended to come mainly from upper social and economic strata of Cuban society. Derived disproportionately from well-educated middle- and upper-class professional and business backgrounds, they brought skills (education, occupational, business, and managerial experience), entrepreneurial values, and substantial amounts of capital that enabled them to prosper and achieve socioeconomic success—in less than one generation—a speed that is virtually unprecedented among American immigrant groups. In less than twenty-five years since their migration, they have become the most affluent of all Hispanics. They have become a major economic force in Miami, Florida, transforming it into an international business and commercial center, especially important in its ties with Latin America. (See Wilson and Portes's article, "Immigrant Enclaves: An Analysis of the Labor Market Experiences of Cubans in Miani" in Part III.) The most recent influx of Cubans—those who left Cuba during the so-called Freedom Flotilla or Mariel Boatlift of 1980—numbered about 125,000. A substantial proportion of this recent migration was comprised of people of working- and lower-class origins (Davis, Haub, and Willette, 1983:23).

Recent Immigration

A recent *Time* cover story entitled "The New Ellis Island," concerning the influx of immigrants into Los Angeles, proclaimed that "Los Angeles is being invaded" (*Time*, 1983). Since 1968, when the provisions of the 1965 Immigration Reform Act went into effect, historic patterns of immigration into the United States have been transformed. This new immigrant wave that is perceived to be "invading" the United States represents one of the most dramatic and far-reaching changes in the ethnic composition of the United States in the twentieth century. Throughout the 1970s, the number of permanent immigrants to the United States increased substantially. By 1980 more than 880,000 legal immigrants were admitted, a number greater than in any year since 1914, the peak year of the "new" immigration. Moreover, estimates of the number of undocumented aliens, or illegal immigrants, entering the United States range from 500,000 to one million annually (Morrison, 1982).

The changes in the national origins of contemporary immigrants are as dramatic as their escalating numbers. Until 1968, immigration to the United States was overwhelmingly European. Today the predominant sources of immigration are Third World nations in Central and South America, the Caribbean, and Asia. Given the declining birth rate of the native American population, legal and illegal entries into the United States almost equal the natural increase in the native-born population. Some demographers estimate that, if current trends in birth rates and immigration rates continue, a century from now 40 percent of the population will be comprised of post-1980 immigrants and their descendants—at least 80 percent of whom will be Hispanic, Caribbean, or Asian—thus altering radically the racial and ethnic composition of the United States (Bouvier, 1981).

Any effort to consider both the short- and long-term implications of these changes in the ethnic composition of American society must consider them within the context of at least two basic factors: (1) recent structural changes in the American economy and (2) the patterns of ethnic and racial relations that have previously been manifested in the American experience. In Parts III and IV we will examine the nature of intergroup relations in, and ethnic adaptations to, American society. We will also speculate on how these recent trends and patterns may affect future patterns of race and ethnicity in the United States.

6

A Theory of the Origin of Ethnic Stratification

Donald L. Noel

While a great deal has been written about the nature and consequences of ethnic stratification, there have been few theoretical or empirical contributions regarding the causes of ethnic stratification.[1] It is the purpose of this paper to state a theory of the origin of ethnic stratification and then test it by applying the theory to an analysis of the origin of slavery in the United States. A number of recent contributions have clarified our knowledge of early Negro-white stratification[2] but there has been no attempt to analyze slavery's origin from the standpoint of a general theoretical framework. The present attempt focuses upon ethnocentrism, competition, and differential power as the key variables which together constitute the necessary and sufficient basis for the emergence and initial stabilization of ethnic stratification.

Ethnic stratification is, of course, only one type of stratification. Social stratification as a

Reprinted from Social Problems 16 (Fall, 1968): 157–72, by permission of The Society for the Study of Social Problems and the author. © The Society for the Study of Social Problems.

Author's note: It should be emphasized that the present paper attempts only to explain the *origin* of ethnic stratification. The author and Ernest Barth are currently engaged in an effort to construct a general theory of ethnic stratification which answers a number of sociological questions in addition to that of origin.

generic form of social organization is a structure of social inequality manifested via differences in prestige, power, and/or economic rewards. Ethnic stratification is a system of stratification wherein some relatively fixed group membership (e.g., race, religion, or nationality) is utilized as a major criterion for assigning social positions with their attendant differential rewards.

Prior to the emergence of ethnic stratification there must be a period of recurrent or continuous contact between the members of two or more distinct ethnic groups. This contact is an obvious requisite of ethnic stratification, but it is equally a requisite of equaltarian intergroup relations. Hence, intergroup contact is assumed as given and not treated as a theoretical element because in itself it does not provide a basis for predicting whether ethnic relations will be equalitarian or inequalitarian (i.e., stratified). Distinct ethnic groups can interact without super-subordination.[3] Factors such as the nature of the groups prior to contact, the agents of contact, and the objectives of the contacting parties affect the likelihood of an equalitarian or inequalitarian outcome but only as they are expressed through the necessary and sufficient variables.[4]

The Theory and Its Elements

In contrast to intergroup contact *per se*, the presence of ethnocentrism, competition, and differential power provides a firm basis for predicting the emergence of ethnic stratification. Conversely, the absence of any one or more of these three elements means that ethnic stratification will not emerge. This is the essence of our theory. Each of the three elements is a variable but for present purposes they will be treated as attributes because our knowledge is not sufficiently precise to allow us to say what degrees of ethnocentrism, competition, and differential power are necessary to generate ethnic stratification. Recognition of the crucial importance of the three may stimulate greater efforts to precisely measure each of them. We shall examine each in turn.

Ethnocentrism is a universal characteristic of autonomous societies or ethnic groups. As introduced by Sumner the concept refers to that ". . . view of things in which one's own group is the center of everything, and all others are scaled and rated with reference to it."[5] From this perspective the values of the in-group are equated with abstract, universal standards of morality and the practices of the in-group are exalted as better or more "natural" than those of any out-group. Such an orientation is essentially a matter of in-group glorification and not of hostility toward any specific out-group. Nevertheless, an inevitable consequence of ethnocentrism is the rejection or downgrading of all out-groups to a greater or lesser degree as a function of the extent to which they differ from the in-group. The greater the difference the lower will be the relative rank of any given out-group, but any difference at all is grounds for negative evaluation.[6] Hence, English and Canadian immigrants rank very high relative to other out-groups in American society *but* they still rank below old American WASPs.[7]

Ethocentrism is expressed in a variety of ways including mythology, condescension, and a double standard of morality in social relations. Becker has labeled this double standard a "dual ethic" in which in-group standards apply only to transactions with members of the in-group.[8] The outsider is viewed as fair game. Hence, intergroup economic relations are characterized by exploitation. Similarly, sexual relations between members of different groups are commonplace even when intermarriage is rare or prohibited entirely. The practice of endogamy is itself a manifestation of and, simultaneously, a means of reinforcing ethnocentrism. Endogamy is, indeed, an indication that ethnocentrism is present in sufficient degree for ethnic stratification to emerge.[9]

Insofar as distinct ethnic groups maintain their autonomy, mutual ethnocentrism will be preserved. Thus Indians in the Americas did not automatically surrender their ethnocentrism in the face of European technological and scientific superiority. Indeed, if the cultural strengths (including technology) of the out-group are not relevant to the values and goals of the in-group they will, by the very nature of ethnocentrism, be negatively defined. This is well illustrated in the reply (allegedly) addressed to the Virginia Commission in 1744 when it offered to educate six Indian youths at William and Mary:

> Several of our young people were formerly brought up at Colleges of the Northern Provinces; they were instructed in all your sciences; but when they came back to us, they were bad runners, ignorant of every means of living in the woods, unable to bear either cold or hunger, knew neither how to build a cabin, take a deer or kill an enemy, spoke our language imperfectly, were therefore neither fit for hunters, warriors, or counsellors; they were totally good for nothing. We are, however, not the less obliged by your kind offer, though we decline accepting it; and to show our grateful Sense of it, if the Gentlemen of Virginia will send us a Dozen of their Sons we will take great care of their education, instruct them in all we know, and make Men of them.[10]

Ethnocentrism in itself need not lead to either interethnic conflict or ethnic stratification, however. The Tungus and Cossacks have lived in peace as politically independent but economically interdependent societies for several centuries. The groups remain racially and culturally dissimilar and each is characterized by a general ethnocentric preference for the in-group. This conflict potential is neutralized by mutual respect and admission by each that the other is superior in certain specific respects, by the existence of some shared values and interests, and by the absence of competition due to economic complementarity and low population density.[11]

The presence of competition, structured along ethnic lines, is an additional prerequisite for the emergence of ethnic stratification. Antonovsky has suggested that a discriminatory system of social relations requires both shared goals and scarcity of rewards,[12] and competition here refers to the interaction between two or more social units striving to achieve *the same scarce goal* (e.g., land or prestige). In the absence of shared goals members of the various ethnic groups involved in the contact situation would have, in the extreme case, mutually exclusive or nonoverlapping value hierarchies. If one group is not striving for a given goal, this reduces the likelihood of discrimination partly because members of that group are unlikely to be perceived as competitors for the goal. In addition, the indifference of one group toward the goal in effect reduces scarcity—i.e., fewer seekers enhance the probability of goal attainment by any one seeker. However, if the goal is still defined as scarce by members of one group they may seek to establish ethnic stratification in order to effectively exploit the labor of the indifferent group and thereby maximize goal attainment. In such a situation the labor (or other utility) of the indifferent group may be said to be the real object of competition. In any event the perceived scarcity of a socially valued goal is crucial and will stimulate the emergence of ethnic stratification unless each group perceives the other as: 1) disinterested in the relevant goal, *and* 2) nonutilitarian with respect to its own attainment of the goal.

In actuality the various goals of two groups involved in stable, complex interaction will invariably overlap to some degree and hence the likelihood of ethnic stratification is a function of the arena of competition. The arena includes the shared objects(s) sought, the terms of the competition, and the relative adaptability of the groups involved.[13] Regarding the objects (or goals) of competition the greater the number of objects subject to competition, the more intense the competition. Moreover, as Wagley and Harris observe, "It is important to know the objects of competition, for it would seem that the more vital or valuable the resource over which there is competition, the more intense is the conflict between the groups."[14] Barring total annihilation of one of the groups, these points can be extended to state that the more intense the competition or conflict the greater the likelihood—other things being equal—

that it will culminate in a system of ethnic stratification. In other words, the number and significance of the scarce, common goals sought determine the degree of competition which in turn significantly affects the probability that ethnic stratification will emerge.

The terms of the competition may greatly alter the probability of ethnic stratification, however, regardless of the intensity of the competition. The retention of a set of values or rules which effectively regulates—or moderates—ethnic interrelations is of particularly crucial significance. If a framework of regulative values fails to emerge, or breaks down, each group may seek to deny the other(s) the right to compete with the result that overt conflict emerges and culminates in annihilation, expulsion, or total subjugation of the less powerful group. If, in contrast, regulative values develop and are retained, competition even for vital goals need not result in ethnic stratification—or least the span of stratification may be considerably constricted.[15]

Even where the groups involved are quite dissimilar culturally, the sharing of certain crucial values (e.g., religion or freedom, individualism, and equality) may be significant in preventing ethnic stratification. This appears to have been one factor in the enduring harmonious relations between the Cossacks and the Tungus. The influence of the regulative values upon the span of ethnic stratification is well illustrated by Tannenbaum's thesis regarding the differences between North American and Latin American slavery.[16] In the absence of a tradition of slavery the English had no established code prescribing the rights and duties of slaves and the racist ideology which evolved achieved its ultimate expression in the Dred Scott decision of 1857. This decision was highly consistent with the then widely held belief that the Negro "had no rights which the white man was bound to respect. . . ." By contrast the Iberian code accorded certain rights to the Latin American slave (including the right to own property and to purchase his freedom) which greatly restricted the extent of inequality between free man and slave.[17]

In addition to the regulative values, the structural opportunities for or barriers to upward mobility which are present in the society may affect the emergence and span of ethnic stratification.

Social structural barriers such as a static, nonexpanding economy are a significant part of the terms of competition and they may be more decisive than the regulative values as regards the duration of the system. Finally, along with the goals and the terms of competition, the relative adaptive capacity of the groups involved is an aspect of competition which significantly affects the emergence of ethnic stratification.

Wagley and Harris assume that ethnic stratification is given and focus their analysis on the adaptive capacity of *the minority group* in terms of its effect upon the span and the duration of ethnic stratification. Thus they view adaptive capacity as:

> those elements of a minority's cultural heritage which provide it with a basis for competing more or less effectively with the dominant group, which afford protection against exploitation, which stimulate or retard its adaptation to the total social environment, and which facilitate or hinder its upward advance through the socioeconomic hierarchy.[18]

We shall apply the concept to an earlier point in the intergroup process—i.e., prior to the emergence of ethnic stratification—by broadening it to refer to those aspects of any ethnic group's sociocultural heritage which affect its adjustment to a given social and physical environment. The group with the greater adaptive capacity is apt to emerge as the dominant group[19] while the other groups are subordinated to a greater or lesser degree—i.e., the span of the stratification system will be great or slight—dependent upon the extent of their adaptive capacity relative to that of the emergent dominant group.

The duration, as well as the origin and span, of ethnic stratification will be markedly influenced by adaptive capacity. Once a people have become a minority, flexibility on their part is essential if they are to efficiently adjust and effectively compete within the established system of ethnic stratification and thereby facilitate achievement of equality. Sociocultural patterns are invariably altered by changing life conditions. However, groups vary in the alacrity with which they respond to changing conditions. A flexible minority group may facilitate the achievement of equality or even dominance by readily accepting modifications of their heritage which will promote efficient adaption to their subordination and to subsequent changes in life conditions.

Competition and ethnocentrism do not provide a sufficient explanation for the emergence of ethnic stratification. Highly ethnocentric groups involved in competition for vital objects will not generate ethnic stratification unless they are of such unequal power that one is able to impose its will upon the other.[20] Inequality of power is the defining characteristic of dominant and minority groups, and Lenski maintains that differential power is the foundation element in the genesis of any stratification system.[21] In any event differential power is absolutely essential to the emergence of ethnic stratification and the greater the differential the greater the span and durability of the system, other things being equal.

Technically, power is a component of adaptive capacity as Wagley and Harris imply in their definition by referring to "protection against exploitation." Nevertheless, differential power exerts an effect independent of adaptive capacity in general and is of such crucial relevance for ethnic stratification as to warrant its being singled out as a third major causal variable. The necessity of treating it as a distinct variable is simply demonstrated by consideration of those historical cases where one group has the greater adaptive capacity in general but is subordinated because another group has greater (military) power. The Dravidians overrun by the Ayrans in ancient India and the Manchu conquest of China are illustrative cases.[22]

Unless the ethnic groups involved are unequal in power, intergroup relations will be characterized by conflict, symbiosis, or a pluralist equilibrium. Given intergroup competition, however, symbiosis is unlikely and conflict and pluralism are inevitably unstable. Any slight change in the existing balance of power may be sufficient to establish the temporary dominance of one group and this can be utilized to allow the emerging dominant group to perpetuate and enhance its position.[23]

Once dominance is established the group in power takes all necessary steps to restrict the now subordinated groups, thereby hampering their effectiveness as competitors,[24] and to institutionalize the emerging distribution of rewards and opportunities. Hence, since power tends to beget power, a slight initial alteration in the distribution of power can become the basis of a stable inequalitarian system.

We have now elaborated the central concepts and propositions of a theory of the emergence and initial stabilization of ethnic stratification. The theory can be summarized as follows. When distinct ethnic groups are brought into sustained contact (via migration, the emergence and expansion of the state, or internal differentiation of a previously homogeneous group), ethnic stratification will invariably follow if—and only if—the groups are characterized by a significant degree of ethnocentrism, competition, *and* differential power. Without ethnocentrism the groups would quickly merge and competition would not be structured along ethnic lines. Without competition there would be no motivation or rationale for instituting stratification along ethnic lines. Without differential power it would simply be impossible for one group to achieve dominance and impose subordination to its will and ideals upon the other(s).

The necessity of differential power is incontestable but it could be argued that neither competition or ethnocentrism is dispensable. For example, perhaps extreme ethnocentrism independent of competition is sufficient motive for seeking to impose ethnic stratification. Certainly ethnocentrism could encourage efforts to promote continued sharp differentiation, but it would not by itself motivate stratification unless we assume the existence of a *need* for dominance or aggression. Conversely, given sociocultural differences, one group may be better prepared for and therefore able to more effectively exploit a given environment. Hence, this group would become economically dominant and might then perceive and pursue the advantages (especially economic) of ethnic stratification quite independent of ethnocentrism. On the other hand, while differential power and competition alone are clearly sufficient to generate stratification, a low degree of ethnocentrism could readily forestall *ethnic* stratification by permitting assimilation and thereby eliminating differential adaptive capacity. Ethnocentrism undeniably heightens awareness of ethnicity and thereby promotes the formation and retention of

ethnic competition, but the crucial question is whether or not some specified degree of ethnocentrism is *essential* to the emergence of ethnic stratification. Since autonomous ethnic groups are invariably ethnocentric, the answer awaits more precise measures of ethnocentrism which will allow us to test hypotheses specifying the necessary degree of ethnocentrism.[25]

Given the present state of knowledge it seems advisable to retain both competition and ethnocentrism, as well as differential power, as integral elements of the theory. Our next objective, then, is to provide an initial test of the theory by applying it to an analysis of the genesis of slavery in the seventeenth century mainland North American colonies.

The Origin of American Slavery

There is a growing consensus among historians of slavery in the United States that Negroes were not initially slaves but that they were gradually reduced to a position of chattel slavery over several decades.[26] The historical record regarding their initial status is so vague and incomplete, however, that it is impossible to assert with finality that their status was initially no different from that of non-Negro indentured servants.[27] Moreover, while there is agreement that the statutory establishment of slavery was not widespread until the 1660's, there is disagreement regarding slavery's emergence in actual practice. The Handlins maintain that "The status of Negroes was that of servants; and so they were identified and treated down to the 1660's."[28] Degler and Jordan argue that this conclusion is not adequately documented and cite evidence indicating that some Negroes were slaves as early as 1640.[29]

Our central concern is to relate existing historical research to the theory elaborated above, *not* to attempt original historical research intended to resolve the controversy regarding the nature and extent of the initial status differences (if any) between white and Negro bondsmen. However, two findings emerging from the controversy are basic to our concern: 1) although the terms servant and slave were frequently used interchangeably, whites were never slaves in the sense of serving for life and conveying a like obligation to their offspring; and 2) many Negroes were not slaves in this sense at least as late as the 1660's. Concomitantly with the Negroes' descent to slavery, white servants gained increasingly liberal terms of indenture and, ultimately, freedom. The origin of slavery for the one group and the growth of freedom for the other are explicable in terms of our theory as a function of differences in ethnocentrism, the arena of competition, and power via-à-vis the dominant group or class.[30]

Degler argues that the status of the Negro evolved in a framework of discrimination and therefore, "The important point is not the evolution of the legal status of the slave, but the fact that discriminatory legislation regarding the Negro long preceded any legal definition of slavery."[31] The first question then becomes one of explaining this differential treatment which foreshadowed the descent to slavery. A major element in the answer is implied by the Handlins' observation that "The rudeness of the Negroes' manners, the strangeness of their languages, the difficulty of communicating to them English notions of morality and proper behavior occasioned sporadic laws to regulate their conduct."[32] By itself this implies a contradiction of their basic thesis that Negro and white indentured servants were treated similarly prior to 1660. They maintain, however, that there was nothing unique nor decisive in this differential treatment of Negroes, for such was also accorded various Caucasian outgroups in this period.[33] While Jordan dismisses the Handlins' evidence as largely irrelevant to the point and Degler feels that it is insufficient, Degler acknowledges that "Even Irishmen, who were white, Christian, and European, were held to be literally 'beyond the Pale,' and some were even referred to as 'slaves'."[34] Nevertheless, Degler contends that the overall evidence justifies his conclusion that Negroes were generally accorded a lower position than any white, bound or free.

That the English made status distinctions between various out-groups is precisely what one would expect, however, given the nature of ethnocentrism. The degree of ethnocentric rejection is primarily a function of the degree of difference, and Negroes were markedly different from the dominant English in color, nationality, language, religion, and other aspects of culture.[35] The differential treatment of Negroes was by no means entirely due to a specifically anti-Negro *color* prejudice. Indeed, color was not initially the most important factor in determining the relative status of Negroes; rather, the fact that they were non-Christain was of major significance.[36] Although beginning to lose its preeminence, religion was still the central institution of society in the seventeenth century and religious prejudice toward non-Christians or heathens was widespread. The priority of religious over color prejudice is amply demonstrated by analysis of the early laws and court decisions pertaining to Negro-white sexual relations. These sources explicitly reveal greater concern with Christian-non-Christian than with white-Negro unions.[37] During and after the 1660's laws regulating racial intermarriage arose but for some time their emphasis was generally, if not invariably, upon religion, nationality, or some basis of differentiation other than race *per se*. For example, a Maryland law of 1681 described marriages of white women with Negroes as lascivious and "to the disgrace not only of the English but also [sic] of many *other Christian* Nations."[38] Moreover, the laws against Negro-white marriage seem to have been rooted much more in economic considerations than they were in any concern for white racial purity.[39] In short, it was not a simple color prejudice but a marked degree of ethnocentrism, rooted in a multitude of salient differences, which combined with competition and differential power to reduce Negroes to the status of slaves.[40]

Degler has noted that Negroes initially lacked a status in North America and thus almost any kind of status could have been worked out.[41] Given a different competitive arena, a more favorable status blurring the sharp ethnic distinctions could have evolved. However, as the demand for labor in an expanding economy began to exceed the supply, interest in lengthening the term of indenture arose.[42] This narrow economic explanation of the origin of slavery has been challenged on the grounds that slavery appeared equally early in the Northern colonies although there were too few Negroes there to be of economic significance.[43] This seemingly decisive point is largely mitigated by two considerations.

First, in the other colonies it was precisely *the few* who did own slaves who were not only motivated by vested interests but were also the men of means and local power most able to secure a firm legal basis for slavery.[44] The distribution of power and motivation was undoubtedly similar and led to the same consequences in New England. For the individual retainer of Negro servants the factual and legal redefinition of Negroes as chattel constitutes a vital economic interest whether or not the number of slaves is sufficient to vitally affect the economy of the colony. Our knowledge of the role of the elite in the establishment of community mores suggests that this constitutes at least a partial explanation of the Northern laws.[45] In addition, the markedly smaller number of Negroes in the North might account for the fact that "although enactments in the Northern colonies recognized the legality of lifetime servitude, no effort was made to require all Negroes to be placed in that condition."[46] We surmise that the laws were passed at the behest of a few powerful individuals who had relatively many Negro servants and were indifferent to the status of Negroes in general so long as their own vested interests were protected.

The explanation for the more all-encompassing laws of the Southern colonies is rooted in the greater homogeneity of interests of the Southern elite. In contrast to the Northern situation, the men of power in the Southern colonies were predominantly planters who were unified in their need for large numbers of slaves. The margin of profit in agricultural production for the commercial market was such that the small landholder could not compete and the costs of training and the limitations on control (by the planter) which were associated with indentured labor made profitable exploitation of such labor increasingly difficult.[47] Hence, it was not the need for labor *per se* which was critical for the establishment of the comprehensive Southern slave system but rather the requirements of the emerging economic system for a particular kind of labor. In short, the Southern power elite uniformly needed slave labor while only certain men of power shared this need in the North and hence the latter advocated slave laws but lacked the power (or did not feel the need) to secure the all-encompassing laws characteristic of the Southern colonies.

There is a second major consideration in explaining the existence of Northern slavery. Men do not compete only for economic ends. They also compete for prestige and many lesser objects, and there is ample basis for suggesting that prestige competition was a significant factor in the institutionalization of slavery, North and South. Degler calls attention to the prestige motive when he discusses the efforts to establish a feudal aristocracy in seventeenth century New York, Maryland, and the Carolinas. He concludes that these efforts failed because the manor was "dependent upon the scarcity of land."[48] The failure of feudal aristocracy in no way denies the fundamental human desire for success or prestige. Indeed, this failure opened the society. It emphasized success and mobility for "it meant that wealth, rather than family or tradition, would be the primary determinant of social stratification."[49] Although the stress was on economic success, there were other gains associated with slavery to console those who did not achieve wealth. The desire for social prestige derivable from "membership in a superior caste" undoubtedly provided motivation and support for slavery among both Northern and Southern whites, slaveholders and nonslaveholders.[50]

The prestige advantage of slavery would have been partially undercut, especially for nonslaveholders, by enslavement of white bondsmen, but it is doubtful that this was a significant factor in their successfully eluding hereditary bondage. Rather the differential treatment of white and Negro bondsmen, ultimately indisputable and probably present from the very beginning, is largely attributable to differences in ethnocentrism and relative power. There was little or no ethnocentric rejection of the majority of white bondsmen during the seventeeth century because most of them were English.[51] Moreover, even the detested Irish and other non-English white servants were culturally and physically much more similar to the English planters than were the Africans. Hence, the planters clearly preferred white bondsmen until the advantages of slavery became increasingly apparent in the latter half of the seventeenth century.[52]

The increasing demand for labor after the mid-seventeenth century had divergent consequences for whites and blacks. The colonists became increasingly concerned to encourage immigration by counteracting "the widespread reports in England and Scotland that servants were harshly treated and bound in perpetual slavery" and by enacting "legislation designed to improve servants' conditions and to enlarge the prospect of a meaningful release, a release that was not the start of a new period of servitude, but of life as a free-man and landowner."[53] These improvements curtailed the exploitation of white servants without directly affecting the status of the Africans.

> Farthest removed from the English, least desired, [the Negro] communicated with no friends who might be deterred from following. *Since his coming was involuntary, nothing that happened to him would increase or decrease his numbers.* To raise the status of Europeans by shortening their terms would ultimately increase the available hands by inducing their compatriots to emigrate; to reduce the Negro's term would produce an immediate loss and no ultimate gain. By mid-century the servitude of Negroes seems generally lengthier than that of whites; and thereafter, the consciousness dawns that the blacks will toil for the whole of their lives. . . .[54]

The planters and emerging agrarian capitalism were unconstrained in a planter-dominated society with no traditional institutions to exert limits. In this context even the common law tradition helped promote slavery.[55]

Ethnocentrism set the Negroes apart but their almost total lack of power and effective spokesmen, in contrast to white indentured servants, was decisive in their enslavement. Harris speaks directly to the issue and underscores the significance of (organized) power for the emergence of slavery:

> The facts of life in the New World were such . . . that Negroes, being the most defenseless of all the immigrant groups, were discriminated against and exploited more than any others. . . . Judging from the very nasty treatment suffered by the white indentured servants, it was obviously not sentiment which prevented the Virginia planters from enslaving their fellow Englishmen. They undoubtedly would have done so had they been able to get away with it. But such a policy was out of the question as long as there was a King and a Parliament in England.[56]

The Negroes, in short, did not have any organized external government capable of influencing the situation in their favor.[57] Moreover, "there was no one in England or in the colonies to pressure for the curtailment of the Negro's servitude or to fight for his future."[58]

The Negroes' capacity to adapt to the situation and effectively protest in their own behalf was greatly hampered by their cultural diversity and lack of unification. They did not think of themselves as "a kind." They did not subjectively share a common identity and thus they lacked the group solidarity necessary to effectively "act as a unit in competition with other groups."[59] Consciousness of shared fate is essential to effective unified action but it generally develops only gradually as the members of a particular social category realize that they are being treated alike despite their differences. "People who find themselves set apart eventually come to recognize their common interests," but for those who share a subordinate position common identification usually emerges "only after repeated experiences of denial and humiliation."[60] The absence of a shared identification among seventeeth century Negroes reflected the absence of a shared heritage from which to construct identity, draw strength, and organize protest. Hence, Negroes were easily enslaved and reduced to the status of chattel. This point merits elaboration.

We have defined adaptive capacity in terms of a group's sociocultural heritage as it affects adjustment to the environment. Efficient adaptation may require the members of a group to modify or discard a great deal of their heritage. A number of factors, including ethnocentrism and the centrality of the values and social structures requiring modification, affect willingness to alter an established way of life.[61] Even given a high degree of willingness, however, many groups simply have not possessed the cultural complexity or social structural similarity to the dominant group necessary to efficient adaptation. Many Brazilian and United States Indian tribes, for example, simply have not had the knowledge (e.g., of writing, money, markets, etc.) or the structural similarity to their conquerors (e.g., as regards the division of labor) necessary to protect themselves from exploitation and to achieve a viable status in an emerging multiethnic society.[62]

By comparison with most New World Indians the sociocultural heritage of the Africans was remarkably favorable to efficient adaptation.[63] However, the discriminatory framework within which white-Negro relations developed in the seventeenth century ultimately far outweighed the cultural advantages of the Negroes vis-à-vis the Indians in the race for status.[64] The Negroes from any given culture were widely dispersed and their capacity to adapt *as a group* was thereby shattered. Like the Negroes, the Indians were diverse culturally but they retained their cultural heritage and social solidarity, and they were more likely to resist slavery because of the much greater probability of reunion with their people following escape. Hence, Negroes were preferred over Indians as slaves both because their cultural background had better prepared them for the slave's role in the plantation system (thus enhancing the profits of the planters) and because they lacked the continuing cultural and group support which enabled the Indians to effectively resist slavery.[65] By the time the Africans acquired the dominant English culture and social patterns *and* a sense of shared fate, their inability to work out a more favorable adaptation was assured by the now established distribution of power and by the socialization processes facilitating acceptance of the role of slave.[66]

Conclusion

We conclude that ethnocentrism, competition, and differential power provide a comprehensive explanation of the origin of slavery in the seventeenth century English colonies. The Negroes were clearly more different from the English colonists than any other group (*except* the Indians) by almost any criterion, physical or cultural, that might be selected as a basis of social differentiation. Hence, the Negroes were the object of a relatively intense ethnocentric rejection from the beginning. The opportunity for great mobility characteristic of a frontier society created an arena of competition which dovetailed with this ethnocentrism. Labor, utilized to achieve wealth, and prestige were the primary objects of this competition. These goals were particularly manifest in the Southern colonies, but our analysis provides a rationale for the operation of the same goals as sources of motivation to institutionalize slavery in the Northern colonies also.

The terms of the competition for the Negro's labor are implicit in the evolving pattern of differential treatment of white and Negro bondsmen prior to slavery and in the precarious position of free Negroes. As slavery became institutionalized the moral, religious, and legal values of the society were increasingly integrated to form a highly consistent complex which acknowledged no evil in the "peculiar institution."[67] Simultaneously, Negroes were denied any opportunity to escape their position of lifetime, inheritable servitude. Only by the grace of a generous master, not by any act of his own, could a slave achieve freedom and, moreover, there were "various legal structures aimed at impeding or discouraging the process of private manumission."[68] The rigidity of the "peculiar institution" was fixed before the Negroes acquired sufficient common culture, sense of shared fate, and identity to be able to effectively challenge the system. This lack of unity was a major determinant of the Africans' poor adaptive capacity as a group. They lacked the social solidarity and common cultural resources essential to organized resistance and thus in the absence of intervention by a powerful external ally they were highly vulnerable to exploitation.

The operation of the three key factors is well summarized by Stampp:

> Neither the provisions of their charters nor the policy of the English government limited the power of colonial legislatures to control Negro labor as they saw fit. . . . Their unprotected condition encouraged the trend toward special treatment, and their physical and cultural differences provided handy excuses to justify it. . . . [t]he landholders' growing appreciation of the advantages of slavery over the older forms of servitude gave a powerful impetus to the growth of the new labor system.[69]

In short, the present theory stresses that *given* ethnocentrism, the Negroes' lack of power, and the dynamic arena of competition in which they were located, their ultimate enslavement was inevitable. The next task is to test the theory further, incorporating modifications as necessary, by analyzing subsequent accommodations in the pattern of race relations in the United States and by analyzing the emergence of various patterns of ethnic stratification in other places and eras.

ENDNOTES

1. The same observation regarding social stratification in general has recently been made by Gerhard Lenski, *Power and Privilege*, New York: McGraw-Hill, 1966, p. ix.

2. See Joseph Boskin, "Race Relations in Seventeenth Century America: The Problem of the Origins of Negro Slavery," *Sociology and Social Research*, 49 (July, 1965), pp. 446–455, including references cited therein; and David B. Davis, *The Problem of Slavery in Western Culture*, Ithaca: Cornell U., 1966.

3. A classic example is provided by Ethel John Lindgren, "An Example of Culture Contact Without Conflict: Reindeer Tungus and Cossacks of Northwest Manchuria," *American Anthropologist*, 40 (October–December, 1938), pp. 605–621.

4. The relevance of precontact and of the nature and objectives of the contacting agents for the course of intergroup relations has been discussed by various scholars including Edward B. Reuter in his editor's "Introduction" to *Race and Culture Contacts*, New York: McGraw-Hill, 1934, pp. 1–18; and Clarence E. Glick, "Social Roles and Types in Race Relations in Andrew W. Lind, editor, *Race Relations in World Perspective*, Honolulu: U. of Hawaii, 1955, pp. 239–262.

5. William G. Summer, *Folkways*, Boston: Ginn, 1940, p. 13. The essence of ethnocentrism is well conveyed by Catton's observation that "Ethnocentrism makes us see out-group behavior as deviation from in-group mores rather than as adherence to out-group mores." William R. Catton, Jr., "The Development of Sociological Thought" in Robert E. L. Faris, editor, *Handbook of Modern Sociology*, Chicago: Rand McNally, 1964, p. 930.

6. Williams observes that "in various *particular* ways an out-group may be seen as superior" insofar as its members excel in performance vis-à-vis certain norms that the two groups hold in common (e.g., sobriety or craftsmanship in the production of a particular commodity). Robin M. Williams, Jr., *Strangers Next Door*, Englewood Cliffs, N.J.: Prentice-Hall, 1964, p. 22 (emphasis added). A similar point is made by Marc J. Swartz, "Negative Ethnocentrism," *Journal of Conflict Resolution*, 5 (March, 1961), pp. 75–81. It is highly unlikely, however, that the out-group will be so consistently objectively superior in the realm of shared values as to be seen as generally superior to the in-group unless the in-group is subordinate to or highly dependent upon the out-group.

7. Emory S. Bogardus, *Social Distance*, Yellow Springs: Antioch, 1959.

8. Howard P. Becker, *Man in Reciprocity*, New York: Praeger, 1956, Ch. 15.

9. Endogamy is an overly stringent index of the degree of ethnocentrism essential to ethnic stratification and is not itself a prerequisite of the emergence of ethnic stratification. However, where endogamy does not precede ethnic stratification, it is a seemingly invariable consequence. Compare this position with that of Charles Wagley and Marvin Harris who treat ethnocentrism and endogamy as independent structural requisites of intergroup hostility and conflict. See *Minorities in the New World*, New York; Columbia, 1958, pp. 256–263.

10. Quoted in T. Walker Wallbank and Alastair M. Taylor, *Civilization: Past and Present*, Chicago: Scott, Foresman, 1949, rev. ed., Vol. 1. pp. 559–560. The offer and counter-offer also provide an excellent illustration of mutual ethnocentrism.

11. Lindgren, *op. cit.*

12. Aaron Antonovsky, "The Social Meaning of Discrimination," *Phylon*, 21 (Spring, 1960), pp. 81–95.

13. This analysis of the arena of competition is a modification of the analysis by Wagley and Harris, *op. cit.*, esp. pp. 263–264. These authors limit the concept "arena" to the objects sought *and* the regulative values which determine opportunity to compete and then partly confound their components by including the regulative values, along with adaptive capacity and the instruments necessary to compete, as part of the "terms" of competition.

14. *Ibid.*, p. 263. They suggest that competition for scarce subsistence goals will produce more intense conflict than competition for prestige symbols or other culturally defined goals.

15. Discussing the ideological aspect of intergroup relations, Wagley and Harris note that equalitiarian creeds have generally not been effective in preventing ethnic stratification. *Ibid.*, pp. 280 ff. The operation of ethnocentrism makes it very easy for the boundaries of the in-group to become the boundaries of adherence to group values.

16. Frank Tannenbaum, *Slave and Citizen: The Negro in the Americas*, New York: Random House, 1963.

17. *Ibid.*, esp. pp. 49 ff. Marvin Harris has criticized Tannenbaum's thesis arguing that the rights prescribed by the Iberian code were largely illusory and that there is no certainty that *slaves* were treated better in Latin America. Harris in turn provides a functional (economic necessity) explanation for the historical difference in treatment of *free* Negroes in the two continents. See Marvin Harris, *Patterns of Race in the Americas*, New York: Walker, 1964, esp. Chs. 6 and 7.

18. Wagley and Harris, *op. cit.*, p. 264.

19. This point is explicitly made by Tamotsu Shibutani and Kian M. Kwan, *Ethnic Stratification: A Comparative Approach*, New York: Macmillan, 1965, p. 147; see also Ch. 9.

20. This point is made by Antonovsky, *op. cit.*, esp. p. 82, and implied by Wagley and Harris in their discussion of the role of the state in the formation of

minority groups, *op. cit.*, esp. pp. 240–244. Stanley Lieberson's recent modification of Park's cycle theory of race relations also emphasizes the importance of differential power as a determinant of the outcome of intergroup contacts. See "A Societal Theory of Race and Ethnic Relations," *American Sociological Review*, 26 (December, 1961), pp. 902–910.

21. Lenski, *op. cit.*, esp. Ch. 3.

22. See Wallbank and Taylor, *op. cit.*, p. 95; and Shibutani and Kwan, *op. cit.*, pp. 129–130.

23. See *ibid.*, esp. Chs. 6, 9, and 12; and Richard A. Schermerhorn, *Society and Power*, New York: Random House, 1961, pp. 18–26.

24. Shibutani and Kwan observe that dominance rests upon victory in the competitive process and that competition between groups is eliminated or greatly reduced once a system of ethnic stratification is stabilized, *op. cit.*, pp. 146 and 235, and Ch. 12. The extent to which competition is actually stifled is highly variable, however, as Wagley and Harris note in their discussion of minority adaptive capacity and the terms of competition, *op. cit.*, pp. 263 ff.

25. The issue is further complicated by the fact that the necessary degree of any one of the three elements may vary as a function of the other two.

26. The main relevant references in the recent literature include Carl N. Degler, *Out of Our Past*, New York: Harper and Row, 1959 and "Slavery and the Genesis of American Race Prejudice," *Comparative Studies in Society and History*, 2 (October, 1959), pp. 49–66; Stanley M. Elkins, *Slavery: A Problem in American Institutional and Intellectual Life*, Chicago: U. of Chicago, 1959; Oscar and Mary F. Handlin, "Origins of the Southern Labor System," *William and Mary Quarterly*, 3rd Series, 7 (April, 1950), pp. 199–222; and Winthrop D. Jordan, "Modern Tensions and the Origins of American Slavery," *The Journal of Southern History*, 28 (February, 1962), pp. 18–30, and *White over Black*, Chapel-Hill: U. of North Carolina, 1968. See also Boskin, *op. cit.*, and "Comment" and Reply" by the Handlins and Degler in the cited volume of *Comparative Studies . . .*, pp. 488–495.

27. Jordan, *The Journal . . .*, p. 22.

28. Handlin and Handlin, *op. cit.*, p. 203.

29. Degler, *Comparative Studies . . .*, pp. 52–56 and Jordan, *The Journal . . .*, pp. 23–27 and *White over Black*, pp. 73–74. Also see Elkins, *op. cit.*, pp. 38–42 (esp. fns. 16 and 19).

30. Our primary concern is with the emergence of Negro slavery but the theory also explains how white bondsmen avoided slavery. Their position vis-à-vis the dominant English was characterized by a different "value" of at least two of the key variables.

31. Degler, *Out of Our Past*, p. 35. Bear in mind, however, that slavery was not initially institutionalized in law or in the mores.

32. Handlin and Handlin, *op. cit.*, pp. 208–209.

33. *Ibid.* They note that "It is not necessary to resort to racist assumptions to account for such measures; . . . [for immigrants in a strange environment] longed . . . for the company of familiar men and singled out to be welcomed those who were most like themselves." See pp. 207–211 and 214.

34. Jordan, *The Journal . . .*, esp. pp. 27 (fn 29) and 29 (fn. 34); and Degler, *Out of Our Past*, p. 30.

35. Only the aboriginal Indians were different from the English colonists to a comparable degree and they were likewise severely dealt with via a policy of exclusion and annihilation after attempts at enslavement failed. See Boskin, *op. cit.*, p. 453; and Jordan, *White over Black*, pp. 85–92.

36. The priority of religious over racial prejudice and discrimination in the early seventeenth century is noted in *ibid.*, pp. 97–98 and by Edgar J. McManus, *A History of Negro Slavery in New York*, Syracuse: Syracuse U., 1966, esp. pp. 11–12.

37. Jordan, *The Journal . . .*, p. 28 and *White over Black*, pp. 78–80.

38. Quoted in *ibid.*, pp. 79–80 (emphasis added). Also see pp. 93–97, however, where Jordan stresses the necessity of carefully interpreting the label "Christian."

39. See Handlin and Handlin, *op. cit.*, pp. 213–216; and W. D. Zabel, "Interracial Marriage and the Law," *The Atlantic* (October, 1965), pp. 75–79.

40. The distinction between ethnocentrism (the rejection of out-groups *in general* as a function of in-group glorification) and prejudice (hostility toward the members of a *specific* group because they are members of that group) is crucial to the controversy regarding the direction of causality between discrimination, slavery, and prejudice. Undoubtedly these variables are mutually causal to some extent but Harris, *op. cit.*, esp. pp. 67–70, presents evidence that prejudice is primarily a consequence and is of minor importance as a cause of slavery.

41. Degler, *Comparative Studies . . .*, p. 51. See also Boskin, *op. cit.*, pp. 449 and 454 (esp. fn. 14); Elkins, *op. cit.*, pp. 39–42 (esp. fn. 16); and Kenneth M. Stampp, *The Peculiar Institution*, New York: Knopf, 1956, p. 21. The original indeterminancy of the Negroes' status is reminiscent of Blumer's "sense of group position" theory of prejudice and, in light of Blumers' theory, is consistent with the belief that there was no widespread prejudice toward Negroes prior to the institutionalization of slavery. See Herbert Blumer, "Race Prejudice as a Sense of Group Position," *Pacific Sociological Review*, 1 (Spring, 1958), pp. 3–7.

42. Handlin and Handlin, *op. cit.*, p. 210. Differential power made this tactic as suitable to the situation of Negro bondsmen as it was unsuitable in regard to white bondsmen.

43. Degler acknowledges that the importance of

perpetuating a labor force indispensable to the economy later became a crucial support of slavery but he denies that the need for labor explains the origin of slavery. His explanation stresses prior discrimination which, in the terms of the present theory, was rooted in ethnocentrism and differential power. See *Comparative Studies . . .* , including the "Reply" to the Handlins, "Comment"; and *Out of Our Past*, pp. 35–38 and 162–168.

44. Elkins, *op. cit.*, pp. 45 (esp. fn. 26) and 48.

45. Historical precedent is provided by the finding that "The vagrancy laws emerged in order to provide the powerful landowners with a ready supply of cheap labor." See William J. Chambliss, "A Sociological Analysis of the Law of Vagrancy," *Social Problems*, 12 (Summer, 1964), pp. 67–77. Jordan, *White over Black*, pp. 67 and 69, provides evidence that the economic advantages of slavery were clearly perceived in the Northern colonies.

46. Elkins, *op. cit.*, p. 41 (fn. 19).

47. By the 1680's "The point had clearly passed when white servants could realistically, on any long-term appraisal, be considered preferable to Negro slaves." *Ibid.*, p. 48.

48. Degler, *Out of Our Past*, p. 3. Also see Hubert M. Blalock, Jr., *Toward a Theory of Minority Group Relations*, New York: Wiley, 1967, 1967, pp. 44–48.

49. Degler, *Out of Our Past*, p. 5; see also pp. 45–50. Elkins, *op. cit.*, esp. pp. 43–44, also notes the early emphasis on personal success and mobility.

50. Stampp, *op. cit.*, pp. 29–33, esp. 32–33. Also see J. D. B. DeBow, "The Interest in Slavery of the Southern Non-Slaveholder," reprinted in Eric L. McKitrick, editor, *Slavery Defended: The Views of the Old South*, Englewood Cliffs, N.J.: Prentice-Hall, 1963, pp. 169–177.

51. Stampp, *op. cit.*, p. 16; and Degler, *Out of Our Past*, pp. 50–51. Consistent with the nature of ethnocentrism, "The Irish and other aliens, less desirable, at first received longer terms. But the realization that such discrimination retarded 'the peopling of the country' led to an extension of the identical privilege to all Christians." Handlin and Handlin, *op. cit.*, pp. 210–211.

52. Elkins, *op. cit.*, pp. 40 and 48; and Handlin and Handlin, *op. cit.*, pp. 207–208.

53. *Ibid.*, p. 210.

54. *Ibid.*, p. 211 (emphasis added). That the need for labor led to improvements in the status of white servants seems very likely but Degler in *Comparative Studies . . .* effectively challenges some of the variety of evidence presented by the Handlins, *op. cit.*, pp. 210 and 213–214 and "Comment."

55. Elkins, *op. cit.*, pp. 38 (fn. 14), 42 (fn. 22), 43 and 49–52; and Jordan, *White over Black*, pp. 49–51.

56. Harris *op. cit.*, pp. 69–70.

57. The effectiveness of intervention by an external government is illustrated by the halting of Indian emigration to South Africa in the 1860's as a means of protesting "the indignities to which indentured 'coolies' were subjected in Natal, ..." See Pierre L. van den Berghe, *South Africa, A Study in Conflict*, Middletown: Wesleyan U., 1965, p. 250.

58. Boskin, *op. cit.*, p. 448. Also see Stampp, *op. cit.*, p. 22; and Elkins, *op. cit.*, pp. 49–52.

59. Shibutani and Kwan, *op. cit.*, p. 42. See also William O. Brown, "Race Consciousness Among South African Natives," *American Journal of Sociology*, 40 (March, 1935), pp. 569–581.

60. Shibutani and Kwan, *op. cit.*, Ch. 8, esp. pp. 202 and 212.

61. See the discussions in Brewton Berry, *Race and Ethnic Relations*, Boston: Houghton-Mifflin, 1965, 3rd ed., esp. pp. 147–149; Shibutani and Kwan, *op. cit.*, esp. pp. 217 f; and Wagley and Harris, *op. cit.*, pp. 40–44.

62. *Ibid.*, pp. 15–86 and 265–268.

63. *Ibid.*, p. 269; Harris, *op. cit.*, p. 14; and Stampp, *op. cit.*, pp. 13 and 23.

64. The Indians were also discriminated against but to a much lesser extent. The reasons for this differential are discussed by Jordan, *White over Black*, pp. 89–90; and Stampp, *op. cit.*, pp. 23–24.

65. Harris, *op. cit.*, pp. 14–16, an otherwise excellent summary of the factors favoring the enslavement of Negroes rather than Indians, overlooks the role of sociocultural support. The importance of this support is clearly illustrated by the South African policy of importing Asians in preference to the native Africans who strenuously resisted enslavement and forced labor. Shibutani and Kwan, *op. cit.*, p. 126. Sociocultural unity was also a significant factor in the greater threat of revolt posed by the Helots in Sparta as compared to the heterogeneous slaves in Athens. Alvin W. Gouldner, *Enter Plato*, New York: Basic Books, 1965, p. 32.

66. Shibutani and Kwan, *op. cit.*, esp. Chs. 10–12. Stampp observes that the plantation trained Negroes to be slaves, not free men, *op. cit.*, p. 12. Similarly, Wagley and Harris note that the Negroes were poorly prepared for survival in a free-market economic system even when they were emancipated, *op. cit.*, p. 269.

67. Davis asserts that while slavery has always been a source of tension, "in Western culture it was associated with certain religious and philosophical doctrines that gave it the highest sanction." *Op. cit.*, p. ix.

68. Wagley and Harris, *op. cit.*, p. 124.

69. Stampp, *op. cit.*, p. 22.

7

An American Dilemma

Gunnar Myrdal

The Negro Problem as a Moral Issue

There is a "Negro problem" in the United States and most Americans are aware of it, although it assumes varying forms and intensity in different regions of the country and among diverse groups of the American people. Americans have to react to it, politically as citizens and, where there are Negroes present in the community, privately as neighbors.

To the great majority of white Americans the Negro problem has distinctly negative connotations. It suggests something difficult to settle and equally difficult to leave alone. It is embarrassing. It makes for moral uneasiness. The very presence of the Negro in America[a]; his fate in this country through slavery, Civil War and Reconstruction; his recent career and his present status; his accommodation; his protest and his aspiration; in fact his entire biological, historical and social existence as a participant American represent to the ordinary white man in the North as well as in the South an anomaly in the very

Abridged from "Introduction," pp. 927–929, 1021–1022 in AN AMERICAN DILEMMA: THE NEGRO PROBLEM AND MODERN DEMOCRACY, Twentieth Anniversary Edition by Gunnar Myrdal, Copyright © 1944, 1962 by Harper & Row, Publishers, Inc. Reprinted by permission of Harper & Row, Publishers, Inc.

[a]The word *America* will be used in this [article] as a synonym for continental United States.

structure of American society. To many, this takes on the proportion of a menace—biological, economic, social, cultural, and, at times, political. This anxiety may be mingled with a feeling of individual and collective guilt. A few see the problem as a challenge to statesmanship. To all it is a trouble.

These and many other mutually inconsistent attitudes are blended into none too logical a scheme which, in turn, may be quite inconsistent with the wider personal, moral, religious, and civic sentiments and ideas of the Americans. Now and then, even the least sophisticated individual becomes aware of his own confusion and the contradiction in his attitudes. Occasionally he may recognize, even if only for a moment, the incongruence of his state of mind and find it so intolerable that the whole organization of his moral precepts is shaken. But most people, most of the time, suppress such threats to their moral integrity together with all of the confusion, the ambiguity, and inconsistency which lurks in the basement of man's soul. This, however, is rarely accomplished without mental strain. Out of the strain comes a sense of uneasiness and awkwardness which always seems attached to the Negro problem.

The strain is increased in democratic America by the freedom left open—even in the South, to a considerable extent—for the advocates of the Negro, his rights and welfare. All "pro-Negro"

121

forces in American society, whether organized or not, and irrespective of their wide differences in both strategy and tactics, sense that this is the situation. They all work on the national conscience. They all seek to fix everybody's attention on the suppressed moral conflict. No wonder that they are often regarded as public nuisances, or worse—even when they succeed in getting grudging concessions to Negro rights and welfare.

At this point it must be observed that America, relative to all the other branches of Western civilization, is moralistic and "moral-conscious." The ordinary American is the opposite of a cynic. He is on the average more of a believer and a defender of the faith in humanity than the rest of the Occidentals. It is a relatively important matter to him to be true to his own ideals and to carry them out in actual life. We recognize the American, wherever we meet him, as a practical idealist. Compared with members of other nations of Western civilization, the ordinary American is a rationalistic being, and there are close relations between his moralism and his rationalism. Even romanticism, transcendentalism, and mysticism tend to be, in the American culture, rational, pragmatic and optimistic. American civilization early acquired a flavor of enlightenment which has affected the ordinary American's whole personality and especially his conception of how ideas and ideals ought to "click" together. He has never developed that particular brand of tired mysticism and romanticism which finds delight in the inextricable confusion in the order of things and in ineffectuality of the human mind. He finds such leanings intellectually perverse.

These generalizations might seem venturesome and questionable to the reflective American himself, who, naturally enough, has his attention directed more on the dissimilarities than on the similarities within his culture. What is common is usually not obvious, and it never becomes striking. But to the stranger it is obvious and even striking. In the social sciences, for instance, the American has, more courageously than anywhere else on the globe, started to measure, not only human intelligence, aptitudes, and personality traits, but moral leanings and the "goodness" of communities. This man is a rationalist; he wants intellectual order in his moral set-up; he wants to pursue his own inclinations into their hidden

haunts; and he is likely to expose himself and his kind in a most undiplomatic manner.

In hasty strokes we are now depicting the essentials of the American *ethos.* This moralism and rationalism are to many of us—among them the author of this book—the glory of the nation, its youthful strength, perhaps the salvation of mankind. The analysis of this "American Creed" and its implications have an important place in our inquiry. While on the one hand, to such a moralistic and rationalistic being as the ordinary American, the Negro problem and his own confused and contradictory attitudes toward it must be disturbing; on the other hand, the very mass of unsettled problems in his heterogeneous and changing culture, and the inherited liberalistic trust that things will ultimately take care of themselves and get settled in one way or another, enable the ordinary American to live on happily, with recognized contradictions around him and within him, in a kind of bright fatalism which is unmatched in the rest of the Western world. This fatalism also belongs to the national *ethos.*

The American Negro problem is a problem in the heart of the American. It is there that the interracial tension has its focus. It is there that the decisive struggle goes on. This is the central viewpoint of this treatise. Though our study includes economic, social, and political race relations, at bottom our problem is the moral dilemma of the American—the conflict between his moral valuations on various levels of consciousness and generality. The "American Dilemma," referred to in the title of this book, is the ever-raging conflict between, on the one hand, the valuations preserved on the general plane which we shall call the "American Creed," where the American thinks, talks, and acts under the influence of high national and Christian precepts, and, on the other hand the valuations on specific planes of individual and group living, where personal and local interests; economic, social, and sexual jealousies; considerations of community prestige and conformity; group prejudice against particular persons or types of people; and all sorts of miscellaneous wants, impulses, and habits dominate his outlook.

The American philosopher, John Dewey, whose immense influence is to be explained by his rare gift for projecting faithfully the aspirations and possibilities of the culture he was born into, in the maturity of age and wisdom has written a book on *Freedom and Culture*, in which he says:

> Anything that obscures the fundamentally moral nature of the social problem is harmful, no matter whether it proceeds from the side of physical or of psychological theory. Any doctrine that eliminates or even obscures the function of choice of values and enlistment of desires and emotions in behalf of those chosen weakens personal responsibility for judgment and for action. It thus helps create the attitudes that welcome and support the totalitarian state.

We shall attempt to follow through Dewey's conception of what a social problem really is.

Valuations and Beliefs

The Negro problem in America would be of a different nature, and, indeed, would be simpler to handle scientifically, if the moral conflict raged only between valuations held by different persons and groups of persons. The essence of the moral situation is, however, that the conflicting valuations are also held by the same person. *The moral struggle goes on within people and not only between them. As people's valuations are conflicting, behavior normally becomes a moral compromise. There are no homogeneous "attitudes" behind human behavior but a mesh of struggling inclinations, interests, and ideals, some held conscious and some suppressed for long intervals but all active in bending behavior in their direction.*

The unity of a culture consists in the fact that all valuations are mutually shared in some degree. We shall find that even a poor and uneducated white person in some isolated and backward rural region in the Deep South, who is violently prejudiced against the Negro and intent upon depriving him of civic rights and human independence, has also a whole compartment in his valuation sphere housing the entire American Creed of liberty, equality, justice, and fair opportunity for everybody. He is actually also a good Christian and honestly devoted to the ideals of human brotherhood and the Golden Rule. And these more general valuations—more general in the sense that they refer to all human beings—are,

to some extent, effective in shaping his behavior. Indeed, it would be impossible to understand why the Negro does not fare worse in some regions of America if it were not constantly kept in mind that behavior is the outcome of a compromise between valuations, among which the equalitarian ideal is one. At the other end, there are few liberals, even in New England, who have not a well-furnished compartment of race prejudice, even if it is usually suppressed from conscious attention. Even the American Negroes share in this community of valuations: they have eagerly imbibed the American Creed and the revolutionary Christian teaching of common brotherhood; under closer study, they usually reveal also that they hold something of the majority prejudice against their own kind and its characteristics.

The intensities and proportions in which these conflicting valuations are present vary considerably from one American to another, and within the same individual, from one situation to another. The cultural unity of the nation consists, however, in the fact that *most Americans have most valuations in common* though they are arranged differently in the sphere of valuations of different individuals and groups and bear different intensity coefficients. This cultural unity is the indispensable basis for discussion between persons and groups. It is the floor upon which the democratic process goes on.

In America as everywhere else people agree, as an abstract proposition, that *the more general valuations—those which refer to man as such and not to any particular group or temporary situation—are morally higher.* These valuations are also given the sanction of religion and national legislation. They are incorporated into the American Creed. The other valuations—which refer to various smaller groups of mankind or to particular occasions—are commonly referred to as "irrational" or "prejudiced," sometimes even by people who express and stress them. They are defended in terms of tradition, expediency or utility.

Trying to defend their behavior to others, and primarily to themselves, people will attempt to conceal the conflict between their different valuations of what is desirable and undesirable, right or wrong, by keeping away some valuations from awareness and by focusing attention on others. For the same opportune purpose, *people will twist and mutilate their beliefs of how social reality actually is.* In our study we encounter whole systems of firmly entrenched popular beliefs concerning the Negro and his relations to the larger society, which are bluntly false and which can only be understood when we remember the opportunistic *ad hoc* purposes they serve. These "popular theories," because of the rationalizing function they serve, are heavily loaded with emotions. But people also want to be rational. Scientific truth-seeking and education are slowly rectifying the beliefs and thereby also influencing the valuations. In a rationalistic civilization it is not only that the beliefs are shaped by the valuations, but also that the valuations depend upon the beliefs.

＊　　　＊　　　＊

When we thus choose to view the Negro problem as primarily a moral issue, we are in line with popular thinking. It is as a moral issue that this problem presents itself in the daily life of ordinary people; it is a moral issue that they brood over it in their thoughtful moments. It is in terms of conflicting moral valuations that it is discussed in church and school, in the family circle, in the workshop, on the street corner, as well as in the press, over the radio, in trade union meetings, in the state legislatures, the Congress and the Supreme Court. The social scientist, in his effort to lay bare concealed truths and to become maximally useful in guiding practical and political action, is prudent when, in the approach to a problem, he sticks as closely as possible to the common man's ideas and formulations, even though he knows that further investigation will carry him into tracts uncharted in the popular consciousness. There is a pragmatic common sense in people's ideas about themselves and their worries, which we cannot afford to miss when we start out to explore social reality. Otherwise we are often too easily distracted by our learned arbitrariness and our pet theories, concepts, and hypotheses, not to mention our barbarous terminology, which we generally are tempted to mistake for something more than mere words. *Throughout this study we will constantly take our starting point in the ordinary man's own ideas, doctrines, theories and mental constructs.*

In approaching the Negro problem as primarily a moral issue of conflicting valuations, it is not implied, of course, that ours is the prerogative of pronouncing on *a priori* grounds which values are "right" and which are "wrong." In fact, such judgments are out of the realm of social science, and will not be attempted in this inquiry. Our investigation will naturally be an analysis *of* morals and not *in* morals. In so far as we make our own judgments of value, they will be based on explicitly stated value premises, selected from among those valuations actually observed as existing in the minds of the white and Negro Americans and tested as to their social and political relevance and significance. Our value judgments are thus derived and have no greater validity than the value premises postulated.

A White Man's Problem

Although the Negro problem is a moral issue both to Negroes and to whites in America, we shall in this book have to give *primary* attention to what goes on in the minds of white Americans. To explain this direction of our interest a general conclusion from our studies needs to be stated at this point. When the present investigator started his inquiry, his preconception was that it had to be focused on the Negro people and their peculiarities. This is understandable since, from a superficial view, Negro Americans, not only in physical appearance, but also in thoughts, feelings, and in manner of life, seemed stranger to him than did white Americans. Furthermore, most of the literature on the Negro problem dealt with Negroes: their racial and cultural characteristics, their living standards and occupational pursuits, their stratification in social classes, their migration, their family organization, their religion, their illiteracy, delinquency and disease, and so on. But as he proceeded in his studies into the Negro problem, it became increasingly evident that little, if anything, could be scientifically explained in terms of the peculiarities of the Negroes themselves.

As a matter of fact, in their basic human traits the Negroes are inherently not much different from other people. Neither are, incidentally, the white Americans. But Negroes and whites in the United States live in singular human relations with each other. All the circumstances of life—the "environmental" conditions in the broadest meaning of that term—diverge more from the "normal" for the Negroes than for the whites, if only because of the statistical fact that the Negroes are the smaller group. The average Negro must experience many times more of the "abnormal" interracial relations than the average white man in America.[a] The more important fact, however, is that practically all the economic, social, and political power is held by whites. The Negroes do not by far have anything approaching a tenth of the things worth having in America.

It is thus the white majority group that naturally determines the Negro's "place." All our attempts to reach scientific explanations of why the Negroes are what they are and why they live as they do have regularly led to determinants on the white side of the race line. In the practical and political struggles of effecting changes, the views and attitudes of the white Americans are likewise strategic. The Negro's entire life, and, consequently, also his opinions on the Negro problem, are, in the main, to be considered as secondary reactions to more primary pressures from the side of the dominant white majority.

The Negro Community as a Pathological Form of an American Community

The value premise for this Part is derived from the American Creed. America was settled largely by persons who, for one reason or another, were dissatisfied with conditions in their homelands and sought new opportunities. Until 1921 the nation welcomed immigrants almost unreservedly. They came from everywhere and brought with them a diversity of institutions and cultural patterns. It was natural that the "melting pot," "Americanization"— or, to use a more technical term, "assimilation"—became a central element in the American Creed. To make a homogeneous nation out of diverse ethnic groups, the immigrants were to abandon their cultural "peculiarities"—or to contribute them to American culture

as a whole, as some would have it—and to take on the cultural forms of America. There could be diversity, to be sure, but this diversity was not to have a strictly ethnic basis; individuals should be free to be part of any community they wished. Ideally, Americanization was to take place immediately, or, rather, in the five years required to achieve citizenship. But it was realistically recognized that in some cases it might require two or three generations.

Negroes have been living here for over three hundred years, and practically all of the ancestors of present-day Negroes came to this country more than a hundred years ago. It is probable that, on the average, Negroes have been Americans longer than any immigrant group except the British. They should be well assimilated by now. Negroes, however, together with the Orientals and, to some extent, Indians and Mexicans, have not been allowed to assimilate as have European immigrants. There is intense resistance on the part of the white majority group to biological amalgamation; and the lower caste status of Negroes is rationalized to prevent miscegenation. Negroes have been segregated, and they have developed, or there have been provided for them, separate institutions in many spheres of life, as, for instance, in religion and education. Segregation and discrimination have also in other ways hampered assimilation. Particularly they have steered acculturation so that the Negroes have acquired the norms of lower class people in America.

Negro institutions are, nevertheless, similar to those of the white man. They show little similarity to African institutions. In his cultural traits, the Negro is akin to other Americans. Some peculiarities are even to be characterized as "exaggerations" of American traits. Horace Mann Bond has characterized the American Negro as a "quintessential American." Even the "exaggeration" or intensification of general American traits in American Negro culture is explainable by specific caste pressures. In his allegiances the Negro is characteristically an American. He believes in the American Creed and in other ideals held by most Americans, such as getting ahead in the world, individualism, the importance of education and wealth. He imitates the dominant culture as he sees it and in so far as he can adopt it under his

[a]This is less true, of course, in communities where the ratio between the number of Negroes and the number of whites diverges sharply from the average ratio of one to ten for the whole nation.

conditions of life. For the most part he is not proud of those things in which he differs from the white American.

True, there has developed recently a glorification of things African, especially in music and art, and there was a back-to-Africa movement after the First World War. But this is a reaction to discrimination from white people, on the one hand, and a result of encouragement from white people, on the other hand. Thus, even the positive movement away from American culture has its source in that culture. Negro race pride and race prejudice serve to fortify the Negro against white superiority. *In practically all of its divergences, American Negro culture is not something independent of general American culture. It is a distorted development, or a pathological condition, of the general American culture.* The instability of the Negro family, the inadequacy of educational facilities for Negroes, the emotionalism in the Negro church, the insufficiency and unwholesomeness of Negro recreational activity, the plethora of Negro sociable organizations, the narrowness of interests of the average Negro, the provincialism of his political speculation, the high Negro crime rate, the cultivation of the arts to the neglect of other fields, superstition, personality difficulties, and other characteristics traits are mainly forms of social pathology which, for the most part, are created by the caste pressures.

This can be said positively: *we assume that it is to the advantage of American Negroes as individuals and as a group to become assimilated into American culture, to acquire the traits held in esteem by the dominant white Americans.* This will be the value premise here. We do not imply that white American culture is "higher" than other cultures in an absolute sense. The notion popularized by anthropologists that *all* cultures may be good under the different conditions to which they are adaptations, and that no derogatory association should *a priori* be attached to primitive cultures, is a wholesome antidote to arrogant and erroneous ideas closely bound up with white people's false racial beliefs and their justification of caste. But it does not gainsay our assumption that *here, in America,* American culture is "highest" in the pragmatic sense that adherence to it is

practical for any individual or group which is not strong enough to change it.

*   *   *

America's Opportunity

The conquering of color caste in America is America's own innermost desire. This nation early laid down as the moral basis for its existence the principles of equality and liberty. However much Americans have dodged this conviction, they have refused to adjust their laws to their own license. Today, more than ever, they refuse to discuss systematizing their caste order to mutual advantage, apparently because they most seriously mean that caste is wrong and should not be given recognition. They stand warmheartedly against oppression in all the world. When they are reluctantly forced into war, they are compelled to justify their participation to their own conscience by insisting that they are fighting against aggression and for liberty and equality.

America feels itself to be humanity in miniature. When in this crucial time the international leadership passes to America, the great reason for hope is that this country has a national experience of uniting racial and cultural diversities and a national theory, if not a consistent practice, of freedom and equality for all. What America is constantly reaching for is democracy at home and abroad. The main trend in its history is the gradual realization of the American Creed.

In this sense the Negro problem is not only America's greatest failure but also America's incomparably great opportunity for the future. If America should follow its own deepest convictions, its well-being at home would be increased directly. At the same time America's prestige and power abroad would rise immensely. The century-old dream of American patriots, that America should give to the entire world its own freedoms and its own faith, would come true. America can demonstrate that justice, equality and cooperation are possible between white and colored people.

In the present phase of history this is what the world needs to believe. Mankind is sick of fear and disbelief, of pessimism and cyncism. It needs the youthful moralistic optimism of America. But empty declarations only deepen cyncism.

Deeds are called for. If America in actual practice could show the world a progressive trend by which the Negro became finally integrated into modern democracy, all mankind would be given faith again—it would have reason to believe that peace, progress and order are feasible. And Amer- ica would have a spiritual power many times stronger than all her financial and military re- sources—the power of the trust and support of all good people on earth. *America is free to choose whether the Negro shall remain her liability or become her opportunity.*

8

The Declining Significance
of Race

William Julius Wilson

Race relations in the United States have undergone fundamental changes in recent years, so much so that now the life chances of individual blacks have more to do with their economic class position than with their day-to-day encounters with whites. In earlier years the systematic efforts of whites to suppress blacks were obvious to even the most insensitive observer. Blacks were denied access to valued and scarce resources through various ingenious schemes of racial exploitation, discrimination, and segregation, schemes that were reinforced by elaborate ideologies of racism.

But the situation has changed. However determinative such practices were in the previous efforts of the black population to achieve racial equality, and however significant they were in the creation of poverty-stricken ghettos and a vast underclass of black proletarians—that massive population at the very bottom of the social class ladder plagued by poor education and low-paying, unstable jobs—they do not provide a meaningful explanation of the life chances of black Americans today. The traditional patterns of interaction between blacks and whites, particularly in the labor market, have been fundamentally altered.

Reprinted from an article that appeared in *Society*, Jan./Feb. 1978 by permission of the author and The University of Chicago Press. © 1978 by The University of Chicago Press.

New and Traditional Barriers

In the pre-Civil War period, and in the latter half of the nineteenth through the first half of the twentieth century, the continuous and explicit efforts of whites to construct racial barriers profoundly affected the lives of black Americans. Racial oppression was designed, overt, and easily documented. As the nation has entered the latter half of the twentieth century, however, many of the traditional barriers have crumbled under the weight of the political, social, and economic changes of the civil rights era. A new set of obstacles has emerged from basic structural shifts in the economy.

These obstacles are therefore impersonal, but may prove to be even more formidable for certain segments of the black population. Specifically, whereas the previous barriers were usually designed to control and restrict the entire black population, the new barriers create hardships essentially for the black underclass; whereas the old barriers were based explicitly on racial motivations derived from intergroup contact, the new barriers have racial significance only in their consequences, not in their origins. In short, whereas the old barriers portrayed the pervasive features of racial oppression, the new barriers indicate an important and emerging form of class subordination.

It would be shortsighted to view the traditional forms of racial segregation and discrimination as having essentially disappeared in contemporary America; the presence of blacks is still firmly resisted in various institutions and social arrangements, for example, residential areas and private social clubs. However, in the economic sphere class has become more important than race in determining black access to privilege and power. It is clearly evident in this connection that many talented and educated blacks are now entering positions of prestige and influence at a rate comparable to or, in some situations, exceeding that of whites with equivalent qualifications. It is equally clear that the black underclass is in a hopeless state of economic stagnation, falling further and further behind the rest of society.

Three Stages of American Race Relations

American society has experienced three major stages of black-white contact, and each stage embodies a different form of racial stratification structured by the particular arrangement of both the economy and the polity. Stage one coincides with antebellum slavery and the early postbellum era and may be designated the period of *plantation economy and racial-caste oppression*. Stage two begins in the last quarter of the nineteenth century and ends at roughly the New Deal era, and may be identified as the period of *industrial expansion, class conflict, and racial oppression*. Finally, stage three is associated with the modern, industrial, post-World War II era which really began to crystallize during the 1960s and 1970s, and may be characterized as the period of *progressive transition from race inequalities to class inequalities*. The different periods can be identified as the preindustrial, industrial, and modern industrial stages of American race relations, respectively.

Although this abbreviated designation of the periods of American race relations seems to relate racial change to fundamental economic changes rather directly, it bears repeating that the different stages of race relations are structured by the unique arrangements and interaction of the economy and polity. More specifically, although there was an economic basis of structured racial inequality in the preindustrial and industrial periods of race relations, the polity more or less interacted

with the economy either to reinforce patterns of racial stratification or to mediate various forms of racial conflict. Moreover, in the modern industrial period race relations have been shaped as much by important economic changes as by important political changes. Indeed, it would not be possible to understand fully the subtle and manifest changes in race relations in the modern industrial period without recognizing the dual and often reciprocal influence of structural changes in the economy and political changes in the state. Thus different systems of production and/or different arrangements of the polity have imposed different constraints on the way in which racial groups have interacted in the United States, constraints that have structured the relations between racial groups and that have produced dissimilar contexts not only for the manifestation of racial antagonisms, but also for racial group access to rewards and privileges.

In contrast to the modern industrial period in which fundamental economic and political changes have made the economic class position of blacks the determining factor in their prospects for occupational advancement, the preindustrial and industrial periods of black-white relations have one central feature in common: overt efforts of whites to solidify economic racial domination (ranging from the manipulation of black labor to the neutralization or elimination of black economic competition) through various forms of judicial, political, and social discrimination. Since racial problems during these two periods were principally related to group struggles over economic resources, they readily lend themselves to the economic class theories of racial antagonisms that associate racial antipathy with class conflict.

Although racial oppression, when viewed from the broad perspective of historical change in American society, was a salient and important feature during the preindustrial and industrial periods of race relations in the United States, the problems of subordination for certain segments of the black population and the experience of social advancement for others are more directly associated with economic class in the modern industrial period. Economic and political changes have gradually shaped a black class structure, making it increasingly difficult to speak of a single or uniform black experience. Although a small elite population of free, propertied blacks did in fact exist during the pre-Civil War period, the interaction between race and economic class only assumed real importance in the latter phases of the industrial period of race relations; and the significance of this relationship has grown as the nation has entered the modern industrial period.

Each of the major periods of American race relations has been shaped in different measure both by the systems of production and by the laws and policies of the state. However, the relationships between the economy and the state have varied in each period, and therefore the roles of both institutions in shaping race relations have differed over time.

Antebellum South

In the preindustrial period the slave-based plantation economy of the South allowed a relatively small, elite group of planters to develop enormous regional power. The hegemony of the southern ruling elite was based on a system of production that required little horizontal or vertical mobility and therefore could be managed very efficiently with a simple division of labor that virtually excluded free white labor. As long as free white workers were not central to the process of reproducing the labor supply in the southern plantation economy, slavery as a mode of production facilitated the slaveholder's concentration and consolidation of economic power. And the slaveholders successfully transferred their control of the economic system to the political and legal systems in order to protect their class interest in slavery. In effect, the polity in the South regulated and reinforced the system of racial caste oppression, depriving both blacks and nonslaveholding whites of any meaningful influence in the way that slavery was used in the economic life of the South.

In short, the economy provided the basis for the development of the system of slavery, and the polity reinforced and perpetuated that system. Furthermore, the economy enabled the slaveholders to develop a regional center of power, and the polity was used to legitimate that power. Since nonslaveholding whites were virtually powerless both economically and politically, they had very little effect on the developing patterns of race

relations. The meaningful forms of black-white contact were between slaves and slaveholders, and southern race relations consequently assumed a paternalistic quality involving the elaboration and specification of duties, norms, rights, and obligations as they pertained to the use of slave labor and the system of indefinite servitude.

In short, the pattern of race relations in the antebellum South was shaped first and foremost by the system of production. The very nature of the social relations of production meant that the exclusive control of the planters would be derived from their position in the production process, which ultimately led to the creation of a juridical system that reflected and protected their class interests, including their investment in slavery.

Workers' Emerging Power

However, in the nineteenth century antebellum North the form of racial oppression was anything but paternalistic. Here a more industrial system of production enabled white workers to become more organized and physically concentrated than their southern counterparts. Following the abolition of slavery in the North, they used their superior resources to generate legal and informal practices of segregation that effectively prevented blacks from becoming serious economic competitors.

As the South gradually moved from a plantation to an industrial economy in the last quarter of the nineteenth century, landless whites were finally able to effect changes in the racial stratification system. Their efforts to eliminate black competition helped to produce an elaborate system of Jim Crow segregation. Poor whites were aided not only by their numbers but also by the development of political resources which accompanied their greater involvement in the South's economy.

Once again, however, the system of production was the major basis for this change in race relations, and once again the political system was used to reinforce patterns of race emanating from structural shifts in the economy. If the racial laws in the antebellum South protected the class interests of the planters and reflected their overwhelming power, the Jim Crow segregation laws of the late nineteenth century reflected the rising power of white laborers; and if the political power of the planters were grounded in the system of producing in a plantation economy, the emerging political power of the workers grew out of the new division of labor that accompanied industrialization.

Class and Race Relations

Except for the brief period of fluid race relations in the North between 1870 and 1890 and in the South during the Reconstruction era, racial oppression is the single best term to characterize the black experience prior to the twentieth century. In the antebellum South both slaves and free blacks occupied what could be best described as a caste position, in the sense that realistic chances for occupational mobility simply did not exist. In the antebellum North a few free blacks were able to acquire some property and improve their socioeconomic position, and a few were even able to make use of educational opportunities. However, the overwhelming majority of free northern Negroes were trapped in menial positions and were victimized by lower-class white antagonism, including the racial hostilities of European immigrant ethnics (who successfully curbed black economic competition). In the postbellum South the system of Jim Crow segregation wiped out the small gains blacks had achieved during Reconstruction, and blacks were rapidly pushed out of the more skilled jobs they had held since slavery. Accordingly, there was very little black occupational differentiation in the South at the turn of the century.

Just as the shift from a plantation economy to an industrializing economy transformed the class and race relations in the postbellum South, so too did industrialization in the North change the context for race-class interaction and confrontation there. On the one hand, the conflicts associated with the increased black-white contacts in the early twentieth century North resembled the forms of antagonism that soured the relations between the races in the postbellum South. Racial conflicts between blacks and whites in both situations were closely tied to class conflicts among whites. On the other hand, there were some fundamental differences. The collapse of the paternalistic bond between blacks and the southern business elite

cleared the path for the almost total subjugation of blacks in the South and resulted in what amounted to a united white racial movement that solidified the system of Jim Crow segregation.

However, a united white movement against blacks never really developed in the North. In the first quarter of the twentieth century, management attempted to undercut white labor by using blacks as strikebreakers and, in some situations, as permanent replacements for white workers who periodically demanded higher wages and more fringe benefits. Indeed, the determination of industrialists to ignore racial norms of exclusion and to hire black workers was one of the main reasons why the industrywide unions reversed their racial policies and actively recruited black workers during the New Deal era. Prior to this period the overwhelming majority of unskilled and semiskilled blacks were nonunionized and were available as lower-paid labor or as strikebreakers. The more management used blacks to undercut white labor, the greater were the racial antagonisms between white and black labor.

Moreover, racial tension in the industrial sector often reinforced and sometimes produced racial tension in the social order. The growth of the black urban population created a housing shortage during the early twentieth century which frequently produced black "invasions" or ghetto "spillovers" into adjacent poor white neighborhoods. The racial tensions emanating from labor strife seemed to heighten the added pressures of racial competition for housing, neighborhoods, and recreational areas. Indeed, it was this combination of racial friction in both the economic sector and the social order that produced the bloody riots in East Saint Louis in 1917 and in Chicago and several other cities in 1919.

In addition to the fact that a united white movement against blacks never really developed in the North during the industrial period, it was also the case that the state's role in shaping race relations was much more autonomous, much less directly related to developments in the economic sector. Thus, in the brief period of fluid race relations in the North from 1870 to 1890, civil rights laws were passed barring discrimination in public places and in public institutions. This legislation did not have any real significance to the white masses at that time because, unlike in the pre-Civil War North and the post-Civil War South, white workers did not perceive blacks as major economic competitors. Blacks constituted only a small percentage of the total population in northern cities; they had not yet been used in any significant numbers as cheap labor in industry or as strikebreakers; and their earlier antebellum competitors in low-status jobs (the Irish and German immigrants) had improved their economic status in the trades and municipal employment.

Polity and Racial Oppression

For all these reasons liberal whites and black professionals, urged on by the spirit of racial reform that had developed during the Civil War and Reconstruction, could pursue civil rights programs without firm resistance; for all these reasons racial developments on the political front were not directly related to the economic motivations and interests of workers and management. In the early twentieth century the independent effect of the political system was displayed in an entirely different way. The process of industrialization had significantly altered the pattern of racial interaction, giving rise to various manifestations of racial antagonism.

Although discrimination and lack of training prevented blacks from seeking higher-paying jobs, they did compete with lower-class whites for unskilled and semiskilled factory jobs, and they were used by management to undercut the white workers' union movement. Despite the growing importance of race in the dynamics of the labor market, the political system did not intervene either to mediate the racial conflicts or to reinforce the pattern of labor-market racial interaction generated by the system of production. This was the case despite the salience of a racial ideology system that justified and prescribed unequal treatment for Afro-Americans. (Industrialists will more likely challenge societal racial norms in situations where adherence to them results in economic losses.)

If nothing else, the absence of political influence on the labor market probably reflected the power struggles between management and workers. Thus legislation to protect the rights of black workers to compete openly for jobs would have conflicted with the interests of white workers, whereas legislation to deny black participation in any kind of industrial work would have conflicted with the interest of management. To repeat, unlike in the South, a united white movement resulting in the almost total segregation of the work force never really developed in the North.

But the state's lack of influence in the industrial sector of private industries did not mean that it had no significant impact on racial stratification in the early twentieth century North. The urban political machines, controlled in large measure by working-class ethnics who were often in direct competition with blacks in the private industrial sector, systematically gerrymandered black neighborhoods and excluded the urban black masses from meaningful political participation throughout the early twentieth century. Control by the white ethnics of the various urban political machines was so complete that blacks were never really in a position to compete for the more important municipal political rewards, such as patronage jobs or government contracts and services. Thus the lack of racial competition for municipal political rewards did not provide the basis for racial tension and conflict in the urban political system. This political racial oppression had no direct connection with or influence on race relations in the private industrial sector.

In sum, whether one focuses on the way race relations were structured by the system of production or the polity or both, racial oppression (ranging from the exploitation of black labor by the business class to the elimination of black competition for economic, social, and political resources by the white masses) was a characteristic and important phenomenon in both the preindustrial and industrial periods of American race relations. Nonetheless, and despite the prevalance of various forms of racial oppression, the change from a preindustrial to an industrial system of production did enable blacks to increase their political and economic resources. The proliferation of jobs created by industrial expansion helped generate and sustain the continuous mass migration of blacks from the rural South to the cities of the North and West. As the black urban population grew and became more segregated, institutions and organizations in the black community also developed, together with a business and professional class affiliated with these institutions. Still, it was not until after World War II (the modern industrial period) that the black class structure started to take on some of the characteristics of the white class structure.

Class and Black Life Chances

Class has also become more important than race in determining black life chances in the modern industrial period. Moreover, the center of racial conflict has shifted from the industrial sector to the sociopolitical order. Although these changes can be related to the more fundamental changes in the system of production and in the laws and policies of the state, the relations between the economy and the polity in the modern industrial period have differed from those in previous periods. In the preindustrial and industrial periods the basis of structured racial inequality was primarily economic, and in most situations the state was merely an instrument to reinforce patterns of race relations that grew directly out of the social relations of production.

Except for the brief period of fluid race relations in the North from 1870 to 1890, the state was a major instrument of racial oppression. State intervention in the modern industrial period has been designed to promote racial equality, and the relationship between the polity and the economy has been much more reciprocal, so much so that it is difficult to determine which one has been more important in shaping race relations since World War II. It was the expansion of the economy that facilitated black movement from the rural areas to the industrial centers and that created job opportunities leading to greater occupational differentiation in the black community (in the sense that an increasing percentage of blacks moved into white-collar positions); and it was the intervention of the state (responding to the pressures of increased black political resources and to the racial protest movement) that removed many artificial discrimination barriers by municipal, state, and federal civil rights legislation, and that contributed to the more liberal racial policies of the nation's labor unions by protective union legislation. And these combined political and economic changes created a pattern of black occupational upgrading that resulted, for example, in a substantial drop in the percentage of black males in the low-paying service, unskilled laborer, and farm jobs.

However, despite the greater occupational differentiation within the black community, there are now signs that the effect of some aspects of structural economic change has been the closer association between black occupational mobility and class affiliation. Access to the means of production is increasingly based on educational criteria (a situation which distinguishes the modern industrial from the earlier industrial system of production) and thus threatens to solidify the position of the black underclass. In other words, a consequence of the rapid growth of the corporate and government sectors has been the gradual creation of a segmented labor market that currently provides vastly different mobility opportunities for different segments of the black population.

On the one hand, poorly trained and educationally limited blacks of the inner city, including that growing number of black teenagers and young adults, see their job prospects increasingly restricted to the low-wage sector, their unemployment rates soaring to record levels (which remain high despite swings in the busines cycle), their labor force participation rates declining, their movement out of poverty slowing, and their welfare roles increasing. On the other hand, talented and educated blacks are experiencing unprecedented job opportunities in the growing government and corporate sectors, opportunities that are at least comparable to those of whites with equivalent qualifications. The improved job situation for the more privileged blacks in the corporate and government sectors is related both to the expansion of salaried white-collar positions and to the pressures of state affirmative action programs.

In view of these developments, it would be difficult to argue that the plight of the black underclass is solely a consequence of racial oppression, that is, the explicit and overt efforts of whites to keep blacks subjugated, in the same way that it would be difficult to explain the rapid economic improvement of the more privileged blacks by arguing that the traditional forms of racial segregation and discrimination still characterize the labor market in American industries. The recent mobility patterns of blacks lend strong support to the view that economic class is clearly more important than race in predetermining job placement and occupational mobility. In the economic realm, then, the black experience has moved historically from economic racial oppression experienced by virtually all blacks to economic subordination for the black underclass. And as we begin the last quarter of the twentieth century, a deepening economic schism seems to be developing in the black community, with the black poor falling further and further behind middle- and upper-income blacks.

Shift of Racial Conflict

If race is declining in significance in the economic sector, explanations of racial antagonism based on labor-market conflicts, such as those advanced by economic class theories of race, also have less significance in the period of modern industrial race relations. Neither the low-wage sector nor the corporate and government sectors provide the basis for the kind of interracial job competition and conflict that plagued the economic order in previous periods. With the absorption of blacks into industrywide labor unions, protective union legislation, and equal employment legislation, it is no longer feasible for management to undercut white labor by using black workers. The traditional racial struggles for power and privilege have shifted away from the economic sector and are now concentrated in the sociopolitical order. Although poor blacks and poor whites are still the main actors in the present manifestations of racial strife, the immediate source of the tension has more to do with racial competition for public schools, municipal political systems, and residential areas than with the competition for jobs.

To say that race is declining in significance, therefore, is not only to argue that the life chances of blacks have less to do with race than with economic class affiliation, but also to maintain that racial conflict and competition in the economic sector—the most important historical factors in the subjugation of blacks—have been substantially reduced. However, it could be argued that the firm white resistance to public school desegregation, residential integration, and black control of central cities all indicate the unyielding importance of race in the United States. The

argument could even be entertained that the impressive occupational gains of the black middle class are only temporary, and that as soon as affirmative action pressures are relieved, or as soon as the economy experiences a prolonged recession, industries will return to their old racial practices.

Both of these arguments are compelling if not altogether persuasive. Taking the latter contention first, there is little available evidence to suggest that the economic gains of privileged blacks will be reversed. Despite the fact that the recession of the early 1970s decreased job prospects for all educated workers, the more educated blacks continued to experience a faster rate of job advancement than their white counterparts. And although it is always possible that an economic disaster could produce racial competition for higher-paying jobs and white efforts to exclude talented blacks, it is difficult to entertain this idea as a real possibility in the face of the powerful political and social movement against job discrimination. At this point there is every reason to believe that talented and educated blacks, like talented and educated whites, will continue to enjoy the advantages and privileges of their class status.

My response to the first argument is not to deny the current racial antagonism in the sociopolitical order, but to suggest that such antagonism has far less effect on individual or group access to those opportunities and resources that are centrally important for life survival than antagonism in the economic sector. The factors that most severely affected black life chances in previous years were the racial oppression and antagonism in the economic sector. As race declined in importance in the economic sector, the Negro class structure became more differentiated and black life chances became increasingly a consequence of class affiliation.

Furthermore, it is even difficult to identify the form of racial contact in the sociopolitical order as the source of the current manifestations of conflict between lower-income blacks and whites, because neither the degree of racial competition between the have-nots, nor their structural relations in urban communities, nor their patterns of interaction constitute the ultimate source of present racial antagonism. The ultimate basis for current racial tension is the deleterious effect of basic structural changes in the modern American economy on black and white lower-income groups, changes that include uneven economic growth, increasing technology and automation, industry relocation, and labor market segmentation.

Fighting Class Subordination

The situation of marginality and redundancy created by the modern industrial society deleteriously affects all the poor, regardless of race. Underclass whites, Hispano Americans, and Native Americans all are victims, to a greater or lesser degree, of class subordination under advanced capitalism. It is true that blacks are disproportionately represented in the underclass population and that about one-third of the entire black population is in the underclass. But the significance of these facts has more to do with the historical consequences of racial oppression than with the current effects of race.

Although the precentage of blacks below the low-income level dropped steadily throughout the 1960s, one of the legacies of the racial oppression in previous years is the continued disproportionate black representation in the underclass. And since 1970 both poor whites and nonwhites have evidenced very little progress in their elevation from the ranks of the underclass. In the final analysis, therefore, the challenge of economic dislocation in modern industrial society calls for public policy programs to attack inequality on a broad class front, policy programs—in other words—that go beyond the limits of ethnic and racial discrimination by directly confronting the pervasive and destructive features of class subordination.

9

The American Indian:
Historical Background

Nancy Oestreich Lurie

Thanks to work by generations of archeologists, ethnologists and historians, there is an enormous literature for intensive study of the prehistoric and historic cultures of the North American Indians and the effects of Euro-American influences on Indian life.[1] This paper seeks only to provide a brief and general chronology of significant phases in the history of Indian-white contact as a background in understanding contemporary Indian life.

Discovery and Early Contact

It is commonly but incorrectly assumed that Indian societies, before Europeans arrived, were stable, and that they had existed in idyllic and unchanging simplicity since time immemorial, until Europeans made their first landfall and began disrupting and ultimately destroying native life. We now know, on the contrary, that their societies were developing and changing in important ways long before first contact. Archeological evidence reveals that prior to the discovery of America by Europeans, widespread trade routes stretched over the entire continent. Many of our important highways follow trails long familiar to the Indians. Furthermore, pottery, burial prac-

tices, grave goods, earthworks and other clues uncovered by the archeologist clearly show that new ideas arose in many different places and diffused to neighboring areas to be adapted to different natural environments, further elaborated and passed on yet again. Religion, economic practices, and artistic and utilitarian productions were all subjected to the process. By the time of significant European contact along the east coast in the late sixteenth and early seventeenth centuries, a simple hunting and gathering economy was already giving way to a food production economy in the vast area south of the Great Lakes from the Mississippi River to the Atlantic Ocean. Domesticated corn, beans, squash and possibly other food plants as well as tobacco were in a process of northward spread from the lower Mississippi valley. They had undoubtedly been introduced from Mexican sources about one A.D., but by a process and routes not yet fully understood.

When Europeans first arrived, tribes in the northern Great Lakes region had only begun to experiment with gardening as a supplement to a diet based primarily on hunting and gathering, while tribes in the Southeast had already achieved populous, permanent settlements exhibiting marked social and material complexities as natural concomitants to the development of food production. The spread of cultural complexity

Reprinted from *The American Indian Today*, Stuart Levine and Nancy Oestreich Lurie, eds., by permission of the publisher, Everett Edwards, Inc., and the editors.

was paced to some extent by the gradual selection of ever hardier varieties of what has been essentially a semi-tropical plant complex, but which now had to survive even shorter growing seasons. Warmer coastal regions permitted a somewhat faster diffusion of gardening than colder inland regions and in some cases peoples already accustomed to raising crops moved northward, displacing groups still largely dependent on hunting.

The establishment of permanent European settlements along the eastern seaboard and St. Lawrence River in the early seventeenth century required the assistance of Indians in providing food, information and skills to survive the first years in a new environment. As the fur trade took on importance, and with it competition among European nations for control of North America, the Indian tribes enjoyed a good deal of bargaining power and learned to use it astutely in their own interests in regard to both commercial and military activities. For many eastern tribes, it was the long period of the fur trade and not the aboriginal past which is recalled as a golden age.

Although the popular view is that a rapid demise was the fate of all Indians, generally it was the more fully agricultural and rigidly structured tribes which went under quickly and completely in the face of early European contact. Located close to the coasts to begin with and hemmed in by mountains or hostile tribes at their backs, these societies bore the first brunt of intense white competition for desirable land. Their more populous villages and accompanying social norms had developed prior to the advent of Europeans, which may have made for a certain inflexibility in adaptivness. It should be borne in mind that in the seventeenth century, the difference in political and technological complexity between Indians and little groups of colonists was not so great as to suggest immediately to the tribes and powerful alliances of tribes that Europeans posed a serious threat to their future. Certainly, the relatively large and compact Indian villages with their gardens and stored surpluses of food were highly vulnerable both to new epidemic diseases and scorched earth campaigns in times of open hostilities when their continued presence in the region became a nuisance to the colonists. Thus, only remnants remain of once

formidable alliances of tribes along the eastern seaboard, and many tribes noted as powerful and culturally sophisticated in the early British, French and Spanish chronicles have disappeared completely.

Further inland, the tribes were less fully committed to complexities attendant upon food production. They apparently benefitted from the greater flexibility and mobility of a hunting ethos as well as from the fact that Europeans were more interested in their country for furs than for colonization. Moreover, the nascent alliances and confederacies which had begun to develop inland were influenced and shaped in response to the Europeans who sought trade and friendship. These tribes accepted, made adaptations, and recognized as inevitable and even desirable that Europeans should be on the scene. When demand for their land eventually developed, as had happened so quickly on the coast, the inland Indians had established clear patterns for looking after their own interests as societies distinct from those of Europeans, despite their long association and extensive trade and more than occasional acceptance of white in-laws.

Beyond the St. Lawrence to the Arctic Circle, there are still groups of people, Indian and Eskimo, who are essentially hunters. Even where ecological conditions might have eventually permitted aboriginal plant domestication, their contact with Europeans occurred before there was an intervening native food producing stage. In many instances, contact with outsiders has been so recent that the first encounters involved immediate introduction to features of highly industrialized society. Thus, there are Indian and Eskimo people who rode in airplanes before they even saw an automobile.[2] Some groups are still able to subsist largely off the land but have availed themselves rapidly and selectively of alien items to make the life of the hunter more efficient and comfortable: repeating rifles, gasoline "kickers" for canoes, even radios. Some are as fully committed to the fur trade as a way of life as the Indians of the eastern woodlands in the seventeenth and eighteenth centuries, while for others the fur trade is in its terminal stage, and they face painful adjustments experienced earlier by other groups living in a market economy.

Gardening also diffused into the Prairie and

Plains region from Mississippian sources in aboriginal times, but was largely confined to river bottom lands where bone or stone implements could turn the loose soil. The people built substantial villages of timber-framed, mud covered lodges and settled down to the elaboration of existence permitted by food production. The open plains, where coarse grass matted the earth, were exploited in brief, organized forays to take buffalo in quantity by such means as driving herds over cliffs. Having only dogs as beasts of burden, Indian people found the Plains dangerous, with uncertain and widely spaced sources of water. Only scattered bands of hunters wandered there on occasion.

Important contact with European people occurred only after the Plains had been made habitable for many tribes by the introduction of the horse. As herds of wild Spanish horses spread north, techniques of horsemanship diffused from Spaniard to Indian. Raiding for tamed animals from tribe to tribe became an important and exciting aspect of existence. The great herds of buffalo which a hunter approached on foot with trepidation could now be exploited efficiently from horseback. The buffalo suddenly became an abundant and dependable food supply and source of housing, utensils and clothing as horses became available to more and more tribes. Some tribes were more or less pushed into the Plains as the pressure of white settlement forced one Indian group against another, but the Plains clearly attracted tribes to a new and exciting way of life as well. The gaudily befringed Indian in warbonnet astride his horse is the archetype of the American Indian all over the world, and we note with wonder the spectacular history of his distinctive way of life. It was made possible by native adaptations of an animal of European origin, achieved astonishing complexity to govern and give deep psychic and esthetic satisfaction to the life of large encampments, and collapsed with the disappearance of the buffalo in the short span of less than 200 years, roughly from 1700 to 1880. By then, the repeating rifle and commercial hunting, which hastened the demise of the buffalo, the windmill, barbed wire and the steel plow transformed the Plains into a rich grazing and grain area, no longer "The Great American Desert" of the early maps, fit only for Indians.

In the Southwest, agriculture had diffused directly from Mexico and stimulated elaborations of social life even earlier than in the Southeast, beginning perhaps about 1000 B.C. Changes in climate and invasions of hunter-raiders from the North saw shifts of settlements, abandonment of old villages and building of new ones before Europeans first visited the pueblos in 1539. Archeological studies show that the settled people of the Southwest, pueblos and other gardening villagers, had long exchanged items and ideas among themselves. Although actual relations with the Spaniards were frequently strained, they readily took over from the Spaniards a host of new objects, skills, plants, animals and ideas to make them peculiarly their own. Learning early the futility of overt aggression against the better armed Spaniards, the pueblo peoples particularly have developed passive resistance to a fine art in dealing with strangers in their midst—even holding hordes of modern tourists at arm's length with bland pleasantries while doing a brisk trade in hand crafts and fees for taking pictures.

The pueblos' once troublesome neighbors, the former raiders today designated as Navaho and Apache, successfully incorporated elements of sedentary Indian cultures into their more mobile life in aboriginal times, and eventually they too made judicious selections from Euro-American culture, reworking and molding them to fit their own cultural predilections. The Southwestern Indians in general retain more obvious and visible symbols of their "Indianness" and for many white observers these are the only "real" Indians left. However, their modern material culture is far from aboriginal, distinctive though it may be. Like Indian groups throughout the country, the important criteria of identity rest in intangible attitudes, values, beliefs, patterns of inter-personal relations.

As in the East, native social and material elaboration in the West tended to thin out toward the North, limited by environmental factors. In the Great Basin, tiny bands of roving gatherers maintained a bare subsistence level of existence. Nevertheless, even some of the simple Basin societies were attracted by the horse-buffalo complex of the Plains and in an incredibly short time the Comanche, for example, had ventured out to become a Plains tribe *par excellence*.

North of the Basin, the relatively greater richness of the environment permitted the Plateau Indian to live much as the more favored northern hunters east of the Mississippi, even to enjoying a fur trade era, although of briefer duration. Gardening never reached this region in aboriginal times, but after contact the horse became important to many of the Plateau peoples.

In the West, there were several unusual situations where nature furnished dependable "crops" which man could harvest without first having sown. In Central California, huge stands of oak accounted for regular supplies of acorns which the Indians converted into a nutritious flour by ingenious techniques of leaching out the bitter and somewhat toxic tannic acid. On the coast, enormous shell mounds are evidence of once large permanent settlements supported in large part by easily gathered mollusks. Many of the California Indians took quite readily to the ministrations of Spanish friars who began arriving in 1769, and set up mission compounds where they introduced the Indians to agricultural and other skills. Crowded together in the new villages, the Indians proved tragically susceptible to new diseases. The eventual discovery of gold, the influx of lawless miners, and competition by the United States for control of California, in which Indian property and rights were often identified with Hispano-American interests, contributed to a rapid and widespread disorganization and decline among many of the California groups. The picture is, in fact, strikingly similar to the rapid depopulation and disruption of native life on the east coast.

Along the Northwest Coast from Oregon to Alaska, an abundance and variety of marine life and a northerly climate mitigated by the warm Japanese Current created ideal conditions for population growth and social elaboration which could be promoted in most places only through the development of food production. The peoples in this region had regularly traded, visited and fought among themselves when first European contacts were made by sailing ships out of Russia, England and the United States in the late eighteenth century. Trade soon flourished in which sea otter and other pelts were exchanged for both utilitarian and novelty items. The Northwest Coast peoples quickly earned a reputation for sharp bargaining and scant concern for the welfare of hapless seamen wrecked on their shores as they busily plundered ships' cargoes. An impressive way of native life became further enriched. Already skilled in working cedar with simple tools and clever methods of steaming, bending and sewing boards, the Indians soon appreciated that totem poles, storage boxes, house posts, masks and other objects could be enlarged and more ornately embellished with metal tools. However, indiscriminate slaughter of the peltry animals brought a rapid close to the coastal trade. Unlike the eastern tribes which foraged further and further west for fresh beaver areas, even to pushing out the resident tribes, the Northwest Coast people had no place else to go. The arrival of Lewis and Clark in 1806 heralded the opening of overland routes of settlement from the east and encroachment of farmers, miners and loggers. The latter adaptations of the Coastal Indians have tended to center in fishing both for their own support and as commercial enterprise.

If we take a broad view of the entire continent from the end of the sixteenth century until well into the nineteenth century, we find that white contact stimulated new ideas, introduced new goods and even greatly accelerated the pace of cultural change in some cases. However, whites arrived on a scene where changes, experimentation, movements of people and diffusion of goods and ideas were already taking place. For the vast majority of tribes, there was time to develop attitudes and adaptations about the presence of whites which involved negotiation and selective borrowing of items rather than absorption into white culture and society. Exposure to similar opportunities to change, furthermore, did not lead to cultural homogeneity throughout the continent, since different Indian societies in different kinds of environments made different selections and adaptations in regard to white culture. The multiplicity of languages and local cultural identity persisted. When, from place to place, the nature of contact changed to one of intense competition for right to the land, the Indians were clearly at a disadvantage. However, even as their power to bargain waned, the various Indian groups continued to adapt to maintain their ethnic integrity. Because they made massive borrowings of European material items, which tended to be similar from place to place—guns, textiles, household utensils and tools—white people generally assumed they would soon gracefully phase out their social and cultural distinctiveness. However, we are still waiting for them to vanish.

Treaties and Reservations

When the United States and Canada finally emerged as the national entities controlling North America, increasingly determined to remain at peace with one another, Indian societies were obliged to deal exclusively with one or the other of these governments and were bereft of the opportunity to play the familiar game of favored nation in war and trade among competing powers—France, Spain, Britain and the young United States. Both Canada and the United States derive their Indian policies from guidelines which were already being laid down in the mid-seventeenth century in New England and Virginia. In the face of overwhelming defeat, the depleted and demoralized tribes in these areas were offered and accepted small parcels of land—the first reservations—secured to them by treaties. These guaranteed homelands and other considerations, in the way of goods and religious and practical teachings, were to be compensation for the vast domains they relinquished. The Indians, in turn, pledged themselves to peace and alliance with the local colonies in case of war with hostile tribes or European enemies. In Virginia, in 1646, the regrouped remnants of the once powerful Powhatan Confederacy agreed in their treaty to pay a small annual tribute in furs to the colony, an interesting portent of things to come for their Indian neighbors to the West, as the fur trade was just beginning to loom importantly to the British.[3]

As the scattered and often competitive British colonies began to recognize their common interests in opposition to the French in the North and both Spain and France to the South, Indian policy became more firmly structured. By 1755, negotiations with Indians, particularly in regard to land, became the exclusive prerogative of the Crown acting through properly designated representatives. A northern and a southern superintendency were set up to regulate trade and undertake necessary diplomacy with the Indians. After the American Revolution, the southern superintendency ceased to exist as a British concern and the northern superintendency was moved from the area of New York State to Canada.

Canadian colonial governors handled Indian affairs locally until 1860 when responsibility in Ontario and Quebec was given directly to the Province of Canada. In 1867, the British North America Act placed Indian affairs under the jurisidiction of the Government of Canada. During the ensuing years, administrative headquarters were shifted between various Offices and Branches of the Government, but policy itself tended to remain relatively consistent. Whenever possible, Canada dealt with tribes by treaty, including as many tribes under a common treaty as could be induced to sign in any particular region. Reserves were located in the tribes' homelands or in nearby, ecologically similar areas, the process being repeated from region to region as national interest in regard to allocation of land expanded west and north. Canada made its last treaty with some of the far northern Indians in 1923. A system to encourage understanding of modern principles of government provides for election of a chief and headmen in each "Band," the Canadian term for locally autonomous Indian groups. The number of headmen is determined by population size, with roughly one headman per 100 people. For some bands, such as the Iroquois groups along the southern border of Canada, this system is an uncomfortable imposition on their own patterns of semi-hereditary leadership, while for bands in the northern Territories, it has given a formal structure to an old system of leadership based on individual ability. The Canadian government has always cooperated with religious denominations in sharing responsibility for Indian affairs, especially in regard to education.

A few Canadian bands were by-passed in treaty negotiations and special provisions have been made for them to qualify for "Treaty Indian" benefits as well as conform to limitations placed on full citizenship by Treaty Indian status. A basic objective has been to encourage Indian people to declare themselves "nontreaty" as individuals and be accepted as full-fledged citizens. After 1950, most of the limitations on citizenship were lifted, even for Treaty Indians, in the hope of hastening the day when Indians would become assimilated. The Canadian government, however, has been generally more tolerant than the United States of ethnic distinctiveness and more agreeable to protecting Indian rights to their lands as defined by treaties.

Eskimo affairs, until 1966, were considered a separate concern, centering more in matters of trade and welfare than in questions of land. At present an effort is underway to consolidate and regularize Indian and Eskimo administration, stressing new experiments in economic development of native communities.

Perhaps the most distinctive feature of Canadian Indian history is the explicit recognition of old communities of stabilized Indian-white mixture, designated *Metis*. This is a sociological and not an official concept; the Metis are simply an ethnic group like Ukranians or French Canadians, sharing none of the benefits of Indian status. They are considered different from Indians both by themselves and the Indian people who also represent some white admixture in the genealogies. In some cases, the actual kinship between certain Indian and Metis families is known to both sides. Since Metis are generally found in the western Provinces and Territories, where there are large Indian populations, and suffer the same disabilities of isolation and inadequate education and perhaps even lower social status in the Canadian class system, there is an increasing tendency to group Metis and Indians in Canadian discussions of problems of poverty, employment, education and the like. The extent to which Metis and Indians themselves are interested in making common cause remains debatable.

The picture in the United States is much more complicated. In the first place there were and are more Indian people representing greater diversity of languages, cultures and ecological adaptations. Encroachment of whites on Indian land has always been a much more acute problem. After France ceased to be a consideration in the struggle for control of North America, many tribes allied themselves with the British against the Americans in the Revolution and War of 1812, or maintained a wary neutrality during these conflicts, waiting to see how they would turn out. Few tribes declared themselves clearly on the side of the Americans. Thus, from the start, American negotiations for land frequently followed recent hostile engagements with the tribes involved. The settlers' fears of disgruntled and warlike Indians, perhaps not yet entirely convinced they were defeated, gave added impetus to a policy designed to move Indian tribes far from the lands they ceded. In Canada, the relatively smaller populations of both Indians and whites as well as a history of friendlier relationships permitted comparatively easier negotiations for land and establishing reserves close to areas opening up for settlement.

Eventually, there was no place left to move Indians and the United States was also obliged to set up reservations in tribal homelands. Added to these many complications was the fact that in time American policy had to be adjusted to old Spanish arrangements in the Southwest where land grants established Indian title, a plan analogous but not identical to the British plan of treaties and reservations.

Following British precedent, the United States made Indian affairs a concern of the central government, but actual procedures were left vague. The Third Article of the Constitution merely empowered Congress to "regulate commerce with foreign nations, and among the several states, and with the Indian tribes." At first, administration was carried out through a system of government authorized trading posts, reminiscent of the British superintendencies. The army handled problems of hostile Indians. Peace negotiations and land sales, including arrangements for reservations, were carried out by special treaty commissions appointed as need demanded. The idea prevailed, as it had since colonial times, that changes in sovereignty over land did not abrogate the rights of possession of those who occupied the land, and that Indians should be recompensed for land which they relinquished. This concept was enunciated in the Northwest Ordinance confirmed in 1789 and extended to cover the tribes in the Louisiana Purchase in 1804. By the time the United States acquired Alaska, we had begun to equivocate on this philosophy, and questions of Indian and Eskimo land remain somewhat confused.[4]

The fact that the United States pledged itself to pay Indians for their lands at a time when there was virtually no national treasury has given comfort to those historians who would see the founding fathers imbued with the noblest of ideals. Cynics point out that it was cheaper and easier than trying to drive the Indians out by force. The price paid across the continent averaged well under ten cents an acre, and the government expected to recoup quickly by sale of land in large blocks to speculators at $1.25 an acre minimum. Moreover the debt on each treaty usually was paid under an annuity plan extending over thirty years. On the other hand, many of the tribes were not entirely naive and held out for payment in specie rather than the uncertain paper issued by banks in the early days of the republic.

Although successive efforts were made to establish a firm line between Indian and white holdings east of the Mississippi River, settlement continued to encroach on the Indian area, necessitating renegotiation of the boundary. By 1824, the demands of settlers, competition from illegal, private traders, and the diminishing returns of the fur trade led the government to abandon the trading business as basic to Indian affairs and concentrate on the land business. The Bureau of Indian Affairs was set up under the Department of War. When the Department of Interior was established in 1849 and Indian affairs were placed under its aegis, most of the eastern tribes had become located much as we find them today.

A few tribes on the seaboard occupy state reservations or are simply old Indian settlements, legacies of the colonial past which could be ignored. Along the Appalachians, particularly toward the southern end and elsewhere in the Southeast, there are isolated communities which identify themselves as Indian, such as the numerous Lumbee of North Carolina and adjoining states and the Houma of Louisiana. Their tribal affiliations are vague, because these people are the descendants of fugitive remnants of many tribes driven from the coasts, white renegades and, in some cases, runaway Negro slaves. These people are, in effect, Metis, but popular and official thinking in the United States has tended to more rigid classification than in Canada. Thus, rejected as white and reluctant to be considered Negro, the American Metis stress their identity as Indian. Those Indian societies which maintained a clear and unbroken tradition of tribal identity and stood in the path of settle-

ment were exhorted, negotiated with and paid to move further west during the period of the 1820's and 1830's.

The United States entered into numerous treaties with these tribes and though it tried to deal with blocs of tribes as was done in Canada, this proved inexpedient. Both tribesmen and treaty commissioners tried to outmaneuver each other by devious diplomatic ploys. The Indians could play for delay in land sales by noting boundaries which had only Indian names and were unknown to the whites, so that final settlement would depend on formal surveys. The whites attempted to play one tribe off against another, and even one subband within a tribe against another, in the hope of leaving intransigent factions so isolated and unprotected that they would be forced to capitulate when their neighbors moved out. And then the factions would rally and claim the treaty had to include all parties with an interest to the land in question. Since treaties had to be ratified by Congress and the work of the commissioners was hampered by both budget allocations for their time and the desire to get back to Washington before Congress recessed, the Indians won compromises. The commissioners could afford to be philosophical as these loose ends could always be tied up in the next round of negotiations. There is little doubt that the Indian tribes hoped to make the best of what could only be a bad bargain, but to stick to that bargain once made, whereas the treaty makers from Washington took the treaties lightly, striving toward a final goal of general Indian removal to the less choice land west of the Mississippi acquired in the Louisiana Purchase.

Thus we find representatives of eastern tribes scattered from Nebraska to Oklahoma: Potawatomi, Winnebago, Miami, Shawnee, Kickapoo, Ottawa, Creek, Choctaw, Chickasaw, Cherokee, Seminole and others even including members of the League of the Iroquois such as Cayuga and Seneca. However, bands or small clusterings of families of many of these tribes managed to return to their homelands or held out against removal, arguing either the illegality of the treaty under which they were to move or misrepresentation by the government as to the quality of the new land or the terms whereby they and their possessions were to be transported. In some cases, this determination led to creation of reservations for them in their homelands, as in the cases of the Eastern Cherokee and Seminoles. Others, including some of the Potawatomi and Winnebago, were granted homesteads as individuals where it was hoped that they would become absorbed into the general rural white population. Popular indignation about the injustice shown one band of Potawatomi in Michigan led to the establishment of a small reservation for them under state jurisdiction. A group of Mesquakie (Fox) picked out and purchased their own land and applied for reservation status. Perhaps the most bizarre instance was the band of Kickapoo who just kept on going west and sought sanctuary in northern Mexico where they remain to this day, preserving many features of nineteenth century woodland Indian culture. In many cases, particularly in the Southeast, little groups simply managed to maintain themselves as Indian neighborhoods on property they were able to purchase, little noticed and bothering no one.

Several Iroquois tribes or portions of them who did not flee to Canada after the Revolution were granted their reservations in New York State by treaties signed during Washington's administration. Of these, the Oneida were induced to move to Wisconsin in the early 1830's along with the Stockbridge, a highly acculturated Algonkian group drawing its membership from remnants of coastal tribes, primarily the Mahicans. In Wisconsin, Michigan and Minnesota we find a number of tribes, Menomini, bands of Ojibwa and others who by various delaying tactics finally managed to get reservations in their homelands.[5]

There is no question that when it was a matter of the larger national interest, defined as the demands of settlers or speculators, the government made every effort to remove the Indians.[6] Humanitarians such as Jefferson expressed the hope that if Indian people conformed to the habits of rural whites they might remain in possession of what land they would need for this purpose, but if they would not change their ways, the only alternative was forceful persuasion and removal. The rationale for dispossession of the Indians has usually conformed to a logic summed up by Theodore Roosevelt in the late nineteenth century, "this great continent could not have been kept as nothing but a game preserve for squalid savages."[7] The myth of the hunter Indian, incapable or unwilling to rouse himself from the sloth of ancestral tradition in the face of new opportunities and the model afforded by civilized man, remains with us today. On close inspection, the problem seems to be less the Indian's inability to adapt than the unorthodoxy of his adaptations. Western cultures have a different history; our traditions evolved out of a stage of feudal peasantry which the Indians by-passed. So Indians react in unexpected but perfectly logical ways to our ideas and artifacts.

The essential problems which arise in the confrontation of different cultural systems, each changing and adapting its own way, are well illustrated in the fate of the Cherokee, who became literate as a result of exposure to the European idea of writing, but hit upon a syllabary rather than an alphabet to best convey the vagaries of their own tongue in written symbols. By the early nineteenth century, the Cherokee and other groups in the Southeast had built upon their growing aboriginal commitment to agriculture with new crops and implements brought by the Europeans. They were successfully self-sustaining from small farmsteads to large plantations, with many acres under cultivation and large herds of horses and cattle. But they wished to maintain themselves as distinct Indian societies, while acknowledging allegiance to the United States.

Decisions sympathetic to this outlook were expressed by the Chief Justice of the Supreme Court, John Marshall, in 1831 (The Cherokee Nation v. The State of Georgia) and 1832 (Samuel A. Worcester v. The State of Georgia) but had little effect in protecting the Cherokee or any Indian tribes from private interests and states bent on their dispossession. Frontier statesmen, particularly during the administration of Andrew Jackson, could argue that Indians were different and therefore still clearly savage and a danger. Congress, as the body duly authorized to deal with Indian affairs, simply went around Marshall's decisions. It carried out the will of local states in regard to unwanted Indians, and provided for treaties and removals.

It must be noted that not all the proponents of the plan of Indian removal were motivated by selfish interests. There were missionaries and others who felt that removal of Indian tribes from the corrupting and demoralizing influences of frontier riff-raff would be in the Indians' best interest and allow them to establish a new and better life. However, even the kindest construction placed on this view must admit to its shortsightedness. Already resident on the land in the west were tribes whose intersts were not consulted before newcomers were moved among them. They were often considerably less than hospitable. Furthermore, it was becoming obvious that the Plains area would not remain forever the habitation of buffalo hunters. By the time pioneers were spreading out into the Plains, instead of bypassing them on the way to the gold fields or fertile valleys of the west coast, there was really no place left to move Indians. There was also the danger that the plan of one, and later two, large Indian Territories in the West would allow tribes to see the advantages of alliance and make common cause against the white man. Therefore, most of the native tribes west of the Mississippi were placed in reservations which are separated from one another yet in or near the original homelands. In contrast, large numbers of eastern Indians were clustered in Oklahoma.[8]

By 1849, when the Bureau of Indian Affairs was shifted from the Department of War to the newly created Department of the Interior, the eastern tribes had been "pacified," although troops were occasionally called in to round up returnees and get them back to their western reservations. The real problem, however, was the Plains Indians, who at this time were in the very midst of their great cultural florescence and were formidable and enthusiastic warriors. The efforts of Interior to get these tribes on reservations by negotiation, conciliation and persuasion were often confounded by the outlook of the War Department, which considered all Indians hostile, dangerous, and fair game. An unfortunate term, "ward," used by Marshall in his 1831 decision was revived. Marshall only intended a rough analogy in endeavoring to explain the responsibility of the federal government to protect Indian tribes against unauthorized usurpation of their lands: "Their relation to the United States resembles that of ward to his guardian." Because the Bureau "sometimes became the uneasy and unhappy buffer between Indians and the U.S. Army,"[9] it was decided in 1862 to designate the Indian tribes as "wards" of the Indian Bureau rather than let them be considered simply as "enemies" over whose fate the army would have jurisdiction to make decisions. Unfortunately, and without ever really having legal sanction, the term "ward" took on administrative connotations by which the Bureau exercised incredible control over the lives and property of individuals, much as a guardian would act for minor and even hopelessly retarded children.

The End of the Treaty Period

As noted, Canada took its Indian treaties more seriously from the start and has continued to respect them. In the United States, although important hostilities such as Little Big Horn and Wounded Knee were yet to come, it was apparent by 1871 that the process of "pacification" would continue at a rapid pace. The need to make treaties with so many different tribes and the embarassment of making new treaties every time the demands of settlement required reduction of Indian acreage suggested to policy makers that Indian tribes were not really "nations" entitled to the respect and formality of treaties. Treaties required the unwieldy and expensive process of mutual agreement—albeit the United States held the greater power in dictating terms—and Senate ratification. Terms of existing treaties would be obeserved as long as the government found it practicable, but after 1871 no more treaties were made with Indian tribes. Instead, "agreements" were negotiated which were worded much like treaties and mistaken for treaties by many Indians, but which were administratively more expedient and not as binding in legalistic and even moral terms as far as the government was concerned. Champions of Indians' rights long endeavored to pique the conscience of the nation by pointing to our bad faith in entering into solemn treaties, "the highest law of the land," which we did not intend to keep.

It was the period from the 1870's to the 1920's during which the worst abuses occurred in regard to administration of Indian affairs. Most Indian people were denied the vote, had to obtain passes to leave the reservation and were prohibited from practicing their own religions, sometimes by force. Leadership and management of community affairs smacking of traditional forms and functions were either discouraged or ignored as proper representations of community interest. Children were dragooned off to boarding schools where they were severely punished if they were caught speaking their own languages. While these things all happened, shortage and rapid turnover of Bureau personnel, administrative apathy and occasional enlightenment at the local administrative level meant that the regulations were not always rigorously enforced. And the Indian societies themselves took a hand in playing off administrators, missionaries and other whites against each other to keep them busy while Indian people held the line in their determination to remain Indian. The ubiquity of factionalism in Indian societies which is so regularly deplored by those people, Indian and white, who are sincerely interested in helping Indian people make a better life, may actually have acted as an important mechanism of social and cultural survival for Indian groups. No outsider could gain total dominance for his programs aimed in one way or another at reducing Indian distinctiveness. This suggestion, while admittedly speculative, seems worth bearing in mind when we turn to the contemporary scene where there seems to be a striving for common goals, in which factionalism for its own sake in avoiding undesirable goals may be giving way to what are really healthy differences of opinion based on habitual wariness in working toward positive objectives.

Attempts at Reform

Educated Indian people and their philanthropic white friends during the nineteenth century were generally as committed as the government to the view that the Indians' only hope was social and cultural assimilation into white society. The reservation system *per se* as well as the widespread peculation and dereliction in duty of reservation personnel were held responsible for impeding Indians in their course toward "civilization." This view tended to ignore the many non-reservation communities in the east which remained almost defiantly Indian, even where government experiments in granting stubborn "returnees" homesteads scattered among white neighbors did not automatically result in Indian assimilation or

break-down of a sense of community. If their conservatism in language, religion and other aspects of culture was noted at all, it was viewed optimistically as inevitably temporary. Ironically, one of the major measures of reform promoted by humanitarians turned out to exacerbate rather than alleviate Indians problems. This was the Indian Allotment Act of 1887. It was actually protested by some far-seeing people who recognized the opportunities it afforded for a tremendous Indian landgrab, but these voices were drowned out by those who considered themselves the Indians' true friends, righteously supported by those who stood to gain from the Allotment Act as predicted by the pessimists.[10]

The idea of allotment was that Indians could be assimilated into the white rural population in the space of a generation by granting them private property. Each individual was to receive his own acreage, usually coming to about 180 acres per family unit, and land left over after all allotments were made was to be thrown open to sale, the proceeds used to build houses and barns and to buy stock and equipment for the Indians to become farmers.

However, even by 1887, subsistence farming by individual families was giving way to large scale, single crop enterprises. Although allotments remained tax free for a period of twenty-five or thirty years, Indian people were not adequately informed nor technically prepared for managing farms. The result was that many of the allotments were lost through tax default or sold to pay debts which far-seeing whites had allowed Indians to run up against the day they would gain patents-in-fee to their land. Although the necessity for more protective provisions was soon recognized by the government, an unexpected complication rendered much of the land useless to its Indian owners. Some time between 1900 and 1910, a rapid decrease in Indian population leveled off and a steady rise set in. Original allotments were divided among increasing numbers of heirs. Given American laws of inheritance, there developed a common situation in which an individual might own forty or more acres, but as scattered fractions of land inherited from a number of ancestors who had received allotments. The easiest course was for the Indian Bureau simply to rent the land out in large parcels to white agriculturalists and stockmen and divide the proceeds among the many heirs. Some people could live on their rent money alone, often supporting less fortunate relatives as well. But, in most cases, rent money brought only a few dollars a year and a living was eked out by wage labor in planting and harvest seasons, forays to the cities to work in factories, and exploitation of the growing tourist industry in terms of sale of handcrafts and public dance performances.

As regulations on Indian movement off the reservations tended to relax, especially if people left to seek work, Indian people became increasingly better informed on the myriad opportunities to earn a living in industrial America besides the drudgery of farming. However, Indian communities persisted even where the allotment process had drastically reduced the land base. Indian people seemed to join circuses and wild west shows, seek out areas where relatively high wages were paid for crop work, or find their way to industrial employment in the cities in a manner reminiscent of hunting, trading or war expeditions. They drifted back home periodically to seek help from relatives if they were broke or to share the spoils of the "hunt" with their kinsmen until it was necessary to forage again. They took to automobiles as enthusiastically as many had taken to ponies at an earlier time, becoming commuters to cities or other places where they could find work, returning daily or weekly or seasonally or by whatever schedule was practical. Some people spent most of their lifetimes in the city, but returned home to their tribesmen upon retirement. And these patterns persist today. Unlike the usual migrants, Indian people do not seem to perceive urban work as a break with the rural past, but merely as an extension of the peripheries of the territory which can be exploited economically. It is difficult to escape the conclusion that Indian people were "rurban" long before anyone coined the term or saw the industrial blending of city and country life as the direction in which the nation as a whole was to move.

Although Indian groups, with their characteristic close communal life, were persisting and increasing in size, the national outlook stressed rugged individualism and private enterprise. Both policy and administration of Indian affairs were oriented toward assimilating Indians as individuals into the general population. Tribal enterprises and industries were introduced only where the overwhelming argument of certain natural resources militated against allotment in severalty. Thus a few tribal forests and fishing grounds provided regular employment and income on the reservation, but even in these cases Indian people were given little voice or purposeful training in management of tribal business. Beyond that, a number of areas escaped allotment either because the terrain made it impractical for subsistence farming or the problems created by allotment elsewhere had become apparent and the plan was simply shelved before more remote areas were included under it.

Other efforts to reform Indian administration gradually got around to matters of practical welfare. The Indian Bureau had always been a political pork barrel, appointments to various posts being handed out to party stalwarts. The pay was poor, but there were opportunities to shave budgets for personal gain. Allotment opened more opportunities to bribe officials to declare Indians "competent" to sell their land. The scandals of peculation, the complaints of sincere employees that the uncertainty of their jobs made it impossible to carry out decent programs, and the clear evidence of honest but unqualified and emotionally callous personnel all led to demands for improvement. Doctors and teaching staffs were put on civil service in 1892, and by 1902 all Bureau employees were on civil service except the Commissioner and Assistant Commissioner.

At the time of the First World War most of the Indian population was still without the vote and also not subject to conscription, but a surprising number of young men volunteered for the armed services and were recognized for remarkable heroism. This stirred the nation from complacency about Indian problems and in 1924 the franchise was extended to all Indians. Significantly, one Indian view, which found expression among tribes all over the country, considered the right to vote a pretty shabby reward and no more than further evidence of national disregard for Indian rights as established by treaties. The implication was that Indians volunteered in America's defense as loyal allies as pledged in treaties rather than as patriotic citizens.[11]

However, few white Americans were aware

of this reaction to their magnaminous gesture, and concerned people continued efforts to understand why Indians had not yet been granted their proper place as assimilated Americans and to search for better means of accomplishing this end. The results of extensive investigation of Indian affairs by the Brookings Institution were published in 1928,[12] setting forth in concise and depressing detail just how bad things really were among Indian people under the federal jurisdiction, and suggesting means of improving the situation.

Although committed to the entrenched view that assimilation of Indians was both desirable and inevitable, the Brookings Report noted that this would take time and the settling of many just grievances harbored by the tribes before trust and cooperation could be expected of them. Throughout the Report we begin to see indications of a changing perspective on Indians' problems in the recommendations reached by objective investigators. For example, in speaking of administration as "leadership," the Report says:

This phrase "rights of the Indian" is often used solely to apply to his property rights. Here it is used in a much broader sense to cover his rights as a human being living in a free country. . . . The effort to substitute educational leadership for the more dictatorial methods now used in some places will necessitate more understanding of and sympathy for the Indian point of view. Leadership will recognize the good in the economic and social life of the Indians in their religion and ethics, and will seek to develop it and build on it rather than to crush out all that is Indian. The Indians have much to contribute to the dominant civilization, and the effort should be made to secure this contribution, in part because of the good it will do the Indians in stimulating a proper race pride and self-respect.[13]

Serious efforts to implement the Brookings recommendations were delayed as the nation entered the depression of the 1930's. With the election of Franklin D. Roosevelt and appointment of John Collier, Sr. as Indian Commissioner, a "New Deal" was also in store for Indian people. Collier's thinking went beyond the Brookings recommendations both in revising administrative procedures and in philosophy. He endea-

vored to set up mechanisms for self government which would allow Indian communities to bargain as communities with the government and the larger society. He sought to teach them about a host of opportunities for community improvement and let them choose accordingly—revolving loan funds, tribal enterprises, resource development, land acquisition, tribal courts, educational programs. In many ways Collier's plan was inappropriate: too "Indian" for some tribes, not "Indian" enough for others, and characterized by unwarranted urgency and hard sell in some instances. For all that, Indian people recognized in large measure that Collier really understood what their grievances were about even if his methods were sometimes less than satisfactory or if Bureau personnel on the local level were often incapable of throwing off old habits of mind and behavior in carrying out the intent of the new administration. Where Collier and Indian people were in agreement was in the objective of restoring not the Indian culture of any past period but the kind of conditions and relationships which existed prior to the "ward" philosophy of Indian administration, a period when Indian people could still select and adapt innovations to find satisfactory patterns of their own for community life. Above all, Collier understood the need to secure an adequate land base for meaningful social experimentation and development.

Collier's administration and philosophy . . . were short-lived as views Congress would be willing to support. They were in effective operation for seven years at most. The Indian Reorganization Act was passed in 1934, time was required to inform Indian people and allow them to make decisions in regard to it, and by 1941 the nation was at war. Domestic programs, including those of the Indian Bureau, were naturally made secondary to the war effort. Wartime prosperity brought temporary alleviation of economic problems for many Indian communities. Collier remained in office until 1946, but it was becoming increasingly apparent that his administrative ideas were losing popularity with Congress.[14] After the war, when servicemen and factory workers returned home, Indian population, like that of the rest of the nation, had increased. Programs just started before the war had not been able to keep pace with the added pressures on the still limited sources of income of the reservations. Since the "Indian problem" suddenly loomed larger than ever, the easy explanation was Collier's revolutionary departure from the time-honored Indian policy of assimilation.

Because Indian people showed a marked aptitude for industrial work during the war, and it was obvious they would not succeed as farmers, the solution was simple. Relocate them in urban centers, preferably in each case as far from the home reservation as possible, and legislate the reservations out of existence so that Indian people could not run home when things got tough or share their good fortune periodically with kinsmen who lacked the gumption to get out on their own.

Like the grand scheme of 1887 to solve the Indians' problems by the simple expedient of allotment in severalty, the relocation-reservation termination plan of the 1950's was out of date for its time in terms of national, social and economic trends. If the ideal of the Allotment Act was to ensconce Indian people in a kind of average, small farm middle-class, which was actually disappearing, the ideal of the policy of the 1950's was primarily to get the government out of the Indian business and scant attention was paid to where Indian people might be able to fit in American life. Indian people opposed the policy of the 1950's, arguing for the alternative of community development through local industries and beefing up the long neglected educational programs. This, Indian people argued, would enable them to plan and manage intelligently in their own behalf community development and tribal enterprises. It would also make it possible for those individuals who wished to assimilate to enter the larger society at a decent economic and occupational level.

At the very time that suburbs were burgeoning, commuting was a way of life for much of the nation, and far sighted people were anticipating greater segmentation of industrial operations and dispersing them to where the people live, Indian policy was based on models of concentrating population in large urban centers. Like the rural myth of the nineteenth century, mid-twentieth century policy promoted the myth of the "melting pot," whereby the ambitious immigrant worked his way out of the poor, ethnic neighbor-

hood by frugality and hard work. Such thinking ignored a number of facts: (1) The agonies which such groups suffered during the period when they were exploited minorities living in urban slums. (2) The loss of a sense of community which such people suffered when, sometimes after repeated moves as a group to different urban neighborhoods, they finally "spun off" into the larger society. (3) The special reliance of Indian people on group identity, group membership and group decisions, which goes beyond anything comparable which the immigrant communities were able to establish. Immigrant communities usually were not communities when they came; their ethnic identities were, to a surprising extent, constructed in America. (4) The increasing difficulty of "making it" economically and socially in an economy which has much less use today for unskilled labor, and a society which sees color so strongly that many of its members still doubt that non-caucasians are really capable of achieving middle-class standards.

The trends of social reform and legislation had taken increasing cognizance of the fact that the individual could no longer hope to go it alone, saving for the rainy days and providing for his old age. Studies of crime and mental health had begun to raise serious questions about the nature of modern, industrialized society in depriving the individual of a sense of community and meaningful engagement in life. But in the 1950's, and to a great extent in the 1960's, it is considered unrealistic, impractical and perhaps even a little silly to suggest, as the Brookings Report did in 1928, that "The Indians have much to contribute to the dominant civilization, and the effort should be made to secure this contribution."[15]

Whether or not Indian people are potential models for satisfactory community life for the nation at large, one thing became clear during the 1950's. They were not happy with the solution to their problems of poverty offered by the government. Furthermore, it was soon obvious that the policy of the 1950's, like allotment in the 1880's, tended to create more new problems rather than solve old ones. By 1960, the presidential candidates of both parties recognized the need to reassess Indian affairs and find new directions for policy. At the same time, Indian people appeared to be more vocal and concerned with exercising a positive influence in regard to legislation affecting them. . . .

ENDNOTES

1. For more intensive study of the subject: William Brandon, *The American Heritage Book of Indians* (New York, 1961; paperback: Dell, 1964): more historical than ethnological. Harold Driver, *Indians of North America* (Chicago, 1961), a scholarly reference book with useful maps. Organized according to topics rather than culture areas. Wendell H. Oswalt, *This Land Was Theirs* (New York, 1966): good treatment of ten representative tribes across the country. Robert F. Spencer, Jesse D. Jennings, *et al.*, *The Native Americans* (New York, 1965): general introductory chapters followed by culture area descriptions and accounts of specific tribes within the areas, written for textbook use. Ruth Underhill, *Red Man's America* (Chicago 1953), also a textbook, and in many ways still the best general introduction to the subject for the beginner. Wilcomb Washburn, ed., *The Indian and The White Man* (Garden City, N.Y., 1964), a fascinating compendium of documents from the period of early contact to the present day, including John Marshall's decisions of 1831 and 1832, and House Concurrent Resolution 108—the termination bill referred to in this paper.

2. A small but revealing incident, illustrative of a kind of hunter's pragmatism, occurred in the Canadian Northwest Territories. When questioned about his first airplane ride, a Slave Indian was clearly enthusiastic but not awe-struck by modern technology—"Good! See moose sign. Come back, go find moose." Personal conversation, June Helm.

3. Nancy Oestreich Lurie, "Indian Cultural Adjustment to European Civilization," in James Morton Smith, ed., *Seventeenth Century America* (Chapel Hill, 1958), 33–60, discusses the Powhatan Confederacy and notes origins of the reservation system in North America.

4. Lurie, "The Indian Claims Commission Act," *The Annals of The American Academy of Political and Social Science* (May, 1957), 56–70, reviews the question of Indian land title, with special reference to an Alaskan case, 64–65.

5. The multitude of treaties in the United States and problems of boundaries are fully set forth in Charles J. Kappler, comp. and ed., *Indian Affairs, Laws and Treaties* (Washington, D.C., Vol. 2, *Treaties*, 1904); and Charles C. Royce and Cyrus Thomas,

"Indian Land Cessions in the United States," *Annual Report* of the Bureau of American Ethnology, Smithsonian Institution, Vol. 18, Pt. 2 (Washington, D.C., 1896–97).

6. *Cf.* William T. Hagan, *American Indians* (Chicago, 1961), for a discussion of Indian rights vs. national interest.

7. Theodore Roosevelt, *The Winning of the West* (New York, 1889–1896), I, 90.

8. There are exceptions, however, as a few multitribe reservations were set up, particularly in the Northwest.

9. *Answers to Questions About American Indians*, Bureau of Indian Affairs (pamphlet), Washington, D.C., 1965, 7. The concept of ward, an equivocal term at best, is often confused with "trusteeship" which has legal meaning and refers to land, not people, in regard to the protective role of the federal government in regard to Indian affairs.

10. Before the general allotment act was passed in 1887, an earlier "pilot" allotment act was passed with specific reference to the Omaha Reservation in Nebraska in 1882. *Cf.* Lurie, "The Lady from Boston and the Omaha Indians," *The American West*, III, 4 (Fall, 1966), 31–33; 80–86.

11. This view of the vote is still found among some Indian people.

12. Lewis C. Merriam and associates, *The Problem of Indian Administration: report on a survey made at the request of the Honorable Hubert Work, Secretary of the Interior*, The Brookings Institution (Baltimore, 1928).

13. *Ibid.*

14. It is an open question whether the Indian Claims Commission Act, passed in 1946, represented the last of the Collier era or the beginning of the termination era. The objective of the act is to provide restitution for Indian grievance, particularly in regard to non-payment or unconscionable consideration for land. However, as sentiment grew in favor of relocation and termination, one argument was that Indian communities would disperse once grievances were settled and only the hope of payment on old debts perpetuated Indian identity. Ideally, claims payments would give Indian people the necessary stake to begin a new life as ordinary citizens far from the reservations. In actual fact, the amounts paid were relatively small on a per capita basis, and Indian communities persisted. Many tribes are still waiting for their claims to be settled.

15. Merriam, *The Problem*, 22–23.

10

Contrasts in the Community Organization of Chinese and Japanese in North America*

Stanford M. Lyman

Race relations theory and policy in North America have for the most part been built upon examination of the experiences and difficulties of European immigrants and Negroes. As a result contrasting ideas and programmes, emphasizing integration for the latter and cultural pluralism for the former, have been generated primarily in consideration of each group's most manifest problems.[1] However, relatively little work has been done to ascertain the conditions under which an ethnic group is likely to follow an integration-oriented or a pluralist-oriented path.[2] Two racial groups found in North America—the Chinese and the Japanese—are likely candidates for the focus of such research, since they have superficially similar outward appearances, a long history as victims of oppression, discrimination, and prejudice, but quite different developments in community organization and cohesion.[3] In this paper an attempt is made to ascertain the distinctive feature of the culture and social organization of the two immigrant groups that played significant

Reprinted from *The Canadian Review of Sociology and Anthropology*, 5:2(1968), by permission of the author and the publisher.

*Revised version of a paper presented at the University of California under the sponsorship of the Committee for Arts and Lectures, August 23, 1966. I am indebted to Herbert Blumer, Jean Burnet and Marvin Scott for criticisms of earlier versions of this paper.

roles in directing the mode of community organization in North America.

There is sound theoretical ground for reconsidering the role of Old World culture and social organization on immigrant communities in North America. Even in what might seem the paradigm case of cultural destruction in the New World—that of the Negro—there is evidence to suggest at least vestiges of cultural survival.[4] In those ethnic communities unmarred by so culturally demoralizing a condition as slavery, there survives what Nathan Glazer calls elements of a "ghost nation," so that despite its fires social life goes on at least in part "beyond the melting pot."[5] American ideology has stressed assimilation, but its society is marked by European, Asian, and some African survivals; Canadian ideology has stressed the "mosaic" of cultures, but at least some of its peoples show definite signs of being Canadianized. The immigrants' cultural baggage needs sociological inspection to ascertain its effects on community organization and acculturation. Fortunately, the Chinese and Japanese communities provide opportunities for this research because of new knowledge about the Old Asian World[6] and extensive material on their lives in North America.

The Chinese

In contrast to the Japanese and several European groups, the Chinese in Canada and the United

States present an instance of unusually persistent social isolation and preservation of Old World values and institutions.[7] To the present day a great many Chinese work, play, eat, and sleep in the Chinese ghettos known throughout North America as "Chinatowns." The business ethics of Chinatown's restaurants and bazaars are institutionalized in guild and trade associations more reflective of nineteenth-century Cathay than twentieth-century North America. Newly arrived Chinese lads work a twelve to sixteen-hour day as waiters and busboys totally unprotected by labor unions. Immigrant Chinese mothers sit in rows in tiny "sweatshops" sewing dresses for downtown shops while infants crawl at their feet. In basements below the street level or in rooms high above the colorfully-lit avenue, old men gather round small tables to gamble at *f' an t' an, p' ai kop piu,* or other games of chance. Above the hubbub of activity in the basements, streets, stores, and sweatshops are the offices of clan associations, speech and territorial clubs, and secret societies. And behind the invisible wall that separates Chinatown from the metropolis the elites of these organizations conduct an unofficial government, legislating, executing, and adjudicating matters for their constituents.

Not every Chinese in Canada or the United States today recognizes the sovereignty of Chinatown's power élite or receives its benefits and protections.[8] At one time San Francisco's "Chinese Six Companies" and Vancouver's Chinese Benevolent Association could quite properly claim to speak for all the Chinese in the two countries. But that time is now past. Students from Hong Kong and Taiwan and Chinese intellectuals, separated in social origins, status, and aspirations from other Chinese, have cut themselves off from their Chinatown compatriots. Another segment of the Chinese population, the Canadian-born and American-born, who have acquired citizenship in the country of their birth, not only exhibits outward signs of acculturation in dress, language, and behaviour, but also grants little if any obeisance to Chinatown's élites. Some of this generation now find it possible to penetrate the racial barrier, and pass into the workaday world of the outer society with impunity. Others still work or reside in Chinatown but are too acculturated to be subject to its private law. Still a few

others are active in the traditional associations seeking power and status within the framework of the old order.

That North America's Chinatowns are not merely creatures of the American environment is indicated by the relatively similar institutionalization of Chinese communities in other parts of the world.[9] The diaspora of Chinese in the last two centuries has populated Southeast Asia, the Americas, Europe, and Africa with Oriental colonies. Should the tourists who today pass along Grant Avenue in San Francisco, Pender Street in Vancouver, and Pell and Mott Streets in New York City, peering at exotic food and art, and experiencing the sights, sounds, and smells of these cities' Chinatowns, be whisked away to Manila, Bangkok, Singapore, or Semarang, or suddenly find themselves in Calcutta, Liverpool or the capital of the Malagasy Republic, they would discover, amidst the unfamiliarity of the several national cultures, still other "Chinatowns" not unlike their North American counterparts. Recognition of the recalcitrance of overseas Chinese to their surroundings takes different forms in different places. In the United States sociologists marvel at their resistance to the fires of the melting pot; in Indonesia the government questions the loyalty of this alien people; in Malaysia native farmers and laborers resent the vivid contrast between their own poverty and Chinese commercial affluence; in Jamaica Chinese are urged to quit their exclusiveness and become part of the larger community. But everywhere the issue is acculturation. Despite more than a century of migration, the Chinese have not fully adopted the culture, language, behaviour—the ways of life—of the countries in which they have settled. Their cultural exclusiveness—especially as it finds its expression in geographically compact and socially distant communities within the host societies' cities—is a world-historical event deserving far more discussion and research than it has yet been given.

The Japanese

The rapid acculturation of the Japanese in North America has been a source of frequent discussion. The fact that "Japan-town" is not as familiar a term to North Americans as "Chinatown" is an unobtrusive measure of this difference between the two peoples. Such local names as "Li'l Tokyo" or "Li'l Yokohama" have been short-lived references for Japanese communities isolated through discrimination, but these have rarely been characterized by such peculiar institutions and private government as are found in the Chinese quarter. Japanese-owned businesses are not organized on the basis of guilds or *zaibatsu;* prefectural associations exist primarily for nostalgic and ceremonial purposes, playing no effective part in political organization in the community; and secret societies like those so prominent among the Chinese are not found in North American Japanese communities. Neither sweatshops nor gambling houses are established institutions of Japanese-American or Japanese-Canadian communities. Indeed, in the geographic sense, the North American Japanese communities show increasing signs of disintegration.

Although overseas Chinese communities exhibit the characteristics of colonization with a superordinate organization to represent them to the larger society, the Japanese are organized on patterns closer to that of a reluctant minority group.[10] The earliest association among immigrant Japanese emphasized defence against prejudice and support for the larger society's laws and customs, and these organizations have been supplanted by even more acculturation-oriented organizations in the second generation. Japanese are the only ethnic group to emphasize geo-generational distinctions by separate nomenclature and a belief in the unique character structure of each generational group. Today the third and fourth generations in North America *(Sansei* and *Yonsei,* respectively) exhibit definite signs of a "Hansen effect"—that is, interest in recovering Old World culture—and also show concern over the appropriate allocation of their energies and activities to things American or Canadian and things Japanese. Ties to a Japanese community are tenuous and find their realization primarily in courtship and marriage and in recreational pursuits.

Although the situation is by no means so clear, overseas Japanese communities outside North America exhibit some patterns similar to and some quite different from those of the continental United States and Canada. In the most

extensive study of acculturation among Japanese in pre-war Kona, Hawaii, the community appeared organized less along Japanese than Hawaiian-American lines. Other studies of Japanese in Hawaii have emphasized the innovative food habits, decline of the patriarch, and changing moral bases of family life. On the other hand, Japanese in Peru, where Japan's official policy of emigration played a significant role in establishing the colony and supervising its affairs, had maintained a generally separate though financially successful and occupationally diversified community until 1942; postwar developments indicate that the Peruvian-born Japanese will seek and obtain increasing entrance into Peruvian society and further estrangement from all-Japanese associations. In Brazil, a situation similar to that of Peru developed: sponsored migration reached great heights during the period of Japan's imperialist development, and, although Brazil welcomed Japanese until 1934, a policy of coerced assimilation motivated by suspicion of Japanese intent led to a closing of many all-Japanese institutions before the outbreak of World War II. In the postwar period, Brazilian-born Japanese indicated a greater interest than their parents had in integration into Brazilian society. In Paraguay, where the first Japanese colony began in La Colmena as recently as 1936, signs of acculturation and community breakdown have been reported by cultural geographers surveying the area.[11] Generally, this cursory survey of overseas Japanese communities suggests that when such communities are not governed by agencies of the homeland and where, as the researches of Caudill and de Vos indicate,[12] Japanese values find opportunity for interpenetration and complementarity with those of the host society (as in the United States and Canada), the speed with which community isolation declines is accelerated.

Contrasts between the Chinese and Japanese have been noticed frequently but rarely researched.[13] As early as 1909 Chester Rowell, a Fresno, California journalist, pointed to the Japanese refusal to be losers in unprofitable contracts, to their unwillingness to be tied to a "Jap-town," and to their geniality and politeness; in contrast he praised the Chinese subordination to contracts and headmen, their accommodation to a ghetto existence, and their cold but efficient and loyal service as domestics. Similar observations were made by Winifred Raushenbush, Robert Park's assistant in his famous race relations survey of the Pacific coast. More recently the late Rose Hum Lee has vividly remarked upon the contrast between the two Oriental groups. Professor Lee asserts that the *Nisei* "exhibit within sixty years, greater degrees of integration into American society, than has been the case with the Chinese, whose settlement is twice as long." Other sociologists have frequently commented on the speed with which Japanese adopted at least the outward signs of Occidental culture and attained success in North America. Broom and Kitsuse summed up the impressive record of the Japanese by declaring it "an achievement perhaps rarely equalled in the history of human migration." More recently, Petersen has pointed to the same record of achievement and challenged sociologists to develop a theory which could adequately explain it as well as the less spectacular records of other ethnic groups.

Although the differences between the Chinese and Japanese in North America have excited more comparative comment than concrete investigation, an early statement by Walter G. Beach deserves more attention that it has received. In a much neglected article[14] Beach observed the contrast between the speed of acculturation of Chinese and Japanese and attributed it to those conditions within and extrinsic to the ethnic groups which fostered either segregation and retention of old world culture traits or rapid breakdown of the ethnic community. Noting that ethnic cultures were an important aspect of the kind of community an immigrant group would form he pointed out that the Chinese came to America "before Chinese culture had been greatly influenced by Western civilization." More specifically, he suggested that "they came from an old, conservative and stationary social organization and system of custom-control of life; and that the great majority came from the lower and least independent social stratum of that life." By contrast, he observed that the Japanese "came at a time when their national political system had felt the influence of Western thought and ambitions." He went on to say: "Japan was recognized among the world's powers, and its people were self-

conscious in respect to this fact; their pride was not in a past culture, unintelligible to Americans (as the Chinese), but in a growing position of recognition and authority among the world's powers." It was because of these differences in culture and outlook, Beach argued, that Japanese tended to resist discrimination more vigorously and to adopt Occidental ways more readily, while Chinese produced a "Chop-suey culture" in segregated communities. Stripped of its ethnocentrism, Beach's analysis suggests that acculturation is affected not only by the action of the larger society upon immigrants, but also, and more fundamentally, by the nature and quality of the immigrant culture and institutions.

The present study specifies and clarifies the features of Japanese and Chinese culture which Beach only hinted at, and details the interplay between Old-World cultures and North American society. Certain key conditions of life in China and Japan at the times of emigration produced two quite different kinds of immigrant social organization. The responses of the American economy and society to Chinese and Japanese certainly had their effects. But these alone did not shape Chinese and Japanese life. Rather they acted as "accelerators" to the direction of and catalysts or inhibitors of the development of the immigrants' own culture and institutions.[15] Prejudices and discrimination added considerable hardship to the necessarily onerous lives of the immigrating Orientals, but did not wrench away their culture, nor deprive them completely of those familial, political, and social institutions which they had transported across the Pacific.[16] The Chinese and Japanese were never reduced to the wretchedness of the first Africans in America, who experienced a forcible stripping away of their original culture, and then a coercive assimilation into selected and subordinated elements of white America. Thus, although both Chinese and Japanese share a nearly identical distinction from the dominant American racial stock, and although both have been oppressed by prejudice, discrimination, segregation and exclusion, a fundamental source of their markedly different rates of acculturation is to be found in the particular developmental patterns taken by their respective cultures[17] in America.

Emigration

The conditions of emigration for Chinese and Japanese reflected respectively their different cultures. The Chinese migrated from a state that was not a nation, and they conceived of themselves primarily as members of local extended kin units, bound together by ties of blood and language and only secondarily, if at all, as "citizens" of the Chinese empire.[18] Chinese emigration was an organized affair in which kinsmen or fellow villagers who had achieved some wealth or status acted as agents and sponsors for their compatriots. Benevolently despotic, this emigration acted to transfer the loyalties and institutions of the village to the overseas community. In the village, composed for the most part of his kinsmen, the individual looked to elders as leaders; in emigrating the individual reposed his loyalty and submitted his fate to the overseas representative of his clan or village. Loans, protection, and jobs were provided within a framework of kin and language solidarity that stretched from the village in Kwangtung to the clan building in "Chinatown." Emigrants regarded their journey as temporary and their return as certain. Abroad the Chinese, as homeless men, never fully accepted any permanence to their sojourn. They identified themselves with their Old-World clan, village, dialect grouping, or secret society whose overseas leaders were recognized as legitimate substitutes for homeland groups. These institutional leaders further insinuated themselves into the overseas immigrant's life by acting as his representative to white society, by pioneering new settlements, and by providing badly-needed goods and services, protection against depredations, and punishments for wrong-doing.

The Japanese emigrant departed from an entirely different kind of society.[19] Japan was a nation as well as a state, and its villages reflected this fact. Village life had long ceased to be circumscribed by kinship, and the individual family rather than the extended kinship group was the locus of loyalty and solidarity. When children departed their homes they left unencumbered by a network of obligations. Unless he had been born first or last, a Japanese son was not obligated as was a Chinese to remain in the home of his parents. After 1868 emigration was sometimes sponsored by the government and certainly encouraged. When Japanese departed the homeland they, like the Chinese, expected only to sojourn, but they were not called back to the home village by the knowledge that a long-patient wife awaited them or that kinsmen fully depended on their return. Moreover, the men who inspired Japanese emigration were not pioneer leaders but exemplary individuals whose singular fame and fortune seemed to promise everyone great opportunity abroad. They did not serve as overseas community leaders or even very often as agents of migration, but only as shining examples of how others might succeed.

Marital Status

The respective marital situation of these two Asian peoples reflected fundamental differences in Chinese and Japanese kinship and profoundly influenced community life overseas. Custom required that a Chinese man sojourn abroad without his wife. A man's return to hearth and village was thus secured, and he laboured overseas in order that he might some day again enjoy the warmth of domesticity and the blessings of children. Abroad he lived a lonely life of labour, dependent on kinsmen and compatriots for fellowship and on prostitutes and vice for outlet and recreation. When in 1882 restrictive American legislation unwittingly converted Chinese custom into legal prohibition by prohibiting the coming of wives of Chinese labourers it exaggerated and lengthened the separation of husbands from wives and, more significantly, delayed for nearly two generations the birth in America of a substantial "second generation" among the immigrant Chinese. Canadian immigration restrictions had a similar consequence.[20] Barred from intermarriage by custom and law and unable to bring wives to Canada or the United States, Chinese men sired children on their infrequent return visits to China, and these China-born sons later partially replenished the Chinese population in North America as they joined their fathers in the overseas venture. Like their fathers the sons also depended on Chinatown institutions. Their lack of independence from the same community controls which had earlier circumscribed the lives of their fathers stood in sharp contrast to the manner of life of the Canadian and American born.

Neither custom nor law barred the Japanese from bringing wives to Canada or America.[21] Within two decades of their arrival the Japanese had brought over enough women to guarantee that, although husbands might be quite a bit older than their wives, a domestic life would be established in America. Japanese thus had little need for the brothels and gambling halls which characterized Chinese communities in the late nineteenth century and which, not incidentally, provided a continuous source of wealth and power to those who owned or controlled them. Japanese quickly produced a second generation in both Canada and the United States, and by 1930 this *Nisei* generation began to claim a place for itself in North America and in Japanese-American and Japanese-Canadian life. The independence and acculturation of the *Nisei* was indicated in their social and political style of life. They did not accept the organizations of their parents' community and established *ad hoc* associations dedicated to civil rights and penetration beyond Canada's and America's racial barrier. Some Japanese immigrants educated one of their children in Japan. These few Japan-educated offspring *(Kibei)* did not enjoy the same status in North America as *Nisei*, and in their marginality and problems of adjustment they resembled the China-born offspring of Chinese immigrants. Educated in Canadian or American schools possessed of Canadian or American culture and values, the *Nisei* found that prejudice and discrimination acted as the most significant obstacle to their success.

Occupations and Locations

Jobs and settlement patterns tended to reinforce and accelerate the different development patterns of Chinese and Japanese communities in America.[22] Except for a small but powerful merchant elite the Chinese began and remained as wage labourers. First employed in the arduous and menial tasks of mining and railroad-building, the Chinese later gravitated into unskilled, clerical and service work inside the Chinese community. Such work necessitated living in cities or returning to cities when unemployment drove the

contract labourers to seek new jobs. The city always meant the Chinese quarter, a ghetto set aside for Chinese in which their special needs could be met and by which the white population could segregate itself from them. Inside the ghetto Old-World societies ministered to their members' wants, exploited their needs, and represented their interests. When primary industry could no longer use Chinese and white hostility drove them out of the labour market and into Chinatown, the power of these associations and their merchant leaders was reconfirmed and enhanced. The single most important feature of the occupation of Chinese immigrants was their tendency to keep the Chinese in a state of dependency on bosses, contractors, merchants—ultimately on the merchant élite of Chinatown.

The Japanese, after a brief stint as labourers in several primary industries then on the wane in western America, pioneered the cultivation of truck crops.[23] Small-scale agriculturalists, separated from one another as well as from the urban anti-Orientalism of the labor unions, Japanese farmers did not retain the kind of ethnic solidarity characteristic of the urban Chinese. Whatever traditional elites had existed among the early Japanese immigrants fell from power or were supplanted. In their place *ad hoc* associations arose to meet particular needs. When Japanese did become labourers and city dwellers they too became segregated in "li'l Tokyos" presided over by Old-World associations for a time. But the early concentration in agriculture and the later demands of the *Nisei* tended to weaken the power even of the city-bred immigrant associations.

Community Power and Conflict

Finally, the different bases for solidarity in the two Oriental communities tended to confirm their respective modes of social organization. The Japanese community has remained isolated primarily because of discriminatory barriers to integration and secondarily because of the sense of congregation among fellow Japanese. The isolated Chinese community is, to be sure, a product of white aversion and is also characterized by congregative sentiments, but, much more than that of the Japanese, it rests on communal foundations. Political life in Chinatown has rarely been tranquil.[24] The traditional clans and *Landsmanschaften* controlled immigration, settled disputes, levied taxes and fines, regulated commerce, and meted out punishments. Opposition to their rule took the form it had taken in China. Secret societies, chapters of or modeled after the well-known Triad Society, took over the functions of law, protection, and revenge for their members. In addition the secret societies owned or controlled the gambling houses and brothels which emerged to satisfy the recreational and sex needs of homeless Chinese men and displayed occasional interest in the restive politics of China. Struggles for power, blood feuds, and "wars" of vengeance were not infrequent in the early days of Chinatown. These conflicts entrenched the loyalties of men to their respective associations. More important with respect to non-acculturation, these intramural fights isolated the Chinese from the uncomprehending larger society and bound them together in antagonistic cooperation. Since the turn of the century, the grounds of such battles have shifted on to a commercial and political plane, but violence is not unknown. Chinatown's organizational solidarity and its intra-community conflicts have thus acted as agents of non-acculturation.

Position and Prospects of the Oriental in North America

The conditions for the political and economic integration of the Chinese appear to be at hand now.[25] This is largely because the forces which spawned and maintained Chinatown are now weakened. The near balancing of the sex ratio has made possible the birth and maturation in America of second and third generation Chinese. Their presence, in greater and greater numbers, poses a serious threat to old-world power élites. The breakdown of discriminatory barriers to occupations and residency brought about by a new assertion of civil rights heralds an end to Chinatown economic and domestic monopoly. The relative openness of Canadian and American society to American-born and Canadian-born Chinese reduces their dependency on traditional goods and services and their recruitment into communal associations. Concomitantly, the *casus belli* of the earlier era disappears and conflict's

group-binding and isolating effect loses force. What remains of Chinatown eventually is its new immigrants, its culturally acceptable economic base—restaurants and shops—and its congregative value for ethnic Chinese. Recent events in San Francisco suggest that the young and newly-arrived immigrants from Hong Kong and Taiwan and the American-born Chinese school drop-outs are estranged from both the Chinatown élites and white America. Many of their activities resemble those of protesting and militant Negro groups.

The Japanese are entering a new phase of relations with the larger society in North America. There is a significant amount of anxiety in Japanese circles about the decline of Japanese values and the appearance of the more undesirable features of Canadian and American life—primarily juvenile delinquency but also a certain lack of old-world propriety which had survived through the *Nisei* generation—among the *Sansei* and *Yonsei*.[26] Moreover, like those Negroes who share E. Franklin Frazier's disillusion with the rise of a black bourgeoisie, some Japanese-Americans are questioning the social and personal price paid for entrance into American society. Scholars such as Daisuke Kitagawa have wondered just how *Nisei* and *Sansei* might preserve elements of Japanese culture in America. At the same time one European Japanophile has bitterly assailed the Americanization of the *Nisei*.[27] Nothing similar to a black power movement has developed among the Japanese, and, indeed, such a movement is extremely unlikely given Japanese-American and Canadian material success and the decrease in social distance between Japanese and white Americans. At most there is a quiet concern. But even such mild phenomena are deserving of sociological attention.

Theortical Considerations

This survey of Oriental community organization suggests the need to take seriously Robert Park's reconsideration of his own race relations cycle. Park at first had supposed that assimilation was a natural and inevitable outcome of race contact marked off by stages of competition, conflict, and accommodation before there occurred the eventual absorption of one people by another.[28] In addition to its faults as a natural history, a criticism so often discussed by other sociologists,[29] Park's original statement of the cycle took no account of what, in a related context, Wagley and Harris refer to as the "adaptive capacity" of the immigrant group.[30] However, Park himself reconsidered the cycle and in 1937 wrote that it might terminate in one of three outcomes: a caste system as was the case in India; complete assimilation, as he imagined had occurred in China; or a permanent institutionalization of minority status within a larger society, as was the case of Jews in Europe. Park concluded that race relations occur as phases of a cycle "which, once initiated, inevitably continues until it terminates in some predestined racial configuration, and one consistent with the established social order of which it is a part."[31] Park's later emphasis on alternative outcomes and his consideration of the peculiar social context in which any ethnic group's history occurs implicitly recall attention to the interplay between native and host society cultures. As Herskovitz's researches on West African and American Negro cultures indicate, the immigrant group, even if oppressed *in transitu*, does not arrive with a cultural *tabula rasa* waiting to be filled in by the host culture. Rather it possesses a culture and social organization which in contact with and in the several contexts of the host culture will be supplanted, inhibited, subordinated, modified or enhanced. Kinship, occupations, patterns of settlement and community organization are each factors in such developments. Assimilation, or for that matter pluralism, is not simply an inevitable state of human affairs, as those who cling to "natural history" models assert, but rather is an existential possibility. Social factors contribute to the state of being of a people and to changes in that state. The Chinese and Japanese communities in America illustrate two modes of development and suggest the need to refine even further our knowledge of the factors which affect whatever mode of development an immigrant group chooses.

ENDNOTES

1. Cf. Horace M. Kallen, *Culture and Democracy in the United States* (New York, 1924) with Gunnar Myrdal, *An American Dilemma* (New York, 1944).
2. See Clyde V. Kiser, "Cultural Pluralism," *The Annals of the American Academy of Political and Social Science*, 262 (March 1949), 118–29. An approach to such a theory is found in William Petersen, *Population* (New York, 1961), pp. 114–49.
3. For an extended analysis see Stanford M. Lyman, "The Structure of Chinese Society in Nineteenth-Century America" (unpublished Ph.D. dissertation, University of California, Berkeley, 1961).
4. Melville Herskovitz, *The Myth of the Negro Past* (Boston, 1958). See also Charles Keil, *Urban Blues* (Chicago, 1966), 1–69.
5. Nathan Glazer, "Ethnic Groups in America: From National Culture to Ideology," in Morroe Berger, Theodore Abel, and Charles H. Page, Editors, *Freedom and Control in Modern Society* (New York, 1954), pp. 158–76, Nathan Glazer and Daniel Patrick Moynihan, *Beyond the Melting Pot: The Negroes, Puerto Ricans, Jews, Italians and Irish of New York City* (Cambridge, 1963).
6. The "knowledge explosion" on China has been prodigious since 1949 despite the difficulties in obtaining first-hand field materials. Much research was inspired by interest in the Chinese in Southeast Asia. See Maurice Freedman, "A Chinese Phase in Social Anthropology," *British Journal of Sociology*, 16, 1 (March 1963), 1–18.
7. Sources for the material reported are Lyman, "The Structure of Chinese Society in Nineteenth-Century America," *passim*; Leong Gor Yun, *Chinatown Inside Out* (New York, 1936), 26–106, 182–235; Calvin Lee, *Chinatown, U.S.A.: A History and Guide* (Garden City, 1955); Stuart H. Cattell, *Health, Welfare and Social Organization in Chinatown, New York City* (New York, August 1962), pp. 1–4, 20–68, 81–185. For the origins of organized labour's hostility to the Chinese see Herbert Hill, "The Racial Practices of Organized Labor—The Age of Gompers and Affair," in Arthur Ross and Herbert Hill, Editors, *Employment, Race, and Poverty: A Critical Study of the Disadvantaged Status of Negro Workers from 1865 to 1965* (New York, 1967), pp. 365–402. For a detailed description of Chinese games of chance see the several articles by Stewart Culin, "Chinese Games with Dice" (Philadelphia, 1889), pp. 5–21; "The Gambling Games of the Chinese in America," *Publications of the University of Pennsylvania, Series in Philology, Literature, and Archeology*, I, 4, 1891; "Chinese Games with Dice and Dominoes," *Report of the United States National Museum, Smithsonian Institution*, 1893, pp. 489–537. The sweatshops of San Francisco's Chinatown are described in James Benet, *A Guide to San Francisco and the Bay Region* (New York, 1963), pp. 73–74.
8. See Rose Hum Lee, *The Chinese in the United States of America* (Hong Kong, 1960), pp. 86–131, 231–51, 363–404. See also *Chinese Students in the*

United States, 1948–1955: A Study in Government Policy (New York, March 1965). For a Canadian-Chinese view of his own generation's adjustment to Chinese and Canadian ways of life see William Wong, "The Younger Generation," Chinatown News, 11, 13 (March 18, 1964), 6–7.

9. Material for the following is drawn from Maurice Freedman and William Willmott, "Southeast Asia, with Special Reference to the Chinese," International Social Science Journal, 13, 2 (1961), 245–70; Victor Purcell, The Chinese in Southeast Asia (London, 1965), Second edition; Jacques Amyot, S. J., The Chinese Community of Manila: A Study of Adaptation of Chinese Familism to the Philippine Environment (Chicago, 1960); Richard J. Coughlin, "The Chinese in Bangkok: A Commerical-Oriented Minority," American Sociological Review, 20 (June 1955), 311–16; Maurice Freedman, Chinese Family and Marriage in Singapore (London, 1957); Donald Willmott, The Chinese of Semarang: A Changing Minority Community in Indonesia (Ithaca, 1960); Shelland Bradley, "Calcutta's Chinatown," Cornhill Magazine, 57 (September 1924), 277–85; Christopher Driver, "The Tiger Balm Community," The Guardian (January 2, 1962); Tsien Tche-Hao, "La vie sociale des Chinois à Madagascar," Comparative Studies in Society and History, 3, 2 (January 1961), 170–81; Justus M. Van der Kroef, "Chinese Assimilation in Indonesia," Social Research, 20 (January 1954), 445–72; Leonard Broom, "The Social Differentiation of Jamaica," American Sociological Review, 19 (April 1954), 115–24.

10. Material for the following is based on Michinari Fujita, "Japanese Associations in America," Sociology and Social Research (January–February 1929), pp. 211–28; T. Obana, "The American-born Japanese," Sociology and Social Research (November–December 1934), pp. 161–5; Joseph Roucek, "Japanese Americans," in Francis J. Brown and Joseph S. Roucek, Editors, One America: The History, Contributions, and Present Problems of Our Racial and National Minorities (New York, 1952), pp. 319–84; Forrest E. la Violette, "Canada and Its Japanese," in Edgar T. Thompson and Everett C. Hughes, Editors, Race: Individual and Collective Behavior (Glencoe, 1958), pp. 149–55; Charles Young, Helen R. Y. Reid and W. A. Carrothers, The Japanese Canadians (Toronto, 1938), edited by H. A. Innis; Ken Adachi, A History of the Japanese Canadians in British Columbia (Vancouver (?) (1958); T. Scott Miyakawa, "The Los Angeles Sansei," Kashu Mainichi (December 20, 1962), Part 2, 1; Harry Kitano, "Is There Sansei Delinquency?," Kashu Mainichi (December 20, 1962), Part 2, 1.

11. For the Japanese in Hawaii, see John Embree, "New and Local Kin Groups Among the Japanese Farmers of Kona, Hawaii," American Anthropologist,

41 (July 1939), 400–7; John Embree "Acculturation Among the Japanese of Kona, Hawaii," Memoirs of the American Anthropological Association, No. 59; Supplement to American Anthropologist, 43, 4:2 (1941); Jutsuichi Masuoka, "The Life Cycle of an Immigrant Institution in Hawaii: The Family," Social Forces, 23 (October 1944), 60–64; Masuoka, "The Japanese Patriarch in Hawaii," Social Forces, 17 (December 1938), 240–8; Masuoka, "Changing Food Habits of the Japanese in Hawaii," American Sociological Review, 10 (December 1945), 759–65; Masuoka, "Changing Moral Bases of the Japanese Family in Hawaii," Sociology and Social Research, 21 (November 1936), 158–69; Andrew M. Lind, Hawaii's Japanese, An Experiment in Democracy (Princeton, 1946). For the Japanese in Peru see Toraji Irie: "History of Japanese Migration to Peru," Hispanic-American Historical Review, 32 (August–October, 1951) 437–52, 648–64; (February 1952), 73–82; Mischa Titiev, "The Japanese Colony in Peru," Far Eastern Quarterly, 10 (May 1951), 227–47. For Japanese in Brazil see J. F. Normano "Japanese Emigration to Brazil," Pacific Affairs, 7 (March 1934), 42–61; Emilio Willems and Herbert Baldus, "Cultural Change Among Japanese Immigrants in Brazil in the Ribeira Valley of Sao Paulo," Sociology and Social Research, 26 (July 1943), 525–37; Emilio Willems, "The Japanese in Brazil," Far Eastern Quarterly, 18 (January 12, 1949), 6–8; John P. Augelli, "Cultural and Economic Changes of Bastos, a Japanese Colony on Brazil's Paulista Frontier," Annals of the Association of American Geographers, 48, 1 (March 1958), 3–19. For Paraguay see Norman R. Stewart, Japanese Colonization in Eastern Paraguay (Washington, D.C., 1967).

12. William Caudill, "Japanese American Personality and Acculturation," Genetic Psychology, Monographs, 45 (1952), 3–102; George de Vos, "A Comparison of the Personality Differences in Two Generations of Japanese Americans by Means of the Rorschach Test," Nagoya Journal of Medicine, 17, 3 (August 1954), 153–265; William Caudill and George de Vos, "Achievement, Culture and Personality: The Case of the Japanese Americans," American Anthropologist, 58 (December 1956), 110–226.

13. Materials in this section are based on Chester Rowell, "Chinese and Japanese Immigrants—a Comparison," Annals of the American Academy of Political and Social Science, 24, 2 (September 1909), 223–30; Winifred Raushenbush, "Their Place in the Sun," and "The Great Wall of Chinatown," The Survey Graphic, 56, 3 (May 1, 1926), 141–5, 154–8; Rose Hum Lee, The Chinese in the United States of America, p. 425; Leonard Broom and John I. Kitsuse, "The Validation of Acculturation: A Condition of Ethnic Assimilation," American Anthropologist, 57 (1955), 44–8; William Petersen, "Family Structure and Social Mobility

Among Japanese Americans." Paper presented at the annual meetings of the American Sociological Association, San Francisco, August, 1967.

14. Walter G. Beach, "Some Considerations in Regard to Race Segregation in California," *Sociology and Social Research*, 18 (March 1934), 340–50.

15. See the discussion in Lyman, "The Structure of Chinese Society in Nineteenth-Century America," pp. 370–77.

16. One difference with respect to hostility toward the Chinese and Japanese had to do with whether either was perceived as an "enemy" people. Although the Chinese were occasionally accused of harboring subversive intentions toward America—(see, e.g. P. W. Dooner, *Last Days of the Republic* (San Francisco, 1880)—it was the Japanese who suffered a half-century of such suspicions. See Jacabus tenBroek, Edward N. Barnhart, and Floyd Matson, *Prejudice, War and the Constitution* (Berkeley, 1954) pp. 11–99; Forrest E. La Violette, *The Canadian Japanese and World War II* (Toronto, 1948). Undoubtedly these deep-seated suspicions led Japanese to try very hard to prove their loyalty and assimilability. In this respect see Mike Masaoka, "The Japanese American Creed," *Common Ground*, 2, 3 (1942), 11; and "A Tribute to Japanese American Military Service in World War II," Speech of Hon. Hiram Fong in the Senate of the United States, *Congressional Record*, 88th Congress, First Session, May 21, 1963, pp. 1–13; "Tributes to Japanese American Military Service in World War II," Speeches of Twenty-four Congressmen, *Congressional Record*, 88th Congress, First Session, June 11, 1963, pp. 1–16; Senator Daniel Ken Inouye (with Lawrence Elliott), *Journey to Washington* (Englewood Cliffs, 1967), pp. 87–200.

17. In the tradition of Max Weber, religion might properly be supposed to have played a significant role in the orientations of overseas Chinese and Japanese. However, certain problems make any adoption of the Weberian thesis difficult. First, although Confucianism was the state religion of China, local villages practiced syncretic forms combining ancestor worship, Buddhism, Christianity, and homage to local deities. Maurice Freedman, *Lineage Organization in Southeastern China* (London, 1958), p. 116. Abroad Chinese temples were definitely syncretic and functioned to support a non-rationalist idea of luck and the maintenance of merchant power. See A. J. A. Elliott, *Chinese Spirit Medium Cults in Singapore* (London, 1955), pp. 24–45; Stewart Culin, *The Religious Ceremonies of the Chinese in the Eastern Cities of the United States* (Philadelphia, 1887); Wolfram Eberhard, "Economic Activities of a Chinese Temple in California," *Journal of the American Oriental Society*, 82, 3 (July–September 1962), pp. 362–71. In the case of Japanese, the Tokug-

awa religion certainly facilitated a limited achievement orientation. Robert Bellah, *Tokugawa Religion: The Values of Preindustrial Japan* (Glencoe, 1957), pp. 107–132. But both in Japan and the United States, Japanese exhibit a remarkable indifference to religious affiliation, even countenancing denominational and church differences within the same nuclear family and relatively little anxiety about religious intermarriage. See Morioka, "Christianity in the Japanese Rural Community: Acceptance and Rejection," *Japanese Sociological Studies. The Sociological Review*, Monograph X (Sept. 1966), 183–98; Lenoard D. Cain, Jr., "Japanese-American Protestants: Acculturation and Assimilation," *Review of Religious Research* 3, 3 (Winter 1962), 113–21; Cain, "The Integration Dilemma of Japanese-American Protestants," Paper presented at the annual meetings of the Pacific Sociological Association, April 5, 1962.

18. For information on nineteenth-century Chinese social organization in the provinces from which North America's immigrants came, see Maurice Freedman, *Chinese Lineage and Society: Fukien and Kwangtung* (New York, 1966); Kung-Chuan Hsiao, *Rural China; Imperial Control in the Nineteenth Century* (Seattle, 1960). On the Chinese as sojourners see Paul C. P. Siu, "The Sojourner," *American Journal of Sociology*, 8 (July 1952), 32–44 and Siu, "The Isolation of the Chinese Laundryman," in Ernest W. Burgess and Donald Bogue, Editors, *Contributions to Urban Sociology* (Chicago, 1964), pp. 429–42. On the role of immigrant associations, see William Hoy, *The Chinese Six Companies* (San Francisco, 1942); Tin-Yuke Char, "Immigrant Chinese Societies in Hawaii," *Sixty-First Annual Report of the Hawaiian Historical Society* (1953), pp. 29–32; William Willmott, "Chinese Clan Associations in Vancouver," *Man*, 64, 49 (March–April, 1964), 33–7.

19. Material for the following is based on George B. Sansom, *Japan: A Short Cultural History* (New York, 1943); Taskashi Koyama, "The Significance of Relatives at the Turning Point of the Family System in Japan," *Japanese Sociological Studies. Sociological Review*, 10 (September 1966), 95–114; Lafcadio Hearn, *Japan: An Interpretation* (Tokyo, 1955), pp. 81–106; Ronald P. Dore, *City Life in Japan: A Study of a Tokyo Ward* (Berkeley, 1958), pp. 91–190; Irene Taeuber, "Family, Migration, and Industrialization in Japan," *American Sociological Review* (April, 1951), pp. 149–57; Ezra F. Vogel, "Kinship Structure, Migration to the City, and Modernization," in R. P. Dore, *Aspects of Social Change in Modern Japan* (Princeton, 1967), pp. 91–112.

20. For discussions of United States restrictive legislation see Mary Coolidge, *Chinese Immigration* (New York, 1909), pp. 145–336; S. W. Kung, *Chinese*

in American Life: Some Aspects of Their History, Status, Problems and Contributions (Seattle, 1962), pp. 64–165. A discussion of both American and Canadian restrictive legislation will be found in Huang Tsen-ming, The Legal Status of the Chinese Abroad (Taipei, 1954). See also Tin-Yuke Char, "Legal Restrictions on Chinese in English Speaking Countries, I," Chinese Social and Political Science Review (January 4, 1933), pp. 479–94. Careful analyses of Canadian legislation are found in Duncan McArthur, "What is the Immigration Problem?," Queen's Quarterly (Autumn 1928), pp. 603–14; three articles by H. F. Angus, "Canadian Immigration: The Law and its Administration," American Journal of International Law, 18, 1 (January 1934), 74–89; "The Future of Immigration into Canada," Canadian Journal of Economics and Political Science, 12 (August 1946), 379–86; Jean Mercier, "Immigration and Provincial Rights," Canadian Bar Review, 22 (1944), 856–69; Hugh L. Keenleyside, "Canadian Immigration Policy and Its Administration," External Affairs (May 1949), pp. 3–11; Bora Laskin, "Naturalization and Aliens: Immigration, Exclusion, and Deportation," Canadian Constitutional Law (Toronto, 1960), pp. 958–77. In general see David C. Corbett, Canada's Immigration Policy: A Critique (Toronto, 1957).

21. For Japanese immigration see Yamato Ichihashi, Japanese in the United States (Stanford, 1932), pp. 401–9; Dorothy Swaine Thomas, Charles Kikuchi, and J. Sakoda, The Salvage (Berkeley, 1952), pp. 3–18, 571–626; H. A. Millis, The Japanese Problem in the United States (New York, 1915); K. K. Kawakami, The Real Japanese Question (New York, 1921); T. Iyenaga and Kenosuke Sato, Japan and the California Problem (New York, 1921); Iichiro Tokutomi, Japanese–American Relations (New York, 1922), pp. 65–88 (translated by Sukeshige Yanagiwara); R. D. McKenzie, Oriental Exclusion (Chicago, 1928). For Japanese immigration to Canada see Young, Reid, and Carrothers, The Japanese Canadians; A. R. M. Lower, Canada and the Far East—1940 (New York, 1941), pp. 61–89; H. F. Angus, Canada and the Far East, 1940–1953 (Toronto, 1953), pp. 99–100. For a statement by a pessimistic Nisei see Kazuo Kawai, "Three Roads, and None Easy," Survey Graphic, 56, 3 (May 1, 1926), 164–6. For further discussions see Tsu-toma Obana, "Problems of the American-born Japanese," Sociology and Social Research, 19 (November 1934), 161–5; Emory S. Bogardus, "Current Problems of Japanese Americans," Sociology and Social Research, 25 (July 1941), 562–71. For the development of new associations among Nisei see Adachi, A History of the Japanese in British Columbia, 1877–1958, pp. 11–14; Better Americans in a Greater America, booklet published by the Japanese American Citizens' League, undated (1967),

24 pp. For an ecological analysis of the distribution and diffusion of achievement orientations among Japanese in America see Paul T. Tagagi, "The Japanese Family in the United States: A Hypothesis on the Social Mobility of the Nisei," revision of an earlier paper presented at the annual meeting of the Kroeber Anthropological Society, Berkeley, California (April 30, 1966).

22. For information on occupations and settlement patterns see Lyman, "The Structure of Chinese Society in Nineteenth-century America," pp. 111–27; Milton L. Barnett, "Kinship as a Factor Affecting Cantonese Economic Adaptation in the United States," Human Organization, 19 (Spring, 1960), 40–6; Ping Chiu, Chinese Labor in California: An Economic Study (Madison, 1963).

23. For the Japanese as agriculturalists see Masakazu Iwata, "The Japanese Immigrants in California Agriculture," Agricultural History, 36 (January 1962), 25–37; Thomas et al., The Salvage, pp. 23–5; Adon Poli, Japanese Farm Holdings on the Pacific Coast (Berkeley, 1944). For farming and fishing communities in Canada see Tadashi Fukutake, Man and Society in Japan (Tokyo, 1962), pp. 146–79. For the rise and decline of urban ghettos among Japanese in the United States see Shotaro Frank Miyamoto, Social Solidarity Among the Japanese in Seattle, University of Washington Publications in the Social Sciences XI, 4 (December 1939), 57–129; Toshio Mori, "Li'l Yokohama" Common Ground, 1, 2 (1941), 54–6; Larry Tajiri, "Farewell to Little Tokyo," Common Ground, 4, 2 (1942) 90–5; Robert W. O'Brien, "Selective Dispersion as a Factor in the Solution of the Nisei Problem," Social Forces, 23 (Dec. 1944), 140–7.

24. On power and conflict in Chinatown see Lyman, "The Structure of Chinese Society in Nineteenth-century America," pp. 272–369. For secret societies see Stanford M. Lyman, "Chinese Secret Societies in the Occident: Notes and Suggestions for Research in the Sociology of Secrecy," Canadian Review of Sociology and Anthropology, 1, 2 (1964), 79–102; Stanford M. Lyman, W. E. Willmott, Berching Ho, "Rules of a Chinese Secret Society in British Columbia," Bulletin of the School of Oriental and African Studies, 27, 3 (1964), 530–9. See also D. Y. Yuan, "Voluntary Segregation: A Study of New Chinatown," Phylon Quarterly (Fall 1963), pp. 255–65.

25. For an extended discussion of the progress in eliminating discrimination in Canada and the United States see Stanford M. Lyman, The Oriental in North America (Vancouver, 1962), Lecture No. 11: "Position and Prospects of the Oriental since World War II." On immigration matters to 1962 see S. W. Kung, "Chinese Immigration into North America," Queen's Quarterly, 68, 4 (Winter 1962), 610–20. Information about Chi-

nese in Canada and the United States is regularly reported in the *Chinatown News*, a Vancouver, B.C. publication and in *East-West*, a San Francisco Journal. For problems of recent Chinese immigrants see *San Francisco Chronicle* (March 18, 1968) 2; for those of American born, *ibid.* (March 19, 1968), 42.

26. On April 15, 1965, in response to a rash of teenage burglaries among Japanese in Sacramento, parents and other interested adults met and discussed how the community might act to prevent delinquency.

27. Daisuke Kitagawa, "Assimilation of Pluralism?" in Arnold M. Rose and Caroline B. Rose, *Minority Problems* (New York, 1965), pp. 285-7. Fosco Maraini has written "The *ni-sei* has generally been taught to despise his Asian roots; on the other hand, all he has taken from the west is a two-dimensional duralumin Christianity, ultra-modernism, the cultivation of jazz as a sacred rite, a California

veneer," *Meeting with Japan*, New York, 1960 (translated by Eric Mosbacher), p. 169.

28. Robert E. Park, "Our Racial Frontier on the Pacific," *Survey Graphic*, 56, 3 (May 1, 1926), 196.

29. Seymour Martin Lipset, "Changing Social Status and Prejudice: The Race Theories of a Pioneering American Sociologist," *Commentary*, 9 (May 1950), 475-9; Amitai Etzioni, "The Ghetto—A Re-evaluation," *Social Forces*, 37 (March 1959), 255-62.

30. Charles Wagley and Marvin Harris, *Minorities in the New World* (New York, 1958).

31. Robert E. Park, "The Race Relations Cycle in Hawaii," *Race and Culture* (Glencoe, 1950), pp. 194-5. For an extended discussion of the race cycle see Stanford M. Lyman, "The Race Relations Cycle of Robert E. Park," *Pacific Sociological Review* 11, 1 (Spring 1968), 16-22.

11

Chicanos in the United States: A History of Exploitation and Resistance

Leobardo F. Estrada
F. Chris García
Reynaldo Flores Macías
Lionel Maldonado

This essay seeks to provide material that will contribute to an understanding of Chicanos[1] in the United States today. The task calls for a historical perspective on the Mexican people within the context of the U.S. political economy.

It is essential to examine first the early and continued influence of Mexicans in the development of what is today the southwestern United States. Unlike those who believe that social, political, and economic influences in the region were largely the result of Anglo penetration, we argue that practices and institutions indigenous to Mexicans were largely taken over by colonizing Anglos.[2] The military conquest of the Southwest by the United States was a watershed that brought about the large-scale dispossession of the real holdings of Mexicans and their displacement and relegation to the lower reaches of the class structure. Anglo control of social institutions and of major economic sectors made possible the subsequent exploitation of Mexican labor to satisfy the needs of various developing economic interests.

Mexicans were not passive actors, simply accepting Anglo domination. Mexican resistance to exploitation has taken a great variety of forms

Reprinted by permission of *Daedalus,* Journal of the American Academy of Arts and Sciences, "American Indians, Blacks, Chicanos, and Puerto Ricans," 110:2 (Spring 1981), Cambridge, MA.

since the conquest, contributing to the maintenance and perpetuation of cultural patterns among Mexicans living in the United States. These cultural patterns include: a national identity built around an "Indian" past; an Indianized Catholicism (*La Virgen de Guadalupe*); racial miscegenation (*mestizaje*—Indian and Spaniard—although almost as many Africans as Spaniards were brought to Middle America during the colonial period); and a regional, single language, Spanish. These patterns and practices, which distinguish the Mexican population from other groups, have persisted even among those who left the Southwest for other regions of the United States.

The Military Conquest

Mexicans were incorporated into the United States largely through military conquest. The period that brought the northern reaches of Mexico under the U.S. flag begins approximately in 1836 with the Battle of San Jacinto, and ends in 1853 with the Gadsden Purchase. The military conquest was preceded by a period of Anglo immigration.

In 1810 Mexico began its struggle to gain independence from Spain, an objective finally achieved in 1821. Mexicans, recognizing the advantage of increasing the size of the population loyal to its cause, granted permission to foreigners in 1819 to settle in its northern area, what is now Texas. Two years later Stephen Austin founded San Felipe de Austin: by 1830, one year after Mexico had abolished slavery, it is estimated that Texas had about twenty thousand Anglo settlers, primarily Southerners, with approximately two thousand "freed" slaves who had been forced to sign lifelong contracts with former owners.[3] This trickle of immigrants soon became an invading horde.

Immigrants into the territories of Mexico were required to meet certain conditions: pledge their allegiance to the Mexican government and adopt Catholicism. The settlers' initial acceptance of these conditions, however, soon turned to circumvention. The distance of the settlements from Mexico's capital city, together with the internal strife common in the period, made enforcement of these settlement agreements difficult, almost impossible. The foreigners' attitudes toward their hosts only aggravated the situation. Eugene C. Barker, a historian, wrote that by 1835 "the Texans saw themselves in danger of becoming the alien subjects of a people to whom they deliberately believed themselves morally, intellectually, and politically superior. Such racial feelings underlay Texan-American relations from the establishment of the very first Anglo-American colony in 1821."[4]

A constellation of factors—attitudes of racial superiority, anger over Mexico's abolition of slavery, defiance of initially agreed-upon conditions for settlement, and an increasing number of immigrants who pressed for independence from Mexico—strained an already difficult political situation. Direct and indirect diplomatic efforts at negotiation failed. The result was the Texas Revolt of 1835–36, which created for Anglo-Texans and dissident Mexicans the so-called independent Texas Republic, which was to exist until 1845. This republic, while never recognized by the Mexican government, provided the pretext for further U.S. territorial expansion and set the stage for the war between Mexico and the United States (1846–48).

Despite significant and conflicting regional interests in the war, imperialist interests allied with proponents for the expansion of slavery carried the day. When the United States granted statehood to Texas in 1845, almost a decade after recognizing it as a republic, war was inevitable; it

was officially declared on May 13, 1846. It has been argued that U.S. politicians and business interests actively sought this war, believing Mexico to be weak, a nation torn by divisive internal disputes that had not been resolved since independence.[5]

When hostilities ended in 1848, Mexico lost over half its national territory. The United States, by adding over a million square miles, increased its territory by a third. Arizona, California, Colorado, New Mexico, Texas, Nevada, and Utah, as well as portions of Kansas, Oklahoma, and Wyoming, were carved out of the territory acquired.

The Treaty of Guadalupe Hidalgo, signed on February 2, 1848, officially concluded hostilities and settled the question of sovereignty over the territories ceded. A new border was established, and the status of Mexicans in the newly acquired U.S. territory was fixed. Mexicans were given one year to decide whether to relocate south of the new border, maintaining their Mexican citizenship, or remain on their native lands, accepting U.S. sovereignty. The treaty explicitly guaranteed that Mexicans who elected to stay in the United States would enjoy "all the rights of citizens of the [United States] according to the principles of the Constitution; and in the meantime shall be maintained and protected in the free enjoyment of their religion without restriction."

Mexican property rights were further defined once the treaty had been approved by both governments. A Statement of Protocol, drafted by U.S. emissaries when the Mexican government reacted strongly to changes unilaterally made by the U.S. Senate, said:

> The American government by suppressing the Xth. article of the Treaty of Guadalupe Hidalgo did not in any way intend to annul grants of lands made by Mexico in the ceded territories. These grants preserve the legal value which they may possess, and the grantees may cause their legitimate [titles] to be acknowledged before the American tribunals.
>
> Conformable to the law of the United States, legitimate titles to every description of property, personal and real, existing in the ceded territories, are those which were legitimate titles under the Mexican law of California and New Mexico up to the 13th of May, 1846, and in Texas up to the 2nd of March, 1836.

163

Subsequent events soon indicated that these "guarantees" were specious.

A final portion of Mexican land was acquired by the United States through purchase. James Gadsden was sent to Mexico City in 1853 to negotiate a territorial dispute arising from the use of faulty maps in assigning borders under the Treaty of Guadalupe Hidalgo. Mexico's dire need for funds to rebuild its war-ravaged economy influenced its agreement to sell more land. Gadsden purchased over 45,000 square miles in what is now Arizona and New Mexico, land the United States wanted for a rail line to California. The Gadsden Purchase territories were in time seen to contain some of the world's richest copper mines.

The importance for the United States of this imperialist war and the later Gadsden Purchase cannot be overstated. Vast tracts of land, rich in natural resources, together with their Mexican and Indian inhabitants, provided conditions very favorable to U.S. development and expansion. The United States had done very well in its "little war" with Mexico.

Dispossession and Displacement

To make matters worse, the social and economic displacement of Mexicans and their reduction to the status of a colonized group proceeded rapidly, in clear violation of the civil and property rights guaranteed both by treaty and protocol. In Texas, a wholesale transfer of land from Mexican to Anglo ownership took place. That process had started at the time of the Texas Revolt and gained momentum after the U.S.-Mexico War. Mexican landowners, often robbed by force, intimidation, or fraud, could defend their holdings through litigation, but this generally led to heavy indebtedness, with many forced to sell their holdings to meet necessary legal expenses. With depressing regularity, Anglos generally ended up with Mexican holdings, acquired at prices far below their real value.[6]

The military conquest, the presence of U.S. troops, racial violence, governmental and judicial chicanery—all served to establish Anglos in positions of power in economic structures originally developed by Mexicans. Anglos adopted wholesale techniques developed by Mexicans in mining, ranching, and agriculture.[7] Because this major transfer of economic power from Mexicans to Anglos varied by region, it is important to say something about each.

Texas, responding to a significant expansion in the earlier Mexican-based cattle and sheep industries, was quick to cater to increased world demands. Acreage given over to cotton also expanded, helped greatly by improvements in transport facilities. These industries helped create and develop the mercantile towns that soon became conspicuous features on the Texas landscape.[8] Mexicans, instead of reaping the economic rewards of ownership, found themselves only contributing their labor. Mexicans were increasingly relegated to the lower ranks of society. By the end of the century, ethnicity, merged with social class, made Mexicans a mobile, colonized labor force.

The social structure of *New Mexico* in the beginning was quite different from that of Texas. The state, sparsely populated, was more densely settled in the north, in and about Santa Fé, than in the south; communal villages with lands granted to each community were common in the north. Communal water and grazing rights were assigned by community councils; only homestead and farming land were privately owned. Southern New Mexico, by contrast, boasted *haciendas* that had been established by grantees. This system consisted of *patrónes*, with settlers recruited to perform the necessary chores. It was a social structure organized on a debt-peonage system.

Anglo penetration into New Mexico after the war was more limited and did not occur on a large scale until the mid-1870s. Indian and Mexican defense of the territory served to keep out many settlers. Only an established U.S. military presence in the area made it at all accessible to Anglo cattlemen and farmers. Encountering a diversified class structure among the resident Mexicans, the Anglos generally chose to associate with the U.S. armed forces, creating a quasimilitary society in the process. By the early 1880s, however, the railroads had helped to stimulate a new economic expansion. There was a further swelling of the Anglo population, and as pressure for land increased, the process of Mexican dispossession also dramatically accelerated.

The dispossession process in New Mexico was achieved in part through taxation. The

Spanish-Mexican traditional practice had been to tax the products of the land. Under the new Anglo regime, land itself was taxed. With agricultural income fluctuating greatly with climatic conditions, fixed land taxes placed severe burdens on both farmers and ranchers. Small-scale subsistence farmers were unprepared and generally unable to raise the capital to meet the newly imposed tax liabilities. The practice of transferring the title on land on which delinquent taxes were owed to the person making such payment caused many Mexicans to lose their land. Fraud, deceit, and manipulation were common. An associate justice of the Court of Private Land Claims wrote:

> A number of grants have had their boundaries stretched and areas marvelously expanded. But this has been done mostly by Yankee and English purchasers and not by the original Mexican owners. Where boundaries were made by natural landmarks, such as a "white rock," and "red hill," or a "lone tree," another rock, hill or tree of like description could always be found a league or two farther off, and claimed to be the original landmark described in the grant documents.[9]

Toward the end of the century, federal policies also operated to dispossess Mexicans of their land. The National Forest Service, for example, began taking over millions of acres from northern villages, which were rarely compensated for their losses. Inhabitants were now compelled to pay grazing fees on land that had originally belonged to the villages. The granting of large tracts of land to the railroads served further to confine Mexicans to increasingly smaller land bases.

The Court of Private Land Claims, established in 1891 to resolve conflicts over land claims in New Mexico, Colorado, and Arizona, existed for thirteen years; its Anglo judges had a very limited knowledge and understanding of Mexican and Spanish landowning laws, traditions, and customs. Their judgments, based on Anglo legal practices, greatly contributed to the dispossessions. In time, Anglos came to own four fifths of the New Mexican grant areas,[10] and this loss of land relegated the vast majority of Mexicans to a bleak economic and social existence.

Twenty or so prominent Mexican families in New Mexico joined with the Anglo interests in banking, ranching, and the railroads, expecting to maintain their own political, economic, and social advantages.[11] The alliance, however, was controlled by the Anglo faction, and was therefore always unequal.[12] In any case, efforts by this small proportion of the original Mexican families to hold on to their advantaged status had no positive effect for the vast majority of Mexicans. As in Texas, ethnicity and class merged, and Mexicans, dispossessed of their holdings, saw them taken by the Anglo elites that dominated the political and economic activities of the society.

Arizona offers the example of the development of a colonial labor force in yet another mode. Arizona, not a separate entity at the time of conquest, was originally part of New Mexico, administered from Santa Fé. The small Mexican population was concentrated in the south, largely in Tucson and Tubac. One of the reasons for the sparseness of the settlements was the failure of the Spanish missionaries to impose Christianity on the nomadic Indian inhabitants; another was the aridity of the soil, which made agricultural pursuits difficult. The presence of the U.S. Army in the 1880s began to have its effects on the region. The Army fought the Indians, allowing the mining of copper and silver to resume; it was soon to become a large-scale economic enterprise. As with other industries, Anglo ownership was the norm; Mexicans contributed their labor, employing the familiar techniques they had developed long before.[13] Railroads accelerated the migration of Anglos and the establishment of new towns. The growth of all these major industries called for a cheap wage labor pool. Mexicans who migrated north, mostly to work in these industries, discovered that the wages they received for tasks identical to their Anglo counterparts were considerably lower. Restricted to menial and dangerous work, and forced to live in segregated areas in the mining and railroad communities that had created their jobs, they felt the indignity of their situation.[14]

California differed from the other regions: New England clipper ships had established very early ties with California; Franciscans, founding missions in the area in the 1830s, forced Christianized Indians into agriculture and manufacturing, to work alongside mulatto and *mestizo* Mexicans.

This labor force helped to make California—economically, politically, and socially distant—independent of Mexico City. Excellent climate and abundant natural resources contributed to make this the most prosperous province in Mexico. Strong ties bound the missions to the *ranchos*. Missions, given large parcels of land to carry out their Christianizing enterprise, were neighbors of private individuals who owned vast tracts of land. Eventually, however, the privately owned *ranchos* established their supremacy throughout the province.

Urban settlements also developed: Monterey was the center of northern California; *el Pueblo de Nuestra Señora, la Reina de los Angeles de Porciúncula*, the economic and social center of southern California. Other towns sprung up around the major forts and missions. The rigid feudal system of *patrón* and *peón*, typical of southern New Mexico, did not develop in California. The class system that emerged was three-tiered: wealthy landowners enjoyed political, economic, and social power, and constituted about 10 percent of the population; artisans, small-scale landowners, vaqueros, herders, and soldiers constituted the bulk of Californian society; Indians and lower class *mestizos* stood at the bottom of the class hierarchy.

A few Anglos had come to Alta California before the U.S.-Mexico War; some were recipients of land grants, and many of them apparently assimilated into Mexican society. After the Texas revolt, however, Anglo foreigners coming to California were more reluctant to mingle or assimilate, and openly showed their antagonism towards Mexicans. The U.S. government was at the same time stepping up its efforts to secure California. In 1842, in fact, the U.S. flag was prematurely raised in Monterey, when Commodore Thomas Jones imagined that the war with Mexico had already begun.

The transfer of land titles from Mexicans to Anglos in California differed significantly from the transfer of title in other areas conquered by the U.S. forces. To begin with, the vast majority of Mexicans did not own land in California. The original *Californios* began to lose title to their lands to better-financed Anglo newcomers very early; there was no possibility of competing with

wealth established through banking, shipping, railroads, and other such enterprises. The holdings of these new elites ran into the hundreds of thousands of acres early in the nineteenth century.[15]

Congress established the Land Commission in 1851 to judge the validity of grant claims made by *Californios* whose titles came down through the Spanish and Mexican periods. The commission served mainly to hasten the process of dispossession. Litigation costs often involved a contingent lawyer's fee of one quarter of the land in question. Some Mexican landowners borrowed money at high interest rates to carry on their legal fights, and frequently found themselves in the end selling their lands to meet their debts. Anglo squatters only added to the burden; they formed associations to apply political pressure favorable to their own interests, and were generally successful in retaining land forcefully taken from Mexicans.[16] Violence and murder in California, as in other parts of the conquered territories, was the order of the day.

Gold discoveries in 1849 in northern California brought a massive influx of Anglo gold-seekers. Although Mexicans had been working claims in the area for some time, those who now arrived entered as laborers. The Anglo-American foreigners, inexperienced and ignorant of mining techniques, depended on the Mexican/Spanish/Indian mining experience in Arizona, northern Mexico, and California for the technical knowledge required to develop mining in California. Large-scale borrowing of mining techniques, tools, and language, not to speak of geological knowledge, took place between 1840 and 1860. The highly prejudiced Anglo miners treated Mexican miners as they did Chinese laborers; illegal taxation, lynchings, robbings, beatings, and expulsion became daily occurrences. Gold-mining lasted only a short time. When it was over, Anglos in great numbers turned to agricultural pursuits. The Mexican and Chinese populations migrated to California's towns to become landless laborers.

Southern California showed a very different face. *Rancheros* managed to hold onto their land for at least a generation after the Gold Rush. But climate, in the end, defeated many of them. Floods, followed by severe droughts, undercut the economy of the region in the 1860s and again in the 1880s. These were not "good times" for California agriculture.

By the turn of the century, Mexicans had been largely dispossessed of their property. Relegated to a lower-class status, they were overwhelmingly dispossessed landless laborers, politically and economically impotent. Lynchings and murder of both Mexicans and Indians were so common that they often went unreported. Long-term residents of the region were reduced to being aliens in their native lands. The common theme that united all Mexicans was their conflict with Anglo society. The dominant society, profoundly racist, found it entirely reasonable to relegate Mexicans to a colonial status within the United States.

Political, Military, and Cultural Resistance

Mexican resistance to Anglo hegemony took many forms. A great deal has been made of what individuals like Tiburcio Vásquez and Joaquín Murrieta were able to do; they, and others like them, became legendary for their resistance to Anglo domination. While many others resorted to the courts, a militarily conquered people, dispossessed and relegated to a subservient economic and political status largely justified by notions of racial inferiority, have seldom been successful in pressing their grievances to any equitable solution through a legal system controlled by the conquerors.

The political resistance that occurred varied from region to region, but almost always involved an accommodating elite who wanted to force the conqueror to stick to the "rules"— to abide by the Constitution, the Treaty of Guadalupe Hidalgo, and the like. In some areas, Mexicans went as delegates to constitutional conventions, winning at least some of the battles that the treaty negotiators had not been able to guarantee. In California, for example, it was significant that the franchise was not limited to white males. Legal recognition of the Spanish language was achieved for various periods in certain areas. Such political victories were won through struggle and resistance, yet they were rarely long-lived. Once there was Anglo control over a region—through military or police action, by economic advantage, or

population size—there was no possibility of such "victories" being sustained.

The military resistance of Mexicans was never "official." Such actions were most often responses to individual or collective Anglo acts of violence against a Mexican, whether through lynching, rape, murder, or arson. The first person hanged in occupied California was a Mexican woman, three months pregnant, who had been raped by a drunken Anglo assailant. Her Mexican lover/husband who killed the Anglo was exiled; she was lynched.

The atrocities of the U.S.-Mexico war, especially along the Texas-Mexican border, continued; the Texas Rangers in time assumed the role once taken by the U.S. Army in Texas. Jacinto Treviño, Joaquín Murrieta, Chino Cortina, and Las Gorras Blancas are all examples of the "people's revolt" continuing well into the early twentieth century. Although Anglos called such men bandits, outlaws ("Mexican outlaws"), and desperados (from *desesperados*—those without hope, those who are desperate), Mexicans considered them heroes, often aiding and abetting their activities, if for no other reason than because they saw them as the only friendly force between themselves and the Anglo gun.

Many Anglos saw the Mexicans as a natural resource of the region that was to be domesticated and exploited. The Mexicans refused such a characterization; their resistance was a struggle to maintain their identity—control over their language, family, art, and religion—that involved them in a continuing relation with Mexico.

Mexico and Its Relative Standing

Mexico, a nation with a long history of striving for social, political, and economic stability, seemed farther from its goal after its war with the United States than ever. The French invasion of Mexico in 1860 and the ensuing political instability only served to exacerbate many of Mexico's problems. When Porfirio Díaz became president of Mexico in 1876, he inaugurated policies that were intended to lead to rapid economic development. Federal government policies encouraged European and U.S. investments in railroads, mining, oil, and agriculture, especially cotton, sugar, coffee, and rubber. The attraction of foreign capital and investment was, however, too successful. By the time of the 1910 Revolution, foreigners owned three quarters of Mexico's mines, more than half of its oil fields, and massive tracts of land. Huge cattle ranches, particularly in northern Mexico, were owned by foreigners. Five major rail lines in northern Mexico, built and owned by U.S. interests, were characteristic foreign investments. Foreigners, in sum, owned more capital in Mexico than its citizens.

It was one thing to be successful in attracting foreign capital; it was another to reap significant benefits from such a policy. The effects of large-scale foreign investment were neither anticipated nor always beneficial to Mexico. The five rail lines, for example, did little to integrate Mexico's national economy. All five ran unerringly north, connecting Mexico's markets and labor supply with ranching and commercial centers in the U.S. Southwest. Mexico's products made their way into the world market economy; they were not intended for internal markets and thus brought no great advantage to Mexicans, whose industrial economy remained massively underdeveloped.

Meanwhile, mechanization in agriculture displaced many Mexican workers; few could be absorbed into the modest industrial sector. Prices for food and related commodities doubled, and in some cases tripled, in the decades just before the 1910 Revolution. Real wages declined; inflation was consistently high. At the same time, Mexico's population was growing rapidly; it increased by 50 percent between 1875 and 1910. Not surprisingly, such pressures led to great discontent and ultimately to the Revolution of 1910. That event, in turn, created a large-scale movement of Mexicans unable to fit into the restricted Mexican economy. Galarza, in his moving autobiography, *Barrio Boy*,[17] tells how Mexicans in the interior were forced from the land, sought work wherever they might find it—generally on the railroads—and gradually made their way northward, along with products extracted from Mexico, with scant compensation.

The U.S. Southwest and Beyond, 1900–1930
Foreign capital investments in Mexico retarded its economic independence. Far more was extracted than was left for internal development. The situation was made even more serious by events within the United States, particularly in the Southwest, where the local economy was developing and expanding. Initial U.S. demands for labor were large, particularly for agriculture, but also for sheep and cattle ranching. Between 1870 and 1900 the land given over to farming increased from 60,000 to nearly a million and a half acres.[18] Protective tariffs for agricultural products helped to expand the acreage under cultivation. The more powerful influence, however, was the effort by the federal government to bring water to arid regions. The Reclamation Act of 1902 significantly bolstered the struggling agricultural economy of the Southwest; the building of dams and reservoirs in the desert-like area created new prospects for a highly labor-intensive agricultural enterprise. Large areas in California, Texas, Arizona, and New Mexico were turned over to the cultivation of cotton, a commodity of increasing demand for the new industrial sectors of the world. When war came in 1914, Allied needs gave additional incentives for such agricultural expansion. Southwestern agriculture diversified; sugar-beet cultivation was another labor-intensive enterprise bolstered by a protective tariff and improved irrigation; California, Colorado, and Utah all profited. Fruits and vegetables—citrus, lettuce, spinach, beans, carrots, dates, cantaloupes, and nuts—became important commodities, particularly in California.

Agriculture played its own procreative role. It helped create industries for the processing, canning, packing, and crating of agricultural products. These tied in nicely with an expanding rail system that first linked east with west, and later, and more pragmatically, crisscrossed the Southwest to transport its products to new markets. Sheep and cattle ranching continued, creating yet new industries in meat processing and shipping.

Mining gained new momentum and new dimensions during this period. The manufacturing of machinery for ore extraction and processing became vitally important, first, with copper in Arizona and New Mexico, then, with quartz in Nevada, Colorado, and Arizona, and later, with petroleum in Texas and California. The petroleum industry had a multiplier effect; it rapidly became a major component in the nation's burgeoning chemical industry.

The lumber industry also grew. Texas, California, Arizona, and New Mexico identified timbercutting very early as a profitable economic activity that called for new modes of processing and distribution. These in turn developed still other industries.

The common denominator for all this rapid growth in the Southwest was the availability of cheap labor. The majority of European immigrants flowing into the United States through New York were absorbed in the industrial economies of the Northeast and Midwest. The Southwest had its own source of readily available and exploitable labor in the colonized Mexicans who filled the lower ranks of the economic order. They were still developing communities throughout the Southwest and would in time become increasingly visible also in the Midwest.

The conditions that greeted new immigrants from Mexico were essentially like those Mexicans already in the United States knew only too well. There was powerful racial hostility; Mexicans were thought to be inferior beings and inherently unassimilable and foreign. Their economic niche was insecure; their work was often seasonal in nature. In agricultural and related pursuits they were forced into a dual-wage system where they received low wages, frequently below those received by Anglos for the same type and amount of work. Many found themselves barred from supervisory positions. The situation in mining and related industries was not much different.

The railroad companies offered only slightly better conditions. By 1908 the Southern Pacific and the Atchison, Topeka, and Santa Fe were each recruiting more than a thousand Mexicans every month. The vast majority worked as section crews, laying track and ensuring its maintenance. The major difference between this industry and others in which Mexicans found work was that it seemed somewhat more stable and less seasonal; wages, however, were uniformly low.[19]

The Southwest was growing; its urban centers—in most instances, expanded versions of earlier Mexican towns—were often inhibited by Mexicans overwhelmingly concentrated in the lower range of the urban occupational structure. The wage differentials common to the rural sector were not as obvious in the urban areas. Access to particular occupations and industries, however, was limited and channeled. There was no mobility out of the unskilled and semiskilled positions in which Mexicans found themselves. They formed a reserve labor pool that could be called up as the situation dictated. When the economy expanded and jobs were created, these might be filled by Mexicans in specific sectors. Contractions of the economy relegated Mexicans quickly to the ranks of the unemployed; it was then they were reminded that they could be technically subject to another "sovereign," Mexico.

Mexicans served the industrial economy in other ways, also. As a reserve labor pool, employers used them as a sort of "strike insurance," much as female and child labor were used to undercut unionizing efforts in other parts of the country. Such policies tended to generate ethnic antagonism between working-class Mexicans and working-class Anglos. Trade union practices, which excluded Mexicans and contributed to their exploitation, also helped to maintain them as a reserve labor pool, forcing them in the end to organize their own unions and associations.

While the beginnings of a middle class among Mexicans is discernible at this time, it is important to emphasize that most of those who made up this incipient class were self-employed in small-scale service businesses (newspapers, retail stores, and the like) while a few were "professionals," mostly elementary and secondary school teachers (in segregated schools). This class was never absorbed into the general economy. Rather, these business ventures tended to be restricted overwhelmingly to the Mexican community. On a social level, members of this emerging middle class encountered substantial barriers to their acceptance in the larger society, further perpetuating the prevailing patterns of residential and social segregation.

The Mexican government regularly lodged formal complaints with the State Department, protesting the abusive treatment its citizens received from industrial, mining, and agricultural enterprises. Those protests went largely unheeded; the U.S. government generally chose not even to verify the assertions, let alone make efforts to correct abuses.

By the early 1920s Mexicans began to settle

outside of the Southwest. Many were recruited by northern manufacturing interests; meat-packing plants and steel mills in the Chicago area; automobile assembly lines in Detroit, the steel industry in Ohio and Pennsylvania; and Kansas City's meat-packing plants. By 1930 about 15 percent of the nation's Mexicans were living outside the Southwest. In addition to the recruitment of Mexicans from northern Mexico and the American Southwest by the industrial sector, many others chose to settle out of the principal migrant agricultural stream. Regular routes had become established that connected South Texas with the Great Lakes and Plains states. Many Mexicans continued their odyssey, following the crops west through the northern tier of states, finally arriving in the Northwest, and then turning south again. Others journeyed from Texas to the South, then north along the Eastern seaboard. Still others went west for agricultural work. Mexicans in California worked the crops north through that state, into the Northwest, and then east through the Mountain states. Many settled out of the migrant stream in areas where they found work.[20]

Migration 1900–1930

No precise figures are available on the number of Mexicans who migrated north (or south) across the paper-made border between Mexico and the United States before 1900. The fact is that the border was open to unrestricted immigration until the creation and organization of the Immigration and Naturalization Service (and the Border Patrol) in 1924. Even then, however, large parts of the 2,000-mile border were unguarded, making the accuracy of all immigration figures somewhat questionable. One estimate is that from 1901 to 1910 approximately 9,300 Mexicans, principally from central and eastern Mexico, came to the United States each year.[21] In the second decade of the century, Mexicans came principally from northeastern and west-central Mexico; it is thought that 1,900 or so came annually between 1911 and 1914. About 2,750 migrated annually from 1915 to 1919. Economic factors and the Revolution of 1910 spurred migration during this period. The third decade witnessed a very heavy Mexican migration to the

United States. Between 1920 and 1924, more than 135,000 Mexicans (about 27,000 on an annual basis) left for the United States. Migration then tapered off to just under 109,000 between 1925 and 1930, about 18,000 per year. In all, about a quarter of a million Mexicans arrived in the United States during the first three decades of the twentieth century. No comparable figures are available on return migration.[22]

Included in the large wave of Mexican immigrants were a number of merchants, landowners, and intellectuals, many of whom had been displaced by the Revolution of 1910. Many settled in Texas; others established themselves in the Midwest, in cities like Kansas City; some went as far north as Milwaukee. Many, continuing with activities they had pursued in Mexico, became entrepreneurs in the United States. A greater number of Spanish-language newspapers, pamphlets, books, and articles appeared; analysis of the political effects of the Mexican Revolution became a staple item of such publications. Many Mexicans who crossed the border at this time, including this group of entrepreneurs, saw themselves as temporary expatriates who would one day return to Mexico when conditions there were more settled.

The population flow from Mexico during these decades represents one of the largest movements of people in the history of the world. The reasons are easily discoverable: there was an active labor recruitment by mining, railroad, and agricultural interests in the American Southwest, who justified their policies by arguing that Mexicans were uniquely suited for work that Anglo workers refused to do. The labor shortage resulting from U.S. involvement in World War I was another reason for the large upturn in demand. Mexico's Revolution of 1910 also induced many to leave. The net result, however, was that economic interests in the Southwest found an abundant source of cheap and exploitable labor.

The United States has been quite deliberate in permitting access to all immigrants except Asians. This policy of unrestricted immigration had significantly furthered national development. Immigrants took jobs in the industrial Northeast and Midwest that natives would not take, frequently at wages that tended to undermine unionizing activities. Immigrants served other purposes as well; for example, they traditionally constituted a disproportionate number of the enlisted men in the U.S. military forces.

Between 1917 and 1924, however, a combination of events caused the open-door policy to be changed, and free access to the United States was thereby ended. The sixty-year struggle of nativists and xenophobes to control the foreign population stimulated restrictionist legislation and promoted Americanization programs. The uneasy peace after World War I nurtured fear and distrust of all that was foreign, ranging from the League of Nations to immigrants. Old Yankee families in New England viewed with some misgivings the rising percentage of foreign-born around them. Organized skilled labor felt that its interests could be protected only by sharply curtailing cheap foreign labor. There were blocs of Southerners, Populists, and Progressives, each with its own reasons, wanting immigration to end.[23]

These groups were successful. Legislation passed in 1924 set national quotas on European immigrants to the United States. The year used as a base for calculating national quotas was 1890, a date chosen with care and deliberation, for in that year many more of the "older" immigrants from Northern and Western Europe had arrived in the United States. The law thus discriminated openly against the "new" immigrants from Eastern and Southern Europe. Justification for restrictive immigration was provided by the detailed study of the Immigration Commission. Appointed in 1907 by President Theodore Roosevelt, and chaired by Senator Dillingham, the commission issued its conclusions in 1911 in an impressive forty-two volume report, which was soon widely quoted. Its principal message was that the new immigration was essentially different from the old and that new immigrants were less capable of being Americanized. Oscar Handlin, critically reviewing the commission and its work, cites the overt bias of the commission's report, beginning with the acceptance of the very assumptions it was ostensibly charged with investigating:

> The old and the new immigration differ in many essentials. The former was . . . largely a movement of settlers . . . from the most progressive sections of Europe. . . . They entered practically every line of activity. . . . Many of them . . . became landowners. . . . They mingled freely with the native Americans and were quickly assimilated. On the other hand, the new immigration has been largely a movement of unskilled laboring men who have come from the less progressive countries of Europe. . . . They have . . . congregated together in sections apart from native Americans and the older immigrants to such an extent that assimilation has been slow.
>
> Consequently the Commission paid but little attention to the foreign-born element of the old immigrant class and directed its efforts almost entirely to . . . the newer immigrants.[24]

The commission's report reflected the racial bias and attitudes of the time. Handlin cites from *The Passing of the Great Race*, the immensely popular book by the distinguished anthropologist Madison Grant on these newer immigrants:

> The new immigration contained a large and increasing number of the weak, the broken, and the mentally crippled of all races drawn from the lowest stratum of the Mediterranean basin and the Balkans, together with hordes of the wretched, submerged populations of the Polish ghettoes. Our jails, insane asylums, and almshouses are filled with human flotsam and the whole tone of American life, social, moral, and political, has been lowered and vulgarized by them.[25]

These beliefs, although vigorously debated in scientific circles, were given validation by their wholesale incorporation in the Dillingham Commission's report. They gave intellectual support for restrictive immigration legislation.[26] If the Rogers Act, passed in 1924, was silent on the matter of Mexican immigrants who continued to arrive in great numbers, there was no comparable reticence by the Dillingham Commission, which had said of Mexicans:

> Because of their strong attachment to their native land, low intelligence, illiteracy, migratory life, and the possibility of their residence here being discontinued, few become citizens of the United States. . . . In so far as Mexican laborers come into contact with native or with European immigrants they are looked upon as inferiors. . . . Thus, it is evident that in the case of the Mexican he is less desirable as a citizen than as a laborer.[27]

The Dillingham Commission, in common with later immigration legislation, officially sanctioned the social and economic niche of Mexicans: they were not good enough for citizenship but certainly acceptable as manual laborers. Why such "tolerance"? To begin with, there was a great social distance between the Mexican of the Southwest and the nativists of the Midwest and Northwest. Also, the continued expansion of the region's economy, particularly in railroads and agriculture, made the availability of a large labor force imperative. Social distance and the emerging economic needs of the Southwest resulted in a lax policy toward Mexican immigration when the country was otherwise obsessed by its restrictionist mood.[28]

The passage of the 1924 Immigration Act made Mexicans conspicuous by their continued free access to the United States. Debate on the issue continued to agitate Congress. A report prepared for the 1928 congressional hearings on Western Hemisphere immigration, which argued against Mexican immigration, suggests how some, at least, saw the Mexican:

> Their minds run to nothing higher than animal functions—eat, sleep, and sexual debauchery. In every huddle of Mexican shacks one meets the same idleness, hordes of hungry dogs, and filthy children with faces plastered with flies, disease, lice, human filth, stench, promiscuous fornication, bastardy, lounging, apathetic peons and lazy squaws, beans and dried chili, liquor, general squalor, and envy and hatred of the gringo. These people sleep by day and prowl by night like coyotes, stealing anything they can get their hands on, no matter how useless to them it may be. Nothing left outside is safe unless padlocked or chained down. Yet there are Americans clamoring for more of these human swine to be brought over from Mexico.[29]

The Indian racial mixture was clearly a part of the cultural perception, little distinction being made between the two. The nativist drive for racial purity, emphasizing the superiority of the "white" race, denigrated the racial mixture characteristic of Latin America generally and of Indian nations like Mexico in particular. Yet no action was taken to curb the flow of Mexican immigrants. The powerful economic arguments for the continued importation of Mexican laborers had been articulated two years earlier before a congressional committee by John Nance Garner, who was to become Franklin Roosevelt's vice president: "In order to allow land owners now to make a profit of their farms, they want to get the cheapest labor they can find, and if they can get the Mexican labor it enables them to make a profit."[30]

At the same time, control of the "immigrant" population came to include measures that could be applied to the domestic Mexican population. The Americanization activities of the early twentieth century spread throughout the country and were used to bleach all vestiges in the national flock. These activities included intensive English instruction—with retribution for those who chose to speak other tongues— and success defined as a capacity to speak as did the English-speaking middle class; and intensive "civic" classes to socialize the "foreign" population. The norm for success became the Anglo middle class, and standardized IQ and achievement tests measured this success. The widespread institution of high schools that traced the population into occupational or college preparatory curricula, with immigrants and racial minorities tracked into the former—when they entered high schools at all— became common. English oral proficiency became a requirement for immigration, as did English literacy for voting. The latter was also aimed at blacks in the South, and spread throughout the United States as a mechanism of social control. Legislation mandating English instruction in the schools and English proficiency as a prerequisite to employment was targeted for various groups in different parts of the country. Segregated Mexican schools were maintained. In the early 1930s, through federal court litigation, segregation based on race was challenged, and segregation based on grouping for language instruction was initiated and legitimated.[31] Statehood for Arizona and New Mexico (which together had been one territory) was denied several times at the beginning of the century, in part because there were too many Mexicans in the territory. References were made to their "mongrel racial character," their inability to speak English, and therefore, presumably, their dubious allegiance to the United States. Despite racial conflict, physical abuse, cultural genocide, and economic exploitation, the Mexican population grew; however, where restrictionists had failed to limit Mexican immigration, the Great Depression succeeded.

The Great Depression and Repatriation

The decade of the Great Depression was another watershed for Mexicans. Social forces during this period significantly shaped the lives of Mexicans and are in many ways still responsible for their status half a century later. The decade began with a massive economic collapse that started late in the 1920s and continued until World War II. There was a major decline in economic activities, with wage rates in both industry and agriculture suffering, and rampant unemployment. With this came a major acceleration of government intervention in social welfare, with bureaucracies developing and expanding to meet the urgent needs of a dislocated populace. There was also a large-scale westward migration out of the Dust Bowl. In the Southwest, this was a time of accelerated rates of concentration into larger and larger units in both agriculture and mining, where increased mechanization led to a further displacement of labor. The industrial sector in the Southwest lagged behind the rest of the nation and could contribute little to absorb either the locally displaced labor or the dust-bowl migrants. These major economic dislocations fell on Mexicans with even greater force than on other groups. Already relegated to a marginal status, Mexicans were particularly vulnerable. The situation worked to eliminate for all practical purposes further northward migration from Mexico.

The Great Depression had another sobering effect: it engendered a collective social atmosphere of insecurity and fear that set the tone in allocating blame for the major social and economic traumas. Mexicans were singled out as scapegoats and made to bear the guilt for some of the ills of the period. It was not long before great numbers of unemployed Mexicans, like other citizens in the country, found themselves on the rolls of the welfare agencies.

One response to the strain placed on limited economic resources throughout the country was the demand for large-scale repatriations. To reduce the public relief rolls and agitation to organize labor, the Mexican became both the scapegoat

and the safety valve in the Southwest. It is estimated that in the early years of the Depression (1929–34) more than 400,000 Mexicans were forced to leave the country under "voluntary repatriation." Those who applied for relief were referred to "Mexican Bureaus," whose sole purpose was to reduce the welfare rolls by deporting the applicants.[32] Indigence, not citizenship, was the criterion used in identifying Mexicans for repatriation.

A 1933 eyewitness account of a Los Angeles repatriation scene suggests the mental frame of those responsible for the program:

It was discovered that, in wholesale lots, they could be shipped to Mexico City for $14.70 per capita. The sum represented less than the cost of a week's board and lodging. And so, about February 1931, the first trainload was dispatched, and shipments at the rate of about one a month have continued ever since. A shipment consisting of three special trains left Los Angeles on December 8. The loading commenced at about six o'clock in the morning and continued for hours. More than twenty-five such special trains had left the Southern Pacific Station before last April.

The repatriation programme is regarded locally as a piece of consummate statecraft. The average per family cost of executing it is $71.14, including food and transportation. It cost one Los Angeles County $77,249.29 to repatriate one shipment of 6,024. It would have cost $424,933.70 to provide this number with such charitable assistance as they would have been entitled to had they remained—a savings of $347,468.40.[33]

Repatriations took place both in the Southwest and Midwest, where Mexicans, recruited to the area by employers with promises of work, had lived since the early twenties. Approximately half of the "returnees" actually were born in the United States.[34] Shipment to Mexico was a clear violation of both their civil and human rights. The Immigration and Naturalization Service, in concert with the Anglo press, identified the Mexican labor migrant as the source of (Anglo) citizen unemployment, for the increase of public welfare costs (and taxes), and as having entered the country "illegally" and in large numbers. The scapegoating tactics of an earlier nativist generation, with its xenophobic memories and myths, were used against the Mexicans. There was a good deal of sentiment also against Mexico's expropriation and nationalization of its oil industry, which U.S. oil companies had once controlled. Repatriation caused widespread dissolution of family and community, and contributed to an even more acute distrust among Mexicans of all government—local, state, or federal.

Some small efforts at organized resistance were made. Strikes and organizational campaigns were started in the agricultural and industrial sector. *La Unión de Trabajadores del Valle Imperial* and *La Confederación de Uniones Obreras Mexicanas* began late in the 1920s to try to ease the blow of the unfolding Depression through labor organizing and self-defense. There were similar, but less successful, efforts made in the mining industry. *La Confederación Regional Obrera Mexicana*, a Mexican industrial union affiliated with the American Federation of Labor, sought to encourage the formation of unions in California.

Mexican consuls, meanwhile, continued to lodge complaints with the federal government, protesting the treatment of Mexican citizens recruited to work in the United States. Official protests by Mexico generally were ignored, and the abuses went unchecked.

Despite all such efforts, the social and economic standing of Mexicans was seriously eroded by the Great Depression. Families were forcibly broken up by the repatriation efforts, as were communities. The overall economic impact of trade union activities was limited, and failed to modify the underlying problem of relegating Mexicans to the lowest levels of the economic system.

World War II to 1960

World War II brought many changes. In the economic upturn that followed, there was a new demand for both industrial and agricultural labor. The movement to the cities accelerated. Regional economic needs and interests reasserted themselves; they were again instrumental in shaping national legislation in the agricultural arena. The bracero program, reestablished in 1942 and patterned after a similar program in effect from 1917 to 1920, was based on a bilateral agreement between Mexico and the United States, and was intended to supply labor for agriculture. The United States underwrote Mexicans' travel costs, insured a minimum wage, and guaranteed their just and equitable treatment. Agricultural interests were required to post a bond for every bracero and to abide by the agreements negotiated by the two governments. The program, in effect, was a federal subsidy of agriculture's labor needs.

Although intended only as a limited-term war measure to meet specific labor shortages in the agricultural sector, the advantages of the bracero program to both countries suggested its continuance. For Mexico, it was a temporary solution for high levels of unemployment, and made for a significant flow of capital to Mexico in wages earned and sent home. For U.S. agriculture, it gave promise of a steady supply of labor that was readily controlled and minimally paid, and for whom no long-term responsibilities were assumed.

The program, extended annually after the war, was formalized in 1951 as Public Law 78. The reasons given for the extension were labor shortages stemming from U.S. involvement in the Korean War; it is better understood as a continuation of the traditional U.S. manipulation and control of the flow of Mexican labor. The program was terminated in 1964, when annual inmigration quotas of 120,000 were established for all the nations of the Western Hemisphere.

Large-scale abuses were common in the program.[35] Mexico protested these abuses, and each time the agreement was renegotiated, sought to protect its citizens from inequitable wages and overt discrimination in working conditions, housing, and general treatment. The U.S. government relinquished the determination of wage rates to the agricultural employers, but continued to take responsibility for contracting and transporting Mexican laborers across the border. Nearly 5 million Mexicans came to the United States as a result of the program. The peak years were from 1954 to 1962, when 70 percent of all Mexicans involved in the program were working in the United States. We have no figures to tell us how many of these laborers returned to Mexico.

A steady flow of undocumented workers paralleled this importation of braceros. The undocumented proved to be a mixed blessing for agricultural interests. On the one hand, they were generally hired for wages substantially below the modest levels that agribusiness established for braceros, and bonds were not required to be posted for them. They were widely used as strikebreakers to thwart unionizing activities in agriculture. But there were obvious drawbacks. A labor pool made up of largely undocumented workers was very unstable. Since such workers were under no binding agreement to any employer, they were free to seek the highest wage, within the restrictions imposed by specific jobs and particular industries, and under the continuous threat that the employer would terminate the job by calling the Immigration and Naturalization Service just before he was to meet the payroll. To the extent that agribusiness failed to establish a uniform wage, there was a constant temptation for undocumented workers to move on in search of better employment. Moreover, since the undocumented worker was not covered by an agreement restricting him to agricultural tasks, he would always be attracted by industrial jobs in cities, where wages and working conditions were generally better. During World War II, the informal agreements between industry and agribusiness that prohibited the hiring of Mexican labor for factory work were in abeyance.

We understand today how an initial bilateral agreement between Mexico and the United States to supply braceros became in time a unilateral program dictated by U.S. agricultural interests, supported by the federal government.[36] Once agricultural employers took control of the bracero program, they sought to expand their control also over the undocumented worker. Agricultural entrepreneurs ended up by transporting undocumented workers to the border where they were immediately rehired as braceros, thereby transforming what was once an unregulated labor supply into a legal and semicontrolled work force bound to the agricultural sector.

After a regulated labor pool was firmly reestablished for agribusiness, in 1954 the Immigration and Naturalization Service vigorously launched "Operation Wetback." Undocumented workers, unstable and intractable as a labor source, were now to be removed. An astonishing 3.8 million Mexican aliens (and citizens) were apprehended and expelled in the next five years. Of the total number deported during that time, fewer than 2 percent left as a result of formal proceedings. The vast majority were removed simply by the *threat* of deportation. "Looking Mexican" was often sufficient reason for official scrutiny. The search focused initially on California and then Texas; it soon extended as far as Spokane, Chicago, St. Louis, and Kansas City.[37]

For urban Chicanos and Mexicans, World War II had effects similar to those for their rural cousins. On the positive side, war industries provided the semblance of occupational opportunity for many, though often in unskilled, semiskilled, and low-level service capacities. Still, the rigid tie between class and ethnicity seemed somewhat weakened.

World War II posed a major dilemma for the United States. In its official pronouncements and acts, the country strongly condemned the racism explicit in Nazism. Yet at the same time, the United States had a segregated military force. This was also a time when President Roosevelt issued Executive Order No. 9066, which authorized the internment of Japanese who were U.S. citizens and whose sole "crime" was living and working on the West Coast.

This contradiction also manifested itself in ugly confrontations between Mexicans and Anglos. The press, for its part, helped to raise feelings against Mexicans. The violent confrontations between servicemen and local police against Mexican residents began late in 1942 and continued until mid-1943. The overt racial bias of the press with regard to Mexicans has been thoroughly documented. It suggests the power of the press in shaping public opinion and in justifying major abuses by law enforcement and military personnel. The so-called zoot suit riots illustrate the power of the press in mobilizing prejudice:

> The zoot-suiters of Los Angeles . . . were predominantly Mexican youth with some Negro disciples, between the ages of sixteen and twenty. They wore absurdly long coats with padded shoulders, porkpie hats completed by a feather in the back, watch chains so long they almost touched the ground, and peg-top trousers tapering to narrow cuffs. . . . at best, as one pundit observed, they were "not characterized primar-

ily by intellect." They formed themselves into bands with flamboyant names: the "Mateo Bombers," "Main Street Zooters," "The Califa," "Sleepy Lagooners," "The Black Legion," and many more. Their targets for physical harm were members of the armed forces, with a special predilection for sailors. The latter fought back with devastating effect. The situation quickly deteriorated to the point that the Navy declared Los Angeles out of bounds. The city council outlawed wearing zoot suits for the duration and the city simmered down.[38]

Some investigators, more objective than the press, have reversed the roles, with the navy on the offensive and the Mexican young obliged to defend themselves. The firsthand accounts show that the police actually encouraged and supported the servicemen's agression. And not only did the police refuse to halt the violence, they often contributed to it.[39]

Another celebrated incident was the so-called Sleepy Lagoon case in 1942. A Mexican youth was killed as the result of gang conflict. A sensationalist press soon gave the incident a wholly false character; it was thought to be the beginnings of an incipient crime wave led by insurgent Mexicans. Public pressure led the police to massive roundups. Twenty-four Mexican youths were arrested; seventeen were indicted and tried for murder. The defendants, beaten by the police and forced to appear in court in their unkempt and disheveled states, received scant sympathy. Despite the lack of tangible evidence, nine were convicted of murder, eight, of lesser crimes. These decisions, reversed two years later by the California District Court of Appeals as a direct result of efforts by outraged civil rights lawyers and activists, tell much of the temper of the times. They also suggest why Chicanos and Mexicans are so suspicious of the U.S. law enforcement and legal systems. Mexicans believe that they consistently receive harsher sentences than Anglos for the same crime. They also believe that this explains their disproportionate representation in U.S. penal institutions.[40]

The Mexican community, in responding to the situation of World War II, acted as it had done in previous times of hostility and exploitation—with organizational efforts and litigation, and occasionally with armed resistance. Unity

Leagues, created in the early 1940s, had as their principal purpose the election of Mexicans to city councils in Southern California communities; they also conducted voter registration drives, attempted fund-raising, and worked to get voters to the polls. The basic theme uniting these leagues was the fight against racial discrimination, particularly in the schools. The League of United Latin American Citizens (LULAC), founded in South Texas in 1928, expanded into a national organization in the post-World War II period, and was soon heavily involved in anti-discrimination activity, again particularly in the educational arena.

A landmark court decision in 1945 (*Méndez v. Westminster School District*) barred *de jure* segregation of Chicano students. A similar legal action in Texas in 1948 was also successfully pressed. The results of both court actions, as well as others during the 1950s, helped set the stage for the Supreme Court's *Brown v. Board of Education* decision in 1954, and clearly established the illegality of the deliberate segregation of Chicano and Mexican school children on the basis of race, and of bilingual education as a partial remedy for segregation. The success of these efforts served to encourage civil rights suits in other areas, notably against job discrimination in New Mexico.[41]

The refusal of local officials in Corpus Christi, Texas, in 1948, to allow the burial of a Chicano war hero in the local "for whites only" cemetery was the specific catalyst for the creation of the G.I. Forum. The Mexican community proudly emphasized two facts: Chicanos received the largest number of Congressional Medals of Honor during World War II, and despite forbidding interrogations by the North Koreans and Chinese during the Korean War, no Chicano soldier ever "broke down." The collective memory of such Chicano military contributions fed the Mexican distaste of continued political gerrymandering, economic exploitation, physical abuse, and cultural repression at home.

The Mexican American Political Association, formed in 1959, had as its goal "the social, economic, cultural and civic betterment of Mexican Americans and all other Spanish-speaking Americans through political action." The association established chapters in voting districts with large concentrations of Mexican residents, and endorsed candidates for public office who could be counted on to work actively for social improvement.

Large numbers of Mexicans migrated to urban centers in the decades after World War II. There was a general optimism that life in the cities would be better than in the rural setting. The cities seemed to hold out the promise of better jobs, more adequate housing, and new educational possibilities. These early migrants to the cities came with visions of expanded opportunities, and believed that if they themselves did not achieve their aspirations, their children surely would. This optimism made tolerable the thwarted aspirations so many of these urban migrants soon came to feel. Since they outnumbered Mexicans already living in the cities, their optimism spread to the larger group.

Many of the postwar organizations were primarily self-protective, mutual-aid associations. They were formed principally to protect their numbers by offering services consistent with Mexican cultural traditions, in effect compensating for services withheld by the larger society. Organizations such as the G.I. Forum and LULAC entered the activist period of the 1950s and 1960s with an organizational base redirected toward activism. Their resources were considerable—a growing constituency, established legitimacy, and a solid leadership core. Their past history of noninvolvement in political affairs, their emphasis on assimilation, or working within the system, and their passive, nonactivist stance, drew criticism in the 1970s. Such groups, however, provided the foundation for attempts to improve the condition of the Mexican people.

The Chicano Movement 1965–1975

In the 1960s and early 1970s, activist, sometimes radical, organizations appeared. These organizations came to be known collectively as the Chicano movement. Often very critical of the basic assumptions of U.S. society, they sought fundamental transformations in the distribution of power in the United States. Many promoted radical alternatives, preferring socialism, for example, to the prevailing economic and political system. Others hoped to create various kinds of alternative or separatist institutions, with alternative schools, community control of law enforcement, health, educational, and political institutions, and the like. They were looking, in short, for a radical and equitable transformation of a racist society. Almost all such groups emphasized the distinctiveness of Mexican culture. They actively promoted Chicano cultural norms and values. Chicano culture represented the common ground that bound together all the members of the group. Political terms such as "Chicano" and *La Raza Nueva* were used to symbolize unity, and were intended to increase the cohesiveness of otherwise diverse elements.

Charismatic leaders appeared. Reies López Tijerina hoped to restore lost Spanish and Mexican land grants in New Mexico through the widely publicized and often dramatic activities of the *Alianza Federal de Pueblos Libres*. Rodolfo "Corky" Gonzáles, former prizefighter and disaffected Democratic party official, organized the Crusade for Justice and established several alternative community institutions in the Denver area. The miserable working conditions of Mexican agricultural laborers became the special concern of the United Farm Workers Organizing Committee, led by César Chávez.

Throughout the Southwest and Midwest, political and educational issues sparked new organizing activity. In Texas, José Angel Gutiérrez and others overthrew the minority Anglo-dominated governments of several South Texas cities and counties, primarily through a third party, *El Partido de La Raza Unida*. To secure educational change, students in secondary schools and colleges formed Chicano organizations to stage massive school walkouts. These organizations served as foci for various kinds of diffused activities; they brought a variety of grievances under a single banner, and made a collective approach to these grievances possible.

Anglo decision-makers, reacting to the politics of direct action and confrontation, were sometimes repressive, sometimes progressive; many of the gains made could be attributed to the "threatening" activities of such militant organizations. The protest groups, however, were often short-lived. They called for a great expenditure of time and effort and involved considerable risk.

The student groups were ideologically **very** diverse: some were moderate-liberal; others were radical. The Mexican American Youth Organization, a precursor in Texas to the *Raza Unida* party, gave José Angel Gutiérrez, Mario Compeán, and others apprenticeship training in community-based and campus-based politics. *El Movimiento Estudiantíl Chicano de Aztlán*, a campus-based organization, was fairly radical and had many chapters throughout the Southwest; it was very active in support of the farm workers' movement and many other nonschool issues. The United Mexican American Students and the Chicano Youth Organization were other prominent student organizations during this period. Although such organizations often worked off-campus, they pushed also for increased recruitment of Chicano students and faculty, for opening new educational opportunities to Chicanos, and for curricula more relevant to Chicano concerns. Many of these demands were embodied in the new Chicano Studies programs developed in many colleges and universities.

The importance of these campus-based organizations cannot be overemphasized. They provided invaluable resources for both on-campus and off-campus activities. Many interacted with both staff and faculty. Student groups were effective agents of political mobilization; they had the idealism, ideological conmitment, and the relatively supportive environment necessary for sustained organizational activities. Many of these campus organizations, however, were unable to contend with the rapid turnover of student populations, with increasing administrative intransigence, and internal division created by law enforcement *provocateurs* and ultraleftist organizations.

Prior to the 1970s there were few Chicano professional associations, which is not surprising, given the small number of Chicano professionals. As the system yielded to pressure, however, and greater numbers of Chicanos became teachers, lawyers, physicians, and business managers, organization became viable. Many started with less than a dozen members; in many of the academic disciplines, the formation of Chicano/Latino caucuses in major Anglo professional organizations was a necessary first step. Public and private foundations, responding to demands for increased numbers of Chicano professionals, provided support to foster organizational activity. Among these were the *Southwest Council de la Raza*, the Mexican American Legal Defense and Educational Fund (MALDEF), and the *National Task Force de la Raza*.

Until 1970, Mexicans were traditionally concentrated in the nonunion ranks of the U.S. economy. Starting in the early 1920s they attempted to form their own unions or to affiliate with unions in Mexico and the United States. The leadership of established industrial unions in this country was never Chicano, although some change is now taking place. Latino workers—Mexicans, Puerto Ricans, and others—are beginning to coalesce in organizations such as the Labor Council for Latin American Advancement.

With the establishment of "national" offices based in Washington, several Chicano organizations began to grow in the mid-1970s. Interorganizational cooperation between Chicanos and Latinos in general has become more common. There have been several attempts to weld "Hispanic" organizations together in some sort of federation, notably the newly created Forum of National Hispanic Organizations and the Hispanic Higher Education Coalition. In the late 1970s such Washington-based groups as the *National Council de la Raza*, MALDEF, and the Mexican American Women's National Association could coordinate to express the common concerns of Chicano organizations.

Chicanos have gravitated toward public employment, having found opportunities there, particularly in lower-status positions, somewhat more open than in the private sector. Organizations within the public sector, such as IMAGE, a nationwide group of employees that seeks to enhance the working conditions and positions of Chicanos and other Latinos with the government, have emerged. Although there are few high-level government officials of Mexican origin, organizations of Latino officials have come into being. The National Association of Latino Elected and Appointed Officials tries to increase communication between Chicano and Latino decision-makers, particularly on the local level. The Congressional Hispanic Caucus, consisting of the six Latino members of Congress, is the group with the highest governmental status at the federal level.

Two broad coalitions of interests make up the major political parties in the United States, and in general, Chicanos have been exploited by both. Many of the successes of the Democratic party can be attributed to the 70 to 90 percent electoral support regularly given by Chicano voters. Minimal rewards, in the form of minor-patronage and policy concessions, have been returned to the Chicano community by the Democratic party, which for the most part has taken the Chicano vote for granted. In very close elections, Democrats have made extravagant promises to Chicanos, but once the election is over, the Anglo Democratic leadership has generally failed to follow through. The Republican party has only limited appeal for Chicanos; Republican leaders have not made a very serious effort to broaden their base by attracting Chicano participation.

Minor parties, including socialist and Marxist-oriented parties, have not been very successful in recruiting Chicanos to their cause. The most successful third party movement for Chicanos, *El Partido de la Raza Unida* (LRUP), at the height of its influence in the early 1970s played a pivotal role in determing the outcome of several local elections, primarily in South Central Texas. In small localities with large Chicano populations, it succeeded in school, town, and county government elections, often stressing the unresponsiveness of the major parties, and arguing for cultural nationalism. The *Partido* provided an alternative that threatened the customary hegemonic position of the major parties. Both the Democratic and the Republican parties reacted by supporting minor institutional reform: they set up "Hispanic" offices within their party organizations, and the Democratic party went so far as to guarantee Chicano representation in its party structure. Conflicts within its own ranks over strategic issues led *La Raza Unida* to fragment into smaller locally based units. Punitive measures sponsored by the State of Texas and specifically aimed at breaking up the *Partido* contributed to its decline. Modifications in electoral laws proved problematic to third parties that attempted to place their candidates on the ballot. By raising the number of required petition-signers or voters received to qualify for inclusion on the ballot, third parties could be excluded.

By the late 1970s the organizational base of the Chicano community had been largely transformed. Many of the more radical and ideological organizations had either disappeared or were mere shadows of their former selves. Leaders who cut their political teeth in such organizations have become part of older, more broadly based organizations or have joined the new professional organizations that continue to advocate, with renewed spirit, specific political reforms. The organizational structure changes as collective and individual political sophistication continues to grow.

Growth and National Visibility

The structural characteristics of the Chicano population suggest why Chicanos have gained national visibility. All demographic description starts by emphasizing the youthfulness of the Chicano population, the median age for Chicanos being seven years younger than the national population. A youthful population is one that will be active for a longer period, with the bulk of its members in an early phase of labor force participation, or only just beginning to prepare for that phase. A youthful population has its future before it; schooling, family formation, and child-rearing are crucial issues. And given their rapid numerical growth, Chicanos must play an increasingly important role in the United States in the next decades.

With journalistic phrases like "people on the move," "awakening giant," "emerging minority," and "sleeping giant," writers have drawn attention to the "sudden" visibility of Chicanos. Some are surprised by this visibility. Even the most casual traveler through the southwestern United States has observed the centuries-old Spanish and Mexican influence on architecture, cuisine, language, art, music, and the very layout of towns and cities. Chicano presence in the Southwest has never been hidden. It is the sudden awareness that Chicanos also reside outside these traditional southwestern enclaves, and that Chicano issues are not simply regional in nature, that has drawn the continuing attention of the mass media. Indeed, the rapid *growth* and continuing *dispersion* of the Chicano population is producing the new national awareness.

The Chicano population has grown substantially over the last decade. Although this growth is attributed in part to improved methods of survey and enumeration by gathering agencies such as the Census Bureau, the greatest part of the increase comes from the real growth of the Chicano population. This growth rate has been conservatively estimated at 2.2 percent per year; a more liberal estimate is 3.5 percent per year. The first figure indicates a doubling of the Chicano population every twenty-five to twenty-seven years; the second, a doubling in less than twenty years.

This phenomenal rate of growth is in stark contrast with decreasing growth rates for the U.S. population as a whole. While U.S. birth rates are stabilizing at just above replacement level, the Chicano population is maintaining the highest rate of growth of all major racial and ethnic groups in the country. Early marriage and the emphasis placed on family accounts for these high fertility rates. Chicano families are generally about 24 percent larger than the average American family, and one in every five Chicano families consists of six or more persons.

There is, however, a trend toward lower birth rates. Younger Chicanas are having fewer children and spacing them out longer over the childbearing years. Still, even among younger and better-educated women, the emphasis on childbearing appears to remain strong; voluntary childlessness among married Chicanas, or those who were married, is virtually unknown.

The high fertility rates of Chicanos suggest major structural differences between them and the Anglo population. Although the Anglo birth rate has decreased owing to later marriages, birth spacing, and the use of contraceptives to synchronize childbearing with the demands of increased female employment, this has not always been the case. From the late 1930s to the early 1940s the United States had high rates of immigration and fertility; the two together produced a period of high population growth. The Chicano population explosion today is in many ways reminiscent of that earlier era, with high rates of immigration (both legal and undocumented) and birth rates. All signs point to a significant growth of the Chicano population in the 1980s.

There is now considerable discussion regarding total Hispanic population growth in the United States and whether this collective group

will overtake blacks as the largest national minority group. Precise projections are impossible, since they depend on how long current high rates of growth in the Hispanic population are sustained. Still, it is now expected that the Hispanic population will become the largest minority in the United States in the foreseeable future. Further, since Chicanos make up the majority—60 percent—of this population group, they will be among the more visible elements in what is increasingly referred to as the "Hispanization" of the United States.

If high birth rates are important, so also is immigration. The century-old relationship between the United States and Mexico continues to affect both nations. Immigrants, natural resources, and profits continue to flow north. Legal immigration from Mexico to the United States at present allows between forty and fifty thousand visas each year for permanent residence. Those looking for "commuter status," which allows them to work in the United States while living in Mexico, have to endure, barring political connections, a three-year waiting period.

Mexican workers caught in Mexico's economic sluggishness are aware that wages in the United States for identical work are sometimes seven times higher than at home, and many are thus led to risk illegal entry. Such illegal entry is only increased by the active recruitment by "coyotes," who transport Mexicans across the border for a fee. Undocumented workers are a significant part of the U.S. labor force, particularly for work that most American citizens regard as demeaning, low paying, dirty, and unstable. Undocumented workers have always come to the United States in circumstances of multiple jeopardy, as minorities unprotected from employer exploitation and abuse. Such conditions continue unabated today.

A majority of the undocumented workers in the United States come as sojourners in search of economic opportunity; few have any desire to remain here as permanent residents. Despite the widespread impression that Mexican undocumented workers come across the border in search of the promised land, corridos, or ballads, by and about them celebrate the less hostile, more familiar ambience they plan to return to.

The flow of immigration, both legal and

undocumented, is extensive: more than a million persons annually are apprehended by the Border Patrol for seeking entry without inspection. Annual deportations, both voluntary and involuntary, continue to increase steadily. These statistics suggest improved enforcement capabilities; they also measure, however crudely, the growth in the number of Mexicans wanting to cross the permeable U.S.-Mexico border. That flow increases in part because of labor force needs. Jobs are available to Mexican migrants largely in the secondary labor market, where the lack of fringe benefits makes these low-paying, seasonal jobs unattractive to domestic workers. The Mexican worker historically has been desirable. Mexicans—particularly without legal rights and privileges—are especially desirable for agribusiness, marginal industries, seasonal work, or in businesses quickly affected by economic downturns.

Although only a small fraction of the undocumented workers come to the United States with any intention of staying, there is no reason to believe that Mexican immigration will cease, at least in the foreseeable future. The flow of nearly a century and a half, responding to the need for labor by U.S. employers, seems to argue against the possibility of immigration being terminated. The growth of the Chicano population, because of higher fertility and continued immigration, is increasingly visible. The continued dispersion of the Chicano population out of the Southwest into the industrial Midwest, particularly into cities like Chicago, Gary, Hammond, Kansas City, Detroit, Flint, and Saginaw, will go on. It is not difficult to understand the attraction of the Midwest: a Chicano worker with a high-school education will earn approximately $4,000 more per year there than his cousin can expect to earn in the Southwest.

Such differentials in income are significant. The Midwest, highly unionized and with a long-established industrial base, is very different from the Southwest, which is only now beginning to unionize, and where light manufacturing is still the rule. In the Southwest, also, labor-intensive industries in agriculture and mining are giving way to high-level service industries in aerospace, electronics, and petrochemicals that require a labor force that is technically trained. This new labor force tends to be made up largely of transplanted Easterners.

Chicanos in the Midwest, Pacific Northwest, Florida, and other parts of the United States need to be seen as a vanguard. Although farther removed from their origins, they still maintain and perpetuate their Mexican heritage. Their entry into an area is almost always followed by the rapid opening of small Chicano businesses that specifically cater to their needs. Spanish-language mass at the Catholic Church typically follows, along with Spanish-language radio programs and bilingual programs in the schools. The taking root of Chicano businesses, services, and traditions produces a Midwestern version of the Southwestern or Mexican environment. The ability of Chicanos to transfer their ethnic preferences from one location to another tells something of the strength and durability of their cultural ties.

Midwestern Chicanos, finding themselves among non-Chicano Latinos, necessarily interact, but not always easily or without hostility and suspicion. New patterns, however, are becoming evident as efforts at cooperative ventures are made. Chicanos in Milwaukee, Chicago, and Detroit, for example, discovering that they face problems very similar to those of other Latinos, seek to create coalitions that form the basis for a national Latino thrust. These contacts have understandably progressed further among Cuban, Puerto Rican, and Chicano leaders at the national level than at the local level, particularly as the strategy of nationally organized coalition-building has spread.

The dispersal of Chicanos has had positive and negative effects, making it obvious that Chicano issues cannot be dealt with simply as a regional (Southwestern) matter. Chicanos now reside in every state in the Union; the 1980s will undoubtedly see almost half the Chicano population residing outside the five southwestern states. Had the dispersal of Chicanos not occurred, most of the southwestern states would be overwhelmingly Chicano. Although the size of population does not automatically translate into political power, political negotiation and coalition-building would have taken very different forms if the Southwest had become a single and greater Chicano enclave.

181

Current Status

Chicanos lag behind the rest of the U.S. population by every measure of socioeconomic well-being—level of education, occupational attainment, employment status, family income, and the like. Some say that Chicanos are no different from other immigrants who arrived in the United States impoverished, and who managed by hard work to gain advantages for their children, taking the first important step toward assimilation. The substantial achievements of the American-born first generation over that of the immigrant generation are thought to be conclusive. Such an optimistic view overlooks major changes in the society and the historical relationship of over a century and a half of racial discrimination and economic exploitation. Although economic expansion and dramatic social change characterized the postwar years, economic contraction and dislocation, possibly exaggerated by the new conservative retrenchment, are the hallmarks of more recent times. When the economy was productive and growing, Chicanos participated in that growth, at least through their labor. A close examination, however, suggests that the modest gains made in average income and occupational status during the 1950s and 1960s were lost in the 1970s. As one scholar explains:

> When the 1975 occupational employment distributions for Anglos and Chicanos are compared to the Labor Department's revised estimates for 1985 employment opportunities, it is clear that the [1975] recession hurt the future income potential of Chicanos as well as their current incomes. In general, the recession has forced Chicanos into occupational groups for which future employment is expected to decline relative to the employment and in which relative wages can be expected to fall as well. Similarly, while Anglos were moving into those occupations that are expected to have the greatest future income potential, Chicanos were moving out, thus losing the ability to share in the expected relative wage increases that growth usually brings. By 1975, only 33 percent of Chicanos were located in expanding occupations. . . . The evidence supports the conclusion that our latest recession had a definite racial bias and that Mexican Americans received more than their share of economic hardship.[42]

Although second-generation and later Chicanos made large gains relative to those of the first generation, such gains did not allow for their thorough absorption into the economic and social structure of U.S. society. The data of the late 1970s suggest how different generations of Chicanos have fared.[43] The median education for second-generation Chicanos was 11.1 years, only two years more than for U.S. born first-generation, but decidedly more than for the immigrant generation (5.8 years).

All generations of Chicano males are underrepresented in white-collar jobs; Mexican-born males are least likely to be found in such positions. Farm labor is the one area where there is a significant difference between the U.S.-born and immigrant Chicano populations.[44] Over 15 percent of Mexican-born men are employed as farm laborers, twice the number for sons of Mexican immigrants, five times the number of third-generation Chicanos. Labor force participation figures, however, also show that second-generation Chicanos had the highest unemployment rate, while the immigrant generation had the lowest. The data on incomes indicate first-generation Chicano familes as having the highest median income, with the second-generation following, and the Mexican-born as having the lowest incomes. The range, however, was not great—about $1,500.

That Mexicans who have resided for the longest time in the United States—second generation—have the highest unemployment rates and only very modest representation in white-collar, professional, and managerial categories suggests the limited structure of opportunity for Chicanos. They are entering the industrial sector at a time when its socioeconomic structure is increasingly tertiary, demanding highly trained personnel in high-technology industries such as aerospace, communications, and the like. Although Chicanos may be making "progress" relative to their immigrant parents, they are actually falling farther behind when looked at in the context of the opportunity structure in an increasingly post-industrial social order and compared to the dominant population. Also, there is evidence that Chicano technical and occupational skills will increasingly limit them to the secondary labor market, with its unfavorable wage rates, limited fringe benefits, and general instability. These conditions do not promise either full equity or full participation for Chicanos in the decades immediately ahead. Still, that the Anglo population growth is at or near a steady state, with its income-generating population increasingly aging, suggests that the younger and expanding Chicano work force will be shouldering a growing and disproportionate burden in the future. Social Security, Medicare, Medicaid, and the myriad of other social programs funded from taxes on the work force will be more and more borne by youthful employed Chicanos.

Historically, Chicanos' economic rewards have been disproportionate to their contribution to U.S. industrial development. Now that the society is increasingly post-industrial, Chicanos find themselves still carrying the burden. The federal government, which played a prominent role throughout the history of Mexicans in the United States, has been repressive, supporting industries and employers, and generally frustrating Chicanos' efforts to advance. Many of the organizations developed by Chicanos were direct responses to these negative influences. The prediction seems to be unremitting governmental policies that will continue to deplete the resources of the Chicano community or leave it as disadvantaged as ever. But Mexico's new wealth, particularly its energy resources, may somewhat alter that prognosis, especially if Mexico retains control over those resources. A nation tends to treat descendants of foreign stock, even a militarily conquered population, with greater responsibility when it is obliged to negotiate with that foreign nation on an equal footing.

Still, the outlook for Chicanos is not very encouraging. Efforts by Chicano organizations to obtain justice and equality, and to share in society's bounties, have not been overwhelmingly successful. Whether these efforts stand a better chance of succeeding when external forces are more active in helping such efforts, only the future can tell.

REFERENCES

This essay is a joint effort by the authors. The listing of names on the title page in no way indicates the extent of contribution. Rather, all four authors contributed equally.

1. The terms "Chicano" and "Mexican" are used interchangeably in this essay, because the U.S. Southwest and northern Mexico were initially a cultural and geographic unit, the border being only an invisible line between the two nations.

2. The term "Anglo" will be used to refer to U.S. residents of European origin. It is used, for convenience, as a generic term for all European immigrants to the United States.

3. Rodolfo Acuña, *Occupied America* (San Francisco: Canfield Press, 1972), p. 11.

4. Eugene C. Barker, *Mexico and Texas, 1821–1835* (New York: Russell and Russell, 1965), p. 52.

5. Acuña, *Occupied America*.

6. Ibid., p. 44ff; Mario Barrera, *Race and Class in the Southwest* (South Bend: University of Notre Dame Press, 1979), pp. 7–33; Matt S. Meier and Feliciano Rivera, *The Chicanos: A History of Mexican Americans* (New York: Hill and Wang, 1972), pp. 88–94.

7. Carey McWilliams, *North From Mexico* (Philadelphia: Lippincott, 1949).

8. Joan W. Moore, with Harry Pachon, *Mexican Americans*, 2d edition (Englewood Cliffs, N.J.: Prentice-Hall, 1976), pp. 13–14.

9. Barrera, *Race and Class in the Southwest*, p. 25.

10. Meier and Rivera, *The Chicanos*, p. 107.

11. Moore, with Pachon, *Mexican Americans*, p. 15.

12. Barrera, *Race and Class in the Southwest*, pp. 23–30.

13. McWilliams, *North From Mexico*.

14. Peter Baird and Ed McCoughan, *Beyond the Border: Mexico and the U.S. Today* (New York: North American Congress on Latin America, 1979); Barrera, *Race and Class in the Southwest*; Meier and Rivera, *The Chicanos*.

15. Ibid.

16. Barrera, *Race and Class in the Southwest*, p. 20.

17. Ernesto Galarza, *Barrio Boy* (South Bend, Ind.: University of Notre Dame Press, 1971).

18. Meier and Rivera, *The Chicanos*, p. 124.

19. Barrera, *Race and Class in the Southwest*, pp. 84–86.

20. Vernon M. Briggs, Jr., Walter Fogel, and Fred H. Schmidt, *The Chicano Worker* (Austin: University of Texas Press, 1977); Meier and Rivera, *The Chicanos*.

21. Manuel P. Servin, "The Pre-World War II Mexican-American: An Interpretation," *California Historical Society Quarterly*, 45 (1966): 325–38.

22. The migration figures at this time are characterized by imprecision. Leo Grebler, for example, in *The School Gap: Signs of Progress* (Advance Report 7, Mexican American Study Project [Los Angeles: Univer-

sity of California Press, 1967]), has figures that are 20 percent higher than Servin's (Ibid.), and Barrera, in *Race and Class in the Southwest*, indicates that a comparison of Mexico's emigration statistics with U.S. immigration figures shows still higher numbers.

23. Oscar Handlin, *Race and Nationality in American Life* (New York: Anchor Books, 1957), pp. 93–94.

24. Ibid., pp. 101–2.

25. Ibid., p. 97.

26. Ibid., pp. 93–138.

27. William Paul Dillingham, *Report of the Immigration Commission*, vol. 1 (Washington, D.C.: Government Printing Office, 1911), pp. 690–91.

28. Acuña, *Occupied America*, pp. 123–50; Baird and McCoughan, *Beyond the Border*, pp. 21–35; Barrera, *Race and Class in the Southwest*, pp. 72–75.

29. "Mexican Immigration: A Report by Roy L. Garis for the Information of Congress," *Western Hemisphere Immigration*, Committee on Immigration and Naturalization, 71st Congress 2d session, 1930, p. 436.

30. Committee on Immigration and Naturalization, *Seasonal Agricultural Laborers from Mexico*, 69th Congress, 1st session, 1926, p. 24.

31. Moore, with Pachon, *Mexican Americans*, p. 40.

32. Meier and Rivera, *The Chicanos*, p. 163.

33. Moore, with Pachon, *Mexican Americans*, pp. 41–42.

34. Ernesto Galarza, *Merchants of Labor: The Mexican Bracero Story* (Santa Barbara, California: McNally-Loftin, 1964).

35. Ibid.

36. Ibid.

37. Ibid.

38. McWilliams, *North From Mexico*, pp. 227–58.

39. Roger Daniels and Harry H. L. Kitano, *American Racism: Explorations of the Nature of Prejudice* (Englewood Cliffs, N.J.: Prentice-Hall, 1970), p. 76.

40. Armando Morales, *Ando Sangrado: I Am Bleeding* (LaPuente, Calif.: Perspectiva Publications, 1972).

41. Meier and Rivera, *The Chicanos*, pp. 242–43.

42. Tim D. Kane, "Structural Change and Chicano Employment in the Southwest: Some Preliminary Changes," *Aztlan*, 45 (1973): 383–98.

43. Ibid., p. 29.

44. Philip Garcia and Lionel Maldonado, "America's Mexicans: A Plea for Specificity," (mimeo); Philip Garcia, "Nativity, Bilingualism and Occupational Attainment among Mexican American Men," (in press). The data summarized here are from a more detailed analysis of the 1970 Decennial Census and the March 1978 Current Population Survey. This section borrows from that more detailed analysis. Chicanos' attainments on selected racial characteristics are presented in terms of Mexican inmigrants, first-generation and subsequent-generation Chicanos.

12

Emergent Ethnicity:
A Review and Reformulation*

William L. Yancey
Eugene P. Ericksen
Richard N. Juliani

The analysis of ethnicity in American sociology has been dominated by an argument between the assimilationist and pluralist perspectives. Both positions have emphasized the cultural origins of ethnic groups. This underlying assumption has never been tested, nor has the structural context of the argument been specified. The assimilationist position is that cultural differences between national origin groups pass through later generations in progressively diluted forms and ultimately disappear in modern society. This position rests on the assumption that the importance of ascribed status and ascriptively oriented relations wane with increasing modernization and the accompanying emphasis on universalism and achievement. As Blau and Duncan (1967:429) write: ". . . a fundamental trend toward expanding universalism characterizes industrial society. Objective criteria of evaluation that are universally accepted increasingly pervade all spheres of life and displace particularistic standards of diverse ingroups, intuitive judgement, and humanistic values not susceptible to empirical verification."

Reprinted from *American Sociological Review* 41 (June 1976), pp. 391–403 by permission of the authors and the publisher.

*Support for this research was received from Temple University, the Center for Studies of Metropolitan Problems, National Institute of Mental Health (Grant #RO1MH25244) and the Institute for Survey Research, Temple University.

In spite of the popularity of this view, we feel there are important theoretical reasons (e.g., Cohen, 1974; Mayhew, 1968) and empirical evidence (e.g., Laumann, 1973, Granovetter, 1974) indicating that it may be false.

The pluralist position, on the other hand, emphasizes the persistence of cultural heritage as the basis of the continued importance of ascriptive groups (Abramson, 1973; Greeley, 1974). Yet these writers have failed to explore the possibility that such differences could be due to structural conditions which each immigrant group and their descendants have encountered. Lieberson notes in criticizing the cultural explanation for the propensity of immigrants from northern and western Europe to engage in agriculture:

Since the new immigrants, using a geographical distinction, came predominently after the great development and settlement of the national agricultural regions, they were not in a position comparable to that of the old immigrants coming during the mid-nineteenth century (1963:63).

Lieberson's position leads to the hypothesis that the behavior of immigrants and their descendants would vary significantly depending on whether they have lived under conditions which generated and/or reinforced an "ethnic community" in the United States. As Kosa (1956) has demonstrated for Hungarians in New York and Toronto, when group members have different American experiences, their attitudes, behavior and valuation of group membership are different.

The monolithic treatment of ethnicity, used in much contemporary empirical research, has not paid attention to differences within an ethnic group. One example of this failure is Duncan and Duncan's (1968) research on occupational mobility by national origin groups. For some groups, differences in the pattern of occupational mobility were found and were described as being characteristic of the entire group. The same differences could have been found if a significant minority within any national origin group had a unique experience in the United States while the remaining of the group shared a more general pattern. The distinctive situation of the subgroup, rather than cultural heritage or possible discrimination as implied by the Duncans would explain group differences. In short, we suggest that it is not only necessary to test for differences between groups, but also to identify those conditions which produce ethnicity and ethnically related behavior.

The contrasting view of ethnicity developed here is that rather than an ascribed constant or a temporarily persistent variable, ethnicity and ethnically based ascription are emergent phenomena. Rather than viewing ethnicity or ascribed status generally as being inevitably doomed by the processes of modernization, we suggest that ethnic groups have been produced by structural conditions which are intimately linked to the changing technology of industrial production and transportation. More specifically, ethnicity, defined in terms of frequent patterns of association and identification with common origins (Haller, 1973; Greeley, 1974), is crystallized under conditions which reinforce the maintenance of kinship and friendship networks. These are common occupational positions, residential stability and concentration, and dependence on common institutions and services. These conditions are directly dependent on the ecological structure of cities, which is in turn directly affected by the processes of industrialization.

We do not wish to suggest that this is a complete model. Our focus is on the American immigrant experience and is limited to the situation which Lieberson (1961) has characterized as superordinate indigenous group and subordinate migrants. The factor of racial and biological distinctiveness has been fully explored in previous statements of ethnic relations. Similarly, we have not examined either the antecedents or consequences of intergroup conflict as a facilitator of intergroup solidarity. There are some cases where ideologically oriented immigrant groups have come to the United States and self-consciously tried to maintain their heritages and, as Glazer observed (1954), ideological groups frequently develop after arrival in the United States. These groups have found a unique, often autonomous place in the American social structure (Hostetler, 1968), and even then there is modification in their ideology and heritage (Handlin, 1961).

This paper is in two sections. The first is a discussion of the historical and ecological conditions leading to the formation and persistence of ethnic communities in cities. The second section focuses on contemporary patterns of urban ethnic groups. Here we discuss the implication of changing ecological conditions for the maintenance and development of ascriptive associations and identification in contemporary American cities.

Occupational Concentration of Immigrants

Systematic evidence (Lieberson, 1963; Hutchinson, 1956) indicates that immigrant cohorts are differentially located in the American occupational structure. Unlike the widely held model of each immigrant cohort moving into the stratification system at its lowest point, pushing up those who had come before them and then being pushed themselves by later arrivals, all groups did not enter at the lowest occupational levels. Lieberson (1963:173) reports that for some ". . . there was a decline in occupational position from first to the second generation." He points out that to understand the occupational concentrations of immigrants it is necessary to consider both the occupational skills which immigrants brought, as well as the specific working opportunities which were available at the time of their arrival.

Ward (1971) described the American economy between 1850 and 1920 as becoming more diversified and industrial, with substantial concentration of expansion in midwestern cities.

Duncan and Lieberson (1970) have shown that in the first part of this period economic expansion occurred in older port cities of Boston, Philadelphia, New York and Baltimore; as well as in midwestern cities located along water transport routes, such as Cincinnati, St. Louis, Chicago and Pittsburgh. In the second part of this period, characterized by Duncan and Lieberson as the age of steam and steel technology, opportunities continued to expand in the older cities, but the most rapid expansion occurred in the midwestern cities convenient for the development of the iron and steel industries. Some of these were new cities, such as Detroit, Buffalo, Cleveland and Milwaukee. Some were older cities such as Chicago and Pittsburgh. New York as the port of entry remained the destination of many immigrants. As shown by Ward (1971) the Germans and Irish, who were earlier immigrants, concentrated in the older cities such as Philadelphia and St. Louis. By contrast, the newer immigrants from Poland, Italy and Russia concentrated in Buffalo, Cleveland, Detroit and Milwaukee, as well as in some of the older cities with expanding opportunities. Different migration patterns occurred for immigrants with and without skills. Davie (1947) has shown that Jewish immigrants with higher skills were more likely than the unskilled to obtain "matching" occupations in America. Rewards for skilled occupations were greater, and the skilled immigrant went to the cities where there were opportunities to practice his trade. Less highly skilled workers went to the cities with expanding opportunities. Thus, the Italian concentration in construction and the Polish in steel were related to the expansion of these industries as these groups arrived (Golab, 1973). The Jewish concentration in the garment industry may have been a function of their previous experience as tailors, but it is also dependent upon the emergence of the mass-production of clothing in the late nineteenth century.

Similarly, the Irish propensity to participate in the urban political bureaucracy may be understood best in terms of the expansion of city governments in the mid-19th century, rather than as an Irish cultural aptitude for coping with bureaucracy as suggested by Glazer and Moynihan (1963).

The choice of residence and occupation was also influenced by the presence of friends and relatives. Their influence can be seen in the connections made between origins and destinations in the process of international migration. Park and Miller (1921) first described the process of "migration chains." In recent years, they have been documented by studies of immigration to New Zealand (Lochore, 1951), to Australia (Borrie, 1954; Price, 1963), and to the United States (MacDonald and MacDonald, 1964), as well as migration within the United States (Goldstein, 1958). In the case of Italians, recent research has suggested that the *padrone* system, which imported contract laborers for industrial agents, was less important than networks of friends and relatives as the mechanism by which migration was structured (Nelli, 1971; Vecoli, 1964).

The occupational concentration of an immigrant cohort provided at least four potential sources for maintaining group solidarity. Given similarity of occupational status, it is likely that a cohort was characterized by similar economic status. To the degree that behavior is associated with economic status, we should expect some similarity of life styles (Kriesberg, 1963). Second, similarity in occupation provided common social and economic interests (Hannerz, 1974). To the degree that occupational position is related to class consciousness, one expects some degree of group solidarity among cohorts (Centers, 1949; Leggett, 1968). Third, immigrants who were concentrated in a single factory or industry should have had a relatively high degree of interpersonal association stemming from their work relationships (Reiss, 1959). Finally, and perhaps most important, during a time when transportation was not available, industrial workers were forced to live near their employment (Pratt, 1911). Each of these factors—life style, class interests, work relationships and common residential areas—facilitated the development of group consciousness.

Residential Concentrations

The expansion of the industrial economy not only provided specific occupational opportunities to cohorts of immigrants destined for different cities, but also altered urban ecology. Industrialization, coupled with the introduction of the electric streetcar in the late 19th century and the automobile and truck in the early 20th century, had major effects upon residence and institutions (Hawley, 1971; Ward, 1971). These changes in urban ecology, in turn, had a direct effect on the relative concentration and autonomy of ethnic settlements as well as upon the formation of ethnic communities and subcultures.

The establishment of immigrant "ghettoes" in cities must be viewed in relation to the stages of development of American cities. Pre-industrial cities have been described by Pirenne (1925) and Sjoberg (1955) where the affluent lived in central locations, the poor on the periphery and tradesmen and craftsmen between the rich and the poor. Manufacturing typically occurred in small establishments which were not particularly concentrated. The journey to work was short. The central location of the affluent gave them maximum access to commercial activities.

The concentric zone model, described by Burgess (1922), referred to a period in which commerce was centralized. In this period the scale of industrial production grew. This was due to the growth of the market and access to raw materials, encouraged by the railroads and technological innovations which made it possible to have large-scale manufacturing. Industries also became more concentrated. It was difficult to transport coal and heavy raw materials except by railroad. The cost of transporting other goods encouraged centralization where access to other industries and markets was maximized. Limited and costly transportation made it necessary for industrial workers to live near where they worked. The advent of the omnibus and streetcar made it possible, however, for higher status workers to live in successive concentric rings of more expensive and new housing (Warner, 1962).

In contrast, the mid-twentieth century city is characterized by the dispersal of commercial and industrial activities made possible by the expanded use of the motor truck, petroleum and electricity as energy sources, and electronic communication. In addition, industrial workers make considerable use of the automobile to get to work, thus loosening the relationship between work and residence.

The popular belief has been that assimilation of immigrant groups began after the establishment of ghettoes in the center of cities. These concentrations supposedly dispersed as immigrants and their descendants became more directly involved in the mainstream of American life. Warner and Burke (1969), however, point out that this process occurred only for a limited time span in American urban history and then only in some cities. Their position is that ". . . most foreign immigrants to American cities never lived in ghettoes and most immigrant ghettoes that did exist were the product of the largest cities and the eastern and southern European immigrants of 1880–1940." Statistical evidence is admittedly fragmentary, but it does suggest that prior to 1880, immigrant groups, mainly Irish, Canadian, British and German, were dispersed throughout the city with concentration only in a few points. Warner and Burke attribute this dispersal to two conditions: (1) the distribution of the limited stock of available housing and (2) the small scale of most urban economic activity. The latter discouraged the formation of purely residential or purely commercial districts.

Ward (1971), in basic agreement with Warner and Burke, argues that residential patterns in American cities of the mid-nineteenth century were transitional between pre-industrial and modern. Because the first major influx of immigrants occurred before either urban employment became centralized or local transportation improved, the residential patterns of the earlier immigrants were not concentrated. However, after about 1850 "the central concentration of urban employment . . . strongly influenced the location and characteristics of the residential areas of new immigrants, most of whom sought low cost housing close to their places of employment" (Ward, 1971:105).

At least one study of the journey to work, in New York City in 1907, documented the fact that low-paid industrial workers were forced by economic pressures to live close to their places of work (Pratt, 1911). Pratt concluded his important, but little known study of ethnic congestion with the statement:

> In view of the fact that our foreign population is the most unskilled, and therefore, the lowest paid, and that it is employed in industries working the longest hours, the tendency to live in congested districts near the workplace cannot

occasion very great surprise. This tendency—and the fact that the aliens form the largest part of our most congested population is admitted—has been frequently seized upon as the explanation of congestion, and hence these theorists have logically enough demanded restriction of immigration as a remedy for congestion. However, if congestion were due to the desire . . . of our alien population to live in congested districts, we should expect those employed within a reasonable distance of Manhattan to make every effort to live there. But this is exactly contrary to the facts . . . the Italians, Jews and Slavic peoples, who have oftenest been indicted for congestion, have proved themselves innocent and their positive unwillingness to live in Manhattan, when escape is offered, is evidence by every group of workers in the factories outside of Lower Manhattan (1911:187).

Before the concentration of large scale employment, work opportunities for immigrants were scattered and their residential locations were correspondingly scattered. In the later period, to the extent that work opportunities were concentrated, the immigrant "ghettoes" were also concentrated.

Some evidence for this interpretation is found in data compiled by Lieberson (1963). In Boston, the indices of segregation for the Irish from native whites for the years 1850, 1855 and 1880 were 20.7, 26.0 and 14.7. The corresponding indices for Germans were 31.0, 38.6 and 30.7. Trends toward residential assimilation were small and did not continue through to 1950 when the corresponding indices of segregation *increased* to 25.5 and 34.8. In contrast to these groups, the Poles, Russians and Italians who arrived later were more segregated in 1880 and 1930. Their indices were 61.5, 53.8 and 73.8, respectively, in 1880 and in 1930 were 50.4 for the Poles, 64.9 for the Russians and 53.5 for the Italians. Similar patterns were found in other cities—although with more limited historical data. Lieberson (1963:14) found that ". . . length of residence in the United States of the immigrant groups and their differences in socioeconomic level were both found to be independently influencing the magnitude of the immigrant groups segregation." While this can be viewed as evidence for the process of assimilation, we suggest that it can best

be interpreted in terms of the ecology of occupations and residence characterizing the city when immigrant residential patterns were established.

The "old" immigrants were never segregated to the same extent as the "new" immigrants. There appears to be somewhat of a principle of what might be called "ecological inertia"; i.e., once a pattern becomes established, its effects can be seen in later years. Or, conversely, interpretation of urban social structure at one point in time requires knowledge of the patterns that came before, as well as the contemporary forces which continue to operate.

The Development of Ethnic Communities

The influence of residential patterns on the development and maintenance of ethnic communities varies with the particular historical period. There is evidence that the institutional character of neighborhoods is related to the nature of informal networks (Foley, 1950). The earliest urban neighborhoods contained the major institutions of work, religion, family, leisure and, to a considerable degree, government and social control (Pirenne, 1925; Sjoberg, 1955). By the middle of the 19th century, American cities were in a transition from the pre-industrial and industrial. While urban neighborhoods may have been institutionally complete, in general the early immigrants dispersed rather than settled in concentrated ghettoes. Thus, few residential areas contained large concentrations of groups, economic or ethnic, which could establish clearly bounded identities (Warner, 1968; Laurie, 1973).

A very different situation occurred when large waves of immigrants were arriving around the turn of the century. The advances in transportation technology and increased specialization of land use had direct consequences for the relative completeness of urban residential areas. Urban neighborhoods were progressively deprived of their total social system characteristics as particular activities were transferred to more specialized areas. The separation of work and residence for upper income workers, and further development of separate industrial, commercial, leisure and residential areas, resulted in the decline of the multiple institutional and functional char-

189

acter of some earlier urban neighborhoods (Warren, 1963).

These trends were particularly characteristic of the newer, outlying areas, the streetcar and automobile suburbs, but not of older, center city neighborhoods. As the journey to work was problematic for the poor, so, presumably, was the journey to other services. Contemporary research indicates that lower status urban residents are more dependent on institutions and services in the immediate neighborhood (Foley, 1950). Similarly, higher attachment to local neighborhoods, institutions and informal networks appears to be associated with lower status (Fried, 1963) as well as length of residence (Kasarda and Janowitz, 1974) and stage in the life cycle (Bell and Boat, 1957). We expect that similar relationships existed in early twentieth century cities.

It is in the older, centrally located neighborhoods where one expects the development and use of a wide range of local institutions such as food stores, bars, schools, churches, mutual aid societies, fraternal associations and newspapers. And it is in these neighborhoods with their local institutions where interpersonal networks develop and are maintained (Fitzpatrick, 1966; Dahya, 1974; Charsley, 1974). A recent investigation of ethnicity in Montreal is indicative of the role of common institutions for the development and maintenance of an ethnic community. Breton found relationships between the size of the immigrant cohort, their ability to speak the native language, the percentage of the group who were manual workers and the institutional completeness of the ethnic community. The latter in turn was found to be closely related to the character of the interpersonal networks. Breton (1964:197) writes: "The institutions of an ethnic community are the origin of much social life in which the people of that community get involved and as a consequence become tied together in a cohesive interpersonal network."

Although usually interpreted in terms of assimilation, Lieberson's (1963) research on ethnic residential patterns can also be seen as strong evidence of the impact of residential concentrations for the maintenance of ethnic solidarity. He found that those groups which were residentially segregated were more sharply differentiated in their occupational composition, more deviant in

patterns of occupational mobility, less likely to become American citizens, less likely to speak English and more likely to be endogamous. This argument suggests that within a national origin group those members who live outside of areas of concentration are more assimilated than those living within areas of concentration.

The effect of the residential community on ethnic membership is directly relevant to the current controversy regarding ethnic endogamy. The classic studies of Kennedy (1944;1952) and Herberg (1955) suggested that increasing patterns of religious endogamy and ethnic exogamy had resulted in a triple melting pot of Catholic, Protestant and Jew. In contrast to these earlier studies, Abramson (1973) has reported that, among Catholics, patterns of national endogamy have been maintained. Endogamy was found to be highest among the Spanish-speaking and Italians and lowest among the Germans and Irish. Because residential propinquity has been shown to influence the selection of marriage partners (Katz and Hill, 1958; Warren, 1966), Kennedy's findings can be interpreted in terms of the lessened residential concentration of national groups. Abramson's apparently contradictory findings are similarly interpretable. Although the evidence is not direct, those groups which Abramson finds to be the most endogamous are also those Lieberson (1963) found to the most segregated.

The argument that ethnic communities became crystallized in American cities in response to the American urban communities in not new. Glazer (1954), Handlin (1961) and Vecoli (1964) have pointed out that some ethnic groups evolved from smaller, more regional bases of organization and identification to larger nationalistic ones after they arrived in America. Nelli (1970:5) concludes his study of Italians in Chicago saying that ". . . community and group consciousness among 'Southerners' in the United States did not cross the Atlantic, but developed in the new homeland." Killian (1970) has pointed out that white southern migrants, although of diverse origins, formed a relatively cohesive hillbilly community in Chicago. Finally, recent research on urban blacks, both historical (Hershberg, 1973) and contemporary (Long, 1974), has refuted the traditional emphasis on black southern culture as the root cause of urban ghetto life. Thus, mounting evidence suggests that the examination of ethnic experience should use the urban American-ethnic community, rather than the place of origin as the principal criterion of ethnic group membership. Integration into the mainstream of American life should refer to the American ghetto rather than the European rural village as the point of departure (Handlin, 1951).

This general view also suggests that much of the substance of ethnic cultures may be the result of a selective process which consists of a constantly evolving interaction between the nature of the local community, the available economic opportunities and the national religious heritage of a particular group. As Gans (1962a) has shown for the Italian community of the Boston West End, those aspects of a group's original heritage which are appropriate adaptations to the American conditions, as well as those which may have been irrelevant, may remain intact. In contrast, those which are inappropriate or lead to unnecessary negative consequences may be expected to die out. Those that come into conflict with existing American institutions may become issues around which ethnic institutions, consciousness and identities are formed. The apparently persisting influence of the Old World traits appears different for different groups. In some cases such as Jewish values (Fuchs, 1968), Italian mutual aid societies (Vecoli, 1964) and Polish and Italian family structures (McLaughlin, 1971), the effect of cultural heritage appears strong; in other instances such as Jewish mutual aid societies (Glanz, 1970) or Italian community cohesion (Nelli, 1971), the new setting appears more important. What is necessary is the identification of the conditions associated with the demise and/or retention of cultural traits.

Ethnicity and Community in Contemporary Society

Large scale immigration from Europe to the United States essentially was cut off in 1924. Since that time the largest distinctive groups of migrants to northern cities have been southern blacks and Puerto Ricans. Two important questions arise. What factors have contributed to the continued salience of ethnicity for descendants of European immigrants? And, what are the differences in ethnicity and community between blacks and Puerto Ricans and European ethnics?

The ecological bases of urban institutions and communities are different today from what they were three-quarters of a century ago. The influence of the concentration of occupation opportunities on the development of working-class neighborhoods has been altered. With the continued development of transportation, the truck and the high-speed expressway in particular, industries are no longer forced to locate in centralized areas or near railroads or rivers. This new flexibility also enables industry to search for relatively low-cost sites away from urban centers. Consequently, industrial firms increasingly have moved from the centralized core of the city to differentiated areas of commercial and industrial activity near the fingers of metropolitan regions. The remaining occupational opportunities, while diminishing, are concentrated in low-wage, less technically advanced and economically more vulnerable industries (Fusfeld, 1969) and in the unskilled service occupations associated with governmental or commercial activities remaining in central locations.

Since the end of World War II, with the advent of widespread automobile use, the close relationship between the location of employment and that of residence has also been greatly loosened. In particular, this is true for the more affluent workers (Hoover and Vernon, 1959). Therefore, while earlier ethnic communities were formed around expanding industrial opportunities, recent ghettoes have been developed at a time when opportunities were leaving central locations.

These changes in the ecology of urban areas removed the structural conditions which supported ethnicity in the past. These changes have produced at least three rather different types of residential communities. The interpersonal networks, their relationship to the urban economy, and the salience and importance of the ethnicity manifested are different in each.

First, there has been the development of what Gans (1962b) has called "quasi-communities." These are upper and middle income suburbs that do not have the institutional, industrial and associational cohesion of earlier residential areas. Second, there are the more recently formed

191

ghettoes of blacks and Puerto Ricans. Finally, there are residual forms of residential communities formed in the earlier part of this century. These are the urban villages studied by Gans (1962a), Whyte (1943) and Young and Willmott (1957). They appear to have some of the characteristics of the older ethnic communities and newer ghettoes.

The urban village, characterized by concentrated networks and organizations among residents of a similar ethnicity, confounds the effects of ethnicity and the effects of community. The classic study of Bethnal Green (Young and Willmott, 1957) illustrates this point. Young and Willmott found that there was a high rate of local interaction, that newly married couples tended to move only a short distance from their parents, that kinship ties were maintained, that there was primary dependence on local institutions, and that personal connections were used to obtain jobs. These behavior patterns are commonly associated with contemporary ethnic communities in the United States. In these neighborhoods, what is commonly viewed as "ethnic behavior" may be a manifestation of community, a reflection of the exigencies of working-class life, and is ethnic only by coincidence. The close correspondence between working-class communities and ethnicity is suggested by Berger's (1960:95) note that: "Our image of working class life is dominated by ethnic motifs." Two detailed investigations of the Boston West End (Gans, 1962a; Fried, 1974) have concluded that even though that area was widely recognized as an Italian community, the effect of the ethnicity was secondary to that of community and class. In the follow-up study of former Bethnal Green residents who had moved to the suburbs, Willmott and Young (1957) found that patterns of interaction had dropped and that the sense of community was not redeveloped. In an American study of visiting patterns with relatives, Klatsky (1974) found that distance was the principal predictor of frequency of contact with relatives. Once distance was controlled, the effects of ethnicity and religion were minor.

The ethnicity found in black and Puerto Rican ghettoes is clearly different from that of the urban village. We have already observed that these communities are removed from the best economic opportunities. Ethnographic research demonstrates that these communities are also characterized by a social organization containing relatively strong informal networks (Liebow, 1967; Valentine, 1968). These networks are not tied to economic opportunities. Sheppard and Striner (1965) have noted:

> Job information is a critical need among Negroes. While labor economists and other social scientists may be the first to know—after employers, perhaps,—that unemployment rates are going down and job opportunities (in certain occupations and industries) are going up, unskilled Negro workers may be the last to know or may never know.

In short, the segregation of these new ethnics from the best economic opportunities is social as well as geographic.

The situation of the contemporary urban white ethnic may be only marginally better. He would have an advantage over the urban black by virtue of his longevity in the urban economy and thus would have access to knowledge and influence which is crucial in obtaining jobs (Granovetter, 1974). But to the extent that the urban villages are located near older, less productive and declining industries, this information is less useful. The research of Gans (1962a) and Granovetter (1974) has demonstrated the negative effect of membership in local networks at the exclusion of ties outside of the neighborhood. With the continued movement of industries from central locations, the provincialism of these neighborhoods and associations can be expected to be increasingly disadvantageous. Thus, the strength of community identification and the quality of life manifested there are, in part, responses to residues of earlier historical periods and, in part, responses to the increasingly more marginal social and economic positions of the white working-class neighborhoods (Howard, 1971).

All of this is not to imply that ethnic behavior can only be maintained in localized communities. Ethnic salience and identification, as transmitted through the family and friends, can be maintained, whether they are in the same neighborhood or not. Moreover, the establishment of ethnic organizations on a cosmopolitan level can reinforce the salience of ethnicity. Etzioni (1959) has examined ethnicity as a factor operating in a variety of contexts from the extreme of a geographically based "totalistic" community with predominantly local patterns of interaction and primary dependence on local institutions to the other extreme of a residentially dispersed group "maintained by communication and active in limited social situations." Examples of the latter are church and synagogue attendance, marching in a Saint Patrick's or Columbus Day parade, voting for a political candidate of a similar ethnicity, or supporting a political cause associated with the country of origin, such as the emigration of Russian Jews to Israel or the reunification of Ireland. This "situational ethnicity" is likely to be found in the more cosmopolitan networks of residents of the "quasi-communities"—such as the post-World War II suburbs. It is clearly different from the ethnicity found in the white urban village or the colonized ghetto.

These observations suggest that ethnicity should not be regarded as an ascribed attribute with only two discrete categories, but as a continuous variable. The effect of ethnic or national heritage will vary depending upon the situation of a group. Indeed, the small amount of explained variance contributed by one's specific ethnic category, observed by Duncan and Duncan (1968) on occupational attainment, could partly be due to the fact that ethnicity was treated as an ascribed trait. Immigrants and sons of immigrants who never lived in an ethnic neighborhood and who have not attended parochial schools were placed in the same category as others for whom the salience of national origin may have been much greater.

Conclusion

Much that has been written about race, ethnicity, social class and community has centered around the issue of the importance of culture in determining life styles. Our review of this literature suggests that much of it is based on empirically untested assumptions about the importance of the portable heritage which a group brings from one generation and place to another. We suggest that a more parsimonious explanation of ethnic and community behavior will be found in the

relationship of the ethnic community to the larger macroscopic structure of the society—particularly in the constraints of occupation, residence and institutional affiliation.

Something of a paradox is found in the position that has been developed here. On the one hand, we have suggested that much of the behavior that is commonly associated with ethnicity is largely a function of the structural situations in which groups have found themselves. On the other hand, we have also argued that ethnicity defined in terms of frequent patterns of association and identification with common origins (Haller, 1973) is generated and becomes crystallized under conditions of residential stability and segregation, common occupational positions and dependence on local institutions and services. More specifically, we are suggesting that, within the structural parameters characterizing urban working-class life generally, ethnic culture—as heritage—is most likely to become crystallized and persist.

In order to resolve these arguments, it is necessary not only to test for the effects of ethnic heritage (Duncan and Duncan, 1968; Greeley, 1971; Laumann, 1973; Abramson, 1973), but also to identify the conditions under which ethnicity is particularly salient. We expect to find ethnic sub-cultures under conditions giving rise to communities in general. Communities are usually viewed as being geographically based, but what is most important appears to be face-to-face interaction (Hillery, 1955; Homans, 1950). It is possible, as Kosa (1956) has shown, for ethnic networks to exist in geographically dispersed groups, yet the effect of ethnicity may be strongest among members who are geographically clustered. In either case, such ethnic networks may depend on the availability of significant others, such as grandmothers who value ethnic culture, and other community members with feelings of obligation and responsibility. People are more or less dependent on their community at various stages of the life cycle; for example, when looking for a job, when a child is born, when a wife goes to work and needs babysitters, when a person becomes old and needs care. These and other day-to-day needs may be served by neighbors, friends or institutions. When these are of the same ethnicity, the likelihood of ethnic behavior and identification with ethnic origins should be greater.

While the appropriate research is yet to be done, several things seem to be relatively clear. First, being a descendant of an immigrant does not necessarily make an individual an ethnic in America. Certain conditions are also necessary. We echo Cohen's (1974:xv) recent statement that: "unless we recognize differences in degree of manifestation we shall fail to make much progress in the analysis of ethnicity. To put it in the idiom of research, ethnicity is a variable." Second, the conditions which generate ethnicity are not created only for immigrants or others with unique origins. They also exist for native-born Americans without a particular foreign heritage. In such cases, communities are likely to be generated that are similar to ethnic communities. Furthermore, we see no reason why such communities as South Boston, Bethnal Green, Harlem or Harlan do not develop some sense of common origin and pride. Finally, it is clear that ethnicity is not dead but much alive today, although it is something very different than the way it has usually been presented. Rather than a constant ascribed trait that is inherited from the past, ethnicity is the result of a process which continues to unfold. It is basically a manifestation of the way populations are organized in terms of interaction patterns, institutions, personal values, attitudes, life styles and presumed consciousness of kind. The assumption of a common heritage as the essential aspect of ethnicity is erroneous. Ethnicity may have relatively little to do with Europe, Asia or Africa, but much more to do with the exigencies of survival and the structure of opportunity in this country. In short, the so-called "foreign heritage" of ethnic groups is taking shape in this country.

13

A Tale of Three Cities: Blacks, Immigrants and Opportunity in Philadelphia: 1850–1880, 1930 and 1970

Theodore Hershberg
Alan N. Burstein
Eugene P. Ericksen

Stephanie Greenberg
William L. Yancey

Significant differences in socioeconomic conditions characterize the experience of black and white Americans. Why and how this happened, and what if anything should be done about it, are among the central questions of our time. Their answers have important implications for public policy. The crux of the matter can be put this way: were the burdens and disabilities faced by black Americans peculiar to their historical experience or were they simply obstacles which every immigrant group entering American society had to overcome?[1]

Reprinted from *A Tale of Three Cities: Blacks, Immigrants and Opportunity in Philadelphia: 1850-1880, 1930 and 1970* by Theodore Hershberg, Alan N. Burstein, Eugene P. Ericksen, Stephanie Greenberg, and William L. Yancy in volume no. 444 of THE ANNALS of the American Academy of Political and Social Science 441 (January 1979) © 1979 by The American Academy of Political and Social Science. Reprinted by permission of the publisher and the authors.

The Philadelphia Social History Project, part of the School of Public and Urban Policy at the University of Pennsylvania, is funded by the Center for Studies of Metropolitan Problems, NIMH (MH 16621); Division of Research Grants, NEH (RC 25568-76-1156); and the Sociology Program, Division of Social Sciences, NSF (SOC76-20069), Theodore Hershberg, principal investigator. Research underway at Temple University is also supported by the Center for Studies of Metropolitan Problems, NIMH (MH-25244), William L. Yancey and Eugene P. Ericksen, co-principal investigators. A special note of thanks is due to the many PSHP Research Associates and to Henry Williams and Richard Greenfield.

Over the years we have come to see how the study of the black experience requires a broader context than gross comparisons of whites with blacks. Recent research has finally recognized that white America consists of diverse groups and that the study of their distinct experiences requires a comparative ethnic perspective. While this constitutes a major advance, what remains conspicuously absent from the literature—especially from the history of blacks in cities—is an awareness that the study of the black experience necessitates an urban perspective as well.[2] Two distinct environments embrace much of Afro-American history: plantation and ghetto.[3] Once the most rural of Americans, blacks are today the most urbanized. Unfortunately, the histories that have been written treat the city in passive terms, as a kind of incidental setting for the subject at hand; in order to learn how the "city" affected blacks it is necessary to construct a history which treats the city in dynamic terms. Such a history would conceive of "urban" as a "process" linking the experience of people to aspects of the particular environment in which they lived.[4] In this essay a comparative ethnic and an urban perspective are combined to further understanding of the black experience.

This essay will focus on Philadelphia's "opportunity structure." Such a term encompasses a wide variety of factors; although much more than the hierarchy of occupations define an opportunity structure, the distribution of occupations is certainly central to the concept and may be considered its most important single attribute. For the sake of brevity, a vertical distribution of occupations will be used as a proxy measure for a group's place in the larger opportunity structure. The term "ecological structure," or the distribution in space of people, housing, jobs, transportation, and other urban elements is understood as the material expression of the opportunity structure. A city's ecological structure can thus be considered as a major determinant of differential "access"—to jobs, housing, transportation, and services. Finally, the term "structural perspective" encompasses both the opportunity structure and its ecological form and is used here to characterize our overall conceptual approach.

The experience of black and white immigrant groups, then, must be understood within a changing urban environment, recognizing the effects that such environment had upon different groups of people at different points in Philadelphia's past. The ecological "rules" that explain important elements of the white immigrant experience do not explain, for most of Philadelphia's history, what happened to blacks. Where blacks were concerned the rules were inoperative, suspended as it were by the force of racism. Racism, particularly its manifestation in discriminatory hiring and housing practices, is the final dimension in the explanatory framework. The subsiding of the worst of racial discrimination in contemporary American life suggests that blacks will at last begin to be treated as other people. But the potential gains will not be realized because other offsetting changes have occurred simultaneously. Philadelphia's opportunity structure has altered radically for the worse, and the ecological manifestations of these changes leave blacks at a severe disadvantage: they find themselves in the wrong areas of the wrong city at the wrong time. Despite the lessening of racial discrimination, major changes in Philadelphia's opportunity and ecological structure prevent today's blacks from experiencing the successes enjoyed by the city's earlier immigrant groups.

Unique Aspects of the Black Experience

Those who argue that the black experience was not unique fall into two categories. The first

explanation of the socioeconomic differentials can be captured in single words—bootstraps—or opportunities. According to this point of view, blacks, like all immigrant groups, had equal access to opportunities. If they took advantage of these opportunities—that is, if they pulled long enough and hard enough on their bootstraps they made it. The bootstraps argument claims that everybody had it tough and that the problems faced by blacks were no tougher than those encountered by other immigrant groups entering American society. The message of this view for contemporary public policy is obvious: if blacks do not have a uniquely discriminatory past, they do not deserve to be the beneficiaries of compensatory legislation in the present.

The second explanation, known as the "Last of the Immigrants," rejects the bootstraps view of the past and concedes that blacks—in cities such as Philadelphia—were the victims of a peculiarly racist past. Such a concession, however, only documents how racist America was "back then," and suggests that time will be sufficient remedy. As late as 1910, the well-meaning holders of this viewpoint remind us, 90 percent of black Americans were rural and 80 percent were southern. Of all American blacks ever to live in cities, the vast majority settled in them after World War II: thus, in demographic terms, blacks can be considered as the last of the immigrants. Although this explanation differs from the notion of bootstraps in its view of the black past, its implications for public policy in the present are identical. We need not undertake any special legislation to ameliorate the condition of blacks today because the same process of assimilation through which European immigrants were integrated into the urban American mainstream will take care of black urban immigrants. Since the process of assimilation worked for other groups, it will work for blacks: all we need to do is stand by and give it time.[5]

The Assimilation Process

Unfortunately, viewing blacks as the last of the immigrants is inaccurate and, in its false optimism, may ultimately prove to be as pernicious as the bootstraps explanation. Assimilation is not a mysterious process rooted in the individual, but is a combination of factors: opportunities available at a given time; housing stock; the nature and condition of the local, regional and national economy; the number of skilled and unskilled positions available in the labor force; the location of jobs; the transportation facilities; the fiscal circumstances of the local government; and the degree of discrimination encountered. Nor is there much validity in dealing with the assimilation process at the individual level; every immigrant group has its specially gifted members who "make it" despite the barriers erected by the host society. The concern here is with the experience of entire groups rather than the exceptionally talented few, and the focus is on the opportunity structure which affected all people and which regulated the degree of group progress.

The experience of blacks and immigrants will be compared at three points in Philadelphia's history. Although blacks were present in the city over the entire period, the reference to three cities reflects temporally distinct waves of immigrants to Philadelphia: the "Old" immigrants—Irish, Germans and British— who settled in the 1840's and 1850's; the "New" immigrants—Italians, Poles and Russian Jews—who arrived in the years between 1885 and 1914; and the "newest" immigrants—blacks—who came in their greatest numbers after 1945 (see Table 1).[6]

What happened to these groups depended not only upon what they brought with them from the Old World and the South—values, language, skills, urban and industrial experience—but what awaited them upon arrival in Philadelphia. It was not only that people with different backgrounds came to the city, but that the structure of opportunities that they found in Philadelphia was different as well; each time period represented a different stage in the city's urban-industrial development. And it was these differences that shaped a wide range of subsequent experience for each immigrant group. A full treatment of these differences would require discussion of a breadth of topics. This essay will focus on the changing opportunity structure and the residential experience of the black and white immigrants who lived in the designated three cities.

According to the accepted notion of the assimilation process, upon arrival in America immigrants settled in densely populated urban ghettoes among friends and neighbors of the same ethnic background. A few, the most success-

ful among them, were able to move out of the ghetto within their own lifetime, but for most others, integration into the fabric of the larger society was the experience of their children and grandchildren. Several generations were required to complete the process. This point of view pervades our culture; we find it embedded in our literature, film and folklore. Its most recent and popular expression is found in Irving Howe's best-selling study, *World of Our Fathers.*[7]

Settlement in dense urban enclaves made sense. It was seen as the logical response of the newcomers to the hostility of the native population and to the strangeness of white Anglo Saxon Protestant culture at the societal core. It was rational as well—when understood as the natural tendency of the immigrants, faced with an unfamiliar new setting—to establish a secure and friendly place, to create a sense of the old Country in the new. A piece of Europe was transplanted in the streets of America.

The pervasiveness of this notion, however, did not rest solely on logic or cultural trappings. With the nation absorbing twenty million immigrants in thirty years at the turn of the last century, some scholars, particularly a group of sociologists at the University of Chicago, undertook major studies of the immigrant experience.[8] Their empirical observations corroborated those of the social reformers who were dealing with the problems of the immigrants, as well as those of the writers and artists who were capturing the immigrant saga in word and on canvas.

Residential Segregation

Sociologists have maintained that the degree of residential segregation is an acceptable indicator of, or a proxy for, assimilation. An ethnically enclosed residential experience insulates a group from important mechanisms of assimilation, limits cross-cultural contacts that affect the socialization of the young, and has serious implications for subsequent experiences such as intermarriage, upward job mobility, and the formation of social ties. Thus, the lower the degree of segregation the greater the likelihood that a group is experiencing assimilation. The accepted notion of the assimilation process found what appeared to be scientific confirmation in the levels of segregation observed for northern and midwestern cities in 1930. Expec-

197

TABLE 1. *Ethnic Composition of Philadelphia: 1850–1970 (as Percent of Total Population)*

	1850	1880	1900	1930	1970
Blacks	4.8	3.6	4.8	11.3	33.6
Ireland*					
Born	17.6	11.9	7.6	2.7	0.4
2nd		15.1	13.6	6.8	1.9
Stock		27.0	21.2	9.4	2.3
Germany					
Born	5.6	6.6	5.5	1.9	0.6
2nd		9.6	9.6	4.8	1.4
Stock		16.2	15.1	6.7	1.9
Great Britain†					
Born		3.8	3.6	1.9	0.4
2nd			4.8	3.2	1.1
Stock			8.4	5.1	1.5
Italy					
Born		0.2	1.4	3.5	1.3
2nd			0.9	5.8	4.0
Stock			2.2	9.3	5.3
Poland					
Born		0.1	0.6	1.6	0.6
2nd			0.3	5.8	1.8
Stock			0.9	7.4	2.4
USSR°					
Born		0.03	2.2	4.5	1.3
2nd			1.3	5.3	3.2
Stock			3.6	9.9	4.5
Total Foreign					
Born	29.0	24.2	22.8	18.9	6.5
2nd		30.4	32.1	31.7	16.6
Stock		54.6	54.9	50.6	23.1
Total Population	408,081	840,584	1,293,697	1,950,961	1,950,098

*Includes Northern Ireland.

†Includes England, Scotland, Wales.

°Includes Russia, Lithuania, Estonia, Latvia.

Note: In 1880, "2nd generation" refers to native-born with *fathers* born in specified country. Native-born with native fathers and foreign-born mothers are classified as native. In 1990, 1930, and 1970, "2nd Generation" refers to native-born with *fathers* born in specified country or, if father is native, with *mother* born in specified country. If parents are born in different foreign countries, birthplace of father determines parentage of native-born. "Stock" includes foreign-born plus 2nd generation.

Sources: Figures for 1850 and 1880 are computed primarily from Philadelphia Social History Project compilations of the United States manuscript censuses of population. In 1880, figures for Italy, Poland, and USSR are taken from published United States Census totals. See Department of the Interior, Census Office, *Census of Population: 1880*, v.I., "Statistics of the Population of the United States at the Tenth Census," (Washington, D.C.: U.S. Government Printing Office, 1883), 540. Figures for 1900, 1930 and 1970 are computed from published United States Census totals. See Department of the Interior, United States Census Office, *Census of Population: 1900*, v.I, pt. 1, "Population," (Washington, D.C.: U.S. Census Office, 1901), 780, 866–905; U.S. Department of Commerce, Bureau of the Census, *Census of Population: 1930*, v.III, pt. 2, "Population," (Washington, D.C.: U.S. Government Printing Office, 1932), 701–708: U.S. Bureau of the Census, *Census of Population: 1970*, v.I, "Characteristics of the Population," pt. 40, Pennsylvania—Section 1, (Washington, D.C.: U.S. Government Printing Office, 1973), 356.

tations based on the accepted model were apparently confirmed by the data: old immigrants from Ireland, Germany and Britain, who had arrived in America in the 1840's and 1850's, were the least segregated residentially (20–30); while new immigrants from Italy, Poland and Russia, who came between 1885 and 1914, were considerably more segregated (50–60).[9] Here was proof— or so it seemed—that an assimilation process was operating in American cities; with the passage of time immigrants were being integrated into the mainstream. When the logic of this argument is applied to the high levels of segregation for urban blacks (70–80) observed in 1970, one is left with a comforting conclusion. With time, these latest newcomers will assimilate, as did earlier groups. The optimistic implications of this viewpoint for public policy are obvious: no legislation need be passed when a social process operates to generate the desired results.

Unfortunately, while the segregation scores are accurate, the interpretation is not. The data on white immigrant residential segregation are cross-sectional for 1930; when cross-sectional data are used to infer historical process they can distort history and lead to an erroneous conclusion. The low scores for the Irish and German immigrants—half the level observed for the Italians, Poles and Russian Jews—are not indicative of change over time from high to low segregation, and thus proof of an assimilation process; rather, they are the *retention* of segregation levels experienced by the Irish and German immigrants upon initial settlement (see Table 2).[10] In other words, the low segregation scores for the old immigrants, the higher scores for the new immigrants, and the highest scores for the blacks are not evidence for the existence of an assimilation process rooted in the individual and responsive to the passage of time, but are a reflection of changing structural conditions that awaited each wave of immigrants who settled in Philadelphia at three different points in time.[11]

The Nineteenth-Century City: 1850–1880
Immigrant ghettoes did not form in the nineteenth century manufacturing city. In simplest terms, no supply of cheap, concentrated housing existed to quarter the thousands of Irish and Germans who poured into the city seeking work in the 1840's and 1850's. As the manufacturing center of America and one of the largest in the Atlantic community, Philadelphia's job market was a magnet not only for immigrants, but for large numbers of native whites from the surrounding countryside.[12] The rapidly expanding population, which doubled between 1840 and 1860, reaching 565,000 by the latter year, far outstripped growth in the city's housing supply.

Thus newcomers found housing wherever they could. Since the large homes which faced each other on the main streets were expensive, most new settlement occurred in the smaller, cheaper houses and shanties that sprang up in sidestreets, lanes and back-alleys. Boarding with other familes was quite common; one household in four took in lodgers. Population expansion in the pre-Civil War years led to sharply increased density, and growth in general was characterized by a "filling-in" process which ensured socioeconomic heterogeneity within a geographically compact city. The Irish and German immigrants, 18 and 6 percent of the 1850 population, respectively, were dispersed across the face of the city.

By 1880, when data are available to identify the American-born children of the immigrants, Irish stock were 30 percent and German stock 16 percent of the city's population. With these data, the residential patterns of the immigrants and their children can be reconstructed in detail. There were five identifiable clusters of Irish stock and one of German stock. However, only one person in five of Irish background and one person in eight of German background lived in such clusters. What is more, even in these areas which represented the heaviest concentrations of Irish and German stock in the city, each group composed only half of the population in their respective clusters.[13]

In 1850, the city's rudimentary transportation system—the horse-drawn omnibus lines which operated over mud and cobblestone streets—was irregular in service and prohibitively expensive for all but the wealthiest. Almost everyone lived within walking distance of their workplaces; indeed, for many at mid-century, home and work

TABLE 2. *Indices of Dissimilarity from Native Whites: 1850, 1880, 1930–1970* (248 Tracts)

	1850	1880	1930	1940	1950	1960	1970
Blacks	47	52	61	68	71	77	75
Puerto Ricans							
Stock						81	82
Ireland							
Born	30	32	28	32	29		
2nd		31					
Stock		31	21			24	28
Germany							
Born	33	36	32	35	31		
2nd		33					
Stock		34	27			25	26
Great Britain							
Born			24	23	22		
Stock			22			21	22
Italy							
Born			59	60	54		
Stock			58			47	48
Poland							
Born			54	55	46		
Stock			55			32	35
USSR							
Born			56	57	54		
Stock			53			50	52
Foreign							
Born	21	26					
2nd		25					
Stock		25					
Other Foreign							
Born		27					
2nd		21					
Stock		24					

Note: See Note for Table 1. "Stock" for 1960 includes foreign-born plus 2nd generation which is defined as for 1900, 1930 and 1970. "Other Foreign-Born" refers to all immigrant groups except Irish and Germans.

Sources: Figures for 1850 and 1880 are computed from Philadelphia Social History Project compilations of the United States manuscript censuses of population. Figures for 1930–1970 are computed from tract-level data taken from the United States censuses.

were not yet separated. Most blue-collar workers appear to have lived within a radius of half a mile of their jobs in 1850 with a median distance of two blocks.[14]

Most jobs were concentrated within the city's historic core. Half of all manufacturing jobs, which accounted for one male worker in two, and an even greater proportion of nonmanufacturing jobs, were found within a few square blocks of Philadelphia's downtown. Industry—the location of manufactuirng jobs—dominated the organization of the city's spatial arrangements. Workers'

residential patterns reflected the spatial characteristics of their industries. For example, the residences of workers in concentrated, centralized industries were clustered in or adjacent to the city's core; those who labored in dispersed industries lived scattered across the city.[15]

Industry was more important than ethnicity in organizing the city's residential patterns. Workers of different ethnic groups employed in the same industry had residential characteristics— segregation, clustering, density and centrality— more in common with each other than with members of their own ethnic group. German leather workers, to choose a representative example of an ethno-industrial type, were distributed over space more like Irish or native-white leather workers than like Germans in other industries. Under conditions of limited transportation and housing availability, workers had more in common residentially with coindustrial workers than with those of common cultural background.[16]

Another way of making this point is to examine the socioeconomic and demographic characteristics of the Irish population who lived in ethnic clusters. If ethnicity rather than industry were determining the organization of residence, the Irish in these areas should have resembled each other; the areas should have been similar pieces from a common cultural nucleus that was prevented from forming by the state of the housing market. Yet, when the areas are empirically examined, they turn out to be thoroughly distinct from each other. The characteristics of the Irish in each of the five clusters match the industrial opportunities available there; thus they differed markedly in occupational structure, unemployment rates, property holding, age and sex structure, household and family types.

The only major exception to the above generalizations were blacks. They were marginal to the rapidly industrializing urban economy of this period, and were considerably more segregated than white immigrants. They had few manufacturing jobs, even though they lived within easy access to more jobs of this type than any other ethnic group. Although the typical black worker lived within one mile of 23,000 manufacturing jobs—half again as many as were accessible to the typical Irish, German or native-white worker—he was refused employment (see Table 3).[17] Racism proved more powerful than the rules that normally governed spatially conditioned job access. In the few instances when blacks did obtain manufacturing jobs, they did not live close to their white coworkers. Rather they tended to live close to one another, regardless of industrial affiliation.[18]

It is fundamental to understand that, as the result of the new industrial order and the emergence of the factory system, all of this occurred within a context of widening occupational opportunity for whites. This is especially significant because the manufacturing sector has traditionally provided the first step up the occupational ladder to new arrivals to the city. Opportunities for upward mobility created by an expanding economy—which provided the bootstraps for the Irish and German immigrants—were so limited for blacks that they were virtually nonexistent. In 1847, for example, less than one-half of one percent of the adult black male workforce could find jobs in the economy's dynamic new sectors such as iron and steel and machine tools. During the antebellum years, blacks were not only excluded from the new and well-paying positions, they were uprooted as well from many of their traditional unskilled jobs, denied apprenticeships for their sons, and prevented from practicing the skills they already possessed.[19] Little changed between 1850 and 1880; although the number and proportion of skilled positions increased siginficantly with the economy's expansion, which benefited the immigrants and especially their American born children, blacks experienced little or no progress (see Table 4). Thus, at least as far back as the mid-nineteenth century, the position of blacks in the city was unlike that of any other group.

Rapid growth in the years between 1850 and 1880 affected Philadelphia's ecological structure. The traditional view of immigrant residential settlement is firmly rooted in the original Park-Burgess notion of concentric zones, in which socioeconomic status of the population increases with increasing distance from the center of the city.[20] It is this model which describes a city with

TABLE 3. *Distribution of Ethnic Groups by Accessibility to Manufacturing Jobs: 1880 (Males, 18+)*

	Blacks	Irish	Irish-2nd	German	German-2nd	Native-Whites	Total
Mean Jobs within 1 mile	23,289	15,179	14,985	18,894	17,863	15,313	16,074

Note: See Table 1.
Source: Figures are computed from Philadelphia Social History Project compilations of the United States manuscript census of manufactures.

TABLE 4. *Occupational Distribution of Males, 18+, by Ethnicity: 1850, 1880 (As Percent of Ethnic Group)*

	Blacks	Irish	German	Foreign-Born∞	Native-Whites**
			1850		
High White Collar and Professional	1.1	1.4	2.6	1.8	8.9
Low White Collar and Proprietary	4.2	11.2	13.6	12.0	23.2
Artisan	17.1	42.1	67.3	49.6	57.0
Specified Unskilled	44.0	11.2	3.9	9.1	6.3
Unspecified Unskilled	33.3	33.9	12.3	27.6	4.3
Totals	4245	25389	10633	36022	51930
(Row %s)	(4.5)	(27.5)	(11.5)	(39.1)	(56.3)
Dissimilarity from all Native-Whites**	67	34	18	26	—

	Blacks	Irish	Irish-2nd	German	German-2nd	Foreign-Born∞	Native-Whites††	Native-Whites**
				1880				
High White Collar and Professional	1.0	1.2	1.7	1.9	1.8	1.5	5.5	4.6
Low White Collar and Proprietary	6.6	18.3	22.4	23.6	26.0	20.5	33.7	31.2
Artisan	14.0	31.8	43.5	57.9	54.0	42.6	42.7	43.8
Specified Unskilled	52.2	19.5	18.4	10.5	13.0	15.8	12.8	13.7
Unspecified Unskilled	26.2	29.2	14.0	6.1	5.2	19.7	5.3	6.7
Totals	9043	38035	21780	26780	12690	64743	105165	139635
(Row %s)	(4.2)	(17.8)	(10.2)	(12.5)	(5.0)	(30.3)	(49.3)	(65.4)
Dissimilarity from Native-Whites of Native-White Parents††	60	31	15	16	12	17	—	—
Dissimilarity from all Native-Whites**	58	28	12	14	10	15	—	—

††Excludes 2nd Generation Irish and Germans.
**Includes 2nd Generation Irish and Germans.
∞Includes Irish and Germans Only.
Note: See Note for Table 1.
Sources: Figures are computed from Philadelphia Social History Project compilations of the United States manuscript censuses of population.

a low status core and a high status periphery, and it is in the low status core that the immigrant ghettoes are to be found. It is clear, however, that such a model did not fit the preindustrial city. In the preindustrial setting, transportation was poor and did not facilitate movement within the city. Since jobs and services were relatively centralized, the most desirable residences were those close to the center of the city. Thus the preindustrial model, postulated by Sjoberg, describes a city in which the most affluent live close to the center while the impoverished live on the periphery.[21]

In 1850, the residential pattern in Phila-delphia could still be partially described by the preindustrial model. But in 1854, the City of Philadelphia merged with twenty-seven other political sub-divisions with Philadelphia County and the greatly enlarged city (it grew from 2 to 130 square miles) rapidly changed; consolidation led to the professionalization of the police and fire departments and the expansion of the public school system. But more importantly for what concerns us here, governmental rationalization facilitated the implementation of critical techno-logical innovations in transportation and building construction. That, in turn, dramatically accele-rated Philadelphia's transition to the modern form.

Iron track was laid in the streets of the city in 1857; when the horse-drawn cars were hauled over the rail instead of street surfaces, the decline in friction made it possible to carry three to four times more passengers than had the omnibus. The effects of this transportation breakthrough were felt after the Civil War. The war brought boom times to certain sectors of the city's economy, but it retarded building construction as it accelerated capital accumulation. By the late 1860's the building industry, spurred by the new transportation technology, exploded in a surge of construction that continued into the twentieth century. The horse-car lines, which carried some 99 million passengers in 1880, led the way to residential and commerical deconcentration, while growth in the city's railroad network led to manufacturing decentralization; though the city's population more than doubled between 1850 and 1880, reaching 845,000 by the end of the period, the rate of building growth after 1870 far surpassed population growth.[22]

Population density declined; the average dwelling by 1880 (roughly 6 persons) contained almost one person less than it had in 1850. The modal housing type shifted from the free-standing or semi-detached three and four story dwelling to the two story row home. Moreover, houses that previously were erected by carpenters on demand were now built by large contractors anticipating the form of the modern tract development. Some 50,000 homes—one-third of the 1880 housing stock—were built in the preceding decade. The ratio of new population to new homes was 8 to 1 in the 1840s; by the 1870s, it had declined to 4 to 1.[23]

The dramatic growth during the latter period did not result in a duplication of the spatial patterns that characterized the 1850 city; the decade of the 1870's can be considered the beginning of modern urban form in Philadelphia. The shuffling of the occupational universe brought about by the process of industrialization—the creation of jobs with new skills and the dilution of others, the emergence of bureaucracy and a managerial class—coincided with the city's ability to accommodate wholly new changes in landuse specialization. Not only did industry and commerce accelerate their carving up of urban space, but social differentiation and spatial differentiation proceeded in tandem. Social differences in work—wages, status and work environments—now began to be mirrored in increasingly homogeneous residential settings. The supervisors and clerks who left the shop floor for wood-paneled offices now sought to leave their older heterogeneous neighborhoods for new residential areas where they could live with people more like themselves. The differentiation of residential areas along class, racial-ethnic and life-cycle lines accelerated. The more affluent Irish and German immigrants and their children started to join native-whites in an exodus from the city's center to new modern neighborhoods developing at its peripheries. Over the ensuing thirty years, large residential areas of cheap concentrated housing in the old city center were vacated, making room for the next wave of immigrants and ensuring that the residential patterns of the new immigrants would be far more segregated than those experienced by the old immigrants.

The Early Twentieth-Century City: 1900–1930

The availability of cheap, old housing concentrated in close proximity to plentiful manufacturing jobs contributed to the considerably higher levels of residential segregation of the Italians, Poles, and Russian Jews who settled in the industrial city of the early twentieth century.[24] The forces set in motion in the 1870's proceeded apace, led by the tract development of the row house, and major changes in transportation technology. The trolleys were electrified in the 1890's, the elevated train and subway were introduced in the early decades of the next century, and the automobile made its appearance shortly thereafter.

The new means of transportation made it possible to open large outlying areas of the city for residential settlement.[25] Unlike building practices in other major cities, Philadelphia's landlords erected few tenements at this time. The row house remained the modal-housing type; in 1915 roughly nine houses in ten were of this architectural form.[26] The emergence of the street car suburbs and the row house ensured the continued decline in residential density. Despite an increase in the city's population to almost two million by 1930, the average density per dwelling fell to 4.2 persons. Philadelphia richly deserved its nickname as "The City of Homes."

The city's economy did not change dramatically over the half century between 1880 and 1930.[27] Its most salient feature remained its diversification. Despite the entrance of some new industries, most notably in the electronics field, Philadelphia's economy was characterized by the same range of activities found in the nineteenth century: textiles, apparel, printing, publishing, foundry, and machines. Two important changes were noticeable in 1930. First, although the number of manufacturing jobs increased 60 percent over the period, it fell as a proportion of all jobs (from 48 to 31 percent) and increased far less rapidly than did the population as a whole; second, changes in transportation and production technologies began to accelerate the shift of manufacturing activity from the city's center to outlying areas. The full impact of these changes, however, would not be felt until the 1960's and 1970's.

The new occupational opportunities that emerged tended to be located in the economy's white-collar sector (see Table 5). By and large, expanding jobs were found in the professional, white collar or service categories; faced with discrimination, language difficulties and limited educational backgrounds, few blacks and immigrants worked in these desirable positions. As a result, "New" immigrants found their occupational opportunities more limited in this period than the "Old" immigrants had encountered in the nineteenth century; improvements in the overall occupational distribution of black workers during these years were at best marginal.

The socioeconomic differentiation of the city's space that resulted from transportation innovation, the decentralization of manufacturing and greater housing availability produced an urban form well described by the Chicago School model of concentric zones. At furthest remove from the center, in the street-car suburbs, lived white-collar and highly skilled "aristocrats of labor"; largely, these groups were composed of native-whites and the successful descendants of Irish, German and British immigrants. Although the automobile suburbs would not emerge until after World War II, roughly one person in seven in Philadelphia was sufficiently well-off to com-

mute regularly to work by auto in 1934 (this is almost the same proportion of the workforce that could afford regular use of the horse-drawn street cars in their "journey-to-work" in 1880).[28]

In the zones surrounding the manufacturing and retailing core lived the bulk of the working classes, largely "new" immigrants and blacks, roughly one-third of whom walked to work. In general, ethnic concentrations were located near concentrations of industrial employment.[29] This is particularly true of the Italian and Polish areas. Workers living in these neighborhoods were over-represented in industrial occupations. Once again, the relationships between the occupational distribution of immigrant groups and the location of their jobs and residences can be seen.[30] The principal exception were Russian Jews who, after initial settlement in South Philadelphia, established neighborhoods in the nonindustrial street-car suburbs in the west and northwestern areas of the city. Workers here were disproportionately found in wholesale and retail rather than industrial jobs.

By 1930 native whites and old immigrants had moved into better jobs and were able to use their greater income to ensure more housing choice; they lived in many different areas of the city characterized by greater housing value and distance from the center. As a result, they were less segregated. The relationship between occupational segregation and residential segregation was a close one. The data suggest that the segregation of newer immigrants was not complete because their occupational segregation was not complete; and, as in the nineteenth century, work location took precedence over the desire to live in an ethnic neighborhood in the residential location decision.

Blacks again stand in sharp contrast. Although they continued to live in and near areas characterized by high industrial concentrations, blacks were excluded from industrial work. Although 80 percent of the blacks in the city lived within one mile of 5,000 industrial jobs, less than 13 percent of the black work force found gainful employment in manufacturing. Blacks earned their livelihood as best they could, concentrating as they had in the last century, in menial, domestic and largely unskilled low-paying occupations (see Tables 5 and 6).

TABLE 5. *Occupational Distribution of Males and Females, 10+, by Ethnicity: 1900, 1930 (As Percent of Ethnic Group)*

	Blacks	Ireland	Germany	Great Britain	Italy	Poland	Russia	White Foreign-Born	2nd Generation Foreign-Born	Native White of Native Parents
					1900					
Professional	1.6	2.8	3.7	5.2	3.5	0.6	2.0	2.5	4.5	7.5
Owners and Executives	1.5	5.6	8.6	8.3	7.0	3.7	12.6	8.0	7.1	9.6
Clerks and Sales	1.0	8.9	8.6	10.4	1.6	2.3	6.9	4.2	13.6	17.4
Trade and Transportation	10.8	11.5	7.0	7.0	6.4	4.4	7.5	6.9	9.9	10.3
Manufacturing	8.2	40.2	54.3	56.2	32.6	55.5	62.8	47.3	49.2	40.4
Domestic and Personal Service	54.1	18.0	11.1	8.2	12.4	4.8	4.5	17.4	8.9	8.8
Laborers	21.6	10.7	4.0	3.2	34.8	25.9	3.0	11.0	4.6	3.4
Agriculture	0.6	1.0	1.0	0.9	1.4	1.4	0.4	1.2	0.7	1.1
Other	0.6	1.3	1.5	0.6	0.3	1.4	0.3	1.5	1.5	1.5
Dissimilarity from Native-Whites of Native-White Parents††	64	18	17	16	35	38	25	23	10	—

			Blacks	White Foreign-Born	Total Native White
				1930	
Professional			2.4	3.9	8.5
Owners and Executives			1.5	13.6	8.6
Clerks and Sales			2.6	9.3	27.8
Trade and Transportation			17.1	7.9	9.3
Manufacturing			12.6	42.8	33.7
Domestic and Personal Service			43.4	12.4	6.0
Laborers			17.6	7.3	2.5
Agriculture			0.6	0.9	0.4
Other			2.1	2.0	3.2
Totals			118890	203692	565481
(Row %)			(13.4)	(22.9)	(63.7)
Dissimilarity from all Native-Whites**			61	26	—

††Excludes 2nd Generation.
**Includes 2nd Generation.
Note: See Note for Table 1.
Sources: Figures are computed from published United States Census totals. See Department of the Interior, United States Census Office, *Census of Population: 1900*, v.II, pt. II, "Population," (Washington, D.C.: U.S. Census Office, 1902), 583, 585; U.S. Department of Commerce, Bureau of the Census, *Census of Population; 1930*, v.IV, "Population," (Washington, D.C.: U.S. Government Printing Office, 1933), 1412–1415.

The Modern City: 1970

Modern Philadelphia bears little resemblance to earlier periods. Technological change has continued to alter urban form and the means of crossing its increasingly inhabited spaces. Automobile suburbs have emerged in all directions and a wide-range of choice characterizes the housing market. Philadelphia's population peaked in 1950 at 2.1 million and was, in 1970, exactly as it had been in 1930: 1.95 million. Population density, however, continued its decline, reaching three persons per dwelling in 1970—almost exactly half of what it had been in 1850.

Significant changes affected the city's econ-

TABLE 6. *Location of Ethnic Populations by Distance from City Center and Access to Industrial Jobs: 1930 (Percent of Foreign Stock Living in Census Tract with the Following Characteristics)*

	Within 3 Miles of City Center	Within 1 Mile of 5,000 or More Industrial Jobs	Of Those who are Within 3 Miles of City Hall, Percent with access to 5,000 or more Industrial Jobs	Of Those who are Beyond 3 Miles of City Hall, Percent with access to 5,000 or more Industrial Jobs
British	.305	.614	.816	.520
Irish	.411	.610	.791	.483
German	.336	.633	.838	.529
Polish	.404	.815	.943	.724
Russian	.565	.537	.778	.223
Italian	.794	.714	.801	.627
Blacks	.786	.799	.882	.489
Native Whites	.393	.593	.803	.472
Total	.469	.643	.829	.473

Note: See Note for Table 1.
Sources: Figures are computed from tract-level data taken from the United States Census.

omy. Some 75,000 manufacturing jobs were lost between 1930 and 1970, and the appearance of new jobs in the service sectors have not made up the loss. In this regard, Philadelphia's experience resembles that of many older industrial cities in the Northeast. Large manufacturing employers have abandoned the city for regions with lower taxes, and a work force of nonunionized labor. The location of the remaining manufacturing activity has changed significantly. The earlier shift in production technology, from coal and steam to electricity, combined with important changes in transportation technology in the post-World War II years, produced a marked decentralization of manufacturing jobs. The advent of the interstate highway system, connecting with urban expressways—and the emergence of the trucking industry—has led to the suburbanization of manufacturing activity in industrial parks in the surrounding SMSA. Of every ten manufacturing jobs in the city, the three-mile ring from the city's center held nine jobs in 1880, six in 1930 and four in 1970 (see Table 7).

These changes have had important consequences for Philadelphia's blacks—the city's most recent immigrants. Their numbers increased from 221,000 in 1930 to 645,000 in 1970, and their proportion of the city's population increased from one-tenth to one-third. Today's blacks inherit the oldest stock of deteriorated housing once inhabited by two earlier waves of immigrants, but the jobs which once were located nearby and provided previous newcomers with avenues for upward mobility are gone. Precisely at the moment in time when the worst of the racist hiring practices in industry appear to have abated, the most recent black immigrants find themselves at considerable remove from the industrial jobs that remain and thus are unable to repeat the essential experience of earlier white immigrants. When understood in light of changes in the city's economy as a whole, especially the decline of manufacturing activity and the demand for unskilled labor, it is plain to see that blacks in 1970 Philadelphia are faced with a very different set of circumstances from those which existed in the nineteenth and early twentieth centuries.

The uniqueness of the black experience can be understood in yet another way. Blacks have always been the most segregated group in Philadelphia; this was true in the years 1850–1880, when blacks constituted but 4 percent of the city's population; in the years 1900–1930, when they were roughly 8 to 12 percent; and in 1970, when 33 percent of the city was black. Thus population size alone cannot explain their consistently higher levels of segregation; indeed, despite the fact that smaller groups requiring less housing

TABLE 7. *Percent Manufacturing Jobs at Given Distances (in Miles) from Center of Philadelphia: 1850–1970*

Distance	1850*			1880†			1930°			1970°		
	#	%	Cum %	#	%	Cum %	#	%	Cum %	#	%	Cum %
0–0.99	30,366	60.9	60.9	78,111	47.2	47.2	52,794	18.8	18.8	32,380	15.7	15.7
1.00–1.99	15,576	31.3	92.2	44,848	27.1	74.3	62,062	22.1	40.9	26,812	13.0	28.7
2.00–2.99	1,353	2.7	94.9	20,521	12.4	86.7	48,582	17.3	58.2	23,305	11.3	40.0
3.00–3.99	192	0.4	95.3	4,634	2.8	89.5	39,596	14.1	72.3	31,143	15.1	55.1
4.00–4.99	387	0.8	96.1	3,806	2.3	91.8	42,404	15.1	87.4	37,536	18.2	73.3
5.00+	1,959	3.9	100.0	13,570	8.2	100.0	35,384	12.6	100.0	55,067	26.7	100.0
Total Jobs:	49,833			165,489			280,823			206,243		

*Center is 3rd and Market.
†Center is 7th and Market.
°Center is 14th and Market.
Sources: Figures for 1850 and 1880 are computed from Philadelphia Social History Project compilations of the United States manuscript censuses of manufactures. Figures for 1930 and 1970 are computed from tract-level data taken from the Pennsylvania Industrial Directory.

are often the most segregated, as the size and proportion of the black population increased over time, so did their segregation from native whites: 47 (1850), 52 (1880), 61 (1930), 75 (1970) (see Table 2). This development is tied to the rapid growth of new suburban housing after World War II; whites settled in these automobile suburbs, and in classic "trickle down" manner, blacks inhabited the older housing vacated by whites.[31]

What sets the contemporary black experience off from that of earlier white immigrants (and earlier black Philadelphians), however, is not simply the consistently higher level of segregation. A new measure of residential experience has been developed that asks what proportion of a typical person's census tract consisted of the same group; for example, what percentage of the population in the typical black person's census tract was black? In this measure of "dominance," the composition of the areal unit is sought. On the other hand, the Index of Segregation asks what percentage of a group would have to move to another location in the city to achieve a distribution throughout each areal unit in the city equal to their proportion of the city's total population.

Using the dominance measure, the striking differences that distinguish blacks from white immigrants can be seen.[32] The typical Irish immigrant in 1880 and the typical Italian immigrant in 1920, for example, shared a similar aspect of their residential experience. When the hypothetical immigrant in each era walked through his neighborhood, what kind of people might he have met? The Irishman in 1880 lived with 15 percent other Irish immigrants, 34 percent Irish stock, 26 percent all foreign born persons and 58 percent all foreign stock. The typical Italian immigrant in 1930 had an almost identical experience. He lived with 14 percent other Italian immigrants, 38 percent Italian stock, 23 percent all foreign born persons and 57 percent all foreign stock.[33] In striking contrast, the typical black in 1970 lived in a census tract in which 74 percent of the population was black (see Table 8). What is more, the "dominance" of blacks has risen steadily since 1850 when it was 11 percent; it was not until 1950, however, that the typical black lived in a census tract with a black majority. Ghettoes are the product of the post-World War II city.

The black residential experience differs from that of white immigrants in yet another important regard. As ethnic occupational segregation decreased over time—that is, as white immigrant groups gained access to a broader range of occupations—their residential segregation decreased. Quite the opposite was true for blacks: despite the occupational desegregation produced in recent decades by the opening of new job opportunities for blacks, their residential segregation has increased over time.

As measured by the Index of Dissimilarity, the differences between the occupational distributions of blacks and native-whites did not fall below 60 percent until 1940 when it reached 52 percent. After 1930, comparisons can be made only with all whites (native and foreign-born

TABLE 8. *Indices of Dominance: 1850, 1880, 1930–1970 (248 Tracts)*

	1850	1880	1930	1940	1950	1960	1970
Blacks	11	12	35	45	56	72	74
Ireland							
Born	24	15	3	2	2		
2nd		19					
Stock		34	8			5	3
Germany							
Born	9	11	4	3	2		
2nd		14					
Stock		25	11			5	3
Great Britain							
Born			4	3	2		
Stock			12			5	3
Italy							
Born			14	13	9		
Stock			38			23	21
Poland							
Born			7	6	4		
Stock			20			9	8
USSR							
Born			14	12	9		
Stock			28			17	14
Foreign							
Born	32	26	23				
2nd		32	34				
Stock		58	57				
Native-White	68	44					
Other Foreign							
Born	7	8					
2nd		7					
Stock		14					

Note: See Notes for Tables 1 and 2.
Sources: See Sources for Table 2.

combined); it fell to 42 percent in 1950, 29 percent in 1960 and 25 percent in 1970. The significance of the relatively sharp decline in occupational dissimilarity between blacks and whites after World War II, especially in the decade of the 1950's however, should not be exaggerated (see Table 9). In a 1975 survey of adult males in the Philadelphia Urbanized Area, blacks reported a mean income of $3,000 below whites even after the effects of age, education and occupation were controlled.[34]

Summary and Conclusions

Systematic data on levels of segregation, as measured by the index of dissimilarity and our measure of ethnic dominance, make clear that a

"Tale of Three Cities" is the story of three distinct waves of immigrants, three distinct opportunity structures and ecological forms, and three distinct settlement patterns. In each of the three cities, immigrants interacted with the urban structure they encountered and produced markedly different residential patterns.

The first city—the industrializing city of the mid-nineteenth century—was settled by large numbers of Irish, Germans and British of the "Old" immigration. They established integrated residential patterns which have persisted throughout the twentieth century.

The second city—the industrial city of the early twentieth century—was home for even greater numbers of Italians, Poles, and Russian Jews of the "New" immigration. The residential

TABLE 9. *Occupational Distribution of Males and Females, 16+, by Ethnicity: 1970 (As Percent of Ethnic Group)*

	Blacks		Puerto Ricans		Whites	
	City	SMSA	City	SMSA	City	SMSA
Professional	7.7	8.1	4.4	5.3	15.1	17.2
Owners and Executives	2.5	2.5	1.4	1.9	7.0	8.8
Clerks and Sales	21.6	20.4	14.7	13.2	32.7	29.9
Trade and Transportation	5.2	5.3	4.3	3.4	3.8	3.4
Manufacturing	30.1	30.1	52.8	49.3	27.6	27.6
Domestic and Personal Service	22.7	23.1	13.8	14.2	8.0	7.8
Laborers	8.0	8.0	6.8	8.4	3.1	3.0
Agriculture	0.6	0.8	0.8	3.9	0.1	0.6
Other	1.7	1.6	0.8	0.5	2.5	1.5
Totals	232,192	279,703	6,270	10,749	525,058	1,570,045
(Row %)	(30.4)	(15.8)	(0.8)	(0.6)	(68.8)	(83.6)
Dissimilarity from *All* whites	24	25	36	37	—	—

*Includes a small number of non-Black non-Whites, i.e., Chinese, etc.
Sources: Figures are computed from published United States Census totals. See U.S. Bureau of the Census, *Census of Population: 1970* v.I, "Characteristics of the Population," pt. 40, Pennsylvania-Section 1, (Washington, D.C.: U.S. Government Printing Office, 1973), 395, 400, 451, 456, 499, 504.

patterns they formed were much more segregated than those of their predecessors. Yet even here the stereotypic notions of settlement and adjustment to conditions in the New World require some qualification. The experience of initial segregation in working and lower class ghettoes and subsequent occupational and residential mobility, as Sam Warner and Colin Burke pointed out, is a limited case in American history: limited to the "New" immigrants in the largest cities at the turn of the last century.[35] And, as the dominance data make clear, most immigrants never lived in ghettoes if they are understood as places inhabited, only or largely, by a single ethnic group.

The third city—"post-industrial" modern Philadelphia—was the destination for thousands of black migrants largely from the Southeast. Their segregation and dominance scores have increased steadily from 1850. Unlike earlier groups, today's blacks live in isolated ghettoes.[36]

Changes in the patterns of ethnic settlement, can only be fully understood within the context of an ecological explanation that focuses upon changes in the housing market, industrial base, transportation, production, and communication technologies. The ecological perspective makes it possible to explain the changing measures of segregation and dominance, important aspects of the ethnic experience, and the uniqueness of the black experience.

The many significant changes in the relationship between work and residence that characterized Philadelphia's growth over the last century had direct implications for the location, character and stability of ethnic communities. Under constraints of expensive transportation and limited housing, industrial affiliation had a greater impact on the residential choice of immigrants than did their ethnicity.

To the degree that specific ethnic neighborhoods were based on their concentration in nearby industrial employment, the stability of these neighborhoods has depended upon the stability of jobs. When contemporary observers seek explanations for stable neighborhoods, for example, they find strong ethnic ties; yet their analyses all too often confuse causes with effects. The strong ethnic ties are themselves the product of stable neighborhoods; the stability of the neighborhood results from the continuing presence of industrial employment opportunities. The black slums in 1970, for example, were located primarily in areas that had no manufacturing jobs in 1930.[37]

This structural view then suggests that the presence of nearby industrial employment reinforces the stability of white ethnic communities, and it is the industrial concentrations of white ethnics rather than ethnic culture or historical accident that underlies resistance to black invasion. Previous research by Burgess and Duncan and Lieberson has suggested that historical accidents or differences in ethnic tolerance for blacks accounts for their differential resistance to black settlement.[38] The results presented here indicate that the frequently expressed stereotypes of resistant Poles, Italians, and fleeing Russian Jews are applicable only when one does not consider the impact of the ecological structure of the city, the position of these groups in the occupational structure, and their location and access to industrial employment. The reason that white ethnics on Chicago's South Side were able for so many years to prevent black residential penetration has more to do with the continued presence of their job opportunities in the nearby stock yards and steel mills than with cultural factors. The lack of adjacent industrial turf explains the rapid racial turnover that characterized Harlem's transition from an upper middle-class suburb to a lower-class slum in the early decades of the twentieth century.[39] These same factors emerge from an examination of the ghettoes of blacks and Puerto Ricans in contemporary Philadelphia; unlike the earlier white ethnic villages, these racial ghettoes have not formed around abundant employment opportunities; they emerged instead in economically depressed residential areas which were abandoned by affluent whites who moved to more distant suburbs seeking greater socioeconomic homogeneity, better schools, and more spacious housing.

A decade ago the *Report of the National Advisory Commission on Civil Disorders* asked why "the Negro has been unable to escape from poverty and the ghetto like the European immigrants?" Their answer stressed historical factors.[40] They pointed to the changing nature of the American economy, to slavery and its legacy of racial discrimination, and to the decline of patronage and services when urban black voters win political power.

To the arguments of the Kerner Commission, three further points can be added. First, it is clear that the changing opportunity structure and the different ecological arrangements of the city provide the basic parameters within which the experience of white ethnics and blacks must be understood. To assume a constant opportunity structure and an unchanging ecological form is to seek explanations for differences in ethnic settlement and adjustment in the cultural origins of ethnic groups and thus to misdirect inquiry from the obvious. Cultural factors come into play only within the larger structure of the urban environment.[41] Second, the impact of housing and industrial location—the constraints that work and residence imposed on earlier inmigrants—are significant. Western European immigrants came at the most propitious time; both the highly skilled Germans and British, and the relatively unskilled Irish, found ample opportunities. Even though the industrial base of the city began to decline at the turn of this century, it is clear that Eastern European immigrants, when compared with post-World War II blacks, settled in what must be considered the "ghettoes of opportunity." Finally, the experience of blacks stands in sharp contrast to that of white ethnics. Not only has their segregation increased over the last century—contrary to the standing theory of assimilation—but it is also clear that blacks have been forced to settle in the oldest industrial and residential areas of the city—areas which have been left behind by the processes of modern urban-industrial development.

There is little to be gained by continuing a debate among advocates of structural and cultural points of view where one is posed to the exclusion of the other. Both play critical explanatory roles. Structural considerations explain well the occupational and residential experience of white immigrants who settled in mid-nineteenth and early twentieth-century Philadelphia; they do not explain the black experience. Here the explanation must be racism. If it is understood as a cultural factor, then culture explains why blacks who lived in Philadelphia at the same time fared so badly despite the twin structural advantages of abundant industrial opportunities and residential location where these opportunities were particularly plentiful. If racial discrimination had been absent in earlier Philadelphia, blacks should have done at least as well if not better than their white immigrant contemporaries.

In modern Philadelphia racism has somewhat abated, but the twin structural advantages of the past have disappeared. Thus structural constraints loom large today; though different from the racial barriers that prevented advancement in the past, they function just as effectively. They retard the economic progress of all groups—blacks and whites alike—who still inhabit the depressed areas of a city with a declining opportunity structure.

Although the Bootstraps and the Last of the Immigrants explanations for the socioeconomic differential that characterize blacks and whites today are of markedly different types, they have the same implications for public policy: do nothing. Both explanations are false and based on a mistaken understanding of our history. Why these points of view persist is important to comprehend. They are accepted in large part because they justify things as they are now. And in legitimating the status quo, these two views demonstrate how what is believed about the past affects the present—not in abstract scholarly logic, but in the material daily life of real people, not only in Philadelphia, but across the nation. Since our sense of history—conscious or not—exercises a real power in the present, it should sensitize us to the dangers of a historical social science.[42] This essay provides an empirically-grounded and interdisciplinary historical perspective so often absent in discussions of contemporary social problems and their solutions.

The Bootstraps explanation looks to the past, but however heroic the sound which comes from praising the courage and stamina of earlier white immigrants, it rings totally untrue when applied to the historical experience of blacks. The Last of the Immigrants explanation looks to the future, but the conditions that blacks face in modern Philadelphia are so different from those which earlier groups found that the analogy is thoroughly inappropriate. Unless major structural changes and perhaps some form of preferential treatment are undertaken at all levels of public and urban policy, it is doubtful that assimilation and economic progress for blacks will be possible. The approaches which blacks utilize to enter the American mainstream will certainly not be the same as those used by white immigrants; of necessity, they may have to be devised in ways yet unanticipated. As a national policy is formulated to revitalize our cities, it must be remembered that racial discrimination, though less pervasive, persists. The challenge is to recognize how our cities have changed and to use this understanding to provide real bootstraps for blacks so that they may indeed become the last of the immigrants.

ENDNOTES

1. This essay is based on the research of five authors, all Research Associates of the Philadelphia Social History Project which collected and made machine-readable the data for the nineteenth century. For further information about the PSHP and its interdisciplinary approach to research see Theodore Hershberg, "The Philadelphia Social History Project: A Methodological History" (Ph.D. diss., Stanford University, 1973), and "The Philadelphia Social History Project: A Special Issue," *Historical Methods* 9 (1976): 2–3. The twentieth-century data were collected by William Yancey and Eugene Ericksen. PSHP data form the basis for Alan N. Burnstein, "Residential Distribution and Mobility of Irish and German Immigrants in Philadelphia, 1850–1880," (Ph.D. diss., University of Pennsylvania, 1975); the nineteenth and twentieth century data were used in Stephanie Greenberg, "Industrialization in Philadelphia: The Relationship between Industrial Location and Residential Patterns, 1880–1930," (Ph.D., diss., Temple University, 1977).

"A Tale of Three Cities" attempts to synthesize the findings reported in these dissertations and in a number of separate journal articles and unpublished papers. Many of these papers will appear in *Toward an Interdisciplinary History of the City: Work, Space, Family and Group Experience in Nineteenth Century Philadelphia*, ed. Theodore Hershberg (New York: Oxford University Press, forthcoming, 1979); hereafter cited as *Interdisciplinary History of the City*.

2. Recent monographs on urban black communities provide an ethnic and racial perspective on the black experience but fail to adequately treat its urban context. See Gilbert Osofsky, *Harlem: The Making of a Ghetto: Negro New York, 1890-1920* (New York: Harper and Row, 1963); Allan H. Spear, *Black Chicago: The Making of a Negro Ghetto, 1890-1920* (Chicago: University of Chicago Press, 1967); Seth M. Scheiner, *Negro Mecca: A History of the Negro in New York City, 1865-1920* (New York University Press, 1965); David M. Katzman, *Before the Ghetto: Black Detroit in the Nineteenth Century* (Urbana: University

of Illinois Press, 1973); John W. Blassingame, *Black New Orleans, 1860–1880* (Chicago: University of Chicago Press, 1973).

An exception is Kenneth L. Kusmer, *A Ghetto Takes Shape: Black Cleveland 1870–1930* (Urbana: University of Illinois Press, 1976). Following in the tradition of W.E.B. DuBois, the *Philadelphia Negro: A Social Study* (Philadelphia, 1899; New York: Schocken Press, 1965) and St. Clair Drake and Horace R. Cayton, *Black Metropolis: A Study of Negro Life in A Northern City* (New York: Harper and Row, 1945), Kusmer discusses how the urban environment affected the collective experiences of blacks in late nineteenth and early twentieth century Cleveland.

3. For an interpretative overview of Afro-American history that develops this theme see August Meier and Elliot Rudwick, *From Plantation to Ghetto*, 3d. ed. rev. (New York: Hill and Wang, 1976).

4. The concept "urban as process" is elaborated in Theodore Hershberg, "The New Urban History," *Journal of Urban History* 5 (November 1978).

5. This point of view is held by many in positions of considerable influence in our society. In discussing the impact of the Bakke case with a black clerk in a Washington, D.C, bookstore, no less than Chief Justice Warren E. Burger was quoted as saying that ". . . his grandparents had come from Europe and were illiterate and it had taken 150 years for his people to improve themselves." Miss Audrey Hair, the bookstore clerk, said: "I asked him if he didn't think 300 years was enough time for my people?" New York *Times*, 5 November 1978, p. 6. The "Last of the Immigrants" explanation is cogently presented by Nathan Glazer, "Blacks and Ethnic Groups: The Difference, and the Political Difference it Makes," in *Key Issues in the Afro-American Experience*, ed. Nathan I. Huggins, Martin Kilson, and Daniel M. Fox (New York: Harcourt Brace Jovanovich, 1971), pp. 193–211. A more popular expression can be found in Irving Kristol, "The Negro Today is Like the Immigrant of Yesterday," New York *Times* Magazine, 11 September 1966.

No particular author is identified with the Bootstraps explanation; rather it is considered endemic in American culture and is associated with a racist interpretation of the black experience; that is, blacks failed because they are racially inferior.

6. Sam Bass Warner has also described "three" Philadelphias: "The Eighteenth-Century Town" of 1770–1780; "The Big City" of 1830–1860; and "The Industrial Metropolis" of 1920–1930; *The Private City: Philadelphia in Three Periods of Its Growth* (Philadelphia: University of Pennsylvania Press, 1968); see also Warner, "If All the World Were Philadelphia: A Scaffolding for Urban History, 1774–1930," *American Historical Review* 74 (October 1968).

A more recent study also identified "three cities": the "commercial" city of the eighteenth and early nineteenth centuries, the "industrial" city of the late nineteenth and early twentieth centuries, and the "corporate" city of the post World War II period; see David Gordon, "Capitalist Development and the History of American Cities," in *Marxism and the Metropolis: Perspectives in Urban Political Economy*, ed. Larry Sawers and William K. Tabb (New York: Oxford University Press, 1978).

The differences here reflect purpose. Warner initially wanted to demonstrate to historians that systematic data were available with which to document the major changes that occurred in the urban environment over the last two centuries. His major purpose in *The Private City*, however, had far less to do with changes in the city's opportunity and ecological structure than with the failures of urban life in a capitalist economy; he attributes urban problems to the pursuit of private profit at the expense of the public good. Where these once coincided in the colonial city, they diverged permanently with the emergence of the urban industrial order in the nineteenth century. Gordon's purpose was to classify cities according to stages in their historical economic development, arguing that urban form and the requirements of capitalism are inextricably linked to each other. Our purpose differs; we wished to characterize the particular kind of economy and environment that awaited the settlement of three temporally distinct waves of immigrants. Thus we have designated our three cities as "The Industrializing City," "The Industrial City," and "The Post-Industrial City."

7. (New York: Harcourt Brace and Jovanovich, 1976).

8. See for example Robert E. Park, "The Urban Community as a Spatial Pattern and a Moral Order," in *The Urban Community*, ed. Ernest W. Burgess (Chicago: University of Chicago Press, 1926); Louis Wirth, *The Ghetto* (Chicago: University of Chicago Press, 1928); Ernest W. Burgess, "Residential Segregation in American Cities," *Annals of the American Academy of Political and Social Science*, 140 (1928): 105–115; Robert E. Park, *Human Communities* (Glencoe, IL: Free Press, 1952).

9. Stanley Lieberson, *Ethnic Patterns in American Cities* (Glencoe, IL: Free Press, 1963). The Index of Segregation expresses the percentage of a group that would have to move to another location in the city to achieve a distribution throughout each areal unit equal to their proportion of the city's total population; the Index measure is often expressed as a whole number

ranging from 0 (no segregation) to 100 (complete segregation). For a detailed explanation of the Index of Segregation, see also Otis Dudley Duncan and Beverly Duncan, "Residential Distribution and Occupational Stratification," *American Journal of Sociology* 60 (1955): 493–503; Otis Dudley Duncan and Beverly Duncan, "A Methodological Analysis of Segregation Indexes," *American Sociological Review* 20 (April 1955); Karl E. Taeuber and Alma F. Taeuber, *Negroes in Cities: Residential Segregation and Neighborhood Change* (Chicago: Atheneum, 1965), pp. 195–245.

10. The dissimilarity scores reported in Table 2 are calculated in the same manner as the Index of Segregation but describe the degree of difference from native-whites as opposed to the remainder of the city's population. The scores reported in Tables 2 and 8, moreover, *are based on identical areal units.*

Tract level data were not collected by the nineteenth-century U.S. Census Bureau. For the 1930 and 1970 censuses, Philadelphia was divided into 404 and 365 tracts respectively. To achieve compatible boundaries, it was necessary to collapse these into 248 tracts. The much smaller PSHP areal units for the nineteenth century—7,100 rectangular grids one and one-quarter blocks square—were aggregated up to the level of the 248 census tracts. Areal compatibility was thus achieved across the entire 120 year period. For information on the construction of the PSHP grid areal unit, see Hershberg, "The PSHP: A Methodological History," pp. 150–87; and "The PSHP: A Special Issue," pp. 99–105.

11. Given the standing notion of the assimilation process, moreover, the decline in residential segregation over the period 1930–1970 is less than might be expected: the greatest decline was found among Polish stock (55% in 1930 to 35% in 1970), but Italian stock fell only slightly (58% to 48%), and Jewish stock did not change (53% to 52%). See Table 2.

12. Bruce Laurie and Mark Schmitz, "Manufacture and Productivity: The Making of an Industrial Base in Nineteenth-Century Philadelphia," in Hershberg, *Interdisciplinary History of the City.*

13. Hershberg, "The PSHP: A Methodological History," pp. 285–323; see especially Tables 21 and 23; A. Burstein, "Patterns of Segregation and the Residential Experience" in Hershberg, "The PSHP: A Special Issue," pp. 105–113.

14. Hershberg, Harold Cox, Richard Greenfield and Dale Light Jr., "The Journey-to-Work: An Empirical Investigation of Work, Residence, and Transportation in Philadelphia, 1850 and 1880," in Hershberg, *Interdisciplinary History of the City.* Although the estimated journey to work doubled between 1850 and 1880, reaching a radius of one mile and a median of one-half mile, the absolute distances involved remained quite short.

15. Greenfield, Hershberg, and William Whitney, "The Dynamics and Determinants of Manufacturing Location: A Perspective on Nineteenth-Century Philadelphia"; Greenberg, "Industrial Location and Ethnic Residential Patterns" both in Hershberg, *Interdisciplinary History of the City.*

16. Greenberg, "Industrialization in Philadelphia."

17. Greenberg, "Industrial Location and Ethnic Residential Patterns," in Hershberg, *Interdisciplinary History of the City;* and Greenberg, "Industrialization in Philadelphia."

18. On the other hand, given black overrepresentation in such service occupations as waiter and porter, their residential pattern was functional: the single large black residential concentration was located adjacent to the city's largest concentration of hotels, restaurants and inns in the downtown area.

19. Hershberg, "Free Blacks in Antebellum Philadelphia: A Study of Ex-slaves, Freeborn and Socioeconomic Decline," *Journal of Social History* 5 (December 1971); and "Free-born and Slaveborn Blacks in Antebellum Philadelphia," in *Slavery and Race in the Western Hemisphere* ed. Eugene Genovese and Stanley Engerman (Princeton: Princeton University Press, 1975).

The characteristic difficulties that blacks faced in finding employment were described by Joshua Bailey, member of the Board of Managers of the Philadelphia Society for the Employment and Instruction of the Poor. Bailey wrote in his diary that "Employers express themselves willing to receive such an one (a young 'colored' man) into their shops, but they cannot dare to do it knowing the opposition such an act would meet from their workmen who will not consent to work with colored persons." (10 January 1853).

The process of adjustment to conditions in the New World was a difficult one for all newcomers—black and white immigrants alike. Yet the historical record makes clear that much about the black experience was different—some times in degree, other times in kind. Blacks were victims of frequent race riots and saw their homes, schools and churches burned again and again. Though legally a free people and citizens, only members of the black race were denied the right to vote in the State of Pennsylvania after 1838. They occupied the worst housing in the Moyamensing slum and suffered from the greatest degree of impoverishment. Their mortality rate was roughly twice that of whites, and the death of black men early in their adult lives was the major reason that blacks were forced, far more often than whites, to raise their children in fatherless families; see F. F. Furstenberg, Jr., Hershberg and J. Modell, "The Origins of the Female-Headed

Black Family: The Impact of the Urban Experience." *Journal of Interdisciplinary History* 6 (September 1975).

For the occupational experience of the white immigrant workforce, see B. Laurie, Hershberg and G. Alter, "Immigrants and Industry," *Journal of Social History* 9 (December 1975) and B. Laurie and M. Schmitz, "Manufacture and Productivity."

20. Robert Park, Ernest W. Burgess, and Roderick D. McKenzie, eds., *The City* (Chicago: University of Chicago Press, 1928).

21. Gideon Sjoberg, "The Preindustrial City," *American Journal of Sociology* 60 (1955): 438–45; Gideon Sjoberg, *The Preindustrial City: Past and Present* (Glencoe, IL: Free Press, 1960).

22. Hershberg, et al., "The Journey-to-Work."

23. Ibid. We do not wish to leave the impression that the decline in population densities over the period was due solely to the increased availability of housing. Declining population densities were also tied to declining fertility, a process experienced over at least the last century in Western Europe and North America.

When the city is divided into concentric rings of roughly one mile, the inner two rings lost population consistently over the period. The first ring fell from 206,000 persons in 1880 to 67,000 in 1970; and in the second ring population fell from 241,000 in 1880 to 135,000 in 1970. Although contemporary population density gradients from the center outward are not level, their smoothing over time is one of the striking changes in urban population structure.

24. For an excellent discussion of the Polish experience in Philadelphia in the first two decades of the twentieth century, and less detailed but useful information on other immigrant groups in the city at the same time, see Carol Golab, *Immigrant Destinations* (Philadelphia: Temple University Press, 1978).

25. Sam Bass Warner, Jr., has described this process for late nineteenth-century Boston, *Street Car Suburbs: The Process of Growth in Boson, 1870–1900* (Cambridge, MA: Harvard University Press, 1962).

26. Golab, *Immigrant Destinations*, p. 153.

27. Greenberg, "Industrialization in Philadelphia," see Chap 6, "Changes in the Location of Jobs Between 1880 and 1930 and the Composition and Stability of Urban Areas in 1930," pp. 139–182.

28. Greenberg, "Industrialization in Philadelphia," Chap 6; Hershberg, *et. al.*, "The Journey-to-Work."

29. Ericksen and Yancey, "Work and Residence in an Industrial City," *Journal of Urban History* (Forthcoming, 1979).

30. The relationship between work and residence was for Polish immigrants in 1915 what it had been for the Irish and German immigrants in the nineteenth century. Golab summarizes their experience in these words: "Each Polish settlement (and there were nine such areas) directly reflected the industrial structure of the neighborhood in which it was located. It was the availability of work that determined the location of the Polish colony, for the Poles were invariably employed in the neighborhoods where they resided." *Immigrant Destinations*, p. 113.

A similar conclusion was reached by E. E. Pratt in his study of immigrant worker neighborhoods: *Industrial Causes of Congestion of Population in New York City* (New York: Columbia University Press, 1911).

31. William Alonso, "The Historic and the Structural Theories of Urban Form: Their Implications for Urban Renewal," in Charles Tilly, ed., *An Urban World* (Boston: Little, Brown, 1974), 442–446.

32. The "dominance" measure not only operates to homogenize the experience of the two earlier waves of white immigrants, it also calls into question too great a reliance on the Index of Segregation as a useful tool to infer social experience. To the extent that cross-cultural contacts are central to our thinking about the socialization of the young and subsequent mobility and assimilation experience, the dominance measure, in getting more directly at who lives near whom, may be a better measure than the Index of Segregation; indeed we have seen that although some groups can be twice as segregated as others—as the new immigrants were compared to the old—they can display identical levels of dominance. Although the thrust of this essay is not methodological, we think it time that the uses of the Index of Segregation, particularly the assumptions that underlie its correlation with a wide range of social behaviors, be carefully reconsidered. We are not claiming that the Index of Segregation is without value, but rather that in many instances it may be (and has been) inappropriately applied. The socioeconomic correlates of the Index of Segregation and our new measure of dominance remain a topic for empirical investigation.

Although when compared to the black experience the differences between the old and new immigrants appear small indeed, there were differences nonetheless. While the dominance measures for the white immigrant groups were approximately equal, this does not mean that they had the same residential *pattern*. In order for the new immigrants, proportionally smaller than the old immigrants, to achieve so much higher measure of segregation than, and measures of dominance equal to the old immigrants, they would have had to be considerably more clustered. Thus, relative to the entire settled area of the city, the residential pattern of the new immigrants must have been much more compact than that of the old. Accordingly, an examination of the dimensions of segregation reveals that while the very localized experiences of the old and new immigrants may have been the same, the old immigrants had access to more diverse areas of the city. See Burstein, "Patterns of Segregation."

33. Golab's description of 1915 immigrant residential patterns corroborates the argument presented here: "No immigrant group in the city ever totally monopolized a particular neighborhood to the extent that it achieved isolation from members of other groups." Golab, *Immigrant Destinations*, p. 112.

34. Ericksen and Yancey, "Organizational Factors and Income Attainment: Networks, Businesses, Unions," unpublished paper (Temple University, 1978). This result is consistent with those reported in many national studies.

The occupational dissimilarity scores are reported at the bottom of each occupational table. The scores can be interpreted in the same manner as the segregation scores: the percent of blacks who would have to shift to another occupational strata in order to approximate the same distribution as whites.

35. Sam Bass Warner and Colin Burke, "Cultural Change and the Ghetto," *Journal of Contemporary History* 4 (1969): 173–187.

36. Puerto Ricans, a much smaller group than blacks, are in fact the most recent immigrants to the city and are also slightly more segregated than blacks, see Table 2.

37. Gladys Palmer, *Recent Trends in Employment and Unemployment in Philadelphia* (Philadelphia: Works Project Administration, Philadelphia Labor Market Studies, 1937).

38. Burgess, "Residential Segregation"; Otis Dudley Duncan and Stanley Lieberson, "Ethnic Segregation and Assimilation," *American Journal of Sociology* 64 (January 1959): 364–74.

39. Gilbert Osofsky, *Harlem: The Making of a Ghetto*. While carefully documenting the real estate boom and bust that followed the construction of the elevated lines which connected Harlem with lower Manhattan, Osofsky overlooked entirely the significance of the work-residence relationship in his explanation of the dramatic changes in Harlem's racial demography.

40. (New York: Bantam Books, 1968); see chapter 9, "Comparing the Immigrant and Black Experience," pp. 278–282. For a convincing critique of the "Last of the Immigrants" theory that focuses on patterns of intra- and inter-generational occupational mobility and supports our argument nicely, see Stephan Thernstrom, *The Other Bostonians: Poverty and Progress in the American Metropolis* (Cambridge, Mass.: Harvard University Press, 1973), chapter 10, "Blacks and Whites," pp. 176–219. "By now . . . ," Thernstrom concluded, somewhat too optimistically in our opinion, "American Negroes may face opportunities and constraints that are fairly analogous to those experienced by the millions of European migrants who struggled to survive in the American city of the late nineteenth and early twentieth centuries. But until very recently, the problems of black men in a white society were different in kind from those of earlier newcomers . . . the main factor that will impede black economic progress in the future will be the forces of inertia that have been called passive or structural discrimination" (pp. 218–219).

41. Yancey, Ericksen and Richard N. Juliani, "Emergent Ethnicity: A Review and Reformulation," *American Sociological Review* 41 (June, 1976): 3.

42. See Stephan Thernstrom, "Further reflections on the Yankee City series: the pitfalls of a historical social science," *Poverty and Progress: Social Mobility in a Nineteenth-Century City* (Cambridge, Mass.: Harvard University Press, 1964), pp. 225–239; and Michael B. Katz, "Introduction," *The People of Hamilton, Canada West: Family and Class in a Mid-Nineteenth Century City* (Cambridge, Mass.: Harvard University Press, 1975), p. 1.

III

Patterns of Assimilation in American Life

The dominant conceptual framework in the analysis of American ethnic and racial relations has been an assimilation model. One of the earliest and most influential statements of the assimilation model was embodied in the classic "race relations cycle" advanced by sociologist Robert E. Park in 1926:

> In the relations of races there is a cycle of events which tends everywhere to repeat itself. . . .The race relations cycle, which takes the form . . . of contacts, competition, accommodation, and eventual assimilation, is apparently progressive and irreversible. Customs regulations, immigration restrictions, and racial barriers may slacken the tempo of the movement; may perhaps halt it altogether for a time, but cannot change its direction; cannot at any rate, reverse it (Park, 1950:150).

According to the assimilation model of intergroup contact, interethnic relations inevitably go through the stages of competition, conflict, accommodation, and assimilation. Park's attempt to formulate generalizations concerning the nature and dynamics of the process of intergroup contact has generated considerable response from social scientists. We have noted above that Noel ("The Origins of Ethnic Stratification") focuses on the first phase of Park's race relations cycle: the *origins* of ethnic stratification. In "A Societal Theory of Race and Ethnic Relations," Stanley Lieberson contends that the Park race relations cycle is inadequate because it fails to recognize that differences in power relations in the original contact situations produce different outcomes in terms of ethnic stratification.

Lieberson distinguishes between two different situations of ethnic stratification: one in which the migrating group is the dominant ethnic group (migrant superordination) and one in which the group residing in the region at the time of contact is dominant (indigenous superordination). In migrant superordination, the economic, political, and cultural institutions of the subjugated indigenous population are undermined. However, because the subordinate indigenous group seeks to maintain its traditional institutions, conflict with the dominant group can persist over long periods of time. This situation, exemplified by Indian-white relations in the United States, is classic colonialism, in which the subordinate group strenuously resists assimilation. (See Steele's article, "The Acculturation/Assimilation Model in Urban Indian Studies.") When the migrating group is subordinate, on the other hand, its decision to enter another society is more likely to be voluntary, and it is much more likely to accept assimilation into the dominant society, as exemplified by the experience of most European immigrants to America.

Most discussions of assimilation in the United States have focused on the adaptation of immigrant groups that have voluntarily entered American society. The experience of black Americans, whose ancestors were involuntarily imported from Africa, does not fall into either contact situation—migrant or indigenous subordination—that Lieberson outlines. Wilson (1973) maintains that slave transfers constitute a third major contact situation, the one in which the power and coercion of the dominant group is greatest. In contrast to colonization, in which the indigenous group, although subordinate, is able to maintain elements of its own culture, slave transfers involve the forcible and involuntary uprooting of people from families and traditional cultures that places them in a much greater dependent relationship with the dominant group (Wilson, 1973:19–20). The extent to which differences between migrant superordination, indigenous superordination, and slave transfers have affected the nature of intergroup relations has been the subject of considerable controversy among social scientists, especially as they have sought to compare the rates of assimilation among different ethnic groups and to develop explanations for the differences that exist.

An important assumption of the assimilation model has been that, as American society became more modernized, ethnic and racial distinctions would eventually disappear or become insignificant. According to this conception, the forces of modernity—democratic and egalitarian political norms and institutions, industrialization, urbanization, and bureaucratization—place increasing emphasis on rationality, impersonality, status by achievement, physical and social mobility, and equal opportunity. Traditional "irrational" social systems, in which social position is based on racial and ethnic origins rather than on individual merit, become increasingly burdensome (and even expensive) to maintain. Thus, the Southern caste system, in which selection was based on the irrational ascriptive criterion of race, was perceived by advocates of an assimilation model as a vestige of a premodern, agrarian society that ultimately and inevitably will be undermined as the modernization process transforms the society by emphasizing a selection process based on merit, credentials, and skills.

This position was nowhere more clearly articulated than in Gunnar Myrdal's *An American Dilemma*, probably the most important book ever written on the subject of American race relations. Published in 1944, *An American Dilemma* became an instant classic and exerted a profound influence on white America by drawing attention to the dynamics of race in American society in a way that had not been accomplished since the elimination of slavery. Myrdal's title reflected his basic thesis: the American creed of "liberty, equality, justice, and fair opportunity" was violated by the subservient status to which black Americans had been relegated. Myrdal felt that the contradiction between white America's deeply felt professions of equality and brotherhood, on the one hand, and its treatment of black people, on the other, presented an "embarrassing" dilemma that made for "moral uneasiness" in the hearts and minds of white Americans. But he also optimistically felt that the primary thrust of American institutions was in a direction that would ultimately undermine the last vestiges of the irrational caste system.

The assumption that the forces of modernization will progressively weaken the ties of race and ethnicity has been questioned, however; see, for example, Bonacich's discussion in "Class Approaches to Ethnicity and Race." In his classic essay, "Industrialization and Race Relations," Herbert Blumer (1965) scrutinized this assumption of the assimilation model. He noted that the projected effects of industrialization are not, in reality, inevitable. An emphasis on rationality may not make job opportunities available to the best qualified individuals irrespective of race; rather, the goal of efficiency and social harmony may impel managers *rationally* to discriminate because to hire minority applicants might disrupt the efficient and harmonious functioning of the enterprise. "*Rational* operation of industrial enterprises which are introduced into a racially ordered society may call for a deferential respect for the canons and sensitivities of that racial order" (Blumer, 1965:233). In other words, modernization and industrialization do not necessarily change the order of majority-minority relations; rather, these processes adapt and conform to existing systems of racial etiquette, as the situation in contemporary South Africa demonstrates. Therefore Blumer contends that changes in race relations in the workplace are brought about not by any inherent dynamic of the modernization process but by forces outside the world of work itself.

Assimilation as Ideology

In general the assimilation model of racial and ethnic contact assumes that the unique and distinctive characteristics of a minority will be erased and the minority group, its culture, its social institutions, and, ultimately, its identity will be absorbed by the dominant group. However, critics of the assimilation model have charged that, in reality, it reflects a "liberal" view of the manner in which racial and ethnic diversity should be resolved. That is, an assimilationist perspective has frequently served an ideological function of specifying how racial and ethnic groups *should* relate to each other, not necessarily a value-free model of the process whereby different racial and ethnic groups actually *do* interact. Therefore, in many circumstances, assimilationist analyses of racial and ethnic relations in American society have served to legitimize the basic ideology of American society as a land of opportunity.

Metzger ("American Sociology and Black Assimilation") points out that, in general, the assimilationist perspective assumes that

> The incorporation of America's ethnic and racial groups into the mainstream culture is virtually inevitable. . . . Successful assimilation, moreover, has been viewed as synonymous with equality of opportunity and upward mobility for the members of minority groups; "opportunity," in this system, is the opportunity to discard one's ethnicity and to partake fully in the "American Way of Life." In this sense, assimilation is viewed as the embodiment of the democratic ethos.

Myrdal's monumental *An American Dilemma* reflected this general liberal notion of how racial and ethnic groups should come together in American society.

As Metzger notes, the basic framework within which Myrdal conceptualized American race relations is perhaps most clearly reflected in his examination of the nature of black culture and community life. To the extent to which black culture diverged from dominant white culture patterns Myrdal considered it a "distorted development, or a pathological condition, of the general American culture." Therefore the primary thrust of black efforts toward institutional change in American society should be toward acquiring the characteristics of the dominant group. "It is to the advantage of American Negroes as individuals and as a group," wrote Myrdal, "to become assimilated into American culture, to acquire the traits held in esteem by the dominant white Americans."

One of the implications of such a model is that frequently the sources of ethnic conflict are perceived to reside not within the structure of society but within the pathological or maladjusted behavior of the minority group. Resolution of ethnic conflict, therefore, involves the process of the minority group adapting to the standards of the majority. As we will note more fully in the introduction to Part IV, the black protest movement of the late 1960s and early 1970s was in many respects a reaction against such an assimilationist stance.

The nature of the assimilation process and the extent to which various racial and ethnic groups should be permitted or permit themselves to be integrated, incorporated, or absorbed into the mainstream of American society has been the source of considerable controversy. In his now classic analysis, *Assimilation in American Life* (1964), Milton Gordon distinguished among three ideologies— Anglo-conformity, the melting pot, and cultural pluralism—that have been used to explain the dynamics of intergroup relations in American life.

The *Anglo-conformity* ideology assumes that an ethnic minority should give up its distinctive cultural characteristics and adopt those of the dominant group. It can be expressed by the formula $A + B + C = A$, in which A is the dominant group and B and C represent ethnic minority groups that must conform to the values and life styles of the dominant group; they must "disappear" if they wish to achieve positions of power and prestige in the society. An ideology of Anglo-conformity seeks a homogeneous society organized around the idealized cultural standards, institutions, and language of the dominant group.

Such a conception of how a minority group should relate to the majority is not unique to the United States. Consider, for example, the statement of an Australian Minister for Immigration concerning the objective of his country's immigration policy:

> It is cardinal with us that Australia, though attracting many different people, should remain a substantially homogeneous society, that there is no place in it for enclaves or minorities, that all whom we admit to reside permanently should be equal here and capable themselves of becoming substantially Australians after a few years of residence, with their children in the next generation wholly so (Oppenheimer, 1966).

For this model to be applicable to majority-minority relations in societies other than the United States the culture-specific term *Anglo-conformity* must be replaced by the more general term *transmuting pot*.

Like Anglo-conformity, the ultimate objective of a *melting pot* policy is a society without ethnic differences. More tolerant than a policy of Anglo-conformity, the melting pot ideal sees ethnic differences as being lost in the creation of a new society and a new people—a synthesis unique and distinct from any of the different groups that formed it. Unlike Anglo-conformity, none of the contributing groups is considered to be superior; each is considered to have contributed the best of its cultural heritage to the creation of a new amalgam. As Ralph Waldo Emerson expressed it in the mid-nineteenth century:

> As in the old burning of the Temple at Corinth, by the melting and intermixture of silver and gold and other metals a new compound more precious than any, called Corinthian brass, was formed; so in this continent—asylum of all nations—the energy of Irish, Germans, Swedes, Poles, and Cossacks and all the European tribes—of the Africans and of the Polynesians—will construct a new race, a new religion, a new state, a new literature (Quoted in Gordon, 1964: 117).

The melting pot ideal can be expressed by the formula $A + B + C = D$, in which A, B, and C represent the different contributing groups and D is the product of their synthesis.

Cultural pluralism, on the other hand, rejects the inevitability of cultural assimilation. The term refers to a system in which different cultures can coexist and be preserved. According to this notion, the strength and vitality of American society is derived from the many different ethnic groups that have made it a "nation of nations." Each group should be permitted to retain its unique qualities while affirming its allegiance to the larger society. It can be expressed by the equation $A + B + C = A + B + C$, in which A, B, and C are each ethnic groups that maintain their distinctiveness over time (Newman, 1973).

The three types that Gordon delineated can be placed on a continuum ranging from lesser to greater minority-group integrity and autonomy. Each type that Gordon delineated would merge imperceptibly with the adjacent type. For example, Anglo-conformity is much closer to the melting pot than it is to pluralism. Moreover, they can be logically extended. Examination of the history of racial and ethnic contact in the United States and throughout the world makes it apparent that Anglo-conformity (the transmuting pot), the melting pot, and pluralism do not exhaust the theoretical possibilities or the historical examples of the consequences of intergroup contact. A policy of genocide, on one extreme, permits less minority autonomy, obviously, than does a policy based on a conception that the process of interethnic contact resembles a transmuting pot. On the other extreme, *separatism,* or complete autonomy for the minority group, comprises a more expansive ideology than pluralism. When all of these types of ideologies are placed on a continuum, the result looks like Figure 1.

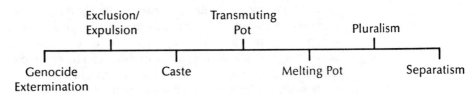

FIGURE 1. *Types of dominant group policies toward racial and ethnic minorities.*

Let us review the range of possible dominant policies toward racial and ethnic minorities. The most repressive dominant-group policy toward a minority group is extermination or *genocide*. The objective of such a policy is to eliminate or substantially reduce the minority group. In essence, members of the minority are told, "Because of your inherent qualities, you have no right to live." The post-World War II International Genocide Convention, which convened in response to the atrocities committed by the Nazi regime between 1933 and 1945, developed the following definition of genocide:

> ...any of the following acts committed with intent to destroy, in whole or in part, a national, ethnic, racial, or religious group as such: (a) Killing members of the group; (b) Causing serious bodily or mental harm to members of the group; (c) Deliberately inflicting on the group conditions of life calculated to bring about its physical destruction in whole or in part; (d) Imposing measures intended to prevent births within the group; (e) Forcibly transferring children of the group to another group (O'Brien, 1968:516).

Because genocide is antithetical to conceptions of the sacredness of human life, the ideology of racism is often developed to explain and to justify genocidal activity. In other words, ideas are advanced that depict the minority group members as subhuman or themselves destructive of human values and human life. With the rationalization or legitimation of racism, annihilation and extinction of the minority group are made to appear morally justified.

The most extreme and notorious modern example of genocide was, of course, the Nazi extermination program, in which Hitler's objective was the systematic extinction of several million Jews and other non-Aryan groups such as Gypsies. In American society, a policy of genocide was one of several pursued by dominant whites in their effort to wrest control of the country's vast lands from the Indians. The slogan "the only good Indian is a dead Indian" was common among frontier whites, who consistently encountered Indian resistance to their continued encroachment on Indian lands. As noted in the introduction to Part II, by the turn of the twentieth century, the Indian population of the United States had been brought to the point of virtual extinction by a combination of Indian susceptibility to European diseases, disintegration of tribal cultures, and an aggressive military policy by the federal government.

Extermination clearly represents the most extreme dominant-group method for dealing with the existence of minorities and the potential for interethnic conflict in a multicultural society. The objective of extermination is to reduce or eliminate contact between majority and minority in order to create an ethnically homogeneous society. A similar rationale underlies the process of expulsion, which involves the ejection of a minority group from areas controlled by the dominant group. Minorities are told, in essence, "Because you differ from us so greatly, you have no right to live among us." Expulsion can be either *direct*—that is, minorities may be forcibly ejected—or it may be brought about by the *indirect* means of harrassment and persecution (Simpson and Yinger, 1972:22–23). There have been numerous examples of this phenomenon in recent history. Nazi Germany sought to achieve a pure "Aryan" people by expelling many minorities from its borders as well as by exterminating them. Historically, British colonial policy in Ireland frequently drove many native Irish off the land to make room for British and Scottish settlers. In American history, the policy of direct expulsion was at no time more pronounced than during the nineteenth century, when increasing numbers of white settlers led to pressures for removal of Indians to areas beyond the Mississippi River. During World War II, 110,000 Japanese-Americans, most of them United States citizens, were forcibly removed from their homes and placed in detention camps in remote areas of the country.

Indirect explusion occurs when harrassment, discrimination, and persecution of a minority become so intense that members "voluntarily" choose to emigrate. Such treatment has led many groups, particularly religious minorities, to seek refuge in the United States. Persecuted Protestant sects were among the earliest European immigrants to the American colonies. The exodus of millions of Jews from Eastern Europe during the late nineteenth and early twentieth century is another example of this process.

Underlying an explusionist policy is the desire to achieve or retain ethnic homogeneity. This may occur not only when an ethnic group is expelled from the society, but also when a host society refuses to admit another group because that group is perceived to threaten the society's basic institutions. In this context, such a policy would be termed *exclusion*. As we noted in the introduction to Part II, between 1917 and 1965 American immigration policy was based on the assumption that some ethnic groups (southern and eastern Europeans and Asians, for example), represented a threat to the social fabric of American society and therefore should be excluded, or their entrance substantially restricted.

A policy of *caste* involves the exploitation of a social category that is excluded from full and equal participation in society. Bonacich suggests that a caste system "depends on exclusiveness rather than exclusion" (Bonacich, 1972:555). Positions of higher prestige, power, and income are reserved exclusively for members of the upper caste. Unlike extermination, expulsion, or exclusion, a caste system accepts the existence of minorities, albeit ambivalently, but subjugates them and seeks to confine them to inferior social positions. The majority group uses its power to maintain a system of social inequality between the minority group and itself.

Slavery, in which the slave's labor was a valuable resource exploited by the slaveowner, is an excellent example of caste in American society. But, as we noted in the introduction to Part II, the system of race relations that endured after slavery also illustrates how such social relations are organized to benefit the dominant group. After a tour of the South at the turn of the twentieth century, a prominent journalist remarked on the exploitive nature of black-white relations:

> One of the most significant things I saw in the South—and I saw it everywhere—was the way in which the white people were torn between their feelings of race prejudice and their downright economic needs. Hating and fearing the Negro as a race (though often loving individual Negroes), they yet want him to work for them; they can't get along without him. In one impulse a community will rise to mob Negroes or to drive them out of the country because of Negro crime or Negro vagrancy, or because the Negro is becoming educated, acquiring property and "getting out of his place"; and in the next impulse laws are passed or other remarkable measures taken to keep him at work—because the South can't get along without him (Baker, 1964:81).

At the other end of the continum is *separatism,* which is the most tolerant and expansive of the majority group policies or practices that we have considered. *Separatism,* like pluralism, implies recognition of social and cultural equality among ethnic groups, and it permits the minority voluntarily to choose to avoid virtually all interaction with the majority. The impulse for separatism frequently has been generated by considerable conflict with the majority group and a desire by a minority group to avoid a recurrence of the discrimination or subjugation to which it has been subjected, but it need not necessarily arise from such conflict. Separate ethnic areas or states have been advocated at various times by spokespersons of a number of different ethnic groups in America—by blacks, Indians, and Germans, among others. Religious groups, such as the Mormons, the Amish, the Hutterites, and the Doukhobors, which have sought to protect their unique identity from the "contaminating" influences of the larger society, have been among the foremost advocates of various separatist plans.

The transmuting pot, melting pot, and pluralism are all assimilation ideologies that imply the intermingling of majority and minority groups in some manner; expulsion, exclusion, caste, and separatism imply some form of minority group separation from the rest of society. But the crucial distinction between ideologies is not based on the issue of separation or integration alone, but on two other interrelated variables as well: whether the separation of the minority group is achieved voluntarily or involuntarily, and whether the minority is relatively autonomous or relatively powerless. Thus, *exclusion* refers to separation by the decision of the majority group, whereas *separatism* means that the minority group has decided voluntarily to place itself apart and is not prevented from doing so by the dominant group.

The case of the American Indian demonstrates that these policies are not mutually exclusive; one or more of them may be embraced simultaneously or in different historical periods. In the early years of the republic, U.S. policy towards American Indians moved from genocide to expulsion and exclusion (the reservation system). Since the late-nineteenth century, the ideology of Anglo-conformity has been predominant, with exclusion an acceptable alternative. For example, as Lurie observed in Part II, the purpose of governmental actions such as the Indian Allotment Act of 1887 was to force Indians to assimilate culturally. Even though many Indians would have welcomed separatism, their confinement to reservations has more closely resembled exclusion, since the reservations have been very substantially controlled by the federal government and other extensions of white society (for example, missionaries and traders).

Neither Anglo-conformity nor exclusion permit Native Americans to exercise free choice. To assimilate or adopt the European-derived norms, values, and cultural standards of the larger American society means to cease being an Indian culturally. On the other hand, to be restricted to the reservation is to have one's life choice and chances severely circumscribed by powerful external forces. Yet in spite of these exigencies, there seems little likelihood that the stubbornly purposeful maintenance of Indian traditions, values, and sense of aloofness from the rest of the society will be surrendered. Even in urban areas, where increasing numbers have migrated since World War II, Indians are resisting assimilation and forming their own ongoing communities, as Steele points out in "The Acculturation/Assimilation Model in Urban Indian Studies."

Dimensions of Assimilation

Gordon recognizes that each of the three theories—Anglo-conformity, melting pot, and cultural pluralism—on which his analysis focused are primarily ideologies; that is, prescriptive models of how the process of intergroup relations in American society *should* proceed. He contends, therefore, that such idealized conceptions are of limited utility in analyzing precisely how diverse ethnic groups in American society have actively interacted with and related to each other.

In "Assimilation in American Life," Gordon argues that in order to accurately assess how extensively different ethnic groups have intermingled, it is essential to recognize assimilation as, not a single phenomenon, but several related but analytically distinct processes. The three most important of these processes are cultural assimilation, structural assimilation, and marital assimilation, each of which "may take place in varying degrees" (Gordon, 1964:71).

Popular discussions of assimilation usually are concerned with *cultural assimilation,* or what Gordon terms *behavioral assimilation* or *acculturation.* This process involves the acquisition by a minority group of the *cultural* characteristics of the dominant group. These include its values, beliefs, language, and behaviors. However, many ethnic groups have become fully acculturated to the mainstream of American culture—that is, they have lost most traces of their ancestral cultures—but still have not been able to achieve full *social* participation in the society. Sharing the same language, norms, and cultural characteristics does not ensure access to informal social organizations, clubs, cliques, and friendship groups. Even sharing membership in secondary groups such as schools, jobs, and community and political organizations does not necessarily provide access to primary-group associations for those who have been culturally assimilated. Thus it is possible for a group to become culturally assimilated but to be unassimilated on the other two dimensions.

Thus it is important to distinguish cultural assimilation from *structural assimilation,* which refers to patterns of social interaction among individuals of different ethnic backgrounds. Structural assimilation occurs on two levels. *Secondary structural assimilation* refers to the ethnic integration of settings characterized by impersonal secondary relationships: jobs, schools, political organizations, neighborhoods, and public recreation. *Primary structural assimilation,* on the other hand, involves personal relationships that are "warm, intimate, and personal" and occur in religious communities, social clubs, friendships involving reciprocal visiting, and families—situations that sociologists refer to as *primary group relations.*

The third subprocess, one that is closely related to and, Gordon maintains, follows from primary structural assimilation, is *marital assimilation,* which refers to intermarriage among different ethnic groups.

Armed with these distinctions, it becomes possible to compare and contrast the relative degree of assimilation or separation of different ethnic groups in American society in a relatively systematic fashion. Considerable research has been directed to developing empirical indicators with which to measure assimilation; among the indicators are years of schooling, income levels, occupational characteristics, segregation indices, and rates of intermarriage. (See Hirschman, 1983, for an excellent review of these efforts).

One of the important issues in terms of Park's original model of the assimilation process, however, is the question of whether rates of assimilation are changing over time. In other words, are there differences between first-generation residents (the immigrants themselves), and second generation (the American-born offspring of immigrants), the third generation (the grandchildren of immigrants), and subsequent generations?

There have been two basic interpretations of the effect of generational differences on ethnicity. *Straight-line theory,* most closely identified with Herbert Gans (see his article, "Symbolic Ethnicity," in Part IV), predicts increasing assimilation with each succeeding generation. According to this model, one would anticipate that English would be more likely to be spoken in the home, that occupational characteristics would be higher, and that there would be higher rates of intermarriage among the second generation than among the first, and, moreover, that these trends toward assimilation would increase with each succeeding generation.

A contrasting model of the assimilation process was proposed by the historian Marcus Lee Hansen. Hansen contended that whereas children of immigrants seek to shed evidence of their foreignness as fully as possible and to "become American," the immigrants' grandchildren—the third generation—seek to rediscover their roots and retain their ethnic distinctiveness. He formulated the notion of the *third generation return:* "What the son wishes to forget the grandson wishes to remember" (Hansen, 1938:9). This model, which has become known as *Hansen's Law,* suggests that increasing assimilation with each succeeding generation is not necessarily inevitable. Instead, there can be variations among generations in rates of assimilation; the third generation, in particular, may identify more closely with their grandparents' ethnic background than did their parents, thus producing elements of a cultural or ethnic revival.

In one of the most celebrated interpretations of American religious life, Will Herberg (1955) employed a variant of Hansen's Law to account for changing patterns of religiosity in America. Herberg argued that because American religious communitites have been so strongly linked to ethnicity, Hansen's model could be extended to explain patterns of religious practice among American ethnic groups. According to Herberg, religiosity was high among the first generation, but because it was perceived as something "foreign" and thus something to escape, it declined among the second generation. For the third generation, however, affiliation with and participation in one of the three broad American religious traditions—Protestantism, Catholicism, and Judaism—provided a socially acceptable way in which to maintain one's ethnic identity in modern society. Therefore, Herberg argued, members of the third generation would tend to have higher rates of participation than their second-generation parents.

Herberg's bold and imaginative interpretation generated considerable controversy. In one important study, Abrahamson (1975) showed that empirical data do not support the three-generations hypothesis as a general interpretation of the process of immigrant adjustment. Analyzing data on the religious beliefs and behavior of ten religioethnic groups, Abrahamson found great variation in generational patterns of religiosity. In general there was little support for the hypothesized decline-and-rise pattern; only one of the ten religioethnic groups in his study (Eastern European Catholics) conformed to the pattern. Although more groups manifested a consistent decline in religiosity over three generations, there were a sufficient number of alternative patterns (for example, an increase in religiosity in the second generation) to preclude unequivocal support for a straight-line interpretation. Abrahamson's study reveals that although ethnicity is still a salient factor affecting religious behavior, the diversity of experiences among American ethnic groups (such as the differences between Irish, Polish, and Italian Catholics) has been so great as to challenge the appropriateness of any general models of immigrant adjustment.

One of Gordon's principal objectives in his 1961 essay, "Assimilation in American Life," was to clarify the confusion that surrounded the term *assimilation*. As noted above, Gordon argued that there was a tendency to use the term in an inclusive way and to ignore the fact that assimilation was a multidimensional phenomenon. Most important, it was essential to distinguish cultural from structural assimilation. He conceded that although extensive cultural assimilation had taken place in American life there was only limited evidence of structural assimilation. For Gordon, a more accurate description of the realities of ethnic relations in American life was *structural pluralism,* in which racial, ethnic, and, in particular, religious categories "retained their separate sociological structures."

To what extent has assimilation proceeded nearly a quarter of a century after Gordon published his classic essay? We will not review all of the voluminous literature on the several dimensions of assimilation here, but we will examine several salient issues suggested by this literature; in particular, those in the articles included in this volume. We will focus especially on the three key areas of socioeconomic status—income levels, occupational status, and educational attainment—as well as residential segregation and patterns of intermarriage.

Socioeconomic Assimilation

By almost any measure, descendants of southern and eastern European immigrants (Italians, Jews, Poles, Greeks, Hungarians) have become structurally assimilated into American life to a degree that would not have been predicted more than twenty years ago when Gordon's classic essay first appeared. Two decades ago one of the strongest and most striking findings in the social science literature dealing with assimilation was the rapid socioeconomic mobility of Jews, who, like most other "new" immigrant groups entering the United States between 1890 and 1915, had arrived virtually penniless (Strodtbeck, 1958). By the 1960s, despite the relatively brief time in which they had resided in the United States, Jews had come to exceed all other ethnic groups on the most common measures of socioeconomic status: median family income, educational attainment, and occupational prestige. The extremely rapid rise in the socioeconomic status of Jews historically contrasted sharply with other "new" immigrant groups (primarily Catholics) who, with Jews, had entered American society in the massive wave of immigration near the turn of the twentieth century. In his essay, "Education and Ethnic Mobility," Stephen Steinberg delineates some of the explanations for these differential rates of mobility.

By the early 1970s, however, Andrew Greeley, the prolific Catholic priest, sociologist, and novelist, was able to celebrate what he characterizes as the "ethnic miracle." Using extensive national social-survey data, Greeley contends that despite their lowly socioeconomic status three generations ago, "the ethnics have made it." The income levels of Irish, German, Italian, and Polish Catholics are today exceeded only by Jews and white Anglo-Saxon Protestants, who in many accounts are defined as the "establishment," or the "core" group to which all other ethnic groups compare themselves. In overall educational achievement, Polish, Italian, and Slavic Catholics still lag somewhat behind the national white average, but when parental educational levels are held constant, Catholic ethnics show higher educational levels than any other ethnic group except Jews. Indeed, Irish Catholics, once among the most despised and unfavorably stereotyped of all European ethnic groups, are today "the richest, best educated, and most prestigious occupationally of any gentile religio-ethnic group." Thus, Greeley concludes, "In a very short space of time, the length of one generation, more or less, the American dream has come true" for European Catholic ethnic groups.

Asians have demonstrated equally striking patterns of social mobility. During the past two decades, especially, there has been a notable change in the perception of Asians in American society. As we noted in the introduction to Part II, Asians, primarily Chinese and Japanese, have been the object of considerable discrimination throughout their history in America. Indeed, so unfavorable were the perceptions of Asians by whites that they were, unlike any European ethnic groups, virtually excluded from immigrating to the United States for more than half a century. Moreover, in one of the most notorious instances of racism in American history, American citizens of Japanese descent were subjected to the humiliation of incarceration in detention camps during World War II.

Today, however, the unfavorable stereotypes that were widely embraced by white Americans before, during, and immediately after World War II have been supplanted by perceptions of Asians as "model minorities," who, despite the discrimination, have demonstrated remarkable patterns of educational, occupational, and financial success (e.g., *Journal of Social Issues*, 1973; Lindsey, 1982; *Newsweek on Campus*, 1984). As Hirschman and Wong point out, the educational levels of Japanese, Chinese, and Filipinos—immigrant as well as native-born—today equal or exceed those of whites. These high levels of educational attainment are particularly pronounced among the younger segments of the population. Moreover, Asians are overrepresented in higher-status occupations, especially the professions. Although their income levels among those of comparable occupational backgrounds tend to be lower than whites, overall income levels for native-born Japanese, Chinese, and Filipino males are about the same as for white males. Nevertheless, Hirschman and Wong caution against generalizing from these selected indices of secondary structural assimilation to other dimensions of assimilation. They conclude that:

> Asian-Americans tend to remain segregated from many sectors of the dominant economy, society, and polity. If the situation of Asian-Americans appears favorable, it is only in reference to greater disadvantages of other minorities. Full equality and participation are still to be achieved.

The patterns of educational, occupational, and financial achievement found among European and Asian ethnic groups are not duplicated among Hispanics and blacks. In "U.S. Hispanics: Changing the Face of America," Davis, Haub, and Willette document the substantial gaps that separate Hispanics from the Anglo population on these dimensions. They anticipate that because there is evidence of increasing Hispanic educational attainments with each succeeding generation, the educational lag between Hispanics and Anglos should narrow in the future. On the other hand, the historic concentration of Hispanics in lower-paid, less-skilled occupations has persisted, and since 1972 the ratio of Hispanic to white income has declined from 71 percent in 1972 to 65 percent in 1983 (see Table 12 in the Statistical Appendix). Moreover, during the same period of time Hispanic poverty increased so that by 1983 28 percent of all Hispanics were officially below the poverty line. However, among Hispanic groups there are obvious disparities, most prominently those between Cubans, whose early migration, especially, was comprised very substantially of middle-class and professional people, and Puerto Ricans, who were much more likely to have had low levels of educational attainment and fewer occupational skills than Cubans.

As we will note more fully in the introduction to Part IV, similar patterns have characterized black socioeconomic status. During the past decades, the black community in general has experienced gains in educational attainment and political participation. Paralleling the decline in income among Hispanics, though, the overall financial condition of black families deteriorated. However, as Wilson notes in his article, "The Black Community in the 1980s" (Part IV), such generalizations obscure the increasing economic divergence within the black community. Wilson contends that the past two decades have been a period in which blacks have had available occupational opportunities unprecedented in the black experience in America. On the other hand, the economic circumstances of the black underclass, and, in particular, female-headed families has grown increasingly acute.

Spatial Assimilation

Each of the dimensions mentioned above—years of schooling, occupational distribution, and income levels—represents social characteristics that in themselves reveal little about the extent of social assimilation, integration, or incorporation of different ethnic groups in a society. In a genuinely pluralistic society with parallel social structures, for example, it is hypothetically possible for two or more ethnic groups to manifest high educational attainment, occupational status, and income levels without substantial physical interaction.

Residential segregation versus intergration has been one of the most frequently examined indices of assimilation. Massey and Mullan ("Processes of Hispanic and Black Spatial Assimilation") have referred to it as *spatial assimilation* and defined it as "the process whereby a group attains residential propinquity with members of a host society." Numerous scholars (e.g., Hershberg, 1979; Lieberson, 1963 and 1980; Marson and Van Valey, 1979; Pettigrew, 1979; Roof, 1979) have shown that there is a close interrelationship between housing, and jobs, educational opportunities, and income. Therefore, an ethnic group's spatial location is a crucial variable affecting its overall socioeconomic position. Massey and Mullan contend that residential location affects "cost and quality of housing, health and sanitary conditions, exposure to crime and violence, quality of services (the most important of which is education), and access to economic opportunity, as well as a host of less tangible factors ranging from the character of one's children's playmates to the kinds of role models they emulate."

In *A Piece of the Pie: Black and White Immigrants Since 1880* (1980), one of the most important studies of American racial and ethnic relations in recent years, Stanley Lieberson undertook an exhaustive comparative analysis of the experiences of blacks and "new" European immigrants in twentieth-century America. His examination of the patterns of residential segregation of blacks and various "new" immigrant groups revealed several important features. First, at the beginning of the period of massive immigration from southern and eastern Europe, blacks living in northern cities were less spatially segregated than the new European groups that were beginning to arrive. Second, the residential segregation of blacks increased during the twentieth century, a process that correspondingly cut them off from participation in most of the activities of the larger community. The position of blacks in northern cities deteriorated from the turn of the twentieth century onward. Moreover, the patterns of residential segregation of blacks and southern European immigrant groups moved in opposite directions: at the same time that the rates of spatial assimilation for blacks were declining, rates were increasing for southern and eastern European immigrants. Thus the deterioration of blacks' position in northern urban areas occurred at precisely the time that the position of immigrant whites was beginning to improve.

As was noted in Part II, the massive migration of blacks out of the South to the North and from rural areas to the nation's cities has been one of the most important demographic shifts in American history. Today, blacks are much more likely to live in metropolitan areas than are whites. Moreover, the percentage of metropolitan blacks who reside in central cities is more than double that of whites, creating the urban racial polarization that is one of the basic racial demographic facts of American life today (Pettigrew, 1979:122).

These patterns of residential segregation are not comparable to the immigrant neighborhoods or enclaves into which "new" immigrant groups congregated around the turn of the century. First, although they were spatially isolated, at no time were immigrant neighborhoods as homogeneous or the spatial isolation as pronounced as in black neighborhoods today. In other words, the spatial isolation of white ethnics was never so extreme as it has been for black Americans for the last half-century. From their examination of the experience of blacks and ethnic groups in Philadelphia, Hershberg et al. ("A Tale Of Three Cities") report:

> The typical Irish immigrant in 1880 and the typical Italian immigrant in 1930... shared a similar aspect of their residential experience. When the hypothetical immigrant in each era walked through his neighborhood, what kind of people might he have met? The Irishman in 1880 lived with 15 percent other Irish immigrants, 34 percent Irish stock, 26 percent all foreign born persons and 58 percent all foreign stock. The typical Italian immigrant in 1930 had an almost identical experience. He lived with 14 percent other Italian immigrants, 38 percent Italian stock, 23 percent all foreign born persons and 57 percent all foreign stock. In striking contrast, the typical black in 1970 lived in a census tract in which 74 percent of the population was black.

Second, as noted above, patterns of ethnic segregation were not enduring but began to break down relatively quickly, whereas the characteristic feature of racial residential segregation since 1940 has been its persistence (Sorensen, Taeuber, and Hollingsworth, 1975; Taeuber, 1983).

One prominent measure that sociologists have developed to determine the extent of residential segregation or spatial isolation is the *index of dissimilarity*. With this measure a score of 100 represents complete racial segregation, in which every city block is 100 percent black and 0 percent white or vice versa; conversely, a score of zero represents a housing pattern in which members of different racial and ethnic groups are distributed in a completely random fashion and each city block has the same percentage of blacks and whites as are found in the city's overall population. The following table shows the means for indices of residential segregation between whites and nonwhites from 1940 to 1980 for the twenty-eight cities that had a black population of more than 100,000 in 1980.

Mean indices of residential segregation

1980	1970	1960	1950	1940
81	87	88	89	87

(Adapted from Taeuber, 1983, and Sorensen, Taeuber, and Hollingsworth, 1975.)

These data demonstrate the very highly segregated residential pattern that has come to characterize American cities during the modern industrial period. Already highly segregated by 1940, the patterns of racial isolation remained relatively stationary during the 1950s and 1960s. In 1970 the average segregation index for the twenty-eight American cities with black populations of more than 100,000 was 87. By 1980 the index had declined by a mere six percentage points to 81, and in some major cities (e.g., Chicago and Cleveland), the index remained above 90 (Taeuber, 1983). Despite the fact that the decline in the '70s was greater than in the preceding three decades, by 1980 the general pattern of spatial isolation for blacks was still more pronounced than for any other racial or ethnic group in American history. Moreover, the modest declines in residential segregation that did occur were so small as to make a substantial increase in spatial assimilation for blacks unlikely in the near future.

One source of this racial polarization has been the increasing suburbanization of American society, especially of the white population, including the white ethnic groups that formerly resided in central cities. The process of suburbanization has involved not only residences, but also schools, churches, synagogues, commercial enterprises, and industry. The suburban movement of business and industry, the effect of which has been to further isolate inner-city residents from access to job opportunities, has been especially important in this regard. In his article, "The Black Community in the 1980s" (Part IV), Wilson points out that during the 1970s, Chicago lost more than 200,000 manufacturing jobs; New York lost 600,000. (Wilson, 1981:39).

A variety of discriminatory mechanisms that we subsumed under the category of attitudinal discrimination in Part I—for example, informal agreements and social pressures, restrictive covenants, neighborhood protection associations, and block-busting practices that serve to exclude racial minorities—have contributed to this pattern of residential segregation. But even if these practices had not been employed, federal government policies would have ensured that the suburban population would be overwhelmingly white and that blacks would be relegated primarily to the inner cities. Most important was the decision by the federal government to permit private enterprise to meet the great demand for housing that had developed during the Depression and World War II. As a result, suburban housing was built almost exclusively for those who could afford to pay, while people unable to meet financing requirements were forced to accept housing vacated by those moving to the suburbs. On the other hand, low-cost, government subsidized housing, which attracted primarily black clientele, was constructed mostly in center cities rather than in the suburbs (Grier and Grier, 1965).

In "A Tale of Three Cities," (Part II) Hershberg et al. note the crucial importance of residential proximity to jobs in American history. For many whites, occupational opportunities have been the primary factor in determining where to live. Blacks, on the other hand, have been circumscribed by racial exclusion. In the nineteenth century, when they resided in close proximity to occupational opportunities, blacks were arbitrarily excluded from jobs. Today, when employment discrimination has declined, they are excluded because their physical distance precludes access to many employment opportunities. Pettigrew assesses the implications of the continuing spatial isolation of black Americans as follows:

> This massive metropolitan pattern of housing segregation has now become the principal barrier to progress in other realms. Indeed, the residential segregation of blacks and whites has emerged as a functional equivalent for the explicit state segregation laws of the past in that it effectively acts to limit the life chances and choices of black people generally (Pettigrew, 1979:124).

Today, despite federal fair-housing legislation, a Supreme Court decision that declared housing discrimination illegal, generally more favorable racial attitudes by whites toward blacks, and a substantial growth in the black middle class, residential segregation still persists on a massive scale in the United States.

But is the residential segregation of blacks a result of racial discrimination or is it a reflection of the generally lower overall class position of blacks? Taeuber and Taeuber have shown that the residential segregation of blacks is not primarily a result of black income levels, which, they maintain, can account for only a small portion of residential segregation. High-income whites and blacks do not live in the same neighborhoods, nor do low-income whites and blacks (Taeuber and Taeuber, 1965). Nevertheless, if, as Wilson argues, class factors have increasingly come to affect the life chances of American racial and ethnic minorities—not merely blacks, but Hispanics and Native Americans, as well—then one should anticipate that these other minorities should experience comparable forms of residential segregation.

However, critics dispute the arguments that the effects of structural economic changes are equally devastating to other contemporary racial and ethnic minorities such as Hispanics and Native Americans. Rather, they argue, because race remains an important determinant of opportunity in American life, other minorities, even those from comparable class locations, have been and will be able to experience social mobility in American society more easily than blacks.

As for the extent to which the pattern and effects of residential segregation of Hispanics (in this case primarily Chicanos) and blacks were comparable, Massey and Mullan ("Processes of Hispanic and Black Spatial Assimilation") found that there were substantial differences in the changing residential patterns of the two groups: "A barrio-centered residential pattern simply does not typify the experience of Hispanics in the same way that a ghetto-centered pattern typifies that of blacks." Blacks who move into previously white neighborhoods find that their presence leads to white flight, but Hispanics do not experience a comparable flight of Anglos as a consequence of their entrance into a neighborhood.

Residential succession (an exodus of current residents) is likely to follow the entry of Hispanics into an Anglo area when the incoming Hispanics are poorly educated and foreign, with low occupational statuses and incomes, and when the tract is near an established black or Hispanic area. In contrast, residential succession follows black entry into an Anglo area no matter what the objective social characteristics of the incoming blacks....Because the Anglo response to Hispanic invasion is not universally one of avoidance and flight, Hispanics are much better able than blacks to translate social into residential mobility.

[Moreover,] the social status required of blacks before they are not threatening to Anglos appears to be significantly higher than that required of Hispanics. In other words, a black lawyer or doctor may be able to move into a mixed neighborhood with other professionals, but a black plumber or bricklayer cannot buy into a working-class Anglo neighborhood. What is required for black spatial assimilation is a quantum leap in social status.

Massey and Mullan conclude that "Anglos avoid blacks on the basis of race, not class," whereas the converse is more likely to be true for Hispanics.

Unlike Wilson, who contends that economic class factors will in the future effect similar life chances for blacks and Hispanics, Massey and Mullen contend that because blacks are unable to translate economic mobility into spatial assimilation in the same manner as Hispanics, "the discrepant patterns of black and Hispanic spatial assimilation portend very different futures for these groups." Because residential integration has strong effects on other patterns of social interaction, such as friendships, marriage, and schooling, the prospects are that blacks are likely to remain "socially and spatially isolated within U.S. society." They therefore dispute the notion that Hispanics can be seen as an underclass in the same way as blacks: "Unlike blacks, [Hispanics] are able to translate social mobility into residential mobility. Hispanics are simply not trapped in the barrio in the same way that blacks are trapped in the ghetto" (870). Therefore, "It is only possible to make the case that race is becoming less salient as a dimension of stratification if one ignores the fact that blacks are segregated by virtue of race, not class."

Marital Assimilation

Gordon maintains that once structural assimilation has occurred, other dimensions of assimilation—most importantly, intermarriage, or what he terms *marital assimilation*— will follow. Marital assimilation, he claims, represents the final outcome of the assimilation process, in which "the minority group (ultimately) loses its ethnic identity in the larger host or core society" (Gordon, 1964:80).

The extent to which marital assimilation has occurred among different ethnic groups has been the subject of considerable research. One of the most celebrated interpretations of intermarriage patterns among white Americans was the "triple melting pot" thesis, which saw intermarriage increasing across ethnic lines but occurring within the three religious communities of Protestants, Catholics, and Jews (Kennedy, 1944, 1954). Although this interpretation was integral to Herberg's discussion (1955) of generational patterns of ethnic identity, discussed above, subsequent analyses have raised a considerable number of questions concerning its validity (Thomas, 1951; Peach, 1980a, 1980b; Hirschman, 1983). Alba's analysis of ethnic marriage patterns ("The Twilight of Ethnicity Among American Catholics,"

Part IV) reveals increasing rates of religious intermarriage, which in turn "point to a decline in the salience of religious boundaries for a good part of the Catholic group." This general inference concerning the waning significance of religious boundaries could also be extended to Protestants, with whom Catholics most frequently intermarry, as well. In other words, religious affiliation is becoming decreasingly significant as a factor influencing mate selection.

Recent analyses suggest that white ethnic groups generally have demonstrated substantial marital assimilation, especially among third and fourth generations and those from higher occupational categories. In national studies of assimilation among American Catholics, Alba (1976 and "The Twilight of Ethnicity") and Alba and Kessler (1979) found that as early as 1963 marriage outside one's ethnic group was extensive. Rates of intermarriage were most pronounced among the third generation and among the youngest adult members of each ethnic group. Similarly, in a study of ethnic consciousness in Providence, Rhode Island, Goering found that among the Irish and Italians only 15 percent of the first generation had married outside their own ethnic group, whereas 63 percent of the third generation had done so (Goering, 1971:382n).

Further evidence of the trend toward greater social and marital assimilation is shown in the rates of intermarriage for American Jews and Japanese. The rate of Jewish intermarriage with non-Jews increased from approximately 3 percent between 1900 and 1940 to nearly one-third (32 percent) between 1966 and 1972 (Massarick, n.d.:10). Since 1976 these rates of Jewish intermarriage have continued to rise (Mayer, 1983: viii). This trend has raised concerns among many Jews that the future of the American Jewish community may be threatened (Mayer and Sheingold, 1979).

Even more dramatic is the increasing rate of marital assimilation among Asians. Tinker (1973) found that more than half the marriages of Japanese were to non-Japanese. Montero (1981), basing his analysis on 1970 census data, found that, except for Native Americans, the rates of intermarriage among Asians was higher than among any other racial group. The following table presents the intermarriage rates by sex among different racial and ethnic categories.

Rates of Intermarriage, by Sex, 1970

	Women	Men
Native Americans	39.0	35.8
Japanese	33.2	11.4
Filipinos	27.2	33.5
Puerto Ricans	18.2	19.4
Mexicans	16.7	16.1
Chinese	12.2	13.5
Blacks	0.7	1.5
Whites	0.3	0.4

(Adapted from Montero, 1981:834)

These data demonstrate that, despite the general trend toward intermarriage among most ethnic categories in American society described above, the marital assimilation of blacks remains very low.

Explanations of Variations in Rates of Ethnic and Racial Assimilation

The social-scientific analysis of race and ethnicity in American life has frequently served as a reflection of social and political controversies within the broader society. As we noted in the introduction to Part I, the research agenda in the field of racial and ethnic relations—issues that have been considered and questions that have been posed—frequently has been drawn from social policy concerns, not from sociological theory alone.

One of the most striking changes in the research agenda in the field of racial and ethnic relations over the past decade has been a shift to a broadly comparative perspective. For some scholars this has led to a crosscultural perspective and has involved examination of the dynamics of race and ethnicity throughout the world (e.g., Burgess, 1978; DeVos and Romanucci-Ross, 1975; Franics, 1976; Glazer and Moynihan, 1975; Gordon, 1978; Henry, 1976; Hecter, 1975; Rose, 1976).

However, the black protest activity of the 1950s and 1960s, which sought to eliminate the chasm historically separating black America from the mainstream of American society, contributed substantially to a resurgence of interest in ethnicity that focused on other ethnic groups as well. Since the late 1970s research dealing with ethnicity in American society has proliferated (e.g., Dinnerstein and Reimers, 1975, 1983; Greeley, 1976; Kinton, 1977; Lieberson, 1980; Mindel and Habenstein, 1976; Patterson, 1978; Seller, 1977; Sowell, 1978, 1980, 1981; Steinberg, 1981). This shift from a focus almost exclusively on black-white relations to an examination of the role of ethnicity in American life was stimulated in part by the conflicts that emerged from blacks' claims for equal participation and opportunity. As Steinberg recently pointed out, "That the ethnic resurgence involved more than nostalgia became clear as racial minorities and white ethnics became polarized on a series of issues relating to schools, housing, local government and control over federal programs" (Steinberg, 1981:50).

The resentments fueled by these conflicts with blacks were reflected in the question frequently posed by white ethnics: "If we made it, why can't they?" If Greeley's characterization of the "ethnic miracle" is correct, if Jews, Poles, Italians, and the Irish today have made it in American society, how have they been able to do so while other groups have not? How do we account for the "extraordinary success story" of Catholics and Jews, who had to overcome poverty, discrimination, illiteracy, and chronic overcrowding in America's urban ghettos?

Arguments over explanations for differences in socioeconomic status—levels of income, educational attainment, and occupational prestige—among American ethnic groups that formerly were debated informally and privately in bull sessions, dinner parties, and cocktail parties have increasingly become the focus of formal inquiry by social scientists, whose interpretations have become part of the public discourse. During the past decade, especially, there have been numerous comparative studies of American ethnic groups: advancing explanations for the differences in achievement levels among American ethnic groups has become a major preoccupation of specialists in the field.

Several explanations for the differences among American ethnic groups have been advanced. Although there are considerable differences among them, they can be divided into two broad categories: those that emphasize qualities and characteristics internal to an ethnic group, and those that emphasize the influence of factors external to an ethnic group, or forces over which members of the group have no control.

Internal Explanations

An internal model conceives an ethnic group's adaptation, adjustment, achievement, or assimilation to be the result primarily of the traits, qualities, or characteristics that the group brings with it—the group's own personality, if you will. The emphasis in this argument is on the inheritance of behavioral traits and characteristics and on continuity of these traits across generations. In other words, proponents believe that groups possess certain identifiable characteristics that are transmitted and perpetuated from generation to generation.

The most simplistic of the internal explanations is a biological or genetic argument; that is, that differences in achievement levels among American ethnic groups reflect different *biological* endowments, and that ethnic groups are endowed with innately different mental, emotional, and moral characteristics, which are *biologically* transmitted from generation to generation.

For instance, during the last decade of the nineteenth century and the first two decades of the twentieth, differences between the political, social, and economic institutions of Anglo-Saxon and non–Anglo-Saxon peoples were "scientifically" attributed to biologically transmitted and relatively immutable "racial" traits. Thus Senator Henry Cabot Lodge, in an 1896 Senate speech condemning continued unrestricted immigration by peoples from southern and eastern Europe, argued that the Anglo-Saxon capacity for democracy was instinctual:

> The men of each race possess an indestructible stock of ideas, traditions, sentiments, modes of thought, an unconscious inheritance from their ancestors, upon which argument has no effect. What makes a race are their mental and, above all, their moral characteristics, the slow growth and accumulation of centuries of toil and conflict. These are the qualities which determine the social efficiency as a people, which makes one race rise and another fall (Lodge, 1896:2819).

Lodge, and most other intellectuals of the day, believed that the "old" immigrants from northern and western Europe (the British, Germans, and Scandinavians) were descended from common ancestors who were "historically free, energetic, and progressive," whereas Slavic, Latin, and Asiatic races were "historically downtrodden, atavistic, and stagnant" (Solomon, 1956:111).

Given these assumptions, which were legitimated as scientifically valid, unrestricted immigration meant the introduction of millions of unassimilable people who lacked the superior instincts of those of northern and western European stock. The absence of these instincts, Lodge believed, would ultimately bring about the "decline of human civilization."

The conceptions of race entertained by Lodge, which were, in one form or another, shared by virtually all American social scientists at the turn of the twentieth century, are radically different from prevailing scientific notions today. Genetic arguments enjoy little legitimacy among contemporary social scientists. The important difference resides in the understanding of the process by which behavioral traits and characteristics are transmitted. Traits that once were considered to be innate and biologically inherited are today conceived to be learned—a product not of the genes but of socialization. Culture, rather than biology, is considered the primary determinant of the traits and characteristics of ethnic groups.

The most prominent contemporary internal explanation attributes an ethnic group's position in a society's stratification system to its *cultural* characteristics: the values, attitudes, beliefs, store of knowledge, customs, and habits learned in the family and the community. That is, some groups possess cultural traits that are quite congruent with the values that make for success in American society—such as high achievement motivation, industriousness, perseverance, future orientation, ability to postpone immediate gratification for later rewards, and so forth. Possession of such values enables groups that have internalized them to succeed, while those lacking them are doomed to failure. Those who have succeeded have done so because of the traits that their cultural tradition bequeathed them, while a group's low socioeconomic status can be attributed to the fact that their cultural inventory did not include the requisite values, attitudes, and personal qualities. An underlying assumption of a cultural interpretation, therefore, is that "American society provides ample opportunity for class mobility and it is [the minority's] cultural institutions—'home and family and community'—that are problematic" (Steinberg, 1981:119). Whether an ethnic group succeeds or fails, it is perceived as being responsible for its own fate. By implication, those who have been less successful than others can ensure their entrance into the mainstream of American society by becoming more fully culturally assimilated; by adopting the cultural values of the dominant group.

Hershberg et al. identified two variants of the cultural argument: the "bootstraps" and "last of the immigrants" explanations. The *bootstraps* explanation for the socioeconomic success of white ethnics and Asians is that they were able to overcome the disabilities with which they were confronted because through hard work, industry, perseverance, self-reliance, and thrift, they exploited as fully as possible the economic opportunity that America afforded. They pulled themselves up by their own bootstraps, without governmental assistance. Thus Greeley contends that when "new" immigrants began their struggle for upward mobility in the first two decades of the twentieth century,

> There were no quotas, no affirmative action, no elaborate system of social services, and heaven knows, no ethnic militancy. There was no talk of reparation, no sense of guilt, no feelings of compassion for these immigrants. . . . Hard work, saving, sacrifice—such is a tentative explanation of the "ethnic miracle."

The other, sometimes complementary, explanation is the *last-of-the-immigrants* argument. According to this argument, ethnic socioeconomic success is only a matter of time and those ethnic groups who have most recently migrated to the nation's cities (Chicanos, Puerto Ricans, American Indians, and, in particular, black Americans) must not be impatient with their present position at the bottom of the economic ladder. In several generations they will inevitably repeat the experience of European ethnic groups and climb into the American economic, educational, and political mainstream. Thomas Sowell, for example, contends that today's patterns of white flight from the central cities to the haven of suburbia are merely repeating the process of ethnic succession that has long been a characteristic feature of America's ethnically diverse cities; ethnic groups who arrive first move when their territory is invaded by a new and "inferior" ethnic group (Sowell, 1981:277–278).

As noted above, in his article, "The Ethnic Miracle," Andrew Greeley subscribes to a cultural explanation in his analysis of the post–World War II socioeconomic achievements of Catholic and Jewish Americans. He contends that these achievements were the consequence of "something in the culture of the immigrants themselves." However, the cultural argument has been nowhere more clearly and effectively articulated than by Thomas Sowell, an economist who has written widely concerning American ethnic groups (Sowell, 1978, 1980, 1981). Sowell's general explanation for the wide variation in the rates of socioeconomic status and achievement among American ethnic groups is that the different values and skills that groups have manifested as part of their cultural inheritance have been crucial in explaining differential rates of achievement. Among the most important of the cultural traits contributing to success is a positive attitude toward "learning and self-improvement," which varied dramatically among different ethnic groups such as Italians and Jews.

The traditional Jewish emphasis on education has often been cited as an explanation for their extremely high levels of achievement. Strodtbeck (1958), for example, argued that Jewish goals, values, and cultural norms were more compatible with the dominant values of American society than was the case for other ethnic groups. In particular, the value of education, learning, and scholarly inquiry was long expressed in the intellectual tradition of orthodox Jewish culture. Jewish immigrants placed a very high prestige on education and educational attainments: the scholar was venerated and accorded respect. As Abraham Cahan wrote in his classic novel of Jewish immigrant life, *The Rise of David Levinsky*, "The ghetto rang with a clamor for knowledge. . . . To save up some money and prepare for college seemed to be the most natural thing to do" (Cahan, 1966:156). By contrast, most Catholic "new" immigrants came from peasant backgrounds where formal education and learning were alien and remote. Southern Italian immigrants, who in many respects were typical of Catholic "new" immigrants, came from a society in which formal education clashed with traditional values. For them, education and learning were regarded as a threat to the integrity and strength of the family. Unlike Jews, Italian parents saw little value in education and did not encourage their children toward educational attainments (Strodtbeck, 1958; Vecoli, 1964).

Chiswick's article, "Immigrants in the U.S. Labor Market" (Part IV), tends to support a cultural or what economists call a *human capital* argument. In a number of studies (Chiswick, 1978, 1979, 1980) Chiswick examined the achievement levels of immigrants compared to nonimmigrants. He found that the economic status of immigrants rose more rapidly than native-born residents. By the time male immigrants have been in the United States for eleven to fifteen years their earnings equal those of the native-born, while the earnings of those in the country for twenty years exceed native-born income levels. Moreover, these trends occur within ethnic catagories. For example, Philippine-born immigrants' earnings ultimately exceed those of Filipino-Americans. These findings suggest that immigration is a selective process, and those possessing certain kinds of personal characteristics—an "immigrant personality"—are most likely to immigrate. Either those who emigrate are more daring and resourceful than nonemigrants to begin with, or the process of emigration itself elicits the traits of initiative, perseverance, tenacity, foresight, and a capacity for hard work.

External Explanations

In contrast to a cultural explanation of ethnic group achievement and assimilation, an *external* or *structural* explanation emphasizes the external constraints, disabilities, limitations, and barriers to which a group is subjected and which serve as obstacles to ethnic-group achievement. Some groups (for example, blacks) have been confronted with substantial barriers that have circumscribed the resources available to them and precluded their full and equal participation in society. As we noted above, there is a range of possible dominant-group policies which, to a greater or lesser degree, serve to limit the options available to a minority group. These can range from policies of extermination to discrimination in many different forms.

A cultural explanation tends to minimize or dismiss the role of external factors, especially in contemporary American society. Sowell, for example, contends that the intergroup animosities and discrimination that existed in American society in the past have lessened in intensity and "in some respects disappeared" (Sowell, 1981:7). Such a perspective presupposes that social structure is blind to group differences and does not play a significant role in affecting patterns of ethnic-group achievement. Put another way, it assumes that the social structure is neutral when it comes to racial and ethnic factors, and that individuals from all ethnic backgrounds have relatively equal opportunities to succeed.

Moreover, a cultural intepretation assumes that external barriers are relatively insignificant in affecting group outcomes since the opportunities of all American ethnic groups have at one time or another been circumscribed in some way. All American ethnic groups, Sowell writes, "have been discriminated against to one degree or another. Yet some of the most successful—such as the Orientals—have experienced worse discrimination than most, and the extraordinary success of Jews has been achieved in the face of centuries of anti-Semitism" (Sowell, 1981:6).

Finally, a cultural model assumes that the distinctive traits and capacities that characterize a group will manifest themselves in spite of harsh and restrictive treatment by other groups. Thus Sowell argues that the characteristics of "working harder and more relentlessly" will overcome even the most pronounced adversity (Sowell, 1981:283).

Each of these assumptions has been vigorously challenged by critics who contend that the structural barriers confronting Chicanos, Puerto Ricans, American Indians, and, in particular, black Americans, have been more severe and repressive than those encountered by "new" immigrants or even by Asians.

The most apparent difference between blacks and "new" immigrants has been the disability of race, which has subjected blacks, in both the South and the North, to discrimination far more severe than experienced by any European ethnic groups. For example, Lieberson's analysis (1980) demonstrates that prejudice and discrimination against blacks in Northern cities intensified rather than diminished during the first few decades of the twentieth century. At the same time that spatial isolation declined for "new" immigrants it increased markedly for blacks. Moreover, the discrimination that blacks encountered in education and employment was never so consistently a feature of the experience of "new" immigrant groups. These findings are reinforced by Hershberg's analysis of Philadelphia, which shows that historically the occupational opportunity structure for blacks has never been as open as that for white immigrants and that, because of increased residential segregation, blacks have been excluded from recent occupational opportunities.

However, the experience of Asians, in particular the Japanese and the Chinese, frequently is cited to support the claim that being nonwhite is not an insurmountable barrier to achievement in American society. In other words, Asian success casts considerable doubt on the notion that nonwhite racial status is inherently a liability to achievement. Indeed, Asians are frequently cited as "model minorities" because they have been able to succeed despite extremely virulent forms of discrimination. They have been able to do so, Sowell writes, because of their cultural traits of "effort, thrift, dependability and foresight, [which] built businesses out of 'menial tasks' and turned sweat into capital" (Sowell, 1981:7).

However, Asians were not forced to endure slavery in this country, nor the extremely derogatory prejudices that endured on a pervasive scale after the elimination of slavery. Moreover, unlike black Americans, the number of Asians in the United States was never so large as to represent a real threat to the existing white population. Even in California, the state in which most Asians have been concentrated, the highest-ever proportion of Japanese in the state's population was 2.1 percent, and the Chinese proportion was even smaller (Peterson, 1971:30). When these extremely small numbers appeared to increase slightly, the perceived threat they represented was reduced by changes in American immigration laws that effectively limited Asian population to an extremely tiny proportion of the total (Lieberson, 1980:368). Moreover, Nee and Wong (1984:20) suggest that the number of blacks who migrated to the West during and after World War II exceeded the small Asian population. Their increased presence, and the greater prejudice toward them on the part of white Americans, lessened the impact of anti-Asian discrimination and thus facilitated Asian-American socioeconomic mobility.

In "Minority Education and Caste," Ogbu contends that there have been qualitative differences between the experiences of the Chinese and Japanese in the United States and the experiences of what he characterizes as *caste minorities*: blacks, Chicanos, Puerto Ricans, and Native Americans. Because Asians have not been subjected to the systematic economic subordination of caste minorities, their academic performance has not been comparably impaired (Ogbu, 1978:21–25).

Ogbu rejects a cultural interpretation of the minority status of blacks and other American minorities. Most cultural explanations, he argues,

> explicitly or implicitly assume that the socioeconomic inequality between blacks and whites is caused, at least in part, by differences in the school performance and educational attainment of the two races [and] that this inequality would largely disappear if only blacks would perform like whites in school (Ogbu, 1978:43–44).

From Ogbu's perspective, however, black inequality has not been caused so much by poor academic performance as poor academic performance is the product of black perceptions that academic achievement will not be rewarded, because of the discriminatory job ceiling that blacks historically have encountered. In other words, Ogbu argues that the absence of high educational aspirations, high achievement motivation, and a future orientation on the part of some minority-group members is a response to external circumstances, to their not-unrealistic perception that their opportunities in the work world have been extremely restricted. Lower school performance is merely a symptom of the broader and more central societal problem of caste. Minority educational achievement will be improved only when there is a dramatic societal commitment to end discrimination in jobs and housing, and more fully to include American minorities in the decision-making process in institutions throughout the whole of American society. "The only lasting solution to the problem of academic retardation," he writes, "is the elimination of caste barriers" (Ogbu, 1978:357).

From a structural perspective, therefore, it is the opportunity structure, not minority values, that accounts for the different socioeconomic positions occupied by different ethnic groups. It is the opportunity structure, not minority values, that must first be changed in order to reduce the inequalities in American society.

The structure of opportunity may be limited by what we have termed attitudinal discrimination, which is motivated by prejudices against racial or ethnic minorities. For example, as noted above, although there is considerable evidence of a decline in attitudinal discrimination in employment, it still remains a potent force perpetuating patterns of residential segregation in America. However, a structural model also focuses on the objective economic circumstances that confront the so-called caste minorities today, and compares them with those that ethnic groups, in particular "new" immigrants, encountered in the past.

William J. Wilson has been among the foremost critics of a cultural perspective. As noted in Part II, in "The Declining Significance of Race," Wilson contends that American race relations can be divided into three periods or stages, each of which reflects changes in blacks' relation to the country's changing economic structure. Wilson acknowledges that in many areas of American life, such as housing, education, and municipal politics, attitudinal discrimination is still pervasive and serves as a barrier to black participation in the mainstream. However, he contends that in the economic sphere, institutional, not attitudinal, discrimination has become the primary source of continuing black inequalities. In the economic life of black Americans, "class has become more important than race in determining black access to privilege and power."

Wilson's thesis is based on the contention that during the modern industrial era black economic status has been influenced by substantial structural economic changes "such as the shift from goods-producing to service-producing industries, the increasing segmentation of the labor market, the growing use of industrial technology, and the relocation of industries out of the central city" that, in themselves, have little to do with race (Wilson, 1981:38). The opportunity structure that blacks today confront in America's urban centers is much different from that faced by "new" immigrants. During the early decades of the twentieth century unskilled labor was in great demand and millions of southern and eastern European immigrants flocked to this country to fill these jobs. However, as a result of changes in the economy, there is no longer a demand for unskilled jobs. Therefore, as Hershberg points out, to adopt a last-of-the-immigrants argument and hold that blacks are merely the most recent arrivals to America's urban industrial areas who will inevitably improve their status is to ignore significant variations in these two vastly different types of urban economies.

As a result of these changes in the economic structure, the structure of the black community has been altered. On the one hand, the black underclass, which lacks education and remains basically unskilled, is becoming increasingly restricted to jobs that are low-paying, nonunion, unskilled, and undesirable. This segment of black society is beset with high rates of unemployment and welfare dependency. On the other hand, "educated blacks are experiencing unprecedented job opportunities in the growing government and corporate sectors, opportunities that are at least comparable to those of whites with equivalent qualifications." This has come about as a result of the expansion of salaried, white-collar positions and pressures resulting from changes in the role of government. Before the modern industrial era, the state merely reinforced patterns of race relations established in the economic sector. Recently, in response to the civil rights movement, the government stands in formal opposition to discriminatory barriers. Indeed, with the enactment of affirmative action programs in the 1960s, government undertook the initiative in combatting discrimination. Thus, the basic economic problems confronting caste minorities in modern America, according to Wilson, are those of institutional discrimination, of the problems created by the existence of a substantial underclass who lack the requisite education and skills for participation in a rapidly changing and technologically sophisticated economy.

As Wilson's analysis demonstrates, a structural interpretation emphasizes the significance of *social-structural* and *class* factors in determining life chances. An ethnic group's initial class position, which involves its control, or lack of control, over economic, political, and educational resources, is considered to be a crucial variable in accounting for its subsequent levels of achievement.

The traditional cultural explanation for the rapid mobility of Jewish immigrants (as contrasted to Catholic "new" immigrants) stressed the high value placed on education, learning, and achievement in the subcultures of immigrants. Steinberg rejects the interpretation that Jewish values are the explanation for their success. Instead, he focuses on the impact of the different social-class backgrounds of entering immigrants. In "Education and Ethnic Mobility" he points out that although Jewish and Catholic "new" immigrants entered the United States with about the same meager amounts of money, their occupational backgrounds were not identical. Immigrant Jews came overwhelmingly from towns and cities of eastern Europe where they had had extensive experience with manufacturing and commerce. More than two-thirds of Jewish immigrants were skilled workers, professionals, or merchants, as opposed to only one-sixth of southern Italians and one-sixteenth of Polish immigrants. More than two-thirds of Italian and three-fourths of Polish immigrants were unskilled laborers or farmers, in contrast to about one-seventh of entering Jews. The skills the Jews brought with them to the United States were needed by an expanding American economy and enabled them to enter at a higher status level than most unskilled immigrants. These occupational backgrounds and experiences of immigrant Jews enabled their children—the second generation—to relatively easily acquire the middle-class skills that were a prerequisite for entrance into the professions, in particular academic pursuits.

Jewish and Catholic "new" immigrants differed on another important characteristic: literacy. About one-fourth of all Jews entering the United States between 1899 and 1910 were unable to read and write, whereas more than half (54 percent) of southern Italians and one-third (35 percent) of Poles were illiterate. Similarly, because many Italians and Poles immigrated to the United States as temporary workers and did not intend to settle permanently in this country, they were much less likely to learn to speak English than were Jews, most of whom were fleeing religious persecution in eastern Europe and did not intend to return there. This stronger commitment to settlement in the United States increased the process of cultural assimilation for Jews. Italians and Poles, whose frames of reference remained in the old country, were much more likely to resist assimilation to American culture, a factor that greatly limited the occupational mobility of the second generation.

Steinberg shows how these background factors affected the occupational mobility of Jews and Catholics within the academic profession. Because academics tend to be drawn from professional, managerial, and small-business backgrounds, individuals whose parents had such characteristics were favored in their access to academic pursuits. Hence, the social class characteristics of Jewish and Catholic "new" immigrants were important influences on their patterns of occupational mobility. Jews did not simply value education and revere learning. As Steinberg points out,

> They were also literate as a group and had cognitive skills to pass on to their children. Conversely, Catholics did not simply place low value on education and occupational mobility but were handicapped by factors related to their peasant origins.

The implication of Steinberg's analysis is that the social-class characteristics of American ethnic groups have played a crucial role in influencing the socio-economic status of their descendants. Such structural dimensions must therefore be an integral part of any explanation for the differential rates of assimilation of American ethnic groups.

14

Assimilation in America: Theory and Reality

Milton M. Gordon

Three ideologies or conceptual models have competed for attention on the American scene as explanations of the way in which a nation, in the beginning largely white, Anglo-Saxon, and Protestant, has absorbed over 41 million immigrants and their descendants from variegated sources and welded them into the contemporary American people. These ideologies are Anglo-conformity, the melting pot, and cultural pluralism. They have served at various times, and often simultaneously, as explanations of what has happened—descriptive models—and of what should happen—goal models. Not infrequently they have been used in such a fashion that it is difficult to tell which of these two usages the writer has had in mind. In fact, one of the more remarkable omissions in the history of American intellectual thought is the relative lack of close analytical attention given to the theory of immigrant adjustment in the United States by its social scientists.

The result has been that this field of discussion—an overridingly important one since it has significant implications for the more familiar problems of prejudice, discrimination, and majority-minority group relations generally—has been largely preempted by laymen, representatives of belles lettres, philosophers, and apologists of various persuasions. Even from these sources the amount of attention devoted to ideologies of assimilation is hardly extensive. Consequently, the work of improving intergroup relations in America is carried out by dedicated professional agencies and individuals who deal as best they can with day-to-day problems of discriminatory behavior, but who for the most part are unable to relate their efforts to an adequate conceptual apparatus. Such an apparatus would, at one and the same time, accurately describe the present structure of American society with respect to its ethnic groups (I shall use the term "ethnic group" to refer to any racial, religious, or national-origins collectivity), and allow for a considered formulation of its assimilation or integration goals for the foreseeable future. One is reminded of Alice's distraught question in her travels in Wonderland. "Would you tell me, please, which way I ought to go from here?" "That depends a good deal," replied the Cat with irrefutable logic, "on where you want to get to."

The story of America's immigration can be quickly told for our present purposes. The white American population at the time of the Revolution was largely English and Protestant in origin, but had already absorbed substantial groups of Ger-

Reprinted by permission from *Daedalus*, Journal of the American Academy of Arts and Sciences, Boston, Massachusetts, Volume 90, Number 2 (Spring 1961), pp. 263–285.

Author's Note: The materials of this article are based on a larger study of the meaning and implications of minority group assimilation in the United States, which I carried out for the Russell Sage Foundation and which was published in *Assimilation in American Life* (New York, 1964).

mans and Scotch-Irish and smaller contingents of Frenchmen, Dutchmen, Swedes, Swiss, South Irish, Poles, and a handful of migrants from other European nations. Catholics were represented in modest numbers, particularly in the middle colonies, and a small number of Jews were residents of the incipient nation. With the exception of the Quakers and few missionaries, the colonists had generally treated the Indians and their cultures with contempt and hostility, driving them from the coastal plains and making the western frontier a bloody battleground where eternal vigilance was the price of survival.

Although the Negro at that time made up nearly one-fifth of the total population, his predominantly slave status, together with racial and cultural prejudice, barred him from serious consideration as an assimilable element of the society. And while many groups of European origin started out as determined ethnic enclaves, eventually, most historians believe, considerable ethnic intermixture within the white population took place. "People of different blood" [sic]—write two American historians about the colonial period, "English, Irish, German, Huguenot, Dutch, Swedish—mingled and intermarried with little thought of any difference."[1] In such a society, its people predominantly English, its white immigrants of other ethnic origins either English-speaking or derived largely from countries of northern and western Europe whose cultural divergences from the English were not great, and its dominant white population excluding by fiat the claims and considerations of welfare of the non-Caucasian minorities, the problem of assimilation understandably did not loom unduly large or complex.

The unfolding events of the next century and a half with increasing momentum dispelled the complacency which rested upon the relative simplicity of colonial and immediate post-Revolutionary conditions. The large-scale immigration to America of the famine-fleeing Irish, the Germans, and later the Scandinavians (along with additional Englishmen and other peoples of northern and western Europe) in the middle of the nineteenth century (the so-called "old immigration"), the emancipation of the Negro slaves and the problems created by post–Civil War reconstruction, the placing of the conquered Indian with his broken culture on government reserva-

tions, the arrival of the Oriental, first attracted by the discovery of gold and other opportunities in the West, and finally, beginning in the last quarter of the nineteenth century and continuing to the early 1920's, the swelling to proportions hitherto unimagined of the tide of immigration from the peasantries and "pales" of southern and eastern Europe—the Italians, Jews, and Slavs of the so-called "new immigration," fleeing the persecutions and industrial dislocations of the day—all these events constitute the background against which we may consider the rise of the theories of assimilation mentioned above. After a necessarily foreshortened description of each of these theories and their historical emergence, we shall suggest analytical distinctions designed to aid in clarifying the nature of the assimilation process, and then conclude by focusing on the American scene.

Anglo-Conformity

"Anglo-conformity"[2] is a broad term used to cover a variety of viewpoints about assimilation and immigration; they all assume the desirability of maintaining English institutions (as modified by the American Revolution), the English language, and English-oriented cultural patterns as dominant and standard in American life. However, bound up with this assumption are related attitudes. These may range from discredited notions about race and "Nordic" and "Aryan" racial superiority, together with the nativist political programs and exclusionist immigration policies which such notions entail, through an intermediate position of favoring immigration from northern and western Europe on amorphous, unreflective grounds ("They are more like us"), to a lack of opposition to any source of immigration, as long as these immigrants and their descendants duly adopt the standard Anglo-Saxon cultural patterns. There is by no means any necessary equation between Anglo-conformity and racist attitudes.

It is quite likely that "Anglo-conformity" in its more moderate aspects, however explicit its formulation, has been the most prevalent ideology of assimilation goals in America throughout the nation's history. As far back as colonial times, Benjamin Franklin recorded concern about the clannishness of the Germans in Pennsylvania, their slowness in learning English, and the establishment of their own native-language press.[3]

Others of the founding fathers had similar reservations about large-scale immigration from Europe. In the context of their times they were unable to foresee the role such immigration was to play in creating the later greatness of the nation. They were not all men of unthinking prejudices. The disestablishment of religion and the separation of church and state (so that no religious group—whether New England Congregationalists, Virginian Anglicans, or even all Protestants combined—could call upon the federal government for special favors or support, and so that man's religious conscience should be free) were cardinal points of the new national policy they fostered. "The Government of the United States," George Washington had written to the Jewish congregation of Newport during his first term as president, "gives to bigotry no sanction, to persecution no assistance."

Political differences with ancestral England had just been written in blood; but there is no reason to suppose that these men looked upon their fledgling country as an impartial melting pot for the merging of the various cultures of Europe, or as a new "nation of nations," or as anything but a society in which, with important political modifications, Anglo-Saxon speech and institutional forms would be standard. Indeed, their newly won victory for democracy and republicanism made them especially anxious that these still precarious fruits of revolution should not be threatened by a large influx of European peoples whose life experiences had accustomed them to the bonds of despotic monarchy. Thus, although they explicitly conceived of the new United States of America as a haven for those unfortunates of Europe who were persecuted and oppressed, they had characteristic reservations about the effects of too free a policy. "My opinion, with respect to immigration," Washington wrote to John Adams in 1794, "is that except of useful mechanics and some particular descriptions of men or professions, there is no need of encouragement, while the policy or advantage of its taking place in a body (I mean the settling of them in a body) may be much questioned; for, by so doing, they retain the language, habits and principles (good or bad) which they bring with them."[4] Thomas Jefferson, whose views on race and attitudes towards slavery were notably liberal and advanced for his time, had similar

doubts concerning the effects of mass immigration on American institutions, while conceding that immigrants, "if they come of themselves...are entitled to all the rights of citizenship."[5]

The attitudes of Americans toward foreign immigration in the first three-quarters of the nineteenth century may correctly be described as ambiguous. On the one hand, immigrants were much desired, so as to swell the population and importance of states and territories, to man the farms of expanding prairie settlement, to work the mines, build the railroads and canals, and take their place in expanding industry. This was a period in which no federal legislation of any consequence prevented the entry of aliens, and such state legislation as existed attempted to bar on an individual basis only those who were likely to become a burden on the community, such as convicts and paupers. On the other hand, the arrival in an overwhelmingly Protestant society of large numbers of poverty-stricken Irish Catholics, who settled in groups in the slums of Eastern cities, roused dormant fears of "Popery" and Rome. Another source of anxiety was the substantial influx of Germans, who made their way to the cities and farms of the mid-West and whose different language, separate communal life, and freer ideas on temperance and sabbath observance brought them into conflict with the Anglo-Saxon bearers of the Puritan and Evangelical traditions. Fear of foreign "radicals" and suspicion of the economic demands of the occasionally aroused workingmen added fuel to the nativist fires. In their extreme form these fears resulted in the Native-American movement of the 1830's and 1840's and the "American" or "Know-Nothing" party of the 1850's, with their anti-Catholic campaigns and their demands for restrictive laws on naturalization procedures and for keeping the foreign-born out of political office. While these movements scored local political successes and their turbulences so rent the national social fabric that the patches are not yet entirely invisible, they failed to influence national legislative policy on immigration and immigrants; and their fulminations inevitably provoked the expected reactions from thoughtful observers.

The flood of newcomers to the westward expanding nation grew larger, reaching over one and two-thirds million between 1841 and 1850 and over two and one-half million in the decade before the Civil War. Throughout the entire period, quite apart from the excesses of the Know-Nothings, the predominant (though not exclusive) conception of what the ideal immigrant adjustment should be was probably summed up in a letter written in 1818 by John Quincy Adams, then Secretary of State, in answer to the inquiries of the Baron von Fürstenwaerther. If not the earliest, it is certainly the most elegant version of the sentiment, "If they don't like it here, they can go back where they came from." Adams declared:[6]

> They [immigrants to America] come to a life of independence, but to a life of labor—and, if they cannot accommodate themselves to the character, moral, political and physical, of this country with all its compensating balances of good and evil, the Atlantic is always open to them to return to the land of their nativity and their fathers. To one thing they must make up their minds, or they will be disappointed in every expectation of happiness as Americans. They must cast off the European skin, never to resume it. They must look forward to their posterity rather than backward to their ancestors; they must be sure that whatever their own feelings may be, those of their children will cling to the prejudices of this country.

The events that followed the Civil War created their own ambiguities in attitude toward the immigrant. A nation undergoing wholesale industrial expansion and not yet finished with the march of westward settlement could make good use of the never faltering waves of newcomers. But sporadic bursts of labor unrest, attributed to foreign radicals, the growth of Catholic institutions and the rise of Catholics to municipal political power, and the continuing association of immigrant settlement with urban slums revived familiar fears. The first federal selective law restricting immigration was passed in 1882, and Chinese immigration was cut off in the same year. The most significant development of all, barely recognized at first, was the change in the source of European migrants. Beginning in the 1880's, the countries of southern and eastern Europe began to be represented in substantial numbers for the first time, and in the next decade immigrants from these sources became numerically dominant.

Now the notes of a new, or at least hitherto unemphasized, chord from the nativist lyre began to sound—the ugly chord, or discord, of racism. Previously vague and romantic notions of Anglo-Saxon peoplehood, combined with general ethnocentrism, rudimentary wisps of genetics, selected tidbits of evolutionary theory, and naive assumptions from an early and crude imported anthropology produced the doctrine that the English, Germans, and others of the "old immigration" constituted a superior race of tall, blonde, blue-eyed "Nordics" or "Aryans," whereas the peoples of eastern and southern Europe made up the darker Alpines or Mediterraneans—both "inferior" breeds whose presence in America threatened, either by intermixture or supplementation, the traditional American stock and culture. The obvious corollary to this doctrine was to exclude the allegedly inferior breeds; but if the new type of immigrant could not be excluded, then everything must be done to instill Anglo-Saxon virtues in these benighted creatures. Thus, one educator writing in 1909 could state:[7]

> These southern and eastern Europeans are of a very different type from the north Europeans who preceeded them. Illiterate, docile, lacking in self-reliance and initiative, and not possessing the Anglo-Teutonic conceptions of law, order, and government, their coming has served to dilute tremendously our national stock, and to corrupt our civic life....Everywhere these people tend to settle in groups or settlements, and to set up here their national manners, customs, and observances. Our task is to break up these groups or settlements, to assimilate and amalgamate these people as a part of our American race, and to implant in their children, so far as can be done, the Anglo-Saxon conception of righteousness, law and order, and popular government, and to awaken in them a reverence for our democratic institutions and for those things in our national life which we as a people hold to be of abiding worth.

Anglo-conformity received its fullest expression in the so-called Americanization movement which gripped the nation during World War I. While "Americanization" in its various stages had more than one emphasis, it was essentially a consciously articulated movement to strip the immigrant of his native culture and attachments and make him over into an American along Anglo-Saxon lines—all this to be accomplished with great rapidity. To use an image of a later day, it was an attempt at "pressure-cooking assimilation." It had prewar antecedents, but it was during the height of the world conflict that federal agencies, state governments, municipalities, and a host of private organizations joined in the effort to persuade the immigrant to learn English, take out naturalization papers, buy war bonds, forget his former origins and culture, and give himself over to patriotic hysteria.

After the war and the "Red scare" which followed, the excesses of the Americanization movement subsided. In its place, however, came the restriction of immigration through federal law. Foiled at first by presidential vetoes, and later by the failure of the 1917 literacy test to halt the immigrant tide, the proponents of restriction finally put through in the early 1920's a series of acts culminating in the well-known national-origins formula for immigrant quotas which went into effect in 1929. Whatever the merits of a quantitative limit on the number of immigrants to be admitted to the United States, the provisions of the formula, which discriminated sharply against the countries of southern and eastern Europe, in effect institutionalized the assumptions of the rightful dominance of Anglo-Saxon patterns in the land. Reaffirmed with only slight modifications in the McCarran-Walter Act of 1952, these laws, then, stand as a legal monument to the creed of Anglo-conformity and a telling reminder that this ideological system still has numerous and powerful adherents on the American scene.

The Melting Pot

While Anglo-conformity in various guises has probably been the most prevalent ideology of assimilation in the American historical experience, a competing viewpoint with more generous and idealistic overtones has had its adherents and exponents from the eighteenth century onward. Conditions in the virgin continent, it was clear, were modifying the institutions which the English colonists brought with them from the mother country. Arrivals from non-English homelands such as Germany, Sweden, and France were simi-

larly exposed to this fresh environment. Was it not possible, then, to think of the evolving American society not as a slightly modified England but rather as a totally new blend, culturally and biologically, in which the stocks and folkways of Europe, figuratively speaking, were indiscriminately mixed in the political pot of the emerging nation and fused by the fires of American influence and interaction into a distinctly new type?

Such, at any rate, was the conception of the new society which motivated that eighteenth-century French-born writer and agriculturalist, J. Hector St. John Crèvecoeur, who, after many years of American residence, published his reflections and observations in *Letters from an American Farmer*.[8] Who, he asks, is the American?

> He is either an European, or the descendant of an European, hence that strange mixture of blood, which you will find in no other country. I could point out to you a family whose grandfather was an Englishman, whose wife was Dutch, whose son married a French woman, and whose present four sons have now four wives of different nations. *He* is an American, who leaving behind him all his ancient prejudices and manners, receives new ones from the new mode of life he has embraced, the new government he obeys, and the new rank he holds. He becomes an American by being received in the broad lap of our great *Alma Mater*. Here individuals of all nations are melted into a new race of men, whose labours and posterity will one day cause great changes in the world.

Some observers have interpreted the open-door policy on immigration of the first three quarters of the nineteenth century as reflecting an underlying faith in the effectiveness of the American melting pot, in the belief "that all could be absorbed and that all could contribute to an emerging national character."[9] No doubt many who observed with dismay the nativist agitation of the times felt as did Ralph Waldo Emerson that such conformity-demanding and immigrant-hating forces represented a perversion of the best American ideals. In 1845, Emerson wrote in his Journal:[10]

> I hate the narrowness of the Native American Party. It is the dog in the manger. It is precisely

opposite to all the dictates of love and magnanimity; and therefore, of course, opposite to true wisdom....Man is the most composite of all creatures....Well, as in the old burning of the Temple at Corinth, by the melting and intermixture of silver and gold and other metals a new compound more precious than any, called Corinthian brass, was formed: so in this continent,—asylum of all nations,—the energy of Irish, Germans, Swedes, Poles, and Cossacks, and all the European tribes,—of the Africans, and the Polynesians,—will construct a new race, a new religion, a new state, a new literature, which will be as vigorous as the new Europe which came out of the smelting-pot of the Dark Ages, or that which earlier emerged from the Pelasgic and Etruscan barbarism. *La Nature aime les croisements.*

Eventually, the melting-pot hypothesis found its way into historical scholarship and interpretation. While many American historians of the late nineteenth century, some fresh from graduate study at German universities, tended to adopt the view that American institutions derived in essence from Anglo-Saxon (and ultimately Teutonic) sources, others were not so sure.[11] One of these was Frederick Jackson Turner, a young historian from Wisconsin, not long emerged from his graduate training at Johns Hopkins. Turner presented a paper to the American Historical Association meeting in Chicago in 1893. Called "The Significance of the Frontier in American History," this paper proved to be one of the most influential essays in the history of American scholarship, and its point of view, supported by Turner's subsequent writings and his teaching, pervaded the field of American historical interpretation for at least a generation. Turner's thesis was that the dominant influence in the shaping of American institutions and American democracy was not this nation's European heritage in any of its forms, nor the forces emanating from the eastern seaboard cities, but rather the experiences created by a moving and variegated western frontier. Among the many effects attributed to the frontier environment and the challenges it presented was that it acted as a solvent for the national heritages and the separatist tendencies of the many nationality groups which had joined the trek westward, including the Germans and Scotch-Irish of the eighteenth century

and the Scandinavians and Germans of the nineteenth. "The frontier," asserted Turner, "promoted the formation of a composite nationality for the American people....In the crucible of the frontier the immigrants were Americanized, liberated, and fused into a mixed race, English in neither nationality nor characteristics. The process has gone on from the early days to our own." And later, in an essay on the role of the Mississippi Valley, he refers to "the tide of foreign immigration which has risen so steadily that it has made a composite American people whose amalgamation is destined to produce a new national stock."[12]

Thus far, the proponents of the melting pot idea had dealt largely with the diversity produced by the sizeable immigration from the countries of northern and western Europe alone—the "old immigration," consisting of peoples with cultures and physical appearance not greatly different from those of the Anglo-Saxon stock. Emerson, it is true, had impartially included Africans, Polynesians, and Cossacks in his conception of the mixture; but it was only in the last two decades of the nineteenth century that a large-scale influx of peoples from the countries of southern and eastern Europe imperatively posed the question of whether these uprooted newcomers who were crowding into the large cities of the nation and industrial sector of the economy could also be successfully "melted." Would the "urban melting pot" work as well as the "frontier melting pot" of an essentially rural society was alleged to have done?

It remained for an English-Jewish writer with strong social convictions, moved by his observation of the role of the United States as a haven for the poor and oppressed of Europe, to give utterance to the broader view of the American melting pot in a way which attracted public attention. In 1908, Israel Zangwill's drama, *The Melting Pot*, was produced in this country and became a popular success. It is a play dominated by the dream of its protagonist, a young Russian-Jewish immigrant to America, a composer, whose goal is the completion of a vast "American" symphony which will express his deeply felt conception of his adopted country as a divinely appointed crucible in which all the ethnic division of mankind will divest themselves of their ancient animosities and differences and become fused into one group, signifying the brotherhood of man. In the process he falls in love with a beautiful and cultured Gentile girl. The play ends with the performance of the symphony and, after numerous vicissitudes and traditional family opposition from both sides, with the approaching marriage of David Quixano and his beloved. During the course of these developments, David, in the rhetoric of the time, delivers himself of such sentiments as these:[13]

> America is God's crucible, the great Melting Pot where all the races of Europe are melting and reforming! Here you stand, good folk, think I, when I see them at Ellis Island, here you stand in your fifty groups, with your fifty languages and histories, and your fifty blood hatreds and rivalries. But you won't be long like that, brother, for these are the fires of God you've come to—these are the fires of God. A fig for your feuds and vendettas! Germans and Frenchmen, Irishmen and Englishmen, Jews and Russians—into the Crucible with you all! God is making the American.

Here we have a conception of a melting pot which admits of no exceptions or qualifications with regard to the ethnic stocks which will fuse in the great crucible. Englishmen, Germans, Frenchmen, Slavs, Greeks, Syrians, Jews, Gentiles, even the black and yellow races, were specifically mentioned in Zangwill's rhapsodic enumeration. And this pot patently was to boil in the great cities of America.

Thus around the turn of the century the melting-pot idea became embedded in the ideals of the age as one response to the immigrant receiving experience of the nation. Soon to be challenged by a new philosophy of group adjustment (to be discussed below) and always competing with the more pervasive adherence to Anglo-conformity, the melting-pot image, however, continued to draw a portion of the attention consciously directed toward this aspect of the American scene in the first half of the twentieth century. In the mid-1940's a sociologist who had carried out an investigation of intermarriage trends in New Haven, Connecticut, described a revised conception of the melting process in that city and suggested a basic modification of the theory of that process. In New Haven, Ruby Jo Reeves Kennedy[14] reported from a study of intermarriages from 1870 to 1940 that there was a distinct tendency for the British-Americans, Germans, and Scandinavians to marry among themselves—that is, within a Protestant "pool"; for the Irish, Italians, and Poles to marry among themselves—a Catholic "pool"; and for the Jews to marry other Jews. In other words, intermarriage was taking place across lines of nationality background, but there was a strong tendency for it to stay confined within one or the other of the three major religious groups, Protestants, Catholics, and Jews. Thus, declared Mrs. Kennedy, the picture in New Haven resembled a "triple melting pot" based on religious division, rather than a "single melting pot." Her study indicated, she stated, that "while strict endogamy is loosening, religious endogamy is persisting and the future cleavages will be along religious lines rather than along nationality lines as in the past. If this is the case, then the traditional 'single-melting-pot' idea must be abandoned, and a new conception, which we term the 'triple-melting-pot' theory of American assimilation, will take its place as the true expression of what is happening to the various nationality groups in the United States."[15] The triple melting-pot thesis was later taken up by the theologian, Will Herberg, and formed an important sociological frame of reference for his anaylsis of religious trends in American society, *Protestant-Catholic-Jew.*[16] But the triple melting-pot hypothesis patently takes us into the realm of a society pluralistically conceived. We turn now to the rise of an ideology which attempts to justify such a conception.

Cultural Pluralism

Probably all the non-English immigrants who came to American shores in any significant numbers from colonial times onward—settling either in the forbidding wilderness, the lonely prairie, or in some accessible urban slum—created ethnic enclaves and looked forward to the preservation of at least some of their native cultural patterns. Such a development, natural as breathing, was supported by the later accretion of friends, relatives, and countrymen seeking out oases of familiarity in a strange land, by the desire of the settlers to rebuild (necessarily in miniature) a society in which they could communicate in the familiar tongue and maintain familiar institutions, and, finally, by the necessity to band together for mutual aid and mutual protection against the uncertainties of a strange and frequently hostile environment. This was as true of the "old" immigrants as of the "new." In fact, some of the liberal intellectuals who fled to America from an inhospitable political climate in Germany in the 1830's, 1840's, and 1850's looked forward to the creation of an all-German state within the union, or, even more hopefully, to the eventual formation of a separate German nation, as soon as the expected dissolution of the union under the impact of the slavery controversy should have taken place.[17] Oscar Handlin, writing of the sons of Erin in mid-nineteenth-century Boston, recent refugees from famine and economic degradation in their homeland, points out: "Unable to participate in the normal associational affairs of the community, the Irish felt obliged to erect a society within a society, to act together in their own way. In every contact therefore the group, acting apart from other sections of the community, became intensely aware of its peculiar and exclusive identity."[18] Thus cultural pluralism was a fact in American society before it became a theory—a theory with explicit relevance for the nation as a whole, and articulated and discussed in the English-speaking circles of American intellectual life.

Eventually, the cultural enclaves of the Germans (and the later arriving Scandinavians) were to decline in scope and significance as succeeding generations of their native-born attended public schools, left the farms and villages to strike out as individuals for the Americanizing city, and generally became subject to the influences of a standardizing industrial civilization. The German-American community, too, was struck a powerful blow by the accumulated passions generated by World War I—a blow from which it never fully recovered. The Irish were to be the dominant and pervasive element in the gradual emergence of a pan-Catholic group in America, but these developments would reveal themselves only in the twentieth century. In the meantime, in the last two decades of the nineteenth, the influx of immigrants from southern and eastern Europe had

begun. These groups were all the more sociologically visible because the closing of the frontier, the occupational demands of an expanding industrial economy, and their own poverty made it inevitable that they would remain in the urban areas of the nation. In the swirling fires of controversy and the steadier flame of experience created by these new events, the ideology of cultural pluralism as a philosophy for the nation was forged.

The first manifestations of an ideological counterattack against draconic Americanization came not from the beleaguered newcomers (who were, after all, more concerned with survival than with theories of adjustment), but from those idealistic members of the middle class who, in the decade or so before the turn of the century, had followed the example of their English predecesors and "settled" in the slums to "learn to sup sorrow with the poor."[19] Immediately, these workers in the "settlement houses" were forced to come to grips with the realities of immigrant life and adjustment. Not all reacted in the same way, but on the whole the settlements developed an approach to the immigrant which was sympathethic to his native cultural heritage and to his newly created ethnic institutions.[20] For one thing, their workers, necessarily in intimate contact with the lives of these often pathetic and bewildered newcomers and their daily problems, could see how unfortunate were the effects of those forces which impelled rapid Americanization in their impact on the immigrants' children, who not infrequently became alienated from their parents and the restraining influence of family authority. Were not their parents ignorant and uneducated "Hunkies," "Sheenies," or "Dagoes," as that limited portion of the American environment in which they moved defined the matter? Ethnic "self-hatred" with its debilitating psychological consequences, family disorganization, and juvenile delinquency, were not unusual results of this state of affairs. Furthermore, the immigrants themselves were adversely affected by the incessant attacks on their culture, their language, their institutions, their very conception of themselves. How were they to maintain their self-respect when all that they knew, felt, and dreamed, beyond their sheer capacity for manual labor—in other words, all that they *were*—was despised or scoffed at in America? And—unkindest cut of all—their own children had begun to adopt the contemptuous attitude of the "Americans." Jane Addams relates in a moving chapter of her *Twenty Years at Hull House* how, after coming to have some conception of the extent and depth of these problems, she created at the settlement a "Labor Museum," in which the immigrant women of the various nationalities crowded together in the slums of Chicago could illustrate their native methods of spinning and weaving, and in which the relation of these earlier techniques to contemporary factory methods could be graphically shown. For the first time these peasant women were made to feel by some part of their American environment that they possessed valuable and interesting skills—that they too had something to offer—and for the first time, the daughters of these women who, after a long day's work at their dank "needletrade" sweatshops, came to Hull House to observe, began to appreciate the fact that their mothers, too, had a "culture," that this culture possessed its own merit, and that it was related to their own contemporary lives. How aptly Jane Addams concludes her chapter with the hope that "our American citizenship might be built without disturbing these foundations which were laid of old time."[21]

This appreciative view of the immigrant's cultural heritage and of its distinctive usefulness both to himself and his adopted country received additional sustenance from another source: those intellectual currents of the day which, however overborne by their currently more powerful opposites, emphasized liberalism, internationalism, and tolerance. From time to time an occasional educator or publicist protested the demands of the "Americanizers," arguing that the immigrant, too, had an ancient and honorable culture, and that this culture had much to offer an America whose character and destiny were still in the process of formation, an America which must serve as an example of the harmonious cooperation of various heritages to a world inflamed by nationalism and war. In 1916 John Dewey, Norman Hapgood, and the young literary critic, Randolph Bourne, published articles or addresses elaborating various aspects of this theme.

The classic statement of the cultural pluralist position, however, had been made over a year

before. Early in 1915 there appeared in the pages of *The Nation* two articles under the title "Democracy *versus* the Melting-Pot." Their author was Horace Kallen, a Harvard-educated philosopher with a concern for the application of philosophy to societal affairs, and, as an American Jew, himself derivative of an ethnic background which was subject to the contemporary pressures for dissolution implicit in the "Americanization," or Anglo-conformity, and the melting-pot theories. In these articles Kallen vigorously rejected the usefulness of these theories as models of what was actually transpiring in American life or as ideals for the future. Rather he was impressed by the way in which the various ethnic groups in America were coincident with particular areas and regions, and with the tendency for each group to preserve its own language, religion, communal institutions, and ancestral culture. All the while, he pointed out, the immigrant has been learning to speak English as the language of general communication, and has participated in the over-all economic and political life of the nation. These developments in which "the United States are in the process of becoming a federal state not merely as a union of geographical and administrative unities, but also as a cooperation of cultural diversities, as a federation or commonwealth of national cultures,"[22] the author argued, far from constituting a violation of historic American political principles, as the "Americanizers" claimed, actually represented the inevitable consequences of democratic ideals, since individuals are implicated in groups, and since democracy for the individual must by extension also mean democracy for his group.

The processes just described, however, as Kallen develops his argument, are far from having been thoroughly realized. They are menaced by "Americanization" programs, assumptions of Anglo-Saxon superiority, and misguided attempts to promote "racial" amalgamation. Thus America stands at a kind of cultural crossroads. It can attempt to impose by force an artificial, Anglo-Saxon oriented uniformity on its peoples, or it can consciously allow and encourage its ethnic groups to develop democratically, each emphasizing its particular cultural heritage. If the latter course is followed, as Kallen puts it at the close of his essay, then,[23]

The outlines of a possible great and truly democratic commonwealth become discernible. Its form would be that of the federal republic: its substance a democracy of nationalities, cooperating voluntarily and autonomously through common institutions in the enterprise of self-realization through the perfection of men according to their kind. The common language of the commonwealth, the language of its great tradition, would be English, but each nationality would have for its emotional and involuntary life its own peculiar dialect or speech, its own individual and inevitable esthetic and intellectual forms. The political and economic life of the commonwealth is a single unit and serves as the foundation and background for the realization of the distinctive individuality of each *nation* that composes it and of the pooling of these in a harmony above them all. Thus "American civilization" may come to mean the perfection of the cooperative harmonies of "European civilization"—the waste, the squalor and the distress of Europe being eliminated—a multiplicity in a unity, an orchestration of mankind.

Within the next decade Kallen published more essays dealing with the theme of American multiple-group life, later collected in a volume.[24] In the introductory note to this book he used for the first time the term "cultural pluralism" to refer to his position. These essays reflect both his increasingly sharp rejection of the onslaughts on the immigrant and his culture which the coming of World War I and its attendant fears, the "Red scare," the projection of themes of racial superiority, the continued exploitation of the newcomers, and the rise of the Ku Klux Klan all served to increase in intensity, and also his emphasis on cultural pluralism as the democratic antidote to these ills. He has since published other essays elaborating or annotating the theme of cultural pluralism. Thus, for at least forty-five years, most of them spent teaching at the New School for Social Research, Kallen has been acknowledged as the originator and leading philosophical exponent of the idea of cultural pluralism.

In the late 1930's and early 1940's the late Louis Adamic, the Yugoslav immigrant who had become an American writer, took up the theme of America's multicultural heritage and the role of these groups in forging the country's national character. Borrowing Walt Whitman's phrase, he described America as "a nation of nations," and while his ultimate goal was closer to the melting-pot idea than to cultural pluralism, he saw the immediate task as that of making America conscious of what it owed to all its ethnic groups, not just to the Anglo-Saxons. The children and grandchildren of immigrants of non-English origins, he was convinced, must be taught to be proud of the cultural heritage of their ancestral ethnic group and of its role in building the American nation; otherwise, they would not lose their sense of ethnic inferiority and the feeling of rootlessness he claimed to find in them.

Thus in the twentieth century, particularly since World War II, "cultural pluralism" has become a concept which has worked its way into the vocabulary and imagery of specialists in intergroup relations and leaders of ethnic communal groups. In view of this new pluralistic emphasis, some writers now prefer to speak of the "integration" of immigrants rather than of their "assimilation."[25] However, with a few exceptions,[26] no close analytical attention has been given either by social scientists or practitioners of intergroup relations to the meaning of cultural pluralism, its nature and relevance for a modern industrialized society, and its implications for problems of prejudice and discrimination—a point to which we referred at the outset of this discussion.

Conclusions

In the remaining pages I can make only a few analytical comments which I shall apply in context to the American scene, historical and current. My view of the American situation will not be documented here, but may be considered as a series of hypotheses in which I shall attempt to outline the American assimilation process.

First of all, it must be realized that "assimilation" is a blanket term which in reality covers a multitude of subprocesses. The most crucial distinction is one often ignored—the distinction between what I have elsewhere called "behavioral assimilation" and "structural assimilation."[27] The first refers to the absorption of the cultural behavior patterns of the "host" society. (At the same time, there is frequently some modification of the cultural patterns of the immigrant-receiving country, as well.) There is a special term for this process of cultural modification or "behaviorial assimilation—namely, "acculturation." "Structural assimilation," on the other hand, refers to the entrance of the immigrants and their descendants into the social cliques, organizations, institutional activities, and general civic life of the receiving society. If this process takes place on a large enough scale, then a high frequency of intermarriage must result. A further distinction must be made between, on the one hand, those activities of the general civic life which involve earning a living, carrying out political responsibilities, and engaging in the instrumental affairs of the larger community, and, on the other hand, activities which create personal friendship patterns, frequent home intervisiting, communal worship, and communal recreation. The first type usually develops so-called "secondary relationships," which tend to be relatively impersonal and segmental; the latter type leads to "primary relationships," which are warm, intimate, and personal.

With these various distinctions in mind, we may then proceed.

Built on the base of the original immigrant "colony" but frequently extending into the life of successive generations, the characteristic ethnic group experience is this: within the ethnic group there develops a network of organizations and informal social relationships which permits and encourages the members of the ethnic group to remain within the confines of the group for all of their primary relationships and some of their secondary relationships throughout all the stages of the life cycle. From the cradle in the sectarian hospital to the child's play group, the social clique in high school, the fraternity and religious center in college, the dating group within which he searches for a spouse, the marriage partner, the neighborhood of his residence, the church affiliation and the church clubs, the men's and the women's social and service organizations, the adult clique of "marrieds," the vacation resort, and then, as the age cycle nears completion, the rest home for the elderly and, finally, the sectarian cemetery—in all these activities and relationships which are close to the core of personality and selfhood—the member of the ethnic group may if he wishes follow a path which never takes him across the boundaries of his ethnic structural network.

The picture is made more complex by the existence of social class divisions which cut across ethnic group lines just as they do those of the white Protestant population in America. As each ethnic group which has been here for the requisite time has developed second, third, or in some cases, succeeding generations, it has produced a college-educated group which composes an upper middle class (and sometimes upper class, as well) segment of the larger groups. Such class divisions tend to restrict primary group relations even further, for although the ethnic-group member feels a general sense of identification with all the bearers of his ethnic heritage, he feels comfortable in intimate social relations only with those who also share his own class background or attainment.

In short, my point is that, while *behavioral assimilation* or acculturation has taken place in America to a considerable degree, *structural assimilation*, with some important exceptions has not been extensive.[28] The exceptions are of two types. The first brings us back to the "triple-melting-pot" thesis of Ruby Jo Reeves Kennedy and Will Herberg. The "nationality" ethnic groups have tended to merge within each of the three major religious groups. This has been particularly true of the Protestant and Jewish communities. Those descendants of the "old" immigration of the nineteenth century, who were Protestant (many of the Germans and all the Scandinavians), have in considerable part gradually merged into the white Protestant "subsociety." Jews of Sephardic, German, and Eastern-European origins have similarly tended to come together in their communal life. The process of absorbing the various Catholic nationalities, such as the Italians, Poles, and French Canadians, into an American Catholic community hitherto dominated by the Irish has begun, although I do not believe that it is by any means close to completion. Racial and quasi-racial groups such as the Negroes, Indians, Mexican-Americans, and Puerto Ricans still retain their separate sociological structures. The outcome of all this in contemporary American life is thus pluralism—but it is more than "triple" and it is more accurately described as *structural pluralism* than as cultural pluralism, although some of the latter also remains.

My second exception refers to the social structures which implicate intellectuals. There is no space to develop the issue here, but I would argue that there is a social world or subsociety of the intellectuals in America in which true structural intermixture among persons of various ethnic backgrounds, including the religious, has markedly taken place.

My final point deals with the reasons for these developments. If structural assimilation has been retarded in America by religious and racial lines, we must ask why. The answer lies in the attitudes of both the majority and the minority groups and in the way these attitudes have interacted. A saying of the current day is, "It takes two to tango." To apply the analogy, there is no good reason to believe that white Protestant America has ever extended a firm and cordial invitation to its minorities to dance. Furthermore, the attitudes of the minority-group members themselves on the matter have been divided and ambiguous. Particularly for the minority religious groups, there is a certain logic in ethnic communality, since there is a commitment to the perpetuation of the religious ideology and since structural intermixture leads to intermarriage and the possible loss to the group of the intermarried family. Let us, then, examine the situation serially for various types of minorities.

With regard to the immigrant, in his characteristic numbers and socio-economic background, structural assimilation was out of the question. He did not want it, and he had a positive need for the comfort of his own communal institutions. The native American, moreover, whatever the implications of his public pronouncements, had no intention of opening up his primary group life to entrance by these hordes of alien newcomers. The situation was a functionally complementary standoff.

The second generation found a much more complex situation. Many believed they heard the siren call of welcome to the social cliques, clubs, and institutions of white Protestant America. After all, it was simply a matter of learning American ways, was it not? Had they not grown up as Americans, and were they not culturally different from their parents, the "greenhorns"? Or perhaps an especially eager one reasoned (like the Jewish protagonist of Myron Kaufmann's novel, *Remember Me To God*, aspiring to membership in the prestigious club system of Harvard

undergraduate social life) "If only I can go the last few steps in Ivy League manners and behavior, they will surely recognize that I am one of them and take me in." But, alas, Brooks Brothers suit notwithstanding, the doors of the fraternity house, the city men's club, and the country club were slammed in the face of the immigrant's offspring. That invitation was not really there in the first place; or, to the extent it was, in Joshua Fishman's phrase, it was a " 'look me over but don't touch me' invitation to the American minority group child."[29] And so the rebuffed one returned to the homelier but dependable comfort of the communal institutions of his ancestral group. There he found his fellows of the same generation who had never stirred from the home fires. Some of these had been too timid to stray; others were ethnic ideologists committed to the group's survival; still others had never really believed in the authenticity of the siren call or were simply too passive to do more than go along the familiar way. All could not join in the task that was well within the realm of the sociologically possible—the build-up of social institutions and organizations within the ethnic enclave, manned increasingly by members of the second generation and suitably separated by social class.

Those who had for a time ventured out gingerly or confidently, as the case might be, had been lured by the vision of an "American" social structure that was somehow larger than all subgroups and was ethnically neutral. Were they, too, not Americans? But they found to their dismay that at the primary group level a neutral American social structure was a mirage. What at a distance seemed to be a quasi-public edifice flying only the all-inclusive flag of American nationality turned out on closer inspection to be the clubhouse of a particular ethnic group—the white Anglo-Saxon Protestants, its operation shot through with the premises and expectations of its parental ethnicity. In these terms, the desirability of whatever invitation was grudgingly extended to those of other ethnic backgrounds could only become a considerably attenuated one.

With the racial minorities, there was not even the pretense of an invitation. Negroes, to take the most salient example, have for the most part been determinedly barred from the cliques, social clubs, and churches of white America. Consequently, with due allowance for internal class differences, they have constructed their own network of organizations and institutions, their own "social world." There are now many vested interests served by the preservation of this separate communal life, and doubtless many Negroes are psychologically comfortable in it, even though at the same time they keenly desire that discrimination in such areas as employment, education, housing, and public accommodations be eliminated. However, the ideological attachment of Negroes to their communal separation is not conspicuous. Their sense of identification with ancestral African national cultures is virtually nonexistent, although Pan-Africanism engages the interest of some intellectuals and although "black nationalist" and "black racist" fringe groups have recently made an appearance at the other end of the communal spectrum. As for their religion, they are either Protestant or Catholic (overwhelmingly the former). Thus, there are no "logical" ideological reasons for their separate communality; dual social structures are created solely by the dynamics of prejudice and discrimination, rather than being reinforced by the ideological commitments of the minority itself.

Structural assimilation, then, has turned out to be the rock on which the ships of Anglo-comformity and the melting pot have foundered. To understand that behavioral assimilation (or acculturation) without massive structural intermingling in primary relationships has been the dominant motif in the American experience of creating and developing a nation out of diverse peoples is to comprehend the most essential sociological fact of that experience. It is against the background of "structural pluralism" that strategies of strengthening intergroup harmony, reducing ethnic discrimination and prejudice, and maintaining the rights of both those who stay within and those who venture beyond their ethnic boundaries must be thoughtfully devised.

ENDNOTES

1. Allen Nevins and Henry Steele Commager, *America: The Story of a Free People* (Boston, Little, Brown, 1942), p. 58.

2. The phrase is the Coles'. See Stewart G. Cole and Mildred Wiese Cole, *Minorities and the American Promise* (New York, Harper & Brothers, 1954), ch. 6.

3. Maurice R. Davie, *World Immigration* (New York, Macmillan, 1936), p. 36, and (cited therein) "Letter of Benjamin Franklin to Peter Collinson, 9th May, 1753, on the condition and character of the Germans in Pennsylvania," in *The Works of Benjamin Franklin, with notes and life of the author*, by Jared Sparks (Boston, 1828), vol. 7, pp. 71–73.

4. *The Writings of George Washington*, collected by W. C. Ford (New York, G. P. Putnam's Sons, 1889), vol. 12, p. 489.

5. Thomas Jefferson, "Notes on Virginia, Query 8"; in *The Writings of Thomas Jefferson*, ed. A. E. Bergh (Washington, The Thomas Jefferson Memorial Association, 1907), vol. 2, p. 121.

6. *Niles Weekly Register*, vol. 18, 29 April 1820, pp. 157–158; see also, Marcus L. Hansen, *The Atlantic Migration, 1607-1860*, pp. 96–97.

7. Ellwood P. Cubberly, *Changing Conceptions of Education* (Boston, Houghton Mifflin, 1909), pp. 15–16.

8. J. Hector St. John Crèvecoeur, *Letters from an American Farmer* (New York, Albert and Charles Boni, 1925; reprinted from the 1st edn., London, 1782), pp. 54–55.

9. Oscar Handlin, ed., *Immigration as a Factor in American History* (Englewood, Prentice-Hall, 1959), p. 146.

10. Quoted by Stuart P. Sherman in his Introduction to *Essays and Poems of Emerson* (New York, Harcourt Brace, 1921), p. xxxiv.

11. See Edward N. Saveth, *American Historians and European Immigrants, 1875–1925*, New York, Columbia University Press, 1948.

12. Frederick Jackson Turner, *The Frontier in American History* (New York, Henry Holt, 1920), pp. 22–23, 190.

13. Israel Zangwill, *The Melting Pot* (New York, Macmillan, 1909), p. 37.

14. Ruby Jo Reeves Kennedy, "Single or Triple Melting-Pot? Intermarriage Trends in New Haven, 1870–1940," *American Journal of Sociology*, 1944, 49:331–339. See also her "Single or Triple Melting-Pot? Intermarriage in New Haven, 1870–1950," *ibid.*, 1952, 58:56–59.

15. Kennedy, "Single or Triple Melting-Pot?... 1870–1940," p. 332 (author's italics omitted).

16. Will Herberg, *Protestant-Catholic-Jew* (Garden City, Doubleday, 1955).

17. Nathan Glazer, "Ethnic Groups in America: From National Culture to Ideology," in Morroe Berger, Theodore Abel, and Charles H. Page, eds., *Freedom and Control in Modern Society* (New York, D. Van Nostrand, 1954), p. 161; Marcus Lee Hansen, *The Immigrant in American History* (Cambridge, Harvard

University Press, 1940), pp. 129–140; John A. Haw-good, *The Tragedy of German-America* (New York, Putnam's, 1940), *passim*.

18. Oscar Handlin, *Boston's Immigrants* (Cambridge, Harvard University Press, 1959, rev. edn.), p. 176.

19. From a letter (1883) by Samuel A. Barnett; quoted in Arthur C. Holden, *The Settlement Idea* (New York, Macmillan, 1922), p. 12.

20. Jane Addams, *Twenty Years at Hull House* (New York, Macmillan, 1914), pp. 231–258; Arthur C. Holden, *op. cit.*, pp. 109–131, 182–189, John Higham, *Strangers in the Land* (New Brunswick, Rutgers University Press, 1955), p. 236.

21. Jane Addams, *op. cit.*, p. 258.

22. Horace M. Kallen. "Democracy *versus* the Melting-Pot," *The Nation*, 18 and 25 February 1915; reprinted in his *Culture and Democracy in the United States*, New York, Boni and Liveright, 1924; the quotation is on p. 116.

23. Kallen, *Culture and Democracy...*, p. 124.

24. *Op. cit.*

25. See W. D. Borrie *et al.*, *The Cultural Integration of Immigrants* (a survey based on the papers and proceedings of the UNESCO Conference in Havana, April 1956), Paris, UNESCO, 1959; and William S. Bernard, "The Integration of Immigrants in the United States" (mimeographed), one of the papers for this conference.

26. See particularly Milton M. Gordon "Social Structure and Goals in Group Relations"; and Nathan Glazer, "Ethnic Groups in America; From National Culture to Ideology," both articles in Berger, Abel, and Page, *op. cit.*,; S. N. Eisenstadt, *The Absorption of Immigrants*, London, Routledge and Kegan Paul, 1954; and W. D. Borrie *et al.*, *op. cit.*

28. See Erich Rosenthal, "Acculturation without Assimilation?" *American Journal of Sociology*, 1960, 66:275–288.

29. Joshua A. Fishman, "Childhood Indoctrination for Minority-Group Membership and the Quest for Minority-Group Biculturism in America," in Oscar Handlin, ed., *Group Life in America* (Cambridge, Harvard University Press, forthcoming).

15

A Societal Theory of Race and Ethnic Relations

Stanley Lieberson

"In the relations of races there is a cycle of events which tends everywhere to repeat itself."[1] Park's assertion served as a prologue to the now classical cycle of competition, conflict, accommodation, and assimilation. A number of other attempts have been made to formulate phases or stages ensuing from the initial contacts between racial and ethnic groups.[2] However, the sharp contrasts between relatively harmonious race relations in Brazil and Hawaii and the current racial turmoil in South Africa and Indonesia serve to illustrate the difficulty in stating—to say nothing of interpreting—an inevitable "natural history" of race and ethnic relations.

Many earlier race and ethnic cycles were, in fact, narrowly confined to a rather specific set of groups or contact situations. Bogardus, for example, explicitly limited his synthesis to Mexican and Oriental immigrant groups on the west coast of the United States and suggested that this is but one of many different cycles of relations between immigrants and native Americans.[3] Similarly, the Australian anthropologist Price developed three phases that appear to account for the relationships between white English-speaking migrants and the aborigines of Australia, Maoris in New Zealand, and Indians of the United States and Canada.[4]

This paper seeks to present a rudimentary theory of the development of race and ethnic relations that systematically accounts for differences between societies in such divergent consequences of contact as racial nationalism and warfare, assimilation and fusion, and extinction. It postulates that the critical problem on a societal level in racial or ethnic contact is initially each population's maintenance and development of a social order compatible with its ways of life prior to contact. The crux of any cycle must, therefore, deal with political, social, and economic institutions. The emphasis given in earlier cycles to one group's dominance of another in these areas is therefore hardly surprising.[5]

Although we accept this institutional approach, the thesis presented here is that knowledge of the nature of one group's domination over another in the political, social, and economic spheres is a necessary but insufficient prerequisite for predicting or interpreting the final and intermediate stages of racial and ethnic contact. Rather, institutional factors are considered in terms of a distinction between two major types of contact situations: contacts involving subordination of an indigenous population by a migrant group, for example, Negro-white relations in South Africa; and contacts involving subordination of a migrant population by an indigenous racial or ethnic group, for example, Japanese migrants to the United States.

After considering the societal issues inherent

Reprinted from *American Sociological Review* 26 (December, 1961):902–910, by permission of the author and the publisher.

in racial and ethnic contact, the distinction developed between migrant and indigenous superordination will be utilized in examining each of the following dimensions of race relations: political and economic control, multiple ethnic contacts, conflict and assimilation. The terms "race" and "ethnic" are used interchangeably.

Differences Inherent in Contact

Most situations of ethnic contact involve at least one indigenous group and at least one group migrating to the area. The only exception at the initial point in contact would be the settlement of an uninhabited area by two or more groups. By "indigenous" is meant not necessarily the aborigines, but rather a population sufficiently established in an area so as to possess the institutions and demographic capacity for maintaining some minimal form of social order through generations. Thus a given spatial area may have different indigenous groups through time. For example, the indigenous population of Australia is presently largely white and primarily of British origin, although the Tasmanoids and Australoids were once in possession of the area.[6] A similar racial shift may be observed in the populations indigenous to the United States.

Restricting discussion to the simplest of contact situations, i.e., involving one migrant and one established population, we can generally observe sharp differences in their social organization at the time of contact. The indigenous population has an established and presumably stable organization prior to the arrival of migrants, i.e., government, economic activities adapted to the environment and the existing techniques of resource utilization, kinship, stratification, and religious systems.[7] On the basis of a long series of migration studies, we may be reasonably certain that the social order of a migrant population's homeland is not wholly transferred to their new settlement.[8] Migrants are required to make at least some institutional adaptations and innovations in view of the presence of an indigenous population, the demographic selectivity of migration, and differences in habitat.

For example, recent post-war migration from Italy and the Netherlands indicate considerable selectivity in age and sex from the total populations of these countries. Nearly half of 30,000 males leaving the Netherlands in 1955 were between 20 and 39 years of age whereas only one quarter of the male population was of these ages.[9] Similarly, over 40,000 males in this age range accounted for somewhat more than half of Italy's male emigrants in 1951, although they comprise roughly 30 per cent of the male population of Italy.[10] In both countries, male emigrants exceed females in absolute numbers as well as in comparison with the sex ratios of their nation. That these cases are far from extreme can be illustrated with Oriental migration data. In 1920, for example, there were 38,000 foreign born Chinese adult males in the United States, but only 2,000 females of the same group.[11]

In addition to these demographic shifts, the new physical and biological conditions of existence require the revision and creation of social institutions if the social order known in the old country is to be approximated and if the migrants are to survive. The migration of eastern and southern European peasants around the turn of the century to urban industrial centers of the United States provides a well-documented case of radical changes in occupational pursuits as well as the creation of a number of institutions in response to the new conditions of urban life, e.g., mutual aid societies, national churches, and financial institutions.

In short, when two populations begin to occupy the same habitat but do not share a single order, each group endeavors to maintain the political and economic conditions that are at least compatible with the institutions existing before contact. These conditions for the maintenances of institutions can not only differ for the two groups in contact, but are often conflicting. European contacts with the American Indian, for example, led to the decimation of the latter's sources of sustenance and disrupted religious and tribal forms of organization. With respect to a population's efforts to maintain its social institutions, we may therefore assume that the presence of another ethnic group is an important part of the environment. Further, if groups in contact differ in their capacity to impose changes on the other group, then we may expect to find one group "superordinate" and the other population "subordinate" in maintaining or developing a suitable environment.

It is here that efforts at a single cycle of race and ethnic relations must fail. For it is necessary to introduce a distinction in the nature or form of subordination before attempting to predict whether conflict or relatively harmonious assimilation will develop. As we shall shortly show, the race relations cycle in areas where the migrant group is superordinate and indigenous group subordinate differs sharply from the stage in societies composed of a superordinate indigenous group and subordinate migrants.[12]

Political and Economic Control

Emphasis is placed herein on economic and political dominance since it is assumed that control of these institutions will be instrumental in establishing a suitable milieu for at least the population's own social institutions, e.g., educational, religious, and kinship, as well as control of such major cultural artifacts as language.

Migrant Superordination

When the population migrating to a new contact situation is superior in technology (particularly weapons) and more tightly organized than the indigenous group, the necessary conditions for maintaining the migrants' political and economic institutions are usually imposed on the indigenous population. Warfare, under such circumstances, often occurs early in the contacts between the two groups as the migrants begin to interfere with the natives' established order. There is frequently conflict even if the initial contact was friendly. Price, for example, has observed the following consequences of white invasion and subordination of the indigenous populations of Australia, Canada, New Zealand, and the United States:

> During an opening period of pioneer invasion on moving frontiers the whites decimated the natives with their diseases; occupied their lands by seizure or by pseudo-purchase, slaughtered those who resisted; intensified tribal warfare by supplying white weapons; ridiculed and disrupted native religions, society and culture, generally reduced the unhappy peoples to a state of despondency

under which they neither desired to live, nor to have children to undergo similar conditions.[13]

The numerical decline of indigenous populations after their initial subordination to a migrant group, whether caused by warfare, introduction of venereal and other diseases, or disruption of sustenance activities, has been documented for a number of contact situations in addition to those discussed by Price.[14]

In addition to bringing about these demographic and economic upheavals, the superordinate migrants frequently create political entities that are not at all coterminous with boundaries existing during the indigenous populations' supremacy prior to contact. For example, the British and Boers in southern Africa carved out political states that included areas previously under the control of separate and often warring groups.[15] Indeed, European alliances with feuding tribes were often used as a fulcrum for the territorial expansion of whites into southern Africa.[16] The bifurcation of tribes into two nations and the migrations of groups across newly created national boundaries are both consequences of the somewhat arbitrary nature of the political entities created in regions of migrant superordination.[17] This incorporation of diverse indigenous populations into a single territorial unit under the dominance of a migrant group has considerable importance for later developments in this type of racial and ethnic contact.

Indigenous Superordination

When a population migrates to a subordinate position considerably less conflict occurs in the early stages. The movements of many European and Oriental populations to political, economic, and social subordination in the United States were not converted into warfare, nationalism, or long-term conflict. Clearly, the occasional labor and racial strife marking the history of immigration of the United States is not on the same level as the efforts to expel or revolutionize the social order. American Negroes, one of the most persistently subordinated migrant groups in the country, never responded in significant numbers to the encouragement of migration to Liberia. The single important large-scale nationalistic effort, Marcus

Garvey's Universal Negro Improvement Association, never actually led to mass emigration of Negroes.[18] By contrast, the indigenous American Indians fought long and hard to preserve control over their habitat.

In interpreting differences in the effects of migrant and indigenous subordination, the migrants must be considered in the context of the options available to the group. Irish migrants to the United States in the 1840's, for example, although clearly subordinate to native whites of other origins, fared better economically than if they had remained in their mother country.[19] Further, the option of returning to the homeland often exists for populations migrating to subordinate situations. Jerome reports that net migration to the United States between the midyears of 1907 and 1923 equalled roughly 65 per cent of gross immigration.[20] This indicates that immigrant dissatisfaction with subordination or other conditions of contact can often be resolved by withdrawal from the area. Recently subordinated indigenous groups, by contrast, are perhaps less apt to leave their habitat so readily.

Finally, when contacts between racial and ethnic groups are under the control of the indigenous population, threats of demographic and institutional imbalance are reduced since the superordinate populations can limit the numbers and groups entering. For example, when Oriental migration to the United States threatened whites, sharp cuts were executed in the quotas.[21] Similar events may be noted with respect to the decline of immigration from the so-called "new" sources of eastern and southern Europe. Whether a group exercises its control over immigration far before it is actually under threat is, of course, not germane to the point that immigrant restriction provides a mechanism whereby potential conflict is prevented.

In summary, groups differ in the conditions necessary for maintaining their respective social orders. In areas where the migrant group is dominant, frequently the indigenous population suffers sharp numerical declines and their economic and political institutions are seriously undermined. Conflict often accompanies the establishment of migrant superordination. Subordinate indigenous populations generally have no alternative location and do not control the numbers of new ethnic populations admitted into their area. By contrast, when the indigenous population dominates the political and economic conditions, the migrant group is introduced into the economy of the indigenous population. Although subordinate in their new habitat, the migrants may fare better than if they remained in their homeland. Hence their subordination occurs without great conflict. In addition, the migrants usually have the option of returning to their homeland and the indigenous population controls the number of new immigrants in the area.

Multiple Ethnic Contacts

Although the introduction of a third major ethnic or racial group frequently occurs in both types of societies distinguished here, there are significant differences between conditions in habitats under indigenous domination and areas where a migrant population is superordinate. Chinese and Indian migrants, for example, were often welcomed by whites in areas where large indigenous populations were suppressed, but these migrants were restricted in the white mother country. Consideration of the causes and consequences of multiethnic contacts is therefore made in terms of the two types of racial and ethnic contact.

Migrant Superordination

In societies where the migrant population is superordinate, it is often necessary to introduce new immigrant groups to fill the niches created in the revised economy of the area. The subordinate indigenous population frequently fails, at first, to participate in the new economic and political order introduced by migrants. For example, because of the numerical decline of Fijians after contact with whites and their unsatisfactory work habits, approximately 60,000 persons migrated from India to the sugar plantations of Fiji under the indenture system between 1879 and 1916.[22] For similar reasons, as well as the demise of slavery, large numbers of Indians were also introduced to such areas of indigenous subordination as Mauritius, British Guiana, Trinidad, and Natal.[23] The descendants of these migrants comprise the largest single ethnic group in several of these areas.

McKenzie, after observing the negligible participation of the subordinated indigenous populations of Alaska, Hawaii, and Malaya in contrast to the large numbers of Chinese, Indian, and other Oriental immigrants, offers the following interpretation:

> The indigenous peoples of many of the frontier zones of modern industrialism are surrounded by their own web of culture and their own economic structure. Consequently they are slow to take part in the new economy especially as unskilled laborers. It is the individual who is widely removed from this native habitat that is most adaptable to the conditions imposed by capitalism in frontier regions. Imported labor cannot so easily escape to its home village when conditions are distasteful as can the local population.[24]

Similarly, the Indians of the United States played a minor role in the new economic activities introduced by white settlers and, further, were not used successfully as slaves.[25] Frazier reports that Negro slaves were utilized in the West Indies and Brazil after unsuccessful efforts to enslave the indigenous Indian populations.[26] Large numbers of Asiatic Indians were brought to South Africa as indentured laborers to work in the railways, mines, and plantations introduced by whites.[27]

This migration of workers into areas where the indigenous population was either unable or insufficient to work in the newly created economic activities was also marked by a considerable flow back to the home country. For example, nearly 3.5 million Indians left the Madras Presidency for overseas between 1903 and 1912, but close to 3 million returned during this same period.[28] However, as we observed earlier, large numbers remained overseas and formed major ethnic populations in a number of countries. Current difficulties of the ten million Chinese in Southeast Asia are in large part due to their settlement in societies where the indigenous populations were subordinate.

Indigenous Superordination

We have observed that in situations of indigenous superordination the call for new immigrants from other ethnic and racial populations is limited in a manner that prevents the indigenous group's loss of political and economic control. Under such conditions, no single different ethnic or racial population is sufficiently large in number or strength to challenge the supremacy of the indigenous population.

After whites attained dominance in Hawaii, that land provided a classic case of the substitution of one ethnic group after another during a period when large numbers of immigrants were needed for the newly created and expanding plantation economy. According to Lind, the shifts from Chinese to Japanese and Portuguese immigrants and the later shifts to Puerto Rican, Korean, Spanish, Russian, and Philippine sources for the plantation laborers were due to conscious efforts to prevent any single group from obtaining too much power.[29] Similarly, the exclusion of Chinese from the United States mainland stimulated the migration of the Japanese and, in turn, the later exclusion of Japanese led to increased migration from Mexico.[30]

In brief, groups migrating to situations of multiple ethnic contact are thus subordinate in both types of contact situations. However, in societies where whites are superordinate but do not settle as an indigenous population, other racial and ethnic groups are admitted in large numbers and largely in accordance with economic needs of the revised economy of the habitat. By contrast, when a dominant migrant group later becomes indigenous, in the sense that the area becomes one of permanent settlement through generations for the group, migrant populations from new racial and ethnic stocks are restricted in number and source.

Conflict and Assimilation

From a comparison of the surge of racial nationalism and open warfare in parts in Africa and Asia or the retreat of superordinate migrants from the former Dutch East Indies and French Indo-China, on the one hand, with the fusion of populations in many nations of western Europe or the "cultural pluralism" of the United States and Switzerland, on the other, one must conclude that neither conflict nor assimilation is an inevitable outcome of racial and ethnic contact. Our distinction, however, between two classes of race and ethnic relations is directly relevant to consideration of which of these alternatives different populations in contact will take. In societies where the indigenous population at the initial contact is subordinate, warfare and nationalism often—although not always—develop later in the cycle of relations. By contrast, relations between migrants and indigenous populations that are subordinate and superordinate, respectively, are generally without long-term conflict.

Migrant Superordination

Through time, the subordinated indigenous population begins to participate in the economy introduced by the migrant group and, frequently, a concomitant disruption of previous forms of social and economic organization takes place. This, in turn, has significant implications for the development of both nationalism and a greater sense of racial unity. In many African states, where Negroes were subdivided into ethnic groups prior to contact with whites, the racial unity of the African was created by the occupation of their habitat by white invaders.[31] The categorical subordination of Africans by whites as well as the dissolution and decay of previous tribal and ethnic forms of organization are responsible for the creation of racial consciousness among the indigenous populations.[32] As the indigenous group becomes increasingly incorporated within the larger system, both the saliency of their subordinate position and its significance increase. No alternative exists for the bulk of the native population other than the destruction or revision of the institutions of political, economic, and social subordination.

Further, it appears that considerable conflict occurs in those areas where the migrants are not simply superordinate, but where they themselves have also become, in a sense, indigenous by maintaining an established population through generations. In Table 1, for example, one can observe how sharply the white populations of Algeria and the Union of South Africa differ from those in nine other African countries with respect to the per cent born in the country of settlement. Thus, two among the eleven African countries for which such data were available[33] are outstanding with respect to both racial turmoil and the high proportion of whites born in the country. To be sure, other factors operate to influence the nature of racial and ethnic relations. However, these data

TABLE 1. *Nativity of the White Populations of Selected African Countries, Circa 1950*

Country	Per Cent of Whites Born in Country
Algeria	79.8
Basutoland	37.4
Bechuanaland	39.5
Morocco[a]	37.1[c]
Northern Rhodesia	17.7
Southern Rhodesia	31.5
South West Africa[b]	45.1
Swaziland	41.2
Tanganyika	47.6
Uganda	43.8
Union of South Africa	89.7

Source: United Nations, *Demographic Yearbook*, 1956, Table 5. Copyright United Nations, 1956. Reproduced by permission.

[a]Former French zone. [b]Excluding Walvis Bay.

[c]Persons born in former Spanish zone or in Tangier are included as native.

Note: Other non-indigenous groups included when necessary breakdown by race is not given.

strongly support our suggestions with respect to the significance of differences between indigenous and migrant forms of contact. Thus where the migrant population becomes established in the new area, it is all the more difficult for the indigenous subordinate group to change the social order.

Additionally, where the formerly subordinate indigenous population has become dominant through the expulsion of the superordinate group, the situation faced by nationalities introduced to the area under earlier conditions of migrant superordination changes radically. For example, as we note earlier, Chinese were welcomed in many parts of Southeast Asia where the newly subordinated indigenous populations were unable or unwilling to fill the economic niches created by the white invaders. However, after whites were expelled and the indigenous populations obtained political mastery, the gates to further Chinese immigration were fairly well closed and there has been increasing interference with the Chinese already present. In Indonesia, where Chinese immigration had been encouraged under Dutch domain, the newly created indigenous government allows only token immigration and has formulated a series of laws and measures designed to interfere with and reduce Chinese commercial activities.[34] Thompson and Adloff observe that,

> Since the war, the Chinese have been subjected to increasingly restrictive measures throughout Southeast Asia, but the severity and effectiveness of these has varied with the degree to which the native nationalists are in control of their countries and feel their national existence threatened by the Chinese.[35]

Indigenous Superordination

By contrast, difficulties between subordinate migrants and an already dominant indigenous population occur within the context of a consensual form of government, economy, and social institutions. However confused and uncertain may be the concept of assimilation and its application in operational terms,[36] it is important to note that assimilation is essentially a very different phenomenon in the two types of societies distinguished here.

Where populations migrate to situations of subordination, the issue has generally been with respect to the migrants' capacity and willingness to become an integral part of the ongoing social order. For example, this has largely been the case in the United States where the issue of "new" vs. "old" immigrant groups hinged on the alleged inferiorities of the former.[37] The occasional flurries of violence under this form of contact have been generally initiated by the dominant indigenous group and with respect to such threats against the social order as the cheap labor competition of Orientals on the west coast,[38] the nativist fears of Irish Catholic political domination of Boston in the nineteenth century,[39] or the desecration of sacred principles by Mexican "zoot-suiters" in Los Angeles.[40]

The conditions faced by subordinate migrants in Australia and Canada after the creation of indigenous white societies in these areas are similar to that of the United States; that is, limited and sporadic conflict, and great emphasis on the assimilation of migrants. Striking and significant contrasts to the general pattern of subordinate immigrant assimilation in those societies, however, are provided by the differences between the assimilation of Italian and German immigrants in Australia as well as the position of French Canadians in eastern Canada.

French Canadians have maintained their language and other major cultural and social attributes whereas nineteenth and twentieth century immigrants are in process of merging into the predominantly English-speaking Canadian society. Although broader problems of territorial segregation are involved,[41] the critical difference between French Canadians and later groups is that the former had an established society in the new habitat prior to the British conquest of Canada and were thus largely able to maintain their social and cultural unity without significant additional migration from France.[42]

Similarly, in finding twentieth century Italian immigrants in Australia more prone to cultural assimilation than were German migrants to that nation in the 1800's, Borrie emphasized the fact that Italian migration occurred after Australia had become an independent nation-state. By contrast, Germans settled in what was a pioneer colony without an established general social order and institutions. Thus, for example, Italian children were required to attend Australian schools and learn English, whereas the German immigrants were forced to establish their own educational program.[43]

Thus the consequences of racial and ethnic contact may also be examined in terms of the two types of superordinate-subordiante contact situations considered. For the most part, subordinate migrants appear to be more rapidly assimilated than are subordinate indigenous populations. Further, the subordinate migrant group is generally under greater pressure to assimilate, at least in the gross sense of "assimilation" such as language, than are subordinate indigenous populations. In addition, warfare or racial nationalism—when it does occur—tends to be in societies where the indigenous population is subordinate. If the indegenous movement succeeds, the economic and political position of racial and ethnic populations introduced to the area under migrant dominance may become tenuous.

A Final Note

It is suggested that interest be revived in the conditions accounting for societal variations in the process of relations between racial and ethnic groups. A societal theory of race relations, based on the migrant-indigenous and superordinate-subordinate distinctions developed above, has been found to offer an orderly interpretation of differences in the nature of race and ethnic relations in the contact situations considered. Since, however, systematic empirical investigation provides a far more rigorous test of the theory's merits and limitations, comparative cross-societal studies are needed.

ENDNOTES

1. Robert E. Park, *Race and Culture*, Glencoe, Ill.: The Free Press, 1950, p. 150.

2. For example, Emory S. Bogardus, "A Race-Relations Cycle," *American Journal of Sociology*, 35 (January, 1930), pp. 612–617; W. O. Brown, "Culture and Race Conflict" in E. B. Reuter, editor, *Race and Culture Contacts*, New York: McGraw-Hill, 1934, pp. 34–47; L. Franklin Frazier, *Race and Culture Contacts in the Modern World*, New York: Alfred A. Knopf, 1957, pp. 32 ff.; Clarence E. Glick, "Social Roles and Types in Race Relations" in Andrew W. Lind, editor, *Race Relations in World Perspective*, Honolulu: University of Hawaii Press, 1955, pp. 243–262; Edward Nelson Palmer, "Culture Contacts and Population Growth" in Joseph J. Spengler and Otis Dudley Duncan, editors, *Population Theory and Policy*, Glencoe, Ill.: The Free Press, 1956, pp. 410–415; A. Grenfell Price, *White Settlers and Native Peoples*, Melbourne: Georgian House, 1950. For summaries of several of these cycles, see Brewton Berry, *Race and Ethnic Relations*, Boston: Houghton Mifflin, 1958, Chapter 6.

3. Bogardus, *op. cit.*, p. 612.

4. Price, *op. cit.*

5. Intra-urban stages of contact are not considered here.

6. Price, *op. cit.*, Chapters 6 and 7.

7. Glick, *op. cit.*, p. 244.

8. See, for example, Brinley Thomas, "International Migration" in Philip M. Hauser and Otis Dudley Duncan, editors, *The Study of Population*, Chicago: University of Chicago Press, 1959, pp. 523–526.

9. United Nations, *Demographic Yearbook*, 1957, pp. 147, 645.

10. United Nations, *Demographic Yearbook*, 1954, pp. 131, 669.

11. R. D. McKenzie, *Oriental Exclusion*, Chicago: University of Chicago Press, 1928, p. 83.

12. See, for example, Reuter's distinction between two types of direct contact in E. B. Reuter, editor, *op. cit.*, pp. 4–7.

13. Price, *op. cit.*, p. 1.

14. Stephen Roberts, *Population Problems of the Pacific*, London: George Routledge & Sons, 1927.

15. John A. Barnes, "Race Relations in the Development of Southern Africa" in Lind, editor, *op. cit.*

16. *Ibid.*

17. Witness the current controversies between tribes in the newly created Congo Republic. Also, for a list of tribes living on both sides of the border of the Republic of Sudan, see Karol Józef Krótki, "Demographic Survey of Sudan" in *The Population of Sudan*, report on the sixth annual conference, Khartoum: Philosophical Society of Sudan, 1958, p. 35.

18. John Hope Franklin, *From Slavery to Freedom*, second edition, New York: Alfred Knopf, 1956, pp. 234–238, 481–483.

19. Oscar Handlin, *Boston's Immigrants*, revised edition, Cambridge, Mass.: The Belknap Press of Harvard University Press, 1959, Chapter 2.

20. Harry Jerome, *Migration and Business Cycles*, New York: National Bureau of Economic Research, 1926, pp. 43–44.

21. See George Eaton Simpson and J. Milton Yinger, *Racial and Cultural Minorities*, revised edition, New York: Harper & Brothers, 1958, pp. 126–132.

22. K. L. Gillion, "The Sources of Indian Emigration to Fiji," *Population Studies*, 10 (November, 1956), p. 139; I. M. Cumpston, "A Survey of Indian Immigration to British Tropical Colonies to 1910," *ibid.*, pp. 158–159.

23. Cumpston, *op. cit.*, pp. 158–165.

24. R. D. McKenzie, "Cultural and Racial Differences as Bases of Human Symbiosis" in Kimball Young, editor, *Social Attitudes*, New York: Henry Holt, 1931, p. 157.

25. Franklin, *op. cit.*, p. 47.

26. Frazier, *op. cit.*, pp. 107–108.

27. Leo Kuper, Hilstan Watts, and Ronald Davies, *Durban: A Study in Racial Ecology*, London: Jonathan Cape, 1958, p. 25.

28. Gillion, *op. cit.*, p. 149.

29. Andrew W. Lind, *An Island Community*, Chicago: University of Chicago Press, 1938, pp. 218–229.

30. McKenzie, *Oriental Exclusion, op. cit.*, p. 181.

31. For a discussion of territorial and tribal movements, see James S. Coleman, "Current Politial Movements in Africa," *The Annals of the American Academy of Political and Social Science*, 298 (March, 1955), pp. 95–108.

32. For a broader discussion of emergent nationalism, see Thomas Hodgkin, *Nationalism in Colonial Africa*, New York: New York University Press, 1957;

Everett C. Hughes, "New Peoples" in Lind, editor, *op. cit.*, pp. 95–115.

33. United Nations, *Demographic Yearbook, 1956* Table 5.

34. B. H. M. Vlekke, *Indonesia in 1956,* The Hague: Netherlands Institute of International Affairs, 1957, p. 88.

35. Virginia Thompson and Richard Adloff, *Minority Problems in Southeast Asia,* Stanford, California: Stanford University Press, 1955, p. 3.

36. See, for example, International Union for the Scientific Study of Population, "Cultural Assimilation of Immigrants." *Population Studies, supplement,* March, 1950.

37. Oscar Handlin, *Race and Nationality in American Life,* Garden City, New York: Doubleday Anchor Books, 1957, Chapter 5.

38. Simpson and Yinger, *op. cit.*

39. Oscar Handlin, *Boston's Immigrants, op. cit.,* Chapter 7.

40. Ralph Turner and Samuel J. Surace, "Zoot-Suiters and Mexicans: Symbols in Crowd Behavior," *American Journal of Sociology,* 62 (July, 1956), pp. 14–20.

41. It is, however, suggestive to consider whether the isolated settlement of an area by a racial, religious, or ethnic group would be permitted in other than frontier conditions. Consider, for example, the difficulties faced by Mormons until they reached Utah.

42. See Everett C. Hughes, *French Canada in Transition,* Chicago: University of Chicago Press, 1943.

43. W. D. Borrie assisted by D. R. G. Packer, *Italians and Germans in Australia,* Melbourne: F. W. Cheshire, 1954, *passim.*

16

The Ethnic Miracle

Andrew M. Greeley

The neighborhood is a 10-square-block area with almost 14,000 people, an average of 39.8 inhabitants per acre—three times that of the most crowded portions of Tokyo, Calcutta, and many other Asian cities. One block contains 1,349 children. A third of the neighborhood's 771 buildings are built on "back lots" behind existing structures; the buildings are divided into 2,796 apartments, with a ratio of 3.7 rooms per apartment. More than three quarters of the apartments have less than 400 square feet. Tenants of the 556 basement apartments stand knee-deep in human excrement when even moderate rainstorms cause plumbing breakdowns. Garbage disposal is a chronic problem—usually, trash is simply dumped in the narrow passageways between buildings. Nine thousand of the neighborhood's inhabitants use outdoor plumbing. The death rate is 37.2 per thousand per year.

These are the poorest of the poor people, making less than three quarters of the income of nonminority-group members in the same jobs. The rates of desertion, juvenile delinquency, mental disorder, and prostitution are the highest in the city here. Social disorganization in this neighborhood, according to all outside observers—even the sympathetic ones—is practically total and irredeemable.

Blacks? Latinos? Inhabitants of some Third World city? No—Poles in Chicago in 1920.

The neighborhood is still there. You drive in from O'Hare airport and see the towering spires of St. Mary of the Angels, St. Stanislaus Kostka, and Holy Trinity. If you turn off at Division Street you will see the manure boxes are gone, and so are the backyard buildings, the outdoor plumbing, the sweatshops over the barns, the tuberculosis, the family disorganization, the violence, and the excessive death rates.

For the most part, the Poles are gone too. Some of them remain, sharing a much more pleasant (and brightly painted) neighborhood with Puerto Ricans. Where have the Poles gone? Farther northwest along Milwaukee Avenue, even out into the suburbs—they are now a prosperous middle class. How have they managed to make it, this most despised of all the white immigrant groups? It is no exaggeration to say that no one really knows, and that the success of the southern and eastern European immigrant groups who frantically crowded into the United States before the First World War is as unexplained as it is astonishing. Indeed, rather than to attempt an explanation, many Americans—including some from those very same ethnic groups—prefer to deny the phenomenon of ethnic success.

Yet the "ethnic miracle" is one of the most

Reprinted with permission of the author from THE PUBLIC INTEREST 45 (Fall 1976), pp. 20–36. © by National Affairs, Inc.

fascinating stories in the history of the United States, an American success story, an accomplishment of the "system" in spite of itself; and while the "ethnic miracle" does not necessarily provide a model for later groups (in fact, it almost certainly does not), it does offer insights into how American society works that social-policy-makers can ill afford to ignore.

"Social Disorganization"?

The neighborhood I described is called the "Stanislowowo" after St. Stanislaus Kotska, its parish church. At one time, it was the largest Catholic parish in the world (40,000 members) in the second largest Polish city in the world. Nobody in the United States between 1900 and 1920 did its parishioners any favors. In five of the years before the First World War, more than one million foreign immigrants poured into the country. They were ignorant, illiterate, and dirty; they spoke little English if any at all; their families, the sociologists of the time assured us, were chronically "disorganized." They had no tradition of freedom and responsibility; they lacked political maturity. They were a bad bet to assimilate into American society.

Was there poverty and suffering in the Stanislowowo and neighborhoods like it? That was largely the fault of the immigrants themselves, Americans were told by their elites. The Dillingham Commission on immigration assured the rest of the country that the Italians were inherently disposed to criminal behavior and that the Polish family lacked stability—both groups were racially inferior. The walls of restrictive immigration legislation were quickly erected after the war to end immigration. Large-scale "Americanization" campaigns were begun to try to teach these illiterate peasants the virtues of good Americans, and there was great hope that the public high schools would mold the children of the immigrants (the parents were beyond hope) into good, loyal, dutiful citizens.

There were no quotas, no affirmative action, no elaborate system of social services, and, heaven knows, no ethnic militancy (although it need not follow that there should not be these things for the more recent immigrants to the big cities of the United States). There was no talk of reparation, no sense of guilt, no feelings of compassion for these immigrants. The stupid, brutal, but pathetic

heroes of Nelson Algren's novels were about as much as most Americans recognized; "Scarface" and "Little Caesar" of the motion pictures were taken to be typical of the Italians who got beyond street cleaning, ditch digging, garbage collection, and waiting on tables. It is safe to say that in the 20th century, no urban immigrants have been so systematically hated and despised by the nation's cultural and intellectual elites. The sterotypes may be more sophisticated now, but they still portray the ethnics as hateful and despicable. Stanley Kowalski has been replaced by Don Corleone, but both still represent the white ethnic as a blue-collar, racist, hard-hat, chauvinistic "hawk"—even though available statistical evidence does not support the myth of the Godfather or the bigot, and lends no credence to the ethnic joke.

Closely related to the thesis of the racial inferiority of the eastern and southern European immigrants was the theory of their cultural inferiority. "Social disorganization" was the explanation of the plight of the Stanislowowians offered by the "Chicago school" of sociology. The cultural values of the immigrants were not able to absorb the shock of the immigration experience and the resultant confrontation with the more "modern" values of the host society. Crime, generational conflict, family disorganization, prostitution, and juvenile delinquency were the effects of this unequal meeting of a peasant and a modern culture. Several generations of scholars, administrators, and social workers were raised on such scholarly books as *The Gang*, *The Gold Coast and the Slum*, and *The Polish Peasant in Europe and America*—which were in whole or in part about the Stanislowowo; much of the reform legislation of the 1930's was designed from that perspective. The problem with the poor was not their poverty but their "social disorganization" and "alienation." Fortunately for the ethnics, they stopped being poor before the reformers could set up high-rise public housing and dependency-producing welfare legislation to "undisorganize" them.

Across the Chicago River from "St. Stan's" is the infamous Cabrini-Green high-rise public housing project, one of the most evil things that good intentions have ever produced—a monstrosity that causes the very "social disorganization" it was designed to eliminate. It is a slum far worse than the author of *The Gold Coast and the Slum* could have imagined, and while the death rate may not be as high as it was in the Stanislowowo in 1901, the human demoralization in Cabrini-Green is far worse. (*Cooley High* of movie fame was once the parochial high school for St. Stan's.) If contemporary welfare, urban renewal, and public housing legislation had existed a half century ago, the Poles might still be poor, and sociologists might still be writing books about how the Polish family structure—one of the strongest in America—is "disorganized."

One need not conclude that there ought to be no government intervention to help and protect the poor. On the contrary, the "ethnic miracle" might have happened more quickly if the government had intervened to prevent discrimination and to facilitate the rise out of poverty. But the "ethnic miracle" at least raises questions as to whether social legislation would be more effective it it were to respect the culture and family life of the poor and fight poverty directly, rather than with most useless attempts to correct "alienation" and "social disorganization." There obviously are individuals and families so badly traumatized by either poverty or misguided efforts to "unalienate" them (or combinations of both) that they cannot cope with problems or urban living without help from society. But the "ethnic miracle" suggests that such help should be aimed at making them think and act not like psychiatrically oriented social workers but rather like the more successful members of their own cultural community.

A half century ago, the "disorganization" models of the "Chicago school" of sociology looked like a big change from the biological racism of the Immigration Commission. In retrospect, and in light of the "ethnic miracle," one is permitted to wonder if in fact the theory of "social disorganization" was not a more subtle but equally pernicious form of "cultural racism"—and one not absent by any means from the reform legislation of the 1960's.

Explanations for Success

The 1920's and 1930's were bad times for the immigrants and their children. The fierce nativism of the 1920's and the grim and frustrating Great Depression of the 1930's kept them pretty much in the poverty of the immigrant neighborhoods.

Only a few managed to claw their way out into middle-class respectability. But in the three decades since the end of the Second World War, an extraordinary economic and social phenomenon has occured: The ethnics have made it. The Italians are now the third richest religio-ethnic group in American society—second only to Jews and Irish Catholics—and the Poles earn almost $1,000 a year more than the average white American in metropolitan areas of the North. In the middle 1940's, the curve of college attendance for young people for both Italians and Poles began to swing upward, so that by the 1960's, Poles and Italians of college age were *more* likely to attend college than the national average for white Americans.

Without anyone's noticing it, those who were doomed to be failures by their race, religion, language, and family backgrounds have now succeeded. Few of them are wealthy, some are still poor; but on the average their incomes are substantially higher than those of other white Americans living in the same cities and regions of the United States. Many Americans reject in principle the possibility of such a miracle; some of the ethnic leaders themselves (in a perhaps unintentional ethnic joke) vigorously deny the success of their own people; yet the data are beyond any reasonable doubt. In a very short space of time, the length of one generation, more or less, the American dream has come true; and some of the people who were children in the Stanislowowo in 1920 have lived to see and to enjoy the achievement of their dream. Even the Stanislowowo has changed for those who remain. The well fed, neatly dressed, scrupulously clean children who troop out of St. Stanislaus Kostka on a spring afternoon—grandchildren, perhaps, of the women who worked 60 hours a week in sweatshops filled with the stench of manure—are clearly the offspring of an affluent society.

There is doubtless much wrong with the United States of America, and we will doubtless hear all about it in the course of the 200th anniversary of the republic; but sometimes things have gone well—despite almost conscious efforts to make them go badly. The success of the eastern and southern European immigrant groups at the turn of the century is one of America's success stories. The achievements of the Jews have been well known for some time; only recently have we discovered that the Italians and the Poles have also done remarkably well. We do not like to admit it. Very few agencies or scholars, whose responsibility it is to study and understand American society, show any interest at all in the extraordinary success story of those against whom the immigration acts of 1920 were directed. It seems that we couldn't care less about finding an explanation.

Perhaps it was the public school—maybe good, solid American education undid the work of a thousand years of oppression and misery. The evidence, however, suggests the opposite. The success of the Polish and the Italians seems to have come *first* in income, then in education, and finally in occupation (and, as we shall see later, they are still impeded somewhat in occupational achievement).[1]

The few scholars who pay any attention to immigration have begun to wonder whether the conventionally understood progression from education through occupation toward economic success is all that helpful a model. Among the Asian immigrants to the United States, and among the Sephardic Jews in Israel, income parity seems to come before educational and occupational parity. In the Sephardic families, for example, with everyone working—husband, wife, and children—equality of family income with the Ashkenazics has already been achieved, although educational and occupational parity lag behind. It would seem very likely that most immigrant groups must first achieve some kind of basic financial success, and only then can they exploit the advantages of educational and occupational mobility and concomitant opportunities for even more dramatic income achievement.

However patriarchal the family structures may have been, the women of the ethnic immigrants went to work from the beginning—long before it became an upper-middle-class fashion. The income of many wage earners in a family no doubt provided an economic base for the ethnics to make their initial breakthrough—which occurred, perhaps, sometime in the early 1950's. (Data on neighborhood concentration of various ethnic communities indicate that the Poles finally began to move out from the center of the city at that time.) But by 1970, the women in Polish and Italian families were no more likely to have jobs than their nonethnic counterparts in the large cities of the North. So the income achievement

of the southern and eastern European Catholics cannot be explained by multiple wage earners in the family—though there is a possibility that many of the men and some of the women may also have second and third jobs.[2]

Education and Income Mobility

The mean education of Polish, Italian, and Slavic Catholics ("Slavic" means non-Polish eastern Europeans) is substantially below the national white average of 11.56 years. The Poles and the Italians have little more than 11 years of education, the Slavs fall under 11 years (Table 1). However, when one looks at educational achievement *given parental educational level*, the Catholic ethnics have higher academic achievement than do British Americans; indeed it is higher than anyone else in the country save for the Jews—and the Italians have an even higher achievement than Jews.

Furthermore, if one considers college attendance by the various age cohorts (an indication of educational decisions made by an ethnic collectivity at a time when a given cohort was of college age), one can see that the slope of college attendance for the three southern and eastern European ethnic groups turned sharply upward in the 1940's; by the 1960's, it had crossed the national average.[3]

While Irish Catholics are not significantly different from British Protestants in occupational achievement, the three more recent Catholic ethnic groups were substantially beneath the national average in occupation and did not make up the difference even when parental education and their

TABLE 1.   Education and Religio-Ethnicity[1]

Religio-Ethnic Group	Years of Education
Jewish	13.9
Irish Catholic	12.8
British Protestant	12.41
German Catholic	11.59
National white average	11.56
German Protestant	11.34
Scandinavian Protestant	11.32
Polish Catholic	11.11
Italian Catholic	11.07
Irish Protestant	10.95
"Amercian" Protestant	10.93
Slavic Catholic	10.84

[1]Source: National Opinion Research Center. [Used by permission.]

own education was taken into account. In other words, the Polish, Slavic, and Italian Catholics were not getting the occupational prestige to which their education seemed to entitle them in comparison with British Protestants.

However, despite their lower occupational achievement, the Catholic ethnic groups (save for the Slavs) earn more money than their British counterparts, and when the pertinent background variables are taken into account these differences become statistically significant. Indeed, the net advantage of Italians over British Protestants in income is higher even than that of the Jews. In other words, while they may not get the kind of jobs their education entitles them to, the Catholic ethnics seem to make more money than their occupational level entitles them to. On the face of it, it would appear that, like Avis, they try harder (Table 2).[4]

In sum, eastern and southern European Catholics do more with their parents' education in terms of their own education than do other Americans, and they also do more with their occupation in terms of income earned than do other Americans. However, they apparently still are not able to convert education into the same level of occupational prestige as that of Jews and British Protestants.

A word should be said in passing about a slightly earlier "ethnic miracle," that of the Irish Catholics, who are the richest, best educated, and most prestigious occupationally of any gentile

TABLE 2. *Real Family Income and Religio-Ethnicity*[1]

Religio-Ethnic Group	1974 Income
Jewish	$14,577
Irish Catholic	13,451
German Catholic	12,543
Italian Catholic	12,473
Polish Catholic	12,257
British Protestant	12,208
National average for whites	11,892
German Protestant	11,500
Slavic Catholic	11,499
Scandinavian Protestant	11,284
Irish Protestant	10,714
"Amercian" Protestant	10,572

[1]Source: National Opinion Research Center. [Used by permission.]

religio-ethnic group—the comparison again being made with their appropriate counterparts, those living in metropolitan regions in the North. Irish-Catholic college attendance for those of college age surpassed the national average as long ago as 1910, and has remained substantially above the average ever since, passing even the Episcopalians in the 1960's. The Irish Catholic income advantage over British Protestants is $1,243 a year (trailing behind the $2,369-a-year advantage of Jews). Many of those who are willing to admit that the Poles and Italians may have achieved rough parity with the rest of the country find the spectacular success of Irish Catholics almost impossible to swallow.

There may be an important social policy hint in the apparent primacy of income in the "assimilation" of the early 20th-century immigrants. Subject to much more careful investigation, *one might take it as a tentative hypothesis that the school is a rather poor institution for facilitating the upward mobility of minority groups—until they first acquire some kind of rough income parity.* The naive American faith that equality of education produces equality of income seems to have been stood on its head in the case of the ethnics. For them, better income meant more effective education.[5]

Nor did the public schools play the critical "Americanization" role that such educators as Dr. James B. Conant expected them to play in the 1940's and 1950's. Even taking into account parents' education and income, the most successful of the ethnics—educationally, occupationally, and economically—went to parochial schools, and they did so at a time when the schools were even more overcrowded than they are today, staffed by even less adequately trained teachers, and administered by an even smaller educational bureaucracy than the very small one that somehow manages to keep the parochial schools going today. Again, a social policy hint: Maybe what matters about schools for a minority group is, as my colleague Professor William McCready has remarked, that "they are *our* schools" (whoever "we" may be).

The Legacy of the Immigrants

So one must still face the puzzle: Despite the virtually unanimous opinion of educated Americans a half century ago, the children and the grand-children of eastern and southern European immigrants have achieved not only economic equality but economic superiority, on the average, in the United States. They were not supposed to be able to do it; to many people it is incredible that they have done it; and to almost everyone the explanation of their success is obscure. Now we see that the ethnics in the quarter century between the end of the Second World War and the end of the Vietnamese War did exactly what the Jews had done in the previous quarter century—and with apparent ease.

How did they manage it? The immigrants themselves were ambitious. Perhaps they were the enterprising and courageous young people in their own societies—and young they were. When we see movies like *Hester Street*, many of us are astonished to discover that the immigrants from eastern and southern Europe were disproportionately young, and either unmarried or just recently married. We all have a recollection of an old grandparent whom we knew during childhood, and without giving the matter much thought, we tend to imagine the immigrants themselves as old—forgetting that the old *babushka* or *mamacita* was once as young as we were.

The immigrants came from a Europe which, as one American historian has remarked, "invited desertion." The population expansion of the middle 19th century had created a land-hungry peasant class for whom there was no room either on the farms or in the cities. They came to the United States seeking the "good life," the kind of life that owning land made possible. They were fully prepared to work hard; indeed, a life of anything but hard work was beyond their comprehension. They would work hard to make money. "All the Italians want is money," remarked an observer around 1910, and like devout practitioners of the Protestant ethic, they would sacrifice to save as much money as they could. In 1905, when Poles were still pouring into the city of Chicago, 15 per cent of the money in Chicago savings-and-loan institutions was already in Polish-owned associations, a remarkable achievement for people who were scarcely off the boat. Credit buying was taboo; "cash money" paid for everything. Desperately poor people themselves, with scores of generations of poverty behind them, the immigrants

could imagine no other way to live besides scrimping, sacrificing, saving. America did them no favors, gave them no special treatment, in fact discriminated against them, forced them into the most menial occupations and the most miserable housing, and exploited them through the most corrupt political structures in the country. Americans hated them, despised them, condemned them, and eventually tried to bar their relatives from joining them; they joked about them, stereotyped them, and tried to change them into "good Americans" by making them ashamed of their own heritages.

The Poles and the Italians, like the Irish and the Jews before them, bitterly resented such treatment, but they did not grow angry at the United States, for even though it did them no favors, it still provided them with two things they would never have had in the old country: personal freedom and the opportunity to convert the hard work they took for granted into economic progress. In the old country, hard work got you nothing; in the United States it got you, or at least your children or their children, a chance.

Hard work, saving, sacrifice—such is a tentative explanation of the "ethnic miracle." Ironically, the Catholic ethnics turned out to be very good at these "Protestant" and "American" traits that the Dillingham Commission thought they could never learn. To work hard, to save, to be ambitious for oneself and one's children—the immigrants needed no "Americanization" to learn that way of life. They came here with a dream; it was not that they expected something for nothing, but rather that their hard work would earn them something. For some of them, for many of their children, and for most of their grandchildren the dream came true.

Is that how it happened? It would seem so, though until much more careful study of the history of immigrant families is done, we will not know for sure. And it should be done in the relatively near future, while some of the immigrants and their oldest children are still alive to be interviewed. But curiously enough, many Americans, including ethnics like Michael Novak, are much more eager to believe that the American dream has not come true for the ethnics. If it hasn't, then there is nothing to explain.

In the process of economic achievement,

have the ethnics "assimilated"? Have they absorbed the values and beliefs and behavior patterns of the host culture? To begin with, they came with many values in common. They were, after all, products of the same white-European, Judaeo-Christian heritage. They learned to speak English quickly, they wore the same clothes, listened to the same radio and television programs, read the same newspapers; and yet a remarkable diversity of values, attitudes, styles, opinions, and behavior has persisted. Affection and authority, for example, are recognizably different in Jewish, Italian, Polish, and Irish families, as are the styles with which they approach politics, the ways in which they consume alcohol, and the ultimate views they hold about human nature and the nature of the universe.

Ethnicity and American Culture

Furthermore, these differences do not seem to diminish with the number of generations ethnics have been in the United States or with the amount of education they have had. In a loose, pluralistic society like the United States, economic success and rather harmonious adjustment to other groups can be achieved while still maintaining a partially distinctive culture. Indeed, such a distinctive culture can be maintained without having to be self-conscious about it. The Irish propensity for politics and alcohol, for example, and the Polish propensity to vote (Poles have the highest voting rates of any American religio-ethnic group) are not affected by ethnic self-consciousness or militancy. The anxiety of the Dillingham Commission and its nativist successors about whether diversity threatened America's "common culture" missed the whole point: In America the common culture validates diversity in theory, if not in practice. You can be anything you want—religiously, culturally, stylistically—so long as you are committed to the fundamental political principles of the republic.

Ethnicity is not a way of looking back to the old world. Most of the immigrants were only too happy to get the hell out of it. Ethnicity is rather a way of being American, a way of defining yourself into the pluralistic culture which existed before you arrived. The last thing in the world the new ethnic upper-middle class wants is to define themselves out of the common American culture. Why should they? America may have done them

no favors, but it still has been better to them than any society their families ever knew.

So the militant ethnic somewhere out there in "middle America"—hard hat on his head and gun in his hand, ready to tear society apart by resisting the advances of the nonwhite immigrants—is almost entirely a fiction of the imagination of liberals and leftists in the media and the academy. The ethnic may not always like some of the things he sees and hears on television, but his standard of living has doubled at least in the last quarter century, so he is not angry at the "American way"; he is not about to do anything to endanger his still precarious respectability and affluence. He may rejoice that the black activisim of the 1960's has legitimated his somewhat more explicit and conscious pride in heritage, but the "ethnic revival" or the "new ethnic militancy" is largely another fiction of the liberal imagination.

Nor has the ethnic turned to the right. He is neither a "rugged individualist" nor a political reactionary, as many left-liberal commentators would so dearly like to believe. On social legislation, the Italian, Polish, and for that matter, Irish Catholics are still left of center, still members of the New Deal coalition. They did not disproportionately defect from the Democratic party to vote against George McGovern, nor were they strong supporters of George Wallace in the 1968 Presidential election. The myth of the massive Polish vote for Wallace is so powerful that it is practically impossible to debunk; yet the Poles were the most likely of all gentile groups to vote for Hubert Humphrey, and substantially less than the six per cent non-Southern vote for Wallace was recorded among Polish Catholics. It would surely be inaccurate to think of the children, grandchildren, and great grandchildren of the ethnics as left-wing liberals or militant integrationists (most militants seem to live in the suburbs), but on virtually every political and social issue facing the country today, the ethnics are either at the center or to the left of it. Their Irish coreligionists are either close to or just behind the Jews on most measures of liberalism. I do not expect such data to be believed, because too many people have too much emotional energy invested in the opposite opinion. The data, nevertheless, are impossible to ignore.

So the "ethnic miracle" was accomplished without the complete loss of values or family structures—and without a right-wing backlash either. Indeed it was accomplished without any notable desertion from the Democratic party. The Stanislowowians and their children and grand-children apparently made it despite their Polish values and family structure.

But is the word "despite" appropriate? Might there be a possibility that there was something in the culture of the immigrants that actually facilitated the "ethnic miracle"? Preliminary but sophisticated research conducted both at the Department of Labor and the National Bureau of Economic Research (NBER) suggests that Catholics and Jews are more successful in American society than Protestants because of some special factor at work in their early childhood—perhaps a closer and more intense attention from parents. As Thomas Juster of the NBER observes, "Economists and other social scientists have recently begun to pay close attention to the possible role of preschool investments in children by parents as it affects subsequent educational attainment ...[and to the] possible influence on earnings of different amounts of parental time spent with preschool or school-age children....Taking account of family background factors like father's and mother's education and occupation, variables for both Jewish and Catholic religious preference have a significant (positive) impact on reported earnings relative to respondents' reporting of Protestant preference....Plausible hypotheses are that they reflect differences in the cultural background to which the respondents were exposed during formative years or differences in the quality or quantity of parental time inputs...."

Not only the Dillingham Commission but even the Protestant ethic has been stood on its head; the familial culture of the ethnics, their stubborn differences in family values, may well have turned out to be an economic asset. In the absence of further research, such a possibility will remain an intriguing speculation.[6]

Status versus Income

Is all well then for the ethnics? Not quite. Their educational mobility is the highest in America, and their income achievement goes beyond what one would expect, given their education and oc-cupation. However, they do not achieve the occupational status appropriate for their education.

Interestingly enough, this discrepancy occurs at the upper end of the educational and prestige hierarchies. Poles and Italians do as well in occupational prestige as anyone else if they do not go to college. However, among those who have attended college, Poles and Italians have notably lower occupational-prestige scores. For those who attended college, the "cost" of being Polish or Italian is about one-third as high as the cost of being black, and more than half that of being Spanish-speaking.

How can one explain this underrepresentation of the college-educated ethnics in the occupational-prestige levels to which their education should entitle them? In the past, many social scientists would have attributed the difference to a lack of energy, or ambition, or "need achievement" among the ethnics. However, the considerable economic achievement of the ethnics makes this explanation implausible. Others would suggest that the ethnics are more likely to devote psychic energy to income than to prestigious occupations—to become insurance brokers, for example, instead of college professors.

James Coleman and his colleagues asked the same question in their study of how blacks and whites maximize their resources in obtaining jobs. Using a technique called "canonical correlations," they concluded that there is a tendency for blacks to seek income in jobs, and whites to seek status. It would appear that British Protestants, Irish Catholics, and Polish Catholics follow exactly the same pattern of "investing" their education into status and income as do Coleman's whites (indeed, to almost the same numerical weights). To paraphrase Coleman, the status attributes of jobs attract British, Irish, and Polish ethnics; the income attributes of jobs attract Italians and Jews. The occupational disadvantage of the Italians relative to their education may be a result of an "over-investment" in income achievement, which parallels that of the Jews. (The Jews have higher occupational status than their education "entitles" them to, but they achieve even higher income than their occupation "entitles" them to.) However, no such strategy exists for the Poles and the Irish, and the substantial underrepresentation of college-educated Poles and the moderate under-representation of college-educated Irish Catholics in higher prestige positions cannot be explained by a differential strategy. Thus the question of discrimination must necessarily remain open, at least for these groups.

Whatever the explanation—and much more careful research than is likely to be done would be required for certainty—it is a matter of everyday observation that Italian, Polish, and even Irish Catholics are largely absent from the world of the elite private universities, the large foundations, the national mass media, the big financial institutions (as opposed to manufacturing corporations), and certain of the intellectually oriented government agencies. At a national meeting concerned with the lack of women and nonwhite scholars this was attributed to the "intellectual inferiority produced by Catholic religious belief." Women and blacks, I was told, are absent because of discrimination, Catholic ethnics because their religion interferes with intellectual achievement. This explanation was offered with a straight face and obvious sincerity.

In fact, since 1960 Catholics have not been underrepresented in those groups pursuing academic careers, finishing dissertations, publishing articles, or even obtaining tenured appointments at the major state universities. The myth of Catholic intellectual inferiority simply will not stand up to examination in the light of valid empirical evidence—at least not for Catholics who are under 35, presumably the grandchildren of the immigrants. (Given where the eastern and southern European immigrants began, what is surprising is not that their children did not become scholars in proportionate numbers but that their grandchildren did.) If a religio-ethnic group is intellectually good enough to get its young people on the faculties of Michigan, Wisconsin, and California but not quite good enough to make it at Columbia, Yale, Harvard, or Chicago, one begins to wonder what subtle criteria for intellectual excellence are being used at the elite private schools.

There would be very few who would question that the lower occupational scores of the blacks who attended college are the result of discrimination. Unless one can come up with solid evidence for another explanation, intellectual honesty should compel one to take very seriously the possibility that the same explanation should be ap-

plied to the lower scores of Polish, Irish, and Italian Catholics.

Recovering the Past

If there is any ethnic militancy at all, it is to be found not in the vast middle and lower reaches of income and occupational prestige but rather among the elite, those college-educated and graduate-school-educated ethnics who bump up against the residual nativism still present in the upper strata of American society. It is not the Slovakian steelworkers but the Michael Novaks who are the most likely to be angry—and with good reason. Or, as far as that goes, it is not the Irish cop or the Irish politician or the Irish attorney who grows angry at elite nativism, for they either do not encounter it or it does not affect them. (The reader may judge for himself whether the author of this article is an angry militant.)

Those of us who stand on the shoulders of the immigrants are ill at ease with our predecessors. Their raw acquisitiveness embarrasses us, and their sacrifices and sufferings cause us pain. It is hard to admit that we owe a great deal to those who came before us. We repress memories of places like the Stanislowowo in the same way we repress memories of such disasters as the Spanish Influenza or the Great Depression; they are too terrible and too close for us to think about very much. It took a long, long time before a movie like *Hester Street* could be made, and it may be another generation or two before the descendants of those brave, strong, ambitious young people who swarmed into this country between 1890 and 1914 will be able to relax sufficiently to place those urban pioneers alongside the other brave people who came over the Appalachian mountains a century earlier to pioneer an unexplored continent. The miracle of the frontier is now a standard part of American mythology. Perhaps by the tricentennial the ethnic miracle will have become one of the respected marvels of the American story.

ENDNOTES

1. The empirical evidence on which this article is based comes from an analysis of a composite file assembled from 12 National Opinion Research Center (NORC) national sample surveys (A complete report

will be published under the title *Ethnicity, Denomination, and Inequality* by Sage Publications, Beverly Hills, California.) The composite sample numbers some 18,000 respondents and, despite serious limitations, still represents the best collection of data currently available on American religio-ethnic groups. The United States Census cannot ask a religious question, and only recently has the Census monthly "Current Population Survey" (CPS) begun to ask an ethnic question intermittently. However, since Polish Jews and Polish Catholics are combined under the rubric "Pole," and Irish Protestants (disproportionately rural southerners and more numerous than Catholics) are combined with Irish Catholics, the CPS data are useful only with respect to Italians. The NORC composite statistics, however, have been compared with the results of the CPS (50,000 respondents). There are only slight variations between the two; in the case of the Italians, a group for which the NORC data and CPS data are roughly comparable, there is virtually no difference in the statistics on education, occupation, and income. Unfortunately, until funding agencies are willing to support better data collection, composite survey data will provide the only available evidence for scholarly investigation.

2. Nor do the 25 years of prosperity between 1945 and 1970 explain the "ethnic miracle," though they obviously created an environment in which such a miracle could occur. For not only did the ethnics improve their income during that quarter century, as did virtually everyone else, but they improved it *disproportionately*. At the end of the quarter century, not only were they better off than in 1945, they had improved their relative position in comparison with the rest of the population. Prosperity, in other words, provided the opportunity for the "ethnic miracle," but the miracle itself was a response to the opportunity.

3. The analytic technique used is a form of dummy-variable multiple-regression analysis in which each ethnic group becomes a dummy variable and is compared with the British Protestant group. The "net differences" among groups are arrived at by adding to the regression equation the dummy variables for region and for metropolitan residence, as well as for the number of years of the mothers' and fathers' education. Subsequent net differences are arrived at by adding individual educational achievement and occupational prestige to the regression equation. This method is somewhat different from that used in *Ethnicity, Denomination, and Equality* and is more "conservative" statistically, permitting estimates of the statistical significance of observed differences. I am grateful to Christopher Jencks for suggesting the technique to me.

College attendance was measured according to the log of the "odds ratio" of attendance to non-attendance for each age cohort. Tests of statistical significance were used to determine that the slope of the three ethnic groups was different from the national slope.

4. Since the analytic technique used in this article is somewhat different from that used in *Ethnicity, Denomination, and Equality*, there are minor differences in the tables between this article and the longer report. In addition, a different technique was used to take into account cost-of-living changes to bring income from surveys taken in the 1960's into line with income reported in surveys taken in the 1970's. Hence, income figures here are slightly higher than those in the longer report.

5. It should be noted that I do not intend to suggest a comparison between the white immigrants of the turn of the century and the more recent nonwhite immigrants to the city. The path of upward mobility which worked for one group at one time does not necessarily work for another group at another time. Comparisons may be interesting and suggestive, but they should not be pushed too far. The Polish immigrants were indeed abject and miserable, unwanted and humiliated—but they were still white. On the other hand, the apparent historical phenomenon of income preceding rather than following education for the ethnics does seem to add weight to the argument of those who presently wonder whether too much has been expected of education as a corrective of social pathology in the last two decades. The experience of the ethnics is interesting in itself; whatever hints for current social policy may be obtained from their study should be considered no more than that—certainly not as blueprints for imitation. Occasionally one hears an ethnic complain "Why can't 'they' work hard like we did?" but the evidence shows that most ethnics are well aware that nonwhites have to put up with greater obstacles. The irony of their comment is aimed not so much at the more recent immigrants but rather at those of the intellectual and cultural elite who despised the ethnics when they were poor, and have contempt for them now that they are middle-class. As the Irishman said, "Where were you when we needed help?"

6. Let it be noted again that while ambition, hard work, and strong family support for achievement may have been the path to upward mobility for the white ethnics, it does not follow that the same path can or must be followed by more recent immigrants. The ethnic miracle is worth studying in itself even if it has no pertinence to more recent social problems or provides only useful insights for considering those problems.

17

Education and Ethnic Mobility:
The Myth of Jewish Intellectualism
and Catholic Anti-Intellectualism

Stephen Steinberg

"If our children don't go to school, no harm results. But if the sheep don't eat, they will die. The school can wait but not our sheep." (An Italian peasant, quoted in Leonard Covello, *The Social Background of the Italo-American School Child*, 1967.)

Horace Mann, the architect of the common school, once described education as "the great equalizer." Implicitly Mann recognized that the schools would function within the context of class inequality, providing the less privileged members of society with opportunities for social and economic advancement. In *Democracy and Education* John Dewey also wrote that "it is the office of the school environment...to see to it that each individual gets an opportunity to escape from the limitations of the social group in which he was born, and to come into living contact with the broader environment."[1] To this day, it is an article of faith in American society that education is the key to material success, and the key to eliminating social inequalities as well.

Consistent with this liberal faith in education, two general assumptions run through the social science literature on education and ethnic mobility. The first is that those ethnic groups that

have taken advantage of educational opportunities have, for that reason, enjoyed comparative mobility and success. The second assumption is that the values of some groups have been conducive to intellectual achievement, whereas other groups have been saddled with anti-intellectual values or other cultural traits that discouraged their children from pursuing educational opportunities. This "theory" is thus a variant of the more general theory of ethnic success discussed earlier.

As before, issue arises not with the fact that ethnic groups vary in educational attainment, but with the assumption that this reflects the operation of cultural factors, such as the degree to which education is valued. How do we know that some ethnic groups value education more highly? Because they have a superior record of educational attainment. Obviously, it is incorrect to infer values from the outcome, and then to posit these values as causal factors. To prove the cultural thesis, it is necessary to furnish independent evidence that some groups placed special value on education, and that this factor operated in its own right as a determinant of educational achievement.

Yet a number of writers have claimed such evidence by pointing to the cultural systems of certain ethnic groups that are thought to be compatible or incompatible with the requirements of modern education. This argument is commonly made with respect to Asians and Jews, both of whom have in fact achieved higher levels of education than most other groups in American society.

Stephen Steinberg, "Education and Ethnic Mobility" from *The Ethnic Myth*. Copyright © 1981 by Stephen Steinberg. Reprinted with the permission of Atheneum Publishers, Inc.

For example, in his book on Japanese-Americans William Petersen begins with the factual observation that "since 1940, the Japanese have had more schooling than any other race in the American population, including whites."[2] He then proceeds to explain the high educational levels of Japanese-Americans as an outgrowth of a particular set of cultural values. On the basis of his examination of the records of Japanese students at Berkeley during the late 1950s and early 1960s, Petersen writes: "Their education had been conducted like a military campaign against a hostile world, with intelligent planning and tenacity.... In a word, these young men and women were squares."[3] Irrespective of Petersen's questionable metaphor (would enterprising Jewish or Italian students be described as waging a military campaign, or is this imagery reserved for the Japanese?), his characterization of such students as "squares" is most revealing. According to Petersen, the "cultural traditions" of Japanese produced diligent, persevering, and industrious students who eschewed the pleasures of the moment in their dogged pursuit of long-range goals. Like the "old-fashioned boys" in Horatio Alger's novels, it is the squares who ultimately triumph.

In her praise of Chinese educational achievement, Betty Sung is even more explicit in tracing this to a specific "cultural heritage." According to Sung:

> Chinese respect for learning and for the scholar is a cultural heritage. Even when a college degree led to no more than a waiter's job, the Chinese continued to pursue the best education they could get, so that when opportunities developed, the Chinese were qualified and capable of handling their jobs. Other minorities have not had the benefit of this reverence for learning.[4]

For Sung, the Chinese reverence for learning is not merely characteristic of Chinese-Americans, but is a product of cultural heritage rooted in centuries of history.

Of course, it is the Jews who are most often acclaimed, in folklore and social science alike, as a "people of the book." The implication here is that Jews owe their intellectual prominence to a reverence for learning that is rooted in their religious culture and that has been passed down through the ages. There is hardly a study of Jews in America that does not cite a "Jewish passion for education" as a major factor, if not *the* major factor, in explaining Jewish mobility. A typical exposition of this idea is found in Marshall Sklare's 1971 book on *America's Jews*:

> Jewish culture embraced a different attitude toward learning from that which characterized the dominant societies of eastern Europe. This Jewish attitude was part of the value-system of the immigrants. It pertains to learning in general, though in the traditional framework it is most apparent with respect to the study of religious subjects.[5]

According to Sklare and numerous others, the high valuation that Jews traditionally placed on religious learning was, in the New World, transferred to secular learning, and with this cultural head start, the children of Jewish immigrants were quick to climb the educational ladder.

A large number of empirical studies have documented Jewish intellectual achievements. It is known that, compared with most other groups, Jews are more likely to go to college, especially highly competitive colleges, to excel once they are there, and to go on to graduate and professional schools. Studies have also shown that Jews are disproportionately represented among the teaching faculties of the nation's college and universities and this is especially so in the leading research institutions.[6] Still other studies have shown that Jews have produced more than their share of eminent scholars and scientists, and of course there has been much preoccupation with the fact that Marx, Freud, and Einstein, three of the towering figures of modern history, have been Jewish.[7] As in the case of Jewish economic success, the fact of Jewish intellectual prominence can hardly be disputed. Rather it is the interpretation of this fact—specifically, the notion that Jewish educational achievements result from a reverence for learning embedded in Jewish history and culture—that is problematic.

An alternative to this cultural theory is a social class theory that does not deny the operation of cultural factors, but sees them as conditional on preexisting class factors. Whereas the cultural theory holds that certain groups placed unusually high value on education, which resulted in greater mobility, the class theory turns this proposition around, and holds that economic mobility occurred first, and that this opened up channels of educational opportunity and engendered a corresponding set of values and aspirations favorable to education. Obviously, education allowed these groups to consolidate and extend their economic gains, but these were gains that initially occurred in the occupational marketplace without the benefit of extensive education.

This is not to deny the well-documented fact that Japanese, Chinese, and Jews all placed high value on education; nor does the class theory deny that reverence for education may be rooted in the traditional belief systems of these groups. Where the class theory differs from the cultural theory is in its emphasis on the *primacy* of class factors. That is to say, it is held that cultural factors have little independent effect on educational outcomes, but are influential only as they interact with class factors. Thus, to whatever extent a reverence for learning was part of the religious and cultural heritage of Asians and Jews, it was activated and given existential significance by their social class circumstances. Without this congruence between culture and circumstance, it is hardly conceivable that these groups could have sustained their traditional value on education, or that it would have actually resulted in higher levels of educational achievement.

The Myth of Jewish Intellectualism

Can Jewish intellectual traditions, rooted in premodern and prescientific systems of thought, explain the academic achievements of Jews in twentieth-century America? This is the question raised by anthropologist Miriam Slater, who did a "content analysis" of Jewish scholarly traditions. Slater shows that the style and content of traditional Jewish scholarship were fundamentally at odds with the requirements of modern secular education, and if anything would have operated as a deterrent to educational achievement in America. For example, whereas shtetl learning involved a ritualistic preoccupation with Talmudic legalisms, Western education is highly pragmatic, innovative, and oriented toward lucrative employment in the marketplace. In Slater's view it was a striving for material success, and not a passion for learning, that spurred Jews up the educational ladder.[8]

Slater is not the first to suggest that the specific content of traditional Jewish education was incompatible with modern secular education. For example, in his study on the historical evolution of science, Lewis Feuer writes of Talmudic scholarship that "this sterile type of 'learning' and disputation was an obstacle to the development of science among Jews, a hurdle they had to surmount."[9] In *World of Our Fathers* Irving Howe also comments that "scholarship often degenerated into abysmal scholasticism. Intellect could be reduced to a barren exercise in distinctions that had long ago lost their reality."[10] A less dispassionate view of traditional Jewish pedagogy is found in Michael Gold's autobiographical novel *Jews Without Money:*

> Reb Moisha was my teacher....What could such as he teach any one? He was ignorant as a rat. He was a foul smelling, emaciated beggar who had never read anything, or seen anything, who knew absolutely nothing but this sterile memory course in dead Hebrew which he whipped into the heads and backsides of little boys.[11]

In his own fashion, Gold concurs with Slater's view that Jewish scholarship was "discontinuous" with secular education in America.

Yet the issue that Slater raises is a spurious one. What sociologists have argued is not that Jewish intellectual traditions were important in and of themselves, but rather that they fostered a positive orientation toward learning that was easily adapted to secular education. In his novel *The Rise of David Levinsky*, Abraham Cahan explores how Old World values were recast in the New World. Formerly a Talmudic scholar in Russia, David Levinsky yearns to go to City College. Gazing at the "humble spires" of a City College building, he thinks to himself: "My old religion had gradually fallen to pieces, and if its place was taken by something else...that something was the red, church-like structure on the southeast corner of Lexington Avenue and Twenty-third Street. *It was the synagogue of my new life.*"[12] This last phrase epitomizes the transfer of a traditional value on learning from religious to secular education which, according to the conventional wisdom, accounts for the rapid economic mobility that Jews experienced in America.

Yet in Cahan's novel, Levinsky never fulfills his ambition to go to City College; instead he makes a fortune as an entrepreneur in the garment industry. Is this mere fiction or does Cahan's character typify the pattern of Jewish mobility? In other words, was it generally the case that Jews achieved economic mobility *before* their children climbed the educational ladder? Indeed, this is the conclusion of a recent study by Selma Berrol on "Education and Economic Mobility: The Jewish Experience in New York City, 1880–1920."[13]

Berrol's inventory of educational facilities in New York City at the turn of the century shows that the schools could not possibly have functioned as a significant channel of mobility. Still in an early stage of development, the public school system was unable to cope with the enormous influx of foreigners, most of whom were in their childbearing ages. Primary grade schools were so overcrowded that tens of thousands of students were turned away, and as late as 1914 there were only five high schools in Manhattan and the Bronx. If only for this reason, few children of Jewish immigrants received more than a rudimentary education.

Berrol furnishes other data showing that large numbers of Jewish students ended their schooling by the eighth grade. For example, in New York City in 1908 there were 25,534 Jewish students in the first grade, 11,527 in the seventh, 2,549 in their first year of high school, and only 488 in their last year.[14] Evidently, most immigrant Jewish children of this period dropped out of school to enter the job market.

Nor could City College have been a major channel of Jewish mobility during the early decades of the twentieth century. Until the expansion of City College in the 1930s and 1940s, enrollments were not large enough to have a significant impact on Jewish mobility. Furthermore, Jewish representation at the college was predominantly German; Berrol estimates that in 1923 only 11 percent of CCNY students had Russian or Polish names.

In short, prior to the 1930s and 1940s, the public schools, and City College in particular, were not a channel of mobility for more than a privileged few. It was not until the expansion of higher education following the Second World War that City College provided educational oppor-tunities for significant numbers of Jewish youth. However, by this time New York's Jewish population had already emerged from the deep poverty of the immigrant generation, and had experienced extensive economic mobility.

It was the children of these upwardly mobile Jews who enrolled in City College during the 1930s and 1940s. For them, education was clearly a channel of mobility, but it accelerated a process of intergenerational mobility that was already in motion, since their parents typically had incomes, and often occupations as well, that were a notch or two above those of the working class in general. As Berrol concluded:

> ...most New York City Jews did not make the leap from poverty into the middle class by going to college. Rather, widespread utilization of secondary and higher education *followed* improvements in economic status and was as much a result as a cause of upward mobility.[15]

The conclusion that economic mobility preceded the Jewish thrust in education is also suggested by Herbert Gutman's analysis of 1905 census data.[16] Gutman did a comparison of two immigrant Jewish neighborhoods on New York's East Side: Cherry Street, one of the section's poorest neighborhoods, made up largely of rank-and-file workers; and East Broadway, a somewhat more prosperous neighborhood largely inhabited by businessmen and professionals. The contrast between the two neighborhoods in terms of the mobility patterns of the next generation is striking. On Cherry Street almost all of the children in their late teens had left school and gone to work, generally at low-status, blue-collar jobs that barely raised them above the level of their parents. However, the children of the more affluent families on East Broadway were making a breakthrough into higher-status white-collar occupations and the professions.

Though Gutman's data are far from conclusive, they are consistent with other historical data suggesting that economic success was a precondition, rather than a consequence, of extensive schooling. There is no evidence to indicate that the children of Jewish rank-and-file workers received more education than other immigrant children of the same social class. If this assumption is correct, then the greater overall success that Jews experienced stems from the fact that Jews had an occupational head start compared to other immigrants, that this resulted in an early economic ascent, which in turn allowed more of their children to remain in school and avail themselves of educational opportunities.

Precisely at the time that Jews were overcoming the poverty of the immigrant generation, there was a vast increase in educational opportunity, another fortuitous wedding of historical circumstance that facilitated Jewish mobility. As the economy matured, the demand increased for a more educated labor force. This set in motion a long series of educational reforms leading to an expansion and overhaul of the nation's educational institutions. Especially in the northern industrial states where Jews were concentrated, there was a trend toward much heavier public investment in schools and colleges. The curricula were also changing away from their classical traditions toward science, vocational training, and professional education, and thus were more compatible with the talents and aspirations of children born outside the upper class.

One ramification of the educational expansion of the period was that teaching itself emerged as a significant profession. Between 1898 and 1920, the number of teachers in the New York City schools increased from 10,008 to 24,235, the largest numerical increase in any profession.[17] And among Russian Jews who graduated from City College between 1895 and 1935, more entered teaching than either medicine or law.[18] But it was not until a second major expansion of higher education after the Second World War that Jews began to show up in large numbers on the faculties of American colleges and universities.[19] Not surprisingly, they tended to enter new and expanding fields in the social and natural sciences. In all these ways, the stages of economic and educational development within the Jewish population coincided with stages of growth and change in American educational institutions.

What conclusion, then, can be drawn concerning the relationship between Jewish cultural values and Jewish educational achievements? It goes without saying that the educational levels that Jews finally attained would not have been possible without a corresponding set of supportive

values that encouraged education, defined college as a suitable channel for social and economic mobility, and idealized intellectual achievement. But were these values distinctively part of a religious and cultural heritage, or were they merely cultural responses of a group that had acquired the economic prerequisites for educational mobility at a time when educational opportunities abounded?

There is a sense in which both these questions can be answered affirmatively. Even if Jews placed no special value on education, their social class position undoubtedly would have led them to pursue educational opportunities anyway. But Jews *did* place a special value on education, and this helped to impart the pursuit of educational opportunities with deeper cultural significance. Given the role of study in Jewish religion, the transfer of these values to secular learning tended to legitimate and sanctify a worldly desire for social and economic improvement. But these values only assumed operational significance in their interaction with a wider set of structural factors, especially the advantageous position of economically mobile Jews and the favorable structure of educational opportunity that they encountered. It was because education carried with it such compelling social and economic rewards that the traditional value on education was activated, redefined, and given new direction.

Had immigrant Jews remained trapped in poverty and deprived of educational opportunities, it is unlikely that Jewish intellectual life would have advanced beyond the archaic scholasticism that immigrant Jews carried over with them from Europe. Conversely, other immigrant groups that started out with less favorable cultural dispositions with respect to education rapidly developed an appetite for education once they achieved a position in the class system comparable to that of Jews a generation earlier.

The Myth of Catholic Anti-Intellectualism

In matters of education, Catholics stand in historical counterpoint to Jews, lagging behind in areas where Jews have excelled. This has sometimes led to invidious comparisons between the two groups. For example, Thomas O'Dea, a leading Catholic scholar, wrote in 1958:

It is doubtful that even the Irish immigrants, perhaps the poorest of the nineteenth-century arrivals to these shores, were much poorer than the eastern European and Russian Jews who came after 1890, except possibly in the worst years of the Irish potato failure in the 1840s. Yet these eastern Jews...have contributed a larger proportion of their children and grandchildren to academic and scholarly life than have Catholic immigrants as a whole.[20]

Having assumed that Catholics and Jews started out in the same place in the class system, O'Dea implicitly dismisses class factors as irrelevant to the question of why Jews have produced a greater number of scholars. As already shown, however, although Jewish immigrants were poor, they had social class advantages in the form of literacy and occupational skills, that resulted in more rapid economic mobility. Thus, O'Dea's unfavorable comparison between Catholics and Jews is based on a false assumption.

Yet O'Dea's failure to consider class factors has been characteristic of nearly half a century of social research, and has resulted in a castigation of Catholicism itself for the underrepresentation of Catholics among the nation's scientists and scholars. For example, in 1931 *Scientific Monthly* published an article on "Scientific Eminence and Church Membership," in which the authors reported that Unitarians were 1,695 times more likely than Catholics to be listed among the nation's eminent scientists. The data seemed to give credence to the popular stereotype of the Catholic Church as a dogmatic and authoritarian institution that restricts free thought and scientific inquiry. The authors thus concluded that "the conspicuous dearth of scientists among Catholics suggests that the tenets of the church are not consonant with scientific endeavor."[21]

Several decades later, in his book on *Anti-Intellectualism in American Life*, Richard Hofstadter also scored Catholics for having "failed to develop an intellectual tradition in America or to produce its own class of intellectuals...."[22] Like earlier writers, Hofstadter automatically assumed that the low level of Catholic representation among scholars is symptomatic of an anti-intellectualism rooted in Catholic religion and culture.

The same inference is made in Kenneth

Hardy's 1974 study of the "Social Origins of American Scientists and Scholars," published in *Science* magazine.[23] Hardy ranked American undergraduate colleges in terms of the "scholarly productivity," as measured by the relative number of their graduates who went on to receive Ph.D.s. Like women's colleges and southern colleges, Catholic colleges turn out to be low in scholarly productivity. Hardy's interpretation of these findings is altogether circular. He assumes ipso facto that those institutions low in productivity are marked by anti-intellectual, antidemocratic, and antihumanitarian values that are antithetical to scholarship. But the only evidence he has that institutions have such retrograde values is that they are low in productivity. On this flimsy basis, he portrays Catholic colleges, as well as women's colleges and southern colleges, as culturally to blame for the fact that relatively few of their students go on to earn Ph.D.s.

A more plausible explanation, however, is that such colleges tend to attract students from less privileged backgrounds who have lower academic qualifications from the start, and who are less likely to aspire to careers that entail graduate education. Indeed, Alexander Astin has shown that it is not the attributes of colleges that determine their productivity of future Ph.D.s, but rather the attributes of the students they recruit.[24] In fact, those Catholic colleges that maintain high entrance standards—for example, Georgetown University, Boston College, Loyola University, and the Catholic University of America—all have above-average records for producing future Ph.D.s. Thus, there is no basis for attributing the generally lower rates of scholarly productivity of Catholic colleges to the intellectual quality of these institutions, much less to a specific set of anti-intellectual values rooted in the Catholic religion.

Why, then, have Catholics produced fewer scholars and scientists than other groups? What was the meshing of culture and circumstance that obstructed educational progress for Catholics? As a first step in addressing this issue, it is necessary to consider the varied ethnic composition of the Catholic population. It makes little sense to treat Catholics as a monolith, especially given the fact that the ethnic groups that made up the nation's Catholic population occupy such different positions in the class system. As Andrew Greeley has shown, Irish and German Catholics rank well above the national average on measures of income, occupation, and education, while Poles, Italians, Slavs, and French are closer to average.[25] These differences themselves suggest that religion may be less important as a factor in explaining social class outcomes than factors associated with the nationality of particular groups. In order to explore this further, it will be useful to focus on Italians, since they constitute the largest Catholic group in the last great wave of immigration, and because Italians have often been singled out as a group whose values are said to be inimical to education.

Most Italian immigrants came from the underdeveloped provinces of Southern Italy, where they worked as landless peasants. This helps to explain not only why Italians were less mobile than other groups, but also why they would have exhibited different attitudes toward education. Obviously, immigrants from peasant backgrounds were not likely to have the same outlook upon education as other immigrants, including Northern Italians, who came from more industrially advanced sectors of their countries of origin. In his book *The Social Background of the Italo-American School Child*, Leonard Covello had this to say about the sources of the Southern Italian's low valuation of formal education:

> As a peasant, unable to perceive things in *abstracto*, and as a man of the soil, he perceived education in association with material benefits. He saw the need to educate his children only insofar as the school provided means for bettering one's economic condition, or for breaking through the caste system. But since few precedents existed where a peasant's son became anything but a peasant, the *contadino* almost never entertained the possibility of his son's becoming a doctor, a lawyer, or embarking on some other professional career.[26]

Given the fact that Italian peasants were tied to the soil, formal education had little value for individual or collective survival.

A more basic reason for the high rate of illiteracy that prevailed among Italian immigrants was that schools were poor or nonexistent. As John Briggs has shown in a recent study, in areas where education was available, illiteracy was far less prevalent. On the basis of a painstaking analysis of educational statistics in the early 1900s, Briggs reached the following conclusion:

> Literacy, then, was closely associated with the quality and quantity of schooling available in southern Italy. The lower social classes had little control over the provision of public schooling. They took advantage of it where it existed. Illiteracy resulted where it was lacking or was offered only under extremely inconvenient circumstances. Clearly, the prevalence of illiteracy among emigrants is not a good criterion of their attitudes toward education, nor is it an indication of the inappropriateness of their traditional culture for their futures as urbanites. Such evidence is better viewed as a measure of past opportunity than as a prediction of future response to schooling.[27]

To whatever extent Southern Italians exhibited negative attitudes toward education, in the final analysis these attitudes only reflected economic and social realities, including a dearth of educational opportunities.

A number of ethnographic studies of Italians in the United States have also found evidence of unfavorable attitudes toward education, and have implicitly chastised Italians for not being more zealous in pursuit of educational opportunities. But, once again, it is necessary to ask whether Italian attitudes toward education were simply a carryover from Europe, as is commonly assumed, or whether they were responses to conditions of Italian life in this country as well.

This issue arises, for example, in interpreting the results of a 1958 study by Richard Otis Ulin on "The Italo-American Student in the American Public School," which was based on a comparison of students from Italian and Yankee backgrounds in Winchester, Massachusetts. Ulin found that the Italian students generally had poorer academic records, and he ascribed this to cultural orientations inherited from Southern Italy. The most important cultural flaw, according to Ulin, is a tendency toward fatalism and an inability to plan for the future. As Ulin writes:

> One can see much of the same Wheel of Fortune attitude that left the South Italian peasant praying for rain but neglecting to dig an irrigation ditch,

hoping for a remittance from America or for a windfall in the national lottery. These are sentiments which are echoed today in the currently popular tune, which interestingly enough, has Italian lyrics, "Che Sera, Sera" ("What Will Be, Will Be").[28]

Aside from Ulin's stereotypical view of the Italian peasant, what evidence is there that his Italian subjects in Winchester exhibit a "wheel of fortune attitude" toward life?

Ulin bases his conclusion on comments by Italian students such as the following: "I know other guys who worked their———off in school and they got good grades and now they got lousy jobs. It's just the way the ball bounces." But Ulin offers no evidence to support his claim that such attitudes are rooted in Southern Italian culture. On the contrary, it could be argued that his Italian subjects are expressing attitudes that are typical of the working class and in all likelihood accurately reflect the world as it actually exists for these working-class students in Winchester, Massachusetts. At least this is what is implied by another student, whom Ulin also construes as expressing a fatalistic attitude:

Listen, they [the teachers] can talk all they want about how everybody in Winchester has an equal chance. Do they think us kids from the Plains have an equal chance? In the pig's eye! The West Side kids get all the breaks. They don't have to work after school. The teachers go out of their way to help them. And if they want to go to college, their old man will give 'em the dough.[29]

What these students appear to be expressing is not a cultural disregard for education, but a recognition of the fact that, unlike their more affluent Yankee peers, their chances of reaching college are slim, and consequently their futures are not likely to depend upon their school performance. Like the men on *Tally's Corner*, they have adjusted their aspirations and their strategies to what they can realistically hope to achieve.

The view that cultural factors explain the low academic achievement of Italians has also been advanced in a study by Fred Strodtbeck that compared Italian and Jewish students on a number of value measures that predict educational performance. The largest differential was on the item:

"Planning only makes a person unhappy because your plans hardly ever work out anyway." Only 10 percent of Jewish students in his sample, but 38 percent of Italians, answered in the affirmative. Strodtbeck interprets such responses as an indication of the extent to which individuals have developed a sense of self-mastery, which he speculates is more often found in Jewish families because they are more democratic, and for this reason produce more motivated, secure, and achieving children. Not only does this interpretation involve a perilous leap from rather scant data, but there is evidence in Strodtbeck's data that what he measured were not ethnic differences, but class differences. When Strodtbeck compared Italian and Jewish students of the same social class background, there was no longer any difference between them.[30] In other words, the reason that the Jews in his original comparison were more likely to exhibit such traits as a future-time orientation, self-mastery, and democratic family relationships was that these qualities are generally characteristic of the middle class, regardless of the ethnic character of the groups involved.

In short, if Italians and other Catholics have not excelled academically, this cannot be blamed on a value system that discouraged education, since these values themselves only reflect the operation of social class factors and the unfavorable structure of educational opportunity that confronts the lower classes generally. As in the case of Jews, Catholics had to secure an economic foothold before their children could make significant advances up the economic ladder. But given the relative disadvantages associated with the peasant origins of most Catholic immigrants, more time was required to establish this foothold. Since the Second World War, however, Catholics have substantially improved their collective position in the class system. On the basis of national surveys extending from 1943 to 1965, one study concluded that:

At the end of World War II, Protestants in the United States ranked well above Catholics in income, occupation, and education; since then Catholics have gained dramatically and have surpassed Protestants in most aspects of status.[31]

If the above historical interpretation is correct

then the fact that Catholics are achieving economic parity with the rest of the population should bring an end to patterns of Catholic underrepresentation among the nation's scholars and scientists.

The Changing Religious Composition of American Higher Education

About a decade ago the Carnegie Commission on Higher Education conducted a massive survey of approximately 60,000 faculty in 303 institutions of higher learning across the nation.[32] From this landmark study it is possible to chart historical trends in the religious background of American scholars and scientists and, indirectly, to test the proposition that Catholicism is inherently anathema to intellectual achievement.

Table 1 reports the religious background of faculty in four different age groups, and of graduate students planning a career in college teaching. In evaluating these figures it should be kept in mind that Catholics make up roughly 26 percent of the national population, Protestants 66 percent, and Jews 3 percent.

The data in Table 1 show unmistakably that there has been a gradual uptrend in Catholic representation over the past several decades. Among the oldest cohort of faculty, Catholics are only 15 percent, but this figure increases among younger age groups to 17, 19, and 20 percent. Among graduate students who plan a career in college

TABLE 1. *The Religious Background of College Faculty of Different Ages (All Institutions)*

Religious background	Age of faculty				Graduate students planning a career in college teaching
	55 or more	45–54	35–44	34 or less	
Protestant	76%	69%	63%	63%	58%
Catholic	15	17	19	20	22
Jewish	5	8	10	10	10
Other	2	3	4	4	4
None	2	3	4	3	6
Total	100%	100%	100%	100%	100%

Source: Stephen Steinberg, *The Academic Melting Pot* (New York: McGraw-Hill, 1974), p. 104. Reprinted by permission of the Carnegie Foundation for the Advancement of Teaching.

teaching, the figure again rises to 22 percent. Since Catholics make up 26 percent of the national population, it is clear that they are rapidly approaching the point of being represented among faculty in the same proportion as in the nation as a whole.

In the case of Jews, the data indicate a pattern of overrepresentation. Though only 3 percent of the national population, Jews were already 5 percent of the oldest cohort of faculty, and this proportion gradually rose to 10 percent, where it has leveled off. The largest increase in Jewish representation occurred with the 45–54 age group, which indicate that Jews made their major breakthrough in college teaching during the expansion of higher education after World War II.

The increasing representation of Catholics and Jews among college faculty has resulted in a proportionate decrease of Protestants. Between the oldest cohort and the youngest, Protestants have gone from being overrepresented to being underrepresented relative to their proportion of the national population. Given the Protestant decrease and the Catholic increase, it can now be said that Catholics and Protestants have achieved parity with each other.

The same trends emerge even more clearly when the ranking universities are examined (this includes seventeen "top" institutions such as Columbia, Harvard, Johns Hopkins, Northwestern, etc.). Jewish representation in these institutions is considerably higher than among colleges and universities generally, and Protestant and Catholic representation is somewhat lower. But the *trend* is even more pronounced than before (see Table 2). That is, Catholic representation in these ranking institutions has steadily increased; there has been a corresponding decrease of Protestants; and the Jewish proportion reached a peak with the expansion of higher education after the Second World War and then leveled off. As far as Catholics are concerned, all the evidence leads to the conclusion that they are belatedly taking their place in American higher education.[33]

Further insight into the different mobility patterns of Protestant, Catholic, and Jewish scholars can be gleaned from data on the class origins of faculty in the Carnegie survey. Respondents were asked about the occupation of their fathers; the category labeled "working class" in-

TABLE 2. *The Religious Background of College Faculty of Different Ages (The 17 Top-Ranking Universities Only)*

Religious background	55 or more	45–54	35–44	34 or less	Graduate students planning a career in college teaching
Protestant	72%	64%	57%	55%	52%
Catholic	10	11	13	16	20
Jewish	12	16	19	18	16
Other	2	3	5	4	5
None	4	6	6	7	7
Total	100%	100%	100%	100%	100%

Source: Stephen Steinberg, *The Academic Melting Pot,* op. cit., p. 107. Reprinted by permission of the Carnegie Foundation for the Advancement of Teaching.

cludes both blue-collar workers and those in low-level white-collar occupations such as clerical and sales workers. The data, reported in Table 3, are consistent with the historical data analyzed above.

In the first place, relatively few Jewish scholars, and many more Catholics, have their origin in the working class. The figure for Jews is 25 percent; for Protestants, 32 percent; for Catholics, 45 percent. What is especially notable is that even among older age cohorts, relatively few Jewish faculty come from working-class backgrounds.

An unusually large number of Jewish faculty had fathers who owned small businesses. Indeed, this is the case of slightly over half the Jews in the oldest age category, and a third of those in the youngest age category. As observed earlier, many Jewish immigrants were able to use their prior experience in commerce as an avenue of economic mobility. The data now indicate that it is the children of these businessmen who went on to become scholars and scientists in disproportionate numbers. On the other hand, the Jewish working class has never been a major source of Jewish scholars.

The pattern is quite the opposite for Catholics. In every age cohort four out of every ten Catholic scholars come from working-class backgrounds, and on the basis of what is known about the occupational concentrations of Catholics in the society at large, it is safe to assume that Catholic scholars are typically coming not

TABLE 3. *Social Class Origins of College Faculty by Religion and Age*

Religious background Father's occupation	Age				
	55 and more	45–54	35–44	34 or less	Total
Protestants					
Professional	26%	22%	22%	25%	23%
Managerial*	13	16	17	20	17
Owner, small business	17	16	15	13	15
Farm	19	14	12	9	13
Working class**	25	32	34	33	32
Total	100%	100%	100%	100%	100%
Catholics					
Professional	10%	14%	13%	16%	14%
Managerial*	19	18	19	22	20
Owner, small business	22	16	17	13	16
Farm	9	6	5	4	5
Working class**	40	46	46	45	45
Total	100%	100%	100%	100%	100%
Jews					
Professional	13%	14%	17%	26%	19%
Managerial*	14	11	13	17	14
Owner, small business	52	45	44	33	41
Farm	2	1	0	1	1
Working class**	19	29	26	23	25
Total	100%	100%	100%	100%	100%

*Includes corporate officials and owners of large businesses.

**Includes skilled and unskilled workers and low-level white-collar workers such as clerical and sales workers. Armed Forces personnel are also included, though they constitute a negligible 1 percent of the sample.

Source: Stephen Steinberg, *The Academic Melting Pot,* op. cit., p. 92. Reprinted by permission of the Carnegie Foundation for the Advancement of Teaching.

from the bottommost strata, but rather from stable working-class occupations that offer an adequate, if marginal, livelihood. This is a more precarious economic base than existed for Jews, which helps to explain the lower representation of Catholics in the academic profession.

Conclusion

Given the disadvantages with which Catholic immigrants started life in America, it is not surprising that they required another generation or two to produce their numerical share of scholars and scientists. Thomas O'Dea is too quick to dismiss immigration and problems of assimilation as factors bearing on "the absence of intellectual life" among Catholics.[34] The fact that the great majority of Catholic immigrants came from peasant backgrounds was of enormous consequence. Not only did high levels of illiteracy slow the pace of cultural adjustment, but Catholic immigrants also lacked the kinds of occupational skills that facilitated economic mobility for other groups. These conditions also presented formidable obstacles to intellectual achievement, especially in light of the class character of American higher education, and the many factors producing a far lower rate of college attendance among lower-class children. However, as Catholics have gradually improved their position in the class system, their children are going to college with greater frequency, and as in every group, a certain number of them pursue academic careers and become scholars of distinction. The scenario is no different for Catholics than for other groups. It has only taken longer to play itself out.

ENDNOTES

1. Quoted in Samuel Bowles and Herbert Gintis, *Schooling in Capitalist America* (New York: Basic Books, 1976), p. 21.

2. William Petersen, *Japanese Americans* (New York: Random House, 1971), p. 113.

3. Ibid., pp. 115–16.

4. Betty Lee Sung, *The Story of the Chinese in America* (New York: Macmillan, 1967), pp. 124–25.

5. Marshall Sklare, *America's Jews* (New York: Random House, 1971), p. 58.

6. Stephen Steinberg, *The Academic Melting Pot* (New York: McGraw-Hill, 1974), chap. 5.

7. Tina Levitan, *The Laureates: Jewish Winners of the Nobel Prize* (New York: Twayne Publishers, Inc., 1960); Nathaniel Weyl and Stefan Possony, *The Geography of Intellect* (Chicago: Henry Regnery, 1913), pp. 123–28.

8. Miriam Slater, "My Son the Doctor: Aspects of Mobility Among American Jews," *American Sociological Review* 34 (June 1969): 359–73.

9. Lewis S. Feuer, *The Scientific Intellectual* (New York: Basic Books, 1963), p. 303.

10. Irving Howe, *World of Our Fathers* (New York: Harcourt Brace Jovanovich, 1976), pp. 8–9.

11. Michael Gold, *Jews Without Money* (New York: Avon Books, 1961; orig. edition 1930), p. 43.

12. Abraham Cahan, *The Rise of David Levinsky* (Colophon Books: New York, 1960), p. 169 (italics added).

13. Selma C. Berrol, "Education and Economic Mobility: The Jewish Experience in New York City, 1880–1920," *American Jewish Historical Quarterly*, March 1976, pp. 257–71.

14. Ibid., p. 261.

15. Ibid., p. 271.

16. Gutman's unpublished data are summarized by Irving Howe in *World of Our Fathers*, op. cit., pp. 141–44.

17. Sherry Gorelick, *Social Control, Social Mobility and the Eastern European Jews: Public Education in New York City, 1880–1924*, unpublished Ph.D. dissertation, Columbia University, 1975 (scheduled for publication by the Rutgers University Press), p. 167. *The World Almanac, 1923* (New York: The Press Publication Co., 1923), p. 549.

18. Gorelick, ibid., p. 165.

19. Steinberg, op. cit., p. 106.

20. Thomas O'Dea, *American Catholic Dilemma* (New York: Sheed & Ward, 1959), p. 87.

21. Harvey D. Lehman and Paul A. Witty, "Scientific Eminence and Church Membership," *Scientific Monthly* 33 (December 1931), pp. 548–49.

22. Richard Hofstadter, *Anti-Intellectualism in American Life* (New York: Random House, 1963), p. 136.

23. Kenneth Hardy, "Social Origins of American Scientists and Scholars," *Science*, vol. 185, August 9, 1974, pp. 497–506. Also, my critique in *Change* magazine, June 1976, pp. 50–51, 64.

24. Alexander Astin, " 'Productivity' of Undergraduate Institutions," *Science* 136 (April 1962); *Predicting Academic Performance in College* (New York: Free Press, 1971), pp. 129–35.

25. Andrew Greeley, *Why Can't They Be Like Us?* (New York: Dutton, 1971), pp. 67–68, "The Ethnic Miracle," *Public Interest*, Fall 1976, pp. 20–36.

26. Leonard Covello, *The Social Background of the Italo-American School Child*, edited with an introduction by Francesco Cordasco (Totowa, N.J.: Rowman and Littlefield, 1972), p. 256.

27. John W. Briggs, *An Italian Passage* (New Haven: Yale University Press, 1978), p. 64.

28. Richard Otis Ulin, "The Italo-American Student in the American Public School," unpublished Ph.D. dissertation, Harvard University, 1958, p. 157.

29. Ibid., p. 156.

30. Fred L. Strodtbeck, "Family Interaction, Values, and Achievement," in Marshall Sklare, *The Jews* (New York: Free Press, 1958), pp. 161–62.

31. Norval D. Glenn and Ruth Hyland, "Religious Prejudice and Worldly Success," *American Sociological Review* 32 (February 1967), pp. 84–85.

32. For methodological details regarding these surveys, see Martin Trow and Oliver Fulton, *Teachers and Students* (New York: McGraw-Hill, 1975), pp. 297–371.

33. Though the Carnegie surveys did not query respondents about their ethnic background, it is safe to assume that the Irish have contributed disproportionately to the Catholic increase, since they have higher levels of income and education in the population at large. See Andrew Greeley, "The Ethnic Miracle," op. cit.

34. O'Dea, op. cit., p. 93.

18

Trends in Socioeconomic Achievement among Immigrant and Native-Born Asian-Americans, 1960–1976*

Charles Hirschman
Morrison G. Wong

Minority status is universally perceived to be associated with an inferior position in the distribution of power and of socioeconomic rewards in the society. Indeed, considerable empirical research over the past ten to fifteen years has documented the wide socioeconomic gap between Blacks, Chicanos, and other minority groups from majority whites (Siegel, 1965; Schmid and Nobbe, 1965; Farley, 1977; Duncan, 1969; Poston and Alvirez, 1973; Poston, Alvirez, and Tienda, 1976; Johnson and Sell, 1976; Featherman and Hauser, 1976; U.S. Commission on Civil Rights, 1978). One of the major conclusions of this body of research is the persistence of discrimination in the process of unequal socioeconomic achievement for minorities and whites.

Asian-Americans, particularly those of Chinese, Filipino, and Japanese origins, are minority groups which exemplify a different pattern. Historically, Chinese and Japanese in the United States have achieved higher socioeconomic attainments than other minorities, and in recent years Asian-American socioeconomic achievements have been equal to or exceeded those of whites (Lyman, 1974; Peterson, 1966, 1971; Kuo, 1979; Hosokawa, 1969; Hsu, 1971; Sung, 1967). The substantial socioeconomic gains of Asian-Americans are more evident in educational and occupational outcomes than in income. Filipino-Americans lag behind Chinese and Japanese socioeconomic levels but show signs of significant advancement in recent years. These achievements have taken place despite a long and sordid history of institutional discrimination against Asians in the United States (Lyman, 1974; Kitano, 1974; Saxton, 1971; Daniels and Kitano, 1970; Saniel, 1967; Sandmeyer, 1973; Bosworth, 1967; Daniels, 1970) and evidence of present-day unequal economic returns to social background (Wong, 1980b; Jibou, 1976-77).

This pattern of minority groups achievement, in spite of considerable institutional obstacles, is not an entirely unknown phenomenon. The most obvious case is that of Jews in North America and Europe, but there are parallels with Chinese in Southeast Asia, Indians in East Africa, and Palestinians in the Middle East. Greeley (1976) includes Catholic Americans as a successful minority. The most common explanation for overachieving minorities is that they possess "middle-class" cultural values such as thrift, perseverance, and commitment to work that are conducive to socioeconomic advancement

From *The Sociological Quarterly* 22:4 (Autumn 1981): pp. 495–514. ©1981 by The Sociological Quarterly. All rights reserved.

*A revised version of a paper presented at the Annual Meetings of the Population Association of America, Denver, Colorado, April 10–12, 1980. This research was supported by a grant from the National Institute of Mental Health (1 ROI 14337-01) and a Duke University Biomedical Research Support Grant. The authors thank Ronald Rindfuss and Scott Grosse for comments on an earlier draft and Teresa Dark for typing the manuscript.

(Rosen, 1959; Peterson, 1971; Hsu, 1971: 114–16; Caudill and DeVos, 1965; Schwartz, 1971). However, the limited empirical evidence on this issue is not supportive of the thesis (Featherman, 1971). A more substantial variant of the cultural perspective posits that kinship networks, ethnic institutions, and a high degree of ethnic solidarity are the most influential factors responsible for the rapid socioeconomic advancement of Asians in America (Li, 1977; Miyamoto, 1972; Light, 1972). However, the fact that Asian-Americans have only succeeded in making substantial socioeconomic progress in the last twenty to thirty years, while cultural orientations and social institutions were presumably the same as that prior to World War II, cautions against the simple acceptance of this interpretation. We argue that cultural variables must be interpreted in light of the structural conditions that give rise to them and maintain them over time.

In an alternative theoretical formulation, Bonacich (1973) argues that the structured position of a "sojourner" community—temporary residence in a hostile environment—promotes ethnic enterprise and solidarity. When resident in multiethnic societies, these groups are labeled "middlemen minorities." With long-term goals fixed upon return to another homeland—even if never realized—an ethnic community can display extraordinary habits of deferred gratification, accumulated savings, and investment in human capital. Furthermore, as unassimilated "outsiders," middlemen minorities are permitted to occupy certain "occupational niches" which are noncompetitive with the dominant group. These positions allow for somewhat higher socioeconomic status than other minority groups, but there remains a ceiling on advancement into positions of authority or institutional power. This perspective has been applied by several authors to account for the relatively high socioeconomic position of the Asians in America (Kitano, 1974; Loewen, 1971; Wong, 1977). The positions which these middleman minorities occupy are precarious and dependent upon the goodwill of the dominant group. They are allowed to achieve, but only so high. In an elaboration of this perspective, Wong (1981), in his description of the Chinese sweatshop industry, argues that the Chinese immigrant entrepreneurs (sweatshop owners) fulfill "middleman" functions by exploiting members of their own ethnic group in the interests of larger firms in the core sector of the economy.

In a recent paper Wilson and Portes (1980) offer a somewhat different interpretation of the ethnic enterprise phenomenon in their "immigrant enclave" model. Drawing upon the Cuban experience in Miami, they posit that the spatially defined minority enclave where businesses are owned by minority group members offers distinct advantages for social mobility. While immigrant entrepreneurs pay very low wages, they offer minority workers opportunities for advancement that are unavailable in the nonenclave economy. This thesis seems to be particularly appropriate to the case of Asian-Americans.

In the present form, we do not attempt to test these alternative theoretical frameworks, rather the objective is to provide a thorough introduction to the structure of socioeconomic patterns and achievements of three Asian-American communities: Chinese, Japanese, and Filipinos, with particular attention to changes from 1960 to 1976. This is a significant period because the 1965 Immigration Act opened the door to renewed immigration from Asia. For this reason, the analysis contrasts the socioeconomic characteristics of both immigrants and native-born Asian-Americans for three dates for which data are available: 1960, 1970, and 1976. In subsequent research we plan to extend the present analysis to directly address the major theoretical alternatives. Before beginning this analysis, a brief history of Asian immigration will be presented so that the present situation may be understood better.

Historical Perspective on Asian Immigration and Settlement in the United States

In the latter half of the nineteenth century Asian migration to the United States was stimulated by the demands for cheap labor, first in California and then in the sugar industry of Hawaii. The Chinese began to arrive in large numbers in the early 1850s as the gold mines of California drew migrants from everywhere. Early Chinese workers played significant roles in the development of numerous industries in California, in the construction of the railroads, and in the mining and agricultural sectors in the Pacific and mountain states.

With fewer resources and a "sojourner" outlook, Chinese immigrants accepted lower wages and were thought to work longer and at a harder pace than native white workers. As employers exploited these differences, bitter and often violent ethnic antagonism erupted between Chinese and white workers (Bonacich, 1973). Pushed by pressures from organized labor and popular racist sentiments, Congress passed the ten-year Chinese Exclusion Act of 1882, which was renewed in 1892 and made permanent in 1902. While this act did not completely eliminate Chinese immigration, it did reduce the numbers of unskilled Chinese laborers (Boyd, 1971a: 48).

Significant Japanese immigration began in the 1880s, first to the sugar plantations of Hawaii, followed by movements to California. Encountering the same anti-Asian sentiments as the Chinese before them, Japanese were restricted from immigrating to the United States by the so-called Gentlemen's Agreement of 1908. The small number of Chinese and Japanese entering the United States after the enactment of these exclusionary policies were further reduced to almost a trickle by the 1924 Immigration Act with its infamous national origins quotas which favored immigrants from Northwestern Europe (Japan was not allocated any immigrant quota).

Filipino immigration began in the early 1920s as barriers were enacted to limit other sources of Asian immigration. Initially classified as American nationals, Filipinos were not restricted by the 1924 Immigration Act. This omission was soon "rectified" by the Tydings-McDuffie Act, better known as the Filipino Exclusion Act, which was passed in 1934.

Immigration from Asia continued on a very modest scale over the next several decades, with a small rise in the years following World War II. In spite of the official policy of exclusion represented by the token quotas of 100–175 annual immigrants from the major countries of Asia, immigration from Asia was still possible for those with family ties to American citizens and for those who were considered refugees.

The major change in U.S. immigration policy came with the 1965 Immigration Act, which eliminated almost eight years of an exclusionary policy toward Asia. With the eradication of the national origin quotas and the emphasis on family reunification and scarce occupational skills, Asian immigrants rose from about 8 percent of all immigrants in the early 1960s to 35 percent in the mid-1970s (Wong and Hirschman, 1981). Current trends suggest not only an increase in the number of "old wave" Asian immigrants (i.e., Chinese, Japanese, and Filipinos) but also a significant migration of "new wave" Asians from other countries such as Korea, India, and Indochina (Wong and Hirschman, 1981).

Growth of Asian-American Minorities

The history of Asian immigration to the United States is partially reflected in the numbers (and percentage foreign-born) of Japanese, Chinese, and Filipinos counted in the decennial censuses of the United States during the twentieth century (table 1). At the turn of the century, there were only about 119,000 Chinese and 85,000 Japanese in the United States. There was no count of Filipinos in 1900, but their number in the U.S. was probably insignificant at the time. In the next two decades, the number of Japanese in the United States more than doubled, while the absolute number of Chinese actually shrank. While net immigration from Japan continued, there appears to have been a greater exodus of return migrants to China than new immigrants arriving. Another important difference was the substantially higher proportion of women among the Japanese immigrant community than among Chinese. With fifteen to twenty males to every female among Chinese in the United States in the late nineteenth and early twentieth century, natural increase (and a second generation community) was minimal (Lyman, 1974:88). The Filipino community only began to grow in the 1920s, but immigration restrictions limited further growth in the following decades.

It was not until after World War II, and especially in the 1950s and 1960s, that substantial growth is evident among the three Asian-American populations. From 1950 to 1976, the Japanese population almost doubled from 326,000 to 621,000, but the Chinese and Filipino populations increased fivefold during the same period and numbered 578,000 and 554,000 in 1976, respectively. This resurgence of growth was initiated by an increase in fertility as the number of young

TABLE 1. *Census Counts of Japanese, Chinese, and Filipinos in the U.S. (Including Hawaii), Sex Ratio, Percent Foreign-Born of Each Population, and All Three Populations as a Percentage of the Total U.S. Population, 1900–1976.*

Census Year	Japanese			Chinese			Filipino			Total as a Percent of U.S. Pop.
	Pop.c	Sex Ratio b %	FB	Pop.c	Sex Ratio b %	FB	Pop.c	Sex Ratio b %	FB a	
1900	85	487	94%	119	1,385	87%	—	—	—	0.3%
1910	153	349	83%	94	926	75%	3	944	—	0.3%
1920	221	160	64%	85	466	64%	27	485	—	0.3%
1930	279	129	43%	102	296	51%	108	706	—	0.4%
1940	285	119	30%	106	224	40%	99	457	—	0.4%
1950	326	109	25%	150	168	50%	123	271	60%	0.4%
1960	464	102	22%	237	133	40%	176	175	50%	0.5%
1970	591	85	21%	435	111	47%	343	123	52%	0.7%
1976 (Survey of income & education)	621	75	28%	578	102	67%	554	85	67%	0.8%
Percent Increase										
1900–1920	159%			−29%			—			
1920–40	29%			24%			267%			
1940–50	14%			41%			24%			
1950–60	42%			58%			43%			
1960–70	27%			84%			95%			
1970–76	5%			33%			62%			

a Filipino immigrants were not classified as foriegn-born until 1950.
b Sex Ratio is the ratio of men per 100 women.
c Population (expressed) in 1000s.
Sources: U.S. Bureau of the Census 1953, table 8; U.S. Bureau of the Census 1963a, table :4; U.S. Bureau of the Census 1963b, table 8; U.S. Bureau of the Census 1973, tables 48 and 190; U.S. Bureau of the Census 1975, table series 91–118; 1976 Survey of Income and Education, Public Use Sample; Schmitt, 1968, p. 121

women in the childbearing years became a larger fraction of the total population (this was most important for the Chinese and Filipino populations). Of even greater importance was the opening of the door to a new wave of Asian immigration after 1965. These changes are reflected in the changing proportion of foreign-born Asian-Americans over the decades. The most settled Asian community has been the Japanese-American population, which has had a majority native-born since 1930. The influx of Japanese immigration after 1965 was fairly modest and the proportion of foreign-born only rose from 20 percent in 1970 to 28 percent in 1976. While the proportion of foreign-born Chinese was reduced over the decades, this trend was reversed in the 1960s with the influx of new Chinese immigrants. In 1976, two-thirds of Chinese and Filipinos in the U.S. were foreign-born.

A closer look at the patterns of recent immigration is presented in table 2, which shows the percentage of foreign-born among the three Asian-American populations for 1960, 1970, and 1976. The historical legacy of immigration trends is imprinted in the changing proportions of foreign-born from older to younger age groups. Recent immigration is most evident by comparing inter-cohort shifts (across columns) and intracohort changes in the proportion foreign-born (looking at changes diagonally) in table 2.

Although immigrants are typically young males, this is not always the case. In 1960, there was a considerably higher proportion of foreign-born Japanese women than men, especially in the young adult ages reflecting in part the large number of Japanese women who married American soldiers stationed in Japan during the postwar years. Although there have been modest increases in the percent foreign-born among the younger Japanese population from 1960 to 1976, the Japanese-American community remains predominantly a native-born population. Immigrants are a very small minority with the Japanese community even after the changes brought by the 1965 reform immigration legislation.

Because of an unbalanced sex ratio and a continued trickle of immigration, a sizeable second generation was slower to develop among the Chinese-American population than other Asian groups. In 1960 and 1970, a majority of Chinese

below age 25 was native-born, but the reverse was true for Chinese men and women above age 15 (see table 2). There is evidence of considerable immigration during the 1960–70 decade. For instance, the percentage foreign-born among 15–24 year-old males was 41 percent in 1960, but the figure for the same cohort ten years later (looking at those age 25–34 in 1970) was 66 percent. Even more dramatic are the changes from 1970 to 1976. During this period, the influx of Chinese immigrants (primarily from Taiwan and Hong Kong) was so substantial as to push the percentage foreign-born figure from 47 percent to 67 percent of the entire Chinese-American population. Indeed, more than eight out of ten Chinese above age 15 in 1976 were foreign-born. The impact of this enormous Chinese immigrant flow has yet to be analyzed.

Comparable patterns are evident among the Filipino population. Although they were more of an immigrant population in 1960 than the Chinese population (and with three males for every female), there were native-born majorities among young Filipinos (below age 25). A major wave of Filipino immigration began after the 1965 Immigration Act, and by 1976 a majority of Filipinos were foreign-born in all age groups except those below age 15.

In the following sections, the socioeconomic differences between native-born and foreign-born males of the three major Asian-American populations relative to whites are explored for the period from 1960 to 1976. (For earlier studies, see Boyd, 1971b; Wilber et al., 1975; and U.S. Commission on Civil Rights, 1978.)

Data and Variables

The analysis of the socioeconomic status and change of immigrant and native-born Americans relative to whites relies on three sources of data: the 1960 Population Census, the 1970 Population Census, and the 1976 Survey of Income and Education (SIE). These three data sources provide sufficient samples of Asian-Americans and a comparison group of whites. All three data sources are available in public use samples (PUS) of unit records of household and individuals. From the .01 sample of the 1960 PUS, we selected all Japanese (N = 1081), Chinese (N = 724), and Filipino (N =

TABLE 2. *Percent Foreign-Born[a] of Japanese, Chinese, and Filipinos in the U.S., by Sex and Age, 1960, 1970, and 1976.*

	Japanese						Chinese						Filipino					
	Male			Female			Male			Female			Male			Female		
Age	1960	1970	1976	1960	1970	1976	1960	1970	1976	1960	1970	1976	1960	1970	1976	1960	1970	1976
0-14	7	5	10	7	5	17	9	19	29	8	19	33	12	19	26	11	21	25
15-24	8	7	16	13	9	17	41	41	52	35	43	38	30	42	54	26	46	61
25-34	12	23	19	41	38	32	52	66	82	51	69	88	53	69	84	51	75	87
35-44	5	15	28	11	48	56	60	60	83	48	62	88	74	68	87	64	69	88
45-54	15	6	6	14	15	38	69	59	80	56	57	87	92	76	57	75	72	69
55-64	65	11	2	74	17	15	68	62	78	59	68	72	92	90	89	80	75	92
65 and above	93	65	68	92	65	72	67	65	87	65	69	89	91	88	100	1	68	99
% FB of Total Population	18	15	18	25	26	35	44	47	65	34	48	69	58	55	65	38	51	68
N[b] (000)	41	39	49	61	83	125	59	106	190	34	98	197	66	101	167	22	78	202

[a]Each cell entry is the percent foreign-born of that particular age-sex-ethnic population; [b]The 1960 and 1970 N's are the census counts and the 1976 figures are the weighted SEI sample.

Sources: U.S. Bureau of the Census, 1963b, tables 3, 4, 5, 8; U.S. Bureau of the Census, 1973, table 190; 1976 Survey of Income and Education, Public Use Tapes.

694) males age 25–64, and a comparison group of white men (N = 3654). From the .01 public use sample of the 1970 Census (15 percent questionnaire, state file), comparable samples were selected (Japanese N = 1271, Chinese N = 1062, Filipino N = 825, white N = 3864). The 1976 SIE, one of the largest national surveys undertaken (over 150,000 households), contained sufficient Asians to select samples of 651 Japanese, 278 Chinese, 315 Filipinos, and 8,740 white men age 25–64 (these are unweighted N's). All SIE data reported in this paper are weighted to provide representative estimates of the U.S. population.

These three data sources were gathered by the U.S. Bureau of the Census with comparable standards of data collection, coding, and preparation of data files. Moreover, by definition all these data files are comparable in terms of universe (although the 1976 SIE was limited to the household population), structure, wording of questions, and methods of data collection. (For more information on the methodological details, see U.S. Bureau of the Census, 1971; 1972; 1977.) We have limited our present analysis to males between the ages of 25 through 64 years. Sex dif-

ferences in socioeconomic achievement are sufficiently complex to require a separate analysis, which we plan to do in a separate study. The age limitation was imposed in order to consider only those individuals in the economically active period of the life cycle (e.g., persons eligible for labor force participation). For the most part, the U.S. Census Bureau used the respondent's self definition to identify racial/ethnic categories. For the 1960, 1970, and 1976 samples, racial/ethnic designation was relatively straightforward, relying on the respondent's (or the person responding on behalf of the household) self-identity for race or ethnicity. The white sample includes Spanish-surnamed and/or individuals of Latin American origin who identified themselves as whites.

Educational attainment was operationally defined as the number of completed years of schooling, ranging from 0 (no schooling) to 18 (6 or more years of college). Relying largely on the major occupational categories, we classified occupations into ten major groupings: professionals, salaried managers, self-employed managers (proprietors), sales workers, clerical workers, craftsmen, operatives, laborers (nonfarm), service, and

TABLE 3. *Mean Years of Schooling of White, Japanese, Chinese, and Filipino Males in the U.S. by Age and Nativity Status, 1960, 1970, and 1976*

Age	Mean Years of Schooling								
	White			Japanese					
				Native-Born			Foreign-Born		
	1960	1970	1976	1960	1970	1976	1960	1970	1976
25–34	11.4	12.4	13.4	12.8	13.7	14.7	14.7	14.9	16.2
35–44	10.8	11.6	12.4	11.9	12.9	13.3	13.6	15.2	14.5
45–54	10.2	11.2	11.9	10.0	12.0	13.2	9.0	13.9	12.5
55–64	8.8	10.4	11.0	8.3	10.3	11.4	7.8	9.6	12.2
Total (25–64)	10.4	11.5	12.3	11.7	12.4	13.2	10.3	14.1	14.8
N[a]	3654	3864	8652	894	1084	592	186	185	59
	Ratio to White Mean								
Age	1960	1970	1976	1960	1970	1976	1960	1970	1976
25–34	100	100	100	112	110	110	129	120	121
35–44	100	100	100	110	111	107	126	131	117
45–54	100	100	100	98	107	111	88	124	105
55–64	100	100	100	94	99	104	89	92	111
Total (25–64)	100	100	100	112	108	107	99	123	120

[a]The N's are from the public use samples of each data source (the 1976 N's are based upon the unweighted data). The Asian-American samples are .01 in the 1960 and 1970 Censuses and .001 for whites. From the 1976 SEI, all Asian-American respondents were selected and .10 of white respondents.

Sources: Public Use Samples of 1960 and 1970 Population Censuses, and the 1976 Survey of Income and Education.

farmers/farm workers. The industrial classification was collapsed into eleven major categories, chosen to represent the major industries that differentiate Asian-American populations from whites. Earnings were measured with reference to the calendar year prior to the census of survey, namely, 1959, 1969, and 1975. For comparison, the earnings data for all years are adjusted for inflation into constant 1975 dollars.

Educational Attainment

One would expect that most older Asian immigrants, like their counterparts from Europe, arrived in the United States with very little formal education. Since education was seen by immigrants as a channel for upward mobility for the children, one would expect a considerable rise in education among second-generation Asian-Americans. One would also expect that more recent immigrants from Asia (post-1965) would be more educated than older (pre-1965) Asian immigrants carrying advanced educational degrees as the criteria for entry into the U.S. These general expectations are confirmed in table 3, which shows mean educational levels by age group for native-born and foreign-born Asian-American

men and for the reference group of white males (95 percent of whom are native-born.)

Asian immigrants above age 55, especially in 1960, had very low educational attainment, considerably less than white Americans. But educational selectivity becomes more apparent among younger age groups, especially in more recent years. By 1960, young Asian immigrants had average educational levels above those of whites. By 1976, young Asian immigrants averaged 14–16 years of formal schooling, exceeding the very high average of 13.4 years of schooling for young white males. Even more impressive were the astounding educational levels of native-born Asian-Americans. Young native-born Japanese and Chinese men had educational attainments of 10–20 percent above the white averages, and native-born Filipino men were quickly catching up. More detailed data by specific level of schooling (not shown here) indicate that in recent years 90 percent of young Chinese and Japanese men have attended college and almost all continue to graduation.

Comparisons within Asian-American populations reveal slightly higher educational levels among Japanese immigrants relative to the native-born, while the reverse is true among Chinese. Young immigrant Filipino men have higher edu-

						Mean Years of Schooling						
		Chinese						Filipino			
	Native-Born			Foreign-Born			Native-Born			Foreign-Born	
1960	1970	1976	1960	1970	1976	1960	1970	1976	1960	1970	1976
13.1	13.8	16.0	11.7	14.4	14.9	11.2	11.6	12.9	12.5	14.1	13.8
12.0	13.2	15.6	9.4	12.1	13.7	10.4	11.2	13.6	8.7	12.7	14.9
9.5	12.4	13.1	6.4	10.7	12.2	6.4	9.3	14.2	6.0	9.7	10.2
6.8	10.5	11.5	5.0	7.8	9.7	7.6	8.2	8.5	5.3	6.4	8.2
11.1	12.8	14.3	8.1	11.8	13.3	9.4	10.8	13.5	7.0	10.7	13.0
283	344	118	435	701	160	110	190	89	573	605	226

						Ratio to White Mean						
1960	1970	1976	1960	1970	1976	1960	1970	1976	1960	1970	1976
115	111	119	103	116	111	98	94	96	110	114	103
111	114	126	87	104	110	96	97	110	81	109	120
93	111	110	63	96	102	63	83	119	59	78	86
77	101	104	57	75	88	86	79	77	60	62	75
107	111	116	78	103	108	90	94	110	67	93	106

cational attainment than comparable native-born Filipino men. Yet these differentials should not obscure the major finding that all three Asian populations are very selective. In 1970, the native-born and foreign-born Chinese and Japanese had attained higher educational levels than whites. In 1976, the native-born and foreign-born population of all three Asian groups had this distinction. We now turn to a consideration of socioeconomic characteristics of the Asian-Americans to see if educational progress has translated into commensurate social and economic positions and rewards.

Occupational Structure

With the exception of an above-average proportion of professionals, native-born Japanese-American men have had an occupational structure very similar to that of whites for the past two decades (index of dissimilarity was only 11.7 in 1976 [table 4]. Although native-born Japanese are also somewhat less likely to be operatives than whites, they are slightly more numerous in agriculture (although this has been a diminishing occupational category for all workers). Foreign-

born Japanese men have a somewhat higher status occupational distribution than either native-born Japanese or whites. Most notable is the very high proportion of immigrant Japanese professionals—more than one-third in both 1970 and 1976. While the occupational structure of native-born Japanese men and white men has converged, the occupational structure difference between foreign-born Japanese and whites has remained fairly dissimilar since 1960.

Occupational patterns among the Chinese population are somewhat more complex to describe. Both native-born and immigrant Chinese have a very high proportion of professionals—considerably higher than that of whites and native-born Japanese (although less than foreign-born Japanese). Native-born Chinese men are also somewhat more highly represented in most white-collar occupations and substantially underrepresented in all blue-collar positions. However, another pattern is evident among immigrant Chinese. They are also concentrated in the professional categories, but they are also overrepresented in the self-employed manager category, and especially in service occupations. In 1960, one-third of immigrant Chinese men were in this latter cat-

TABLE 4. *Occupational Composition of White, Japanese, Chinese, and Filipino Men in the U.S. Experienced Labor Force, Age 25–64,* by Nativity Status, 1960, 1970, and 1976

Occupation	White			Japanese					
				Native-Born			Foreign-Born		
	1960	1970	1976	1960	1970	1976	1960	1970	1976
Professionals	11	16	17	18	20	20	14	36	41
Salaried managers	8	10	16	6	8	16	6	12	11
Self-employed managers	4	4	3	5	3	4	6	1	11
Sales workers	6	7	6	6	5	4	6	7	1
Clerical workers	7	7	5	9	8	4	6	6	2
Craftsmen	25	23	23	22	24	24	10	9	14
Operatives	19	18	16	10	10	7	6	6	11
Laborers-nonfarm	6	5	5	5	10	7	8	11	3
Service workers	6	6	6	4	6	6	13	8	3
Farmers and farm workers	7	4	4	14	5	7	26	3	4
Total[a]	100%	100%	100%	100%	100%	100%	100%	100%	100%
(N)	3323	3726	8263	827	1042	581	178	177	55
Index of dissimilarity[b] with whites	0	0	0	16.4	13.1	11.7	32.4	31.6	31.7

[a]Totals may not add to 100% due to rounding.
[b]Indexes of dissimilarity were computed on more detailed percentage figures than shown above.
Sources: Same as Table 3.

egory. By 1976 more than one quarter of Chinese immigrants were still in service occupations. This occupational category contains waiters, dishwashers, and other petty service jobs in hotels, restaurants, and other entertainment activities. The relatively small number of native-born Chinese in the service sector suggests greater socioeconomic "assimilation" as compared to the foreign-born Chinese. However, native-born Chinese men are different from whites in being overrepresented in the higher status occupations. These differences in occupational structure characteristics have not narrowed but increased over the years.

The Filipino occupational structure contains elements of both the "Asian immigrant" pattern and a concentration in some blue-collar jobs. For instance, immigrant Filipino men have a high proportion in service occupations—similar to Chinese immigrants. The most important change has been the rapid upward shift in the Filipino occupational structure from 1960 to 1976. The proportion of immigrant Filipino men employed as professionals rose from 8 to 23 percent. This rise paralleled a downward decline in the proportion employed in farming. Similar changes have occurred in the occupational structure of native-born Filipino men. Even though there is a higher proportion in the blue-collar occupations (espe-

cially operatives), there is a definite (and strong) upward trend in the Filipino occupational structure.

Industrial Structure and Earnings

The basic patterns and trends of the occupational data are reflected in the industrial composition of the employed male population of the three Asian-American populations by nativity status (table 5). The collapsed industrial sector classification in table 5 is meant to highlight the fundamental differences between Asian-Americans and whites. Agriculture is lumped with mining as extractive industries. Construction, manufacturing, and transportation are the major sectors of the industrial economy. The trade sector was divided into two components: wholesale trade and retail trade. The heterogeneous service sector is broken into five components: (1) business and repair services, (2) laundries, (3) other personal services, (4) professional services, and (5) public administration. The category, laundries, is a very minor one, but it is shown separately because of the historical concentration of Chinese workers in laundry establishments.

Consistent with our prior observations, na-

Chinese						Filipino					
Native-Born			Foreign-Born			Native-Born			Foreign-Born		
1960	1970	1976	1960	1970	1976	1960	1970	1976	1960	1970	1976
25	29	31	15	33	29	11	12	20	8	24	23
9	10	12	5	4	11	1	4	16	1	2	7
7	6	10	17	9	15	—	1	—	1	—	1
8	7	12	3	2	2	—	8	—	1	1	3
13	9	10	5	6	2	10	6	7	3	9	20
14	17	18	3	4	7	24	22	29	9	10	5
11	11	3	15	11	6	18	24	12	14	12	6
4	3	—	1	1	—	12	9	8	10	6	7
7	7	4	34	29	28	14	12	4	26	23	22
1	1	—	2	1	—	10	2	4	27	13	7
100%	100%	100%	100%	100%	100%	100%	100%	100%	100%	100%	100%
227	320	115	408	678	154	72	169	83	486	505	197
26.9	19.4	32.5	44.5	45.6	46.1	20.0	16.4	14.7	43.3	36.4	42.8

tive-born Japanese men have an employment structure most similar to white men, although they have somewhat higher proportions in agriculture, trade, and public administration and a marked deficit in the manufacturing sector. Immigrant Japanese men have higher proportions in professional services and wholesale trade.

Native-born Chinese men are more dissimilar from whites with significantly higher proportions in retail trade, professional services, and public administration. There appears to have been a marked exodus of native-born Chinese out of the manufacturing sector. These basic patterns are more extreme among foreign-born Chinese with almost half employed in retail trade and related small-scale service activities (personal, business). In 1960, 13 percent of immigrant Chinese men worked in laundries, but this has dropped to only 2 percent by 1976.

Filipino men have a much more balanced in-

dustrial distribution with a proportion in manufacturing similar to white men. Immigrant Filipino men are overly represented in professional services and trade, although not to the degree of the Chinese. They are also overrepresented in the agricultural sector, although this sector of employment is declining for all populations.

Mean earnings provide a crude measure of the relative economic success of the Asian-American minorities. The bottom row of table 5 shows mean earnings for three years: 1959, 1969, and 1975. To control for inflation, all figures are converted to constant 1975 dollars (adjustments were made by using the Consumer Price Index). The row below the earnings data shows the ratio of each minority group's earnings to the comparison group of white men for each year.

While the 1960s were generally years of economic progress, the first half of the 1970s were not. Two strong recessions left most earners with

TABLE 5. *Industrial Composition and Mean Earnings of White, Japanese, Chinese, and Filipino Men in the U.S. Experienced Labor Force, by Nativity Status, 1960, 1970, and 1976*

| | White | | | Japanese | | | | | |
| | | | | Native-Born | | | Foreign-Born | | |
Industry	1960	1970	1976	1960	1970	1976	1960	1970	1976
Agriculture & mining	9	7	6	16	12	14	29	14	5
Construction	11	10	10	10	11	7	5	2	2
Manufacturing	32	30	29	18	18	14	11	14	42
Transportation	9	9	9	7	8	5	4	6	2
Wholesale trade	4	6	5	6	5	9	8	13	6
Retail trade	12	12	12	15	13	15	13	8	4
Business & repair services*	7	8	8	6	7	10	5	8	7
Laundries	1	0	0	1	1	0	1	0	0
Other personal services[b]	3	2	2	3	4	2	9	4	2
Professional services	6	10	12	7	11	13	14	30	31
Public administration	6	7	7	11	12	12	1	2	1
Total	100%	100%	100%	100%	100%	100%	100%	100%	100%
(N)	3360	2842	8264	833	3528	582	178	177	55
Index of dissimilarity with whites	0	0	0	18	14	22	39	36	23
Mean earnings[c] (1975$)	10,970	14,104	13,632	10,527	14,880	14,803	7,460	13,240	12,811
Ratio to white mean earnings	100	100	100	96	106	109	68	94	94
(N)	3409	3614	8652	868	1046	592	177	169	59

*Includes finance, insurance, and real estate services.

[b]Includes recreation and entertainment services.

[c]Mean earnings of workers, who received any earnings during the preceding year, in constant 1975 dollars.

Sources: Same as Table 3.

less real purchasing power in 1975 than in 1969. Comparing earnings of Asian-American minorities with whites for these years, several different findings are apparent. First, native-born Japanese, Chinese, and Filipino men (the last group only in 1976) have average earnings roughly equivalent to or higher than white men. However, since the backgrounds of Asian-American men (education and occupation) are generally higher than that of whites, parity of earnings does not indicate similarity of the earnings determination process (for more detail, see Wong, 1980b). Although there has been some closing of the earnings gaps between whites and immigrant Asians over the years, especially for the Japanese, a gap still remains in 1975. This is a topic that deserves further inquiry.

Comparison of Pre- and Post-1965 Immigrants

In much of the preceding discussion, the effects of the 1965 Immigration Act on the number and composition of Asian immigrants have been alluded to, but have not been empirically addressed. With the 1970 Census, it is possible to separate immigrants by year of arrival in the United States. In table 6, the three foreign-born Asian populations are divided into two components, pre-1965 immigrants and post-1965 immigrants, in order to measure differences in occupational and industrial composition, and in earnings attainment.

In all cases there is a dramatic difference in the character of Asian immigration following the 1965 act. The proportion of Asian professionals rises sharply. The most dramatic shift was among Filipino immigrants with a shift from 15 percent to 47 percent in the professional category and a corresponding decline among service workers. Although recent Chinese immigrants continue to find employment in the service sector, this is an exception to the general pattern of an upward shift in the occupational distribution after 1965. The post-1965 Japanese immigrants show signi-

Chinese						Filipino					
Native-Born			Foreign-Born			Native-Born			Foreign-Born		
1960	1970	1976	1960	1970	1976	1960	1970	1976	1960	1970	1976
11	1	0	2	1	0	10	4	4	29	17	8
6	8	5	1	3	1	8	7	9	2	5	6
20	15	8	9	15	15	27	19	24	18	18	16
5	9	9	4	3	4	11	15	19	9	6	2
4	3	23	4	3	2	0	7	1	1	3	5
25	17	12	49	37	42	7	10	8	13	10	15
6	11	6	2	5	8	1	6	7	1	6	9
3	1	0	13	6	2	1	0	0	0	1	0
3	3	3	4	5	2	6	7	2	8	5	10
10	14	19	9	19	18	8	10	17	12	20	17
18	16	14	2	4	7	20	14	9	6	8	9
100%	100%	100%	100%	100%	100%	100%	100%	100%	100%	100%	100%
228	1042	115	413	678	154	73	320	83	491	505	197
39	26	34	54	43	37	23	21	13	33	27	24
11,330	14,874	14,023	7,756	12,169	11,922	7,322	9,474	13,334	6,526	9,832	10,840
103	105	103	71	86	88	67	67	98	59	70	80
266	316	118	402	651	160	99	567	89	532	180	226

TABLE 6. *Occupational Composition, Industrial Composition, and Mean Earnings of Foreign-Born Japanese, Chinese, and Filipino Men, Age 25–64, in the U.S. Experienced Labor Force, by Year of Immigration, 1970.*

	Japanese		Chinese		Filipino	
Occupation	Pre-65	Post-65	Pre-65	Post-65	Pre-65	Post-65
Professionals	29	47	31	40	15	47
Salaried managers	9	17	4	3	3	0
Self-employed managers	2	—	10	4	0	1
Sales workers	5	11	2	3	1	1
Clerical workers	4	9	6	8	7	14
Craftsmen	11	6	5	2	10	12
Operatives	8	1	11	10	14	8
Laborers-nonfarm	18	1	1	1	6	4
Service workers	10	4	29	30	28	9
Farmers and farm workers	4	3	1	0	17	4
Total	100%	100%	100%	100%	100%	100%
(N)[a]	(107)	(70)	(532)	(146)	(363)	(142)
Industry						
Agriculture & mining	21	4	1	1	21	5
Construction	3	0	3	3	5	5
Manufacturing	14	13	15	14	16	22
Transporation	4	9	3	2	6	6
Wholesale trade	8	21	2	6	2	5
Retail trade	9	6	40	25	13	5
Business & repair services[b]	9	6	5	3	4	13
Laundries	0	0	7	3	0	2
Other personal services[c]	6	0	4	6	6	2
Professional services	24	39	14	36	16	31
Public administration	2	3	5	1	10	4
Total	100%	100%	100%	100%	100%	100%
Mean 1969 earnings (1975 $)	$13,432	$12,933	$13,421	$7,516	$10,202	$8,981
(N)[a]	(104)	(65)	(513)	(138)	(395)	(172)

[a]The N for occupation and industry consists of the experienced labor force on April 1, 1970. The (N) for earnings consists of those who received any 1969 earnings.
[b]Includes finance, insurance, and real estate.
[c]Includes entertainment and recreation services.
Source: Public Use Sample of 1970 Population Census, 15% Questionnaire.

ficant gains in the proportion involved in white-collar occupations and a decline in blue-collar occupations.

By industrial sector, the corresponding patterns show declines after 1965 in agriculture (for Japanese and Filipinos) and retail trade (for Chinese) but a strong upward shift in professional services for all Asian immigrants. Despite the higher socioeconomic status of the post-1965 Asian immigrants, their earnings are considerably below that of older immigrants, especially for the Chinese population. Whether this is simply a temporary depression in earnings due to the "entry level" positions (little tenure in jobs) or a more permanent feature is a question for future research.

Discussion

While the evidence of Asian-Americans as "successful minorities" as compared to other minorities dominates the interpretation of Asian-American stratification patterns, the empirical patterns and trends revealed here do not all point in the same direction. Moreover, there are important variations among specific nationality groups and between immigrant and native-born populations.

The most consistent evidence in favor of the successful minorities image is the very high level of educational attainment among Asian-Americans. While older Asian immigrants had lower educational achievement than whites, the pattern has been reversed for several decades; native-born and immigrant Asian-Americans have very high educational attainments. Associated with these educational credentials is a very strong overrepresentation of Asian-Americans in professional occupations. Although we have not examined detailed occupational categories here, most of the Asian-American professionals are in technical careers such as engineering. Other observers have noted that Asian-American success is less visible in positions of institutional power and in political influence (Kuo, 1979).

The most settled of the Asian populations are the Japanese-Americans whose occupational and industrial structures most closely parallel those of whites. The least advantaged Asian minority are the Filipinos, who have recorded considerable progress over the 1960s and early 1970s. Native-born Chinese-Americans have an economic structure which is most dissimilar to that of whites, primarily because almost one-third of Chinese-American men are employed as professionals (almost twice that of whites).

However, despite these signs of "success," there are also signs of an underside of Asian-American economic life in the United States. This is most evident among immigrant Chinese and Filipino men with significant concentrations in retail trade and related petty-service positions (four out of ten immigrant Chinese men). Long hours and low pay are the dominant characteristics of employment in these sectors.

Another sign of inequality is the earnings achievement process. We do not directly analyze this question here but given the above average level of education of Asian-Americans, the equivalent earnings levels of Asian and white men probably indicate unequal reward structures (see Wong, 1980b). Immigrant Asian-Americans receive earnings far below those of whites. This subject requires far more analysis.

In our introduction, we contrasted cultural with structural interpretations of the Asian-American socioeconomic situation. The question is not one that can be resolved by empirical evidence alone. It is impossible to deny that many, if not most, Asian-Americans have strong motivations for upward mobility that is reflected in attitudes and behavior. The fundamental issue, as we see it, is to understand the structural conditions that give rise to such cultural orientations and reinforce their transmission across generations. To deal adequately with these questions would require an in-depth historical study (for good examples of this sort of work, see Lieberson, 1980; Bonacich and Modell, 1980). But our present study does suggest several general observations relevant to the findings reported here and which may be addressed in future research on Asian-American stratification.

The episodic and changing character of Asian immigration is perhaps the most fundamental element in any interpretation of the stratification process. Because of selectivity from the origin as well as the investment of the migration experience itself, immigrants (and their children) are usually motivated to take full advantage of all opportunities and to defer consumption to maximize future mobility. The intense discrimination which early Asian immigrants encountered probably reinforced the typical immigrant perseverance and self-reliance. The virtual halt of Asian immigration for many decades in the twentieth century may have lessened the economic pressures on the resident Asian community and allowed for greater investment in the second generation. (This was coupled with a low level of reproduction which was also favorable for upward mobility; see Uhlenberg, 1972.) The resurgence of Asian immigration after 1965 was quite different from earlier patterns. The most dominant characteristic was a very favorable educational and occupational composition (a classic "brain drain" example) which gave a strong basis for socioeconomic success in the United States. Yet the other side of occupational distribution of immigrants—concentration in services—suggests that not all recent Asian immigrants are entering into the mainstream of the American economy.

Historically, Asians in the United States have been heavily overrepresented in small-scale entrepreneurial—petit bourgeois— activities. This is often coupled with an enclave economy based upon a large concentration of Asian people (e.g., Chinatowns). While the economic rewards from such vocations are probably minimal for all but a few, the ethnic enterprise phenomenon may be a fundamental link in the sponsorship of upward social mobility. The sharp downward decline in service occupations and the retail-trade sector among native-born Asians (especially Chinese) relative to the foreign-born generation suggests a preference for employment in more rewarding positions. The entrepreneurial role may, however, allow for the accumulation of savings to finance the education of children, and perhaps also reinforce cultural orientations favorable to social mobility. This is a hypothesis that deserves further scrutiny.

A final factor is the changes in the relative level of opportunities for Asians in the postwar period, especially in the last two decades. There seems to have been a noticeable lessening of the virulent prejudice that characterized white-Asian relationships early in the twentieth century. Furthermore, the passage of the Civil Rights legislation in the 1960s has created a much more favorable climate for Asian-American socioeconomic achievement.

As a final note, we caution against simple interpretations of the Asian-American socioeconomic progress of the last few decades as a sign of the openness of the American opportunity structure or as an example for other minorities to follow. Part of the recent success may be a reflection of the persistent discrimination of years past, which constrained Asian-Americans into ethnic entrepreneurship. Moreover, Asian-Americans tend to remain segregated from many sectors of the dominant economy, society, and polity. If the situation of Asian-Americans appears favorable, it is only in reference to greater disadvantages of other minorities. Full equality and participation are still to be achieved.

19

Immigrant Enclaves: An Analysis of the Labor Market Experiences of Cubans in Miami[1]

Kenneth L. Wilson
Alejandro Portes

The purpose of this study is to examine the extent to which the phenomenon of self-enclosed minorities modifies general labor processes in the U.S. economy. Empirical data with which to address this question come from a sample of recently arrived Cuban émigrés.

The classic sociological literature on immigrant minorities uniformly portrayed the adaptation process as one in which initial economic hardships and discrimination gave way to gradual acceptance by members of the dominant groups and eventual assimilation. With minor variations, different authors identified the culmination of the process as the entrance of immigrants, or their descendants, into the mainstream of the economy and their cultural fusion with the majority (Handlin 1951; Warner and Srole 1945; Wittke 1952). More recently, Gordon (1961, 1964) distinguished the ideal types of cultural pluralism and Anglo-conformity, but still the overriding theme

Reprinted from the *American Journal of Sociology* 86:2 (September 1980), pp. 135–160, by permission of the authors and the publisher, The University of Chicago Press. Copyright © 1980 by the University of Chicago. All rights reserved.

[1]Data on which this paper is based were collected as part of the ongoing study, "Latin American Immigrant Minorities in the United States," at Duke University. Data collection and analysis were supported by grants MH 23262-02 from the National Institute of Mental Health and SOC75-16151 from the National Science Foundation.

was that of blending in and contributing to national welfare. Thus the major goal of immigration research was to document the barriers to assimilation confronted by various minorities and to orient policy decisions at the national and local levels toward their removal.

During the 1960s and in the wake of militant protests by urban ethnic minorities, a new critical literature arose. Spearheaded by the writings of black authors (Carmichael and Hamilton 1967; Malcolm X 1967), this literature documented the tenacity of barriers against entrance of blacks and other "unmeltable" ethnics into the better-paid and more prestigious occupations. Such scholars as Robert Blauner (1972) took up the theme and went on to explore the historical role played by the exploitation of these groups in the development of the American economy. Borrowing a concept developed by González Casanova (1965) in Mexico, the exploitation of nonwhite minorities was termed "internal colonialism."

The assimilationist and internal colonialist perspectives offered diametrically opposite predictions about the fate of racial and ethnic minorities in the United States. According to the first, gradual learning of the culture and acquisition of occupational skills would open the way for entrance into "middle-class" society; according to the other, cultural assimilation of these groups was irrelevant since their subjection and exploitation in the labor market were preconditions for the continuing growth of U.S. capitalism.

Later research has advanced our knowledge of the role of race and ethnicity in the American class structure. It has, by and large, confirmed the persistence of racial differences in status and income even when cultural skills and past individual attainments are taken into account (Duncan 1969; Jencks 1972; Portes and Wilson 1976; Gordon 1971). Other recent studies have tended to concentrate on the specific manner in which blacks, Chicanos, and other minorities have become inserted into the U.S. labor market and on the historical evolution of their condition. As a consequence, the earlier and broader concepts of internal colonialism and colonized minorities have become progressively abandoned in favor of those of segmented class structure and its variants in the industrial economy: "split" and dual labor markets (Bonacich 1972; Gordon 1972).

Since all these perspectives have been concerned with phenomena at the center of the American political economy, they have neglected others taking place at the fringes but having definite theoretical implications. These pertain to immigrant minorites which remain spatially concentrated in a particular city or region. The distinctive characteristics of these groups are that they are less culturally assimilated than native ethnic minorities, tend to cling to their languages and customs, and frequently do better economically than minorities in the mainstream economy. The resilience and economic achievements of these enclaves do not fit well the predictions of either assimilation theory or internal colonialism. Nor, as we will see, is their case satisfactorily explained by dual labor market theories, as currently developed.

Some recent studies have significantly advanced our understanding of self-enclosed immigrant minorities. Most of these have had, as empirical base, the situation of Asian immigrants (Bonacich, Light, and Wong 1977; Sung 1967). To our knowledge, however, the existence of an enclave labor market distinct from those in the general economy and the factors leading immigrants to remain thus confined have not been systematically explored.

The purpose of the following sections is twofold: first, to describe the historical origins of a different immigrant enclave—Cuban émigrés in Miami; second, to examine whether the members of an enclave labor force can be distinguished empirically from immigrants who have taken jobs in the general economy. Before proceeding to description and analysis, however, we discuss recent theories of the evolution of the U.S. economy and the dual labor market as an appropriate framework for the subsequent analysis.

Dual Labor Markets and Immigration

The Dual Economy

Analyses of the dual economy (Averitt 1968; Galbraith 1971) are based on the recognition that monopolistic tendencies in industry are no longer a statistical anomaly but constitute perhaps *the* defining feature of advanced capitalism. Monopoly firms are governed under competitive conditions. Averitt refers to the monopolistic sector as the "center economy"; Galbraith terms it the "industrial state."

With attention concentrated on long-run stability, center firms tend to gain gradual control of the many contingencies which make the existence of peripheral firms problematic. Center firms are able to make full use of economies of scale and to structure productive organizations which are both geographically dispersed and vertically integrated. These firms have moved in recent years to control their sources of supply in technology and raw materials and their markets. Market control is effected through oligopolistic pricing and through the molding of consumer tastes by mass advertising (O'Connor 1973). To insulate themselves further from market contingencies, monopoly firms develop large cash reserves and stablize their labor force through training programs and promotional ladders or "internal markets" (Edwards 1975).

The notions of dual or segmented labor markets were originally developed independently of the theory of the dual economy. These notions began inconspicuously as a series of empirical observations about ghetto employment (see Doeringer et al. 1969; Baron and Hymer 1968; Ferman 1968). Some of the most consistent findings were that there seemed to be little relationship between investment in human capital—either formal education or job-training programs—and employment. There was a remarkably high level of job instability. For those who averaged 35—40 hours per week, wages were low, often below the poverty line; the discipline in their jobs was often harsh and arbitrary; there appeared to be an absence of ladders to success, most jobs usually providing almost no opportunity for promotion.[2]

In short, central city jobs appeared to be cut off from the rest of the economic system. Individuals, usually minority members, who were caught in these labor markets had little hope for escape. Thus, various investigators were led to postulate the existence of a dual labor market. The primary labor market has the positive characteristics of stability, chances for promotion, high wages, and good working conditions, while the secondary labor market has the negative traits outlined above (Wachtel 1972). Gordon (1971) pursued the implications of this division and found that the predominant proportion of occupational mobility (measured as job changes) was within these labor markets with very little mobility between them.

Over time, it became clear that these findings converged with the emerging theory of the dual economy. The primary labor market corresponds to the center economy, the secondary labor market resides in the periphery. The market power of monopoly firms enables them to pass on increases in costs to consumers and, hence, finance the advantageous condition of their workers. The periphery, being subject to the constraints of competition, must maintain low wages, otherwise firms may be forced into bankruptcy. Low wages and absence of internal ladders of

promotion encourage rapid turnover of workers. For some economists, job instability is the defining characteristic of the secondary labor market (Piore 1975).

Immigrant Workers and Economic Dualism

The contemporary literature on international migration deals primarily with movements sharing two characteristics. First, they are displacements of *labor*, that is, of individuals who migrate with the intention of selling their labor power in places of destination. Second, they tend to occur from less economically developed areas to economically developed centers. Recent historical studies of immigration to the United States and Western Europe have emphasized the increasing importance of immigrant labor in the development of these advanced economies (Rosenblum 1973; Burawoy 1976; Castles and Kosack 1973; Sassen-Koob 1978).

Contemporary immigration to the United States has become fragmented in ways that parallel the situation described by dual labor market theories. On the one hand, immigration laws have moved toward encouraging migration of highly skilled foreign workers and professionals; on the other hand, they have formally barred the less skilled from entry into the country (Keely 1979). Thus, for example, the amended 1965 Immigration Act reserves the third and sixth preference categories for professional, technical, and skilled workers in short supply in the country.

Further, the U.S. Department of Labor maintains a Schedule A of occupations for which there is "a shortage of workers willing, able, qualified, and available." Individuals in these occupations receive special privileges when applying for an immigrant's visa. In recent years, Schedule A occupations have included physicians and surgeons, nurses, speech therapists, pharmacists, and dietitians.

The effect of these regulations has been to encourage a flow of immigration directed to the primary labor market. Highly qualified immigrants find employment in large-scale firms, research institutions, public and private hospitals, universities, and the like (Stevens, Goodman, and Mick 1978). The numerical extent of this flow is not insignificant. In 1977, 62,400 foreign

---

[2]Doeringer and Piore (1971) add the following hypothesis: not only does the secondary labor market possess negative characteristics; it also encourages the development of negative psychological characteristics in the labor force that services the secondary market. Particularly, over time there is a gradual rapprochement between poor working conditions in the secondary labor market and poor work habits of minority workers, such as arriving at work late and general task irresponsibility. The main problem with this hypothesis is that of separating contextual labor market effects from those due to individual work habits. To avoid such overlap, the hypothesis must specify psychological characteristics that endure even when the worker has found a job in the primary labor market. Such a hypothesis would require special data and analysis and is beyond the scope of this paper.

professionals, managers, and technicians were admitted to the United States for permanent residence (U.S. Bureau of the Census 1978, p. 86).

Given existing regulations, it is not surprising that the occupational distribution of *legal* immigrant cohorts in recent years compares favorably with that of the domestic labor force. For example, during the 1970s the percentage of professional and technical workers among occupationally active immigrants has consistently exceeded that in the U.S. civilian labor force (Portes 1978). Nor is it surprising that studies focusing on legal immigration report significant upward occupational mobility after several years (North 1978), absence of discrimination in pay and work conditions (Stevens, Goodman, and Mick 1978; North 1978), and an economic situation equal to or better than that of domestic workers (Chiswick 1978).

On the other hand, a numerically larger flow of immigrants is composed of individuals with few skills who find employment in the low-wage menial occupations identified with the secondary labor market. Low-wage labor immigration bypasses occupational selection procedures of the immigration law through several channels. First, workers in less developed territories under U.S. jurisdiction can generally travel without restrictions to the mainland. The most important case is Puerto Rican migration. Though formally a domestic movement, migration from Puerto Rico has many of the same characteristics as international labor flows from Third World countries (Maldonado 1979).

Second, an immigrant group already in the United States can avail itself of family reunification provisions and other clauses of the present immigration law to continue the movement from the source country. A substantial proportion of Asian immigration, from countries such as Korea, and of legal Mexican immigration appears to be of this type (Bonacich 1978; Alba-Hernandez 1978).

Third, and most important, illegal or undocumented immigration into the United States currently brings in hundreds of thousands of low-skill workers. Though no reliable figures on the magnitude of illegal immigration exist, even the most conservative estimates place it significantly above that of *total* legal immigration. Apprehensions by the U.S. Immigration and Naturalization Service, used as a very rough indicator of the magnitude of the illegal flow, exceeded one million in 1976 and again in 1977 (U.S. Immigration and Naturalization Service 1978). The main source of illegal immigration is Mexico, but increasing flows from the Dominican Republic, the British Caribbean, Columbia, and Central America have also been detected (Cornelius 1977).

Dual labor market writings dealing with recent immigration have focused primarily on the flow directed to the secondary labor market. These studies have dealt, for example, with the situation of Puerto Rican migrants in Boston (Piore 1973), Korean and other Asian immigrants on the West Coast (Bonacich 1978), and undocumented Mexican immigrants throughout the Southwest and Midwest (Barrera 1977; Bustamante 1975). Along with domestic minorities, new immigrant workers are defined as additions to the more vulnerable labor pool destined to the low-wage, unstable occupations of the peripheral economy. Past occupational experience and other investments in human capital count very little for these immigrants because, unlike workers in the primary sector, they are hired primarily because of their vulnerability rather than their skills (Galarza 1977; Bach 1978; Bustamante 1975).

A recent paper by Bonacich (1978) has argued that immigrant entrepreneurs fulfill "middleman" functions by exploiting their own national group in the interest of larger firms in the center economy. With this sole exception, however, the dual labor market literature has not regarded immigrant labor and immigrant economy activity as phenomena deserving special attention. If only by default, these theories define immigrant enterprises as just one more segment of the peripheral economy. The logical derivation from this perspective can be formalized as follows:

1. New immigrant workers will concentrate in the secondary labor market. With the exception of those who gain access to the primary sector, immigrants will share all the characteristics of peripheral employment, including low prestige, low income, job dissatisfaction, and the absence of return to past human capital investments. The situation of workers employed by immigrant enterprises will not differ from those in the larger secondary labor market.

This prediction and the general characterization of "entrapment" in the peripheral economy are contradicted by the experience of at least some immigrant groups. The case of the Japanese (Boyd 1971; Daniels 1971; Peterson 1971) is well known, but other studies have highlighted similar experiences among other national groups such as the Chinese (Sung 1967; Light 1972). For the Koreans, Bonacich notes the proliferation of immigrant businesses and the mobility opportunities that they make available (Bonacich, Light, and Wong 1977).

It should be noted also that the situation of these minorities is not adequately portrayed by aggregate studies of legal immigration. As seen above, the positive characterization of immigrant mobility in these studies is based largely on the arrival of professional, managerial, and skilled talent encouraged by current immigration provisions. The aggregate statistics reflect insertion of these immigrants into the primary labor market, but they fail to capture the distinct phenomenon of immigrant enclaves.

For these last groups, it appears that although new arrivals are forced to work hard for low wages, they do not find upward mobility channels blocked. Many immigrants manage to move up either within existing enterprises or by setting up new businesses. A charted path seems to exist in several of these instances leading from hard labor in the firm of another immigrant to gradual promotion culminating in another business concern.

Some social psychological explanations have been advanced for the economic success of some immigrant minorities (Hagen 1962; Kurokawa 1970; Eisenstadt 1970). A more compelling structural reason, however, appears to be the existence of advantages for enclave enterprises which those in the open competitive sector do not have. Put succinctly, immigrant enterprises might manage to create a workable form of vertical integration by developing ethnically sympathetic sources of supply and consumer outlets. They can organize unorthodox but effective forms of financial and human capital reserves by pooling savings and requiring new immigrants to spell a tour of duty at the worst jobs. These advantages may enable enclave firms to reproduce, albeit imperfectly, some of the characteristics of monopolistic control accounting for the sources of enterprise in the center economy.

A necessary condition for the emergence of an economic enclave is the presence of immigrants with sufficient capital. Capital might be brought from the original country, as is often the case with political exiles (Fagen, Brody, and O'Leary 1968), or accumulated through savings. Individuals with the requisite entrepreneurial skills might be drawn into the immigrant flow to escape economic and political conditions in the source country or to profit by the opportunities offered by a preexisting immigrant "colony" abroad.

Although the data presented below do not permit direct analysis of immigrant firms, they allow a test of an important additional hypothesis 1:

2. *Immigrant workers are not restricted to the secondary labor market. In particular, those inserted into an immigrant enclave can be empirically distinguished from workers in both the primary and secondary labor markets. Enclave workers will share with those in the primary sector a significant economic return to past human capital investments. Such a return will be absent among those in the "open" secondary labor market.*

A review of the recent history of Cuban immigration and the development of the Cuban enclave in Miami is presented next as an introduction to the empirical analysis.

Cuban Immigration and the Development of the Cuban Enclave

The immigrant flow giving rise to the Cuban enclave in Miami has political rather than economic roots. Massive Cuban immigration to the United States began with the advent of Fidel Castro to power in January 1959. The first émigrés, members of the overthrown Batista regime, represented a small minority. As the revolution consolidated, however, it began to implement a populist program contrary to the interest of the dominant classes. Immigration increased as landowners, industrialists, and former Cuban managers of U.S.-owned enterprises left. Others left in anticipation of new measures as the revolution accelerated the transformation of the Cuban class structure; many came to Miami to organize a military force with which to overthrow the Castro government. From mid-1959 to October 1960, approximately 37,000 émigrés came, most of them well to do and many bringing to the United States considerable assets (Thomas and Huyck 1967).

After the defeat of the exile force in the Bay of Pigs in April 1961, the flow of refugees accelerated further and its composition began to diversify, reaching down to the middle classes and even sectors of the urban working class (Clark 1977). By the end of 1962, official figures reported 215,323 Cuban émigrés in the United States.

To process this massive flow, the Kennedy administration established the Cuban Refugee Program (CRP) under the secretary of Health, Education, and Welfare. The arrival of Cuban refugees in Miami was viewed at the time as a source of strain aggravating the depressed economy of the area. Thus, efforts of the Cuban Refugee Emergency Center, established by the CRP in Miami, concentrated on relocating the émigrés throughout communities in the United States. Cuban lawyers were transformed into language teachers and sent to high schools and colleges in the North. Others found widely varied occupations, often with the support of private charity organizations. To insure that relocation proceeded smoothly, the center made emergency welfare aid contingent on acceptance of job offers when available. By 1967, 251,000 Cuban émigrés had registered with the CRP, and 153,000 had been relocated away from Miami. The program was widely regarded in federal circles as a complete success (Thomas and Huyck 1967).

With many ups and downs, which included the establishment of a "family reunification" airlift by agreement of the two governments, the inflow of Cuban émigrés continued during the next decade. At the end of 1976, official figures for Cuban refugee arrivals in the United States totaled 661,934 (U.S. Immigration and Naturalization Service 1977). During this entire period, the relocation program conducted by the Cuban Refugee Center continued. By the early 1970s, there was evidence, however, of a significant return migration to Miami. In 1973, a survey estimated that over 25% of Cubans residing in Miami were returnees from other U.S. locations (Clark 1973). The proportion at present should be, if anything, higher.

Cultural and climatic reasons have obviously much to do with return decisions. More important, however, there is evidence that relocated émigrés used their period in northern areas much as other migrants have used their stay in high-wage industrial regions: as an opportunity for accumulating capital. Small-scale investments by returnees from the North were added to those made with capital brought from Cuba to consolidate an immigrant economic enclave.

Cuban-owned enterprises in the Miami area increased from 919 in 1967 to about 8,000 in 1976. While most of them are small scale, some employ hundreds of workers. Enclave firms tend to concentrate on textiles, leather, furniture, cigar making, construction, and finance. An estimated 40% of the construction companies are Cuban owned, and émigrés control roughly 20% of the local commerical banks (*Time* 1978; Clark 1977). There are also some investments in agriculture, especially sugar cane plantations and sugar mills.

Enclave firms in the service sector include restaurants (a favorite investment for small entrepreneurs), supermarkets, private clinics, legal firms, funeral parlors, and private schools. In 1976, the population of Spanish origin in Dade County (Miami) was estimated at 488,500 or 33% of the total. About 82% of this population is Cuban. Over half of the population in the municipalities of Miami and Hialeah is Cuban (Clark 1977). Numerical concentration and diversity of economic activities allow many immigrants to lead lives restricted almost completely to the enclave. This is especially true among those employed in Cuban-owned firms.

More important, newly arrived émigrés in Miami have an option of economic incorporation not available to other immigrant minorities. It remains to be seen, however, whether their participation in the enclave economy possesses empirically distinct characteristics or whether competitive immigrant-owned enterprises merely reproduce those labor processes associated with the broader peripheral economy.

Method

Data Collection

Data for this study come from a sample of Cuban immigrants interviewed at the point of arrival in the United States during the fall of 1973 and spring of 1974. The sample was reinterviewed three years later during 1976–77. Unlike more established groups of émigrés, recent immigrants usually lack the capital to go into business by themselves and, hence, must join the labor market. They are employed by firms in the primary and secondary markets as well as by enclave enterprises. It is this characteristic which makes the sample suitable for testing the hypotheses above. In all, 590 new immigrants were interviewed during the original survey. All had arrived in the United States via Miami and had stayed in that city.

The first survey met with considerable initial obstacles. The two daily flights or "airlifts" between Cuba and Miami had been suspended just before the beginning of data collection, thus closing the only major source of new immigrants. While Cubans continued to leave via Spain, few could come to the United States since they required a permanent resident's visa. In October 1973, however, Secretary of State Kissinger signed an executive resolution authorizing Cuban exiles in Spain to come to the United States as parolees. Flights were organized to transport those wishing to come. These "family reunion" flights had Miami as their major point of destination.

Through the cooperation of agencies organizing these flights, newly arrived émigrés were contacted and interviewed at their place of residence. No available data on the population of Cuban émigrés exist against which to compare sample results. The U.S. Immigration Service data on Cuban immigrants pertain to those who adjusted their status to that of permanent residents. It takes a minimum of two years before new émigrés can effect this adjustment. Hence, official figures for "new" Cuban immigrants do not pertain to those who actually arrive in the country during a given year. Excluding refusals (6%), the sample is, however, coterminous with the universe of exiles during the survey period since most new arrivals were contacted.

The original sample was limited to males aged 18–60 and not dependent on others. This excludes women, children, and the aged. Restriction of the sample to males in the productive ages was dictated by the many complexities of an exploratory study and the impossibility of dealing adequately with all categories of immigrants. Priority was given to family heads and economically independent individuals who, in this immigrant group, are overwhelmingly adult males.

In 1976–77, three years after the first survey, a follow-up was conducted. Difficulties of tracing respondents are well known and have been the subject of a growing methodological literature (Eckland 1968; McAllister, Butler, and Goe 1973). Difficulties were compounded in this case by the unique characteristics of the sample. On the basis of a series of field techniques and the efforts of a number of people, a total of 427 cases were located and reinterviewed. This represents 72% of the original sample or 76% if respondents who died or left the United States are discounted. Practically all follow-up respondents had stayed in Miami.

A high attrition rate presents a serious challenge to any attempt to correlate U.S. experiences with the characteristics of the original sample as a whole. We assessed the extent of this bias by comparing means for the original and follow-up samples and correlating a "Missing" dummy variable with a series of first-wave predictors of income into a stepwise procedure with "Missing" as the dependent variable.

None of these results indicate the presence of a significant bias. Table 1 presents correlation and regression coefficients linking first-wave predictors with "Missing." Not a single correlation differs significantly from zero. All β weights are small, and the joint amount of variance explained in the "Missing" variable is 2%. While it is still an inferential leap to assume the absence of bias among second-wave variables, these results provide some assurance about the validity of generalizing the findings to the original sample. We interpret results accordingly.

Data Analysis

The ensuing analysis is conducted in two parts. First, we assess the extent to which a range of

TABLE 1. *Correlations and Regressions of First-Wave Variables with Second-Wave Attrition Variable, Cuban Immigrants (1973–77)*

Independent Variables	"Missing"	
	r	β
Father's occupation	−.081	−.093
Father's education	0	.066
Mother's education	−.023	−.019
Size-place of early community of residence	−.055	−.045
Age	.097	.084
Education	−.024	−.029
Main occupation at arrival	−.014	−.007
Knowledge of English at arrival	.015	.055
Income aspirations at arrival	.037	.041
R^2	...	.022

Note.—For dependent variable: missing = 1, nonmissing = 0.

variables differentiates immigrants in the three labor markets: primary, secondary, and enclave. The set of variables selected for this analysis pertains to the work situation and the quality of life the immigrant has experienced in the United States. According to the theoretical discussion above, we expect to find systematic differences in occupational prestige, economic stability, occupational and income satisfaction, perception and experiences of discrimination, interaction with Anglo-Americans, and other related variables between immigrants employed in center and peripheral firms. If hypothesis 2 holds, we would also expect enclave workers to emerge as an empirically distinct group, but approaching some of the characteristics of workers in the primary sector.

For this part of the analysis, we employ discriminant analysis (Van de Geer 1971, pp. 243–72; Klecka 1975). Discriminant analysis allows the specification of a nominal reference variable which is used to extract whatever significant discriminant functions exist in a set of independent variables. The maximum number of functions is one fewer than the number of subpopulations. If fewer than the maximum possible number of discriminant functions are significant, then some of the subpopulations are not empirically distinguishable from each other, at least in regard to the variables included in the analysis.

Second, we examine processes of occupational and income attainment within each labor market.

Independent variables for this analysis are those conventionally included in human capital and status-attainment models of income (Mincer 1970; Sewell and Hauser 1975), plus those representing skills specifically relevant to immigrant populations. If hypothesis 2 holds, immigrants in the secondary labor market will show the least return to prior attainments and human capital, while those in the primary and enclave labor markets will exhibit similar, and higher, levels of return for their past investments. Different processes of attainment will be reflected in significant variations in metric regression coefficients across the three labor markets.

The major problem for the two parts of the analysis is the establishment of criteria for assignment of immigrants to one or another labor market. Identification of those in the enclave is the most straightforward. All immigrants indicating employment in firms owned by Cubans were assigned to the enclave. A total of 143 cases, or 33% of the follow-up sample, were classified as enclave workers.

The division of the rest of the sample into primary and secondary sector is more problematic. Economists have used as criteria both the structural characteristics of occupations and industries and the demographic characteristics of their respective workers (Edwards 1975). Since part of our purpose is to test for differences in the characteristics of immigrant workers, we have used only the first type of criteria for our definition of primary and secondary sectors. Three criteria were employed: (1) The presence of an "internal labor market" or promotional ladder within the industry (Doeringer and Piore 1971); particularly, occupation/industry classifications wherein at least 25% of the workers had "considerable" opportunities for advancement were considered as candidates for the primary labor market (for more detailed information on this criterion see Freedman [1976], appendix C). (2) The median establishment size: occupation/industry classifications within which more than 10% of the workers were employed in firms with more than 1,000 workers were candidates for the primary labor market. (3) Occupation/industry classifications with average wages higher than $6,000 per year were candidates for the primary labor market.

Only those occupation/industry categories

that were high on all three criteria were classified in the primary labor market. In the general U.S. population, this classification would result in 54% of the workers being assigned to the primary labor market (Freedman 1976, p. 21). In our immigrant sample, the corresponding figure is 36% of the follow-up sample.

These criteria represent necessary approximations to the primary/secondary division. Given the characteristics of the labor market in Miami, an area dominated by tourism and small industry (Fagen, Brody, and O'Leary 1968), the likely direction of bias is toward assignment to the primary sector of immigrants actually employed in competitive enterprises. The effect of this error is conservative, since it would attenuate actual differences across labor markets, thus reducing the chances for statistical differences.

Results

1. We first test the hypothesis that immigrants in the dual and enclave labor markets can be empirically distinguished on the basis of their experiences and socioeconomic situation in the United States. For this analysis, a set of the 12 most pertinent independent variables was selected. Four of these are objective indicators: present occupational prestige, measured in Duncan SEI scores; home ownership, an indirect measure of economic stability; number of relatives living in the United States; and objective information about U.S. society. The fourth is a composite index formed by the unit-weighted sum of six items measuring knowledge of political and economic facts. Factor analysis indicated a clear unidimensional structure and a high level of internal consistency.[3]

[3]The U.S. information index is constructed by the sum of correct responses to six factual questions: (1) name of the current vice-president of the United States, (2) name of the governor of the state, (3) knowledge of the meaning of social security, (4) knowledge of the effect of home mortage interest on personal income tax, (5) knowledge of the annual interest rate charged by common credit cards (e.g., "Master Charge"), and (6) knowledge of the approximate interest rates charged by commercial banks on personal loans. These items were entered into a principal components factor analysis. All loadings exceed .45 and the first factor explains 65% of the common variance. Successive factors produce eigenvalues lower than 1.0 Internal consistency, as measured by Cronbach's α, is .691.

The rest of the variables are subjective indicators measuring such attitudes as income satisfaction, desire to change occupations, desire to return to Cuba, and willingness to come to the United States if the experience had to be repeated. Three additional subjective variables are self-reports: opportunities for relating with Anglo-Americans, perceived discrimination against Cubans in the United States, and personal experiences of discrimination. In the subsequent analysis, all variables are coded in agreement with their labels. Variable means and standard deviations are presented in the Appendix.

Results of this analysis are presented in table 2. Included are standardized discriminant function coefficients, relative percentages for each eigenvalue, canonical correlations, and group centroids. Wilks's λ's have been transformed into

TABLE 2. *Discriminant Analysis of Characteristics of Cuban Immigrants in Three Labor Markets Cuban Immigrants (1973–77)*

Variables	First Function	Second Function
Occupational prestige	.14	−.27
Home ownership	.22	−.13
Relatives in United States (N)	.31	.13
Information about U.S. society	.02	−.32
Income satisfaction	−.07	−.57
Desire to change occupations	−.40	−.12
Plans to move to another country	.02	−.35
Would not come to United States if he had to do it over	.10	.25
Would return to Cuba if things changed there	.27	−.04
Opportunities for relating with Anglos	−.70	−.02
Perceived discrimination against Cubans in United States	.33	.07
Personal experiences of discrimination	.13	−.55
Eigenvalue-relative percentage	60.8	39.2
Canonical correlation	.38	.32
χ^2	90.00	36.00
$P<$	0	0
Group centroids:		
"Enclave"	.49	−.02
Primary labor market	−.32	−.30
Secondary labor market	−.25	.52

χ^2s and probability levels are also presented. The analysis yields two significant discriminant functions. Canonical correlations in each case represent the association between the discriminant function and the $m-1$ set of dummy variables representing the m different subgroups. Canonical coefficients for both are modest but not insignificant.

The nature of the two discriminant functions can be gleaned from the standardized coefficients. Disregarding signs for the moment, the first and most important function is defined by opportunities for relating with Anglos, desire to change occupations, perceived discrimination against Cubans, and number of relatives living in the United States. The second discriminant function is defined by income satisfaction, personal experiences of discrimination, plans to move to another country, information about U.S. society, and occupational prestige.

The most important results, however, are the group centroids, for they bear directly on the hypotheses above. These are the average discriminant scores for each group on the two functions. The significant χ^2 for the first function is mostly due to distance in the reduced function space between the enclave group and the other two. In other words, immigrants in the primary and secondary markets are undistinguishable in this function, but both are empirically distinct from immigrants in the enclave. This result clearly supports hypothesis 2 and disconfirms the view of enclave workers as only one segment of the secondary sector.

Looking now at the direction of coefficients, enclave membership appears associated with more relatives living in the United States, lesser opportunities for relating with Anglo-Americans, and stronger inclinations to return to Cuba if political conditions were to change. These results appear predictable. Less predictable, perhaps, membership in the enclave economy is also linked with lesser interest in changing occupations and with higher perceptions of discrimination against Cubans in the United States.

The second discriminant function rearranges the groups differently. In this case, the significant difference in the reduced function space is that between the enclave and primary sector, on the one hand, and the secondary sector, on the other. The difference between the first two groups is

insignificant. Thus, in this second dimension, which is closely defined by variables reflecting occupational and economic conditions, immigrants in the enclave are nearer those in the primary sector. This result again supports hypothesis 2. Predictably, membership in the secondary labor market is associated with lesser income satisfaction, lesser occupational prestige, lesser information about U.S. society, and less willingness to come to the United States if the decision had to be taken again. Surprisingly, however, secondary sector membership is also related to lesser reported experiences of discrimination in the United States.[4]

Taken as a whole, these findings challenge the view that workers confined to an immigrant enclave share in the disadvantages of those in the secondary labor market and are undistinguishable from the latter. The variables available in these data at least suggest that the experiences and economic situation of immigrants can separate those in the enclave economy from those in the "open" labor market along a major axis and bring together enclave and primary workers, in opposition to those in the secondary labor market, along a second.[5]

2. Having established systematic differences in terms of current experiences and situations among the three labor markets, we must examine whether the economic effects of background variables, in particular, past investments in human capital, also differ across them. In this part of the analysis, we compare the effects of predictors

---

[4]A possible explanation is that the low positions occupied by secondary sector workers shield them from confronting barriers in the dominant society which are experienced by immigrants in higher-status occupations, especially those in the center economy.

[5]Another way to display these results is with regression analysis, which has the advantage of being more readily understood. Unfortunately, regression analysis is not suitable for our purposes at this stage. It affords no easy way to assess the empirical distinctiveness among three categories of a nominal variable with reference to a list of dependent variables. However, in order to get a rough assessment of the comparability of our findings with regression results, we turned our hypotheses around and estimated the multiple correlations between the list of variables as independent variables and the three labor markets as three dummy dependent variables. The multiple correlations range from .28 to .37 and are roughly similar to the canonical correlations we report for the discriminant analysis.

conventionally included in human capital and status-attainment models on three dependent variables in each labor market. These dependent variables are principal occupation in Cuba, present occupation in the United States, and present income. Independent variables include father's and mother's education, father's occupation, respondent's education in Cuba, education since arrival in the United States, and age. Occupational variables are coded in Duncan's SEI scores, education in Cuba is coded in years completed and in the United States in completed months, and income is the respondent's present monthly earnings in dollars.

In addition, we include as predicators two variables not generally found in human capital models but indicative of important skills for newly arrived immigrants. One is the index of information about U.S. society described above. The other is an objective test of knowledge of English. This is an index constructed by the sum of correct answers to eight items, each asking the respondent to translate a word or sentence from English into Spanish. As with the U.S. information index, the knowledge-of-English index was constructed after factor analysis had indicated a clear unidimensional structure and high reliability.[6]

All parental variables, education, principle occupation in Cuba, and age were measured during the first interview. All other variables, including items in the information and knowledge-of-English indices, were measured during the second. Income is regressed on independent variables in its natural form since skewness in the distribution does not justify a log transformation. Conclusions would not be altered by such transformation, but it would obscure the substantive interpretation of coefficients. Means and standard deviations of all the variables are presented in the Appendix.

Regressions of income and occupation on independent variables are presented in table 3.

[6]The test is designed to measure English comprehension at elementary and junior high school levels and includes sentences like "There is a horse near the church" and words like "guilt" and "surplus." All item loadings exceed .65 in a principal components factor analysis. The first unrotated factor accounts for 70% of common variances, with no secondary factor having an eigenvalue of 1.0 or higher. Internal consistency (α) for this index is .94.

Figures in the table are metric coefficients; those which meet the standard criterion of exceeding twice their standard errors are enclosed in parentheses. If hypothesis 1 is correct, the pattern of regression results for immigrants in enclave firms should be similar to that of immigrants in the secondary sector. For both groups, effects of human capital and past attainments on occupation and income should be significantly weaker than among immigrants in the primary sector. If hypothesis 2 is correct, on the other hand, enclave and primary sector workers should be similar and register greater returns to their past attainment and skills than those in peripheral firms.

In addition to present occupation and income, we have included occupation in Cuba as a dependent variable to check the possibility that contemporary differences across labor markets are not a result of structural market characteristics in the United States but of individual traits. It is conceivable that systematic differences in the causal relationships among variables predated the arrival of immigrants in the United States and account for those found at present. This would run contrary to dual labor market theory, according to which such differences are due to structural characteristics of the firms where immigrants become employed.

Results in table 3 show a fundamental similarity in determinants of principal occupation in Cuba across the three labor markets. While modest reliable effects are associated with age in one subsample and father's education in another, the major determinant of occupation in all three groups is education. Each year of completed education yields a reliable gain of roughly three SEI prestige points in each subsample. These coefficients are so strong that they quadruple their respective standard errors in all three groups.

Although in Cuba education resulted in a clear occupational return for all immigrants, the same is not true in the United States. Education has sizable positive effects on present occupation for immigrants in the primary and enclave labor markets but not for those in the secondary sector. In terms of the overall pattern of results, past individual attainment and background variables explain roughly one-third of the variance of present occupation in the primary and enclave subsamples but one one-fifth in the secondary sample. The latter figure is due only to the

TABLE 3. *Human Capital Determinants of Income in Three Labor Markets*

Dependent Variables	Father's Occupation	Father's Education	Mother's Education	Education in Cuba	Education in United States	Knowledge of English	Information about U.S. Society	Age	Occupation in Cuba	Present Occupation	R^2
						Enclave					
Occupation in Cuba	−.017	.305	.405	(3.446)	...	...	...	(.550)	...	...	.394
Occupation in United States	−.216	−.677	1.600	(3.296)	.146	−.988	.742	.176	(.183)	...	.333
Present income	1.683	.256	−13.027	−3.212	−.059	−14.462	(51.667)	−2.414	.041	(3.746)	.208
					Primary Labor Market						
Occupation in Cuba	.131	(1.474)	−1.571	(3.158)	...	...	...	.294	...	...	.359
Occupation in United States	.120	.132	−.129	(1.883)	−.154	(1.676)	−.094	.557	(.272)	...	.307
Income	1.178	2.070	−1.803	−2.671	−5.544	9.448	(47.417)	−3.803	1.909	(3.111)	.255
					Secondary Labor Market						
Occupation in Cuba	.100	.483	−.791	(3.237)	...	...	...	.110	...	...	.334
Occupation in United States	−.115	−.543	1.792	.211	.256	−.796	−.712	−.440	(.338)	...	.210
Income	−.977	−3.530	19.575	−9.186	−1.296	.604	6.616	−5.357	1.628	.955	.143

Note.—Numbers are metric regression coefficients. Coefficients exceeding twice their SEs are enclosed in parentheses.

inertial effect of principal occupation in Cuba on present occupation. These results lend clear support to relationships predicted by hypothesis 2.

Stronger evidence against the defintion of enclave enterprises as an extension of the peripheral economy is provided by the regressions of income. Only two individual attainment variables—present occupation and the index of information about U.S. society—have significant effects on income. These effects, however, are quite strong *and* they are limited to the primary and enclave subsamples. Net of other variables, each additional point of occupational prestige represents a reliable gain of over $3.00 per month in both subsamples. More important, each unit change in the six-point information index yields a net gain of $47 per month in the primary sector and $52 in the enclave. Metric coefficients corresponding to information about the United States triple their respective standard errors in both subsamples. In contrast, not a single significant effect of past attainment or human capital indicators on income is found in the secondary labor market. While total explained income variance is modest in all cases, the figure for the secondary subsample is the lowest.

These results reinforce those in the first part of the analysis in showing the similarity of immigrant workers employed in center and enclave firms and their common and systematic differences from those confined to the peripheral sector. Taken as a whole, these findings support dual labor market predictions concerning the different yield of human capital investments in different sectors of the economy but correct their routine assignment of immigrant workers to the secondary labor market. For Cuban immigrants at least, the payoff of education, occupational status, and objective information appears as great among those employed in enclave enterprises as for those working in the mainstream center economy.

Conclusion

The data analysis above has shown the impossibility of automaticaly merging enclave workers into the peripheral economy and the fact that they reproduce, in a number of ways, the characteristics of those in the primary labor market. Strictly speaking, these results cannot be generalized beyond the universe of Cuban émigrés from which they were drawn. Nonetheless, although the Cuban political exodus clearly possesses many unique characteristics, these results are in general agreement with past qualitative and historical analysis of other immigrant groups. The significance of our findings is that they provide, for the first time, quantitative evidence of the empirical distinctness of an enclave labor force and the limitation of dual labor market theories for understanding its character. Additional research is required, however, to test the possibility of generalizing these results to other immigrant minorities.

The literature available in this area seems to agree that the development of immigrant enclaves requires two conditions: first, the presence of immigrants with sufficient capital and initial entrepreneurial skills; second, the renewal of the enclave labor force through sustained immigration (Sung 1967; Bonacich, Light, and Wong 1977). Our hypothesis that the findings above can be replicated for other immigrant minorities is based on the fact that these conditions are not unique to the Cuban case, nor do they appear to require the unique circumstances of a political exodus. Other charted paths seem to exist through which other immigrant groups have fulfilled them, as the case of the Japanese and the more recent one of the Koreans indicate.

Future research in this area must consider not only the situation of individual workers but also the structural characteristics of immigrant enterprises. Such research would help elucidate a contradiction in the existing literature. On the one hand, the economic success of such groups as the Japanese, the Cuban, and the Korean has been noted repeatedly; on the other, the exploitation which immigrant workers suffer at the hand of immigrant entrepreneurs has been stressed.

Bonacich (1973, 1978), for example, analyzes with insight the functions that immigrant entrepreneurs play with respect to larger firms in the center economy. As "middleman minorities," they enact economic directives from above and channel upward profits extracted from the exploitation of their respective groups. Enclave entrepreneurs can help cheapen labor costs for larger firms by the exploitation of the more vulnerable immigrant labor force. This might take the form of either intermediate input production for larger enterprises or a modern "put-out" system in which finished consumer goods, such as clothing, are produced in the enclave under contract for larger manufacturers.

Though speculative at this point, we hypothesize that the contradiction between the image of success and the image of exploitation of immigrant enclaves is more apparent than real. The line of reasoning pursued in the foregoing analysis suggests that the low-wage labor of immigrant workers is what permits survival and expansion of enclave enterprises which, in turn, open new opportunities for economic advancement.

Immigrant entrepreneurs make use of language and cultural barriers and of ethnic affinities to gain privileged access to markets and sources of labor. These conditions might give them an edge over similar peripheral firms in the open economy. The necessary counterpart to these ethnic ties of solidarity is the principle of ethnic preference in hiring and of support of other immigrants in their economic ventures.

The economic expansion of an immigrant enclave, combined with the reciprocal obligations attached to a common ethnicity, creates new mobility opportunities for immigrant workers and permits utilization of their past investments in human capital. Not incidentally, such opportunities may help explain why many immigrants choose to stay in or return to the enclave, forgoing higher short-term gains in the open economy.

Additional research is required to test this interpretation and examine possible differences across immigrant groups. At this point, we note only that this interpreation is in line with the results above insofar as they indicate that enclave workers are not better off initially, but that they are subsequently rewarded for skills and past investments in human capital.

Findings presented in this paper reintroduce a topic not adequately accounted for by theories of immigrant assimilation or internal colonialism, or by recent writings on the dual economy and dual labor markets. While often described in journalistic and qualitative terms, the phenomenon of immigrant enclaves and its theoretical implications have not received sufficient attention in the sociological literature. The results presented above raise perhaps more questions than they answer. Still, the remarkable geographic concentration of this sample and the differences detected for immigrants employed in center, peripheral, and enclave enterprises suggest the significance of the phenomenon and the need for additional research on the topic.

Appendix. *Variable Means and Standard Deviations*

Variable	Mean	SD
Father's occupation (SEI scores)	28.51	20.38
Father's education (years)	6.10	3.21
Mother's education (years)	5.59	2.45
Education in Cuba (years)	8.57	3.67
Education in United States (months)	2.99	5.89
Knowledge of English (correct answers)	2.69	2.74
Information about U.S. society (correct answers)	3.26	1.76
Age (years)	42.20	7.64
Occupation in Cuba (SEI scores)	39.76	24.46
Present occupation (SEI scores)	30.58	21.48
Present income (dollars per month)	647.05	293.71
Home ownership (yes = 1, no = 0)	.14	.35
Relatives in United States (N)	4.39	5.26
Income satisfaction (low = 1 to high = 3)	2.09	.96
Plans to move to another country (yes = 1, no = 0)	.05	.22
Would not come to the United States if he had to do it over (yes = 1, no = 0)	.04	.20
Would return to Cuba if things changed (yes = 1, no = 0)	.72	.45
Opportunities for relating with Anglos (very few = 1 to many = 4)	1.40	1.02
Perceived discrimination against Cubans (yes = 1, no = 0)	.30	.46
Personal experiences of discrimination (never = 0 to frequently = 3)	.76	.96

20

Immigrant And Ethnic Enterprise
in North America

Ivan Light

In the decade 1820–30, 80 percent of free white Americans owned their own means of livelihood (Corey, 1966: 113). This decade was the high-water mark of self-employment in America, and subsequent trends have shown an almost uninterrupted decline. Generations of sociologists have declared that business self-employment in the modern United States has become an economic anachronism which is in the process of disappearance (Light, 1979: 31). Following Marx on this point, they have observed that the progressive concentration of capital reduced the once numerous class of free entrepreneurs that existed in the last century. Indeed, three decades ago C. W. Mills (1951) already showed the steady decline of agricultural and non-agricultural self-employment in the United States between 1870 and 1950:

> A larger number of small businesses are competing for a smaller share of the market. The stratum of urban entrepreneurs has been narrowing, and within it concentration has been going on. Small business becomes smaller, big business becomes bigger (Mills 1951: 24).

After Mills wrote this evaluation the decline of self-employment in the American labor force unambiguously continued until 1973. In that year

Reprinted from *Ethnic and Racial Studies* 7:2 (April 1984) by permission of Routledge & Kegan Paul PLC.

a slim majority of American farmers continued to be self-employed, but less than 7 percent of non-farm workers were self-employed (Ray, 1975). Given these trends, government and business analysts agreed that the probability of self-employment had become poorer than in the past and its rewards correspondingly more meagre (Cingolani, 1973: 8–10; Special Task Force, 1973: 21). In this economic context, social scientists generally concluded that small business self-employment was incompatible with capitalist economic concentration and could be expected to slide into oblivion for this reason (Bottomore, 1966: 50; O'Connor, 1973: 29–30; Horvat, 1982: 11–15; Auster and Aldrich, 1981).

However, on the cultural side, sociologists had to explain the atavistic persistence of entrepreneurial values and ambitions in the American labor force (Chinoy, 1952; Walker and Guest, 1952) as well as the extent of self-employment among the wage-earning population (Lipset and Bendix, 1959: 102–3, 177–81). Given the USA's *laissez-faire* traditions (Meyer, 1953) it was easy to understand entrepreneurial ambitions and frustrated aspirations as cultural residuals of an economically bygone era (Vidich and Bensman, 1960: 305–6). Thus, Riesman (1950) juxtaposed the 'inner-directed' old-fashioned individualism of yesteryear's entrepreneurs with the glad-handed 'other-direction' of corporate executives, finding in this contrast a shift in the modal personality from the former to the latter. In a similar exercise, Miller and Swanson (1958: 123) found that achievement imagery in the American middle class had shifted away from self-employment toward bureaucratic careers in corporate hierarchies. Bell's (1976: 84) analysis of the 'cultural contradictions of capitalism' identified the Puritan tradition as a self-destructive rationality whose adolescent heirs had discarded the disciplines of planning and work in favor of 'voluptuary hedonism.'

Entrepreneurship's protracted decline provided a neat illustration of cultural lag, the belated adjustment of superstructure to changes in production relations (Aronowitz, 1973: 257). A small business economy needed entrepreneurial motivations in its labor force. When the economic basis of small business deteriorated, socialization lagged behind, continuing to produce entrepreneurial ambitions and values in lifelong wage workers (Lynd and Lynd, 1937: 70). The temporary result was a glut of disappointed aspirants for small business self-employment, a situation of imbalance between supply and demand (O'Connor, 1973: 29–30). Ultimately, the market's surplus of aspiring entrepreneurs reached back into the socialization system causing reallocation of motivational resources away from this overpopulated occupation in diminishing demand. As salaried workers corrected their aspirations for realistic prospects, the social origins of American small business owners declined (Newcomer, 1961: 490;

Meyer, 1947: 347; Mills, 1966). By 1952 the 'creed of the individual enterpriser' had become 'a working class preoccupation' (Lipset and Bendix, 1964: 462).

Ethnic and Immigrant Enterprise in America

Taken very generally, cultural lag still offers a satisfactory explanation of what happened to entrepreneurial individualism in twentieth-century America. However, the cultural lag orthodoxy encounters two serious objections, one empirical, the other conceptual. First, as Giddens (1973: 177–8) has observed, the *rate* of decline in self-employment was never so rapid as Marxists had expected even though the direction of change was mostly negative. Moreover, in the specific period 1972–9, 'the number of self-employed Americans rose by more than 1.1 million, reversing decades of steady decreases' (Fain, 1980: 3). This stabilization suggests that a plateau in self-employed population firmly supports an ideology of entrepreneurship among a minority (see Table 1). This conclusion is particularly appealing since Boissevain (1984) has reported that in 1978 'Common Market countries registered a net increase in the number of entrepreneurs and family workers' thus reversing their postwar trend of decline.

Second, cultural lag orthodoxy depends upon a simplifying, inaccurate assumption of homogeneity in economy and labor force. A homogeneous economy means uniformity in industrial

TABLE 1. *Self-employed And Unpaid Family Workers in the United States, 1948–79 (number in thousands)*

1948	1948	1958	1968	1972	1979
Non-agricultural industries					
Total employed	51,975	56,863	72,900	78,929	94,605
Self-employed	6,109	6,102	5,102	5,332	6,652
Percent of total	11.8	10.7	7.0	6.8	7.0
Unpaid family workers	385	588	485	517	455
Percent of total	0.7	1.0	0.7	0.7	0.5
Agriculture					
Total employed	6,309	4,645	3,266	3,005	2,993
Self-employed	4,664	3,081	1,985	1,789	1,580
Percent of total	73.9	66.3	60.8	59.5	52.8
Unpaid family workers	1,318	941	550	467	304
Percent of total	20.9	20.3	16.8	15.5	10.1

Source: T. Scott Fain, 'Self-Employed Americans: Their Number Has Increased,' *Monthly Labor Review* 103 (1980): Table 1, p. 4.

conditions among the various sectors as well as a uniform rate of capitalist concentration in each. Labor force homogeneity means all workers are identical in values, attitudes, skills, employment access, and return on human capital. Both assumptions are unrealistic. The USA economy actually consists of a plurality of sectors which differ in respect to industrial conditions, capitalist concentration, and rates of change. O'Connor's (1973) distinctions between competitive, monopoly and state sectors need attention, and this tripartite division could easily be augmented in the interest of exactitude (reviewed in Kallenberg and Sorenson, 1979). Additionally, the USA labor force consists of unequally situated groups which differ in cultural heritages. At the very least, one must distinguish the immigrant, the nonwhite, and the native white labor force sectors. Workers in these sectors experience differential returns on human capital, rates of under- and unemployment, welfare and legislative support, and career opportunities.

Given variation in the economy and labor force, uneven resolution of cultural lag follows. On the one hand, some business sectors retain contrary-to-trend compatibility with entrepreneurial activities. On the other, some working populations retain atavistic aspirations for business self-employment. In point of fact, immigrant and nonwhite workers cluster heavily in the economy's competitive sector within which, by definition, a small business milieu persists (Waldinger, 1982: 1–2; Zenner, 1982: 474; Auster and Aldrich, 1983). Thus, on structural grounds alone, there is reason to predict that old-fashioned entrepreneurial ideology should remain among immigrant and minority sector workers long after native white workers have resigned themselves to salaried and wage employment in the monopoly and state sectors.

This situation is not really novel. In actual fact, the foreign-born have been overrepresented in American small business since 1880 and probably earlier (Light, 1980: 33; Higgs, 1977: 92). Two explanations seem plausible. The first is disadvantage in the labor market. Such disadvantage causes foreigners to concentrate in small business because they suffer under- and unemployment as a result of poor English, unvalidated educational credentials, discrimination, and so forth (Reitz, 1980: 191). Anyone who is disadvantaged in the labor force derives from this unfortunate situation a special incentive to consider self-employment, and the greater his disadvantage, the greater his incentive. The unemployed apple vendors of the Great Depression epitomize the resourcefulness of workers who, unable to find wage-earning jobs, turn to any and every pitiful self-employment from economic desperation.

However, labor markets' disadvantage cannot be the whole explanation of this phenomenon, because some immigrant and ethnic minority groups have higher rates of urban self-employment ('entrepreneurship') than do others (Goldscheider and Kobrin, 1980: 262–75; Boissevain, 1984; Jenkins, 1984). Given equal disadvantage why do some foreign groups have higher rates than others, and why should the foreign-born in general have higher rates of business self-employment than disadvantaged native minorities, especially blacks (Handlin, 1959: 74)? Native blacks are more disadvantaged than native whites, yet the blacks' rates of business self-employment have been and remain lower than the native whites' rates and much lower than the foreign-born rates despite presumptively higher disadvantage of the blacks (Light, 1972, 1979; Wright et al., 1982: 724).

Orthodox and Reactive Cultural Contexts

The orthodox answer to this issue has fastened upon transplanted cultural endowments of various ethnic minority groups. Derived from Max Weber, this model of entrepreneurship has claimed that individuals introject cultural values in the course of primary socialization. When a group's values and motivations encourage business enterprise, cultural minorities produce socialized adults who prosper in business. The prototype is Weber's (1958a) Protestant sectarians who espoused the values of diligence in a calling, thrift, profit, and individualism. These values and attendant motivations caused adult sectarians to prosper in business. With appropriate adjustments, this model might account for the anomalous and persistent overrepresentation of selected cultural minorities in self-employment. American examples include Jews, Chinese, Japanese, Greeks, Macedonians, West Indians, Dominicans, Gypsies, Iraqi Christians, Lebanese, Koreans, and Arabs.[1] In all such cases, cultural theory has explained business overrepresentation and/or success in terms of intact, unmodified cultural heritages. A fine example is the migration of Gypsy fortunetellers. Before debarkation in New York City, the Gypsies already knew how to tell fortunes, and their cultural baggage included ready-to-use skills (crystal balls, tarot cards, palmistry) other groups simply lacked. Gypsy practice of these skills in the United States only involved the utilization of a cultural tradition for the specific purpose of self-employment (Sway, 1983).

This view has merit, but research in ethnic enterprise has disclosed its inadequacy. In reality, immigration and alien status release latent facilitators which promote entrepreneurship independently of cultural endowments (Turner and Bonacich, 1980: 145, 148). Three facilitators are especially important. The first is psychological satisfaction arising from immigration to a high-wage country from a low-wage country. Immigrants in the United States have recurrently proven willing to accept low money returns, long hours of labor, job-related danger, and domestic penury in order to maintain business self-employment. Relative to their countries of origin, even adverse conditions look good to immigrants and, until fully adapted to the American standard of living, immigrants obtain satisfaction from squalid proprietorships that would not attract native-white wage earners. This is *relative satisfaction*.

A second, much-documented reaction is enhanced social solidarity attendant upon cultural minority status. Chain migrations create immigrant communities with extraordinarily well-developed social networks. Numerous studies have shown that these social networks create resources upon which immigrant co-ethnics can draw for business purposes (Light, 1972; Bonacich, 1973, 1975; Bonacich and Modell, 1980; Wilson and Portes, 1980). 'The cornerstone of an ethnic subeconomy is the communal solidarity of a minority group' (Hraba, 1979: 374). Insofar as reactive solidarity encourages immigrant entrepreneurship, a situation has brought out a collective response which is not cultural in the orthodox sense (Young, 1971). A concrete example is the influence of immigrant *Landsmannschaften* upon business enterprise. Immigrant *Landsmänner* be-

long to a primary group which did not exist as such in their country of origin. Thus, among Japanese of Los Angeles *Hiroshimakenjin* formed a solidaristic subgroup within the metropolitan population—all the brothers hailed from Hiroshima. One the other hand, contemporaneous residents of Hiroshima did not share the sense of local solidarity so the immigrants had obviously created a solidarity abroad that did not exist in Hiroshima, their city of origin (Modell, 1977: 99–117). This is a *reactive* solidarity which required alien status to liberate, and as such is quite different from the practice of fortunetelling by immigrant Gypsies.

The third endowment is sojourning (Siu, 1952). Sojourning arises when immigrants intend to repatriate, and derive from this intention a desire to amass as much money as possible as quickly as possible. As Bonacich (1973) has shown, sojourning implies a battery of entrepreneurial motivations which give middleman minorities an advantage in business competition over nonsojourners. Admittedly, the cultural status of sojourning is uncertain, and the phenomenon arguably arises liturgically as well as situationally (Light, 1979: 33–4). Nonetheless, sojourning is a frequent (but not invariant) accompaniment to international immigration, and its presence provides an economic edge to the foreign born in small business enterprise (Zenner, 1982: 458; Portes, Clark and Lopez, 1981–2: 18).

Light's (1980: 34–6) distinction between reactive and orthodox cultural contexts of entrepreneurship is a new one necessitated by the rapidly growing literature on this topic, but anticipated by earlier writers (Young, 1971). Orthodox and reactive contexts in Light's rubric correspond closely to what Turner and Bonacich (1980: 145, 148) elsewhere identified as cultural and situational variables. In both cases, authors responded to the tendency of ethnic business researchers to 'talk past' real issues on the one hand or, on the other, to engage in 'unnecessary and wasteful polemics' about pseudo-issues (Turner and Bonacich, 1980: 145, 147). Authorities agree that, however named, the conceptual distinctions identified do not necessitate an empirical repugnance because different variables can contribute to the entrepreneurship of the same ethnic groups. Old-fashioned cultural analysis (Belshaw, 1955) stressed only orthodox etiologies, thus creating the erroneous implication that only culturally intact transmission affected entrepreneruship (Freedman, 1959). Conversely, Bonacich's (1973) model of 'middleman minorities' ignored orthodox contributions, focussing only upon reactivities. In Light's (1972) treatment of prewar blacks and Asians in the USA the overrepresentation of Asians in business proprietorships is credited to reactions arising from relative satisfaction and immigrant solidarity *as well as* to rotating credit associations, culturally transmitted institutions fitting the orthodox model (see also Woodrum, Rhodes and Feagin, 1980: 1245).

Orthodox, reactive, or mixed entrepreneurship arises when only-orthodox, only-reactive or mixed orthodox and reactive components of entrepreneurship figure in an empirical analysis. On the face of the available evidence, some groups belong in one, other groups in another category. The crucial evidence arises from two comparisons. On the one hand, the foreign-born in general have been overrepresented in American small business since at least 1880 and are still overrepresented. On the other hand some foreign-born groups have higher rates of business self-employment than do others. For example, Jews have been and remain extraordinarily entrepreneurial whereas Irish have been lower than the foreign-born average (Goldscheider and Kobrin, 1980). The general overrepresentation of the foreign-born betokens a situationally-induced responsiveness to self-employment. This responsiveness is *prima facie* evidence for a reactive model. On the other hand, the higher than average rates of selected foreign-born groups suggest unique cultural endowments. Unique endowments imply cultural heritages transmitted intact, the orthodox cultural model. The best fit of theory and evidence occurs when theory acknowledges the additive possibilities of orthodox and reactive components. On this view, the foreign-born in general experience the reactive entrepreneurship arising from their alien situation, but middleman minorities (Jews, Chinese, Greeks, etc.) add to this reaction their culturally intact heritages of sojourning entrepreneurship (Bonacich and Modell, 1980: Ch. 2). As a result, rates of entrepreneurship are higher among middleman minorities than among the foreign-born

in general, and higher among the foreign-born than among the native-born whites.

Ethnic and Class Resources

Efforts to explain ethnic and immigrant entrepreneurship invariably turn up batteries of special causes. That is, the immigrants developed higher than average rates of entrepreneurship because they drew upon special resources which native groups lacked. In Barth's (1962) terminology these facilities constitute entrepreneurial 'assets' but the term resources is more general and does not lend itself to confusion with financial assets (Light, 1980: 35). *Ethnic resources* are any and all features of the whole group which coethnic business owners can utilize in business or from which their business benefits (Reitz, 1982; Wallman, 1979a: ix; 1979b: 10). Thus, ethnic resources include orthodox cultural endowments, relative satisfaction, reactive solidarities, sojourning orientation, and these four encompass all types of ethnic resources empirically described in the existing literature (cf. Turner and Bonacich, 1980: 152). As such, ethnic resources should be distinguished from class resources. *Class resources* are cultural and material. On the material side, class resources are private property in the means of production and distribution, human capital, and money to invest. On the cultural side, class resources are bourgeois values, attitudes, knowledge and skills transmitted intergenerationally in the course of primary socialization (DiMaggio, 1982: 190–1). An established bourgeoisie equips its youth with appropriate class resources, and, having them, the youth are well endowed to prosper in a market economy. Class resources exist, and sociological theory has amply and basically acknowledged their importance. An analytical dispute has arisen, however, when studies of ethnic entrepreneurship have sought to distinguish ethnic resources from class resources. The mainstream view ignored ethnic resources, assuming that only class resources do or even can exist. On this view, an ethnic bourgeoisie is just a bourgeoisie rather than a bourgeoisie which has unique access to ethnic resources.

In principle, class and ethnic resources might occur singly or in combination. This compatibility yields four basic etiologies: class-only, ethnic-only, class-ethnic mixed, and no resources. A class-only etiology explains ethnic minority or immigrant entrepreneurship strictly on the basis of class origins, property, money, and human capital. Class-only explanation is Type 1 in Table 2. Ethnic-only analysis omits the above, focussing explanation wholly upon ethnic resources such as cultural heritages, reactive solidarities, sojourning, and relative satisfaction. Ethnic-only explanation is Type 2 in Table 2. Mixed analysis combines elements of ethnic and class analysis to suit empirical cases of entrepreneurship. Mixed explanation is Type 3 in Table 2. Since class-only analysis is most compatible with a macro-theory of the economy, the mixed and ethnic-only analytic possibilities signal a newly discovered frontier of theoretical controversy. If the latter types exist, class macro-theory needs adjustment to take into account complexities currently ignored.

The North American literature contains no examples of class-only or ethnic-only resource-mobilizing entrepreneurial subgroups. All the empirical cases are mixed. The evidence thus reduces the theoretical polarities to ideal types. Admittedly some cases of ethnic minority or immigrant entrepreneurship weigh more heavily on one side or the other of this class/ethnic balance. Especially in the past, immigrant entrepreneurship seems to have depended more heavily upon ethnic resources than it currently does. Turn-of-the-century Chinese and Japanese immigrants in California are the best-documented illustrations. Disadvantaged in the general labor market, they turned in extraordinary proportion to self-employment, apparently mobilizing ethnic resources very effectively to this end (Light,

1972; Modell, 1977; Bonacich and Modell, 1980). Post-1970 Asian immigrants in North America continue to mobilize ethnic resources to support business ownership, but the balance has shifted toward money, human capital, and bourgeois culture. Thus, all cases of Asian entrepreneurship have been mixed, but in the last half-century the balance has appreciably swung from ethnic toward class resources (Thompson, 1979).

In contemporary American and Canadian society, immigrant entrepreneurship still combines ethnic and class resources, thus creating an empirical problem of sorting out each contributor and assessing its contribution. Thorny as is this measurement problem the empirical dualism is clear especially in the important cases of political refugees from the Third World. To a substantial extent, Korean, Vietnamese, Taiwanese, Hong Kong, Cuban, and Iranian immigrants now in the United States derived from property-owning upper classes in their countries of origin.[2] Fearing or experiencing sociopolitical turmoil in their homelands, these refugees entered the United States with human capital, money to invest, and bourgeois cultural values. Accordingly, it is no surprise that their involvement in small business has been extensive, their success in it remarkable, and their achievements much celebrated in popular media (Ramirez, 1980). On a class-only model the small business success of these refugees reflects only the class resources they brought with them, and any group of wealthy refugees would have created as many small businesses. Ethnicity conferred nothing: this is the null hypothesis.

TABLE 2. *Ethnic and Class Resources of Entrepreneurship*

| | Resource Basis | | | |
| | Ethnic | | Class | |
	Orthodox	Reactive	Material	Cultural
1. Class-only	O	O	X	X
2. Ethnic-only	X	X	O	O
3. Mixed	X	X	X	X
4. Mixed: class predominant	x	x	X	X
5. Mixed: ethnic predominant	X	X	x	x
6. No resources	O	O	O	O

O = none
x = some
X = much

Class resources indisputably help, but empirical research suggests that a class-only explanation is inadequate. An immigrant bourgeoisie utilizes ethnic resources in supplementation of class resources. The two best-studied examples are Cubans in Miami, and Koreans in Los Angeles.[3] Wilson and Portes (1980; Portes, 1981; Wilson and Martin, 1982) found that about one-third of Cubans in Miami were employed in Cuban-owned business and another fragment were self-employed. For the Cubans returns on human capital were more favorable among the self-employed than among those employed for wages in the competitive sector. Indeed, returns on human capital were equivalent to those in the primary sector. Explaining this success, Wilson and Portes (1980: 315) conclude:

> Immigrant entrepreneurs make use of language and cultural barriers and of ethnic affinities to gain privileged access to markets and sources of labor. . . . The necessary counterpart to these ethnic ties of solidarity is the principle of ethnic preference in hiring and of support of other immigrants in their economic ventures.

Since these resources would be unavailable in Cuba, the Cuban immigrant bourgeoisie acquires access to ethnic resources in Miami where they are members of a cultural minority. To a substantial extent, these reactive resources permit the Cubans to thrive in small business and even to outperform the native whites in this sphere despite the material advantages of the latter.

Bonacich, Light and Wong (1977, 1980; see also Light, 1980; Bonacich and Jung, 1982) have looked into the entrepreneurial success of 60,000 Koreans in Los Angeles. In 1980, approximately 40 percent of employed Korean men headed small firms (Yu, 1982: 54).[4] An additional 40 percent of Koreans worked in these firms so only about 20 percent of the Korean immigrants found employment in non-Korean-owned firms or government agencies. Admittedly, the Korean immigrants were highly educated: on one account nearly 70 percent of men had college degrees compared with only 15 percent of Los Angeles County residents in general. Additionally, the Koreans brought with them sums of capital rarely less than $25,000 and sometimes millions.

On the other hand, these class resources supplemented ethnic resources; they did not exclude them. As among the Cubans in Miami, Koreans in Los Angeles made effective business use of language and cultural barriers distinguishing co-ethnics from the general population, reactive social solidarity, nepotistic hiring, and formal and informal mutual support networks. Additionally, Koreans made some use of rotating credit associations, nationalistic appeals for labor peace, vertical and horizontal integration of firms, informal and formal restraints of trade,[6] and political connections with City Hall developed by leading Korean business organizations. In all these respects, Korean entrepreneurship drew upon ethnic resources not merely upon class resources.

Collectivist and Individualist Styles of Entrepreneurship

Textbook treatments of entrepreneurship have long begun with the economistic assumption that small business owners are individualists. Indeed, the term 'entrepreneurial individualism' remains in general currency as a reflection of this persisting assumption. Underlying the microeconomic theory of the firm are the class resources of the bourgeoisie which provide facilities for individual business owners. In Schumpeter's famous image, these entrepreneurs behave like spectators in a crowded stadium during a rainstorm. Feeling rain, each spectator independently decides to raise his umbrella, and decides to put it away when the sun once again comes out. In this analogy, the material resource is the umbrella, and the cultural resource is the trained wisdom to utilize it properly. But each entrepreneur thinks and acts independently albeit in utilization of class-linked resources.

Accepting Schumpeter's (1934: 81, n.1, 2) class-only model of entrepreneurship,[7] sociology has, however, parted company with neoclassical economics on the issue of consciousness. Insofar as a resource-transmitting bourgeoisie develops self-consciousness, this consciousness becomes a class resource capable of affecting the economic success of members. Thus, elitist studies of the American upper class have long claimed that debutante cotillions, preparatory schools, swank vacation resorts, exclusive suburbs, and stuffy downtown clubs reflect and forge upper-class consciousness (Useem, 1980: 53–8). Group consciousness enhances the chances of individual bourgeois to monopolize access to material and status rewards. For instance, clubs provide a private place to concoct business and political deals or to arrange marriages. Admittedly the importance of bourgeois group consciousness has not been so systematically examined in its economic as in its political ramifications. However, class-only theories of the bourgeoisie have acknowledged the development of an entrepreneurial collectivism which enhances the competitive chances of the individual members of the bourgeoisie. Evaluating two generations of social research on the American business elite, Useem (1980: 58) finds 'internal cohesion' strikingly in evidence. 'Unity is far more extensively developed at the top than anywhere else in the class structure.'

A similar evolution has characterized sociological studies of ethnic business (Jenkins, 1984). Classical sociologists called attention to cultural endowments which governed the style of business ownership, and explained in historical context the transition from merchant to bourgeois. The prototype was, of course, Weber's (1958a) Protestant sectarians whose economic style reflected religio-cultural values. Their disciplined lifestyle caused them to prosper in business, but they were expected to do so as noncooperating individuals standing or falling on individual merits. Of course, there is no denying that under some cultural or situational conditions, small business owners can be individualistic nor that introjected values of hard work, thrift, and economic rationality encourage business survival and success.[8] Bechofer et al.'s (1974) study of Scottish business owners in Edinburgh depicts individualistic business conduct. Jarvenpa and Zenner (1979) reported the same individualism among Scots in the Canadian fur trade. On the other hand, even Weber overstated the extent of individualism among Protestant sectarians and, aware of this error, was more careful (1958b) in some writings. Historical research among Puritan business owners in seventeenth-century New England has not disclosed the expected individualism. On the contrary, Bailyn (1955), Hall (1977), and Griffen

and Griffen (1977: 150) concluded that observantly Calvinist business owners in New England were active participants in commercial networks knit together on the basis of extended kinship and friendship, these networks actually linking ports of origin in the British Isles and New England cities.

In the same sense, cultural treatments of middlemen minorities in North America began with the assumption that cultural subgroups acted out their values in enterprising individualism based upon hard work, thrift, rationality, and self-denial (Auster and Aldrich, 1983). In this model, immigrant entrepreneurs drew upon a cultural tradition, then fanned out into the economy in individualistic search for profitable opportunities. Equipped with cultural resources, co-ethnics knew how to make the most out of such business opportunities as they encountered— but each did so as an isolated individual.

There is, of course, no question that ethnic values and motivations do affect individual behavior. However, ethnic research has shown there exists a largely ignored dimension of collective action which goes beyond individualistic value or motivational effects, important as those are (Leff, 1979). This is the dimension of entrepreneurial collectivism in the ethnic minority (Young, 1971: 140–1; Cummings, 1980). Collective styles of entrepreneurship depend upon group resources in which business owners only participate insofar as they maintain active, adult participation in community life (Herman, 1979: 84). For example, a rotating credit association requires cooperators to establish a reputation for trustworthiness in the ethnic community, and this reputation depends in turn upon active involvement (Light, 1972: Ch. 2). Similarly, an immigrant or ethnic informational network confers benefits upon business owners, but to obtain these benefits an owner needs to belong to the network. Isolates cannot share network information so this ethnic resource only benefits participants in ethnic community networks. Finally, trade guilds may regulate and control internal competition, but the benefits of collusion in restraint of trade accrue to members. Isolates suffer the consequences of collusion by others.

In principle, class and ethnic resources both confer potentialities for individualist or collectivistic styles of business management. As before, however, all empirical cases in the literature have been mixed. For instance, Koreans in Los Angeles have utilized both class and ethnic resources, and these resources have here supported individualistic and there collectivistic entrepreneurship. Taken together, Korean entrepreneurship in Los Angeles is a pastiche of ethnic and class resources and individualist and collectivist styles. On the other hand, the balance of individualism and collectivism in immigrant entrepreneurship appears to have shifted in three generations. Chinese and Japanese immigrants in California at the turn of the century utilized entrepreneurial strategies which were more collectivistic than those currently utilized by Chinese immigrants in Toronto (Chan and Cheung, 1982). In the same manner, Polish, Finnish, Irish, Mormon, and Jewish entrepreneurship appears to have undergone a shift in this century away from an immigrant-generation dependence upon collective resources toward a native-born generation dependence upon individual resources.[9]

Two related changes explain this shifting balance. On the one hand, the competitive sector has become smaller in size and the price of admission higher in response to capitalist concentration. Ethnic collectivism may be less adequate than in the past. On the other hand, upward social mobility has conferred class resources upon native-born ethnics whose progenitors did not have them. Specifically, native-born descendants of immigrant business owners enter the business sector with money, education, and skills their forebears lacked. Possessing class resources, immigrant and ethnic minority entrepreneurs become more individualistic in style. Thus, impoverished immigrants needed to combine their small amounts of capital in rotating credit associations in order to assemble a sum large enough to finance small business. Dependent upon kinsmen and landsmen for initial capital, immigrant business owners could not thereafter operate their businesses as if they were isolated individualists. With personal money to invest, the descendants of these immigrants and contemporary 'new' immigrants no longer need to borrow from kin and friends (Kim, 1977). Therefore, they establish their business enterprises without rotating credit associations, and operate them in a more individual-

ualistic manner.[10] Similarly, poor immigrants did not understand inventories or balance sheets so they turned to kin and friends for advice in business management. Equipped with MBAs, their descendants and North America's new immigrants possess the business skills they need as class resources. Therefore, they do not need to turn for management advice to informal, ethnically linked agencies, and they are free to operate their business enterprises as if they were isolated individuals. In this manner, access to class resources may obviate collectivism in ethnic enterprise—but not exclude it altogether. In Toronto, Thompson (1979) reports, a bipolar business class has actually emerged as a result of these processes. On the one side are the old-fashioned, ethnic-dependent Mom and Pop store owners; on the other, Hong Kong millionaires operating investment corporations. 'The new stratum of entrepreneurial elites differ in both origin and lifestyle from the traditional merchant elites who for years controlled the [Chinese] ethnic community' (Thompson, 1979: 311).

In principle, ethnic and immigrant small business ought to run out of solidarity to exploit because cultural assimilation and higher education undercut the ascriptive solidarities from which immigrant-generation business owners derived the resources to power their business network (Turner and Bonacich, 1980: 157). Much evidence suggests that over generations ethnic resources do decay for this reason (Bonacich and Modell, 1980: Chs 6, 9; Borhek, 1970; Goldscheider and Kobrin, 1980; Montero, 1981). 'Over the long run,' Reitz (1980: 231) observes, 'there is a progressive trend toward abandonment of ethnic group ties for all groups in which long-term experience can be measured.' However, the rate of deterioration has been much slower than sociologists once expected (Wilensky and Lawrence, 1979). The indisputable profitability of ethnic capitalism is an apparent cause of this retardation. Especially relative to equally qualified members of the same ethnic group in the general labor market, owners of ethnic sector business enterprises earn high incomes in business. Big profits make ethnic business attractive (Wilson and Portes, 1980: 314; Sway, 1983; Reitz, 1982; Bonacich and Modell, 1981: 257). Ethnic business owners identify with their ethnic community and participate actively in it. They provide the leadership for ethnic institutions. Ethnic attachments also persist more strongly among wage workers whose workplace is a co-ethnic firm whose language is that of the homeland, not English (Bonacich and Modell, 1980; Reitz, 1980; Woodrum, Rhodes and Feagin, 1980: 1240–52). These two classes often account for between 40 and 80 percent of the total ethnic population. Ethnic-owned businesses 'help prop up other institutions which recruit and maintain ethnic membership' (Reitz, 1980: 223). Ethnicity supports the ethnic economy, and the ethnic economy supports ethnic perpetuation (Bonacich and Modell, 1981: 257).

No Resources Entrepreneurship

The preceding analysis offers a satisfactory account of why equally disadvantaged ethnic and immigrant minorities display unequal rates of entrepreneurship: survival and success depend upon group resources. Groups with more resources outperform groups with less; and groups with class resources are individualistic whereas groups with ethnic resources are collectivistic. On this view, entrepreneurship is highest when disadvantaged immigrant minorities are well endowed with class and ethnic resources; endowment with one or the other is intermediate; and neglible endowment in both class and ethnic resources implies correspondingly low rates of entrepreneurship.

Behind this conclusion lies the assumption that immigrant minorities' rate of business ownership is a fair measure of their entrepreneurship. The rate of business ownership has been operationally defined as self-employed per 1000 in the urban labor force.[11] A major objection to this definition, it is increasingly clear, arises from the inadequacy of published statistics (Karsh, 1977; Light, 1979: 39–40; US Small Business, 1980). 'The Census has a completely nonsociological way of defining "self-employment"' (Wright et al., 1982: 712n). US statistics routinely exclude petty traders without fixed business premises, no-employee firms, illegally operated firms in legitimate industries, and firms producing unlawful goods or services. Since minorities and immigrants bulk very large is such firms, their exclusion from official tabulations results in undercounts of

minority-owned business enterprise as well as theoretical misperception of the whole phenomenon of ethnic entrepreneurship. No one knows how many untabulated firms exist nor what is their distribution among various sectors of the labor force.

The case of native-born black Americans is instructive because blacks are disadvantaged but native-born. All statistical and ethnographic sources have uniformly reported that rates of business self-employment among urban blacks have been and remain lower than among even native-white, let alone the foreign-born (Light, 1972, 1979, 1980). At the same time, ethnographic sources have stressed the importance of 'hustling' as an economic activity among underclass urban blacks (Valentine, 1978; Glasgow, 1980: 9, 90; Light, 1977b). Hustling involves piecing together a livelihood by operating a variety of legal, semi-legal, and sometimes illegal business activities. Legal enterprises of urban blacks include street corner and door-to-door peddling of trinkets, object d'art, junk, salvage, and fire-damaged merchandise. Unlawfully conducted legal enterprises include unlicensed taxicabs, unlicensed pharmacies, unlicensed medical services, welfare cheating, tax-evading labor services and so forth. Illegal enterprise includes gambling administration, pimping, prostitution, narcotics vending, and other victimless crimes (Light 1977a, 1977b). Predatory crimes include armed robbery, burglary, shop-lifting, and all similar activities. All these self-employed activities are entrepreneurial in that they involve risk and uncertain return (Harbison, 1956: 365). Although comprehensive statistics are lacking, there seems little doubt that urban blacks are as overrepresented in marginal legal and unlawfully operated self-employment as crime statistics indicate they are in illegal enterprise and predatory crime. Taken together, this package suggests much higher than average self-employment among economically marginal blacks in unmeasured business at the same time that official statistics reveal much lower than average self-employment in measured business.

Given the presumptively high rates of black self-employment in these undocumented industries, it is improper to conclude that native blacks are less entrepreneurial than other economically disadvantaged immigrants and ethnic minorities.

It rather appears that native-born blacks have elaborated an alternative, heavily illegal, highly individualistic style of coping with protracted economic marginality. Compared to the foreign-born in general, and middleman minorities in particular, native-born blacks are low in ethnic resources of entrepreneurship, but share economic disadvantage (Wong, 1977; Light, 1972: Chs 2, 6–8; Venable, 1972: 30). Compared to native whites, native blacks are high in economic disadvantage, low in class resources of entrepreneurship, but similar in respect to ethnic resources of entrepreneurship. Table 3 documents these contrasts. Low on ethnic resources of entrepreneurship but high in economic disadvantage, native-born blacks were compelled to depend upon class resources in which they have been underendowed for centuries. As an overall result, marginal black enterprises have not broken into the circle of legal, officially enumerated small business enterprises. Their problem has been nonpromotion of their very large class of petty but invisible enterprises such that a visible minority enjoy upward social mobility within the legitimate, competitive sector (Glasgow, 1980: 189). It is in the assistance of upward mobility that ethnic and class resources make themselves appreciably manifest (Gelfand, 1981: 185, 190). Given labor force disadvantage, chronic unemployment or both, any ethnic or immigrant minority resorts to self-employment, but only resources make possible the promotion of marginal enterprises into small businesses whose long-term profitability brings along the social mobility of proprietors, their kin, and their heirs (Wilson and Martin, 1982: 155–7).

Summary and Conclusion

Uneven development has created economic enclaves within which small business can still be profitable. Success in small business requires, however, a combination of class and ethnic resources with some evidence indicating the former have increased their importance in the last generation. Nonetheless, ethnic resources persist, and immigrant and ethnic minority groups are overrepresented in small business in large part because their access to ethnic resources permits them to outcompete native workers. In this comparative respect native whites and blacks are similar but the native blacks lack class resources and additionally suffer labor market disadvantage which gives them a motive to seek self-employment income. Underclass blacks do find this income in the form of hustling, but hustling has by and large failed to create firms that are large and legal enough to achieve visibility in government statistics.

Ethnic resources of entrepreneurship often depend upon premodern values and solidarities. So long as these survive in the ethnic community, co-ethnic business owners are able to utilize them in business, achieving advantage over fully proletarianized, native-born workers among whom blacks are conspicuous. In theory, ethnic capitalism and cultural assimilation should first under-

TABLE 3. *Profiles of Entrepreneurship*

	Comparison groups			
	Middleman Minorities	Foreign-born	Native Blacks	Native Whites
Rotating credit associations	+			
Precapitalist commercial background	+			
Landsmannschaften	+	+		
Extended kinship	+	+		
Relative satisfaction	+	+		
Sojourning	+			
Unpaid family labor	+	+		
Labor force disadvantage	+	+	+	
Ineligible for public welfare	+	+		
Language barrier	+	+		
Special consumer demands	+	+		

cut and then demolish precapitalist solidarities, thus eliminating an ethnic group's competitive edge in small business. In the perspective of history, this self-destruction probably occurs. However, its rate should not be exaggerated. Ethnic enterprises still earn handsome financial returns, and these substantial rewards prop up the ethnicity upon which owners depend for resources. Profitability brakes the rate of deterioration of ethnic solidarity, supports the persistence of ethnic-owned firms in the competitive sector, and perpetuates the whole competitive sector.

ENDNOTES

*An earlier version of this paper was presented at the 10th World Congress of the International Sociological Association, Mexico City, August 19, 1982.

1. See Gelfand, 1981; Chs 4, 5; Goldscheider and Kobrin, 1980; Light, 1972: Ch. 5; Light and Wong, 1975; Wong, 1977; Sassen-Koob, 1981: 30–1; Modell, 1977; Bonacich and Modell, 1981; Lovell-Troy, 1980, 1981; Chock, 1981; Sway, 1983; Sengstock, 1967; Bonacich, Light and Wong, 1977, 1979; Blackistone, 1981; Herman, 1979: 90; Zenner, 1982; Waldinger, 1982; Yu, 1982; Bonacich and Jung, 1982.

2. 'Most of the refugees are ethnic Chinese, most of whom were shopkeepers or businessmen who had little future under a communist system.' 'Bleak outlook for Vietnam refugees,' East/West (San Francisco), June 20, 1979: 1. See also: McMillan, 1982; Rogg, 1971: 480; Chan and Cheung, 1982; Thompson, 1979; Wilson and Portes, 1980.

3. But two recent studies have produced important new documentation. In New York City's garment industry, Waldinger (1982) reported extensive and critically important utilization of ethnic networks among Dominican entrepreneurs. In Los Angeles's taxi industry, Russell (1982) documented the mutual assistance common among Soviet Jews seeking to break into the occupation.

4. A similar situation apparently exists in New York City, site of the second largest Korean settlement in the United States. See Illsoo Kim, 1981: 110; see also 'Faced with prejudice and language difficulties, New York Koreans turn to private business,' Koreatown (Los Angeles), December 14, 1981: 8–9.

5. '$400,000 kye broke,' Joong-ang Daily News (Los Angeles: in Korean), February 20, 1979; Kim, 1981: 210–11.

6. 'Markets agree to cut down on competition,' Korea Times English Section (Los Angeles), November 23, 1981: 1. 'KCCI asks bizmen for more cooperation,' Korea Times English Section, February 6, 1980; 'Fifteen Korean chambers unite,' Koreatown, November 17, 1980; 'Prosperity of shops leads community development,' Korea Times English Section, November 22, 1976.

7. Schumpeter's (1934) views are endorsed in Beveridge and Oberschall, 1979: 207, 225, 229; criticized in Jones and Sakong, 1980: 211; reviewed in Hagen, 1968: 221–7.

8. 'When individuals go into business they must be prepared to lower standards of living and make personal sacrifices until their firms begin to prosper,' Cingolani, 1972.

9. See Chas 4–10 in Cummings (ed.), 1980.

10. In the wake of extremely high interest rates, white Californians began to utilitze the Pandero, a Brazilian rotating credit association, for purposes of home purchase. In this situation, a class-based, individualistic style reverted to old-fashioned collectivism as class resources became inadequate because of high interest rates. See DeWolfe, 1982.

11. Gerry and Birkbeck (1981) and Portes (1981) argue that marginal self-employed of the Third World are 'thinly disguised wage workers' because of their indirect economic dependencies upon big firms. However, Aldrich and Weiss (1981) have shown that a linear relationship exists between employment size and business owners' incomes, and linearity persists in the USA when non-employer firms are introduced. 'Owners without employees are simply the "poorest of the poor" among small capitalists. This group . . . should be assigned to the owner class in future research.'

21

The Acculturation/Assimilation Model in Urban Indian Studies: A Critique

C. Hoy Steele

Introduction

Since World War II, American Indians have been migrating from rural to urban areas faster than any other ethnic or racial group. U.S. Census figures reveal that between 1960 and 1970 Native Americans moved to cities at a rate 4⅓ times that of Blacks and 11½ times that of Whites (U.S. Bureau of the Census, 1972:262).[1] Approximately half the nation's one million Indians now live in cities, a situation somewhat at odds with the popular image of rural, culturally isolated peoples.

Social scientists who have studied this demographic phenomenon have recognized that such an extensive ethnic population shift raises the possibility of significant alterations in cultural adaptation and social organization. Theoretically, the range of these changes is almost infinitely broad: many scholars have proceeded on the *assumption*, however, that the inevitable overall result of Indian urbanization is acculturation or assimilation—that is, absorption—into the larger, non-Indian society.

This is an important issue for at least two reasons. First, Indians have been objects of public interest for several years now—at least to the

extent that the media cover militant Indian actions and books on American Indian history are popular. However, virtually nothing is known about the nature of contemporary Indian communities or the character and substance of Indian–non-Indian relations. Social scientists are but a few steps ahead of the general populace in this regard. Urban Indians were especially ignored until around 1960, and since then only a trickle of studies has appeared. Literally for centuries, Indians have been expected to disappear into the White population. Will the rapid urbanization of the last quarter of a century finally accomplish this, as the acculturation/assimilation model predicts? Or, on the other hand, are other issues more crucial?

The second reason that the nature of Indian urbanization is important is that *acculturation*, *assimilation*, and related terms are frequently employed in the lexicon of the social sciences for the study of ethnic and racial groups of all types. Thus, critical examination of the limitations of these concepts with respect to American Indians may have implications for the study of other minority groups and the general analysis of majority-minority relations.[2] In this article I shall present ethnographic data that seriously question assumptions underlying the acculturation/assimilation models.

From *Proceedings of the 1973 Annual Spring Meeting of the American Ethnological Society* (St. Paul, Minn.: West).

Acculturation or Assimilation—
A Conceptual Tangle

Use of the concepts of acculturation and assimilation has been marked by considerable confusion. Antropologists have focused on acculturation, while sociologists have been preoccupied with assimilation. This reflects the traditional emphases of anthropology and sociology on the analytically separable but intimately related concepts of culture and social structure, respectively. By and large, however, both sets of scholars have been discussing the same phenomenon—the extent to which a minority group dissolves into the majority group. Since anthropologists have exhibited greater interest in Indians, it is not surprising that acculturation is the more frequently used term for Indian social and cultural change.

More recently, acculturation generally has been felt to comprise but one aspect of assimilation. Gordon (1964:71) has developed a schema of seven assimilation variables, of which three— acculturation, structural assimilation, and amalgamation—appear most crucial and have commanded the greatest attention (e.g., see Parenti, 1967). Gordon's usage is paralleled by Roy (1972) and by White and Chadwick (1972), with minor terminological differences. Acculturation, which Gordon also labels cultural or behavioral assimilation, refers to the adoption by one group of the culture traits of another. Structural assimilation, on the other hand, denotes the merger of the social networks of two groups, including their primary groups and social institutions. Finally, amalgamation, which Gordon also calls marital assimilation, denotes biological merger or intermarriage.

According to Gordon, acculturation does not necessarily lead to structural assimilation, but the latter inevitably produces the former. Indeed, once structural assimilation has occurred, all other forms of assimilation follow. "Structural assimilation, then, rather than acculturation, is seen to be the keystone of the arch of assimilation" (Gordon, 1964:81).

In this paper, *assimilation* refers to Gordon's structural assimilation, and *acculturation* corresponds to his cultural or behavioral assimilation. Although I agree with Gordon that assimilation (his structural assimilation) is probably more fundamental, in this discussion I am using the

words together (acculturation/assimilation) in recognition of the predominance of the former term in research on American Indians.

The Acculturation/Assimilation Model

Two basic assumptions appear to underlie the acculturation/assimilation model. The first is that once Indians move to cities, the process of acculturation/assimilation inevitably occurs. This assumption seems to be based on three factors: (1) the small number of Indians in relation to the rest of the urban population; (2) the assumed contrast between reservation and urban life; and (3) the phenomenon of intermarriage between Indians and non-Indians. The second and most important assumption, closely related to the first, is that Indians must acculturate/assimilate if their adaptation to urban life is to be successful.

Indians Will Acculturate/Assimilate

1. The social scientist who begins to examine the phenomenon of Indian urbanization immediately confronts the obvious numerical discrepancy between non-Indians and Indians in the city. Sheer weight of numbers, then, provides one rationale for assuming that movement from a reservation to an urban area necessarily or automatically implies a corresponding change, both in consciousness and behavior, from Indian to White. One scholar, writing about Indians in Spokane, Washington, states, "The assumption made in this study is that the smaller American Indian society will be assimilated into the larger white society . . ." (Roy, 1972:227; see also Price, 1968; White and Chadwick, 1972). It is anticipated that Indians will become absorbed by the dominant society as a teaspoonful of strawberry milkshake becomes absorbed in a large glass of vanilla milkshake. As will be shown below, however, this absorption process is far from automatic.

2. An implicit emphasis in many studies upon the contrast between reservation and urban life may be a second factor influencing the adoption of the acculturation/assimilation model. *Reservation* implies both *rural* and *folk* life. In the literature of the social sciences, these terms frequently are placed in opposition to *urban* (see Redfield, 1947). Most reservations are, in fact, rural by customary standards, and their residents

probably exhibit as many traits of folk societies as can be found in this country. These obvious ecological contrasts between reservation and city, however, tend to obscure equally important linkages. Most significant is the fact that the economic and social systems in which Indians participate include both reservation and city.

The economic aspect of the acculturation/assimilation model is as follows: Indians have failed to adopt normative values of thrift, hard work, and deferred gratification and have remained outside the social patterns of American life; thus, they have failed to develop the economic potential of their reservations. Acculturation (changing their values) and assimilation (participating within the economic system) will, it is thought, result in development.

Joseph Jorgensen (1971) and others—notably Indian political activists—have challenged this view of Indian economic problems. According to Jorgensen, Indian reservations are not isolated from the economic mainstream, but are totally integrated within it through economic exploitation. Even the most isolated Indian reservation is joined with an urban center or centers through the urban center's economic control. The economic problem of the reservation, Jorgensen asserts, is that Indians are indeed "integrated into the national political economy"—as "super-exploited victims" (1971:68–69, emphasis deleted; 84). He cites Bureau of Indian Affairs statistics for 1968 showing that non-Indians received 75 percent, or 127.4 million dollars, of the gross from reservation agriculture, a total of 170 million dollars. They paid Indians only *12 percent* (16 million dollars) of their gross "for exploitation of Indian lands" (1971:82). Indian mining and timber resources are exploited in similar fashion.

As a consequence of the fact that Indians do not control the economic resources on their reservations, they live in chronic poverty. A corollary is that many reservation Indians must either commute to urban areas or make semipermanent migrations to find work. The circle is complete: commerical enterprises with urban headquarters or markets exploit Indian land, siphoning off economic benefits; reservation residents are thus forced to make a choice between moving to urban areas or commuting long distances.

We turn to the sociocultural dynamics of this situation—the social systems in which urban Indians participate. Does the acculturation/assimilation model adequately describe them? Here, we may turn to a case study (Steele, 1972) that focused on Prairie City (pseudonym), Kansas, a city of 125,000 people, and two small reservations less than fifty miles away, Prairie Band Pottawatomi and Kickapoo respectively.

Indians on these reservations are poor; jobs are virtually non-existent; and most reservation land is owned or leased by Whites. Many reservation residents commute daily to work in Prairie City and in the large industrial plants located just outside the city limits. Many former reservation residents now reside in Prairie City. They comprise approximately three-fourths of the one thousand Indians living there.

This situation has resulted in a complex social structure on a primary-group level. Residence in Prairie City rarely removes an Indian from the influence of the reservation, where a high level of locally based tribal participation is maintained. This includes three active native religious groups, annual Pow Wows, frequent dinners and other events, and a high degree of informal visiting. The proximity of the reservations to Prairie City facilitates convenient participation in these events by the urban Indians. Indeed, many Indians in Prairie City have indicated a strong preference for reservation life, but feel they must reside in the city for economic reasons. Likewise, much of the social life of the Prairie City Indian community also includes reservation residents. On Friday nights, for example, one of the most likely places to find a Pottawatomi—young or old, male or female, reservation or urban—is at either of two bowling alleys in Prairie City.

We have seen, then, that the acculturation/assimilation model makes false assumptions about both economic and social systems in which Indians participate. It assumes that underdevelopment, caused by a failure of acculturation/assimilation, is the economic problem of the reservations and that Indians who migrate to cities to look for jobs are probably planning to leave behind their cultural and social patterns. The fact is, however, that the principal economic problem of reservations is exploitation, which results from unequal power, not social and cultural distinctiveness.

The acculturation/assimilation model also assumes that the city is the total environment of the urban Indian, and conversely, that the reservation Indian is not influenced by the city. The fallacies of these notions have been demonstrated with respect to one city and its nearby reservations. Pressures upon an urban Indian to assimilate and acculturate are greatly lessened by the proximity (psychological as well as spatial) of his reservation.

3. If one assumes that Indians in cities inevitably become absorbed by the predominantly White population, one may naturally wish to look for ways of documenting this fact. One indicator of acculturation or assimilation used for many urban Indian studies is intermarriage. Little attention is paid to the non-Indian spouse, since—the reasoning seems to go—Whites are numerically dominant and therefore it is the Indian partner who will lose his or her ethnic identity.[3] This assumption requires closer scrutiny if a poor research design is to be avoided. Indian marriage to non-Indians *may* reflect assimilation/acculturation by the former. This is an empirical question to be determined by research, however; its veracity is not evident *a priori*. Gordon grants that widespread intermarriage (amalgamation) implies prior structural assimilation. "However," he warns,

a vastly important and largely neglected sociological point about mixed marriages, racial, religious, or national, apart from the rate, is in what social structures the intermarried couples and their children incorporate themselves. If Catholic-Protestant intermarried couples live more or less completely within either the Catholic social community or the Protestant social community, the sociological fact of the existence of the particular religious community and its separation from other religious communities remains [1964:130, emphasis deleted]

We may easily substitute "Indian-White" for "Catholic-Protestant."

Most Indians, reservation or urban, are constantly exposed to non-Indians. Indeed, any minority group that receives unequal treatment at the hands of a dominant group must not only be exposed to it but must also learn to adapt to many different kinds of majority-minority inter-

actions. Furthermore, the dominant group controls all forms of mass media. Thus, an Indian marrying a White already knows a great deal about the customs, habits, expectations and values of his or her new partner. A White marrying an Indian, on the other hand, may experience extensive resocialization into a more or less separate subsociety; almost certainly, he or she will have to internalize new norms and meanings.

Let us turn again to our case study. Sufficient data were obtained to comment on eighteen interracial marriages between Indians and non-Indians[4] in and around Prairie City. Three such couples seem to be entirely non-Indian in orientation; in each case both partners appear to have adopted White values, life styles, and primary relations. Six couples are split along racial lines—that is, the Indian partner is more or less active within the Indian community while his or her partner is not. Of the remaining nine couples, five are participants in both the non-Indian and Indian communities. The full extent of their participation in the non-Indian society is unknown, but they are fairly active in the Indian community on a primary group level. For example, a Chicano man whose wife is a well-known Indian dancer sells Indian craft and art work at powwows and is known to many Indians. A White woman and her Pottawatomi husband are inveterate participants in weekend Indian social activities, and she occasionally performs Indian dances.

The remaining four couples present striking examples of non-Indian acculturation and assimilation to *Indian* ways.[5] A Chicano man has been the head of the Pottawatomi Education Committee since its inception. He has demonstrated a thoroughgoing emotional, as well as physical, involvement in the problems of the reservation. He stated once (only half-humorously, I thought) that he wished he were an Indian. A second man, a White, has been learning Pottawatomi from his father-in-law. To his wife's embarrassment, he is more fluent in the language than she. He has also been the more vigorous proponent of their children's participation in Indian dancing. He is widely known and respected by Indians throughout the area.

The other two non-Indians are young White women recently married to young Indian men. Both have immersed themselves in the Indian community; one seems to have cut off most of her relationships with former White associates, while the other has very little remaining family and almost no ties outside the Indian community. Two of these four couples have recently moved from Prairie City to the Pottawatomi reservation, while a third lives just outside the city. The fourth also resides on the Pottawatomi reservation.

Indians Must Acculturate/Assimilate

If one major assumption of many urban Indian studies is that Indians who move to cities *will* become absorbed into the White urban mass, a second seems to be that survival in the city is possible by no other means—that assimilation and acculturation are *prerequisite* to successful urban adjustment (e.g., see Price, 1968; Roy, 1972; White and Chadwick, 1972).

One difficulty with this perspective is that it places the burden of successful adjustment totally on Indians themselves. Implicit is the notion that the city—that is, the dominant society and its institutions—bears no responsibility for facilitating adjustment. Whatever difficulties Indians experience are of their own making. The logic employed is of the type that holds that poor people themselves—not the political and economic institutions of the society—are responsible for poverty. Just as liberal social scientists spoke glibly of "the Negro problem" a decade ago, now we have "the urban Indian problem," if on a smaller scale.

Rarely, in urban Indian studies, are urban social institutions subjected to critical scrutiny. What are realistic possibilities for employment at a living wage in the city? How extensive is discrimination and what forms does it take? What kinds of agencies and organizations provide meaningful assistance to low-income urban immigrants or residents of whatever ethnic group? Another parallel may be drawn with Black-White relations of the volatile sixties. The Kerner Report (Report of the National Advisory Commission on Civil Disorders, 1968) included bold assertions about the racist nature of the society; but its major recommendations amounted to changing Black people instead of restructuring the society. Similarly, the chronic poverty and attendant social problems of American Indians are widely

deplored; no other mistreated ethnic group evokes greater sympathy. Yet social scientific and social policy ideologies simultaneously require conformity to Anglo, middle-class patterns as the price for inclusion of Indians in society's rewards.

Even accepting as reality the intransigence of the dominant group's social institutions and the cultural and class intolerance of the society as a whole, the question must still be asked whether acculturation and assimilation *actually* provide the only roads to successful adaptation to the city. This question leads to consideration of the internal life of the urban Indian population, which most studies fail to examine. It is my belief that this arena can provide a far richer source of social scientific knowledge than the investigation of questions of acculturation and assimilation. Those inquiries, by the nature of the issues posed, neglect more important questions. For example, are traditional Indian values retained in the city? To what extent are primary relations among urban Indians limited to the ethnic group? Does an urban Indian organizational life exist? Is there such a thing as an Indian "community" within the urban world?

My participant observation study of Prairie City, which lasted over a year, revealed interesting answers to these questions, at least for that city. In the remainder of this paper I shall comment upon Indian values, group life, and community in regard to the Indian population of Prairie City.

Repeatedly, and in a variety of ways, Indian people residing in Prairie City expressed adherence to values that they interpreted as uniquely "Indian" and that they advanced as credentials of Indianness. These include the legal criteria of Indian identity set forth by the U.S. Bureau of Indian Affairs—namely, certifiable membership in a recognized tribal group, which is in turn dependent upon blood descent of specified degree (usually one-fourth) from other members of the group. In addition to the legal requirements, there are informal credentials of "Indianness," including strong emphasis upon family life and obligations (especially in regard to the extended family), adherence to the ethic of mutual aid (especially to kin but also to other tribal members and other Indians), and participation in a variety of Indian ceremonies. "Indian" physiognomy and skin color, along with a high percentage of Indian "blood," ability to speak a native language, and observation of matters of etiquette in personal relationships (such as noninterference in the affairs of others) are also valued. Other criteria include rejection of what are commonly regarded as peculiarly Anglo traits of acquisitiveness, some forms of competition, and an exploitative attitude toward nature.[6]

People who share these values come together in a variety of formal and informal activities. I shall discuss only the formal ones. They include a powwow club, a smaller Indian singing and dancing group, all-Indian bowling teams, softball teams and basketball teams, an Indian (mission) Protestant Church as well as Indian religious groups on the reservations, and an Indian Center with numerous programs that have an impact upon, and involve, many Indian people within the city. These are Indian activities by virtue of the fact that, with few exceptions, Indian people are the only participants. For many, primary relations in Prairie City are restricted to these formal groups and to informal association with other Indians. In short, an Indian subsociety exists within Prairie City.

A substantial minority of the Indian population of Prairie City—approximately 25 percent—did not come from nearly reservations but migrated from Oklahoma, Nebraska, the Dakotas, the Southwest, or more distant points. These non-Kansans[7] tend to possess relatively few credentials of Indianness in the eyes of local Indian people.[8] On the other hand, substantial numbers of individuals within this diverse category are rather adept at dealing with White society; thus, they are especially useful to several Indian organizations. The Indian Center of Prairie City, for example, which became the hub of urban Indian activity while I was engaged in field work there, effectively integrated both local and nonlocal constituencies, at leadership levels as well as participant-client levels.

A final factor contributing to the sense of Indian ethnic identity and community in Prairie City is the existence of a network of parallel activities in neighboring towns, cities, and states that provide occasions for Indian people to come together from a wide geographical area. All-Indian bowling, basketball, and softball tourna-

ments are held frequently in neighboring cities, especially in Oklahoma. Pow Wows in the summer and dinner dances during the rest of the year take place throughout the plains states and stimulate frequent travel to distant and nearby places. Every organized group is part of some kind of regional or national network, or both.[9] These networks, added to the factors already mentioned (particularly ties to local reservations) further reinforce Indian identity and a sense of community within the local geographic unit. They are especially useful in helping Indian migrants from states outside Kansas to become part of the Prairie City Indian community.

It is important in this context to clarify the meaning of the term *community*, which may be defined as a "self-conscious social unit and a focus of group identification" (Theodorson and Theodorson, 1969:63).

> Community also implies a certain identification of the inhabitants with the geographic area, . . . a feeling of sharing common interests, and goals, a certain amount of mutual cooperation, and an awareness of the existence of the community in both its inhabitants and those in the surrounding area. [Theodorson and Theodorson, 1969: 64][10]

According to this definition, not all persons within the Indian *population* can be considered part of the Indian *community*. The excluded aggregate consists of those who, either by choice or circumstance, do not participate in the life of the Indian community—that is, they do not associate with other Indians. However, the wide range of Indian activities and the possibility of selective participation in them provide considerable flexibility, which is further enhanced by two facts relating to the earlier discussion of Indian values. First, no single individual can fulfill to the maximum all the criteria for Indian identity. Thus, at some point, everyone is vulnerable to the charge of not being totally Indian. On the other hand, some flexibility of lifestyle has to be recognized, and, in fact, standards often are not applied rigorously. Second, even more important to Indian identity than the possession of cultural criteria (for example, a high percentage of Indian "blood" or the ability to speak a native language) is participation in the life of the community. This participation, more than anything else, identifies someone as "Indian," for it is a public statement of, and pride in, belonging.[11]

Conclusion

We have seen that the acculturation/assimilation model is an inadequate conceptual tool in examining the Indian community of Prairie City, Kansas. This model fails to encompass the total environment of the Indian community, which includes two reservations as well as the city. Its assumptions that Indians will and must become absorbed by the non-Indian urban population have been seriously questioned. The acculturation/assimilation model neglects the role of non-Indians and of urban institutions in the adaptation of Indian people to urban life. Finally, it does not allow for the possibility of the existence of an ongoing urban Indian community, much less aid in its examination.

This study alone does not provide a firm basis for generalizing broadly about the dynamics of majority-minority relations. It suggests, however, that the acculturation/assimilation model be subjected to critical scrutiny prior to its use as a device for understanding minority group adaptation.[12] Future studies hopefully will be more alert to the flexibility and complexity of ethnic identity. As McFee (1972a) has suggested, ethnicity is not a zero-sum game. In the case of the Blackfeet, whom he studied, accommodation to White society did not destroy Blackfeet identity in many cases but produced a "150 percent man," capable of functioning equally well in both Indian and White social systems.

Levy's study (1973) supplies further evidence that ethnicity may be much more dynamic than has been assumed in the past. She found a remarkable ability among the Lubovitcher Hassidim in Brooklyn to manipulate the symbols of their ethnic identity as situationally required. When it is to their advantage to do so, Lubovitchers utilize the benefits of the larger society, but avoid activities that would set them beyond the ethnic boundary. Residence, clothing, the practice of ritual, and especially "the successful manipulation of kinship, marriage, educational institutions, and other types of social relations [can] promote individual goals while simultaneously

preserving the image of Lubovitch to the larger society" (Levy, 1973:29). It also appears likely that ethnic identity may be rekindled after a period of apparent dormancy.[13]

Turning more specifically to the issue of contemporary Indian communities, it is probable that the dynamics of Indian life in and around Prairie City are representative of the hundreds of relatively small urban areas near reservations in which Indians reside (for example, see White's study [n.d.] of Rapid City). Even in major urban areas like Chicago or Oklahoma City, where the Indian population is counted in thousands rather than hundreds, communities probably exist within the Indian population in considerably greater measure than most researchers have noted (see Krutz's study [1973] of Kiowas in San Francisco).

Native Americans probably have little to fear from White culture or the seductiveness of white primary groups and other social institutions; in this generation, too, the predicted Indian demise will be proven wrong. Indeed, Indians frequently assert the superiority of their own cultural and social orientations. What Indians have to fear is White political and economic power. Perhaps scholars interested in the maintenance of Indian identity, particularly those who see that identity as valuable for Indians and non-Indians alike, will recognize this fact, and begin to turn their research sights on governmental institutions and corporate power as they are brought to bear upon Indian communities.

ENDNOTES

1. Between 1950 and 1960 the number of Indians in cities almost tripled, and in the next ten years the urban Indian population more than doubled (U.S. Bureau of the Census, 1969:29; 1972:262).

2. The study of Indian urbanization offers potential rewards to the researcher in other areas as well—for example, urbanization per se, inter-ethnic relations among minority groups, and the effectiveness of urban social institutions in relating to a new group of constituents (see Steele, 1972: Chapter 6).

3. One survey of urban Indian studies (Petit, 1969:156–157) found that only one of the works examined mentioned the possibility that intermarriage could lead to non-Indian as well as Indian assimilation.

4. Two-thirds of the Indians are married to whites; the remainder are married to Chicanos. The

extent of non-Indian acculturation/assimilation is unrelated both to these ethnic differences and to race-sex correlations. Three marriages between Indians and blacks are not included because they present a special case. (See Steele, 1972:113–114, 211.)

5. As Hallowell (1972) has observed, a strict definition of acculturation refers to culture change of groups rather than of individuals. The latter phenomenon is designated *transculturalization* by Hallowell. I have chosen to use the former term because of its greater familiarity and general usage. To my knowledge, no one has yet suggested a term for (structural) assimilation on an individual, rather than a group, basis.

6. This list of values is closely paralleled by the finding of other researchers (cf. Gearing, 1970; McFee, 1972b; M. Wax et al., 1964; R. Wax and Thomas 1961).

7. Two small, contiguous reservations are located on the Kansas-Nebraska border. These reservations (one, Sac and Fox, the other, Iowa) are almost depopulated. People from these tribes living in Prairie City are so few that they are excluded from this discussion.

8. Pottawatomis and Kickapoos are closely related in origin, have lived as neighbors in Kansas for more than a century, and maintain a high rate of intermarriage. They participate in overlapping social systems and, except for minor differences, share a common culture.

9. A conflict over land between the Pottawatomi tribe and the BIA arose in 1970 and continues at this writing. The Pottawatomi have received aid from Indians of other tribes and from other Indian organizations. The Indian network, in other words, has a political dimension as well as social and cultural dimensions.

10. These tests, which the Indian population meets, are more important than the standard of economic independence, which it cannot meet, in specifying the existence of a community (Theodorson and Theodorson, 1969:64).

11. For example, a Kickapoo man once spoke approvingly of a woman who "acted and talked Indian" even though she could pass for a fullblood White and was married to a White.

12. Other articles in this section provide further evidence that caution is required.

13. See Part IV.

22

American Sociology and Black Assimilation: Conflicting Perspectives[1]

L. Paul Metzger

Introduction

The failure of sociologists to anticipate and direct their research attention to new developments in American race relations during the 1960s has been acknowledged by Hughes (1963) and Pettigrew and Back (1967, pp. 714–16). Rossi (1964, pp. 125–26) noted that "it is sadly ironic that as the pace of change in race relations stepped up in the past four years, the volume of social science research has declined during the same period." With the exception of projects sponsored by the federal government—most notably, the so-called Coleman and Moynihan reports (Coleman 1966; Rainwater and Yancey 1967)—significant in terms of their potential impact on national policy but resting on the theoretical foundations of an earlier period of basic research (Tumin 1968, pp. 118–19), the picture Rossi sketched remains relatively unchanged; his call for research into the black movements, the political aspects of racial change, and the role of ethnicity in American life has been met by only a handful of sociologists. Despite two recent studies by Bell (1968) and Levy (1968), the civil rights movement of the

early sixties remains largely uncharted by sociologists. Similarly, the black-power and nationalist movements which succeeded it, as distinct from the earlier Muslim movement (about which there are able accounts by Lincoln [1961] and Essien-Udom [1962]), remain virtually *terra incognita* within the sociological profession.

As an explanation for this failure, Hughes suggests that the concern with professionalism among sociologists has impaired their capacity to empathize with the movements of lower strata; Pettigrew and Back (1967, p. 706) refer to the timidity of foundations, the obstacles placed in the way of race-relations research by diehard white segregationists, and "a sociological bias in race relations toward studying the static and segregation-making elements." It is the thesis of this paper that the failure can be attributed in part to the theoretical framework through which most American sociologists have viewed race relations in the United States. This framework, it is believed, rests essentially on the image of American society which has been set forth by American liberalism, wherein the minority problem is defined in the narrow sense of providing adequate, if not equal, opportunity for members of minority groups to ascend as individuals into the mainstream culture. America, in this view, is the land of opportunity through competitive

Reprinted from the *American Journal of Sociology* 76 (Jan., 1971), pp. 627–647, by permission of the author and the publisher. Copyright © 1971 by the University of Chicago Press.

struggle in the marketplace; it can, and will, provide opportunities for all to gain just rewards for their individual merit. (American liberalism differs with American conservatism largely over the issue of whether the opportunities already present are adequate and takes its reformist cast from its recognition that they are not.)

Sociologists, by and large, have accepted this image of Horatio Alger in the Melting Pot as the ideal definition of American society. Although they have repeatedly documented the discrepancy between social reality and cultural myth in America, they have also taken the view that the incorporation of America's ethnic and racial groups into the mainstream culture is virtually inevitable. (Similar tendencies can be discerned in the field of social stratification, according to Pease, Form, and Rytina 1970). Successful assimilation, moreover, has been viewed as synonymous with equality of opportunity and upward mobility for the members of minority groups; "opportunity," in this system, is the opportunity to discard one's ethnicity and to partake fully in the "American Way of Life"; in this sense, assimilation is viewed as the embodiment of the democratic ethos.

The convergence of liberal and sociological thought in the area of race relations is striking and raises serious questions about the "value-free" character of sociological inquiry in this area.[2] This is particularly the case since the equation of assimilationist with democratic values in minority-majority relations is by no means universal even within Western culture (Schermerhorn 1959). The right of national self-determination has played a significant role in the liberal-democratic movement in Europe, and as Myrdal (1944, p. 50) noted, "the minority peoples of the United States are fighting for status in the larger society; the minorities of Europe are mainly fighting for independence from it."

Equally remarkable perhaps, is the fact that assimilationist values, with their connotations of elitism and a monocultural society, have come under as little attack as they have from either liberal or radical social criticism in the United States. The philosophy of democratic cultural pluralism has had, in fact, able spokesmen in America, most notably during the period of World War I (Bourne 1964) and the twenties

(Kallen 1924), but the issue of ethnic pluralism has not been a central preoccupation of the American Left until the recent emergence of the black-power movement. This can be traced, perhaps, to the ascendancy in the thirties of Marxian modes of thought in Left circles and the resulting preoccupation with economic and political questions, on one hand, and working-class solidarity, on the other.

The aim of this paper is to examine some of the major arguments which have appeared in the sociological literature in support of the view that the outcome of race relations in the United States will be the integration or assimilation[3] of the Negro into the American mainstream. The widespread and uncritical acceptance of these arguments by sociologists, it is believed, has contributed heavily to the void in race-relations research which has been noted above, as well as to the tendency to regard black-nationalist movements as "extremist" (Glazer and Moynihan 1963, p. 78), "escapist" (Morsell 1961, p. 6), and essentially deviant-pathological phenomena.[4] It will be pointed out that some of the components of a revised perspective on American race relations can already be found within the sociological literature and that a new perspective will include (1) abandoning the idea that racial assimilation in the form of gradual absorption of black Americans into the middle-American mainstream is necessarily either inevitable or desirable from the standpoint of democratic values, (2) a recognition that forces producing ethnicity as well as forces favoring assimilation are operative in American society today and that a realistic analysis of the ethnic and racial situation will take both into account, (3) a more balanced view of "black pluralism" (Killian 1968, p. 135) than thus far appeared in the work of most sociologists. In short, it is argued that a rethinking of the theory of eventual assimilation will open up prospects for a more pertinent and realistic assessment of minority problems, particularly race problems, in the United States.

The arguments favoring eventual assimilation will be grouped under two headings: (1) those which rest on assertions about the nature of the dominant white American society, (2) those which rest on assertions about the nature of minority groups and experience within this society.

Arguments from the Nature of the Dominant White Society

Central to the view of those sociologists who have taken the position that racial assimilation is the key to the American racial problem are certain beliefs about the nature of modern society in general, and American society in particular, which imply that prejudice, discrimination, and racist institutions are incompatible with the major features of modern social organization and hence will eventually "wither away." These assertions have taken various forms, but the common thread running through them has had several consequences: (1) the liberal optimism of most sociologists with respect to the possibility of peaceful and orderly change in the direction of racial integration[5]; (2) the belief that the major locus of institutional racism lay in the South, as a kind of underdeveloped area, the modernization of which would remove most of the institutional supports of racism; (3) the belief that the vestigial remains of racism in the urbanized and industrialized North would disappear as the educational, economic, and occupational status of both blacks and whites improved in the direction of greater affluence and security for all. Clearly, this perspective ill equipped sociologists for the racial crises of the sixties, a period of rapid economic growth and high prosperity which nonetheless witnessed heightened racial tension, urban ghetto violence on an unprecedented scale, and marked racial polarization (National Advisory Committee on Civil Disorders 1968).[6]

Robert E. Park and the Race Relations Cycle

In 1926, one of the most famous and influential statements of the theory of eventual assimilation was made by Robert E. Park (1950, pp. 149–50): "In the relations of races there is a cycle which tends everywhere to repeat itself. . . . The race relations cycle which takes the form . . . of contacts, competition, accommodation and eventual assimilation, is apparently progressive and irreversible. . . . Racial barriers may slacken the tempo of the movement, but cannot change its direction. . . . The forces which have brought about the existing interpenetration of peoples are so vast and irresistible that the resulting changes assume the character of a cosmic process." The universality and inevitability of this "cosmic

process" along with other formulations of race-relations cycle theories have long since been questioned by many sociologists,[7] but the acceptance of some form of melting-pot theory as descriptive of American society has been strongly maintained nonetheless.[8]

An ambiguity with respect to Park's (1950) views on the eventual assimilation of the American Negro should be noted. In 1913, for example, he wrote:

> Under conditions of secondary contact, that is to say, conditions of individual liberty and individual competition, characteristic of modern civilization, depressed racial groups *tend to assume the form of nationalities* [italics mine]. A nationality, in this narrower sense, may be defined as the racial group which has attained self-consciousness, no matter whether it has at the same time gained political independence or not. . . . The fundamental significance of the nationality movement must be sought in the effort of subject races to substitute, for those supplied to them by aliens, models based on their racial individuality and embodying sentiments and ideals which spring naturally out of their own lives. . . . In the South . . . the races seem to be tending in the direction of a bi-racial society, in which the Negro is gradually gaining a limited autonomy. [Pp. 219–20]

Frazier (1947, p. 269) noted that even up to "about 1930, Park's sociological theory in regard to race relations did not go beyond the thesis of a bi-racial organization." Hence, if Park believed in the eventual assimilation of races in the United States, his attention as an observer in the contemporary situation was strongly focused on the emergence of a black "national consciousness." Insofar as he regarded the growth of such a consciousness as a stage in the process leading to eventual assimilation, however, his cycle theory can be regarded as one of the more potent influences in the direction of viewing assimilation as a natural and inevitable process in the evolution of modern society.[9]

An American Dilemma

If Gunnar Myrdal (1944) was critical of the "do-nothing (laissez faire)" presuppositions which he detected in the work of American sociologists (including Park) and the subsequent tendency of the latter to "ignore practically all possibilities of modifying—by conscious effort—the social effects of the natural forces" (p. 1050), his classic opus remained very much within the assimilationist tradition. The author of *An American Dilemma* wrote that "we assume it is to the advantage of American Negroes as individuals and as a group to become assimilated into American culture, to acquire the traits held in esteem by the dominant white Americans" (p. 929).[10]

Myrdal discerns no structual impediment in American society to the realization of an assimilationist program: the race problem is a moral problem "in the heart of the American" (p. xlvii); and "America is free to choose whether the Negro shall remain her liability or become her opportunity" (p. 1022). This decidedly nonsociological approach to the problem is justified, according to Myrdal, because "there is evidently a strong unity in this nation and a basic homogeneity and stability in its valuations. Americans . . . have something in common: a social ethos, a political creed. It is difficult to avoid the judgment that this "American Creed" is the cement in the structure of this great and disparate nation" (p. 1). Furthermore, "the conquering of color caste in America is America's own innermost desire. . . . The main trend in its history is the gradual realization of the American Creed" (p. 1021).[11] The creed is carried, Myrdal believed, by the "huge institutional structures" of the society, through which "a constant pressure is brought to bear on race prejudice, counteracting the natural tendency for it to spread and become more intense. . . . The ideals thereby gain fortification of power and influence in society. This is a theory of social self-healing that applies to the type of society we call democracy" (p. 80).

Despite his hortatory tone and his call for national planning, social legislation, and social engineering on the part of an enlightened leadership, however, Myrdal had relatively few concrete suggestions for policy with respect to the race problem beyond his faith in the power of concerted educational effort (pp. 48–49) to break down the already-crumbling walls of the "caste beliefs and valuations" which he believed lay at the heart of white racism.[12] The race problem would be solved simply by moving the society

further in the course on which it was already set—that of welfare capitalism—which would require no major reorganization of its economic and political institutions. In the process, the South, as the major locus of the racial problem and "itself a minority and a national problem" (p. 1010), would take its place in the mainstream of the American polity.[13]

At the level of social determinants, Myrdal suggested that the forces of modernization in the South—industrialization, urbanization, the spread of literacy—were themselves powerful mechanisms for the elimination of racism in America. This theme frequently recurs in the post-Myrdal writings on race, and is especially emphasized by Arnold Rose (1956, p. 75): "The conditions which led to the development of the caste system in the nineteenth century are no longer with us. . . . New forces have arisen which make the caste system increasingly less desirable and useful to the dominant white group in the South or any other section of the country: These include industrialization, automation, the leadership of the United States in the free Western world, rising educational levels among both whites and Negroes. . . . These changes . . . *have made a mere hollow shell of tradition*" (italics mine).[14]

Hence, the belief that racism is incompatible with the major features of modern social organization has roots which go far deeper than Myrdal's liberal optimism and ethical-philosophical idealism. It is, in fact, rooted in what is perhaps the major theme of modern sociological theory—the shift, in Cooley's terms, from "primary" to "secondary" relations as the basis of social order.

The Sociological Traditions

In the course of their presentation of the case for the inevitability of desegregation, Simpson and Yinger (1959, p. 389) note that "in the approach to desegregation that we are taking, one can perceive a major recurring theme of sociological theory. Here is Sir Henry Maine's idea of the shift from status to contract. Here is an illustration of the perceptiveness of Simmel's work . . . concerning the influence of a money economy. Here is much of Toennies and Weber and Durkheim. Parsons and others who use the structural-functional approach have caught this fundamental orientation in such a way as to make it more readily applicable to such . . . problems as the one with which we are concerned."[15]

Thus, it is no surprise that Parsons (1966, p. 739) states that the major theoretical reason for asserting that conditions are ripe in America for the full "inclusion" of the Negro is that "the universalistic norms of the society have applied more and more widely. This has been true of all the main bases of particularistic solidarity, ethnicity, religion, regionalism, state's rights, and class. . . . Today, more than ever before, we are witnessing an acceleration in the emancipation of individuals of all categories from these diffuse particularistic solidarities." Whether phrased in terms of the Parsonian pattern variables, the older formulations of Durkheim, Cooley, or Toennies, or Myrdal's American creed, it is clear that this tradition of sociological theory views ethnicity as a survival of primary, quasi-tribal loyalties, which can have only a dysfunctional place in the achievement-oriented, rationalized, and impersonal social relationships of the modern, industrial-bureaucratic order.

That the tenets of this theoretical tradition necessarily imply the inevitable disappearance of "particularistic solidarities," however, has been put to a major theoretical test in the recent work of Van den Berghe (1967). Rather than assuming, with the Myrdal-Parsons school, that race relations per se tend to disappear in gesellschaft-like societies, he asserts that they merely shift their form from "paternalistic" to "competitive." In the latter case, there is declining contact between racial castes, segmentation into ghettoes, and economic competition between racial groups. Although Van den Berghe (1967) asserts that racial cleavages in competitive societies "constitute one of the major sources of strain and disequilibrium in such systems" (p. 30), he makes no judgment as to their ultimate disappearance and states that a possible outcome is the "Herrenvolk democracy . . . in which the excerise of power and suffrage is restricted, *de facto* and often *de jure*, to the dominant group" (p. 29).

Van den Berghe's formulation is one of the few attempts in the literature to link the persistence of racial cleavages in competitive modern societies to the essential structure of such societies, and thus represents a major theoretical departure from the tradition discussed in this section. It is a departure which permits the description of

America as a "socially pluralistic" society along racial lines despite its *cultural* homogeneity (pp. 34–36), which views racial cleavage and conflict as inherent in the nature of competitive society (pp. 30–31) and sees racism[16] as central to, rather than a "hollow shell" within, the Western cultural tradition (pp. 11–18). As such, it provides a perspective for the analysis of racial consciousness and conflict which is lacking in the orthodox Myrdal-Parsons schema.

White Gains and White Resistance

Mounting white resistance, North and South, to the black movement in the sixties forced sociologists to reassess the role of racism in the American social fabric, and, in doing so, they have introduced (or reapplied) concepts which echo Van den Berghe's theoretical analysis. Killian (1968), for example, in *The Impossible Revolution?* writes that "the theme of white supremacy has always been an integral and pervasive feature of the American system" (p. 16)[17] and adds, "it is the challenge to white adjustment in the social order that provides the greatest revolutionary potential" (p. 22). By virtue of his exclusion from a "white man's country" (p. 26), the black, says Killian, is "in the process of becoming an ethnic group" (p. 137), a development which is a radical challenge to the assimilationist ideal in America and which, hence, is fraught with the potential for a revolutionary confrontation.

The notion that specifiable "gains" accrue to whites by virtue of the subordination of blacks was introduced by Dollard (1937) and suggests that white resistance to racial change rests on something more than cultural lag or Myrdalian moral schizophrenia. As such, it is a valuable corrective to the notion that racism is "dysfunctional" or "deviant" within the wider culture. Heer (1959) and Glenn (1963, 1965, 1966) have offered both theoretical and empirical support for this notion, and Glenn writes : "Negro-white antagonism in the United States is and will long remain a matter of realistic conflict. Negroes cannot advance without the loss of traditional white benefits and it is unlikely that most of the whites who benefit . . . will willingly allow Negro advancement. This is not to say that race prejudice and social discrimination are strictly or even largely an expression of economic rationality [1966, p. 178] . . . nor should the many known and possible dysfunctions of discrimination be overlooked. However. . . the tradition of discrimination against Negroes apparently receives continuous reinforcement from the present self-interests of the majority" (1963, pp. 447–48). To the extent, however, that the theory of white gains conceives of white resistance in terms of benefits to individuals, or categories of individuals, it tends to find its place within a social psychological rather than a social structural perspective. Hence, there is not, as yet, a systematic exploration by American sociologists of the possibly latent and positive functions of racism in sustaining the "equilibrium" of the American social system.

Summary

Two perspectives on the features of modern society as they bear on the question of racial assimilation have been presented here. The first, which has occupied the place of a conventional orthodoxy in America sociology since World War II, takes the position that racism is a carry-over from the past which is bound to wither and decay and that, as a consequence, the gradual assimilation of the races can be expected. In the sense that the American creed is viewed as normatively constituent of American society, this perspective suggests a consensus model of racial change and relegates the stresses and strains of the process to a secondary place, as a kind of by-product of inevitable and healthful social trends—the rear-guard response of a dying tradition. The second perspective suggests that racism is integral in American society, that it is central to the culture and interests of the white majority, and that its breakdown will only occur through a protracted process of social conflict and at least some degree of restructuring of the existing institutional arrangements of the society. The gradual emergence of the elements of such a perspective can be noted in the sociological literature in the sixties, although there is little doubt that the first perspective continues to hold sway as a kind of official orthodoxy within the sociological establishment (see, e.g. Parsons 1966, Hauser 1966a, and Pettigrew 1969). An earlier prototype of the second perspective has been present in the Marxian analysis of the race problem.[18]

The affinity of these two perspectives with liberal and radical ideological stances, respectively, on the race problem is apparent (Horton 1966). Our purpose here, however, is neither to claim more abstract-truth value for one or the other (although we believe that the credibility of the first has been seriously put to the test by the racial events of the sixties) nor to condemn both on grounds of their ideological "contamination."[19] Like many sociological theories, these perspectives are schema which serve to point to differing aspects of a complex and probably contradictory reality. What is problematic, we believe, is the overwhelming acceptance, until recently, of the assimilationist perspective among sociologists and the claim that it is supported by social science evidence (Pettigrew 1969) in a way in which the second perspective—which can be referred to as "pluralistic"—is not. In our view, neither the accumulated evidence of social science research nor developments in American race relations in the sixties can support this view. Moreover, the acceptance of the assimilationist perspective has played a large role in shaping the direction of empirical research on race relations[20] and in inhibiting the development of research efforts pertinent to the last decade. Beyond pointing to the ideologically liberal presuppositions which have permeated this perspective, the further specification of factors which can account for its acceptance is a problem in the sociology of knowledge, which is beyond the scope of this paper.

Arguments from the Nature of American Minority Groups

If sociologists who have favored the assimilation-integration perspective have taken a benign view of the capacity and willingness of American society to achieve racial assimilation, they have also supported their position through a common set of assumptions about American minorities in general and blacks in particular. These assumptions can be stated as follows: American minorities (especially blacks) desire assimilation into main stream America. As far as the white ethnic immigrant groups are concerned, there have been no insuperable obstacles in either their socio-cultural characteristics or their ideologies which have prevented their assimilation; in this respect,

345

their most relevant traits have been those which they shared with lower-class groups in American society as a consequence of their having entered the society at the lower rungs of the class hierarchy. They have shared the majority commitment to the American creed, and the rate of their assimilation is directly proportional to their access to the socializing agencies of the dominant culture. The conventional position on the assimilation of white ethnics was well stated by Warner and Srole (1945, p. 295) when they wrote: "The future of American ethnic groups seems to be quite limited; it is likely that they will be quickly absorbed. When this happens, one of the great epochs of American history will be ended, and another, that of race, will begin" (p. 295).

With the exception of the distinctiveness of his castelike position in the South and his unique visibility, the position of the Negro, it has been believed, is similar. In the words of Kristol (1966), "the Negro today is like the immigrant yesterday," and if his special history and status in American society have subjected him to unusually severe barriers to full participation, his absorption can be expected nonetheless. The remainder of this section will discuss some questions which arise concerning this view of black assimilation in the light of the recent reassessment by social scientists of the assimilation process and the nature of black culture in American society.

The Assimilation of White Ethnic Immigrants

If the assimilation of blacks is predicted on the analogy of their position with that of the white ethnic groups, serious problems arise if the assimilation of the latter has been, in fact, much less extensive than has been commonly supposed. Such is the conclusion of recent analyses of ethnicity in American society. As early as fifteen years ago, Glazer (1954, p. 172) noted that a kind of ethnic consciouness, part "nostalgia" and part "ideology," was observable among the descendants of immigrant groups, which consciousness performs, "some functions, and even valuable functions, in American life." Gordon (1964) distinguishes between structural assimilation (participation in the dominant society at the primary group level) and acculturation (acquisition of the culture of the dominant group). He argues that

the latter process has been rapid on the part of minorities in American society, but that the former has and will remain limited for the foreseeable future (except in the "intellectual sub-society"). In the sense that primary social participation for most people remains limited by ethnic boundaries, the United States, argues Gordon, can be described as structurally pluralistic along ethnic, racial, and religious lines. Glazer and Moynihan (1963) note the differential response and resistance of diverse minorities to Americanizing influences and state that the ethnic group is more than a survival of traditional immigrant culture; it is, they claim, a product of the impact of American life on such culture, a "new social form" (p. 16). They go beyond Gordon in emphasizing the ethnic influence in secondary (occupational, political) as well as primary spheres. Greeley (1969, p. 7) doubts that even the acculturation process has been as thorough as Gordon claims and has called for (1964) a reassessment of the ethnic group as a source of identity, interest-group formation, and subcultural differentiation in American society.

In view of the emphasis placed by these writers on ethnicity in contemporary American society, it is surprising, perhaps, that they have not explicitly addressed themselves to a reassessment of the assimilation-integration perspective as it applies to the black American. If the white minorities have legitimately preserved an ethnic identity, should not the blacks propose to do the same? In this connection, the views of these writers are squarely in the assimilationist tradition, Glazer and Moynihan (1963, p. 52), for example, write that "it is not possible for Negroes to view themselves as other ethnic groups viewed themselves . . . because the Negro is only an American, and nothing else. He has no values and culture to guard and protect." In a similar vein, Gordon (1964, p. 114) writes of the black community that "dual social structures are created solely by the dynamics of prejudice and discrimination rather than being reinforced by ideological commitment of the minority itself." Both these studies, in short, are concerned with the survival or transformation of *prior* ethnic identities in America rather than with the generation of *new* ones, or, in Singer's (1962) terms, "ethnogenesis." Moreover, they fail to raise the question of what the meaning and content of racial assimilation can be in a society which remains ethnically plural. In the words of Harold Cruse (1967, p. 9), "Although the three main power groups—Protestants, Catholics, and Jews—neither want nor need to become integrated with each other, the existence of a great body of homogenized, inter-assimilated white Americans is the premise for racial integration. Thus, the Negro integrationist runs afoul of reality in pursuit of an illusion, the 'open society'—a false front that hides several doors to several different worlds of hyphenated Americans."

The Problem of Black Culture

If the American Negro has been considered "100 percent American" by sociologists, the divergence of his culture from the middle-class norm has at the same time been heavily examined and documented. The prevailing sociological view was stated by Myrdal (1944, p. 928): "American Negro culture is not something independent of general American culture. It is a distorted development, or a pathological condition of the general American culture." The view that the race problem is a white man's problem here becomes coupled with the view that the black has been unable to create an authentic subculture in America, owing to his oppression and powerlessness, and, hence, that his condition is to be diagnosed as one of a pervasive social pathology.

It is beyond the scope of this paper to review the reassessment of this perspective which is currently under way in the social sciences, but two observations can be made. First, this reassessment, no doubt stimulated by the efforts of black intellectuals (e.g., Ellison 1966; Cruse 1967) to question the "social pathology" interpretation of black culture, has been mainly evident in the work of the so-called urban anthropologists rather than that of sociologists. Their application of ethnographic techniques to the study of the culture of the black ghetto contrasts with the usual practice of sociologists of compiling statistical indexes of social disorganization. Particularly notable in this respect have been the works of Keil (1966) and Hannerz (1969), as well as the theoretical attack mounted by Valentine (1968) on the theory of the "culture of poverty." Recent

essays by Blauner (1969), and McCarthy and Yancey (1971, pp. 648–72) make an overdue shift of sociological attention in this direction. Ellison's (1966, p. 302) comment that "in Negro culture, there is much of value for America as a whole. What is needed are Negroes to take it and create of it the uncreated consciousness of their race" might well serve as a major leitmotiv of this reassessment on the part of both the scholarly and the black communities.

Second, the sociological emphasis on the pathologies of the black community produced a tendency among sociologists in the sixties to view the major barriers to racial integration as residing in the sociocultural characteristics of the black minority itself rather than in the racism of the dominant society. Whether phrased in the form of demographic characteristics (Hauser 1966b)[21] or the social disorganization which is believed to spring, in part, from these and, in part, from the "heritage" of prejudice and discrimination (rather than from the current institutional functioning of the society itself), these views have harmonized nicely with the benign orthodox analysis of American society outlined earlier. They have led to considerably less optimistic prognoses for the rapid assimilation of the Negro than were characteristic of the fifties (e.g., Broom and Glenn 1965, pp. 187–91) and have led to charges, especially on the part of black activists, that social scientists were simply providing a new apologia for the racial status quo in America. In any case the view that black culture contains positive elements that can form the basis of black ethnic consciousness which can and should be preserved is a challenge of major dimensions to the orthodox sociological image of the black community and black culture in America.

Note on the Caste Hypotheses

Through the work of Dollard (1937), Davis, Gardner, and Gardner (1941), and Warner (1936), the concept of caste became, during the forties, an almost standard tool for the analysis of American race relations. The caste hypothesis acknowledged that the race problem could not be regarded as merely another instance of the minorities problem in the United States, owing to the unique position of the Negro in the overall system of stratification. Moreover, at least in the statement of Warner, the caste hypothesis viewed racial development (especially in the South) as tending toward "parallelism" (Warner 1936, p. 235), or, in Park's terms, a "biracial society." Within the conventional sociological literature, then, there has been available a conceptual framework which was not assimilationist in its premise but which has not been adequate to account for or foresee the racial crisis of the past decade.

Several reasons for the failure of the caste hypothesis in this respect can be noted. First, it described a system of racial accommodation in which the permanent status subordination of the black caste was believed to lie in a system of folkways and mores which both castes accepted as inevitable and unalterable. Hence, it was attacked by both Myrdal (1944) and Cox (1948) for failing to take into account the dynamic forces which were altering the traditional Southern pattern of "race etiquette," for exaggerating the extent of black compliance with this system, and for neglecting the role of force and violence in maintaining it. Second, the thesis of a biracial society was incompatible with the liberal-assimilationist ethos and (if only implicitly) was rejected by those sociologists who shared this ethos and feared the possibility—which Warner, in his 1936 statement, neglected—of the interracial conflict which was latent in a structure of caste parallelism. Finally, the caste concept was applied, even by the Warner school, largely to the South; hence it was compatible with the view of the Northern Negro as the "new immigrant" whose problems, in their essentials, were no different from those of the earlier white immigrants whose assimilation was proceeding apace.

An urgent need in the current analysis of American race relations is a conceptual framework which recognizes, as the caste hypothesis does, the unique status of the black in America but which views this status, as the caste hypothesis does not, as a dynamic force with the potential for transforming the black community and black personality in the direction of becoming a major-change agency in American society. Singer's (1962, p. 423) concept of "ethnogenesis . . . the process whereby a people, that is, an ethnic group, comes into existence" remains the major effort along these lines in American sociology.

Conclusion

Three major conclusions emerge from this survey of the role of the assimilation-integration perspective in the study of American race relations:

1. The belief that racial assimilation constitutes the only democratic solution to the race problem in the United States should be relinquished by sociologists. Beyond committing them to a value premise which compromises their claim to value neutrality, the assimilationist strategy overlooks the functions which ethnic pluralism may perform in a democratic society. Suggestions as to these functions are found in the writings of Gordon (1964, pp. 239–41), Greeley (1964,; 1969, pp. 23–30), and Etzioni (1959, pp. 260–62). The application of this perspective to the racial problem should result in the recognition that the black power and black nationalist movements, to the extent that they aim at the creation of a unified and coherent black community which generates a sense of common peoplehood and interest, are necessarily contrary neither to the experience of other American minorities nor to the interests of black people. The potential for racial divisiveness—and in the extreme case, revolutionary confrontation—which resides in such movements should also be recognized, but the source of this "pathological" potential should be seen as resting primarily within the racism of the wider society rather than in the "extremist" response to it on the part of the victimized minority.

2. To abandon the idea that ethnicity is a dysfunctional survival from a prior stage of social development will make it possible for sociologists to reaffirm that minority-majority relations are in fact group relations (Blumer 1958a) and not merely relations between prejudiced and victimized individuals. As such, they are implicated in the struggle for power and privilege in the society, and the theory of collective behavior and political sociology may be more pertinent to understanding them than the theory of social mobility and assimilation. Although general theories of minority-majority relations incorporating notions of power and conflict can be found in the writings of sociologists (e.g., Schermerhorn 1964; Lieberson 1961), it is only recently, in the work of Killian (1968) and Oppenheimer (1969), that such perspectives have found

their way into sociologists' analyses of the American racial situation.

3. To abandon the notion that assimilation is a self-completing process will make it possible to study the forces (especially at the level of cultural and social structure) which facilitate or hinder assimilation or, conversely, the forces which generate the sense of ethnic and racial identity even within the homogenizing confines of modern society. On the basis of an assessment of such forces, it is certainly within the province of sociological analysis to point to the possibilities of conscious intervention in the social process (by either the majority or the minority group) to achieve given ends and to weigh the costs and consequences of various policy alternatives. These functions of sociological analysis, however, should be informed by an awareness that any form of intervention will take place in a political context—that intervention itself is in fact a political act—and that the likelihood of its success will be conditioned by the configuration of political forces in the society at large. Without this awareness—which is nothing more than an awareness of the total societal context within which a given minority problem has its meaning—sociological analysis runs a very real risk of spinning surrealistic fantasies about a world which is tacitly believed to be the best of all possible worlds. Whether the call of sociologists for racial assimilation in American society as it is currently organized will fall victim to such a judgment remains to be seen.

ENDNOTES

1. I wish to express my appreciation to Mrs. Saundra Hudson for her assistance in providing background material for this article, and to Vassar College for a grant which helped to make its preparation possible. Appreciation is also due Lilo Stern and James Moss for their comments on an earlier draft.

2. Horton (1966) has stated that "the liberal tendency of American sociology . . . is particularly marked in the sociological analysis of the Negro question. . . . The liberal fate of minorities, including Negroes, is basically containment through socialization to dominant values" (pp. 707–8). He goes on to argue that "contemporary liberalism . . . is a variant of conservative order theory" (p. 707).

3. The terms "integration" and "assimilation" are not necessarily synonymous. Integration, especially as it was used in the fifties, can have the limited meaning of "desegregation" (particularly de jure) and, sociologically, need not be followed by assimilation in the usual sense of cultural merger. Most sociologists have seemingly assumed, however, that desegregation would be followed by the gradual movement of blacks into mainstream American culture, and that racial characteristics would gradually lose their significance as determinants of social status and identity, and it is this assumption which is called into question here (see also Gordon 1964, pp. 246–47). The tendency for sociologists to use the two terms interchangeably is apparent in the writings of Hauser (1966a, 1966b).

4. For a different view, see Gregor (1963, p. 431), who writes that "Negro proletarian radicalism has stood, largely mute, beyond the pale of American intellectual life." An effective rationale for the study of such movements has been made by Record (1956).

5. Even in the sixties, after the appearance of solidly organized white resistance in the South (Vander Zenden 1959a, 1959b, 1965) sociologists gave voice to this optimism in uninhibited terms. Rose, for example, wrote (1965, p. 7) "there could be no doubt that the races were moving rapidly toward equality and desegregation by 1964. . . . The change had been so rapid . . . that this author ventures to predict—if current trends continue—the end of all legal segregation and discrimination to a mere shadow in two decades. These changes would not mean that there would be equality between the races within this time . . . but the dynamic social forces creating inequality will, if the present trends continue, be practically eliminated in three decades."

6. The emergence of the black movement in the sixties and the racial crises which followed forced sociologists to acknowledge, ex post facto, the resistance of American society to racial integration. They were quick to apply the retrospective wisdom that social change entails strain and conflict and that racial conflict may have positive functions (Himes 1966). Mounting black pressure was accounted for, again ex post facto, by an application of reference-group theory in the form of the notion of "relative deprivation" (Pettigrew and Back 1967, pp. 694–96). It should be noted that insofar as this theory assumes that the black movement is the product of actual *gains* made by blacks since World War II, it is open to question since the extent of black gains, especially vis-à-vis whites, in this period is not clear. On the negative side, for example, residential segregation increased in American cities between 1930 and 1960 (Hauser 1966b, pp. 76–77), and there was virtually no change in the ratio of nonwhite to white family income between 1947 and 1964 (Fein, 1966, p. 122). Moynihan points out (1966, p. 189) that the acknowledged growth of the black middle class may not be accompanied by improvement

in the condition of the black lower-class majority and, in *The Negro Family: The Case for National Action*, claims that the black family is in a state of decline (Rainwater and Yancey 1967). Wright (1967), citing comparative data from the U.S. Census, disputes the notion of the rapid socio-economic advance of the Negro since World War II. Finally, Wilhelm and Powell (1964) find the roots of the black movement not in Negro advance, but *retrogression:* "With the onset of automation, the Negro is moving out of his historical state of oppression into uselessness. . . . He is being removed from economic participation in white society"; and his nascent nationalism constitutes a "quest for identity" (pp. 3–6). In short, the theory of relative deprivation as an account of black unrest has yet to be adequately tested.

7. Berry (1958, pp. 128–49) provides a useful and critical survey of Park and others' cycle theories. Etzioni (1959) presents a systematic critique of Park's views in the context of his review of Wirth's *The Ghetto* (1928). He points out that there is no a priori reason for regarding assimilation as the inevitable outcome of culture contact, and that Park's theory, because it fails to specify the temporal span of and conditions producing each phase, can accommodate any observation and hence is untestable.

8. For a statement of the theory of the "triple melting pot," which presents the case for the disappearance of the ethnicity of the white immigrant groups within the wider structure of American religious pluralism (itself compromised by the ecumenical movement and a shared commitment to the "American Way of Life" as a quasi-religious ideal), see Herberg (1955, particularly chap. 2).

9. The fact that an earlier generation of American sociologists did not regard the assimilation of the American Negro as anything like an immediate prospect and viewed the emergence of a sense of collective unity as an outcome of the Negro's status in American society is apparent in E. B. Reuter's *The American Race Problem* (1927). In chap. 16, Reuter traces the history of, and analyzes the "growth of race consciousness," and concludes that "the continued growth of a Negro nationlistic spirit in America is perhaps inevitable" (p. 429).

10. It is to the credit of Myrdal that he recognized that this assumption was indeed a "value premise" (p. 929) and not the statement of a "natural force" or an "inevitable social process." This distinction frequently is blurred in the sociological literature, as, for example, when Herberg (1955, p. 23) writes that the "perpetuation of ethnic differences is altogether out of line with the logic of American reality." This "logic" would seem to amount to little more than the power of an entrenched social myth.

11. For a critique of Myrdal's view that the "strain toward consistency" produced by the psychological and moral discomforts of the dilemma is a major motive force in the direction of realization of the American creed, see Medalia (1962).

12. In his emphasis on beliefs and attitudes, Myrdal's analysis had an affinity with the social psychological interpretation of race relations which has been so pronounced in American social science. Blumer (1958*b*) refers to this interpretation as the "prejudice-discrimination axis" and characterizes it as follows: "It rests on a belief that the nature of relations between racial groups results from the feelings and attitudes which these groups have toward each other. . . . It follows that in order to comprehend and solve problems of race relations it is necessary to study and ascertain the nature of prejudice" (p. 420). It is probable that the search for the determinants of prejudice and discrimination in attitudinal sets, personality structure, or role-specific behavior has inhibited the development of a social structural perspective on race relations in American sociology. The work of Lohman and Reitzes (1952, 1954) offered some corrective, but the lead they offered has not been followed.

13. Ralph Ellison (1966, pp. 298–99) writes that *"An American Dilemma . . .* is the blueprint for a more effective exploitation of the South's natural, industrial, and human resources. . . . In the positive sense, it is the key to a more democratic and fruitful usage of the South's natural and human resources; and in the negative, it is the plan for a more efficient and subtle manipulation of black and white relations—especially in the South."

14. Similar statements can be found in Simpson and Yinger (1954, 1958, 1959) and Rose (1965). The hypothesis that urbanization constitutes a major impetus to racial integration and equalization has been challenged on theoretical grounds by Killian and Grigg (1966) and Howard and Brent (1966); Blalock (1959) found little support for it in an analysis of Southern census data and comments that "urbanization in the South has at least in part taken a form which is compatible to that developed in certain colonial territories. . . . It is . . . entirely possible that as the South continues to urbanize, at least in the early stages . . . non-whites may remain in the most unskilled positions. . . . A constant or even an increasing gap may be maintained" (pp. 147–48).

15. Greeley (1964), a proponent of the view that the ethnic group, which he defines as a "semi-gemeinschaft collectivity" (p. 108), remains a significant element in modern social structure, suggests that the gemeinschaft-gesellschaft tradition poses a "danger that sociologists, impressed with the tremendous increase in gesellschaft, would rule out the possibility of the survival of

gemeinschaft, at least beyond the level of the nuclear family" (p. 107).

16. Van den Berghe defines racism as "any set of beliefs that organic, genetically transmitted differences are intrinsically associated with the presence or absence of certain socially relevant abilities or characteristics" (p. 11).

17. Westie (1965, pp. 537–38) also notes that "a wealth of sociological evidence suggests that in many social situations in America, it is not the person who behaves in a prejudiced manner who is deviant, but rather, the non-prejudiced person who refues to discriminate. . . . People with no dilemma in Myrdal's sense seem to experience another type of dilemma; a conflict between their endorsement of democratic action and yet another normative system, which exists in the majority of American local communities; the system which says that one ought to be prejudiced and out to discriminate."

18. For an effective, if neglected, analysis of American race relations in the Marxian tradition, see Cox (1948). As noted above, Marxism failed to supply a corrective to the assimilationist bias of both American social science and American social criticism. In fact, the overall impact of Marxian thought has been to relegate ethnicity to the status of "false consciousness"; national and ethnic sensibility is viewed as an out-growth of the culture of capitalism and as a stratagem of the bourgeoisie for dividing and weakening the working-class movement. For the orthodox Marxist, minorities and minority problems, as such, will disappear with the cessation of class oppression. The strengths of the Marxian interpretation of racism lie in its linking of this pattern to the total structure of the society of which it is a part and its insistence that the race problem has determinants in the economic institutions and the struggle for power and privilege in the society. The viable elements of the Marxian perspective can be retained even as the simplistic account of the race problem as a reflex of the class struggle has been, correctly, rejected.

19. We agree with Horton (1966, p. 713) when he writes that "the error of the sociologist is not that he thinks politically and liberally about his society, but that he is not aware of it."

20. The main trends of this research prior to the 1960s have been thoroughly summarized in the invaluable papers of Drake (1957) and Blumer (1958b).

21. The hypothesis that there is a direct correlation between economic discrimination and Negro population increase has been put to empirical test by Blalock (1956) and Glenn (1963), whose data do not clearly support it.

23

Processes of Hispanic and Black Spatial Assimilation[1]

Douglas S. Massey
Brendan P. Mullan

Recent theory and reseach have overlooked spatial aspects of assimilation and stratification. While sociologists have long recognized a relationship between social and spatial mobility, we go further to stress that spatial assimilation is an essential step in the process of assimilation, with important ancillary effects on stratification. The socioeconomic position of any group cannot be understood apart from its spatial location in society.

Assimilation is the process by which a group comes to resemble, on a variety of dimensions, some larger society of which it is a part. Gordon (1964) has divided this process into seven distinct phases. The first is acculturation. During this phase a group acquires the language and cultural practices of the host society. It is the least problematic step in the assimilation process, and most groups complete it within two generations. The second stage is structural assimilation, the

large-scale entrance of a group into primary relationships with members of the host society. It may occur concurrently with acculturation, subsequent to it, or not at all. According to Gordon, this is the crucial step in the process of assimilation. Once structural assimilation has occurred, all other phases of assimilation (marital, identificational, behavioral receptional, attitudinal receptional, and civic) follow automatically.

However, this scheme does not consider spatial elements in the assimilation process. Assimilation does not occur in a vacuum. Groups and individuals interact in a physical world. We suggest that spatial assimilation is a necessary intermediate step between acculturation and other types of assimilation. Spatial elements strongly affect nearly all stages of assimilation subsequent to acculturation. For example, research has shown residential propinquity to be a primary determinant of such variables as friendship (Whyte 1956), prejudice (Deutsch and Collins 1951; Jahoda and West 1951; Allport 1954; Works 1961), and marriage (Bossard 1932; Kennedy 1943; Koller 1948; Catton and Smircich 1964; Hanson, Marble, and Pitts 1972; Peach 1981), all mentioned by Gordon as elements of assimilation which are contingent on prior acculturation. If a group is not physically integrated within a society, structural assimilation, and consequently the subsequent stages of assimilation, will be

Reprinted from the *American Journal of Sociology* 89:4 (January 1984), pp. 836–873 by permission of the author and the publisher, The University of Chicago Press. Copyright © 1984 by the University of Chicago. All rights reserved.

[1] We would like to thank Stanley Lieberson, Barrie Morgan, and three anonymous reviewers for their helpful comments, and Ruth Deuel for her able programming assistance. This research was supported, in part, by National Science Foundation grant SPI-7914866; the grant is gratefully acknowledged.

exceedingly difficult. Spatial assimilation thus provides a mechanism relating acculturation to other types of assimilation. In order to comprehend the process of assimilation, one must first explicate the nature of spatial assimilation.

By *spatial assimilation*, we mean the process whereby a group attains residential propinquity with members of a host society. In the United States, it has generally involved the movement of minority groups out of established racial or ethnic neighborhoods into a larger urban environment inhabited primarily by "nonethnic" native whites (Cressy 1938; Ford 1950; Kiang 1968). The dynamic force behind this process is social mobility. As Park noted long ago, changes in education, income, and occupational status are usually followed by changes in location (1926, p. 9). Over the years, many studies have documented the association between social and spatial mobility (cf. Lieberson 1963; Nelli 1970; Ward 1971; Thernstrom 1973; Esslinger 1975; Kobrin and Goldscheider 1978). Indeed, this association appears to have grown stronger over time (Burstein 1981).

The reasons for the relationship between socioeconomic advancement and spatial mobility are not hard to understand. Opportunities and resources vary geographically. To take advantage of them, people move. In a profound way, where one lives plays a large role in determining one's life chances. A list of important variables determined by residential location includes the cost and quality of housing, health and sanitary conditions, exposure to crime and violence, quality of services (the most important of which is education), and access to economic opportunity, as well as a host of less tangible factors ranging from the character of one's children's playmates to the kinds of role models they emulate. Thus in urban society, socioeconomic advancement tends to be accompanied by spatial movement aimed at bettering personal or familial circumstances.

In achievement-oriented societies like the United States, this bond between social and physical mobility is created and reinforced through acculturation. According to Brian Berry (1973, p. 50):

As growth has taken place, links between social and spatial mobility have been reinforced by a

peculiarly American social dynamic. . . . The drive for achievement is a variable of key importance within the "mainstream" American culture— a culture in which status and self-respect come from what a person does, in the material world, rather than from his ancestry or his holiness. Social and spatial mobility are built into and interrelated within individuals' nervous systems as a result of the attitudes and pressures of the culture. . . . Earnings must be spent on the best possible homes and material possessions in the best possible neighborhoods. Any increase in job or financial status must be matched by a move to a better neighborhood in which the new and higher-status life style may be pursued.

In other words, a logical outgrowth of acculturation is the progressive spatial integration of an ethnic group within society at large, with the degree and kind of integration being determined by the objective socioeconomic characteristics the group has achieved (see Timms 1971).

This theoretical perspective suggests three specific hypotheses which we will test using data on racial and ethnic groups in selected U.S. cities: (1) The average socioeconomic status of minority members is higher in areas of recent entry composed primarily of majority members than in established ethnic or racial neighborhoods. (2) The average socioeconomic status of minority members varies directly with distance from an established ethnic or racial neighborhood. (3) The probability of contact with majority members is positively related to a minority's average socioeconomic status.

Spatial mobility is not only a key component in the process of assimilation; it also has important feedback effects on social mobility itself and is therefore an important element in social stratification—that is, the process by which socioeconomic inequality is generated. Because social and economic resources vary geographically, patterns of spatial assimilation have a clear impact on the opportunities for socioeconomic advancement. Barriers to spatial mobility are barriers to social mobility. This line of reasoning is particularly relevant to the recent debate on "the declining significance of race" (Wilson 1978). During the 1970s, a variety of scholars made the case that race was becoming less important as a dimension of stratification in U.S. society (Banfield 1970; Featherman and Hauser 1978; Sowell 1981). However, notably lacking in this debate has been serious attention to the effects of persistent racial residential segregation. Given the important impact of residential location on individual life chances, racial segregation, to the extent that it exists, cannot be ignored as a salient dimension of stratification in the United States.

For example, institutionalized discrimination has led to racially segregated housing markets which constrain the ability of black buyers to realize their locational aspirations (see Helper 1969; Pearce 1979). As a result, blacks pay more than whites for housing of comparable quality (Kain and Quigley 1975; Jackman and Jackman 1980; Villemez 1980). Residential segregation thus lowers the discretionary income of blacks compared with whites earning the same annual income. Insofar as it restricts their ability to escape high-crime ghetto areas, segregation also forces blacks to bear a disproportionate share of the economic losses stemming from urban crime (Hindelang 1976; Lee 1981). In addition, blacks are more likely to absorb costs associated with illness and loss of life, since black neighborhoods have higher mortality rates than white ones (Kitagawa and Hauser 1973). Social mobility is further impaired by inferior education within racially segregated inner-city schools, which results directly from residential segregation (Coleman, Kelly, and Moore 1975; Farley 1978). Finally, to the extent that black ghettos house a "culture of poverty" (Lewis 1965; Banfield 1970), the spatial confinement of blacks within them insures that poverty will be passed from generation to generation.

This paper elaborates on these issues by documenting the mechanisms which generate racial segregation in U.S. cities. This goal is accomplished by comparing patterns of black and Hispanic spatial assimilation. Previous studies have shown widespread differences between these groups in the level and pattern of segregation (see Grebler, Moore, and Guzman 1970; Massey 1979a, 1979b, 1981; Lopez 1981). In general, black segregation is far greater than that of Hispanics and is less likely to be affected by such factors as social class, suburbanization, and generation (native vs. foreign birth for Hispanics; northern vs. southern birth for blacks). Thus we anticipate fundamental differences between black and Hispanic spatial assimilation. Assuming that non-Hispanic whites (henceforth called Anglos) are more likely to avoid living near blacks than near Hispanics, these differences can be precisely specified in terms of four hypotheses concerning the relative ability of each group to achieve spatial assimilation in U.S. society: (4) Areas of black settlement display a higher probability of Anglo population loss and subsequent turnover (i.e., residential succession) than areas of Hispanic settlement. (5) Blacks are less able than Hispanics to translate socioeconomic achievements into spatial separation from an established racial/ethnic area. (6) Blacks are less able than Hispanics to convert socioeconomic achievements into residential proximity with Anglos. (7) Consequently, at any time, the probability of black contact with Anglos (i.e., the extent of spatial assimilation) is less than the probability of Hispanic contact with Anglos.

The hypotheses are examined in the ensuing paragraphs using data on blacks and Hispanics in selected U.S. cities.

Data

Any study of residential succession requires comparable areal units at two census dates. Seven SMSAs containing significant Hispanic populations and having similar census tract grids in 1960 and 1970 were selected for analysis: Tuscon, El Paso, Sacramento, Denver, San Diego, San Francisco–Oakland, and Los Angeles. Only in five southwestern states were data on Hispanics available for census tracts at both dates, and only these seven SMSAs simultaneously contained enough Hispanics and grids similar enough to sustain analysis.[2] Unfortunately, these constraints led to a data set more representative of the urban conditions of Hispanics than blacks. Therefore, comparisons between these groups focus on Los Angeles, an SMSA with large concentrations and established communities of both groups.

In order to establish comparabilities between 1960 and 1970 census tracts, the investigators inspected maps and consulted Census Bureau lists relating the two sets of tracts to one another.

[2]In the New York SMSA, Puerto Ricans were enumerated by census tract in both 1960 and 1970, but this urban area is the subject of a separate study.

When tracts were not comparable because of a boundary redefinition, an attempt was made to aggregate several tracts into a larger unit that was the same in both years. In the few cases for which comparability could not be established, tracts were excluded from analysis. A single 1960–70 data file was created by combining published data for 1960 tracts with data taken from the Fourth Count Summary Tapes for 1970.

A major problem in combining 1960 and 1970 data is that the Hispanic population was defined differently at the two dates. In 1960, data published for census tracts defined Hispanics as persons of Spanish surname; in 1970 they were defined as persons of Spanish language *plus* those of Spanish surname but not of Spanish language. Within census tracts this change creates the erroneous impression of a loss in Anglo population and gain in Hispanic population between 1960 and 1970, a shift in ethnic composition due solely to the different definitions. Within areas of Hispanic settlement there is therefore a bias toward the identification of succession tracts. Fortunately, it is conservative with respect to the findings of this paper. A more detailed documentation of this bias and its effects appears in Massey (1983).

These difficulties reflect a broader conceptual problem inherent in any study of ethnic segregation. The ambiguities involved in defining "Hispanics" imply that some persons of Hispanic ancestry might be excluded entirely from the "Hispanic" population. For example, in this study, people who did not have a Spanish surname and did not come from a household where Spanish was spoken would be counted as "Anglos," even if their grandparents were born in Mexico. However, it is virtually impossible for someone of black ancestry to be classifed as white. While ethnicity is an ambiguous concept that provides some individuals with a choice of ethnic affiliations, race is an ascriptive concept over which an individual has little control. It is therefore always possible to argue that ethnic segregation might be greater, and residential succession more prevalent, were a broader definition to be employed. Since this problem does not arise in studying black segregation, apparent differences between blacks and Hispanics can always be questioned as artifacts of the definition chosen.

While this competing hypothesis cannot be eliminated, the widely divergent patterns of black and Hispanic spatial assimilation found in this study render it implausible, even if one makes liberal allowances for discrepancies between the census definition and the true population of Hispanics. Moreover, the 1970 definition of Hispanics used in this paper (that based on language and surname) is the most inclusive available, giving a larger "Hispanic" population than other alternatives (Siegel and Passel 1979). Ultimately, however, the ambiguity of identification is an intrinsic characteristic of ethnicity, one which broadens the parameters of assimilation and sets Hispanics distinctly apart from blacks in their dealings with U.S. society, a fact which is clearly reflected in our results.

Methods of Analysis

In earlier work (Massey 1983), the analytic scheme of Taeuber and Taeuber (1965) was used to analyze the dynamics of Hispanic and black segregation. Their procedure classifies census tracts according to the type of interethnic change over a decade shown by shifts in the number and percentage of different groups in each tract. When applied over all census tracts in an urban area, it measures the prevalence of succession and classifies tracts according to their stage in the succession process. However, some classifications made using this method proved ambiguous in Hispanic areas, since they were often made on the basis of intercensal changes in the percentage Hispanic, changes that were highly suspect given the shift in definitions (Massey 1983). Therefore, a simpler classification scheme based only on absolute changes was developed. This scheme is presented in table 1.

In using this scheme to classify tracts, we took care not to confound processes of black and Hispanic succession. Tracts containing 250 or more Hispanics and fewer than 250 blacks were considered separately from those containing 250 or more blacks and fewer than 250 Hispanics. The former are referred to as "Hispanic tracts" while the latter are called "black tracts." Census tracts containing 250 or more of both groups—called "mixed tracts"—were not classified.

This scheme was applied in a sequential and hierarchical manner to classify tracts according to type of interethnic or interracial change between

TABLE 1. *Classification Scheme Used to Measure the Incidence of Residential Succession within Areas of Hispanic and Black Settlement*

Tract Classification	
A. Hispanic tracts:	In 1970, fewer than 250 blacks and more than 250 Hispanics
1. Established	Hispanics exceed 60% of population in both 1960 and 1970
2. Invasion	Hispanics fewer than 250 in 1960; more than 250 in 1970
3. Succession:	Hispanic population growing; Anglo population falling
3.1. Early	Percentage Hispanic less than 20%
3.2. Middle	Percentage Hispanic more than 20% and less than 40%
3.3. Late	Percentage Hispanic more than 40%
4. Growth	Hispanic population growing; Anglo population growing
5. Displacement	Hispanic population falling; Anglo population growing
6. Decline	Hispanic population falling; Anglo population falling
B. Black tracts:	In 1970, fewer than 250 Hispanics and more than 250 blacks
1. Established	Blacks exceed 60% of population in both 1960 and 1970
2. Invasion	Blacks fewer than 250 in 1960; more than 250 in 1970
3. Succession:	Black population growing; Anglo population falling
3.1. Early	Percentage black less than 20%
3.2. Middle	Percentage black more than 20% and less than 40%
3.3. Late	Percentage black more than 40%
4. Growth	Black population growing; Anglo population growing
5. Displacement	Black population falling; Anglo population growing
6. Decline	Black population falling; Anglo population falling

1960 and 1970. First, tracts were defined as either Hispanic, black, mixed, or non-Hispanic/black. The former two sets were then classified as either established or invasion areas. Tracts that were 60% minority at both dates were considered to be established areas. Those that contained fewer than 250 minority members in 1960 but more than that number in 1970 were called invasion areas. If not classifiable as invasion or established areas, tracts were entered into one of four remaining categories. Succession tracts gained minority members but lost Anglos over the decade. Growth tracts experienced a gain in both groups, while declining tracts showed a loss in both groups. Finally, displacement tracts gained Anglos but lost minority members. The definitional problems mentioned earlier obviously bias Hispanic tracts toward the identification of invasion and succession areas.

Prevalence of Hispanic and Black Succession

The scheme of table 1 was applied to classify census tracts in the data set in order to shed light on our fourth hypothesis, that black areas have a greater chance of Anglo loss and turnover than

Hispanic areas. Table 2 presents tracts in each of the seven SMSAs grouped by type of residential change observed between 1960 and 1970.

This table reveals important contrasts between patterns of black and Hispanic segregation. First, blacks are confined to a much smaller share of each SMSA's residential areas than are Hispanics. While 77% of all tracts contained at least 250 Hispanics, the comparable figure for blacks was only 27%. The contrast was especially marked in Los Angeles, where 78% of all tracts contained Hispanics but only 23% contained blacks. Second, Hispanics were considerably less likely than blacks to be living in an established area. Only in El Paso did such tracts constitute an important share of Hispanic tracts. Overall, only 4% of Hispanic tracts were established areas, compared with 49% of black tracts. Again the contrast was particularly noteworthy in Los Angeles, which contains the well-known barrio of East Los Angeles as well as the Watts ghetto. While 61% of black tracts in this city were established racial areas, only 4% of Hispanic tracts could be classified as established ethnic areas. A barrio-centered residential pattern simply does not typify the experience of

TABLE 2. *Classification of Census Tracts by Type of Residential Change in Seven Southwestern SMSAs: 1960–70 (%)*

	Hispanic Tracts								Black Tracts		
	Tucson	El Paso	Sacramento	Denver	San Diego	San Francisco-Oakland	Los Angeles	Total	San Francisco-Oakland	Los Angeles	Total
Established tract	13.5	40.0	.0	.0	.0	.0	4.3	3.8	26.7	61.1	48.8
Succession tract:	27.0	45.7	27.4	29.7	10.8	28.0	27.8	26.4	18.4	24.0	22.0
Late	13.5	42.8	3.2	11.7	.6	1.8	11.0	8.9	11.7	23.1	19.0
Middle	2.7	2.9	12.9	10.6	5.1	10.1	10.5	9.5	.0	.9	.6
Early	10.8	.0	11.3	7.4	5.1	16.1	6.3	8.0	6.7	.0	2.4
Invasion:	37.8	2.8	50.0	58.5	73.4	54.4	53.7	54.5	15.0	10.2	11.9
Anglo gain	16.2	2.8	37.1	29.8	46.8	30.4	26.2	29.2	3.3	.0	1.2
Anglo loss	21.6	.0	12.9	28.7	26.6	24.0	27.5	25.3	11.7	10.2	10.7
Other tracts:	21.6	11.5	22.6	11.7	15.8	17.6	14.2	15.2	13.3	4.6	7.8
Growth	21.6	8.6	14.5	8.5	13.3	17.1	13.1	13.6	.0	.9	.6
Displacement	.0	.0	.0	1.1	.0	.0	.3	.2	8.3	.9	3.6
Decline	.0	2.9	8.1	2.1	2.5	.5	.8	1.4	5.0	2.8	3.6
Total black or Hispanic tracts (N)	37	35	62	94	158	217	743	1,346	44	108	152
Mixed Hispanic-black tracts (N)	11	11	26	14	26	125	165	378	125	156	290
Total tracts with Hispanics or blacks (N)	48	46	88	108	184	342	908	1,724	169	273	442
Percentage of all tracts in SMSA	96.0	100.0	81.5	69.7	82.9	70.0	77.5	76.9	34.6	23.3	26.6

357

Hispanics in the same way that a ghetto-centered pattern typifies that of blacks.

Table 2 also reveals differences in the dynamics of black and Hispanic segregation. Although Hispanic tracts are somewhat more likely than black tracks to be undergoing residential succession, they are more evenly distributed between stages and are more likely than black areas to be in the earliest stages of succession. Only 11% of black succession tracts are classified as being within the early stage, compared with 30% of Hispanic succession tracts. This pattern is consistent with Massey's (1983) results which showed that when succession occurs in Hispanic areas, it happens at a much slower pace than in black areas. Given the dearth of established Hispanic areas and the slower pace of neighborhood transition, it seems reasonable to conclude that Hispanic succession, when it occurs, stabilizes at a much lower minority proportion than does black succession. Finally, given the direction of prevailing biases, the prevalence of Hispanic residential succession is probably overstated by the data in table 2. If anything, the contrast between patterns of black and Hispanic succession is greater than our figures indicate.

Perhaps the greatest contrast between the two minority groups lies in the relative importance of invasion areas. Among Hispanic tracts, invasion is the model category in all SMSAs save El Paso. In five of the seven, the percentage of invasion areas is 50% or more; and across all seven the figure is 55%. In contrast, only 12% of black tracts were classified as invasion areas. The relative frequency of invasion tracts in Los Angeles was 54% for Hispanics and 10% for blacks. Inspection of tract maps for that SMSA revealed that black invasion areas were invariably located on the periphery of established black areas, while Hispanic invasion areas could be found throughout the city. Black penetration of Anglo areas is apparently limited to a minority of tracts adjacent to existing black areas, thereby accounting for their relative paucity.

Table 2 also shows that invasion by Hispanics is far less likely to be followed by Anglo population loss than is invasion by blacks. In Los Angeles, for example, a tract had about a 50–50 chance of gaining Anglos following invasion by Hispanics. Given the fact that the definitional

change biases the data toward finding an Anglo loss, this figure must be regarded as conservative. After invasion by blacks, no tracts in Los Angeles showed an Anglo increase over the decade. Thus, while succession may be initiated when an Anglo area is penetrated by Hispanics, it is clearly not inevitable or even likely.

These results verify our fourth hypothesis. Black areas display a much higher probability of Anglo loss and subsequent turnover than do areas of Hispanic settlement. Indeed, when the proportion of invasion tracts which experienced an Anglo gain is added to the proportions of growth and displacement tracts, we obtain the total share of tracts which showed an Anglo increase. Across all SMSAs, this figure is 43% for Hispanic tracts, but only 8% for black tracts. The presence of Hispanics does not seem to render a residential area unattractive to Anglo settlement in the same way as the presence of blacks does.

Socioeconomic Correlates of Succession

The ecological perspective that spatial assimilation should accompany social mobility led to our first hypothesis that the average socioeconomic status of minority members should be higher in areas composed primarily of Anglos than in established ethnic or racial neighborhoods. This broad proposition in turn leads to two specific hypotheses regarding the socioeconomic concomitants of succession. First, leaders in the process of spatial assimilation should be later-generation Hispanics of high SES (Park 1926; Duncan and Lieberson 1959; Taeuber and Taeuber 1965). Thus we hypothesize that within invasion areas, Hispanics will be of high SES and predominantly native stock, but that these indicators will decline progressively through the various stages of succession to an established Hispanic area. Second, from previous research on residential succession, we expect Hispanics within invasion tracts to resemble socioeconomically the Anglos that live there (Duncan and Duncan 1957; Taeuber and Taeuber 1965). As residential succession proceeds we also expect dissimilarity between Anglos and Hispanics to increase, as lower-status Hispanics move into the formerly high-status neighborhood.

The four panels of figure 1 confirm these hypotheses by plotting socioeconomic indicators

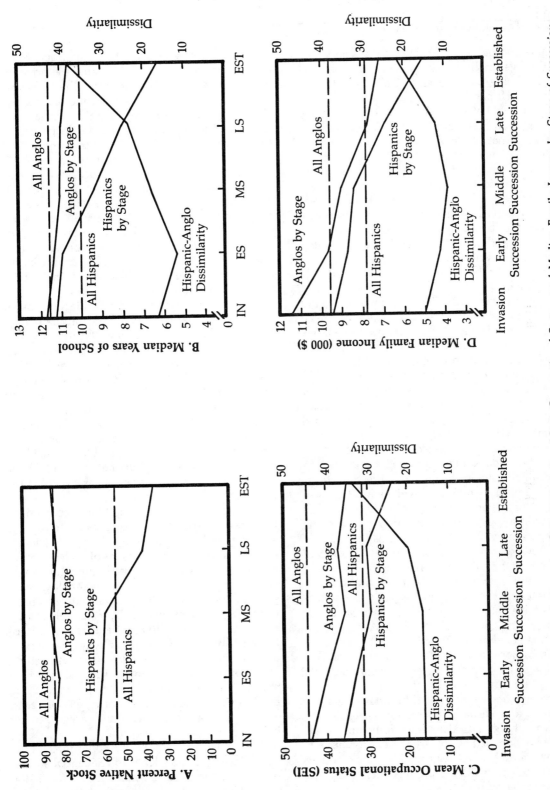

FIGURE 1. Percentage Native Stock, Median Education, Mean Occupational Status, and Median Family Income by Stage of Succession: Five Southwestern SMSAs, 1970.

by stage of succession, using data aggregated for the five smallest SMSAs in the data set (the omissions are San Francisco-Oakland and Los Angeles). Hispanics in invasion tracts are more likely to be of native stock (native born of native parents) than Hispanics in general; and the percentage of native stock declines with each succeeding stage in the succession process. Moreover, in terms of education, income, and occupational status, Hispanics in invasion tracts are well above the average for Hispanics as a whole. Indeed, their education and income place them just under the average for Anglos. All three indicators of SES show nearly monotonic declines across stages of succession. Within established areas, Hispanic SES is considerably below the level for Hispanics as a whole.

As hypothesized, Hispanics and Anglos are of similar socioeconomic status in invasion areas. We measured degree of similarity using the index of dissimilarity, which ranges from a minimum of zero (for identical sooioeconomic distributions) to a maximum of 100 (where there is no overlap between distributions). It gives the proportion of people who would have to change their socioeconomic status to achieve equality. Hispanic-Anglo dissimilarity is in the neighborhood of 15 within invasion tracts. It tends to decline slightly in the early and middle succession stages and then to rise dramatically during the late succession stage. The figures also show that while education and occupational status of Anglos in invasion areas are about average for that group, Anglo income is considerably above average. This fact implies that upwardly mobile Hispanics tend to locate within economically exclusive Anglo areas.

Figure 2 compares selected socioeconomic correlates of succession in Hispanic and black tracts using data combined for the San Francisco-Oakland and Los Angeles SMSAs. Average education is not shown since Hispanics display considerably more variation in schooling than blacks, a fact which exaggerates stage-of-succession effects among the former relative to the latter. (Taken separately, however, the educational correlates of black and Hispanic succession replicate the patterns of fig. 1.) Also, since only one black tract was classified as an early succession area in the two SMSAs, and it proved to be an outlier on all indicators, this tract has been excluded from the figures for blacks.

Patterns observed for Hispanic tracts replicate those in other SMSAs, and patterns for blacks are generally similar, but with some interesting differences. First, socioeconomic dissimilarity between blacks and Anglos displays no clear trend as succession progresses. Inspection of the socioeconomic distributions (not shown) reveals that growing socioeconomic dissimilarity in the later stages of Hispanic succession occurs because high-status Anglos tend to remain in succession areas as they fill up with low-status Hispanics. For blacks, dissimilarity does not increase because Anglo losses are taken disproportionately from high-status groups. Consequently, as black succession proceeds, the socioeconomic distributions of blacks and Anglos tend to shift downward together.

A second difference is that black invasion areas are not characterized by the unusually high levels of Anglo income that typify Hispanic invasion tracts. Lower income levels in black invasion tracts probably result from the fact that they are located on the periphery of established black areas. They are thus universally inner-city areas, unlike Hispanic invasion tracts which are found also in suburban neighborhoods. The fact that black settlers are restricted to residential areas in and around existing black neighborhoods means that they do not generally have access to economically exclusive areas within the larger urban environment.

Thus both Hispanics and blacks conform to hypotheses derived from ecological notions of spatial assimilation. In both cases, leaders in the assimilation process are persons of high socioeconomic status who enter predominantly Anglo areas containing residents of a similar class background. Both groups attempt to assimilate spatially in roughly the same way and presumably for the same reasons. The difference is that invasion of an area by blacks almost always renders it unattractive to further Anglo settlement, setting off a process of residential succession which results in the rapid transition to an established black area. However, in at least 50% of cases, entry of Hispanics into an Anglo area does not initiate residential succession.

In order to specify the conditions under which Hispanic entry leads to residential succession, we performed a discriminant function analysis of Hispanic invasion tracts within the Los

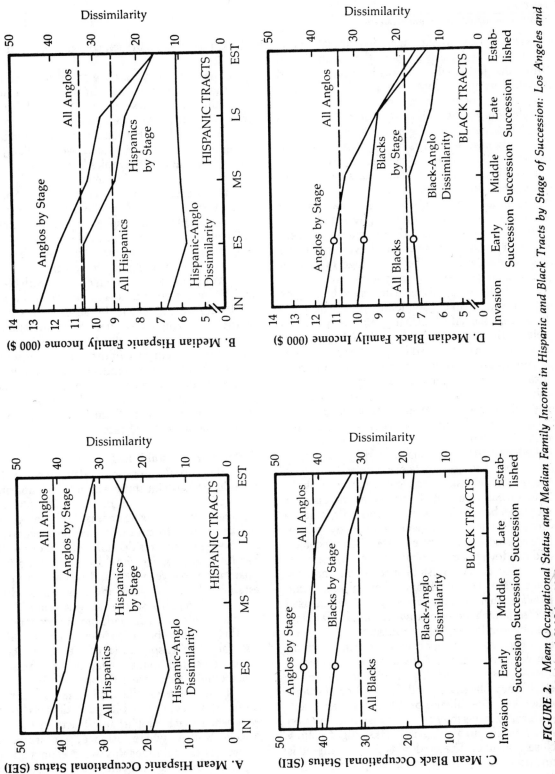

FIGURE 2. *Mean Occupational Status and Median Family Income in Hispanic and Black Tracts by Stage of Succession: Los Angeles and San Francisco–Oakland SMSAs, 1970.*

Angeles SMSA, attempting to discriminate socio-economically between tracts that gained and those that lost Anglo residents between 1960 and 1970. Los Angeles contained 399 Hispanic invasion tracts, of which 195 gained and 204 lost Anglos during the 1960s. Because of the change in the definition of Hispanics, some tracts are probably misclassified as having lost Anglos. To the extent that differences between the two sets of tracts exist, such a bias will attenuate the discriminating power of the function.

Our leading hypotheses in this analysis stem from the ecological notion that physical distance between groups should reflect prevailing perceptions of social distance. The lower the social status and the larger the percentage of foreign stock among incoming Hispanics, the greater should be the social distance perceived by Anglos and the more likely avoidance on their part. However, the effect of Hispanic entry into a neighborhood should be conditioned by its distance from an established Hispanic or black area. If Anglos seek to minimize contact with minorities, the threat of unmanageable residential turnover is greater, or at least more salient, the closer the neighborhood is to an established black or Hispanic neighborhood. Thus Anglo avoidance of an invasion area should vary inversely with distance to established black or Hispanic areas.

When invasion tracts are divided into those that gained and those that lost Anglos during the 1960s, mean values of SES variables and distance measures behave in expected ways. Hispanics in areas which lost Anglos were more likely to be of foreign stock, had lower educations and incomes, and had lower occupational statuses. These areas were also closer to established black and Hispanic areas. The significant canonical correlation indicates that these variables can indeed be used to discriminate between invasion areas that were gaining and losing Anglo residents.

The two most important factors in determining whether a Hispanic invasion area gained or lost Anglos were the distance of a tract from an established black area and the level of Hispanic education. The salience of the first variable suggests that Anglos may perceive Hispanic invasion to be more threatening if blacks might follow closely behind. The credibility of this threat is underscored by the very large proportion of

black tracts which, in fact, contain Hispanics (see table 2).

These results verify the social distance perspective of human ecology. In addition to stating that Anglo loss is less likely to follow Hispanic than black invasion, we can specify the conditions under which Hispanic succession tends to be initiated. Residential succession is likely to follow the entry of Hispanics into an Anglo area when the incoming Hispanics are poorly educated and foreign, with low occupational statuses and incomes, and when the tract is near an established black or Hispanic area. In contrast, residential succession follows black entry into an Anglo area no matter what the objective social characteristics of the incoming blacks.

With rising socioeconomic status, both blacks and Hispanics attempt spatial assimilation. Hispanics are more successful because, as their social status rises, Anglos evaluate them in terms of achieved more than ascribed status, as is consistent with the theory we outlined in our introductory section. However, blacks fail in their attempt to assimilate spatially; no matter what their achieved social characteristics, Anglos avoid residential proximity with them because of the ascribed characteristic of race.

Distance from Established Areas

According to the reasoning developed in the introduction, social status should vary not only by stage of succession but also by physical distance from established areas. If Hispanics and blacks attempt to translate their socioeconomic achievements into residential mobility out of the barrio or ghetto, we should observe a positive relationship between SES and distance from an established area, as stated in hypothesis 2. However, the foregoing section suggests that blacks should have a more difficult time in accomplishing this mobility than Hispanics. They should be less able than Hispanics to convert their status attainments into spatial separation from established ethnic/racial areas (hypothesis 5).

Figure 3 plots estimated relationships between status attainment variables and distance from established black or Hispanic tracts in the Los Angeles SMSA, where distance is measured as before. These relationships were estimated by regressing distance on average characteristics of

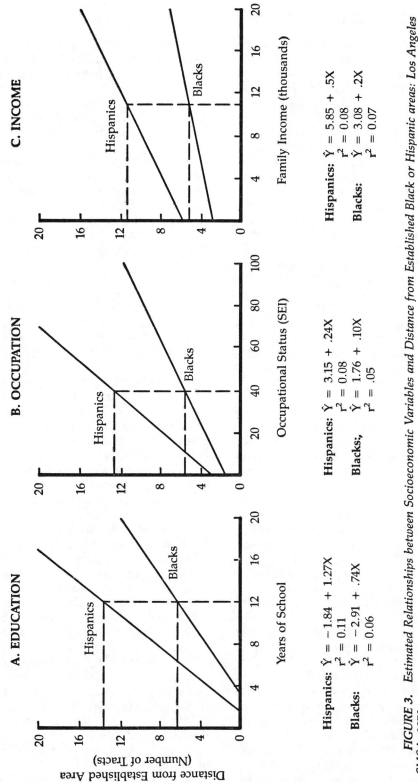

A. EDUCATION

Years of School

Hispanics: $\hat{Y} = -1.84 + 1.27X$
$r^2 = 0.11$
Blacks: $\hat{Y} = -2.91 + .74X$
$r^2 = 0.06$

B. OCCUPATION

Occupational Status (SEI)

Hispanics: $\hat{Y} = 3.15 + .24X$
$r^2 = 0.08$
Blacks:, $\hat{Y} = 1.76 + .10X$
$r^2 = .05$

C. INCOME

Family Income (thousands)

Hispanics: $\hat{Y} = 5.85 + .5X$
$r^2 = 0.08$
Blacks: $\hat{Y} = 3.08 + .2X$
$r^2 = 0.07$

Distance from Established Area (Number of Tracts)

FIGURE 3. Estimated Relationships between Socioeconomic Variables and Distance from Established Black or Hispanic areas: Los Angeles SMSA, 1970.

Patterns of Assimilation in American Life

Hispanic and black populations within census tracts. For blacks, the regression is across all tracts which contain black residents (including "mixed" tracts). Similarly, for Hispanics the regression is across all tracts containing Hispanic residents (again including "mixed" tracts).

The panels of figure 3 confirm our two hypotheses. For both groups social status is positively related to distance from an established area, but the lesser ability of blacks to achieve spatial separation from established areas is at once evident. For example, figure 3A shows that the expected location of a hypothetical population of black high school graduates is about six tracts from an established black area, while the expected location of an equivalent Hispanic population is 13 tracts from an established Hispanic area. Similarly, figure 3B indicates that blacks with an occupational status of 40 (roughly that of a skilled blue-collar worker) would be able to live only five tracts away from the ghetto, but Hispanics of the same occupational status would be 13 tracts away from the barrio. Finally, whereas an average income of $11,000 would let a group of blacks settle about five tracts from the ghetto, it would let a group of Hispanics settle 11 tracts from the barrio. In short, because the Anglo response to Hispanic invasion is not universally one of avoidance and flight, Hispanics are much better able than blacks to translate social into residential mobility.

Probabilities of Intergroup Contact

If spatial assimilation follows from social mobility, we should find a positive relationship between socioeconomic status and spatial assimilation (hypotheses 3). Moreover, if Anglos avoid residential proximity with blacks more than with Hispanics, blacks should be less able to convert status attainments into spatial assimilation (hypothesis 6). In this context, spatial assimilation is defined operationally as the proportion of Anglos within any Hispanic or black tract. This quantity is the second term on the righthand side of equation (1), which is weighted across tracts to compute the city-wide probability of intergroup contact. By regressing it, across tracts, on overall characteristics of Hispanics or blacks in the same tracts, we estimate the effects of socioeconomic variables on spatial assimilation with Anglos. Because the dependent variable has a limited

range, we employ the logit transformation (Hanushek and Jackson 1977, p. 200). Also, to avoid confounding the effects of blacks and Hispanics being in the same tract, we exclude mixed areas and estimate regressions separately over black and Hispanic tracts. The results of this analysis are presented in figure 4 for the Los Angeles SMSA.

The three panels of figure 4 confirm our hypotheses. First, blacks are clearly less able to convert achievements into assimilation. While a group of black high school graduates could expect to reside in a tract that was 27% Anglo, a similarly educated Hispanic population could expect to live in a tract that was 91% Anglo. Results for occupational status and income are similar. With an occupational status of 40 (skilled blue collar), the probability of Anglo contact is 35% for blacks but 87% for Hispanics; and at a family income of $11,000 (about the median for Los Angeles in 1970), the likelihood of black-Anglo interaction was 18% compared with an 81% chance of Hispanic-Anglo interaction. In short, middle- and working-class Hispanics could expect to reside in a tract that was predominantly Anglo, but middle- and working-class blacks could not. At all but very high levels of socioeconomic status, blacks reside in predominantly black areas.

These figures also support our third hypothesis, that socioeconomic status is related positively to degree of spatial assimilation. No matter which measure of SES is chosen, the probability of contact with Anglos rises for both blacks and Hispanics with rising SES. Interestingly, the estimated slope coefficients for blacks actually exceed those for Hispanics. The rate at which status attainments are converted into contact with Anglos is actually greater for blacks than for Hispanics. What differs, by a considerable margin, is the intercept. It simply costs blacks a great deal more capital—human and financial—before they are able to achieve any significant contact with Anglos. The social status required of blacks before they are not threatening to Anglos appears to be significantly higher than that required of Hispanics. In other words, a black lawyer or doctor may be able to move into a mixed neighborhood with other professionals, but a black plumber or bricklayer cannot buy into a working-class Anglo neighborhood. What is required for

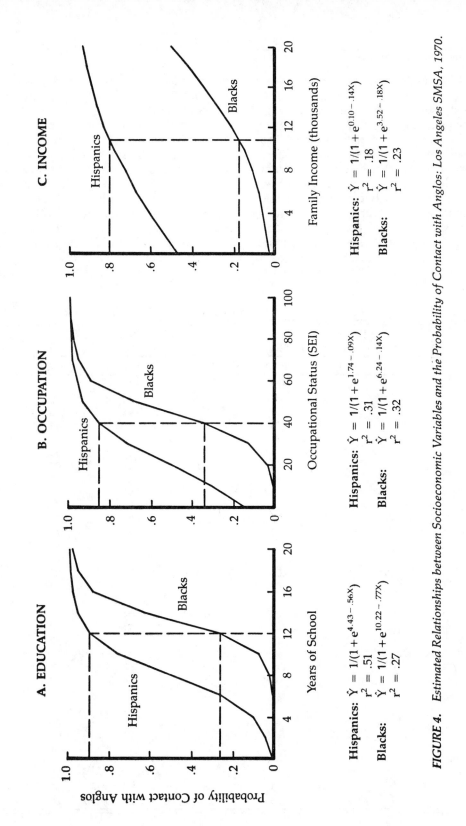

FIGURE 4. *Estimated Relationships between Socioeconomic Variables and the Probability of Contact with Anglos: Los Angeles SMSA, 1970.*

black spatial assimilation is a quantum leap in social status.

The end result of such differential processes of assimilation is that, within any city at any time, blacks are more spatially isolated from Anglos than are Hispanics (hypothesis 7). To measure spatial isolation we used the P^* index described earlier. It gives the probability of residential contact between two groups and is an asymmetric measure of segregation, depending not only on the residential strategies of blacks, Hispanics, and Anglos but also on their proportions of the total population. Thus the probability of Anglos interacting with blacks may be very different from the probability of blacks interacting with Anglos, especially if one group is much larger than the other (Lieberson 1980).

Probabilities of intergroup contact calculated using formula (1) are presented in table 3 for the years 1960 and 1970. In general, there was little change in these probabilities over the decade. Anglos were always extremely likely to be living in residential areas with other Anglos. In 1970 the average Anglo in the seven SMSAs lived in a tract that was 81% Anglo, compared with a figure of 87% in 1960. However, the probability of Anglo contact with blacks was very low—2% in 1960 and 3% in 1970. Anglos also displayed a

TABLE 3. *Probabilities of Intergroup Contact in Seven Southwestern SMSAs: 1960 and 1970*

	Probability of Anglo Interaction with:		Probability of Black Interaction with:		Probability of Hispanic Interaction with:	
	1960	1970	1960	1970	1960	1970
Tucson:						
Anglos	.87	.82	.42	.50	.47	.47
Blacks	.02	.02	.24	.18	.06	.04
Hispanics	.10	.15	.31	.30	.44	.46
El Paso:						
Anglos	.70	.58	.42	.44	.32	.27
Blacks	.02	.03	.11	.08	.03	.02
Hispanics	.27	.38	.46	.47	.46	.47
Sacramento:						
Anglos	.89	.84	.60	.55	.78	.73
Blacks	.02	.03	.23	.27	.05	.06
Hispanics	.06	.09	.09	.12	.11	.16
Denver:						
Anglos	.93	.88	.28	.29	.67	.66
Blacks	.01	.02	.54	.56	.08	.05
Hispanics	.05	.09	.15	.13	.23	.27
San Diego:						
Anglos	.92	.84	.46	.32	.73	.71
Blacks	.02	.02	.47	.45	.10	.06
Hispanics	.05	.12	.15	.19	.15	.19
San Francisco–Oakland:						
Anglos	.87	.79	.38	.32	.75	.66
Blacks	.04	.05	.50	.54	.09	.09
Hispanics	.06	.11	.06	.09	.12	.19
Los Angeles:						
Anglos	.89	.81	.21	.16	.58	.52
Blacks	.02	.03	.65	.71	.08	.06
Hispanics	.07	.14	.09	.09	.31	.38
Average:						
Anglos	.87	.81	.40	.37	.61	.57
Blacks	.02	.03	.39	.40	.07	.05
Hispanics	.09	.15	.19	.20	.26	.30

fairly low probability of residential contact with Hispanics, but the average was nonetheless several times the probability of contact with blacks. Probabilities of black contact with Anglos illustrate the asymmetries alluded to before. The 1970 probability of black contact with Anglos was 37%, many times its Anglo-black complement. The average black had roughly a 40% chance of living near another black, and a 20% chance of living near a Hispanic. Consistent with our hypotheses, Hispanics were considerably less isolated from Anglos than were blacks. Indeed, the average Hispanic in 1970 was actually more liekly to live near an Anglo than near another Hispanic. The probability of Hispanic contact with Anglos was 57%, compared with a 30% chance of interaction with other Hispanics. Like Anglos, Hispanics were unlikely to live near blacks. The probability was only 5% in 1970.

The contrast between blacks and Hispanics is attenuated when figures are averaged over all seven SMSAs. Many SMSAs have very small black populations so that the probability of black-black interaction is low and black-Anglo interaction high because of composition effects alone. In Los Angeles, however, both groups constitute sizable minorities, and here blacks' spatial isolation from Anglos is pronounced. The average black in Los Angeles has a 71% chance of living near another black but only a 16% chance of living near an Anglo. In contrast, the average Hispanic is still more likely to live near Anglos than near other Hispanics. The likelihood of Hispanic-Anglo contact was 52%, compared with a probability of Hispanic-Hispanic contact of only 38%. Thus Hispanics are over three times as likely as blacks to live near Anglos.

Discussion and Conclusion

Results for Hispanics have consistently supported the ecological theory of assimilation put forth in the introduction to this paper. Spatial assimilation occurs as Hispanics of high socioeconomic status enter predominantly Anglo areas located throughout the urban environment. Hispanic SES is positively related to distance from an established area and to probability of contact with Anglos. Our estimated structural model of Hispanic assimilation implies that increases in education, occupational status, and income will lead to geographic mobility which promotes spatial assimilation with Anglos. Increases in these variables also increase spatial assimilation directly by lessening the social distance from Anglos and thus lowering Anglo resistance to Spanish settlement.

But the spatial assimilation of Hispanics does have problematic aspects. Entry of Hispanics into an Anglo area is followed by Anglo population loss in about half of all cases. Whether an invasion area gains or loses Anglos is determined by the social status of the entering Hispanics and the distance of the area from established black and Hispanic neighborhoods. However, once begun, residential sucession proceeds slowly and stabilizes at a relatively low proportion Hispanic. Established Hispanic areas are therefore relatively uncommon.

In contrast, blacks face strong barriers to spatial assimilation which cause them to be spatially isolated from both Anglos and Hispanics, in spite of the fact that blacks themselves conform to predictions from the ecological theory of assimilation. Blacks within invasion areas possess relatively high levels of education, income, and occupational status compared with those in other neighborhoods; and black SES is positively related to distance from an established black area and to probability of contact with Anglos. Indeed, the slopes governing these relationships are even stronger than for Hispanics.

It is not blacks that contradict our theory of spatial assimilation, but Anglos. Increasing black social status apparently does not reduce the social distance that Anglos perceive between themselves and blacks. Areas of potential black settlement are restricted to tracts adjacent to existing black neighborhoods, and entry of blacks into these areas is almost always followed by residential succession, no matter what the objective socioeconomic characteristics of the entering blacks. In a sense, the ghetto follows upwardly mobile blacks as they attempt to assimilate spatially. As a result, they are less able than Hispanics to put distance between themselves and established areas, and they are less able to convert status attainments into spatial assimilation with Anglos. Thus our simultaneous equations model of black spatial assimilation shows that blacks face relatively stronger impediments to integration with Anglos at every stage in the process. The direct effects of social status variables on assimilation are fewer and generally weaker than for Hispanics. Blacks also convert status attainments into Anglo contact with less efficiency than Hispanics. Moreover, in estimated equations relating SES variables to distance from established areas and probability of Anglo contact, the intercepts are generally lower for blacks than for Hispanics, indicating the handicap with which blacks begin the process of spatial assimilation. The outcome of such measurable differences in spatial processes of assimilation is a high degree of black-Anglo segregation within cities at any time, in contrast to the more moderate degree of segregation between Hispanics and Anglos.

Both the Hispanic and black models of spatial assimilation suggest that Hispanics parallel the behavior of Anglos in avoiding residential contact with blacks. In the Hispanic model, direct as well as indirect effects of Hispanic socioeconomic status are quite strongly negative with respect to the probability of Hispanic-black contacts. In the black model, black social status variables have no direct effect on the likelihood of contact with Hispanics, and the indirect effects are negative. The reason the level of segregation between Hispanics and blacks is lower than that between Anglos and blacks is probably that Hispanics have fewer socioeconomic resources than Anglos with which to realize their locational aspirations.

Our results stress the need to incorporate spatial elements into theories of assimilation. We have argued that spatial assimilation is a necessary precursor to other forms of assimilation, with strong effects on patterns of friendship, marriage, and prejudice among different groups. If this view is valid, the discrepant patterns of black and Hispanic spatial assimilation portend very different futures for these groups. After more than 200 years in the United States, blacks remain socially and spatially isolated within U.S. society. In contrast, Hispanic assimilation is very much an ongoing process. Our results contradict the view that these groups are similarly disadvantaged minorities trapped in declining urban areas from which escape is unlikely, a view recently put forth by the President's Commission for a National Agenda for the Eighties (1980, p. 17): "Although the assimilation process had enabled earlier immigrants or their offspring to use the city as a launching pad, a growing proportion of poor blacks and Hispanics had been left behind, and sizeable proportions have become part of a nearly permanent urban underclass." If there is an underclass in the United States, Hispanics cannot be considered "permanent" members of it in the same way as blacks. Our results point consistently to an ongoing process of assimilation among Hispanics circa 1970. Unlike blacks, they are able to translate social mobility into residential mobility. Hispanics are simply not trapped in the barrio in the same way that blacks are trapped in the ghetto.

Our results also underscore the need to incorporate spatial elements into theories of stratification. Because so many important variables relevant to individual life chances are spatially determined, barriers to spatial mobility are barriers to social mobility. Our structural models of Hispanic and black assimilation represent a first step toward this goal, linking status attainment theory to the ecological model. These two traditions have developed along separate lines within sociology, notwithstanding the obvious interplay between socioeconomic and ecological processes. Our results demonstrate how the two perspectives can be fruitfully combined to shed light on processes of ethnic stratification in U.S. society.

The relevance of spatial processes to stratification is clearly illustrated in the current controversy over "the decling significance of race." It is only possible to make the case that race is becoming less salient as a dimension of stratification if one ignores the fact that blacks are segregated by virtue of race, not class. Because rising social status does not allow blacks to assimilate spatially in the manner of other groups, they are isolated within all-black or largely black neighborhoods confined to a minority of residential areas located disproportionately within declining inner-city areas. Because of racial residential segregation, they pay exorbitant prices for low-quality housing, suffer higher rates of mortality and morbidity, and are disproportionately victims of urban crime. Social mobility is impaired by the low quality of public education within segregated schools and is further stifled when racial segregation forces blacks of all classes to raise their children within a "culture of poverty." Finally, as changes in the U.S. economy continue to shift jobs away from central cities to suburban and nonmetropolitan areas (a trend especially true for blue-collar jobs), blacks find themselves increasingly isolated from sources of employment in the United States. In short, as long as residential segregation is imposed on blacks in U.S. cities, race cannot be ignored as a salient dimension of stratification in American society.

24

Minority Education and Caste

John U. Ogbu

Lower school performance among American minorities is an adaptation maintained by two processes: First, minorities are forced by the caste system to occupy social and occupational positions that do not require high educational credentials; second, a job ceiling and other caste barriers generate doubts among minorities about the value of education and of working hard to succeed in school when they do not expect to get jobs and wages commensurate with their training and abilities in comparison with whites. These two processes do not, however, fully account for the adaptation. They do not, for example, explain why some minority group members, who do not consciously evaluate their schooling in terms of the job ceiling, still do poorly in school. Nor do they account for the inadequate performance of young minority children who are not old enough to understand the meaning of the job ceiling on such minority institutions as the family and the status mobility system, as well as on the nature of the skills or personal attributes required for competence in the social and occupational positions to which minorities have traditionally been restricted.

Reprinted from John U. Ogbu, *Minority Education and Caste* by permission of the author and publisher, Academic Press, Inc.

Caste Barriers, Divergent Cultural Elements, and School Performance

In this section, I consider two examples of how the caste system shapes black indigenous institutions, status mobility and family patterns, and how these in turn influence black school performance.

The evolution of some black cultural elements that diverge from those emphasized by the public schools is attributable to the physical and social segregation of blacks in the ghettos, a process begun during slavery. After emancipation, the slave quarters in the old southern towns became restricted black residential areas. In the newer southern towns and in the North, residential segregation is more nearly complete, resulting in larger ghettos (Drake 1968:112). . . .

Caste barriers generated many sociocultural and economic features within the ghettos that further differentiate them from white residential areas. For example, although a ghetto is not a slum, a large part of a black ghetto usually has many features of a slum—poor-quality housing, overcrowding, high rents, and so on—all of which converge to undermine the physical well-being of its residents (Forman 1971). Another distinguishing feature is that a ghetto has two sets of institutions: caretaker institutions (e.g., welfare and economic, legal, communication, education, and political institutions) controlled by members of the dominant caste; and indigenous institutions (e.g., family and kinship, social class, religious, and voluntary associations) which have developed because its residents have been excluded from participating in similar institutions among the dominant caste. Ghetto culture also develops its own forms of folklore, literature, music, dialect, and self-image. Since the dominant caste controls the caretaker institutions, blacks participate in such institutions mostly in the role of clients; they do not easily establish parallel institutions in these areas because they lack the power and other resources to do so.

How the caste system shapes indigenous black institutions can be illustrated with two examples, both of which are relevant to black school performance: the black status mobility system and the family. . . . Although social classes exist within the two castes, these two systems of social class are not equal because blacks have less access to the resources for class mobility. Here I describe the way in which the caste system affects the social mobility of blacks, i.e., their status mobility system, and its implications for black school performance.

Caste Barriers and the Black Status Mobility System

In addition to retarding the development of the middle-class sector of the black community, the American caste system has fostered different patterns of social mobility for blacks and whites. Basically, the same criteria for self-betterment or social mobility are found within the class systems of the two castes. These are good education, good jobs, income, housing, and the like. Traditionally, however, members of the two castes have been required by the caste system to use different approaches to achieve these goals. Among whites, the approved method emphasizes individual efforts in more or less open and fair competition. Their status mobility system thus encourages the development of such personal qualities as independence, foresight, initiative, industriousness, and individualistic competitiveness. For blacks, on the other hand, achieving a good education, desirable occupations, good incomes, adequate housing, and the like has traditionally required more than individual efforts. Blacks desiring self-betterment have had to depend

on members of the dominant white group who, as individuals or organized groups, controlled the access to such things. Furthermore, because the amount of these resources available to blacks is proportionately more limited than the amount available to whites, blacks cannot obtain them on the basis of ability in open competition. The more limited opportunities for status mobility among blacks calls for stiffer competition than occurs among whites. This situation has resulted in a commonly held belief among blacks that if blacks and whites are found holding equivalent jobs, especially if they are high status jobs, the blacks are probably twice as qualified as the whites; when blacks live in a predominantly white neighborhood, they are probably twice as wealthy or twice as good as their white neighbors, and so on. The point of the present discussion is that the stiffness of the competition for such limited resources has forced blacks to develop three types of responses to the situation: withdrawal from the competition altogether; reliance on the patronage of individual whites or white organizations; or reliance on cooperative efforts of organized groups (e.g., civil rights organizations). Black experience over many generations showed that reliance on white patronage was the most effective approach to self-betterment, though reliance on organized civil rights efforts is becoming increasingly important.

The reliance on white patronage has encouraged such personal qualities as dependency, compliance, and manipulation, which are quite different from the qualities of initiative, competitiveness, and perseverance which the white approach to self-betterment encourages them to develop. The influence of caste barriers on the evolution of some black qualities is suggested in the following description by Shack (1970):

> Real and potential coercive force at the disposal of the Whites summarily denied Black parents and by extension their children also, opportunities for engaging in the kinds of positive social [and techno-economic] experiences which give rise to that focal value which underlies the conception of a mechanistic, controllable universe. A substantive norm evolved for Black people which stressed the manipulation of persons and things, actually and symbolically, through verbal and nonverbal forms of behavior. Tradition-

ally, manipulative behavior has been stereo-typically expressed in the story book caricatures of Uncle Tom and Brer Rabbits, or say, the humble, grinning Pullman Porter. On the current scene [1970s], some forms of Black militancy with the threatening virtuperative rhetoric of ritually condemning the White world represents a variation on the traditional stereotypical theme. For neither Uncle Tom, the grinning porter, nor the black militant ever gain *control* over the situation at hand; it is rather that they *manipulate* Whites whom they confront to avoid thrashing, to gain a gratuity, or to gain public exposure which might result in a token reward. These institutionalized cultural mechanisms serve the function of enabling temporary adjustment to situations over which Blacks are, or believe themselves to be, powerless to control [pp. 24–25].

Shack goes on to point out that this adjustive behavior spills over into the school setting:

In the school situation, the flight from learning involves employment of similar verbal and behavioral manipulative techniques to which Black children resort in adjusting to their day-to-day relation with teachers [who represent the dominant caste to them]. It is an extension of the adult cultural pattern of manipulating uncontrollable situations; it is a part of a much wider cultural pattern which historically started off in a particular direction of development and the momentum derived from the Black experience has carried it on [p. 25].

But black children's school behavior is not just a spillover of adult adjustive behavior; *it is a part of the training of black children for their survival in the American caste system.* Since blacks achieve high status by renouncing those behaviors which are functional for whites (e.g., academic competition), black children must learn this captive behavior in school as they also learn it in their families and peer groups. This is not, however, to say that blacks are not competitive; they are. The point is that the American caste system which encourages one mode of status mobility for whites and another for blacks forces blacks to channel their competitiveness into areas not regarded as the domain of white competitiveness, such as sports or physical and verbal dueling.

This diversion of black competitiveness into non-academic realms is what Clark (1972:43) has called *compensatory competition.*

Caste Barriers and the Black Family

In American society, the traditional orientation of the family is basically patriarchal; that is, the father is accorded the role of titular head and is expected to be responsible for the family's subsistence and protection. The woman is responsible for childbearing and caring for the young children during their early years.[1] Among blacks, marginal participation in the economic system, especially the marginal participation of black men, has resulted in a different form of family adaptation: a tendency for the woman to be the dominant person in the household. The development of this pattern began during slavery, when black men had no independent economic status. The black woman, on the other hand, partly because of her procreative value and partly because she was sometimes taken as a concubine by the white master, acquired higher social and economic advantages that made her the head of the household in which her children were born and raised. The dominant position of the female in the household remained after emancipation because caste barriers prevented the men from advancing beyond their marginal position in the economic system. The evidence supporting this point of view comes from the fact that the incidence of female-headed households tends to be highest in the poorest sections of the ghetto, that is, among those who are economically worst off. The economic insecurity of the black male reinforces the dominant position of the black female in the family. The economic system of American society thus functions differently with respect to white and black families: it strengthens the authority of white men and emasculates black men.

The influence of caste barriers in shaping the ghetto system of status mobility, family structure, and other indigenous institutions directly contributes to educational adaptation. The restriction of black parents largely to low-level and menial social and occupational roles and their traditional lack of opportunity to advance above these positions through their own abilites, education, or other efforts probably prevents them from training their children effectively to develop competitive attitudes and persistent efforts toward schoolwork. The social and economic emasculation of the black male ensures both that a large number of black children grow up in households without the full benefit of the role models provided by two-parent families and that they will grow up in poverty with all its consequences for school learning.

The Job Ceiling and the Development of School-Related Skills

It is well known that black and white children differ in the linguistic, cognitive, and motivational skills they possess when they first come to school. This difference has been used to explain why black children do less well in school than white children. It has also been said that black children differ from white middle-class children in these skills because black parents do not socialize their children in the same way as white middle-class parents. This explanation, which I shall call the *failure-of-socialization hypothesis*, had an enormous influence on the compensatory education and other programs begun in the 1960s to help black children do better in school. However, these programs have been relatively ineffective in eliminating the assumed black "deficits" in linguistic, cognitive, and motivational skills.

The problem with the failure-of-socialization hypothesis and with various studies of black socialization is that they focus almost exclusively on the process of socialization and pay little attention to the *objective* of socialization, why a particular form of the skill being studied should be transmitted. They rarely ask: Why should black parents transmit to their children *the same* linguistic, cognitive, and motivational skills as white parents, using the *same* techniques, when as adults black and white children are destined to occupy different status positions? A more adequate study of socialization will have to take into account the fact that socialization is also immensely influenced by the needs of the wider society; it does not depend simply on the ability and capability of individual parents to raise their children.

Job Ceiling, Competence, and Personal Attributes

Alex Inkeles's writings on the role of socialization in producing competent people in society suggest how we can begin to understand the consequences of the job ceiling and other caste barriers on the types of skills or personal attributes that black parents as agents of socialization transmit to their children. According to Inkeles (1968b:85), each society has its role repertoire which determines the pattern of behavior expected of typical status incumbents. The role repertoire, therefore, determines the qualities the incumbents must have. These qualities are "what the individuals in the culture must learn and be if they are to meet the role demands" set for them by their society and they are acquired through the process of socialization. Hence, for Inkeles as for myself, there are two important tasks of socialization study: first, *to identify the qualities* demanded for effective role performance in the society of its segment under study, and then to *study how these qualities are transmitted* to the younger generation. Inkeles introduces the concept of *competence* as the linkage between socialization and the status positions in society. Competence—the end product of socialization—is defined by him as "the ability to attain and perform valued social roles" (1968a:52). Socialization, on the other hand, is the formative process of competence, its objective being to produce competent people. Both competence and socialization vary from culture to culture according to variation in role repertoire.

According to Inkeles (1968a:65), American society defines competence as

> the ability to work at gainful and reasonable remunerative employment, to meet the competition of those who would undo us while yet observing the rules for such competition as set down by society, and to manage one's own affairs, to achieve some significant and effective participation in community and political life, and to establish and maintain a reasonably stable home and family life.

It is evident from what has been said so far that this type of competence described by Inkeles does not fit the status position of blacks in American society. It is the competence associated with the status position of white middle-class people, which requires certain kinds of personal qualities transmitted to white middle-class children in their socialization. Among these qualities, Inkeles tells us (1968a:66), are the ability to tell and manage time, a certain kind of language skill, level of information, motive, and cognitive modes.

If American society unevenly distributes socially valued status positions between two castes, does it seem logical for society to expect the two to possess the same kinds of competence and hence the same types of personal qualities or attributes? We should not expect blacks and whites to have the same socialization practices and experiences, because they are not being prepared for roles requiring the same kinds of competence. My guess is that given different forms of competence requiring different personal attributes or qualities, the socialization processes of the two castes probably differ, although they may be equally valid. It makes no sense to judge black socialization in terms of white socialization without first establishing that both are directed toward producing the same kind of competence. With this background, I next focus on language, motivation, and cognition for illustrative purposes. I argue that when blacks differ from whites in these or other skills it is probably because their status positions require variant forms of the skills in question, not because black parents have failed in their socialization duty.

Command of Language

Until recently, it was not generally known that black children had difficulty learning to read in school because they possessed a separate English dialect which interferes with their attempts to read standard English. This phenomenon was not recognized until lately because social scientists tended to study black speech behavior as a deviation from the speech behavior of the white middle class rather than as a system in its own right and a phenomenon related to black lower-caste status. Baratz and Baratz (1970) pointed out that under prevailing American sociopolitical ideology, social scientists tend to confuse legal equality with sameness and therefore judge black behavior by white middle-class standards:

> The application of this misinterpretation of egalitarian principle to social science data has often

left the investigator with the unwelcome task of describing [black] behavior not as it is, but rather as it deviates from the normative system defined by the White middle class [pp. 113–114].

Thus social scientists, particularly educational psychologists, generally labeled black students as "verbally deprived" (see Bereiter 1965; Bereiter *et al.* 1966; Bereiter and Engelman 1966; C. Deutsch 1964; M. Deutsch *et al.* 1967; C. Deutsch Whiteman and Deutsch (1968). Many of the efforts in the 1960s to explain why black children were failing in school, especially in reading skills, and what solution were needed to prevent that failure were based on the notion of verbal deprivation. The myth of verbal deprivation is described by Labov (1972) as follows:

> Black children from the ghetto area are said to receive little verbal stimulation, to hear very little well-formed language, and as a result are impoverished in their means of verbal expression. They cannot speak complete sentences, do not know the names of common objects, cannot form concepts or convey logical thoughts [p. 201].

The same educational psychologists blamed the phenomenon of verbal deprivation on black parents and their methods of language training for their children. It was said that these parents did not provide their children with the same kind and amount of verbal stimulation as did their white counterparts in the suburbs.

Field studies by linguists and anthropologists have now provided sufficient evidence for rejecting the concept of verbal deprivation on the grounds that it is inapplicable to black children in the ghetto. These scholars have conducted careful studies of the structure and function of everyday conversations (vernacular speech) of black ghetto residents in various cities, such as Chicago, Detroit, and New York, and have come to the following conclusions: that blacks possess a separate English dialect which is a normal and well-formed language system like the standard English dialect of the white middle-class; that black children acquire this black English dialect in a normal way, much as white children acquire the white English dialect; and that black children are not verbally deprived. Summarizing the present position of linguists and anthropologists on the matter, Labov (1972) states that:

> The most careful statement of the situation as it actually exists might read as follows: Many features of prononication, grammer, and lexicon are closely associated with black speakers—so closely as to identify the great majority of black people in the Northern cities (as well as in the South generally) by their speech alone [p. 7].

The identification of blacks with a particular speech pattern is the basis of the social reality of their language skills. These studies show that black children, far from being verbally deprived, receive a good deal of verbal stimulation. Labov (1972) points out that

> the concept of verbal deprivation has no basis in social reality. In fact, black children in the urban ghettos receive a great deal of verbal stimulation, hear more well-formed sentences than middle-class children, and participate fully in a highly verbal culture. They have the same basic vocabulary, possess the same capacity for conceptual learning, and use the same logic as anyone else who learns to speak and understand English [p. 201].

But the English dialect ghetto children learn and use is different from that learned and used by their white middle-class peers (Stewart 1970:367).

Linguists have also gone on to explain why a separate English dialect exists, in spite of opposition to the idea from teachers, principals, and civil rights leaders (Labov 1972:7). Partly to forestall any possible misuse of the concept for "a racist" cause, Stewart (1970) warns linguists that "quite objective and innocently made statements about dialect differences between whites and [blacks] might be interpreted by white racists as evidence of [black] cultural backwardness or mental inferiority, or even seized upon by black racists as evidence of some sort of mythical Negro 'soul' [p. 356]." Consequently, Stewart and others have tried to trace the origins of the black English dialect from the eighteenth-century West African pidgin English dialect, through the evolution of the latter into the Creole English dialect of the plantation South and the process of

decreolization following emancipation, leading finally to the present-day form (Stewart 1968, 1970; see also Dillard 1972). Labov (1972:66) acknowledges the validity of some aspects of the Creole hypothesis of Stewart and other historical dialectologists but emphasizes the fusion of southern and northern Black English dialects in the evolution of the present-day ghetto dialect.

These and other accounts of the evolution of the ghetto dialect may be sufficient to dispel potential opposition to and misuse of the concept; but they hardly touch upon the influence of caste barriers in creating and perpetuating the separate dialect. Moreover, the Creole hypothesis almost overstresses the persistence of the grammatical structure of West African pidgin English so as to suggest that its resistance to change is responsible for the present-day dialect. The evidence offered by Stewart and others, however, strongly suggests the need to explore the influence of caste barriers in the evolution and perpetuation of this dialect. This evidence indicates that during slavery the Creole dialect came into being because caste barriers limited contacts between black speakers of pidgin English and white speakers of standard English. The same forces limited the process of decreolization after emancipation. The influence of racial isolation on black language patterns during slavery is well described by Stewart when he points out that house slaves quickly acquired a "more standard variety of English than the Creole of the field hands," as did the educated blacks of the period (1970:360). Labov (1972) describes an interesting case of fourteen present-day black and white individuals whose racial identities could not be established on the basis of their speech patterns. These individuals were

> blacks raised without any black friends in solidly white areas; whites raised in areas dominated by black cultural values; white Southerners in Gullah-speaking territory; blacks from small northern communities untouched by recent migration; college-educated blacks who reject the northern ghetto and the South alike [p. 10].

It seems likely that if blacks had not been isolated from whites during slavery they would have given up their dialect to acquire standard English just as the Chinese gave up their own pidgin

English and learned standard English. The Creole dialect evolved on the plantations because of racial isolation, not because the grammatical structure of West African pidgin English resisted change. Caste barriers resulting in racial isolation also account for the incompleteness of decreolization after emancipation. If social mobility in American society requires standard English, as Stewart (1970:361) suggests, then the caste barriers which have traditionally limited social mobility among blacks have also limited their opportunities to acquire standard English. A more complete account of the evolution and persistence of present-day black English must examine the problem in the context of the American caste system.

These findings—the existence of a separate black dialect and its acquisition in a normal way by ghetto children—have led linguists and anthropologists working in the field to suggest that the failure of black children to learn to read at the same pace and with the same ease as their white middle-class peers is caused by interference from their own dialect when they are trying to use standard English. Baratz (1970), for instance, writes that

> When the middle-class child starts the process of learning to read, his problem is primarily one of decoding the graphic representations of a language he already speaks. The disadvantaged black child must also "translate" them into his own language. This presents him with an almost insurmountable obstacle since the written words frequently do not go together in any pattern that is familiar or meaningful to him [p. 20].

The more difficult task of ghetto children in learning to read is compounded by the fact that neither their teachers nor their schools recognize that they come to school with an essentially *different* English dialect, different both structurally and functionally from the standard English they have to learn to read. In fact, teachers and other school personnel are likely to label black English as pathological, lazy, disordered, or sloppy (Baratz 1970; Labov 1972; Stewart 1970).

Cognitive Skills

Cognitive function refers to both the forms and styles of thinking characteristic of individuals

(Inkeles 1968a:61). Thinking may be concrete, abstract, or both as Bruner, Piaget, Vernon, and others have indicated. Cognitive modes of functioning are an important quality for effective participation in any society; and contemporary technological societies emphasize the abstract and related forms more than the concrete. The dominant social sciences' view of the past two decades has been that children acquire their cognitive skills and styles in the course of interacting with their environment, the latter being narrowly defined to mean parental, familial, and neighborhood factors. I have already pointed out the inadequacy of this concept and suggested another way of looking at environment that would include such features of the wider society as economic systems, sociopolitical organization, and the like. Ultimately, it is these broader features—the macroenvironment—which determine cognitive skills and styles required for competence by role incumbents. The family, the peer groups, and even the schools—the microenvironments—are only channels or instruments through which the adaptive cognitive repertoire of a society or a segment of it is transmitted in each generation.

Blacks and whites have been shown to differ in their cognitive skills as measured by intelligence tests (Baugham 1971; Dreger 1973; Jensen 1969). The lower performance of blacks is usually explained in terms of the failure-of-socialization hypothesis. But efforts to resocialize black children to develop white middle-class forms of cognitive skills have not proved successful. These efforts failed primarily because the hypothesis upon which they were based assumed that blacks and whites ought to have the *same* cognitive skills acquired in the *same* way, despite the fact that the status positions of the two castes are *different* and probably require *different* cognitive adapations.

I suggest that the cognitive differences between blacks and whites are attributable primarily to the fact that the two groups have traditionally occupied different and unequal positions in both the occupational and sociopolitical structures of American society. The low and menial roles to which blacks have been restricted require and stimulate the development of cognitive and other skills different from those associated with the more desirable positions open to whites. The fact that blacks have had only limited access to white-collar, technical, managerial, and professional positions and have been confined to unskilled and menial labor for generations has probably meant that they have not had the same opportunities as whites to develop those ways of conceptualizing, thinking, and speaking demanded by the former positions. Scientific analysis, control, and exploitation of the physical environment, large-scale and long-range planning and execution require the type of thinking characteristic of the Western middle class. But this class did not always possess those cognitive skills, at least not to the same degree. Participation in these activities not only requires them but also stimulates their development. In the case of blacks, we find that their initial and arbitrary exclusion from these activities was based on their lower-caste status, not their lack of the requisite mental capacities and processes. The menial social positions to which they have been confined required and stimulated different forms of cognitive skills, which black parents as agents of socialization under the caste system, transmit to their children.

Cognitive Styles

Studies of cultural differences in cognitive styles are becoming popular. Group differences in cognitive styles are sometimes explained in terms of genetic differences (Jensen 1969), but most often they are explained in terms of differences in socialization styles (Berry 1966; Cohen 1969; Ramirez and Casteneda 1974; Witkin *et al.* 1954, 1962) and occasionally in terms of differences in ecological factors (Berry 1971; Dawson 1967). I focus here on the socialization hypothesis as it applies to black Americans.

Witkin, who initiated the study of cognitive styles during World War II, distinguished between two polar styles of thinking—the global and the articulated. People with the articulated style of thinking are able to differentiate and organize features of their environments and approach tasks more objectively than those with the global style. According to Witkin *et al.* (1962), the two types of cognitive styles arise from differences in socialization styles: articulated or field-independent people are raised by parents who use child-

rearing practices typical of well-educated white middle- and upper-middle-class parents; global or field-dependent people are raised by parents who do not use such childrearing techniques.[2]

In her Pittsburgh study, Cohen (1969) also identifies two polar cognitive styles, which she calls analytical and relational. People with analytical cognitive styles function well in formal organizational settings such as schools and use the analytic approach in abstracting information from a stimulus situation, whereas those characterized by a relational style are most descriptive in their approach to a stimulus, tend to relate mainly to the global features of the situation, and are more self-centered in their orientation to reality. Cohen's analytic and relational styles are, in fact, equivalent to Witkin's articulated (field-independent) and global (field-dependent) styles. Like Witkin, Cohen suggests that her polar types originate from difference in socialization styles. People with analytic cognitive styles are raised in more formally organized family and peer settings, while those with relational styles are raised in "shared-function" primary groups. Careful reading of Cohen's presentation suggests that formally organized group socialization characterizes the white middle class while the shared-function primary group socialization is typical of the lower class and disadvantaged minorities.

Ramirez and Castañeda (1974) argue that Anglo-Americans and Mexican-Americans of Texas have different cognitive styles: Anglo-Americans are field independent; Mexican-Americans are field dependent. Like Witkin and Cohen, they trace the differences in cognitive styles to differences in socialization styles: "Socialization styles, including teaching approaches, the nature of rewards, and characteristics of the relationship between 'teacher' and learner, which children experience at home, differ from culture to culture. Values and socialization styles determine or affect development of cognitive styles in children [p. 60]."

None of these studies of differences in cognitive styles in the United States has attempted to examine the way in which groups' positions in the wider society affect their characteristic cognitive styles. But we find that those reported to be global, field dependent, relational, and concrete in their cognitive styles are found primarily in subordinate groups, such as women (Witkin *et al.* 1962), members of shared-function primary groups (i.e., lower class) (Cohen 1969), Mexican-Americans (Ramirez and Castañeda 1974), blacks (Jensen 1969), and Jewish boys from mother-dominated, father-emasculated families (Castelo and Peyton 1973). In other words, the socialization pattern that produces global, field-dependent, relational, and concrete thinking is associated with subordinate status. The competence associated with the different (and usually unequal) power and technoeconomic positions occupied by different groups based on sex, class, and caste status requires different types of cognitive styles. Differences in socialization styles are determined by the need to transmit cognitive styles adaptive to the different positions. Socialization processes show us *how* the adaptive cognitive styles are acquired or transmitted, not why they exist in the population.

I do not deny that there are group differences in cognitive styles. My contention, however, is that the explanations of why they occur are inadequate. Studies of cognitive styles, though becoming popular, are as yet few, poorly conceptualized, and culture bound. Many of their conclusions are premature and unwarranted.[3]

Achievement Motivation

Research on achievement motivation among blacks reveals an interesting paradox. Black children do not have a lower interest in education than white children (Katz 1967; Mingione 1965; Rosen 1959). At the same time, they do not perform as well as whites in the intellectual tasks of the classroom (Katz 1967:144). Why is there a lack of motivation to perform in the classroom among black children? Almost all explanations point to the failure of black socialization as the ultimate cause. Here I discuss two variants of the failure-of-socialization hypothesis because they are directly related to the issue of competence in a caste society.

Inkeles (1968a), Riessman (1962), and Cloward and Jones (1963) attribute the lack of motivation to perform in the classroom to culture conflict. They argue that the competence goals of the schools are probably different from the competence goals to which black families have socialized their children. They suggest that to eliminate the conflict and increase black motivation to

perform in the classroom, the goals of education should be modified to make them more compatible with the values, goals, and learning styles of black children. But they do not say exactly what they consider these values, goals, and learning styles to be. Their main point is that since black parents are not able to socialize their children to acquire the white middle-class attributes that fit successful learning in the schools, the schools should modify their approach to fit the qualities or skills possessed by black children. One wonders, however, how this modification would prepare black children to participate competently as adults in a technological society requiring white middle-class qualities and competence.

In my view, Katz (1967) identifies the problem more correctly as *the lack of the will to learn*, but I think that he incorrectly explains it in terms of the failure-of-socialization hypothesis. He states:

> I think that the crux of the matter is the differential capacity of children from different social backgrounds for vigorous and sustained efforts on tasks that are not consistently interesting and attractive and which offer no immediate payoff, either positive or negative. In this view, effective scholastic motivation is largely reducible to self-control—*an outcome of socialization processes involving the internalization of standards of excellence and of affect-mediating evaluation response to one's own performance* [p. 140; emphasis added].

He then suggests a new experimental approach to the study of the socialization of motivational competence. The results of the experience show that children who perform the experimental task correctly and have good academic records are less self-critical than those who also perform the experimental task correctly but have poor academic records. The results of the experiment show that ghetto children who fail in school may come from homes with high achievement standards but that their standards are so stringent and rigid as to be utterly dysfunctional [p. 161]. Self-criticism is an effective mechanism for self-discouragement, which, according to Katz the children have internalized in the course of their socialization.

In explaining why black students usually express about the same scholastic interests and aspirations as white students but perform less well in school, Katz argues that the majority of black parents teach their children to aspire to high educational goals and lay down verbal rules and regulations about classroom behavior, the transgression of which they punish severely. However, they do not teach their children the instrumental behavior necessary for achieving their educational goals (1967:174).

As in other instances, the failure-of-socialization hypothesis confuses the process of transmitting a given skill or personal quality that exists or is emphasized in a society or group with the reason why a particular form of the skill exists at all. We know from studies cited by Katz (1967) and others that the quality noticeably absent from black students is seriousness and perseverance in their schoolwork. At the same time, there are reports that these students are very skilled at manipulating the system. It is reasonable to infer that in the course of their socialization black children learn manipulative skills but do not learn skills that enable them to be serious and persevering in schoolwork. The reason for this failure to learn lies partly in the effect of the job ceiling on their perceptions of schooling and partly in the form of status mobility or paths for self-improvement the caste system fosters among them.

Both of these phenomena force blacks to rely on white patronage to achieve jobs and other necessities of life. And competence in winning their objectives through patronage requires the skills of dependence, compliance, and manipulation. Thus the caste system requires blacks to renounce such white motivational skills as autonomy, independence, initiative, and competitiveness in order to "make it" in the wider society. Under the caste system, black parents perform their socialization task competently by transmitting to their children the motivational skills adaptive to their status positions as dictated by both the job ceiling and their status mobility.

The failure-of-socialization hypothesis leads to a gross misconception of the development of personal qualities or attributes. It fails to separate the reason *why* a particular skill or attribute or its variant form is characteristic of a society or its segment from a different question, the question of *how* the skill is transmitted to each generation. Skills or personal qualities dominant in a given population are functionally adaptive for its mem-

bers. Conversely, skills only marginally present or entirely absent are not functionally adaptive. Socialization is the process by which an already existent skill or its variant is transmitted to the younger generation; socialization does not by itself generate the skills thus transmitted. This assertion is well illustrated by reference to differences between blacks and whites in reading skills.

The fact that American society rewards blacks and whites differently for reading and language proficiency, for example, contributes to the difference between the two groups in their reading performance. Although both blacks and whites are required to learn reading and other associated skills, for whites, proficiency in these skills is a passport to professional and white-collar jobs, financial rewards and social prestige; for blacks, it is not—at least not to the same extent. The higher proficiency of whites in reading and associated skills does not result merely from the fact that white parents do more to encourage their children to read than black parents. White parents encourage their children more because in their own experience *as a group*, proficiency in reading leads to good jobs and other rewards in adult life. In other words, proficiency in reading is functionally adaptive for whites. This is a strong incentive for white parents to encourage their children and for the children to strive to acquire good reading habits and skills as well as to demonstrate their proficiency in test situations as they begin to perceive the importance of reading to their future roles in adult life. The situation is quite different for black parents and children, to whom society offers less incentive to acquire and express proficiency in reading. This analysis can be extended to other skills such as mathematical skills, which are taught and measured in the schools.

The Educational Performance of Indians, Mexican-Americans, and Puerto Ricans

Thus the job ceiling against blacks contributes to their lower school performance in many ways and helps to prepare them educationally for primarily low-status and menial jobs. The same argument can be made in regard to Indians, Mexican-Americans, and Puerto Ricans. American society and its school systems maintain as they do in the case of blacks, that these groups need good educations to obtain the better jobs and social position enjoyed by Anglos. But neither society nor the schools provide them with the real opportunity to do so. The schools provide them with inferior education, and society uses the job ceiling to prevent them from benefiting more fully from their education (Education: Carter 1970; National Advisory Council on Indian Education 1974. Employment opportunities: Schmidt 1970). The policies and practices within schools prepare most of them primarily for low-status social and occupational positions in life. The devices by which the schools accomplish this are the same mechanisms, both gross and subtle, that schools with a majority of black students use in preparing blacks for inferior roles. A number of studies have documented these mechanisms in predominantly Indian schools (National Council on Indian Education 1974); in predominantly Mexican-American schools (Carter 1970; Grebler *et al.* 1970; Parsons 1965; Sanchez 1965; USCCR 1971a, 1972, 1973a, 1974b; U.S. Senate, Select Committee 1970a); and in schools in which Puerto Ricans are in the majority (Moore 1964; U.S. Senate Select Committee 1970b).

The Job Ceiling and Perception of Schooling

Besides its influence on the educational policies and practices of Indian, Mexican-American, and Puerto Rican schools, the job ceiling also affects the way these minorities perceive their schooling and their efforts in school. Although this problem has not been systematically studied, we can safely assume that these groups know and believe that they do not have chances for employment, advancement on the job, good wages, and other benefits of education equal to those of Anglos. They also know and believe that the primary reason for this lack of equal opportunity is discrimination against them. The fact that we do not have ethnographic or other documentation of how they perceive their schooling in relation to the job ceiling does not mean that the two are unrelated. In any case, one recent study suggests a possible unconscious link between them.

The study in question is that of Blair (1971, 1972), who investigated the employment and schooling experiences of Mexican-Americans in Santa Clara County, California. He compared the benefits, measured by wages, received by Anglo-Americans and Mexican-Americans of the same levels of education. He compared two paired groups of Mexican-Americans and Anglo-Americans based on areas of residence. One pair lived in predominantly Mexican-American barrios, and the other pair lived outside the barrios. In each case, Blair found that the Mexican-American group earned lower wages than the Anglo-American group, when the two groups had the same level of education. Among those living in the barrios, the Anglo-Americans earned $880 more per year than Mexican-Americans with the same level of education; among those living outside the barrios, the Anglo-Americans earned $1713 more. Blair calls the wage differential a "schooling penalty" against the Mexican-Americans. He points out that the average difference in the wages, the *schooling penalty*, is equivalent to what an average person in the county would expect to earn by acquiring an additional 2½ years of schooling. The study also shows that this schooling penalty is greater for younger Mexican-Americans than for older members of the group (Blair 1971:82–85).

What is an even more significant aspect of Blair's findings is that the schooling penalty is greater for Mexican-Americans who graduate from high school or college than for those who drop out short of graduation. That is, Mexican-Americans who stay long enough or persevere hard enough to graduate from high school or college experience a greater earning gap between them and their Anglo peers, whereas Mexican-Americans who drop out of high school or college experience less of a gap. Blair notes that in this way the caste system is transmitting different messages to Anglo and Mexican-American students. To the Anglo student the message is consistent with the American ideology that more education and hard work in school lead to greater self-improvement: It tells the Anglo student that he can expect increasing rewards from society if he stays long enough and works hard enough in school to obtain a high school diploma or a college degree. The Mexican-American student as well as castelike minority students in general receive the contrary message that they can expect to earn wages a little closer to what their Anglo peers earn if they drop out of school rather than stay long enough and work hard enough to obtain a high school diploma or college degree. Blair suggests that Mexican-American and other castelike minority people probably realize, albeit unconsciously, that additional schooling or graduation from high school or college brings less returns, when compared with the resources and effort they have to invest in the schooling. Perhaps because of these contradictory messages, castelike minority students adjust differently to schooling than do the Anglo students. Without implying that minority students should drop out of school, Blair says:

> This explanation of the dropout phenomenon would put less emphasis on sociocultural determinants of school-taking behavior, such as childhood conditioning of parents' SES [socioeconomic status], students' motivations and aspirations, educational quality, and academic ability [at the same time recognizing their partial role]. It would, instead, place greater stess on the observed fact of real ethnic money-wage [and job] discrimination in the employment market for equal age and school-attainment qualifications.
>
> Apparently, only efforts to ensure that employers and unions pay employed Mexican-Americans of given school attainment and age the same money as their Euro-American counterparts and provide equal access to the same kind of work will close the ethnic income gap and equalize return investment in schooling [1972:98–99].

In other words, because the job ceiling (with its attendant income ceiling) stultifies the schooling efforts of minority people, the remedy lies in eliminating the job and income ceiling, not in changing the minority people.

That Indians, Mexican-Americans and Puerto Ricans, like blacks, perceive and react to the barriers against them in future employment and social positions probably accounts for the commonly observed phenomenon which Carter calls "mental withdrawal" (1970). Caste-minority children may or may not lag behind in the first two or three grades, but during the intermediate grades, their performance begins to drop sharply, while that of Anglo children increases (see Carter 1970:178; Fuchs and Havighurst 1973:126; Sexton 1972). Bryde (cited in Fuchs and Havighurst 1973) reports that among Indians a sharp drop in achievement begins to occur at about grade 6 or

grade 7, at the age of puberty, when the children become more aware of the "Indianness" and begin to feel more alienated, with the result that they lose self-confidence. They subsequently stop trying to do well in school, and thus their achievement drops. Fuchs and Havighurst argue (1973:128ff) that the drop in the Indian children's school achievement occurs well before the age of puberty, and they go on to explain this in terms of environmental factors, such as family background and culture conflict.

Carter (1970: 136–137) has reviewed various explanations of the phenomenon of declining achievement among Mexican-Americans, which he says is associated with "mental withdrawal." His preferred explanation links it to the nature of the education system or school itself. He seems to imply that the children do relatively well in the early grades because at that stage school curriculum and authority structure are flexible enough to make them enjoy school. From the intermediate grades, however, the curriculum becomes progressively more rigidly defined and controlled, and school becomes less relevant to children. At this point, their background becomes the crucial factor as to whether their academic achievement will drop or go up. He explains the ability of middle-class children to maintain or increase their achievement by saying that a middle-class background provides them the kind of support, reinforcement, and reward that generates increased academic achievement; the lower-class and minority children's background, on the other hand, fails to provide such stimuli, resulting in a drop in the academic achievement of lower-class children. Anglo middle-class children apparently persevere in school and do well, even though schooling per se is essentially uninteresting and unrewarding, according to this explanation, because their parents teach them to expect their reward in "future social success." In contrast, "poor parents may not support the idea that school is a series of steps that must be climbed regardless of the boredom or unpleasantness involved, nor are they able to guarantee their children significant future social rewards for perseverance in and graduation from school [Carter 1970:137]."

Although Carter's explanation has some merit, it fails to explain why non-middle-class, immigrant peasant minorities, including those from Mexico, do well in school and do not exhibit "mental withdrawal." Any explanation of the success of such immigrant children and the failure of Indian, Mexican-American, and Puerto Rican children, must account for the fundamental difference between the latter groups and the Anglo-American middle class in terms of experience with regard to jobs and social position under the caste system. If Anglo-American middle-class parents teach their children that they should persevere in school regardless of the boredom and unpleasantness involved *because they will be rewarded in the future with desirable social positions and jobs*, the behavior [teaching] of these parents is motivated by a belief system derived from the actual experience of white middle-class people which they "naturally" transmit to their children. If the Anglo-American middle-class children accept their parents' advice or teaching and behave accordingly, it is also because they know from the experiences of their parents and other adults in their communities that their success in school will surely bring social and occupational rewards. Now the experiences of Indian, Mexican-American, and Puerto Rican parents are different: Education has not usually brought the same desirable social and occupational rewards; and there is no reason to expect that the different experiences of the minority-group parents *will generate the attitudes, beliefs, and teaching about schooling* characteristic of Anglo-American middle-class parents. Nor does one have to be a member of the Anglo-American middle-class to share its attitudes, beliefs, and behavior. Immigrant parents, whether or not they are of middle-class background, tend to have similar instrumental attitudes, partly because they want their children to be educated in order to get better jobs than their parents and partly because they have not become disillusioned by repeated failure to achieve self-improvement through education because of caste barriers.

It should be added that children do not always persevere in school simply because their parents teach them to do so; nor do children always give in to peer-group pressures because their parents fail to teach them about future rewards through perseverance in school. Immigrant parents whose children achieve school success may have no good understanding of how American schools operate and may lack the knowledge of Anglo-American middle-class parents to teach their children what is required to succeed in American schools. Immigrant parents are not relevant models of school success or failure for their children. What is significant is not what these parents (or any other parents) can teach their children but what both parents and children believe or expect they can gain from their educational efforts. Castelike minority children, on the other hand, learn from the experiences of their parents and other adult members of their communities that education does not always lead to good social and occupational positions in adult life and that the reason for this is that they are members of caste minorities, that they are Indians, Mexican-Americans, Puerto Ricans, or blacks. As they get older, they are likely to compare their future chances with those of their Anglo-American peers, and they are likely to ask why they should work as hard now in school for smaller future rewards. Under these conditions they are more susceptible to peer-group influences than Anglo-American middle-class children. In other words, peer influence or pressure becomes an important link to school failure only when mental withdrawal from schoolwork has already taken place because of perceived limited future chances for employment opportunities and other benefits supposedly based on school success or education.

ENDNOTES

1. I am fully aware of the vast changes in sex roles now taking place among white Americans. While these changes may substantially reduce the dominance of the white male in the family, they do not invalidate my claim here that the caste system has functioned to create a black family pattern in which the female has tended to be the more dominant. Nor am I concerned with the political aspect of changing sex roles, such as whether the family should be male dominated, female dominated, or egalitarian.

2. Most cross-cultural studies use the terms *field-independence* and *field-dependence* to represent the two polar types of cognitive style identified by Witkin, although *field-independence* and *field-dependence* refer primarily to perceptual styles (See Cole and Scribner 1974:82).

3. There is a curious but dangerous parallel in the policy implications of Jensen's theory and the theories

of some of his opponents. Referring to the work of Jensen (advocate of genetic basis of cognitive differences) and of Ramirez (advocate of the cultural basis of cognitive differences), De Avila and Havassy (1975) note this parallel:

> While the Jensen and Ramirez positions imply very different causal explanations, functionally speaking their arguments run the risk of being reduced to the same position regarding the educational approach to be taken with Mexican-American children. That is, Ramirez's position that Mexican-American children are field-sensitive [i.e., field-dependent, global, relational, etc.] and consequently not receptive to learning abstract problem-solving strategies is much the same, at the practical level, as Jensen's position—that the intellectual capabilities of Mexican-Americans [and blacks] are limited to Level 1 [i.e., the level of concrete, non-analytical thinking] because of genetic endowment. Both arguments suggest a curriculum for Mexican-American students which eliminates or minimizes tasks requiring the abstract manipulations of impersonal data [p. 250].

Ramirez bases his research partly on Witkin and partly on the work of Lesser, Fifer, and Clark (see Stodolsky and Lesser 1971). The latter found that there are ethnic differences in the mean scores for verbal, reasoning, numerical, and spatial portions of the intelligence test they administered to Chinese, Jewish, black, and Puerto Rican children in New York and Boston. Although they disclaimed any attempt to relate their finds on ethnic cognitive styles to school ability or learning styles, their findings have been used to argue the case against school integration (see Weinberg 1970:375). Potential misuse of the findings on ethnic differences in cognitive styles is as likely by well-meaning school personnel as by racist "expert" psychologists. I think that the potential for this misuse is most likely to occur when no adequate explanation for the differences is provided, as in the case of Lesser and his associates. In none of their writings on this particular study have they examined the possible influence of historical and social structural forces on the test performance of their groups. The fact that Jewish children did best on tasks of verbal ability but not on tasks of space conceptualization, while for Chinese children the reverse was true might be due to several factors not mentioned in their interpretation. For example, (a) Jewish literary background, their relative fluency in English—the language in which the test was given—and the relative absence of architectural (and constructional) investment in Jewish ghettos during the Diaspora; and (b) the difference between the Chinese and English languages and the relative lack of fluency in English among some Chinese children, which partly accounts for the tendency among Chinese-Americans as a group to go into fields of science where there is less need for English usage than other skills (e.g., those involving space conceptualization).

IV

Race and Ethnicity in 1980s America

In 1965, in an introduction written for a series of essays entitled "The Negro American" in the scholarly journal *Daedalus*, President Lyndon Johnson wrote: "Nothing is of greater significance to the welfare and vitality of this nation than the movement to secure equal rights for Negro Americans" *(Daedalus*, 1965:743). Johnson's crucial role in achieving passage of the landmark 1964 Civil Rights Act and the 1965 Voting Rights Act; and his War on Poverty program are ample evidence that his support was not merely rhetorical.

Johnson spoke these words at the zenith of personal and national attention to the status of blacks in America. Three years later the commission he had appointed to investigate the causes of the civil disorders sweeping American cities during the late 1960s—disorders that claimed a toll of over 100 lives and millions of dollars in property damage—attributed the primary responsibility for the outbreaks to white racism and concluded that "there can be no higher claim on the Nation's conscience" than to eliminate "deepening racial division" by a "compassionate, . . . massive, and sustained" commitment of resources and energy (National Advisory Commission on Civil Disorders, 1968).

Yet Johnson, by that time preoccupied with the escalation of the war in Vietnam, ignored the commission's recommendations, just as his successor, Richard Nixon, disputed its basic conclusions. Thus during the 1970s, despite several significant private and governmental efforts to implement programs to achieve racial equality, the status of blacks no longer occupied the prominence in the American consciouness that it did in 1965. The policy of "benign neglect" that Daniel P. Moynihan urged Richard Nixon to adopt toward blacks appears to have been realized. As the editors of a 1981 issue of *Daedalus* devoted to American racial minorities wrote, "It is a measure of the distance we have traveled in sixteen years that is almost unthinkable to imagine any white politician today making such a statement as Johnson's in 1965, giving such primacy to the issue of racial equality" *(Daedalus*, 1981: vi). Nor, I might add, is it likely today for a national commission, comprised primarily of white Americans, to so unequivocally call for massive action to address the continuing problems afflicting black America.

If there was a decline in attention to blacks since the late '60s, there was also a corresponding surge of interest in ethnicity and a reassertion of the importance of ethnic pluralism during the same period. The heightened cultural and political self-awareness that characterized the black protest movement of the 1960s extended in the 1970s to Hispanics, Native Americans, Asians, and, especially, to white ethnics—those descendants (primarily Catholic) of southern and eastern Europeans who had migrated to the United States in massive numbers between 1890 and 1915. As the nation's preoccupation with blacks waned, interest in ethnicity became increasingly fashionable.

Demographic Changes in the 1970s

In order to comprehend the dynamics of ethnic relations during the 1970s (and to anticipate the nature of ethnic relations in the future), it is useful to examine briefly some of the demographic changes that occurred during that time. Table 1 of the Statistical Appendix provides the basic data for several broad racial and ethnic categories. Primarily because of increased Asian and Latin immigration and relatively lower birth rates among whites, the white percentage of the population is lower today than at any time since the Civil War; blacks, Asians, American Indians, and Hispanics now comprise more than one-fifth (20.3 percent) of the American people.

Blacks, the nation's largest racial minority, increased by approximately four million to a total of twenty-six and a half million, or more than the entire population of Canada or of Sweden, Denmark, Norway, Finland, and Iceland combined. As in 1970, blacks continued to live overwhelmingly in urban areas, especially in the nation's largest cities. Today New York City has a black population of more than one and three-quarters million, more than any other city in the world and more than any state in the country. Chicago has more blacks than Mississippi or South Carolina; and Philadelphia more than Arkansas and Kentucky combined (Pettigrew, 1979). For the first time in this century, there was little change in the percentage of blacks (53 percent) who lived in the South. Although some blacks were still migrating from the South to the North and West, their numbers were nearly balanced by blacks who were moving into this region.

During the 1970s, the number of Hispanics (which, as you recall is a general rubric including several extremely disparate national and ethnic categories) increased by more than five million, or more than 61 percent. This is an increase that was greater both proportionately and numerically than the black population, which grew by 17 percent. Earlier predictions were that by 1990 Hispanics would exceed the number of blacks in the country. These predictions now seem exaggerated, but the increase in the Hispanic population was substantial. California had the greatest number of Hispanics: more than four and a half million, or about 31 percent of the 14.6 million enumerated in 1980. Texas and New York together accounted for a comparable number, thus bringing the Hispanic populations in these three states alone to more than three-fifths of Hispanics in the country overall. Reflecting its historical role as the nation's—indeed the world's—most ethnically diverse city, New York City remained the American city with the largest

Hispanic population. Today blacks and Hispanics together comprise more than 42 percent of New York's population.

Among the most striking demographic changes of the 1970s was the growth of the Asian population, which nearly doubled between 1970 and 1980. During the 1970s the number of Koreans increased by 412 percent; the number of Chinese and Filipinos by 125 percent; and the number of Chinese by 85 percent. The number of Chinese and Filipinos both surpassed the Japanese, who in 1970 had been the largest Asian ethnic group. Moreover, more than one-third million Asian Indians and more than one-quarter million Vietnamese, neither of whom had previously been enumerated separately, helped to swell the number of Asians to more than three and a half million. Regionally, Asians were concentrated in the West, especially in California, which had more Chinese, Japanese, Filipinos, Koreans, and Vietnamese than any other state.

The increase in immigration in the past two decades is a result of three factors. First was the passage of the Immigration Reform Act of 1965, which dramatically changed the underlying rationale of America's immigration policy. The previous law, which had been enacted in 1924, had established immigration quotas for each country based on the assumption that some people (such as the British, who were allocated more than 65,000 of the 150,000 annual quotas) were more assimilable and hence more desirable than others (such as the Italians, who were granted a quota of fewer than 6,000, or the Greeks, whose quota was 310). Reflecting the racist assumptions on which it was based, immigration laws excluded most Asians completely.

Enacted at the height of what Gans termed the equality revolution of the 1960s (Gans, 1968), the 1965 law abolished the old national-origins quota system, increased the annual quota to 170,000, placed a limit of 20,000 for each country, and, for the first time, established a limit (120,000) on immigration from the Western Hemisphere. It also established preferences for those who would be reunited with their families, for those with occupational skills needed in the United States, and for those emigrating for political reasons.

Since 1968 (when the 1965 immigration law actually went into effect) the annual number of permanent immigrants increased substantially. During this period, the number of legal immigrants averaged nearly 437,000, compared to 282,000 in the decade prior to 1965. In 1980, more than 880,000 immigrants were legally admitted, a number greater than in any year since 1914. Given the declining birth rate of the native-born American population, immigrants now comprise a greater percentage of the nation's total population growth than they have since the first two decades of the twentieth century—approximately 25 percent of the population increase, in contrast to 6 percent in 1940.

Even more dramatic than the increase in numbers, however, were the changes in the immigrants' countries of origin. Until the enactment of the 1965 law, immigrants into the United States had historically been overwhelmingly from European countries. Today the predominant sources of immigration are Asia, Central and South America, and the Caribbean. European immigration declined from nearly three-fifths of the total (59 percent) during the 1950s to one-eighth (12 percent) in 1978. Similarly, Asian immigration increased from 6 percent to 42 percent, and immigrants from the Western Hemisphere (not including Canadians) rose from 23 percent to 41 percent. In 1978 the leading countries of origin for immigrants to the United States were Mexico, the West Indies, Vietnam, the Philippines, Cuba, Korea, Dominican Republic, China, and India, in that order. As Polenberg recently pointed out, by 1976 the United States "was receiving fewer immigrants from Italy and Greece combined than from India alone, fewer from Germany than from Thailand, fewer from Ireland than from Egypt, and fewer from Poland than from Trinidad and Tobago" (Polenberg, 1980:282).

Moreover, the settlement patterns of this "new immigrant wave" differ from previous flows into the United States. Whereas previous immigrants settled primarily in the industrial states of the northeast and midwest (New York, Illinois, New Jersey, Pennsylvania), immigrants today are much more dispersed geographically. States with the largest foreign-born populations in 1980 were California, New York, Florida, Illinois, and Texas (U.S. Bureau of the Census, 1982:14–19).

The changes in America's immigration laws have affected the occupational composition of the present immigrant population as well as the country of origin. Today the range of immigrants' occupations much more closely resemble those of the native population than have immigrant populations in the past. Whereas a preponderance of immigrants during the first two decades of the twentieth century was unskilled blue-collar workers, preference today for those with skills needed by the United States has meant that immigrants entering are much more highly educated than earlier. (See Hirschman and Wong's article, "Trends in Socioeconomic Achievement among Immigrant and Native-Born Americans, 1960–1976," for confirmation of this trend among Asian immigrants.) Physicians, nurses, scientists, architects, artists, entertainers, engineers, and others with highly technical skills have contributed to a "brain drain," first from Europe and later from Third World nations that can least afford to lose their skills. (More than half the physicians in New York City's municipal hospitals today are graduates of foreign medical schools, for example.) The preference for skills has meant that unlike the peak years of American immigration between 1840 and 1920, it has become almost impossible for unskilled laborers to gain entrance unless they can claim a close family relationship or refugee status. It has also meant that the less highly skilled have increasingly resorted to illegal means to enter the country. Throughout the 1970s about a million illegal aliens were apprehended annually, and it has been estimated that about 500,000 so-called undocumented aliens still enter each year (Fallows, 1983:101–102).

Refugees represent the second major factor contributing to the swell of immigrants entering the United States. Determining who can enter the country as a refugee is essentially a political judgment, made by the federal government. Given that there are an estimated thirteen million political and economic refugees in the world today under the government's definition, the moral and political pressures to admit refugees are considerable. Although refugees from more than 100 different nations have been admitted, official government policy has given special treatment to those fleeing communism, and the vast majority to enter the United States in the past two decades have been from Cuba and Vietnam. By 1981, nearly a million Cubans and more than 400,000 Vietnamese had been admitted—both groups coming from nations where American-supported governments had been supplanted by communist regimes. But the refugee quotas established under the 1965 law and its revisions have proved inadequate to respond both to the global refugee pressures and to the specific pressures represented by groups such as the Cubans and the Vietnamese. In some instances, as in the case of the Vietnamese, special laws were passed to enable the president to respond to emergency situations. In others, such as the case of the Cuban "Freedom Flotilla" in 1980, the political power of the Cuban-American community and the propagenda value of thousands fleeing Fidel Castro's regime permitted a *de facto* circumvention of the law.

However, as indicated by the cases of the Haitians and the Salvadorans, whose plight has been less widely publicized, the admission of refugees for political reasons does not apply to non-communist regimes, even those that are equally oppressive. Thus in 1984 the Reagan administration planned to offer legal status and citizenship opportunities to more than 100,000 Cubans who entered the United States during the Freedom Flotilla but failed to extend the same privileges to 7,200 Haitian refugees who had fled their nation in small boats at approximately the same time (Pear, 1984:1). Nor has there been a groundswell of support for those fleeing government-sponsored terror in El Salvador or for admitting the basically unskilled Haitians seeking to escape poverty and the reactionary regime of "Baby Doc" Duvalier.

Massey (1981:58) and Portes ("Illegal Immigration and the International System") suggest that a third factor contributing to the recent increase in immigrants has been the emergence of an international pattern of migration between low and high income countries starting in the 1960s (see also Piore, 1979). This pattern has contributed to the rise in legal immigration to the United States, but it has had a particular impact on illegal immigration, especially from Mexico and the Caribbean. According to Charles Keely, one of the leading experts on contemporary immigration, "the most recent and soberest assessments indicate that there are between 3.5 and 5 million people living in the United States illegally" (Kelly, 1982:41).

Traditionally, historians and social scientists have used a dualistic, "push-pull" model to explain immigration to the United States (e.g., Handlin, 1951; Jones, 1960; Taylor, 1971; Sellers, 1977; Dinnerstein and Reimers, 1981). They have enumerated numerous push factors, such as population increases, economic deprivation, and religious and political repression, that impel people to leave their homelands. They have also identified pull factors such as economic opportunity and abundance, and freedom of religious and political expression, that have lured immigrants to the United States.

A widespread assumption concerning the newest immigrant wave is that, as in the past, migration pressures—the push factors—are internal to those countries. The United States has been perceived in the past to influence these migration pressures only to the extent that it offers a beacon of hope for emigrants to escape lives of economic impoverishment or political repression. Thus, the push factors that have impelled people to emigrate are the consequence of policies, practices, and social arrangements that the United States has been relatively powerless to control or influence.

However, this traditional push-pull model is inadequate to explain forces stimulating immigration today. Pull factors, though greatly influenced by the pervasiveness of the mass media in even the remotest corners of the world, remain *qualitatively* the same as ever: the U.S. has been, and remains, the epitome of economic abundance, affluence, and opportunity in people's minds. But starting after World War II, the push factors producing immigration no longer lay largely outside U.S. influence. In the past quarter-century, the United States has emerged as the world's dominant economic, political, and military power. This transformation has reshaped international relations as well as expanded U.S. influence on the internal affairs of many of the world's states. The major difference between immigration today and in the past, then, is the economic and political impact of the United States in those countries that have been among the major sources of immigration. In other words, the increased numbers of immigrants entering the United States are an indirect—and sometimes direct—consequence of American policies and practices. And furthermore, American ideas and actions—economic, social, and political—have created or contributed to the creation of conditions that have led to the uprooting of people in many societies, a number of whom have immigrated to the United States as a result.

Alejandro Portes' article, "Illegal Immigration and the International System," supports this interpretation. Portes contends that, paradoxically, it is Third World economic *development,* not underdevelopment, that has contributed significantly to the growing pressures for emigration. The American model of economic development, with its emphasis on consumerism and consumption, and American economic forces have transformed the social structures of many developing societies. Simultaneously, unemployment, underemployment, and income inequalities preclude access by the majority of the population of developing countries to these consumer goods. Portes writes, "In the eyes of the Mexican worker, the United States stands as the place where the benefits of an advanced economy, promised but not delivered by the present national development strategy, can be turned into reality." Thus, ironically, the very forces generated by the American economic system and exported extensively to the economic life of Third World societies, have been instrumental in attracting the massive influx of immigrants to the United States.

Two implications can be drawn from this interpretation. First, given the thrust of the modernization process and the impact of American political and economic power throughout the world, that the United States will continue to attract immigrants—legal and illegal—from Third World sources appears inevitable. This continuation of immigration for the foreseeable future will likely reinforce and recreate the ethnic diversity that, almost from its very founding, has characterized American society. Second, although migration pressures are manifested in different ways in different countries, they frequently derive their impetus from American economic and political power abroad. Thus comprehension of the dynamics of American immigration today cannot begin at America's borders. Rather, it must encompass the examination of the migration pressures in immigrant-exporting countries as well. To achieve this, contemporary immigration to the United States must be conceptualized more broadly as an integral component and consequence of the highly interrelated economic and political system of societies in the modern world.

The Ethnic Revival

This "new immigrant wave" became a significant phenomenon just when ethnicity and the celebration of America's ethnic diversity became more fashionable than ever before in the country's existence. The main theme of the ethnic revival of the 1970s was the rediscovery and reassertion of the importance and value of cultural pluralism with a concomitant rejection of Anglo-conformity and melting-pot conceptions, both of which ultimately envision an ideal society as culturally homogeneous rather than culturally diverse. Blacks, Chicanos, Puerto Ricans, Native Americans, and Asians each asserted their cultural distinctiveness and rejected what they perceived as efforts to impose on them the culture of the white middle class.

Each of these assertions of cultural identity and distinctiveness can be seen as efforts at ethnic mobilization—"the process by which a group organizes along ethnic lines in pursuit of collective political ends" (Nagel and Olzak, 1982:127). Nagel's "The Political Mobilization of Native Americans" provides an explanation for the emergence of recent tribal, pan-tribal, and pan-Indian movements. She, like Enloe, sees such movements as responses to external stimuli; in particular, to policies of the American federal government that control resources available to Indians.

However, the primary impetus for the ethnic revival of the 1970s came from the so-called white ethnics. Spokespersons for the ethnic revival maintained that the movement represented a spontaneous and broadly based reassertion of ethnic pride, not only of intellectuals but of the frequently ignored, unarticulated, and pervasive sentiments of working-class ethnics as well. Michael Novak, the grandson of Slovakian immigrants and author of *The Rise of the Unmeltable Ethnics* (1971), was one of the foremost proponents of the new ethnicity. He identified two basic elements in the movement: a sensitivity to and appreciation of the importance of ethnic pluralism; and a self-conscious examination of one's own cultural heritage (Novak, 1971:17). Another prominent spokesman, Andrew Greeley, the prolific Irish-American sociologist, priest, and novelist, noted several ways in which this ethnic "consciousness raising" was expressed: increased interest in the literary, intellectual, and artistic culture of one's ethnic background; visits to one's ancestral homeland; and increased use of one's ancestral language (Greeley, 1975:149–151).

The case for a broadly based ethnic revival was supported by considerable impressionistic evidence. In 1969, for the first time, the Census Bureau asked Americans about their ethnic backgrounds. Those interviewed were given seven choices from which to select: German, English, Irish, Spanish, Polish, Italian, and Russian (and "mixed" or "other"). Thirty-eight percent of the respondents (equivalent to 75 million Americans) placed themselves in one of the seven categories. Three years later, when the Census Bureau conducted a similar survey, Americans appeared much more conscious of, or willing to indicate, their affiliation with an ethnic group. This time nearly 50 percent (equivalent to 102 million) identified with a specific national group. Moreover, during the late 1960s and early 1970s numerous ethnic groups developed organizations, such as the Italian-American Civil Rights League, that were designed to combat negative perceptions of their group. Such self-consciously ethnic organizations also mobilized to obtain the increasing financial resources from the federal government and private foundations in order to fund activities to rekindle or awaken ethnic consciousness. In 1972 the Ethnic Heritage Studies Act provided federal government sanction to the ethnic revival by providing financial assistance to promote ethnic studies. The Act gave, in the words of one of its sponsors, "official recognition to ethnicity as a positive constructive force in our society today" (quoted in Polenberg, 1980:246).

The notion of an ethnic revival was also reflected in increased academic attention to ethnicity. History, literature, and sociology courses that had focused almost exclusively on black Americans during the 1960s broadened their scope to include other ethnic groups in the 1970s. Indeed, student enrollments declined in black studies courses and there were instances in which ethnic courses supplanted race courses completely. The increasing salience of ethnicity during the decade was also symbolized by the founding of several journals devoted to its analysis: *Ethnicity* (1974), *Journal of Ethnic Studies* (1974), *Ethnic and Racial Studies* (1978), *MELUS* (Multiethnic Literature in the United States) (1975), and most recently, the *Journal of American Ethnic History* (1981). Finally, one of the most salient indices of the decade's rediscovery of ethnicity was publication in 1980 of the *Harvard Encyclopedia of American Ethnic Groups,* the most comprehensive resource available on the subject today. Publication of the *Encyclopedia* under the aegis of the nation's most prestigious university press reflects the primacy that ethnicity has been accorded over the last decade.

What are the reasons for this resurgence of ethnicity during the '70s? Foremost was the impact that the black protest movement had on the self-definition of other ethnic groups, in particular white ethnics. On the one hand, the emphasis on black pride and on understanding black culture, stimulated by the civil rights movement of the late '50s and '60s, led many white ethnics to consider their own heritages more closely. Then the "roots phenomenon" among white ethnics both reflected and was stimulated by the celebrated television saga "Roots," which was based on Alex Haley's attempt to trace and recreate his origins on the African continent.

On the other hand, spokespersons for white ethnics criticized what they perceived to be the myopia of the white, liberal, basically Protestant, Establishment. They contended that liberal academics and journalists, especially, were oblivious to the discrimination to which white ethnics historically had been subjected, and tended to portray white ethnics as the primary source of racism towards blacks. For many white ethnics, who felt that they had been the object of derision by liberals, such charges reinforced their perception that the conditions of their lives had not been given the same sympathetic treatment as was given to blacks, Chicanos, Puerto Ricans, and Native Americans. Novak contends that from the white liberal perspective, the latter were "legitimate" minorities but that the idea of white ethnics as minorities was unacceptable. The white ethnic's perspective, Novak wrote, was that "he is being asked to pay the entire price of the injustices done to blacks—he who is living on the margin himself—while those who are enriched pay nothing" (Novak, 1975:112). Thus the ethnic revival was in some respects a defensive response to external pressures, particularly in its opposition to an increasingly strident black protest movement, rather than a positive, liberating affirmation of identity.

In another sense, however, the movement had little to do with factors external to the white ethnic groups, but was derived from the very success of these groups' adaptation to American society. By the 1970s the fourth generation of the southern and eastern European immigrants were entering adulthood. As the distance from their ancestral roots increased, their identification with them weakened. The decline of the ancestral language, the dispersion of ethnic neighborhoods, the decreasing participation in and identification with the traditional religious community (primarily among Catholics, especially those under thirty years of age), and the increased rates of ethnic intermarriage contributed to the dwindling of a meaningful ethnic identity.

Another major factor was what Greeley termed the "ethnic miracle," which we discussed in Part III. The increased economic, educational, and occupational mobility Greeley documented indicates that white ethnics have moved into the mainstream of American society, where their identification with their ethnic origins has become increasingly remote.

Moreover, there is considerable evidence that ethnicity as a source of social cohesion is decreasing, especially among the third and fourth generations. In "Symbolic Ethnicity," Herbert Gans disputes the notion of an enduring ethnic revival, arguing that cultural and social assimilation continue to take place in American society. Ethnicity is no longer rooted in group membership or cultural patterns but instead has become symbolic, a matter of choice, an ethnicity of "last resort." In his study of an Italian-American community in Boston in the 1960s, Gans did not find ethnicity to be increasing. Instead, he found a straight-line decline in ethnicity over three generations. That is, ethnicity was less significant in each succeeding generation (Gans, 1962). More recently, a study by Sandberg showed a constant decline in ethnic consciousness, identification, and cohesion among Polish-Americans in Los Angeles; by the fourth generation, ethnicity had ceased to play an important role in their lives (Sandberg, 1974). These findings are reinforced by the patterns of increased rates of ethnic intermarriage, which were discussed in Part III.

Yet, paradoxically, at precisely the moment that white ethnics have become the most fully assimilated into American society, culturally and socially, their interest in and identification with their ethnic roots has also become the most pronounced. In *The Ethnic Myth,* Stephen Steingberg argued that ". . . the impulse to recapture the ethnic past is a belated realization that ethnicity is rapidly diminishing as a significant factor in American life" (Steinberg, 1981:73). Although neither is especially sympathetic to the notion of an ethnic revival, both Irving Howe (1977) and Herbert Gans ("Symbolic Ethnicity") suggest another source of the surge of interest in things ethnic. In an interpretation reminiscent of Herberg's (1955) explanation of the surge of religiosity a generation earlier, they find that ethnicity provides a fashionable, socially acceptable source of personal identity in an increasingly homogenized America. In Howe's words,

> We are all aware that our ties with the European past grow increasingly feeble. Yet we feel uneasy before the prospect of becoming "just Americans." We feel uneasy before the prospect of becoming as undistinguishable from one another as our motel rooms are, or as flavorless and mass-produced as the bread many of us eat (Howe, 1977:18).

Thus, although there appears to be widespread interest today among many Americans in retrieving or maintaining a sense of ethnic identity (what Gans called *symbolic ethnicity),* precisely how deep and enduring the ethnic revival will remain is problematic (for a similar interpretation, see Hirschman, 1983).

Finally, Lieberson's "A New Ethnic Group in the United States" suggests that a substantial number of Americans have no sense of ethnic group identity other than a general notion that they are American. The European origins of these unhyphenated whites, as Lieberson characterizes them, is either so remote or so mixed that they are able to define themselves, in true melting pot or transmuting pot fashion, only as American. Lieberson's article raises the intriguing question of whether his findings herald the continual decline of ethnicity among people of European extraction. Or, if ethnicity is situational and emergent, is it more likely that unhyphenated whites will coalesce into novel ethnic groupings fully derived from the American experience in the future?

The Status of Blacks in America

There can be little doubt that the rise of black militancy was one of the most momentous developments of the turbulent 1960s. Each year during the decade, the scale of racial conflict and violence escalated. In retrospect, the beginnings appear relatively subdued. In 1960, the most dramatic events involved drugstore sit-ins in Greensboro, North Carolina, a tactic that quickly spread throughout the South. In the following years, the pace and intensity of protest increased dramatically. Civil disorders engulfed cities throughout the country, with great loss of property and lives. In the heated climate of those years, four of the most important figures in the movement for black equality were the victims of assassins' bullets. Two of them, Malcolm X and Martin Luther King, Jr., were black; two, John Kennedy and Robert Kennedy, were white.

Between 1960 and 1970, the goals and means of the black protest movement underwent substantial changes. As is characteristic of much social change, yesterday's radicalism became today's moderation. Many ideologies and tactics that came to be defined as moderate would have appeared unthinkably radical to concerned individuals—black and white—a decade earlier. Joseph C. Hough, Jr., has characterized this as the "stretching of the extremism spectrum":

> About 1953 I had my first conversation with [a friend in the South] about race relations, and he and I agreed that while the Negro deserved a better chance in America, we must be careful to oppose two kinds of extremists—the NAACP and the Ku Klux Klan. In 1955, we had another conversation, and again we agreed that Negroes ought to be able to attend desegregated public schools, but that we should oppose two kinds of extremes—White Citizens Councils and Martin Luther King. In 1966, this same friend said to me, "If we could get the good whites and the good Negroes to support Martin Luther King, perhaps we could put the brakes on these SNCC and CORE people and also put a stop to this ridiculous revival of the Ku Klux Klan (Hough, 1968:224–225).

By the late 1960s, the forms and direction of black protest had shifted from the moderate civil rights movement to a more militant black power movement. The civil rights movement of the 1950s and early 1960s had been based essentially on an order model of society; the primary goal had been integration into the mainstream of the dominant society, and the primary means were nonviolent. And, as Skolnick (1969) pointed out, the civil rights movement "operated for the most part on the implicit premise that racism was a localized malignancy within a relatively healthy political and social order; it was a move to force American morality and American institutions to root out the last vestiges of the 'disease' " (Skolnick 1969:31).

The fundamental ideological thrust of the black power movement, on the other hand, derived from a conflict model of societal functioning. In response to the intransigence and unresponsiveness of white America, articulate black spokes-persons increasingly questioned the capacity of traditional goals and means to ensure the dignity and autonomy of black people in a white society. After the Kerner Commission's report was published in 1968, militancy among black people, particularly among the young, increased even further. Perhaps the most important shift in attitudes among America's blacks was the growing recognition that the racial problems were national and could not be confined to the South; that nonviolence was merely a *tactic* in a power struggle and in many instances was useless to obtain black equality and autonomy; and that racism was rooted in the society's institutions. Consequently, the primary efforts of the black power movement were to obtain a more equitable distribution of power in the many institutional spheres of American life, to search for new ideological forms, or cultural alternatives, to those of white America.

For black Americans, however, the 1960s were a decade of progress: during this period blacks experienced their greatest gains since their emancipation in 1865. These gains were brought about by the unprecedented efforts of federal, state, and local governments and private organizations to remove inequalities and redress injustices that had for years relegated black Americans to second-class citizenship.

Most visible and dramatic were the legal changes made by the federal government. For the first time in American history the three branches of the federal government acted in concert on behalf of black Americans. The Supreme Court, whose *Brown v. The Board of Education* decision had outlawed segregated schools in 1954, substantially extended the implications of the *Brown* decision, and symbolized the beginning of a new era for blacks. It outlawed state laws prohibiting racial intermarriage and racial discrimination in the rental and sale of private and public property. Moreover, it decisively rejected efforts by local school districts to evade its desegregation rulings, and unanimously supported school busing as one means of achieving that goal. President Lyndon Johnson, a Southerner, provided the most unequivocal moral and political support of black aspirations of any president in American history. Through his leadership, the Congress enacted legislation that outlawed discrimination in public accommodations, employment, housing, voting, and education. In addition, his Great Society economic programs provided federal funds to enhance occupational and educational opportunities for blacks.

By the end of the 1960s black Americans, particularly the better educated and more highly skilled, had made substantial gains both economically and educationally. One of the best indices of these changes was black median family income, which in 1959 was only half of white median family income. By 1964 it had risen to 54 percent of white income and by 1969, reflecting the economic expansion and prosperity that characterized the decade, as well as national efforts to reduce black inequalities, it had risen to 61 percent. Thus, although problems remained acute for poorly educated and unskilled black Americans, the efforts of the 1960s had clearly produced some impressive advances.

However, the civil rights movement, which during the 1960s had generally displayed consensus concerning both goals and tactics despite internal differences, was now in disarray. Part of the reason for this was the movement's very success in achieving impressive legislative and judicial victories in the '60s. But the disarray also reflected the fact that for many black Americans the optimism of the early '60s had been shattered by the failure of these legislative changes to institute meaningful changes in their lives. It became increasingly apparent that the abolition of legal barriers to public accommodations and suburban housing, for example, did not address the essential problems of a substantial portion of the black population. The erosion of the fragile consensus among blacks was symbolized by the outbreaks of the civil disorders of the late '60s, which did little to allay conscious and unconscious white anxieties concerning black demands for substantial changes in the status quo. As many whites grew weary of what they perceived as government support for lawlessness, and tired of the constant media attention to blacks, the conservative mood of the country increased, contributing to the 1968 election of Richard Nixon to the presidency.

By the early 1970s, the impetus and fervor of the black power movement was spent. The frequency of mass social unrest dramatically declined during the decade. American involvement in Indochina formally ended and the civil disorders that rent many American cities during the 1960s did not recur on a equally massive scale. The sense of concern for social justice affecting many white Americans was replaced by an indifference, even an aversion, to the problems of racial minority groups in the country. Indeed, the activism of the so-called concerned generation of the 1960s was replaced by a stance of benign neglect.

Compared to the progress achieved during the 1960s, the decade of the '70s was, at best, a period during which the rate of black advance slowed appreciably; at worst it was a time of retrogression and retrenchment.

The most dramatic advances for blacks during the 1970s were in the political arena. The tactics of public confrontations, boycotts, and demonstrations, which in the late 1950s and early '60s had been successful in effecting social change, were supplanted in the 1970s by more traditional political activity. "Politics is the civil-rights movement of the 1970s," said Maynard Jackson, the black mayor of Atlanta (Sitkoff, 1981:229). Such a stance was possible because of the increase in black political strength brought about by the Voting Rights Act of 1965, which provided federal protection for blacks' efforts to register and vote in states throughout the South. The percentage of Southern blacks registered to vote increased from 35 percent in 1964 to 65 percent in 1969. In Alabama the increase was from 19 to 61 percent; in Mississippi from 7 to 67 percent; and in Georgia from 27 to 60 percent (Polenberg, 1980:192).

The increases in black voters throughout the South substantially increased black political representation. In 1964 there were only 103 blacks holding elected offices (ranging from local school board member to president) among the nearly half-million elected officials in the entire country. By 1970 this number had increased to 1,400 and by 1984 to 5,600, two-thirds of them in the South. Moreover, the number of black mayors had increased from *none* in 1965 to over 200 in 1984, including four of the nation's six largest cities—Los Angeles, Chicago, Philadelphia, and Detroit. Finally, by 1984 the Congressional Black Caucus, comprised of black members of the House of Representatives, claimed a membership of twenty-one out of the 435 seats in that body.

Because of their strategic location in the major metropolitan areas of key industrial states, the combined voting strength of blacks represents a possible balance of power in close elections. This was demonstrated first in 1960, when

John Kennedy's narrow victory over Richard Nixon was due to the substantial margin he obtained from black voters in the industrial Northeast and Midwest. It was even more noteworthy in the 1976 election, when over 90 percent of more than six and a half million black voters opted for Jimmy Carter. Carter owed his victory margin in most of the Southern as well several Northern states— and thus his election as a whole—directly to the overwhelming support of black voters. Although his legislative record did not match his campaign promises to blacks, Carter appointed more black officials to the judiciary and to prominent positions in the executive branch of the federal government than all previous presidents combined. Finally, the increasing significance of black political power was made abundantly clear in 1984, when Jesse Jackson's candidacy electrified the black community and was instrumental in registering thousands of new black voters.

Yet despite these highly visible changes, by 1984 blacks still remained only about 1 percent of all elected officials in the country, a percentage not even closely approximately their nearly 12 percent of the total population. In the South, where blacks comprise more than 20 percent of the population, only 3 percent of the elected officials were black. Moreover, in many instances the political power that black elected officials do have today is limited by the fact that they are politically isolated. And given the exodus of white middle-class residents and businesses to the suburbs, they have gained political power without the financial resources with which to provide the jobs and services (educational, medical, police and fire protection) that their constituents most urgently need.

During the 1970s, blacks also experienced substantial gains in education. By 1975 almost identical percentages of blacks and whites (87% vs. 86%) aged 5–20 were enrolled in school; among people 25–34 the median number of school years completed by blacks was only slightly less than that for whites (12.00 for blacks vs. 12.60 for whites). In 1960 only 33 percent of blacks aged 20–24 had completed high school compared to 61 percent of whites. By 1978 73 percent of blacks and 85 percent of whites had done so. In 1960 only 4 percent of blacks and 12 percent of whites aged 24–34 had completed four or more years of college; but by 1978 comparable figures were 11 percent for blacks and 25 percent for whites. And although the black high-school dropout rate remained higher than that of whites, there was a substantial reduction in the percentage black dropouts, from 22 percent in 1968 to less than 17 percent in 1978 (compared to a decline of 11.9% to 11.3% for whites). Furthermore, a steadily increasing percentage of blacks began attending college, so that by 1977 the percentage enrolled was nearly proportional to the black population as a whole, a striking increase over the college attendance rates of blacks in the mid-'60s (Jones, 1981).

However, these statistics obscure substantial qualitative differences in black educational achievement. Ironically, black students in the South today are far more likely to attend racially integrated elementary and secondary schools than are black students in the North. Because of the patterns of residential segregation in most American cities, 70 percent of black children outside the South attend schools that are comprised predominantly of minority children. The situation is most acute in the nation's twenty-six largest cities, where three-fourths of all black children attend schools that have greater than 90 percent minority enrollment. This pattern of marked racial isolation has led to the increasing use of busing to achieve racially balanced schools. But even in circumstances where there is over-whelming evidence of state responsibility for the creation and support of the residential segregation that created racial imbalance in public schools to begin with, there has also been extraordinarily heated resistance to busing. The impor-tance of this resistance is reflected in the spate of recent Congressional proposals to restrict the courts' use of busing as a remedy for metropolitan segregation.

The narrowing of the gap in college attendance between blacks and whites obscures the fact that although black students are today found in a much wider range of educational institutions than ever before (including the nation's most selective colleges and universities), a disproportionately large percentage attend two-year junior and community colleges, and about one-third attend historically black colleges. Blacks now comprise nearly 11 percent of students enrolled in four-year colleges and universities in the United States, but they received less than 7 percent of the bachelor's degrees awarded in 1975/76. The disparity becomes even more marked at the graduate and professional levels: in 1975/76 blacks represented less than 6 percent of the graduate school enrollments, 4.5 percent of professional school enrollment, and received less than 4 percent of the doctorates awarded (Jones, 1981). Clearly, there have been significant educational advances for blacks during the past decade, but whether the educational improvements can be translated into higher economic status remains problematic.

Thus the trends in both the political and educational arenas indicate qualified improvements for black Americans. However, no such progress took place in the economic sphere, perhaps the most important institutional category. The eco-nomic gains of the 1960s were eroded by inflation, two recessions, and changes by the Nixon administration in programs that had provided job training and placement for blacks. Thus during the 1970s the income gap separating black and white widened substantially. After rising from 50 percent in 1959 to 61 percent in 1969 the ratio of median family income between blacks and whites had declined again to 56 percent in 1983. The gap in terms of absolute dollars nearly tripled, from a difference of $3,800 in 1969 to more than $11,000 in 1982.

With the exception of three years during the 1970s, the annual black unem-ployment rate has been at least double that for whites since 1954. In 1983 it stood at nearly 18 percent (17.8%) of the black labor force. The National Urban League, whose research division continually surveys black households, contends that the official unemployment rate substantially underrepresents real unemploy-ment because it does not include discouraged workers who have dropped out of the labor force entirely. Thus the Urban League's Hidden Unemployment Index, which includes such individuals, placed the 1980 unemployment figure at 25 percent—a figure equal to the national rate at the height of the great depres-sion of the 1930s (Hill, 1981). In addition, the official unemployment rate for black teenagers stood at nearly 40 percent throughout most of the decade, again more than double the rate for whites. But these figures are national averages and obscure the variations among different cities, in some of which, the Urban League estimates, the jobless rate for black teenagers may be as high as 80 percent. Thus the overall economic status of blacks Americans appears to have deteriorated during the '70s.

However, as Wilson ("The Black Community in the 1980s") points out, this deterioration in economic status was not felt uniformly throughout the black community. During the 1970s, middle-class blacks made impressive economic advances. The number of blacks in professional and managerial positions increased to two and a half times what it had been in 1965. Indeed, between 1975 and 1980 the largest gains in black employment were in higher-status occupations. During this period the number of blacks employed increased by 1.3 million, over half of them in managerial, professional, and craft jobs (Hill, 1981:22). Moreover, Wilson notes that prior to 1960 the ratio of black income to white income actually decreased as educational attainment increased, but that this pattern has now been reversed: the higher the black educational level, the more closely incomes approximate those of whites. In fact, in 1978 black males who graduated from college earned, on average, slightly more than comparable whites.

However, Wilson argues, as a result of changes in economic conditions, a segmented labor market has emerged. As a consequence, there is today a growing division among blacks between the middle class and an impoverished underclass that lacks education and job skills, is characterized by high rates of unemployment and welfare dependency, and is isolated residentially from employment opportunities. The jobs available to the underclass are what Moore ("Minorities in the American Class System") has termed *peripheral*—unskilled, low-paying, undesirable, nonunionized, and without much prospect for advancement. Therefore, the underclass has not only been unable to participate in the progress experienced by the black middle class, but its social and economic position has deteriorated. Although the black underclass is a legacy of racial discrimination, it is class and not racial factors that are primarily responsible for sustaining the underclass today. Lacking the necessary training and job skills for positions in the modern economy, members of the underclass are instead the victims of broad economic and technological changes in American society. Even if all racial prejudice and discrimination were eliminated, the black underclass would still lack the necessary qualifications with which to participate in the mainstream of the economy and would continue to be found primarily in the low-paying, unskilled sector where unemployment is extremely high. In the economic sphere institutional, not attitudinal, discrimination has become the primary source of continuing black inequalities.

Thus the economic problems confronting black Americans are those of structural discrimination. The thrust of Wilson's thesis is that major attention must be directed not only to the removal of racial barriers (which he acknowledges still confront blacks in education, politics, and especially in housing) but to the very structure of the American economy and its inability to provide opportunity for a substantial segment of its population. However, as Moore's analysis of the situation for urban Chicanos, Puerto Ricans, and American Indians demonstrates, structural discrimination transcends the specific situation of blacks. It extends to other racial-ethnic minorities who have been increasingly isolated from education and job skills and locked into poverty areas of cities whose employment opportunities have markedly diminished over the past two decades. The challenge for American society in the next decade, therefore, is not only to ensure that the barriers of racial discrimination continue to recede, but that class barriers now precluding minority access to economic opportunities are also eliminated.

The Future of Race and Ethnicity in American Life

At the 1963 March on Washington, Martin Luther King, Jr., delivered one of the most memorable speeches ever uttered by an American. In this address he spoke of his dream for the future:

> I have a dream . . . of that day when all God's children, black men and white men, Jews and Gentiles, Protestants and Catholics, will be able to join hands and sing in the words of that old Negro spiritual, "Free at last! Free at last! Thank God almighty, we are free at last.

Within two years of his historic address two of the most far reaching pieces of federal legislation to help black Americans realize this dream—the 1964 Civil Rights Act and the 1965 Voting Rights Act—were enacted. Moreover, as noted above, the predominant thrust of public policy during the late 1960s was to undermine and deny the legitimacy of the forces of ethnic and racial particularism—to eliminate the formal barriers that had previously relegated certain racial and ethnic groups to second-class citizenship. These efforts were suffused with an optimism that racial and ethnic criteria would cease to be salient issues in American life, that the dream of racial and ethnic equality of which King had so eloquently spoken would be realized.

Today, more than twenty years after King's historic address, despite the repudiation of racist ideologies and substantial changes in many facets of society, race and ethnicity remain prominent features of American life. Civil rights legislation and well-intentioned commitments on the part of many whites have not eliminated controversies over racial and ethnic matters. For example, social programs such as affirmative action, busing, and bilingual education, all of which were implemented in order to remedy the effects of past discrimination and to achieve greater equity among racial and ethnic groups, have been denounced by scholars and politicians who contend that they contravene the very goals of equality for which they were enacted. Indeed, far from withering away, debates concerning what constitutes a racially and ethnically just society, and what are the appropriate mechanisms with which to achieve it, show little sign of diminishing in intensity.

In his article, "Models of Pluralism: The New American Dilemma," Milton Gordon seeks to clarify the assumptions undergirding two contrasting models of the racially and ethnically just society. He characterizes these stances as *liberal pluralism* and *corporate pluralism*. Advocates of both positions espouse equality as a prime objective toward which American society should strive. However, they differ in their definition of the word *equality*. For the liberal pluralist it is equality of opportunity whereas it is equality of results for the corporate pluralist. Gordon contrasts the positions of these two conceptions of racial and ethnic relations on six different dimensions and delineates some of the assumptions that underlie the various conceptions of equality being debated in American society today. His analysis suggests that even if many of the social, economic, and political inequalities separating racial and ethnic groups today are successfully eliminated in the future, the debate over the proper role of race and ethnicity in American life is likely to continue.

25

Immigrants in the U.S. Labor Market

Barry R. Chiswick

In recent years, the increased internationalization of the American economy has apparently become an important feature of the United States labor market, an importance that is expected to grow in the coming decades. To the casual observer, it would seem that Filipino doctors and nurses staff inner-city hospitals; restaurants depend on Mexican kitchen help; taxis are driven by Arabs, Iranians, and West Indians; and South Asian and East Asian restaurants and groceries are appearing in ever-increasing numbers.

These perceptions are well grounded in the substantial changes that have occurred in immigration. This transformation has two dimensions: the relative increase in the number of immigrants and the dramatic change in the countries of origin of these immigrants. To discern the role of immigrants in the labor market, we need both to understand these demographic changes and to consider the labor market characteristics—including earnings—of the immigrants.

Number and Countries of Origin
The United States experienced high rates of immigration around the turn of the century. The annual

number of immigrants per thousand population in the decade 1901–10 was 10.4, that is, 10 immigrants per year per one thousand persons in the country (Table 1). As a consequence of tighter restrictions on Asian immigration, the disruption of trans-Atlantic travel during World War I, the adoption of literacy requirements in 1917, severe restrictions on southern and eastern European immigration in the 1920s—national origins quota acts of 1921 and 1924—and the Great Depression of the 1930s, immigration fell sharply. During the 1930s, only 0.4 immigrants entered per year per thousand population, and emigration among the foreign born exceeded immigration.

TABLE 1. *Annual Number of Immigrants Per One Thousand U.S. Population, 1861–1978*

Period	Rate*	Period	Rate*
1861–70	6.4	1931–40	0.4
1871–80	6.2	1941–50	0.7
1881–90	9.5	1951–60	1.5
1891–1900	5.3	1961–70	1.7
1901–10	10.4	1971–74	1.9
1911–20	5.7	1975–78	2.2
1921–30	3.5	—	—

Source: U.S. Bureau of the Census, *Statistical Abstract of the United States: 1980,* 101st ed. (Washington, DC: Government Printing Office, 1980), Table 131, p. 91.

*Rate is the annual number of immigrants per one thousand population in the years shown.

From Barry R. Chiswick, "Immigrants in the U.S. Labor Market, *The Annals* 460 (March 1982), pp. 64–72. Copyright © 1981 by the American Academy of Political and Social Science. Reprinted by permission of Sage Publications, Inc.

Immigration started increasing after World War II and has grown relative to the population ever since. This arose in part as a consequence of successive waves of refugees: Europeans from the displaced person camps in the 1940s, Hungarian freedom fighters in 1956–57, Cubans since 1959, and Southeast Asians since 1975. In addition, the numerical ceilings on nonrefugee Eastern Hemisphere immigration were increased with the 1965 amendments to the Immigration and Nationality Act, the same amendments that eliminated the national origins quota system and the discrimination against Asians. Relative to the population, immigration increased fivefold from the trough of the 1930s to the late 1970s, but this ratio was still only one-fifth of the ratio of immigrants to population in the first decade of this century (Table 1).

Most immigrants are young adults, and the slow rate of immigration from the middle 1920s through the late 1940s meant an aging foreign-born component of the labor force. The recent increases in immigration and the retirement of an earlier generation of immigrants mean that the foreign-born component of the labor force is growing and becoming younger.

Even more dramatic than the increase in numbers is a historic shift in immigration by country of origin (Table 2). During the 1950s, over half of the immigrants were from Europe, predominantly northern and western Europe. Canada and Mexico were also important sources. The rest of the world—Asia, Africa, Oceania, and Latin America—supplied about one-fifth of the immigrants. As a consequence of the abolition of the national origins quota system, together with Cuban and Southeast Asian refugee flows, the source countries have changed sharply. In the period of 1971–78, Europe and Canada accounted for 23 percent of the immigrants rather than the 68 percent in the 1950s, while the Mexican share increased from 12 percent to 15 percent. Asians accounted for one-third and other parts of the Western Hemisphere—

TABLE 2. *Immigrants by Country of Last Permanent Residence, 1820–1978 (in percentages)*

Country	Period			
	1820–1978	1951–60	1961–70	1971–78
Europe	74.4	52.7	33.8	19.0
Austria-Hungary	8.9	4.1	0.8	0.4
Germany	14.3	19.0	5.7	1.7
Great Britain	10.1	7.8	6.3	3.0
Ireland	9.7	2.3	1.1	0.3
Italy	10.9	7.4	6.4	3.4
USSR	6.9	0.02	0.1	0.8
Asia	5.9	6.1	12.9	33.4
China and Hong Kong	1.5	1.0	3.3	5.0
Korea	0.5	0.2	1.0	5.9
Philippines	0.8	0.8	3.0	7.8
Vietnam	0.2	0.1	0.1	3.1
America	18.6	39.6	51.7	45.1
Canada	8.4	15.0	12.4	3.9
Cuba	1.1	3.1	6.3	6.7
Mexico	4.4	11.9	13.7	15.2
West Indies	1.5	1.2	4.0	5.8
Africa	0.3	0.6	0.9	1.6
All Other	0.8	1.0	0.8	0.9
Total	100.0	100.0	100.0	100.0

Source: U.S. Bureau of the Census, *Statistical Abstract of the United States: 1980*, 101st ed. (Washington, DC: Government Printing Office, 1980), Table 134, p. 93.

Note: Not all country categories are included within continent categories. Detail may not add to total because of rounding.

excluding Canada and Mexico—accounted for over one-quarter of the immigrants in 1971–78.

Criteria for Legal Immigration

Under current law the criteria for entry of legal immigrants to the United States are primarily based on kinship ties. The immediate relatives of U.S. citizens—spouse, minor children, and parents—can enter the United States and are not subject to numerical limitation. In recent years, they have numbered about 125,000. There is now an annual worldwide ceiling of 270,000 visas for other types of immigrants, with an annual 20,000 visa limit for each independent country, of which at least 216,000 visas are reserved for other relatives of U.S. citizens and of resident aliens. At most, 54,000 visas are reserved for the skill-based occupational preferences—professionals and other skilled workers. However, about two-thirds of the occupational preference visas are used by the spouses and minor children of the workers who receive labor certification.

The Refugee Act of 1980 raised the annual quota of refugees to 50,000 per year and removed the restriction that a refugee had to be fleeing either a Communist regime or the general area of the Middle East. As in the past, the attorney general and the president have the authority to parole into the United States additional refugees in emergency situations, and indeed, about 125,000 Cuban "freedom flotilla" refugees were accepted just months after the passage of the act. It is largely due to emergency admissions of refugees that annual legal immigration to the United States has substantially exceeded the total of 400,000 envisioned in the 1965 legislation.[1]

Illegal Immigration

It is generally believed that there has also been a substantial increase in illegal immigration to the United States in the past few decades. It is difficult to obtain reliable data on illegal aliens since this population has an obvious incentive to avoid revealing its identity. The number of deportable aliens located by the Immigration and Naturalization Service (INS) increased nearly 15-fold in two decades—from 70,684 in 1960 to 110,371 in 1965; 345,353 in 1970; 766,600 in 1975; and in excess of one million since 1977.[2] Of the nearly 1.1 million apprehensions in fiscal year 1978, 90 percent were Mexican nationals who "entered without inspection" (EWIs), that is, they slipped across the border; three percent were Mexican nationals who either violated their visas or entered with fraudulent visas; two percent were non-Mexicans who entered without inspection; and six percent were non-Mexicans who were visa abusers or used fraudulent documents. Of the Mexican nationals apprehended, only 22 percent were women and children.

These data are not representative of the illegal alien population residing in the United States. Apprehensions are a function not simply of the flow of illegal aliens but also of INS enforcement policies. Apprehensions per million dollars of enforcement resources are greater if these resources are concentrated along the Mexican border—hence a large number of male Mexican EWIs appear in the data. Since there are virtually no costs incurred by the illegal alien from having been arrested near the U.S.-Mexican border at the time of entry, in contrast to apprehension after having penetrated further into the United States, many believe current policy involves a virtual revolving door with little net deterrent effect.

The stock of illegal aliens residing in the United States at any one time is a function not just of successful entry, but also of the re-emigration of illegal aliens. Studies done in Mexican villages suggest that there is much to-and-fro migration and that many of these migrants view illegal employment in the United States as temporary.[3] The extent of return-and-repeat illegal immigration is probably less for non-Mexican nationals, since they incur greater costs in illegal entry. A recent preliminary report prepared by the U.S. Bureau of the Census concluded that there were at least 3.5 million but probably less than six million illegal aliens in the United States, with Mexican nationals constituting about half of the illegal alien population.[4]

The data on the growth in apprehensions support the contention of many that the flow of illegal aliens from Mexico and elsewhere has increased sharply in the past two decades. Several reasons have been offered for this development. Perhaps first and foremost is that Mexico and other countries in Central America and the Caribbean are experiencing rapid increases in their young adult populations spurred by high birthrates and falling infant mortality rates in recent decades. The increased competition for jobs is encouraging search for work elsewhere. Modern communications and transportation have provided the information and means for migrating, legally or otherwise, to places where there are job opportunities better than those available in the home country, even if these jobs offer low wages by the standards of the host country.

In addition, during the period 1942–64 thousands of Mexican farm workers were temporarily employed in the United States during the harvest in the bracero program. After this program was phased out in the middle 1960s, some Mexican workers continued the cyclical—temporary—work pattern, but now their status was that of illegal alien.[5] Also, the 1965 amendments introduced numerical limits on immigration from the independent countries in the Western Hemisphere, limits that were apparently imposed in response to growing immigration from Mexico and the Caribbean. As a consequence, immigration queues have formed for Mexico and some Caribbean islands where the supply of immigrants exceeds the number of visas available.

The Productivity of Immigrants

The productivity of adult immigrants in the labor market can be compared with the productivity of the adult native-born population. In the fairly competitive labor markets that exist in the United States, productivity can be approximated by earnings—that is, wage, salary, and self-employment income—and occupational status. To provide a structure for this comparison, it is useful to think in terms of two characteristics of immigrants: the degree of favorable self-selection for labor market success and the extent of the transferability of their skills.

International migration is determined by the costs and benefits from moving from one country to another, the resources to finance the investment in moving and relocating, and the legal barriers to leaving the country of origin and entering the country of destination. International migrants can be classifed by a trichotomy: eco-

nomic migrants, tied—kinship—migrants, and refugees. Economic migrants have as a primary consideration in the benefit-and-cost calculations their earnings in the origin and the destination. Tied or kinship migrants are persons whose migration decision is heavily influenced by the migration decision of a family member rather than by their own economic opportunities. Refugee migration decisions are heavily influenced by concerns for the safety of one's person or property, with more narrowly defined economic opportunities at best playing a minor role.[6]

Economic migrants are, therefore, more intensely self-selected for their economic success in the destination and they can be expected to receive the largest economic gain from moving. They tend to be more able, aggressive, ambitious, and entrepreneurial. Earnings potential in the destination is less relevant for tied movers and for refugees, since other considerations affect the migration decision. Economic migrants tend to be young adults, whereas groups of tied movers and refugees are more likely to include middle-aged workers. Economic migrants are likely to have more highly transferable skills than either tied movers or refugees, since economic benefits are their primary motivation. Family members and refugees whose skills may be of little value in the United States—for example, Vietnamese lawyers—make the move for other than economic reasons. This suggests that, other things being the same, economic migrants will have an easier adjustment and be more successful in the U.S. labor market than will refugees and tied movers.

These considerations help put into focus the labor market experiences of immigrants. Immigrants initially experience downward occupational mobility, but their occupational status increases with the number of years in the United States. Studies using longitudinal data on occupational status in the 1970 Census of Population indicate that male immigrants who have been in the United States less than five years are in lower-status occupations than their preimmigration occupations. With the passage of time in the United States, however, the occupational status of immigrants rises more rapidly than the occupational status of the native born.[7] The initial downward mobility results from the less-than-perfect international transferability of skills, whereas the more rapid subsequent upward mobility results from the adjustment of previously acquired skills to the U.S. labor market. The U-shaped pattern is shallow for immigrants with highly transferable skills (immigrants from developed English-speaking countries), deeper for economic migrants with less transferable skills (immigrants from non-English-speaking countries), and deepest for refugees, since their skills are the least transferable (Cubans and Vietnamese).

In terms of earnings, immigrants on average do well in comparison with the native born.[8] According to the 1970 Census of Population, native-born and foreign-born adult white men had approximately the same earnings, $9700, in 1969. This similarity in earnings arose from offsetting effects. The foreign born had one year less schooling—10.8 years instead of 11.9 years—but were less likely to live in low earnings areas, such as the South and rural places. Perhaps most interesting is the relation between earnings and duration of residence. On arrival, white male immigrants earn less than similarly situated native-born men, that is, men of the same schooling, age, marital status, and place of residence, but their earnings rise sharply at first and then increase more slowly with duration of residence. Earnings parity with the native born is reached by immigrants who have been in the United States 11 to 15 years, and thereafter the foreign born have higher earnings. For example, among adult white men, the foreign born who have been in the United States for 20 years earn six percent more than the native born, other things being the same.

When earnings analyses for men are done within race/ethnic groups, for example, comparing white immigrants with white natives, Mexican immigrants with native-born Mexican-origin men, several notable patterns emerge. First, within each of five race/ethnic groups—white, Mexican, black, Filipino, and Japanese—the earnings of economic migrants reach those of the native born, other things being the same, at 11 to 15 years of residence in the United States, with the foreign born who have been in the United States more than 15 years having higher earnings. Second, schooling and country-of-origin labor

market experience have smaller positive effects on earnings in the United States among economic migrants than among the native born. Third, refugees have lower earnings than economic migrants, and schooling and country-of-origin labor market experience have smaller effects on their earnings. Fourth, although earnings rise sharply with U.S. experience for refugees, an earnings parity with the native born either never occurs or takes much longer than for economic migrants.

Although it is difficult to differentiate economic migrants and tied movers in most data sets, some studies have attempted to make this differentiation, with interesting results. Women who accompany their husbands in international migrations are more likely to be tied movers than are women who migrate as single persons. In analyses of census data, the former have lower earnings, about three percent lower among white women. Other data have shown that seven years after immigration, those who immigrated under the kinship preferences have significantly lower earnings than those who immigrated under the occupational preferences.[9] Among native-born internal migrants within the United States, those who are tied movers tend to have higher unemployment rates and lower earnings.[10]

If there is a more intense favorable self-selection of immigrants, one would expect that to some extent this would be transmitted to their native-born children. There would, however, presumably be a "regression to the mean," that is, the effect would diminish with each successive generation. Data from the 1970 Census of Population and the National Longitudinal Survey of adult men suggests that, other things being equal, including race or ethnic origin, second-generation American men—native born with foreign-born parents—earn five to ten percent more than American men with both parents native born. Comparing third-generation white male Americans with those whose four grandparents were born in the United States reveals that the earnings of the former are about the same or up to four percent higher, depending on the number of foreign-born grandparents—roughly one percentage point per foreign-born grandparent!

There tend, however, to be differences by race and ethnic background in the levels of education and earnings among first- and second-generation Americans. Mexican-origin men, for example, have lower levels of schooling and, taking into account schooling level, lower earnings than other white men. Indeed, Mexican-origin men earn 15 to 25 percent less than Anglos, and the difference does not appear to diminish with the number of generations that the person's family has lived in the United States.

Labor Market Characteristics of Illegal Aliens

There are also some data on the labor market characteristics of illegal aliens. In 1975 David North and Marion Houstoun administered an extensive questionnaire to 800 apprehended illegal aliens who had worked in the United States for at least two weeks. Analyses of these data offer interesting findings and indicate that the data do not support the view that illegal aliens are locked into low-wage, dead-end jobs.[11]

Most of these illegal aliens were in the United States for only a short period of time—as the average length of stay was only two years. The occupational distribution in the United States of the apprehended illegal aliens from Mexico was very similar to that of Mexican immigrants who had been in the United States less than five years, as reported in the 1970 Census. The occupational distribution of the illegal aliens seemed to increase with the level of development of the country of origin, but the increase was smaller than the increase in the occupational distribution of legal immigrants.

Although the federal minimum wage in 1975 was $2.10 per hour for nonfarm work and $1.80 per hour for farm work, the average wage of the Mexican illegal aliens was $2.34 per hour; the wage averaged $3.05 per hour for other Western Hemisphere illegal aliens and $4.08 per hour for the Eastern Hemisphere illegal aliens.

As is the case among legal immigrants, earnings among the illegal aliens were higher for those with more schooling and more labor-market experience in the country of origin; this was true for Mexican as well as other illegal aliens. For both Mexican and non-Mexican apprehended illegal aliens, earnings rise with the duration of U.S. residence, particularly during the first few years.

Conclusion

Immigrants are playing, and are increasingly going to play, an important role in the U.S. labor market. Whereas earlier waves of immigrants were predominantly from Europe and Canada, the absolute and relative numbers of immigrants from these areas have declined, with immigration from Latin America, the Caribbean, and Asia growing sharply. Overall, immigrants appear to adapt very well to the U.S. labor market. There are, however, variations in economic success by level of schooling, motive for migrating, and country of origin.

A better understanding of these trends and differences in economic adjustment is important for immigration policy formation. Since neither a completely open door nor a completely closed door is a realistic policy alternative, immigration policy should be based on a consideration of the impacts of alternative numbers of immigrants, criteria for rationing immigrations visas, and levels of enforcement of immigration law.

ENDNOTES
1. Since 1959, when Castro came to power, over one million Cubans have immigrated to the United States, and since 1975 over one-half million Southeast Asians have been admitted.

2. Apprehensions dipped below one million in 1980, apparently because of a moratorium on interior enforcement to facilitate taking the 1980 census and because of a diversion of INS resources to register Iranian students and refugees in the Cuban "freedom flotilla." The data are from U.S. Department of Justice, *1978 Statistical Yearbook: Immigration and Naturalization Service* (Washington, DC: Government Printing Office, 1980), Table 23.

3. See, for example, Wayne Cornelius, "Mexican Migration to the United States: The View from Rural Sending Communities," mimeographed (Cambridge: Migration and Development Study Group, Massachusetts Institute of Technology, 1976).

4. Jacob S. Siegel, Jeffrey S. Passel, and J. Gregory Robinson, "Preliminary Review of Existing Studies of Illegal Residents in the United States," mimeographed (Washington, DC: U.S. Bureau of the Census, 1980).

5. In 1960, for example, 427,240 Mexicans and 20,000 workers of other nationalities entered the United States on temporary work permits as agricultural laborers. In 1979, less than 14,000 agricultural laborers and woodsmen were admitted, primarily from the

West Indies. These data include multiple admissions of the same individuals. U.S. Bureau of the Census, *Statistical Abstract of the United States: 1980,* 101st ed. (Washington, DC: Government Printing Office, 1980), Table 140, p. 96.

6. One needs to be careful to avoid confusing motives for migrating with the preference category used to enter a country. Refugee migration movements often include many economic migrants and tied movers, and economic migrants may use kinship ties as a mechanism for gaining entry into a country.

7. See Barry R. Chiswick, "A Longitudinal Analysis of the Occupational Mobility of Immigrants," in *Proceedings of the 30th Annual Winter Meeting, Industrial Relations Research Association* ed. Barbara Dennis (Madison, WI: IRRA, 1978), pp. 20–27; David S. North, *Seven Years Later: The Experiences of the 1970 Cohort of Immigrants in the U.S. Labor Market* (Washington, DC: Linton, 1978), pp. 102–13; Barry Stein; "Occupational Adjustment of Refugees: The Vietnamese in the United States," *International Migration Review* 13: 24–45 (Spring 1979).

8. Unless noted otherwise, the empirical findings reported in the rest of this section are based on detailed research findings in Barry R. Chiswick, "The Economic Progress of Immigrants: Some Apparently Universal Patterns," in *Contemporary Economic Problems 1979* ed. William Fellner (Washington, DC: American Enterprise Institute, 1979), pp. 359–99; idem, *An Analysis of the Economic Progress and Impact of Immigrants* (Chicago: Department of Economics and Survey Research Laboratory, University of Illinois—Chicago Circle, 1980), chs. 3–12.

9. North, *Seven Years Later,* pp. 102–4, B–9.

10. Jacob Mincer, "Family Migration Decisions," *Journal of Political Economy,* 86: 749–74 (Oct. 1978).

11. David S. North and Marion F. Houstoun, *The Characteristics and Role of Illegal Aliens in the U.S. Labor Market: An Exploratory Study* (Washington, DC: Linton, 1976); Barry R. Chiswick, "Illegal Aliens in the U.S. Labor Market" (Paper presented at Sixth World Congress, International Economics Association, Mexico City, Aug. 1980).

26

Illegal Immigration and the International System: Lessons From Recent Legal Mexican Immigrants To the United States*

Alejandro Portes

To assess the foreign policy implications of a new immigration policy, one must first understand its domestic implications for the countries involved. My purpose in this paper is to examine the internal significance of illegal or undocumented immigration for the countries where it originates, as a necessary background against which to evaluate the Carter Administration's proposed policies. For this purpose, I will present data from an ongoing study of Mexican immigration, one addressing at least some of the questions generally asked about the nature of the movement. On the basis of these data and other recent studies, I will analyze (briefly) the Administration's policies for dealing with this illegal flow.

Reprinted from SOCIAL PROBLEMS 26:4 (April 1979): 425–438, by permission of the The Society for the Study of Social Problems and the author. © The Society for the Study of Social Problems.

*Paper presented at the session on "Undocumented Mexican Workers" meetings of the Society for the Study of Social Problems, San Francisco, September 1978. This is a modified version of a statement originally delivered at the hearings on "Undocumented Workers: Implications for U.S. Policy in the Western Hemisphere" held by the U.S. House Subcommittee on Inter-American Affairs, Washington, D.C., July 26, 1978. The data are part of the project "Latin American Immigrant Minorities in the United States," supported by grants MH 27666-03 from the National Institute of Mental Health and SOC 77-22089 from the National Science Foundation.

It is important to begin by clarifying what illegal immigration is *not*. It is not, first of all, a flow coming from a single country. The overwhelming representation of Mexico in apprehension statistics is, in part, a function of the development practices of the Border Patrol, which tends to concentrate its efforts along the southern border. Although Mexican immigrants are certainly a majority of the illegal or undocumented population, the proportional representation of other countries—especially those from the Caribbean—is not insignificant (Office of the U.S. Attorney General, 1978). A relatively novel twist in Caribbean immigration is furnished by Dominican workers who are reported to enter the United States surreptitiously by crossing the Mona passage into Puerto Rico. Illegal immigration, then, should not be conceived simply as a process involving only Mexico and the United States, but as one originating in several peripheral societies.

Second, illegal immigration is not only caused by "push" forces in the original countries, but by the needs and demands of the receiving economy. The relative stability of the illegal flow, year after year, cannot be attributed to an impoverished alien population "overwhelming" the U.S. borders; it must be acknowledged that this flow of immigrants fulfills important needs for agricultural and urban industrial firms in the United States. Clearly, the persisting relationship illegal immigration creates is a symbiotic one, simultaneously fulfilling concealed but nonetheless real economic needs—on both sides of the border (see Portes, 1977a, b; Bach 1978b).

Third, illegal immigration is not primarily a movement of economic "refugees" in search of welfare, but one of workers in search of job opportunities. The illegal flow is, above all, a displacement of labor. More specifically, it is a displacement of low-wage labor, advantageous for many enterprises.

Fourth, illegal immigration is not necessarily permanent. Available studies of Mexican immigration at its points of origin, as well as data from this study, suggest that there is a significant proportion of return migration. The dominant stereotype concerning illegal immigration still couples the image of "impoverished masses overwhelming the border" with the idea that those who cross the gates of the land-of-plenty do so never to return. But empirical research suggests that many illegal immigrants do return and the the process is a complex one often involving cyclical entries and departures from the United States (see Cornelius, 1978). Reasons for this pattern are not difficult to understand once one realizes that, although work-opportunities and wages are higher in the United States, the money saved from wages can be used for consumption or reinvestment at much higher rates in the country of origin.

The aspects of illegal immigration just reviewed are not, however, the only commonly-held ideas about the nature of illegal immigration. They are merely the ones most convincingly clarified by past research. The following results begin to address a fifth and so far underresearched aspect—the socioeconomic backgrounds and present characteristics of the immigrants themselves.

The Study
The data presented below come from a study of 822 documented Mexican immigrants interviewed at the point of arrival in the United States during 1972–73. Interviews were conducted in Spanish immediately after completion of immigration formalities. Interviews took place over a nine-month period at border check points in El Paso and Laredo. These are the two major ports of entry along the Texas border, and second and third, respectively, for Mexican immigrants in the nation.

Because of the exploratory nature of the study, the sample was limited to males in the economically productive ages, 18 to 60. Among Mexican immigrants, this group can be assumed to comprise the majority of family heads and self-supporting individuals. Immigrants were interviewed on a first-come basis during regular office hours. A few who crossed at night could not be interviewed. The refusal rate was less than 2 percent.

Statistical comparisons show that this sample is unbiased with respect to the universe of Mexican immigrants during fiscal year 1973 in such characteristics as average age, occupation and education. Because of the geographic location of field sites, the sample does overestimate immigrants originating in central and eastern Mexico and destined for Texas, Arizona, New Mexico and Illinois, and underestimates those originating in western Mexico and destined for California. Except for the latter limitation, the sample appears generally representative of legal Mexican immigration.

The question then is, what relevance does this sample have for illegal immigration? Several past studies have noted the intimate relationship between undocumented Mexican immigration to the United States. The reason is that illegal immigrants can frequently manage to regularize their status through the "family reunification" provision of the 1965 Immigration Law. According to the previous studies, legal Mexican immigration differs from most immigrant flows in the past because most of the people involved are not first-comers, but already *de facto* residents of the United States (see Stoddard, 1976).

Results from the present study confirm this impression. Fully 43.7 percent of the sample came outside immigration quota limits as spouses of U.S. citizens (IR-1 visas). An additional 4.7 percent came as children of U.S. citizens (IR-2 visas). The Immigration and Naturalization Service does not break down figures on quota immigrants from the Western Hemisphere (SA-1 visas) by specific categories. Our belief is, however, that most of the 46.5 percent of quota immigrants in the sample received visas as spouses or immediate relatives of U.S. permanent residents.

When asked, 61.5 percent said they had resided previously in the United States. That figure is probably an underestimate, because some respondents might have been reluctant to report prior (illegal) entry: collating responses to a number of other relevant questions, we arrived at an estimate that 69.9 percent of the sample could be reliably regarded as having resided in the United States for extended periods prior to documented entry.

The point of these figures is that the study of legal Mexican immigration is, to a large extent, identical to that of *prior* illegal immigration. No claim is made that former illegal immigrants identified in this manner are representative of the total illegal population. They represent, however, an important and so far unresearched sector of that universe. Their characteristics ideally should be compared with those of illegals identified by other means, such as official apprehensions. Still, the present data offer an initial glimpse of those immigrants who have not only succeeded in remaining in the United States, but have consolidated their position through legal entry.

Results

Everyone concerned with the process believes that illegal immigration occurs because of economic reasons: immigrants come to take advantage of the superior economic opportunities offered by a developed economy. The usual companion impression is that illegal immigrants must come from the most impoverished and backward sectors of their country of origin. In the specific case of Mexico, undocumented migration to the United States has, for decades, been associated with the plight of a largely illiterate and dispossessed rural population (Briggs, 1978; Santibanez, 1930). The dominant image held of surreptitious border crossers has been that they are peasants, frequently unemployed at home and coming to perform agricultural work in the United States.

Tables 1 to 7, drawn from the present sample, afford the opportunity to test these assertions. First, there is no doubt that immigration from Mexico occurs for economic reasons. Asked for their main reason for coming to the U.S., 49.5

percent of immigrants in the sample responded in terms of work, wages and living conditions. This percentage equals those for all other response categories put together. Further, when asked what they considered was the major problem confronting Mexico, 61.1 percent mentioned poverty, unemployment, high prices and other economic difficulties (Table 1).

The hypothesis that immigrants come predominantly from rural communities is examined in Table 2 by comparing their community of origin (main locality of residence before age 16) with those of the overall population of Mexico. As seen in Table 2 the immigrant sample as a whole and immigrants with prior residence in the United States are more "urban" than the original population. In Mexico, 58 percent of the population lived in communities of less than 10,000 in 1970; so did 37.3 percent of all immigrants and 43.6 percent of immigrants with prior U.S. residence. Forty-eight percent of the formerly undocumented immigrants, however, came from urban communities of 20,000 or more; and the figure for the total Mexican population is only 35 percent.

A related notion is that illegal immigrants are destined primarily to small agricultural communities in the United States. This rural-to-rural migration pattern has figured prominently in most prior descriptions of the flow (Santibanez, 1930; Buroway, 1976). Table 3 presents the size-distribution of communities where immigrants intended to reside. Only 15.5 percent of the total sample and 16.4 percent of immigrants with prior U.S. residence planned to live in communities of 10,000 or less. At the other extreme, fully 73 percent of both formerly undocumented immigrants and of the total sample planned to reside in cities of 100,000 or more; of these, 54 and 46 percent, respectively, planned to live in cities of over half a million. Clearly, these immigrants not only come from cities in Mexico, far more than the majority intend to seek residence in metropolitan areas of the United States.

A third characteristic imputed to illegal Mexican immigrants is that they are either illiterates or come from the least educated sectors of the source population. In one of the best available studies, Samora (1971) found that 28 percent of apprehended *mojados* had never attended school.

TABLE 1. *Salience of Economic Problems for Recent Mexican Immigrants to the United States 1972–73*

Main Reason for Coming to the U.S.	%	Major Problem Confronting Mexico at Present	%
Reunite with family	28.3	No Major Problems	7.5
Work, wages, better living conditions	49.5	*Economic Problems:* Poverty, unemployment, high prices, housing, etc.	61.1
Education for self and children	9.7	*Legal and Political Problems:* Corruption, inefficient bureaucracy, antiquated laws, lack of democracy, etc.	13.7
Self-improvement in general, achieve independence	4.3		
To learn more	1.7		
Likes the U.S.	2.9	*Class Inequality:* Indifference of the rich, exploitation of the people, control by those on top	1.8
Other reasons	3.7		
Total	100.0 (N = 818)[1]	*Educational Problems:* Lack of schools, teachers, illiteracy, etc.	7.0
		Crime Problems: Thieves, alcoholism, prostitution, drugs, etc.	6.3
		Other Problems	2.6
		Total	100.0 (N = 732)[2]

[1]Missing data = 4.
[2]Excludes 90 people who did not know or did not answer.

TABLE 2. *Size-Class of Community of Origin of Mexican Immigrants and Distribution of Total Mexican Population*

Population	Immigrant's Community of Origin, 1972–73[1]		Mexico-1970[2] %
	Prior Residence in the U.S. %	Total Sample %	
9,999 or less	43.6	37.3	57.7
10,000–19,999	8.3	7.1	7.1
20,000–99,999	20.2	20.5	12.0
100,000 or more	27.9	35.1	23.2
Totals	100.0 (N = 564)	100.0 (N = 808)[3]	100.0 (N = 48,381,547)

[1]Source: Project data.
[2]Source: U.N., *Demographic Yearbook,* 1971–Table 10. Copyright United Nations, 1971. Reproduced by permission.
[3]Missing data = 14.

TABLE 3. *Size-Class of Community of Destination of Mexican Immigrants, 1972–73*

Population of Intended U.S. Community of Residence	Immigrants with Prior U.S. Residence %	Total Sample %
9,999 or less	16.4	15.5
10,000–19,999	1.8	1.8
20,000–99,999	9.0	9.8
100,000–499,999	18.7	26.5
500,000 or more	54.1	46.4
Totals	100.0 (N = 567)	100.0 (N = 812)[1]

[1]Missing data = 10.

Similarly, North and Houstoun (1976) reported that 43.5 percent of their sample of apprehended Mexican immigrants had received 4 years of education or less. These conclusions can again be examined on the basis of the present data. Figures in Table 4 compare various indicators of educational attainment for the immigrants studied and for the Mexican population. As seen in Table 4, the proportion of illiterates among such immigrants is much lower than for all adult Mexicans. Similarly, the percentages of immigrants (both the total set and those with prior U.S. residence) who completed primary education or had at least some secondary education is almost twice as high as the corresponding figure for the adult Mexican population. Clearly, while these immigrants by no means belong to the university-trained elite, they are from among those in the working class who have had at least some access to formal schooling and, in the process, acquired modest educational credentials.

Finally, there is the question of occupational background. Again, the stereotype is that illegal Mexican immigrants are predominantly landless peasants and agricultural workers. In 1970, close to 40 percent of Mexican's economically active population was employed in the agrarian sector, so the proportion among illegal immigrants should if anything, be higher. Table 5 presents data on occupational sector for our immigrant sample.

TABLE 4. *Education of Mexican Immigrants and Comparative Figures for the Mexican Population*

Education	Mexican Immigrants-1973		Mexican Population
	Prior Residence in the U.S. %	Total Sample %	15 Years of Age and Older–1970 %
Percent Illiterate (less than 2 years of formal schooling)	3.4	3.0	21.9[1]
Percent Completing Primary School or Higher	58.7	65.4	31.0[1]
Percent with Some Secondary Schooling	26.6	32.4	15.2
Percent Completing Secondary School or Higher	5.3 (N = 563)	5.5 (N = 806)[2]	4.7

[1]Male Population only.
[2]Missing data = 16.

TABLE 5. *Last and Next-to-Last Sector of Employment of Mexican Immigrants, 1972–73*

	Last Occupation		Next-to-Last Occupation	
	Immigrants with Prior U.S. Residence %	Total Sample %	Immigrants with Prior U.S. Residence %	Total Sample %
Sector				
Out of labor market	1.9	6.1	6.7	15.2
Agriculture, Fishing, Mining	12.2	11.2	18.3	16.3
Manufacturing	29.3	24.0	22.7	17.9
Construction	17.3	15.1	15.5	13.0
Transport, Commerce, and Related Services	15.4	18.4	18.2	18.7
Personal Services	23.9	25.2	18.6	18.9
Totals	100.0	100.0	100.0	100.0
	(N = 566)	(N = 808)[1]	(N = 555)	(N = 794)[2]

[1]Missing data = 14.
[2]Missing data = 28.

(Last and next-to-last occupations are included because immigrants with prior residence in the United States probably were last employed in *this* country. By asking a question concerning employment prior to the last one, we hoped to approximate their original occupation. Results are, however, similar in both cases.)

Only 12 percent (both of the total sample and of these immigrants with prior U.S. residence) were *last* employed in agriculture and other extractive activities. In contrast, a fourth of both samples were last employed in manufacturing, while transport, commerce and personal services had employed an additional two-fifths. *Next*-to-last employment was in agriculture and other extractive industries for nearly 20 percent of these formerly undocumented immigrants, but much higher percentages had been in manufacturing and service occupations instead; in fact the latter category was the next-to-last occupation of over a third of the total sample and of those with prior U.S. residence. It should also be noted that rates of reported *un*employment decreased significantly in the period from next-to-last to last occupation, and were especially low among former illegal immigrants (1.9%).

A related question is that of what occupations these immigrants originally had. The relevant data are presented in Table 6. Frequencies for main and next-to-last occupations are pre-sented. (Main occupation refers to the job the immigrant declared he had mostly pursued as an adult.) Results for both variables are again similar. Agricultural labor represents 12 percent of the distribution for main occupations and close to a fifth for next-to-last occupation. But the modal category in both cases is "skilled and semiskilled urban worker," followed by that of "unskilled worker and urban service laborer." Close to half of the immigrants declared skilled and semiskilled trades as their main occupation, and a third had such trades as their next-to-last occupation. Roughly a fourth of the sample, finally, reported unskilled and minor urban service occupations as main and next-to-last occupations.

These results contradict the common impression that illegal Mexican immigrants are mostly rural workers. Most men in the sample are manual workers, but in urban-based occupations. And most of these immigrants, whether formerly undocumented or new arrivals, do not intend to pursue farm occupations in the United States. Table 7 compares the occupational distribution for the total U.S. population with: (a) the universe of immigrants arriving in 1974; (b) the total legal Mexican immigration during that year; and (c) formerly undocumented immigrants in the sample.

Among all legal immigrants to the United

TABLE 6. *Main and Next-to-Last Occupation of Mexican Immigrants, 1972–73*

Occupational Level	Main Occupation		Next-to-Last Occupation	
	Immigrants with Prior U.S. Residence %	Total Sample %	Prior U.S. Residence %	Total Sample %
Out of labor market	2.5	6.5	6.5	15.1
Agricultural laborer	12.5	11.6	17.7	15.5
Minor urban service laborer and unskilled worker	24.7	21.4	29.6	25.0
Semi-skilled and skilled urban worker	50.5	46.2	34.3	31.1
Intermediate urban service and white-collar worker	8.2	12.5	11.2	12.3
Manager and Professional	1.6	1.8	0.7	1.0
Totals	100.0 (N = 556)	100.0[1] (N = 799)	100.0 (N = 554)	100.0[2] (N = 796)

[1]Missing data = 23.
[2]Missing data = 26.

States in recent years (i.e., those from all nations), the percentage of professionals and technicians has been higher than that among the total U.S. population. This has not been the case, however, for Mexican immigrants, among whom the proportion of highly-trained occupations is insignificant. This trend again confirms the distinct character of Mexican immigration and its ability to bypass occupational certification requirements of the Immigration Law by taking advantage of family reunion provisions.

Farm work is not, however, the modal *intended* occupation for Mexican immigrants. For the total 1974 Mexican immigrant cohort, Table 7 shows that the proportion of farm laborers is 4 percent, essentially the same as for total immigration during the year. Among sample immigrants with prior U.S. residence, the proportion increases to 11 percent, but it is still a minority. The bulk of Mexican immigrants concentrates in the category of nonfarm laborer—unskilled and semiskilled urban workers. Other substantial percentages are found in the categories of service workers and of craftsmen and operatives, all urban-based occupations. This holds true both for the universe of legal Mexican immigrants and for our sample of formerly undocumented ones.

Several caveats are clearly in order at this point. First, these results refer only to Mexican immigration. As seen above, illegal immigration comes at present from several countries. Second, the data for illegal immigrants refer only to a sample of those who have regularized their situation in the United States. Such a group cannot be taken as representative of the total population of illegal Mexican immigrants. Studies based on interviews of apprehended illegals, such as those by Samora (1971) and North and Houstoun (1976), report findings in closer agreement with the generalized image of illegal immigration. The relative numerical significance of the different immigrant profiles emerging from alternative research and sampling strategies remains to be determined.

Nevertheless, it is still remarkable how systematically the present sample differs from the conventional image of illegal immigration. To summarize, most of these immigrants with prior residence in the United States came from cities in Mexico and were bound for metropolitan areas in the United States. Most were literate and, as a whole, exceeded the educational attainment of the source population. Only one-eighth had worked mostly as farm laborers or in related activities; the vast majority were concentrated in urban occupations—manufacturing and service. *Intended* first occupations in the United States were also overwhelmingly urban.

TABLE 7. *Occupational Distribution of Active U.S. Labor Force, Total Fiscal Year 1974 Immigrants, Total Mexican Immigrants, and Immigrants with Prior U.S. Residence*

Category	U.S.–1970[1]	Declared First Occupation in the U.S.		
		FY 74[2] Immigrants	FY 74[2] Mexican Immigrants	Mexican Immigrants with Prior U.S. Residence 1972–73[3]
Professional, Technical, and Kindred	14.1	23.5	2.2	0.8
Managers and Proprietors	14.1	6.1	1.4	0.6
Farmers and Farm Managers	3.0	—	—	—
Clerical and Sales	12.7	10.7	3.5	4.9
Craftsmen and Kindred	20.9	13.2	7.7	18.5
Operatives	17.9	11.9	7.9	
Service Workers Including Private Household	8.2	17.8	27.5	11.9
Laborers, except Farm	7.3	12.1	45.4	52.7
Farm Laborers	1.8	4.7	4.4	10.6
Total	100.0	100.0	100.0	100.0

[1]As percentage of the occupationally active population. Source: *U.S. Census, Current Population Report-Persons of Spanish Origin in the U.S.-Series P–20, No. 380, 1975.*

[2]As percentage of occupationally active immigrants. Source: U.S. Immigration and Naturalization Service, *1975 Annual Report.*

[3]Recoded occupational category estimates for comparison with census classification Source: Project data.

Given the probable importance of the universe represented by these immigrants, one must then ask why results are so different from conventional expectations. To answer, one must entertain a perspective contrasting markedly with that held by most scholars and by the general public.

Immigration and Development

Some reasons why the background of these undocumented immigrants differs from usual expectations can be found in a closer examination of Mexican society itself. Usual "economic dualist" views divide the country into a modern-urban Mexico and a rural-traditional Mexico, and assign illegal immigration to the latter. And the common corollary is that "as modernity overcomes tradition" the sources of the illegal flow will progressively be eliminated.

The above data suggest that a substantial proportion of illegal immigration comes from social groups already modernized, already living in cities and having above-average education. I will argue that the sources of this illegal immigration are not to be found in a backward and traditional rural economy but in the very contradictions accompanying Mexican *development.*

To summarize an argument made before, the process of capitalist industrialization in Mexico has been marked by four major contradictions. First, it mobilized a rural population, cutting traditional ties to the land without offering opportunities for alternative employment. The Mexican revolution, largely fought on the "agrarian question" (Womack, 1968), put many previously isolated peasants in contact with the benefits of modern urban civilization. Neither the triumph of the revolution nor the dominant economic strategy followed afterwards succeeded in responding to the new needs for mass employment.

In a country like Mexico, open and declared unemployment is a luxury; few really have access to the system of social security which might subsidize periods of enforced idleness. In 1969, only 20.9 percent of the economically active population (EAP) was covered by Mexican social security (Economic Commission for Latin America, 1974). Thus, it is not surprising that in the 1970 census declared unemployment amounted to only 3.8 percent of the EAP. Much more significant are the figures on disguised unemployment and on underemployment, representing people who must somehow survive with neither minimally remunerated nor stable employment. Twelve percent of the Mexican EAP was estimated to be in conditions of disguised unemployment and an additional 35–40 percent was underemployed in 1970. Together, they amount to almost half of the labor force (Urquidi, 1974; Alba, 1978).

Second, Mexico has experienced the contradiction of a sustained rate of economic growth coupled with an increasingly unequal distribution of national income. During the last three decades, the average annual rate of growth in national GNP has been 6 percent. During the same period, inequality in the distribution of income has not decreased, it has increased—substantially. By 1973, Mexico had a GNP per capita of (U.S.) $774. The top 5 percent of the population had 29 percent of the national income, and the top 20 percent received 57 percent of the national income. At the other extreme, the poorest 20 percent received an income share of only 4 percent (United Nations, 1974). Eighteen percent of the population had annual incomes of less than (U.S.) $75 (cf. Portes and Ferguson, 1977).

Third, Mexico has absorbed an increasingly modern culture and the modern cult of advanced consumption, while denying the mass of the population the means to participate even minimally in it. As in the advanced countries, the mass media have made sure that the attractions of modern consumerism reach the most remote corners of the country. Especially in urban areas, people are literally bombarded with advertising for new products and the presumed benefits that their acquisition would bring. But underemployment and a highly unequal income distribution actually deny access to these goods to the majority of the population (Eckstein, 1977; Alba, 1978).

This situation, which has been labelled the syndrome of "modernity-in-underdevelopment," provides an appropriate background for interpreting some of the findings in this study. It is not surprising that a sizable proportion of undocu-

mented immigrants are neither rural nor illiterate, but come from cities and have above-average education and occupational training. These groups are most susceptible to the emigration alternative for they are most exposed to the contradictions between the desire to consume and the impossibility of doing so. The urban working class, especially its most literate groups, are more closely integrated into modern Mexican society than into the remaining enclaves of subsistence agriculture. For this reason, they are most subject to the contradictions of the system.

Fourth, Mexico faces the contradiction between a formally nationalistic government policy and an international reality of increasing dependence involving control of the Mexican economy by foreign sources. Approximately half of the 400 largest industries in Mexico are foreign-owned, predominantly by U.S. corporations. Over 25 percent of industrial production, especially in the most technologically advanced and dynamic branches, is generated by multinational companies. There are more subsidiaries of major U.S. multinationals in Mexico than in any other Latin American country and these foreign companies are buying up an increasing number of domestic firms (Vaupel and Curhan, 1977).

Mexican foreign trade is entirely dominated by the United States, which accounted, in 1976, for 62 percent of the imports and received 56 percent of the exports. Mexican external public debt, which in 1955 represented 54 percent of foreign exchange earnings, had surpassed 160 percent by 1970 (Bach, 1978a).

This extreme external dependence has two major effects on the process of labor emigration. First, Mexican industrialization, carried out under foreign auspices, has been based on importation of capital-intensive technology. The success in productivity of this strategy has been impressive. Manufacturing far outdistances agriculture at present as the most important and most dynamic sector of the economy. Practically all consumer goods now sold in Mexico are produced domestically and the share of manufactured products among total exports is the highest for Latin America. These successes have not been shared, however, by the mass of the population since so few are employed by the industries. Manufacturing absorbs approximately one-fifth of the economically active population, having increased its share by only 5 percent since the early days of the Revolution. The urban *service* sector, not manufacturing, is the one in which employment has increased most rapidly during the last three decades (Cumberland, 1968). The increasing production of domestic goods, coupled with failure to widen the consumer market through employment in the industrial sector, has aggravated, in turn, the other contraditions of the system.

Second, the presence and influence of the United States have accelerated the modernization of Mexican culture and the spread of the cult of consumption. The North has come to appear to be the land where contradictions plaguing Mexico at present can be solved, at least for the individual. Massive emigration to the United States must be regarded as the natural response of part of the Mexican working class to conditions created *for them*, rather than *by them*. Efficient industry coupled with widespread underemployment, diffusion of modern styles of consumption coupled with high concentration of income in higher social classes, both are processes which cannot be understood apart from recognition of the heavy presence in Mexico of foreign, mostly U.S., capital and technology.

In the eyes of the Mexican worker, the United States stands as the place where the benefits of an advanced economy, promised but not delivered by the present national development strategy, can be turned into reality. It is only natural that many trek North in search of the means to acquire what transnational firms and the mass media have so insistently advertised for years. The individual immigrant data presented above and the analysis of the Mexican economic situation in this section have converged and show that illegal immigration has been propelled not by failure of development strategies, but by their success. The movement does not occur because Mexico is poor and stagnant, but precisely because it has developed rapidly—in one particular direction. The main implication is that we in the United States should not expect that illegal immigration will fade away as Mexico becomes less rural and more developed. Instead, if Mexican development proceeds along the lines it has followed in the past, we must expect more, not less, pressures at the southern border.

Policy Proposals

Mexican immigration is not only the most sizable component of the illegal flow, but the one for which more information is available. With necessary modifications, I believe that the essentials of the situation just described apply to other countries from which undocumented immigrants come. Caribbean nations, especially the Dominican Republic, have also begun a process of economic development based on import-substitution industrialization, importation of capital-intensive technology, and mobilization of the rural population into urban areas.

The Carter Administration's proposals to deal with illegal immigration consist in essence, of three measures: 1) amnesty for illegal aliens who can prove continuous residence in the U.S. since 1970; 2) five-year work permits without unemployment and social security benefits for those coming after that date; and 3) strict enforcement of the border to prevent continuation of illegal entries. A great deal of attention has been focused on the first two provisions (see Portes, 1978), but it is the third one that is most important to any analysis of the foreign policy implications of these proposals. I will not discuss here the means proposed to close the border, but rather, the purpose. Also, I will not advance an alternative policy, but will only comment on the implications of the existing border enforcement proposal.

There are two ways of looking at the actors or contenders involved in the Administration's proposed policies. The more apparent one is to conceive of two nation-states, the United States and Mexico (or other source country), which have opposite interests. The decision to enforce the border is then taken to defend the interest of one national community even at the expense of the other. A second way of considering the process is to view the different nation-states not as separate entities, but as integral components of the same overarching international system. This world-system contains and indeed depends on the existence of national borders and national states, but both the nation-states and their borders function within the constraints imposed by the international totality.

In the specific case of international labor migration, the fundamental cleavage in the world-system is not between national states, but between social classes. Classes cut across national borders and may have interests contrary to those of the rest of the respective national populations. One could speak of capital and labor as the two relevant classes, but that is too general. Actually, there are four subclasses or class sectors primarily involved in the process: (a) foreign and domestic capital owners in Mexico (and the Mexican *state*); (b) competitive-sector enterprises in the United States; (c) unemployed and underemployed Mexican workers from rural and, as seen above, urban areas; and (d) workers in the United States who serve as an actual or potential labor force to competitive firms. Women and racial and ethnic minorities are disproportionately represented in this labor market.

Owners and managers in Mexico and the Mexican government are placed in the same category here because their interest in labor emigration is ultimately the same. Primarily, this is not an interest in would-be emigrants as an economic resource, but as a political threat. The contradictions of Mexican development and the mass of unemployed and underemployed are serious causes of concern for the future of the social order. This is especially true in a country which not so long ago witnessed popular revolutionary forces bring down an aristocratic regime. Emigration to the North functions in this situation as a welcome and important resource to maintain social peace and meliorate the tensions of economic growth without equality. For the Mexican state, the remittances (savings) sent by emigrants to the United States also represent an increasingly important means of counteracting balance-of-payments difficulties (Cornelius and Diez-Canedo, 1976).

Employers of illegal labor in the United States are not, by and large, major corporations but smaller competitive firms dependent for profits on holding down the costs of labor. In areas where illegals concentrate, many such firms have come to depend on this kind of labor for their very survival (North and Houstoun, 1976; Marshall, 1975). As stated above, illegal immigration thus establishes a symbiotic relationship among owners on both sides of the border, one in which the political legitimation needs of some and the

economic labor-saving needs of others are served by the same process.

For the mass of Mexican workers, the best alternative in the long run is obviously a major transformation of the dominant economic order. No one lives in the long run, however, and in the here-and-now emigration to the United States offers many the best chance for fulfillment of their aspirations. As a respondent in Dinerman's recent study of emigrants from a village community in Lake Patzcuaro stated—he did not get too worried when money became scarce because "he could always go North" (Dinerman, 1978).

Illegal immigration does not pose an immediate threat to middle-class nonmanual workers, to artisans and highly skilled workers, and in general to workers organized in strong unions in the United States. The reason is that illegal labor has neither sought nor gained entry into the mainstream of the American economy. No evidence exists that major corporations have knowingly hired a substantial number of undocumented immigrants. The class of workers in the United States most directly affected by illegal labor competition is precisely the class that is least organized and least able to articulate its interests: the largely female and nonwhite competitive labor sector. In areas where illegal immigrants concentrate, the situation is further confused by the fact that the apparent economic opposition between undocumented and domestic minority workers is tempered by cultural, ethnic and language affinities. To this day, many local unions and ethnic organizations are not certain whether they should oppose and denounce illegal immigrants, embrace them as part of the same community, or adopt some intermediate attitude.

In principle, the Administration's proposals appear progressive for they would strengthen the bargaining hand of domestic workers in the competitive sector, while forcing Mexico and other exporting countries to face their reality without the safety valve of emigration. Out of that situation, presumably, significant structural changes in the direction of equality might result. The configuration of class forces just outlined suggests, however, that the border enforcement clause will be difficult to maintain without a parallel program of regulated access to immigrant labor. On the other hand, border enforcement may be possible in the short run because the amnesty program, also part of the Administration's plan, would turn undocumented workers already in the country into a *de facto* immigrant contract labor force. What we must recognize, however, is that once this group is absorbed the same pressures can be expected to reassert themselves.

Neither the needs of employers of low-wage labor in the United States nor the class structure of Mexican society are likely to change significantly in the near future. The American state, at the center of the contemporary world economy, makes decisions affecting different sectors of American society not only directly but indirectly, through their repercussions in other nations integrated into the same system. It is in this sense that what appears on the surface as "foreign policy" is still domestic policy if we see it from the vantage point of the reality of the international economic system. The U.S. government cannot reasonably ignore the serious threats to political and economic stability that would be posed *in Mexico* by strict enforcement of the border. It can no more do so than ignore the opposition of a politically powerful sector of domestic employers. Despite the apparent intentions of the Administration and the probable eventual support of organized labor, it is not likely that the program as conceived will survive.

International labor migration thus represents a process remarkable for the contradictions between its determinants and the policy measures formulated to control it. The flow of illegal immigration is not an autonomous phenomenon of peripheral countries, but originates in the character of their externally-shaped development. The economic hegemony exercised by the United States over these countries produces patterns of industrialization within them which increase rather than decrease the pressure on their working classes. Conversely the evolution of the world economy has produced an increasing reliance on foreign sources of cheap labor in the advanced capitalist nations. Precisely because the laborers have been made redundant in their own countries, they can be hired cheaply to counterbalance high wages for the domestic working class. Attempts to prevent such long run structural processes by administrative decisions to "close the border" or reduce the size of the "traditional" rural sector in the nations from which such workers flow are just alternative forms of official fantasy. Policies thus far formulated to deal with illegal immigration highlight the continuing gap between the reality of an internationalized political economy and the national standpoint from which its consequences are interpreted. Flows of capital and of labor are interrelated, international, and influenced by profit and wage levels and by persisting trends in the shares of wealth available to various social classes in the constituent nations of the world economy.

27

The Twilight of Ethnicity Among American Catholics of European Ancestry

Richard D. Alba

The vitality of ethnicity in advanced industrial societies like that of the United States recently has become accepted generally as a fact, although there has been little consensus about the reasons for it. With some oversimplification, two basic explanations can be discerned. According to one, ethnicity is rooted in primordial sentiments that throb beneath the veneer of an industrial order. That is, ethnic communities and cultures serve vital human needs because they provide enduring personal identities amid the social flux of a rapidly changing society and also provide communities of solidarity that are larger than face-to-face groups and are smaller than the whole society. According to the other explanation, ethnicity flourishes along the lines of fracture in the stratification order, revitalized if not recreated by the struggle over access to privilege. Ethnicity is reinforced by common socioeconomic position that may be imposed from outside a group by majority groups seeking to solidify their privileges; or it may emerge from a group's natural history, as the peculiarities of the opportunities open to it and the disabilities inherent in its culture lead to a rough congruence between group membership and social class position.

The Catholic ethnic groups of European origins, the focus of this article, hold a position of strategic importance for evaluating these recent understandings of ethnicity in the United States. This is not to deny the variations among them in culture, American experience, and socioeconomic success, but some common features stand out in most treatments of them.[1] They are generally believed to persist in strong ethnic affiliations, a persistence which has been seen from the vantage points of both explanations. In the main, the Catholic groups came from underdeveloped rural areas of Europe and were often recruited from the poorest strata of these societies. With some notable exceptions, they tended to settle in the major urban areas of the Northeast and the Midwest, where they clustered together in intensely ethnic communities that retain an ethnic character even today. This concentration gave rise to a view of Catholic ethnics as having merely transplanted their peasant solidarities from rural Europe to urban America—a view that seemed to explain their apparent lack of mobility. This lack is ascribed to cultural values finely attuned to the needs of survival in rural Europe, but incapacitating in urban, industrial America. Indeed, groups like the Poles and Italians have come to occupy a peculiar place in the iconography of inequality in America, often used by the mass media in symbolic evocations of working-class life. Were these and other Catholic groups to be assimilating, that fact would indicate a clear need for a reevaluation of our current assumption about ethnicity's vitality.

The Catholic groups are comparatively recent settlers in the United States. There were few Catholics in the former colonies at the end of the eighteenth century.[2] The Catholic population grew rapidly through immigration during the nineteenth century and the first few decades of the twentieth. The Irish were the first large Catholic group to arrive, their immigration swelling to a flood during the famine years in the 1840s and 1850s. There were also many Catholics among the immigrants from Germany, and they too began coming in large numbers around the middle of the nineteenth century. Later in the nineteenth century, immigration from southern and eastern Europe began in earnest, bringing many Polish and other eastern European Catholics and those from Italy. This so-called new immigration reached a crescendo during the early years of the twentieth century, before being stifled by the restrictive immigration laws of the 1920s. There has not been a mass immigration of European Catholics since then.

Characteristics of Catholic Ethnic Groups Today

To arrive at an assessment of the current situation of the Catholic groups, it is necessary to use national survey data, since the Census does not ask about religion. For this article, I have used the National Opinion Research Center's (NORC) annual General Social Survey, combining the surveys for the years 1973–78 to make certain that statistics are based on ample numbers of individuals.[4] Some important characteristics of the Catholic groups are shown in Table 1, which also shows the same characteristics of all white Protestants and of Protestants of British ancestry for purposes of comparison. Religion in Table 1, it should be noted, is the religion in which an individual was raised.

In terms of numbers, individuals who were raised as Catholics make up slightly more than a quarter of the adult American population. The vast majority of this group is composed of persons who trace their ancestry to European nations, and among them is a sizable minority who do not identify themselves in terms of a single nationality. The NORC survey asks the respondent to name the "countries or part of the world" from which his or her ancestors came. In the event that more than one country is named, the respondent is asked to indicate the country to which he or she feels "closer." Still, many respondents cannot make such a choice or cannot name any country in response to the first question, and for these the survey yields no information about

TABLE 1. *Selected Characteristics of Major Catholic Ethnic Groups of European Ancestry*

	Percentage of Population	Percentage Not Identified Ethnically	Percentage Third Generation or Later†	Percentage in Urban North‡	Percentage Who Attended College	Percentage With Multiple Ancestry
All white Catholics*	25.9	11	62	38	31	30§
Italian	4.3	—	34	53	29	20
German (including Austrian)	3.8	—	79	33	26	31
Irish	3.6	—	85	42	42	41
Polish	2.1	—	52	52	25	20
All white Protestants*	56.7	25	88	13	31	36§
British (English, Welsh, Scotch)	13.4	—	88	16	46	39

Source: National Opinion Research Center's General Social Surveys, 1973–78.
Note: Combined N = 8984.
*Religion is religion raised.
†Generation is available only for the 1977 and 1978 surveys.
‡The urban North is defined as the large urban areas and their suburbs in the Northeast and the Midwest.
§For each religious group, the percentage base includes only those who are ethnically identified to aid comparability to percentages among nationality categories.

national background. This is true for over 11 percent of white Catholics, most of whom name more than one country—there are few who do not name any. Since this lack of an ethnic identification is likely to be associated with many generations of family residence in the United States, the bulk of this minority is probably descended from northern and western European ancestors.

Of those who are ethnically identified, either because their ancestry is from a single country or because they feel closer to one country, four Catholic groups are especially prominent in size. The largest of these is composed of Italian-Americans, who make up over 4 percent of the American population and nearly 17 percent of white Catholics. The second and third largest are composed, respectively, of those from German-speaking countries and of those from Ireland. Each of these groups accounts for nearly 4 percent of the American population and about 14 percent of white Catholics. Polish-Americans constitute the last of the four major groups; they are slightly more than 2 percent of the American population and 8 percent of the Catholic population.[5]

Several simple indices roughly delineate the current situations of these major Catholic groups. One is generational distance from the point of immigration, with each new generation likely to represent another step in processes of assimilation. The first generation is the immigrant one itself; the second generation is born in America of immigrant parents; the third and fourth generations have immigrant grandparents and great-grandparents, respectively. The generational distribution of the major Catholic groups conforms to their order of arrival, but indicates that most adult members of these groups are within living memory of the immigrant experience. Although large proportions of Irish and German Catholics, as well as of British Protestants, belong to the third and later generations, the modal generation of the two Catholic groups is the third, while nearly three quarters of British Protestants belong to the fourth or a later generation. A smaller proportion of Polish Catholics belongs to these later generations, and the smallest proportion of all, one third, is found among Italian Catholics. Even in the 1970s, more than half of adult Italian-Americans are the children of immigrants.

In contrast with Protestant Americans, the major Catholic groups of European origins are concentrated in the large cities of the Northeast and the Midwest and in their suburbs. The concentration is greatest for the two most recently arrived groups, Polish and Italian Catholics, and is least for German Catholics, who are unusual among the Catholic groups because they settled in rural America in large numbers. But even they are more concentrated in the urban North than are American Protestants or those of British ancestry. This urban concentration is important because for the better part of this century, these places experienced tremendous economic growth, with profound consequences for the Catholic groups that we shall soon see.

Two last indices bear directly on assimilation. Although assimilation can be thought of as having several dimensions, two stand out; acculturation and structural—or social—assimilation. Acculturation may involve only the taking on of some of the cultural traits of the host society—perhaps only those that are minimally necessary for participation in the economic and political institutions of the host society. It need not imply the dissolution of ethnic communities or the waning of ethnic identities. Structural assimilation, on the other hand, the entry into socially intimate relations like friendship and marriage with individuals from outside the ethnic group, has profound consequences for ethnic group life. At the extreme, large-scale structural assimilation usually signifies the disappearance of ethnic boundaries that constrain social relations and the imminent full assimilation of an ethnic group.[6]

I have used educational attainment—more specifically, the percentage of a group's members who attend college—as an index of acculturation. It serves as an index in two senses, since educational institutions promote the acculturation of those who pass through them and also tend to select for the best educational credentials those individuals who already are acculturated.[7] Obviously, educational attainment holds another significance: it is closely related to subsequent occupation and income. Within the range of educational attainment, college attendance represents a crucial threshold.

In the aggregate, the educational differences among ethnic groups seem to indicate serious disadvantages for most of the major Catholic groups. To be sure, there is not a statistically significant difference in the college attendance rates of British Protestants and Irish Catholics, the most successful of all the Catholic groups in this, as in other ways.[8] But the other major Catholic groups are distinctly less likely than these two groups to have been to college. The relative lack of success of Italian and Polish Catholics reflects the comparative recency of their arrival in America and, according to a familiar argument, the education-hobbling values they brought with them from rural Europe. The educational attainment of German Catholics is probably hindered by their lower concentration in the urban areas of the North.

Of the various forms that structural assimilation can take, interethnic marriage looms large. Not only does it involve an enduring relationship across ethnic boundaries between two individuals, but it generally leads to some degree of social intimacy between their families and means that their children will be raised in an ethnically heterogeneous milieu. A direct measure of interethnic marriage is not available in the NORC data, but an indirect one, resulting from intermarriages in preceding generations, is, namely, the percentage of a group's members who report multiple national ancestry. This too is reported in Table 1.

Clearly indicated in the pattern of multiple ancestry is the relative salience of ethnic boundaries among the more recently arrived Catholic groups. Only one fifth of those who identify themselves as Polish and Italian Catholics trace their ancestry to more than one country, while two fifths of Irish Catholics and British Protestants do; German Catholics fall in between these two poles. In the case of British Protestants—as is true to a lesser extent of Irish and German Catholics—the extent of multiple ancestry is underestimated greatly in Table 1 because many others who could trace a part of their ancestry to this group undoubtedly are included among the individuals who are unable to give a single ethnic identification.

The Trajectory of Assimilation

So far, this portrait of the Catholic groups seems familiar, but it is too static. For the two indices of assimilation, the aggregate group differences in Table 1 are misleading and fail to reveal the powerful dynamics affecting the Catholic groups and bringing about a convergence between them and others in America. These dynamics are traceable in two ways: by generations and by age. The significance of generations has been noted already, but time measured in generations is not the only kind of time that correlates with assimilation processes. Changes in the nature of the opportunities available to the members of a group—that result, for example, from a waning of prejudice toward its members—generally are visible in differences among age categories. That is, as these historical shifts occur, the opportunities available to an individual who matures, say, 20 years later than another are different from what they were for the earlier person, even when both belong to the same generation.

The changes occurring among the Catholic groups are illustrated in Table 2. This table gives a crude sense of the magnitude of change through a comparison of two birth cohorts in each group, those born before World War I and those born after World War II. The changes associated with generations are not represented directly. They are represented indirectly, however, since the younger members of each group, those born after World War II, are more likely to belong to the third or fourth generations than are its older members.

The trends in Table 2 are sharply etched. In terms of educational attainment, few among the German, Italian, and Polish Catholics born before World War I had attended college—only about 1 out of 10 in each group. This proportion compares with over a quarter of the older Irish Catholics and nearly two fifths of British Protestants. But nearly everything has changed among those born after World War II. About half the Irish, Italian, and Polish Catholics have attended college, the same proportions as found among British Protestants. Only Germans, the Catholic group least concentrated in urban areas, deviate from this rate—about one third of them have attended college. The younger members of the urban Catholic groups, in other words, have caught up.[9]

Convergence is visible also in multiple ancestry. In the older group, there are virtually no Italian Catholics and very few Polish ones with ethnically mixed ancestry. More substantial pro-

TABLE 2. *Change by Birth Cohort of Selected Characteristics of Major Catholic Ethnic Groups*

	Birth Cohort	Percentage Not Identified Ethnically	Percentage Who Attended College	Percentage With Multiple Ancestry	Percentage Who Married Inter-religiously*
All white Catholics	Before WWI	8	15	17	30
	After WWII	12	42	41	44
Italian	Before WWI	—	6	2	21
	After WWII	—	49	40	40
German	Before WWI	—	12	21	41
	After WWII	—	32	38	51
Irish	Before WWI	—	26	27	18
	After WWII	—	59	52	40
Polish	Before WWI	—	11	7	20
	After WWII	—	51	41	35
All white Protestants	Before WWI	25	21	25	11
	After WWII	25	39	42	24
British	Before WWI	—	38	35	9
	After WWII	—	52	43	24

Source: National Opinion Research Center's General Social Surveys, 1973–78.
Note: Combined N = 8984.
*Based on the religions in which respondents and their spouses were raised.

portions of the older German and Irish Catholics— about one fifth and one quarter, respectively— have mixed ancestry, and the largest proportion is found unsurprisingly among British Protestants, over one third of whom have mixed ancestry. But profound changes are visible in the younger group. Two fifths of Italian and Polish Catholics born after World War II report mixed ancestry, a proportion which is repeated among German Catholics and British Protestants. Fully half of those identified as Irish Catholics have ancestry other than Irish as well.

It should be remembered at this juncture that multiple ancestry lags by a generation after intermarriage, and thus the rates of multiple ancestry in Table 2 are likely to be considerably lower than the rates of intermarriage for the same groups. And by the evidence of a survey of American Catholics collected in 1963, they are. Generally speaking, large majorities of the third- and fourth-generation members of the major Catholic groups and of their youngest members also had married across ethnic boundaries. Among

those who were 30 years old or younger in 1963, for example, 82, 74, 65, and 69 percent of Irish, German, Polish, and Italian Catholics, respectively, had intermarried.[10]

The Significance of the Trends in College Attendance and Intermarriage

What are we to conclude about the positions of the major Catholic groups in American society? The enormous differences between the older and younger cohorts in Table 2 demonstrate beyond the shadow of a doubt a growing ethnic convergence, but it would be wrong to infer from that fact the disappearance of ethnic differentiation in the near future. In the case of educational attainment, the current equality in rates of college attendance need not imply the complete disappearance of educational and other socioeconomic differences. It may well be that the groups that have only recently entered higher education in large numbers, such as the Italians and Poles, are more concentrated than others in two-year colleges and in less prestigious public colleges and universities.

Some hesitation is also necessary in drawing conclusions about acculturation. A widely held position is that the acculturation of the Catholic groups, as indeed of many other American ethnic groups, has occurred in terms of a public American culture—and note that we speak here of secular, not religious, culture—but that behind an Americanized facade, ethnic subcultures quietly live on, receiving their chief expression in terms of the values concerned with home, family and community. The extensive research of Andrew Greeley demonstrates that some cultural differences among aggregate ethnic categories are visible in current survey data,[11] although this demonstration is not as conclusive as it seems at first sight because aggregate categories contain considerable numbers of less acculturated older persons and those from the first and second generations. Still, some ethnic cultural variation is compatible with growing educational equality.

Yet this growing equality should not be left without some recognition that it does clearly imply profound cultural change. The Italians, the most intensively studied of the Catholic groups, provide a compelling illustration. They frequently have been portrayed as bearers of cultural values that inhibit educational achievement. Indeed, the starkest of these portraits, drawn from the life of the group in America and in the Mezzogiorno and containing some spillover from descriptions of Italian-American organized crime, have resonated with echoes of the "culture of poverty." Amoral familism, fatalism, and a constricting loyalty to the family above all else—these and other overlapping concepts suggest a group that is tied to the lower rungs of the social ladder by its cultural chains.[12] Projected against this background, the increase in the rate of college attendance among Italian Catholics looks stunning. One cannot escape concluding that a decline in adherence to the core values of the ethnic subculture has happened, since it is at the very center of this core, in the emphasis on certain family values, that a key impediment is located.

In addition, a profound weakening of ethnic boundaries seems indicated by the rising rates of intermarriage that are visible behind the patterns of multiple ancestry in Table 2, although it must be acknowledged that we ought to know more about the consequences of intermarriage than we do. The most often studied type of intermarriage is interreligious marriage, but its consequences are likely to be different from those of marriage across nationality boundaries, since American culture firmly supports membership in some religious denomination, and family pressures tend to bring about the conversion of one spouse to the religion of the other.

Even though interreligious marriage serves as in indicator of weakening religious boundaries, detachment from religious group membership is not its usual consequence. The limited evidence about marriage across nationality lines suggests that it entails quite a different outcome. For one thing, this kind of intermarriage appears to go hand in hand with the attenuation of ethnic subcultures, since ethnicity has a weaker relation to specific attitudes and behaviors among the intermarried and those with multiple ancestry than it does among those who marry within their own ethnic group. Also, interethnic marriage is linked to a broader relaxation of ethnic boundaries, since the personal networks of intermarried individuals, and also of individuals with multiple national ancestries, include friends and relatives drawn from a wider ethnic spectrum than found in the more ethnically homogeneous networks of the in-married.[13]

The final piece of evidence about the meaning of interethnic marriage lies in the pattern of intermarriage itself, in the matrix of who marries whom. The expectations that flow from the familiar notion of "social distance" would lead one to suspect that when individuals marry across ethnic boundaries, they usually choose partners from one of the few groups that are culturally and socially close to their own. But in fact this happens only to a minor degree, at least among marriages between partners from the Catholic groups of European origins.[14] In the main, then, intermarriage between members of these Catholic groups functions like a "melting pot."

The emergence of separate melting pots within religious boundaries was the thesis of the most prominent essay on ethnicity of the 1950s—Will

Herberg's *Protestant-Catholic-Jew.* In Herberg's view, ethnicity was an enduring feature of American life, but it was destined to transmute itself before reaching a stable form. Rising rates of intermarriage across nationality lines but within religious boundaries would weaken ethnicity based on national ancestry while strengthening ethnicity based on religious group membership. In the case of Catholics, intermarriage would bring about a Pan-Catholic group by submerging national cultural differences and giving rise to a uniform American Catholicism.

Speaking against the emergence of a Pan-Catholicism, however, are the increasing rates of interreligious marriage depicted in Table 2. Over 40 percent of Catholics born after World War II have married individuals not raised as Catholics, with the vast majority of these marriages to persons raised as Protestants. Increases in interreligious marriage have occurred among all four major Catholic ethnic groups, although in every case recent rates are still a considerable distance from those obtainable if religious boundaries lost their meaning altogether. Since Catholics are only a quarter of the population, three quarters of them would marry non-Catholics if this happened.

Nevertheless, the increasing rate and substantial magnitude of interreligious marriage on the part of Catholics point to a decline in the salience of religious boundaries for a good part of the Catholic group. These facts suggest that the most significant aspect of rising rates of marriage across nationality lines is that they signal a general decline in the importance of ethnic and religious boundaries for Catholics of European descent.

Does this decline mean the complete submergence of ethnic identity? It would appear not, on the basis of the evidence in Table 2. Despite the extent of intermarriage, the proportion of Catholics who lack an ethnic identification has risen only modestly between the older and younger cohorts and remains at a low level even among those born after World War II, only 12 percent of whom do not identify with some nationality group. But just because the vast majority of Catholics retain some ethnic identification does not mean that we should conclude that little has changed. Ethnic identities are likely to be far more circumscribed in scope and practice for individuals in ethnically heterogeneous milieus, such as the intermarried, than they are for individuals in ethnically homogeneous ones.

The great extent of intermarriage among young Catholics in juxtaposition with their retention of some ethnic identification seems in accord with Herbert Gans's notion of "symbolic ethnicity." Briefly, Gans suggests that ethnicity has become increasingly peripheral to the lives of many upwardly mobile members of ethnic groups. But they do not relinquish ethnic identity entirely; rather, they adapt it to their current circumstances, selecting from an ethnic heritage a few symbolic elements that do not interfere with the need to intermix socially with persons from a variety of ethnic backgrounds. This symbolic identification with the ethnic group allows individuals to construct personal identities that contain some ethnic "spice," but it reflects an ethnicity in disarray. One key to the character of symbolic ethnicity is its voluntaristic nature, so that the symbolic elements differ from one individual to another, removing the basis for group cohesion.[15]

Conclusion

Ethnicity, then, appears to be subsiding among the Catholic ethnic groups, although not disappearing entirely. At this juncture, one may wonder where this leaves the widely accepted belief in an "ethnic resurgence" among Catholic, as among other, ethnic groups. My own suspicion is that this ethnic resurgence was more in the eyes of beholders than it was in events among the Catholic ethnics and, moreover, that the increased visibility of ethnicity was paradoxically a product of the same forces sapping ethnicity's vitality. During the 1970s, ethnicity could be celebrated precisely because assimilation had proceeded far enough that ethnicity no longer seemed so threatening and divisive. Ethnicity was made more visible by the penetration of Catholic ethnics into positions of prominence in American life.

To understand the reasons for the increasing assimilation of the Catholic ethnic groups, it is important to recognize the significance of the fact that the Catholic groups entered American society as voluntary immigrants; they were not incorporated forcibly through conquest and enslavement, as were Blacks and some other minority Americans. Their mode of entry was so fateful because, simply put, immigrant groups have had greater freedom than others to determine where they settle and what occupations they pursue.[17]

The greater latitude afforded immigrant groups combined in the case of some of the major Catholic groups with peculiarities of time, place, and circumstance to promote their social mobility and eventually their assimilation. Three of the major Catholic groups, the Irish, Italians, and Poles, and a number of smaller ones settled in the major cities of the Northeast and the Midwest; their mobility was spurred by the economic dynamism of these places over a good part of the nineteenth and twentieth centuries. Economic dynamism is a key because the changes in the occupational structure that accompany advancing industrialization generate a large-scale mobility that does not have a zero-sum character. Expansion of the middle and upper levels of the occupational hierarchy allows the children of those at lower levels to rise without having to displace the children of those at higher ones. Many children and grandchildren of immigrants were beneficiaries of this sort of structural mobility; as they moved upward, the equal-status contact between them and others that resulted made ethnic boundaries seem less and less meaningful.

There were, of course, many other contingencies that affected the assimilation of the Catholic groups. Without any pretense of exhaustiveness, a few must be mentioned.

The assimilation of the Catholic groups was made easier by the great distance of American shores from their European homelands, preventing a back-and-forth movement that would have periodically renewed ethnic sentiments and loyalties. For similar reasons, assimilation was made easier by the restrictive immigration laws of the 1920s, which eliminated mass immigration as a continuing source of revitalization for ethnic communities.

The order in which groups came was also consequential. That later Catholic groups were preceded by the Irish, who were able to garner a strong measure of political power by virtue of their command of the English language and their familarity with political institutions derived from English models, probably created channels of

mobility for the later groups that would have been harder to open otherwise.

And lastly, there were many idiosyncrasies in group cultures or in the opportunities in a specific place at a specific time that helped to shape ethnic mobility. One need not subscribe to all the mythology surrounding the Mafia, for example, to acknowledge that organized crime has provided a ladder of mobility for some Italians and members of some other groups.

Ethnicity appears to be nearing twilight among the Catholic ethnic groups whose forebears immigrated to the United States in the nineteenth and early twentieth centuries. The approach of this twilight is deceptive, for a fading glow from the intense ethnicity of the earlier part of the century remains. And it is a twilight which may never turn into night. For the foreseeable future, some individuals will retain strong affiliations with the Catholic groups, and immigrants will replace a few of those whose affiliations have lapsed. But the Catholic ethnic groups, so prominent a feature of the American social landscape for the better part of this century, seem destined as groups to recede into the background, at the same time that many Americans descended from these groups, still tinged by the ethnicity of their ancestors, move into the social heartland of America.

ENDNOTES

1. Two introductions to ethnicity among American Catholics are as follows: Harold Abramson, *Ethnic Diversity in Catholic America* (New York: John Wiley & Sons, 1973); and Andrew Greeley, *The American Catholic: A Social Portrait* (New York: Basic Books, 1977) (hereafter cited as *The American Catholic*). Also important, even though limited to New York City, is Nathan Glazer and Daniel Patrick Moynihan, *Beyond the Melting Pot* (Cambridge: The M.I.T. Press, 1970).

2. Greeley, *The American Catholic*, p. 35.

3. Sources for immigration statistics are as follow: *Historical Statistics of the United States, Colonial Times to 1970*, part I (Washington: U.S. Department of Commerce, 1975), pp. 105–6; and *Statistical Abstract of the United States, 1979* (Washington: U.S. Department of Commerce, 1979), pp. 89–90.

4. The combined surveys yield a total of 8984 cases with racial, religious, and nationality information. It should be noted that the sampling universe for these surveys is limited to the English-speaking popula-

tion, and consequently, Spanish-speaking Americans are underrepresented. This is not a matter of concern for this article, which focuses on Catholics of European ancestry.

5. With the exception of Italian-Americans, the literature devoted to these groups is sparse. Two studies of Irish Catholics are as follows: Andrew Greeley, *That Most Distressful Nation* (Chicago: Quadrangle, 1972); and Marjorie Fallows, *Irish Americans* (Englewood Cliffs, NJ: Prentice-Hall, 1979). On Polish Catholics, there are as follow: Helena Znaniecki Lopata, *Polish Americans* (Englewood Cliffs, NJ: Prentice-Hall, 1976); and Neil Sandberg, *Ethnic Identity and Assimilation: The Polish American Community* (New York: Praeger, 1974). To my knowledge, there is no contemporary sociological study of German-Americans. The literature on Italian-Americans is too large to be cited fully here. Two classics are as follow: William F. Whyte, *Street Corner Society* (Chicago: University of Chicago Press, 1943); and Herbert Gans, *The Urban Villagers* (New York: The Free Press, 1962). Another useful essay is by Joseph Lopreato, *Italian Americans* (New York: Random House, 1970).

6. These are, simplified for my purposes, the familiar concepts from Milton Gordon's *Assimilation in American Life* (New York: Oxford University Press, 1964), ch. 3.

7. This is as true of the Catholic educational system as it is of others. See Andrew Greeley and Peter Rossi, *The Education of Catholic Americans* (Chicago: Aldine, 1966).

8. See Greeley, *The American Catholic*, ch. 3.

9. That the Catholic ethnics are now very mobile is argued persuasively by Greeley in *The American Catholic*, ch. 3.

10. Richard Alba, "Social Assimilation Among American Catholic National-Origin Groups," *Am. Soc. Review*, 41: 1030–46 (Dec. 1976) (hereafter cited as "Social Assimilation").

11. For example, see Greeley, *The American Catholic*.

12. Edward Banfield, *The Moral Basis of a Backward Society* (New York: The Free Press, 1958); Richard Gambino, *Blood of My Blood* (New York: Doubleday, 1974), ch. 8; and Carmi Schooler, "Serfdom's Legacy: An Ethnic Continuum," *Am. J. Soc.*, 81: 1265–86 (May 1976).

13. Richard Alba, "Ethnic Networks and Tolerant Attitudes," *Public Opinion Quarterly*, 42: 1–16 (spring 1978); and Alba, "Social Assimilation."

14. Richard Alba and Ronald Kessler, "Patterns of Interethnic Marriage Among American Catholics," *Social Forces*, 57: 1124–40 (June 1979).

15. Herbert Gans, "Symbolic Ethnicity: The Future of Ethnic Groups and Cultures in America," *Ethnic and Racial Studies*, 2: 1–20 (Jan. 1979).

16. For data on the growing representation of Catholics in the academic world, see Stephen Steinberg, *The Academic Melting Pot* (New York: McGraw-Hill, 1974).

17. Robert Blauner, *Racial Oppression in America* (New York: Harper & Row, 1972), ch. 2.

28

Symbolic Ethnicity:
The Future of Ethnic Groups
and Cultures in America*

Herbert J. Gans

Introduction
One of the more notable recent changes in America has been the renewed interest in ethnicity, which some observers of the American scene have described as an ethnic revival. This paper argues that there has been no revival, and that acculturation and assimilation continue to take place. Among third and fourth generation 'ethnics' (the grand and great-grand children of Europeans who came to America during the 'new immigration'), a new kind of ethnic involvement may be occuring, which emphasizes concern with identity, with the feeling of being Jewish or Italian, etc. Since ethnic identity needs are neither intense nor frequent in this generation, however, ethnics do not need either ethnic cultures or organizations; instead, they resort to the use of ethnic symbols. As a result, ethnicity may be turning

Reprinted from *Ethnic and Racial Studies* 2:1 (January 1979) by permission of Routledge & Kegan Paul Ltd., publishers.

*A longer version of this paper appears in Herbert J. Gans, Nathan Glazer, Joseph R. Gusfield and Christopher Jencks, eds, *On the Making of Americans: Essays in Honor of David Riesman*. Philadelphia: University of Pennsylvania Press, 1979. The paper was originally stimulated by S. N. Eisenstadt's talk at Columbia University in November 1975 on 'Unity and Diversity in Contemporary Jewish Society'. For helpful comments on an earlier draft, I am grateful to Harold Abramson, Richard Alba, James Crispino, Nathan Glazer, Milton Gordon, Andrew Greeley, William Kornblum, Peter Marris, Michael Novak, David Riesman, Paul Ritterband, Allan Silver and John Slawson.

into symbolic ethnicity, an ethnicity of last resort, which could, nevertheless, persist for generations.

Identity cannot exist apart from a group, and symbols are themselves a part of culture, but ethnic identity and symbolic ethnicity require very different ethnic cultures and organizations than existed among earlier generations. Moreover, the symbols third generation ethnics use to express their identity are more visible than the ethnic cultures and organizations of the first and second generation ethnics. What appears to be an ethnic revival may therefore only be a more visible form of long-standing phenomena, or of a new stage of acculturation and assimilation. Symbolic ethnicity may also have wider ramifications, however, for David Riesman has suggested that 'being American has some of the same episodic qualities as being ethnic.'[1]

Acculturation and Assimilation[2]
The dominant sociological approach to ethnicity has long taken the form of what Neil Sandberg aptly calls straight-line theory, in which acculturation and assimilation are viewed as secular trends that culminate in the eventual absorption of the ethnic group into the larger culture and general population.[3] Straight-line theory in turn is based on melting pot theory, for it implies the disappearance of the ethnic groups into a single host society. Even so, it does not accept the values of the melting pot theory, for it implies the

disappearance of the ethnic groups into a single host society. Even so, it does not accept the values of the melting pot theorists, since its conceptualizers could have, but did not, use terms like cultural and social liberation from immigrant ways of life.

In recent years, straight-line theory has been questioned on many grounds. For one thing, many observers have properly noted that even if America might have been a melting pot early in the 20th century, the massive immigration from Europe and elsewhere has since then influenced the dominant groups, summarily labelled White Anglo-Saxon Protestant (WASP), and has also decimated their cultural, if not their political and financial power, so that today America is a mosaic, as Andrew Greeley has put it, of subgroups and subcultures.[4] Still, this criticism does not necessarily deny the validity of straight-line theory, since ethnics can also be absorbed into a pluralistic set of subcultures and subgroups, differentiated by age, income, education, occupation, religion, region, and the like.

A second criticism of straight-line theory has centered on its treatment of all ethnic groups as essentially similar, and its failure, specifically, to distinguish between religious groups like the Jews and nationality groups like the Italians, Poles etc. Jews, for example, are a 'peoplehood' with a religious and cultural tradition of thousands of years, but without an 'old country' to which they owe allegiance or nostalgia, while Italians, Poles and other participants in the 'new immigration' came from parts of Europe which in some cases did not even become nations until after the immigrants had arrived in America.

That there are differences between the Jews and the other 'new' immigrants cannot be questioned, but at the same time, the empirical evidence also suggests that acculturation and assimilation affected them quite similarly. (Indeed, one major difference may have been that Jews were already urbanized and thus entered the American social structure at a somewhat higher level than the other new immigrants, who were mostly landless labourers and poor peasants.) Nonetheless, straight-line theory can be faulted for virtually ignoring that immigrants arrived here with two kinds of ethnic cultures, sacred and secular; that they were Jews from Eastern—and Western—Europe, and Catholics from Italy, Poland and elsewhere. (Sacred cultures are, however, themselves affected by national and regional considerations; for example, Italian Catholicism differed in some respects from German or Polish, as did Eastern European Judaism from Western.)

While acculturation and assimilation have affected both sacred and secular cultures, they have affected the latter more than the former, for acculturation has particularly eroded the secular cultures which Jews and Catholics brought from Europe. Their religions have also changed in America, and religious observance has decreased, more so among Jews than among Catholics, although Catholic observance has begun to fall off greatly in recent years. Consequently, the similar American experience of Catholic and Jewish ethnics suggests that the comparative analysis of straight-line theory is justified, as long as the analysis compares both sacred and secular cultures.

Two further critiques virtually reject straight-line theory altogether. In an insightful recent paper, William Yancey and his colleagues have argued that contemporary ethnicity bears little relation to the ancestral European heritage, but exists because it is functional for meeting present 'exigencies of survival and the structure of opportunity', particularly for working class Americans.[5] Their argument does not invalidate straight-line theory but corrects it by suggesting that acculturation and assimilation, current ethnic organizations and cultures, as well as new forms of ethnicity, must be understood as responses to current needs rather than only as departures from past traditions.

The other critique takes the reverse position; it points to the persistence of the European heritage, argues that the extent of acculturation and assimilation has been overestimated, and questions the rapid decline and eventual extinction of ethnicity posited by some straight-line theorists. These critics call attention to studies which indicate that ethnic cultures and organizations are still functioning, that exogamous marriage remains a practice of numerical minorities, that ethnic differences in various behavior patterns and attitudes can be identified, that ethnic groups continue to act as political interest groups, and that ethnic pride remains strong.[6]

The social phenomena which these observers identify obviously exist; the question is only how they are to be interpreted. Straight-line theory postulates a process, and cross-sectional studies do not preempt the possibility of a continuing trend. Also, like Yancey, *et al.*, some of the critics are looking primarily at poorer ethnics, who have been less touched by acculturation and assimilation than middle class ethnics, and who have in some cases used ethnicity and ethnic organization as a psychological and political defense against the injustices which they suffer in an unequal society.[7] In fact, much of the contemporary behaviour described as ethnic strikes me as working class behaviour, which differs only slightly among various ethnic groups, and then largely because of variations in the structure of opportunities open to people in America, and in the peasant traditions their ancestors brought over from the old country, which were themselves responses to European opportunity structures. In other words, ethnicity is largely a working-class style.[8]

Much the same observations apply to ethnic political activity. Urban political life, particularly among working class people, has always been structured by and through ethnicity, and while ethnic political activity may have increased in the last decade, it has taken place around working class issues rather than ethnic ones. During the 1960s, urban working class Catholic ethnics began to politicize themselves in response to black militancy, the expansion of black ghettoes, and governmental integration policies which they perceived as publicly legitimated black invasions of ethnic neighbourhoods, but which threatened them more as working class homeowners who could not afford to move to the suburbs. Similarly, working and lower-middle class Catholic ethnics banded together in the suburbs to fight against higher public school taxes, since they could not afford to pay them while they were also having to pay for parochial schools. Even so, these political activities have been *pan-ethnic*, rather than ethnic, since they often involved coalitions of ethnic groups which once considered each other enemies but were now united by common economic and other interests. The extent to which these pan-ethnic coalitions reflect class rather than ethnic interests is illustrated by the 1968 election campaign of New York City's Mario

Proccaccino against John Lindsay. Although an Italian, he ran as a 'candidate of the little people' against what he called the 'limousine liberals'.

The fact that pan-ethnic coalitions have developed most readily in conflicts over racial issues also suggests that in politics, ethnicity can sometimes serve as a convenient euphemism for anti-black endeavors, or for political activities that have negative consequences for blacks. While attitude polls indicate that ethnics are often more tolerant racially than other Americans, working class urban ethnics are also more likely to be threatened, as home-owners and jobholders, by black demands, and may favor specific anti-black policies not because they are 'racists', but because their own class interests force them to oppose black demands.

In addition, part of what appears as an increase in ethnic political activity is actually an increase in the visibility of ethnic politics. When the pan-ethnic coalitions began to copy the political methods of the civil rights and anti-war movements, their protests became newsworthy and were disseminated all over the country by the mass media. At about the same time, the economic and geographic mobility of Catholic ethnic groups enabled non-Irish Catholic politicians to win important state and national electoral posts for the first time, and their victories were defined as ethnic triumphs, even though they did not rely on ethnic constituents alone, and were not elected on the basis of ethnic issues.

The final, equally direct, criticism of straight-line theory has questioned the continued relevance of the theory, either because of the phenomenon of third-generation return, or because of the emergence of ethnic revivals. Thus, Marcus Hansen argued that acculturation and assimilation were temporary processes, because the third generation could afford to remember an ancestral culture which the traumatic Americanization forced the immigrant and second generations to forget.[9] Hansen's hypothesis can be questioned on several grounds, however. His data, the founding of Swedish and other historical associations in the Midwest, provided slender evidence of a widespread third generation return, particularly among non-academic ethnics. In addition, his theory is static, for Hansen never indicated what would happen in the fourth generation, or what processes were involved in the return that would enable it to survive into the future.[10]

The notion of an ethnic revival has so far been propounded mostly by journalists and essayists, who have supplied impressionistic accounts or case studies of the emergence of new ethnic organizations and the revitalization of old ones.[11] Since third and fourth generation ethnics who are presumably participating in the revival are scattered all over suburbia, there has so far been little systematic research among this population, so that the validity of the revival notion has not yet been properly tested.

The evidence I have seen does not convince me that a revival is taking place. Instead, recent changes can be explained in two ways, neither of which conflict with straight-line theory: (1) Today's ethnics have become more visible as a result of upward mobility; and (2) they are adopting the new form of ethnic behavior and affiliation I call symbolic ethnicity.

The Visibility of Ethnicity

The recent upward social, and centrifugal geographic, mobility of ethnics, particularly Catholics, has finally enabled them to enter the middle and upper middle classes, where they have been noticed by the national mass media, which monitor primarily these strata. In the process they have also become more noticeable to other Americans. The newly visible may not participate more in ethnic groups and cultures than before, but their new visibility makes it appear as if ethnicity had been revived.

I noted earlier the arrival of non-Irish Catholic politicians on the national scene. An equally visible phenomenon has been the entry of Catholic ethnic intellectuals into the academy, and its flourishing print culture. To be sure, the scholars are publishing more energetically than their predecessors, who had to rely on small and poverty-stricken ethnic publishing houses, but they are essentially doing what ethnic scholars have always done, only more visibly. Perhaps their energy has also been spurred in part by the need, as academics, to publish so that they do not perish, as well as by their desire to counteract the anti-

ethnic prejudices and the entrenched vestiges of the melting pot ideal which still prevail in the more prestigious universities. In some cases, they are also fighting a political battle, because their writings often defend conservative political positions against what they perceive—I think wrongly—as the powerful liberal or radical academic majority. Paradoxically, a good deal of their writing has been nostalgic, celebrating the immigrant culture and its Gemeinschaft at the same time that young Catholic ethnics are going to college partly in order to escape the restrictive pressures of that Gemeinschaft. (Incidentally, an interesting study could be made of the extent to which writers from different ethnic groups, both of fiction and non-fiction, are pursuing nostalgic, contemporary or future-oriented approaches to ethnicity, comparing different ethnic groups, by time of arrival and positon in the society today, on this basis.)

What has happened in the academy has also happened in literature and show business. For example, although popular comedy has long been a predominantly Eastern European Jewish occupation, the first generation of Jewish comic stars had to suppress their ethnicity and even had to change their names, much as did the first generation of academic stars in the prestigious universities. Unlike Jack Benny, Eddie Cantor, George Burns, George Jessel and others, the comics of today do not need to hide their origins, and beginning perhaps with Lenny Bruce and Sam Levinson, comics like Buddy Hackett, Robert Klein, Don Rickles and Joan Rivers have used explicitly Jewish material in entertaining the predominantly non-Jewish mass media audience.

Undoubtedly, some of the academics, writers and entertainers have undergone a kind of third generation return in this process. Some have re-embraced their ethnicity solely to spur their careers, but others have experienced a personal conversion. Even so, an empirical study would probably show that in most cases, their ethnic attitudes have not changed; either they have acted more publicly and thus visibly than they did in the past, or in responding to a hospitable cultural climate, they have openly followed ethnic impulses which they had previously suppressed.

Ethnicity in the Third Generation

The second explanation for the changes that have been taking place among third generation ethnics will take up most of the rest of this paper; it deals with what is happening among the less visible population, the large mass of predominantly middle class third and fourth generation ethnics, who have not been studied enough either by journalists or social scientists.[12]

In the absence of systematic research, it is even difficult to discern what has actually been happening, but several observers have described the same ethnic behavior in different words. Michael Novak has coined the phrase 'voluntary ethnicity'; Samuel Eisenstadt has talked about 'Jewish diversity'; Allan Silver about 'individualism as a valid mode of Jewishness', and Geoffrey Bock about 'public Jewishness'.[13] What these observers agree on is that today's young ethnics are finding new ways of being ethnics, which I shall later label symbolic ethnicity.

For the third generation, the secular ethnic cultures which the immigrants brought with them are now only an ancestral memory, or an exotic tradition to be savored once in a while in a museum or at an ethnic festival. The same is true of the 'Americanization cultures', the immigrant experience and adjustment in America, which William Kornblum suggests may have been more important in the lives of the first two generations than the ethnic cultures themselves. The old ethnic cultures serve no useful function for third generation ethnics who lack direct and indirect ties to the old country, and neither need nor have much knowledge about it. Similarly, the Americanization cultures have little meaning for people who grew up without the familial conflict over European and American ways that beset their fathers and mothers: the second generation which fought with and was often ashamed of immigrant parents.

Assimilation is still continuing, for it has always progressed more slowly than acculturation. If one distinguishes between primary and secondary assimilation, that is, out of ethnic primary and secondary groups, the third generation is now beginning to move into non-ethnic primary groups.[14] Although researchers are still debating just how much intermarriage is taking place, it is rising in the third generation for both Catholic ethnic groups and Jews, and friendship choices appear to follow the same pattern.[15]

The departure out of secondary groups has already proceeded much further. Most third generation ethnics have little reason, or occasion, to depend on, or even interact with, other ethnics in important secondary group activities. Ethnic occupational specialization, segregation, and self-segregation are fast disappearing, with some notable exceptions in the large cities. Since the third generation probably works, like other Americans, largely for corporate employers, past occupational ties between ethnics are no longer relevant. Insofar as they live largely in the suburbs, third generation ethnics get together with their fellow homeowners for political and civic activities, and are not likely to encounter ethnic political organizations, balanced tickets, or even politicians who pursue ethnic constituencies.

Except in suburbs where old discrimination and segregation patterns still survive, social life takes place without ethnic clustering, and Catholics are not likely to find ethnic subgroups in the Church. Third generation Jews, on the other hand, particularly those who live in older upper-middle class suburbs where segregation continues, if politely, still probably continue to restrict much of their social life to other Jews, although they have long ago forgotten the secular divisions between German (and other Western) and Eastern European Jews, and among the latter, the division between 'Litwaks' and 'Galizianer'. The religious distinction between German Reform Judaism, and Eastern European Conservatism has also virtually disappeared, for the second generation that moved to the suburbs after World War II already chose its denomination on status grounds rather than national origin.[16] In fact, the Kennedy-Herberg prediction that eventually American religious life would take the form of a triple melting-pot has not come to pass, if only because people, especially in the suburbs, use denominations within the major religions for status differentiation.

Nevertheless, while ethnic ties continue to wane for the third generation, people of this generation continue to *perceive* themselves as ethnics, whether they define ethnicity in sacred or secular terms. Jews continue to remain Jews because the sacred and secular elements of their culture are strongly intertwined, but the Catholic ethnics also retain the secular or national identity, even though it is separate from their religion.[17]

My hypothesis is that in this generation, people are less and less interested in their ethnic cultures and organizations—both sacred and secular—and are instead more concerned with maintaining their ethnic identity, with the feeling of being Jewish, or Italian, or Polish, and with finding ways of feeling and expressing that identity in suitable ways. By identity, I mean here simply the socio-psychological elements that accompany role behavior, and the ethnic role is today less of an ascriptive than a voluntary role that people assume alongside other roles. To be sure, ethnics are still identified as such by others, particularly on the basis of name, but the behavioral expectations that once went with identification by others have declined sharply, so that ethnics have some choice about when and how to play ethnic roles. Moreover, as ethnic cultures and organizations decline further, fewer ethnic roles are prescribed, thus increasing the degree to which people have freedom of role definition.

Ethnic identity can be expressed either in action or feeling, or combinations of these, and the kinds of situations in which it is expressed are nearly limitless. Third generation ethnics can join an ethnic organization, or take part in formal or informal organizations composed largely of fellow-ethnics; but they can also find their identity by 'affiliating' with an abstract collectivity which does not exist as an interacting group. That collectivity, moreover, can be mythic or real, contemporary or historical. On the one hand, Jews can express their identity as synagogue members, or as participants in a consciousness-raising group consisting mostly of Jewish women. On the other hand, they can also identify with the Jewish people as long-suffering collectivity which has been credited with inventing monotheism. If they are non-religious, they can identify with Jewish liberal or socialist political cultures, or with a population which has produced many prominent intellectuals and artists in the last 100 years. Similar choices are open to Catholic ethnics. In the third generation, Italians can identify through membership in Italian groups, or by

strong feelings for various themes in Italian, or Neapolitan or Sicilian culture, and much the same possibilities exist for Catholics whose ancestors came over from other countries.

Needless to say, ethnic identity is not a new, or third generation phenomenon, for ethnics have always had an ethnic identity, but in the past it was largely taken for granted, since it was anchored to groups and roles, and was rarely a matter of choice. When people lived in an ethnic neighborhood, worked with fellow ethnics, and voted for ethnic politicans, there was little need to be concerned with identity except during conflict with other ethnic groups. Also, the everyday roles people played were often defined for them by others as ethnic. Being a drygoods merchant was often a Jewish role; restaurant owners were assumed to be Greek; and bartenders, Irish.

The third generation has grown up without assigned roles or groups that anchor ethnicity, so that identity can no longer be taken for granted. People can of course give up their identity, but if they continue to feel it, they must make it more explicit than it was in the past, and must even look for ways of expressing it. This has two important consequences for ethnic behavior. First, given the degree to which the third generation has acculturated and assimilated, most people look for easy and intermittent ways of expressing their identity, for ways that do not conflict with other ways of life. As a result, they refrain from ethnic behavior that requires an arduous or time-consuming commitment, either to a culture that must be practiced constantly, or to organizations that demand active membership. Second, because people's concern is with identity, rather than with cultural practices or group relationships, they are free to look for ways of expressing that identity which suit them best, thus opening up the possibility of voluntary, diverse or individualistic ethnicity. Any mode of expressing ethnic identity is valid as long as it enhances the feeling of being ethnic, and any cultural pattern or organization which nourishes that feeling is therefore relevant, providing only that enough people make the same choice when identity expression is a group enterprise.

In other words, as the functions of ethnic cultures and groups diminish and identity becomes the primary way of being ethnic, ethnicity takes on an expressive rather than instrumental function in people's lives, becoming more of a leisure-time activity and losing its relevance, say, to earning a living or regulating family life. Expressive behavior can take many forms, but it often involves the use of symbols—and symbols as signs rather than as myths.[18] Ethnic symbols are frequently individual cultural practices which are taken from the older ethnic culture; they are 'abstracted' from that culture and pulled out of its original moorings, so to speak, to become stand-ins for it. And if a label is useful to describe the third generation's pursuit of identity, I would propose the term symbolic ethnicity.

Symbolic Ethnicity

Symbolic ethnicity can be expressed in a myriad of ways, but above all, I suspect, it is characterized by a nostalgic allegiance to the culture of the immigrant generation, or that of the old country; a love for and a pride in a tradition that can be felt without having to be incorporated in everyday behavior. The feelings can be directed at a generalized tradition, or at specific ones: a desire for the cohesive extended immigrant family, or for the obedience of children to parental authority, or the unambiguous orthodoxy of immigrant religion, or the old-fashioned despotic benevolence of the machine politician. People may even sincerely desire to 'return' to these imagined pasts, which are conveniently cleansed of the complexities that accompanied them in the real past, but while they may soon realize that they cannot go back, they may not surrender the wish. Or else they displace that wish on churches, schools, and the mass media, asking them to recreate a tradition, or rather, to create a symbolic tradition, even while their familial, occupational, religious and political lives are pragmatic responses to the imperatives of their roles and positions in local and national hierarchical social structures.

All of the cultural patterns which are transformed into symbols are themselves guided by a common pragmatic imperative: they must be visible and clear in meaning to large numbers of third generation ethnics, and they must be easily expressed and felt, without requiring undue interference in other aspects of life. For example, Jews have abstracted rites de passage and individual

holidays out of the traditional religion and given them greater importance, such as the bar mitzvah and bas mitzvah (the parallel ceremony for 13 year old girls that was actually invented in America). Similarly, Chanukah, a minor holiday in the religious calendar, has become a major one in popular practice, partly since it lends itself to impressing Jewish identity on the children. Rites de passage and holidays are ceremonial; and thus symbolic to begin with; equally important, they do not take much time, do not upset the everyday routine, and also become an occasion for family reunions to reassemble family members who are rarely seen on a regular basis. Catholic ethnics pay special attention to saint's days celebrating saints affiliated with their ethnic group, or attend ethnic festivals which take place in the area of first settlement, or in ethnic churches.

Consumer goods, notably food, are another ready source for ethnic symbols, and in the last decades, the food industry has developed a large variety of easily cooked ethnic foods, as well as other edibles which need no cooking, for example, chocolate matzōhs which are sold as gifts at Passover. The response to symbolic ethnicity may even be spreading into the mass media, for films and television programs with ethnic characters are on the increase. The characters are not very ethnic in their behavior, and may only have ethnic names—for example, Lt. Colombo, Fonzi, or Rhoda Goldstein—but in that respect, they are not very different from the ethnic audiences who watch them.

Symbolic ethnicity also takes political forms, through identification or involvement with national politicians and international issues which are sufficiently remote to become symbols. As politicians from non-Irish ethnic backgrounds achieve high state or national office, they become identity symbols for members of their group, supplying feelings of pride over their success. That such politicians do not represent ethnic constituencies, and thus do not become involved in ethnic political disputes only enhances their symbolic function; unlike local ethnic politicians, who are still elected for instrumental bread-and-butter reasons, and thus become embroiled in conflicts that detract from their being symbols of ethnic pride.

Symbolic ethnicity can be practiced as well through politically and geographically even more distant phemomena, such as nationalist movements in the old country. Jews are not interested in their old countries, except to struggle against the maltreatment of Jews in Eastern Europe, but they have sent large amounts of money to Israel, and political pressure to Washington, since the establishment of the State. While their major concern has undoubtedly been to stave off Israel's destruction, they might also have felt that their own identity would be affected by such a disaster. Even if the survival of Israel is guaranteed in the future, however, it is possible that as allegiances toward organized local Jewish communities in America weaken, Israel becomes a substitute community to satisfy identity needs. Similar mechanisms may be at work among other ethnic groups who have recently taken an interest in their ancestral countries, for example the Welsh and Armenians, and among those groups whose old countries are involved in internal conflict, for example the Irish, and Greeks and Turks during the Cyprus war of 1973.

Old countries are particularly useful as identity symbols because they are far away and cannot make arduous demands on American ethnics; even sending large amounts of money is ultimately an easy way to help unless the donors are making major economic sacrifices. Moreover, American ethnics can identify with their perception of the old country or homeland, transforming it into a symbol which leaves out its domestic or foreign problems that could become sources of conflict for Americans. For example, most American Jews who support Israel pay little attention to its purely domestic policies; they are concerned with its preservation as a state and a Jewish homeland, and see the country mainly as a Zionist symbol.

The symbolic functions of old countries are facilitated further when interest in them is historical; when ethnics develop an interest in their old countries as they were during or before the time of the ancestral departure. Marcus Hansen's notion of third-generation return was actually based on the emergence of interest in Swedish history, which suggests that the third generation return may itself only be another variety of symbolic ethnicity. Third generations can obviously attend to the past with less emotional risk than first and second generation people who are still trying to

escape it, but even so, an interest in ethnic history is a return only chronologically.

Conversely, a new symbol may be appearing among Jews: the Holocaust, which has become a historic example of ethnic group destruction that can now serve as a warning sign for possible future threats. The interest of American Jews in the Holocaust has increased considerably since the end of World War II; when I studied the Jews of Park Forest in 1949-1950, it was almost never mentioned, and its memory played no part whatsoever in the creation of a Jewish community there. The lack of attention to the Holocaust at that time may, as Nathan Glazer suggests, reflect the fact that American Jews were busy with creating new Jewish communities in the suburbs.[19] It is also possible that people ignored the Holocaust then because the literature detailing its horrors had not yet been written, although since many second generation American Jews had relatives who died in the Nazi camps, it seems more likely that people repressed thinking about it until it had become a more historical and therefore a less immediately traumatic event. As a result, the Holocaust may now be serving as a new symbol for the threat of group destruction, which is required, on the one hand, by the fact that rising intermarriage rates and the continued decline of interest and participation in Jewish religion are producing real fears about the disappearance of American Jewry altogether; and on the other hand, by the concurrent fact that American anti-semitism is no longer the serious threat to group destruction that it was for first and second generation Jews. Somewhat the same process appears to be taking place among some young Armenians who are now reviving the history of the Turkish massacre of Armenians some sixty years later, at a time when acculturation and assimilation are beginning to make inroads into the Armenian community in America.

I suggested previously that ethnicity per se had become more visible, but many of the symbols used by the third generation are also visible to the rest of America, not only because the middle class people who use them are more visible than their poorer ancestors, but because the national media are more adept at communicating symbols than the ethnic cultures and organizations or earlier generations. The visibility of symbolic ethnicity provides further support for the existence of an ethnic revival, but what appears to be a revival is probably the emergence of a new form or acculturation and assimilation that is taking place under the gaze of the rest of society.

Incidentally, even though the mass media play a major role in enhancing the visibility of ethnicity, and in communicating ethnic symbols, they do not play this role because they are themselves ethnic institutions. True, the mass media, like other entertainment industries, continue to be dominated by Jews (although less so than in the past), but for reasons connected with anti-semitism, or the fear of it, they have generally leaned over backwards to keep Jewish characters and Jewish fare out of their offerings, at least until recently. Even now, a quantitative analysis of major ethnic characters in comedy, drama and other entertainment genres would surely show that Catholic ethnics outnumber Jewish ones. Perhaps the Jews who write or produce so much of the media fare are especially sensitive to ethnic themes and symbols; my own hypothesis, however, is that they are, in this case as in others, simply responding to new cultural tendencies, if only because they must continually innovate. In fact, the arrival of ethnic characters followed the emergence and heightened visibility of ethnic politics in the late 1960s, and the men and women who write the entertainment fare probably took inspiration from news stories thay saw on television or read in the papers.

I noted earlier that identity cannot exist apart from a group and that symbols are themselves part of a culture, and in that sense, symbolic ethnicity can be viewed as an indicator of the persistence of ethnic groups and cultures. Symbolic ethnicity, however, does not require functioning groups or networks; feelings of identity can be developed by allegiances to symbolic groups that never meet, or to collectivities that meet only occasionally, and exist as groups only for the handful of officers that keep them going. By the same token, symbolic ethnicity does not need a practiced culture, even if the symbols are borrowed from it. To be sure, symbolic culture is as much culture as practiced culture, but the latter persists only to supply symbols to the former. Indeed, practiced culture may need to persist, for

some, because people do not borrow their symbols from extinct cultures that survive only in museums. And insofar as the borrowed materials come from the practiced culture of the immigrant generation, they make it appear as if an ethnic revival were taking place.

Then, too, it should be noted that even symbolic ethnicity may be relevant for only some of the descendents of the immigrants. As intermarriage continues, the number of people with parents from the same secular ethnic group will continue to decline, and by the time the fourth generation of the old immigration reaches adulthood, such people may be a minority. Most Catholic ethnics will be hybrid, and will have difficulty developing an ethnic identity. For example, how would the son of an Italian mother and Irish father who has married a woman of Polish-German ancestry determine his ethnicity, and what would he and his wife tell their children? Even if they were willing, would they be able to do so; and in that case to decide their children's ethnicity, how would they rank or synthesize their diverse backgrounds? These questions are empirical, and urgently need to be studied, but I would suggest that there are only three possibilities. Either the parents choose the single ethnic identity they find most satisfying, or they become what I earlier called pan-ethnics, or they cope with diversity by ignoring it, and raise their children as non-ethnic.

The Emergence of Symbolic Ethnicity

The preceding observations have suggested that symbolic ethnicity is a new phenomenon that comes into being in the third generation, but it is probably of earlier vintage and may have already begun to emerge among the immigrants themselves. After all, many of the participants in the new immigration were oppressed economically, politically and culturally in their old countries, and could not have had much affection even for the village and regions they were leaving. Consequently, it is entirely possible that they began to jettison the old culture and to stay away from ethnic organizations other than churches and unions the moment they came to America, saving only their primary groups, their ties to relatives still left in Europe, and their identity. In small town America, where immigrants were a numerically unimportant minority, the pressure for immediate acculturation and assimilation was much greater than in the cities, but even in the latter, the seeds for symbolic ethnicity may have been sown earlier than previously thought.

Conversely, despite all the pressures toward Americanization and the prejudice and discrimination experienced by the immigrants, they were never faced with conditions that required or encouraged them to give up their ethnicity entirely. Of course, some of the earliest Jewish arrivals to America had become Quakers and Episcopalians before the end of the nineteenth century, but the economic conditions that persuaded the Jamaican Chinese in Kingston to become Creole, and the social isolation that forced Italians in Sydney, Australia, to abolish the traditional familial male-female role segregation shortly after arriving, have never been part of the American experience.[20]

Some conditions for the emergence of symbolic ethnicity were present from the beginning, for American ethnics have always been characterized by freedom of ethnic expression, which stimulated both ethnic diversity, and the right to find one's own way of being ethnic that are crucial to symbolic ethnicity. Although sacred and secular ethnic organizations which insisted that only one mode of being ethnic was legitimate have always existed in America, they have not been able to enforce their norms, in part because they have always had to compete with other ethnic organizations. Even in ethnic neighborhoods where conformity was expected and social control was pervasive, people had some freedom of choice about ethnic cultural practices. For example, the second generation Boston Italians I studied had to conform to many family and peer group norms, but they were free to ignore ethnic secondary groups, and to drop or alter Italian cultural practices according to their own preference.

Ethnic diversity within the group was probably encouraged by the absence of a state religion, and national and local heads of ethnic communities. For example, American Jewry never had a chief rabbi, or even chief Orthodox, Conservative and Reform rabbis, and the European practice of local Jewish communities electing or appointing local laymen as presidents was not carried across the ocean.[21] Catholic ethnics had to obey the cardinal or bishop heading their diocese, of course, but in those communities where the diocese insisted on an Irish church, the other ethnic groups, notably the Italians, kept their distance from the church, and only in parochial schools was there any attempt to root out secular ethnic patterns. The absence of strong unifying institutions thus created the opportunity for diversity and freedom from the beginning, and undoubtedly facilitated the departure from ethnic cultures and organizations.

Among the Jews, symbolic ethnicity may have been fostered early by self-selection among Jewish emigrants. As Liebman points out, the massive Eastern European immigration to America did not include the rabbis and scholars who practiced what he called an elite religion in the old countries; as a result, the immigrants established what he calls a folk religion in America instead, with indigenous rabbis who were elected or appointed by individual congregations, and were more permissive in allowing, or too weak to prevent, deviations from religious orthodoxy, even of the milder folk variety.[22] Indeed, the development of a folk religion may have encouraged religious and secular diversity among Jews from the very beginning.

Still, perhaps the most important factor in the development of symbolic ethnicity was probably the awareness, which I think many second generation people had already reached, that neither the practice of ethnic culture nor participation in ethnic organizations were essential to being and feeling ethnic. For Jews, living in a Jewish neighborhood or working with Jews every day was enough to maintain Jewish identity. When younger second generation Jews moved to suburbia in large numbers after World War II, many wound up in communities in which they were a small numerical minority, but they quickly established an informal Jewish community of neighborly relations, and then built synagogues and community centers to formalize and supplement the informal community. At the time, many observers interpreted the feverish building as a religious revival, but for most Jews, the synagogue was a symbol that could serve as a means of expressing identity without requiring more than occasional participation in its activities.[23] Thus, my observations among the second generation Jews of Park Forest and other suburbs led me to think as far back as the mid 1950s that among Jews, at least, the shift to symbolic ethnicity was already under way.[24]

The Future of Ethnicity

The emergence of symbolic ethnicity naturally raises the question of its persistence into the fifth and sixth generations. Although the Catholic and Jewish religions are certain to endure, it appears that as religion becomes less important to people, they, too, will be eroded by acculturation and assimilation. Even now, synagogues see most of their worshippers no more than once or twice a year, and presumably, the same trend will appear, perhaps more slowly, among Catholics and Protestants as well.

Whether the secular aspects of ethnicity can survive beyond the fourth generation is somewhat less certain. One possibilty is that symbolic ethnicity will itself decline as acculturation and assimilation continue, and then disappear as erstwhile ethnics forget their secular ethnic identity to blend into one or another subcultural melting pot. The other possibility is that symbolic ethnicity is a steady-state phenomenon that can persist into the fifth and sixth generations.

Obviously, this question can only be guessed at, but my hypothesis is that symbolic ethnicity may persist. The continued existence of Germans, Scandinavians, and Irish after five or more generations in America suggests that in the larger cities and suburbs, at least, they have remained ethnic because they have long practiced symbolic ethnicity.[25] Consequently, there is good reason to believe that the same process will also take place among ethnics of the new immigration.

Ethnic behavior, attitudes, and even identity are, however, determined not only by what goes on among the ethnics, but also by developments in the larger society, and especially by how that society will treat ethnics in the future; what costs it will levy and what benefits it will award to them as ethnics. At present, the costs of being and feeling ethnic are slight. The changes which the immigrants and their descendants wrought in America now make it unnecessary for ethnics to surrender their ethnicity to gain upward mobility, and today ethnics are admitted virtually everywhere, provided they meet economic and status requirements, except at the very highest levels of the economic, political, and cultural hierarchies. Moreover, since World War II, the ethnics have been able to shoulder blacks and other racial minorities with the deviant and scapegoat functions they performed in an earlier America, so that ethnic prejudice and 'institutional ethnism' are no longer significant, except again at the very top of the societal hierarchies.

To be sure, some ethnic scapegoating persists at other levels of these hierarchies; American Catholics are still blamed for the policies of the Vatican, Italo-Americans are criticized for the Mafia, and urban ethnics generally have been portrayed as racists by a sometime coalition of white and black Protestant, Jewish, and other upper-middle class cosmopolitans. But none of these phenomena, however repugnant, strike me as serious enough to persuade many to hide their ethnicity. More important but less often noticed, white working class men, and perhaps others, still use ethnic stereotypes to trade insults, but this practice serves functions other than the maintenence of prejudice or inequality.

At the same time, the larger society also seems to offer some benefits for being ethnic. Americans increasingly perceive themselves as undergoing cultural homogenization, and whether or not this perception is justified, they are constantly looking for new ways to establish their differences from each other. Meanwhile, the social, cultural and political turbulence of the last decade, and the concurrent delegitimation of many American institutions have also cast doubt on some of the other ways by which people identify themselves and differentiate themselves from each other. Ethnicity, now that it is respectable and no longer a major cause of conflict, seems therefore to be ideally suited to serve as a distinguishing characteristic. Moreover, in a mobile society, people who move around and therefore find themselves living in communities of strangers, tend to look for commonalities that make strangers into neighbors, and shared ethnicity may provide mobile people with at least an initial excuse to get together. Finally, as long as the European immigration into America continues, people will still be perceived, classified, and ranked at least in part by ethnic origin. Consequently, external forces exist to complement internal identity needs, and unless there is a drastic change in the allocation of costs and benefits with respect to ethnicity, it seems likely that the larger society will also encourage the persistence of symbolic ethnicity.

Needless to say, it is always possible that future economic and political conditions in American society will create a demand for new scapegoats, and if ethnics are forced into this role, so that ethnicity once more levies social costs, present tendencies will be interrupted. Under such conditions, some ethnics will try to assimilate faster and pass out of all ethnic roles, while others will revitalize the ethnic group socially and culturally if only for self-protection. Still, the chance that Catholic ethnics will be scapegoated more than today seems very slight. A serious economic crisis could, however, result in a resurgence of anti-semitism, in part because of the affluence of many American Jews, in part because of their visibly influential role in some occupations, notably mass communications.

If present societal trends continue, however, symbolic ethnicity should become the dominant way of being ethnic by the time the fourth generation of the new immigration matures into adulthood, and this in turn will have consequences for the structure of American ethnic groups. For one thing, as secondary and primary assimilation continue, and ethnic networks weaken and unravel, it may be more accurate to speak of ethnic aggregates rather than groups. More important, since symbolic ethnicity does not depend on ethnic cultures and organizations, their future decline and disappearance must be expected, particularly those cultural patterns which interfere with other aspects of life, and those organizations which require active membership.

Few such patterns and organizations are left in any case, and leaders of the remaining organizations have long been complaining bitterly over what they perceive as the cultural and organizational apathy of ethnics. They also criticize the resort to symbolic ethnicity, identifying it as an effortless way of being ethnic which further threatens their own persistence. Even so, attacking people as apathetic or lazy, or calling on

them to revive the practices and loyalties of the past have never been effective for engendering support, and reflect instead the desperation of organizations which cannot offer new incentives that would enable them to recruit members.

Some cultural patterns and organizations will survive. Patterns which lend themselves to transformation into symbols and easy practice, such as annual holidays, should persist. So will organizations which create and distribute symbols, or 'ethnic goods' such as foodstuffs or written materials, but need few or no members and can function with small staffs and low overheads. In all likelihood, most ethnic organizations will eventually realize that in order to survive, they must deal mainly in symbols, using them to generate enough support to fund other activities as well.

The demand for current ethnic symbols may require the maintenance of at least some old cultural practices, possibly in museums, and through the work of ethnic scholars who keep old practices alive by studying them. It is even possible that the organizations which attempt to maintain the old cultures will support themselves in part by supplying ethnic nostalgia, and some ethnics may aid such organizations if only to assuage their guilt at having given up ancestral practices.

Still, the history of religion and nationalism as well as events of recent years, should remind us that the social process sometimes moves in dialectical ways, and that acculturative and assimilative actions by a majority occasionally generate revivalistic reactions by a minority. As a result, even ethnic aggregates in which the vast majority maintains its identity in symbolic ways will probably always bring forth small pockets of neo-traditionalism—of rebel converts to sacred and secular ways of the past. They may not influence the behavior of the majority, but they are almost always highly visible, and will thus continue to play a role in the ethnicity of the future.

Symbolic Ethnicity and Straight-line Theory
The third and fourth generation's concern with ethnic identity and its expression through symbols seem to me to fit straight-line theory, for symbolic ethnicity cannot be considered as evidence either of a third generation return or a

revival. Instead, it constitutes only another point in the secular trend that is drawn, implicitly, in straight-line theory, although it could also be a point at which the declining secular trend begins to level off and perhaps straightens out.

In reality, of course, the straight-line has never been quite straight, for even if it accurately graphs the dominant ethnic experience, it ignores the ethnic groups who still continue to make tiny small bumps and waves in the line. Among these are various urban and rural ethnic enclaves, notably among the poor; the new European immigrants who help to keep these enclaves from disappearing; the groups which successfully insulate themselves from the rest of American society in deliberately-enclosed enclaves; and the rebel converts to sacred and secular ways of the past who will presumably continue to appear.

Finally, even if I am right to predict that symbolic ethnicity can persist into the fifth and sixth generations, I would be foolish to suggest that it is a permanent phenomenon. Although all Americans, save the Indians, came here as immigrants and are thus in one sense ethnics, people who arrived in the seventeenth and eighteenth centuries, and before the mid-nineteenth century 'old' immigration, are, except in some rural enclaves, no longer ethnics even if they know where their emigrant ancestors came from.

The history of groups whose ancestors arrived here seven or more generations ago suggests that eventually, the ethnics of the new immigration will be like them; they may retain American forms of the religions which their ancestors brought to America, but their secular cultures will be only a dim memory, and their identity will bear only the minutest trace, if that, of their national origin. Ultimately, then, the secular trend of straight-line theory will hit very close to zero, and the basic postulates of the theory will turn out to have been accurate—unless of course by then America, and the ways it makes Americans, has altered drastically in some now unpredictable manner.

ENDNOTES

1. Personal communication. Incidentally, David Riesman is now credited with having invented the term ethnicity as it is currently used. (Hereafter, I shall omit personal communication footnotes, but most of the individuals named in the text supplied ideas or data through personal communication.)

2. For reasons of brevity, I employ these terms rather than Gordon's more detailed concepts. Milton Gordon, *Assimilation in American Life*, New York, Oxford University Press, 1964, Chapter 3.

3. Neil C. Sandberg, *Ethnic Identity and Assimilation: The Polish-American Community*, New York, Praeger, 1974. The primary empirical application of straight-line theory is probably still W. Lloyd Warner and Leo Srole, *The Social Systems of American Ethnic Groups*, New Haven, Yale University Press, 1945.

4. See e.g., Andrew Greeley, *Ethnicity in the United States*, New York, Wiley, 1974, Chapter 1.

5. W. Yancey, E. Ericksen and R. Juliani, 'Emergent Ethnicity: A Review and Reformulation', *American Sociological Review*, Vol. 41, June 1976, pp. 391–403, quote at p. 400.

6. The major works include Greeley, op. cit.; Harold J. Abramson, *Ethnic Diversity in Catholic America*, New York, Wiley, 1973; and Nathan Glazer and Daniel P. Moynihan, *Beyond the Melting Pot*, Cambridge, MIT Press, 2nd ed. 1970.

7. Class differences in the degree of acculturation and assimilation were first noted by Warner and Srole, op. cit.; for some recent data among Poles, see Sandberg, op. cit.

8. Herbert J. Gans, *The Urban Villagers*, New York, Free Press, 1962, Chap. 11. See also Dennis Wrong, 'How Important is Social Class', in Irving Howe, ed. *The World of the Blue Collar Worker*, New York, Quadrangle, 1972, pp. 297–309; William Kornblum, *Blue Collar Community*, Chicago, University of Chicago Press, 1974; and Stephen Steinberg, *The Academic Melting Pot*, New Brunswick, Transaction Books, 1977.

9. Marcus L. Hansen, *The Problems of the Third Generation Immigrant*, Rock Island, Ill., Augustana Historical Society, 1938; and 'The Third Generation in America', *Commentary*, Vol. 14, November 1952, pp. 492–500.

10. See also Harold J. Abramson, 'The Religioethnic Factor and the American Experience: Another Look at the Three-Generations Hypothesis', *Ethnicity*, Vol. 2, June 1975, pp. 163–177.

11. One of the most influential works has been Michael Novak, *The Rise of the Unmeltable Ethnics*, New York, Macmillan, 1971.

12. Perhaps the first, and now not sufficiently remembered, study of third-generation Jews was Judith Kramer and Seymour Leventman, *The Children of the Gilded Ghetto*, New Haven, Yale University Press, 1961.

13. Geoffrey Bock, 'The Jewish Schooling of American Jews', unpublished Ph.D. Dissertation, Graduate School of Education, Harvard University, 1976.

14. The notion of primary assimilation extends Gordon's concept of marital assimilation to include movement out of the extended family, friendship circles and other peer groups. In describing marital assimilation, Gordon did, however, mention the primary group as well. Gordon, op. cit. p. 80.

15. The major debate at present is between Abramson and Alba, the former viewing the amount of intermarriage among Catholic ethnics as low, and the latter as high. See Abramson, 'Ethnic Diversity in Catholic America', op. cit.; and Richard Alba, 'Social Assimilation of American Catholic National-Origin Groups', *American Sociological Review*, Vol. 41, December 1976, pp. 1030–1046.

16. See e.g., Marshall Sklare and Joseph Greenblum, *Jewish Identity on the Suburban Frontier*, New York, Basic Books, 1967; Herbert J. Gans, 'The Origin and Growth of a Jewish Community in the Suburbs: A Study of the Jews of Park Forest', in Marshall Sklare, ed., *The Jews: Social Pattern of an American Group*, New York, Free Press, 1958, pp. 205–248, and Herbert J. Gans, *The Levittowners*, New York, Pantheon, 1967, pp. 73–80. These findings may not apply to communities with significant numbers of German Jews with Reform leanings. There are few Orthodox Jews in the suburbs, except in those surrounding New York.

17. Sandberg, op. cit. and James Crispino, *The Assimilation of Ethnic Groups: The Italian Case*, New York, Center for Migration Studies, 1979.

18. My use of the word symbol here follows Lloyd Warner's concept of symbolic behavior. See W. Lloyd Warner, *American Life: Dream and Reality*, Chicago, University of Chicago Press, 1953, Chapter 1.

19. See Nathan Glazer, *American Judaism*, Chicago, University of Chicago Press, 2nd ed. 1972, pp. 114–115.

20. On the Jamaica Chinese, see Orlando Patterson, *Ethnic Chauvinism*, New York, Stein and Day, 1977, Chapter 5; on the Sydney Italians, see Rina Huber, *From Pasta to Pavlova*, St. Lucia, University of Queensland Press, 1977, Part 3.

21. For a study of one unsuccessful attempt to establish a community presidency, see Arthur A. Goren, *New York Jews and the Quest for Community*, New York, Columbia University Press, 1970.

22. Charles S. Liebman, *The Ambivalent American Jew*, Philadelphia, Jewish Publication Society of America, 1973. Chapter 3. Liebman notes that the few elite rabbis who did come to America quickly sensed they were in alien territory and returned to Eastern Europe. The survivors of the Holocaust who came to America after World War II were too few and too late to do more than influence the remaining Jewish orthodox organizations.

23. Gans, The Origin of a Jewish Community in the Suburbs, op. cit.

24. See Herbert J. Gans, 'American Jewry: Present and Future', *Commentary*, Vol. 21, May 1956, pp. 422–430, which includes a discussion of 'symbolic Judaism'.

25. Unfortunately, too little attention has been devoted by sociologists to ethnicity among descendants of the old immigration.

29

A New Ethnic Group
in the United States

Stanley Lieberson

It is the thesis of this paper that there is a major and extraordinarily important ethnic shift underway in the United States: the growth and expansion of a new white ethnic group. This new white group is characterized by several features.

There is a recognition of being white, but lack of any clearcut identification with, and/or knowledge of, a specific European origin. Such people recognize that they are not the same as some of the existing ethnic groups in the country such as Greeks, Jews, Italians, Poles, Irish, and so forth. The vast bulk of persons meeting these conditions are of older Northwestern European origins, but there are also some persons from newer European sources of immigration shifting into this group. Indeed, for reasons to be given below, I would expect more to do so in the years ahead.

There is some difficulty in finding an appropriate name for this group. The term WASP is inappropriate for two reasons: first, it is often used in a pejorative sense; second, it is not clear that this new group is restricted to persons of Anglo-Saxon origin or to Protestants. For lack of

A revised and abridged verson of a paper in April, 1984 at the SUNY-Albany Conference on Ethnicity and Race in the Last Quarter of the 20th Century. This is part of a larger Social Science Research Council Census Monograph project supported by the Russell Sage Foundation, which will be co-authored by Lawrence Santi. His assistance, as well as that of Mark Scarbecz and Mary C. Waters is gratefully acknowledged. A special debt is owed to Guy E. Swanson, who suggested the term *unhyphenated whites*.

an appropriate alternative, I will refer to this group as *unhyphenated whites*—as distinguished from all whites. Note that my thesis is not that the term *unhyphenated whites* means the elimination of some other specific ethnic groups such as, say, Germans. It is perfectly appropriate to recognize that there are some persons of German ancestry who would declare themselves to be German-American or some such variant, and that there would be others of German ancestry who would fit into the unhyphenated white category.

This conclusion about a new ethnic group stems from several factors that are not as widely appreciated as they might be. First, there is a tendency to see ethnic and racial categories as static, unchanging entities—a perception that is probably correct in the short term, but radically in error when viewed from a long-range, historical perspective. To be sure, it is widely recognized that the degree of identification with an ethnic group may fluctuate over time as a function of various social conditions. But less clearly understood is the fact that the group categories themselves may shift over time and, moreover, short-term vacillations in identification may well be hiding strong long-term shifts. Second, the understanding of the mechanisms that permit shifts in ethnic classification and identification is inadequate. Third, there are fundamental causes of changes that have not been recognized. Finally, there are data that are at least consistent with this thesis about a newly forming ethnic

443

group, but they have not been interpreted in this way.

Ethnic and Racial Groups in Flux

Racial and ethnic groups are not merely static entities, but also products of labelling and identification *processes* that change and evolve over time. Differentials in fertility, mortality, and migration are not the only forces responsible for the expansion or decline in their numbers. Beyond this, gradual shifts occur in the sets and subsets of groups found in a society such as to lead to both new combinations and new divisions. This continuous process of combining and recombining means that the very existence of a given group is not be be taken for granted; groups appear and disappear. Ethnic groups such as Mexicans or Puerto Ricans are essentially very recent in nature, resulting from interethnic contacts only since the expansion of Europe into the New World. In similar fashion, the Coloured population in South Africa is a recent group. But it would be the case for many older ethnic groups as well; the English ethnic population in the United Kingdom, for example, is obviously a hybridized population descending from contact and expansion involving a number of groups.

These processes can be so gradual that they may run for hundreds of years before anything close to a complete shift occurs (an estimate that is probably conservative). Ethnic origin, from this point of view, is both a status and a process. At any given time, we are most likely to see the state of affairs reported by the population—it is less easy to see the process of ethnic change that is also going on. Indeed, some of the difficulties that researchers and census takers experience in using data on racial and ethnic groups reflect the processes of ethnic and racial change themselves. Part of the difficulty in asking people about their ethnic or racial origins is actually due to a social fact that is telling us something about the flux in the concepts and identifications themselves.

In short, when examining the racial and ethnic groups found in a given society, there is a tendency to take for granted their existence. In fact, a given racial or ethnic group does not go back to the origins of the human species. Rather, each ethnic group was created out of dynamic processes that took place over periods far longer than a given individual's lifespan. Just as various species in the plant and animal worlds are continuously changing—even though it is normally possible to point to this species or that—so, too, ethnic groups are under continuous flux in terms of their birth, maintenance, and decline. If people are asked for their ethnic ancestry at a given time, they are apt to give answers that largely fit into the rubrics established and conventional at the time. Responses that do not fit these rubrics tend to be viewed as errors, or as failures of the enumeration instrument, or of the enumerator, or what have you. And that is often the case. But in addition, there is a continuous flux in the categories themselves and in who defines himself or herself (or is defined by others) as belonging in these categories. In this manner, there are shifts in racial and ethnic populations. Because we are dealing with populations, it is perfectly possible, particularly at some intermediate stage of change, for some persons of X ancestry to identify themselves as belonging to ethnic group X while an increasing proportion with X ancestry are now reporting themselves as Y.

Mechanisms of Shift

How might the ethnic/racial origins reported in a country shift without being the result of differentials in birth, death, and international migration? No matter what causal force underlies the change (and we shall see that there are many), untimately it must operate through a limited number of mechanisms. There are really four main ways of thinking about a respondent's ancestry. One deals with the true ancestral origins for a given respondent, i.e., what we would learn about the respondent if roots could be traced back to some specific temporal point. We can call this the *true ancestral origin* or AO_t. The second are the origins that the respondent *believes* to be his or her ancestral origins at a given specified point in time. In most cases, then, AO_b is the only indicator available of AO_t. It is an imperfect indicator, but nevertheless one would hope that there is some reasonably strong association between reported and actual ancestral origins. The third and fourth measures refer to *identification.* This is either self-identification *(SI)*, or what a person declares as the group(s) he/she identifies with; *or* the ethnic label imposed on the person by others *(OI)*.

These four variables are actually oversimplified in the sense that there are subsets of each that could be considered in greater detail than is possible here. Even AO_t, the true ancestral origins, is more complicated than it might seem at first glance. If it were possible to trace somebody's ancestry backwards in time, there would be no "natural" stopping point at which one could say, "At last, here is this person's ancestry." One could always go further back and find earlier combinations of characteristics that led to the ones just recognized. The only natural stopping points are really societal ones. In a study of the ancestral origins of the United States population, chances are the investigator is interested in the defined ancestral roots at the time of arrival in the New World. However, for ancestors who were here prior to the expansion of Europe in the sixteenth century, we would simply want to know what the ancestors were at that time rather than earlier, e.g., Indian tribes rather than origins at the time these peoples crossed into the New World much earlier. Therefore conclusions about ancestral origins—if we were to imagine the capability of actually determining each person's true roots as far back in time as we wanted—would depend on where one decided to stop. In similar fashion, then, beliefs about ancestral origins would also have certain complications that depended on the "generational span" covered by ancestors in the information passed on to offspring. One source of distortion, then, is the societal process of intergenerational transmission. Under any circumstance, if it were possible for an investigator to correctly trace the actual ancestral history of each respondent as far back as relevant, there is no doubt that the information obtained in such a manner would differ in many cases from what was reported as the respondent's ancestral origins. Presumably there is some sort of correlation between reported and true origins, but who can say how close it is?

Because the self-identification reported to others can be affected by both the audience and the social context, there are several subtypes of *SI*. Indeed, private self-identification can even be totally different from any public declaration of ethnic identification. As a matter of fact, ethnic or racial cases of "passing" are exactly that— situations where someone's publicly declared identification is intentionally different from the person's private self-identification. At the very least, we can say that the social context may affect both an individual's self-identification *and* the identification reported to someone else.

As for the identification imposed by others, *OI*, it is almost certain that parents will be a powerful force since in most cases it is from them that one obtains at least the initial sense of self-identification. However, this is not a simple, cut-and-dried matter. More than one single message may be conveyed to the offspring even from within the family, particularly if parents have different identifications. Beyond this, outsiders can have certain notions of who one is that are at variance with the identification learned at home. In turn, individuals can be swept into social movements and other events during their lifetime that end up redefining their self-identification. The power of outside identifications can range enormously. The Pass Laws of South Africa and the policies of Nazi Germany represent extreme versions of this, where in effect the state will not allow certain options at all. Thus persons of partial Jewish ancestry were suddenly identified as Jews by the State in a way that could not be avoided. The current use of a self-enumeration procedure in the United States Census gives respondents considerable freedom to report their own identification. However, this complete freedom does not mean that reported origins or identification is a free-floating matter, since self-identification is still affected by the identification placed on the individual by others and this in turn affects the voluntary response in a census or any other context.

Societal forces are more than simply *imposed*, pure and simple, on the population. And, of course, it is these forces that are especially important to consider in studying self-identification and response in a country such as the United States. (Incidentally, until very recently, there was not complete freedom for respondents in the United States to declare whatever ancestry they wanted. Instructions to enumerators indicated very specific rules about accepting certain responses from persons of mixed, non-white origins. Likewise, there used to be various state laws that defined blacks in very specific descent terms.) In other words, self-identification is a complicated variable, affected by a variety of societal forces. Pass Laws and completely laissez-faire policies may represent the extremes of political forces, but the actual responses in laissez-faire situations are not without their strong informal pressures. For example, the response a person of mixed-white origins receives, based on his or her distinctive surname, may well lead to the less visible and unidentified origin fading.

In summary, one can visualize obtaining four items of information for each respondent: self-identification (vaguely defined, since there would be contextual effects on the SI that is reported); AO_b, which refers to what the respondent believes is his or her ancestral origin; AO_t, the historically *true* origins at the time the various ancestors arrived in the New World or, if Native Americans, at the outset of the sixteenth century; and OI, the identification imposed by others. One can also visualize measuring the association between various pairings of these attributes. There is, for example, the linkage between true ancestral origins and what one believes them to be; the association between self-identification and believed origins; and the linkage between self-identification and true origins. Presumably there are positive associations between each of these pairs, but it is an open question—and one not readily answered—as to how strong they would be. In the case of self-identification and believed origins, for example, I think we can expect a fairly strong linkage, if only because modifications in one of these will tend to modify the other; if not within one's lifespan, then at least in the course of a few generations. If SI and AO_b are highly linked, such that shifts in one lead to shifts in the other, it would mean that changes in self-identification will cause the association between *believed* and *true* ancestry to drift apart and become progressively weaker. Thus the linkage between self-identification and true ancestral origins, as well as the linkage between true and believed origins, should get progressively weaker over time.

Given these distinctions, it is clear that many studies of race and ethnic relations are truncated or warped to some unknown degree. If one examines the assimilation of, say, persons of

Italian ancestry, then those that either do not identify or are not aware of their Italian ancestry are fully lost. Such a subset of the population with Italian ancestry is almost certain to differ from the entire set of persons who could have accurately reported themselves of that origin. The loss or truncation is certainly affected by the research instrument. The 1980 U.S. census and 1979 Current Population Survey conducted by the census both allowed for multiple responses, but the National Opinion Research Center studies of ethnic origin in the General Social Survey and earlier census surveys did not.

Two Forms of Change

Changes in ethnic grouping can occur either within the life span of a respondent or intergenerationally. It is easy to visualize a variety of ways through which changes of the latter type can take place. If there is intermarriage and interbreeding, then the lineage of the descendants becomes more complicated with each passing generation. The potential of dropping off and simplifying ethnic matters becomes great. Even endogamous mating does not necessarily avoid simplification when there are Old World geographic complications and subtleties that can be lost in each succeeding generation. For example, the descendants of Swiss-Germans do not always know that their ancestors drew a sharp distinction between Swiss-German (as opposed to being German-German) nor do they always know that being Swiss does not convey any ethnic ancestry at all. Boundary changes, incorrect and/or oversimplified knowledge of various settings, confusion, and the like all affect intergenerational continuity even in relatively simple settings.

Schools and religious institutions may or may not serve to reinforce and maintain ethnic identification. Much of this depends on governmental policies. In some countries, for example, linguistic differences between the ethnic groups lead to separate schools and these, in turn, mean setting off an ethnic marker for each child at a very early age. (Obviously de jure ethnic/racial school segregation can and does occur for other reasons as well.) In the United States, the existence of public schools and the mixture of ethnic groups found within some of the denominations offering private schooling (e.g., Roman Catholics and Lutherans) probably does less to maintain specific ethnic identity among white groups than occurs in some other nations.

It is by no means inevitable that a full and correct transmission of ethnic ancestry will occur through the family. First, there are distortions through the increasingly common circumstances in which many children spend part or all of their life in a household with at least one of the parents absent through divorce, desertion, or death. Intergenerational knowledge can easily be affected in situations where one or both parents die before their offspring reach adulthood; children are abandoned; or children are raised by relatives on one side of the family. Beyond this, there are also circumstances where promiscuity may literally lead to ignorance of one parent's origins. Finally, there is the possibility of intentional discontinuities between parents and children, in which parents attempt to hide certain ethnic origins or in some other way de-emphasize certain knowledge.

In addition, there are children with only a modest interest in their ancestral origins, children who do not focus on the topic. Others become interested too late to obtain accurate information from parents who, by then, are deceased. To be sure, such a situation presupposes a special type of society, one where a significant number of children are not that interested in the answer *and* one where it is not automatically learned regardless of a child's initial interest. In similar fashion, there may be parents who have little or no interest in discussing ancestral histories with their offspring. In all of this, of course, we can visualize an intergenerational shift in largely one direction: from knowledge to ignorance, from detail to blur. Thus, unless exceptional effort is made, it is unlikely for knowledge about ancestral origins to be reclaimed in later generations. Such events mean that some members of later generations will be unable to provide any ethnic identification at all, but it also means badly warped responses that are either totally or largely inaccurate on the part of others. Questions on ancestry, for *some* respondents, begin to approximate a sociological form of the ink blot test.

Ethnic identification may also change *within* someone's lifespan through a variety of ways. One force is analogous to the intergenerational simplifying process, except here within someone's own lifespan a complicated ancestral history slowly changes and is simplified by forgetting or unlearning some parts of it. Even some details of a relatively simple ancestral history can be distorted and changed during a person's lifetime. In either case, we would find a deterioration in the detail with which ancestral history is reported. Certainly, too, there is the question of self-identification, particularly after people reach an age where they are removed from parental pressures and control. At such a point, certain changes in self-identification are freer to come out.

The identification imposed by others on a given respondent will also influence intragenerational changes. It is my impression that regions of the country vary considerably in the degree to which residents can "spot" or identify members of different groups. If this impression is correct (or if for other reasons someone experiences variation in the degree to which others are attuned to ethnic ancestry), then the identification imposed by others affects the propensity for someone to identify himself or herself in a certain manner.

Causes

What social forces cause shifts in identification, ancestral knowledge, and in the categories themselves? By contrast, what keeps such shifts from occurring in other contexts? As a general rule, one should recognize that social organization and ethnic delineations tend to be linked. Changes in the identification of groups, by either others or themselves, in the long run affect the organizational structure of racial and ethnic populations. On the other hand, changes in the organizational structure of racial and ethnic populations generate new identifications (again by themselves or imposed by others) that reflect their structural positions within the society. A series of forces can thus be visualized as operating to affect identification, the known ancestral origins, and the ethnic categories found in a population. Needless to say, they are not always mutually exclusive in any given context.

1. It is important to recognize that social pressures towards shift are sometimes of an idiosyncratic nature. Ryder (1955) has demonstrated this rather nicely for Canada with respect to

residents of German ethnic origin during World War II. The sharp, downward decline in the numbers reporting themselves as German suggested a definite misreporting and reflected the unpopularity of being German. In this case (and in others below), we can see how such changes might be especially likely for persons of mixed ethnic origins; it would simply be a matter of emphasizing one origin at the expense of another. If a historically idiosyncratic or unique feature were to operate for a relatively long time, there is a strong chance that the consequence would be a shift in self-identification and knowledge of ancestral origin, which would then persist even if the cause was later to disappear. This is because of the natural drift mechanism described below.

2. An ethnic ranking system means that members of some groups enjoy prestige and various advantages, whereas others face handicaps or even punishments. This suggests that, other things being equal, there will be a net change toward the direction that generates positive rewards and prestige, and away from those categorizations and classifications that generate disadvantages and lower status. Insofar as groups differ in their prestige and in the real advantages and disadvantages that perceived membership offers, one might expect subtle and less-than-subtle shifts towards more desirable, or less disadvantaged, origins at the price of others. This could occur for those without any claims to such ancestries, and certainly for those of mixed ancestry. Thus under some circumstances, ethnic origins will be lost, identifications changed, and perhaps new nomenclature used as a device for avoiding social disadvantages. A nice example of the latter, by the way, is the use of *Czech* as an ethnic identifyer in the United States instead of *Bohemian*, the latter having certain unfavorable connotations in an earlier period.

To be sure, this is not the only response possible to such a ranking and reward system. Responses of a far different nature involve combatting disadvantages through legislation, protests, group organization, and the like. Acquiescence is another response, not unknown at least for the short-term. It is only possible to speculate, at this point, whether ancestral loss is less likely during periods of intense, organized effort by a group to alter its disadvantaged situation.

During such periods ethnic awareness is likely to be intensified and reinforced by organized efforts; slight or partial shifts away from the group identification are also likely to be branded as betrayals or traitorous acts. (Under such circumstances, by the way, a different form of distortion can occur: the de-emphasis of other ancestries among the mixed members of groups aroused to protest and combat their disadvantaged situation.) But overall, where there is ethnic shift, it is in the direction towards groups that provide more advantageous positions in the ethnic hierarchy.

3. The very opposite factor to that discussed above is a natural drift mechanism; namely, indifference to one's ethnic origin, which leads to the loss of detailed or even partially accurate information on ancestry. Once this occurs, it is unlikely for details to be recovered in later generations, although there is the possibility via grandparents or other relatives such as aunts and uncles. Hence, for the most part, any de-emphasis or loss of interest in ethnic origins leads to permanent losses of information and, as a consequence, possibly newer and vaguer and simpler identification schemes. In that sense, change can occur only in the direction towards distortion or new delineations.

One feature of this drift is that it is more likely to occur in some directions than in others. As a general rule, voluntary drifts in identification are never towards greater disadvantages, but either maintain or improve one's position within the system. The drift is limited to shifts toward memberships and identifications that are beneficial, or at least not harmful. Hence it is unlikely for people to give up distinctions that are beneficial by merging or joining them with categories that are beneath them in prestige and/or other rewards. A broader and vaguer ethnic delineation may then develop, if it is not disadvantageous when compared with the more precise ancestral delineations that previous generations would have given. As we shall see below, this is what I believe is going on with respect to the development of a new unhyphenated-white ethnic group.

4. Government and other major institutions vary over time, and between societies, in how much formal attention they pay to ethnic/racial

categories. But it is unlikely that the subject will be totally ignored in any multiethnic situation. As a consequence, at least some formal bureaucratic rules and definitions are always used and that such rules will be too simple to take into account the entire range of ethnic/racial complexities and the existing array of self-identifications is virtually guaranteed. Furthermore, the rules almost certainly deviate from the reality in the direction of meeting the needs of the dominant population and/or the organizations themselves (Petersen, 1969). This means that governmental and other organizational forms of control affect the ethnic delineation process. Because various organizational processes formally identify ethnic lineage, they can leave less room for distortion than there could be otherwise (except when the distortions are in the governmental delineations themselves, such as when one-sixteenth black and fifteen-sixteenths white is defined as "black"). But organizational forms of control are relevant because they offer advantages to some identifications and disadvantages to others. For example, being on Indian tribal rolls can provide certain rewards in the United States at this time, so there is an incentive to remain on such rolls and to be sure that one's offspring (in the case of persons of mixed origins) are aware of their Indian heritage.

Governmental and other institutional delineations of racial and ethnic categories (and the criteria for inclusion) are almost certain to differ from all the subtle permutations and combinations of identification and ancestry held by the populations themselves. The net effect is a massive set of distortions due to these influences, combined with efforts by members of different groups to adjust to these delineations (in order to take advantage of the rewards from some categories and to escape the handicaps of others).

5. Also affecting the shifts, and their direction, is the nature of the identification system. This can be visualized as ranging from a totally coercive system, where identification is imposed on the individual by the government or some other institution, to the other extreme, where identification is voluntary and completely a matter of self-declaration. As noted earlier, South Africa, with its Pass Laws, and Germany during the Nazi era, represent one such extreme on the *coercive-voluntary continuum*. The laissez-faire

disposition toward race in Brazil represents the other extreme. The United States is somewhere between an imposed coercive system and a purely voluntaristic one. In addition, there have been fluctuations over time, as in the cases of blacks and American Indians. For most white groups in the United States, however, ethnic/ancestral affiliations are in principle voluntary; i.e., there is no governmental or other *formal* institutional constraint on the affiliation claimed. Likewise, the civil rights legislation at present encourages some persons to maintain particular identifications, at least in certain contexts, in order to enjoy special programs and considerations.

6. Intergroup conflicts have consequences for labelling and identification. Certainly the dominant group's interaction with subordinate groups has a direct impact on the organization of the subordinates. The terms *Native American* or *American Indian* are examples of this, involving a new classification scheme (new in the sense of post-European conquest) that incorporates within it ethnic groups (tribes) whose sense of oneness is a function only of the presence of the white groups and the fact that they share a common condition. In that sense, the ethnic lines and boundaries are to be viewed as floating—as a function of the interactions with other groups and, particularly, the behavior of the dominant groups toward them. In similar fashion, any sense of a common bond among the various black ethnic groups of South Africa must be a function of the behavior directed toward them by the dominant white population and, as a consequence, the common situation that they find themselves in. Another example in the United States is the newly developing Latino identification for various groups descending from Spanish-speaking ancestors.

An important reason for the shift of ethnic identification is also possible simply because the scale and nature of the contact is different. This is particularly striking for migrant peoples who originally saw themselves in their homelands as members of a given town or, at best, province or region. In the context of the United States, however, they find themselves in contact with others from the same national homeland who, although different, still have far more in common with them than do the vast bulk of persons with whom they now co-exist. Moreover, these persons are all given a common label by the larger society, for whom these distinctions are of no interest. This was an important force among many immigrant groups to the United States who had identified with a much narrower unit prior to emigration.

In this case, the ecological-demographic context is significant: numerically smaller groups are less likely to be singled out as distinctive by the dominant group. But of course this hinges in part on the distinctiveness of the group (cultural, physical, spatial isolation, religious, and the like), the number of other groups present, and the importance to the dominant group of making specific distinctions. But the dominant group also has a propensity to simplify the situation and description of subordinate groups. The errors and distortions made by the dominant group, insofar as they are of consequence for the life chances of the groups subjected to these actions, do in the long run affect the identifications of the groups themselves and tend to draw them into new bonds.

7. Internal group pressures, although a necessary product of some of these other forces, themselves merit at least brief separate mention. In the course of interethnic/racial conflicts, groups often generate elaborate rituals and pressures to maintain members' identification. Self-identification becomes a central part of the socialization process and becomes defined in the context of respect for parents, extended family, and friends. These thrusts toward group identification are really no different from those exerted by the larger society or nation to maintain allegiance to itself or, on the other hand, the loyalties that other groups in conflict attempt to promote (e.g., labor unions, teams, etc.) Aside from the powerful pull of primary-group ties, there is also a glorification of the group through such mechanisms as learning of a noble history, belief in its special and unique qualities, tales of heroes who sacrificed much for it, and the like. Such developments, at least for the short run, can well reduce inter- and intragenerational shifts.

Empirical Consequences

The above analysis suggests that censuses and other survey data on racial and ethnic groups are characterized by all sorts of volatile and erratic qualities. These and other inconsistencies need not be interpreted as *errors* in either enumeration procedures or in respondent behavior, although such errors cannot be ruled out. Rather, such difficulties may well reflect the flux outlined above in the nature of race and ethnic relations in the society. It is not easy to deal with this topic as an empirical problem. The birth of new ethnic groups, and the shifts among others, do not necessarily occur overnight in a cataclysmic fashion. Although the rates of change are probably not linear, they are probably more gradual than sudden. For example, it is rather unlikely that a vast segment of the population of England awoke one day to discover they were neither Saxons nor Normans nor Angles nor Jutes, but were rather English. Likewise there is now evidence supporting the contention that a new white ethnic group is evolving in the United States.

Two important statistical developments are noteworthy. The U.S. government asked a straight ethnic-origins question in the 1980 decennial census as well as in important sample surveys taken in recent years. The population was asked, "What is this person's ancestry?" Multiple entries were accepted and recorded. In addition, the census asked separate questions on Spanish/Hispanic origin or descent and one that seemed to elaborate on the old color or race question. Second, the General Social Survey (GSS), conducted by the National Opinion Research Center, has been asking a question on ethnic origin since 1972. Its question construction and treatment of multiple entries are of interest to us because they are different from that found in the census, and hence can provide additional clues as to what is going on. The NORC surveys asked, "From what countries or part of the world did your ancestors come?" If more than one country was named, the respondent was asked to indicate the one they felt closest to. If they couldn't decide, then they were recorded separately without any group entered.

Both the 1980 census and the 1979 current population survey accepted *American* as an ethnic ancestry response, but it was discouraged and collected only as a response of last resort. First of all, the use of *American* as a suffix, as in Mexican-American, Italian-American, and so forth was rejected by the census in their coding procedures. A Mexican-American response was counted as Mexican, likewise Italian-American was shortened to Italian, and so on. Even more significantly, the 1979 CPS, which was based on interviews (in contrast to the mail-back procedure in 1980) explicitly instructed its interviewers as follows:

> Some persons may not identify with the foreign birthplace of their ancestors or with their nationality group and may report the category "American." If you have explained that we are referring to the nationality group of the person or his or her ancestors before their arrival in the United States, and the person *still* says that he or she is "American," then print "American." (Italics added.)

American was also discouraged in the 1980 census with the instructions specifying that "Ancestry (or origin or descent) may be viewed as the nationality group, the lineage, or the country in which the person or the person's parents or ancestors were born before their arrival in the United States."

Nevertheless, out of a total United States population of 226.5 million in 1980, there were an estimated 13.3 million who gave "American" or "United States" as their ancestry. Just under 6 percent of the population could not name any specific ancestries—or chose not to; in the 1979 survey, the percentage was slightly higher, 6.3 (U.S. Bureau of the Census, 1983, Table E: 4). To appreciate the importance of this number, consider three additional facts. First, "American" is a major ethnic response, ranking fifth in the nation. To be sure, it trails by a massive amount the 50 million reporting English, the 59 million indicating German, the 40 million with Irish ancestry, and the 21 million who indicated black (the actual number indicating black on the census *race* question is nearly 8 million greater than the number obtained on this ethnic item). But "American" narrowly edges out such groups as French and Italian, and, by much greater margins, exceeds other leading ancestry responses such as Scottish, Polish, Mexican, American Indian, and Dutch (see U.S. Bureau of the Census, 1983: 2).

Second, there is a strong bias against the "American" response. The decision to exclude American as an acceptable multiple response is understandable, even though other multiethnic responses were accepted and recorded by the Census Bureau in both 1979 and 1980. One assumes that many persons used the word "American" along with another ancestry response only as a way of indicating that they were true-blue citizens of the United States, being neither sojourners nor of questionable loyalty. But certainly, there may have been respondents who indicated themselves as, say, Irish-Americans or some such, not for this reason but in order to convey the complexity of their mixed ancestry and/or the limits of their identification with the group specified. In this regard, the figures for various specific groups combine persons who made such a response exclusively with those who picked the specified group in addition to one or in some cases, two other groups. In 1980, for example, there were 40 million persons recorded as having Irish ancestry; only 25.7 percent of these reported Irish ancestry exclusively (10.3 million) whereas nearly 30 million of these included at least one other ethnic group. Now obviously many of the mixed Irish respondents would pick Irish if they were forced to select only one group, but it is clear that there are more members of the Irish than the American ethnic group in the United States. Nevertheless, it is also clear that these census procedures work toward an undercount of the population who call themselves unhyphenated white or the equivalent.

Finally, a large number of respondents do not report any ancestry, about 23 million respondents in both 1979 and 1980; in effect, about one-tenth of the entire population. It is reasonable to assume that at least some of these would be classified as part of this new group of white Americans who are unable to specify any ethnic ancestry.

The General Social Survey (GSS) conducted by the National Opinion Research Center is relevant to these results. From 1972 through the census year of 1980, there were 1,288 respondents who could not name *any* country at all when asked, "From what countries or part of the world did your ancestors come?" This amounts to 10.7 percent of those responding to the question. In addition, there were 339 who selected "America" in response to the ancestral geography question used in the GSS. Thus about 13.5 percent of the American population could name no country or simply took the America response. The percentage unable to name any country is larger than all but the respondents indicating German, England and Wales, black, and those unable to choose a preference between countries. Both the census and the NORC approaches indicate substantial segments of the population who are unable to specify a conventional ethnic response.

Whites are only about 45 percent of the respondents indicating "American" on the GSS, and they are about 74 percent of the much larger number who cannot name *any* ancestral country. Between these two categories, it means that 9.2 percent of the entire population are whites who are either unable to report an ancestral nation or indicate simply that they are American. Confining ourselves to NORC survey data only for whites, one finds that the unhyphenated-white component amounts to 10 percent of all whites in the period between 1972 and 1980. Thus the number of whites responding as either Americans or unable to name any ancestry is an important component of the entire white population of the United States.

At this point, there are three issues to address. First, is there further evidence that a significant part of the white population is in what might be thought of as an ethnic flux leading toward a new American ethnic group? Second, who are these people who report themselves as American in the census or are unable to indicate any country in the GSS survey? Finally, what are the trends with respect to the unhyphenated white group in the future?

Evidence of Flux

There are two separate indications of enormous flux in the ethnic responses among many whites. These come from comparisons of ethnic responses obtained for the same individuals a year apart and the generational makeup of "Americans" and other new residual responses.

Inconsistency

A rare test of consistency and shift was provided by the Current Population Surveys conducted by the Bureau of the Census in 1971, 1972, and 1973. Not only was there a certain degree of overlap in the respondents interviewed in each year with those interviewed in the preceding, but in each case respondents were asked to report their ethnic origin. The same question was asked in March of each year: "What is ...'s origin or descent?" Of special interest here is the fact that the same people were matched in adjacent years. Hence we have a rare opportunity to "match" the ethnic origin reported for the same person a year later.

There is remarkably low consistency in the ethnic origins reported for persons one year later: *in only 65 percent of the cases was the same ethnic response obtained for the respondent one year later.* In other words, in fully one-third of the match ups, a different response was obtained one year later. These inconsistencies in part reflect procedural difficulties related to the manner in which the data were collected, but intergroup differences in the level of inconsistency suggest that something else is going on—something that might be a true flux or vacillation in the ethnic responses that some people are giving. The degree of fluidity varied greatly between groups in a manner that is quite consistent with the theoretical perspective discussed above. Consistency ranged from nearly 80 to more than 95 percent for Poles, Cubans, Italians, Mexicans, blacks, and Puerto Ricans. On the other hand, the consistency was much lower for white groups from Northwestern Europe, the so-called old European stocks who have many ancestors going back a large number of generations in the United States. Little more than half of the respondents giving English, Scottish, or Welsh in 1971 reported a similar response a year later. Thus inconsistency varies in a systematic way: the older-stock white populations from Northwestern Europe, containing substantial components with many generations of residence in the United States, have much lower levels of consistency than either blacks or whites from relatively more recent sources of immigration such as Italy and Poland.

Such a pattern of inconsistency is exactly what one might expect if flux within the white population increases by generations of residence in the United States. This would be compatible with the simple hypothesis that there is a decline in the ties and knowledge of ancestral homelands such that knowledge of—and identification with—such origins declines sharply, if all factors are held constant.

Generational Comparisons

It is one matter to hypothesize that an increase in the confusion and uncertainty about ancestral origins (as well as perhaps indifference) is a pathway to the development of a new ethnic conception; it is another matter to provide evidence of such a claim. However, the evidence is fairly convincing on this matter.

The NORC survey permits a distinction in terms of four generations, applying the procedure described by Alba and Chamlin (1983). Some 57 percent of the entire U.S. population is at least fourth generation, i.e., the United States is the country of birth for themselves, both of their parents, and all four of their grandparents. Among unhyphenated whites (those unable to name any ancestral country or those choosing "American"), 97 percent were at least fourth generation. Thus unhyphenated whites make up fully 16 percent of all Americans with at least four generations' residence in the country, and therefore about 20 percent of the non-black population with at least four generations' residence in the United States. By contrast, new unhyphenated whites are one percent or less of the third, second and first generations. This sharp difference by generation—with such small percentages for earlier generations—suggests that the data are quite meaningful. One would be suspicious if many of the immigrants or their offspring were unable to state the countries or part of the world from which their ancestors came, and/or if the American response was given after only such a short generational stay in the United States.

An added hypothesis about ethnic origins is suggested by the distinctive regional distribution of these unhyphenated whites. Compared with all whites, unhyphenated whites are especially likely to be found in the South, particularly in the South Atlantic states. Thirty-eight percent of all unhyphenated whites are found in the South Atlantic states, and 67 percent are in the entire South. By contrast, only about 30 percent of the entire white population surveyed by NORC lives in the South. The distribution of unhyphenated

whites, in varying degrees throughout the rest of the nation, is less than other whites. This difference from the rest of the country could reflect several different forces:

1. The historically large black population of the South could lead to a relative deemphasis of ethnic distinctions.
2. The white ethnic composition of the South is of proportionately greater numbers of various Northwestern European origins. Perhaps they are especially likely to shift, after taking into account their number of generations in the country.
3. The relative absence of significant new European immigration has meant that there is less renewal of ethnic ties for older groups and less regeneration of ethnic issues for them in the sense of reminding the older groups of white subdivisions.
4. On the other hand, regional differences could simply reflect the fact that proportionately more of the whites found in a particular region are of 4 or more generations' residence. It is certainly true that there has been only moderate migration to the South for quite some time. So it might well be that the average length of generations within the 4-plus category is greater among those in the South.

The available data are not really adequate to evaluate most of these interpretations. But one can at least compare the distribution of all 4-plus generation whites in the United States with that for unhyphenated whites. Among all whites in the United States, about 53 percent have at least four generations of residence in the country. By contrast, 80 percent of whites in the South have 4-plus generations of residence in the country. This reflects the fact that various white immigrant groups have not, for the most part, found the South an attractive destination. A much larger segment of the Southern white population can trace its ancestry back for a longer span. The concentration of unhyphenated whites in the 4-plus generation category, coupled with the fact that 4-plus generation whites are more likely to be found in the South, would lead one to expect that there would be proportionately more unhyphenated whites in the South. But the concentration is even greater: two-thirds of unhyphenated whites are found in the South, whereas half of all 4-plus generation whites are located in this part of the country (67 versus 46 percent).

Characteristics

Neither the census nor the GSS data allow for determination of the true ancestral origins (AOt) of those reporting themselves as unhyphenated white. Indeed, as the surveys are now constructed, all one can obtain is either some belief about such origins (AOb), some declaration of self-identification, or a mixture of the two. This means that one of the more interesting questions cannot be answered at this time, to wit, the ancestral origins of those who become unhyphenated whites.

Nevertheless, the census and GSS do permit examination of some of the social characteristics of this population, which in turn, can be compared with the entire white population. The data below are drawn from various GSS data sets obtained between 1972 and 1980.

Not only is the new white ethnic population disproportionately located in the South, but it is especially concentrated in rural areas. In the United States as a whole, 33 percent of all unhyphenated whites are located in what NORC refers to as *Open Country.* By contrast, 17 percent of all whites are located in the open country. This is more than a reflection of regional differences and the former's concentration in the South. Some 27 percent of all whites living in the South are found in open country; by comparison 42 percent of unhyphenated whites living in the South are in these rural areas. It is not easy to determine whether these are areas with relatively little ethnic heterogeneity and where shift is thereby encouraged. All of this is speculative at this point.

The vast majority of unhyphenated whites were raised as Protestant (87 percent) when compared with all whites in the country (64 percent). Although Roman Catholics are clearly less likely to report themselves in this category (8 percent compared with 29 percent of the total white population), it is significant that the category is not exclusively Protestant. If the theoretical exposition presented earlier is valid, one may speculate that the Roman Catholic component will increase in the years ahead, particularly with generational

changes. Among those giving either of the unhyphenated white responses, less than 0.5 percent reported themselves as having been raised as Jews.

As a general rule, the unhyphenated white population tends to be of lower socioeconomic status (SES) than the entire white population in the United States. Unhyphenated whites also have considerably lower levels of educational attainment. For example, 15 percent of all whites had four or more years of college, compared with 4 percent of unhyphenated whites. By contrast, 19 percent of the latter had no more than seven years of schooling, compared with 7 percent of all whites. Also noteworthy are some important occupational differences, with the proportion of unhyphenated whites in professional-technical occupations amounting to less than half that found for all whites. There is a massive difference in the opposite direction with respect to concentration in the relatively unskilled operatives-transport category.

The overall occupational prestige score for all whites is 40.7 and 38.9, respectively, for men and women. For purposes of calibration, it is about 31 for black men and women. The score for unhyphenated white men, 36.0, falls just about midway between all white men and black men; the mean prestige score for unhyphenated women is 33.6, considerably closer to the level for black women than all white women. In the ten-word vocabulary test used by NORC, the average number of correct responses for all whites is 6.17, compared with 4.54 for unhyphenated whites. This is the lowest score obtained for any of the larger populations specified as part of a general study of the topic, being very slightly lower than the level obtained for blacks. The general cross-tabulation between educational attainment and vocabulary for the entire population was used to determine the expected number for unhyphenated whites that takes into account their lower educational levels and the obvious influence of education on vocabulary. Using this variant of standardization, one would have expected 5.22 correct words for unhyphenated whites; thus their actual level is even lower than would be expected after taking their levels of education into account.

In regard to conventional political labels, there are only modest differences between whites as a whole and this new ethnic group. About the same percentages are Democrats (subclassified as "strong" or "not very strong"), independents of one sort or another, or Republicans (likewise subdivided). At most, the differences between all whites and unhyphenated whites in any of these categories is no more than 3 percentage points. In similar fashion, there are only modest differences between them in their self-conception along liberal-conservative lines. The biggest gap is rather modest, with 40 percent of all whites and 44 percent of unhyphenated whites describing themselves as "moderate." There are some bigger differences with respect to specific political issues, but for the most part the new unhyphenated white group is not distinctive in conventional political terms.

On the normative issues that were considered, somewhat larger gaps turned up, but for the most part they are hardly of the magnitude to suggest a strikingly unique subset of whites. There are some differences with respect to values for children. Given a list of characteristics, subjects were asked to select the most desired characteristic for a child to have. The three most common ones picked by all whites in the country were honesty (39 percent of those able to choose one characteristic), sound judgement (17 percent), and obeys parents (13 percent). By contrast, these characteristics were picked by 41, 12, and 21 percent of unhyphenated whites as the most desirable. Admittedly, the new ethnic population tends to favor obedience more than do whites generally (a difference of 8 percentage points) and are less concerned about sound judgement, but the gaps are not terribly great. In fact, about 40 percent of both groups pick honesty as the most important characteristic. Of course this type of measure is not necessarily a good substitute for observing actual behavior. More of a gap turns up on some specific political issues, suggesting that unhyphenated whites are more conservative than the total white population. The former are more likely to think that too much is being spent to improve conditions of blacks (41 versus 29 percent for all whites) and are less likely to object to the level of military spending (19 versus 28 percent thinking too much is spent). There is a particularly large difference with respect to the civil liberties question; that is, whether a communist should be allowed to make

a speech. Two-thirds of unhyphenated whites thought a communist should *not* be able to, whereas close to 60 percent of all whites thought just the opposite. (Persons who did not respond or indicated "don't know" and the like are excluded from the computations). On the other hand, the gap is very small (4 percentage points) between unhyphenated whites and all whites with respect to favoring the death penalty. In short, the results are mixed with regard to the attitudinal-normative qualities of the new white group. On some dimensions they are very close to all whites and on others there are moderate to fairly large differences.

A Final Note

In recent years, considerable attention has been given to two related theses about white ethnic groups in the United States:

1. The rediscovery and re-emphasis of ethnic identification among white groups in recent years. Presumably the assertions of black pride and black awareness served as a catalyst for this new emphasis among white ethnic groups.
2. The presumed failure of the ethnic melting pot to work as advertised and believed for many years.

It may well be that the melting pot is beginning to work in a different way than has been discussed in the literature. Instead of different groups acting increasingly alike, perhaps a *new* population is in process of forming. Whether this is the case requires much more evidence than is possible to present here. The strongest evidence will come from the 1990 census, when it will be possible to make longitudinal comparisons; specifically, whether there is an increase in the unhyphenated white response for each age- and generational-specific cohort as it ages. At the present time, the proportions giving such responses seem to be concentrated in the older age groups, but with data for one period it is impossible to separate the age, cohort, and period effects.

A second issue pertains to meaning of the responses. Given the relatively low SES positions held by the unhyphenated white population (as measured with NORC data) there is always the possibility that people giving these responses are selective on various characteristics and are not truly representative of a new ethnic thrust. In this regard, the two subsets of the population defined as unhyphenated white with NORC data—those reporting themselves as American as opposed to those unable to name a group—do differ on some dimensions. For example, the specifically American subset appear to be *relatively* higher in SES, less likely to reside in the South, and more Catholic compared to the other subset. But they are still different from all whites. Obviously, this deserves more examination. Under any circumstance, it would be helpful to understand why the population giving these responses are relatively concentrated in lower SES positions. Further clues may well develop when the census data on American whites are examined. The concentration in the South, in my estimation, is less of a puzzle since it is more a matter of choosing and evaluating several plausible explanations for the fact. However, an evaluation of these different causal forces may well help provide important clues about what factors are generating this new ethnic group in America.

30

The Political Mobilization of Native Americans[1]

Joane Nagel

In many regards American Indians are unlikely candidates for political mobilization.[2] This is not due to a paucity of grievances, rather, the surprising aspect of Indian mobilization stems from the "artificiality"[3] of Indian ethnicity. Historically "Indian" has been a content-free, ascriptive designation that has always included religiously, culturally, and linguistically diverse and historically separate and factious groups. The several hundred remaining American Indian tribes in the U.S. represent dozens of distinct language groups and are geographically dispersed across the continent. In light of this heterogeneity, Guillemin has described the designation of "Indian" as racist in recognition of its purely external character—a label applied to religiously and culturally varied peoples for the convenience of an outside group.[4]

Faced with such diversity and with an alternating, often divisive U.S. Indian policy, until the past two decades, American Indians seemed destined to follow one of two paths: assimilation or annihilation. There was evidence for both outcomes. The threat of physical extinction from war and disease in the last century and the current continued poor standard of living characterizing Indians as a category[5] have been sources of denunciation and alarm. However, with the stabilization and growth of the American Indian population in this century, fears of physical annihilation have given way to concern over "cultural genocide" in the face of intermarriage (both among Indian tribes and with non-Indians), religious conversion, native language loss, and an increasingly urban population.[6]

Surprisingly, in spite of the poor health and economic condition of the American Indian population as a whole and in spite of the tendencies toward language loss and exogamy, American Indians have been neither annihilated nor assimilated. In fact there is strong evidence of just the opposite—a cultural and ethnic revitalization and mobilization. During the past two decades there has emerged a reaffirmation of Indian identity, a cultural renaissance, and a political awakening. As Thomas notes, American Indians are forming "a new ethnic group...a new 'nationality' in America"—the Native American.[7] Out of a linguistically and culturally diverse "convenience" category has emerged a political movement characterized by organizations and collective action designed to articulate and address various grievances of specific tribes and/or of Indians generally. What is interesting about this mobilization is that it appears to be occurring simultaneously along three ethnic boundaries: tribal, pan-tribal, and pan-Indian.

Indian mobilization is along *tribal* lines when

Reprinted from *Social Science Journal* 19:3 (July 1982) by permission.

it involves organization and action by members of one tribe in pursuit of tribal goals. An example would be the litigation or protest activities of a single tribe regarding tribal rights, e.g., the 1975 Menominee action in Wisconsin involving a land claim disputed by the Alexian Brothers.[8] Mobilization is along *pan-tribal* lines when it involves organization and action by members of more than one tribe acting on the basis of tribal affiliation in pursuit of tribal or pan-tribal goals. An example would be the coordination of activities or protests by several tribes concerning an issue of interest to them all. The Council of Energy Resource Tribes (CERT) represents one such pan-tribal organization and mobilization effort. Mobilization is along *pan-Indian* lines when it involves organization and action by individual Indians on the basis of Indianness and in pursuit of pan-Indian goals. An example would be the organization of Indians from various tribes on the basis of Native Americanness (not in the role of representatives of particular tribes) such as the National Indian Youth Council or the American Indian Movement.

The three-tiered mobilization of American Indians may be considered a reflection of two external forces. First, the shift upward in scale of organization from tribal to either pan-tribal or pan-Indian levels can be seen as the result of the competitive advantage accrued large-scale organizations in modern economic and political arenas.[9] That is, small-scale organizations are less able to successfully participate in, influence, or extract resources from large-scale economic and political organizations. One reason for this seems to be the limited resources available to small-scale organizational units. Thus, in an attempt to expand resources, small units often cooperate or federate. An example is the United Tribes of Oklahoma and Kansas, a consortium of small tribes organized for several purposes, one of which is the acquisition of federal funds. The skilled personnel required to write and administer government grants as well as community size restrictions attached to certain programs (e.g., mobile medical units, winterization) places small, solitary tribes at a disadvantage in applying and qualifying for funding. The United Tribes is a pan-tribal solution to these external constraints.

A second reason for the multi-tiered pattern of Indian mobilization seems to flow directly from the shifting character of U.S. Indian policy. In this case, the split between tribally-based mobilization and mobilization on the basis of the larger Native American identity (pan-Indian) can be seen as a result of a two-pronged policy historically pursued by the U.S. government—a policy that vacillated between 1) recognition of tribes as geo-political units and thus the foci of various government programs and legislation, and 2) insistence that Indianness was the relevant ethnic distinction for political policy purposes. An example of the duality can be seen in the area of U.S. Indian education policy. The boarding school design for Indian education in the late nineteenth and early twentieth centuries promoted *pan-Indianism* inasmuch as the schools served as the meeting place for Indians of diverse backgrounds and insofar as the assimilative, English-language emphasis of the schools provided a common basis, albeit coercively enforced, for intertribal communication. On the other hand, education policies after the 1930s that focused on reservation educational development and that hence carried a tribal emphasis (e.g., the 1967 Bilingual Education Act), have contributed to *tribal* mobilization.[10]

It can be argued then, that the various levels of American Indian mobilization that have evolved during the past few decades have been, to a great extent, shaped by the political and economic contexts within which Indian mobilization has occurred. In other words, the tribal, pan-tribal, or pan-Indian organizational forms are responses to a particular incentive structure largely determined by U.S. Indian policies.

This vision of Indian mobilization as a tactical reaction to political policies and rules of access is consistent with the resource mobilization model of social movements.[11] According to this view, the timing and extent of social movement mobilization is heavily dependent upon resources (personnel, leadership, money, facilities) available in the environment. To the extent that resources are politically controlled (as in the case of American Indians), then political policies are enormously powerful in their ability to dictate the rules for resource acquisition. Successful mobilization strategies are those that "fit" the blueprints for access and influence drawn up by the political center. The United Tribes version of pan-tribal mobilization described above is one such mobilization pattern. The Native American Rights Fund is another example of a strategically efficacious organizational design in response to federal legal policies (e.g., regarding legal claims and litigation).

Thus, American Indian mobilization can be seen as the result of two complementary processes—one originating from below within Indian communities and one originating from above within the political center. The impetus from below flows from the nature and extent of Indian grievances and from the skills and abilities of Indian mobilizers. The impetus from above is that contained in the design of government policies that control the resources available to Indians and that specify the rules of access and allocation. The impetus from below determines *if* mobilization will occur. The impetus from above determines the *shape* the mobilization will take.

The remainder of this paper highlights different periods of U.S. Indian policy history in an attempt to point out the effects of various policies on the formation of Indian organizations and on subsequent patterns of mobilization. The paper ends with a discussion of the implications of the multi-level shape of American Indian mobilization.

A Brief History of Indian Policy and Mobilization

U.S. Indian policy history can be roughly divided into four periods since 1880:[12]

1880–1933	Assimilation and Incorporation
1933–1946	Indirect Rule
1946–1960	Termination
1960–1980	Economic Development and Self-Determination

Each of these periods will be discussed in order to illustrate the ways in which U.S. Indian policies have shaped American Indian mobilization. Of particular interest are the ways in which these policies have contributed to variations in tribal, pan-tribal, and pan-Indian organization.

1880–1933: Assimilation and Incorporation

By the 1880s, the U.S.-Indian wars had ended, most Indian reservations had been created, and the federal government began a policy of penetration and incorporation. Policies centered on the alienation of Indian lands, the assimilative education of Indian youth, and the creation of Indian citizens. 1885 marked the first in a series of judicial decisions extending state and federal criminal and civil jurisdiction into Indian reservations. The Dawes Act of 1887, otherwise known as the General Allotment Act (GAA), began the process of dismantling reservation land by permitting the deeding of land parcels to individual tribal members rather than to tribes. American Indian land holdings dropped from 140 million acres in 1887 to 32 million acres in the mid-1920s.[13] A related strategy of assimilation was pursued through the establishment of Indian boarding schools in the late 1880s. In 1924 the Indian Citizenship Act was passed, providing citizenship status, and thus, at least symbolically, incorporating Indians as individuals into the American political system.

All of these policies were implicit or explicit denials of the uniqueness and separateness of Indians and of Indian tribes. The land, education, and citizenship policies all attempted to undermine tribal economic, social, and political integrity and to establish a material and ideological foundation for assimilation. The land policies of the GAA greatly weakened tribal organization and viability and set in motion the trend toward Indian urban migration which served as the demographic basis for future *pan-Indianism*. The boarding schools provided the educated, acculturated, multi-lingual leadership[14] that led ultimately to the creation of a series of urban Indian organizations beginning with the Society of American Indians (1912) and culminating in a variety of *pan-Indian* and *pan-tribal* organizations by the 1960s.[15] The mobilizing effect of education (though certainly not planned by the architects of Indian education) has been noted by Indian scholars. Deloria comments that the "first [political] movement of any note was that triggered by the Indian graduates of the government boarding schools."[16] The Citizenship Act, though not enforced for many years after its passage, provided the legislative basis for later definitions and enactments of *pan-Indian* political interests, for example, the "Indian vote."[17]

1933–1946: Indirect Rule

The 1933 appointment of John Collier as the Commissioner for Indian Affairs and the passage of the 1934 Howard-Wheeler or Indian Reorganization Act (IRA), shifted the focus of U.S. policy from the individual back to the tribe via a strategy of indirect rule. The IRA stopped the land break-up and provided for the adoption of tribal constitutions and the election of tribal chairmen. Thus, the tribe became an intermediate link between the individual Indian and the government. As Guillemin notes, as a result of the IRA "many of today's tribal governments have an identical political structure and articulate in precisely the same way with the central government."[18] This standardization of tribal organization and U.S. government linkage produced "a recognition of shared political fate" that ultimately spurred *pan-tribal* organizational development.[19] For instance, the National Congress of American Indians (NCAI) was formed in 1944—an outgrowth of U.S. government sponsored meetings designed to elucidate and facilitate the implementation of the IRA.[20] Tribal boundaries, weakened by the Allotment Act, were thus revitalized and linked by pan-tribal associations.

Witt describes the mobilizing impact of one series of conferences convened by the BIA in 1935 for the purpose of explaining the Indian Reorganization Act.

> The policies of the Collier Administration and the Howard-Wheeler Act brought about external pressures for tribal and inter-tribal communication unknown to that degree in previous history . . . [The conference] resulted, in many cases, in the first face-to-face interaction of tribes culturally and geographically remote . . . [and] produced dynamic situations.[21]

1946–1960: Termination

With the establishment of the Indian Claims Commission (ICC) in 1946, U.S. Indian policy entered a period known as "termination." The purpose of the ICC was to settle Indian claims against the government in order to begin the process of terminating the unique relationship between the federal government and the various tribes and thus to pave the way for Indian assimilation. Four years later, the Navajo-Hopi Rehabilitation Program was initiated. It was the first in a new series of "relocation" programs designed to move Indians from reservations to urban areas where government centers assisted them in finding work, housing and other services.[22] In order to facilitate relocation efforts, the BIA conducted a number of manpower training programs and Congress passed the 1956 Indian Vocational Education Act.

American Indian organizational development during this period showed a predictable increase in the number of urban *pan-Indian* organizations. The important NCAI continued to flourish. The relocation policy of establishing Indian centers in urban areas and shifting large numbers of Indians to those areas promoted urban Indian mobilization. As Thomas notes, "pan-Indian communities . . . [formed] around Indian centers" in urban areas and the organizations that emerged were similarly pan-Indian in membership and leadership.[23] Thus, by the late 1950s there was a substantial urban Indian population complemented by an urban pan-Indian organizational network. The reservations had been reorganized and connected through a pan-tribal organizational network. And so the organizational infrastructure was in place when the mobilizing policies of the most recent period were implemented.

1960–1980: Economic Development and Self-Determination

The 1960s was a period of much ethnic and political mobilization in the U.S. This was no accident. The programs of Johnson's Great Society were directly responsible. The resource mobilization model of social movements cited above is dramatically descriptive of this period. The War on Poverty programs of the 1960s injected massive resources into a nascent Native American movement and the result was Red Power.

In the 1960s, the BIA's urban relocation programs continued and were complemented by a variety of War on Poverty programs targeted toward Indians (as well as other groups). These included: the Manpower Development and Training Act, the Elementary and Secondary Education Act (Head Start, Teacher Corps, VISTA), and the Area Redevelopment Act. The BIA instituted an Indian Industrial Development Plan and HEW created an Office of Indian Progress. A National Council on Indian Opportunity was established in 1968 and the Office of Economic Opportunity established Indian Desks within the agency. Officer reports that

> by the end of FY 1965, 10 Job Corps Conservation Centers had been approved for Indian reservations, 55 Indian communities had applied for assistance under the National Youth Corps Program, another 20 had requested funds for Operation Head Start, and 26 applications had been approved for Community Action Programs.[24]

During the 1960s the BIA tripled assistance to Indian college students, and in the period from 1965 to 1973, over $1 billion was spent on various programs for Indians.[25] Steiner reports mixed reactions among Indians to the War on Poverty: "to the Sioux [it] was a hypocritical apology for the misery that the white man had caused."[26]

While the long-term economic benefits of the 1960s can be debated, the organizational implications were enormous. Steiner comments that for many Indians the War on Poverty was "a stomping ground for their political coming of age."[27] During this period two other important pan-Indian political organizations were formed: the National Indian Youth Council (NIYC) (another legacy of government Indian educational programs) and the American Indian Movement (AIM). Both organizations were comprised of young, educated, urban Indians and both employed more activist strategies than earlier organizations. In 1965, the NIYC participated in a "fish-in" in the state of Washington, and in 1969 AIM took part in the occupation of Alcatraz Island. AIM continued as an active participant in Indian protest actions throughout the 1970s.[28]

The 1970s were characterized by an expansion of Indian legislation aimed at economic development. Examples include the BIA's Indian Business Development Fund and the Alaska Native Claims Settlement Act, both of 1971, the 1972 Indian Education Act, Reservation Acceleration Program, and the inclusion of reservation courts

and police forces under the Law Enforcement Assistance Act, the 1974 Indian Financing Act, and the 1975 Indian Self-Determination and Educational Assistance Act.[29]

Pan-Indian organizations also appear to have expanded during this period. AIM, established in 1968, was reported to have 70 local chapters by 1972.[30] In 1975 what might be interpreted as one organizational response to self-determination policy emerged: CERT reportedly requested assistance from OPEC in developing its energy resources.[31]

The period of the 1960s and 1970s is most clearly illustrative of the tripartite mobilizing impact of U.S. Indian policies. Some of the programs of the Office of Economic Opportunity encouraged organizations along *tribal lines* (e.g., Head Start), some encouraged *pan-tribal* organization (e.g., certain area redevelopment programs), and yet others supported *pan-Indianism* (e.g., Upward Bound, Job Corps). Further, the Nixon administration's renunciation of termination policies and its emphasis on Indian self-determination strongly buttressed tribal boundaries while encouraging pan-tribal cooperative efforts (e.g., in economic development), and while simultaneously reinforcing pan-Indian universalism (e.g., in BIA hiring or educational assistance policies). Thus, both OEO and Nixon administrative policies provided incentives for mobilization along all three boundaries.

Discussion

The above brief synopsis of U.S. Indian policy illustrates the shifting character of the federal government's orientation toward Indians. The evolution of supra-tribal large-scale organizations (both pan-tribal and pan-Indian) as well as the continued viability of the smaller tribal units stem from this vacillation.

Policies that specifically reinforced *tribal* organization and promoted tribal-level mobilization included: the Reservation Acceleration Program, the Law Enforcement Assistance Act, the Alaska Native Claims Settlement Act—all of which were passed or implemented in the early 1970s and which served to stimulate the instruction in Indian languages on reservation schools and in schools with large Indian student populations, thus emphasizing tribal identifications; the 1934 Indian Reorganization Act which resulted in the political restructuring of many Indian tribes and provided a new vitality and legitimacy to the tribal unit.

Policies that specifically reinforced *pan-tribal* organization and promoted pan-tribal-level mobilization included: again the IRA which contributed to the creation of a pan-tribal organizational network (e.g., the NCAI and the National Association of Tribal Chairmen) through implementation policies; the establishment of the 1946 Indian Claims Commission which similarly promoted pan-tribal organizations designed to organize and present tribal claims (e.g., the Native American Rights Fund); the various programs of the 1960s (e.g., under OEO) and those continuing into the present that encourage pan-tribal grant application and administration due to size restrictions and the competitive advantage afforded such combined undertakings; and the 1975 Indian Self-Determination and Educational Assistance Act which reasserted tribal integrity and thus opened the way for pan-tribal efforts at resource development (e.g., CERT).

Policies that specifically reinforced *pan-Indian* organization and promoted pan-Indian-level mobilization included: the 1887 General Allotment Act which resulted in the alienation of tribal land and the beginning of urban migration that was accelerated by the relocation programs of the 1950s; various education policies (e.g., the boarding schools) whose intent was acculturation and assimilation, and the scholarship programs that were less coercive, but similar in design; and the hiring policies of the BIA (e.g., Indian preference) that tend to promote pan-Indianism in that Indianness is the basis for hiring rather than tribal affiliation.[32]

The multi-level pattern of the American Indian movement is likely to continue as a mobilization form. First, because U.S. government policy remains divided in its mobilizing effect on Indian action; second, because of the divisions among Indians—demographically, ethnically, and politically; and third, because of the strategic utility of a flexible and multi-tiered organizational framework. Such flexibility also has its costs, the greatest of which are, no doubt,

the conflicts among Indians regarding interests and strategies that such multi-level mobilization inevitably fosters.

ENDNOTES

1. This research was supported, in part, by grants from the University of Kansas General Research Fund (No. 3448-20-0038) and the National Science Foundation (No. SES-8108314). I wish to thank Norman Yetman for his comments on an earlier version of this paper.

2. Mobilization is defined as the process by which a group acquires resources and assures their delivery in pursuit of collective ends. See Charles Tilly, *From Mobilization to Revolution* (Reading, MA: Addison-Wesley Publishing Company, 1978), p. 69; Anthony Oberschall, *Social Conflict and Social Movements* (Englewood Cliffs, NJ: Prentice-Hall, Inc., 1973), p. 102; Amitai Etzioni, "Mobilization as a Macro-sociological Conception," *British Journal of Sociology*, vol. 19 (1968), p. 243.

3. Crawford Young, *Politics in the Congo* (New Haven: Yale University Press, 1965), pp. 242–46.

4. Jeanne Guillemin, "American Indian Resistance and Protest," in *Violence in America*, edited by H. Graham and T. Gurr (Beverly Hills: Sage Publications, 1979), pp. 287–306.

5. American Indians remain among the poorest and most unhealthy of all Americans, with an infant mortality rate 1½ times the national average, a life expectancy 10 years below the national average, and a median income 40 percent of the national average. Vincent Parillo, *Strangers to These Shores* (Boston: Houghton-Mifflin, 1980), pp. 247–48.

6. By 1970, 45 percent of American Indians lived in cities, less than one-third reported a non-English mother tongue, and among married Indians, one-third in the cities and one-sixth in rural areas reported having white spouses, with intermarriage among tribal groups still higher. HEW, *A Study of Selected Socio-Economic Characteristics of Ethnic Minorities Based on the 1970 Census, Volume 3, American Indians* (Washington, D.C.: Government Printing Office, 1974).

7. Robert K. Thomas, "Pan-Indianism," in *The American Indian Today*, edited by Stuart Levine and Nancy O. Lurie (Deland, FL: Everett/Edwards, 1968), pp. 77–85.

8. George Spindler and Louise Spindler, "Identity, Militancy and Cultural Congruence: The Menominee and Kainai," *Annals* (March 1978), pp. 73–85.

9. Joseph Hraba and Eric Hoiberg, "Freedom and Folk Identity in Modern Life," Mimeographed paper (Department of Sociology, Iowa State University,

1982); Michael Hannan, "The Dynamics of Ethnic Boundaries in Modern States," in *National Development and the World System*, edited by J. Meyer and M. Hannan (Chicago: University of Chicago Press, 1979).

10. While established in the nineteenth century, American Indian boarding schools still exist and educate considerable numbers of students. I am grateful to Stanley L. Sorkin for pointing out their continued role in Indian education.

11. Oberschall, *op. cit.*; John McCarthy and Mayer Zald, *The Trend of Social Movements in America: Professionalization and Resource Mobilization* (Morristown, NJ: General Learning Press, 1973); Bruce Fireman and William Gamson, "Utilitarian Logic in the Resource Mobilization Perspective," in *The Dynamics of Social Movements*, edited by M. Zald and J. McCarthy (Cambridge: Winthrop, 1979), pp. 8–44.

12. J. G. Jorgensen, "A Century of Political Economic Effects on American Indian Society, 1880–1980," *The Journal of Ethnic Studies*, vol. 6 (1978), p. 1.

13. Jorgensen, *op. cit.*, p. 16.

14. These characteristics of pan-Indian leaders (educated, acculturated, urban-based) represent a pattern that is reproduced among nationalist and subnationalist leaders in many countries. See Donald Horowitz, "Three Dimensions of Ethnic Politics, World Cultural Movements and Ethnic Change," *Annals* (September 1977), p. 6; M. Yinger and G. Simpson, "The Integration of Americans of Indian Descent," *Annals* (March 1978), p. 137.

15. Hazel W. Hertzberg, *The Search for an American Indian Identity: Modern Pan-Indian Movements* (Syracuse: Syracuse University Press, 1971).

16. Vine Deloria, Jr., *The Indian Affair* (New York: Friendship Press, 1975), p. 43.

17. Stanley Steiner, *The New Indians* (New York: Harper and Row, 1969), p. 235.

18. Guillemin, *op. cit.*, p. 295.

19. Guillemin, *op. cit.*, pp. 296–97.

20. Shirley Witt, "Nationalistic Trends Among American Indians," in *The American Indian Today*, edited by Stuart Levine and Nancy O. Lurie (Deland, FL: Everett/Edwards, 1968), pp. 56, 77–85.

21. Witt, *op. cit.*, pp. 59–60.

22. Jorgensen, *op. cit.*, p. 24; Steiner, *op. cit.*, p. 180.

23. Thomas, *op. cit.*, p. 81; Sol Tax, "The Impact of Urbanization on American Indians," *Annals* (March 1978), p. 121.

24. J. E. Officer, "The Bureau of Indian Affairs Since 1945: An Assessment," *Annals* 436 (March 1978), p. 121.

25. Donald T. Berthrong, *The American Indian: From Pacifism to Activism* (St. Louis, MO: The Forum Press, 1973), p. 10; Robert Havighurst, "Indian Education Since 1960," *Annals* (March 1978), pp. 13, 22.

26. Steiner, *op. cit.*, p. 195.

27. Steiner, *op. cit.*, p. 210.

28. Jorgensen, *op. cit.*, pp. 31–37.

29. R. V. Butler, "The Bureau of Indian Affairs: Activities Since 1945," *Annals* (March 1978), pp. 50, 58–59; Vine Deloria, Jr., "Legislation and Litigation Concerning American Indians," *Annals* (March 1978), pp. 86, 88; Alan Sorkin, "The Economic Basis of Indian Life," *Annals* (March 1978), pp. 1, 7–10; Havighurst, *op. cit.*, p. 22; Jorgensen, *op. cit.*, p. 40; Officer, *op. cit.*, p. 70.

30. Deloria, 1974, *op. cit.*, p. 46.

31. "American Indians—Struggling for Power and Identity," *New York Times Magazine* (February 11, 1979).

32. The utility of this hiring policy has been much criticized in that Indians have historically occupied lower level, non-policy-making positions within the BIA. See Officer, *op. cit.*, pp. 61–72.

31

U.S. Hispanics:
Changing the Face of America

Cary Davis
Carl Haub
JoAnne Willette

The 1980 census counted 14.6 million persons of Spanish origin in the United States, 6.4 percent of the then total population of 226.5 million. Hispanics are the second largest U.S. minority after blacks (11.7 percent in 1980) and the fastest growing. Fueled by the relatively high fertility of most Hispanic groups and increasing immigration, both legal and illegal, their numbers grew by about 265 percent from 1950 to 1980, compared to just under 50 percent for the total U.S. population. If immigration to the U.S. were to continue at the recent estimated total of about one million a year (legal plus illegal, Hispanics plus Asians and all others), Hispanics could number some 47 million and comprise 15 percent of the population by the year 2020, displacing blacks as the country's largest minority.

Thirty years ago, Spanish Americans consisted primarily of a few million Mexican Americans living in the Southwest, some of whom traced their ancestry back to the original Spanish-colonial and Indian inhabitants of that area. Today the umbrella term "Hispanic" covers a diverse population, still concentrated in a few states, but found throughout the nation: Mexican Americans, now beginning to move from their traditional base in the Southwest; Puerto Ricans,

From *Population Bulletin*, 38:3 (June 1983) by permission of the authors and Population Reference Bureau, Inc.

mainly concentrated in New York and New Jersey; Cubans headquartered in Florida; and recent arrivals from at least 16 other Spanish-speaking countries of Latin America and Spain itself.

Like other immigrant groups before them, Hispanics are beginning to change the face of America, making their distinctive contributions to the neighborhoods in which they live. But with their growing numbers, they are also encountering the hostility historically accorded almost all newly arriving ethnic groups. Some predict that Hispanics will eventually assimilate into the American "melting pot" as the Irish, Italians, and Polish did before them. Others feel their very numbers and common language could delay assimilation and create a "Hispanic Quebec" within the United States. Hispanics also face a special problem in gaining acceptance—the presence among them of a large and growing number of illegal immigrants from Mexico and other Central and South American countries. And as America's latest great wave of immigrants, they are learning that newcomers start out at the bottom. U.S. Hispanics as a group are much less educated, much poorer, occupy lower rungs on the occupational ladder, and are much more likely to be unemployed than the non-Hispanic population. But some Hispanics, particularly Cubans, are beginning to catch up and the evidence suggests that future generations of U.S. Hispanics will too.

This *Bulletin* looks at where U.S. Hispanics

are today, demographically and socioeconomically, and what their numbers are likely to be over the next few decades. We begin with outlining the problems of defining who is included in this increasingly visible and influential segment of the U.S. population.

Who Are the Hispanics?

While "Hispanic" has become a convenient way to refer to Americans of Spanish heritage, the catchall term masks a variety of ethnic, racial, national, and cultural backgrounds. And within the U.S., the various "Hispanic" groups tend to be separated geographically and in their way of life. The four categories used by the U.S. Census Bureau are now most frequently taken to encompass the "Spanish-origin" or Hispanic population. These are, first, Mexican Americans, or "Chicanos," the largest group, living mostly in the Southwest. Many of these are not immigrants but "Hispanos" who trace their ancestry back to the Spanish colonialists and Indians who were the original inhabitants of the American Southwest. Next are Puerto Ricans, an intermixture of Spanish, Indian, and black, who, as U.S. citizens at birth, are not subject to immigration restrictions. Cubans, the smallest group, assumed numerical importance as an ethnic group in the U.S. after the 1959 Cuban Revolution. The "Other Hispanic" category, now the second largest of the four groups, covers people from other Spanish-speaking countries of Latin America and from Spain. Many Hispanos also place themselves in this category on Census Bureau questionnaires. *Not* included among Hispanics are immigrants from non-Spanish-language Latin American countries such as French-speaking Haitians and Portuguese-speaking Brazilians.

Population Growth and Ethnic Mix

The Hispanic population of the U.S. numbers at least 15 million as of 1983, plus an uncounted number of illegal immigrants. The growth of this population began with the 1848 Treaty of Guadalupe Hidalgo in which Mexico ceded to the U.S. the territory which is now Texas, New Mexico, Arizona, California, Nevada, Utah, and part of Colorado. Many Hispanics in the U.S. Southwest

thus trace their ancestry to Mexico in a very direct way. But the vast majority of today's Mexican-origin population is the result of immigration in the 20th century, beginning in the early 1900s with immigrants lured north to work in the farmlands of California and to build the railroads of the Southwest. This first immigration wave ended during the depression of the 1930s with the deportation of over 400,000 Mexicans, but picked up again during the 1940s with the *bracero* program. Designed to bring temporary workers north to alleviate U.S. labor shortages during World War II, the program brought in 4.8 million Mexicans before its demise in 1964.[3] Fueled by legal and illegal immigration plus relatively high fertility, the Mexican-American population has continued to grow, but its share of the total U.S. Hispanic population has been reduced to 60 percent from about 70 percent in 1950 with the influx of Puerto Ricans, Cubans, and "Other Hispanics" since then.

Puerto Ricans have had free access to the U.S. mainland as U.S. citizens since the Jones Act of 1917, long before the island became a Commonwealth with a unique relationship to the U.S. in 1952, after being a U.S. territory since the Spanish-American War of 1898. Less than 70,000 Puerto Ricans had settled on the mainland by the time of the 1940 census, however. But in the 1950s alone, job opportunities and the advent of regular and cheap plane service between San Juan and New York City attracted a net influx of half a million Puerto Ricans to the mainland, primarily New York City—a tremendous flow for a country with a 1950 population of 2.2 million.[4]

Fewer than 50,000 Cubans lived in the U.S. before Castro overthrew the regime of Fulgencio Batista in 1959, many of them making cigars in Florida or New York City.[5] The first post-revolutionary wave of exiles brought about 260,000 largely affluent, professional Cubans to the U.S. before air traffic between the two countries was temporarily ended, following the 1962 missile crisis. A refugee airlift agreed upon by Castro and the Johnson Administration in 1965 brought in 344,000 more Cubans before Castro cut off emigration in 1973. Thousands more arrived clandestinely by small boat or through Mexico or Spain in the following years, climaxed by the mass influx of 125,000 Cubans in the

Mariel boatlift which Castro permitted from April to September 1980.

Stimulated by changes in U.S. immigration law, numbers of immigrants from all other Spanish-speaking countries have increased dramatically from about 33,000 arriving in 1950–54 to nearly 300,000 in 1975–79, according to the Immigration and Naturalization Service (INS).[6] These countries taken together have now replaced Mexico as the largest supplier of new legal immigrants to the U.S.

Growth Since 1950

With heavy immigration added to relatively high fertility, the U.S. Hispanic population has soared since 1950. While the total U.S. population grew by just under 50 percent from 1950 to 1980, the increase for Hispanics was about 265 percent, as seen in Table 1. The black population—the country's other significant minority—accounted for 9.9 percent of the U.S. population in 1950 and increased its share to 11.7 percent by 1980. In the same period, the Hispanic population went from about 2.7 to 6.4 percent of the U.S. total, making it without question the country's fastest-growing minority.

The 1950, 1960, and 1970 figures for Hispanics shown in Table 1 are estimates which attempt to make up for some of the deficiencies in the data for this population. Collection of data on all Hispanics began only with the 1970 census. The

TABLE 1. *Total U.S. and Hispanic Population: 1950–1980 (Numbers in millions)*

Year	Total U.S. Population	Hispanics	Hispanic Population Increase in Preceding Decade	Hispanic Percent of U.S. Population
1950	151.3	4.0	—	2.7
1960	179.3	6.9	2.9	3.9
1970	203.2	10.5	3.6	5.2
1980	226.5	14.6	4.1	6.4

Sources: U.S. population: Bureau of the Census, various census reports; Hispanic population: JoAnne Willette, et al, *The Demographic and Socioeconomic Characteristics of the Hispanic Population in the United States: 1950–1980*, report to the Department of Health and Human Services by Development Associates, Inc., and Population Reference Bureau, Inc., January 18, 1982.

census count for Hispanics in 1970, based on the Spanish-origin question, was 9.1 million.[7] Using this as a base, the Census Bureau projected that the 1980 count would be 13.2 million.[8] The actual count (based on the 1980 Spanish-origin question) turned out to be 14.6 million—1.4 million higher.[9] The difference was probably due to better reporting by Hispanics in 1980. The census was preceded by a well orchestrated campaign to improve minority cooperation and coverage, the Spanish-origin question was much improved and appeared early in the questionnaire sent to every household in the country, and the very awareness of Hispanics as a population had probably increased since 1970. Another part of the story may be the increased number of illegal immigrants during the 1970s, some of whom—reassured of anonymity— were willing to answer the questionnaire. It has now been estimated that the 1980 census count of 226.5 million for the total U.S. population included at least 2 million illegal immigrants, with about 1.3 million from Latin American countries.

Starting from the 1980 Spanish-origin count of 14.6 million, the Hispanic population estimates shown in Table 1, prepared by the Population Reference Bureau for the U.S. Department of Health and Human Services, were derived by projecting the population back to 1950, using INS data on legal immigrants by country of birth and assumptions about Hispanic mortality based on available estimates. This procedure increases the 1970 figure from the original Spanish-origin census count of 9.1 million to 10.5 million. The estimates for the three decades indicate that the U.S. Hispanic population grew from about 4 million in 1950 to 14.6 million in 1980 and that the numbers added rose from about 2.9 million during the 1950s to about 4.1 million in the 1970s.

The ethnic mix of Hispanics has changed. Mexican Americans, the overwhelming majority before 1950, accounted for only 60 percent by 1980, with 8.7 million persons (see Table 2). Persons of Spanish origin from countries other than Mexico, Cuba, or Puerto Rico now number 3 million and account for one in every five Hispanics, a factor which lends even more diversity to this growing minority. Puerto Ricans rank third with a count of 2 million and 14 percent of the 1980 Hispanic population, and the 803,000 Cubans put them in fourth place with 6 percent.

Age and Sex Composition

Hispanics as a whole are younger, on average, than both the general U.S. population and blacks. In 1980, the median age for the Hispanic population was 23, compared to 30 for the total U.S. population and 25 for the black population. (The median marks the point at which half the population is younger and half is older.) Nearly one-third (32 percent) of Hispanics were younger than 15 and only 5 percent were 65 or older. By contrast, only 23 percent of all Americans were under 15 and 11 percent were age 65 or older.[10]

The youthfulness of the Hispanic population is due both to relatively high fertility and heavy immigration of young adults. These effects can be seen in the shape of the age-sex structure of the Hispanic population as of the 1980 census, which contrasts with the structure of the total U.S. population. The relatively large proportion of children in the Hispanic population reflects both the larger than average family sizes of Hispanics

TABLE 2. *U.S. Hispanic Population, by Type: 1980*

Type	Number (in thousands)	Percent	States with Largest Concentrations
Total Hispanic	14,609	100.0	California, Texas, New York
Mexican American	8,740	59.8	California, Texas, Illinois
Puerto Rican	2,014	13.8	New York, New Jersey, Illinois
Cuban	803	5.5	Florida, New Jersey, New York
Other Hispanic	3,052	20.9	California, New York, New Mexico

Source: Bureau of the Census, "Persons of Spanish Origin by State: 1980," *1980 Census of Population*, Supplementary Report, PC80-S1-7, August 1982.

and the fact that a substantial proportion of immigrants are in the prime childbearing ages; in the last half of the 1970s, more than one-third of legal immigrants from Spanish-speaking countries were aged 20-34,[11] and this is undoubtedly also true of illegal immigrants.

As the baby boom generation passes out of the childbearing ages, succeeding U.S. birth cohorts will become smaller and smaller, if the U.S. rate of childbearing remains near the current low level of 1.8 children per woman. Among Hispanics, by contrast, continuing replenishment of the childbearing population through immigration, plus a fertility rate still about 2.5 children per woman—well above "replacement" level—guarantees larger cohorts of children for some time to come.

Relative youthfulness and large proportions of children are evident among the Mexican-American, Puerto Rican, and "Other Hispanic" populations. Mexican-Americans have the highest fertility of all Hispanic groups. However, the Cubans' age composition is radically different. Bulges in the age 40–59 and 15–24 age categories reflect the young and middle-aged Cubans who arrived in the 1960s and early 1970s and their children. Moreover, Cubans' current fertility rates are very low. Because Cubans are just 6 percent of all U.S. Hispanics, their low fertility (even lower than the national average) and much older age (a median of 41 years in 1980) are outweighed in statistics on all Hispanics.

Where Hispanics Live

Today there are Hispanics in every state of the U.S., including Vermont (which had the fewest in 1980, 3,304), and the outlying states of Alaska (9,507), and Hawaii (71,263). But Hispanics still cluster in certain states and metropolitan areas, where they have become a powerful—even dominating—influence. California, with 4.5 million Hispanics, was home to almost one of every three Spanish-origin residents counted in the 1980 census. Add in Texas, with nearly 3 million Hispanics, and New York state, with 1.7 million, and 63 percent of the Hispanic population in 1980 has been accounted for. Florida, with 858,000 Hispanics, ranked fourth in number of Hispanics. Only five other states had more than 250,000 Hispanics apiece in 1980—Illinois, New Jersey, New Mexico, Arizona, and Colorado. Together, these nine states contained 85 percent of the U.S. Hispanic population—12.4 million (see Table 3).

Hispanics made up 19 percent of the population in California, the nation's most populous state, and 21 percent in Texas, the third most populous state. They were almost 10 percent of the population in New York, the second most populous state. New Mexico's population has the highest proportion of Hispanics—37 percent—and they make up 26 percent of Arizona's population and 12 percent in Colorado.

Hispanics of different origins are even more geographically concentrated. In 1980, 73 percent of the 8.7 million Mexican Americans lived in California and Texas alone and another 10 percent in the other three southwestern states of Arizona, Colorado, and New Mexico. Illinois, with more than 400,000, was the only state outside the Southwest with a sizable number of Mexican Americans. Fully 61 percent of the 2 million Puerto Ricans lived in New York and New Jersey, and another 6 percent in Illinois. Florida was home to nearly 59 percent of the 803,000 Cubans counted in the 1980 census and this one state became even more the Cuban center when an estimated 120,000 of the "Marielitos" later chose to resettle there.

The 3 million Hispanics in the "Other Hispanic" group were more scattered, but still only seven states had more than 100,000 each of this fourth group. In California, with the largest number (753,000), there were sizable communities of Salvadorans, Guatemalans, and Nicaraguans. New York, also with more than half a million "Other Hispanics," has attracted many Dominicans, Colombians, and Ecuadorans. Other Hispanics are also becoming increasingly evident in the Miami and Chicago areas. The "Other Hispanics" in New York, New Jersey, Florida, and Illinois are mostly immigrants from Central and South American countries, while it is likely that the "Other Hispanics" in Texas, New Mexico, and Colorado are largely Hispanos who preferred not to identify themselves as Mexican Americans in the census. California's "Other Hispanics" are a mixture of Hispanos and Central and South Americans.

Though the proportion of all Hispanics living in the nine most Hispanic states increased from 82 percent to 85 percent between 1970 and 1980 (see Table 3), the 1980 census actually showed that Hispanics are becoming less regionally concentrated. The proportion of Mexican Americans living in the five southwestern states dropped from 87 to 83 percent between 1970 and 1980, and the proportion of Puerto Ricans in New

TABLE 3. *Top Nine States in Hispanic Population: 1970 and 1980 (States with 250,000 or more Hispanics in 1980)*

State	Rank	1970 Number of Hispanics	Percent Distribution	Rank	1980 Number of Hispanics	Percent Distribution
United States, total	—	9,072,602[a]	100.00	—	14,608,673	100.0
California	1	2,369,292	26.1	1	4,544,331	31.1
Texas	2	1,840,648	20.3	2	2,985,824	20.4
New York	3	1,351,982	14.9	3	1,659,300	11.4
Florida	4	405,036	4.5	4	858,158	5.9
Illinois	5	393,204	4.3	5	635,602	4.4
New Jersey	7	288,488	3.2	6	491,883	3.4
New Mexico	6	308,340	3.4	7	477,222	3.3
Arizona	8	264,770	2.9	8	440,701	3.0
Colorado	9	225,506	2.5	9	339,717	2.3
Total in nine top states		7,447,266	82.1		12,432,738	85.1

Source: Bureau of the Census, "Persons of Spanish Origin by State," *1980 Census of Population,* Supplementary Report, PC80-S1-7, August 1982.

[a]Unadjusted 1970 Spanish-origin total which differs from 1970 total in Table 2. See text for explanation.

York, New Jersey, and Illinois declined from 80 to 67 percent. On the other hand, the percentage of Cubans living in Florida rose from 46 to 59 percent during the 1970s and the share of "Other Hispanics" living in California and New York went up from 28 to 43 percent.

City Dwellers

Though perceived by many as rural, Hispanics are a highly urban population. Fully 88 percent live in metropolitan areas, according to the 1980 census, compared to 75 percent of the general population and 81 percent of blacks.[12] Moreover, 50 percent of U.S. Hispanics live in the central cities of metropolitan areas. This is far

more than the 30 percent of the general population living in central cities.

Table 4 lists the 29 of the nation's 318 Standard Metropolitan Statistical Areas where Hispanics numbered more than 100,000 in 1980. Over 3½ million lived in the Los Angeles and New York areas alone—almost one-quarter of all Hispanics in the U.S. Mexican Americans are the largest Hispanic group in most of the 29 SMSAs listed in Table 4. However, Cubans are the most metropolitan of Hispanics; virtually 100 percent are metro dwellers in the four states with the most Cubans (Florida, New Jersey, New York, and California).

Miami is the undisputed Cuban center. Over

TABLE 4. *Standard Metropolitan Statistical Areas with 100,000 or More Hispanics in 1980*

Standard Metropolitan Statistical Area[a]	Hispanics in SMSA	Hispanics in Central City	Largest Hispanic Group and Its Percent of All Hispanics in SMSA
Los Angeles-Long Beach, CA	2,065,727	866,689	Mexican, 80%
New York, NY-NJ	1,493,081	1,405,957	Puerto Rican, 60%
Miami, FL	581,030	194,087	Cuban, 70%
Chicago, IL	580,592	422,061	Mexican, 64%
San Antonio, TX	481,511	421,774	Mexican, 93%
Houston, TX	424,901	281,224	Mexican, 88%
San Francisco-Oakland, CA	351,915	115,864	Mexican, 54%
El Paso, TX	297,001	265,819	Mexican, 95%
Riverside-San Bernardino-Ontario, CA	289,791	81,671	Mexican, 87%
Anaheim-Santa Ana-Garden Grove, CA	286,331	145,253	Mexican, 81%
San Diego, CA	275,176	130,610	Mexican, 83%
Dallas, Ft. Worth, TX	249,613	159,778	Mexican, 89%
McAllen-Pharr-Edinburg, TX	230,212	86,393	Mexican, 96%
San Jose, CA	226,611	140,574	Mexican, 78%
Phoenix, AZ	198,999	115,572	Mexican, 89%
Denver-Boulder, CO	173,362	94,933	Mexican, 63%
Albuquerque, NM	164,200	112,084	Other Hispanic, 56%
Brownsville-Harlingen-San Benito, TX	161,632	116,076	Mexican, 86%
Corpus Cristi, TX	158,123	108,175	Mexican, 96%
Fresno, CA	150,820	51,489	Mexican, 93%
Jersey City, NJ	145,163	41,672	Puerto Rican, 38%
Newark, NJ	132,356	61,254	Puerto Rican, 47%
Philadelphia, PA-NJ	116,280	63,570	Puerto Rican, 68%
Oxnard-Simi Valley-Ventura, CA	113,241	64,223	Mexican, 89%
Tucson, AZ	111,418	82,189	Mexican, 90%
Nassau-Suffolk, NY	101,418	[b]	Puerto Rican, 49%
Sacramento, CA	101,692	39,160	Mexican, 77%

Sources: Bureau of the Census, "Standard Metropolitan Statistical Areas and Standard Consolidated Statistical Areas: 1980," *1980 Census of Population*, Supplementary Report, PC80-S1-5, October 1981; and Cheryl Russell, "The News About Hispanics," *American Demographics*, March 1983, p. 17.

[a]A Standard Metropolitan Statistical Area (renamed Metropolitan Statistical Area as of July 1983) is a county with a central city (or urbanized area) of at least 50,000 population, plus adjacent counties that are economically linked with that county.

[b]Does not contain a central city.

half the country's Cuban Americans live in the Miami area where Cubans make up 70 percent of Hispanics. The Cuban influence has transformed Miami from a resort town to a year-round commercial center with linkages throughout Latin America and a leading bilingual cultural center. The Los Angeles area is the Mexican-American metropolitan capital. Mexicans comprise 80 percent of Hispanics in the area, 22 percent of the total population, and one-fifth of all Mexican Americans in the country. San Antonio, however, where Mexican Americans make up 93 percent of Hispanics and are also the population majority in the central city, can claim to be the first large U.S. city with a Mexican-American mayor—Henry Cisneros, elected in 1981. Puerto Ricans began flowing into New York City during the 1950s and, with 43 percent of all Puerto Ricans in the country, the New York metropolitan area is still the hub of Puerto Rican life on the mainland.

Fertility

Although immigration may appear to be the major spur to the growth of the U.S. Hispanic population, an estimated two-thirds of that growth actually stems from Hispanics' relatively high fertility, combined with mortality that is probably no higher than that of non-Hispanics. The available data suggest that the fertility of Hispanic women as a group—though lower than it was two decades ago—is about 60 percent higher than the non-Hispanic average and 50 percent higher than the average for all U.S. women. It is also higher than black fertility. Mexican-American women have the highest fertility among Hispanics, while Cuban women's fertility is far below even that of non-Hispanic women.

Hispanic fertility is difficult to estimate because accurate counts of the "true" Hispanic population are still so elusive and systematic registration of births by Hispanic origin began only in 1978 and so far covers only 22 states (though an estimated 90 percent of the Hispanic population). One clue, however, is the "child-woman ratio," or the number of children under age five per 1,000 women aged 15-44, calculated from the 1980 census. As seen in Table 5, this ratio was 462 for Hispanic women, 55 percent higher than the ratio of 298 for non-Hispanic

TABLE 5. Child-Woman Ratio and Percentage of Children Among Hispanics, Non-Hispanics, and Blacks: 1980

Population	Children Aged 0–4 per 1,000 Women Aged 15–44	Percent of Population under Age 15
Hispanic	462	32.0
Non-Hispanic	298	22.0
Black	366	28.7

Source: Bureau of the Census, "Age, Sex, Race, and Spanish Origin of the Population by Regions, Divisions, and States: 1980," *1980 Census of Population*, Supplementary Report, PC80-S1-1, 1981.

women of childbearing age and 26 percent higher than the black ratio of 366. Also, as already noted, 32 percent of the total Hispanic population counted in the 1980 census were children under age 15. This compares with 29 percent in the black population and 22 percent among all non-Hispanics.

Table 6 shows birth rates and fertility rates for 1979 that could be computed by the National Center for Health Statistics (NCHS) for nine of the 19 states where births were by then being recorded by Hispanic origin of mother and father. The most recently published from birth registration information, these 1979 rates cover less than 60 percent of the Hispanic population and exclude the heavily Hispanic states of Texas and New Mexico, which, along with Georgia, began

TABLE 6. Birth Rates and Fertility Rates, by Hispanic Origin: Nine States, 1979

Ethnic Group	Births per 1,000 Population	Births per 1,000 Women Aged 15–44
All origins	15.6	66.7
Non-Hispanic	14.7	63.2
All Hispanic	25.5	100.5
Mexican-American	29.6	119.3
Puerto Rican	22.6	80.7
Cuban	8.6	39.7
Other Hispanic	25.7	95.9

Source: Stephanie J. Ventura, "Births of Hispanic Parentage, 1979," *Monthly Vital Statistics Report*, Vol. 31, No. 2, Supplement, May 1982.

Note: The nine states are Arizona, California, Colorado, Florida, Illinois, Indiana, New Jersey, New York, and Ohio.

registration of births by Hispanic origin only in 1980. The "crude" birth rate for all Hispanics of 25.5 births per 1,000 population was 73 percent higher than the birth rate of 14.7 per 1,000 of the non-Hispanic population. However, the gap was less when measured by the number of births per 1,000 women of childbearing age (15–44), a more accurate measure of fertility. Here the 100.5 rate for Hispanic women as a whole was 59 percent higher than the rate of 63.2 for non-Hispanic women, but only 51 percent higher than the rate of 66.7 births per 1,000 among all women aged 15–44 in the nine reporting states. The latter results tally well with results from the Census Bureau's June 1980 Current Population Survey. Among the 36,000 women aged 18–44 included in the nationwide sample, there were 107 births per 1,000 Hispanic women in the 12 months preceding the survey.[13] This rate was also 51 percent higher than the rate for all women—71—and it was 27 percent higher than the black rate of 84.

The Mexican-American rate of 119.3 births per 1,000 women aged 15–44 shown in Table 6 is the highest among the four Hispanic groups. The rates for Puerto Ricans (80.7) and "Other Hispanic" women (95.9) are also much higher than the rates for non-Hispanics (63.2) and for all women (66.7). The Cuban rate of 39.7 is far below all others. Stephanie Ventura, author of the NCHS report, attributes this partly to the relatively older age of Cuban women in Florida (more of those aged 15–44 are in the low-fertility years of 35–44 than are their Mexican and Puerto Rican counterparts), but it probably also reflects the low family-size preferences of the relatively affluent and better educated Cuban population.[14]

Reasons for Higher Hispanic Fertility
Except for Cubans, Hispanics have less education, lower family incomes, and are much more likely to be living in poverty than the general U.S. population, as we shall see later. This undoubtedly explains much of their higher fertility, for these factors are correlated with relatively high fertility among all U.S. groups. The Census Bureau's June 1980 survey, for example, found a rate of 94 births per 1,000 women in families with incomes under $5,000 per year compared to just 49 per 1,000 women in families with incomes of $25,000 and over. The NCHS found that only 47

percent of all Hispanic women and 37 percent of Mexican-American women reported to have had a birth in 1979 and completed at least 12 years of schooling, compared to 78 percent among the non-Hispanic mothers and 77 percent among Cubans. Ventura comments that these lower levels of schooling among non-Cuban Hispanics were partly due to "the relatively larger proportion of births to teenagers among Hispanic mothers."[15] Fully 19 percent of Hispanic women in the study who had a birth in 1979 were under age 20, compared to 15 percent for all mothers. The proportion of teenage births for Mexican women was 20 percent and a still higher 23 percent for Puerto Rican women.

Traditional preferences for large families in the countries from which most Hispanics originate probably also play a role. Cuba currently has an exceptionally low fertility rate for a developing country—just 1.8 births per woman, the same as that of the U.S.[16] Puerto Rico's rate of 2.7 is considerably higher, but still well below the Latin American average of 4.3 births per woman. More typical is Mexico's experience. At the beginning of the 1970s, Mexico's fertility rate was over 7 births per woman. However, in less than a decade it has dropped to about 4.7 births per woman in the wake of a vigorous government family planning program.[17] Other Latin American countries have now launched family planning programs to reduce population growth and it is probable that many recent Hispanic immigrants to the U.S. have had some experience with contraception.

To judge from a 1979 survey of 2,100 women of childbearing age living on the U.S. side of the Mexican border, contraceptive use is quite high among Hispanics in the U.S., but not so high as for non-Hispanics. Some 66 percent of the currently married Hispanic women surveyed were using contraception, compared to 75 percent among "Anglos" (white, non-Hispanic).[18] However, the differences were not significant among women under 35, which suggests that younger Hispanic married women may be about as likely to practice contraception as their non-Hispanic counterparts. Never-married Hispanic women were only half as likely to be using contraception as single Anglo women, however, though equal proportions in both groups (12 percent) reported that they were sexually active.

Closing the Gap

Although Hispanic fertility is still well above the national average, there is evidence that it has been falling in concert with that of all U.S. women since the mid-1950s. This suggests that the gap should eventually be closed.

Using census data on "own children," demographers Robert Rindfuss and James Sweet calculated that Hispanic women's fertility dropped by 25 percent between 1955 and 1969. A study by the Centers for Disease Control noted a similar decrease from 1970 to 1977 among Spanish-surnamed women in Texas.[19] Data from the Census Bureau's Current Population Survey displayed in Table 7 show that the decline continues. In 1973, Hispanic married women aged 30–34 reported that they had had 3.3 births to date; by 1981, the average for such women was down to 2.5. In 1981, these women still expected to have an average of 2.8 children during their lifetime, compared to 2.2 for all married women aged 30–34. But young Hispanic married women aged 18–24 in 1981 said they expected an average of 2.3, virtually the same as the 1981 national average of 2.2 for all married women aged 18–24.

Thus, the fertility of U.S. Hispanic women as a group—now probably about 2.5 births apiece—is likely to continue to decline. Actual convergence with the U.S. national average may be somewhat delayed, however, as each year

brings a new wave of legal and illegal immigrants reared in traditions of somewhat larger families. From a demographic standpoint, it is also significant that Hispanic fertility is still well above the "replacement" level of about two children per woman needed to stop population growth in the long run, and may remain above that level for some time to come.

Family and Marital Status

Hispanics are less likely than the general U.S. population to be living in married-couple families and much more likely to be in families headed by a single parent, almost always the mother. But in both respects they fare much better than blacks.

In 1981, as Table 8 shows, 73 percent of the nation's 3.2 million Hispanic families were headed by a married couple, compared to 82 percent of all families and just 54 percent of black families. Fifty-two percent of Hispanic families had children living at home—higher than the 41 percent among all families.

Single parents with children under 18 comprised 18 percent of all Hispanic families. This was three-quarters higher than the proportion among all families (10 percent) but well below the proportion among blacks (31 percent). Fully 16 percent of Hispanic families in 1981 were maintained by a woman alone, compared to 9 percent among all families. Puerto Rican families are far

TABLE 7. *Births to Date and Total Births Expected in Lifetime, Hispanic and All Married Women: 1973, 1975, 1978, 1981 (Numbers are births per currently married women)*

Year and Group	Total, aged 18–34		Women 18–24		Women 30–34	
	Births to Date	Lifetime Births Expected	Births to Date	Lifetime Births Expected	Births to Date	Lifetime Births Expected
Hispanic women						
1973	2.1	3.0	1.1	2.6	3.3	3.8
1975	1.9	2.7	1.0	2.2	3.0	3.2
1978	1.8	2.6	1.1	2.4	2.8	3.0
1981	1.9	2.6	1.1	2.3	2.5	2.8
All women						
1973	1.7	2.5	0.9	2.3	2.6	2.8
1975	1.6	2.3	0.8	2.2	2.4	2.6
1978	1.5	2.3	0.8	2.2	2.2	2.4
1981	1.5	2.2	0.9	2.2	2.0	2.2

Source: Carolyn C. Rogers, "Fertility of American Women: June 1981," *Current Population Reports*, Series P-20, No. 378, April 1983, Table 1.

TABLE 8. *Hispanic, Black, and All Families: 1981*

Family Type and Presence of Own Children under 18	Hispanic	Black	All Families
All families			
Number (in thousands)	3,235	6,317	60,309
Percent	100.0	100.0	100.0
Married-couple families	73.1	53.7	81.7
With own children	51.7	30.7	41.3
No own children	21.5	23.0	40.4
Single-parent/ child families	18.2	30.6	10.4
Mother and own children	16.3	28.9	9.3
Father and own children	1.9	1.8	1.1
Other families	8.7	15.7	7.8

Source: Bureau of the Census, "Household and Family Characteristics: March 1981," *Current Population Reports*, Series P-20, No. 371, May 1982, Tables 12 and 13.

more likely than other Hispanic families to be maintained by a woman—40 percent were in 1979, versus just 15 percent among Mexican Americans and 17 percent among other Hispanics, including Cubans.[25]

Because of their higher fertility, Hispanic family households are larger than the national average. In 1981, Hispanic families averaged 3.9 persons each, compared to 3.3 among all families and 3.7 for blacks.[26]

Marital Status

Although Hispanics marry as readily as all Americans, they are somewhat more likely to separate or divorce, which explains their higher proportion of female-headed families. Fourteen percent of Hispanic women aged 15 and over were separated or divorced in 1981—more than the 10 percent for all women this age but, again, lower than the proportion among black women, which was nearly 20 percent (Table 9). In the same year there were 146 divorced Hispanic women for every 1,000 Hispanic women who were married and living with their husbands.[27] For all women, the ratio was 129, and for black women, 289. On the other hand, 53 percent of Hispanic women over 15 were married and living with their husbands in 1981, very close to the 55 percent among all women. Hispanics tend to marry somewhat earlier than other Americans do. In 1981, about 25 percent of Hispanic women under age 20 were or had been married, compared to 15 percent among all teenage women and only 7 percent among black women under 20.

Thus, while the marital experience of Hispanics is more similar to the U.S. average than that of blacks, Hispanics are somewhat more likely to dissolve their marriages. This leads in turn to somewhat higher proportions of female-headed households, which is a factor in Hispanics' lower family incomes, as noted later.

TABLE 9. *Marital Status of Hispanic, Black, and All Persons Aged 15 and Over: 1981 (Numbers in percent)*

Marital Status	Hispanic		Black		All Persons	
	Males	Females	Males	Females	Males	Females
Total	100.0	100.0	100.0	100.0	100.0	100.0
Never married	34.0	26.0	41.0	33.7	29.4	22.5
Married, spouse present	55.2	52.6	41.1	32.8	60.2	54.8
Married, spouse absent	5.2	7.8	7.0	11.4	2.8	3.7
Separated	2.5	6.4	5.8	10.1	1.9	2.9
Other	2.6	1.4	1.2	1.2	0.9	0.8
Widowed	1.6	6.0	3.7	12.7	2.3	11.9
Divorced	4.0	7.7	7.3	9.5	5.3	7.1

Source: Bureau of the Census, "Marital Status and Living Arrangements: March 1981," *Current Population Reports*, Series P-20, No. 372, 1982, Table 1.

Immigration

Hispanics' increasing visibility on the American scene reflects a striking shift in the pattern of immigration to the U.S. From 1930 to 1960, Europeans still dominated the immigrant influx— 41 percent from Northern and Western Europe, and 17 percent from Southern and Eastern Europe. Latin Americans made up only 15 percent of total legal immigration. Since 1960, Latin Americans have averaged 40 percent of the total. By 1975–79, they were up to 42 percent, outpacing legal immigrants from Asia (39 percent) and Europe (down to 13 percent).[28] The total numbers have also been rising. Immigration and Naturalization Service (INS) statistics put the number of Hispanic immigrants entering the country legally at 956,000 during the 1950s, 1.3 million in the 1960s, and 1.4 million in the 1970s. Added to this is a growing, if unknown, number of illegal immigrants arriving from Latin America.

This shift in the origins of immigrants has had all the more impact on the makeup of the U.S. population because net immigration has become an increasingly important part of annual population growth as fertility has declined. In 1981, for example, it has been estimated that natural increase (births minus deaths) accounted for 57 percent of population growth; 43 percent was contributed by 1.2 million immigrants— 480,000 legal immigrants, 217,000 refugees, and an estimated 500,000 illegal immigrants.[29]

Behind the shift are some stark demographic and economic figures. Latin America's labor force is growing by 4 million a year; that of Mexico and the rest of Central America by 1.2 million a year. Forty percent of their current work force is unemployed or working only a few hours a week or days in the year.[30] Per capita income for all Latin America was $2,063 in 1981. For the U.S.—even as the recession deepened—it was $12,530.[31]

Equally important in the shift to Latin American predominance among immigrants was the change in the U.S. policy signaled by passage of the Immigration and Nationality Act of 1965, which came into force in 1968. Responding to an increased influx of Latin American immigrants, this imposed for the first time a numerical limit on legal immigration from the Western Hemisphere—120,000 annual arrivals, admitted on a first-come, first-served basis. At the same time, Eastern Hemisphere countries became subject to a 170,000 overall ceiling, plus a 20,000 annual per-country limit based on a complicated preference system which stressed job skills and reunification with close family members already in the U.S. This abolished a quota system in effect since the 1920s that had favored immigrants from Northern and Western Europe.

The result was an increase in the percentage of legal immigrants from non-European countries. It also left many would-be Mexican migrants to the U.S. without legal means of entry, coming as it did just after Congress had ended the *bracero* program which, at its peak, had brought to the U.S. over 400,000 temporary Mexican workers annually.[32] Without the visa preference system, there was little control over legal admissions of Latin Americans. To change this and put Latin America on an "equal footing" with the rest of the world, the U.S. in 1977 extended the visa preference system and the 20,000 per-country annual limit to the Western Hemisphere. This put the most severe restriction ever on immigration from the Western Hemisphere and probably stimulated illegal immigration of persons who did not qualify for a preference or refused to wait out the many years it often now takes to gain clearance.

In 1978, the hemisphere quotas were replaced with a single worldwide ceiling of 290,000, later changed to 270,000 excluding refugees, with no more than 20,000 from any one country. Immediate relatives of U.S. citizens are admitted in addition to the 270,000 limit, however, which raised the total of legal immigrants to 480,000 in 1981, for example. Another component of the legal influx are refugees, for which quotas are set annually under the terms of the Refugee Act of 1980; 140,000 refugee slots were allocated in 1982. The 125,000 Cubans of the Mariel boatlift, along with 10,000 Haitians who also sought refuge in the U.S. during 1980, were admitted under still another category as special "entrants."

The growing share of Latin Americans among immigrants has aroused public concern about the impact on American standards and values of an ethnically and culturally distinct group endowed with socioeconomic characteristics perceived as inferior to those of the "average" American. Forgotten are the similar concerns voiced at the turn of the century when immigrants from Southern and Eastern Europe began to outnumber those from Northern and Western Europe. The degradation of U.S. society predicted at that time has obviously not come to pass.

One issue unique to Hispanics, however, is that they share a common language. This has helped them develop a group identity and increased leverage in demands for special attention and services. It has also provoked a negative response from those who fear the U.S. will be forced into bilingualism, or at least the sort of linguistic factionalism most recently evident in Canada. In 1981, now retired Senator S. I. Hayakawa proposed a resolution to amend the U.S. Constitution to make English the country's official language. Voters in Dade County, Florida, where Miami is located, in November 1980 overturned a countywide policy of bilingualism adopted in 1973.

In numbers is strength, however. Thus Hispanics are likely to continue to dominate immigration to the U.S. to the disadvantage of white non-Hispanics and blacks from other countries who currently make up little of the flow. The U.S. became more ethnically and culturally diverse as the result of earlier shifts in the profile of immigrants and this can be expected to occur again with the increase in Hispanics. Legitimate questions remain about the costs and benefits of reorganizing society and how fast that should happen. More easily influenced by policymakers than fertility and mortality—the other two variables that shape a country's population growth and composition—immigration is likely to remain a much debated issue in the U.S. for some time to come.

Legal Immigration Diversity

Each of the four Hispanic groups has its own unique immigration history and, once arrived, has generally settled in different regions of the U.S., as we have seen. There are also differences in the amount that immigration has contributed to each group's growth since 1950—almost all for Cubans and "Other Hispanics," and very little since the 1960s for the Puerto Ricans.

Data on legal immigration for Mexicans, Cubans, and Other Hispanics are drawn from INS records. Puerto Ricans, who have unrestricted access to the U.S., do not appear in INS records. To estimate their net migration one must use a residual procedure involving two Puerto Rican census counts and registration of births and deaths for the decade they span. Drawing on these two sources, Table 10 shows immigration into the U.S. of each of the four groups for the three decades from 1950 to 1980.

During the 1950s, Puerto Ricans accounted for half of all Hispanic immigration, providing the U.S. with a net gain of nearly half a million. This movement, with one of every six Puerto Ricans moving to the U.S. during the decade, ranks as one of the most dramatic voluntary exoduses on record. It was driven by the promise of jobs—any jobs—as an escape from the island's stagnant agrarian economy, cheap plane fares, and the freedom of entry accorded Puerto Ricans as U.S. citizens.

A sharp rise in immigration in the last half of the 1950s boosted Mexican immigration to almost 300,000 for the decade. The number grew by about 140,000 in each of the next two decades, yielding a total for the 1970s of just under 570,000. Mexico ranked as the largest single

TABLE 10. *Hispanic Immigration into the U.S., by Ethnic Group: 1950–1980*

Ethnic Group	1950–59		1960–69		1970–79	
	Number of Migrants	Percent of Total	Number of Migrants	Percent of Total	Number of Migrants	Percent of Total
Mexican	293,000	30.7	431,000	33.2	567,000	40.8
Cuban	71,000	7.4	249,000	19.2	278,000	20.0
Puerto Rican	480,000	50.2	222,000	17.1	41,000	3.0
Other Hispanic	112,000	11.7	397,000	30.6	503,000	36.2

Sources: Mexican, Cuban, Other Hispanic: Immigration and Naturalization Service annual reports 1950–1979, Table 9; Puerto Rican: Estimated from Puerto Rican census and vital statistics.

contributor to U.S. legal immigration over this 20-year span and accounted for over 40 percent of all Hispanic immigration.

Cuban immigration also grew dramatically over the three decades. Although the INS statistics shown in Table 10 add to 527,000 Cuban immigrants for 1960–80, the actual number of Cuban arrivals was close to 640,000, with over 70 percent occurring during the 1960s. Such large numbers of Cubans could only enter the U.S. by assigning them special status as political refugees or "parolees." But the INS records such individuals' entries only when their status is adjusted to "immigrant."

Touched off by Castro's rise to power in 1959, Cuban legal immigration subsequently rose and fell in concert with shifts in both U.S. and Cuban government policies, as we have seen— surging in the first years after the revolution and in the late 1960s and early 1970s, ebbing after the 1962 missile crisis and following Castro's cutoff of emigration in 1973. The latest and largest influx of Cubans into the U.S. began when an April 1980 rush on the Peruvian embassy in Havana by a crowd demanding asylum drew a sudden response from Castro that whoever wanted to leave the island was welcome to go. By December 1980, 125,000 had arrived in the U.S., transported in a flotilla of boats sent to collect them from the port of El Mariel. These refugees were set off from their predecessors not only by their numbers but also by their socioeconomic characteristics. Most stemmed from "urban working and lower class origins," as had Cubans arriving in the early 1970s, while the first waves of post-revolutionary refugees had been "displaced bourgeoisie"—well educated, middle and upper class professionals and businesspeople alienated by the new regime.[33]

One ramification of the timing of the Mariel boatlift, which began just after completion of the 1980 census, was to undermine the relevancy of census data on the Cuban population. Close to 15 percent of the 1981 U.S. Cuban population was not in residence at the time of the April 1, 1980, census.

Comparing the 1980 census count of Cubans (803,000) with the number estimated to have emigrated to the U.S. from 1959 up to the census date (670,000) indicates that some 80 percent of the 1980 population are first-generation immi-

grants. The Mariel arrivals would, of course, further increase this percentage.

The Other Hispanics are shown in Table 10 to have had the largest gain in immigration over the 30-year interval. From 112,000 and 12 percent of Hispanic immigration in the 1950s, they grew to 503,000 and 36 percent of the total in the 1970s, putting them into second place after Mexicans in their contribution to Hispanic immigration for the decade. For the 1975–79 period, they were actually in first place, as noted earlier. Of course, this total represents immigration from 16 separate nations. The largest contingents come from the Dominican Republic, Colombia, Argentina, and Ecuador, joined, in recent years, by growing numbers of escapees from the political turmoil in Nicaragua and El Salvador. This increase in Other Hispanic immigration partly reflects growing population pressures in the countries from which they come. Current population growth in these 16 countries averages over 2 percent a year—a rate at which a population doubles in just 35 years. This alone foretells for this group an ever-growing dominance in Hispanic legal immigration totals.

After holding first place during the 1950s, Puerto Rican net immigration dwindled to just 41,000 and 3 percent of the total in the 1970s. Why was this? With an island population of less than 2.4 million in 1960 and fertility on the decline, it would have been impossible for Puerto Rico to continue to export half a million residents each decade. But other factors also played a role. For one, pressure on the home job market was relieved by the exodus of earlier emigrants. Economic opportunities may still have been brighter in the U.S. but not enough to warrant the wrench of leaving home. Deciding to stay was also made more feasible by increases in U.S. government welfare support, combined with remittances from family members who had ventured to the mainland.

Unique to Puerto Rican immigration, however, is the fact that the net migration figures mask a large movement of people back and forth from the island, which unrestricted entry to the U.S. permits. Puerto Ricans have been characterized as having "one foot on the mainland and one on the island." Detailed figures for the 1970s show a net flow back to Puerto Rico of people aged 35 and over and older children aged 5–19, but this was offset by a larger net influx into the U.S. of persons aged 20–29 and children under age five. This suggests that young adults are lured to the U.S. with their children by the prospect of better economic opportunities and later choose to return to the island.

Sex and Age of Legal Immigrants

The characteristic ages and sex of 1950–80 immigrants, which helped shape the age-sex composition of the 1980 resident Hispanic population, also varied among the four groups. Women consistently outnumbered men among immigrants from Cuba and Other Hispanic countries, as has been true of immigrants to the U.S. generally since the 1930s. Fifty-seven percent of new arrivals among Other Hispanics during the 1950s were women—a high proportion which reflects the pattern of rural-to-urban migration in Latin America where women also outnumber men. By the 1970s this figure had declined somewhat to 54 percent.

Among Cuban immigrants, the proportion of women was 53 percent in the 1950s and 1960s, just before and after the 1959 Castro takeover, and rose to 55 percent in the 1970s. In this case the predominance of women came about because young men of conscription age were not allowed to emigrate. The sex ratio of Cuban immigrants in the 1980s will have changed with the addition of the Marielitos, 70 percent of whom were men.[34]

Among Mexican and Puerto Rican immigrants, by contrast, men have been more numerous. For Mexicans, the male share was 53 percent during the 1950s, followed by a decline to 50–51 percent in the next two decades. This pattern probably reflects job opportunities in the Southwest. Many legal immigrants in the 1950s may have been former *braceros* or their relatives who knew of job opportunities for men in the U.S.

Among Puerto Ricans, the proportion of men was 54 percent during the 1950s, 56 percent in the 1960s, and 73 percent in the 1970s. The 1970s figure must be viewed cautiously since it is based on such a small net immigration total. Even so, the increasing predominance of males is obvious. This could be because Puerto Ricans can come to the U.S. freely, without the hurdles that face all other Hispanic legal immigrants, and

men are thus easily able to come temporarily to take a job without uprooting an entire family.

Two-thirds of immigrants arriving from Mexico and "Other Hispanic" countries from 1950 to 1980 were between the ages of 15 and 44. This is typical of most migrant streams, for this is the stage of life when one can expect to profit most from a move to a place promising better economic opportunities. As might be expected, such migrants bring with them a sizable number of young children.

Puerto Rican movement during the 1970s, as noted, stands out for its net influx of migrants aged 20–29 and net emigration at ages above 35. The pattern was similar, if less pronounced, in the earlier decades.

Cuban immigrants of the 1950s were mostly in the typical young adult ages but much older in the two decades after the revolution. Thirty-three percent in the 1960s and 45 percent in the 1970s were over age 44. Seventeen percent of the Cuban women who immigrated from 1960 to 1980 were 65 and over, much higher than the 7.1 percent of Cuban women this age counted in the U.S. in the 1980 census. Demographers Sergio Diaz and Lisandro Perez point out some reasons for the older, more female Cuban immigration before the Mariel boatlift: "The Cuban government generally prohibited the emigration of males eligible for military conscription. Also persons of working age had to spend time in agricultural labor before being allowed to leave the country. There were no such restrictions for the elderly, a dependent population the revolutionary government was not particularly eager to keep."[35]

Illegal Immigration

Illegal immigration—hard to measure but thought to be on the increase—looms large in any assessment of the impact of recent Hispanic immigration to the U.S. Not all illegal immigrants are Hispanics, of course, but the majority probably are. Their motives are no different from those of legal immigrants; most come seeking jobs or to escape political and social turmoil at home. Unfortunately, these legitimate interests often conflict with the interests of current citizens.

Who Are They?

Illegal or undocumented aliens are classified as persons crossing the border "without inspection" or with fraudulent documents, or overstaying a work or study visa. This definition rules out Puerto Ricans, with free access as U.S. citizens, and most Cubans, who have been accorded special refugee status because of the political overtones attached to their movements to the U.S. Thus the undocumented Hispanic population is made up almost entirely of Mexicans and Other Hispanics.

An estimated 50-60 percent of all illegal aliens are Mexicans,[36] stimulated by the closeness of the border, a long history of moving back and forth to fill the heavy labor needs of the Southwest's agriculture, and erratic U.S. policies. Mexicans were deported when jobs grew scarce during the 1930s and courted again with the *bracero* program as labor became short during World War II. Through the *bracero* program was viewed as a way to stop illegal immigration, it actually served to step up the influx as word got round of jobs to be had across the border. By the 1950s the domestic labor supply was back up to full force and the INS set out to staunch the illegal flow with "Operation Wetback." (Many Mexicans waded clandestinely across the Rio Grande; hence, "wetback.") At the same time, however, U.S. employers were still allowed to hire illegal entrants who managed to get through. Further illegal Mexican immigration was practically guaranteed by the ending of the *bracero* program in 1964 and institution of the 120,000 hemispheric ceiling on immigration in 1968 and 20,000 per-country limit in 1977. Currently, with unemployment again high in the U.S., there is renewed pressure for control of the influx from Mexico, just as pressure mounts on the other side to escape Mexico's deteriorating economy and devalued peso.

Much of the illegal movement from Mexico into the U.S. is offset by return migration. Workers come north, find jobs, and eventually return to home and family. The Southwest has been the traditional destination for Mexican migrants but many now make their way as far north as Chicago and Detroit. The farther the search for a job and the more urban the job is, the less likely it is that an undocumented Mexican will move back and forth across the border.

A substantial portion of other illegal immigrants are from such countries as Guatemala, El Salvador, the Dominican Republic, Colombia, Ecuador and Peru. Many of these are now also crossing the Mexican border. Undocumented "Other Hispanics," however, more typically enter with a temporary work visa and stay past the expiration date, sticking to large cities to avoid detection. Many Dominicans enter through Puerto Rico. They obtain travel passes to the island and are virtually unidentifiable among Puerto Ricans in legal transit to the U.S. "Other Hispanic" illegal aliens are more likely than Mexicans to remain in the U.S. once here.

How Many?

In the early 1970s, estimates of the number of illegal aliens living in the U.S. ranged from 2 to 12 million. Recently a consensus has grown for an estimate of 3.5 to 6 million, as given in a 1981 report prepared by Census Bureau demographer Jacob Siegel and colleagues for the Select Commission on Immigration and Refugee Policy.[37] The latest light comes from a Census Bureau study, unveiled in April 1983, which estimated that just over 2 million undocumented persons were included in the 1980 total census count of 226.5 million.[38] This does not reveal how many undocumented residents were missed by the census, but it is difficult to imagine that it was even as many as the number counted because the Census Bureau made a concerted effort to enumerate the undocumented population and to reach all segments of the Hispanic community.

Of the 2 million, 1.3 million, or 64 percent, were estimated to be from Latin America. Mexicans alone numbered 931,000. All other Latin American countries with legal immigration to the U.S. also turn up in the estimate of illegal aliens enumerated in the 1980 census but none made a substantial contribution.

That the number of illegal aliens arriving each year may be increasing is suggested by figures on deportable aliens apprehended by the INS. This number grew from 420,000 in 1971 to over a million each year in 1977 through 1979, followed by a slight drop to 976,000 in 1981 and 970,000 in 1982.[39] Most apprehensions occur at the Mexico border where the INS concentrates such efforts. From January through April 1983, there were 377,000 apprehensions at the border, a 46 percent increase over the same period in 1982.[40] Apprehensions, however, are not an accurate count of the actual number of illegal aliens entering each year since the same person may be apprehended more than once in a year. Nor do they record movements out of the country. Estimates of the annual *net* increase in the total undocumented population of the U.S. range from below 100,000 up to 500,000.[41]

Education

Younger Hispanic adults spend more time in school than their elders did, as is now true for all racial and ethnic groups in the U.S. But Hispanics still lag behind blacks and far behind whites as a whole in average educational attainment—the key to economic and occupational progress. Some Hispanic groups are more educated than others, however, which reflects differences in immigration histories more than ethnic attitudes toward education.

Cubans, still dominated by the middle-class and professional people who were the first to flee the Castro regime, tend to be better educated than other Hispanics. So, too, are recent legal immigrants from Central and South America. The Mexican-American family whose roots in the U.S. go far back in history, typically progressed from little education among earlier generations to several college graduates and advanced degree-holders among the latest generations. However, educational attainment for Mexican Americans as a whole reflects the much lesser schooling of the majority who are recent legal and illegal immigrants. Average educational attainment is also low for Puerto Ricans in the U.S., partly stemming from the constant flow back and forth between the island and the mainland. Public education in Puerto Rico suffers from scant funding—just $694 per pupil in 1977—below the $900 of Arkansas which ranked lowest of the U.S. states on this score.[45] Children transferred to schools in the U.S. must usually drop to grades lower than the average for their age and often have their schooling disrupted by moves back to the island; some 20,000 pupils a year were transferred back and forth between Puerto Rico and New York City alone during the 1970s. Frustration with the public school system in Puerto Rico prompts many middle- and upper-class professionals to place their children in private schools.

School Enrollment Progress

Hispanics' lesser involvement in education begins early. In 1981, only 25 percent of Spanish-origin three- and four-year-olds were enrolled in school compared to some 36 percent of both blacks and whites as a whole.[46] These early education programs include public and private nursery schools and Head Start, which are particularly important for children from disadvantaged backgrounds.

Between ages 5 and 15, nearly all Hispanics along with blacks and whites attend school, but the gap widens again from age 16 when students are able to leave school legally in most states. In 1981, school enrollment among Hispanics was 83 percent for 16- and 17-year-olds compared to some 91 percent for blacks and whites, and only 38 percent at ages 18 and 19, in contrast to roughly one-half for blacks and whites. Some 36 percent of Hispanics aged 18 and 19 were not enrolled in school and were also not high school graduates, i.e., they were dropouts. This was more than double the figure for whites of that age (16 percent) and almost double that of blacks (19 percent).

Hispanics' high dropout rates are partly due to the fact that many are enrolled in grades below the average for their age, where they can be bored, feel out of place, and be labeled slow learners. In 1976, about 9 percent of Mexican-American and Puerto Rican 8-to-13 years-olds were at least two years behind their "expected" grade in school, compared to 5 percent of white non-Hispanics; at ages 14–20, the figures were 25 percent for Hispanics versus just 9 percent for non-Hispanic whites.[47] In New England in the early 1970s, 50 percent of Hispanics were at least two grades behind and only 12 percent were in their "expected" grade.[48] Delay is particularly serious for transfer students from Puerto Rico; in Boston, for example, students aged 17–19 who were in senior high school in Puerto Rico are often placed in the sixth or seventh grade.

Not surprisingly, Hispanics are much less likely to graduate from high school than other groups, and the percentage of Hispanic high school graduates who go on the college dropped from 35.4 percent to 29.9 percent between 1975 and 1980.[49]

High School and College Completion

Hispanics aged 25 and over are increasingly likely to be at least high school graduates, like blacks and all white adults, but the gap remains wide, as seen in Figure 1. In 1981, 46 percent of

Hispanic males, for example, had completed four years of high school or more, up from 33 percent in 1970, but the figure for black males was 53 percent and for white males as a whole, 72 percent. However, younger Hispanics are catching up. Among those aged 25 to 34 in 1981, 57 percent had completed high school. Mexican Americans and Puerto Rican males have made some gains in high school completion since 1960, according to a study by the U.S. Commission on Civil Rights, but still trailed behind other Hispanic groups as well as blacks and all whites in 1976.[50] There is another gap in high school completion between metropolitan and nonmetro-politan Hispanics; in 1979, only 36 percent of Hispanic adult men living in nonmetropolitan areas had finished high school, compared to 44 percent of Hispanic men in metropolitan areas.[51]

Scholastic Aptitude Test scores reveal the poorer preparation of Hispanic high school graduates who do go on the college. Among entering freshmen in 1979, the average on the verbal part of the test was 356 (out of a possible 800) for Puerto Ricans and 372 for Mexican Americans compared to 442 for non-Hispanic whites, and 387 for Puerto Ricans and 413 for Mexican Americans in math versus 482 for non-Hispanic whites.[52]

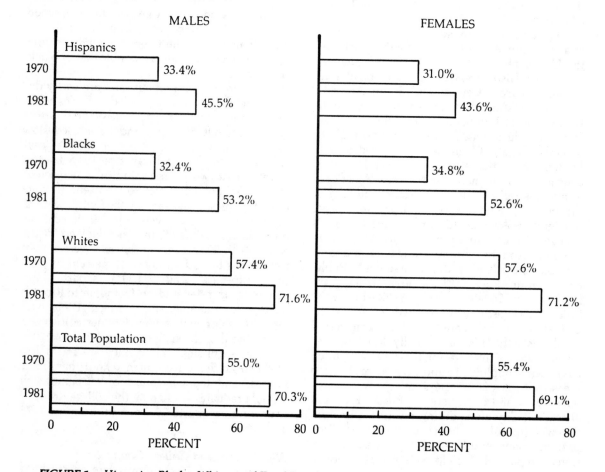

FIGURE 1. *Hispanics, Blacks, Whites, and Total Population Aged 25 and Over Who Completed Four Years of High School or More: 1970 and 1981 (Source: Bureau of the Census, "Population Profile of the United States: 1981," Current Population Reports, Series P-20, No. 374, 1982, Table 6–3.)*

Hispanic college enrollment doubled from one-quarter million to half a million between 1972 and 1981, but still made up only 4.8 percent of total college enrollment in 1981.[53] Once in college, Hispanics are far more likely than other college students to drop out; 57 percent of Hispanic males and 54 percent of Hispanic females fail to graduate, compared to 34 percent of all white males and females.[54] Figures in 1981 for adults 25 years and over who had completed at least four years of college were only 10 percent for males and 6 percent for females among Hispanics, compared to 22 percent for all white males and 14 percent for white females, and 8 percent for both black males and females.[55] Part of the reason for this disparity is that Hispanic students primarily attend two-year colleges. In 1980, 54 percent of Hispanics enrolled in college, compared to 36 percent of all white students, were attending two-year colleges.[56]

Why the Educational Lag?

Whether or not he or she was born in the U.S. makes a difference in a Hispanic's educational attainment. Demographers A. J. Jaffe, Ruth Cullen and Thomas Boswell found from 1970 census data that Hispanics born in the U.S. generally attend school longer than their foreign-born parents.[57] Another research team found even greater educational progress between second- and third-generation Mexican Americans.[58] Thus, like other immigrant groups before them, U.S. Hispanics' educational attainment should improve in time. Meanwhile, there are barriers, as Jaffe and his colleagues point out. "Cultural reinforcement" is one. A constant influx of new arrivals keeps Latin cultural values and the Spanish language alive among Mexican Americans in the Southwest, Puerto Ricans in the Northeast, and even Cubans in Florida, washed by the wave of Marielitos in 1980. A Mexican-American professional in California described how "macho" values can hinder education: "If you drop out [to father a child] or to buy a car, you're a big man. But when I came home with my Ph.D., my friends acted like they didn't know me."[59] Early pregnancy and marriage, poverty which forces teenagers prematurely into the labor force, and the problems of over-crowded, poorly equipped big-city schools which most Hispanics attend also boost dropout rates and discourage education. And like blacks and unlike earlier immigrant groups, Hispanics in the U.S. and in its schools have suffered from the discrimination accorded dark-skinned people.

Lack of English clearly retards Hispanics' general educational progress. In 1978, 26 percent of Hispanics in public elementary and secondary schools spoke little or no English.[60] On the other hand, use of Spanish is not necessarily a barrier to education, as proven by Cubans. Though educational levels are generally higher for those who grew up speaking English at home, Cubans, who outpace other Hispanics in high school achievement tests and college entrance, are also most likely to speak Spanish at home. This suggests that factors like more parental education and higher family income determine educational progress more than use of Spanish.[61]

Use of Spanish, however, is an issue in the current controversy over federal funding of bilingual education. Federally funded bilingual programs, in which a student is taught academic subjects in his native language until he can master English, began in 1968 in order to speed school progress for pupils who enter school speaking little or no English. They still cover less than half of Hispanic students in that category, funding was cut from $167 million in fiscal year 1981 to $138 million in 1982, and research has not yet shown that the programs have clearly achieved their purpose.[62] Critics claim that they slow down students' learning of English and foster the use of Spanish which hinders Hispanics' assimilation into the mainstream of U.S. society and could create an "Hispanic Quebec" in the U.S. A widely publicized report of the Twentieth Century Fund, issued in May 1983, recommended that federal bilingual funds be spent instead on teaching English to non-English-speaking children, and asserted: "Although this nation has become more aware of the value of ethnic identities, anyone living in the U.S. who is unable to speak English cannot fully participate in our society."[63]

Employment and Occupation

From poor education to poor economic and professional standing is but a short step. Though Hispanics' economic status has improved in recent decades, they remain clustered in low-paying blue-collar and semi-skilled jobs in fields like construction and manufacturing that suffer high seasonal or cyclical unemployment and thus earn far less and are more likely to be unemployed and live in poverty than the white population as a whole. Again, however, Cubans and Central and South Americans fare better than Mexican Americans and Puerto Ricans, especially women.

Economist Dennis Roth of the Congressional Research Service points out that Hispanic women aged 20 and over were almost as likely as all adult women to be working or seeking work in 1980 (48.8 percent compared to 51.3 percent) and the labor force participation rate for Hispanic men (85.2 percent) was *higher* than the rate for all adult men (79.4 percent).[64] But this comparison is misleading. As seen in Table 11, within specific age groups, Hispanic women's rates were generally 7.5 to 12 percentage points lower than those of all adult women and Hispanic men had rates slightly less than those of the total male population, except at ages 20–24 and 55 and over. The overall rates for Hispanics were pushed up because Hispanics are generally younger than the average for the total population and younger adults are more likely to be in the labor force.

Between 1973 and 1981, the number of Hispanic women in the work force surged by 82 percent, outpacing the increase among all

TABLE 11. *Labor Force Participation Rates of Hispanics and All U.S. Adults, by Sex: 1980*

Age Group	Percent in Labor Force			
	All Men	Hispanic Men	All Women	Hispanic Women
Total, 20 and over	79.4	85.2	51.3	48.8
20–24	86.0	88.2	69.9	57.1
25–34	95.3	93.5	65.4	53.9
35–44	95.5	94.1	65.5	56.0
45–54	91.2	91.0	59.9	52.0
55–64	72.3	72.5	41.5	32.9
65 and over	19.1	19.4	8.1	4.9

Source: Dennis M. Roth, "Hispanics in the U.S. Labor Force: A Brief Review," in Congressional Research Service, *The Hispanic Population of the United States: An Overview*, report prepared for the Subcommittee on Census and Population of the House Committee on Post Office and Civil Service (Washington, D.C.: Government Printing Office, 1983) Table 1, p. 60.

women, Roth points out. This was mainly due to an increase in the number of Hispanic women of working age because of continued immigration. But, except for Puerto Ricans, Hispanic women's labor force participation rate also went up nearly 9 percentage points—slightly more than that of all women. Meanwhile, the rate for Puerto Rican men dropped more than 8 percentage points, while remaining about the same for Hispanic men as a whole. Roth attributes the drop in rates for Puerto Rican men and women to the declining economy in New York City. In 1979, one-half of all mainland Puerto Ricans of working age lived in New York where total employment had dropped by 13 percent between 1969 and 1977. By 1982, only 51 percent of adult Puerto Ricans in the U.S. were in the labor force, compared to some 62 percent of Cubans and Mexican Americans and similar proportions of blacks and all whites.[65] This was primarily due to the low 37 percent of Puerto Rican women who were working or looking for work; among all other women, including Mexican Americans and Cubans, the figure was about 50 percent.

In an earlier review of Hispanics' work experience, Bureau of Labor Statistics economist Morris Newman suggests that Puerto Rican women's low labor force participation rate may also be a lingering cultural trait—women in Puerto Rico are much less likely to work outside the home than women in the U.S. But this is true of all Latin nations, and yet Mexican women once in the U.S. join the work force in proportions equal to that of all other U.S. women, although they are no more educated and have more children than Puerto Rican women, on average.[66]

Unemployment and Underemployment
Hispanics' jobless rate is typically 40 to 50 percent higher than the overall unemployment rate, though not so high as that of blacks, which is usually double the national rate. In the last quarter of 1982, for example, when unemployment rates climbed to the highest levels since the depression of the 1930s, 15.2 percent of Hispanic workers and 20.4 percent of black workers over age 20 were out of work, while the overall unemployment rate for adults was 10.7 percent.[67]

As might be expected, Puerto Ricans have the highest unemployment rate among Hispanics and Cubans the lowest. Roth credits Cubans' lower rate to their better education and older age—60 percent of Cuban workers are over 35 compared to 36 percent of Puerto Ricans—and joblessness is usually lower among more mature, stable, experienced older workers.

A study by the U.S. Commission on Civil Rights of minorities' work experience from 1971 to 1980 shows that Hispanic men and women—along with blacks and non-Hispanic white women—are more likely to be underemployed than "majority" non-Hispanic white men, as well as having higher unemployment rates.[68] Both Hispanic men and women are more likely than "majority" males to have to accept parttime work when they would rather work full time. Hispanic men are also more likely to be employed on and off, receive poverty wages, and be overeducated for their jobs, while more Hispanic women than any other minority group are paid inequitably.

Occupation

In 1981, as in earlier years, Hispanic workers were more concentrated in lower paid, lesser skilled occupations than the overall work force. More than 75 percent of employed Mexican-American, Puerto Rican, and Cuban women were clerical workers, machine operators or "non-

transport operatives," or service workers—three of the lowest paid occupations—compared to less than two-thirds of all women workers (see Table 12). Although the large percentage of Hispanic women employed in clerical positions is similar to that of all working women, their heavy concentration in operatives jobs—dressmakers, assemblers, packers, graders, and the like—is striking. Nearly 30 percent of Cuban women, about one-quarter of Puerto Rican women, and more than one-fifth of Mexican American women worked at these jobs in 1981, compared to one-tenth of all women. Interestingly, Puerto Rican and Cuban women were less likely than women in general to work in services—as cleaners, housekeepers, and restaurant helpers, etc.

Among men, Cubans were nearly as likely as all men to be employed in professional and technical jobs or as managers and administrators—27 compared to 31 percent. The percentages for Mexican Americans (12.0) and Puerto Ricans (15.4) in these two highest paid fields were less than half or barely half the Cuban rate, probably due mostly to their relative youthfulness and low educational attainment. Puerto Rican men were most likely to work in nontransport operatives jobs (21 percent), with large proportions also employed as service workers and craft workers.

TABLE 12. *Occupations of Hispanic and All Workers, by Sex: 1981 (Number in percent of total workers, by sex)*

Occupation	All workers		Total Hispanics		Mexican-American		Puerto Rican		Cuban	
	Men	Women	Men	Women	Men	Women	Men	Women	Men	Women
Professional and technical	15.9	17.0	7.7	8.8	5.7	8.0	8.5	11.6	12.9	9.9
Managers, Administrators	14.6	7.4	7.8	4.7	6.3	4.3	6.9	6.1	14.5	5.5
Sales	6.1	6.8	3.1	5.1	2.6	5.2	2.6	3.0	6.2	4.9
Clerical	6.3	34.7	6.4	31.9	5.0	32.4	13.1	36.4	9.4	31.9
Craft and kindred workers	20.7	1.9	20.1	2.4	20.9	2.5	15.4	2.5	20.7	2.2
Operatives, except transport	11.1	9.7	18.9	22.0	20.2	21.6	20.6	25.8	12.5	29.7
Transport equipment operatives	5.5	0.7	6.6	0.4	6.8	0.5	6.2	0.5	6.6	—
Nonfarm laborers	7.1	1.3	10.9	1.6	12.7	2.2	8.5	0.5	7.4	1.1
Service workers	8.9	19.4	13.3	21.4	12.2	21.1	17.6	13.1	9.4	14.8
Farm workers	3.9	1.1	5.2	1.6	7.5	2.5	0.3	0.5	0.4	—

Source: Roth, "Hispanics in the U.S. Labor Force" (See Table 11), Tables 5 and 6.

Among Mexican-American and Cuban men, craft jobs were most prevalent, with services and operatives jobs also employing many individuals. Mexican-Americans are often stereotyped as farmworkers but, in fact, only 8 percent of employed Mexican-American men were recorded as farmworkers in 1981. However, this was double the 4 percent for all male workers in the U.S. Probably, also, the actual number of Mexican-American farmworkers is understated in the Census Bureau's Current Population Survey which collects these data; illegal immigrants, many of whom work in the fields, probably avoid interviews and migrant farmworkers are hard to locate.[69]

Though Hispanics remain under-represented in the more skilled, higher paying occupations, their occupational status has improved since 1973—the earliest year for which suitable data are available—though more for women than men. Between 1973 and 1981, the proportion of Hispanic men employed as professionals, technicians, managers, and craft workers (which includes often well-paid jobs as construction workers and mechanics) rose slightly from 32 percent to 36 percent and the percentage of machine operators and farmworkers declined. For women there was a similar but more marked shift, plus an increase in clerical workers.

Hispanics have been sharing these shifts with all U.S. workers as lower skilled blue-collar jobs lose out to automation and white-collar office jobs increase. However, Roth notes that "generally speaking, Hispanics improved their labor market status relative to the improvement made by all workers," and observes: "It does appear that Hispanics will be able to further improve their occupational status in the U.S. if past trends continue."[70] Marked improvement, however, will require a gain in Hispanics' educational attainment rapid enough both to narrow the gap with increasingly highly educated white non-Hispanics and to meet the demands of the high-technology age.

Income and Poverty

If Hispanic workers improved their occupational status relative to all workers in the U.S. during the 1970s, this gain has not yet shown up in

TABLE 13. *Median Income of Hispanic, Black, and White Families: 1972–1981 (in constant 1981 dollars)*

Year	Median Family Income			Hispanic Family Incomes as Percent of White Income
	Hispanic	Black	White	
1972	17,790	14,922	25,107	71
1973	17,836	14,877	25,777	69
1974	17,594	14,765	24,728	71
1975	16,140	14,835	24,110	67
1976	16,390	14,766	24,823	66
1977	17,141	14,352	25,124	68
1978	17,518	15,166	25,606	68
1979	18,255	14,590	25,689	71
1980	16,242	13,989	24,176	67
1981	16,401	13,266	23,517	70

Source: Bureau of the Census, "Money Income and Poverty Status of Families and Persons in the United States: 1981 (Advance Data from the March 1982 Current Population Survey)," *Current Population Reports*, Series P-60, No. 134, July 1982, Table 3.

family income statistics. In 1972, the median Hispanic family income was 71 percent of the median for white families, as seen in Table 13, which measures Hispanic-white differentials in median family income since 1972 in constant 1981 dollars. In 1981, the median for Hispanic families ($16,401) was still just 70 percent of the median for white families as a whole ($23,517) after two years of recession had reduced real incomes for all families. Hispanics fare better than blacks, however, whose median family income in 1981 ($13,266) was just 56 percent of the median for white families, down from 59 percent in 1972. Like blacks, Hispanics' family income must stretch further than that of white families for family sizes are generally larger. Hispanics' relative youthfulness also depresses family income statistics—younger householders, in general, earn less than older ones.

Hispanics do better when both husband and wife work. In 1981, the median family income for such families was $23,641, or 80 percent of the median of $29,713 of all married-couple white families with the wife in the labor force.[71] The biggest difference in Hispanic-white family income levels comes in female-headed families. In 1981, 23 percent of Hispanic families were headed by a female alone—double the 12 percent among all white families—and their median income ($7,586) was just 60 percent of the median income of $12,508 of female-headed families among all whites.

Cubans, as might be expected, have the highest incomes of all Hispanic groups. In 1979, their median family income was $17,538, 86 percent of the white median of $20,502. This was close to double the Puerto Rican median of $9,855, which was the lowest among Hispanic families and well below the black family median of $11,644.[72] Mexican-American and Central and South American families had intermediate and similar median incomes—$15,171 and $15,470, respectively.

Poverty

In 1981, close to 800,000 Hispanic families, 24 percent of all Hispanic families in the U.S., were classified as "poor" by the Census Bureau, compared to 8.8 percent of all white families (see Table 14). The Census Bureau's poverty threshold varies by family size and age of the "householder" and is adjusted annually for inflation. It is based only on money income and does not take account of the benefits received by many low-income persons such as food stamps, Medicaid and Medicare, and housing aid. (In 1981, the average poverty threshold for a family of four was $9,287). On this score, too, Hispanics do better than blacks; nearly 31 percent of black families fell below the poverty threshold in 1981.

TABLE 14. *Poverty Rate of Hispanic, Black, and White Families: 1973–1981*

Year	Percent of Families below Poverty Level			Ratio of Hispanic to White Poverty Rate
	Hispanic	Black	White	
1973	19.8	28.1	6.6	3.0
1974	21.2	26.9	6.8	3.1
1975	25.1	27.1	7.7	3.3
1976	23.1	27.9	7.1	3.3
1977	21.4	28.2	7.0	3.1
1978	20.4	27.5	6.9	3.0
1979	20.3	27.8	6.9	2.9
1980	23.2	28.9	8.0	2.9
1981	24.0	30.8	8.8	2.7

Source: Bureau of the Census, "Money Income and Poverty Status: 1981" (See Table 13), Table 15.

Also the rise in the poverty rate was a little less for Hispanics than for other families from 1979 to 1981 as the recession deepened and unemployment rose. However, Hispanic families were still 2.7 times as likely as all white families to be living in poverty in 1981, only marginally improved from the differential in 1973 (3.0) when poverty statistics for the Hispanic population were first calculated.

Thus the statistics for the past decade show Hispanics as a group still trailing well behind the general U.S. population on all measures of social and economic well-being. But a decade is hardly time enough to measure genuine progress. The higher educational attainment of younger Hispanics holds out hope that more Hispanics in general, and not just Cubans, will be joining the higher paid, white-collar work force in the future. And as they do, income levels should increase and unemployment rates fall, along with poverty rates. Even with their present income lag behind the general U.S. population, Antonio Guernica and Irene Kasperuk note in *Reaching the Hispanic Market Effectively* that "Hispanics in the United States are the wealthiest Hispanics in the world. The opportunity for economic improvement is the primary reason why legal and illegal Hispanic immigration to the United States continues unabated."[73]

Hispanics in America's Future

"The one demographic trend above all others that will mold the future of the Hispanic community through the 1980s and beyond is its numerical growth," Guernica and Kasperuk also assert.

The table at the bottom of Figure 2 presents two sets of projections from 1980 to 2000 and 2020 for the total U.S. population and the four main racial and ethnic groups—white non-Hispanics, blacks, Hispanics, and Asians and Others. The chart at the top shows Hispanic population growth based on these projections. The projections are *not* predictions of U.S. population growth; rather, they present population size as it might be in 2000 and 2020, given reasonable assumptions about our fertility, mortality, and immigration experience in this 40-year period.

The first set of projections assumes that

FIGURE 2. *Population 1980 and as Projected for 2000 and 2020: Hispanics, Total U.S. Population, and Four Main Racial/Ethnic Groups*

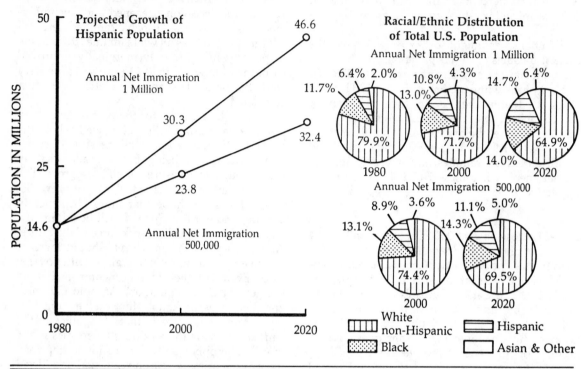

Racial/ethnic Group	1980		2000		2020	
	Number (millions)	Percent of Total	Number (millions)	Percent of Total	Number (millions)	Percent of Total
			Annual net immigration = 500,000			
Total U.S. population	226.5	100.0	267.4	100.1	291.5	100.0
White non-Hispanic	181.0	79.9	198.9	74.4	202.7	69.5
Black	26.5	11.7	35.2	13.1	41.7	14.3
Hispanic	14.6	6.4	23.8	8.9	32.4	11.1
Asian and other	4.4	2.0	9.5	3.6	14.7	5.0
			Annual net immigration = 1 million			
Total U.S. population			279.1	100.0	316.9	100.0
White non-Hispanic			200.3	71.7	205.6	64.9
Black			36.4	13.0	44.4	14.0
Hispanic			30.3	10.8	46.6	14.7
Asian and other			12.1	4.3	20.3	6.4

Source: Leon F. Bouvier and Cary B. Davis, *The Future Racial Composition of the United States* (Washington, D.C.: Demographic Information Services Center of the Population Reference Bureau, 1982).

annual net immigration to the U.S. will average 500,000 a year. This is below the net immigration average of 600,000 per year in 1979–81 when refugees from Southeast Asia and the sudden influx of Cubans and Haitians in 1980 inflated the number admitted legally to the U.S. But it is about what the average might be if the Simpson-Mazzoli bill were passed with a 425,000 per-year cap on annual immigrants and was rigorously implemented, and allowance is made for refugees. The assumption of 1 million net immigration per year in the second set of projections may appeal to those who wish to add net illegal immigration of at least 500,000 a year—the upper limit of recent net illegal immigration estimates. Both sets of projections assume that the fertility of all racial/ethnic groups will converge in 2030 at the current national average of 1.8 children per woman; for Hispanics, the starting point (1980) was set at about 2.6 children per woman.

With net immigration at 500,000 per year, the Hispanic population is projected to grow to about 32 million and 11 percent of the total U.S. population in 2020. With net immigration at 1 million a year, Hispanics could number some 47 million and nearly 15 percent of the total in 2020, overtaking blacks as the country's largest minority. If all immigration had ceased in 1980, we project that Hispanics would number 24 million in 2020. This is a substantial 9.4 million increase over the 14.6 million of 1980 which would be due solely to the natural increase (births minus deaths) stemming from Hispanics already in the U.S. in 1980, but far below what the totals would be with the addition of immigrants arriving after 1980 and their subsequent natural increase.

How likely are these projections to materialize? Potential fluctuations in immigration (as well as fertility) make this impossible to tell. Although net immigration of Puerto Ricans dwindled to a trickle in the 1970s, their immigration remains unrestricted and could surge upward again if the island's economy deteriorates and prospects in the U.S. improve. Refugee influxes from Cuba depend on the vagaries of Cuban—and U.S.— policy. While immigration from Mexico and other Spanish-speaking countries of Latin America does fall under the control of U.S. immigration law, the open-ended family reunification clause currently allows for more arrivals than the 20,000 per-country annual limit. This will change if the Simpson-Mazzoli bill passes into law in the form approved by the Senate, but there remains the murky question of illegal immigration.

The ethnic mix of the Hispanic population should remain relatively stable for the remainder of this century, although Hispanics from countries other than Mexico, Cuba, and Puerto Rico may increase their share of the population somewhat. Here, too, the big unknowns are unregulated immigration from Puerto Rico and illegal immigration, as well as changes in the U.S. immigration law.

Whatever their future numbers, Hispanics are already a growing force in American society. There are now nine Hispanic Congressmen* (though no Senators), one state governor (Toney Anaya of New Mexico), Hispanic mayors in Denver, Miami and San Antonio, and groups like the Southwest Voter Registration Project in San Antonio are working to get out more of the Hispanic vote. Only 30 percent of Hispanics of voting age cast ballots in the 1980 presidential election, compared to the national figure of 59 percent—down from 38 percent in 1972. Hispanics' political and social influence is marshaled by such organizations as the Mexican-American Legal Defense and Educational Fund (MALDEF), the National Council of La Raza, and the League of United Latin American Citizens. There are 13 TV stations and 118 radio stations broadcasting full time in Spanish and another 100 or more scheduling ten or more hours each week in Spanish. And U.S. business has discovered the Hispanic market; J. Walter Thompson and other leading advertising agencies now have Hispanic units; Safeway, Jewel and other supermarket chains stock Hispanic culinary specialties; and Mattel markets a Hispanic version of the Barbie doll.

Many questions about the impact of the growing Hispanic population will only be answered with the passage of time. Will Hispanics assimilate into the U.S. "melting pot" as other immigrant ethnic groups have before them? How much of their identity as a group will they wish to maintain? Whatever the outcome, their arrival has changed the face of America once again.

REFERENCES

Editor's note: Portions of this article—and some accompanying references—have been deleted from this reprinting, by permission of authors and publisher.

***

3. Select Commission on Immigration and Refugee Policy, *U.S. Immigration Policy and the National*

*The nine Congressmen are: Robert Garcia (D-New York), Kika de la Garza (D-Texas), Henry Gonzales (D-Texas), Manual Lujan, Jr. (R-New Mexico), Matthew Martinez (D-California), Solomon Ortiz (D-Texas), Bill Richardson (D-New Mexico), Edward Roybal (D-California), Estaban Torres (D-California).

4. U.S. Commission on Civil Rights, *Puerto Ricans Interest* (Washington, DC: Government Printing Office, March 1981).

in the Continental United States: An Uncertain Future (Washington, DC: 1976).

5. Perez, Lisandro, "Cubans," in *Harvard Encyclopedia of American Ethnic Groups* (Cambridge, MA: Belknap Press of Harvard University, 1980).

6. Unpublished tables of immigrants by country of birth, 1950–1979, obtained from Immigration and Naturalization Service, Statistics Branch.

7. Bureau of the Census, "Persons of Spanish Origin: 1970."

8. Bureau of the Census, "Persons of Spanish Origin in the United States: March 1980 (Advance Report)," *Current Population Reports*, Series P-20, No. 361, May 1981, Table 1.

9. Bureau of the Census, "Persons of Spanish Origin by State: 1980," *1980 Census of Population*, Supplementary Report PC80-S1-7, August 1982.

10. Bureau of the Census, *1980 Census of Population, General Population Characteristics*, PC80-1B, various state issues.

11. Immigration and Naturalization Service, annual reports, various issues.

12. Bureau of the Census, *State and Metropolitan Area Data Book: 1982*, August 1982, Table A.

13. O'Connell, Martin and Carolyn Rogers, "Differential Fertility in the United States: 1976–1980," *Family Planning Perspectives*, Vol. 14, No. 5 (September/October 1982) Table 1, p. 283.

14. Ventura, Stephanie J., "Births of Hispanic Parentage, 1979," *Monthly Vital Statistics Report*, Vol. 31, No. 2, Supplement, May 1982, p. 2, and personal communication, June 1983.

15. Ventura, "Births of Hispanic Parentage," p.3

16. Popluation Reference Bureau, *1983 World Population Data Sheet* (Washington, DC: 1983).

17. Instituto Mexicano del Seguro Social, *Fecundidad y Uso de Metodos Anticonceptivos en Mexico* (Mexico City: May 1981).

18. Rochat, Roger W., et al, "Family Planning Practices Among Anglo and Hispanic Women in U.S. Counties Bordering Mexico," *Family Planning Perspectives*, Vol. 13, No. 4 (July/August, 1981).

19. Rindfuss, Ronald R. and James S. Sweet, *Postwar Fertility Trends and Differentials in the United States* (New York: Academic Press, 1977); and Centers for Disease Control, *Texas Fertility, 1950–1977: Childbearing Patterns and Trends* (Atlanta: 1980).

***

25. Bureau of the Census, "Persons of Spanish Origin in the United States: March 1979," *Current Population Reports*, Series P-20, No. 354, 1980, Table 18.

26. Bureau of the Census, "Household and Family Characteristics: March 1981," *Current Population Reports*, Series P-20, No. 371, 1982, Table 18.

27. Bureau of the Census, "Marital Status and Living Arrangements: March 1981," *Current Population Reports*, Series P-20, No. 372, 1982, Table C.

28. Bouvier, Leon F., "Immigration and its Impact on U.S. Society," *Population Trends and Public Policy*, No. 2 (Washington, DC: Population Reference Bureau, 1981).

29. Murphy, Elaine M. and Patricia Cancellier, "Immigration: Questions and Answers," Population Reference Bureau, 1982, p. 1.

30. Fox, Robert W., Inter-American Development Bank, personal communication, June 1983.

31. Population Reference Bureau, *1983 World Population Data Sheet*.

32. Barberis, Mary, "Hispanic America," *Editorial Research Reports*, Vol. 11, No. 4 (July 30, 1982) pp. 561–562.

33. Diaz-Briquets, Sergio and Lisandro Perez, "Cuba: The Demography of Revolution," *Population Bulletin*, Vol. 36, No. 1 (April 1981).

34. Department of Health and Human Services, Cuban-Haitian Task Force, *Monthly Extract Data Report for March 1981*, 1981, Table 7.

35. Diaz-Briquets and Perez, "Cuba," p. 31.

36. Teitelbaum, Michael S., "Right Versus Right: Immigration and Refugee Policy in the United States," *Foreign Affairs*, Vol. 59, No. 1 (Fall 1980) p. 23.

37. Siegel, Jacob S., et al, "Preliminary Review of Existing Studies of the Number of Illegal Residents in the United States," Bureau of the Census, prepared for the staff of the Select Commission on Immigration and Refugee Policy, January 30, 1981.

38. Warren, Robert and Jeffrey Passel, "Estimates of Illegal Aliens from Mexico Counted in the 1980 United States Census," paper presented at the annual meeting of the Population Association of America, Pittsburgh, April 1983.

39. Immigration and Naturalization Service, *1979 Statistical Yearbook*, Table 23, and personal communication, June 1983.

40. Pear, Robert, "Immigration Reform is Alive and Well," *The New York Times*, May 22, 1983.

41. Heer, David, "What is the Annual Net Flow of Undocumented Mexican Immigrants to the United States?" *Demography*, Vol. 16, No. 3 (August 1979) pp. 417–422; Charles B. Keely, "Illegal Immigration," *Scientific American*, Vol. 246, No. 3 (March 1982) p. 41; and Teitelbaum, "Right Versus Right," p. 25.

***

45. Bonilla, Frank and Ricardo Campos, "A Wealth of Poor: Puerto Ricans in the New Economic Order," *Daedalus*, Spring 1981, p. 163.

46. Bureau of the Census, "School Enrollment—Social and Economic Characteristics of Students: October 1981 (Advance Report)," *Current Population Reports*, Series P-20, No. 373, February 1983.

47. National Center for Education Statistics (NCES), *The Condition of Education for Hispanic Americans* (Washington DC: 1981) Table 2.21.

48. U.S. Commission on Civil Rights, *Puerto Ricans*, p. 101.

49. Magallan, Rafael J., "Hispanics: Resume/Overview," *CASE Currents*, Council for Advancement and Support of Education, April 1983, p. 9.

50. U.S. Commission on Civil Rights, *Social Indicators of Equality for Minorities and Women* (Washington DC: 1978).

51. Fratoe, Frank A., *The Education of Nonmetro Hispanics*, Rural Development Research Report No. 31 (Washington, DC: U.S. Department of Agriculture, Economic Research Service, 1981) Table 4.

52. Duran, Richard P., *Hispanics' Education and Background: Predictors of College Achievement* (New York: College Entrance Examination Board, 1983) p. 59.

53. Bureau of the Census, "School Enrollment: October 1981."

54. Magallan, "Hispanics: Overview," p. 9.

55. Bureau of the Census, "Population Profile of the United States: 1981," *Current Population Reports*, Series P-20, No. 374, September 1982, Table 6-3.

56. Magallan, "Hispanics: Overview," p. 9.

57. Jaffe, A. J., Ruth M. Cullen, and Thomas D. Boswell, *The Changing Demography of Spanish Americans* (New York: Academic Press, 1980) p. 33.

58. Grebler, L., J. W. Moore, and R. C. Guzman, *The Mexican-American People* (New York: The Free Press, 1970) p. 149.

59. Quoted in Marilyn Chase, "Latins Rise in Numbers in U.S. But Don't Win Influence or Affluence," *Wall Street Journal*, June 9, 1982.

60. NCES, *Condition of Education for Hispanic Americans*.

61. Duran, *Hispanics' Education and Background*, p. 109; and Susan H. Boren, "Education of Hispanics: Access and Achievement," in Congressional Research Service, *The Hispanic Population of the United States:*

An Overview, report prepared for the Subcommittee on Census and Population of the House Committee on Post Office and Civil Service (Washington, DC: Government Printing Office, 1983) pp. 26–27.

62. Boren, "Education of Hispanics," pp. 21–23; and David Fernandez, Mexican-American Legal Defense and Educational Fund, personal communication, May 1983.

63. Twentieth Century Fund, *Making the Grade* (New York: 1983).

64. Roth, Dennis M., "Hispanics in the U.S. Labor Force: A Brief Examination," in Congressional Research Service, *Hispanic Population of the United States*, p. 59.

65. U.S. Department of Labor, Bureau of Labor Statistics, *Employment and Earnings*, January 1983, Table 45.

66. Newman, Morris J., "A Profile of Hispanics in the U.S. Work Force," *Monthly Labor Review*, Vol. 101, No. 12 (December 1978) p. 5.

67. Urquhart, Michael A. and Marilyn A. Hewson, "Unemployment Continued to Rise in 1982 as Recession Deepened," *Monthly Labor Review*, Vol. 106, No. 2 (February 1983) Table 3, p. 8.

68. Gordon, Henry A., Constance A. Hamilton, and Havens C. Tipps, *Unemployment and Underemployment Among Blacks, Hispanics, and Women* (Washington DC: U.S. Commission on Civil Rights, 1982) pp. 56–57.

69. Newman, "Profile of Hispanics in the U.S. Work Force," p. 11.

70. Roth, "Hispanics in the U.S. Labor Force," pp. 69, 72.

71. Bureau of the Census, "Money Income and Poverty Status of Families and Persons in the United States: 1981 (Advance Data from the March 1982 Current Population Survey)," *Current Population Reports*, Series P-60, No. 134, July 1982, Table 1.

72. Bureau of the Census, "Persons of Spanish Origin in the United States: March 1980 (Advance Report)," *Current Population Reports*, Series P-20, No. 361, May 1981, Table 5.

73. Quoted in Cheryl Russell, "The News About Hispanics," *American Demographics*, Vol. 5, No. 3 (March 1983) p. 24.

32

The Black Community in the 1980s: Questions of Race, Class, and Public Policy

William Julius Wilson

Civil rights supporters are puzzled by recent developments in the black community. Despite the passage of antidiscrimination legislation and the creation of affirmative action programs, they sense that conditions are getting worse not better for the vast majority of black Americans. This perception emerges because of the constant flow of pessimistic reports concerning the sharp rise in black unemployment, the substantial decline of blacks in the labor force, the steady drop in the black–white family income ratio, the consistent increase in the percentage of Blacks on the welfare roles, the remarkable growth of the single-parent households, and the persistent problems of black crime and black victims of crime. The perception is reinforced by the almost uniform cry among black leaders that not only are conditions deteriorating, but white Americans have abandoned the cause of Blacks as well. In the face of these developments, there are noticeable signs

Reprinted from "The Black Community in the 1980s: Questions of Race, Class, and Public Policy" by William Julius Wilson in vol. no. 454 of THE ANNALS of the American Academy of Political and Social Science. © 1981 by the American Academy of Political and Social Science.

Note: An extended and somewhat different version of this article, under the title "Barriers to Labor Market Access: Questions of Class, Race, and Public Policy," appeared in *Adherent: A Journal of Comprehensive Employment Training and Human Resources Development*, 7(2) (Dec. 1980).

that demoralization has set in among many Blacks who have come to believe that "nothing really works" and among many whites who are otherwise committed to social reform.

However, a careful review of the issues makes it immediately clear that significant variations in the black experience tend not to be noted or appreciated and that the differing effect of policy programs on different segments of the black population are usually not specified. In this article, these issues are examined within the context of a broader framework of macroeconomic and political change. In the process I hope to focus on a series of mounting problems that are not receiving serious attention, but that have profound implications for the structure of the black community and for the future of race relations in America.

Changing Definitions of the Problem

In the mid-1960s, a series of insightful articles were written by black and white intellectuals that raised the questions about the direction and goals of the black protest movement.[1] Basically, the authors of these articles made it clear that from 1955 to 1965, the chief objectives of the Civil Rights movement were to integrate public accommodations and to eliminate black disfranchisement. These were matters of constitutional rights and basic human dignity, matters that affected Blacks and other minorities exclusively and therefore could be defined and addressed simply as problems of civil rights. However, these authors noted that despite the spectacular victories in the area of civil rights, by the latter half of the 1960s, a more complex and fundamental set of problems had yet to be attacked—problems of jobs, education, and housing that affected not only Blacks, but other minorities and Whites as well.

A consistent theme running throughout these articles is that in the period from 1955 to 1965, all Blacks, regardless of their station in life, were concerned about the banning of discrimination in public accommodations and in voting. As Bayard Rustin observed, "Ralph Bunche was as likely to be refused service in a restaurant or a hotel as any illiterate sharecropper. This common bond prevented the latent class differences and resentments from being openly expressed."[2] However, it did not take long to realize that the group that had profited the most from the civil rights legislation up to 1965 were middle-class Blacks—Blacks who had competitive resources such as steady incomes, education and special talents. As Kenneth Clark argued in 1967, "The masses of Negroes are now starkly aware of the fact that recent civil rights victories benefited a very small percentage of middle-class Negroes while their predicament remained the same or worsened."[3]

What these observers were telling us in the mid-1960s is that a close examination of ghetto black discontent, most dramatically revealed in the riots of that period, revealed issues that transcended the creation and implementation of civil rights laws. "To the segregation by race," Bayard Rustin observed in 1967, "was now added segregation by class, and all the problems created by segregation and poverty—inadequate schooling, substandard and overcrowded housing, lack of access to jobs and job training, narcotics and crime—were greatly aggravated."[4] In short, for ghetto Blacks the issue of human rights is far more important than the issue of civil rights. The late Martin Luther King, Jr., recognized this point in 1968 when shortly before his death he asked, "What good is it to be allowed to eat in a restaurant if you can't afford a hamburger?"[5] It would not be unfair to suggest that he was probably influenced by the thoughts of Bayard

Rustin who, four years earlier in his now classic article "From Protest to Politics," phrased the matter in much the same way: "What is the value of winning access to public accommodations for those who lack money to use them?"[6]

Thus the removal of artificial racial barriers would not enable poor Blacks to compete equally with other groups in society for valued resources because of an accumulation of disadvantages flowing from previous periods of prejudice and discrimination, disadvantages that have been passed on from generation to generation. Basic structural changes in our modern industrial economy have compounded the problems of poor Blacks because education and training have become more important for entry into the more desirable and higher-paying jobs and because the increased reliance on labor-saving devices has contributed to a surplus of untrained black workers. In short, once the movement faced these more fundamental issues, argued Rustin in 1964, "it was compelled to expand its version beyond race relations to economic relations, including the role of education in society."[7]

During the same period in which problems of structural inequality were being raised, scholars such as Kenneth Clark and Lee Rainwater were also raising important issues about the experiences of inequality.[8] Both scholars sensitively examined the cumulative effects of chronic subordination and racial isolation on life and behavior in the urban ghettos. As Kenneth Clark put it, "The symptoms of lower-class society affect the dark ghettos of America—low aspirations, poor education, family instability, illegitimacy, unemployment, crime, drug addiction, and alcoholism, frequent illness and early death."[9] And whether the focus was on the social and psychological dimensions of the ghetto, as in the case of Clark's study, or on the analysis of ghetto family patterns, as in the case of Rainwater's study, facts of ghetto life "that are usually forgotten or ignored in polite discussions"[10] were vividly described and carefully analyzed.

Indeed, what was both unique and important about Clark and Rainwater's studies was that their discussions of the experiences of inequality were inextricably tied to their discussions of the structure of inequality. Thus in reading their works one received a clear understanding of how the economic and social situations into which so many poor Blacks are born produce modes of adaptation and the creation of subcultural patterns that take the form of a "self perpetuating pathology."[11] In other words, and in sharp contrast to approaches that simply "blame the victim" or which use a "culture of poverty" thesis to explain group disadvantages, the works of Clark and Rainwater not only presented a sensitive portrayal of the destructive features of ghetto life, they also provided a comprehensive analysis of the deleterious structural conditions that produce these features.

However, arguments stressing economic relations in determining the structure of inequality and in significantly influencing the experiences of inequality began to compete with a new definition, description, and explanation of the black condition. This new approach, proclaimed as the "black perspective," revealed an ideological shift from interracialism to racial solidarity. It first gained currency among militant black spokesmen in the late 1960s and became a theme in the writings of young black intellectuals by the early 1970s. Although the "black perspective" represented a variety of views and arguments on issues of race, the trumpeting of racial pride and self-affirmation was common to all the writings and speeches on the subject. Thus interracial cooperation and integration were being challenged by the ideology of racial solidarity; and the rhetoric of black militancy, symbolized by the cry of "Black Power," gradually moved from expressions of selective to generalized hostility toward Whites.

The complex factors associated with this shift in emphasis cannot be reviewed in full detail in a short article, but I would like to point out that the declining support for interracialism and the rising emphasis on black solidarity in the late 1960s was typical of a pattern that had been repeated throughout the history of dominant-subordinate group relations in multiethnic societies. Perhaps Robert Merton comes closest to providing the theoretical explanation for this shift when he states that "when a once powerless collectivity acquires a socially validated sense of growing power, its members experience an intensified need for self-affirmation. Under such conditions, collective self-glorification, found in some measure among all groups, becomes a predictable

and intensified counterresponse to long standing belittlement from without."[12] Few would deny the fact that the black liberation movement in the late sixties and early seventies was marked by an avowed effort to minimize effects of subordinate status through a strong emphasis on black pride, black identity, and black cultural heritage. And in this atmosphere of race chauvinism a series of studies written by scholars proclaiming a "black perspective" appeared.[13]

The arguments set forth in these studies made it clear that a substantial and fundamental shift in both the tone and focus of race relations scholarship was occurring. Consistent with the emphasis on black glorification and the quest for self-affirmation, arguments maintaining that some aspects of ghetto life were pathological (in the sense that the logical outcome of racial isolation and class subordination is that individuals are forced to adapt to the realities of the ghetto community and are therefore seriously impaired in their ability to function in any other community) were categorically rejected in favor of those emphasizing black community strengths. And arguments proclaiming the deterioration of the poor black family were dismissed in favor of those extolling the "virtues" and "strengths" of black families. Thus behavior described as pathological by some scholars was reinterpreted as functional by the black perspective proponents—functional in that Blacks were displaying the ability to survive and flourish in a ghetto milieu. Ghetto families were described as resilient and were seen as creatively adapting to an oppressive racist society. The net effect of these revisionist studies, designed to "liberate" the social sciences from the influence of "racism," is that black achievement was emphasized at the expense of devoting sufficient and warranted attention to the consequences and ramifications of oppression, including the psychological damage emanating from chronic subordination.

Also consistent with the dominant focus on racial solidarity in the writings of the black perspective proponents was an emphasis on "we" versus "they" and "Black" versus "White." Since the emphasis was solely on race, little attention was paid to the internal differences within the black community. Moreover, since the problems were defined in racial terms very little discussion was devoted to problems with the economy and the need for economic reform. This is why Orlando Patterson was led to proclaim in a latter analysis that black ethnicity had become "a form of mystification, diverting attention from the correct kinds of solutions to the terrible economic condition of the group" thereby making it difficult for Blacks to see "how their fate is inextricably tied up with the structure of the American economy."[14]

Meanwhile, during this period of black glorification, significant developments were occurring in the black community that were related both to changes in the economy and in the laws and policies of the state. These changes prompted some writers to revive the arguments postulating the centrality of economic relations, to once again stress the deteriorating conditions of life in the ghetto and their behavioral consequences, and to return to the discussion of public policy that involves matters of both race and economic class position.[15] In the next three sections, I shall attempt to document some of these developments.

Internal Changes in the Black Community Since 1960

Although the black population is often regarded as a monolithic socio-economic group by social scientists and social commentators alike, since the end of World War II, and especially since 1960, Blacks have become increasingly differentiated along occupational lines. The proportion of employed black workers from 1960 to 1978 increased 10.7 percent and 9.6 percent in professional and technical positions and in clerical jobs, respectively, and decreased 13.4 percent and 5.0 percent in service workers and laborer jobs and in farm worker jobs, respectively.[16]

However, these occupational changes only partly demonstrate the nature of internal change within the black population. The major problem is that occupational data on employed workers, which reveal substantial progress in the movement of black workers from lower-paying to higher-paying positions, fail to capture the relative decline in the economic position of poor Blacks during the last decade—a growing number of whom are either unemployed, underemployed or outside the labor force altogether. Thus in

order to more completely describe the range of experiences in the black community, I should like to conceptualize a black class structure that includes a middle class represented by white-collar workers, a working class represented by semiskilled operatives, and a lower class represented by unskilled laborers and service workers. Within the lower class is an underclass population, a heterogenous grouping at the very bottom of the economic class hierarchy. This underclass population includes those lower-class workers whose income falls below the poverty level, the long-term unemployed, discouraged workers who have dropped out of the labor market, and the more or less permanent welfare recipients.[17]

Although the underclass constitutes the more impoverished segment of the lower class, I shall attempt to show that even full-time "lower-class" workers increasingly face structural barriers in advanced industrial society that trap them in menial, dead-end jobs. Nonetheless, the concept of "underclass" depicts a reality that is not fully captured in using the more general designation of "lower-class." For example, unlike other families in the black community, the head of the household in underclass families is almost invariably a woman. The distinctive characteristics of the underclass are also reflected in the large number of unattached adult males who have no fixed address, who live mainly on the streets, and who roam from one place of shelter to another.

Problems of Employment and Unemployment

The question of what happens to individuals who are trapped in depressed areas and are therefore denied access to the normal channels of economic opportunity and mobility takes on even greater meaning for the black poor today than in previous years. Poor black Americans, heavily concentrated in inner cities, have experienced a worsening of their economic position on the basis of nearly all the major labor-market indicators. As revealed in Table 1, the unemployment rates for both black men and black women from 1955 to 1978 have increased more rapidly at all age levels than those of comparable Whites, with black teenage unemployment showing the sharpest increase—from 13.4 percent in 1955 to 34.4 percent in 1978 for men, and from 19.2

TABLE 1. *Unemployment Rates by Race, Sex, and Age, Selected Years, 1955–78 (in Percentages)*

Race, Sex, and Age	1955	1965	1973	1978
White men				
16–19	11.3	12.9	12.3	13.5
20–24	7.0	5.9	6.5	7.6
25 and over	3.0	2.5	2.4	3.0
White women				
16–19	9.1	14.0	13.0	14.4
20–24	5.1	6.3	7.0	8.3
25 and over	3.7	3.6	3.7	4.5
Black and other men*				
16–19	13.4	23.3	26.9	34.4
20–24	12.4	9.3	12.6	20.0
25 and over	8.0	5.5	4.2	6.3
Black and other women*				
16–19	19.2	31.7	34.5	38.4
20–24	13.0	13.7	17.6	21.3
25 and over	6.9	6.4	6.1	8.2

Source: U.S. Department of Labor, *Monthly Labor Review* (Washington, DC: U.S. Government Printing Office, Oct. 1979).

*"Black and other men" and "Black and other women" are United States Census Bureau designations and are used in those cases where data are not available solely for Blacks. However, because about 90 percent of the population designated by "Black and other men and women" is black, statistics reported for this category generally reflect the conditions of the black populations.

percent in 1955 to 38.4 percent in 1978 for women. The unemployment rates for Blacks age 20 to 24 also reached very high proportions in 1978—20 percent for men and 21.3 percent for women—extending a trend of increasing joblessness that began in the mid-1960s. The significant rise in unemployment for younger Blacks stands in sharp contrast to the slight change in the rate of unemployment for Blacks 25 years old and over. Still, even the older Blacks had unemployment rates above those of their white counterparts.

The severe problems of joblessness for black teenagers and young adults are also seen in the data on changes in the male civilian labor-force participation rates. The percentage of black males who were in the labor force fell from 45.6 in 1960 to 30.8 in 1977 for those 16 and 17 years old, from 71.2 to 57.8 for those 18 and 19, and from 90.4 to 78.2 for those 20 to 24. Even Blacks 25 to 34 years old experienced a decline in labor-force participation; however, the drop was not nearly as steep as that recorded by younger Blacks— from 96.2 percent to 90.4 percent. Whereas black

males are dropping out of the labor force in significant numbers, white males have either maintained or slightly increased their rate of participation since 1960—from 46.0 to 53.8 for those 16 and 17 years old, from 69.0 to 65.8 for those 18 and 19, from 87.8 to 86.8 for those 20 to 24, and from 97.7 to 96.0 for those 25 to 34.[18]

But even unemployment rates and labor-force participation rates do not reveal the real depth of joblessness among younger Blacks. If we consider the ratio of the employed civilian population to the total civilian noninstitutional population, that is, the employment population ratio, we find that less than 30 percent of all black male teenagers and only 62 percent of all black young adult males 20 to 24 years old were employed in 1978. In short, the problem of joblessness for young black men has reached castastrophic proportions.[19]

Finally, the bleak employment picture for young Blacks is further demonstrated by the data on work experience in any given year. Whereas the proportion of white male teenagers 16 to 19 years old and young adults 20 to 24 years old with work experience has changed very little from 1966 to 1977 and the proportion of white female teenagers and young adults with work experience has increased,[20] the proportion of young Blacks with work experience has decreased from 67.3 to 47.2 percent for black male teenagers, from 90.1 to 76.7 percent for young adult black males, from 48.9 to 37.5 percent for black female teenagers, and from 67.2 to 63.6 percent for young adult black females.[21]

Thus the combined indicators of unemployment, labor-force participation, employment-population ratios, and work experience reveal a disturbing picture of black joblessness, especially among younger Blacks. If the evidence presented in recent longitudinal research is correct, then black youth joblessness will have a long-term harmful effect on their chances in the labor market.[22] For all these reasons, a significant segment of the black population is in danger of being permanently locked out of the mainstream of the American occupational systems. It cannot be overemphasized that the increasing black youth joblessness is a problem primarily experienced by lower-income Blacks; for example, 67 percent of unemployed black teenagers living at home in 1977 were from families with incomes of less than $10,000. And among those unemployed teenagers living at home and not enrolled in school, 75 percent were from families with less than $10,000 incomes and 41 percent were from families with less than $5000 income.[23]

The high incidence of joblessness among Blacks as a group is partly related to the fact that they constitute a disproportionate percentage of workers employed in the lowest-paying jobs, such as service work and unskilled labor—jobs that have high turnover and are susceptible to unemployment. Nonetheless, this fact alone cannot account for the rapid deterioration of the position of poor Blacks in the labor market; nor can their employment problems be adequately explained in terms of racial discrimination. These issues will be further clarified by considering the effect of basic shifts in the economy on the life chances of lower-class Blacks. But first let me pay special attention to changes that are occurring in poor black families, changes that have accompanied their worsening economic plight and that

could have long-term effects on their future employment prospects.

The Economic Crisis and the Poor Black Family

In 1969, black median family income was 61 percent that of Whites; by 1976 it had dropped to 59 percent; by 1977 to 57 percent; and by 1978, it had risen slightly to 59 percent, but was still below the ratio of 1969. However, it should be pointed out that the ratio of black to white median family income in male-headed homes was 72 percent in 1969, rose to 80 percent in 1976, declined to 75 percent in 1977, then climbed back up to 80 percent in 1978.[24]

What should be underlined, therefore, is that the overall relative decline in black family income since 1969 has been accompanied by the sharp increase in female-headed homes during this period—from 28 percent in 1969, to 37 percent in 1976, to 39 percent in 1977, and finally to a staggering 40 percent in 1978.[25] And when we take into account the fact that the median income of black male-headed families ($15,678) in 1978 was $9690 more than the median income of black female-headed families, it becomes clear why the recorded black-to-white family income ratio has declined in recent years. By 1978, the proportion of all poor black families headed by women had reached 74 percent.[26]

The class-related features of black female-headed households cannot be overemphasized. I have already stated that what is distinctive about underclass black families is that the head of the household is almost invariably a woman. The powerful connection between class background and the structure of the black family is further revealed in the data presented in Table 2. Whereas 80.3 percent of all black families with incomes of less than $4000 and 63.8 percent with incomes between $4000 and $6999 were headed by women in 1978, only 15.3 percent of those with incomes between $16,000 and $24,999 and 7.7 percent with incomes of $25,000 and more were headed by women. In metropolitan areas the differences in the proportion of black families with female heads was even greater, with extremes of 85.1 percent for those whose incomes were below $4000 and 7.6 percent for those whose income

TABLE 2. *Proportion of Families by Race, Income Level, Female Head, and Metropolitan Residence in 1978*

Subject	All Families (in Percentages)	Female Heads (in Percentages)	Families in Metropolitan Areas (in Percentages)	Metropolitan Families with Female Heads (in Percentages)
Black				
Under $4000	15.9	80.3	71.1	85.1
$4000 to $6999	16.2	63.8	74.7	71.2
$7000 to $10,999	18.3	46.2	74.8	50.7
$11,000 to $15,999	16.7	28.9	76.3	31.8
$16,000 to $24,999	19.2	15.3	82.7	15.4
$25,000 and over	13.4	7.7	88.5	7.6
White				
Under $4000	4.3	42.1	53.3	50.2
$4000 to $6999	4.7	27.6	56.2	33.7
$7000 to $10,999	12.7	19.5	57.7	21.8
$11,000 to $15,999	16.9	13.4	59.9	16.7
$16,000 to $24,999	28.8	7.2	66.0	8.5
$25,000 and over	29.5	2.9	75.4	3.1

Source: U.S. Bureau of the Census, *Current Population Reports*, Consumer Income, Series P-60, no. 123 (Washington, DC: U.S. Government Printing Office, 1980).

were $25,000 and more. Although, as shown in Table 2, the factor of race is clearly associated with the difference in the makeup of black and white families, the relationship between type of family and level of income is much stronger among Blacks than among Whites.

Reflecting the rise in black female-headed families, the proportion of black children living with both parents has decreased sharply from 64 percent in 1970, to 56 percent in 1974, and finally, to 48.5 percent in 1978.[27] An extremely high percentage of black children who do not live with both parents are impoverished. More specifically, 41.2 percent of all black children under 18 years old and 42.5 percent of all black children under 6 years old were living in families whose incomes were below the poverty level in 1978. Even more startling, 32.1 percent of all black children under 18 years old and 33.6 percent of all black children under 6 years old were living in female-headed families whose incomes were below the poverty level. Finally, if we focus on black families below the poverty level, 78 percent of all poor black children under 18 years old and 79 percent of all poor black children under 6 years old lived in female-headed homes in 1978.[28]

Thus the problem for female-headed families

is not simply the absence of fathers.[29] The problem is that an overwhelming number of these families are impoverished. Given the fact that most of these families are more or less permanent recipients of welfare, unless a serious program of economic reform is introduced, the odds are extremely high that the children in these families will be permanently trapped in the underclass.

The findings in this section and the ones presented in the previous sections have profound implications for both the future of race relations in this country and for the internal structure of the black community. They also raise serious questions about existing policy programs that have been designed to address matters of racial inequality.

In the next section, I should like to take a critical look at these programs and suggest why they have not sufficiently addressed the problems and experiences of underclass Blacks. In the process I hope to show that the problems of poor Blacks are closely related to changes in the modern American economy.

Issues of Race, Class, and Public Policy

Since World War II, political changes in the government and structural changes in the economy have both contributed to a gradual and continuous process of deracialization in the economic sector—in other words, a process in which racial distinctions gradually lose their importance in determining individual mobility in the United States. The expansion of the economy, on the one hand, facilitated the movement of Blacks from southern rural areas to the industrial centers of the nation and created job opportunities leading to greater occupational differentiation within the black community. On the other hand, the state, instead of reinforcing the racial barriers that were created during previous periods, has, in recent years, promoted racial equality. Partly in response to the pressure of increased black political resources—resources that were a result of the growing concentration of Blacks in large industrial cities—and partly in response to the pressures of black protest movements—pressures which in many ways were a manifestation of greater black political strength—the state has consistently intervened in behalf of Blacks with the enactment and enforcement of antidiscrimination legislation. In short, a combination of economic and political changes created greater economic mobility opportunities for a substantial segment of the black population.

The curious paradox, however, is that whereas economic growth since World War II enabled many Blacks to experience occupational mobility, recent structural shifts in the economy have diminished mobility opportunities for others. And whereas antidiscrimination legislation has removed many racial barriers, not all Blacks are in a position to benefit from them. Indeed the position of the black underclass has actually deteriorated during the very period in which the most sweeping antidiscrimination legislation and programs have been enacted and implemented. The net effect is a growing bifurcation between the "haves" and "have nots" in the black community.

Thus while poor Blacks are recording rising levels of employment, declining labor-force participation rates, sharp drops in employment-population ratios, and decreasing proportions with work experience, the number of Blacks in professional and managerial positions climbed to more than 1.8 million by the second quarter of 1980, over two and a half times the number in 1965 (728,999).[30] Moreover, whereas prior to the late 1960s, the ratio of black income to white income actually decreased as educational attainment increased, today the reverse seems to be the case, especially for younger black males. In 1978, 25- to 29-year-old black males who graduated from high school earned on the average only 79 percent as much as their white counterparts—$9995 for Blacks and $12,678 for Whites—whereas those who graduated from college actually earned on the average more than comparable Whites—$15,217 for Blacks and $14,013 for Whites.[31]

The failure to recognize these profound differences in the black experience, differences based on economic class position, often leads to policies that do not address the specific needs and concerns of those Blacks who are the most disadvantaged. For example, it has been argued in many quarters, and with rising insistence, that there should be a more vigorous enforcement of affirmative action programs to reverse the decline in the black-white family income ratio. However, as I have attempted to show, the recent relative decline in black family income is largely due to the growth of female-headed families, an overwhelming percentage of whom are impoverished. And, as I shall argue in more detail, affirmative action programs, which have helped to enhance the economic position of the more trained and educated Blacks, are not really designed to address the unique economic problem of poor Blacks. Indeed, even if all racial discrimination in labor-market practices were eliminated, unless there were a serious attempt to address the problems of structural barriers to decent jobs, the economic position of poor Blacks would not improve significantly. I shall elaborate briefly on this argument.

People who argue that current racial bias is the major cause of the deteriorating plight of the black poor not only have a difficult time explaining the simultaneous economic progress of more privileged Blacks, but they also fail or in some cases refuse to recognize how the fate of poor Blacks is inextricably connected with the structure and functioning of the modern American economy. The net effect is that policy programs are recommended that do not confront the fundamental causes of poverty—underemployment and unemployment. In other words, policies that do not take into account the changing characteristics of the national economy—including its rate of growth and the nature of its variable demand for labor; the factors that affect industrial employment, such as profit rates, technology, and unionization; and patterns of institutional and individual migration that are a result of industrial transformation and shifts—will not effectively handle the economic dislocation of poor Blacks.

It cannot be overemphasized that poor Blacks are particularly vulnerable to structural economic changes beyond racial considerations such as the shift from goods-producing to service-producing industries, the increasing segmentation of the labor market, the growing use of industrial technology, and the relocation of industries out of the central city. All of these changes have profoundly altered the character of the labor market in the central cities. As John D. Kasarda has put it:

> The central cities have become increasingly specialized in jobs that have high educational prerequisites just at the time that their resident populations are increasingly composed of those with poor educational backgrounds. As a result, inner-city unemployment rates are more than twice the national average and even higher among inner-city residents who have traditionally found employment in blue-collar industries that have migrated to suburban locations.[32]

The extent to which white-collar jobs are replacing blue-collar positions in central cities is illustrated in the data on the number of jobs in five selected occupational categories in 18 older northern cities (Table 3). Whereas the professional, technical, and clerical employment increased by 291,055 positions from 1960 to 1970, blue-collar employment—craftsmen, operatives, and laborers—decreased by 749,774 positions. And the overwhelming majority of the jobs lost were the higher-paying blue-collar positions: craftsmen and operatives. There is also some indication that the blue-collar jobs decline in large northern cities has accelerated. During the decade of the 1970s, Chicago lost more than 200,000 jobs, mostly in manufacturing. New York City lost 600,000 jobs during the 1970s despite the fact that the number of white-collar, professional, managerial, and clerical jobs increased in Manhattan.[33]

In considering these job shifts, it should be emphasized that roughly 60 percent of the unemployed Blacks in the United States reside in the central city, mostly within the cities' low-income areas. Conversely, there is much more dispersion among unemployed Whites, as approximately 40 percent live in suburban areas and an additional 30 percent reside in nonmetropolitan areas. Furthermore, the proportion of black men employed as laborers and service workers—occupational categories with a higher than average jobless ratio—is twice that of white workers employed in these jobs. In the final analysis, the lack of economic opportunity for lower-class Blacks means that they are forced to remain in economically depressed ghettos and their children are forced to attend inferior ghetto schools. This gives rise to a vicious circle as ghetto isolation and inferior opportunities in education reinforce their disadvantaged position in the labor market and contribute to the growing gap in the economic resources of the haves and have nots in the black community.

TABLE 3. *Number of Jobs in Five Occupational Categories in Eighteen Northern Cities, 1960–70*

Occupation	1960	1970	Change
Professional and technical	1,018,663	1,222,650	203,987
Clerical	1,833,483	1,920,551	87,068
Craftsmen	1,099,584	904,231	−195,353
Operatives	1,673,811	1,188,200	−485,611
Laborers	320,074	251,264	−68,810

Source: From John D. Kasarda, "The Implications of Contemporary Redistribution Trends for National Urban Policy," in *Handbook of Contemporary Urban Life*, ed. David Street (San Francisco: Jossey-Bass, 1978) used w/permission.

Note: "Figures are for eighteen SMSA central cities in the Northeast and North Central regions that had populations of at least 50,000 each before 1900 and did not annex more than 5 percent of their population between 1960 and 1970. The data were computed from metropolitan place-of-work reports from the 1960 and 1970 censuses." Ibid.

Given these basic economic realities, it is instructive to examine race-oriented policies and programs such as affirmative action. Of all the programs created to improve the economic position of Blacks, none has received as much attention as affirmative action. However, whereas affirmative action programs have contributed to the recent occupational mobility of trained and educated Blacks, they are not designed to break down color-blind barriers created by the shift from goods-producing to service-producing industries, the relocation of industries, the segmentation of the labor market, and the growth of technology and automation.

Furthermore, affirmative action programs are irrelevant to the problem of labor surplus in low-wage industries. Many of the dead-end and low-paying jobs in these industries do not generate racial competition between black and white workers because they are not in high demand and are now identified as "minority jobs." Because fewer black and white workers are willing to accept an economic arrangement that consigns them to dead-end, menial, and poorly paid jobs, low-wage service and manufacturing industries have increasingly used immigrant labor, including illegal aliens or undocumented workers from Mexico and other Latin American countries, to control labor problems and keep wages depressed.

If race-oriented policies are not designed to deal with the deteriorating economic condition of poor Blacks, then more attention has to focus on programs of economic reform. Everything from growing unemployment to the growth of female-headed families can be traced to economic dislocation. As Lee Rainwater observed 14 years ago, unemployed men are more likely to abandon their families than are employed men.[34] Indeed, the female-headed pattern in the ghetto symbolizes the poverty-striken nature of the underclass. To repeat, the main problem is that the lower-class black family is in the throes of an economic depression and the rising percentage of female-headed families is one of the symptoms, not the cause, of that problem.

However, if a program of economic reform is to be meaningful, it has to be directed at improving the job prospects of both poor black men and poor black women. And considering the fact that most poor black families are now headed by women, it would even be advisable to include the creation of publicly financed day-care centers in this reform program so that women can avail themselves of job opportunities if and when they develop.

In suggesting the need for economic reform, I am fully aware that it will be more successful if it can generate conditions that guarantee sustained full employment. I am also aware of the difficulty entailed in trying to create such conditions. Unlike several other capitalist democracies, the United States does not have a system of central government planning to further economic growth, establish long-range industrial policy, and outline labor-market projections and to design land use, regional distribution of resources, and educational development. Accordingly, the government response to economic fluctuations is much more likely to be determined by short-term political considerations, to reflect the interests of the more powerful and organized groups in society, and therefore to underrepresent the interests of the poor and the unemployed.

Moreover, even many of those committed to social reform have yet to recognize that current discrimination is not as central to the plight of the black poor as is the problem of economic dislocation. We only need to consider the fact that in the latter half of the 1970s, articulate black and white supporters of equal rights expressed far more concern and devoted far more attention to the *Bakke* case than to the Humphrey Hawkins full-employment bill.[35] If the nation is to avert serious domestic problems in the future, a shift in emphasis will soon have to occur. And a first step in that direction is to recognize what the problem is and where it is concentrated.

ENDNOTES

1. Bayard Rustin, "From Protest to Politics: The Future of the Civil Rights Movement," *Commentary* (Feb. 1964); idem, "A Way Out of the Exploding Ghetto," *New York Times Magazine* (13 Aug. 1967); idem, "The Lessons of the Long Hot Summer," *Commentary* (Oct. 1967); Tom Kahn, "Problems of the Negro Movement," *Dissent* 11:108–38 (winter 1964); and Kenneth B. Clark, "The Present Dilemma of the Negro" (Paper presented at the Annual Meeting of the Southern Regional Council, Atlanta, Georgia, 2 Nov. 1967) (hereafter cited as "The Present Dilemma of the Negro").

2. Rustin, "The Lessons of the Long Hot Summer."

3. Clark, "The Present Dilemma of the Negro," p. 8.

4. Bayard Rustin, "The Blacks and the Unions," *Harper Magazine*, May 1971.

5. Martin Luther King, Jr., "Showdown for Non-Violence," *Look*, 32:23–25 (16 April 1978).

6. Rustin, "From Protest to Politics."

7. Ibid.

8. Kenneth B. Clark, *Dark Ghetto: Dilemmas of Social Power* (New York: Harper & Row, 1965) (hereafter cited as *Dark Ghetto*); and Lee Rainwater, "Crucible of Identity: The Negro Lower-Class Family," *Daedalus*, 95:172–216 (winter 1966).

9. Clark, *Dark Ghetto*, p. 27.

10. Rainwater, p. 173.

11. Clark, *Dark Ghetto*, p. 81.

12. Robert K. Merton, "Insiders and Outsiders: A Chapter in the Sociology of Knowledge," *Am. J. Soc.*, 78:18–19 (July 1972).

13. See, for example, Joyce Ladner, ed., *The Death of White Sociology* (New York: Random House, 1973); Robert B. Hill, *The Strength of Black Families* (New York: Emerson Hall, 1972); Nathan Hare, "The Challenge of a Black Scholar," *Black Scholar*, 1:58–63 (Dec. 1969); Abd-l Hakim Ibn Alkalimat (Gerald McWorter), "The Ideology of Black Social Science," *Black Scholar*, 1:28–35 (Dec. 1969); Robert Staples, "The Myth of the Black Matriarchy," *Black Scholar*, 2:9–16 (Feb. 1970); and idem, *The Black Family: Essays and Studies* (Belmont CA: Wadsworth Publishing Co., 1971).

14. Orlando Patterson, *Ethnic Chauvinism: The Reactionary Response* (New York: Stein & Day, 1977), p. 155.

15. William Julius Wilson, *The Declining Significance of Race: Blacks and Changing American Institutions*, 2nd ed. (Chicago: University of Chicago Press, 1980) (hereafter cited as the *The Declining Significance of Race*); Lewis M. Killian, "Conflicting Definitions of the Racial Crisis in the United States" (Paper presented at the New York Sociological Society, Albany, New York, 19 Oct. 1979); and Carl Gehrsman, "A Matter of Class," *The New York Times Magazine* (5 Oct. 1980), pp. 24, 92–105.

16. U.S. Department of Commerce, *Statistical Abstract of the United States* (Washington, DC: U.S. Government Printing Office, 1979).

17. A more detailed discussion of the black structure is presented in Wilson, see footnote 15.

18. U.S. Department of Labor, *Employment and Training Report of the President* (Washington, DC: U.S. Government Printing Office, 1978). The figures reported for Blacks were those for "Black and Other Males."

19. U.S. Department of Labor, *Monthly Labor Review* (Washington, DC: U.S. Government Printing Office, Oct. 1979).

20. For white male teenagers, the percentage with work experience was 75.9 percent in 1966 and 73.8 percent in 1977; for white female teenagers, it was 59.8 percent in 1966 and 64.8 percent in 1977. For white young adult males, it was 93.8 percent in 1966 and 93.2 percent in 1977; for white young adult females, in was 69.8 percent in 1966 and 79.0 percent in 1977. U.S. Department of Labor, *Monthly Labor Review* (Washington DC: U.S. Government Printing Office, Oct. 1979).

21. U.S. Department of Labor, *Monthly Labor Review* (Washington, DC: U.S. Government Printing Office, Oct. 1979).

22. Brian Becker and Stephen Hills, "Today's Teenage Unemployed—Tomorrow's Working Poor?" *Monthly Labor Review*, Jan. 1979, pp. 69–71.

23. U.S. Department of Labor, *Monthly Labor Review* (Washington DC: U.S. Government Printing Office, Oct. 1979).

24. Based on calculations from U.S. Bureau of the Census, "Money Income and Poverty Status of Families and Persons in the United States: 1978," *Current Population Reports*, Series P-60, no. 120 (Washington, DC: U.S. Government Printing Office, 1979) (hereafter cited as *Current Population Reports*, P-60, no. 120); U.S. Bureau of the Census, "Money Income and Poverty Status of Families and Persons in the United States: 1977," *Current Population Reports*, Series P-60, no. 116 (Washington, DC: U.S. Government Printing Office, 1978); U.S. Bureau of the Census, "The Social and Economic Status of the Black Population in the United States, 1970," *Current Population Reports*, Series P-23, no. 38 (Washington DC: U.S. Government Printing Office, 1971).

25. Ibid.

26. *Current Population Reports*, P-60, no. 120.

27. U.S. Bureau of the Census, "The Social and Economic Status of the Black Population in the United States, 1974" *Current Population Reports*, Series 23, no. 54 (Washington DC: U.S. Government Printing Office, 1975); and U.S. Bureau of the Census, "Money Income of Families and Persons in the United States: 1978," *Current Population Reports*, Series P-60, no. 123 (Washington DC: U.S. Government Printing Office, 1980). It should be pointed out that of the one-parent black families with children in 1979, only six percent were maintained by fathers. Thus to speak of single-parent black families is to speak of female-headed families.

28. U.S. Bureau of the Census, "Characteristics of the Population Below the Poverty Level: 1978," *Current Population Reports*, Series P-60, no. 124 (Washington, DC: U.S. Government Printing Office, 1980).

29. There is considerable research documenting the important role of the extended family pattern—that is, the role of the grandmother or other relatives in the household—as opposed to the nuclear family norm of the middle class, in rearing and socializing black children. See, for example, Elmer P. Martin and Joanne Mitchell Martin, *The Black Extended Family* (Chicago: University of Chicago Press, 1978); and David M. Schneider and Raymond T. Smith, *Class Differences in American Kinships* (Ann Arbor: University of Michigan Press, 1978).

30. U.S. Department of Labor, *Employment and Earnings* (Washington, DC: U.S. Government Printing Office, 18 July 1980); and U.S. Department of Labor, *Employment and Training Report of the President* (Washington, DC: U.S. Government Printing Office, 1978).

31. The average income of black and white females in now comparable at both the high school and college levels. For year-round full-time workers the average income of black female college graduates in 1978 was 97 percent ($12,945) that of comparable white females ($13,344), and the average income of black female high school graduates was 98 percent ($9138) that of white female high school graduates ($9293). Since all of these figures are below those of comparable black and white men, it would appear that the job-market problems of black women are more related to sexual than to racial status. U.S. Bureau of the Census, "Money Income of Families and Persons in the United States: 1978," *Current Population Reports*, Series P-60, no. 123 (Washington DC: U.S. Government Printing Office, 1980).

32. John D. Kasarda, "Urbanization, Community, and the Metropolitan Problem," in *Handbook of Contemporary Urban Life*, ed. David Street (San Francisco, CA: Jossey-Bass Publication, 1978).

33. John D. Kasarda, "The Implications of Contemporary Redistribution Trends for National Urban Policy," *Social Science Quarterly* (in press).

34. Rainwater.

35. For a more detailed discussion of this argument, see William Julius Wilson, *The Declining Significance of Race*; and "The Declining Significance of Race: Myth or Reality," in *The Declining Significance of Race? A Dialogue among Black and White Social Scientists*, ed. Joseph R. Washington, Proceedings of the Fifth Annual Symposium of the Afro-American Studies Program (Philadelphia, PA: University of Pennslyvania, 1979), pp. 1–20.

33

Minorities in the American Class System

Joan W. Moore

No dream is so dear to Americans as the possibility of a society that is completely open to ambitious people. But when we wake, the realities of class and race are difficult to face. Perhaps this is why we are so willing to leave the study of realities to specialists—and to draw from them the kind of uneasy compromise that we call public policy. But ambiguity has its uses: we must be free to tell children that hard work and education will find their reward. Young blacks and Chicanos must be persuaded to wait another generation, always another generation.

But the problems of class and race are too important to leave to the specialists; we should be at least faintly aware of the main categories of professional polemic and wishful thinking, because the present situation is embarrassing and unpleasant, for at least four reasons. First, obsolete and monolithic paradigms still dominate much of the professional thinking, masking the realities. Second, our share of minority people is growing so rapidly that they will soon be a majority in certain areas. Third, the political climate is such that blacks, Chicanos, Puerto Ricans, and Native Americans will be left to themselves to win their own way. And fourth, the surge of hope and

Reprinted by permission of *Daedalus*, Journal of the American Academy of Arts and Sciences, 110:2 (Spring 1981), Cambridge, MA.

practical results won by all four minorities in the 1960s is well remembered.

Biracialism and Other Delusions
The first and most deceptive of the paradigms that mask reality is the assumption that America's minorities and all their problems are simply a question of "black" and "white." For most Americans, "race" means black people and white people, as does "minority." This narrow biracial assumption is enshrined in the U.S. census, where it does great mischief. We are given statistics based on "white" and "nonwhite," and most people read nonwhite as black. Minorities that don't fit this assumption are counted as exceptions and tossed into a residual category—into "other colored," as in the past; "other nonwhite," as used now for Native Americans and Koreans; or into both categories, as is done now for Puerto Ricans. Mexican Americans have so baffled the classifications of the census that they were moved back and forth from a racial ("other nonwhite") category in 1930 to a kind of ethnic group ("persons of Spanish mother tongue") in 1940. An even more ambiguous classification—"white persons of Spanish surname"—was used in 1950 and 1960. In 1970 it was "persons of both Spanish surname and Spanish mother tongue."[1] In 1980 Chicanos, Puerto Ricans, and other Hispanics became a kind of superethnic group, listed along

with other national descent groups and also in a category by itself. Sometimes (but rarely) the census tabulates them as a race, along with white, black, and other nonwhite. This grudging and inconsistent acknowledgment that Chicanos and Puerto Ricans are something other than simple ethnic groups (like Greeks or Italians) is a consequence of the biracialist paradigm. It is not a harmless assumption. It is built into the way the census and the nation constructs reality.

But the census is a model of realism by contrast with the social science professionals. At least the census (and some other federal agencies) troubled to collect systematically the available data on non-black minorities. Academic social scientists have been extraordinarily blind to Chicanos, Puerto Ricans, Native Americans, and other nonblacks. Generations of textbooks on "intergroup relations" have discussed only blacks. Generations of doctoral dissertations, community studies, and policy monographs have equated "minority" with "black." By contrast, there is only a very sparse literature on other minorities in the class system, and as we shall see, it has greatly impoverished the thinking on class and race in the United States.

From the beginning, an Alice-in-Wonderland quality pervaded thought about the American class system and how such a system absorbs or excludes minorities. The dominant sociological paradigm is based on the idea that America is a nation of immigrants. It was assumed that economic opportunity would forever expand and forever provide mobility up the ladder. In the process, all but vestigial and trivial meanings of non-American origins would vanish. It was believed that this upward struggle would create a kind of cohesiveness in the society, because everyone subscribed to the same set of goals.[2]

The process was seen as very nearly inevitable. In the 1940s a detailed timetable was developed for the assimilation of each ethnic/racial group through its mobility in the class system. A later generation of sociologists found a ranking in the current socioeconomic attainment of various ethnic groups that corresponded roughly to the distinction between the "old" (Western European) and the "new" (Eastern and Southern European) immigrants. Latin Americans (Chicanos and Puerto Ricans) and West Indians (black) trailed

well behind.[3] Some economists have even tried, rather unconvincingly, to project such status attainments into the future, to estimate how long it will take blacks to catch up,[4] like the earlier timetable for assimilation. Class was believed to absorb ethnicity, a conception that was widely accepted for some important reasons only remotely related to science. It was a very nice idea, and romantically comforting: we all grow together in a new land and achieve our dearest aspirations. It offered the comforts of both rationality and morality to the most conservative white people. And, of course, it certified the importance and moral worth of certain American institutions such as the educational system, which, it now appears, do not work very well at present and did not work very well in the past. But back in the forties, these quibbles went unnoticed.

Even then there was the nagging exception of American blacks; it was obvious that the class system was not working in the same fashion for black people. They were seen as separate and apart, locked into a castelike system that had been convincingly demonstrated in a series of classic studies, primarily of life in the South. This caste system was unpleasant, but understandable, in the terms of life in the American South. So understandable, in fact, that when coupled with the biracial assumption, social scientists generally overlooked their inability to apply the caste system to any other racial groups or minorities. Every group was somehow an exception. The American Indians were an exception: according to popular belief, they lived mostly on reservations and were a "special" population. When Puerto Ricans began to arrive on the mainland in large numbers, they also were seen as "special." But the exceptionalism used to explain Indians and Puerto Ricans was much less excusable for the millions of Mexican Americans in the Southwest. Mexicans were neither a caste, nor did they fit into the assimilation timetable (even though they were classified as similar to the Mediterranean Catholic immigrants). This minority came to the United States by conquest, not by slavery or immigration. Their status varied immensely from place to place in the conquered territory. Sometimes the conquering Americans displaced the elite Mexicans; in other areas they simply married and joined them. Sometimes they fitted the resident Mexicans into a new industrial system and then found it necessary to import even more. In some cities, old Mexican families retained their status in the very top layers of the upper class; in California, some "old" families are firmly intermarried with the most powerful industrial and financial interests. But Western history is a tiny specialty of American history, and the nation's social scientists knew little of this. When the last great waves of European immigration coincided with the revolution-inspired emigration from Mexico after 1910, Mexicans were treated as just another late ethnic arrival in the panorama of American assimilation. Few noticed that not until after World War II did Mexican patterns of settlement in the United States begin to bear any resemblance to those of the European immigrants who settled in the urban industrial North. The analogy with the older ethnics was just too thin, and there were just too many Chicanos for exceptionalism to work very well.

Interestingly, the academic myths about minorities were destroyed not by more and better research, but by the ethnics themselves. Minority activism of the 1960s not only attacked social and economic barriers directly, but their intellectuals destroyed the melting pot concept. New models were borrowed from the former colonies of European countries. To the ethnic intellectuals, the situation of American blacks, Indians, and Chicanos seemed to be similar to that of colonial and postcolonial situations. To complete the paradigm, Puerto Rico *was* very nearly still a colony. While this "internal colonialism" model had some flaws, the resemblance was striking. The analogy drew attention to the long-standing structures and emergent social structures that were very easy to ignore under the discredited ethnic-assimilationist idea—and too narrowly conceptualized under the race and caste analogy.[5] (Generally, these paradigms were congruent with Marxist-Leninist conceptions. Although they tended to emerge first in a cultural-nationalist context, the new approaches probably encouraged extensive exploration of Marxist theories among many minority social scientists.) Certainly the flaws in these old paradigms were very obvious by this time. The search for new models also profited from concurrent attempts to reconceptualize the economic opportunity structure.

But the old models are slow to die. The caste paradigm clearly no longer fits the facts of the 1970s and 1980s, even for blacks. Yet the idea of caste and the ethnic-assimilationist model continues to suit a large group of social scientists who find the ferment of the 1960s repugnant. The ethnic-assimilationist model fits extremely well with the neoconservative emphasis on "pure" market factors as an explanation of status mobility, and on cultural factors as an explanation of failure. Thus Nathan Glazer and Daniel Patrick Moynihan, for example, argue, in a sophisticated version of the old "cultural deprivation" theory, that there is nothing special in the current circumstances of blacks, Chicanos, Puerto Ricans, and Native Americans that cannot be subsumed under the ordinary factors that help or hinder white ethnics from mobility in the labor market. This is a view that condemns minority activism and use of the political system for the direct redistribution of jobs, housing, and other essentials. They charge that all such activity assumes that the ideal of equality of opportunity has failed—and, they claim, it has not. Therefore, such activism is a serious threat to core American values and norms—perhaps even more of a threat than the activities of the crook who uses deviant means to attain success, but does not try to legitimate or excuse his methods. This controversy about the ability of minorities to fade eventually into the mainstream occupational and class structure is far from disinterested or academic. It is often personal, often bitter, and has direct policy consequences.[6]

The Parodox of Place: Old Minorities in New Places

This bitterness about minorities has roots deep in American culture—so deep they cannot be explored here. They reach into the early American idea of faraway people as romantic. This spiritualized gloss lay heavy on the people living in the remnants of Southern plantation feudalism. It created the happy exotics of John Steinbeck's *Cannery Row* and the noble, stoic Red Men living on the reservations in the faraway Southwest. We thought of the Puerto Ricans as fascinating, content in our remote island colony. It was a gloss thick enough to hide the realities of subordination. Only when these minorities left the stage and the novels and their traditional geographic and social places and moved right next door to us in the city did the subordination flower into its true ugliness, highly visible to both the happy exotics and the urban middle-class Anglos. Then conservative social scientists could argue that nothing but ideology hindered these urban newcomers from advancing, just as did the European greenhorns of past generations. The media could prod all the latent fears of the urban middle classes about the depredations (and costliness) of these new barbarians. Immediately after World War II in the large American cities, the fates of the four minorities began to converge, and naive romanticism was dead.

By the 1970s all of these minorities were predominantly city-dwellers. Most blacks (81% by 1970) lived in the cities, and almost half lived outside the South by 1975. Most Mexican Americans (81%) lived in metropolitan areas, and 13 percent had moved out of the five Southwestern states in which they had traditionally lived (the border states and Colorado). More than a third of the nation's Puerto Ricans lived not in Puerto Rico, but on the mainland, and 95 percent of these were crowded into cities. Even the Indians were leaving their reservations; half of them lived in urban areas by the mid-1970s. Each group moved geographically and socially in a different manner, but all did so primarily after World War II.[7]

The most openly "managed" migration was that of American Indians. In 1950 only 16 percent of Native Americans lived in cities. The enormous movement in the following decades was the result of the relocation policy of the Bureau of Indian Affairs. Poverty on the reservations led to the policy of "off-reservation" employment in the Employment Assistance Act of 1956. Well intentioned it may have been, but the net result is that the vast majority did badly in urban labor markets and became poor in the cities as well as on the reservations. In some ways they are worse off: the Indian population is such a small fraction of the large cities that it has been generally difficult for them to establish their own institutions and to maintain a strong community life. Some observers think this migration is restless, with some return migration, and much back-and-

forth movement. By the late 1970s some experts were predicting a stabilization of urban communities and a revival of tribal patterns in cities like New York. Others continue to see nothing but disintegration.[8]

Back-and-forth migration also characterizes the Puerto Rican movement to cities of the mainland. This also was highly managed, although the mechanism is less overt than in the case of the Indians. Active labor recruiting and contracting brought large numbers of Puerto Rican workers to New York and other cities in the years after World War II. New low-cost air transportation helped make the shift possible. The Puerto Rican government cooperated actively. Operation Bootstrap itself, with its emphasis on high-technology, capital-intensive development, also tended to push out unskilled workers.[9]

Chicanos were not new to the cities of the Southwest; in fact, many of these cities were founded by Mexican immigrants. But they *seemed* to appear in large numbers in the cities, especially in California, after World War II. With this came a gradual awareness of both their very large numbers and their concentration in urban centers. The 1930s and 1940s were times of massive federal and state management. Mexicans were deported in the 1930s, imported in the 1940s as agricultural braceros, and deported, once again, in large numbers in the 1950s. Federal management is still a critical factor in the endless struggle over undocumented Mexican workers. Mexican workers flocked into Southwestern cities because of labor opportunities there during and after World War II. This consolidation of urban settlements coincided with a mass movement out of the oppressive environment in Texas. This movement went largely to California, although increasing numbers of Chicanos are leaving the Southwest and moving into the Midwest, particularly into the great chain of industrial cities from southeastern Wisconsin through Chicago to Detroit. At the same time, enormous numbers of undocumented workers and their families are settling in the more traditional areas of the Southwest. How many is a subject of great controversy, but the correct answer would be in the millions.[10]

The "Great Migration" of black Americans from the South started even earlier, early in the twentieth century. In 1910 almost 90 percent lived in the South, 65 percent of these in rural areas. Labor recruiters spurred the movement to the North as early as the 1920s in a search for large numbers of naive strikebreakers. At the onset of World War II, only 23 percent of the black population lived outside the South (most of them in the Northeast and north central regions). As did many other Americans, blacks began to move west in great numbers after 1940, in response to the many industrial jobs created in the Sunbelt by the war and by later economic development. The movement out of the South was overwhelmingly a movement to the cities; 95 percent of the non-Southern blacks lived in cities in the late 1960s. But the pattern slowed considerably by the mid-1970s. Not only did the north central regions and the Northeast begin to lose blacks, but the black population of the South began to grow again.[11]

What, then, did this movement from traditional places mean for these four minorities? Most significantly, it meant that their life circumstances began to converge. All four groups were locked into cities, in some cases, into the same cities. Significant portions of all four groups were locked also into the poverty areas of these cities, areas that had poor institutional services and poor housing—precisely the services and circumstances that to a large degree determine the life chances of minority group members.

Generally, this is described as the process of *ghettoization*, the term most commonly used for blacks in Northern cities. Harold Rose finds that ghetto formation in the Old South depended on legalized segregation, with urban areas set aside for blacks; in the North, the newcomers took over "used" housing in areas of the inner city. More recently, however, these regional differences have begun to vanish.[12] The recent awareness of the growth of the black middle class has led many specialists to question whether ghettoization is not an obsolete concept for a significant number of middle-class urban blacks. But many blacks with substantial incomes still seek out residential areas within the central city, frequently adjacent to black ghettos. Recent real estate inflation may have priced them out of any hope of moving to the suburbs in many cities. What has been interpreted as black suburbanization, according to Rose, is not a middle-class or integrated pattern. Rather, blacks migrating from the South frequently choose to live on the outskirts of large cities in a life-style and setting closer to their rural Southern origins. Even within the metropolitan rings, some enclaves of blacks, communities dating from the turn of the century, are found in industrial "satellites." But neither small towns nor the industrial satellites, although geographically suburban, represent living conditions that are any better than the ghettos of the central city. Whether middle-class blacks can migrate to the suburbs and actually become part of the receiving community (as opposed to segregated "ghettolets," a term coined by Rose) must await the data of the 1980 census.[13]

But is ghettoization a valid concept for the other minorities? There is little doubt that it applies to mainland Puerto Ricans. Incoming Puerto Ricans not only were segregated in the old tenements of New York and other cities, but they even shared many of the living spaces of blacks, as on the edges of Harlem in New York. The concept is less valid for urban Indians, even though they tend to live in subcommunities in poorer areas of the city. It is difficult to think of ghettoization in regard to such a comparatively small number of people.

It is with Mexican Americans that the concept of ghettoization is most questionable. At least in the Southwest, Chicano residential segregation from Anglos and from blacks is markedly different because of two historical factors. First, many Southwestern cities were founded by Mexicans. Current prevailing residential patterns reflect many decades during which new Anglos competed with original Mexicans for space. In reverse, waves of newcomer Mexicans are displacing Anglos. Second, many of these cities grew by annexation or absorption of outlying areas. Frequently these areas included traditional Mexican settlements, many of them near work sites. These patterns contribute to a lower level and a more variable pattern of residential segregation, often (as in San Diego or the San Fernando Valley near Los Angeles) to a scattering of older small and medium-sized barrios in a veritable sea of Anglo housing, often very new.[14]

It seems unlikely that big cities will have one big mixed ghetto in the future. Blacks and Chicanos in the Southwest have been segregated from each other and from Anglos at about the same degree for decades, and the pattern appears to be stable. In the Snowbelt cities, black and Hispanic ghettos tend to be adjacent and to blur around the edges, but they appear not to have merged. Although a single huge ghetto is not likely, the living situations of all four minorities have striking similarities. There is, in addition, a growing feeling that their interests may very well be the same. A focus of this interest is, of course, the urban industrial labor market.

Changes in the Structure of Opportunity

Earlier we noted how the massive shift of minority people away from the traditional places made difficulties for the theorists. Urban poverty is meaner and less easily sentimentalized than rural poverty. It is strange that this sentimentalization continues: the Southern caste system and the struggles of Cesar Chavez for his farm workers still attract wide interest. In their time the Chicano Brown Berets and the Black Panthers drew much less interest. The riots of the 1960s were, somehow, the last straw. In policy terms, wide interest in improving the opportunity structure has given way to a neoconservative emphasis on economic development. Yet, there is the special difficulty that economic development tends to erode away at the bottom of business cycles, just when it is most needed. In terms of importance, the rise and fall of economic development schemes are much less critical to American minorities than the structural factors at work in the modern labor marketplace.

Opportunity and Geography

A simple and pointed way to begin is to ask whether minorities are in the right places for today's jobs. In answering, two points should be made. The first is that job opportunities are declining in the North—the target of much minority movement and an area much affected by business cycles[15]—and increasing in the South and West. Most of the job growth in these areas is in the new complex of industries closely tied to federal needs in aerospace and military goods. These are fast-growing high-wage industries, and their rate of expansion over twenty years was 180 percent in the South, compared to a national growth of 92 percent.[16] Minorities leaving the South and Southwest are missing such opportunities, even though others may benefit. But, actually, it is much more likely that minorities who remain in these areas will benefit from the darker side of Sunbelt growth. Certain low-paying manufacturing jobs also increased in the nonunionized South, although they declined elsewhere in the nation. Thus cheap labor (leftover minorities and undocumented workers) allowed the Sunbelt "to capture a significant share of the low-wage manufacturing industries, and in some activities [the South] now accounts for as much as 60 to 70 percent of the national employment in these low-wage portions of manufacturing."[17] Thus the widely hailed shift to the Sunbelt probably has not benefited the four minorities.

The second point, the so-called mismatch hypothesis, argues that blue-collar manufacturing jobs are leaving the central city for the white-collar suburbs just as blue-collar minorities are migrating to those central cities. The hypothesis seems to fit the facts that suburban jobs grew disproportionately between 1960 and 1970 and that there are increasing rates of minority unemployment in the central city. The mismatch idea is especially appealing because the solution appears to be simple: transport central city residents to suburban jobs or relocate segregated minority workers to the suburbs.

Unfortunately, the evidence is not very convincing. There is no simple relationship between the growth of suburban manufacturing jobs and the recent growth of urban unemployment. Worse yet, there is evidence that the mismatch hypothesis is based on wrong information: jobs in the central city were undercounted, and with few exceptions, increased and show signs of continued increase.[18] Furthermore, government and service are the two growth sectors of the economy that disproportionately hire minority workers. Both areas are disproportionately growing in the central cities.[19] Semiskilled and unskilled employment increased enough in the 1960s for all resident central city workers.[20] And in the early 1970s blue-collar work actually continued to increase in the central cities more than in the suburbs.[21] Simple observation of the Chinatown sweatshops in Manhattan suggests that low-wage employers locate near their labor supply. At least one study shows that suburban employers who need low-wage workers are forced to bus their workers—surely an uneconomic activity.[22] Thus, though job opportunities in the central city have not been great, they also have not disappeared—yet unemployment *has* risen. Why this is happening will be a large part of our discussion.

Opportunity and the Shifting Structure of Jobs

Structural changes in the job market have been critical for minority employment, let alone minority advancement. Both the type of job and the nature of competition for the jobs have changed over the past forty years. More jobs are white collar and tend to demand either a college degree or a high-school diploma, although the upper-level jobs (professions) are expected to increase rather more slowly in the 1980s. Service occupations will expand. Blue-collar jobs will grow more slowly, and farm jobs will continue to decline.[23]

This changing shape of the opportunity structure looks more and more middle class. Yet the long-heralded "revolution of the middle class" may be a long time coming. Much of the white-collar expansion has involved women, many of them second earners, who are entering the labor force in unprecedented numbers. And when the revolution does come, it may continue to leave the American minorities behind. The large number of highly educated Americans means that jobs will require higher and higher levels of education, and all four minorities lag far behind Anglos in education, especially college education. "By 1978 one out of four college graduates held a job traditionally filled by someone with less schooling."[24] As this trend continues, minorities will find "credentialism" even more frustrating. It is an endless game of "catch-up." At the other end, jobs that traditionally go to uneducated people probably would expand fast enough to match the supply of poorly educated workers *if* employers were concerned only with skill. Almost certainly, however, employers will continue to discriminate.

These occupational shifts accompanied the expansion of the government, trade, and service sectors of the economy. Trade and service occupations are expected to continue to grow relatively fast during the 1980s because service industries are less likely to need fewer workers because of increased efficiency through either technology or management.[25] It is considered much less likely that the government sector will grow. This is unfortunate because government tends to hire minorities. Most of the expansion in government employment took place at state and local levels, and the slight decline after 1975 was seen as the harbinger of a more general decline that would result from public resistance to taxation. Without acknowledging the vulnerability of public employment, William Wilson in *The Declining Significance of Race*, a recent and important analysis of class and race, sees public employment as a critical factor in the employment of minorities.

Opportunity and the Segmented Labor Market

A job is not necessarily an opportunity: it may be badly paid and meaningless. Some "opportunity structures" consist of a lifetime of bad jobs. The essential question for minorities is just *how* the market for jobs operates. Until recently, most labor economists assumed a kind of mass of job seekers lined up for employers in exact order of qualification: the first best qualified person in the queue, regardless of ethnicity or other irrelevant factors, would be selected for the best job. Irrational employers who insisted on discriminating would, in the long run, pay for their discrimination. This comfortable belief in employer rationality has crumbled in the face of a great deal of evidence that nothing of the sort happens. Instead of one labor market, there are actually several. In technical terms, the labor market is "segmented."

Segmented, or "dual labor market," theorists argue that the labor market operates differently for different types of employers. Employers offering "good" jobs (relatively high wages, good working conditions, fringe benefits, security, a chance for advancement, and due process) recruit in markets that are different from those used by the more marginal employers. The primary core enterprises are heavily capitalized, concentrated, and unionized, at least partly as a consequence of the restructuring of industry and jobs through the unionism of the old CIO and the effective labor legislation it helped shape. On the other side of the market, employers of secondary labor are highly competitive with one another. Not only can they pay the lowest possible acceptable wage, but they may structure their work force as they please. A vast number of these enterprises systematically evade wage-and-hour laws, as proved to be the case with 83 percent of the garment manufacturers recently inspected in California.[27]

These marginal employers seek employees who make minimal demands. Teenage workers in the fast-food chains will work for minimum wages and are happy with an occasional free Saturday night as a "reward" in the weekly negotiations for a work schedule. Ex-offenders will work to satisfy a parole requirement. But many adults actively reject such jobs, and this leads to continual complaints by low-wage employers about labor shortages. They turn to pools of workers that make fewer demands. "Employers were actively engaged in recruiting new workers from the American South, Puerto Rico, the Caribbean, Latin America and elsewhere...from backward, rural areas, who were unfamiliar with modern industry, illiterate in their own language, and could not speak English."[28] Decades of such recruitment have greatly helped in producing the racial mix of today's cities. Southern blacks, Chicanos settling out of the migrant stream, new Mexican immigrants, and Puerto Ricans from the Island undemandingly accept the wages and working conditions that make them attractive to marginal or exploitative employers. A number of studies show that during the 1960s Southern black migrants fresh to the North were more likely to be working than blacks born in the North. Their attitudes were different: the newcomers were exploitable, docile workers; the Northern-born were demanding and skeptical.[29]

This distinction between labor markets is critical for minorities. Only the core sector offers "opportunity" in the usual sense—a decent job that offers advancement, a career. However, core-sector employers, since they pay more for workers anyway (and are less competitive with one another), do discriminate. This does not usually involve open prejudice but rather credentialism, a problem for minorities. Marginal and low-wage employers in the secondary labor market are looking for cheap, docile workers, and they consistently recruit them both in the inner city and in outside labor markets. Foundries and

tanneries in the North, for example, recruited Mexicans in Texas in the 1920s and Puerto Ricans in the 1950s. Thus the operations of marginal employers have implications not only for minorities already on the scene, but also for their competitors. These are the "newest" of the urban minorities—the Koreans, Thais, Samoans, and Chinese—and this competition has implications for the future of American cities.

Opportunity and the Government

During the past twenty years, government actions have improved the opportunity structure for minorities in several ways. But government action also has its negative twists. First, it has created jobs, but these jobs are vulnerable to the political winds of change. Second, a large portion of government employment for minorities (at least for blacks, for whom it is documented) is in delivering services to poor minority clientele.[30] This kind of employment provokes jokes about "poverty pimps" and "welfare colonialism," but this function of the welfare state is of major importance to minority professionals. (In this sense, the contemporary welfare state differs from its long-standing prototype, the Bureau of Indian Affairs, which was notably reluctant to employ Indians in routine administrative positions.)

Government is also important in pressuring both its bureaus and agencies and industry to hire minorities through affirmative action. But, as Wilson notes, the benefits tend to accrue primarily in "higher paying jobs of the expanding service-producing industries in both the corporate and the government sectors."[31] Thus they operate to proletarianize the minority poor even further. In addition, there are those who argue that, for blacks, affirmative action is almost entirely responsible for the gains in middle-class jobs, and there is little noticeable softening in the discriminatory hiring practices of "good" employers.

The Overall Impact of Changes

The four minorities have moved out of their traditional social and geographic places into the peculiar world of late twentieth century industrialism, a very different opportunity structure from that found by earlier immigrants. Most observers focus on two particular shifts in this structure: first, government is now important in both opening access to, and in creating, opportunities; second, minorities are moving to the wrong places—that is, to places and industries at a time when those places and industries are losing their viability.

There is little doubt about the importance of government in opening and creating job opportunities, and little question that it is a new effect and generally very beneficial for minorities and for their entry into the middle class. Of course, "qualified" minorities have always done better, but in earlier days that "better" was not very good, and government action appears to have made the major difference.

There is less clarity about the importance of opportunity shifts in creating an urban minority underclass. Theorists of the segmented labor market and some community studies of Chicano and black poor people suggest other factors.[32] The most important is the "generational hypothesis." This model sees a continuous influx of naive and unskilled beginners who take exploitative jobs. Despite the inadequacy of their earnings, they and their children survive and cope, in a tripartite economy that includes welfare and illegal sources of income in addition to wages. Later we will trace some more implications of this generational hypothesis for the urban underclass. But first, generally speaking, how much progress have the minorities made during the last twenty years?

The Question of Progress
Rather than coping with sophisticated definitions, we will deal only with the widely used social indicators of income and occupational attainment. Do these indicators show that life is improving for minorities in the American class system? Almost surely the answer is Yes. Most black, Chicano, Puerto Rican, and Indian males, at least, have improved their position in the past twenty years. But they still continue to lag behind Anglo males in both occupational and income attainment (according to a measure of change between 1959 and 1975). Beyond such wide generalizations, the question of improvement is very doubtful. Even the data base is questionable, largely because of the notorious inability of the U.S. census to find low-achieving minority males.

Some of the best work has been done by the U.S. Commission on Civil Rights, in an analysis that used ratios extensively. Thus "progress" is shown by their finding that between 1959 and 1975 minority males came notably closer to Anglo males in earnings (see Table 1A). In 1959 black males earned on the average 52 percent of what Anglo males earned; by 1975 they had moved up to 65 percent. Much less progress is shown for women, even Anglo women. Measured against Anglo males, women in general earned *less* on the average in 1975 than they earned in 1959. Black women are the only exception.

There is another point to remember when comparative earnings are examined. Who is really receiving and using this income? Does the income of a minority worker and that of an Anglo worker mean the same thing at home? The answer is No. It is characteristic of minorities that there are *more* people per household, and each member of the average minority family thus shares less from the wages of the wage-earner (Table 1B). It is in the family that individuals learn values and act out their values and lifestyles. This differential experience probably has an impact on the labor market behavior of the minority poor.

But the size of the household is not the only difference. Anglo workers tend to be better educated, to have jobs with more prestige, to work more weeks per year and more hours per week, and to be younger. In addition, the income levels among states of residence may vary considerably.[33] These factors can be controlled statistically by the use of a hypothetical earnings ratio, which estimates what each minority subgroup might have earned *if* these six work-related characteristics were the same as those of the average majority males. When these factors are controlled, the results show that earnings would be closer to parity, but there is still a gap. Compare Table 1A for "reality" with Table 1C for the earnings possible if the minorities were as "qualified" as Anglos. Thus some portion of the earnings gap between minorities and Anglos is explainable by differences in individual qualification and characteristics of the typical job, but discrimination probably accounts for the remaining difference.

Statistical manipulation also is used to explain *away* all of the observed differences between minorities and Anglos, as is basically done, for instance, by neoconservative Edward Banfield

TABLE 1. *Earnings and Household Per Capita Income Ratios, Four Minorities and Majority Males, by Sex, 1959–60 and 1975–76.*

	Male		Female	
	1959	1975	1959	1975
A. Observed Mean Earnings Ratios for Those with Earnings				
Black	0.52%	0.65%	0.29%	0.43%*
Mexican American	0.64	0.65	0.33	**0.31**
Puerto Rican	0.60	0.72	0.42	**0.41**
American Indian/Alaskan Native	0.54	0.73	0.36	**0.35**
Majority	1.00	1.00	0.50	**0.45**
B. Median Household Per Capita Income Ratios				
Black	0.46%[a]	0.52%[a]	0.27%[b]	**0.20%[b]**
Mexican American	0.50	**0.49**	0.29	**0.28**
Puerto Rican	0.59	**0.50**	0.49	**0.29**
American Indian/Alaskan Native	0.32	0.57	0.26	0.30
Majority	1.00	1.00	0.75	**0.59**
C. Hypothetical Mean Earnings Ratios for Those with Earnings				
Black	0.71%	0.85%	0.47%	0.61%**
Mexican American	0.84	**0.82**	0.48	0.48
Puerto Rican	0.87	0.98	0.55	0.57
American Indian/Alaskan Native	0.73	0.92	0.53	0.54
Majority	1.00	1.00	0.57	0.57

Source: Derived from U.S. Commission on Civil Rights, *Social Indicators for Minorities and Women*, pp. 50, 54. Figures representing a decline in relative status between 1959 and 1975 are in boldface.

[a]All households
[b]Female-headed households

*Interpreted as follows: In 1975 black females earned, on the average, 43 percent of the majority male average earnings.

**Interpreted as follows: In 1975 black females would have earned, on the average, 61 percent of the majority male average earnings if they had possessed work-related characteristics similar to those of majority males.

when he contrasts the "statistical Negro" with the "Census Negro." Banfield argues that "when all non-racial factors are controlled for . . . the Statistical Negro is indistinguishable from the white." This is done, for example, by calculating a birth rate for blacks that excludes women who have lived on Southern farms. This conceit (the Statistical Negro) comes up with a black birth rate that is the same as white.[34] Of course, it is impossible to justify the exclusion of a socially significant fraction of any group. Analogously, one might exclude all white males who live in suburbs, or all Mexican Americans born in Mexico, or perhaps all Indian women living on reservations. The point remains: a departure from descriptive data drawn from the census or some other broad-based source makes possible the manipulation of results to emphasize progress or problems.

What, then, do these three tables show about minority progress? The answer must be equivocal. Most subgroups of minority males are improving somewhat compared with Anglo males, especially if they have the same work-related characteristics. There is less progress if we look at per capita income on the basis of households: on that measure, all four minorities earn only about half the salaries of Anglo males. Women and female-headed households fare much worse; there is simply no case for progress at all, except a mild improvement for black women. Even when the work-related characteristics are controlled, women do badly—and worse than before. Whatever else the fabled American melting pot can do, it does not yet melt women. And it is accepting minority women even less readily than it did sixteen years ago.

But medians and means tell only part of the story. The two ends, top and bottom, of the income distribution curves for minorities may be very different indeed. Wilson argues that, for black people, both the top of the curve and the bottom are rather strange, and findings from the U.S. Civil Rights Commission bear him out. College educated black men very nearly match (80%) the earnings of comparable Anglos, but college educated black women reach only 65 percent of the earnings of college-educated Anglo men. Other minorities do much worse. College-educated Indian and Hispanic men and Mexican American women fall somewhere in between the "observed" and "hypothetical" ratios (reported in Table 1A and 1C). College-educated Puerto Rican and Indian women do very badly—and it must be remembered that even black men and Chicano women (the highest achieving) were only a third as likely to complete college as are Anglo men.[35] The top 10 percent of the minority earners thus earn notably less than the top 10 percent of the Anglo wage earners.[36]

At the bottom end, it is enough to say that minority families are from two to five times as likely as Anglo families to be living in poverty.[37] Here the figures rapidly become meaningless, because a number of state and federal supportive measures build an income "floor" high enough so that minority poor are not significantly poorer than Anglos.

Minorities and Classes: Some Special Issues

Unfortunately, these aggregate measures tell us very little about the processes that affect the subgroups of people who reach certain occupations and use the income. And, of course, it has little to do with the experience of these people. What, then, is the impact on American minorities and on American society?

Elites: The Neglected Theme

Even coupling the word *elite* with the word *minority* sounds like a bad joke. American experiments in appointing black men and women to high offices are hesitant and trivial: every appointment is still a "first" and something remarkable, and such appointments rarely go to the still largely unknown and untried Chicanos, Puerto Ricans, and Native Americans. Black appointments usually symbolize the growing importance of minorities (at least of blacks) to the fortunes of major political parties. In the corporate world, the alleged new movement toward corporate responsibility has produced almost nothing. In 1976 a study of five thousand positions on boards of directors or positions of authority showed only fifteen blacks, a tiny number indeed, but a substantial increase from an unbelievable *two* persons in 1970. This study did not try to measure the Mexican Americans, Puerto Ricans, or Indians in positions of national leadership, although there are very few.[38]

But behind this dismal picture there are some interesting changes. Blacks listed in *Who's Who in America* in 1924–25 and in 1974–75 show a very great change (no other minority was studied). The earlier base of achievement was a castelike black subsystem of segregated churches, colleges, and universities. After fifty years, the *Who's Who* listings show greater participation in national organizations.[39] But these listings still are peculiar: entertainers and sports figures account for almost a third of the black achievers in the 1970s. There is little relationship to national leadership, for black leaders are largely symbolic. Unless such celebrity is converted to another kind of achievement (such as Jackie Robinson's), it is transient and even somewhat questionable.[40]

In the lower, but still important, policy-making positions of the federal civil service (grades 14 to 18), minorities (blacks) were less grossly underrepresented. Social welfare bureaucracies have 6.6 percent black leaders. But in other bureaucracies, blacks were only 2.7 percent.[41] This rather peculiar distribution of policy-making blacks should be remembered in considering their much larger presence in local government elites. The black mayor is a phenomenon of the 1970s, along with the "black politician class."[42] Yet demographic shifts of blacks to the cities do not quite explain the increase in black elected officials. Few of the cities with black mayors have populations that are more than half black. Nor is the black electorate growing very rapidly, even after the mobilization of the civil rights movement of the 1960s; black voter participation dropped drastically in the North and West between 1964 and 1976.[43]

To follow the mystery of the black mayors a bit farther: many of the cities with black mayors are "distressed"—a bit of urbanist jargon summarizing the more obvious signals of deterioration. These include fiscal problems, many of them caused by the need to provide more public service at higher costs against a fixed or even declining local resource base.[44] Under such circumstances, it is difficult to see the new black politician class as a move toward some kind of vague community control. The old-fashioned organized political party has given way to a set of bureaucracies that are quite dependent on federal politics.[45] Black politicians must not only find substitutes for strong local power bases, but also usually lack strong bases with local white-controlled corporate powers. Many of these cities have "weak mayor" institutions, and thus the political problems of the mayors may be severe.[46] In sum, the new black politician class, especially in troubled cities, is a sad reminder of some of the more cynical black prophets of the 1960s: "The immediate authority is loyalist Black, and the ultimate authority is the white. . . . The Government will allow community control, as long as it determines the framework, philosophy, hiring policies and finances."[47]

Even if the black political elite is thin, no other minority has approached even this level of electoral leadership in local government. A few Puerto Ricans are visible in the New York metropolitan area, but they have gathered virtually no political strength anywhere else, even in Chicago, where their numbers are considerable. Native Americans are invisible in urban politics.

The pattern for Chicanos is rather different because of their historical roots. In certain parts of the nation they were not even outsiders. Rather, as in New Mexico, the peculiarities of the Anglo conquest gave upper-status Hispanics political visibility on the state and local levels. Not only do they elect many local officials in the more obscure counties of New Mexico, but they continue to be represented on the state level as well. In other states, especially California, political representation was never restored after the conquest. Even by 1980 the vast Chicano population of Los Angeles had no elected representation at the city or county level, and very little in the state legislature. Chicano urban politics in California

started in the environment of progressive "nonpartisan" reforms, a style that tended to work against the development of the machine-style politics typical of Eastern cities. In the late 1970s the large number of foreign-born Mexicans also clouded the political picture.

It is yet too early, even in 1980, for the black political elite to represent much more than a platform for rhetoric. This is also probably true for the Puerto Ricans. Chicano elites are in a far more equivocal position. Many remnants of the old colonial forms, including the colonial exclusion, still bedevil the few political elite.

The Middle Classes: Bitter Controversy

Minority middle-class citizens always face two sharp dilemmas: first, individual attainments may be at the expense of the poor masses of their own group; second, they may either ally with, or dissociate themselves from, minority causes. Nearly every person in the minority elite shows some kind of conflict or estrangement over the problem of identification. The two Hispanic groups were blessed (or cursed) with a strong middle class already in place. Each traced its growth to the early colonialism of the Spanish conquest, and neither doubted its superiority to the *peones*, an opinion generally shared by the incoming Anglo conquerors. One of the long-standing consequences was a pattern for social acceptability by the dominant Anglos that for a century kept upwardly mobile Texas and California Chicanos resolutely claiming "pure" Spanish ancestry.

Neither the blacks nor the Native Americans could gain acceptance through such social fictions, nor could more than a handful pass as white. For both, the dominating passion was a desire not to be confused with lower-class people having lower-class traits. The pervasive context of race prejudice even in 1899 prompted W. E. B. DuBois to write, "As a class they feel strongly the centrifugal forces of class repulsion among their own people, and, indeed, are compelled to feel it in sheer self defense. . . . They shrink from all such display as will expose them to the veiled insult and deprivation which the masses suffer."[48] A similar Indian pattern often involved a middle class deeply involved with the administration of Indian lands. Often it led to patterns of intermarriage.[49] By the 1950s, E. Franklin Frazier saw the "black bourgeoisie" as people who lived in a world of make-believe, struggling for status in a segregated and artificial "Society" based on nothing more substantial than "the crumbs of philanthropy, the salaries of public servants, and what could be squeezed from the meager earnings of Negro workers."[50] This was a caricature of the white society from which they were barred, but to which this quasi-middle-class black community yearned to belong. Frazier's vivid portrayal of the fantasy world enraged many American blacks.[51]

The life-styles of the black, Puerto Rican, Chicanos, and Indian bourgeoisie no longer much interest social scientists. The "social whirl" may persist, but its symbolic meaning has declined significantly since the middle of the 1960s. At least in part, this is a result of the civil rights movement, which emphasized racial solidarity across class lines. At least in its black version, many middle-class people worked in the front lines. For blacks (and also to a somewhat lesser extent for Chicanos), the movement consciously attempted to legitimate stereotyped lower-class physical and cultural attributes. Thus class distinctions lost some of their nastiest edges. By 1980 it was less necessary for the middle class to dissociate itself from the lower classes.

But the controversy has shifted elsewhere. The new question is whether discrimination and institutionalized racism remain viable diagnoses of the acknowledged problems of minorities. The fury generated by Frazier started all over again with Wilson's *The Declining Significance of Race*. Wilson puts the question simply enough: Do Americans discriminate against blacks—or is it that they simply discriminate against lower-class people? He argues that in our contemporary industrial society, the overt and explicit efforts by whites to subjugate blacks do not really account for the lack of black progress. In essence, he argues that black work-related characteristics and the segmented labor market together limit black access. Wilson does not deal with the racism built into the schools and the housing segregation that generate and preserve these work-related characteristics. Nor does he acknowledge the remaining income disparities suffered by middle-class as well as lower-class blacks.[52]

Much of the controversy over Wilson's book turns on his unwillingness to accept affirmative action as the major factor in black progress. Wilson implies that, since college-educated blacks earn incomes close to that of whites, "benign neglect" would not affect their progress. For Wilson, affirmative action is only one factor. Other experts argue that affirmative action is the *sine qua non*, and they see Wilson's arguments as jeopardizing not only affirmative action programs, but also policy decisions designed to help the poor of the inner city. It may be true that government policies of the 1960s helped black and Hispanic middle classes more than they helped the poor (a charge hotly disputed by Sar Levitan and others).[53] Yet, some real aid was received by the poor. Its importance is obscured by Wilson's argument just at a time when market solutions to poverty have become political orthodoxy.

Wilson's argument has its own little twist. He fails to note that a major portion of black middle-class attainment rests on middle-class occupations that involve service to the poor—presumably the black poor. By 1976 almost 54 percent of all black professionals, administrators, and technicians were working for the government, mostly on the state and local level. Almost all of these jobs were in education, social welfare, housing, health, and community development.[54] Education accounts for 32.2 percent of all such jobs, more than any other category. This is a very large increase since 1960, both in the numbers involved and also in the concentration in public social welfare work.

There is good reason to believe that the base of other minorities is much the same. The *Trabajadores de la Raza* are the Hispanic counterpart of the National Association of Black Social Workers, and very nearly as old. Almost ten thousand Hispanic professionals are working in the Elementary and Secondary Education Act's Title VII bilingual education programs.

The criminal justice system also is becoming a major source of professional jobs for minorities, at the same time that the proportion of minorities in the prisons is increasing: minorities have begun to get jobs as police and probation officers, correctional guards, and parole officers. The minority stake in this billion-dollar "growth industry" is increasing. Taxpayer revolts that threaten the welfare bureaucracies do not threaten the criminal justice system. Criminal justice jobs increased by 59 percent between 1965 and 1976 as new prisons were built in the third great wave of prison-building in the United States.[55]

In earlier days, new ethnic groups used the urban political machines for movement into the class system—a famous example is the Irish policeman. But Steven Erie sees the new minority "welfare economy" as a distinctly different way of using the local political system. There may be more payoff in terms of jobs, but there is far less overall control. Clients get their favors from an impersonal bureaucracy that happens to be staffed by fellow minority group members rather than local wardheelers. It is funded in the state capital or in Washington, and local minority bureaucrats have no influence at that level. Erie thinks this remote-control effect explains the lowered voting rates of minority citizens in recent years.[56]

Minority businesses usually have a small and shaky minority foundation. Black and Hispanic business enterprise traditionally has built on the special tastes and needs of a community and on the existence of segregation itself. Some small Chicano food enterprises have grown into large and successful corporations, but most such opportunities have been preempted by earlier arrivals. Mom-and-Pop *tiendas* and restaurants survive in many ethnic enclaves from the South Bronx to East Los Angeles, but small enterprises are hard-pressed to compete with fast-food chains and supermarkets. The decline of the black-owned insurance companies is a cautionary tale. Thirteen of the thirty-eight black insurance companies founded before 1940 and doing business in 1944 disappeared by 1975 and must be presumed defunct. Their dependence on small policies made them fatally less efficient than large companies.[57]

Overall, then, middle-class status attainments are tenuous. The fragility of this base (affirmative action and fellow ethnics) is easily overestimated in the glow of new accomplishment. And unfortunately, this base is deeply intertwined with government and politics, and is thus vulnerable both to the winds of changing policy and the willingness of the general population to pay substantial taxes. In some ways it is narrower than before: in their time, Irish policemen and Italian sanitation workers served the entire city. It is more common now for minority

workers to serve minority areas. The last change is very slow and paradoxical: as minorities increasingly are identified with the big city itself, the cities are beginning to be seen as minority places.

The American Underclass: Is It a Proletariat?

The word *proletariat* derived from the Latin *proles*, "offspring." In Roman society it was the class "regarded as contributing nothing to the state except offspring."[58] "Underclass" is a trendy term for an ancient concept and now describes people who are marginal to the labor force, who move in and out of dead-end jobs, and may live on the income generated through transfer payments. They make up a surplus labor force that (unlike the reserves of teenagers and the second-earner women) is a kind of community, bounded either by its position at the bottom or margins of the economy, and in America, by virtue of the bonds of ethnicity or race. Because of race, they are also unacceptable, and thus disqualified to work for some employers.[59]

The important connotation in both "underclass" and "proletariat" is the idea of permanency. The dual labor market implies such a permanence. Unskilled, but hardworking, "peasants" are recruited by urban employers (and by institutional brokers like the Bureau of Indian Affairs) who need docile labor for dead-end jobs, where every tiny margin of profit can be squeezed out of the worker by evading normal benefit payments and paying substandard wages. Some of these workers are sojourners and will return home—to Mexico, rural Texas, Puerto Rico, small Southern towns, and the reservations—but many or even most will remain in the city.[60] Their children often do miserably in the inadequate central city schools. They drop out, and may be functionally illiterate even after ten years of school. They find themselves unqualified for jobs in an increasingly demanding, credential-inflated, core-sector labor market. They are resentful and unwilling to take the "slave jobs" held by their parents until they are well into their thirties or even forties.

Some of these second generation children will make their way into core-sector jobs, often through family connections with unionized trades like upholstery and meat-cutting, which at one time were open to Chicanos in such cities as Los

Angeles. Or there may be public help in the form of carefully designed employment and training programs. Others will accept the slave jobs of their parents. There are, however, some successes in the secondary labor market. Yet, careful examination shows how very limited are the "good" jobs. And perhaps more important, there is always an endless supply of docile first-generation immigrants.

Of the groups considered here, only the Mexicans have "undocumented" immigrants among their newcomers. There has been a substantial attempt to get American policymakers to think of such immigrants as an "external proletariat" that goes home to villages in Mexico. The worker is pictured as a normal young male venturing forth into American markets in search of wages.[61] It is true that most of those deported by the Immigration and Naturalization Service fit this profile. Such men are highly visible in the car washes and restaurants of the Southwest and in the huge chain hotels. But there is also good evidence that the undocumented include many women, some of them the huge army of unnoticed and uncounted maids in private homes. There are also many families, and people of a wide range of ages and skills.[62] The process of proletarianization is not the least bit speculative for many of these people. A 1975 Texas law debars education at public expense for the children of undocumented aliens unless they pay tuition—in Houston, a prohibitive $172 per month. Although the law is under heavy assault from some civil rights groups, in 1980 approximately one hundred thousand children were kept out of the public school system.[63] The children of a notably familistic population are being pushed into an inevitable proletarian future. The idea that low-wage Mexicans "go home to Mexico for Christmas" was popular in California in the 1920s, and is an interesting way of allowing society (and the practical men of the county governments) to deny the reality of the millions of Mexican Americans living permanently in their midst.

Black, Chicano, Puerto Rican, and Indian newcomers tend to live close to their compatriots in relatively clear-cut urban enclaves. Second-generation young men gather in groups and give themselves emotional and psychological support in a defeating world. The street life-style that develops has been semi-institutionalized in metropolitan barrios and ghettos throughout the nation. The gangs have existed in some areas since the 1920s and in other areas are just beginning. It is a life-style that provides opportunities for income through the illegal sale of drugs and narcotics, petty gambling, or other victimless crimes. At home, it is possible to survive in the tripartite economy—occasional jobs in the secondary labor market, unemployment benefits or welfare, or both, and illegal marketing—from which they and other people in the household draw income.

But this street life-style does not necessarily mean one is an outcast or rebel. Black gang boys in Chicago help their mothers at home far more than white gang boys.[64] Chicano gang boys also tend to be integrated into family and community networks. This interaction with the "square" community was fundamental to much of the self-help activity among minority prisoners in the early 1960s and 1970s, and its pervasiveness buttressed much of the community and family support for the community-based gang and ex-prisoner programs during the same period. In the minority ghettos and barrios, the ambivalence toward problem youngsters is not that of the romantic for "rebels," nor is it a tolerance for deviants. It is simply that, statistically, so many respectable, traditional, religious, first-generation black, Mexican, and Puerto Rican families have such sons. Further, even though their personal and network resources are considerably depleted by repeated trips to prison, many of these boys do settle down ultimately to more or less conventional life-styles.[65]

The problems of the second generation repeat in subsequent generations. It becomes more and more difficult to sustain the sense of morale in a minority community, the sense that degradation has not overtaken the community. The feeling of being an underclass grows, both internally and externally. Ironically, it is more difficult to sustain morale if the new workers entering a community differ from the existing minority population, as, for example, when black neighborhoods in New York must also accommodate Puerto Rican and Dominican immigrants. To the old residents—the immigrants from the rural South—the community appears to be deteriorating. The newcomers do not at all resemble themselves when they were new and young. But in the barrios of East Los Angeles, the flow of new Mexican workers from Mexico confirms the sense of worth of the old workers and the validity of their demands upon their children. Mainland Puerto Ricans probably keep up their morale both by virtue of the influx of "new" Puerto Ricans and by substantial visiting and return migration.

It is also in the lower levels of the American class system that female-headed households begin to be significant. Writers on class are quite reasonably accused of providing a "theory of white males." There always have been more black women in the labor force than other minority women, but, ironically, other groups are catching up. (More than half of the black women in this nation worked in 1977, compared with 47.4% of the white women.) More important, when one talks about "the American poverty class," to a large extent one is talking about households headed by women.[66] In 1976 women headed one quarter of the poor Native American households and a third of the poor black households.[67] Some critics argue that these statistics are spurious and that the males are concealed.[68] But it is still true that female-headed households are far more likely to be poor, and this is especially true of minority households. More precisely, minority female households are five times more likely to be poor than Anglo households.[69] Furthermore, as noted in Table 1, minority women did not make many gains during the last twenty years. It is some small comfort that, as some studies suggest, there is more barter economy in female Puerto Rican and black households than the average minority household with a male head. Possibly female adaptation to the underclass is quite different from that of men. This, in turn, has some unexplored implications about the long-standing controversy over the effects of life in a female-headed household.[70]

The Meaning of Class and Race

It is ironic that the great diversity of American minorities is just now beginning to be noticed— just as their cultures and diversity are beginning to be lost in the urban industrial world that has characterized America since World War II. Their fate is now inextricably linked both to that industrial world and to the cities themselves. An immigrant history becomes an industrial, urban history, modified more or less by federal and local actions and by the economic climate for the urban industrial base. The real architect of the minority underclass, the marginal employer, will surely continue to import docile, cheap labor. The children of these workers will perpetuate themselves, being changed only in small numbers by the same crippled and inept institutions. This may be an unpleasant prospect, but then, nothing useful is gained by pretending, either in academia or in Washington, that the traditional ladders of a mythic past continue to work.

The euphoria generated during the 1960s and the early 1970s emerged from a sense of progress. Progress meant both movement out of traditionally oppressive places in society and frontal attacks on the agents of traditional oppression. Chicano farm workers thought of the farm worker movement as an economic struggle. Its other Chicano and Anglo supporters usually thought of it as a status struggle against traditional oppression, like the black civil rights struggle in the South and the militant Native American reawakening. But once these movements ran up against the tough bastions of the central city, they began to run out of steam—and just as important, out of support from nonminority sympathizers. For themselves, minorities see the struggle in the cities as critical. The victories to date are so valuable, however, that the present minority agenda is simply to continue that battle and consolidate that apparent progress.

Interestingly, nostalgia for the old lost places is still important. Indians and Puerto Ricans particularly are nostalgic for what has been lost by the migration away from "home." If the social and economic oppression is alleviated and the "New South" becomes something more than a public relations expression, if the reservations could become self-sustaining, if Puerto Rico could hire its own natives, if Mexico could channel its natural resources efficiently enough to sustain a reasonable standard of living, if the rural Southwest could overcome generations of discrimination and limited local opportunities—then there might be less deadly certainty about the issue of these four minorities in the American class system. Those who wished to live in their homes could do so—and with decency.

The truth is that the notion of regenerating the traditional places is nothing much more than daydreaming. It is the urban, industrial world that is the future locale for most American minorities. In turn, they will become a numerical majority in many cities. To the extent that the industrial and institutional bases of these settings can be restructured, there is reason to hope. If they continue unchanged, the prospect is not encouraging.

REFERENCES

I wish to thank A. Moore, S. Erie, J. Long, R. Meadows, F. Mittelbach, H. Pachon, and D. Vigil for critical comments on an early draft of this essay and for help in locating sources outside my field. Criticisms from other contributors to this issue were also very helpful. Burton Moore provided invaluable editorial advice.

1. The "biracialist assumption," often noted in discussions among Hispanics, is so labeled by Clara Rodriguez from a Puerto Rican point of view. *The Ethnic Queue in the U.S.: The Case of the Puerto Ricans* (San Francisco: R and E Research Associates, 1974). Margo Conk (personal communication) notes: "The history of racial classification in the census goes back to the Three Fifths Compromise, which mandated that slaves be counted separately from free people for legislative apportionment in Congress. Questions on place of birth were added in 1850; in 1890, a question on the respondents' ability to speak English was added, and was modified by 1920 to include a question on 'mother tongue.' The purpose of all of these questions was to separate the population into white and nonwhite, and native white and foreign white populations. Any smaller group which did not fit into these gross distinctions was forced into one or another category. The bureau invented 'other colored' in 1890, which came to include Indians, Chinese, Japanese, Mexicans (1930 only), Korean, Filipinos, and Hindus (1930). See U.S. Bureau of the Census, *Population and Housing Inquiries in the U.S. Decennial Census, 1790–1970* (Washington, D.C.: U.S. Government Printing Office, 1973); Leon Truesdell, *The Development of Punch Card Tabulation in the Bureau of the Census, 1890–1940* (Washington, D.C.: U.S. Government Printing Office, 1965)." The erratic history of Hispanic identifiers is discussed in *Cuantos Somos: A Demographic Study of the Mexican-American Population*, Charles H. Teller, et al. (eds.) (Austin:

University of Texas, Center for Mexican American Studies, 1977).

2. As discussed by Jessie Bernard in *Sociology of Community* (Glenview, Ill.: Foresman, 1973). This is, of course, in ironic contrast to the Marxian view that class distinctions are inherently conflictful.

3. W. Lloyd Warner and Leo Srole, *The Social System of American Ethnic Groups* (New Haven: Yale University Press, 1945). See Beverly and Otis Dudley Duncan, "Minorities and the Process of Stratification," *American Sociological Review*, 33 (June 1968): 356–64; David Featherman, "The Socio-Economic Achievement of White Religio-Ethnic Subgroups," *American Sociological Review*, 36 (April 1971): 207–22; and David Featherman and Robert Hauser, *Opportunity and Change* (New York: Academic Press, 1978) for the documentation of ethnic differences in status attainment. There are anomalies: the "new" Russian (Jewish) origin persons were relatively well off, and "old" Irish-origin persons lag behind, for example.

4. For an example of this logic: in 1971, 19 percent of nonwhites were poor, with incomes below $3000. The last time that high a proportion of whites was poor was in 1951—twenty years earlier. Thus, the implication goes, it may take nonwhites another twenty years to reach the current poverty level of whites. These time-gap analyses can become very elaborate, and while always interesting analytic devices, they can produce very spurious results for the unwary reader. They do *not* tell us how long it will take for minorities to catch up, just how many years they are behind. For a recent illustration, see Anne Horowitz, "The Pattern and Causes of Changes in White-Nonwhite Income Differences: 1947–1972," in *Patterns of Racial Discrimination: VII Employment and Income*, George M. Von Furstenberg, et al. (eds.) (Lexington, Mass.: Lexington Books, 1974).

5. This tradition includes works such as Frantz Fanon, *The Wretched of the Earth* (New York: Grove Press, 1963); Albert Memmi, *The Colonizer and the Colonized* (Boston: Beacon Press, 1965); Kenneth Clark, *Dark Ghetto* (New York: Harper and Row, 1965); Joan W. Moore, "Internal Colonialism; The Case of the Mexican Americans," *Social Problems*, 17 (Spring 1970): 463–72; Robert Blauner, *Racial Oppression in America* (New York: Harper and Row, 1972); Edward Murguia, *Assimilation, Colonialism, and the Mexican American People* (Austin: University of Texas Press, 1975); Mario Berrera, *Race and Class in the Southwest* (South Bend: University of Notre Dame Press, 1979); William Tabb, *The Political Economy of the Black Ghetto* (New York: W. W. Norton, 1970). See Joan W. Moore, "American Minorities and 'New Nation' Perspectives," *Pacific Sociological Review*, 19 (October, 1976): 447–67, for a critique.

6. See Thomas Sowell, "Ethnicity in a Changing

America," *Daedalus*, Winter, 1978, pp. 213–38; Nathan Glazer and Daniel P. Moynihan, *Ethnicity* (Cambridge, Mass: Harvard University Press, 1975); and Nathan Glazer, *Affirmative Discrimination* (New York: Basic Books, 1975) for variations on this theme.

7. This section was developed from materials prepared by Pauli Taylor-Boyd.

8. Estelle Fuchs and Robert J. Havighurst, *To Live on This Earth: American Indian Education* (New York: Anchor Books, 1972); Alan L. Sorkin, *The Urban American Indian* (Lexington, Mass: Lexington Books, 1978); Joseph H. Stauss and Lawrence Clinton, "The Bureau of Indian Affairs, Adult Vocational Training Program: Success by Whose Criteria?" in *Chicanos and Native Americans: The Territorial Minorities*, Rudolph O. de la Garza (ed.) (Englewood Cliffs, N.J.: Prentice Hall, 1972). Samuel Stanley and Robert K. Thomas, "Current Social and Demographic Trends among North American Indians," in *Annals*, 436 (March, 1978); 111–20. For New York, B. Hawk, personal communication.

9. Antonia Pantoja, "Puerto Rican Migration," cited in Rodriguez, *The Ethnic Queue*, pp. 74–75.

10. See Joan W. Moore, *Mexican Americans* (Englewood Cliffs, N.J.: Prentice Hall, 1975).

11. See Richard L. Morrill and O. Fred Donaldson, "Geographical Perspectives on the History of Black America," in *Black America: Geographic Perspectives*, Robert T. Ernst and Lawrence Hugg (eds.) (New York: Anchor Books, 1976); and Thomas A. Clark, *Blacks in Suburbs* (New Brunswick, N.J.: Rutgers University Press, 1979).

12. Harold M. Rose, "The Origin and Pattern of Development of Urban Black Social Areas," in Ernst and Hugg, *Black America*.

13. Suburbanization of blacks is dealt with in Clark, *Blacks in Suburbs*; Harold M. Rose, *Black Suburbanization: Access to Improved Quality of Life or Maintenance of the Status Quo?* (Cambridge, Mass.: Ballinger Publishing Co., 1976); and Robert W. Lake, "Racial Transition and Black Homeownership in American Suburbs," in *Annals*, 441 (January 1979): 142–56.

14. See Moore, *Mexican Americans*.

15. Bennett Harrison and Edward Hill, "The Changing Structure of Jobs in Older and Younger Cities," in *Central City Economic Development*, Benjamin Chinitz (ed.) (Cambridge, Mass: Abt Books, 1979); B. L. Weinstein testimony in "Regional Impact of Current Recession," Hearings before the Subcommittee on Fiscal and Intergovernmental Policy of the Joint Economic Committee, U.S. Congress, October 16, 1979.

16. Alfred J. Watkins and David C. Perry, "Regional Change and the Impact of Uneven Urban Development," in *The Rise of the Sunbelt Cities*, David C. Perry and Alfred J. Watkins (eds.) (Beverly Hills, Calif: Sage Publications, 1977). See also Kirkpatrick Sale, *Power Shift* (New York: Vintage, 1975), esp. pp. 46–48; and George Sternlieb and James W. Hughes (eds.), *Post-Industrial America: Metropolitan Decline and Inter-Regional Job Shifts*, (New Brunswick, N.J.: Center for Urban Policy Research, 1976).

17. Watkins and Perry, "Regional Change."

18. William Grigsby et al. (eds.), *Re-Thinking Housing and Community Development Policy* (Philadelphia: University of Pennsylvania Press, 1977) p. 67ff.

19. Bennett Harrison, *Urban Economic Development: Suburbanization, Minority Opportunity and the Condition of the Central City* (Washington, D.C.: The Urban Institute, 1974), p. 27ff.

20. Charlotte Fremon argues that the new central city jobs were being taken by commuters from the suburbs: *Central City and Suburban Unemployment Growth* (Washington, D.C.: The Urban Institute), cited in Harrison, Ibid.

21. Franklin James, "Recession and Recovery in Urban Economics," unpublished paper cited in Grigsby et al. (eds.), *Re-Thinking Housing*.

22. Ibid., p. 128.

23. Denis F. Johnston, "The U.S. Labor Force in a Changing Economy: Implications for Manpower Policy and Research," in *Manpower Research and Labor Economics*, Gordon I. Swanson and Jon Michaelson (eds.) (Beverly Hills, Calif: Sage Publications, 1979).

24. Marcia Freedman, "The Competition for Good Jobs," unpublished ms., 1979, p. 3.

25. Johnston, "The U.S. Labor Force."

26. William Wilson, *The Declining Significance of Race* (Chicago: University of Chicago Press, 1978). Between 1960 and 1970 government workers increased from 15.4 percent to 17.7 percent of the labor force, with a peak in 1975 of 19.1 percent and a slight decline by 1978 to 18.4 percent. These figures are drawn from Bureau of Labor Statistics monthly *Employment and Earnings* reports, summarized in *Statistical Abstracts*, pp. 412–16, and differ slightly from those utilized by Wilson, though they show the same trends. Reference 41 gives an analysis of the minority patterns in government employment.

27. As discussed in Chicano Pinto Research Project, *Final Report*, 1979.

28. Michael Piore, "Conceptualization of Labor Market Reality" in *Manpower Research and Labor Economics*, Swanson and Michaelson (eds.), p. 111. This discussion of the segmented labor market also draws on David Gordon, *Theories of Poverty and Underemployment* (Lexington, Mass.: D.C. Heath, 1972); and Marcia Freedman, *Labor Markets: Segments and Shelters* (Montclair, N.J.: Allanheld, Osmun, 1976).

29. Larry H. Long in "Reply to Norton," *American Sociological Review*, 44 (February, 1979): 179–81,

cites half a dozen statistical studies of this "generational" pattern and a handful of attitudinal ones.

30. Steven P. Erie and Michael K. Brown, "Social Policy and the Emergence of the Black Social Welfare Economy," paper presented at National Conference for Public Administration, 1979.

31. Wilson, *Declining Significance of Race*, p. 110.

32. For the barrios, see Joan W. Moore et al., *Homeboys: Gangs, Drugs and Prison in the Barrios of Los Angeles* (Philadelphia: Temple University Press, 1978). For the ghetto, see Bettylou Valentine, *Hustling and Other Hard Work* (New York: The Free Press, 1978).

33. The researchers used a multiple regression technique by which mean values for majority males on each of the six salient variables (educational attainment, prestige score for the occupation, mean income for the worker's state, number of weeks worked during the preceding year, number of hours worked in the week preceding the census date of April 1, and age) were substituted for the observed value of each variable, retaining the "minority coefficient" (or b value) for each variable in the equation. Appendix B. Commission on Civil Rights, *Social Indicators*.

34. Edward Banfield, *The Unheavenly City* (Boston: Little, Brown, 1968) p. 70.

35. Thus the college completion ratios were as follow: black males 0.32; Mexican American males 0.32; Puerto Rican males 0.18; American Indian/Alaskan Native males 0.24; black females 0.32; Mexican American females 0.15; Puerto Rican females 0.12; American Indian/Alaskan Native females 0.12; majority females 0.65. Commission on Civil Rights, *Social Indicators*, p. 14.

36. A. Wohlstetter and S. Coleman, "Race Differences in Income," in *Racial Discrimination in Economic Life*. A. Pascal (ed.) (Lexington, Mass: Lexington Books 1972), cited in Anne Horowitz, "The Pattern and Causes of Changes in White-Nonwhite Income Differences: 1947–1972," in *Patterns of Racial Discrimination*, George M. Von Furstenberg et al. (eds.).

37. Commission on Civil Rights, *Social Indicators*, p. 62.

38. Thomas R. Dye in *Who's Running America?* (Englewood Cliffs, N.J.: Prentice-Hall, 1979) studied the one hundred largest corporations in each epoch, the twenty-five largest banks, the twenty largest transportation, utilities, and communications corporations, and the ten largest insurance companies. Blacks appointed to corporate boards in the 1970s were primarily men who were executives of black organizations, e.g., Vernon Jordan of the National Urban League and Vivian W. Henderson, president of Clark College in Atlanta.

39. Stanley Lieberson and Donna K. Carter, "Making It in America: Differences between Eminent Blacks and White Ethnic Groups," *American Sociological Review*, 44 (June, 1979): 347–66.

40. One of the more vitriolic attacks on such leaders labels them "eunuch leaders," appointed by whites, members of a leadership that excludes those who can "muster people," i.e., blacks with large followings but lower-class styles of leadership. Nathan Hare, *Black Anglo Saxons* (New York: Collier, 1965).

41. Michael K. Brown and Steven P. Erie, "Administrative Power and the Black Social Welfare Economy: The Political Legacy of the War on Poverty" (presented at ASPA meetings, 1980). Blacks formed 25.2 percent of the total work force in federal social welfare agencies in 1977, and only 14.6 percent of other agencies. Social welfare agencies include DHEW, DOL, VA, HUD, and CSA.

42. The phrase is from Martin Kilson, "Blacks and Neo-Ethnicity in America," in Glazer and Moynihan, *Ethnicity*, p. 257. The census publication on the social and economic status of blacks notes that the surge in elected black officials (from 103 in 1964 to 3503 in 1975) is the first such surge since Reconstruction (1869–1901). U.S. Bureau of the Census, *The Social and Economic Status of the Black Population in the United States: An Historical View, 1790-1978*, p. 148. No such surge has appeared for Hispanics.

43. Erie and Brown, "Social Policy." Black voter participation in the North and West dropped by 16.7 percent, that of whites by 10.4 percent. In the South, black voter participation increased by 4.5 percent, while that of whites declined by 0.6 percent.

44. Eric L. Stowe, "Urban Issues in the Late 1970s: A Metropolitan Perspective," in *The Need for a National Urban Policy: Occasional Papers in Housing and Community Affairs*, Robert Paul Boynton (ed.), vol. 4 (Washington, D.C.: U.S. Department of Housing and Urban Development: Office of Policy Development and Research, July 1979), p. 182. Urban fiscal stress varies widely: some states support public social services at a higher level than others; larger and older cities have higher costs by virtue of scale and quality of infrastructure items, e.g., sewers. Western and some Southern cities have been able to alleviate some stress by annexing new revenue-generating territories, but most Northern and Midwestern cities have been hemmed in by the suburbs.

45. Steven P. Erie, "Two Faces of Ethnic Power: Comparing the Irish and Black Experiences," *Polity*, 13 (2) (Winter 1980): 261:84.

46. Mack Jones, "Black Political Empowerment in Atlanta: Myth and Reality," and Herrington Bryce, et al., "Housing Problems of Black Mayor Cities," *Annals*, 439 (September, 1976); 90–117 and 80–89.

47. W. E. Anderson, "Revolutionary Black Nationalism and the Pan-African Idea," in *The Black 70s*, Floyd B. Barbour (ed.) (Boston: Porter Sargent Publisher, 1970), p. 101.

48. *The Philadelphia Negro*, p. 177, cited in Gunnar Myrdal, *An American Dilemma* (New York: Harper and Row, 1944) p. 1388.

49. Stanley and Thomas, "Current Social and Demographic Trends"; Murray Wax in *Indian Americans* (Englewood Cliffs, N.J.: Prentice-Hall, 1971) discussed the "Mixedbloods" who served as middlemen in reservation BIA agencies and whose descendants are some of the urban middle class.

50. E. Franklin Frazier, *Black Bourgeoisie* (New York: The Free Press, 1956), p. 234.

51. See, for example, Floyd McKissick's and Oliver Cox's introductions to Nathan Hare's *Black Anglo Saxons*. Cox argues that these caricatures should be seen as "vital solutions to social situations" (p. 19), and McKissick sees them as a "response to the demands of a schizophrenic white society which requires that they think and act white in order to survive but continue to reject them because they are Black" (p. 12).

52. See *The Caste and Class Controversy*, Charles V. Willie (ed.) (Bayside, N.Y.: General Hall, 1979), especially Charles Paine, "On the Declining—and Increasing—Significance of Race," and Thomas F. Pettigrew, "The Changing—Not Declining—Significance of Race."

53. Sar Levitan, *The Promise of Greatness* (Cambridge, Mass.: Harvard University Press, 1975).

54. Brown and Erie, "Administrative Power," p. 20.

55. *Jericho*, 19 (Winter 1979–80): 12. Eight hundred and eighty-four new correctional facilities were under construction or proposed, at an average cost of $7.69 million. *Jericho*, 18 (Fall, 1979): 12.

56. Erie, "Two Faces of Ethnic Power."

57. Data on Negro life insurance firms are from Joseph A. Pierce, *Negro Business and Business Education* (Westport, Conn.: Negro Universities Press, 1947), p. 325, and U.S. Bureau of the Census, *The Social and Economic Status of the Black Population*, p. 80; data on ownership structure are from p. 78.

58. *Oxford English Dictionary*.

59. See Anthony Giddens, *The Class Structure of Advanced Societies* (New York: Harper & Row, 1975), esp. p. 215 ff, for a history of this concept. The concept became fuzzier (as Marcia Freedman notes—unpublished ms.) as the term was adopted by mass media writers. It began to connote the "disreputable poor" rather than those struggling for survival, as in the *Time* cover story (August 29, 1977), which embodied Banfield's "lower class" stigma.

60. There is considerable variation in the rate of return. For the more easily traced Indians, 37 percent of the Navajos who migrated to Los Angeles between 1952 and 1961 were back on the reservation a few years later (Fuchs and Havighurst, *To Live on This Earth*, p. 277). Back-and-forth "sojourns" also characterize the patterns of many urban Indians, Southern-born blacks, Puerto Ricans, and Texas Mexicans. School dropouts also vary widely. One estimate places the Indian dropout rate in some cities as high as 80 percent (Sorkin, *The Urban American Indian*, p. 89).

61. Thus Daniel Bell (in Glazer and Moynihan, *Ethnicity*, p. 152) use the term "external proletariat" to refer to "large foreign minorities who are at the bottom rungs of the society and are effectively excluded from participation in the political life of the host countries." He is talking about European guest workers, but the concept (and the guest worker analogy) have been utilized heavily in discussions of Mexican undocumented workers, especially by Wayne Cornelius.

62. M. D. Van Arsdol, Jr., Joan W. Moore, and Susan H. Paulvir, "Social and Labor Force Characteristics of Undocumented Aliens Resident in Los Angeles County," (U.S.C. Population Laboratory, *Final Report*, 1979).

63. *The New York Times*, March 13, 1980.

64. James Short and Fred Strodtbeck, *Group Process and Gang Delinquency* (Chicago: University of Chicago Press, 1965).

65. This description is drawn from a 1979 study, funded by the National Institute on Drug Abuse (R01 DAO 1849–01), The Department of Labor (#21-06-78-18), and the Center for the Study of Metropolitan Problems, of Chicano "hard core" former gang members, all ex-offenders, and their families. See also Moore, et al., *Homeboys*, chapter 1. Marcia Freedman's "Work and the Underclass" (unpublished manuscript) and Bettylou Valentine's *Hustling and Other Hard Work* have also informed it.

66. Joan R. Acker, "Women and Stratification: A Case of Intellectual Sexism," *American Journal of Sociology*, 78 (January, 1973): 936–44.

67. Special tabulations of the Survey of Income and Education provided through the courtesy of Jose Hernandez.

68. Thus Bettylou Valentine argues that, because a minimal level of living requires more income than can be provided by welfare (work and hustling supply the missing cash), "women and children help to hide the men" whenever surveys or censuses are taken, to protect the source of income that men represent. *Hustling and Other Hard Work*, p. 124.

69. U.S. Commission on Civil Rights, *Social Indicators*, p. 62.

70. Carol Stack, *All Our Kin* (New York: Harper and Row, 1974), and for Puerto Ricans, Pablo Navarro

Hernandez, "The Structure of Puerto Rican Families in a Context of Migration and Poverty: An Ethnographic Description of a Number of Residents in El Barrio, New York City," Ph.D. dissertation, Teachers College, Columbia University, 1978.

34

Models of Pluralism: The New American Dilemma

Milton M. Gordon

Over a generation ago, Gunnar Myrdal, in his monumental study of this country's greatest and most salient issue in race relations—what was then referred to as "the Negro problem"—wrote of an "American dilemma"—the gap and implicit choice between the religious and political ideals of the American Creed which called for fair and just treatment of all people, regardless of race, creed, or color, and the overt practices of racial discrimination and prejudice directed by Whites toward Blacks which took place in the daily life of the American people. Thus this country stood at a crossroads whence it could choose to follow the existing pathway of racial discrimination and hostility or, conversely, make the decision to honor its best ideals and eliminate differential treatment of its people on the basis of race. The tension of this choice, declared Myrdal, existed not only between Americans of varying attitudes and persuasion, but also within the heart of the individual citizen.[1]

It is my contention that, at least at the level of formal governmental action, the United States of America, in the three and one half decades

since Myrdal published his great study, has moved decisively down the road toward implementing the implications of the American Creed for race relations, that this is a most important step (although it obviously does not remove all aspects of racially discriminatory treatment and prejudice from the institutions and private social relations of everyday American life), and that, with respect to racial and ethnic relations, America now faces a *new dilemma*—a dilemma which is oriented toward a choice of the *kind of group pluralism* which American governmental action and the attitudes of the American people will foster and encourage. After a brief discussion of the first part of this contention, I will turn to an explication of the components which make up each of these types of pluralism in the racial and ethnic arena.

Judicial Decisions

The great watershed event in the treatment of race in American society in the twentieth century was the *Brown* v. *Board of Education of Topeka* decision of the Supreme Court in 1954 dealing with state governmental action (and, also, by extension, municipal government action, since municipalities are legally creations of the state) in the racial area, and the companion *Bolling* v. *Sharpe* case dealing with the action of

Reprinted from "Models of Pluralism: The New American Dilemma," by Milton M. Gordon in vol. no. 454 of THE ANNALS of the American Academy of Political and Social Science. © 1981 by the American Academy of Political and Social Science.

the federal government in this area. Using the "equal protection of the laws" clause of the Fourteenth Amendment in the former case and the "due process of law" clause of the Fifth Amendment in the latter, the Court unanimously held that segregation of children in the public schools violated the Constitution of the United States. By implication, all other governmental action establishing segregation by race was also interpretable as unconstitutional. Thus the entire structure of "Jim Crow" laws segregating public facilities in the South by race and prohibiting racial intermarriage was now clearly without legal underpinning.

Although it took over a decade for successive case litigation to dismantle the formal Jim Crow apparatus (which had rested on the now repudiated *Plessy* v. *Ferguson* decision of 1896), and although many southern states dragged their feet in implementing educational and other forms of desegregation, the decisive implications of the *Brown* and the *Bolling* cases were clear from the start. No longer was the black man or woman, or anyone of a nonwhite racial category, to be designated by any branch of American government to receive rights and privileges inferior or separate from those of the white population. The Constitution was now declared to be racially impartial, a decision presumably reviving and endorsing the famous words of the remarkable Justice Harlan in his lonely dissent to the *Plessy* decision a half century earlier: "Our Constitution is color-blind, and neither knows nor tolerates classes among citizens."[2]

New Legislation and Aftermath

The impact of these momentous decisions of the Supreme Court in the 1950s was extended and solidified in the 1960s by several pieces of congressional legislation which Nathan Glazer has characterized as marking a "national consensus" on how to deal with racial and ethnic matters.[3] These were the Immigration Act of 1965 which removed all racial and national origins or ethnic considerations from our method of selecting immigrants for admission to the United States, and the Civil Rights Act of 1964 and the Voting Rights Act of 1965 which put the power of the federal government behind efforts to eliminate racial and ethnic discrimination in employment, voting, public accommodations, public facilities, and education. Instead of ushering in a new period of increased racial harmony and rapid peaceable integration, however, all of these events served to constitute a prelude to the outbreak of an unprecedented series of race riots in our major cities, the rise of black militancy, black cultural nationalism, and the "black power" movement, and through a sequence of presidential executive orders and later Supreme Court decisions, the emergence of the "affirmative action" procedure as a compensatory device for past discrimination and as a technique for ensuring mandated percentages of Blacks or other non-Whites in employment and access to higher education, together with court-ordered busing to effect racial integration in the public schools.

The reasons for these somewhat unanticipated developments are not wholly clear, although most informed observers point to at least three considerations: (1) the fact that the new gains in the political and civic rights of Blacks had little or no impact on the income and employment problems of the larger number of the black "underclass"—those unemployed and underemployed blacks living under cruel and depressing conditions in the urban ghettos; (2) the delaying tactics used by many of the southern states to frustrate the Supreme Court's decisions forbidding racial segregation and discrimination; and (3) psychological processes revolving around the phenomenon of the "revolution of rising expectations" and the inevitable general frustration following the initial euphoria produced by the promises of a new era implicit in the *Brown* decision.

This rather drastic turnabout in the nature of government's role in dealing with racial issues— most of which took place in the 1970s—has created its own set of tensions both within the general population and among the intellectual and political leadership of the nation, produced by different convictions concerning the wisdom and desirability of such measures as government-mandated affirmative action procedures and school busing across neighborhood district lines. During this period, also, the United States underwent a substantial growth in its Hispanic population of Mexican and Puerto Rican origin, together with the arrival of a significant number of Cuban refugees. The burgeoning size and political salience of Hispanic peoples have raised the issue of government-mandated bilingual education in the public schools for children whose home language is not English, to the point of implicit support by at least one Supreme Court decision and explicit support by the federal Department of Education and some state governments. This issue is also hotly debated in the educational world and elsewhere and is the occasion for sharply divided opinion.

A New Dilemma

It is clear, then, that America now faces a new dilemma in the area of racial and ethnic relations—one markedly different from that described by Myrdal in that the dilemma which Myrdal presented identified two divergent paths, one of them supported by the finest ideals of religious and civic morality, the other buttressed not by any well-understood moral and religious conviction, but by destructive and hateful practices arising out of the worst impulses in humankind. In the new American dilemma, however, which centers on the proper role of government in dealing with racial and ethnic relations, proponents of both sides can claim in good faith to derive their respective positions from standard moral and religious systems, one side emphasizing principles of equal treatment and individual meritocracy, the other principles that call upon group compensation for undeniable past injustices. It is my conviction that this controversy and the important choices involved can be discussed most expeditiously and with the optimum possibility for producing a useful, well-considered national debate rather than a simple emotional dismissal of one side or the other, in the larger context of types of pluralism and the choice of which type of pluralist society is most appropriate and most beneficial for a nation composed of many ethnic groups—and specifically, for the United States of America.

The Nature of Pluralism

What, indeed, is racial and ethnic pluralism? In its most generic aspects it refers to a national society in which various groups, each with a psychological sense of its own historical peoplehood, maintain some structural separation from each other in intimate primary group relationships and in certain aspects of institutional life and thus create the possibility of maintaining, also, some cultural patterns which are different from those of the "host" society and of other racial and ethnic groups in the nation. I have referred to these two dimensions as "structural pluralism" and, in the term suggested by Horace Kallen, "cultural pluralism."[4] Note that I use the phrase "create the possibility of maintaining" in reference to variations in cultural patterns. I use this construction advisedly, since racial and ethnic pluralism can exist without a great deal of cultural diversity; it cannot exist at all, however, without structural separation.

As I interpret the American historical experience, using these analytical distinctions, and also bringing into play the role of both the Anglo-conformity and the "melting pot" ideas, the dominant pattern with regard to our country's racial and ethnic diversity has been a composite consisting of a great deal of persistent structural pluralism, cultural pluralism in the case of the first generation of immigrants, and the overwhelming dominance of Anglo-conformity with regard to the cultural patterns of the second and successive generations, although not to the exclusion of the retention of symbolic elements of the ancestral tradition[5] and, of course, with the maintenance of religious differences from the original Protestant norm, that is, Roman Catholicism and Judaism (although both in Americanized form)—and all of this spiced up with a little and flavorful bit of "melting pot."[6]

Liberal and Corporate Pluralism

The new element in the situation—the one which creates the dilemma of choice currently before the American people—is the role of government in racial and ethnic relations, together with ethical and philosophical issues revolving around ideas of just rewards and whether to treat persons as individuals or as members of a categorically defined group. In combination, these issues point to the delineation of two alternative theoretical patterns or models of a racially and ethnically plural society, in which the issues of cultural and structural differences figure, but are now joined by other dimensions in order to incorporate the new considerations. I have called the two patterns thus distinguished *liberal pluralism* and *corporate pluralism*.[7] I wish now to portray and analyze these alternative models of pluralism in somewhat systematic form. For that purpose, I am denoting six dimensions with which to compare and contrast the two theoretical types of racial and ethnic pluralistic societies. These are (1) legal recognition and differential treatment, (2) individual meritocracy and equality of opportunity versus group rewards and equality of condition, (3) structural separation, (4) cultural differences, (5) area exclusivism, and (6) institutional monolingualism versus institutional bilingualism or multilingualism. I shall now proceed to a consideration of these two differing types of pluralism using these dimensions.

Legal Recognition and Differential Treatment

In liberal pluralism, government gives no formal recognition to categories of people based on race or ethnicity (and, of course, religion, which may be considered a possible component of ethnicity). Furthermore, it provides no benefits to nor exerts any penalty from any individual because of his or her racial or ethnic background. It does not stipulate segregation, nor does it formally promote integration, but allows individuals of all racial and ethnic groups to work things out by themselves on the basis of freedom of choice. It may, however, intervene legally through legislation or executive orders to *prevent* discrimination in such areas as employment, education, voting, public facilities, and public accommodations. But such prevention is focused on *specific acts which can be proven to be discriminatory* and not on the promotion of integration through direct governmental action. Thus a fair employment commission's investigation and adjudication of a complaint of racial discrimination in a particular firm, agency, or educational institution would fall within the framework of liberal pluralism, while an industry-wide investigation to ascertain and change particular percentages of racial and ethnic percentages of employees would not.

It is plausible to suggest that the just described pattern within the framework of "liberal plural-ism" has been the general ideal and goal of the American experience, and that although, in practice, America has at times miserably failed to live up to this ideal—notably, though not exclusively, in the case of Blacks—nevertheless, recent advances in the race relations area have brought us close to full implementation of this set of desired patterns in the relationship of the American government toward its citizens.[8]

Corporate pluralism, on the other hand, envisages a nation where its racial and ethnic entities are formally recognized as such—are given formal standing as groups in the national polity—and where patterns of political power and economic reward are based on a distributive formula which postulates group rights and which defines group membership as an important factor in the outcome for individuals. In widely varying degrees, nations like Belgium, the Netherlands, Switzerland, Canada, the Soviet Union, and Lebanon contain some aspects of a corporate pluralism model. In the United States, recently introduced measures, such as government-mandated affirmative action procedures in employment, education, and stipulated public programs, and court-ordered busing of school children across neighborhood district lines to effect racial integration, constitute steps toward the corporate pluralist idea. Many proponents of these measures support them simply as transitional and compensatory devices to rectify the effects of past racial discrimination; however, it is not clear what formulas would be used to measure the designated completion of the process and whether, in fact, these procedures, if left in place for any length of time, would not simply become eventually a permanent part of the national pattern of operation.

Individual Meritocracy and Equality of Opportunity versus Group Rewards and Equality of Condition

These are basic philosophical ideas of equality and attribution which also definitely distinguish the two types of pluralism from each other. In liberal pluralism, the unit of attribution for equity considerations is always and irrevocably the individual. The individual gets what he deserves in economic and political rewards on the basis of his merit and accomplishment. Both in theory and practice, considerations of compassion and the need for basic minimal rewards usually shore up the bottom end of the scale, but above this minimal line individual merit prevails. Equality for citizens is defined as equality of opportunity (and, of course, equality before the law), but not in terms of results or condition, a matter which is left to the myriad workings of the competitive process. Racial and ethnic factors, in this paradigm, should play no role at all in the distributive process, either positive or negative. Proponents of this model insist that it represents traditional American ideals and the principles of the Enlightenment on which the American republic was founded.

Corporate pluralism postulates a reward system, both economic and political, which gives legitimacy to the standing and stake of racial and ethnic groups in the distributive process. Political bodies, such as legislatures, judiciaries, municipal councils, and even executive offices, must reflect, to a substantial degree, the numerical weight of the various racial and ethnic groups in the total population. In the economic arena, economic justice is not achieved until the income and occupational distributions of the various groups are approximately equal, and business, professional and government units of significant size must each, individually, show a pattern of reward of differential income, power, and status to its employees which mirrors the national population distribution of racial and ethnic groups. Presumably, *within* the required ratios, individual merit considerations will be operative. Proponents of this system argue that, at the very least, it is necessary to institute such a model of rewards for a time in order to allow a minority group which has suffered heavy discrimination in the past to catch up with the other groups with any reasonable degree of rapidity. In this system also, equality is defined as equality of condition rather than simply equality of opportunity.

Structural Separation

Liberal pluralism's formula for the resolution of structural issues—deciding what cliques, clubs, and institutions to belong to—is strictly laissez faire. Its message to the minority group member is, "If you want to form your own ethnically enclosed network of primary group relations, and your separate institutional life, go ahead.

That's your business. If you don't want to, that's equally all right. If you want to marry across racial or ethnic lines, there is no legal bar. The policy in all these matters is strictly 'hands off.'"

In the American historical experience, this policy, where it was implemented (it was, of course, distinctly not implemented in the southern states for Blacks and Whites until recently), gave members of racial and ethnic minorities the maximum amount of freedom of choice in these matters. Of course, we are referring here to government policy only. In the northern states, physical intimidation and custom did what government did not attempt to do: keep people of different races apart. Second-generation immigrants (most first-generation immigrants, quite understandably, wanted to stay within their own ethnic enclaves for primary group relations) who ventured out of the ethnic social network and looked for some "neutral" social structure found that the only alternative structures were white Protestant Anglo-Saxon in nature and reluctant or unwilling to let them in, anyway. The opening up of primary group networks, after all, requires two favorable decisions, one by the aspiring entrant, the other by the gatekeeper of the social structure in which one is seeking entrance. But as far as government was concerned, except for the now defunct Jim Crow laws, the gates were legally open, and private attitudes determined the outcome.

In the case of corporate pluralism, the situation is somewhat different. Structural separation is not necessarily legally mandated, but the logic of the reward system stipulating that group membership plays a large role in educational access, occupational placement, income, political power, and similar matters places distinct pressure on members of particular racial and ethnic groups to stay within the group for marriage, close personal friendship, institutional life, and social identity. After all, if a significant portion of one's rational interests are likely to be satisfied by emphasis on one's ethnicity, then one might as well stay within ethnic boundaries and at the same time enjoy the social comforts of being among "people of one's own kind," where prejudice and discrimination toward oneself are not present. Moving across ethnic boundaries to engage in significant interethnic social relationships is likely to lead to social marginality in a society where ethnicity and ethnic identity are such salient features. Thus the logic of corporate pluralism is to emphasize structural separation.

Cultural Differences

Very much as in the case of structural issues, liberal pluralism allows members of minority groups the maximum amount of freedom to make as much or as little as they please of their ancestral cultural heritage. There are no "bonus points" for perpetuating it and no penalties for drawing away from it. Groups and individuals from within the group can make their own decisions on these matters.

There are, of course, boundaries which indicate that a certain value consensus for all groups within the national framework is expected. The attempt to introduce polygamy in the American historical experience failed because it violated this consensus. No projected set of alternative values which advocated violence, murder, or theft as desirable patterns of behavior would obviously be tolerated. But within the normal range of nondestructive behavior, much variation is allowed, and conflicts over what norms shall constitute public policy are usually settled through the usual political processes—that is, the ballot box and judicial decisions. Or if the numbers are not great and civic policy is not essentially threatened, alternative value and behavior patterns are institutionalized as allowable exceptions or variations. An American case in point would be the provisions made in national legislation for conscientious objectors to war and military service, which stem, institutionally, from the value systems of British-descended Quakers and several religious sects of German origin whose ancestors were once immigrants to America. The issue of monolingualism versus bilingualism is also, of course, a cultural one, but it is so important in itself that I am considering it separately below.

Corporate pluralism, on the other hand, places a distinct positive value on cultural diversity and encourages its perpetuation. Its viewpoint is that the preservation of its own ancestral cultural patterns by each racial and ethnic group is both an institutional right and a positive virtue. From this perspective, the culture of the nation is seen as a mosaic of subcultural patterns interacting in an overall framework of integration and harmony, thus providing a richer cultural life for the nation than is possible where one standard set of cultural patterns, established by the majority, constitutes the norm. Thus members of diverse racial and ethnic groups are encouraged to lay considerable emphasis on developing and honoring their own ancestral heritage even in successive generations of the original group.

Area Exclusivism

In the liberal pluralist model, no racial or ethnic group is able to lay legal claim to a particular piece of territory within the nation and to exclude people of other identities from access or residence. This is the case both in terms of large segments of national territory and in terms of particular neighborhoods in a specific community. Thus area exclusivism is legally forbidden. Area concentration, however, which reflects the voluntary choices of members of a particular racial or ethnic group to live in the same neighborhood or to settle in a particular city, is well within the liberal framework and is likely to occur, as the American experience has shown. However, if dubiously legal or extralegal attempts (that is, the once but on longer legally permissible "restrictive covenant," real estate brokerage practices, and physical intimidation) are made to exclude members of other groups from living in a particular neighborhood or portion of the city, then the principles of liberal pluralism are flagrantly violated. It is clear that American practices in this area, although improving, still have a long way to go to achieve full implementation of these principles.

Corporate pluralism does not demand area exclusivism, but is more tolerant of it as a possible variant arrangement in the domain of racial and ethnic relations. Its emphasis on group identity and group rights makes it less insistent on the principle of free access in travel or residence to any physical portion of the national collectivity, regardless of race, color, or creed.

Institutional Monoligualism versus
Institutional Bilingualism or Multilingualism

On the language issue, liberal pluralism and corporate pluralism stand at opposite poles. Liberal pluralism insists on institutional monolingualism—that is, that there shall be only one standard language in the nation, that this language shall be the publicly mandated language of the educational system and all legal documents and procedures, and that no other language shall have any public standing. This viewpoint does not sanction hostility to the teaching or learning of other languages as supplementary options, it does not militate against voluntary retention of other languages as taught in the home or in private supplemental schools, and in fact, may encourage bilingualism or multilingualism for cultural or pragmatic purposes. But it makes one language the standard of the nation and allows no other to assume any official status. It is a clearly delineated position which, in fact, has been basically the American position, historically and up to the very recent present, at which time is has been challenged by proponents of mandatory bilingual education in the public schools for children who are language handicapped as a result of coming from a non-English-speaking home.

Corporate pluralism, on the other hand, supports official or institutional bilingualism or multilingualism. Its position is that the various racial and ethnic groups have the right and, indeed, should be encouraged to retain their ancestral languages, that there is no reason why there must be only one official language, and that all members of the national polity should be encouraged, perhaps even compelled, to become bilingual or multilingual. The large growth in numbers and political activism of the Hispanic population in the United States and the consequent demand for bilingual education in the public schools have brought aspects of this issue to the fore in recent years in the American context. Canadian society, with its English-speaking and French-speaking populations, is an example of an institutionally bilingual nation with its attendant controversies which are still in the process of attempted resolution.

Conclusion
The preceding six dimensions serve to define the differences between liberal pluralism and corporate pluralism. By their conceptualization and use I have tried to make it clear that there is now an important dilemma before the American people and that this dilemma is not simply a choice between isolated and fragmented policies, but rather that there is an inherent logic in the relationship of the various positions on these public issues which makes the choice one between two patterns—two overall types of racial and ethnic pluralism each with distinctly different implications for the American way of life. Those who favor the liberal form of pluralism emphasize in their arguments the ethical and philosophical value of the idea of individual meritocracy and the notion that current generations should not be expected to pay for the sins of their fathers—or at least, those who lived here before them, whether genetically related or not. They also point to functional considerations such as the possibility that measures such as forced busing and affirmative action to ensure group quotas will create white backlash and serve as continuing major irritants in the relationships between racial and ethnic groups. Those who favor policies which fall, logically, under the rubric of corporate pluralism emphasize, in return, the moral and philosophical position which posits group rights as well as individual rights, and the need for major compensatory measures to make up for the massive dimensions of racial discrimination in the past.

And so the argument is joined. This article has been written with the distinct conviction that the argument is a momentous one and that its resolution, in whatever form, will be best served by as much intellectual clarity, thoughtfulness, and good will as we can all muster in the process. Certainly, what the American people decide about this patterned complex of issues in the last 20 years of the twentieth century will have much to do with determining the nature, shape, and destiny of racial and ethnic relations in America in the twenty-first century which will then follow.

ENDNOTES
1. Gunnar Myrdal, with the assistance of Richard Sterner and Arnold Rose, *An American Dilemma* (New York, Harper and Brothers, 1944), particularly, chs. 1 and 45.

2. Supreme Court of the United States, 163 U.S. 537 (1896).

3. Nathan Glazer, *Affirmative Discrimination* (New York: Basic Books, 1975), ch. 1.

4. Milton M. Gordon, *Assimilation in American Life* (New York: Oxford University Press, 1964); see also my *Human Nature, Class, and Ethnicity* (New York: Oxford University Press, 1978).

5. See Herbert J. Gans, "Symbolic Ethnicity: The Future of Ethnic Groups and Cultures in America," in *On the Making of Americans: Essays in Honor of David Riesman*, eds. Herbert J. Gans, Nathan Glazer, Joseph R. Gusfield, and Christopher Jencks (Philadelphia: University of Pennsylvania Press, 1979).

6. See Milton M. Gordon, *Assimilation in American Life*, passim.

7. Milton M. Gordon, "Toward A General Theory of Racial and Ethnic Group Relations," in *Ethnicity: Theory and Experience*, eds. Nathan Glazer and Daniel P. Moynihan (Cambridge, MA: Harvard University Press, 1975). This paper is reprinted in my *Human Nature, Class, and Ethnicity*. The terms "liberal pluralism" and "corporate pluralism" were chosen because they appear to me to portray accurately and nonperjoratively the salient and historically appropriate characteristics of each type of pluralist society. It is true that many liberals today support measures which fall in the "corporate" variety of pluralism. But there has been a longer historical association of the term "liberal" with those measures and conditions which I am grouping under the term "liberal pluralism."

8. See Nathan Glazer, *Affirmative Discrimination*, ch. 1, for a presentation of such a viewpoint.

Statistical Appendix

TABLE 1. *Racial and Hispanic Population in the United States, 1970–1980*

	Number (in thousands)		Percent Distribution	
	1980	1970	1980	1970
TOTAL	226,546	203,212	100.0	100.0
White	188,341	177,749	83.2	87.5
Black	26,488	22,580	11.7	11.1
American Indian, Eskimo, and Aleut	1,418	827	0.6	0.4
Asian and Pacific Islander	3,501	1,539	1.5	0.8
Chinese	806	435	0.4	0.2
Filipino	775	343	0.3	0.2
Japanese	701	591	0.3	0.3
Asian Indian	362	NA	0.2	—
Korean	355	69	0.2	0.0
Vietnamese	262	NA	0.1	—
Hispanics*	14,609	9,073	6.4	4.5
Mexican-American	8,740	4,532	3.9	2.2
Puerto Rican	2,014	1,429	0.9	0.7
Cuban	803	544	0.4	0.3
Other	3,051	2,566	1.3	1.2
Other	6,757	517	3.0	0.3

NA—Not available
*—Hispanics included in white, black and "other" categories
Source: Bureau of the Census, *Census of Population;* Supplementary Reports.

TABLE 2. United States Population of Indians, Chinese, Japanese, Filipinos, Koreans, and Puerto Ricans

	Indian	Chinese	Filipino	Japanese	Korean	Puerto Rican[2]
1890	248,253	107,448		2,039		
1900	237,196	89,863		24,236		
1910	276,927	71,531	160	72,157		
1920	244,437	61,639	5,603	111,010		
1930	343,352	74,954	45,208	138,834		
1940	345,252	77,504	45,563	126,947		
1950	357,499	117,629	61,636	141,768		301,375
1960[1]	523,591	237,292	176,310	464,332		892,513
1970[1]	792,730	435,062	343,060	591,290	69,130	1,429,396
1980[1]	1,418,195	806,027	774,640	700,747	354,529	2,013,945

[1]The 1960, 1970 and 1980 census data include Hawaii and Alaska.
[2]Data on persons of Puerto Rican parentage were first collected in the 1950 census.
Source: Bureau of the Census, *Historical Statistics of the United States,* p. 9; Bureau of the Census, *1970 Census of Population,* Subject Reports, American Indians, p. 5; Puerto Ricans, p. xi; Japanese, Chinese, and Filipinos in the United States, p. 148; Bureau of the Census, *1960 Census of Population, Characteristics of the Population,* vol. 1, part 1, p. 145. Bureau of the Census, *1980 Census of Population,* Supplementary Reports, "Race of Population by States: 1980," pp. 6–14.

TABLE 3. Total Persons and Spanish Origin Persons by Type: 1980 and 1970

United States	1980	1970	Percent Distribution 1980	Percent Distribution 1970
Total persons	226,545,805	203,211,926	100.0	100.0
Persons of Spanish origin	14,608,673	9,072,602	6.4	4.5
Persons not of Spanish origin	211,937,132	194,139,324	93.6	95.5
Spanish origin	14,608,673	9,072,602	100.0	100.0
Mexican	8,740,439	4,532,435	59.8	50.0
Puerto Rican	2,013,945	1,429,396	13.8	15.8
Cuban	803,226	544,600	5.5	6.0
Other Spanish	3,051,063	2,566,171	20.9	28.3

Source: Bureau of the Census, *1980 Census of Population:* Supplementary Report: "Persons of Spanish Origin by State," p. 3.

TABLE 4. *American Population, by Ancestry—Selected Characteristics*

Ancestry	Total (1,000)	Median Age (years)	Percent Foreign Born	Percent Native of Foreign or Mixed Parentage[1]	Percent High School Graduates[1]	Percent Completed 1 Year or More of College[1]	Number of Families (1,000)	Median Family Income
Total population[2]	216,613	30.3	5.4	10.9	68.7	31.5	59,001	$15,764
Total, reported at least one specific ancestry	179,078	30.3	6.2	12.6	70.7	33.2	48,552	16,224
Reported single ancestry group[3]	96,496	34.6	10.4	16.9	66.0	29.5	31,243	15,456
English	11,501	40.4	3.8	6.2	75.7	37.8	4,039	16,891
French	3,047	36.2	5.1	15.3	66.4	26.6	1,080	15,571
German	17,160	37.1	4.0	10.7	72.2	30.2	6,196	17,531
Irish	9,760	39.0	2.7	10.4	69.5	30.4	3,174	16,092
Italian	6,110	42.3	13.1	44.1	61.5	22.4	2,134	16,993
Polish	3,498	46.0	10.8	40.3	61.6	25.4	1,205	16,977
Scottish	1,615	43.5	10.5	14.2	79.9	45.9	736	20,018
Spanish	9,762	23.5	30.3	25.1	41.4	16.6	2,453	10,607
Reported multiple ancestry groups[4]	82,582	24.5	1.2	7.6	78.2	39.0	17,309	17,810
American Indian and other group(s)	7,847	23.4	.4	2.4	61.7	20.6	1,706	13,641
Dutch and other group(s)	6,759	27.3	1.0	4.2	68.2	28.1	1,457	15,868
English and other group(s)	28,503	27.1	.9	5.7	81.4	43.7	6,344	18,680
French and other group(s)	11,000	24.5	1.0	6.8	76.8	38.1	2,244	17,048
German and other group(s)	34,489	23.0	.6	5.9	80.2	38.8	6,889	18,375
Irish and other group(s)	33,992	25.7	.5	4.5	75.1	34.7	7,112	16,860
Italian and other group(s)	5,622	17.7	.6	9.9	84.5	41.8	733	17,833
Polish and other group(s)	4,923	20.3	1.6	13.9	84.3	46.0	897	19,968
Scottish and other group(s)	12,590	32.2	1.0	6.1	81.2	44.2	3,086	19,148

[1]Covers persons 25 years old and over.

[2]Includes responses indicating "American," religious groups, and persons who did not report or whose ancestry is not shown separately.

[3]Includes other single ancestry groups not shown separately.

[4]Includes other multiple ancestry groups not shown separately. Persons reporting multiple ancestry groups may be included in more than one multiple ancestry category; total is the number of persons reporting multiple ancestry groups.

Source: U.S. Bureau of the Census, *Statistical Abstract, 1983;* U.S. Bureau of the Census, *Current Population Reports,* series P-23, No. 116, and unpublished data.

TABLE 5. *Total Resident Population by Race for Selected Years: 1790 to 1978*

Year	Millions of Persons		Percent Black of Total
	Total	Black	
1790	3.9	0.8	19.3
1860	31.4	4.4	14.1
1870	39.8	5.4	13.5
1890	62.9	7.5	11.9
1900	76.2	8.8	11.6
1910	92.2	9.8	10.7
1920	106.0	10.5	9.9
1930	123.2	11.9	9.7
1940	132.2	12.9	9.7
1950	151.3	15.0	9.9
1960	179.3	18.9	10.5
1970	203.2	22.6	11.1
1980	226.5	26.5	11.7

Source: U.S. Bureau of the Census. *The Social and Economic Status of the Black Population in the United States: An Historical Overview, 1970–1978.* 1979, pp. 9, 170; U.S. Bureau of the Census, *1980 Census of Population, Supplementary Report,* "Race of Population by States: 1980," p. 6.

TABLE 6. Racial Distribution of the Population, by Region for Selected Years: 1790 to 1980

Area and Race	1790	1870	1910	1940	1960	1970	1980
BLACK							
United States, millions	1	5	10	13	19	23	26
Percent, total	100	100	100	100	100	100	100
South	91	91	89	77	60	53	53
North	9	9	10	22	34	39	38
Northeast	9	4	5	11	16	19	18
North Central	—	6	6	11	18	20	20
West	—	—	1	1	6	8	9
WHITE							
United States, millions	3	34	82	118	159	178	188
Percent, total	100	100	100	100	100	100	100
South	40	23	25	27	27	28	31
North	60	74	67	62	56	54	50
Northeast	60	36	31	29	26	25	22
North Central	—	38	36	33	30	29	28
West	—	3	8	11	16	18	19
BLACK AS A PERCENT OF THE TOTAL POPULATION							
United States	19	13	11	10	11	11	12
South	35	36	30	24	21	19	19
North	3	2	2	4	7	8	9
Northeast	3	1	2	4	7	9	9
North Central	—	2	2	4	7	8	8
West	—	1	1	1	4	5	5

Source: U.S. Bureau of the Census, *The Social and Economic Status of the Black Population in the United States: An Historical Overview, 1790–1978.* 1979, p. 13, and U.S. Bureau of the Census, *1980 Census of Population, Supplementary Reports,* "Race of Population by States: 1980," pp. 6–9.

TABLE 7. Black Population of Selected States by Rank in 1980: 1980 and 1970

United States Regions States [100,000 or More Black Population]	1980 Rank	1980	1970	Change, 1970 to 1980		Percent Distribution	
				Number	Percent	1980	1970
United States	. . .	26 488 218	22 580 289	3 907 929	17.3	100.0	100.0
Northeast	. . .	4 848 786	4 344 153	504 633	11.6	18.3	19.2
Massachusetts	24	221 279	175 817	45 462	25.9	0.8	0.8
Connecticut	25	217 433	181 177	36 256	20.0	0.8	0.8
New York	1	2 401 842	2 168 949	232 893	10.7	9.1	9.6
New Jersey	16	924 786	770 292	154 494	20.1	3.5	3.4
Pennsylvania	11	1 047 609	1 016 514	31 095	3.1	4.0	4.5
North Central	. . .	5 336 542	4 571 550	764 992	16.7	20.1	20.2
Ohio	10	1 076 734	970 477	106 257	10.9	4.1	4.3
Indiana	21	414 732	357 464	57 268	16.0	1.6	1.6
Illinois	4	1 675 229	1 425 674	249 555	17.5	6.3	6.3
Michigan	9	1 198 710	991 066	207 644	21.0	4.5	4.4
Wisconsin	27	182 593	128 224	54 369	42.4	0.7	0.6
Missouri	19	514 274	480 172	34 102	7.1	1.9	2.1
Kansas	28	126 127	106 977	19 150	17.9	0.5	0.5
South	. . .	14 041 374	11 969 961	2 071 413	17.3	53.0	53.0
Maryland	14	958 050	699 479	258 571	37.0	3.6	3.1
District of Columbia	20	448 229	537 712	−89 483	−16.6	1.7	2.4
Virginia	12	1 008 311	861 368	146 943	17.1	3.8	3.8
North Carolina	7	1 316 050	1 126 478	189 572	16.8	5.0	5.0
South Carolina	15	968 146	789 041	159 105	20.2	3.6	3.5
Georgia	5	1 465 457	1 187 149	278 308	23.4	5.5	5.3
Florida	6	1 342 478	1 041 651	300 827	28.9	5.1	4.6
Kentucky	23	259 490	230 793	28 697	12.4	1.0	1.0
Tennessee	18	725 949	621 261	104 688	16.9	2.7	2.8
Alabama	13	995 623	903 467	92 156	10.2	3.8	4.0
Mississippi	17	887 206	815 770	71 436	8.8	3.3	3.6
Arkansas	22	373 192	352 445	20 747	5.9	1.4	1.6
Louisiana	8	1 237 263	1 086 832	150 431	13.8	4.7	4.8
Oklahoma	26	204 658	171 892	32 766	19.1	0.8	0.8
Texas	3	1 710 250	1 399 005	311 245	22.2	6.5	6.2
West	. . .	2 261 516	1 694 625	566 891	33.5	8.5	7.5
Colorado	30	101 702	66 411	35 291	53.1	0.4	0.3
Washington	29	105 544	71 308	34 236	48.0	0.4	0.3
California	2	1 819 282	1 400 143	419 139	29.9	6.9	6.2

Source: U.S. Bureau of the Census, *1980 Census of Population, Supplementary Reports:* Race of Population by States: 1980, p. 12.

TABLE 8. American Indian Population of Selected States by Rank in 1980: 1980 and 1970

United States Regions States [15,000 or More American Indian Population]	1980 Rank	1980	1970	Change, 1970 to 1980		Percent Distribution	
				Number	Percent	1980	1970
United States	. . .	1 361 869	792 730	569 139	71.8	100.0	100.0
Northeast	. . .	76 574	49 466	27 108	54.8	5.6	6.2
New York	10	38 117	28 355	9 762	34.4	2.8	3.6
North Central	. . .	246 456	151 287	95 169	62.9	18.1	19.1
Illinois	20	15 833	11 413	4 420	38.7	1.2	1.4
Michigan	8	39 702	16 854	22 848	135.6	2.9	2.1
Wisconsin	13	29 318	18 924	10 394	54.9	2.2	2.4
Minnesota	12	34 841	23 128	11 713	50.6	2.6	2.9
North Dakota	16	20 119	14 369	5 750	40.0	1.5	1.8
South Dakota	7	45 081	32 365	12 716	39.3	3.3	4.1
Kansas	21	15 254	8 672	6 582	75.9	1.1	1.1
South	. . .	369 497	201 222	168 275	83.6	27.1	25.4
North Carolina	5	64 519	44 406	20 113	45.3	4.7	5.6
Florida	18	18 981	6 677	12 304	184.3	1.4	0.8
Oklahoma	2	169 297	98 468	70 829	71.9	12.4	12.4
Texas	9	39 374	17 957	21 417	119.3	2.9	2.3
West	. . .	669 342	390 755	278 587	71.3	49.1	49.3
Montana	11	37 153	27 130	10 023	36.9	2.7	3.4
Colorado	19	17 726	8 836	8 890	100.6	1.3	1.1
New Mexico	4	104 634	72 788	31 846	43.8	7.7	9.2
Arizona	3	152 610	95 812	56 798	59.3	11.2	12.1
Utah	17	19 158	11 273	7 885	69.9	1.4	1.4
Washington	6	58 159	33 386	24 773	74.2	4.3	4.2
Oregon	14	26 587	13 510	13 077	96.8	2.0	1.7
California	1	198 095	91 018	107 077	117.6	14.5	11.5
Alaska	15	21 849	16 276	5 573	34.2	1.6	2.1

Source: Bureau of the Census, *1980 Census of Population, Supplementary Reports:* "Race of Population by States: 1980," p. 12.

TABLE 9. Population of the United States, by Metropolitan-Nonmetropolitan Residence, Race, and Spanish Origin: 1960 to 1980 (Numbers in thousands. Resident population.)

Race and Residence	1980	1970	Change, 1970 to 1980	Percent Change		Percent Distribution	
				1970-80	1960-70	1980	1970
All races	226,505	203,302	23,203	11.4	13.3	100.0	100.0
Metropolitan areas	169,405	153,694	15,711	10.2	16.6	74.8	75.6
In central cities	67,930	67,850	80	0.1	6.5	30.0	33.4
Outside central cities	101,475	85,843	15,631	18.2	26.7	44.8	42.2
Nonmetropolitan areas	57,100	49,608	7,492	15.1	6.8	25.2	24.4
White	188,341	177,749	10,592	6.0	11.9	100.0	100.0
Metropolitan areas	138,044	133,574	4,469	3.3	14.0	73.3	75.1
In central cities	47,014	53,100	−6,086	−11.5	0.1	25.0	29.9
Outside central cities	91,029	80,474	10,555	13.1	26.1	48.3	45.3
Nonmetropolitan areas	50,297	44,175	6,122	13.9	7.8	26.7	24.9
Black	26,488	22,580	3,908	17.3	19.7	100.0	100.0
Metropolitan areas	21,474	17,872	3,602	20.2	31.6	81.1	79.1
In central cities	15,301	13,546	1,755	13.0	33.2	57.8	60.0
Outside central cities	6,173	4,326	1,847	42.7	26.4	23.3	19.2
Nonmetropolitan areas	5,014	4,708	306	6.5	−5.3	18.9	20.9
Spanish origin	14,606	9,073	5,533	61.0	(NA)	100.0	100.0
Metropolitan areas	12,793	7,826	4,967	63.5	(NA)	87.6	86.3
In central cities	7,351	4,825	2,526	52.4	(NA)	50.3	53.2
Outside central cities	5,443	3,001	2,441	81.3	(NA)	37.3	33.1
Nonmetropolitan areas	1,813	1,246	566	45.4	(NA)	12.4	13.7

Source: U.S. Bureau of the Census, *Current Population Reports*, "Population Profile of the United States: 1981," Series P-20, No. 374, p. 23.

TABLE 10. Top Nine States in Hispanic Population: 1970 and 1980 (States with 250,000 or more Hispanics in 1980)

State	1970			1980		
	Rank	Number of Hispanics	Percent Distribution	Rank	Number of Hispanics	Percent Distribution
United States, total	—	9,072,602	100.00	—	14,608,673	100.0
California	1	2,369,292	26.1	1	4,544,331	31.1
Texas	2	1,840,648	20.3	2	2,985,824	20.4
New York	3	1,351,982	14.9	3	1,659,300	11.4
Florida	4	405,036	4.5	4	858,158	5.9
Illinois	5	393,204	4.3	5	635,602	4.4
New Jersey	7	288,488	3.2	6	491,883	3.4
New Mexico	6	308,340	3.4	7	477,222	3.3
Arizona	8	264,770	2.9	8	440,701	3.0
Colorado	9	225,506	2.5	9	339,717	2.3
Total in nine top states		7,447,266	82.1		12,432,738	85.1

Source: Bureau of the Census, *1980 Census of Population:* Supplementary Report: "Persons of Spanish Origin by State," PC80-S1-7, August 1982.

TABLE 11. Black population as percent of the total population of the twelve largest U.S. cities,* 1920, 1950, 1970, 1980

	1920†	1950†	1970	1980
New York	2.7	9.8	21.1	25.2
Los Angeles	2.7	10.7	17.9	17.0
Chicago	4.1	14.1	32.7	39.8
Philadelphia	7.4	18.3	33.6	37.8
Houston	24.6	21.1	25.7	27.6
Detroit	4.1	16.4	43.7	63.1
Dallas	15.1	13.2	24.9	29.4
San Diego	1.2	4.5	7.6	8.9
Phoenix	3.7	6.0	4.8	4.8
Baltimore	14.8	23.8	46.4	54.8
San Antonio	8.9	6.7	7.6	7.3
Indianapolis	11.0	15.0	18.0	21.8

*These were the twelve largest cities in the United States in 1980.
†Figures pertain to "nonwhite" population.
Sources: U.S. Census of 1920; U.S. Census of 1950; U.S. Bureau of the Census, *Negroes in the United States, 1920–1932,* Washington, D.C.: U.S. Government Printing Office, 1935; "Characteristics of the Population," *Statistical Abstract of the United States, 1972,* pp. 21–23; *Statistical Abstract of the United States, 1984,* pp. 28–30.

TABLE 12. Standard Metropolitan Statistical Areas with 100,000 or More Hispanics in 1980

Standard Metropolitan Statistical Area[a]	Hispanics in SMSA	Hispanics in Central City	Largest Hispanic Group and Its Percent of All Hispanics in SMSA
Los Angeles-Long Beach, CA	2,065,727	866,689	Mexican, 80%
New York, NY-NJ	1,493,081	1,405,957	Puerto Rican, 60%
Miami, FL	581,030	194,087	Cuban, 70%
Chicago, IL	580,592	422,061	Mexican, 64%
San Antonio, TX	481,511	421,774	Mexican, 93%
Houston, TX	424,901	281,224	Mexican, 88%
San Francisco-Oakland, CA	351,915	115,864	Mexican, 54%
El Paso, TX	297,001	265,819	Mexican, 95%
Riverside-San Bernardino-Ontario, CA	289,791	81,671	Mexican, 87%
Anaheim-Santa Ana-Garden Grove, CA	286,331	145,253	Mexican, 81%
San Diego, CA	275,176	130,610	Mexican, 83%
Dallas-Ft. Worth, TX	249,613	159,778	Mexican, 89%
McAllen-Pharr-Edinburg, TX	230,212	86,393	Mexican, 96%
San Jose, CA	226,611	140,574	Mexican, 78%
Phoenix, AZ	198,999	115,572	Mexican, 89%
Denver-Boulder, CO	173,362	94,933	Mexican, 63%
Albuquerque, NM	164,200	112,084	Other Hispanic, 56%
Brownsville-Harlingen-San Benito, TX	161,632	116,076	Mexican, 86%
Corpus Cristi, TX	158,123	108,175	Mexican, 96%
Fresno, CA	150,820	51,489	Mexican, 93%
Jersey City, NJ	145,163	41,672	Puerto Rican, 38%
Newark, NJ	132,356	61,254	Puerto Rican, 47%
Philadelphia, PA-NJ	116,280	63,570	Puerto Rican, 68%
Oxnard-Simi Valley-Ventura, CA	113,241	64,223	Mexican, 89%
Tucson, AZ	111,418	82,189	Mexican, 90%
Nassau-Suffolk, NY	101,418	[b]	Puerto Rican, 49%
Sacramento, CA	101,692	39,160	Mexican, 77%

Sources: Bureau of the Census, "Standard Metropolitan Statistical Areas and Standard Consolidated Statistical Areas: 1980," *1980 Census of Population,* Supplementary Report, PC80-S1-5, October 1981; and Cheryl Russell, "The News About Hispanics," *American Demographics,* March 1983, p. 17.

[a]A Standard Metropolitan Statistical Area (renamed Metropolitan Statistical Area as of July 1983) is a county with a central city (or urbanized area) of at least 50,000 population, plus adjacent counties that are economically linked with that county.

[b]Does not contain a central city.

TABLE 13. *Median Family Income 1947 to 1983 (in Current Dollars)*

	Median Income					Median Income Ratio		
Year	All Races	White	Black and Other Races	Black	Hispanic	Black & Other Races (to White)	Black (to White)	Hispanic (to White)
1947	3,031	3,157	1,614	NA	NA	0.51	NA	NA
1948	3,187	3,310	1,768	NA	NA	0.53	NA	NA
1949	3,107	3,232	1,650	NA	NA	0.51	NA	NA
1950	3,319	3,445	1,869	NA	NA	0.54	NA	NA
1951	3,709	3,859	2,032	NA	NA	0.53	NA	NA
1952	3,890	4,114	2,338	NA	NA	0.57	NA	NA
1953	4,233	4,392	2,461	NA	NA	0.56	NA	NA
1954	4,173	4,339	2,410	NA	NA	0.56	NA	NA
1955	4,418	4,613	2,544	NA	NA	0.55	NA	NA
1956	4,783	4,993	2,628	NA	NA	0.53	NA	NA
1957	4,971	5,166	2,764	NA	NA	0.54	NA	NA
1958	5,087	5,300	2,711	NA	NA	0.51	NA	NA
1959	5,417	5,643	2,917	2,812	NA	0.54	0.50	NA
1960	5,620	5,835	3,233	NA	NA	0.55	NA	NA
1961	5,737	5,981	3,191	NA	NA	0.53	NA	NA
1962	5,956	6,237	3,330	NA	NA	0.53	NA	NA
1963	6,249	6,548	3,465	NA	NA	0.53	NA	NA
1964	6,569	6,858	3,839	3,725	NA	0.56	0.54	NA
1965	6,957	7,251	3,994	3,885	NA	0.55	0.54	NA
1966	7,500	7,792	4,674	4,491	NA	0.60	0.58	NA
1967	7,974	8,274	5,141	4,920	NA	0.62	0.59	NA
1968	8,632	8,937	5,590	5,360	NA	0.63	0.60	NA
1969	9,433	9,794	6,190	6,001	NA	0.63	0.61	NA
1970	9,867	10,236	6,516	6,279	NA	0.64	0.61	NA
1971	10,285	10,672	6,714	6,440	NA	0.63	0.60	NA
1972	11,116	11,549	7,106	6,864	8,183	0.62	0.59	0.71
1973	12,051	12,595	7,596	7,269	8,715	0.60	0.58	0.69
1974	12,902	13,408	8,578	8,006	9,540	0.64	0.60	0.71
1975	13,719	14,268	9,321	8,779	9,551	0.65	0.62	0.67
1976	14,958	15,537	9,821	9,242	10,259	0.63	0.59	0.66
1977	16,009	16,740	10,142	9,563	11,421	0.61	0.57	0.68
1978	17,640	18,368	11,754	10,879	12,566	0.64	0.59	0.68
1979	19,661	20,502	12,380	11,644	14,569	0.60	0.57	0.71
1980	21,028	21,904	13,843	12,674	14,716	0.63	0.58	0.69
1981	22,388	23,517	14,598	13,266	16,401	0.62	0.56	0.70
1982	23,433	24,603	15,211	13,598	16,230	0.62	0.55	0.66
1983	24,580	25,757	15,887	14,506	16,956	0.61	0.56	0.65

NA: Not Available
Sources: U.S. Bureau of the Census, *Current Population Reports*, Series P-60, 1948–1984; and U.S. Bureau of the Census, *The Social and Economic Status of the Black Population in the United States: An Historical Overview, 1790–1978*, 1979, p. 31.

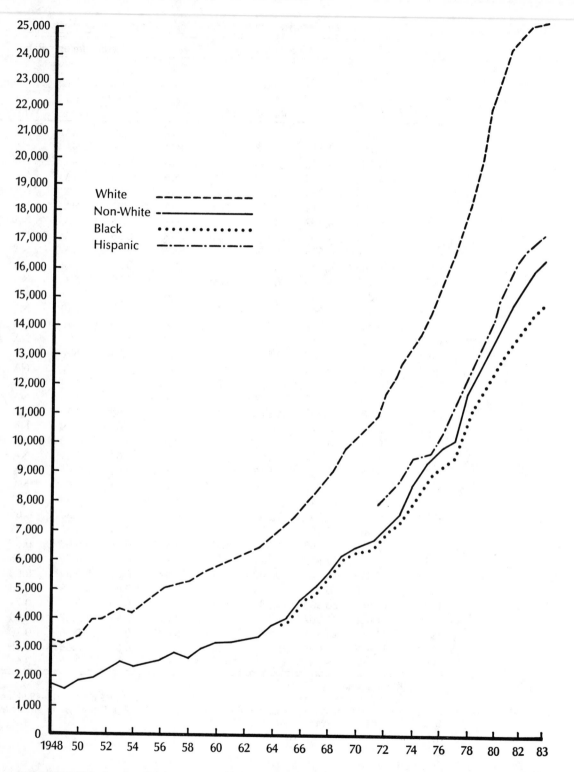

FIGURE 1. *Median Family Income for White, Non-White, Black, and Hispanics 1948–1983 (Source: Table 13)*

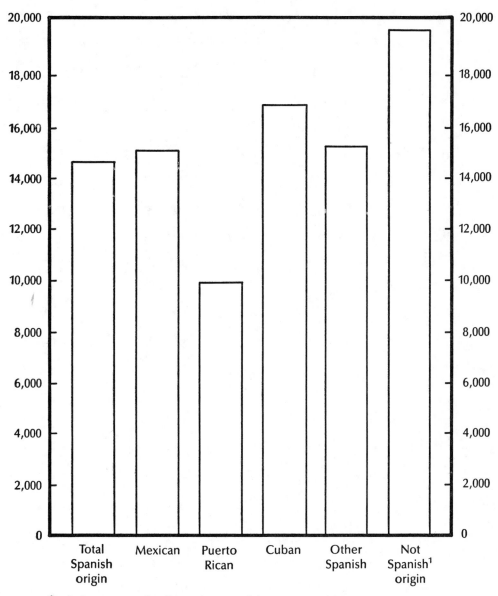

¹Includes persons who did not know or did not report origin.

FIGURE 2. *Median Income in 1979 of Spanish-Origin Families, by Type of Spanish Origin (Source: U.S. Bureau of the Census. Persons of Spanish Origin in the United States: March 1978. Current Population Reports. Series P-20, No. 339.)*

TABLE 14. *Unemployment Rates for Persons 16 Years Old and Over: 1948–1983*

Year	Unemployment Rate (Annual Averages)		Ratio: Black and Other Races to White
	Black and Other Races	White	
1948	5.9	3.5	1.7
1949	8.9	5.6	1.6
1950	9.0	4.9	1.8
1951	5.3	3.1	1.7
1952	5.4	2.8	1.9
1953	4.5	2.7	1.7
1954	9.9	5.0	2.0
1955	8.7	3.9	2.2
1956	8.3	3.6	2.3
1957	7.9	3.8	2.1
1958	12.6	6.1	2.1
1959	10.7	4.8	2.2
1960	12.2	4.9	2.1
1961	12.4	6.0	2.1
1962	10.9	4.9	2.2
1963	10.8	5.0	2.2
1964	9.6	4.6	2.1
1965	8.1	4.1	2.0
1966	7.3	3.3	2.2
1967	7.4	3.4	2.2
1968	6.7	3.2	2.1
1969	6.4	3.1	2.1
1970	8.2	4.5	1.8
1971	9.9	5.4	1.8
1972	10.0	5.0	2.0
1973	8.9	4.3	2.1
1974	9.9	5.0	2.0
1975	13.9	7.8	1.8
1976	13.1	7.0	2.0
1977	13.1	6.2	2.2
1978	11.9	5.2	2.3
1979	11.3	5.1	2.2
1980	13.1	6.3	2.1
1981	14.2	6.7	2.1
1982	17.3	8.6	2.0
1983	17.8	8.4	2.1

Source: U.S. Bureau of the Census, *The Social and Economic Status of the Black Population in the United States: An Historical Overview, 1790–1978,* 1979, pp. 69, 209; and *Economic Report of the President,* 1984.

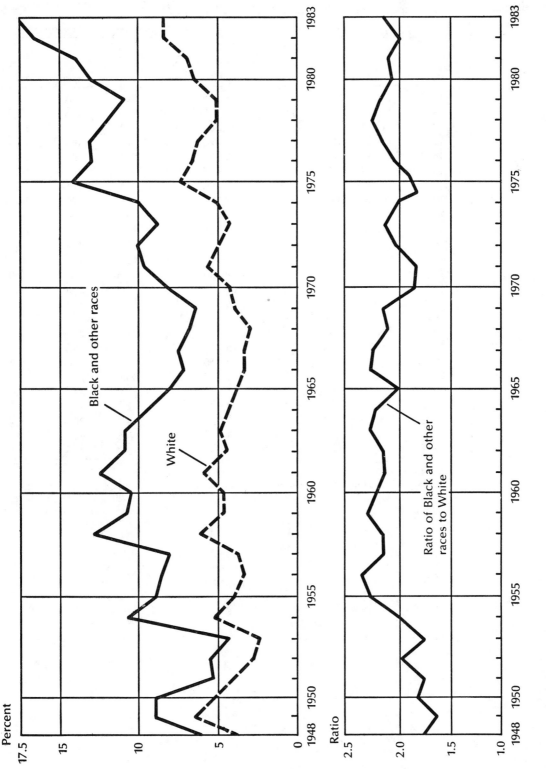

FIGURE 3. Unemployment Rates: 1948 to 1983 (Annual averages) (Source: Table 14)

TABLE 15. *Persons Below the Poverty Level 1959–1983 (as of the Following Year)*

Year	Number (thousands)				Percent Below the Poverty Level			
	Black & Other Races	Black	Hispanic	White	Black & Other Races	Black	Hispanic	White
1959	10,430	9,927	NA	28,336	53.3	55.1	NA	18.1
1960	11,524	NA	NA	28,309	55.9	NA	NA	17.8
1961	11,738	NA	NA	27,890	56.1	NA	NA	17.4
1962	11,953	NA	NA	26,672	55.8	NA	NA	16.4
1963	11,198	NA	NA	25,238	51.0	NA	NA	15.3
1964	11,098	NA	NA	24,957	49.6	NA	NA	14.9
1965	10,689	NA	NA	22,496	47.1	NA	NA	13.3
1966	9,220	8,867	NA	19,290	39.8	41.8	NA	11.3
1967	8,786	8,486	NA	18,983	37.2	39.3	NA	11.0
1968	7,994	7,616	NA	17,395	33.5	34.7	NA	10.0
1969	7,488	7,095	NA	16,659	31.0	32.2	NA	9.5
1970	7,936	7,548	NA	17,484	32.0	33.5	NA	9.9
1971	7,780	7,396	NA	17,780	30.9	32.5	NA	9.9
1972	8,257	7,710	2,414	16,203	31.9	33.3	22.8	9.0
1973	7,831	7,388	2,366	15,142	29.6	31.4	21.9	8.4
1974	7,970	7,467	2,575	16,290	29.5	31.4	23.0	8.9
1975	NA	7,545	2,991	17,770	NA	31.3	26.9	9.7
1976	NA	7,595	2,783	16,713	NA	31.1	24.7	9.1
1977	NA	7,726	2,700	16,416	NA	31.3	22.4	8.9
1978	NA	7,625	2,067	16,259	NA	30.6	21.6	8.7
1979	NA	8,050	2,921	17,214	NA	31.0	21.8	9.0
1980	NA	8,579	3,491	19,699	NA	32.5	25.7	10.2
1981	NA	9,173	3,713	21,553	NA	34.2	26.5	11.1
1982	NA	9,697	4,301	23,517	NA	35.6	29.6	12.0
1983	NA	9,885	4,249	23,974	NA	35.7	28.4	12.1

NA: Not Available.

Sources: U.S. Bureau of the Census, *The Social and Economic Status of the Black Population in the United States: An Historical Overview, 1790–1978,* 1979, pp. 49, 202; and U.S. Bureau of the Census, *Current Population Reports,* Series P-60, No. 140, 1983, p. 21; Series P-60, No. 145, 1984, p. 20.

TABLE 16. Poverty Rate of Hispanic, Black and White Families 1959, 1966–1983 (Percent of Families below poverty level)

Year	Black Poverty Rate (% of All Black Families)	Hispanic Poverty Rate (% of All Hispanic Families)	White Poverty Rate (% of All White Families)	Ratio of Black to White Poverty Rate	Ratio of Hispanic to White Poverty Rate
1959	48.1	NA	15.2	3.2	NA
1966	35.5	NA	9.3	3.8	NA
1967	33.9	NA	9.0	3.8	NA
1968	29.4	NA	8.0	3.7	NA
1969	27.9	NA	7.7	3.6	NA
1970	29.5	NA	8.0	3.6	NA
1971	28.8	NA	7.9	3.7	NA
1972	29.0	NA	7.1	4.1	NA
1973	28.1	19.8	6.6	4.3	3.0
1974	26.9	21.2	6.8	4.0	3.1
1975	27.1	25.1	7.7	3.5	3.3
1976	27.9	23.1	7.1	3.9	3.3
1977	28.2	21.4	7.0	4.0	3.1
1978	27.5	20.4	6.9	4.0	3.0
1979	27.8	20.3	6.9	4.0	2.9
1980	28.9	23.2	8.0	3.6	2.9
1981	30.8	24.0	8.8	3.5	2.7
1982	33.0	27.2	9.6	3.4	2.8
1983	32.4	26.1	9.7	3.3	2.7

NA: Not Available

Sources: Bureau of the Census, "Money Income and Poverty Status of Families and Persons in the United States 1981: Advance Data from the March Current Population Survey," *Current Population Reports,* Series P-60, No. 134, July 1980, Table 15; Series P-60, No. 145, 1984, Table 15, p. 20.

TABLE 17. *Black Elected Officials, by Office, 1970–1984*

Year	Total	U.S. and State Legislatures	Regional City and County Offices	Law Enforcement	Education
1970	1,472	182	715	213	362
1972	2,264	224	1,108	263	669
1973	2,621	256	1,264	334	767
1974	2,991	256	1,602	340	793
1975	3,503	299	1,878	387	939
1976	3,979	299	2,274	412	994
1977	4,311	316	2,497	447	1,051
1978	4,503	316	2,595	454	1,138
1979	4,584	315	2,647	486	1,136
1980	4,890	326	2,832	526	1,206
1981	5,014	343	2,863	549	1,259
1982	5,115	342	2,951	563	1,259
1983	5,606	400	3,222	607	1,377
1984	5,700	410	3,283	636	1,371

Source: Joint Center for Political Studies, *National Roster of Black Elected Officials*, Washington, D.C., annual. Reprinted by permission.

TABLE 18. *Years of School Completed by Age and Race 1940–1982*

Age and Year	All Persons					Black Persons				
	Percent Not High School Graduates		Percent with 4 Years of High School or More		Median School Years Completed	Percent Not High School Graduates		Percent with 4 Years of High School or More		Median School Years Completed
	Total	With Less Than 5 yrs. of School	Total	College, 4 yrs. or More		Total	With Less Than 5 yrs. of School	Total	College, 4 yrs. or More	
25 years and over:										
1940	75.5	13.7	24.5	4.6	8.6	92.7	42.0	7.3	1.3	5.7
1950	65.7	11.1	34.3	6.2	9.3	87.1	32.9	12.9	2.1	6.8
1960	58.9	8.3	41.1	7.7	10.6	79.9	23.8	20.1	3.1	8.0
1970	47.7	5.5	52.3	10.7	12.1	68.6	14.6	31.4	4.4	9.8
1980	31.4	3.4	68.6	17.0	12.5	48.8	9.2	51.2	7.9	12.0
1981	30.3	3.3	69.7	17.1	12.5	47.1	7.9	52.9	8.2	12.1
1982	29.0	3.0	71.0	17.7	12.6	45.1	7.3	54.9	8.8	12.2
25–29 years:										
1940	61.9	5.9	38.1	5.9	10.3	88.4	27.7	11.6	1.6	7.0
1950	49.5	4.7	52.8	7.7	12.0	80.4	16.8	22.2	2.7	8.6
1960	39.3	2.8	60.7	11.1	12.3	62.3	7.0	37.7	4.8	9.9
1970	26.2	1.7	73.8	16.3	12.6	44.6	3.2	55.4	6.0	12.1
1980	14.6	.8	85.4	22.5	12.9	23.4	.6	76.6	11.5	12.6
1981	13.7	.7	86.3	21.3	12.8	22.7	.5	77.3	11.5	12.6
1982	13.8	.8	86.2	21.7	12.8	19.0	.7	81.0	12.6	12.7

Source: U.S. Bureau of the Census, *Statistical Abstract, 1984*, p. 144.

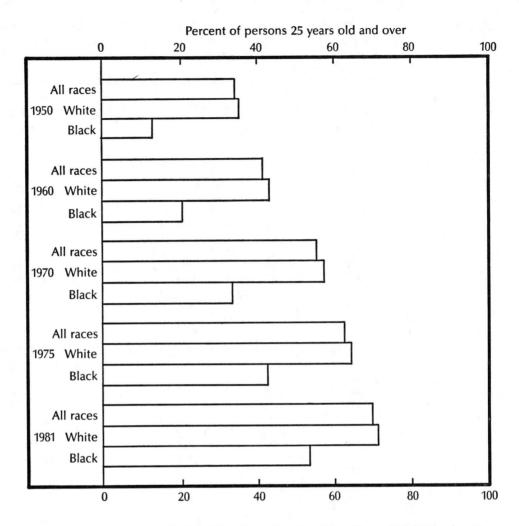

FIGURE 4. Percent of Adults Who Have Completed Four Years of High School or More 1950–1981 (Source: U.S. Bureau of the Census, *Statistical Abstract,* 1983, p. 133.)

TABLE 19. Immigration to the United States 1820–1980 (From 1820 to 1867, figures represent alien passengers arrived; from 1868 through 1891 and 1895 through 1897, immigrant aliens arrived; from 1892 through 1894 and 1898 to the present time, immigrant aliens admitted.)

Year	Number of Persons	Year	Number of Persons	Year	Number of Persons	Year	Number of Persons
1820–1980	49,655,952						
1820	8,385						
1821–1830	143,439	1861–1870	2,314,824	1901–1910	8,795,386	1941–1950	1,035,039
1821	9,127	1861	91,918	1901	487,918	1941	51,776
1822	6,911	1862	91,985	1902	648,743	1942	28,781
1823	6,354	1863	176,282	1903	857,046	1943	23,725
1824	7,912	1864	193,418	1904	812,870	1944	28,551
1825	10,199	1865	248,120	1905	1,026,499	1945	38,119
1826	10,837	1866	318,568	1906	1,100,735	1946	108,721
1827	18,875	1867	315,722	1907	1,285,349	1947	147,292
1828	27,382	1868	138,840	1908	782,870	1948	170,570
1829	22,520	1869	352,768	1909	751,786	1949	188,317
1830	23,322	1870	387,203	1910	1,041,570	1950	249,187
1831–1840	599,125	1871–1880	2,812,191	1911–1920	5,735,811	1951–1960	2,515,479
1831	22,633	1871	321,350	1911	878,587	1951	205,717
1832	60,482	1872	404,806	1912	838,172	1952	265,520
1833	58,640	1873	459,803	1913	1,197,892	1953	170,434
1834	65,365	1874	313,339	1914	1,218,480	1954	208,177
1835	45,374	1875	227,498	1915	326,700	1955	237,790
1836	76,242	1876	169,986	1916	298,826	1956	321,625
1837	79,340	1877	141,857	1917	295,403	1957	326,867
1838	38,914	1878	138,469	1918	110,618	1958	253,265
1839	68,069	1879	177,826	1919	141,132	1959	260,686
1840	84,066	1880	457,257	1920	430,001	1960	265,398
1841–1850	1,713,251	1881–1890	5,246,613	1921–1930	4,107,209	1961–1970	3,321,677
1841	80,289	1881	669,431	1921	805,228	1961	271,344
1842	104,565	1882	788,992	1922	309,556	1962	283,763
1843	52,496	1883	603,322	1923	522,919	1963	306,260
1844	78,615	1884	518,592	1924	706,896	1964	292,248
1845	114,371	1885	395,346	1925	294,314	1965	296,697
1846	154,416	1886	334,203	1926	304,488	1966	323,040
1847	234,968	1887	490,109	1927	335,175	1967	361,972
1848	226,527	1888	546,889	1928	307,255	1968	454,448
1849	297,024	1889	444,427	1929	279,678	1969	358,579
1850	369,980	1890	455,302	1930	241,700	1970	373,326

Year	Number of Persons	Year	Number of Persons	Year	Number of Persons	Year	Number of Persons
1851–1860	2,598,214	1891–1880	3,687,564	1931–1940	528,431	1971–1980	4,493,314
1851	379,466	1891	560,319	1931	97,139	1971	370,478
1852	371,603	1892	579,663	1932	35,576	1972	384,685
1853	368,645	1893	439,730	1933	23,068	1973	400,063
1854	427,833	1894	285,631	1934	29,470	1974	394,861
1855	200,877	1895	258,536	1935	34,956	1975	386,194
1856	200,436	1896	343,267	1936	36,329	1976	398,613
1857	251,306	1897	230,832	1937	50,244	1976,TQ	103,676
1858	123,126	1898	229,299	1938	67,895	1977	462,315
1859	121,282	1899	311,715	1939	82,998	1978	601,442
1860	153,640	1900	448,572	1940	70,756	1979	460,348
						1980	530,639

From 1869 to 1976, the data are for fiscal years ended June 30. Prior to fiscal year 1869, the periods covered are as follows: from 1820–1831 and 1843–1849, the years ended on September 30—1843 covers 9 months; from 1832–1842 and 1850–1867, the years ended on December 31—1832 and 1850 cover 15 months. For 1868, the period ended on June 30 and covers 6 months. The transition quarter (TQ) for 1976 covers the 3-month period, July-September 1976. Beginning October 1, 1976, the fiscal years ended on September 30.

Source: U.S. Immigration and Naturalization Service, *1980 Statistical Yearbook of the Immigration and Naturalization Service*, p. 1.

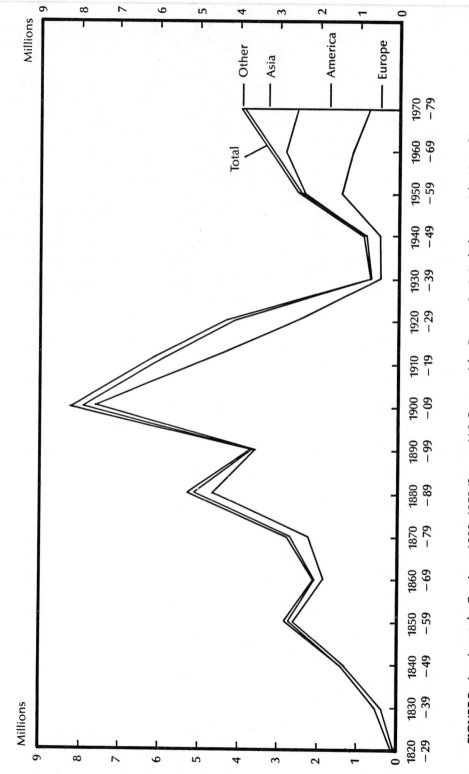

FIGURE 5. Immigrants by Continent 1820–1979 (Source: U.S. Bureau of the Census, Statistical Abstract of the United States, 1981–1983, p. 87)

TABLE 20. *Immigrants, by Country of Last Permanent Residence: 1820 to 1979 (In thousands, except percent. For years ending June 30 except, beginning 1977, ending September 30. Data prior to 1906 refer to country from which aliens came. Because of boundary changes and changes in list of countries separately reported, data for certain countries throughout.)*

Country	1820-1979, total	1951-1960, total	1961-1970, total	1971-1979, total	1975	1976	1977	1978	1979	Percent 1820-1979	Percent 1961-1970	Percent 1971-1979
Total	**49,124**	**2,515.5**	**3,321.7**	**3,962.5**	**386.2**	**398.6**	**462.3**	**601.4**	**460.3**	**100.0**	**100.0**	**100.0**
Europe	**36,267**	**1,325.6**	**1,123.4**	**728.2**	**72.8**	**73.0**	**74.0**	**76.2**	**64.2**	**73.8**	**33.8**	**18.4**
Austria[1] ⎫	4,316 ⎧ 67.1	20.6	9.1	.5	.5	.5	.5	.5	8.8	.6	.2
Hungary ⎭	⎨ 36.6	5.4	5.8	.6	.6	.5	.6	.5		.2	.1
Belgium	204	18.6	9.2	4.7	.4	.5	.5	.6	.6	.4	.3	.1
Czechoslovakia	138	.9	3.3	5.0	.3	.3	.3	.4	.5	.3	.1	.1
Denmark	364	11.0	9.2	3.9	.3	.4	.4	.4	.4	.7	.3	.1
Finland	33	4.9	4.2	2.3	.2	.2	.2	.3	.3	.1	.1	.1
France	754	51.1	45.2	22.7	1.8	2.0	2.7	2.7	2.9	1.5	1.4	.6
Germany[1]	6,985	477.8	190.8	67.9	5.9	6.6	7.4	7.6	7.2	14.2	5.7	1.7
Great Britain[2]	4,914	195.5	210.0	121.5	12.2	13.0	14.0	16.4	15.5	10.0	6.3	3.1
Greece	661	47.6	86.0	87.7	9.8	8.6	7.8	7.0	5.9	1.3	2.6	2.2
Ireland[3]	4,724	57.3	37.5	10.6	1.1	1.0	1.0	.9	.8	9.6	1.1	.3
Italy	5,300	185.5	214.1	123.9	11.0	8.0	7.4	7.0	6.0	10.8	6.4	3.1
Netherlands	360	52.3	30.6	9.5	.8	.9	1.0	1.2	1.2	.7	.9	.2
Norway	856	22.9	15.5	3.5	.4	.3	.3	.4	.4	1.7	.5	.1
Poland[1]	520	10.0	53.5	32.5	3.5	3.2	3.3	4.5	3.9	1.1	1.6	.8
Portugal	453	19.6	76.1	93.3	11.3	11.0	10.0	10.5	7.1	.9	2.3	2.4
Soviet Union[1] [4]	3,376	.6	2.3	28.4	4.7	7.4	5.4	4.7	1.9	6.9	.1	.7
Spain	262	7.9	44.7	37.4	2.6	2.3	5.6	4.3	3.3	.5	1.3	.9
Sweden	1,273	21.7	17.1	5.8	.5	.6	.6	.6	.8	2.6	.5	.1
Switzerland	350	17.7	18.5	7.7	.7	.8	.8	.9	.9	.7	.6	.2
Yugoslavia	116	8.2	20.4	28.5	2.9	2.3	2.3	2.2	1.9	.2	.6	.7
Other Europe	310	10.8	9.2	16.4	1.3	2.0	2.0	2.5	1.8	.6	.3	.4
Asia	**3,038**	**153.3**	**427.8**	**1,352.1**	**129.2**	**146.7**	**150.8**	**243.6**	**183.0**	**6.2**	**12.9**	**34.1**
China[5]	540	9.7	34.8	96.7	9.2	9.9	12.5	14.5	12.3	1.1	1.0	2.4
Hong Kong	[6]200	15.5	75.0	109.5	12.5	13.7	12.3	11.1	16.8	.4	2.3	2.8
India	182	2.0	27.2	141.4	14.3	16.1	16.8	19.1	18.6	.4	.8	3.6
Iran	[6]48	3.4	10.3	34.9	2.2	2.6	4.2	5.9	8.3	.1	.3	.9
Israel	[6]90	25.5	29.6	34.2	3.5	5.2	4.4	4.5	4.3	.2	.9	.9
Japan	411	46.3	40.0	45.4	4.8	4.8	4.5	4.5	4.5	.8	1.2	1.1
Jordan	[6]41	5.8	11.7	24.0	2.3	2.4	2.9	3.2	3.2	.1	.3	.6
Korea	[6]276	6.2	34.5	235.4	28.1	30.6	30.7	28.8	28.7	.6	1.0	5.9
Lebanon	[6]58	4.5	15.2	37.3	4.0	5.0	5.5	4.8	4.8	.1	.5	.9
Philippines	[7]431	19.3	98.4	312.7	31.3	36.8	38.5	36.6	40.8	.9	3.0	7.9
Turkey	386	3.5	10.1	11.1	1.1	1.0	1.0	1.0	1.3	.8	.3	.3
Vietnam	[8]133	2.7	4.2	129.3	2.7	2.4	3.4	87.6	19.1	.3	.1	3.3
Other Asia	244	9.0	36.7	140.3	13.2	16.2	14.1	22.0	20.3	.5	1.2	3.5
America	**9,248**	**996.9**	**1,716.4**	**1,778.3**	**174.7**	**169.2**	**223.2**	**226.5**	**197.1**	**18.8**	**51.7**	**44.9**
Argentina	[9]97	19.5	49.7	27.2	2.8	2.7	3.1	4.1	3.1	.2	1.5	.7
Brazil	[9]59	13.8	29.3	16.4	1.4	1.4	1.9	2.2	1.8	.1	.9	.4
Canada	4,125	378.0	413.3	156.2	11.2	11.4	18.0	23.5	20.2	8.4	12.4	3.9
Colombia	[9]156	18.0	72.0	66.0	6.4	5.7	8.2	10.9	10.5	.3	2.2	1.7

continued

TABLE 20 *continued*

Country	1820-1979, total	1951-1960, total	1961-1970, total	1971-1979, total	1975	1976	1977	1978	1979	Percent		
										1820-1979	1961-1970	1971-1979
Cuba	[10]539	78.9	208.5	249.7	25.6	28.4	66.1	27.5	14.0	1.1	6.3	6.3
Dominican Republic	[10]235	9.9	93.3	130.8	14.1	12.4	11.6	19.5	17.5	.5	2.8	3.3
Ecuador	[9]91	9.8	36.8	44.0	4.7	4.5	5.2	5.7	4.4	.2	1.1	1.1
El Salvador	[9]50	5.9	15.0	28.4	2.4	2.4	4.4	5.9	4.5	.1	.4	.7
Guatemala	[9]44	4.7	15.9	22.2	1.9	2.0	3.7	4.1	2.6	.1	.5	.6
Haiti	[10]89	4.4	34.5	49.8	5.0	5.3	5.2	6.1	6.1	.2	1.0	1.3
Honduras	[9]37	6.0	15.7	14.8	1.4	1.3	1.6	2.7	2.5	.2	.5	.4
Mexico	2,177	299.8	453.9	583.7	62.6	58.4	44.6	92.7	52.5	4.4	13.7	14.7
Panama	[9]51	11.7	19.4	19.8	1.7	1.8	2.5	3.3	3.5	.1	.6	.5
Peru	[9]52	7.4	19.1	25.1	2.3	2.6	3.9	5.1	4.0	.1	.6	.6
Other West Indies	758	29.8	133.9	237.4	22.3	19.6	27.1	34.6	33.5	1.5	4.0	6.0
Other America	695	99.2	106.2	106.9	8.9	9.3	16.1	18.6	16.4	1.4	3.2	2.7
Africa	**142**	**14.1**	**29.0**	**66.7**	**5.9**	**5.7**	**9.6**	**10.3**	**11.2**	**.3**	**.9**	**1.7**
Australia and												
New Zealand	**123**	**11.5**	**19.6**	**21.6**	**1.8**	**2.1**	**2.5**	**2.6**	**2.5**	**.3**	**.6**	**.5**
All other	**309**	**14.0**	**5.7**	**15.8**	**1.8**	**1.9**	**2.2**	**2.2**	**2.3**	**.6**	**.2**	**.4**

[1]1938–1945, Austria included with Germany; 1899–1919, Poland included with Austria-Hungary, Germany, and Soviet Union.
[2]Beginning 1952, includes data for United Kingdom not specified, formerly included with "Other Europe."
[3]Comprises Eire and Northern Ireland.
[4]Europe and Asia.
[5]Beginning 1957, includes Taiwan.
[6]Prior to 1951, included with "Other Asia."
[7]Prior to 1951, Philippines included with "All other."
[8]Prior to 1953, data for Vietnam not available.
[9]Prior to 1951, included with "Other America."
[10]Prior to 1951, included with "Other West Indies."
Source: U.S. Bureau of the Census, *Statistical Almanac of the United States, 1982–1983,* p. 89.

Bibliography

The articles reprinted in this volume are drawn from a wide range of sources and reflect many different reference formats. I have attempted to provide some uniformity of reference style. Where the references are numbered in the original publication, I have placed them at the end of each article ("Endnotes"). Where the system of identifying references by last name of author, year of publication, and page numbers (for example, Bonacich, 1972:553) has been used, I have placed all reference sources in this bibliography. An asterisk (*) next to a citation in this bibliography indicates that the selection or portions of it are reprinted in this volume.

Abrahams, R. 1967, Revised edition. *Deep Down in the Jungle.* Hatboro, Pa.: Folklore Associates.

Abramson, Harold J. 1971. "Ethnic Diversity Within Catholicism: A Comparative Analysis of Contemporary and Historical Religion." *Journal of Social History* 4.

_____. 1973. *Ethnic Diversity in Catholic America.* New York: Wiley.

_____. 1975. "The Religioethnic Factor and the American Experience: Another Look at the Three-Generations Hypothesis." *Ethnicity* 2:2 (June).

Alba, Francisco. 1978. "Mexico's International Migration as a Manifestation of Its Development Pattern." *International Migration Review* 12 (Winter).

Alba, Richard D. 1976. "Social Assimilation Among American Catholic National Origin Groups." *American Sociological Review* 41 (December).

*_____. 1981. "The Twilight of Ethnicity among American Catholics of European Ancestry." *Annals of the American Academy of Political and Social Sciences* 454 (March).

Alba, Richard D., and Chamlin, Mitchell B. 1983. "A Preliminary Examination of Ethnic Identification among Whites." *American Sociological Review* 48:240–247.

Aldrich, Howard, and Weiss, Jane. 1981. "Differentiation Within the U.S. Capitalist Class." *American Sociological Review* 46.

Alexander, R. D. 1971. "The Search for an Evolutionary Philosophy of Man." *Proceedings of the Royal Society of Victoria* 84.

Allen, Robert L. 1970. *Black Awakening in Capitalist America.* Garden City, N.Y.: Doubleday.

Allport, Gordon W. 1958. *The Nature of Prejudice.* Garden City, N.Y.: Doubleday.

Almaguer, Tomas. 1974. "Historical Notes on Chicano Oppression." *Aztlan* 5 (Spring/Fall).

Alvarez, Rodolfo. 1973. "The Psycho-Historical

and Socioeconomic Development of the Chicano Community in the United States." *Social Science Quarterly* 53 (March).

Amin, Samir. 1974. *Accumulation on a World Scale: A Critique of the Theory of Underdevelopment.* New York: Monthly Review Press.

Anderson, Patrick. 1976. "On Working Closely with Jimmy Carter." *New York Times* (July 19).

Appel, J. J. 1961. "Hansen's Third-Generation 'Law' and the Origins of the American Jewish Historical Society." *Jewish Social Studies* 23.

Aronowitz, Stanley. 1973. *False Promises.* New York: McGraw Hill.

Association of Black Sociologists. 1978. "Statement." *ASA Footnotes* (December).

Astin, A., and Panos, R. J. 1969. "The Educational and Vocational Development of College Students." Washington, D.C.: American Council on Education.

Auster, Ellen, and Aldrich, Howard. 1984. "Small Business Vulnerability, Ethnic Enclaves, and Ethnic Enterprise." In Robin Ward, ed., *Ethnic Business in Britain.* Cambridge: Cambridge University Press.

Averitt, Robert T. 1968. *The Dual Economy: The Dynamics of American Industry Structure.* New York: Norton.

Bach, Robert L. 1978a. "Foreign Policy Implications of Recent Trends in Mexican Immigration." Testimony presented before the Committee on International Relations, U.S. House of Representatives, May 24.

_____. 1978b. "Mexican Immigration and the American State." *International Migration Review* 12 (Winter).

Bailey, Thomas A. 1934. *Theodore Roosevelt and the Japanese-American Crisis.* Stanford: Stanford University Press.

Bailyn, Bernard. 1955. *The New England Merchants in the Seventeenth Century.* Cambridge, Mass.: Harvard University Press.

Baker, Ray Stannard. 1964. *Following the Color Line: American Negro Citizenship in the Progressive Era.* New York: Harper Torchbooks.

Banfield, Edward C. 1970. *The Unheavenly City.* Boston: Little, Brown.

Banton, Michael. 1974. "1960: A Turning Point in the Study of Race Relations." *Daedalus* 103:40–41.

Baran, Paul and Sweezy, Paul. 1966. *Monopoly Capital.* New York: Monthly Review Press.

Barash, D. P. 1977. *Sociobiology and Behavior.* New York: Elsevier.

Baratz, Joan C. 1970. "Teaching Reading in the Urban Negro School System." In F. Williams, ed., *Language and Poverty: Perspectives on a Theme.* Chicago: Markham.

Baratz, Stephen S., and Baratz, Joan C. 1968. "Negro Ghetto Children and Urban Education: A Cultural Solution." *Bulletin of the Minnesota Council for the Social Studies* (Fall). (Reprinted in 1969 in *Social Education* 33.)

_____. 1969. "The Social Pathology Model: Historical Bases for Psychology's Denial of the Existence of Negro Culture." APA Paper. Washington, D.C.

_____. 1970. "Early Childhood Intervention: The Social Science Base of Institutional Racism." *Harvard Educational Review* 40.

Barkow, J. H. 1978. "Culture and Sociobiology," *American Anthropologist* 80:1.

Baron, Harold M. 1968. "Black Powerlessness in Chicago." *Transaction* 6 (1).

Baron, Harold M., and Bennett Hymer. 1968. "The Negro Worker in the Chicago Labor Movement." In *The Negro and the American Labor Movement,* ed. J. Jacobson. Garden City, N.Y.: Doubleday.

Barrera, Mario. 1977. "Class Segmentation and Internal Colonialism: A Theory of Racial Inequality Based on the Chicano Experience." Mimeographed. San Diego: University of California.

Barth, Ernest A. T., and Noel, Donald L. 1972. "Conceptual Frameworks for the Analysis of Race Relations: An Evaluation." *Social Forces* 50 (March).

Barth, Frederick. 1962. *The Role of Entrepreneur in Social Change in Northern Norway.* Bergen: Norwegian Universities Press.

Barth, Fredrick, ed. 1969. *Ethnic Groups and Boundaries.* Boston: Little, Brown.

Basil, Anne. 1969. *Armenian Settlements in India.* West Bengal: Armenian College.

Baughman, E. Earl. 1971. *Black Americans.* New York: Academic Press.

Bechofer, Frank; Elliott, Brian; Rushforth, Monica; and Bland, Richard. 1974. "Small Shopkeepers: Matters of Money and Meaning." *Sociological Review* 22.

Becker, Gary. 1957. *The Economics of Discrimination.* Chicago: University of Chicago Press.

Becker, Howard. 1956. *Man in Reciprocity.* New York: Praeger.

Bell, Daniel. 1975. *The Cultural Contradictions of Capitalism.* New York: Basic Books.

Bell, Inge Powell. 1968. *CORE and the Strategy of Non-Violence.* New York: Random House.

Bell, Wendell. 1954. "A Probability Model for the

Measurement of Ecological Segregation." *Social Forces* 32:357–364.

Bell, Wendell, and Boat, M. 1957. "Urban Neighborhoods and Informal Social Relations." *American Journal of Sociology 62*.

Belshaw, Cyril. 1955. "The Cultural Milieu of the Entrepreneur." *Explorations in Entrepreneurial History 7*.

Bender, E. I., and Kagiwada, G. 1968. "Hansen's Law of 'Third-Generation Return' and the Study of American Religio-Ethnic Groups." *Phylon 29*.

Benedict, Barton. 1958. "Family Firms and Economic Development." *Southwest Journal of Anthropology* 24:19–24.

Bereiter, C. 1965. "Academic Instruction and Preschool Children." In R. Cobin and M. Crosby, eds., *Language Programs for the Disadvantaged*. Champaign, Ill.: National Council of Teachers of English.

Bereiter, Carl, and Engelman, Siegfried. 1966. *Teaching Disadvantaged Children in Preschool*. Englewood Cliffs, N.J.: Prentice-Hall.

Berelson, Bernard, and Salter, Patricia J. 1946. "Majority and Minority Americans: An Analysis of Magazine Fiction." *Public Opinion Quarterly 10*.

Berg, E. J. 1966. "Backward-sloping Labor Supply Functions in Dual Economies—the Africa Case." In I. Wallerstein, ed., *Social Change: The Colonial Situation*. New York: Wiley.

Berger, Bennett M. 1960. *Working Class Suburb*. Berkeley: University of California Press.

Berreman, Gerald D. 1969. "Caste in India and the United States." In J. Roach, L. Gross, and O. Gursslin, eds., *Social Stratification in the United States*. Englewood Cliffs, N.J.: Prentice-Hall.

*_____. 1972. "Race, Caste, and Other Invidious Distinctions in Social Stratification." *Race* 13 (April).

Berry, Brian J. L. 1973. *The Human Consequences of Urbanization*. New York: St. Martin's.

Berry, Brewton. 1958. *Race and Ethnic Relations*. New York: Harper and Row.

Berry, J. W. 1966. "Temne and Eskimo Perceptional Skill." *International Journal of Psychology 1*.

_____. 1971. "Ecological and Cultural Factors in Spatial Perceptual Development." *Canadian Journal of Behavioral Science 3*.

Bettelheim, Charles. 1970. "Economic Inequalities Between Nations and International Solidarity." *Monthly Review* 22:19–24.

Beveridge, Andrew A., and Oberschall, Anthony R. 1979. *African Businessmen and Development in Zambia*. Princeton, N.J.: Princeton University Press.

Bierstedt, Robert. 1948. "The Sociology of Majorities." *American Sociological Review* 13 (December).

Bigelow, R. 1968. *The Dawn Warriors*. Boston: Little, Brown.

Billingsley, A. 1968. *Black Families in White America*. Englewood Cliffs, N.J.: Prentice-Hall.

Blackistone, Kevin B. 1981. "Arab Entrepreneurs Take Over Inner City Grocery Stores." *Chicago Reporter* 10.

Blair, Philip M. 1971. *Job Discrimination and Education: An Investment Analysis*. New York: Praeger.

_____. 1972. "Job Discrimination and Education." In M. Carnoy, ed., *Schooling in a Corporate Society: The Political Economy of Education in America*. New York: David McKay.

Blalock, H. M., Jr. 1956. "Economic Discrimination and Negro Increase." *American Sociological Review* 21 (October).

_____. 1962. "Occupational Discrimination: Some Theoretical Propositions." *Social Problems* 9 (Winter).

_____. 1967. *Toward a Theory of Minority-Group Relations*. New York: Wiley.

Blassingame, John W. 1972. *The Slave Community: Plantation Life in the Antebellum South*. New York: Oxford University Press.

Blau, Peter M. 1964. *Exchange and Power in Social Life*. New York: Wiley.

_____. 1977. *Inequality and Heterogeneity*. New York: Free Press.

Blauner, Robert. 1969. "Black Culture: Myth or Reality?" In N. E. Whitten, Jr., and J. F. Szwed, eds., *Afro-American Anthropology*. New York: Free Press.

_____. 1969. "Internal Colonialism and Ghetto Revolt." *Social Problems* 16 (Spring).

_____. 1972. *Racial Oppression in America*. New York: Harper and Row.

_____. n.d. "Marxist Theory, Nationality, and Colonialism." Unpublished manuscript.

Bloom, Leonard, and Riemer, Ruth. 1949. *Removal and Return*. Berkeley: University of California Press.

Blumer, Herbert. 1954. "What is Wrong with Social Theory?" *American Sociological Review* 19 (February).

_____. 1958. "Race Prejudice as a Sense of Group Position." *Pacific Sociological Review* 1 (Spring).

_____. 1958. "Research on Racial Relations: The United States of America." *International Social Science Bulletin* 10 (1).

_____. 1965. "Industrialisation and Race Relations." In G. Hunter, ed., *Industrialisation and Race Relations: A Symposium*. Institute of Race Relations. New York: Oxford University Press.

Boissevain, Jeremy. 1984. "Small Entrepreneurs in Contemporary Europe." In Robin Ward, ed., *Ethnic Business in Britain*. Cambridge: Cambridge University Press.

Bonacich, Edna. 1972. "A Theory of Ethnic Antagonism: The Split Labor Market." *American Sociological Review* 37 (October).

_____. 1973. "A Theory of Middleman Minorities." *American Sociological Review* 38 (October).

_____. 1975. "Abolition, the Extent of Slavery and the Position of Free Blacks: A Study of Split Labor Markets in the United States, 1830–1863." *American Journal of Sociology* 81:601–628.

_____. 1975. "Small Business and Japanese American Ethnic Solidarity." *Amerasia Journal* 3.

_____. 1976. "Advanced Capitalism and Black/White Relations in the United States: A Split Labor Market Interpretation." *American Sociological Review* 41:34–51.

_____. 1978. "Korean Immigrant Small Business in Los Angeles." In Roy S. Bryce-Laporte, ed., *Sourcebook on the New Immigration*. New Brunswick, N.J.: Transaction Books.

_____. 1978. "U.S. Capitalism and Korean Immigrant Small Business." Mimeographed. Riverside, Cal.: University of California.

_____. 1979. "The Past, Present, and Future of Split Labor Market Theory." *Research in Race and Ethnic Relations* 1.

*_____. 1980. "Class Approaches to Ethnicity and Race." *Insurgent Sociologist* 10 (Fall).

_____. 1980. "The Development of U.S. Capitalism and Its Influence on Asian Immigration." Unpublished manuscript.

Bonacich, Edna, and Hirata, Lucie Cheng. 1979. "International Labor Migration: A Theoretical Orientation." Unpublished manuscript.

Bonacich, Edna, and Jung, Tae Hwan. 1982. "A Portrait of Korean Small Business in Los Angeles: 1977." In Eui-Young Yu, Earl H. Phillips, and Eun Sik Yang, eds., *Koreans in Los Angeles*. Los Angeles: Koryo Research Institute and Center for Korean-American and Korean Studies, California State University.

Bonacich, Edna, Light, Ivan H., and Wong, Charles Choy. 1977. "Koreans in Business." *Society* 14 (September/October):54–59.

Bonacich, Edna, and Modell, John. 1980. *The Economic Basis of Ethnic Solidarity: Small Business in the Japanese-American Community*. Berkeley: University of California Press.

Bonnett, Aubrey W. 1980. "An Examination of Rotating Credit Associations Among Black West Indian Immigrants in Brooklyn." In Roy S. Bryce-Laporte, ed., *Sourcebook on the New Immigration*. New Brunswick, N.J.: Transaction Books.

Borhek, J. T. 1970. "Ethnic Group Cohesion." *American Journal of Sociology* 76.

Borrie, W. D. 1954. *Italians and Germans in Australia*. Melbourne: Chesire.

Bossard, James H. S. 1932. "Residential Propinquity as a Factor in Marriage Selection." *American Journal of Sociology* 38:219–224.

Bosworth, Allen R. 1967. *America's Concentration Camps*. New York: W. W. Norton.

Bottomore, T. B. 1966. *Classes in Modern Society*. New York: Pantheon.

Bourne, Randolph S. 1964. *War and the Intellectuals: Collected Essays, 1915–19*, ed. Carl Resek. New York: Harper and Row.

Boyd, Monica. 1971a. "Oriental Immigration: The Experience of the Chinese, Japanese, and Filipino Population in the U.S." *International Migration Review* 5 (Spring):48–61.

_____. 1971b. "The Chinese in New York, California, and Hawaii: a Story of Socioeconomic Differentials." *Phylon* 32 (2):195–206.

Brace, C. Loring and Livingstone, Frank B. 1971. "On Creeping Jensenism." In C. L. Brace, G. R. Gamble, and J. T. Bond, eds., *Race and Intelligence*. Washington, D.C.: American Anthropological Association.

Breton, Raymond. 1964. "Institutional Completeness of Ethnic Communities and the Personal Relations of Immigrants." *American Journal of Sociology* 70.

Briggs, Vernon M. 1978. "Labor Market Aspects of Mexican Migration to the United States in the 1970s." In Stanley R. Ross, ed., *Views Across the Border: The United States and Mexico*. Albuquerque: University of New Mexico Press.

Broom, Leonard, and Glenn, Norval D. 1965. *Transformation of the Negro American*. New York: Harper and Row.

Bryce-Laporte, Roy Simon. 1969. "The American Slave Plantation and Our Heritage of Communal Deprivation." *American Behavioral Scientist* 4 (March-April).

Bryde, John S. 1970. *The Sioux Indian Student: A*

Study of Scholastic Failure and Personality Conflict. Vermillion, S.D.: Dakota Press.

Burgess, Ernest W. 1922. "The Determination of Gradients in the Growth of the City." *Proceedings of the American Sociological Society* 18.

Burgess, M. Elaine. 1978. "The Resurgence of Ethnicity: Myth or Reality?" *Ethnic and Racial Studies* 1:3 (July).

Buroway, Michael. 1976. "The Functions and Reproduction of Migrant Labor: Comparative Material from Southern Africa and the United States." *American Journal of Sociology* 81 (March).

Burstein, Alan N. 1981. "Immigrants and Residential Mobility: The Irish and Germans in Philadelphia, 1850–1880." In Theodore Hershberg, ed., *Philadelphia: Work, Space, Family, and Group Experience in the 19th Century.* New York: Oxford University Press.

Bustamante, Jorge A. 1975. "Espaldas mojadas: Materia prima para la expansión del capital norteamericano." *Cuadernos del Centro de Estudios Sociologicos,* no. 9 (Mexico, D.F.).

Cahan, Abraham. 1966. *The Rise of David Levinsky.* New York: Harper Torchbooks. (Originally published in 1917.)

Carmichael, Stokely, and Hamilton, Charles V. 1967. *Black Power: The Politics of Liberation in America.* New York: Vintage Books.

Carter, Thomas P. 1970. *Mexican Americans in School: A History of Educational Neglect.* New York: College Entrance Examination Board.

Castells, Manuel. 1975. "Immigrant Workers and Class Struggles in Advanced Capitalism: The Western European Experience." *Politics and Society* 5 (1):33–66.

Castles, S., and Kosack, G. 1973. *Immigrant Workers and Class Structure in Western Europe.* London: Oxford University Press.

Cator, W. L. 1936. *The Economic Position of the Chinese in the Netherlands Indies.* Chicago: University of Chicago Press.

Catton, William R., and Smircich, R. J. 1964. "A Comparison of Mathematical Models for Effects of Residential Propinquity on Mate Selection." *American Sociological Review* 29:522–529.

Caudill, William, and DeVos, George. 1956. "Achievement, Culture and Personality: The Case of the Japanese Americans." *American Anthropologist* 58.

Centers, Richard. 1959. *Psychology of Social Classes.* Princeton, N.J.: Princeton University Press.

Chagnon, N. A., and Irons, W., eds. 1978. *Evolu-tionary Biology and Human Social Behavior.* North Scituate, Mass.: Duxbury Press.

Chan, Janet B. L., and Cheung, Yuet-Wah. 1982. "Ethnic Resources and Business Enterprise: A Study of Chinese Business in Toronto." Paper presented at the Annual Meeting of the American Sociological Association, San Francisco, September 6.

Charsley, S. R. 1974. "The Formation of Ethnic Groups." In A. Cohen, ed., *Urban Ethnicity.* London: Tavistock.

Child, Irwin L. 1943. *Italian or American? Second Generation in Conflict.* New Haven, Conn.: Yale University Press.

"The Children of Immigrants in Schools." 1911. *Reports of the Immigration Commission,* vol. 1. Washington, D.C.: U.S. Government Printing Office.

Chinoy, Ely. 1952. "The Tradition of Opportunity and the Aspirations of Automobile Workers." *American Journal of Sociology* 57.

Chiswick, Barry. 1978. "The Effect of Americanization on the Earnings of Foreign-born Men." *Journal of Political Economy* 86:897–921.

*_____. 1982. "Immigrants in the U.S. Labor Market." *The Annals of the American Academy of Political and Social Sciences* (March).

Chock, Phyllis P. 1981. "The Greek-American Small Businessman: A Cultural Analysis." *Journal of Anthropological Research* 37.

Cingolani, Cindy. 1973. "Avoiding Management Pitfalls." *Bank of America Small Business Reporter* 11 (5).

Clark, Juan M. 1973. "Los Cubanos de Miami: Cuántos son y de dónde provienen." *Ideal* 2 (January): 17–19.

_____. 1977. "The Cuban Exodus: Why?" Mimeographed. Miami: Cuban Exile Union.

Clark, Kenneth B. 1965. *Dark Ghetto.* New York: Harper and Row.

_____. 1972. *A Possible Reality: A Design for the Attainment of High Academic Achievement for Inner-City Students.* New York: Marc Corporation.

Cleaver, Eldridge. 1968. *Soul on Ice.* New York: McGraw-Hill.

Cloward, Richard A., and Jones, J. A. 1963. "Social Class Educational Attitudes and Participation." In A. H. Passow, ed., *Education in Depressed Areas.* New York: Teachers Press.

Cohen, Abner. 1969. *Custom and Politics in Urban Africa: A Study of Hausa Migrants in Yoruba Towns.* Berkeley: University of California Press.

_____. 1974. "Introduction." In A. Cohen, ed., *Urban Ethnicity*. London: Tavistock.

Cohen, Rosalie A. 1969. "Conceptual Styles, Culture Conflict, and Nonverbal Test of Intelligence." *American Anthropologist* 71.

Cole, Michael, and Scribner, Sylvia. 1974. *Culture and Thought: A Psychological Introduction*. New York: Wiley.

Coleman, James S. 1966. *Equality of Educational Opportunity*. Washington, D.C.: U.S. Government Printing Office.

Coleman, James S., Kelly, Sara D., and Moore, John A. 1975. *Trends in School Segregation, 1968-1973*. Washington, D.C.: Urban Institute.

Collins, A. Michael. 1975. "Minority Income and Employment: Issues and Efforts." In N. R. Yetman and C. H. Steele, eds., *Majority and Minority: The Dynamics of Racial and Ethnic Relations*. Boston: Allyn and Bacon.

Corey, Lewish. 1966. "The Middle Class." In Reinhard Bendix and Seymour Lipset, eds., *Class Status, and Power,* 2d ed. Glencoe, Ill.: Free Press.

Corneluis, Wayne A. 1977. "Undocumented Immigration: A Critique of the Carter Administration's Policy Proposals." *Migration Today* 5 (October).

_____. 1978. "Mexican Migration to the United States: Causes, Consequences, and U.S. Responses." Center for International Studies, Migration and Development Group, Massachusetts Institute of Technology, July.

Cornelius, Wayne A., and Diez-Canedo, Juan. 1976. "Mexican Migration to the United States: The View from Rural Sending Communities." Center for International Studies, Migration and Development Group, Massachusetts Institute of Technology, June.

Coughlin, Richard J. 1960. *Double Identity: The Chinese in Modern Thailand*. Hong Kong: Hong Kong University Press.

Counts, George Sylvester. 1922. "The Selective Character of American Secondary Education." *Supplementary Educational Monographs* 19. Chicago: University of Chicago Press.

Cox, Oliver C. 1948. *Caste, Class and Race*. New York: Doubleday.

Cressey, Paul F. 1938. "Population Succession in Chicago." *American Journal of Sociology* 44:56–59.

Crevecoeur, Hector St. John de. 1957. *Letters From an American Farmer*. New York: E. P. Dutton. (Originally published in 1782.)

Cruse, Harold. 1967. *The Crisis of the Negro Intellectual*. New York: Morrow.

_____. 1968. *Rebellion or Revolution?* New York: Apollo Editions.

Cumberland, Charles. 1968. *Mexico: The Struggle for Modernity*. New York: Oxford University Press.

Cummings, Scott A. 1980. "Collectivism: The Unique Legacy of Immigrant Economic Development." In Scott Cummings, ed., *Self-Help in Urban America*. Port Washington, N.Y.: Kennikat Press.

Dahrendorf, Ralf. 1959. *Class and Class Conflict in Industrial Society*. Stanford, Cal.: Stanford University Press.

Dahya, Badr. 1974. "Pakistani Ethnicity in Industrial Cities in Britain." In A. Cohen, ed., *Urban Ethnicity*. London: Tavistock.

Daniels, Roger. 1966. *The Politics of Prejudice*. Gloucester, Mass.: Petter Smith.

_____. 1972. *Concentration Camps USA: Japanese Americans and World War II*. New York: Holt, Rinehart and Winston.

Daniels, Roger, and Kitano, Harry H.L. 1970. *American Racism*. Englewood Cliffs, N.J.: Prentice-Hall.

Davie, Maurice. 1947. *Refugees in America*. New York: Harper.

Davis, Allison, Gardner, Burleigh B., and Gardner, Mary R. 1941. *Deep South*. Chicago: University of Chicago Press.

*Davis, Cary, Haub, Carl, and Willette, Joanne. 1983. "U.S. Hispanics: Changing the Face of America," *Population Bulletin* 38:3 (June).

Davis, David Brian. 1966. *The Problem of Slavery in Western Culture*. Ithaca, N.Y.: Cornell University Press.

_____. 1975. *The Problem of Slavery in the Age of Revolution*. Ithaca, N.Y.: Cornell University Press.

Dawkins, R. 1976. *The Selfish Gene*. London: Oxford University Press.

Dawson, J.L.M. 1967. "Cultural and Physiological Influences Upon Spatial Perceptual Processes in West Africa." *International Journal of Psychology* 2.

De Avila, Edward A., and Havassy, Barbara E. 1975. "Piagetian Alternative to IQ: Mexican-American Study." In N. Hobbs, ed., *The Future of Children*, vol. 2, Issues in the Classification of Children. San Francisco: Jossey-Bass.

Degler, Carl N. 1971. *Neither Black Nor White*. New York: Macmillan.

Department of Economics, University of Natal. 1961. "Studies of Indian Employment in Natal." *Natal Regional Survey*, vol. 11. Cape Town: Oxford University Press.

Desai, Rashmi. 1963. *Indian Immigrants in Britain*. London: Oxford University Press.

Despres, Leo A. 1969. "Differential Adaptations and Micro-Cultural Evolution in Guyana." *Southwestern Journal of Anthropology* 25 (Spring).

Deutsch, C., and Deutsch, M. 1968. "Theory of Early Childhood Environment Programs." In R. Hess and R. Bear, eds., *Early Education: Current Theory, Research and Action*. Chicago: Aldine Publishing.

Deutsch, Martin, and Associates. 1967. *The Disadvantaged Child: Selected Papers of Martin Deutsch and Associates*. New York: Basic Books.

Deutsch, Morton, and Collins, Mary C. 1951. *Interracial Housing: A Psychological Evaluation of a Social Experiment*. Minneapolis: University of Minnesota Press.

De Vos, George, and Romanucci-Ross, Lola. 1975. *Ethnic Identity: Cultural Continuities and Change*. Palo Alto, Cal.: Mayfield.

De Vos, George, and Wagatsuma, Hiroshi. 1966. *Japan's Invisible Race: Caste in Culture and Personality*. Berkeley: University of California Press.

DeWolfe, Evelyn. 1982. "Fund Pools Blocked by Postal Law." *Los Angeles Times,* February 21, VII.

Dillard, J. L. 1972. *Black English: Its History and Usage in the United States*. New York: Random House.

———. (In press.) *Black English in the United States*. New York: Random House.

Dimaggio, Paul. 1982. "Cultural Capital and School Success: The Impact of Status Culture Participation on the Grades of U.S. High School Students." *American Sociological Review* 47.

Dinerman, Ina R. 1978. "Patterns of Adaptation among Households of U.S.-bound Migrants from Michoacan, Mexico." *International Migration Review* 12 (Winter).

Dinnerstein, Leonard, and Reimers, David M. 1975, 1983. *Ethnic Americans: A History of Immigration and Assimilation*. New York: Harper and Row.

Doeringer, Peter B., Geldman, Penny, Gordon, David M., Piore, Michael J., and Reich, Michael. 1969. "Urban Manpower Programs and Low-Income Labor Markets: A Critical Assessment." Mimeographed. Washington, D.C.: Manpower Administration, Department of Labor.

Doeringer, Peter B., and Piore, Michael J. 1971. *Internal Labor Markets and Manpower Analysis*. Lexington, Mass.: D. C. Heath.

Dollard, John. 1937. *Caste and Class in a Southern Town*. New Haven, Conn.: Yale University Press.

Dotson, Floyd, and Dotson, Lillian. 1967. "Indians and Coloureds in Rhodesia and Nyasaland." In M. L. Barron, ed., *Minorities in a Changing World*. New York: Knopf.

Doxley, G. V. 1961. *The Industrial Colour Bar in South Africa*. Cape Town: Oxford University Press.

Drake, B. St. Clair. 1957. "Recent Trends in Research on the Negro in the United States." *International Social Science Bulletin* 9 (4).

———. 1968. "The Ghettoization of Negro Life." In L. A. Ferman, J. L. Kornbluh, and J. A. Miller, eds., *Negroes and Jobs*. Ann Arbor: University of Michigan Press.

Dreger, Ralph Mason. 1973. "Intellectual Functioning." In K. S. Miller and R. M. Dreger, eds., *Comparative Studies of Blacks and Whites in the United States*. New York: Seminar Press.

Du Bois, W. E. B. 1961. *The Souls of Black Folk*. Greenwich, Conn.: Fawcett.

Duncan, Beverly, and Duncan, Otis D. 1968. "Minorities and the Process of Stratification." *American Sociological Review* 33.

Duncan, Beverly, and Lieberson, Stanley. 1970. *Metropolis and Region in Transition*. Beverly Hills, Cal.: Sage.

Duncan, Otis Dudley. 1969. "Inheritance of Poverty or Inheritance of Race?" In Daniel P. Moynihan, ed., *On Understanding Poverty: Perspectives from the Social Sciences*. New York: Basic.

Duncan, Otis Dudley, and Duncan, Beverly. 1957. *The Negro Population of Chicago*. Chicago: University of Chicago Press.

Duncan, Otis Dudley, and Lieberson, Stanley. 1959. "Ethnic Segregation and Assimilation." *American Journal of Sociology* 64.

Dyson-Hudson, R., and Smith, E. A. 1978. "Human Territoriality, An Ecological Reassessment." *American Anthropologist* 80:1.

Eckland, Bruce K. 1968. "Retrieving Mobile Cases in Longitudinal Surveys." *Public Opinion Quarterly* 32: 51–64.

Eckstein, Susan. 1977. *The Poverty of Revolution: The State and the Urban Poor in Mexico*. Princeton, N.J.: Princeton University Press.

Economic Commission for Latin America. 1974. "Economic Survey of Latin America, Part 3." United Nations Document E/CN.12/974/Add. 3.

Edwards, Richard C. 1975. "The Social Relations of Production in the Firm and Labor Market Structure." In R. C. Edwards, M. Reich, and D. M. Gordon, eds.,

Labor Market Segmentation. Lexington, Mass.: D.C. Heath.

Egerton, John. 1970. "Black Executives in Big Business." *Race Relations Reporter* 17 (October).

———. 1972. "Blacks on Corporate Boards Multiply." *Race Relations Reporter* (November).

Eisenstadt, S. N. 1970. "The Process of Absorbing New Immigrants in Israel." In S. N. Eisenstadt, ed., *Integration and Development in Israel.* Jerusalem: Israel University Press.

Eitzen, D. Stanley. 1971. "Two Minorities: The Jews of Poland and the Chinese of the Philippines." In N. R. Yetman and C. H. Steele, eds., *Majority and Minority.* Boston: Allyn and Bacon.

Eitzen, D. Stanley, and Yetman, Norman R. 1977. "Immune From Racism? *Civil Rights Digest* 9 (Winter).

Elkins, Stanley M. 1959. *Slavery: A Problem in American Institutional and Intellectual Life.* Chicago: University of Chicago Press.

Ellison, Ralph. 1966. *Shadow and Act.* New York: New American Library.

Emmanuel, Arghiri. 1972. *Unequal Exchange: A Study of the Imperialism of Free Trade.* New York: Monthly Review Press.

Engelhardt, Tom. 1971. "Ambush at Kamikaze Pass." *Bulletin of Concerned Asian Scholars* 3 (Winter–Spring).

*Enloe, Cynthia. 1981. "The Growth of the State and Ethnic Mobilization: The American Experience." *Ethnic and Racial Studies* 4:2 (April).

Essien-Udom, E. U. 1962. *Black Nationalism: The Search for Identity in America.* Chicago: University of Chicago Press.

Esslinger, Dean R. 1975. *Immigrants and the City: Ethnicity and Mobility in a Nineteenth Century Midwestern Community.* Port Washington, N.Y.: Kennikat Press.

Etzioni, Amitai. 1959. "The Ghetto: A Re-evaluation." *Social Forces* 37 (March).

Fagen, Richard R., Brody, Richard A., and O'Leary, Thomas. 1968. *Cubans in Exile.* Stanford, Cal.: Stanford University Press.

Fain, T. Scott. 1980. "Self-Employed Americans: Their Number Has Increased." *Monthly Labor Review* 103.

Fallows, James. 1983. "Immigration." *The Atlantic* 252:5 (November).

Fanon, Frantz. 1968. *The Wretched of the Earth.* New York: Grove.

Farley, Reynolds. 1977. "Trends in Racial Inequalities: Have the Gains of the 1960s Disappeared in the 1970s?" *American Sociological Review* 42:189–207.

———. 1978. "School Integration in the United States." In Frank D. Bean and W. Parker Frisbie, eds., *The Demography of Racial and Ethnic Groups.* New York: Academic Press.

Feagin, Joe R., and Feagin, Clairece Booher. 1978. *Discrimination American Style.* Englewood Cliffs, N.J.: Prentice-Hall.

Featherman, David. 1971. "The Socioeconomic Achievements of White Religio-ethnic Subgroups: Social and Psychological Explanations." *American Sociological Review* 36:207–222.

Featherman, David, and Hauser, Robert. 1976. "Changes in the Socioeconomic Stratification of the Races, 1962–1973." *American Journal of Sociology* 82:462–483.

———. 1978. *Opportunity and Change.* New York: Academic Press.

Fein, Rashi. 1966. "An Economic and Social Profile of the Negro American." In T. Parsons and K.B. Clark, eds., *The Negro American.* Boston: Houghton Mifflin.

Ferguson-Davie, C. J. 1952. *The Early History of Indians in Natal.* Johannesburg: South African Institute of Race Relations.

Ferman, Louis A. 1968. "The Irregular Economy: Informal Work Patterns in the Ghetto." Mimeographed. Ann Arbor: University of Michigan.

Fishman, Joshua, Nahirny, Vladimir C., Hofman, John E., and Hayden, Robert G. 1966. *Language Loyalty in the United States.* The Hague: Mouton.

Fitzpatrick, Joseph P. 1966. "The Importance of Community in the Process of Immigrant Assimilation." *International Migration Review* 1.

Flaming, Karl H., et al. 1972. "Black Powerlessness in Policy-Making Positions." *The Sociological Quarterly* 13 (Winter).

Fogel, Robert William, and Engerman, Stanley L. 1974. *Time on the Cross: The Economics of American Negro Slavery.* Boston: Little, Brown.

Foley, Donald L. 1950. "The Use of Local Facilities in a Metropolis." *American Journal of Sociology* 56.

Foner, Laura, and Genovese, Eugene, eds. 1969. *Slavery in the New World.* Englewood Cliffs, N.J.: Prentice-Hall.

Fong, Ng Bickleen. 1959. *The Chinese in New Zealand.* Hong Kong: Hong Kong University Press.

Ford, Richard G. 1950. "Population Succession in Chicago." *American Journal of Sociology* 56.

Forman, Robert E. 1971. *Black Ghettos, White Ghettos, and Slums.* Englewood Cliffs, N.J.: Prentice-Hall.

Fox, R., ed. 1975. *Biosocial Anthropology.* New York: Wiley.

Francis, E. K. 1976. *Interethnic Relations: An Essay in Sociological Theory.* New York: Elsevier.

Frank, Andre Gunder. 1967. *Capitalism and Underdevelopment in Latin America.* New York: Monthly Review Press.

_____. 1969. *Latin America: Underdevelopment or Revolution?* New York: Monthly Review Press.

Frazier, E. Franklin. 1947. "Sociological Theory and Race Relations." *American Sociological Review* 12 (June).

Freedman, Marcia. 1976. *Labor Markets: Segments and Shelters.* New York: Universe.

Freedman, Maurice. 1959. "The Handling of Money: A Note on the Background to the Economic Sophistication of the Overseas Chinese." *Man* 59.

Fried, Marc. 1963. "Grieving for a Lost Home." In L. S. Duhl, ed., *The Urban Condition.* New York: Basic Books.

_____. 1974. *The World of the Urban Working Class.* Cambridge, Mass.: Harvard University Press.

Friedman, Samuel. 1969. "How is Racism Maintained?" *Et Al.* 2 (Fall).

Fuchs, Estelle, and Havighurst, Robert J. 1973. *To Live on This Earth: American Indian Education.* Garden City, N.Y.: Doubleday.

Fuchs, Lawrence H. 1968. *American Ethnic Politics.* New York: Harper and Row.

Furnivall, J. S. 1948. *Colonial Policy and Practice.* Cambridge: Cambridge University Press.

_____. 1956. *Colonial Policy and Practice.* New York: New York University Press.

Fusfeld, Daniel R. 1969. "The Basic Economics of the Urban and Racial Crisis." Ann Arbor: Research Seminar on the Economics of the Urban and Racial Crisis, University of Michigan.

Galarza, Ernesto. 1977. *Farm Workers and Agri-Business in California, 1947-1960.* Notre Dame, Ind.: University of Notre Dame Press.

Galbraith, John Kenneth. 1971. *The New Industrial State.* New York: Mentor.

Gallo, Patrick J. 1974. *Ethnic Alienation: The Italian-American.* Cranbury, N.J.: Fairleigh Dickinson University Press.

Gambino, Richard. 1974. *Blood of My Blood: The Dilemma of the Italian-Americans.* New York: Doubleday.

Gans, Herbert. 1962a. *The Urban Villagers.* New York: Free Press.

_____. 1962b. "Urbanism and Suburbanism and Ways of Life: A Re-evaluation of Definitions." In A. Rose, ed., *Human Behavior and Social Processes.* Boston: Houghton Mifflin.

_____. 1968. "Social Protest of the 1960's Takes the Form of the Equality Revolution." *New York Times Magazine,* November 3.

*_____. 1979. "Symbolic Ethnicity: The Future of Ethnic Groups and Culture in America." *Ethnic and Racial Studies* 2 (January).

Garis, Roy L. 1927. *Immigration Restriction.* New York: Macmillan.

Gearing, Fred. 1970. *The Face of the Fox.* Chicago: Aldine Publishing.

Geertz, Clifford. 1963. *Peddlers and Princes.* Chicago: Chicago University Press.

_____. 1963. "The Integrative Revolution: Primordial Sentiments and Civil Politics in New States." In Clifford Geertz, ed., *Old Societies and New States.* New York: Free Press.

Gelfand, Mitchell Brian. 1981. "Chutzpah in El Dorado: Social Mobility of Jews in Los Angeles, 1900–1920." PhD Dissertation, Carnegie-Mellon University, Pittsburgh, Pa.

Genovese, Eugene D. 1975. *Roll, Jordon, Roll: The World the Slaves Made.* New York: Pantheon Books.

Gerry, Chris, and Birkbeck, Chris. 1981. "The Petty Commodity Producer in Third World Cities: Petit-Bourgeois or Disguised Proletarian?" In Frank Bechofer and Brian Elliott, eds., *The Petite Bourgeoisie.* New York: St. Martin's Press.

Geschwender, James. 1978. *Racial Stratification in America.* Dubuque, Iowa: William C. Brown.

Giddens, Anthony. 1973. *The Class Structure of the Advanced Societies.* New York: Harper and Row.

Gillion, K. L. 1962. *Fiji's Indian Immigrants.* Melbourne: Oxford University Press.

Gittler, Joseph B. 1956. *Understanding Minority Groups.* New York: Wiley.

Glanz, Rudolf. 1970. *Jew and Italian: Historic Group Relations and the New Immigration (1881–1924).* New York: Klau.

Glasgow, Douglas G. 1980. *The Black Underclass.* San Francisco: Jossey-Bass.

Glazer, Nathan. 1954. "Ethnic Groups in America."

In M. Berger, T. Abel, and C. Page, eds., *Freedom and Control in Modern Society*. New York: Van Nostrand.

———. 1955. "Social Characteristics of American Jews, 1654–1954." *American Jewish Yearbook* 56. Philadelphia, Pa.: The American Jewish Committee and The Jewish Publication Society of America.

Glazer, Nathan, and Moynihan, Daniel Patrick. 1963. *Beyond the Melting Pot*. Cambridge, Mass.: MIT Press and the Harvard University Press.

———. 1970. *Beyond the Melting Pot* 2d ed. Cambridge, Mass.: MIT Press.

———. 1975. *Ethnicity: Theory and Experience*. Cambridge, Mass.: Harvard University Press.

Glenn, Norval D. 1963. "Occupational Benefits to Whites from Subordination of Negroes." *American Sociological Review* 28 (June).

———. 1965. "The Role of White Resistance and Facilitation in the Negro Struggle for Equality." *Phylon* 26 (June).

———. 1966. "White Gains from Negro Subordination." *Social Problems* 14 (Fall).

Glyn, Andrew, and Sutcliffe, Bob. 1971. "The Critical Condition of British Capital." *New Left Review* 66.

———. 1972. *British Capitalism, Workers and the Profit Squeeze*. Hammondsworth, Eng.: Penguin.

Goering, John M. 1971. "The Emergence of Ethnic Interests: A Case of Serendipity." *Social Forces* 49 (March).

Goffman, Erving. 1961. *Asylums*. New York: Doubleday.

Golab, Caroline. 1973. "The Immigrant and the City: Poles, Italians, and Jews in Philadelphia, 1870–1920." In A. F. Davis and M. H. Haller, eds., *The Peoples of Philadelphia*. Philadelphia: Temple University Press.

Goldscheider, Calvin, and Kobrin, Frances. 1980. "Ethnic Continuity and the Process of Self-Employment." *Ethnicity* 7.

Goldstein, Sidney. 1958. *Patterns of Mobility, 1910–1950*. Philadelphia: University of Pennsylvania Press.

Gonzalez-Casonova, Pablo. 1965. *Le democracia en Mexico*. Mexico, D.F.: Era.

Gordon, David M. 1971. *Class Productivity and the Ghetto*. Ph.D. dissertation, Harvard University.

———. 1972. *Theories of Poverty and Underemployment*. Lexington, Mass.: D. C. Heath.

*Gordon, Milton M. 1961. "Assimilation in America: Theory and Reality." *Daedalus* 90:2 (Spring).

*———. 1964. *Assimilation in American Life*. New York: Oxford University Press.

———. 1978. *Human Nature, Class, and Ethnicity*. New York: Oxford University Press.

*Gordon, Milton M. 1981. "Models of Pluralism: The New American Dilemma." *The Annals of the American Academy of Political and Social Sciences* 454 (March).

Gourman, Jack. 1967. *The Gourman Report*. Phoenix, Az.: The Continuing Education Institute.

Graham, Hugh Davis, and Gurr, Ted Robert. 1969. *Violence in America: Historical and Comparative Perspectives*. A Report Submitted to the National Commission on the Causes and Prevention of Violence. Washington, D.C.: U.S. Government Printing Office.

Granovetter, Mark. 1974. *Getting a Job: A Study of Contacts and Careers*. Cambridge, Mass.: Harvard University Press.

Gray, Lois. 1975. "Jobs Puerto Ricans Hold in New York City." *Monthly Labor Review* 98 (October).

Grebler, L., Moore, J. W., and Guzman, Ralph, eds. 1970. *The Mexican-American People, The Nation's Second Largest Minority*. New York: Free Press.

Greeley, Andrew M. 1964. "American Sociology and the Study of Immigrant Ethnic Groups." *International Migration Digest* 1 (Fall).

———. 1969. *Why Can't They Be Like Us?* New York: Institute of Human Relations Press.

———. 1971, 1975. *Why Can't They Be Like Us?* New York: E. P. Dutton and Company.

———. 1972. "The New Ethnicity and Blue Collars." *Dissent* 19.

———. 1974. *Ethnicity in the United States: A Preliminary Reconnaissance*. New York: Wiley.

*———. 1976. "The Ethnic Miracle." *The Public Interest* 45 (Fall).

———. 1976. *Ethnicity, Denomination, and Inequality*. Beverly Hills, Cal.: Sage.

———. 1977. *The American Catholic: A Social Portrait*. New York: Basic Books.

———. 1978. *Ethnicity, Denomination and Inequality*. Beverly Hills, Cal.: Sage.

———. 1978. "Group Formation and the Cultural Division of Labor." *American Journal of Sociology* 84:293–318.

Greeley, Andrew M., and Rossi Peter. 1966. *The Education of Catholic Americans*. Chicago: Aldine.

Greene, P. 1978. "Promiscuity, Paternity and Culture." *American Ethnologist* 5:1.

Gregor, A. James. 1963. "Black Nationalism: A

Preliminary Analysis of Negro Radicalism" *Science and Society* 27 (Autumn).

Grier, Eunice, and Grier, Scott. 1965. "Equality and Beyond: Housing Segregation in the Great Society." *Daedalus* 95 (Winter).

Griffen, Saily, and Griffen, Clyde. 1977. "Family and Business in a Small City: Poughkeepsie, N.Y., 1850–1880." In Tamara Hareven, ed., *Family and Kin in Urban Communities, 1700–1930.* New York: New Viewpoints.

Grimshaw, Allen D. 1959. "Lawlessness and Violence in America and Their Special Manifestations in Changing Negro-White Relationships." *Journal of Negro History* 44 (January).

Grodzins, Morton. 1966. *Americans Betrayed: Politics and the Japanese Evacuation.* Chicago: University of Chicago Press. (Reprinting of 1956 edition.)

Guest, Avery M., and Weed, James A. 1976. "Ethnic Residential Segregation: Patterns of Change." *American Journal of Sociology* 81.

Gutkind, Lee. 1975. *The Best Seat in Baseball, But You Have To Stand!* New York: Dial Press.

Gutman, Herbert G. 1976. *The Black Family in Slavery and Freedom, 1750–1925.* New York: Pantheon Books.

Hagen, Everett E. 1962. *On the Theory of Social Change: How Economic Growth Begins.* Homewood, Ill.: Dorsey.

_____. 1968. *The Economics of Development.* Homewood, Ill.: Richard D. Irwin.

Hall, Peter Dobkin. 1977. "Family Structure and Economic Organization: Massachusetts Merchants, 1700–1850." In Tamara Hareven, ed., *Family and Kin in Urban Communities, 1700–1930.* New York: Viewpoints.

Haller, Mark H. 1973. "Recurring Themes." In A. F. David and M. Haller, eds., *The Peoples of Philadelphia.* Philadelphia: Temple University Press.

Hallowell, A. Irving. 1972. "American Indians, White and Black: The Phenomenon of Trans-Culturalization." In H. M. Bahr, B. A. Chadwick, and R. C. Day, eds., *Native Americans Today: Sociological Perspectives.* New York: Harper and Row. (Reprinted from *Current Anthropology* 4 December 1963.)

Hamilton, Gary. 1978. "Pariah Capitalism: A Paradox of Power and Dependence." *Ethnic Groups* 2:1–15.

Hamilton, W. D. 1964. "The Genetical Evolution of Social Behavior." *Journal of Theoretical Biology* 7.

Handlin, Oscar. 1951. *The Uprooted.* New York: Grossett and Dunlap.

_____. 1957. *Race and Nationality in American Life.* Garden City, N.Y.: Doubleday.

_____. 1959. *The Newcomers: Negroes and Puerto Ricans in a Changing Metropolis.* Cambridge, Mass.: Harvard University Press.

_____. 1961. "Historical Perspectives on the American Ethnic Group." *Daedalus* 90.

Hannerz, Ulf. 1969. *Soulside.* New York: Columbia University Press.

_____. 1974. "Ethnicity and Opportunity in Urban America." In A. Cohen, ed., *Urban Ethnicity.* London: Tavistock.

Hansen, Marcus Lee. 1938. *The Problem of the Third Generation Immigrant.* Rock Island, Ill.: Augustana Historical Society.

_____. 1952. "The Third Generation in America." *Commentary* 14.

Hanson, P. O., Marble, D. F., and Pitts, F. 1972. "Individual Movement and Communication Fields." *Regional Science Perspectives* 2.

Hanushek, Eric A., and Jackson, John E. 1977. *Statistical Methods for Social Scientists.* New York: Academic Press.

Harbison, Frederick. 1956. "Entrepreneurial Organization as a Factor in Economic Development." *Quarterly Journal of Economics* 70.

Harris, Donald J. 1972. "The Black Ghetto as a Colony: A Theoretical Critique and Alternative Formulation." *Review of Black Political Economy* 2.

Harris, Marvin. 1964. *Patterns of Race in the Americas.* New York: Walker.

Hartung, J. 1976. "On Natural Selection and the Inheritance of Wealth." *Current Anthropology* 17:4.

Hauser, Philip M. 1966. "Next Steps on the Racial Front." *Journal of Intergroup Relations* 5 (Autumn).

_____. 1966. "Demographic Factors in the Integration of the Negro." In T. Parsons and K. B. Clark, eds., *The Negro American.* Boston: Houghton Mifflin.

Hauser, Robert M., and Featherman, David L. 1977. *The Process of Stratification: Trends and Analyses.* New York: Academic Press.

Hawley, Amos. 1971. *Urban Society: An Ecological Approach.* New York: Ronald Press.

Hechter, Michael. 1975. *Internal Colonialism: The Celtic Fringe in British National Development.* London: Routledge & Kegan Paul.

_____. 1976. "Ethnicity and Industrialization." *Ethnicity* 3:3.

Heer, David M. 1969. "The Sentiment of White

Supremacy: An Ecological Study." *American Journal of Sociology* 64 (May).

Helper, Rose. 1969. *Racial Policies and Practices of Real Estate Brokers.* Minneapolis: University of Minnesota Press.

Heneman, H. G., and Yoder, Dale. 1965. *Labor Economics.* Cincinnati, Ohio: Southwestern.

Henry, Frances. 1976. *Ethnicity in the Americas.* Chicago: Aldine.

Henry, J. 1965. "White People's Time, Colored People's Time." *Transaction* (March-April)

Henry, Jeanette. 1967. "Our Inaccurate Textbooks." *The Indian Historian* 1 (December).

Herberg, Will. 1955. *Protestant-Catholic-Jew.* New York: Doubleday.

———. 1960. *Protestant-Catholic-Jew* rev. ed. Garden City, N.Y.: Anchor.

Herman, Harry Vjekoslav. 1979. "Dishwashers and Proprietors: Macedonians in Toronto's Restaurant Trade." In Sandra Wallman, ed., *Ethnicity at Work.* London: Macmillan.

*Hershberg, Theodore, Burstein, Alan N., Ericksen, Eugene P., Greenberg, Stephanie, and Yancey, William L. 1979. " A Tale of Three Cities: Blacks, Immigrants and Opportunity in Philadelphia: 1850–1880, 1930 and 1970." *The Annals of the American Academy of Political and Social Science* 441 (January).

Hershberg, Theodore, Modell, John, and Furstenberg, Frank. 1973. *Family Structure and Ethnicity: A Historical and Comparative Analysis.* Philadelphia Social History Project, University of Pennsylvania.

Herskovits, M. 1938–39. "The Ancestry of the American Negro." *American Scholar.* (Reprinted in *The New World Negro.* Bloomington: Indiana University Press, 1966.)

———. 1941. *The Myth of the Negro Past.* New York: Harper and Brothers.

Higgs, Robert. 1977. *Competition and Coercion.* Cambridge: Cambridge University Press.

Higham, John. 1965. *Strangers in the Land.* New York: Atheneum.

Hill, Robert B. 1981. "The Economic Status of Black Americans." In *The State of Black America.* New York: National Urban League.

Hillery, G. A. 1955. "Definitions of Community: Areas of Agreement." *Rural Sociology* 20.

Himes, Joseph. 1966. "The Functions of Racial Conflct." *Social Forces* 46 (September).

Hindelang, Michael J. 1976. *Criminal Victimization in Eight American Cities.* Cambridge, Mass.: Ballinger.

Hirschman, Charles. 1983. "America's Melting Pot Reconsidered." *Annual Review of Sociology* 9.

Hobsbawm, Eric. (1977). "Some Reflections of 'The Break-up of Britain.' " *New Left Review* 105:3–23.

Hoetink, H. 1967. *Caribbean Race Relations.* London: Oxford University Press.

Hollingsworth, L. W. 1960. *The Asians of East Africa.* London: Macmillan.

Homans, George. 1950. *The Human Group.* New York: Harcourt, Brace.

Hoover, Edgar M., and Vernon, Raymond. 1959. *Anatomy of a Metropolis.* Cambridge, Mass.: Harvard University Press.

Horton, John. 1966. "Order and Conflict Theories of Social Problems as Competing Ideologies." *American Journal of Sociology* 71 (May).

Horvat, Branko. 1982. *The Political Economy of Socialism.* Armonk, N.Y.: M. E. Sharpe.

Hoselitz, Bert F. 1963. "Main Concepts in the Analysis of the Social Implications of Technical Change." In B. F. Hoselitz and W. E. Moore, eds., *Industrialization and Society.* UNESCO: Mouton.

Hosokawa, Bill. 1969. *Nisei: The Quiet Americans.* New York: William Morrow.

Hostetler, John. 1968. *Amish Society.* Baltimore: Johns Hopkins University Press.

Hough, Joseph C., Jr. 1968. *Black Power and White Protestants: A Christian Response to the New Negro Pluralism.* New York: Oxford University Press.

Howard, John. 1971. "Public Policy and the White Working Class." In I. Horowitz, ed., *The Use and Abuse of Social Science.* New Brunswick, N.J.: Transaction Books.

Howard, Perry, and Brent, Joseph, III. 1966. "Social Change, Urbanization, and Types of Society." *Journal of Social Issues* 22 (January).

Howe, Irving. 1977. "The Limits of Ethnicity." *The New Republic* (June 25).

Hraba, Joseph. 1979. *American Ethnicity.* Itasca, Ill.: F. E. Peacock.

Hsu, Francis L. K. 1971. *The Challenge of the American Dream: The Chinese in the United States.* Belmont, Cal.: Wadsworth.

Hughes, Everett C. 1963. "Race Relations and the Sociological Imagination." *American Sociological Review* 28 (December).

Hutchinson, Edward P. 1956. *Immigrants and Their Children.* New York: Wiley.

Hutchison, Emilie J. 1968. *Women's Wages.* New York: AMS Press.

Ichihashi, Yamato. 1932. *Japanese in the United States*. Stanford, Cal.: Stanford University Press.

Inkeles, Alex. 1968a. "Social Structure and the Socialization of Competence." *Harvard Educational Review*, Report Series 1.

_____. 1968b. "Society, Social Structure and Child Socialization." In J. A. Clausen, ed., *Socialization and Society*. Boston: Little, Brown.

Issacs, Harold R. 1963. *The New World of Negro Americans*. New York: Viking.

_____. 1975. "Basic Group Identity: the Idols of the Tribe." In Nathan Glazer and Daniel P. Moynihan, eds., *Ethnicity and Experience*. Cambridge, Mass.: Harvard University Press.

Iwata, Masakazu. 1962. "The Japanese Immigrants in California Agriculture." *Agricultural History* 36 (January).

Jackman, Mary R., and Jackman, R. W. 1980. "Racial Inequalities in Home Ownership." *Social Forces* 58:1221–1234.

Jacobson, Robert L. 1971. "Black Enrollment Rising Sharply, U.S. Data Show." *Chronicle of Higher Education* (October).

Jahoda, Marie, and West, Patricia S. 1951. "Race Relations in Public Housing." *Journal of Social Issues* 7:132–139.

Jarvenpa, Robert, and Zenner, Walter P. 1979. "Scot Trader/Indian Worker Relations and Ethnic Segregation: a Subarctic Example." *Ethnos* 44.

Jencks, Christopher. 1972. *Inequality: A Reassessment of the Effects of Family and Schooling in America*. New York: Harper and Row.

Jenkins, Richard. 1984. "Ethnicity and the Rise of Capitalism." In Robin Ward, ed., *Ethnic Business in Britain*. Cambridge: Cambridge University Press.

Jenks, Jeremiah W., and Lauck, V. Jett. 1912. *The Immigration Problem*. New York: Funk and Wagnalls.

Jensen, Arthur R. 1968. "Social Class and Verbal Learning." In M. Deutsch, I. Katz, and A. R. Jensen, eds., *Social Class, Race and Psychological Development*. New York: Holt.

_____. 1969. "How Much Can We Boost I.Q. and Scholastic Achievement?" *Harvard Educational Review*, Reprint Series No. 2.

Jessepe, Lester L. 1972. "Our Story: The Prairie Band Pottawatomi Indians (How to Survive When the Government Tries to Steal Everything You Have)." Mimeographed. Mayetta, Kan.

Jiobu, Robert M. 1976–77. "Earnings Differentials between Whites and Ethnic Minorities: The Cases of Asian-Americans, Blacks, and Chicanos." *Sociology and Social Research* 61 (1).

Johnson, Charles S. 1934. *Shadow of the Plantation*. Chicago: University of Chicago Press.

Johnson, Michael P., and Sell, Ralph R. 1976. "The Cost of Being Black: A 1970 Update." *American Journal of Sociology* 82:183–190.

Jones, Faustine C. 1981. "External Crosscurrents and Internal Diversity: An Assessment of Black Progress, 1960–1980." *Daedalus* 110:2 (Spring).

Jones, James M. 1972. *Prejudice and Racism*. Reading, Mass.: Addison-Wesley.

Jones, Leroy, and Sakong, I. 1980. *Government, Business and Entrepreneurship in Economic Development: The Korean Case*. Cambridge, Mass.: Harvard University Council on East Asian Studies.

Jones, Maldwyn Allen. 1960. *American Immigration*. Chicago: University of Chicago Press.

_____. 1976. *Destination America*. New York: Holt, Rinehart and Winston.

Jorgensen, Joseph G. 1971. "Indians and the Metropolis." In J. O. Waddell and O. M. Watson, eds., *The American Indian in Urban Society*. Boston: Little, Brown.

Kain, John F., and Quigley, J. M. 1975. *Housing Markets and Racial Discrimination: A Microeconomic Analysis*. New York: National Bureau of Economic Research.

Kalleberg, Arne L., and Sorenson, Aage B. 1979. "The Sociology of Labor Markets." *Annual Review of Sociology* 5.

Kallen, Horace. 1924. *Culture and Democracy in the United States*. New York: Boni and Liveright.

Karsh, Norman C. 1977. *What Is a Small Business?* Washington, D.C.: Small Business Administrations.

Kasarda, John D., and Janowitz, Morris. 1974. "Community Attachment in Mass Society." *American Sociological Review* 39.

Katz, Alvin M., and Hill, Ruben. 1958. "Residential Propinquity and Marital Selection: A Review of Theory, Method and Fact." *Marriage and Family Living* 20.

Katz, Irwin. 1967. "Socialization of Academic Achievement in Minority Group Children." In D. Levine, ed., *Nebraska Symposium on Motivation*. Lincoln, Neb.: University of Nebraska.

Keely, Charles B. 1979. *U.S. Immigration: A Policy Analysis*. New York: Population Council.

_____. 1982. "Illegal Migration." *Scientific American* 246:3 (March).

Keil, Charles. 1966. *Urban Blues*. Chicago: University of Chicago Press.

Kemnitzer, Luis S. 1969. "Reservation and City as

Parts of a Single System: The Pine Ridge Sioux." Unpublished paper presented at meetings of the Southwestern Anthropological Association.

Kennedy, Rose J. 1943. "Premarital Propinquity and Ethnic Endogamy." *American Journal of Sociology* 48.

Kennedy, Ruby Jo Reeves. 1944. "Single or Triple Melting Pot? Intermarriage Trends in New Haven, 1870–1940." *American Journal of Sociology* 49.

_____. 1952. "Single or Triple Melting Pot? Intermarriage in New Haven, 1870-1950." *American Journal of Sociology* 58.

Keyes, C. F. 1976. "Toward a New Formulation of the Concept of Ethnic Group." *Ethnicity* 3:3.

Kiang, Y. C. 1968. "The Distribution of Ethnic Groups in Chicago, 1960." *American Journal of Sociology* 74:292–295.

Killian L. M. 1968. *The Impossible Revolution?* New York: Random House.

_____. 1970. *White Southerners.* New York: Random House.

Killian, Lewis M., and Grigg, Charles. 1966. "Race Relations in an Urbanized South." *Journal of Social Issues* 22 (January).

Kim, Hyung-Chan. 1977. "Ethnic Enterprises Among Korean Immigrants in America." In Hyung-Chan Kim, ed., *The Korean Diaspora*. Santa Barbara, Cal.: ABC-CLIO.

Kim, Illsoo. 1981. *New Urban Immigrants: The Korean Community in New York*. Princeton, N.J.: Princeton University Press.

King, Cameron H., Jr. 1908. "Asiatic Exclusion." *International Socialist Review* 8 (May).

King, Martin Luther, Jr. 1964. *Why We Can't Wait.* New York: Harper and Row.

_____. 1967. *Where Do We Go From Here? Chaos or Community*. New York: Harper and Row.

Kinton, Jack. 1977. *American Ethnic Revival*. Aurora, Ill.: Social Service and Sociological Resources.

Kitagawa, Evelyn M., and Hauser, Philip M. 1973. *Differential Mortality in the United States*. Cambridge, Mass.: Harvard University Press.

Kitano, Harry H. L. 1969. *Japanese Americans: The Evolution of a Subculture*. Englewood Cliffs, N.J.: Prentice-Hall.

_____. 1974. "Japanese Americans: The Development of a Middleman Minority." *Pacific Historical Review* 43:4.

Klatsky, Sheila R. 1974. "Patterns of Contact with Relatives." Rose Monograph Series. Washington, D.C.: American Sociological Association.

Klecka, William R. 1975. "Discriminant Analysis." In N. H. Nie et al., eds., *Statistical Package for the Social Sciences*. 2d ed. New York: McGraw-Hill.

Klineberg, Otto. 1963. "Children's Readers: Life is Fun in a Smiling, Fair-Skinned World." *Saturday Review* (February).

Kluegel, James R., and Smith, Eliot R. 1982. "Whites' Beliefs about Black Opportunity." *American Sociological Review* 47:4 (August).

Kobrin, Frances E., and Goldscheider, Calvin. 1978. *The Ethnic Factor in Family Structure and Mobility*. Cambridge, Mass.: Ballinger.

Koenig, Samuel. 1942. "The Socioeconomic Structure of an American Jewish Community." In I. Graeber and S. H. Britt, eds., *Jews in a Gentile World*. New York: Macmillan.

Koller, Marvin R. 1948. "Residential Propinquity of White Males at Marriage in Relation to Age and Occupation of Males, Columbus, Ohio, 1938 and 1946." *American Sociological Review* 13:613–616.

Kosa, John. 1956. "Hungarian Immigrants in North America: Their Residential Mobility and Ecology." *Canadian Journal of Economics and Political Science* 22.

Kramer, Judith. 1970. *The American Minority Community*. New York: Thomas Y. Crowell.

Kriesberg, Louis. 1963. "Socio-Economic Rank and Behavior." *Social Problems* 10.

Kristol, Irving. 1966. "The Negro Today is Like the Immigrant Yesterday." *New York Times Magazine* (September 11).

Kronus, Sidney. 1971. *The Black Middle Class*. Columbus, Ohio: Merrill.

Krutz, Gordon V. 1973. "Compartmentalization as a Factor in Urban Adjustment: The Kiowa Case." In J. O. Waddell and O. M. Watson, eds., *American Indian Urbanization*. Lafayette, Ind.: Purdue Research Foundation.

Kuo, Wen H. 1979. "On the Study of Asian-Americans: Its Current State and Agenda." *Sociological Quarterly* 20.

Kuper, Leo. 1965. *An African Bourgeoisie*. New Haven, Conn.: Yale University Press.

Kuper, Leo, and Smith, M. G. 1969. *Pluralism in Africa*. Berkeley and Los Angeles: University of California Press.

Kurokawa, Minako. 1970. *Minority Responses*. New York: Random House.

Labov, William. 1967. "The Logic of Nonstandard Dialect." In J. Alatis, ed., *School of Languages and Linguistics Mongraph Series 22*. Washington, D.C.: Georgetown University.

_____. 1972. *Language in the Inner City: Studies in the Black English Vernacular.* Philadelphia: University of Pennsylvania Press.

Larrick, Nancy. 1965. "The All-White World of Children's Books." *Saturday Review* (September 11).

Laumann, Edward O. 1973. *Bonds of Pluralism.* New York: Wiley.

Laurie, Bruce G. 1973. "Fire Companies and Gangs in Southwark: The 1840's." In A. F. Davis and M. Haller, eds., *Peoples of Philadelphia.* Philadelphia: Temple University Press.

Lazerwitz, B., and Rowitz, L. 1964. "The Three-Generation Hypothesis." *American Journal of Sociology* 69.

Lee, Barret A. 1981. "The Urban Unease Revisited: Perceptions of Local Safety and Neighborhood Satisfaction among Metropolitan Residents." *Social Science Quarterly* 62:611–629.

Leff, Nathaniel. 1978. "Industrial Organization and Entrepreneurship in the Developing Countries: The Economic Groups." *Economic Development and Cultural Change* 26.

Leggett, John C. 1968. *Class, Race, and Labor.* New York: Oxford University Press.

Legum, Colin. 1967. "Color and Power in the South African Situation." *Daedalus* 96 (2) (Spring).

Lemarchand, Rene. 1975. "Ethnic Genocide." *Society* 12 (2) (January-February).

Lenin, V. I. 1939. *Imperialism: The Highest State of Capitalism.* New York: International Publishers.

_____. 1964. "Imperialism and the Split in Socialism." In *Collected Works* vol. 23 (August 1916–March 1917). Moscow: Progress.

_____. (1968). *National Liberation, Socialism, and Imperialism: Selected Writings.* New York: International Publishers.

Lenski, G. 1961. *The Religious Factor.* Garden City, N.Y.: Doubleday.

_____. 1966. *Power and Privilege.* New York: McGraw-Hill.

Leon, Abram. 1970. *The Jewish Question: A Marxist Interpretation.* New York: Pathfinder.

Levine, Gene N., and Montero, Darrel M. 1973. "Socioeconomic Mobility Among Three Generations of Japanese Americans." *Journal of Social Issues* 29 (2).

Levine, Lawrence W. 1977. *Black Culture and Black Consciousness.* New York: Oxford University Press.

Levy, Charles J. 1968. *Voluntary Servitude: Whites in the Negro Movement.* New York: Appleton-Century-Crofts.

Levy, Sydelle. 1973. "Shifting Patterns of Ethnic Identification." Unpublished paper presented at the annual meeting of the American Ethnological Society, Wilmington Beach, N.C. (March).

Lewis, Oscar. 1965. *La Vida.* New York: Vintage.

Li, Peter S. 1977. "Ethnic Businesses among Chinese in the United States." *Journal of Ethnic Studies* 4:3.

*Lieberson, Stanley. 1961a. "A Societal Theory of Race and Ethnic Relations." *American Sociological Review* 26 (December).

_____. 1961b. "The Impact of Residential Segregation on Ethnic Assimilation." *Social Forces* 40.

_____. 1963. *Ethnic Patterns in American Cities.* New York: Free Press.

_____. 1973. "Generational Differences Among Blacks in the North." *American Journal of Sociology* 79.

_____. 1980. *A Piece of the Pie: Blacks and White Immigrants Since 1900.* Berkeley and Los Angeles: University of California Press.

Lieberson, Stanley, Dalto, Guy, and Johnston, Mary Ellen. 1975. "The Course of Mother-Tongue Diversity in Nations." *American Journal of Sociology* 81.

Liebow, Elliot. 1967. *Tally's Corner.* Boston: Little, Brown.

Light, Ivan. 1972. *Ethnic Enterprise in America.* Berkeley, Cal.: University of California Press.

_____. 1977a. "The Ethnic Vice District, 1880–1944." *American Sociological Review* 44.

_____. 1977b. "Numbers Gambling: A Financial Institution." *American Sociological Review* 43.

_____. 1979. "Disadvantaged Minorities in Self-Employment." *International Journal of Comparative Sociology* 20.

_____. 1980. "Asian Enterprise in America." In Scott Cummings, ed., *Self-Help in Urban America.* Port Washington, N.Y.: Kennikat Press.

*_____. 1984. "Immigrant and Ethnic Enterprise in North America." *Ethnic and Racial Studies* 7:2 (April).

Light, Ivan H., and Wong, Charles. 1975. "Protest or Work: Dilemmas of the Tourist Industry in American Chinatowns." *American Journal of Sociology* 80.

Lincoln, C. Eric. 1961. *The Black Muslims in America.* Boston: Beacon.

Lind, Andrew. 1958. "Adjustment Patterns Among Jamaican Chinese." *Social and Economic Studies* 7 (June).

_____. 1968. *An Island Community.* New York: Greenwood.

Lindgren, E. J. 1938. "An Example of Culture Contact Without Conflict: Reindeer Tungus and Cossacks of Northwest Manchuria." *American Anthropologist* 40 (October–December).

Lipset, Seymour, and Bendix, Reinhard, eds. 1953. "Social Mobility." In *Class, Status, and Power*. Glencoe, Ill.: Free Press.

———. 1959. *Social Mobility in Industrial Society*. Berkeley and Los Angeles: University of California Press.

Litwak, Leon. 1961. *North of Slavery: The Negro in the Free States, 1790–1860*. Chicago: University of Chicago Press.

Lochore, R. A. 1951. *From Europe to New Zealand*. Wellington: A. A. and A. W. Reed.

Lodge, Henry Cabot. 1896. Speech in the United States Senate, *Congressional Record*. 54th Congress, Second session (March 16).

Loewen, James W. 1971. *The Mississippi Chinese: Between Black and White*. Cambridge, Mass.: Harvard University Press.

Lohman, J. D., and Reitzes, D. C. 1952. "Note on Race Relations in Mass Society." *American Journal of Sociology* 58 (November).

———. 1954. "Deliberately Organized Groups and Racial Behavior." *American Sociological Review* 19 (June).

Long, Larry H. 1974. "Poverty Status and Receipt of Welfare Among Migrants and Non-Migrants in Large Cities." *American Sociological Review* 39.

Lopez, Manuel Mariano. 1981. "Patterns of Interethnic Residential Segregation in the Urban Southwest." *Social Science Quarterly* 62:50–63.

Lovell-Troy, Lawrence A. 1980. "Clan Structure and Economic Activity: The Case of Greeks in Small Business Enterprise." In Scott Cummings, ed., *Self-Help in Urban America*. Port Washington, N.Y.: Kennikat Press.

———. 1981. "Ethnic Occupational Structures: Greeks in the Pizza Business." *Ethnicity* 8.

*Lurie, Nancy Oestreich. 1965. "The American Indian: Historical Background." In S. Levine and N. O. Lurie, eds., *The American Indian Today*. Deland Fla.: Everett/Edwards.

*Lyman, Stanford M. 1968. "Contrasts in the Community Organization of Chinese and Japanese in North America." *Canadian Review of Sociology and Anthropology* 5:2.

———. 1968. "The Race Relations Cycle of Robert E. Park." *Pacific Sociological Review* 11 (Spring).

———. 1974. *Chinese Americans*. New York: Random House.

Lynd, Robert S., and Lynd, Helen M. 1937. *Middletown in Transition*. New York: Harcourt Brace.

McAllister, Ronald J., Butler, Edgar W., and Goe, Steven J. 1973. "Evolution of a Strategy for the Retrieval of Cases in Longitudinal Research." *Social Science Research* 58:37–47.

MacDonald, John S., and MacDonald, Leatrice. 1964. "Chain Migration, Ethnic Neighborhood Formation and Social Networks." *Milbank Memorial Fund Quarterly* 42.

McFee, Malcolm. 1972. "The 150% Man, a Product of Blackfeet Acculturation." In H. M. Bahr, B. A. Chadwich, and R. C. Day, eds., *Native Americans Today: Sociological Perspectives*. New York: Harper and Row.

———. 1972. *Modern Blackfeet: Montanans on a Reservation*. New York: Holt, Rinehart and Winston.

McLaughlin, Virginia Yans. 1971. "Patterns of Work and Family Organization Among Buffalo's Italians." *Journal of Inter-disciplinary History* 2.

McLemore, S. Dale. 1973. "The Origins of Mexican American Subordination in Texas." *Social Science Quarterly* 53 (March).

———. 1983. *Racial and Ethnic Relations in America* 2nd ed. Boston: Allyn and Bacon.

McMillan, Penelope. 1982. "Vietnamese Influx: It's Chinatown with Subtitles." *Los Angeles Times*, February 14: II.

McWilliams, Carey. 1945. *Prejudice; Japanese-Americans*. Boston: Little, Brown.

Mahajani, Usha. 1960. *The Role of Indian Minorities in Burma and Malaya*. Bombay: Vora.

Malcolm X. 1967. *Malcolm X on Afro-American History*. New York: Merit Publishers.

Maldonado, Edwin. 1979. "Contract Labor and the Origins of Puerto Rican Communities in the United States." *International Migration Review* 13 (Spring):103–121.

Mandel, Ernest. 1972. "Nationalism and the Class Struggle." *International Socialist Review* 33:18–23, 38–39.

Marshall, Ray. 1975. "Economic Factors Influencing the International Migration of Workers." Paper presented at the Conference on Contemporary Dilemmas of the Mexican-United States Border. San Antonio: The Weatherhead Foundation.

Marson, Wilfred G., and van Valey, Thomas L. 1979. "The Role of Residential Segregation in the Assimilation Process." *The Annals of the American Academy of Political and Social Sciences* 441 (January).

Mason, Philip. 1970a. *Patterns of Dominance.* London: Oxford University Press.

———. 1970b. *Race Relations.* London: Oxford University Press.

Massarik, Fred. n.d. "Intermarriage: Factors for Planning." National Jewish Population Study. New York: Council of Jewish Federation and Welfare Funds.

Massey, Douglas S. 1979a. "Effects of Socioeconomic Factors on the Residential Segregation of Blacks and Spanish Americans in the U.S. Urbanized Areas." *American Sociological Review* 44:1015–1022.

———. 1979b. "Residential Segregation of Spanish Americans in United States Urbanized Areas." *Demography* 16:653–664.

———. 1981. "Dimensions of the New Immigration to the United States and the Prospects for Assimilation." *Annual Review of Sociology.*

———. 1981. "Hispanic Residential Segregation: A Comparison of Mexicans, Cubans, and Puerto Ricans." *Sociology and Social Research* 65:311–322.

———. 1983. "Residential Succession: The Hispanic Case." *Social Forces* 61:825–834.

*Massey, Douglas S., and Mullan, Brendan P. 1984. "Processes of Hispanic and Black Spatial Assimilation." *American Journal of Sociology* 89:4 (January).

Mathews, Fred H. 1964. "White Community and Yellow Peril." *Mississippi Valley Historical Review* 50 (March).

Mayer, Egon. 1983. "Children of Intermarriage." New York: American Jewish Committee.

Mayhew, Leon. 1968. "Ascription in Modern Societies." *Sociological Inquiry* 38.

Maynard Smith, J. 1964. "Group Selection and Kin Selection." *Nature* 201:4924.

Medalia, Nahum Z. 1962. "Myrdal's Assumptions on Race Relations: A Conceptual Commentary." *Social Forces* 40 (March).

Memmi, Albert. 1967. *The Colonizer and the Colonized.* Boston: Beacon.

Mercer, Jane R. 1972. "I.Q.: The Lethal Label," *Psychology Today* 6 (September).

*Merton, Robert K. 1949. "Discrimination and the American Creed." In R. M. MacIver, ed., *Discrimination and the National Welfare.* New York: Institute for Religious and Social Studies and Harper and Row.

*Metzger, L. Paul. 1971. "American Sociology and Black Assimilation: Conflicting Perspectives." *American Journal of Sociology* 76 (January).

Meyer, Kurt. 1947. "Small Business as a Social Institution." *Social Research* 14.

———. 1953. "Business Enterprise: Traditional Symbol of Opportunity." *British Journal of Sociology* 4.

Miller, Daniel R., and Swanson, Guy E. 1958. *The Changing American Parent.* New York: John Wiley.

Miller, Randall M., and Marzik, Thomas D. 1977. *Immigrants and Religion in Urban America.* Philadelphia: Temple University Press.

Millis, H. A. 1915. *The Japanese Problem in the United States.* New York: Macmillan.

Mills, C. W. 1951. *White Collar.* New York: Oxford University Press.

———. 1966. "The Middle Classes in Middle-Sized Cities." In Reinhard Bendix and Seymour Martin Lipset, eds., *Class, Status, and Power* 2nd ed. New York: Free Press.

Mincer, Jacob. 1970. "The Distribution of Labor Incomes: A Survey with Special Reference to the Human Capital Approach." *Journal of Economic Literature* 8: 1–26.

Mindel, Charles H., and Habenstein, Robert W. 1976. *Ethnic Families in America: Patterns and Variations.* New York: Elsevier.

Mingione, A. 1965. "Need for Achievement in Negro and White Children." *Journal of Counseling Psychology* 29.

Miyamoto, Samuel F. 1972. "An Immigrant Community in America." In Hilary Conroy and T. Scott Miyakawa, eds., *East Across the Pacific.* Santa Barbara, Cal.: CLIO Press.

Miyamoto, Shotaro F. 1939. "Social Solidarity Among the Japanese in Seattle." *Publications in the Social Sciences* 11 (December). Seattle: University of Washington.

Modell, John. 1969. "Class or Ethnic Solidarity: The Japanese American Company Union." *Pacific Historical Review* 38 (May).

———. 1977. *The Economics and Politics of Racial Accommodation: The Japanese of Los Angeles, 1900–1942.* Urbana: University of Illinois Press.

Moles, I. N. 1968. "The Indian Coolie Labour Issue." In *Attitudes to Non-European Immigration.* Melbourne: Cassell Australia.

Montero, Darrell. 1981. "The Japanese Americans: Changing Patterns of Assimilation Over Three Generations." *American Sociological Review* 46.

Moore, Alexander. 1964. *Realities of the Urban Classroom.* Garden City, N.Y.: Doubleday.

Moore, Joan W. 1970. "Colonialism: The Case of the Mexican Americans." *Social Problems* 17 (Spring).

———. 1976. "American Minorities and 'New

Nation' Perspectives." *Pacific Sociological Review* 19:4 (October).

*_____. 1981. "Minorities in the American Class System. *Daedalus* 110:2 (Spring).

Moore, Robert. 1972. "Race Relations in the Six Counties: Colonialism, Industrialization, and Stratification in Ireland." *Race* 14 (July).

Morrison, Thomas K. 1982. "The Relationship of U.S. Aid, Trade, and Investment to Migration Pressures in Major Sending Countries." *International Migration Review* 16 (Spring).

Morsell, John A. 1961. "Black Nationalism." *Journal of Intergroup Relations* 3 (Winter).

Moynihan, Daniel Patrick. 1966. "Employment, Income and the Ordeal of the Negro Family." In T. Parsons and K. B. Clark, eds., *The Negro American*. Boston: Houghton Mifflin.

*Myrdal, Gunnar. 1944. *An American Dilemma: The Negro Problem in Modern Democracy*. New York: Harper and Row.

*Nagel, Joane. 1982. "Political Mobilization of Native Americans." *Social Science Journal* 19:3 (July).

Nagel, Joane, and Olzak, Susan. 1982. "Ethnic Mobilization in New States and Old States: An Extension of the Competition Model." *Social Problems* 30:2 (December).

Nairn, Tom. 1975. "The Modern Janus." *New Left Review* 94:3–29.

National Advisory Commission on Civil Disorders. 1968. *Report*. Washington, D.C.: Government Printing Office.

National Advisory Council on Indian Education. 1974. *First Annual Report*. Washington, D.C.: U.S. Government Printing Office.

Nee, Victor G., and Nee, Brett DeBary. 1974. *Longtime Californ': A Documentary Study of an American Chinatown*. Boston: Houghton Mifflin.

Neils, Elaine M. 1971. *Reservation to City*. University of Chicago: Department of Geography, Research Paper No. 131.

Nelli, Humbert S. 1970. *The Italians in Chicago: 1880–1930*. New York: Oxford University Press.

Newcomer, Mabel. 1961. "The Little Businessman: A Study of Business Proprietors in Poughkeepsie, N.Y." *Business History Review* 35.

Newman, William M. 1973. *American Pluralism: A Study of Minority Groups and Social Theory*. New York: Harper and Row.

Niebuhr, H. Richard. 1929. *Social Sources of Denominationalism*. New York: Henry Holt.

*Noel, Donald L. 1968. "A Theory of the Origin of Ethnic Stratification." *Social Problems* 16 (Fall).

_____. 1972. *The Origins of American Slavery and Racism*. Columbus, Ohio: Charles E. Merrill.

North, David S., and Houston, Marion F. 1976. "The Characteristics and Role of Illegal Aliens in the U.S. Labor Market: An Exploratory Study." Washington, D.C.: Linton.

_____. 1978. "Seven Years Later: The Experiences of the 1970 Cohort of Immigrants in the U.S. Labor Market." Mimeographed. Report to the Employment and Training Administration. Washington, D.C.: Department of Labor.

Novak, Michael. 1971. *The Rise of the Unmeltable Ethnics*. New York: Macmillan.

_____. 1974. "The New Ethnicity." *The Center Magazine* VII:4 (July/August).

_____. 1975. "Black and White in Catholic Eyes." *New York Times Magazine* (November 16).

O'Brien, William V. 1968. "International Crimes." In D. L. Sills, ed., *International Encyclopedia of the Social Sciences*. New York: Macmillan.

O'Conner, James. 1973. *The Fiscal Crisis of the State*. New York: St. Martin's Press.

O'Dea, Thomas. 1958. *American Catholic Dilemma*. New York: Sheed and Ward.

Office of the U.S. Attorney General. 1978. "Illegal Immigration: President's Program." Washington, D.C., February.

*Ogbu, John U. 1978. *Minority Education and Caste: The American System in Cross-Cultural Perspective*. New York: Academic Press.

Olsen, Jack. 1968a. "The Black Athlete—A Shameful Story." *Sports Illustrated* (July 22).

_____. 1968b. *The Black Athlete*. New York: Time-Life Books.

Olsen, Marvin E. 1968. *The Process of Social Organization*. New York: Holt, Rinehart, and Winston.

Oppenheimer, Martin. 1969. *The Urban Guerrilla*. Chicago: Quadrangle Books.

_____. (1974). "The Sub-Proletariat: Dark Skins and Dirty Work." *Insurgent Sociologist* 4:7–20.

Opperman, Hubert. 1966. "Australia's Immigration Policy." Paper delivered to the Youth and Student Seminar, Canberra, Australia (May 28).

Palmer, Mabel. 1957. "The History of the Indians in Natal." *Natal Regional Survey* vol. 10. Cape Town: Oxford University Press.

Palmer, P. C. 1966. "Servant Into Slave: The Evolution of the Legal Status of the Negro Laborer in Colonial Virginia." *South Atlantic Quarterly* 65 (Summer).

Paredes, J. Anthony. 1971. "Toward a Reconceptualization of American Indian Urbanization: A Chippewa Case." *Anthropological Quarterly* 44 (October).

Parenti, Michael. 1967. "Ethnic Politics and the Persistence of Ethnic Identification." *American Political Science Review* 61 (September).

Park, Robert E. 1926. "The Urban Community as a Spatial Pattern and a Moral Order." In Ernest W. Burgess, ed., *The Urban Community*. Chicago: University of Chicago Press.

_____. 1928. "Human Migration and the Marginal Man." *American Journal of Sociology* 33.

_____. 1939. "The Nature of Race Relations." In E. T. Thompson, ed., *Race Relations and the Race Problem*. Durham, N.C.: Duke University Press.

_____. 1950. *Race and Culture*. Glencoe, Ill.: Free Press.

Park, Robert E., and Miller, Herbert A. 1929. *Old World Traits Transplanted*. New York: Harper.

Parker, S. 1976. "The Precultural Basis of the Incest Taboo." *American Anthropologist* 73:2.

Parsons, Talcott. 1954. *Essays in Sociological Theory*. Glencoe, Ill.: Free Press.

_____. 1966. "Full Citizenship for the Negro American?" In Talcott Parsons and K. B. Clark, eds., *The Negro American*. Boston: Houghton Mifflin.

Parsons, Talcott, and Shils, Edward A. 1954. *Toward A General Theory of Action*. Cambridge, Mass.: Harvard University Press.

Parsons, Theodore W., Jr. 1965. "Ethnic Cleavage in a California School." Ph.D. thesis, Stanford University.

Pascal, Anthony H., and Rapping, Leonard A. 1970. *Racial Discrimination in Organized Baseball*. Santa Monica, Cal.: Rand Corporation.

Patterson, Orlando. 1977. *Ethnic Chauvinism: The Reactionary Impulse*. New York: Stein and Day.

Peach, Ceri. 1981. "Ethnic Segregation and Ethnic Intermarriage: A Reexamination of Kennedy's Triple Melting Pot in New Haven, 1900–1950." In Ceri Peach, ed., *Ethnic Segregation in Cities*. London: Croom Helm.

Pear, Robert. 1984. "Cuban Aliens, but Not Haitians Will Be Offered Residency Status." *New York Times*, February 12.

Pearce, Diana M. 1979. "Gatekeepers and Homeseekers: Institutional Factors in Racial Steering." *Social Problems* 26:325–342.

Pease, John, Form, William, and Rytina, Joan. 1970. "Ideological Currents in American Stratification Literature." *American Sociologist* 5 (May).

Peterson, William. 1966. "Success Story, Japanese-American Style." *New York Times Magazine,* January 9.

_____. 1969. "The Classification of Subnations in Hawaii: An Essay in the Sociology of Knowledge." *American Sociological Review* 34:863–877.

_____. 1971. *Japanese Americans: Oppression and Success*. New York: Random House.

Petit, Patrick F. 1969. "A Preliminary Investigation of the Migration and Adjustment of American Indians to Urban Areas." M. A. Thesis, Department of Sociology, University of Kansas, Lawrence.

Petras, Elisabeth M. 1980. "Toward a Theory of International Migration: The New Division of Labor." In R. S. Bryce-Laporte, ed., *Sourcebook on the New Immigration*. New Brunswick, N.J.: Transaction Books.

Petras, James F. 1975. "Sociology of Development or Sociology of Exploitation?" Paper presented at the Meeting of the American Sociological Association, August.

Pettigrew, Thomas F. 1969. "Racially Separate or Together?" *Journal of Social Issues* 25 (January).

_____. 1979. "Racial Change and Social Policy." *The Annals of the American Academy of Political and Social Science* 441 (January).

Pettigrew, Thomas F., and Black, Kurt W. 1967. "Sociology in the Desegregation Process: Its Use and Disuse." In P. F. Lazarsfeld, W. H. Sewell, and H. L. Wilensky, eds., *The Uses of Sociology*. New York: Basic Books.

Pinkney, Alphonso. 1969. *The Black Americans*. Englewood Cliffs, N.J.: Prentice-Hall.

Piore, Michael J. 1973. "The Role of Immigration in Industrial Growth: A Case Study of the Origins and Character of Puerto Rican Migration to Boston." Mimeographed. Cambridge, Mass.: Massachusetts Institute of Technology.

_____. 1975. "Notes for a Theory of Labor Market Stratification." In R. C. Edwards, M. Reich, and D. M. Gordon, eds., *Labor Market Segmentation*. Lexington, Mass.: D. C. Heath.

_____. 1979. *Birds of Passage: Migrant Labor and Industrial Societies*. Cambridge: Cambridge University Press.

Pirenne, Henri. 1925. *Medieval Cities: Their Origins and the Revival of Trade*. Princeton, N.J.: Princeton University Press.

Pitt-Rivers, Julian. 1967. "Race, Color, and Class in Central America and the Andes." *Daedalus* 92:2 (Spring).

Piven, Frances F., and Cloward, Richard A. 1971. *Regulating the Poor*. New York: Pantheon.

Polenberg, Richard. 1980. *One Nation Divisible: Class, Race and Ethnicity in the United States since 1938.* New York: Viking.

Portes, Alejandro. 1977a. "Why Illegal Migration? A Structural Perspective." Durham, N.C.: Latin American Immigration Project Occasional Papers, Duke University.

_____. 1977b. "Labor Functions of Illegal Aliens." *Society* 14 (September-October).

_____. "Towards a Structural Analysis of Illegal Immigration." *International Migration Review* 12 (Winter).

_____. 1977. "Migration and Underdevelopment." *Politics and Society* 8:1.

*_____. 1979. "Illegal Immigration and the International System, Lessons from Recent Legal Mexican Immigrants to the United States." *Social Problems* 26:4 (April).

_____. 1981. "Modes of Structural Incorporation and Present Theories of Labor Immigration." In Mary M. Kritz and Charles B. Keely, eds., *Global Trends in Migration: Theory and Research on International Population Movements.* New York: Center for Migration Studies of New York.

Portes, Alejandro, Clark, Juan M., and Lopez, Manuel M. 1981–82. "Six Years Later: the Process of Incorporation of Cuban Exiles in the United States: 1973–1979." *Cuban Studies* 11–12.

Portes, Alejandro, and Ferguson, D. Frances. 1977. "Comparative Ideologies of Poverty and Equity: Latin American and the United States." In I. L. Horowitz, ed., *Equity, Income, and Policy: Comparative Studies in Three Worlds of Development.* New York: Praeger.

Portes, Alejandro, and Kenneth L. Wilson. 1976. "Black-White Differences in Educational Attainment." *American Sociological Review* 41 (June): 414–431.

Poston, Dudley, and Alvirez, David. 1973. "On the Cost of Being a Mexican American." *Social Science Quarterly* 53:695–709.

Poston, Dudley, Alvirez, David, and Tienda, Marta. 1976. "Earnings Differences between Anglo and Mexican-American Male Workers in 1960 and 1970: Changes in the 'Cost' of Being Mexican-American." *Social Science Quarterly* 57:618–631.

Pratt, E. E. 1911. *Industrial Causes of Congestion of Population in New York City.* New York: Columbia University Press.

President's Commission for a National Agenda for the Eighties. 1980. *Urban America in the Eighties: Perspectives and Prospects.* Washington, D.C.: Government Printing Office.

Price, Charles A. 1963. *Southern Europeans in Australia.* Melbourne: Oxford Universtiy Press.

_____. 1969. "The Study of Assimilation." In John A. Jackson, ed., *Migration.* London: Cambridge University Press.

Price, John A. 1968. "The Migration and Adaptation of American Indians to Los Angeles." *Human Organization* 27 (Summer).

Raab, E., and Lipset, S. M. 1962. "The Prejudiced Society." In E. Raab, ed., *American Race Relations Today.* New York: Doubleday.

Rainwater, Lee, and Yancey, William L. 1967. *The Moynihan Report and the Politics of Controversy.* Cambridge, Mass.: M.I.T. Press.

Ramirez, Anthony. 1980. "Cubans and Blacks in Miami." *Wall Street Journal,* May 29.

Ramirez, Manuel, and Castaneda, Alfredo. 1974. *Cultural Democracy, Bicognitive Development and Education.* New York: Academic Press.

Rawick, George P. 1972. *From Sundown to Sunup: The Making of the Black Community.* Westport, Conn.: Greenwood Press.

Ray, Robert N. 1975. "A Report on Self-Employed Americans in 1973." *Monthly Labor Review* 98.

Record, Wilson. 1956. "Extremist Movements Among American Negroes." *Phylon* 17 (March).

_____. 1973. "Can Sociology and Black Studies Find a Common Ground?" Paper presented at Black Cultural Forum, Portland, Ore.

Redfield, Robert. 1947. "The Folk Society." *American Journal of Sociology* 52 (January).

Reich, Michael. 1971. "The Economics of Racism." In D. M. Gordon, ed., *Problems in Political Economy.* Lexington, Mass.: D. C. Heath.

Reiss, Albert. 1959. "Rural-urban and Status Differences in Interpersonal Contacts." *American Journal of Sociology* 65.

Reitz, Jeffrey G. 1980. *The Survival of Ethnic Groups.* Toronto: McGraw-Hill.

_____. 1982. "Ethnic Group Control of Jobs." Paper presented at the Annual Meeting of the American Sociological Association, San Francisco, September 6.

Reports of the Immigration Commission, 41 vols. 1970. Washington, D.C.: U.S. Government Printing Office. (Reprinted by Arno Press, New York.)

Reports of the Industrial Commission on Immigration, vol. 15. 1901. Washington, D.C.: U.S. Government Printing Office.

Reuter, Edward B. 1927. *The American Race Problem.* New York: Crowell.

Rex, John. 1970. *Race Relations in Sociological Theory*. New York: Schocken.

Riesman, David. 1950. *The Lonely Crowd: A Study of the Changing American Character*. New Haven, Conn.: Yale University Press.

Riessman, Frank. 1962. *The Culturally Deprived Child*. New York: Harper.

Riis, Jacob. 1957. *How the Other Half Lives*. New York: Hill and Wang.

Rinder, Irwin D. 1958-9. "Strangers in the Land: Social Relations in the Status Gap." *Social Problems* 6 (Winter).

Rischin, Moses. 1962. *The Promised City: New York Jews, 1870–1914*. Cambridge, Mass.: Harvard University Press.

Rogg, Eleanor. 1971. "The Influence of a Strong Refugee Community on the Economic Adjustment of Its Members." *International Migration Review* 5.

Roof, Wade Clark. 1979. "Race and Residence: The Shifting Basis of American Race Relations." *The Annals of the American Academy of Political and Social Science* 441 (January).

Rose, Arnold. 1956. "Intergroup Relations vs. Prejudice: Pertinent Theory for the Study of Social Change." *Social Problems* 4 (October).

_____. 1965. "The American Negro Problem in the Context of Social Change." *The Annals of the American Academy of Political and Social Science* 357 (January).

Rose, Jerry D. 1976. *Peoples: The Ethnic Dimension in Human Relations*. Chicago: Rand McNally.

Rosen, Bernard C. 1959. "Race, Ethnicity, and the Achievement Syndrome." *American Sociological Review* 24 (February).

Rosenblum, Gerald. 1973. *Immigrant Workers: Their Impact on American Labor Radicalism*. New York: Basic Books.

Rossi, Peter. 1964. "New Directions for Race Relations Research in the Sixties." *Review of Religious Research* 5 (Spring).

Roy, Prodipto. 1972. "The Measurement of Assimilation: The Spokane Indians." In H. M. Bahr, B. A. Chadwick, and R. C. Day, eds., *Native Americans Today: Sociological Perspectives*. New York: Harper and Row.

Rubinow, Israel. 1907. "The Economic Condition of Jews in Russia." *Bulletin of the Bureau of Labor* 72. Washington, D.C.: U.S. Government Printing Office.

Russell, Raymond. 1982. "Ethnic and Occupational Cultures in the New Taxi Cooperatives of Los Angeles." Paper presented at the Annual Meeting of the American Sociological Association, San Francisco, September 6.

Russo, N. J. 1969. "Three Generations of Italians in New York City: Their Religious Acculturation." *International Migration Review* 3.

Ryan, William. 1971. *Blaming the Victim*. New York: Pantheon Books.

Ryder, Norman B. 1955. "The Interpretation of Origin Statistics." *Canadian Journal of Economics and Political Science* 21:466–479.

Sahlins, M. 1976. *The Use and Abuse of Biology*. Ann Arbor: University of Michigan Press.

Samora, Julian. 1971. *Los Majodos: The Wetback Story*. Notre Dame, Ind.: University of Notre Dame Press.

Sandberg, Neil C. 1974. *Ethnic Identity and Assimilation: The Polish American Community*. New York: Praeger.

Sandhu, Kermal Singh. 1969. *Indians in Malaya*. Cambridge: Cambridge University Press.

Sandmeyer, E. C. 1973. *The Anti-Chinese Movement in California*. Chicago: University of Illinois Press.

Saniel, J., ed. 1967. *The Filipino Exclusion Movement, 1929–1935*. Quecon City: Institute of Asian Studies.

Sanjian, Avedis K. 1965. *The Armenian Communities in Syria Under Ottoman Dominion*. Cambridge, Mass.: Harvard University Press.

Santibanez, Enrique. 1930. *Ensayo Acerca de la Immigracion Mexicana a Estados Unidos*. San Antonio, Tex.: The Clegg Co.

Sassen-Koob, Saskia. 1978. "The International Circulation of Resources and Development: The Case of Migrant Labour." *Development and Change* 9:509–545.

_____. 1981. "Exporting Capital and Importing Labor: The Role of Caribbean Migration to New York City." New York: Center for Latin American and Caribbean Studies, Occasional Papers No. 28, New York University.

Saul, John S. 1979. "The Dialectic of Class and Tribe." *Race and Class* 20:347–372.

Saveth, Edward N. 1948. *American Historians and European Immigrants*. New York: Columbia University Press.

Saxton, Alexander. 1971. *The Indispensable Enemy: Labor and the Anti-Chinese Movement in California*. Los Angeles: University of California Press.

Schermerhorn, Richard A. 1959. "Minorities: European and American." *Phylon* 20 (June).

_____. 1964. "Toward a General Theory of Minority Groups." *Phylon* 25 (September).

_____. 1970. *Comparative Ethnic Relations: A Framework for Theory and Research.* New York: Random House.

_____. 1974. "Ethnicity in the Perspective of Sociology of Knowledge." *Ethnicity* 1 (April).

Schmid, Calvin F., and Nobbe, Charles E. 1965. "Socioeconomic Differentials among Non-white Races." *American Sociological Review* 30.

Schmidt, Fred H. 1970. "Spanish Surnamed American Employment in the Southwest: A Study Prepared for the Colorado Civil Rights Commission Under the Auspices of the Equal Employment Opportunity Commission." Washington, D.C.: U.S. Government Printing Office.

Schmitt, Robert C. 1968. *Demographic Statistics of Hawaii: 1778–1965.* Honolulu: University of Hawaii Press.

Schneider, John, and Eitzen, D. Stanley. 1979. "Racial Discrimination in American Sport: Continuity or Change?" *Journal of Sport Behavior* 2 (August).

Schuman, Howard. 1969. "Sociological Racism." *Transaction* 7 (2) (December).

Schumpeter, Joseph. 1934. *The Theory of Economic Development,* trans. Redvers Opie. Cambridge, Mass.: Harvard University Press.

Schwartz, Audrey J. 1971. "The Culturally Advantaged: A Study of Japanese-American Pupils." *Sociology and Social Research* 55.

Seller, Maxine. 1977. *To Seek America: A History of Ethnic Life in the United States.* Englewood, N.J.: Jerome S. Ozer.

Sengstock, Mary Catherine. 1967. "Maintenance of Social Interaction Patterns in an Ethnic Group." Ph.D. dissertation, Washington University.

Sewell, William H., and Robert M. Hauser. 1975. *Education, Occupation, and Earnings: Achievement in the Early Career.* New York: Academic Press.

Sexton, Patricia Cayo. 1972. "Schools: Broken Ladder to Success." In F. Cordasco and E. Bucchiono, eds., *The Puerto Rican Community and Its Children on the Mainland: A Source Book for Teachers, Social Workers, and Other Professionals.* Metuchen, N.J.: Scarecrow Press.

Shack, William A. 1970. "On Black American Values in White America: Some Perspectives on the Cultural Aspects of Learning Behavior and Compensatory Education." Paper prepared for the Social Science Research Council, Sub-Committee on Values and Compensatory Education.

Sheppard, Harold, and Striner, Herbert E. 1966.

Civil Rights, Employment and Social Status of American Negroes. Kalamazoo, Mich.: Upjohn Institute.

Shibutani, Tamotsu, and Kwan, Kian M. 1965. *Ethnic Stratification.* New York: Macmillan.

Shockley, John. 1974. *Chicano Revolt in a Texas Town.* Notre Dame, Ind.: University of Notre Dame Press.

Siegel, Jacob S., and Passel, Jeffrey S. 1979. "Coverage of the Hispanic Population of the United States in the 1970 Census: A Methodological Analysis." *Current Popluation Reports,* ser. P-23, no. 82. Washington, D.C.: U.S. Government Printing Office.

Siegel, Paul M. 1965. "On the Cost of Being a Negro." *Sociological Inquiry* 35.

Simpson, George E., and Yinger, J. Milton. 1954. "The Changing Pattern of Race Relations." *Phylon* 15 (December).

_____. 1958. "Can Segregation Survive in an Industrial Society?" *Antioch Review* 18 (March).

_____. 1959. "The Sociology of Race and Ethnic Relations." In R. K. Merton, L. Broom, and L. S. Cottrell, Jr., eds., *Sociology Today.* New York: Basic Books.

_____. 1972. *Racial and Cultural Minorities: An Analysis of Prejudice and Discrimination* 4th ed. New York: Harper and Row.

Singer, L. 1962. "Ethnogenesis and Negro Americans Today." *Social Research* 29 (Winter).

Sitkoff, Harvard. 1981. *The Struggle for Black Equality: 1945–1980.* New York: Hill and Wang.

Siu, Paul. 1952. "The Sojourner." *American Journal of Sociology* 8 (July).

Sjoberg, Gideon. 1955. "The Preindustrial City." *American Journal of Sociology* 60.

_____. 1960. *The Preindustrial City.* New York: Free Press.

Skolnick, Jerome. 1969. *The Politics of Protest. A Staff Report to the National Commission on the Causes and Prevention of Violence.* Washington, D.C.: U.S. Government Printing Office.

Smith, Michael G. 1965. *The Plural Society in the British West Indies.* Berkeley and Los Angeles: University of California Press.

Smith, M. W. 1940. "The Puyallup of Washington." In R. Linton, ed., *Acculturation in Seven American Indian Tribes.* New York: Appleton-Century.

Smith, Robert J. 1980. "The Concept of Ethnocide." Unpublished paper.

Smith, Timothy L. 1978. "Religion and Ethnicity in America." *American Historical Review* 83 (December).

Sowell, Thomas. 1978. *Essays and Data on Ameri-*

can Ethnic Groups. Washington, D.C.: Urban Institute.

_____. 1980. Ethnic America. New York: Basic Books.

_____. 1981. Markets and Minorities. New York: Basic Books.

Special Task Force to the Secretary of Health, Education, and Welfare. 1973. Work in America. Cambridge, Mass.: MIT Press.

Spicer, Edward H. 1962. Cycles of Conquest. Tucson: University of Arizona Press.

_____. 1969. A Short History of the Indians of the United States. New York: Van Nostrand Reinholdt.

Stampp, Kenneth M., et al. 1968. "The Negro in American History Textbooks." Negro History Bulletin 31 (October).

State Board of Control of California. 1922. California and the Oriental. Sacramento: California State Printing Office.

Steele, C. Hoy. 1972. "American Indians and Urban Life: A Community Study." Ph.D. dissertation, Department of American Studies, University of Kansas, Lawrence.

*_____. 1973. "The Acculturation/Assimilation Model in Urban Indian Studies: A Critique." Revised paper presented at American Ethnological Society, Wilmington Beach, N.C., March.

Stein, Howard F., and Hill, Robert F. 1977. The Ethnic Imperative: Examining the White Ethnic Movement. State College: Pennsylvania State University Press.

*Steinberg, Stephen. 1974. The Academic Melting Pot: Catholics and Jews in American Higher Education. New York: McGraw-Hill.

*_____. 1981. The Ethnic Myth: Race, Ethnicity, and Class in America. New York: Atheneum.

Stevens, Rosemary, Goodman, Louis W., and Mick, Stephen S. 1978. The Alien Doctors: Foreign Medical Graduates in American Hospitals. New York: Wiley.

Stewart, William. 1970. "Toward a History of American Negro Dialect." School of Languages & Linguistics Monograph Series 22. Washington, D.C.: Georgetown University.

Stocking, George W. 1968. Race, Culture, and Evolution: Essays in the History of Anthropology. New York: Free Press.

Stoddard, Ellwyn R. 1976. "A Conceptual Analysis of the 'Alien Invasion': Institutionalized Support of Illegal Mexican Aliens in the U.S." International Migration Review 10 (Summer).

Stodolsky, Susan, and Lesser, Gerald. 1971.

"Learning Patterns in the Disadvantaged." Harvard Educational Review Reprint Series No. 5.

Stonequist, E. V. 1935. "The Problem of the Marginal Man." American Journal of Sociology 41.

_____. 1937. The Marginal Man. New York: Charles Scribner's Sons.

Strodtbeck, Fred L. 1958. "Family Interaction, Values and Achievement." In M. Sklare, ed., The Jews: Social Patterns in An American Group. New York: Free Press.

Stryker, Sheldon. 1959. "Social Structure and Prejudice." Social Problems 6 (Spring).

Sung, Betty Lee. 1967. Mountain of Gold: The Story of the Chinese in America. New York: Macmillan.

Sutherland, Edwin H., and Cressey, Donald R. 1970. Criminology. Philadelphia: Lippincott.

Suttles, Gerald D. 1968. The Social Order of the Slum. Chicago: University of Chicago Press.

Sway, Marlene. 1983. "Gypsies as a Middleman Minority." Ph.D. dissertation, University of California, Los Angeles.

Syzmanski, Albert. 1976. "Racial Discrimination and White Gain." American Sociological Review 41 (June).

Tabb, William. 1970. The Political Economy of the Black Ghetto. New York: Norton.

Taeuber, Karl. 1983. "Racial Residential Segregation, 28 Cities, 1970–1980." CDE Working Paper 83–12, University of Wisconsin, Madison.

Taeuber, Karl E., and Taeuber, Alma F. 1965. Negroes in Cities. Chicago: Aldine.

Task Force on the Administration of Military Justice in the Armed Forces. 1972. Report. Washington, D.C.: U.S. Government Printing Office.

Taylor, D. Garth, Sheatsley, Paul B., and Greeley, Andrew M. 1978. "Attitudes Toward Racial Integration." Scientific American 238 (June).

Taylor, Philip. 1971. The Distant Magnet: European Emigration to the U.S.A. New York: Harper and Row.

Teague, Bob. 1968. "Charlie Doesn't Even Know His Daily Racism Is a Sick Joke." New York Times Magazine (September 15).

Theodorson, George A., and Theodorson, Achilles G. 1969. A Modern Dictionary of Sociology. New York: Thomas Y. Crowell.

Thernstrom, Stephan. 1973. The Other Bostonians: Poverty and Progress in the American Metropolis 1880–1970. Cambridge, Mass.: Harvard University Press.

Thernstrom, Stephan, ed. 1980. *Harvard Encyclopedia of American Ethnic Groups*. Cambridge, Mass.: Harvard University Press.

Thomas, Dorothy Swaine, and Nishimoto, Richard S. 1969. *The Spoilage: Japanese American Evacuation and Resettlement*. Berkeley: University of California Press.

Thomas, John F., and Earl E. Huyck. 1967. "Resettlement of Cuban Refugees in the United States." Paper presented at the annual meeting of the American Sociological Association, San Francisco.

Thomas, Robert K. 1966. "Powerless Politics." *New University Thought* 4 (Winter).

Thompson, Richard H. 1979. "Ethnicity vs. Class: Analysis of Conflict in a North American Chinese Community." *Ethnicity* 6.

Thompson, Virginia, and Adloff, Richard. 1955. *Minority Problems in Southeast Asia*. Boston: Beacon Press.

Thurow, Lester C. 1969. *Poverty and Discrimination*. Washington, D.C.: Brookings Institution.

Time. 1975. "America's Rising Black Middle Class." June 17.

_____. 1978. "Hispanic Americans: Soon the Biggest Minority." Special Report (October 16), pp.48–61.

Timms, Duncan. 1971. *The Urban Mosaic*. New York: Cambridge University Press.

Tinker, John N. 1973. "Intermarriage and Ethnic Boundaries: The Japanese American Case." *Journal of Social Issues* 29:2.

Tumin, Melvin M. 1968. "Some Social Consequences of Research on Racial Relations." *American Sociologist* 4 (May).

_____. 1969. *Comparative Perspectives on Race Relations*. Boston: Little, Brown.

Turner, Jonathan H., and Bonacich, Edna. 1980. "Toward a Composite Theory of Middleman Minorities." *Ethnicity* 7.

Tuttle, William M., Jr. 1974. *Race Riot: Chicago in the Red Summer of 1919*. New York: Atheneum.

Uhlenberg, P. 1972. "Demographic Correlates of Group Achievement: Contrasting Patterns of Mexican-Americans and Japanese-Americans." *Demography* 9.

United Nations. 1974. "Report on the World Social Situation—Social Trends in the Developing Countries, Latin America and the Caribbean." U.N. Document E/CN.5/512/Add. 1, 1974.

U.S. Bureau of the Census. 1953. U.S. Census of the Population: 1950. Special Reports, *Nonwhite Population by Race*. Washington, D.C.: U.S. Government Printing Office.

_____. 1963a. U.S. Census of the Population: 1960. *Characteristics of the Population*. Part I. U.S. Summary. Washington, D.C.: U.S. Government Printing Office.

_____. 1963b. U.S. Census of the Population: 1960. Subject Reports. *Nonwhite Population by Race*. Final Report PC(2)-1C. Washington, D.C.: U.S. Government Printing Office.

_____. 1969. *Statistical Abstract of the United States* 90th ed. Washington, D.C.: U.S. Government Printing Office.

_____. 1971. *One in a 100: A Public Sample of Basic Records From the 1960 Census: Description and Technical Documentation*. Washington, D.C.: U.S. Government Printing Office.

_____. 1972. U.S. Census of the Population: 1970. *General Population Characteristics*. Final Report PC(1)-B1 United States Summary. Washington, D.C.: U.S. Government Printing Office.

_____. 1972. *Public Use Samples of Basic Records From the 1970 Census: Description and Technical Documentation*. Washington, D.C.: U.S. Government Printing Office.

_____. 1973. *U.S. Census of the Population: 1970. Characteristics of the Population*. Vol. 1, Part I. U.S. Summary Section 2. Washington, D.C.: U.S. Government Printing Office.

_____. 1975. *Historical Statistics of the United States*. Washington, D.C.: U.S. Government Printing Office.

_____. 1977. Technical Documentation for the 1976 Survey of Income and Education. Mimeo. Washington, D.C.: Data User Services, Bureau of the Census.

_____. 1978. *Statistical Abstract of the United States*. Washington, D.C.: U.S. Government Printing Office.

_____. 1979. *The Social and Economic Status of the Black Population in the United States: An Historical View, 1790–1978*. Series P-23 (80). Washington, D.C.: U.S. Government Printing Office.

U.S. Commission on Civil Rights. 1961. *Report: Justice 5*. Washington, D.C.: U.S. Government Printing Office.

_____. 1971. *Ethnic Isolation of Mexican Americans in the Public Schools of the Southwest*, Report I: Mexican-American Study Project. Washington, D.C.: U.S. Government Printing Office.

BIBLIOGRAPHY

_____. 1972. *The Excluded Student: Educational Practices Affecting Mexican-Americans in the Southwest,* Report III: Mexican-American Study Project.

_____. 1973. *Teachers and Students,* Report V: Mexican-American Education Study, Differences in Teacher Interaction with Mexican-American and Anglo Students. Washington, D.C.: U.S. Government Printing Office.

_____. 1974. Toward Quality Education for Mexican-Americans, Report VI: Mexican-American Education Study. Washington, D.C.: U.S. Government Printing Office.

_____. 1978. *Social Indicators of Equality for Minorities and Women.* Washington, D.C.: U.S. Government Printing Office.

_____. 1982. Census of Population and Housing, Provisional Estimates of Social, Economic and Housing Characteristics. Washington, D.C.: U.S. Government Printing Office.

_____. 1983. Ancestry of the Population by State: 1980. Supplementary Report, PC80-S1-10. Washington, D.C.: U.S. Government Printing Office.

U.S. Immigration and Naturalization Service, 1977. *Cubans Arrived in the United States by Class of Admission, January 1, 1959–September 3, 1976.* Special Reports. Washington, D.C.: INS Statistics Branch.

_____. 1978. *Annual Report 1977.* Washington, D.C.: U.S. Government Printing Office.

U.S. Senate, Select Committee. 1970a. *Hearing Before the Select Committee on Equal Educational Oppoutunity,* Part 4: Mexican-American Education. Washington, D.C.: U.S. Government Printing Office.

_____. 1970b. *Hearing Before the Select Committee on Equal Educational Opportunity,* Part 8: Equal Educational Opportunity for Puerto Rican Children. Washington, D.C.: U.S. Government Printing Office.

U.S. Small Business Administration, Office of Advocacy. 1980. *The Small Business Data Base.* Washington, D.C.: U.S. Small Business Administration.

Useem, Michael. 1980. "Corporations and the Corporate Elite." *Annual Review of Sociology* 6.

Urquidi, Victor L. 1974. "Empleo y Explosion Demografica." *Demografia y Economia* 8(2).

Valentine, Bettylou. 1978. *Hustling and Other Hard Work.* New York: Macmillan.

Valentine, Charles A. 1968. *Culture and Poverty.* Chicago: University of Chicago Press.

Van de Geer, John P. 1971. *Introduction to Multivariate Analysis for the Social Sciences.* San Francisco: W. H. Freeman.

van den Berghe, Pierre L. 1963. "Dialectic and Functionalism: Toward a Theoretical Synthesis." *American Sociological Review* 28 (October).

_____. 1965, 1967b. *South Africa: A Study in Conflict.* Middletown, Conn.: Wesleyan University Press.

_____. 1966. "Paternalistic Versus Competitive Race Relations: An Ideal-Type Approach." In B. E. Segal, ed., *Racial and Ethnic Relations.* New York: Crowell.

_____. 1967a. *Race and Racism: A Comparative Perspective.* New York: Wiley.

_____. 1970. *Race and Ethnicity.* New York: Basic Books.

_____, ed. 1974. *Class and Ethnicity in Peru.* Leiden: Brill.

_____. 1978a. *Race and Racism: A Comparative Perspective* 2nd ed. New York: John Wiley and Sons.

_____. 1978b. *Man in Society.* New York: Elsevier.

*_____. 1978c. "Race and Ethnicity: A Sociobiological Perspective." *Ethnic and Racial Studies* 1:4 (October).

_____. 1981. *The Ethnic Phenomenon.* New York: Elsevier.

_____ and Barash, D. P. 1977. "Inclusive Fitness and Human Family Structure." *American Anthropologist* 79:4.

Van der Horst, Sheila T. 1965. "The Effects of Industrialization on Race Relations in South Africa." In G. Hunter, ed., *Industrialization and Race Relations.* London: Oxford University Press.

van der Kroef, Justus M. 1953. "The Eurasian Minority in Indonesia." *American Sociological Review* 18 (October).

Vander Zanden, James. 1959a. "Desegregation and Social Strains in the South." *Journal of Social Issues* 15 (4).

_____. 1959b. "A Note on the Theory of Social Movements." *Sociology and Social Research* 44 (September-October).

_____. 1965. *Race Relations in Transition: The Segregation Crisis in the South.* New York: Random House.

Vaupel, James, and Curhan, Joan. 1973. *The World's Multinational Enterprises: A Sourcebook of Tables.* Boston: Harvard Business School.

Vecoli, Rudolph J. 1964. "Contadini in Chicago: A Critique of the Uprooted." *Journal of American History* 51.

Venable, Abraham S. 1972. *Building Black Busi-*

ness: An Analysis and a Plan. New York: Earl G. Graves.

Vidal, David. 1980. "Hispanic Newcomers in City Cling to Values of Homeland." *New York Times,* May 11.

Vidich, Arthur, and Bensman, Joseph. 1960. *Small Town in Mass Society.* Garden City, N.Y.: Doubleday Anchor Books.

Villemez, Wayne J. 1980. "Race, Class, and Neighborhood: Differences in the Residential Return on Individual Resources." *Social Forces* 59:414–430.

Wachtel, Howard M. 1972. "Capitalism and Poverty in America: Paradox or Contradiction?" *American Economic Review* 62:187–194.

Wagley, Charles, and Harris, Marvin. 1958. *Minorities in the New World.* New York: Columbia University Press.

Waldinger, Roger. 1982. "Immigrant Enterprise and Labor Market Structure." Paper presented at the Annual Meeting of the American Sociological Association, San Francisco, September 6.

Walker, Charles and Guest, Robert. 1952. *The Man on the Assembly Line.* Cambridge, Mass.: Harvard University Press.

Wallerstein, Immanuel. 1966. *Social Change: The Colonial Situation.* New York: Wiley.

_____. 1976. *The Modern World-System.* New York: Academic Press.

Wallman, Sandra. 1979a. "Foreword." In Sandra Wallman, ed., *Ethnicity at Work.* London: Macmillan.

_____. 1979b. "The Scope for Ethnicity." In Sandra Wallman, ed., *Ethnicity at Work.* London: Macmillan.

Walton, John. 1975. "Internal Colonialism: Problems of Definition and Measurement." In W. A. Cornelius and F. Trueblood, eds., *Latin American Urban Research* vol. 5. Beverly Hills, Cal.: Sage.

Ward, David. 1971. *Cities and Immigrants: A Geography of Change in Nineteenth Century America.* New York: Oxford University Press.

_____. 1968. *The Private City.* Philadelphia: University of Pennsylvania Press.

Warner, Sam Bass, and Burke, Colin. 1969. "Cultural Change and the Ghetto." *Journal of Contemporary History* 4.

Warner, W. Lloyd. 1936. "American Caste and Class." *American Journal of Sociology* 32 (September).

Warner, W. Lloyd and Srole, Leo. 1945. *The Social Systems of American Ethnic Groups.* New Haven, Conn.: Yale University Press.

Warren, Bruce L. 1966. "A Multiple Variable Approach to the Assortative Mating Phenomenon." *Eugenics Quarterly* 13.

Warren, Ronald L. 1963. *The Community in America.* Chicago: Rand McNally.

Washburn, Wilcomb. 1964. *The Indian and the White Man.* New York: Anchor Books.

_____. 1975. *The Indian in America.* New York: Harper and Row.

Wax, Murray L. 1971. *Indian Americans: Unity and Diversity.* Englewood Cliffs, N.J.: Prentice-Hall.

Wax, Murray L., Wax Rosalie H., and Dumont, Robert B., Jr. 1964. "Formal Education in an American Indian Community." *Supplement to Social Problems* (Spring).

Wax, Rosalie H., and Thomas, Robert K. 1961. "American Indians and White People." *Phylon* 22 (Winter).

Weber, Max. 1958a. *The Protestant Ethnic and the Spirit of Capitalism.* New York: Scribner.

_____. 1958b. "The Protestant Sects and the Spirit of Capitalism." In Hans H. Gerth and C. W. Mills, eds., *From Max Weber.* New York: Oxford University Press.

_____. 1963. *The Sociology of Religion.* Boston: Beacon Press.

Weinberg, M. 1970. *Desegregation Research: An Appraisal* 2d ed. Bloomington, Ind.: Phi Delta Kappa.

Wertheim, W. F. 1964. *East-West Parallels: Sociological Approaches to Modern Asia.* The Hague: W. van Hoeve.

Westie, Frank R. 1965. "The American Dilemma: An Empirical Test." *American Sociological Review* 26 (August).

White, Lynn C., and Chadwick, Bruce A. 1972. "Urban Residence, Assimilation and Identity of the Spokane Indian." In H. M. Bahr et al., eds., *Native Americans Today: Sociological Perspectives.* New York: Harper and Row.

White, Robert A. n.d. "The Development of Collective Decision-Making in an American Indian Community: The Politics of an Urban Indian Ethnic Community." Unpublished manuscript.

Whiteman, M., and Deutsch, M. 1968. "Social Disadvantage as Related to Intellectual and Language Development." In M. Deutsch, I. Katz, and A. R. Jensen, eds., *Social Class, Race and Psychological Development.* New York: Holt.

Whyte, William Foote. 1943, 1955. *Street Corner Society.* Chicago: University of Chicago Press.

Whyte, William H., Jr. 1956. *The Organization Man*. New York: Simon & Schuster.

Wilber, George L., Jaco, Daniel E., Hagan, Robert J., and del Fierro, Alfonso C., Jr. 1975. *Minorities in the Labor Market* vol 2: Orientals in the American Labor Market. Lexington, Ky.: University of Kentucky.

Wilcox, Preston. 1970. "Social Policy and White Racism." *Social Policy* 1 (May/June).

Wilensky, Harold L., and Lawrence, Anne T. 1979. "Job Assignment in Modern Societies: A Reexamination of the Ascription-Achievement Hypothesis." In Amos H. Hawley, ed., *Societal Growth*. New York: Free Press.

Wilhelm, Sidney M. 1970. *Who Needs the Negro?* Cambridge, Mass.: Schenkman.

————, and Powell, Elwin H. 1964. "Who Needs the Negro?" *Transaction* 1 (September-October).

Willard, Myra. 1967. *History of the White Australia Policy to 1920*. London: Melbourne University Press.

Williams, Eric. 1944. *Capitalism and Slavery*. Chapel Hill, N.C.: University of North Carolina Press.

Williams, Robin M. 1964. *Strangers Next Door: Ethnic Relations in American Communities*. Englewood Cliffs, N.J.: Prentice-Hall.

————. 1966. "Some Further Comments on Chronic Controversies." *American Journal of Sociology* 71 (May).

Willie, Charles V. 1978. "The Inclining Significance of Race." *Society* 15:5 (July/August).

————. 1979. *Caste and Class Controversy*. Bayside, N.Y.: General Hall.

Willmott, W. E. 1966. "The Chinese in Southeast Asia." *Australian Outlook* 20 (December).

Wilson, E. O. 1975. *Sociobiology, The New Synthesis*. Cambridge, Mass.: Belknap.

*Wilson, Kenneth L., and Portes, Alejandro. 1980. "Immigrant Enclaves: An Analysis of the Labor Market Experience of Cubans in Miami." *American Journal of Sociology* 86:2 (September).

————, and Martin, W. Allen. 1982. "Ethnic Enclaves: A Comparison of the Cuban and Black Economics in Miami." *American Journal of Sociology* 88:1 (July).

Wilson, William J. 1973. *Power, Racism, and Privilege: Race Relations in Theoretical and Sociohistorical Perspectives*. New York: Macmillan.

*————. 1978. *The Declining Significance of Race*. Chicago: University of Chicago Press.

————. 1978. "The Declining Significance of

Race: Revisited but not Revised." *Society* 15:5 (July/August).

*————. 1981. "The Black Community in the 1980s: Questions of Race, Class, and Public Policy." *Annals of the American Academy of Political and Social Science* 454 (March).

Wirth, Louis. 1928. *The Ghetto*. Chicago: University of Chicago Press.

Witkin, H. A., Lewis, H. B., Hertzman, M., Machover, K., Meissner, P. B., and Wapner, S. 1954. *Personality Through Perception*. New York: Harper.

Witkin, H. A., Patterson, H. F., Goodenough, D. R., and Karp, S. A. 1962. *Psychological Differentiation*. New York: Wiley.

Wittke, Carl. 1952. *Refugees of Revolution: The German Forty-eighters in America*. Philadelphia: University of Pennsylvania Press.

————. 1953. "Immigration Policy Prior to World War I." In B. M. Ziegler, ed., *Immigration: An American Dilemma*. Boston, D. C. Heath.

Wolff, Kurt H. 1950. *The Sociology of Georg Simmel*. Glencoe, Ill.: Free Press.

Wolpe, Harold. 1970. " Industrialism and Race in South Africa." In Sami Zubaida, ed., *Race and Racialism*. London: Tavistock.

Womack, John. 1968. *Zapata and the Mexican Revolution*. New York: Vintage Books.

Wong, Charles Choy. 1977. "Black and Chinese Grocery Stores in Los Angeles' Black Ghetto." *Urban Life* 5.

Wong, Morrison G. 1977. "The Japanese in Riverside, 1890 to 1945: A Special Case in Race Relations." Ph.D. dissertation, University of California, Riverside.

————. 1980a. "Changes in Socioeconomic Status of the Chinese Male Population in the United States from 1960 to 1970." *International Migration Review* 14:4.

————. 1980b. "The Cost of being Chinese, Japanese, and Filipino in the United States: 1960, 1970, and 1976." Unpublished manuscript.

————. 1981. "Chinese Sweatshops in the United States: A Look at the Garment Industry." In Ida H. Simpson and Richard L. Simpson, eds., *Research in the Sociology of Work* vol. 2. Greenwich, Conn.: JAI Press.

Wong, Morrison G., and Hirschman, Charles. 1983. "The New Asian Immigrants." In William C. McCready, ed., *Culture, Ethnicity and Identity: Current Issues in Research*. New York: Academic Press.

Woodrum, Eric, Rhodes, Colbert, and Feagin, Joe R. 1980. "Japanese American Economic Behavior: Its

Types, Determinants and Consequences." *Social Forces* 58.

Woodward, C. Vann. 1957. *The Strange Career of Jim Crow.* New York: Oxford University Press.

Works, Ernest. 1969. "The Prejudice-Interaction Hypothesis from the Point of View of the Negro Minority Group." *American Journal of Sociology* 67:47–52.

Wright, E. O., Costello, Cynthia, Hachen, David, and Sprague, Joey. 1982. "The American Class Structure." *American Sociological Review* 47.

Wright, Nathan. 1967. "The Economics of Race." *American Journal of Economics and Sociology* 26 (January).

*Yancey, William L., Ericksen, Eugene P., and Juliani, Richard N. 1976. "Emergent Ethnicity: A Review and Reformulation." *American Sociological Review* 41 (June).

Yarwood, A. T. 1964. *Asian Immigration to Australia.* London: Cambridge University Press.

_____. 1968. *Attitudes to Non-European Immigration.* Melbourne: Cassell Australia.

Yetman, Norman R. 1970. *Life Under the "Peculiar Institution."* New York: Holt, Rinehart and Winston.

_____. 1975. "The Irish Experience in America." In H. Orel, ed., *Irish History and Culture.* Lawrence, Kan.: University Press of Kansas.

_____. 1983. "The 'New Immigrant Wave.' Migration Pressures and the American Presence." Paper presented at the meetings of the American Studies Association, Philapelphia, November.

_____. 1984. "Ethnic Pluralism in the 1970s." *American Studies in Scandinavia* 16:2.

Yetman, Norman R., and Eitzen, E. Stanley. 1971, 1975, 1982. "Racial Dynamics in American Sport: Continuity and Change." In N. R. Yetman and C. H. Steele, eds., *Majority and Minority: The Dymanics of Race and Ethnicity in American Life* 3 eds. Boston: Allyn and Bacon.

Yinger, J. Milton. 1968. "Prejudice: Social Discrimination." In D. L. Sills, ed., *International Encyclopedia of the Social Sciences.* New York: Macmillan.

Young, Frank W. 1971. "A Macrosociological Interpretation of Entrepreneurship." In Peter Kilby, ed., *Entrepreneurship and Economic Development.* New York: Free Press.

Young, Michael, and Willmott, Peter. 1957. *Family and Kinship in East London.* London: Routledge and Kegan Paul.

Yu, Eui-Young. 1982. "Occupation and Work Patterns of Korean Immigrants." In Eui-Young Yu, Earl H. Phillips, and Eun-Sik Yang, eds., *Koreans in Los Angeles.* Los Angeles: Koryo Research Institute and Center for Korean-American and Korean Studies, California State University.

Zenner, Walter P. 1982. "Arabic-Speaking Immigrants in North America as Middlemen Minorities." *Ethnic and Racial Studies* 5.

List of Contributors

Richard D. Alba is Associate Professor of Sociology and Director of the Center for Social and Demographic Analysis at the State University of New York, Albany.

Gerald D. Berreman is Professor of Anthropology at the University of California, Berkeley.

Edna Bonacich is Professor of Sociology at the University of California, Riverside.

Alan N. Burstein is a financial consultant in Chicago, Illinois.

Barry R. Chiswick is a professor in the Department of Economics and a research professor at the Survey Research Laboratory, University of Illinois, Chicago Circle.

Cary Davis is Research Demographer at the Population Reference Bureau.

Cynthia Enloe is Professor of Government at Clark University.

Eugene P. Ericksen is Associate Professor of Sociology at Temple University.

Leobardo F. Estrada is Associate Professor of Architecture and Urban Planning at the University of California, Los Angeles.

Herbert J. Gans is Professor of Sociology at Columbia University and Senior Research Associate at the Center for Policy Research.

F. Chris Garcia is Professor of Political Science and Dean of the College of Arts and Sciences at the University of New Mexico.

Milton M. Gordon is Professor of Sociology at the University of Massachusetts, Amherst.

Andrew M. Greeley, priest, novelist, and sociologist, is Professor of Sociology at the University of Arizona and affiliated with the National Opinion Research Center.

Stephanie Greenberg is a research analyst with the Mountain States Telephone and Telegraph Company.

Carl Haub is Director of Demographic and Policy Analysis of the Population Reference Bureau.

Theodore Hershberg is Assistant to the Mayor of Philadelphia for Strategic Planning and Policy Development.

Charles Hirschman is Professor of Sociology at Cornell University.

Richard N. Juliani is Associate Professor of Sociology at Villanova University.

Stanley Lieberson is Professor of Sociology at the University of California, Berkeley.

Ivan Light is Professor of Sociology at the University of California, Los Angeles.

Nancy Oestreich Lurie is Curator of Anthropology at the Milwaukee Public Museum and Adjunct Professor of Anthropology at The University of Wisconsin, Milwaukee.

Stanford Lyman is Professor of Sociology at the New School for Social Research.

Reynaldo Flores Macias is Assistant Professor of Education at the University of Southern California.

Lionel Maldonado is Associate Professor of Sociology at the University of Wisconsin, Parkside.

Douglas S. Massey is Assistant Professor of Sociology at the University of Pennsylvania.

Robert K. Merton is University Professor Emeritus and Special Service Professor at Columbia University.

L. Paul Metzger is Associate Professor of Sociology at the State University of New York, New Paltz.

Joan W. Moore is Professor of Sociology at the University of Wisconsin, Milwaukee.

Brendan P. Mullan is a doctoral candidate in demography at the University of Pennsylvania.

Gunnar Myrdal has been a distinguished professor at numerous American and European universities, has served on various Swedish governmental and international committees, and was awarded the Nobel Prize for Economics in 1974.

Joane Nagel is Associate Professor of Sociology at the University of Kansas.

Donald L. Noel is Professor of Sociology at the University of Wisconsin, Milwaukee.

John Ogbu is Professor of Anthropology at the University of California, Berkeley.

Alejandro Portes is Professor of Sociology at the Johns Hopkins University.

C. Hoy Steele is president of Hoy Steele Associates, a California-based conflict mediation firm.

Stephen Steinberg is Professor of Sociology and Urban Studies at Queens College and the Graduate Center of the City University of New York.

Pierre van den Berghe is Professor of Sociology and Anthropology at the University of Washington.

JoAnne Willette is Senior Research Specialist at Development Associates, Inc.

Kenneth L. Wilson is Associate Professor of Sociology and Social Psychology at Florida Atlantic University.

William J. Wilson is Lucy Flower Professor of Urban Sociology at the University of Chicago.

Morrison G. Wong is Assistant Professor of Sociology at Texas Christian University.

William L. Yancey is Professor of Sociology at Temple University.

Norman R. Yetman is Professor of Sociology and American Studies at the University of Kansas.